NIGEL CALDER'S CRUISING HANDBOOK

A Compendium for Coastal and Offshore Sailors

"He who goes to sea for pleasure
would go to hell to pass the time!"

—Anonymous

NIGEL CALDER'S CRUISING HANDBOOK

A Compendium for Coastal and Offshore Sailors

NIGEL CALDER

International Marine / McGraw-Hill
Camden, Maine • New York • Chicago • San Francisco • Lisbon • London
Madrid • Mexico City • Milan • New Delhi • San Juan • Seoul • Singapore
Sydney • Toronto

Other Books by Nigel Calder

Boatowner's Mechnical and Electrical Manual: How to Maintain, Repair, and Improve Your Boat's Essential Systems, 2nd edition

The Cruising Guide to the Northwest Caribbean: The Yucatan Coast of Mexico, Belize, Guatemala, Honduras, and the Bay Islands of Honduras

Cuba: A Cruising Guide

Marine Diesel Engines: Maintenance, Troubleshooting, and Repair, 2nd edition

Refrigeration for Pleasure Boats: Installation, Maintenance, and Repair

Repairs at Sea

International Marine
A Division of The ***McGraw-Hill*** *Companies*

10 9 8 7 6 5 4

Acknowledgments for the use of previously published material begin on page xv.

Library of Congress Cataloging-in-Publication Data
Calder, Nigel.
[Cruising handbook]
Nigel Calder's cruising handbook : a compendium for coastal and offshore sailors / Nigel Calder.
p. cm.
Includes bibliographical references and index.
ISBN 0-07-135099-3 (alk. paper)
1. Sailing—Handbooks, manuals, etc. 2. Sailboats—Handbooks, manuals, etc.
I. Title: Cruising handbook. II. Title.
GV811.C333 2001
797.1´24—dc21 00-054102

Questions regarding the content of this book should be addressed to
International Marine
P.O. Box 220
Camden, ME 04843
www.internationalmarine.com

Questions regarding the ordering of this book should be addressed to
The McGraw-Hill Companies
Customer Service Department
P.O. Box 547
Blacklick, OH 43004
Retail customers: 1-800-262-4729
Bookstores: 1-800-722-4726

This book is printed on 45# New Era Matte by Courier Westford
Design by Geri Davis, The Davis Group
Production management by Janet Robbins
Edited by Jonathan Eaton, Constance Burt, Molly Mulhern, and D. A. Oliver
Line drawings by Jim Sollers unless otherwise noted
Graphs and weather drawings by Nancy Benner
Part opener and heading photo by PhotoDisc
Page layout by Kristen Goble, PerfecType
Registered trademarks are found on page 573

To Terrie, who humors my addiction to sailboats
in spite of the fact that she would rather explore the world
from behind the wheel of a minibus.

CONTENTS

PART TWO: CRUISING SKILLS

PREFACE

In 1971, as a footloose English hippie, I met a wild nineteen-year-old American. Keen to impress her, I suggested we "borrow" my brother's 28-foot sailboat, fittingly named *Wallop*, and spend a week exploring England's east coast. Terrie took a look at a small-scale chart of the region, which included most of the North Sea and its European coastline, and said, "Why don't we go to Amsterdam?"

"Well, OK," I answered, a little hesitantly, concealing the fact that while I had done a fair amount of dinghy sailing, I had virtually no offshore experience and almost no navigational skills.

"Let's go."

We rounded up a crew of landlubbers, filled the bilges with bottles of homemade beer, drank a few toasts, and headed out the Crouch estuary. The first North Sea swells found me hunched over the chart table, poring over the piloting chapters in a well-thumbed copy of Eric Hiscock's *Cruising under Sail*, alternately reading and retching.

Hiscock got us to Amsterdam, at which point Terrie said she needed to go ashore to make a phone call. Fifteen minutes later, a Dutch boyfriend showed up on the dock and she was gone! There was nothing in Hiscock to help me deal with that crisis. Fortunately, it was soon resolved: Terrie was back the next day (the Dutch guy had a full-time job, which made life rather boring), and we have been cruising together ever since.

Hiscock's book and its companion piece, *Voyaging under Sail* (combined into a single volume in 1980), were seminal works not just for us, but also for generations of cruising sailors. In fact, his books have been popular enough to spawn an entire genre. This book of mine is just the latest entry in the field. So you might well ask, "Why another one?"

The answer is that, although many of the skills required to sail a boat are the same today as they were fifty years ago when Hiscock first started writing, the boats in which today's sailing is done are a far cry from those of Hiscock's day, as indeed is the equipment used to sail, pilot, and navigate them. It is this, I feel, that makes another stab at the subject worthwhile.

As irresponsible as it was, Terrie, I, and our landlubberly crew could set off with nothing more than a basic understanding of how to sail a boat, and still successfully cruise around northern Europe (we did, however, get run down by a freighter on the way home, but that's another story . . .). We simply could not have done it in most modern boats.

So my hope is that I can demystify the desirable attributes of modern cruising boats, walk the reader through modern cruising systems and equipment, and summarize those skills that we have found necessary or useful to happily cruise for the past thirty years.

My qualifications for writing such a book include decades of experience with the technical side of cruising, an appreciation of the benefits of the best of modern technology, and years of family cruising. Even so, despite the fact that Terrie and I have many miles of blue-water passagemaking behind us, I need to acknowledge that we are no great sailors. Terrie gets very seasick, and I chum the water from time to time. In common with most of the people who read this book, we have never crossed an ocean—and maybe never will. The longest open-water passage we have made is 600 miles—across the Gulf of Mexico—although we have now done this eighteen times, often in midwinter in unpleasant conditions. As cruisers, we are fairly typical of mainstream or "wanna-be" cruisers—I believe I am coming from the same place most of my readers would like to be!

In writing this book, I have tried to be as objective as I know how but, inevitably, this is a more subjective book than *Boatowner's Mechanical and Electrical Manual* and my other technical books. When it comes to stripping down a winch or overhauling a toilet, there is essentially a right way and the wrong ways. However, when it comes to determining a suitable keel configuration for a cruising boat, there is a range of choices, all of which may be right in different circumstances.

I make no attempt to explore all of the options—the book would be too unwieldy and, in any case, I don't have the knowledge base. Instead, I frequently resort to explaining my choices and the reasons for them, and then leave it to you, the reader, to bounce your own ideas off the (I hope, coherent) framework provided.

In short, what follows is a potpourri of both objective and subjective information distilled over three decades of fooling around in and ruminating about cruising boats. This information has worked for Terrie and me. I hope it works as well for you and, in the process, helps you to have as much fun as we have had.

Nigel Calder
Alna, Maine
April 2001

ACKNOWLEDGMENTS

This book was an enormous project. I never could have completed it without a lot of help from numerous people. In particular, I want to express special thanks to naval architect Jay Paris, who read the first half of the manuscript (much of it several times) and made innumerable valuable suggestions; and to Jon Eaton, Molly Mulhern, Constance Burt, D. A. Oliver, Janet Robbins, and the production crew at International Marine for doing their usual superb job, as well as being a pleasure to work with at all times. The excellent line drawings are by Jim Sollers.

Patience Wales at *Sail* magazine, George Day at *Blue Water Sailing*, and Chuck Hawley of West Marine also read the manuscript and made many suggestions for improvements.

John (Jake) Crump, our buddy and perennial crew member from the United Kingdom, spent several weeks helping me create the artwork for the book, including being hosed down by the children (for foul-weather-gear shots) and put through all kinds of contortions. As usual, he never lost his sense of humor.

Numerous boatbuilders contributed information and artwork, specifically Newport R&D (the Alerion Express), Bavaria Yachts, Beneteau USA, Cabo Rico, Caliber Yachts, Catalina, Hallberg-Rassy, Hunter Marine, Island Packet, J-Boats, Malö, Northshore Marine (Vancouver), Oyster Yachts, Pacific Seacraft, Rival-Bowman, Royal Passport, Sabre Yachts, and Saga Yachts. Special thanks are due to Bill Bolan (Island Packet), Les Davies (Rival-Bowman), Garry Hoyt (Newport R&D), Don Kohlmann (Pacific Seacraft), Allan Poole (Saga Yachts), Magnus Rassy (Hallberg-Rassy), Ann Stirlen (Cabo Rico), Rachel Sweeney (Beneteau USA), and Liz Whitman (Oyster Yachts).

A number of naval architects supplied me with helpful information, notably Dave Gerr (who gave permission to use several tables and graphs from his excellent books), David Cooper, Bill Crealock, Bob Johnson, Hans Leander, Chuck Paine, Bob Perry, and Carl Schumacher.

Kathy Weishampel of Harken USA provided some dynamite illustrations, as did photographer Patrick Roach. Other illustrations came from Kevin Alston (Glacier Bay), Avon Marine, Jenifer Clark (Jenifer Clark's Gulfstream Analysis), Kim Dowling, Bill Drake (Marinco), Bill Full, Arild Jensen (Statpower), Andy Kruse (SW Wind-power), Peter O'Connell (Navtec), Paratech Anchor, Everett Pearson (TPI), James Rhodes (for Taylor Made Environmental), Timothy Rulon and John Vogel (NOAA), Donald Scott (Scott Boomlock), Tim Seymour, Spurs Marine, Martin Van Breems (Dutchman Boombrake), and Heidi Rabel.

Additional help or input came from Bob Adriance (BoatU.S.), Keith Buzzel (Yale Cordage), Jim Dodez (KVH), G. P. Foster (the Cordage Institute), Tom Hale of the American Boat and Yacht Council (ABYC), and John Kibbee (New England Ropes).

Several cruising sailors in the Bahamas and elsewhere tolerated me putting them through various cruising routines while I shot roll after roll of film, including John and Barbara Gayford on *Island Way*, and Rod and Joan Kennan on *Columbine*. But first and foremost is the Rublee family on *Southern Cross*—Mark, Jamie, Ethan, Joelle, and Madeline—who have star billing at numerous points in this book. With great good humor, they ran aground, kedged off, dragged anchors, set and took down sails, and even posed on the toilet! We had a wonderful time cruising in company with them and look forward to doing it again soon.

Some of the material in this book has been adapted from my articles published in *Sail* magazine, *Ocean Navigator*, *Professional Boatbuilder*, and *Yachting Monthly*. Beth Leonard and *Sail* kindly gave me permission to quote extensively from her article published in the August 2000 issue.

There are many others who contributed in innumerable ways. I know I have overlooked some that I should specifically thank—my apologies.

Finally, and above all, there are Terrie and our children—Pippin and Paul. The only way I know to process the huge amount of information assembled for this book is to immerse myself in the project, twelve to sixteen hours a day, seven days a week, sometimes for months on end. For a significant part of the last two years, despite having an office in our house and sometimes never leaving the property for weeks at a time, they have seen little of me. They almost never complain. I believe they know they are the most wonderful family in the world.

Chapter epigraphs are reprinted with permission as follows:

Page 2, quote by Bill Shaw, in *Desirable and Undesirable Characteristics of Offshore Yachts*, edited by John Rousmaniere. Courtesy of the Cruising Club of America.

Page 2, quote by Dave Gerr, *The Nature of Boats*. Camden, ME: International Marine, page 124.

Pages 116 and 195, quotes by Eric Hiscock, *Cruising under Sail*, published by International Marine.

Page 155, quote by Bob Griffith, *Blue Water*, published by Sail Books, pages 70 and 71.

Page 237, quotes by Olin Stephens in *Desirable and Undesirable Characteristics of Offshore Yachts*, edited by John Rousmaniere. Courtesy of the Cruising Club of America.

Page 237, quote by David Thomas, in *The Complete Offshore Yacht*. Courtesy of *Yachting Monthly*.

Page 237, quote by John Neal, notable sailor and educator.

INTRODUCTION

When Terrie and I first started cruising, the cruising community was quite small, the boats were relatively small, the boat systems were rudimentary, and most cruisers were operating on a shoestring budget. In the past several decades not only has there been an explosion in the number of cruisers, but the average size of the boats has steadily increased, the complexity of these boats has risen dramatically, and the disposable income of the people sailing them has increased substantially.

The net result is that while the core values that people seek through cruising remain fundamentally unchanged, the mechanism for finding these values and the kind of lifestyle associated with cruising have changed radically. There has been a considerable shift from an emphasis on self-sufficiency in simple boats to a dependence on a complex web of systems, many of which rely on elements external to the boat (e.g., global positioning systems [GPS], satellite-based communications systems, and emergency position-indicating radio beacons [EPIRBs]).

An unfortunate side effect of these changes is that the ante has been substantially raised on the entry-level skills required to get into cruising. It is noteworthy that many of these skills have little to do with sailing and, in fact, are primarily concerned with keeping lifestyle-related systems functional.

This book is not about the core values that underlie cruising—they are presupposed. Nor is it about lifestyle issues—there are many other books and publications covering these matters. Instead, this book is designed to provide an understanding of what kinds of boats and boat systems will meet today's cruising aspirations, and to explain the skills necessary to cruise successfully in those boats. Insofar as it meets these objectives, this book should enable those who want to go cruising to "ante up" in today's cruising world.

To meet the objectives, the first half of the book concentrates on the practical—and quite technical—matters that are increasingly important in selecting and setting up a boat for cruising, including the following:

- numeric parameters that help determine a monohull boat's suitability for cruising (I have no experience with multihulls and so am not qualified to make judgments about them; this is the only part of the book that is monohull-specific)
- factors influencing workable deck and interior layouts and organization
- the suitability of different boat systems in cruising applications
- how these systems should be installed to ensure long-term, trouble-free operation
- ultimately, criteria for determining whether a given boat will meet the needs that arise out of specific cruising aspirations

The second half of the book focuses on the skills necessary for successful cruising, whether coastal or offshore, including

- boat-handling skills
- core navigational expertise
- anchoring and associated techniques
- understanding weather and dealing with heavy weather
- specific issues associated with long-term and long-distance cruising

In short, this book is a primer covering the technical and practical side of modern cruising boats, and the skills necessary to safely and enjoyably sail them. I have written it to be complementary to *Boatowner's Mechanical and Electrical Manual*, which deals with the maintenance side of these boats (there is minor overlap on systems issues). My hope is that it proves useful to various people:

- prospective coastal and offshore boat buyers
- those contemplating cruising, whether coastal or world-girdling

- naval architects, boatbuilders, surveyors, and other marine professionals: there are many ideas, refined through years of cruising experience, that may help improve boats, maximize customer satisfaction, and minimize disappointment

I hope this book has sufficient depth to be of interest to experienced cruisers; I probably learned as much researching and writing it as my readers will learn reading it!

However, before getting into the nitty-gritty, a couple of general observations need to be made. The first is that the kinds of boat systems most people hanker after these days do not come cheap. In addition, the expectations that people now bring with them to cruising have not only tremendously upped the entry cost, but also have upped the entry-level skills required to operate and maintain a boat. *None of this is necessary.* The Hiscocks circled the globe several times in boats with systems and amenities that would be considered simply unacceptable by many cruisers today; nevertheless, they did it, and had a wonderful life in the process.

Despite the fact that I make my living writing about the technical side of boating, Terrie and I know from personal experience how little it takes to cruise and to enjoy it. *If you are just getting started with only a limited budget, it is a profound mistake to set your sights too high on the boat and systems side. It is much better to focus on a simple, seaworthy boat and rig; to go out and have fun; and to learn through experience along the way.* When you can afford it, buy a new boat and load it up with gadgets.

Even today, we still see couples cruising into far-flung anchorages on lovely, seaworthy older boats that have minimal systems, with the whole package costing, maybe, $10,000 to $20,000. The nature of this book is such that I look at all the systems and complexities with which many modern cruising sailors customize their boats; however, this should not lead you to lose sight of the big picture: *if you can't afford this level of sophistication, then don't sweat it—enjoy what you can afford.*

The second point that should be made is that even if you can afford all the toys, it must always be remembered that the one given about any system—especially an electrical system—is that it may fail catastrophically. In theory, what distinguishes a sailboat from a powerboat is its ability to keep going with nothing but the wind as its motive power; things need to be kept this way. The farther offshore it is intended to take a boat, the more important it is to ensure that nothing compromises this basic capability. In particular, whatever powered sail-handling devices are installed, it should always be possible to raise and lower, and reef and trim, sails by hand, and there should be both the tools and the knowledge to navigate without electricity and electronics.

To enjoy cruising, there should also be a state of mind that says, "No matter how much we paid for our systems toys, and no matter how much we enjoy the benefits they bring, we can still do without them." Too many cruisers spend too much time and money in far-flung corners of "paradise" chasing parts and labor to fix nonessential equipment and, in the process, undermining the quality of the lifestyle they have adopted, as well as unwittingly assaulting the core values that underlie this lifestyle.

To get the most from cruising, you need to have a clear picture of what it is you are looking for when you go cruising and what your lifestyle expectations are. Once you have these two in mind, this book should help you to choose a boat that meets your aspirations; to determine the level of complexity with which you are comfortable when fitting out that boat; and, at this level of complexity, to see that the systems are set up to function in a trouble-free fashion. Given such a boat, this book then helps you to develop the skills necessary to sail it safely, responsibly, and happily. Beyond that, it is up to you!

PART 1
THE BOAT

When the going gets tough, it's essential to have a boat that will comfortably handle the conditions. (Ladd 53 Scorpio yacht; Patrick Parsons photo, courtesy Harken)

CHAPTER ONE

A BOAT FOR CRUISING

"The classic specifications for the design of a good cruising boat contain the elements of ease of handling, crew safety, good steering control, balance, ample stability, speed, and accommodations that are both functional and comfortable."

BILL SHAW, YACHT DESIGNER, IN *Desirable and Undesirable Characteristics of Offshore Yachts*

"If comfortable motion is at all important to you, you ought to consider some of the 'heavier' and more traditional designs on the market."

DAVE GERR, YACHT DESIGNER, *The Nature of Boats*

"You can survive bad weather with sailing skills in an otherwise unsuitable vessel, but you have a much better chance of coming through in one piece if the yacht herself is capable of coping alone."

A *Yachting World* READER IN A LETTER TO THE EDITOR, OCTOBER 1999

This book is about cruising boats and the skills needed to sail them. As such, it makes sense to begin by determining the fundamental design features that result in a suitable boat, perhaps even an ideal boat, for cruising. But this is much easier said than done, inasmuch as there are a large number of factors to be considered, many of them contradictory.

Every boat is the result of a series of compromises that differ according to the priorities of the decision-maker. At one extreme, performance under sail may be the overriding concern; at another, gunkholing in shallow anchorages may be the primary interest. These differing priorities should result in very different boats (if the yacht designer does his or her job).

In trying to illuminate the options facing cruisers, the best I can do is outline some of the key issues, illustrating them by explaining the logic behind the choices that Terrie, my wife, and I made when we decided to buy and partially customize our present boat. In the process, I look at a number of commonly quoted or easily calculated nondimensional parameters (i.e., valid for comparisons of boats of different sizes) that can be applied to any boat, and explain how they can be used to help make informed decisions. I hope that a reader with different priorities than ours can use my presentation and these parameters to extrapolate the information and concepts necessary to refine his or her own thinking.

It is important when reading this and other chapters relating to boat design and systems (chapters 1 through 5) to remember that my focus tends to be on the ocean-cruising end of the spectrum. Moreover, Terrie and I have certain limitations: Terrie gets very seasick, while I have a bad back; we sail short-handed; and we have done most of our cruising with young children on board. We need a boat that is easy to handle, is comfortable in a seaway, can take care of itself for long periods of time, and is forgiving enough to take a sudden squall in stride without getting knocked flat or creating a dangerous situation. In essence, if you do what Terrie and I did, you will end up with a boat optimized for a particular kind of world cruising. This introduces a certain "spin" that leads to a certain kind of boat and is far more demanding on boats, equipment, and systems than are the needs of weekend and coastal cruisers. It also significantly drives up the cost and complexity of boats to a level that puts them beyond the reach of most sailors.

It is not my intention to drive people out of sailing—quite the opposite! In using what is in many ways from a design perspective a "worst-case" scenario, my intention is to bring into focus the complex issues surrounding the selection of a boat for less demanding applications.

I hope I haven't presented my prescriptions as dogma. I want my readers to get enough of a handle on these parameters to put their own spin on them and, in so doing, to define the kind of boat that best fits their own cruising plans, needs, and budget. The various graphs and tables in this chapter are presented in such a way that you can enter the numbers for any boat and then draw broad conclusions about its suitability for use from a weekend cruiser-racer to a long-term offshore cruiser.

BASIC DESIGN PARAMETERS

Almost all cruising boats, including world-girdling boats, spend the majority of time either anchored out, on a mooring, or secured to a dock. At such times, the boat is little more than a floating condominium. It is natural to want to make it as comfortable a floating home as possible. This requires space and, as a result, yacht designers and boatbuilders are always under pressure to create as much volume as possible in any given design.

Volume nowadays typically translates into a wide beam, carried as far aft as possible, with high freeboard. The boatowner will sometimes want to take this floating home into relatively shoal anchorages, which requires a shallow draft. To get a beamy boat with little draft, the boat must have a flat bottom.

Although this boat will probably not spend much of its life at sea, the boatbuilder and boatowner are still going to want it to perform reasonably well. A couple of keys to maximizing performance are keeping the overall weight (and thus the displacement) as low as possible (lightweight construction), and minimizing wetted surface area by using the least keel area necessary to achieve reasonable upwind performance (a *fin keel*), together with the smallest rudder size and supporting structure needed to maintain control (a smallish *spade rudder*).

The kind of boat taking shape should be familiar; it is seen at every major boat show. There is nothing wrong with this boat; it is built to fit a certain formula that is market-driven and,

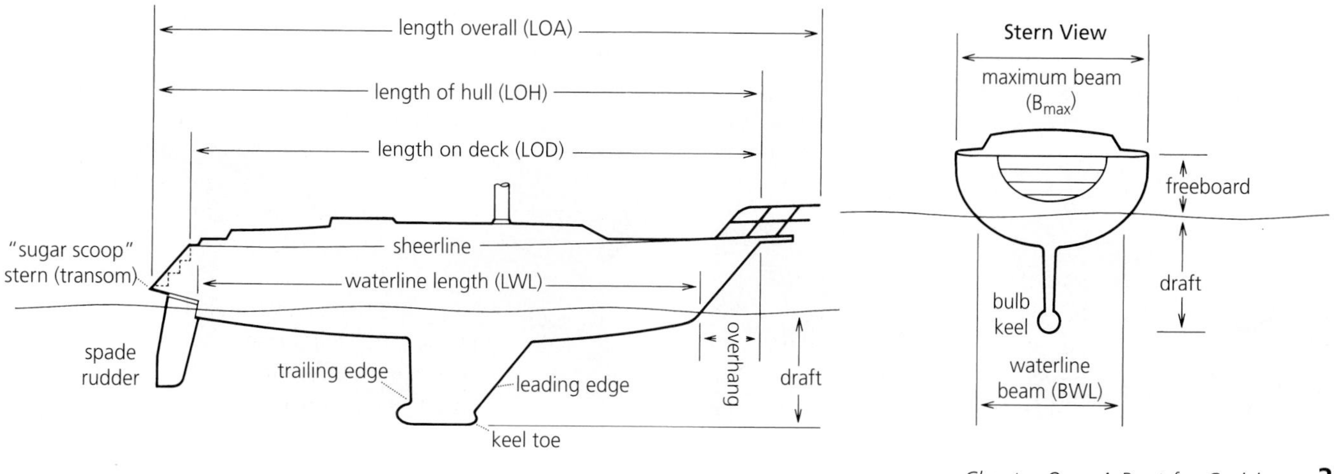

Boat terminology.

by and large, it does an excellent job of fitting this formula.

When it comes to cruising boats—indeed, any boat that may be used offshore—we have to add at least one more criterion to the mix: the ability to safely deliver the crew—with all its stores and belongings—to its chosen destination in the worst conditions that might be encountered, at an acceptable speed, and with as little discomfort as possible.

Among other things, this translates into a boat that is reasonably fast but with an easy motion at sea (a *seakindly* boat), that tracks well and has a light helm, that is *stiff* enough to carry sufficient sail area to keep moving to windward in heavy weather, and that has—in an extreme situation—the ability to claw off a lee shore under sail alone in heavy seas and gale-force winds. It must, of course, be built strongly enough to survive the gale.

Length–Beam Ratio

Just about any boat can be pushed to windward in smooth water, but when things start to get rough, it requires a lot more power to counteract the boat's windage and motion. Power requires sail area. Sail area requires a stiff boat; that is, one that resists *heeling*: all the sail area in the world won't do any good if the boat rolls over and lies on its side!

One way to achieve stiffness is to increase *beam*. As the boat heels, the immersed volume shifts rapidly to leeward, keeping the boat more or less upright; this is known as *form stability*.

A lightweight, beamy boat generally has excellent form stability. However, when the going gets tough, the wide flat sections, combined with the relatively light weight, are not only likely to make it pound and roll uncomfortably—as Dave Gerr writes in *The Nature of Boats*, "light boats with high initial stability simply must have a vicious, snappy roll"—but also will tend to cause its keel to stall out. If the boat has a relatively shallow draft and minimal lateral surface area in the keel and rudder, it will offer little resistance to making leeway as it stalls out. If it also has high freeboard, the windage will simply exacerbate problems.

In other words, many of those features designed to improve comfort at the dock or on the hook and to ensure a sprightly performance in relatively protected waters can become a handicap. A less extreme design approach is needed. The first thing is to reconsider the wide beam, a point reinforced by yacht designer Chuck Paine, who had this to say: "Naval architects have known for centuries that a given bulk can be most easily driven across the interface of sea and sky if it is stretched into the longest, most sharp-ended shape possible" (*Yachting Monthly*, U.K., Jan. 1996).

Yacht designer Bob Perry concurs: "All else being equal, the skinnier boat will be the better boat. Narrow boats are easier to push through the water. . . . The narrow boat is an easier boat to balance, and therefore will have better manners under sail" (*Blue Water Sailing*, Sept. 1998).

The *beaminess* of a boat can be quantified by calculating its *length–beam ratio* (LBR), a number obtained by dividing the length by the beam. Often the *length overall* (LOA)—in this case, it should not include a protruding bow pulpit—and the *maximum beam* (B_{max}) are used, although I prefer to use the *waterline length* (LWL) and *waterline beam* (BWL).

$$LBR = \frac{LOH}{B_{max}} \text{ or } \frac{LWL}{BWL}$$

The two different formulas produce quite different values; therefore, when comparing

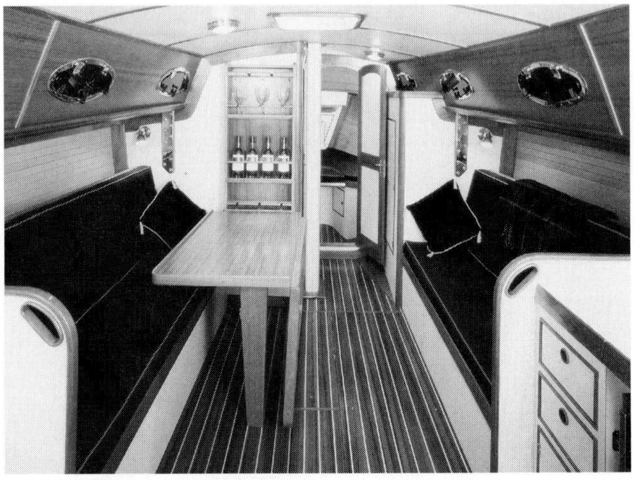

Two very different approaches to beam, interior volume, and other design parameters. Both boats are 38 feet in length, but that's about all they have in common. (Left, courtesy Hunter Marine; right, Billy Black photo, courtesy Newport R&D)

boats, it is essential to use the same methodology to derive the numbers.

For example, our present boat—a Pacific Seacraft 40—has an LOH (excluding the bow pulpit) of 40.33 feet (12.28 m) and a B_{max} of 12.42 feet (3.78 m), giving a length–beam ratio using these numbers of

$$40.33 \div 12.42 = 3.25$$

(Note that the inverse ratio is sometimes given by dividing the beam by the length, in which case we get a *beam–length ratio* of $12.42 \div 40.33 = 0.308$.) However, if we use the LWL (31.25 ft./9.52 m) and BWL (11.33 ft./3.45 m), we get a *waterline length–beam ratio* of

$$31.25 \div 11.33 = 2.76$$

As mentioned previously, for comparison purposes, it is preferable to use the LWL and BWL to derive a length–beam ratio; however, although the LWL is commonly published, the waterline beam is almost never published. As a result, yacht designer Roger Marshall suggests in *The Complete Guide to Choosing a Cruising Sailboat* that a way to use available data is to work with the LWL and ($B_{max} \times 0.9$), which approximates the BWL on many boats. (However, on a range of boats that I looked at, this factor varied from as low as 0.75 to as high as 1.00, so it is a fairly crude approximation.) When we apply these numbers to the Pacific Seacraft 40, we get

$$LWL \div (B_{max} \times 0.9) = 31.25 \div (12.42 \times 0.9) = 2.80$$

This is close to the actual waterline length–beam ratio (2.76).

Lower length–beam ratios indicate proportionately more beam, higher ratios indicate less beam. A *higher ratio is desirable both in terms of windward performance in difficult conditions and as an indicator of handling characteristics and seakindly behavior.*

However, this is not the whole picture. Beam affects stability on a *cubic* basis; that is, *any increase in beam has a disproportionate effect on stability*. If the length–beam ratio is kept constant as length increases, the increase in beam needed to maintain a constant ratio produces a disproportionate increase in stability. For example, a 36-foot (10.96 m) LWL boat with a 3:1 ratio will have a 12-foot (3.65 m)

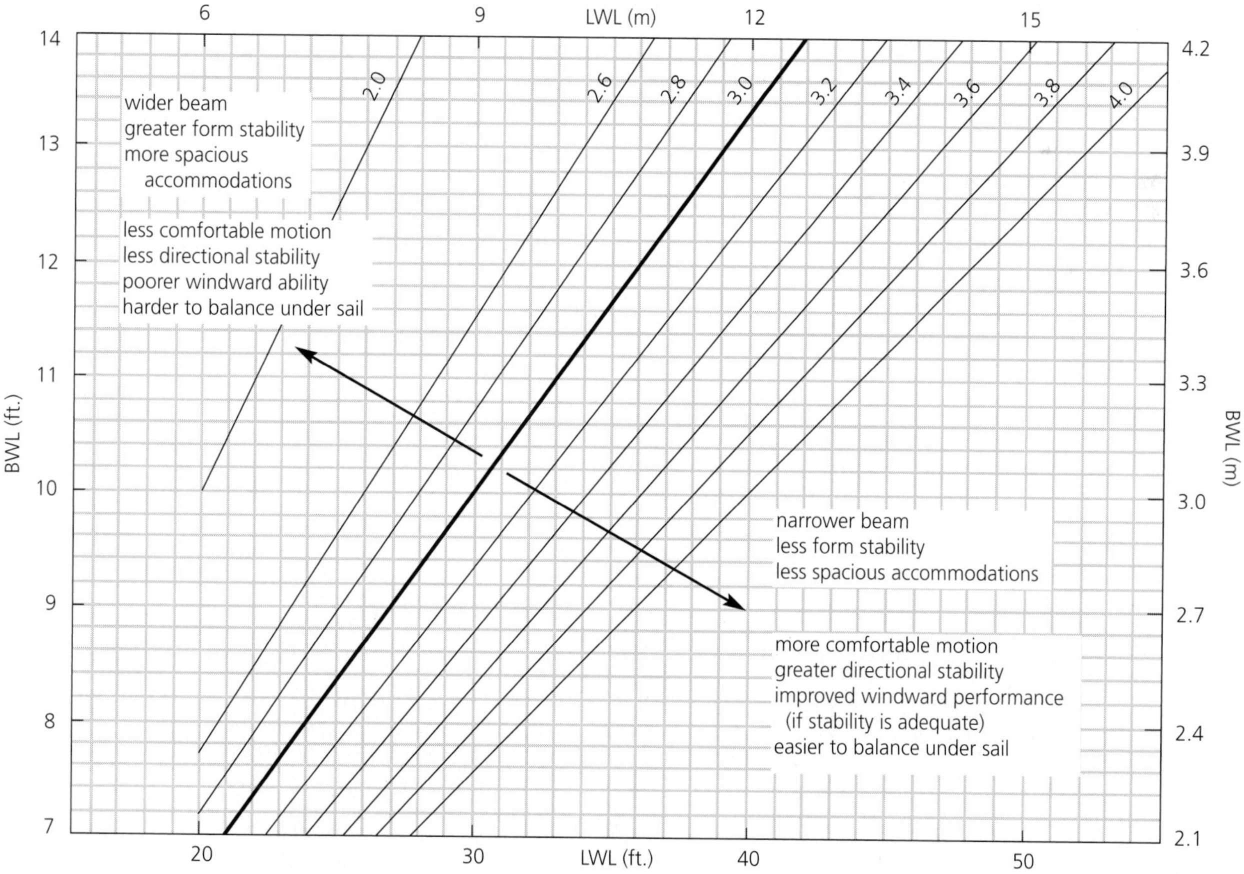

Waterline Length–Beam Ratios. To derive the length–beam ratio, enter the graph with the LWL and BWL. This graph can also be used with length of hull (LOH) and maximum beam (B_{max}) to derive the length–beam ratio commonly used in published literature.

Summarizing Table of Key Parameters of a Selection of Contemporary U.S.

	BOAT DATA											
Boat	LOH, ft.	LWL, ft.	B_{max}, ft.	BWL, ft.	LWL/BWL	Draft, ft.	Ballast, lb.	SA, sq. ft.	WPA, sq. ft.	Displ., lb.	LPI, lb.	LSW
Alerion Express 38	38.42	30.08	10.83	9.75	**3.09**	**5.83**	4,200	690	205	12,400	1,094	10,535
Bavaria 38	38.10	32.30	13.00	11.70	2.76	6.10	5,500	676	265	16,097	1,410	16,097
Bavaria 42	42.50	36.60	13.00	11.70	**3.13**	6.40	6,820	821	300	18,523	1,598	19,580
Beneteau 381	37.80	32.83	12.92	11.63	2.82	**5.33**	4,740	585	267	14,991	1,424	14,991
Beneteau 411	40.40	36.92	13.00	11.70	**3.16**	**5.58**	5,500	697	302	17,196	1,612	17,934
Bowman 42	41.40	32.17	12.58	11.32	2.84	**5.75**	6,900	796	255	21,469	1,359	21,570
Cabo Rico 38	38.00	29.25	11.50	10.35	2.83	**5.00**	7,800	778	212	21,000	1,130	21,000
Cabo Rico 40	40.60	32.17	12.67	11.40	2.82	**5.25**	10,400	909	257	26,800	1,369	26,800
Caliber 40LRC	39.10	32.50	12.66	11.39	2.85	**5.08**	9,500	739	259	21,600	1,382	21,600
Catalina 400 MK II	40.50	36.50	13.50	12.15	**3.00**	6.75	7,250	800	310	19,700	1,655	19,700
Catalina 42 Mk II	41.80	36.00	13.83	12.45	2.89	**6.00**	8,300	796	314	20,500	1,672	20,500
Halberg-Rassy 39	40.10	32.34	12.35	11.12	2.91	6.07	8,400	809	252	22,050	1,341	20,000
Hunter 380	37.10	32.00	12.58	11.32	2.83	6.50	5,400	739	254	15,000	1,352	15,000
Hunter 420	42.50	37.83	13.83	12.45	**3.04**	**4.92**	7,400	825	330	20,200	1,757	20,200
Island Packet 380	37.80	32.00	13.17	11.85	2.70	**4.58**	9,000	756	266	21,000	1,415	22,000
Island Packet 40	39.30	34.00	12.92	11.63	2.92	**4.67**	10,000	774	277	22,800	1,475	22,800
J-42	42.00	35.58	12.17	10.95	**3.25**	6.50	7,000	872	273	19,700	1,454	18,312
Malö 39	39.40	31.68	12.35	11.12	2.85	**5.91**	7,700	750	246	19,404	1,314	19,580
Malö 42	42.10	34.80	13.10	11.79	2.95	6.40	12,100	960	287	29,767	1,531	30,360
Oyster 42	41.80	33.75	12.83	11.55	2.92	**6.00**	8,090	786	273	26,600	1,454	24,660
Pacific Seacraft 40	40.33	31.25	12.42	11.18	2.80	6.08	8,600	846	245	24,000	1,303	22,800
Royal Passport 41	39.50	33.58	12.67	11.40	2.94	**5.75**	8,536	851	268	22,690	1,429	22,690
Sabre 402	40.20	34.00	13.33	12.00	2.83	7.33	7,240	822	286	18,500	1,522	19,500
Saga 43	43.30	38.92	12.00	10.80	**3.60**	6.25	7,800	952	294	20,000	1,568	20,000
Starlight 39	39.33	31.75	12.50	11.25	2.82	6.83	7,119	749	250	19,749	1,333	19,749
Sweden Yachts 390	39.00	31.52	12.71	11.44	2.76	7.39	6,930	841	252	16,800	1,345	16,800
Vancouver 38	38.00	30.50	12.00	10.80	2.82	**5.58**	8,198	680	231	22,378	1,229	22,378
Average	40.01	33.44	12.68	11.41	2.93	5.92	7,645	789	268	20,404	1,427	20,264

Note: All boat data are as supplied by the boat manufacturers.

LOH = Length of Hull
LWL = Length at Waterline (Waterline Length)
B_{max} = Maximum Beam
BWL = Approximate Waterline Beam calculated as ($B_{max} \times 0.9$)
SA = Sail Area
WPA = Approximate Waterplane Area calculated assuming BWL = ($B_{max} \times 0.9$)
Displ.= Published Nominal Displacement
LPI = Pounds Per Inch Immersion using Approximate Waterplane Area
LSW = Light Ship Weight

LPS or AVS = Limit of Positive Stability or Angle of Vanishing Stability, as calculated by:
ISO = International Standards Organization
IMS = International Measurement System
O = Other
STIX = ISO Stability Index
DLR = Displacement–Length Ratio
BDR = Ballast–Displacement Ratio
SADR = Sail Area–Displacement Ratio
PIN/LSW = Personal Increment Number as a decimal fraction of Light-Ship Weight

and European Boats between 38 and 42 Feet in Length

				CALCULATED PARAMETERS											
				Displ. A = LSW + 2,500 lb.				Displ. B = LSW + 3,750 lb.				Displ. C = LSW + 5,000 lb.			
Capsize Screening Value	LPS or AVS	LPS or AVS Method	STIX Number	DLR	BDR	SADR	PIN/LSW	DLR	BDR	SADR	PIN/LSW	DLR	BDR	SADR	PIN/LSW
1.98	***123***	IMS		214	***0.32***	19.9	0.24	234	0.29	18.7	0.36	***255***	0.27	***17.7***	0.47
2.06	118	ISO		246	***0.30***	***15.4***	***0.16***	***263***	0.28	14.7	0.23	***279***	0.26	14.1	0.31
1.93	***131***	ISO		201	***0.31***	***16.7***	***0.13***	212	0.29	***16.1***	***0.19***	224	0.28	***15.5***	0.26
2.10			37.9	221	0.27	13.9	***0.17***	236	0.25	13.2	0.25	***252***	0.24	12.7	0.33
1.99			37.0	181	0.27	14.9	***0.14***	192	0.25	14.3	0.21	203	0.24	13.8	0.28
1.81	***135***	ISO	40.1	***323***	0.29	***15.2***	***0.12***	***340***	0.27	14.7	***0.17***	***356***	0.26	14.3	0.23
1.67				419	***0.33***	***15.1***	***0.12***	442	***0.32***	14.6	***0.18***	464	***0.30***	14.2	0.24
1.70	***135***	O		***393***	***0.35***	***15.3***	***0.09***	410	***0.34***	14.9	***0.14***	426	***0.33***	14.5	***0.19***
1.82	***138***	O		***313***	***0.39***	14.1	***0.12***	***330***	***0.37***	13.7	***0.17***	***346***	***0.36***	13.2	0.23
2.00	111	ISO	42.0	204	***0.33***	***16.2***	***0.13***	215	***0.31***	***15.6***	***0.19***	227	0.29	***15.1***	0.25
2.03	114	ISO		220	***0.36***	***15.7***	***0.12***	232	***0.34***	***15.2***	***0.18***	244	***0.33***	14.7	0.24
1.82	***122***	ISO		***297***	***0.37***	***16.2***	***0.13***	***313***	***0.35***	***15.6***	***0.19***	***330***	***0.34***	***15.1***	0.25
2.04	***126***	O		238	***0.31***	***17.5***	***0.17***	***255***	0.29	***16.7***	0.25	***272***	0.27	***16.0***	0.33
2.04	***127***	O		187	***0.33***	***16.4***	***0.12***	197	***0.31***	***15.9***	***0.19***	208	0.29	***15.3***	0.25
1.88	***136***	O		***334***	***0.37***	14.3	***0.11***	***351***	***0.35***	13.8	***0.17***	***368***	***0.33***	13.4	0.23
1.83	***143***	O		***287***	***0.40***	14.3	***0.11***	***302***	***0.38***	13.9	***0.16***	***316***	***0.36***	13.5	0.22
1.85	***133***	IMS		206	***0.34***	18.4	***0.14***	219	***0.32***	***17.7***	***0.20***	231	***0.30***	***17.1***	0.27
1.84	***134***	ISO	46.2	***310***	***0.35***	***15.2***	***0.13***	328	***0.33***	14.7	***0.19***	***345***	***0.31***	14.2	0.26
1.68	***132***	ISO	***57.4***	***348***	***0.37***	14.9	0.08	***361***	***0.35***	14.6	***0.12***	***375***	***0.34***	14.2	***0.16***
1.77	***140***	O		***315***	***0.30***	13.9	***0.10***	***330***	0.28	13.5	***0.15***	***344***	0.27	13.1	***0.20***
1.76	***143***	O		***370***	***0.34***	***15.7***	***0.11***	***388***	***0.32***	***15.2***	***0.16***	407	***0.31***	14.7	0.22
1.79	***128***	O		***297***	***0.34***	***15.8***	***0.11***	***312***	***0.32***	***15.3***	***0.17***	***326***	***0.31***	14.8	0.22
1.98	119	IMS		***250***	***0.33***	***16.7***	***0.13***	***264***	***0.31***	***16.1***	***0.19***	***278***	***0.30***	***15.6***	0.26
1.77	***123***	IMS		170	***0.35***	19.1	***0.13***	180	***0.33***	18.4	***0.19***	189	***0.31***	***17.8***	0.25
1.85	***138***	O	51.5	***310***	***0.32***	***15.1***	***0.13***	***328***	***0.30***	14.6	***0.19***	***345***	0.29	14.1	0.25
1.99	117	ISO		***275***	***0.36***	18.7	***0.15***	***293***	***0.34***	***17.9***	0.22	***311***	***0.32***	***17.2***	0.30
1.71	***135***	O		***391***	***0.33***	12.7	***0.11***	411	***0.31***	12.3	***0.17***	431	***0.30***	12.0	0.22
1.88				279	0.33	15.8	0.13	294	0.32	15.3	0.19	309	0.30	14.7	0.26

Nigel Calder's recommended values for an approximately 40-foot (12 m) offshore cruiser (in bold italic above):

LWL/BWL = 3.00 or higher
draft = 6.0 ft. or less
DLR = 250–400
BDR = 0.30 or higher
SADR = 15.0–18.0
PIN/LSW = 0.20 or less
Capsize Screening Value = below 2.0
LPS = over 120
STIX # for a 40 ft. boat = over 40. (Note: STIX criteria subject to change)

For coastal cruising, you might want to shift these numbers in a higher performance direction, notably a lower DLR, higher SADR, higher capsize screening value, and lower LPS or AVS. For a racer-cruiser, you will likely want to do all these things, plus increase the draft and the BDR.

BWL, whereas a 48-foot (14.62 m) boat with the same ratio will have a 16-foot (4.87 m) beam; the 48-foot boat will be considerably stiffer, even though it has the same ratio.

This means that if two boats have the same length–beam ratios, the one with the longer waterline is likely to have greater stability and sail-carrying ability, and better performance to windward. Or, put another way, as length increases, the same relative sail-carrying ability can be maintained with a proportionately narrower beam and, therefore, a higher length–beam ratio. As a result, to improve stability and sail-carrying ability, shorter boats need proportionately more beam, resulting in lower length–beam ratios. Consequently, there is no absolute length–beam ratio "magic number" that can be used for comparing boats; length must also be considered: the shorter a boat's LWL, the lower its length–beam ratio is likely to be.

Nevertheless, in the kind of boat range under consideration (basically, 35–45 ft., or 10.7–13.7 m), for a comfortable offshore cruiser I like to see a waterline length–beam ratio of 3.00 or higher (using LWL ÷ [B_{max} × 0.9]). Shorter boats may have a lower ratio; longer boats should have a higher ratio. In a sampling of contemporary boats (see the summarizing table on pages 6–7), the only boat below 40-foot (12 m) LOA that has a ratio of more than 3.00 is the Alerion Express 38. At 40 feet and greater, many of those boats that follow the current fashion of short overhangs (which maximizes the LWL) have ratios of 3.0 and higher, whereas more traditional cruising boats, with longer overhangs, mostly do not. The Pacific Seacraft 40, for example, has a waterline length–beam ratio of 2.80. This is the price paid for its long overhangs combined with the beam needed to provide a more spacious interior, compared to cruising-boat designs of a generation ago.

Many older but nonetheless highly successful cruising boats in this same size range have waterline length–beam ratios of 3.0 and above (based on LWL ÷ [B_{max} × 0.9]). Steve Dashew, the designer of the Deerfoot and Sundeer series of boats, has taken the length–beam ratio to extremes. His boats commonly have ratios of 4:1, 5:1, and up. This is all to the good except that, because of the relatively narrow beam, the boat has to be longer and the costs start to soar for a reasonable interior volume. He writes in the second edition of the *Offshore Cruising Encyclopedia* that he and Linda, his wife and partner, decided to see how small a boat they could design that would contain their minimum requirements, as well as accommodating two guests for a week or two a year. They arrived at a 56-foot length! Unfortunately, however desirable, such a boat is beyond the budget of most cruisers—not only up front, but also in terms of mooring and dockage fees, gear-replacement costs, maintenance (e.g., more boat length to haul and bottom to paint), and so on.

Keel Types

A narrower beam results in less form stability, which can translate into greater heeling when on the wind. To counteract this tendency to heel, it is necessary to put a lot of weight down low. In its extreme form, this results in the 14-foot (4.26 m) fin keels, with massive lead bulbs, seen on some narrow racing boats.

Clearly, such a keel is not practical on a cruising boat, but the principle is the same—to get as much weight as possible as low as possible. How low is primarily a function of where it is intended to cruise. In general, a 6-foot (1.83 m) draft is acceptable, still allowing access to most of the world's finest cruising grounds. However, a boat specifically intended for cruising in the Bahamas or other areas with substantial areas of shoal water might be designed with less draft, whereas one intended for Pacific cruising might have a deeper draft. A cruiser-racer, with an emphasis on racing, is likely to exceed 6 feet, trading access to some cruising grounds for improved racing performance.

For a given draft, the use of a *bulb keel* keeps the weight as low as possible. A *wing keel* does the same, but needs to be carefully designed if it is not to foul lines and seaweed or get stuck in the mud in a grounding. A wing keel is shaped much like a Bruce anchor! Wing keels originated as a rule-beating device in the America's Cup, and have since become something of a fad. Despite their popularity, I doubt that any advantage over a bulb keel outweighs the significant disadvantages in a cruising environment. On our new boat, we chose a bulb keel with a draft of 5 feet, 2 inches (1.57 m) rather than the standard deep keel of 6 feet, 1 inch (1.85 m). We get a significantly reduced draft with a small loss of windward performance (and still run aground!).

The advent of bulb and wing keels has fairly settled the old debate about whether it is preferable to have internal or external ballast: the bulb or wing must be external (it is very difficult to mold them into fiberglass). Clearly, lead, with its great density, should always be used as the ballast material (as opposed to iron,

Left: *A modern wing keel. Although wing keels have performance benefits, they can be a distinct liability in a grounding.* Below: *A wing-keeled boat stuck on a coral reef. It proved extremely difficult to get off, and was ultimately rescued at the expense of the wings on the keel.*

which is sometimes used to save cost regardless of the fact that it only has a little more than 60 percent of the density of lead).

Displacement Calculations

Let's discuss various performance ratios that use displacement as one of the parameters. These ratios seem easy enough to calculate until you realize that although the single largest component of the displacement of a boat—the ballast weight—is a fixed number, the overall displacement is something of a moving target.

To be of most use, the displacement number used to determine these ratios should approximate the weight of the boat with all normal equipment and crew onboard, the tanks half filled, and the lockers half full of food and beverages (what you would expect to find about midway through a cruise). This is known as *half-load displacement* (HLD). In reality, boatbuilders use everything from this number to a "lightly loaded" formula (two people with no mention of "nonstandard" gear and equipment, minimal stores onboard, and tanks half full) to the construction weight of the boat with nothing onboard (the "dry weight" or *light-ship weight*), or even the designed weight (which is almost always exceeded during the building process, often by a substantial amount).

Our Pacific Seacraft 40's published displacement of 24,000 pounds (10,909 kg) has the boat loaded for light local sailing. This includes the tanks half full, with some gear and supplies onboard—that is, a nominal half-load displacement of a stock factory boat. The boat includes, for example, two Group 27 batteries, at approximately 100 pounds (45 kg) each. The total amp-hour capacity of the batteries is about 200 amp-hours, which is not enough for long-term cruising (for more on this, see A Balanced System in chapter 4). In reality, most owners upgrade the system to a minimum 400-amp-hour battery bank and usually add an inverter and other equipment. The weight escalates rapidly.

I performed a rough-weight audit on our boat and discovered that our heavy-duty DC system (a total of 700 amp-hours of battery capacity, two alternators, cabling, DC to AC inverter, wind generator, and solar panels) weighs in at approximately 800 pounds (364 kg), of which probably less than half is included in the manufacturer's published displacement. We also have between 400 and 500 pounds (182–227 kg) in ground tackle. The water tanks, when half full, weigh 700 pounds (318 kg), the diesel 200 pounds (91 kg). The dinghy and outboard, plus fuel, weigh 250 pounds (114 kg); the wind vane and autopilot 60 pounds (27 kg). This comes to about 2,500 pounds (1,136 kg)—much of which is found on any offshore cruising boat, all of which is added before the first crew member steps onboard, and less than half of which is included in the published displacement figure. Then there are all kinds of tools and spares.

Ground tackle on Nada. *This represents a lot of weight, most of it stored well forward.*

People weigh an average of 160 pounds (73 kg). Clothes, books, and gear (including dishes, cutlery, and galley utensils) weigh in at approximately 100 pounds (45 kg) per person. Food and beverages are about 6 pounds (2.7 kg) per person per day; that is, 200 pounds (91 kg) per person for a moderate cruising range. When these numbers are added to the weight of nonstandard equipment, the total added weight for a crew of four is soon up to approximately 4,000 pounds (1,818 kg). When I checked with Bill Crealock (the designer of the Pacific Seacraft 40), I found the total added weight in his "light local sailing" condition is 1,200 pounds (544 kg).

To be fair to Pacific Seacraft, most designers and manufacturers don't even attempt to approximate half-load displacement. Most published displacement figures are based on some form of light-ship weight (see the sidebar), which includes little more than the boat, and does not always include even such basic items as sails, minimum ground tackle, and legally required safety equipment. Too often, these numbers are derived from calculations made by the designer rather than from the actual build weight, which almost always exceeds the calculated weight (the longer a boat is in production, the more the weight tends to increase as upgrades and changes are made). In going beyond light-ship weight, manufacturers such as Pacific Seacraft are often stacking the deck against themselves in terms of making comparisons with other boats.

Recently, I saw a set of figures for a popular cruiser-racer that showed a listed displacement of 28,500 pounds (12,955 kg), an actual weight from the builder with a full set of cruising "options" of 34,500 pounds (15,682 kg), and a fully loaded weight of 39,500 pounds (17,955 kg)! Clearly, for coastal cruising these numbers are likely to be lower; nevertheless, the point remains the same: accurate displacement figures depend on a realistic assessment of weight.

With this is mind, for coastal cruising, a minimum of 2,500 pounds (1,136 kg) should be added to most published displacement figures to get a ballpark half-load displacement; for offshore cruising, 3,750 pounds (1,705 kg) should be added. Most long-term cruisers and liveaboards add *considerably* more weight than this (it would not be unreasonable to increase the coastal weight to 3,750 pounds and the offshore to 5,000 pounds—1,705 and 2,273 kg); weight-conscious cruiser-racers may add less. The Calculating a Personal Increment Number sidebar (page 13) explains how to refine these numbers. *(continued on page 14)*

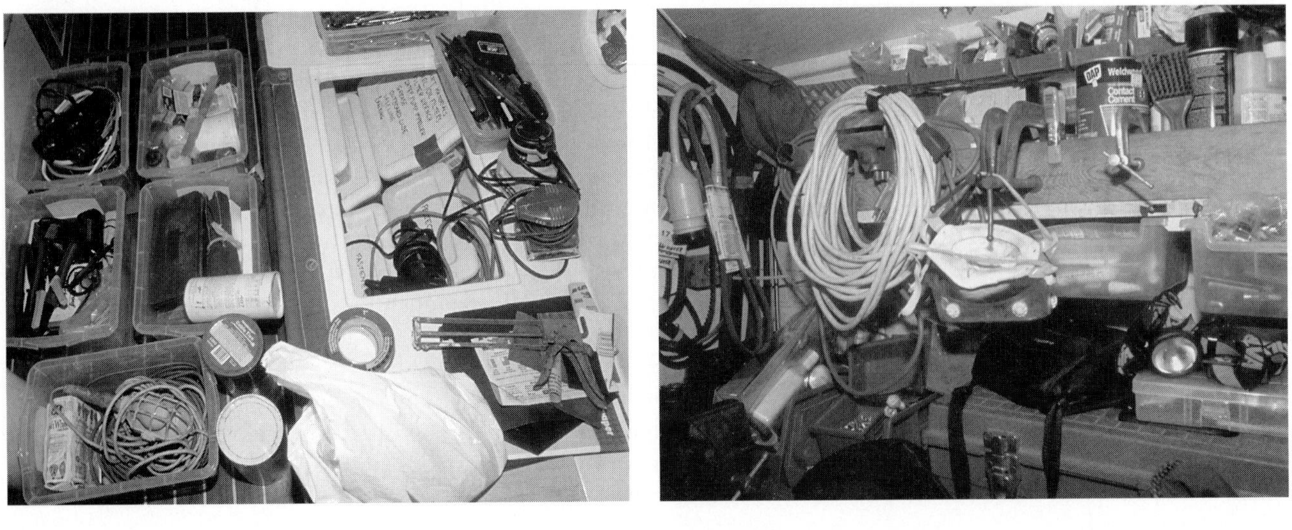

Left: *The tools and spare parts on* Nada. *Because the boat is new, we carry relatively few spares.* Right: *On an older boat you would expect to find many more spares!*

THE DISPLACEMENT MINEFIELD

In the text, I refer to two displacement conditions—light ship and half load. In reality, there are many more in use, *which makes all displacement-based parameters suspect as a basis for comparing boats*. Nevertheless, because of the emphasis on displacement-based performance parameters in boating literature, it is important to make the effort to derive the best possible ballpark figures.

Some manufacturers weigh their boats and obtain accurate numbers; others simply estimate the weight. Estimating is a process fraught with possible errors. I have spent many hours talking to designers and builders trying to nail down accurate numbers for some boats, and still have only marginal confidence in their answers. This is frustrating because it is not that difficult to derive the numbers. Once a boat has been launched, its displacement can be calculated fairly accurately by simply measuring how low it is floating in the water—its real-life draft rather than the designed draft—and then entering this measurement in a computerized lines plan with the appropriate software. An additional 5 percent should be included in the calculated weight of a new boat to allow for "weight growth" over time (e.g., water absorption by the hull).

In Europe, some standardization is occurring through the International Standards Organization (ISO, the European standards-setting body, whose standards form the basis for Recreational Craft Directives [RCDs]), inasmuch as there is a standard (ISO/DIS 8666:2:1999, "Small Craft—Principal Data") that defines displacement in essentially a light-ship condition (known as a *light-craft condition* [LCC]; it adds the weight of spars, rigging, and sails to the factory weight of the boat, although it generally does not include the weight of roller reefers, in-mast reefing, anything other than the basic sail plan, and any other nonstandard gear). When you see displacement numbers for European boats and U.S. boats that have been CE-certified, it is often the LCC that has been used. It likely may become something of an industry standard in the United States because it minimizes displacement and, as one boatbuilder wrote to me, "if we use any other loading condition . . . we will make our performance ratios look worse by comparison with our competitors."

There is another loading condition (*minimum-sailing condition* [MSC]) required in Europe for stability and Stability Index (STIX) calculations (explained later in this chapter). The MSC calculation includes the addition to the LCC of some basic gear, a life raft on offshore boats, and 165 pounds (75 kilograms) per crew member. It still does not include groceries and other supplies, and the tanks are all empty; therefore, it does not in any sense equate with a half-load condition.

Yet another loading condition is used by the International Measurement System (IMS), which replaced the former International Offshore Rule (IOR), to rate many contemporary racing boats. This condition, which is known as *displacement in measurement trim*, does not include the weight of most gear, sails, tankage, and crew. As best as I can determine, it is broadly comparable to the LCC used in Europe.

Where does this leave us when trying to compare one boat to another? It seems fair to assume that, unless stated to the contrary (e.g., in Pacific Seacraft's literature), published displacement is in some form of light-ship, light-craft, minimum-sailing, or measurement-trim condition. For example, in an article by yacht designer Jim Taylor in the July 2000 issue of *Sail* magazine, he describes a number of performance parameters that use displacement. Only in a footnote do you discover that he is using IMS measurement trim (i.e., not even any sails onboard) for displacement!

Although the differences among light-ship, light-craft, minimum-sailing, and measurement-trim conditions are of critical interest to racers, in terms of the kind of gear that will be added by most cruisers (coastal or offshore) and the ultimate half-load or full-load displacement of a cruising boat, they are not that significant and, to a considerable extent, can be ignored.

My own feeling is that for coastal cruising in a boat that will be relatively lightly equipped and provisioned, in most cases it is not unfair to arbitrarily add 2,500 pounds (1,136 kg) to the published displacement figures to get a more realistic half-load number. For offshore work, the published displacement number should be increased by 3,750 pounds (1,705 kg); for longer-term cruising, the published displacement can be increased by 3,750 pounds for coastal cruising and 5,000 pounds for offshore (1,705 and 2,273 kg). If it can be ascertained that the manufacturer has already included some of your payload in the published displacement figure, then whatever has been included can be considered when doing the addition.

Of course, these numbers have to be adjusted in light of the boat, the add-on equipment, and your cruising style. For example, Carl Schumacher was kind enough to share with me his calculations for the lovely Alerion Express 38. The published displacement of 10,250 pounds (4,659 kg) is based on IMS measurement trim, which includes two batteries and 275 pounds (125 kg) of ground tackle and basic safety equipment. His half-load calculation adds the following:

sails	120 lb. (54.55 kg)
dinghy	40 lb. (18.18 kg)
water (½ full—30 gal.)	259 lb. (117.73 kg)
fuel (½ full—12.5 gal.)	89 lb. (40.45 kg)
food (2 people)	40 lb. (18.18 kg)
gear (2 people)	100 lb. (45.45 kg)
books	+ 20 lb. (9.09 kg)
Total	668 lb. (303.64 kg)

(*continued next page*)

If the light-ship payload (275 lb./125 kg) is added to the half-load extras, we get 943 pounds (429 kg) for the total half-load payload. This is nowhere near the 2,500 or 3,750 pounds (1,136–1,705 kg) that I suggest should be added. The number reflects Carl's assumptions about the kind of use to which the boat will be put. If we add all kinds of bells and whistles and then load up the Alerion Express for an extended coastal or world cruise (which is not what he had in mind when he designed the boat), his numbers will have to be significantly adjusted.

Now contrast this with Jay Paris's calculations for the Paris 43 (see below), which is specifically designed for extended cruising. The light-ship weight includes shore power, hot and cold pressure water, and so on. Beyond this, his half-load payload adds 3,780 pounds (1,718 kg); his full-load payload adds 6,660 pounds (3,027 kg). These numbers reflect a fairly accurate payload in world-girdling cruising trim.

Paris 43: An Example of a Realistic Displacement Calculation (Courtesy Jay Paris)

Light-Ship Weight, lb. (kg)	
hull	2,950 (1,341)
decks and house	1,672 (760)
joiner work	1,338 (608)
hull and deck fittings	550 (250)
rig	1,135 (516)
propulsion	872 (396)
ship's systems	525 (239)
electrical	980 (445)
ship's outfit	1,350 (614)
paint	329 (150)
margin and soakage	+ 319 (145)
Light Ship, less Ballast	12,020 (5,464)
Ballast–Lead	10,900 (4,955)
Ballast–Trim	+ 300 (136)
Light-Ship Weight*	23,220 (10,555)
Payload, lb. (kg)	
crew (4 @ 180)	720 (327)
crew effects (4 @ 45)	180 (82)
owner's outfit @ ½	360 (164)
optional gear, spares, tools @ ½	630 (286)
fresh water (½ @ 180 gal.)	750 (341)
food @ ½	360 (164)
beverages @ ½	180 (82)
galley stores @ ½	30 (14)
LPG @ ½	20 (9)
diesel (½ @ 120 gals)	430 (195)
ship's stores @ ½	+ 120 (55)
Half-Load Payload	3,780 (1,718)
Light-Ship Weight	+ 23,220 (10,555)
Half-Load Displacement**	27,000 (12,273)
Additional Payload:	
Owner's Outfit @ ½	360 (164)
Optional Gear, Spares, Tools @ ½	630 (286)
Consumables @ ½	+ 1,890 (859)
Additional Payload	2,880 (1,309)
Half-Load Payload	+ 3,780 (1,582)
Full-Load Payload	6,660 (3,027)
Light-Ship Weight	+ 23,220 (10,555)
Full-Load Displacement***	29,880 (13,582)

* This is the designer's calculated weight. The build weight could still differ substantially from these numbers (generally on the heavy side!) if the builder does not adhere closely to the design specifications.

** This is the displacement on which the LWL is based; on most boats, the LWL is based on a more "nominal" calculation of payload.

*** The boat will float 1.9 in. below its LWL. Note that this displacement includes 8,010 lb. (3,641 kg) of removables (the full-load payload of 6,660 lb. plus ship's outfit of 1,350 lb., 3,027 plus 614 kg)!

For more information on the Paris 43, see pages 259–60.

As with any statistics, you can make the numbers prove a variety of different points of view. The only effective way to use them when comparing boats is to honestly assess *how you intend to use a boat*, in terms of both amenities and supplies. Then calculate what kind of weight this will add, including all the nonstandard equipment—extra batteries, inverter, microwave, in-mast reefing, windlass, additional ground tackle, AC generator, air conditioning, and so on—and the amount of water and diesel tankage you require. From this, you can derive what I call a *personal increment number* (PIN) (see the sidebar on page 13). The PIN is a function of your intended cruising lifestyle; as such, it will be relatively consistent *regardless of what boat you use to achieve that lifestyle*.

Next, look at boats that interest you and attempt to discover the light-ship, light-craft, minimum-sailing-trim, measurement-trim, or similar displacement number (which may well be the published displacement number). To this, add your half-load PIN to derive a half-load displacement number *as you will use the boat*. Even with this methodology, you still penalize those boats that come with a longer list of standard equipment (often heavier-displacement boats) because some of this equipment has to be added to boats that don't already have it (often lighter-displacement boats), increasing the add-on weight.

Now that you have a realistic sense of the displacement of a boat *as you will use it*, you can plug that number into several important performance formulas, using the graphs provided. From your perspective, as a basis for comparing boats, this makes the resulting ratios far more useful than the published ratios.

CALCULATING A PERSONAL INCREMENT NUMBER (PIN)

Only you can determine the style of cruising to which you would like to become accustomed! The following table helps you calculate the weight penalty. To use it, select all those items you intend to have onboard, and tally the weight to derive your PIN. Use the PIN to modify published displacement numbers to derive a more accurate one as *you* will use any given boat.

Remember, some equipment may be included in the published displacement number for one boat but not for another, so a certain amount of sleuthing is necessary to derive reasonably accurate half-load and full-load displacement numbers.

Nominal Light-Ship Weight Estimate
Published Displacement ______
Payload included in displacement over and above light ship (source: designer/builder/importer) – ______
Nominal Light-Ship Weight ______

Weight Corrections and Upgrades to Boat (see table notes 1–7 for examples):

1. deck and hull fittings[1] ______
2. rig[2] ______
3. propulsion[3] ______
4. systems[4] ______
5. electrical[5] ______
6. electronics[6] ______
7. ship's outfit[7] ______

Total Corrections and Upgrades to Boat ______ ______

Half-Load Payload:

Additional Sails (light wind and storm) ______
Optional Outfit (e.g., tools, spares) ______
Owner's Outfit (e.g., books, charts, manuals) ______
Miscellaneous (e.g., snorkel and dive gear) ______
Crew (160 lb./73 kg per person) ______
Crew Effects (50 lb./23 kg per person) ______
Crew's Outfit (50 lb./23 kg per person)[8] ______
Half of Consumables:
food and beverages (6 lb./2.7 kg per person per day times half endurance) ______
galley stores (4 lb./1.8 kg per person per week times half endurance) ______
stove fuel (5 lb. + 1 lb./2.3 + 0.5 kg per person per week times half endurance) ______
ship's stores (e.g., cleaners, finishes, and other) ______
freshwater (8.33 lb. per gal./1.00 kg per L times half tankage) ______
diesel (7.13 lb. per gal./0.86 kg per L times half tankage) ______

Half-Load Payload ______ + ______
Half-Load PIN (Weight Corrections and Upgrades plus Half-Load Payload) ______

Full-Load Payload:
Add the other half of the Consumables ______ + ______
Full-Load PIN (Half-Load PIN plus additional consumables) ______

To find the half-load or full-load displacement for any given boat, add the half-load or full-load PIN to the nominal light-ship weight.

Source: adapted from a table, courtesy Jay Paris.
Notes:
[1]Includes dodger, bimini, cockpit table, wind-vane steering.
[2]Includes roller reefing, in-mast or in-boom reefing, additional mast-mounted winches, electric winches, downwind and spinnaker poles.
[3]Includes additional filters, bow thruster.
[4]Includes powered windlass, saltwater washdown pump, watermaker, refrigeration upgrade (especially cold plates, which are heavy), air conditioning, trash compactor.
[5]Includes additional batteries, inverter, alternator upgrades, additional cabling, wind generator, solar panels, microwave, AC generator.
[6]Usually includes all electronics, radar.
[7]Includes ground tackle, mooring lines, fenders, dinghies, outboards, safety gear (including a life raft), barbecue grill.
[8]Includes bedding, dishes and cutlery, pots and pans.

Ballast Ratio

Once you have determined a half-load displacement number that more or less approximates how you will use a boat, it can be used in several performance ratios, the first of which is the *ballast ratio* (BR); that is, the ballast weight as a function of the boat's overall weight (displacement). The ballast ratio is derived by dividing the ballast weight by the displacement:

$$BR = \frac{ballast\ weight}{displacement}$$

The higher the ballast ratio, the heavier is the keel relative to the rest of the boat and, all else being equal, the stiffer the boat. However, all else is not equal! Given two boats with the same ballast ratio, one might have lead ballast in a bulb on a deep fin keel and the other might have internal iron ballast with a shoal draft. The former will be substantially stiffer. As such, the ballast ratio can be used only as a very broad indicator of a boat's stability; in fact, its utility is significantly limited to comparing boats with a similar hull form and draft.

If, instead of calculating a real-life half-load displacement, you use published displacement numbers to calculate a ballast ratio, remember that the displacement number is almost always low. When the displacement is underestimated, the lighter the weight of a boat relative to the load it will carry, the more the ballast ratio is distorted upward; published ballast ratios on lightweight boats often have to be taken with a *huge* grain of salt.

With these caveats in mind, we can say that the lower limit for the ballast ratio of a 35- to 45-foot (10.7–13.7 m) cruising boat at a realistic half-load displacement should be around 0.30, with ratios up to 0.40 possible on modern boats on which the hull weight has been minimized by the use of high-tech construction techniques and materials. However, at these higher ballast ratios, the penalty for a stiffer boat is a less comfortable motion.

Using published displacement figures, just about all modern boats have a ballast ratio higher than 0.30. However, when I looked at a sampling of modern boats to assess numbers that more realistically approximate coastal cruising trim, a number of the lighter boats dropped below this threshold; in offshore cruising trim, even more fell below it (see the summarizing table on pages 6–7).

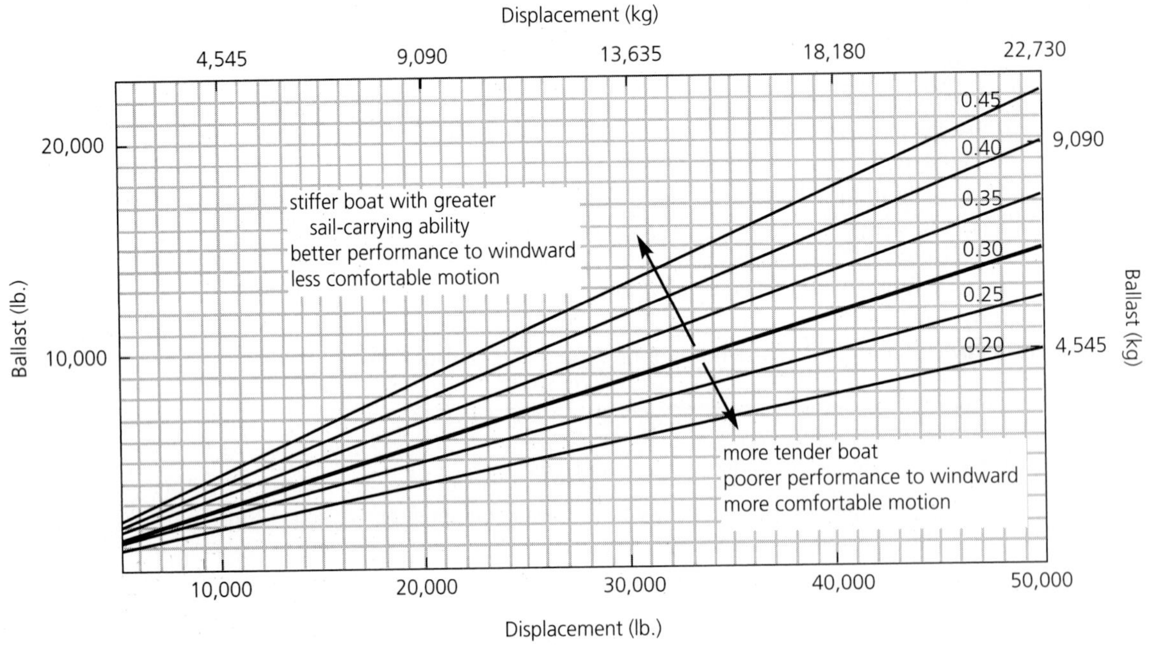

Ballast Ratios. To derive the ballast ratio, enter the graph with a realistic half-load displacement and the ballast weight.

The standard Pacific Seacraft 40 has an 8,600-pound (3,909 kg) keel on a boat with a published displacement of 24,000 pounds (10,909 kg; light local sailing). These numbers give a nominal ballast ratio of 0.36. We have a shoal-draft option (5 feet, 2 inches or 1.57 m) with a ballast weight of 8,880 pounds (4,036 kg) and a published displacement of 24,280 pounds (11,036 kg; again, light local sailing), for a nominal ballast ratio of 0.37. The light-ship weight is 22,800 pounds (10,364 kg)—23,080 pounds (10,491 kg) with the shoal-draft option. If we arbitrarily add 2,500 pounds (1,136 kg) to the light-ship weight, we get ballast ratios of 0.34 and 0.35, respectively; with a 3,750-pound (1,705 kg) payload, these ratios drop to 0.32 and 0.33; and with a 5,000-pound (2,273 kg) payload, we get 0.31 and 0.32.

Water Ballast

Another way to achieve stability is with water ballast. This is becoming popular on the racing circuit and on some cruising boats. Water tanks are placed on both sides of the boat—as far outboard as possible when heeled—with one tank empty and one full. When sailing upwind, whenever the boat is tacked, the water is moved to the windward side (either through gravity before tacking, or by the use of a pump after tacking). In effect, this results in hundreds of pounds of movable ballast placed at its most effective location. Of course, if something goes wrong and the water ends up on the leeward side, it has the exact opposite effect, increasing the heel angle.

At one end of the spectrum, water ballast is now being used on some high-tech, lightweight (and expensive) cruising boats (notably Chuck Paine's Bermuda series); at the other end, it is being used on trailerable sailboats (although in this case, the water is generally in a centerline tank where it simply increases displacement and is not moved from side to side). Nevertheless, water ballast still has a long way to go before it gains widespread acceptance with mainstream cruisers. I, for one, would be reluctant to make a significant part of the stability of my vessel dependent on functioning pumps. However, given its undoubted effectiveness, if water ballast can be proved reliable over time in the most demanding situations, we can expect to see more cruising boats using it.

Displacement–Length Ratio

As discussed previously, the addition of a substantial amount of weight to a boat with light-

Water-ballasted Kanter 53 from the design office of Chuck Paine. (Tim Seymour photo, courtesy Chuck Paine)

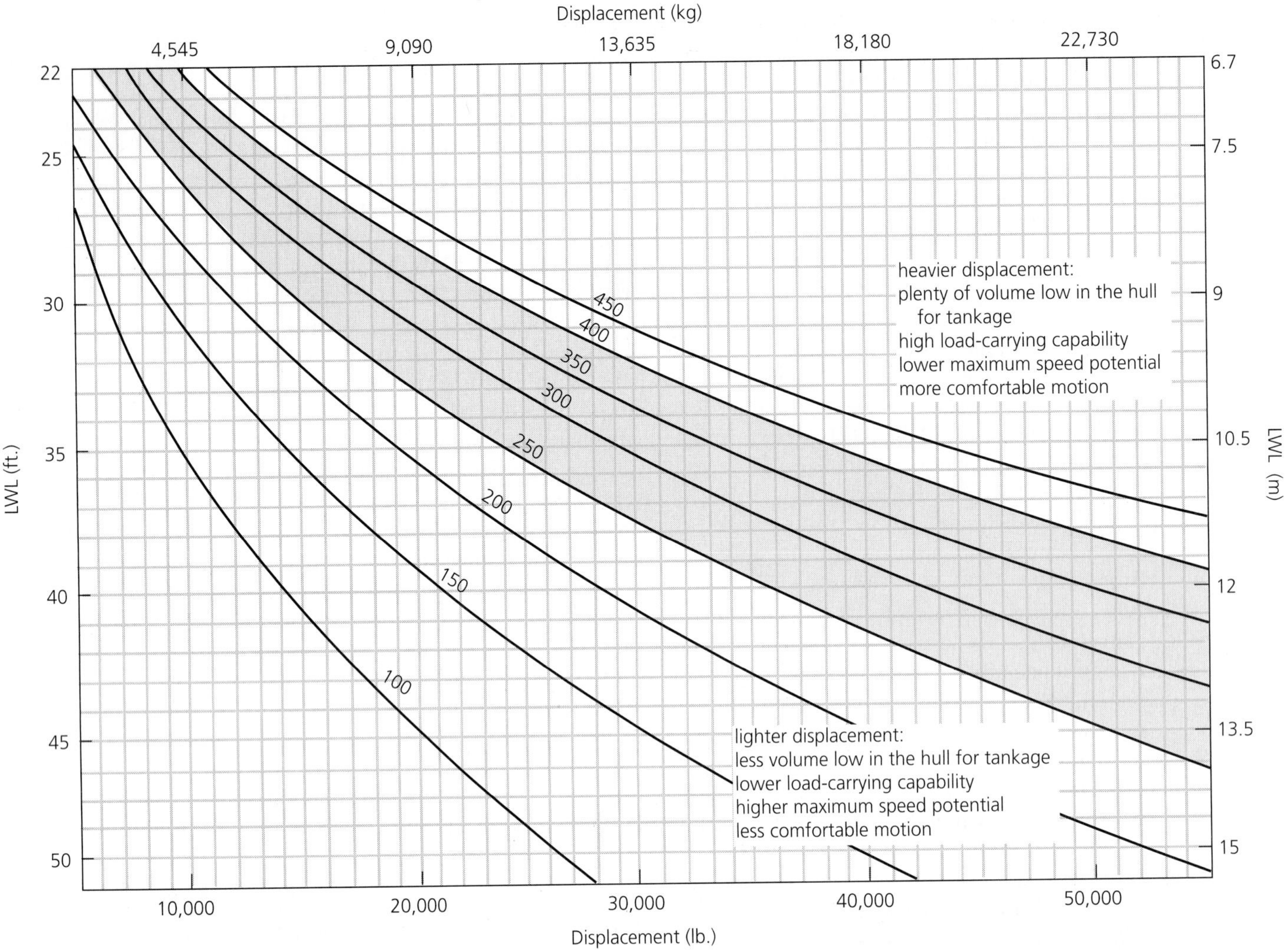

Displacement–Length Ratios. To derive the displacement–length ratio, enter the graph with a realistic half-load displacement and the LWL. Note: shaded portion represents Nigel Calder's recommended range for an approximately 40-foot (12 m) cruising boat.

weight construction has a disproportionately greater impact on the numbers and on the boat's performance than the addition of the same weight to a heavier boat. The farther it is intended to voyage offshore and the longer the voyage, the greater the load the boat is likely to have to carry. In general, a moderate- to heavy-displacement boat can absorb the load better than a light-displacement boat; the former also has a more comfortable motion in a seaway.

Another formula—the *displacement–length ratio* (DLR)—can be used to quantify a boat's "heaviness" independently of its length and, to some extent, its load-carrying capability relative to other boats. The formula is

$$\text{DLR} = \frac{\textit{displacement in long tons}}{(0.01 \times \textit{LWL})^3}$$

where 1 long ton = 2,240 lb.

Because the formula uses displacement, remember that artificially low displacement numbers will skew the figures, *with those for lightweight boats being skewed significantly more than those for heavier boats*. To make realistic comparisons among boats *as you will use them*, plug your PIN into the displacement number before calculating displacement–length ratios. The graph then enables you to determine a ratio that will reflect your usage more accurately than the published number.

Extremely lightweight boats may have a displacement–length ratio below 100; older cruising boats commonly exceed 400 (for some contemporary examples, see the summarizing table on pages 6–7). The higher the ratio, the greater is the volume below the waterline, which translates into comfortable interiors with plenty of fuel and water capacity, but often with a significant performance penalty.

A good range for contemporary cruising boats is between 250 and 400 (using a realistic half-load displacement number). However, Chuck Paine, using expensive high-tech construction and water ballast, brings his Bermuda series boats in at below 200; Steve and Linda Dashews' Deerfoots and Sundeers are also below 200, with some under 100.

Let's look at the Pacific Seacraft 40:

half-load displacement (light ship + 3,750 lb.) = 26,550 lb.

$$\frac{26,550}{2,240} = 11.85 \text{ long tons}$$

$$LWL = 31.25$$

$$(0.01 \times LWL)^3 = 0.0305$$

Therefore:

$$DLR = \frac{11.85}{0.0305} = 389$$

(as opposed to the published figure of 355)

This is definitely at the heavy end for a contemporary boat, although it is mostly because of the boat's relatively short LWL (and long overhangs), which tend to skew the numbers upward. This is also the case for most older designs, especially those designed to the Cruising Club of America (CCA) rule. Many modern boats, especially those influenced by the IMS rule, have almost no overhangs, so the LWL is close to the LOA. If the same design philosophy were used on the Pacific Seacraft 40, with the displacement kept constant, the displacement–length ratio would decrease from 389 to 185—which just goes to show that these numbers are nothing more than a broad guide.

In fact, with a PIN of 3,750 pounds (1,705 kg), the boat sinks almost 3 inches (76 mm), which—because of its long overhangs—increases its LWL by more than 9 inches (228 mm), bringing the displacement–length ratio back down to 362. For the rough-and-ready purposes of comparing boats, I believe this "sinkage factor" can be ignored, particularly because an accurate lines plan (which is unlikely to be available) is needed to calculate it. However, remember that the longer the overhangs and the shallower the angle between the overhangs and the surface of the water, the more the displacement–length ratio will be distorted upward by adding weight without considering its impact on the waterline.

Overhangs

So why not get rid of the Pacific Seacraft's overhangs? In addition to the fact that they are integrally related to a certain aesthetic concept, overhangs are important on an offshore boat for providing reserve buoyancy at the bow and the stern. An overhang at the stern also helps to dampen the pitching when the bow rises to waves.

The bow of a cruising boat is generally expected to carry a substantial amount of weight, mostly in the form of ground tackle—as mentioned previously, we have two anchors and a fair amount of chain, plus 300 feet (91 m) of ⅝-inch (16 mm) nylon rode; this adds up to about 400 pounds (182 kg) in weight. With little or no overhang, "the topsides near the bow are much more vertical than normal; reserve buoyancy (hull volume above the waterline) is lowered and with it resistance to pitching" (Killing, *Yacht Design Explained*). When pounding into waves, a fine bow with no overhang tends to go through the waves, which may prove faster but results in a lot of water over the decks and a wet boat. A bow with some flare and overhang tends to lift to the waves and ride over them. The bow with flare and overhang also tends to have a larger working platform for handling the ground tackle. The overhang has the added benefit of keeping the anchor from banging into the topsides when it is hauled up.

The length of the overhangs can be expressed in terms of the ratio of their combined length to that of the hull. Roger Marshall recommends a value between 0.15 and 0.20 as a reasonable target on a cruising boat. In other words,

$$\frac{(LOH - LWL)}{LOH} = 0.15 \text{ to } 0.20$$

where

LOH = length of hull (the LOA, excluding any bow pulpit but including a sugar-scoop stern or reverse transom)

LWL = waterline length

For the Pacific Seacraft 40, we have

LOH = 40.33 feet (12.28 m)

LWL = 31.25 feet (9.52 m)

Therefore:

$$\frac{LOH - LWL}{LOH} = 0.225$$

This is on the high side—it reflects the boat's long (by today's standards) overhangs.

Short overhangs are nothing new: the Bristol Channel cutter, a design dating back over 100 years and still popular in various contemporary forms (e.g., the Pardeys' Seraffyn), has almost no overhangs.

Half Angle of Entrance

The fineness of a bow is often quantified by yacht designers using the *half angle of entrance*. This is the angle formed between the centerline of the boat and the waterline at the bow (i.e., half of the angle formed by the bow at the waterline) when looking down on the boat from above (i.e., in plan view). The narrower this angle, the lower a hull's resistance is likely to be, but the more cramped the accommodations are in the forward part of the boat.

Most architects have settled on a half angle of entrance of about 22 degrees as an appropriate compromise for a cruising boat; most contemporary racing boats are below 20 degrees. In general, the longer a boat, the lower its angle of entrance is. The Pacific Seacraft 40 has a half angle of entrance of 25 degrees, which is on the high side. On one of the Dashews' designs, the half angle of entrance is as little as 10½ degrees, but this is on an 80-foot boat designed for a cruising couple!

Ideally, the bow sections incorporate some curvature in place of the large flat sections of many modern boats. The flat panels can flex in a seaway, and often contribute to uncomfortable pounding; they also can be surprisingly noisy.

To minimize the water that comes aboard, it is preferable to have a relatively high bow. A conventional *sheerline* will then curve down to a point about two thirds of the way aft so that any water that does come aboard is rapidly shed without invading the cockpit area. This profile has the added benefit of lowering the sheerline in the boarding area, making it easier to get in to and out of dinghies, and to hoist supplies aboard from a dinghy (something you don't think about until the first time you have to do it). We end up with "classic" lines, which just go to show that there is a good reason for these lines!

The high freeboard found on a number of high-volume boats is a real handicap when cruising.

Waterplanes and Immersion

It is often useful to know by how much a boat will settle in the water with the addition of stores and people. This is expressed in terms of the weight it will take to set the boat down by 1 inch (25 mm) on its waterline, or *pounds per inch of immersion*.

The yacht designer who designed the boat should have this number, but it can be approximated by multiplying the LWL (in feet) by the beam *at the waterline* (not B_{max}) in feet, and then multiplying this by a factor that considers the tapering of the waterline toward the bow and stern (0.70 is a good average). The resulting number (in square feet and called the *waterplane area*) is then multiplied by 5.33 (the weight, in pounds, of 1 square foot of seawater 1 inch deep) to give pounds per inch of immersion.

$$\textit{pounds per inch of immersion} = LWL \times BWL \times 0.70 \times 5.33$$

For example, the Pacific Seacraft 40 has an LWL of 31 feet, 3 inches (31.25 ft.) and a BWL of 11 feet, 4 inches (11.33 ft.; if the BWL is not available, use [$B_{max} \times 0.9$]):

$$31.25 \times 11.33 \times 0.70 = 248 \text{ ft.}^2$$
$$248 \text{ ft.}^2 \times 5.33 = 1{,}322 \text{ lb./in.}$$

(The metric equivalent is kilograms per centimeter of immersion. The formula is: LWL ×

BWL × 0.70 × 10.27, where LWL and BWL are in meters.)

As the boat sinks and the waterline lengthens, this number increases, but not by much.

Many people mistakenly believe that the pounds-per-inch-of-immersion number indicates a boat's load-carrying capability. It is simply a function of the waterplane area. Two boats of very different design, construction, and load-carrying capabilities but with the same waterplane area will have the same number.

Load-carrying capability is a function of stability, freeboard, the strength of construction, and displacement. Regardless of the pounds-per-inch-of-immersion number, if a lightweight, lightly constructed boat is made to carry a load for which it is not designed, its ballast ratio, displacement–length ratio, and sail area–displacement ratio will radically change for the worse (see the following section). Stability may suffer, the boat will pound and pitch, and—ultimately—the hull and rig will be subjected to stresses for which they were not designed.

Sinkage Factor

In *The Nature of Boats*, Dave Gerr states that "as a rough guide, average yachts can be allowed to . . . sink . . . below their design waterlines a . . . total of one percent of their waterline length" (this book is a treasure trove of nautical esoterica). This statement needs to be qualified by saying that added weight has an increasingly negative performance effect the lighter is a boat, so at lower displacement–length ratios, the degree of *sinkage* should be kept well below 1 percent of the LWL.

The Pacific Seacraft 40 has an LWL of 31 feet, 3 inches, which is 375 inches (9.52 m); 1 percent is 3.75 inches (95 mm), which represents a payload of 4,958 pounds (2,254 kg). With a payload of 3,750 pounds (1,705 kg), we will put our boat down by 2.8 inches (71.1 mm) over the light-ship waterline and 1 inch (25.4 mm) over the factory waterline. In anticipation of our cruising load, we asked the factory to paint the waterline 2 inches (50 mm) higher.

Another way to look at sinkage is to express it as a function of the LSW. I would suggest that a good target is to keep the PIN below 20 percent of the LSW. Looking at our Pacific Seacraft 40, the LSW is 22,800 pounds (10,364 kg).

$$22{,}800 \times 0.20 = 4{,}560 \text{ lb. } (2{,}073 \text{ kg})$$

Pounds per inch of immersion is 1,322 pounds (601 kg), resulting in a sinkage of 3.45 inches (87.6 mm), which is just under 1 percent of the LWL.

If we look at the Hunter 380, a relatively lightweight boat, we see it has a LSW of 15,000 pounds (6,818 kg; see the summarizing table on pages 6–7). Twenty percent of 15,000 is 3,000 pounds (1,364 kg); pounds per inch of immersion is 1,352 (615 kg), resulting in a sinkage of 2.22 inches (55.8 mm), which is just over 0.5 percent of the LWL.

Comfort Factor

Years ago, Ted Brewer, a well-known yacht designer, developed a formula for what he called his "motion comfort ratio," which he gets by

$$\text{motion comfort ratio} = \frac{\text{displacement (lb.)}}{0.65 \times (0.7\ LWL + 0.3\ LOA) \times beam^{1.33}}$$

In general, motion comfort increases with length; a corollary to this is that a larger boat can have a lower displacement–length ratio than a smaller boat—and, as a result, a better performance—but still have the same motion comfort. For example, in *Cruising Sailboat Kinetics* naval architect Danny Greene calculates that the heavy-displacement Mason 37 (displacement–length ratio of 441) has the same motion comfort ratio as the lightweight Deerfoot 62 (displacement–length ratio of 159).

In *The Nature of Boats*, Dave Gerr simplified this formula to describe how the waterplane area can be used to determine a "comfort factor." He writes: "One excellent indicator of how comfortable a boat will be in a seaway is her rate of heave—how fast she bobs straight up and down. A rapid heave means many quick vertical accelerations that will keep you hanging onto things for support when you'd much prefer to be relaxing. A boat with a slow heave has a solid, shippy feel."

The rate of heave can be inferred from a graph that shows the "waterplane for comfortable heave." The graph is entered with the waterplane area on the side and the displacement on the bottom in long tons of 2,240 pounds (1,018 kg). In theory, boats that lie above the line have a quicker, more uncomfortable heave; those on or below the line have a slower, more comfortable heave—although designers of lightweight boats will dispute this!

Looking at the Pacific Seacraft 40, it has a waterplane area of 248 square feet (23 sq. m)

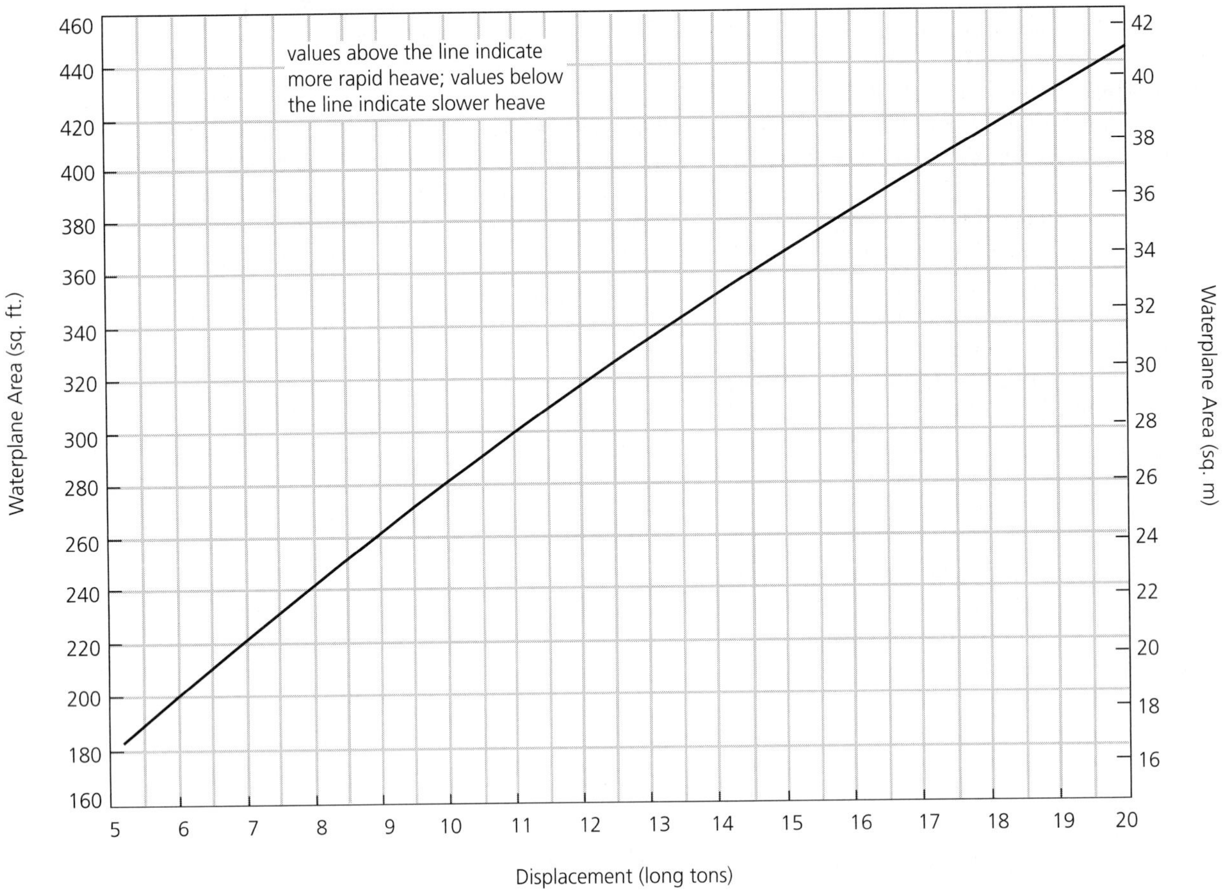

Waterplane for Comfortable Heave. (Excerpted from Dave Gerr, The Nature of Boats, *courtesy Dave Gerr)*

and a half-load weight (i.e., light ship plus 3,750 pounds or 1,705 kg) of 26,550 pounds (12,068 kg), which equals 11.85 long tons; the fully loaded weight could be as high as 12.41 long tons. Both sets of numbers put it well below Gerr's curve. Many modern boats are on the high side of the line, although some shift to the low side if 2,500 or 3,750 pounds (1,136–1,705 kg) of equipment and supplies are arbitrarily added to the published displacement figures to more nearly replicate real-life half-load cruising displacement. (One of the reasons I like this graph is because those manufacturers who come up light on the displacement numbers by fudging the figures get penalized when looking at the comfort factor!)

Sail Area–Displacement Ratio

It is commonly assumed that a moderately heavy-displacement boat, especially one loaded with stores, will be a dog to sail. This is often the case, but need not necessarily be so. As long as the boat is given adequate sail area to compensate for the weight, and *as long as it is stiff enough to stand up under this sail area*, there is no reason for it not to have excellent performance.

The key new parameter is the *sail area–displacement ratio* (SADR), which is calculated (for a sloop or cutter) by determining the nominal area of the mainsail and the *foretriangle* in square feet, and dividing that sum by the boat's displacement in cubic feet taken to the two-thirds power (i.e., use a calculator to raise the cubic footage to the 0.67 power). The equation is as follows:

$$\text{SADR} = \frac{[(I \times J) \div 2] + [(P \times E) \div 2]}{(\text{displacement in cubic feet})^{2/3}}$$

where

I = the height of the foretriangle

J = the horizontal distance from the forward side of the mast to the bottom of the headstay

P = the hoist of the mainsail

E = the foot of the mainsail

The full mizzen is sometimes included with ketches and yawls; other times, only half of its area is counted. When comparing boats, it is important to use the same convention.

Seawater weighs 64 pounds per cubic foot; therefore, the Pacific Seacraft 40, with a half-load displacement of 26,550 pounds (12,068 kg), displaces 415 cubic feet (26,550 ÷ 64). If this is squared, we get 415 × 415 = 172,225, the cube root of which is 55.64. According to some of the Pacific Seacraft literature, the boat's sail area is 1,032 square feet, giving a sail area–displacement ratio of 1,032 ÷ 55.64 = 18.5. However, this number is achieved by including the staysail, which is an improper use of the formula (in other literature, the staysail is excluded). Without the staysail, the sail area drops to 846 square feet and the sail area–displacement ratio to 15.2. A ratio of 15 to 16 is considered acceptable for a traditional cruising boat; 17 to 19 is typical for performance cruisers; and 20 to 22 is on the high side.

In conditions where both the staysail and headsail are flown, the Pacific Seacraft has a fair amount of sail power, *as long as the boat is stiff enough to carry the sail area* (it is of no use if the boat can't carry it without excessive heeling). In a boat test conducted in relatively heavy weather, *Yachting Monthly* magazine commented that the "Pacific Seacraft 40 gives a sprightly performance, mainly due to its large sail area." However, if the staysail is taken out of the picture (which it will be quite often, especially when off the wind), in light airs (which are encountered by cruisers far more often than heavy weather) the basic sail plan is likely to leave the boat underpowered, especially when loaded for cruising; decent light-air sails will be needed.

Again, it is important to use a realistic displacement number. Not only do boatbuilders commonly exaggerate the sail area of their boats (see the Sail Area Measurements sidebar on page 23), they also use some form of light-ship displacement. Taken together, these result in completely unrealistic sail area–displacement ratios. If the numbers are reworked using 100 percent of the sail area and a realistic half-load displacement, it is not uncommon for the sail area–displacement ratio to drop by three full points (e.g., from 17.0 to 14.0; see the summarizing table on pages 6–7). The graph on page 22 can be used to plug realistic sail area and displacement numbers into the calculation, thereby deriving a realistic ratio for any given boat. A good target range for a cruising boat is an SAD ratio of between 15 and 18 at half-load displacement: 15 will emphasize security over performance; 18 will improve performance but require more attention to sail handling (especially reducing the sail area if the wind pipes up).

Stability Curves and Ratio

Stability Curves

Many of the aforementioned factors influence a boat's *stability curve*, otherwise known

It takes a fair amount of sail area to ensure that heavier-displacement boats maintain a sprightly performance; Nada *under downwind working canvas.*

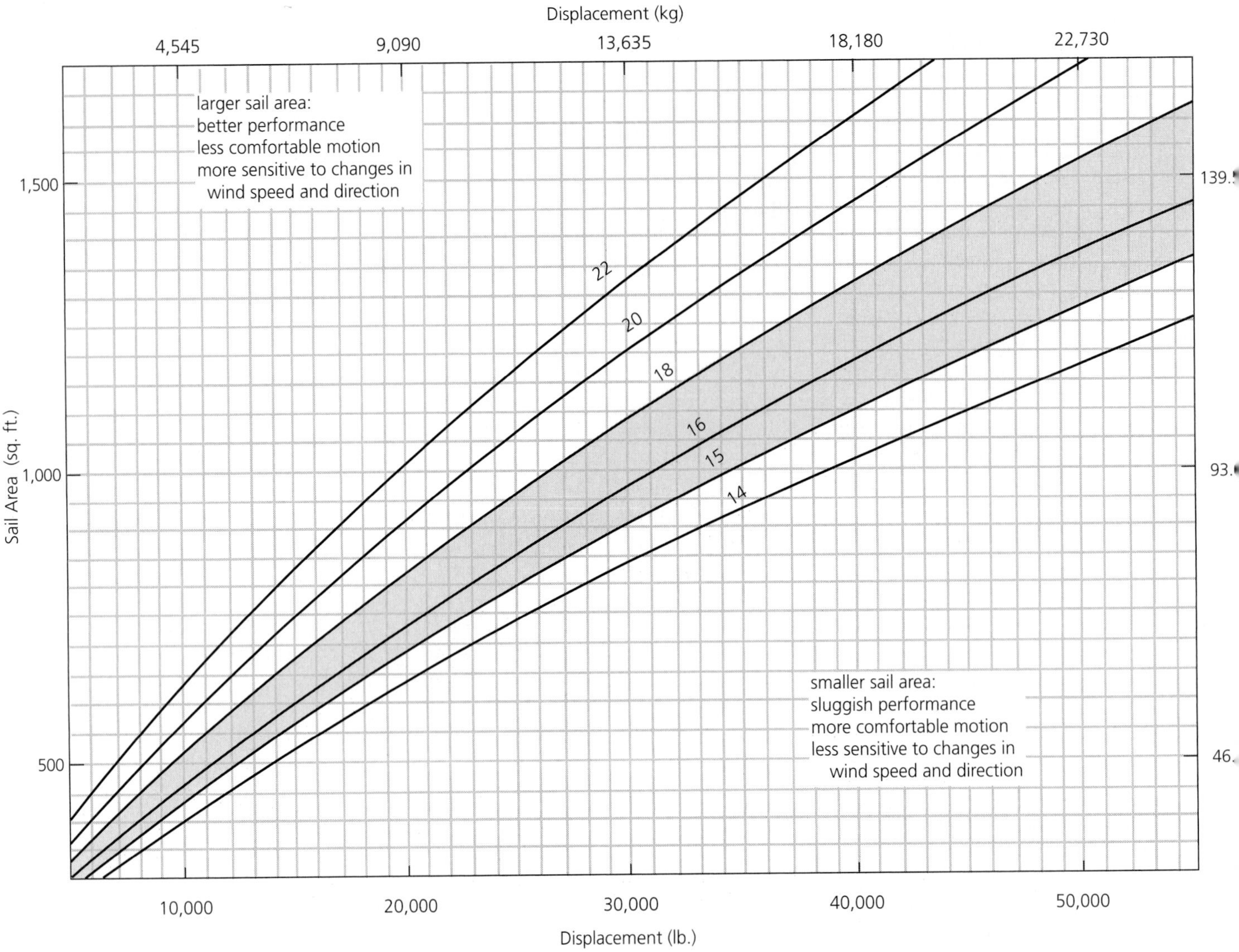

Sail Area–Displacement Ratios. To derive the sail area–displacement ratio, enter the graph with an accurate sail area and a realistic half-load displacement. Note: shaded portion represents Nigel Calder's recommended range for an approximately 40-foot (12 m) cruising boat.

as its GZ *curve*. A stability curve is developed by calculating or measuring the forces needed to heel a boat, and then using accurate data describing the hull's shape to develop a curve that will show, among other things, the point at which the boat has its maximum resistance to heeling (the *point of maximum stability*) and the point at which it will roll over and turn upside down (the *limit of positive stability*, LPS, also known as the *angle of vanishing stability*, AVS, and the *point of no return*).

Depending on how the calculations are made, it is possible to come up with significantly different numbers for the same boat. Unfortunately, the IMS and the ISO have different methodologies that, in turn, may differ from independent calculations. For this reason, it is important to use the same criteria when comparing boats.

Given that the European Union (EU) is requiring some type of stability testing for all new boats, we can expect most boats (both European and U.S.) to be tested to the ISO standard in the near future, which will provide a measure of consistency. However, a couple of caveats need to be remembered. On the one hand, the stability test is conducted in a lightly loaded condition (MSC; factory-installed equipment onboard plus an estimate for crew weight), which tends to understate the stability of a boat loaded down with cruising stores. On the other hand, the test is to some extent done on the "honor system"; therefore, it is quite possible for a builder to have a boat tested with, say,

SAIL AREA MEASUREMENTS

Sail area measurement is another gray area that some boatbuilders like to fudge. As stated in the text, for comparison purposes, it should be 100 percent of the area of the foretriangle (defined as [I × J] ÷ 2) plus the nominal area of the main (defined as [P × E] ÷ 2). It is not uncommon for the staysail area to be included with a cutter or for the overlap on a headsail that is more than 100 percent of the foretriangle to be added in; neither should be included when comparing boats.

As for the mainsail, in the past some boatbuilders calculated the area based on the triangle formed by connecting the clew of the sail by a straight line to the head of the sail at the mast (which is how it should be done for comparison purposes). This excludes any roach area from the calculation, thereby understating the actual area of many mainsails (in particular, fully battened mainsails). Therefore, today whenever there is a roach, there is a tendency to include this (it makes the numbers look better). However, in the case of a hollow leach (commonly used with roller-furling mains), I doubt that the loss of sail area is ever considered!

The following numbers are derived from the literature for a popular cruising boat:

I = 45.44 feet (13.85 m)
J = 12.99 feet (3.96 m)
P = 38.50 feet (11.74 m)
E = 15.09 feet (4.60 m)

Using these numbers, 100 percent of the foretriangle equals (I × J) ÷ 2 = (45.44 × 12.99) ÷ 2 = 295.13 square feet (27.42 sq. m); the nominal area of the mainsail equals (P × E) ÷ 2 = (38.50 × 15.09) ÷ 2 = 290.48 square feet (26.98 sq. m). Therefore, the nominal sail area (i.e., 100 percent foretriangle + main) equals 295.13 + 290.48 = 585.61 square feet (54.40 sq. m).

The literature for this boat gives the mainsail area as 337.5 square feet (31.35 sq. m; this must include a fully battened main with a substantial amount of roach) and a total sail area (150 percent genoa) of 750.3 square feet (69.70 sq. m; as opposed to the 585.6 sq. ft./54.70 sq. m, derived by using more traditional means of calculating the sail area).

As with other parameters, when comparing boats, it is important to ensure that the same methodology was used to determine the numbers. If possible, the I, J, P, and E numbers should be obtained, and the calculations worked from them.

a deep-draft keel and hanked-on sails, which will maximize the stability rating. He or she may then sell the boat with a shoal-draft keel and roller-furling sails, which significantly reduce its stability. As always, for accurate comparisons, it is important to find out on what basis the numbers have been derived.

Regardless of the way in which the calculations are run, a beamy, lightweight boat that relies primarily on form stability for its stiffness will reach both its point of maximum stability and its LPS or AVS well before the deeper-draft, narrower-beam boat that relies more on ballast weight for stiffness. If either boat capsizes, the beamy, lightweight boat will more likely remain upside down, as is well illustrated by some of the current crop of single-handed, round-the-world racers, which are quite stable in the inverted position.

"The way beam is used in combination with displacement and center of gravity is the crux of the stability question," writes Olin Stephens, the famous yacht designer. "The worst of all combinations is large beam with a light-displacement, shoal-bodied hull having necessarily limited ballast that is too high" (quoted in Rousmaniere, *Desirable and Undesirable Characteristics of Offshore Yachts*).

If a boat will always be used in protected waters where there will never be breaking waves large enough to capsize it (for more on this, see chapter 11), the farthest the wind will ever knock it down is 90 degrees, so any LPS or AVS above this will provide security against a capsize. But if a boat is intended for extended cruising where it runs the risk of getting caught in extreme conditions that may roll it, it should have an LPS or AVS of at least 120 degrees (a number of experienced cruiser-writers recommend 130 degrees). This number is chosen because if such a boat is inverted, in theory, it will take about two minutes before another wave rights it, which is the longest most people can hold their breath. With an LPS or AVS of 100 degrees, the boat will remain inverted for five minutes; at 140 degrees, the inversion time is minimal. For coastal cruising, where the probability of encountering seas large enough to roll the boat is very low, I consider an LPS or AVS as low as 115 degrees to be acceptable.

Longer boats are less likely to capsize than shorter boats. To take this into account, the IMS developed a *stability index number* (not to be confused with the ISO's STIX number; see pages 26–27), which is derived by adjusting the

	VALIANT 40	SABRE 402
maximum stability	62°	57°
limit of positive stability	125°	114°
stability ratio	4.560	2.333
stability index	133.2	118.5

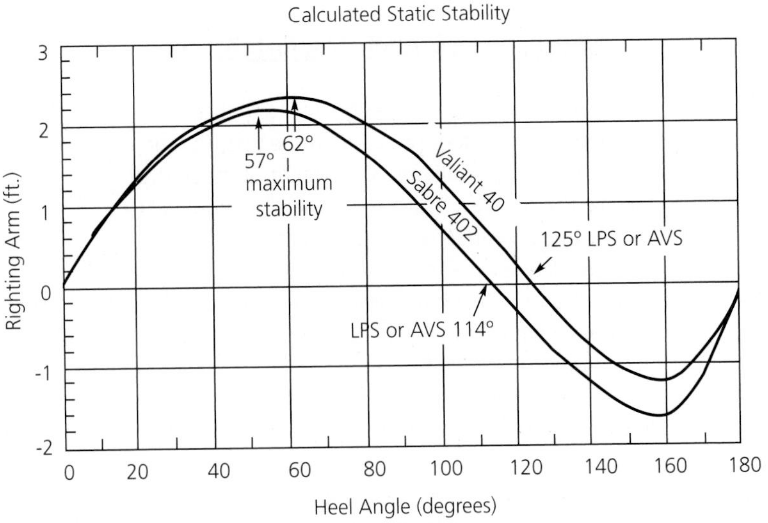

IMS stability curves for a Valiant 40 and a Sabre 402. (Courtesy US Sailing)

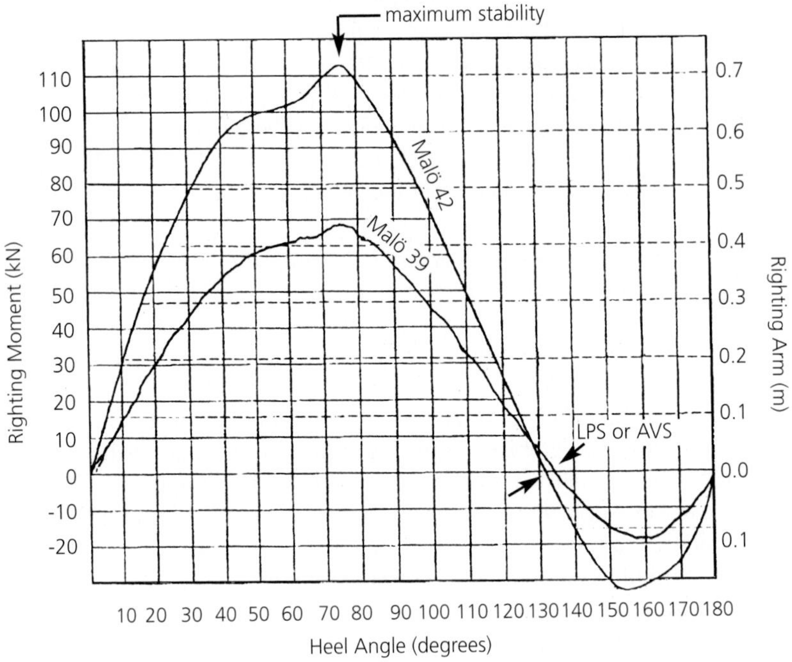

ISO stability curve for Malö 39 and Malö 42 in minimum sailing condition. (Courtesy Malö Yachts)
Note that although these are two very similar designs, the Malö 42 has a significantly higher maximum stability. This demonstrates that it takes a lot more energy to roll over a big boat than it does a little one.

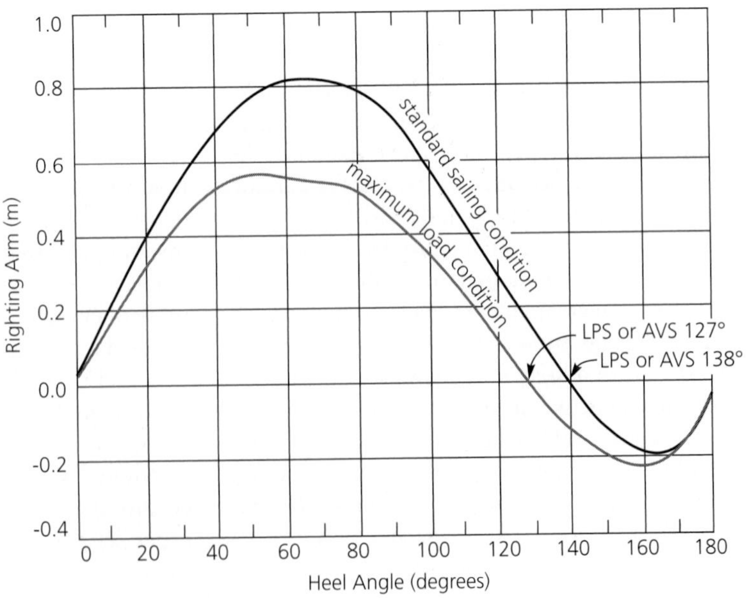

The effect of loading on a boat's stability, here a Starlight 39. (Courtesy Rival Bowman Yachts)
Note that both the maximum stability and the LPS or AVS are lowered in the maximum load condition.

LPS or AVS for a boat's beam–displacement ratio and size. The adjusted number is useful for comparing the relative stability of different boats. For offshore work, the Stability Index Number should be at least 120.

The Pacific Seacraft 40 has not yet been measured under the IMS or ISO system (both of which exclude the beneficial effect of the superstructure on the calculation), but it has been measured with the superstructure and cockpit included in the calculations (a more realistic assessment). This produces a point of maximum stability of 65 degrees and an LPS or AVS of 143 degrees (these numbers would be lower using the IMS and ISO methodologies); both numbers are on the high end for modern boats.

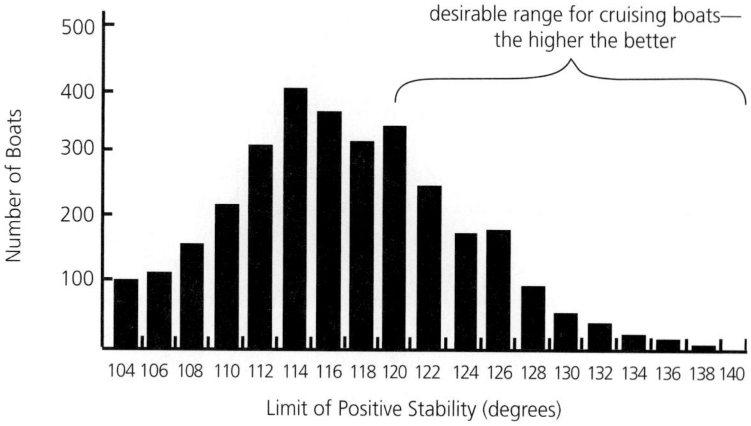

Stability Ratio

Another interesting way of comparing boats is to take the area under the positive portion of the stability curve, which represents the amount of energy necessary to capsize the boat, and divide it by the area under the negative part of the curve, which represents the energy required to return an inverted boat to the point at which it will right itself. The ratio of these two areas—the *stability ratio*—is a measure of the relative stability of the boat, both upright and capsized: the higher the number, the better. On a cruising boat, it should be at least 3.0, and preferably higher; the farther it is intended to go offshore, the higher it should be. I don't have the ratio for the Pacific Seacraft 40, but my guess is that it is above 10.0.

Water ballast raises an interesting question. Given the possibility that in a worst-case scenario it may all end up on the "wrong" side of the boat, should the stability numbers be run with the assumption that the ballast is contributing to or detracting from the boat's stability? The IMS simply assumes there is no water ballast onboard. Studies done by yacht designers at Sparkman and Stephens show that even if the water ballast is on the wrong side, as long as it is kept within generally accepted limits (i.e., with the water ballast all on one side, it induces no more than a 10-degree heel), it has a limited effect on a boat's point of maximum stability, and actually increases its LPS or AVS.

Stability curves and ratios are useful as a guide for selecting offshore boats, but they need to be put in perspective. The curves are based on a static calculation, and do not consider the dynamic forces at work in conditions of heavy-breaking seas when a knockdown is most likely to occur. According to one school of thought, a boat with relatively low freeboard and a deep keel will have significantly less wave-loading area than one with high freeboard and, therefore, will be less likely to roll. According to another school of thought, a lightweight boat with high freeboard and a shallow keel will be more likely to skid sideways before the wave, dissipating the wave's energy, thereby forestalling a capsize!

The stability curve and ratio are also based on some form of light-ship displacement. The addition of cruising stores and gear has a significant effect, with weight somewhat above or anywhere below the boat's center of gravity increasing stability, and anything well above the center of gravity decreasing stability. The higher the added weight on the boat, the more deleterious is the effect; the lighter the boat relative to the weight, the more deleterious is the effect. Factors such as a radar antenna sited high on the mast; roller-reefing headsails; an outboard motor stowed on the rail; and dinghies, anchors, ground tackle, and other gear commonly placed well above the waterline all have a significant negative impact on the numbers. We have all this stuff on our boat!

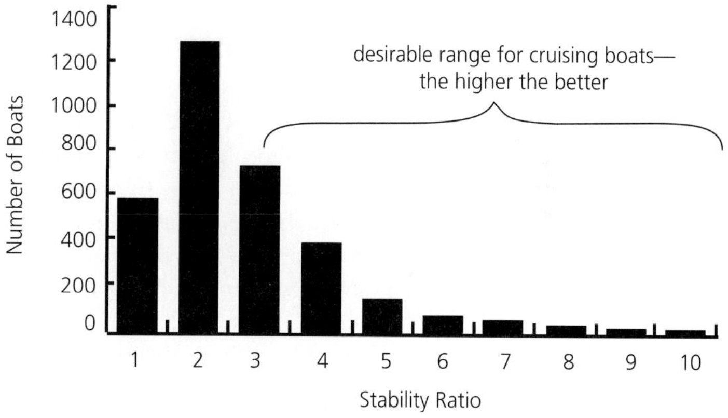

LPS or AVS and Stability Ratio of all the boats currently measured under IMS rules.

In *Adlard Coles' Heavy Weather Sailing*, Peter Bruce reports that the addition of in-mast furling and a roller-reefing headsail to one 28.5-foot (8.68 m) "production cruising yacht" reduced its LPS or AVS from 127 to 96 degrees, which is a potentially life-threatening reduction. Although this is an extreme case (the reduction in LPS or AVS caused by similar gear on a larger boat of significantly heavier displacement is more likely to be on the order of 3 to 4 percent), cruising sailors need to be aware of the effect that additional weight can have on stability, especially weight placed high up, and then make sure that any given boat can handle the cruising load without a serious loss of performance or stability. Every effort must be made to keep heavy weights low in the boat.

Capsize Screening Value and STIX Number

After the disastrous 1979 Fastnet race, in which numerous boats got repeatedly rolled and fifteen people lost their lives, a long, hard look was taken at the stability issue. It was acknowledged by many yacht designers that the IOR, which dominated yacht design in the 1970s and 1980s and under which many of the participating boats were designed, was actually promoting the development of unsafe boats (non-IOR boats built before 1975 survived the race with few problems). Much work went into developing a simple formula that would weed out the worst excesses resulting from attempts to "beat" the rule. The formula that was developed is known as the *capsize screening formula*, which is intended to assess both "the risk of being unduly easily capsized and the risk of sticking in the inverted position for an extended period of time" (USYRU/SNAME Joint Committee on Safety from Capsizing).

The *capsize screening value* (CSV) for any boat is found by dividing the cube root of the boat's displacement volume (in cubic feet) into its B_{max} (in feet).

$$CSV = \frac{B_{max}}{\sqrt[3]{displacement\ volume}}$$

The higher the resulting number is above a value of 2.0, the greater the likelihood is that the boat will be unduly prone to capsize; if it is below 2.0, it should be safe offshore. However, because the capsize screening value is a function of displacement and beam, any two boats with the same displacement and beam have the same value. This is true even if, for example, one boat has a heavily ballasted deep-fin keel and the other has a centerboard and internal ballast, in which case the former is, in fact, much more stable.

In 2001, the ISO was still working (and had been working since 1992) on a more sophisticated *stability index* (STIX) that considers a greater number of variables. Until this work is completed, the existing capsize screening value (despite its shortcomings) is a useful indicator of stability. The Pacific Seacraft 40 has a half-load displacement of 26,550 pounds (12,068 kg; light ship plus 3,750 pounds or 1,705 kg), which is 415 cubic feet (11.75 cu. m). The cube root of 415 is 7.46; the B_{max} is 12.42 feet (3.78 m). The capsize screening value is 12.42 divided by 7.46, which equals 1.66—well below the target of 2.0—confirming the boat's high degree of capsize resistance. If we use the light-ship displacement to work the numbers (this is a worst-case scenario in terms of the capsize screening value), we get a value of 1.75, which is still well below the target of 2.0.

Once the STIX standard gets completed, it may provide a more comprehensive means of comparing boats than the current capsize screening value (although this is by no means certain—the standards-writing process is both political and controversial). However, previous drafts of the STIX standard gave a score of 30 or more, which resulted in an "A" rating—the rating for oceangoing boats—on boats with an LPS or AVS as low as 95 degrees, despite the fact that these boats were clearly not suitable for extended ocean voyaging.

After a well-publicized sinking in a Bay of Biscay (off the coasts of France and Spain) gale of an A-rated boat with an LPS or AVS of 110, the STIX score for an A rating was raised to 32; raising the LPS or AVS to 120 is under discussion. Given that longer boats inherently score higher than shorter boats—regardless of the number that the STIX committee finally determines is appropriate for an A rating—for oceangoing cruising, it may make sense to set a minimum score of 35 or maybe even 40. For coastal cruising, a minimum STIX number of 30 will provide a greater degree of security than the current 23. It, too, should be increased for boats more than 40 feet long.

If the conditions get nasty enough, any boat can be rolled (see chapter 11), and the survival of the crew is going to be significantly affected by how fast the boat will right itself. Only boats that are likely to recover in a minute or two should be considered for blue-water cruising;

hence, the need for an LPS or AVS of 120 or higher, a capsize screening value of 2.0 or lower, and a STIX rating well above 32.

At the end of the day, it must always be remembered that no indices can substitute for an objective analysis of the qualities of a boat. It will always be possible to design and build boats that score highly on a given test, and yet are temperamental and potentially unseaworthy in the open ocean. As with all other numeric parameters, the recommended LPS or AVS, capsize screening value, and STIX number are nothing more than useful indicators of the suitability of a boat for cruising; they are not guarantors.

EU CATEGORIES FOR RATING BOATS

The EU has four categories for rating boats:

Category A: Offshore Ocean. Boats designed for extended offshore passages.

Category B: Offshore Coastal. Boats designed for coastal cruising with offshore passages of up to 500 miles.

Category C: Inshore. Boats that cruise along the coast within 10 miles of land and four hours passage time of a safe harbor or refuge.

Category D: Sheltered Waters. Boats that operate in daylight only in estuaries, inshore or inland, within an hour of a safe harbor or refuge.

Maintaining Control

Given the foregoing discussion, within the context of available production and semiproduction boats, the kind of boat that I recommend for extended cruising has a moderately heavy displacement, a modest beam by today's standards, and a substantial lead keel set well below the hull. The hull must be easy and stable on the helm and, in particular, easily controlled when hard-pressed. The farther offshore the boat is designed to go and the longer the passages, the more important are these behavioral characteristics. It is one thing to take a skittish boat for an afternoon race around the buoys; it is quite another to take that same boat on a week-long, heavy-weather, open-ocean passage.

To maintain helm balance, it is important that there be a balance between the bow and the stern sections of the boat so that as the boat heels, there is no dramatic imbalance in the underbody or underwater shape. Chuck Paine had this to say: "Proper offshore yachts should exhibit a reasonable balance between the bow and stern sections, and they should derive their stability from a low center of gravity rather than flat sections. Yachts of this type are blissful steerers" (quoted in *The Complete Offshore Yacht*).

The lower the length–beam ratio, the more important it is to maintain hull balance when a boat is heeled. Unfortunately, the IOR produced a trend in which the beamier a boat got, the less the hull was balanced when heeled. When such a boat is heeled, the resulting asymmetry in the underwater shape lifts the stern and drives the bow down, at which point the rudder starts to come out of the water, causing it to ventilate and lose its effectiveness just when it is most needed. The net result is a tendency to round up and broach—a common enough image on the racing circuit, but not the kind of behavior we want from a cruising boat. "Beam," Bill Crealock told me, "is one of the principal enemies of balance."

Any control problems are exacerbated by a small fin keel and minimal spade rudder. These rely on boat speed to generate sufficient hydrodynamic lift, which in turn makes the keel or rudder remarkably efficient despite its small size. But take away that speed, and the small keel and rudder become increasingly ineffective. While there is no need to have the full-length keel of the traditional heavy-displacement cruising boat, there is no doubt that a moderately long keel adds significantly to the controllability and directional stability of a boat, especially at lower speeds.

IOR broach. (Courtesy Patrick Roach)

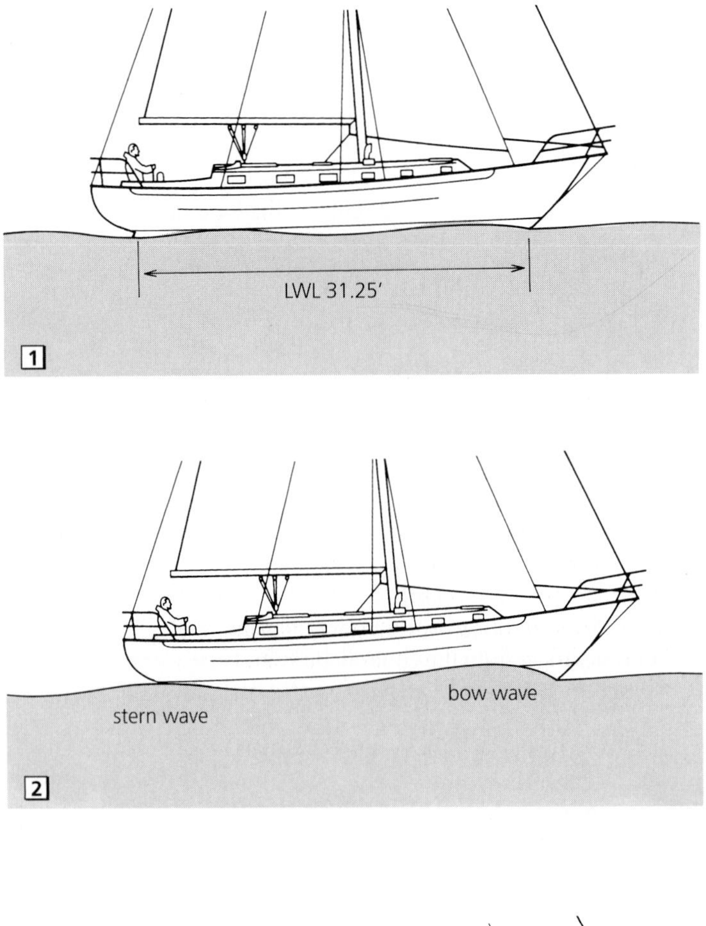

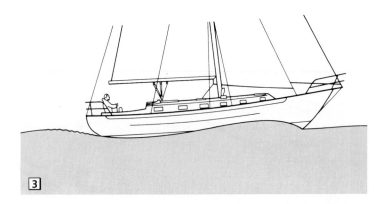

Bow and stern waves: 1. Pacific Seacraft 40 at less than nominal hull speed. 2. Pacific Seacraft 40 at a little above nominal hull speed (approximately 7.8 knots). Although the stern wave has moved aft of the static LWL, the shape of the buttocks is such that the stern is still well supported, effectively extending the LWL. 3. Pacific Seacraft 40 at well above nominal hull speed (approximately 8.5 knots). The stern wave has moved well aft of the stern, which is now dropping into the trough of the bow wave. It takes a tremendous amount of energy to keep the boat moving at this speed.

To quote David Thomas, a well-known British yacht designer of both racing and cruising boats: "A racing yacht, which is usually sailing at optimum speed, can manage with a small high lift, high aspect ratio fin of low lateral area. To sail slowly under full control, and to be able to leave the helm for short periods, a fin of probably twice the area is needed. The same applies to the rudder, which can be too small, but not too big!" (*Complete Offshore Yacht*). The price, of course, is an increase in wetted surface area and resistance, with some loss of maneuverability with the long keel.

There is another very important but frequently overlooked consideration. The farther offshore you intend to sail, the more important it is to have an effective wind vane or autopilot (or both). There are few things worse than having to hand-steer on a long passage. A skittish boat is going to prove difficult to impossible for either a wind vane or an autopilot to handle. When the conditions get really rough and the time comes to heave-to or to adopt other survival strategies, it may be that the fin keeler simply won't heave-to or lie ahull comfortably, under her own devices (see chapter 11). This situation could be life-threatening with a tired, shorthanded crew and the need to keep someone on the helm and the boat sailing to maintain a semblance of control.

Directional stability is an essential feature—not a luxury—on a cruising boat (the best single indicator is a high length–beam ratio).

Speed–Length Ratio

This is a good point at which to try and put speed into perspective. Cruising boats are displacement boats (i.e., boats that generally do not get up on a plane). As they move through the water, they create waves. There is a natural, physical relationship between the speed at which waves move and the distance from crest to crest (a *wavelength*) such that

$$\sqrt{wavelength} \times 1.34 = wave\ speed$$

where wavelength is in feet and wave speed is in knots

This is a "fact of nature" that simply must be considered when designing boats. The bow wave of a boat is moving with the boat. Because of the physical relationship between wave speed and wavelength, the faster a boat moves, the faster the bow wave moves and, consequently, the farther apart it is from its second crest. At some point, this distance—the wavelength—is such that there is a crest at the bow and another at the stern. If a boat goes faster, the wave crest at the stern moves farther aft, dropping the stern into the bow-wave's trough so that the boat is now attempting to "climb" its bow wave. For heavy-displacement boats, which create large bow waves, more power than can normally be generated by sails or an engine is needed; as a result, many sailboats generally do not go this fast.

The boat begins to sink into the trough of the bow wave at the point when the crest of the stern wave moves aft of the aft end of the boat's waterline—in other words, at that point when the wavelength exceeds the LWL of the boat. Consequently, the "maximum speed" of many heavy-displacement boats, commonly termed *hull speed*, is generally on the order of 1.34 times the square root of the LWL. As this speed is approached, *wave-making drag* increases dramatically and continues to rise disproportionately to any increase in speed. Ever-increasing amounts of power are required for small incremental increases in speed.

The net result of the physical laws governing wave-making is that the maximum speed of a displacement boat is substantially determined by its LWL: the longer it is, the faster the boat will go. What is important is not the static LWL, but rather the sailing LWL, which is particularly significant on boats with long and low overhangs. When the boat is at speed, the LWL may increase substantially and the maximum speed will rise accordingly.

This relationship between a boat's speed and its length is often stated in terms of the *speed–length ratio* (SLR), for which the formula is as follows:

$$SLR = \frac{boat\ speed}{\sqrt{LWL}}$$

where boat speed is in knots and LWL is in feet

Buttocks, Diagonals, and Aft Sections

This picture needs to be qualified. As a displacement boat approaches its nominal hull speed (i.e., $1.34 \times \sqrt{LWL}$), factors such as the flatness of the hull's underbody or run aft and

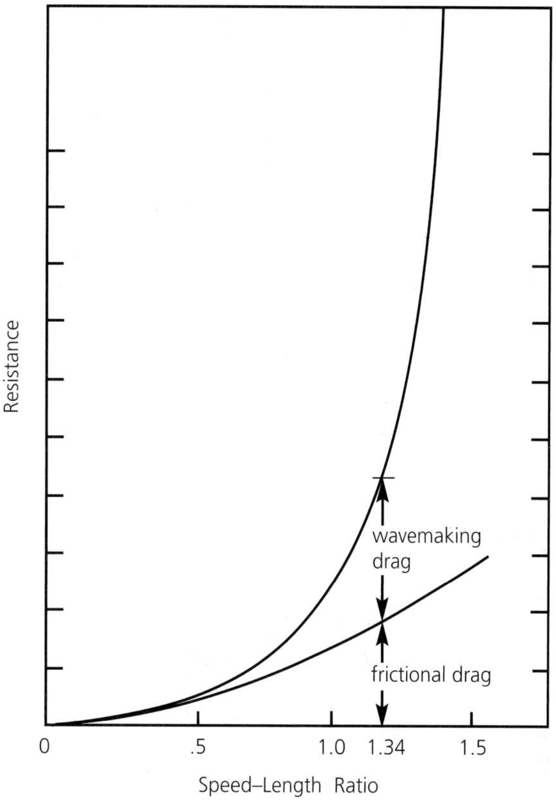

Curves of frictional and wave-making drag as a function of speed for a heavy displacement boat.

the buoyancy in the stern play a significant part in determining the boat's actual maximum speed.

The flatness of the run is quantified by some designers using a *quarter-beam buttock angle*. This can be visualized by imagining a slice through the hull, parallel to its centerline but offset from the centerline by a distance equal to approximately one quarter of the boat's B_{max}. What is primarily of interest is the point at which this line breaks the surface of the water aft and rises to the aft end of the boat. A *buttock angle* (the angle this line makes with the surface of the water) of 15 degrees or less maximizes the boat's effective waterline and, hence, its speed potential.

The buttock angle is easy to see on a boat with a *sugar-scoop stern*—it is demonstrated by the short section of hull that emerges from the water and leads up to the aft edge of the sugar scoop. It is almost always 15 degrees or less. It is not always so easy to pick out with a transom or canoe stern. Sometimes it helps to get a copy of the lines plan from the yacht designer, which often shows this specific line and its intersection with the waterline.

A lines plan also shows the *diagonals*, which are (perhaps) even more significant than the buttock lines. Diagonals are slices through the hull starting at the centerline and sloping downward to intersect the hullside more or less at right angles

Pacific Seacraft 40 (top) *and Alerion Express 38* (bottom) *buttocks lines. (Top drawing courtesy W. E. B. Crealock; bottom drawing courtesy Carl Schumacher)*

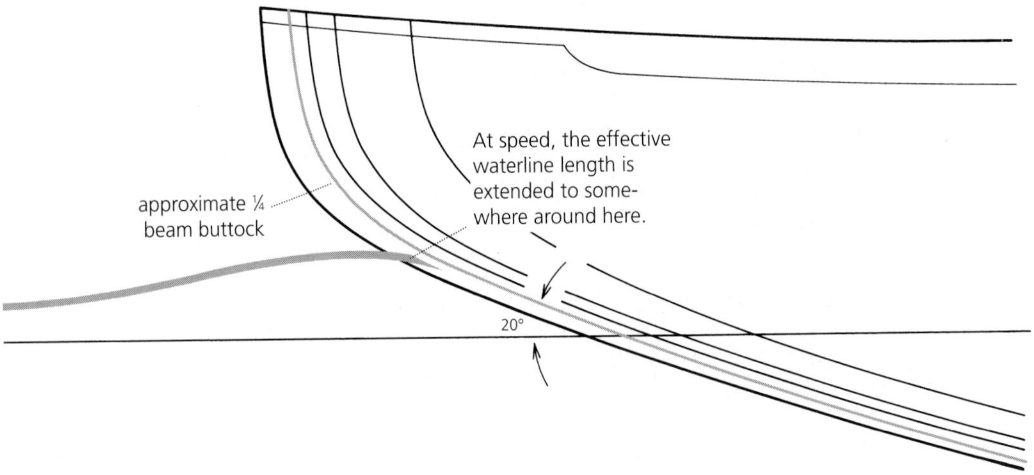

At speed, the effective waterline length is extended to somewhere around here.
approximate ¼ beam buttock
20°

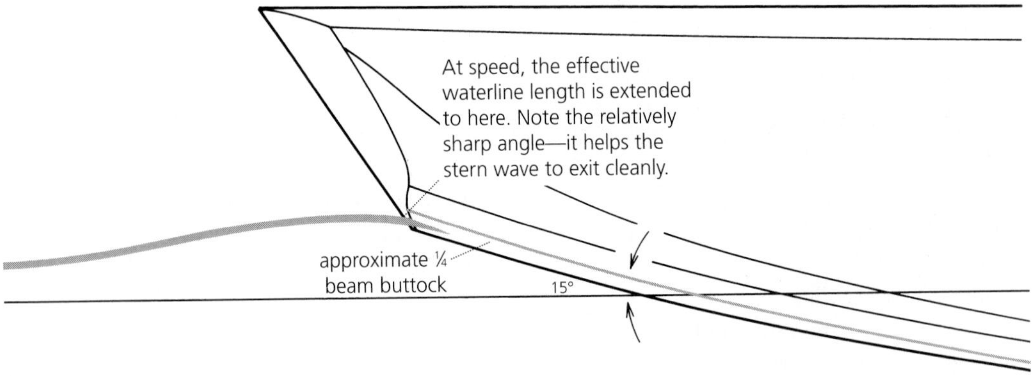

At speed, the effective waterline length is extended to here. Note the relatively sharp angle—it helps the stern wave to exit cleanly.
approximate ¼ beam buttock
15°

(somewhat akin to a segment of an orange). The diagonals crudely approximate the flow of water along the hull at different heel angles. Just as with the buttock lines, a straight run aft increases the boat's effective waterline at speed and, in so doing, maximizes the boat's speed potential.

To be most effective in maximizing speed potential, especially downwind, favorable buttock and diagonal lines need to be combined with flat beamy sections well aft. This reduces any tendency to squat as the stern wave moves aft. In large following seas, this hull shape—especially if combined with a low displacement–length ratio, which minimizes the amount of water that must be pushed aside as the boat moves ahead, which in turn minimizes wave making—allows a boat to surf down wave faces. At that point, the boat temporarily becomes a planing vessel, breaking free of the physical constraints on a displacement boat, and achieving speeds far above its nominal hull speed. Driven hard, such boats often average speeds from 1.5 to 2.0 times the square root of their LWL, with much higher intermittent speeds. In contrast, a boat with little buoyancy aft and buttock and diagonal lines that angle up sharply from the waterline tends to squat, creating a large stern wave. This results in substantial wave-making drag well before the boat's speed is up to 1.34 times the square root of the LWL.

The modern sugar-scoop stern more or less automatically carries the buttock and diagonal lines all the way aft at a favorable angle; whereas, with a canoe stern and some others, it is a real challenge to work favorable buttock angles and diagonals into the overall design of the stern. Our Pacific Seacraft 40 does it better than most canoe sterns. Bill Crealock told me he invested a lot of

A Catalina 42 doing close to 8 knots under power (speed–length ratio of about 1.34). The crest of the stern wave is just behind the aft end of the boat. Note how cleanly it breaks away from the sugar-scoop transom and how little wake the boat makes.

Saga 35 at about 7.5 knots. Again, the crest of the stern wave is just behind the aft end of the boat, breaking cleanly away, and the boat is making remarkably little fuss. (Courtesy Saga Yachts)

A 43-foot (13 m) double-ender doing 6½ knots (speed–length ratio of about 1.2). Despite having a similar LWL to the Catalina 42 and a longer LWL than the Saga 35, and traveling a knot or more slower, the lack of buoyancy in the stern and quarter-beam buttock lines that angle sharply upward are causing the boat to squat and make considerable waves. It will take a huge amount of power to get this boat up to 8 knots.

Island Packet 420, a moderately heavy-displacement cruising boat, close reaching at 8 knots (speed–length ratio of about 1.3). The boat is sailing pretty much on its quarter-beam buttock line; the stern wave is starting to crest right at the transom. (Courtesy Island Packet)

Nada at 7¼ knots (speed–length ratio of about 1.3). A significant stern wave is starting to build, reflecting the substantial displacement of this boat. Despite having a canoe stern, there is sufficient buoyancy aft and the buttock lines are sweet enough for the boat not to squat and for the stern wave to exit cleanly. However, unlike the Catalina 42, at 8 knots (a speed–length ratio of 1.43), this stern wave will start to crest and break: wave-making drag will increase dramatically.

time in getting it right. But if it is so hard to do, why have the canoe stern? In truth, it is more of an aesthetic statement than anything else, except in ultimate survival conditions when running off before breaking seas. In that situation, the canoe stern offers a significantly smaller target to the waves than a large transom or a sugar-scoop stern.

At the other end of the design spectrum, lightweight hulls with beamy aft sections are taken to extremes in many single-handed round-the-world racing boats designed to maximize performance in the heavy-weather, downwind conditions that dominate an east-about circumnavigation in the southern oceans. With their super-light and beamy hulls, high ballast and sail area–displacement ratios, and wide flat sections aft, they achieve speeds and daily runs unheard of in the past. As a result, these features are reflected in contemporary racing boats and increasingly in cruising boats, albeit in a modified form. (Note, however, that similarly high daily runs are also achieved by the Whitbread 60s by using narrow, light-displacement hull forms with deep keels. Although a beamy aft section is currently fashionable, it is by no means the only way to go fast.)

The net result is that we need to modify the popular conception that hull speed equals 1.34 times the square root of the LWL. According to Chuck Paine, "When the displacement–length ratio of a hull is reduced to around 200, the speed–length ratio multiplier climbs from 1.34 to around 1.50 or so, and at a displacement–length ratio of 100, to over 2.00" (*Yachting Monthly*, Jan. 1996). In *The Propeller Handbook*, Dave Gerr published his own formula for using a boat's displacement–length ratio to determine its maximum speed–length ratio:

$$maximum\ practical\ SLR = \frac{8.26}{(DLR)^{0.311}}$$

To work this out requires a scientific calculator. Luckily, Dave produced a graph from this formula, which I've reproduced in chapter 5 (see the figure on page 196).

Speed versus Comfort

A wide stern with full sections above the waterline improves downwind and reaching speed. This sounds great, but the downside to this hull shape and design approach is that it can make a boat cranky and skittish, sometimes resulting in what is known as the *tricycle effect*: the bow, lacking buoyancy, digs in, while the stern rises; the boat tips down and sideways, similar to a tricycle rolling over. The rudder loses its grip on the water and the boat rounds up uncontrollably. It's one thing to operate a temperamental racing boat with a large, gung-ho crew of "deck apes" who are allowed to bring nothing more than a toothbrush onboard (with the handle cut off); it's quite another for a short-handed, "mom-and-pop" crew to load such a boat with cruising stores and take it offshore.

On a cruising boat, it is a fundamental mistake to gear the concept of fast passagemaking to maximizing the absolute speed potential of a boat at the expense of ease of handling, comfortable motion, stability, security, and other highly desirable attributes. Exhilarating performance can be fun in the short term but extremely fatiguing in the long term.

Instead, the goal should be to achieve good sustained performance in all kinds of conditions in an environment that is as relaxing and as much fun as it can be. As Bill Crealock told me: "Speed on passage is quite different from speed around the buoys. A small crew should be able to sail an offshore cruiser to its full potential without exhaustion." Some compromises need to be made with respect to the boat's maximum speed potential; nevertheless, with proper design and modern materials, it should be possible to make these compromises and still—in favorable wind conditions—achieve boat speeds exceeding $1.34 \times \sqrt{LWL}$.

We have, for example, driven our own Pacific Seacraft 40 (by today's standards, a heavy-displacement boat) for hours on end at an average speed of 1.5 times the square root of the LWL. There is no question that many modern cruising boats in our size range achieve higher speed–length ratios than we can (and sail closer to the wind when going to windward), but not—I believe—with the same level of comfort, sense of security, and ease of handling. There is no other 40-foot boat in which I would rather weather a gale or storm.

Looking at longer boats, we get into the realm of what are sometimes referred to as *cruising sleds*. With waterline length–beam ratios of 3.5 and higher, ballast ratios often above 0.40, displacement–length ratios around 100, sail area–displacement ratios frequently well above 20, the characteristic plumb (or near plumb) stem, and beam carried well aft to a sugar-scoop stern, these boats can easily knock off 200-mile days, with a fair degree of comfort even when bashing to windward. (However, Bob Perry, the designer of a number of such boats, notes that "if you reduce the displacement and keep the waterline long, the

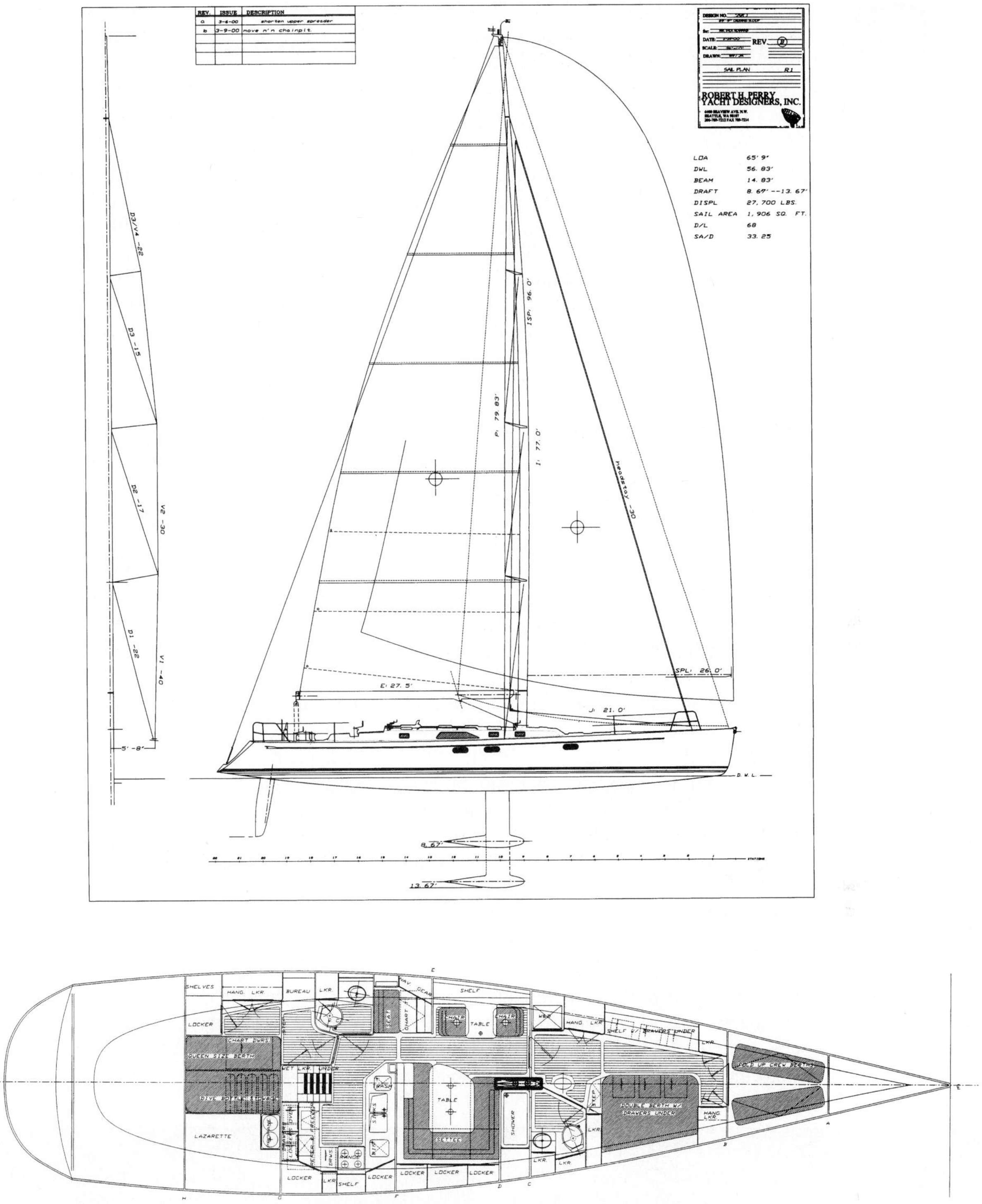

inevitable result is that you eliminate your fore and aft rocker and the boat will pound when going to windward.") They are light on the helm with excellent directional stability—in short, they are wonderful boats.

Unfortunately, to get the interior volume necessary for a couple to cruise in comfort, with adequate tankage and stores, the lowest practical length limit on this style of boat is about 50 feet (for a Dashew design, 56 feet). In addition to the fact that there are times when a boat this size (or its tackle) may be hard to handle, there is the question of cost, both up front and in terms of ownership. Such a boat is out of reach for most of us but, if you can afford it, go for it!

66-foot "cruising sled" from the drawing board of Bob Perry. (Courtesy Bob Perry)

GETTING DOWN TO DETAILS

So far, I have outlined some broad design parameters that I think should govern the choice of a hull type as the platform on which to build cruising dreams. These parameters were largely determined by the requirement to have a secure boat that combines good overall performance with an easy, controllable motion in any conditions, and which has the ability to sail off a lee shore when the chips are down. It is time now to add a number of details.

Construction Materials

I won't delve into the relative merits of different boatbuilding materials—fiberglass, wood, steel, and aluminum—partly because there are several books on the subject, but mostly because the typical cruising sailor is not in a position to make this choice. Almost all of us are driven by economic necessity to buy new or used, production or semicustom boats from boatbuilders who use fiberglass exclusively. End of story!

Fiberglass construction materials and methods have undergone continuous improvement during the past thirty years. Some of the changes minimize the chances of osmotic blisters; some result in stronger, lighter hulls; and some are geared to complying with increasingly stringent environmental regulations, specifically those controlling the emission of *volatile organic compounds* (VOCs) during construction.

The curse of osmotic blisters has dogged the fiberglass boatbuilding industry for many years. In the process of getting a handle on the problem, many boatbuilders and owners have been badly hurt. Today, with new boat construction using vinylester resins and epoxy *barrier coats*, it is reasonable to expect a ten-year, blister-free warranty from a boatbuilder, and to anticipate no problems at the end of the warranty period. Nevertheless, I continue to see production boats fewer than five years old with incipient blistering—which, frankly, is disgraceful.

When buying a new boat, check the resin used in its construction. *Orthophthalic polyesters* are the cheapest, with the worst properties (in addition to their susceptibility to osmotic blistering, they have relatively low strength and elasticity, and are susceptible to stress-cracking); *isophthalic polyesters* are significantly better (stronger, more flexible, and less prone to osmotic blistering); and *vinylester* and *epoxy resins* are the best (lighter, stronger, more flexible, and seemingly immune to osmotic blistering). Vinylesters and epoxies are, of course, much more expensive. Ideally, epoxy—or, at the very least, vinylester—will be used as a barrier coat on the outside of the boat.

When it comes to purchasing older boats, it is definitely a case of "buyer beware." If the boat has never experienced a blistering problem, it probably never will; however, if it has had blisters, it clearly is predisposed to osmotic blistering. The buyer needs to be certain that repair jobs were done by professionals using recognized techniques, and that the hull was then thoroughly barrier-coated. Otherwise, the problem may recur.

So far as VOCs are concerned, the current pressure to keep down emissions during the build process is leading more boatbuilders to complete hull and deck layups inside a *vacuum bag*, which traps VOCs released by the resin and reduces the need for other VOC-emitting solvents. In con-

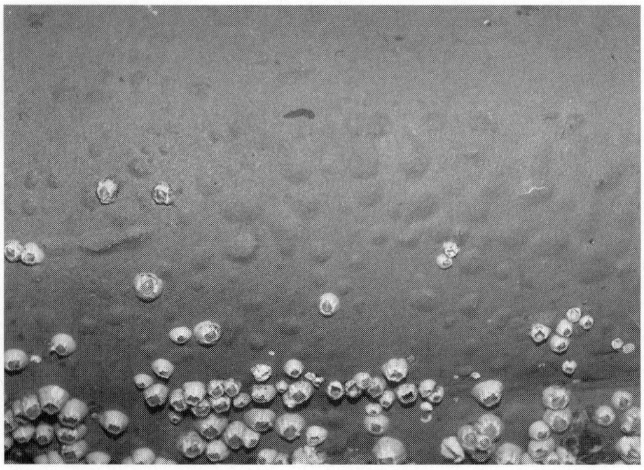

Left: *Osmotic blisters on a boat that is less than a year old; in this case, caused by improper catalyzing of a fairing compound.* Right: *Serious osmosis on another relatively new boat. The manufacturer had a run of problems that resulted in numerous blistered boats.*

Nada's bonded-in copper ground plane.

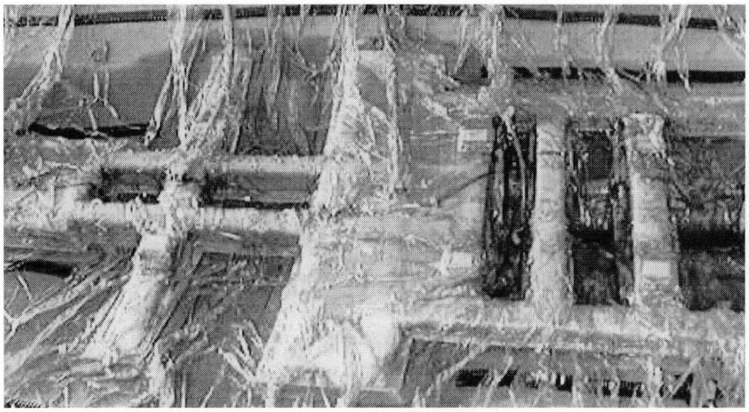

Vacuum-bagging a structural grid for a SCRIMP hull. (Courtesy TPI Composites, Inc.)

ventional vacuum-bagging, the resin is applied before the bag is put on. Another process—the *Seemann Composites Resin Infusion Molding Process* (SCRIMP)—reduces emissions even more by laying the hull fabric up without any resin, adding the vacuum bag, and then injecting the resin. In addition to minimizing VOC releases, this approach to boatbuilding results in higher fabric–resin ratios than in a wet layup, which increases strength and reduces weight—two significant benefits for the boat buyer.

At the time of this writing, the U.S. Environmental Protection Agency (EPA) is considering declaring styrene—a component of most boatbuilding resins—a carcinogen. If this happens, it will increase the pressure on boatbuilders to employ vacuum bags, SCRIMP, and other emissions-trapping technologies. This is likely to have a beneficial fallout for the boat-buying public, although there is a learning process associated with these technologies—avoid buying the first or second boat produced after a boatbuilder switches to new construction methods!

Before leaving the subject of hull construction, it is worth noting that when buying a new boat, it is a good idea to have a substantial area of copper foil and/or screen bonded into the inside of the hull, with a couple of strips protruding in the area of the navigation station. The copper makes an excellent *ground plane* for single sideband (SSB) and other electronics, particularly on a boat that does not have an external ballast keel to serve the same purpose.

(Note: For a technical treatment of cruising boat scantlings, consult Dave Gerr's *Elements of Boat Strength*.)

Cored Hulls and Decks

In recent years, weight-saving technologies have revolutionized racing-boat construction. In particular, S-glass, carbon fiber, and Kevlar can be combined with epoxy resins to produce spectacularly lightweight yet immensely strong structures. Unfortunately, these technologies are still too expensive to be applied to mainstream cruising boats; however, the price of many "exotic" fabrics has been coming down, so we are likely to see much greater use. One technology that has long been affordable is the use of end-grain balsa or foam to produce cored hulls and decks. Properly designed and constructed, these are stronger and lighter than solid hulls and decks.

End-grain balsa and the various foams have different properties. Balsa, for example, excels in terms of compression strength, shear strength, and lack of distortion when hot, which is particularly important in decks (some of the foams get soft at high temperatures). However, the foams have better fatigue strength and better resistance to crack propagation. Balsa is also less resistant to water penetration or contamination with gasoline, oil, and diesel than the foams. Choosing an appropriate core material is a complex subject best left to yacht designers and boatbuilders.

Whatever core is chosen, *a rigid adherence to correct installation procedures is critical to its long-term integrity*. In fact, from the boatowner's perspective, this is more important than the specific core material used. Cored boats should only be bought from quality boatbuilders who have a proven history of successful core use. The key is to ensure a full-strength bond between the core and the outer and inner skins over the entire surface area of the core.

An important contribution to a successful core installation is the use of a vacuum bag (or SCRIMP); however, if not enough resin is applied, or the resin is allowed to "kick off" too soon, or the vacuum bag is not properly installed, there may still be poor, resin-starved areas between the skins and the core. None of this will be visible to the boat buyer (or a surveyor) and it may be decades before problems show up, but when they do, they will be incredibly expensive to fix. Consequently, I reiterate that to avoid long-term problems, people buying a cored hull must be satisfied that the boatbuilder is doing the job right.

For the same panel strength as a solid laminate, a cored hull or deck has significantly thinner total laminations than the noncored hull, which results in sometimes substantial weight savings. However, the cored laminates are spread over both sides of the core so that the exterior laminate is *considerably* thinner (i.e., well under half the thickness) than the noncored hull laminate.

Even so, the nature of a cored hull is such that this thin laminate may have better impact resistance in some situations than the noncored laminate, but what happens if the boat hits a relatively pointed object or grinds on a coral head for a while? The thin laminate is more easily punctured or holds up for proportionately less time than the heavier, noncored laminate. Therefore, regardless of weight considerations—and even if it is not required for engineering purposes—the outer skin on a cruising boat needs to be strong enough to withstand some abuse. Ideally, impact resistance will be substantially increased with a layer of Kevlar cloth somewhere in the layup.

Cores are also prone to damage from water penetration, usually around poorly installed through-hulls or hardware. Balsa, in particular, is susceptible to rot. In cold climates, water in the laminate then freezes over the winter, expanding and cracking the skins from the core, allowing the water to penetrate farther the next season. If the vicious cycle continues for long, extensive structural damage occurs. Unfortunately, this kind of damage is difficult to detect until it is well advanced, at which point repair bills are likely to be horrendous. There are many saturated cored decks out there for which the repairs, if carried out, cost about as much as the total value of the boat.

Core damage from running aground. The hull puncture was quite small, but the core damage extensive. The boatyard has been cutting one square after another from the outer skin, looking for the limit of the damage.

Protecting the Core

This doesn't mean that cores and other modern advances should be rejected in a cruising boat; simply, they must be viewed with the usual long-term skepticism. For this reason, I am not comfortable with any core below the waterline, where the contribution to weight savings is the least important. Above the waterline, a cored hull has significant benefits (in addition to the weight savings, it provides excellent sound and heat insulation) as long as the outer laminate is thick enough to have reasonable puncture and abrasion resistance, and as long as the core itself is totally protected from water penetration in the event of anything short of a hull failure.

Protecting the core comes down to ensuring that no through-hulls or fasteners pass directly through it, so that there is no potential path for water entry. Typically, when a through-hull penetrates the core, the boatbuilder seals the surface of the core with epoxy and then beds the through-hull in the usual manner. This is not adequate; that through-hull may be subjected to severe stresses (e.g., if stood on or hit by a heavy piece of gear), which flex the hull laminate, crack the epoxy, and open up the bedding compound. Water can then migrate undetected into the core.

The only foolproof way to protect the core is to remove it completely in the area of the through-hull and to seal the inner laminate to the outer laminate, thus encapsulating the otherwise exposed edge of the core. If the boatbuilder knows where all the through-hulls will go, this can be done at the molding stage by cutting away the core in the through-hull area before laminating in the inner skin. Otherwise, it can be done when installing the through-hull by cutting an oversized hole through the inner laminate and core down to the outer skin. The resulting cavity is then either filled with a fiberglass "mishmash" and glassed over before drilling the hole for and installing the through-hull (as on our boat), or additional laminations are put in to bond the inner skin down to the outer skin, creating a single skin through which the through-hull is installed.

Core-protection strategies.

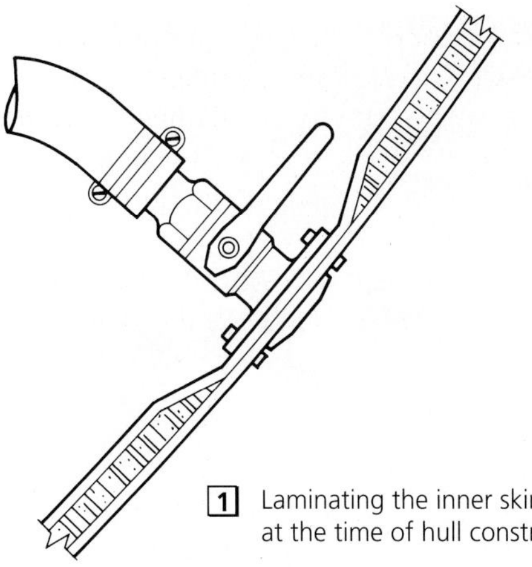

[1] Laminating the inner skin to the outer at the time of hull construction.

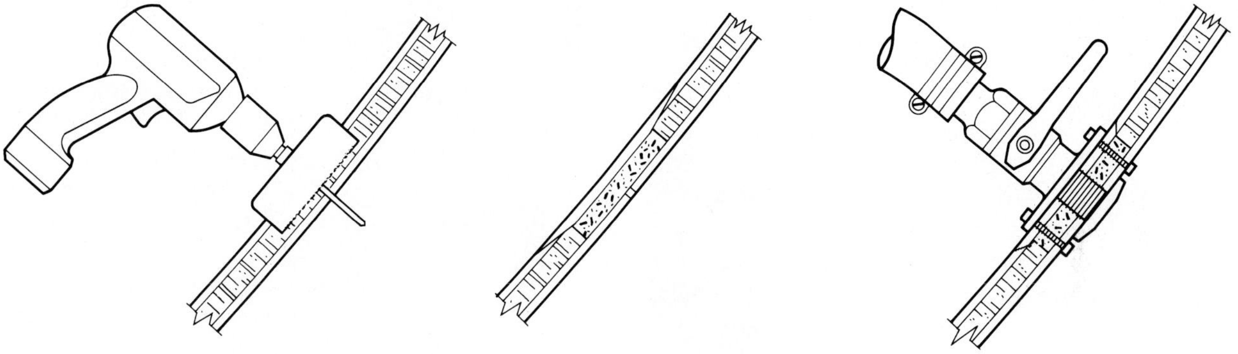

[2] Drill an oversize hole through the inner skin and the core, fill with mishmash, glass over, and install the through-hull through this.

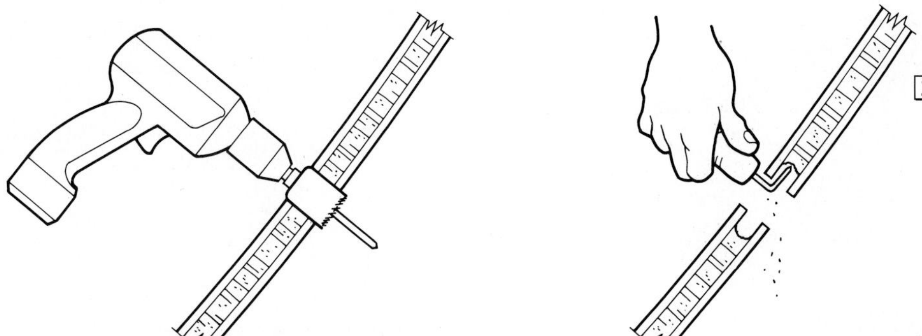

[3] Drill for the through-hull, ream out the core around the hole, or better yet, clean it out with an oversize router bit, fill the cavity with an epoxy paste, and install the through-hull. If the through-hull is held with fasteners, the epoxy plug needs to extend beyond the fasteners.

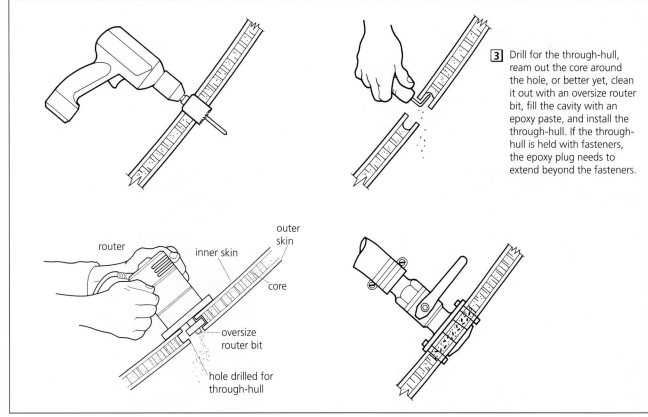

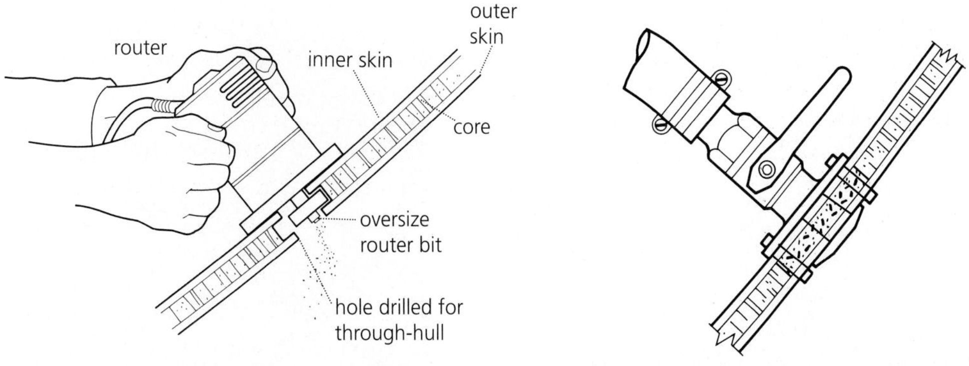

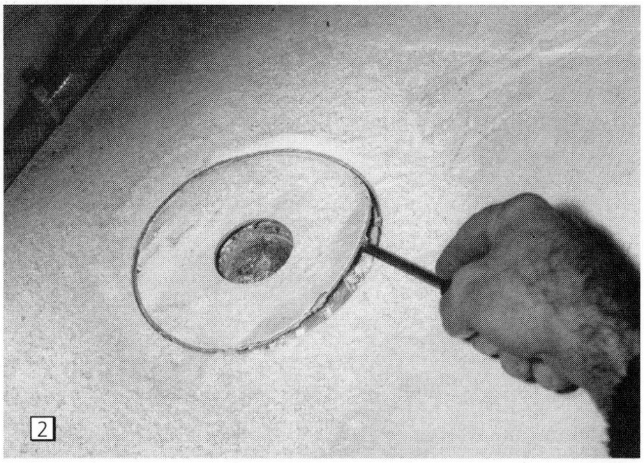

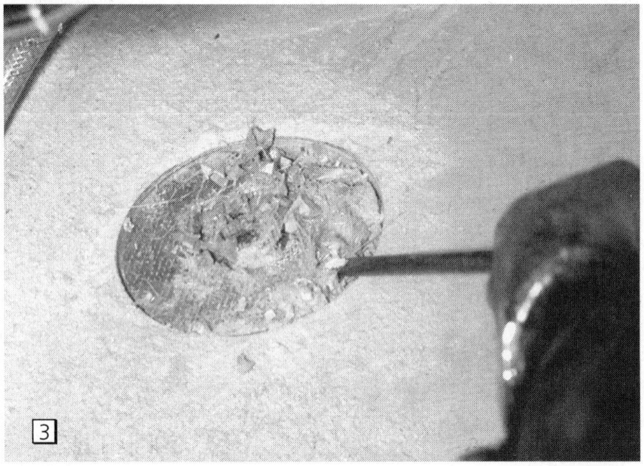

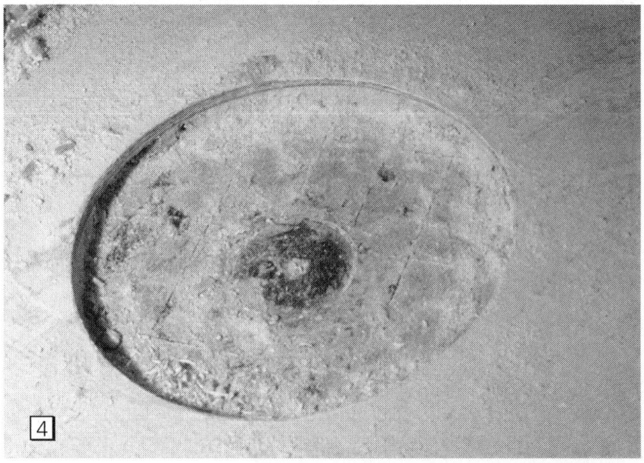

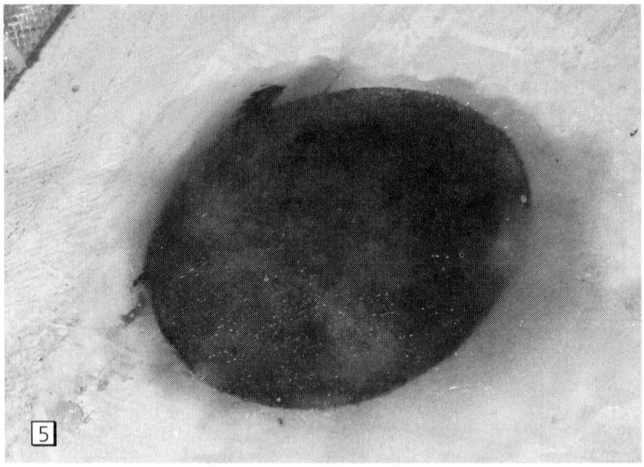

Through-hull installation on Nada. 1. *A 6-inch-diameter hole is drilled through the inner skin and core.* 2. *The inner skin is pried out.* 3. *The core is dug out.* 4. *The resulting cavity.* 5. *This cavity is filled with mish-mash . . .* 6. *and glassed over, at which time the through-hull is . . .* 7. *installed as normal.*

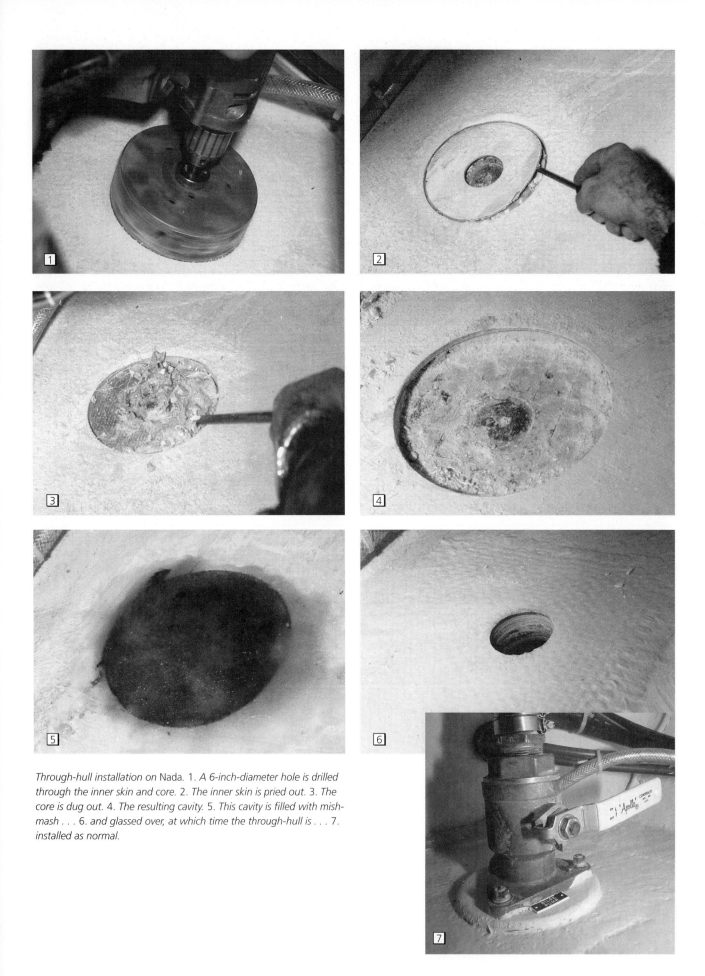

A third approach to core protection is often used. After the hole is drilled for a through-hull or fastener, the core is dug out around the hole and then the cavity is filled with epoxy paste. If done correctly, this effectively seals the edge of the hole and provides a load-bearing epoxy plug for the fitting. However, too often the core is removed with the bent tip of a file handle or maybe a bent nail in the chuck of an electric drill, making a poor job of digging out the core and filling the cavity. For this reason, I am not an advocate of this approach. If it is used, a better job results when the core is removed with a large router bit. Note that if a seacock is held in place with fasteners (rather than threaded onto its through-hull), *it is important to dig out enough of the core and create a large enough epoxy plug for the fasteners to go through the plug and not the core* (this takes considerable digging—it is rarely done).

Cored Decks

Cored decks are more of a problem than cored hulls. The arguments in favor of a core are compelling (because decks are high, the weight savings improve performance, and the additional stiffness reduces the interior framing, which decreases construction costs and increases headroom); however, the tremendous number of through-deck fasteners used to attach hardware—and the high loads imposed on much of the hardware—make it very difficult to guarantee the long-term integrity of the core. High-stress areas are generally given plywood inserts that, among other benefits, minimize the flexing of the skins and, therefore, the likelihood of seals around fasteners getting breached. But ultimately, it is impractical to provide a foolproof long-term seal to either these inserts or the core at all points of penetration.

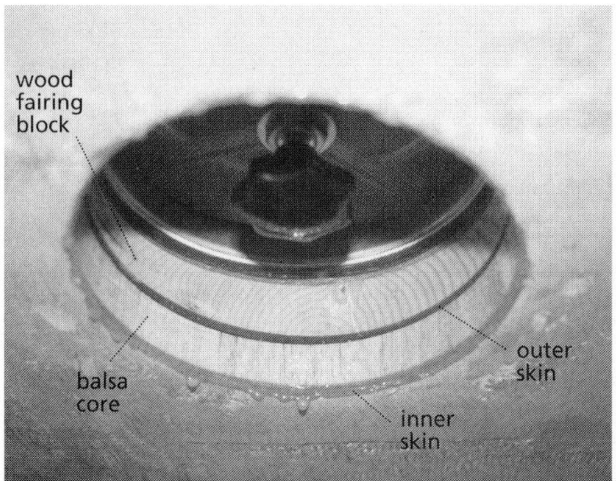

Cutout for a mushroom ventilator. Note the exposed balsa core—it needs to be well sealed.

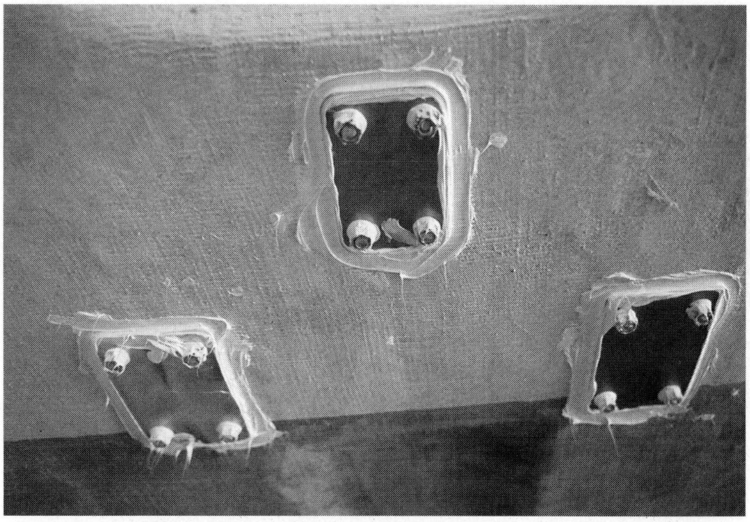

Substantial backing plates spread hardware stresses and minimize the chance of leaks developing. My preference is to not bed the backing blocks. This way, if a leak develops at the deck level, it is possible for the water to make it into the boat and sound the alarm, rather than being trapped in the core.

Substantial backing plates on the underside of hardware spread stresses and minimize the chances of seals being breached. Tests sponsored by *Yachting Monthly* and conducted by Marlow Ropes Research and Development Department after the Fastnet disaster highlight the fact that, in general, metal backing plates do a better job of spreading loads than wood (thick fiberglass also works well).

If seals get breached, anything that prevents the accumulation of standing water around through-deck fasteners will help minimize water ingress and core damage. In particular, the molding-in of raised bosses for winches, rope clutches, genoa and staysail tracks, water and diesel fills, chainplate attachment points, hatches, and so on is an excellent feature. Beyond this, the boatowner is, to a large extent, dependent on the quality of the hardware installation. If there are any signs of leaks (e.g., water in the boat or rust stains emanating from fasteners), the relevant fasteners should be pulled, the core checked (and dried out and sealed if necessary), and the fasteners re-bedded.

In my opinion, backing blocks should not be bedded to the underside of a deck. That way, if a fastener develops a leak, there is a reasonable chance of water coming through to the cabin, alerting the boatowner. The resultant drip, however annoying, is preferable to the water migrating undetected into the deck core, causing long-term damage.

Hull-to-Deck Joints

The hull-to-deck joint is one of the most critical structural elements on a boat, both from an engineering perspective and for preventing frustrating leaks. Too many boats, especially inexpensively constructed boats, have joints that

Left: *Any kind of a flush-mounted fastener through a cored deck, particularly on a highly loaded part, is an invitation for eventual moisture penetration of an improperly sealed core.* Right: *Raised moldings wherever fasteners penetrate the core help minimize moisture ingress.*

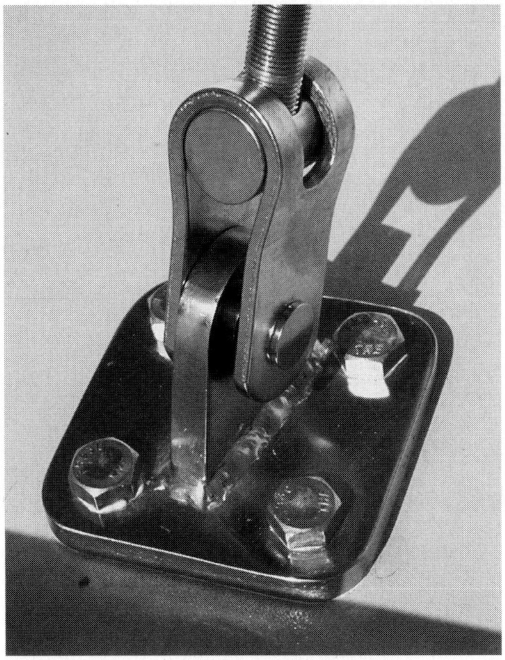

open up over time. I have seen joints that are held together with nothing more than bedding compound, joints that are fastened with pop rivets and self-tapping screws, and joints that appeared to be held together with little more than a plastic rubbing strake!

This is totally unacceptable in a cruising boat. Joint failures threaten the structural integrity of the boat and, ultimately, the safety of the crew, not to mention that they are extremely expensive to repair.

A well-constructed cruising boat typically has a substantial mating surface between the hull and the deck, which is usually established by bonding a flange to the hull side and setting the deck on this shelf. Adhesive sealant is applied to the flange (3M's 5200 polyurethane adhesive sealant is the most popular) and then the deck is through-bolted to the shelf using ¼-inch (6 mm) stainless steel fasteners on 6-inch (150 mm) centers; the result is almost bulletproof.

Stainless steel self-tapping screws are sometimes used as a substitute for bolts (the screws can be installed in a fraction of the time). However, this should be a matter for concern. These screws have nowhere near the cross-sectional area of a similarly sized bolt and, therefore, significantly less strength; in addition, threads tapped into fiberglass are weak and prone to failure (the pressure of the screws tends to delaminate the fiberglass rather than cut effective threads). What is more, stainless steel self-tapping screws are notoriously prone to crevice corrosion and failure if water penetrates the screw holes.

Another approach for the hull-to-deck joint is to bond the hull and deck together by laying in several layers of fiberglass. As long as an adequate layup is used, this too is almost bulletproof. Whichever approach is used, the hull-to-deck joint—particularly any fasteners, including fasteners for stanchions and other hardware that pass through this area—*should be readily accessible for inspection and repairs*. Unfortunately,

A well-engineered hull-to-deck joint. (Courtesy Pacific Seacraft)

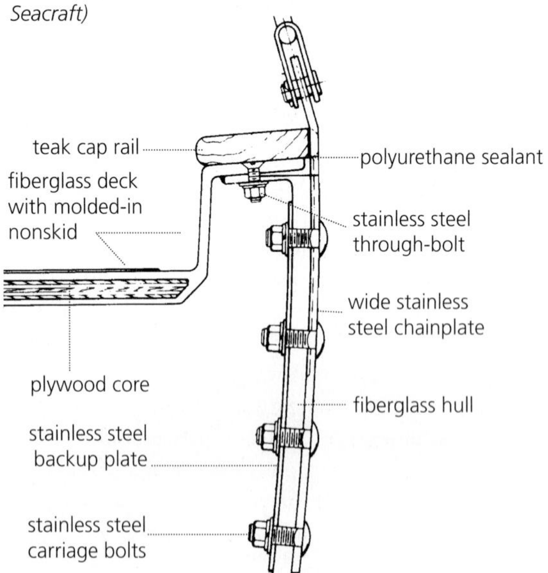

the trend on modern boats is to make this joint almost completely inaccessible.

Structural Reinforcements

Yacht designers design and boatbuilders build a boat for a given set of conditions. Few boats are taken more than 20 miles offshore or out of range of coastal weather reports. If foul weather is brewing, the boatowner will have warning enough to find shelter. As a result, there is no reason to expect that the majority of boats will ever encounter heavy weather or have to survive gale-force or stronger winds with their concomitant sea states. It follows that there is no reason to build for such conditions, particularly because it substantially drives up the cost of a boat and negatively impacts some aspects of performance. It makes no sense for either the builder or the customer.

However, anyone who ventures more than a day or two offshore faces the risk of being caught in a gale. If you intend to cross oceans, it is not a matter of "if" but rather "when." The average production sailboat, which was not designed for these conditions, almost always comes through OK—thousands have gone around the world in all kinds of conditions. But then there are some that don't make it. Speaking for myself, if I am to go offshore, I won't bet the life of my family on a boat not purpose-built for the task.

Of particular note is that the modern fiberglass boat derives a significant part of its overall strength and rigidity from its bulkheads and interior joiner work. These are frequently structural elements but, to work in this respect, they have to remain attached to the hull at all times. During the 1979 Fastnet race, the extreme conditions caused bulkheads and other interior structures to come loose on several boats.

There are many lightweight "cruising" boats that would also start to come apart if faced with the kind of wracking that takes place in a severe gale, or even when pounding to windward in rough seas. Structural integrity in these situations requires hull-to-bulkhead joints that are made using properly prepared plywood. (This is critical: If the plywood is not sealed in the area of the bond prior to bonding, it will soak up the resin used to bond it in place, resulting in a glue-starved joint prone to failure. For sealing and bonding, epoxy or vinylester resins are much stronger than polyester). The *tabbing* (fiberglass strips used to make the bond) must cover an adequate surface area on both the hull side and the bulkhead, and must contain a sufficient number of layers of fiberglass layup (I'm no engineer, so I can't define "adequate" or "sufficient," but I like to see a 4- to 6-inch-wide contact area, and I know that a layer of 18-ounce roving is better than the single thin layer of fiberglass mat frequently used).

Bulkhead on Nada *being prepared for bonding to the deck structure.*

Given properly bonded bulkheads and other structural elements, a cruising-boat hull and deck should be rigid enough to barely flex under the kind of weight and pressure applied by an average person. If hull or deck panels can be flexed, I would have qualms about taking the boat out to sea. This admittedly imprecise and subjective "flex test" rules out many lightly built boats as unsuitable for offshore cruising. There will be many boats that pass the test but that still have not-so-easy-to-detect structural deficiencies, which is why a competent marine surveyor should always inspect a boat before a purchase is consummated (see chapter 6).

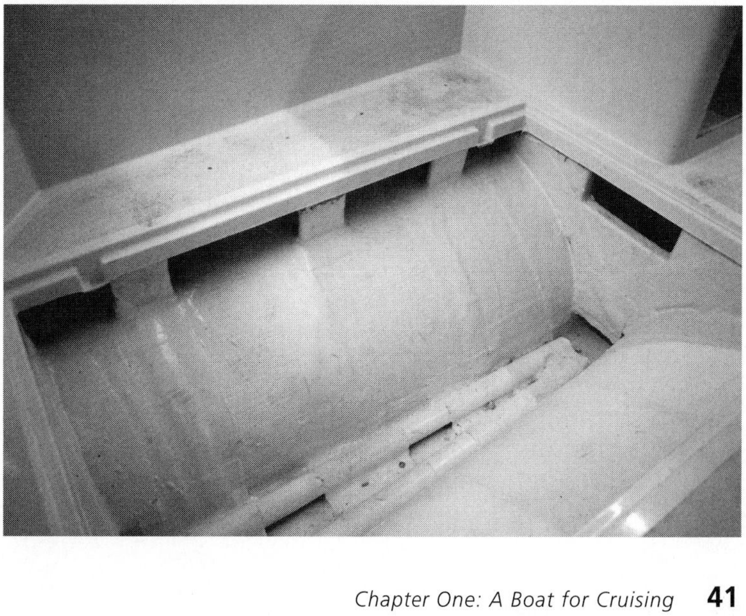

Excellent bonding of interior bulkheads and other components.

The keel and skeg arrangement on Nada *is such that however distressing a grounding such as this may be (Terrie is looking a little stressed out!), little or no damage will be done to the boat.*

As added insurance, at the design stage, it is often possible to seal a bulkhead up forward, and maybe one aft, to the hull to create watertight compartments. This is particularly beneficial up forward because it is the most likely area of impact damage. On an increasing number of modern boats, a watertight bulkhead is combined with a reinforced "crash zone" down the centerline of the boat from a little above the waterline aft toward the keel—an excellent design feature.

Keels

For a cruising boat, it should always be assumed that at some point the boat will be run aground *hard!* The keel and hull need to be designed to minimize the shock-loading to the boat, with adequate strength to ensure that no damage occurs. When we ordered our new Pacific Seacraft, one of my design specifications was the ability to hit a rock pile at 8 knots with nothing more than cosmetic damage. I think the manufacturer thought I was joking; I was not.

Much of the force will be taken out of a grounding if the likely point of contact (the leading edge and *toe* of the keel) forms a gentle curve. In its most extreme form, this results in the kind of entry exhibited by traditional, long-keeled boats. Our old William Atkin *Ingrid* (a Colin Archer derivative) was like this, and took many severe groundings (including an 8-knot impact with a rock pile) with nothing more than a few scratches. On another occasion, we ran over a submerged telephone pole at 6½ knots without making a mark.

However, this kind of profile maximizes the underwater wetted surface area, impacting light-air performance, while the resulting long keel inhibits maneuverability. Not surprisingly, this hull form is no longer fashionable. I would argue that a reasonable compromise between this and the contemporary racing-derived fin keel is a cutaway forefoot leading to a keel that has a leading edge angled well away from the vertical, with a well-rounded forefoot (keel toe) to the ballast (the most likely point of impact).

Nada*'s keel being installed. Note the swept-back leading edge, the rounded toe, the wide root area (which spreads the shock load of a grounding), and the sloping angle at which the keel joins the boat's keel stub (which also helps spread shock loads to the hull without unduly stressing the keel bolts): all are desirable features in a cruising boat.*

Keel with a relatively narrow root. Any kind of grounding will impart a severe shock load. Note the crack at the front edge of the keel-to-hull joint caused by a grounding that we, on Nada, *would consider all in a day's cruising!*

Typically, the boat with this kind of an entry has an external ballast keel—which can easily be in the optimum shape of a bulb—fastened to a keel stub built down below the hull's canoe body. If the contact surface of the keel stub slopes down from forward to aft and is given a substantial surface area, even severe impact loads will be transmitted to the hull without damage.

What is not acceptable, in my opinion, is a deep, narrow fin keel with a near-vertical leading edge and a narrow width (*root*) at the point of attachment to the hull. The keel itself will be prone to bending, while shock loads will be absorbed over a relatively small surface area on the hull. As often as not, a hard knock will result in structural damage that may cause flooding and, in any event, will require the keel to be removed before repairs can be made (the boat frequently has to be torn apart to remove tanks that are obstructing access to the keel bolts). The kind of incident that merely gets the adrenaline flowing on a well-found cruising boat results in expensive damage at best and a possible foundering at worst.

Keel Bolts and Stainless Steel Fasteners

Whatever the keel shape, if the ballast is external, it needs to be fastened in a bulletproof manner. There are two issues here: ensuring that the keel bolts and the floors through which they pass are engineered to take the loads, which should be taken care of by the yacht designer; and ensuring that the bolts will hold up over the long term—I am not sure anybody is taking care of this.

I consider the common practice of casting stainless steel J-bolts into ballast keels to be a matter for concern. Most stainless steels are notoriously subject to crevice corrosion when placed in a damp environment deprived of oxygen (i.e., *anaerobic*). These are precisely the conditions likely to be found at the interface between a lead keel and the hull to which it is fastened, particularly after a few years if the boat has taken some knocks and the joint has cracked, allowing water to penetrate. At this time, because the keel bolts are cast into the lead, there is no way to check for corrosion other than x-raying or dropping the keel in its entirety, something that in practice is never done. I can't help wondering if the boatbuilding industry is creating a problem that will come back to haunt us all in the future.

Of the commonly used grades of stainless steel, 304 is the most likely to corrode; 316 and 317 have significantly better corrosion resistance, while various proprietary alloys (e.g., Aquamet 22) are better still. If stainless steel is used for keel bolts, it should be 316 or something more corrosion resistant, although I still prefer seeing Monel or silicon bronze. In addition, I would like to see a resurrection of the old practice of tapping the keel bolts into the lead so that they can be periodically withdrawn and inspected; if necessary, a heavy steel plate can be cast into the ballast and then drilled and tapped to take the bolts. Another way of making the bolts removable is to cast pockets into the base of the lead for nuts, drill clear through the keel for the bolts, and run the bolts down from inside the boat to the nuts. On our new boat, I had intended to see that we at least got Monel J-bolts; unfortunately, it slipped my mind at a critical moment and we ended up with the standard installation. We'll have to see how it does.

Stainless steel J-bolts cast into Nada's *keel: I much prefer to see the bolts installed in a way that makes them removable.*

A more general issue concerns the widespread use of stainless steel in modern boatbuilding, particularly the near-universal use of stainless steel for deck hardware and fasteners. Any time this stainless steel is put in a damp deoxygenated environment, it has the potential to develop crevice corrosion. These are precisely the conditions found when water penetrates the deck or hull surrounding a fastener.

Too many people think the rust stain dribbling down the cabinside from the base of a piece of hardware or down the hullside from a chainplate bolt is simply cosmetic. It may be, but then again there may be an active corrosion cell significantly damaging the fastener. On an offshore boat, it is my opinion that critical, highly loaded fasteners (e.g., those on winches, turning blocks, and chainplates) should be pulled and inspected every ten years (or at least a sampling of them). In addition to properly bedding and backing them, using 316 stainless steel in place of the more common 304 significantly reduces the chances of corrosion. The fasteners themselves still need to be readily accessible, as opposed to the common practice of hiding them behind joinerwork and cabin liners.

Rust stains emanating from a series of chainplate bolts; these are almost certainly not just cosmetic stains.

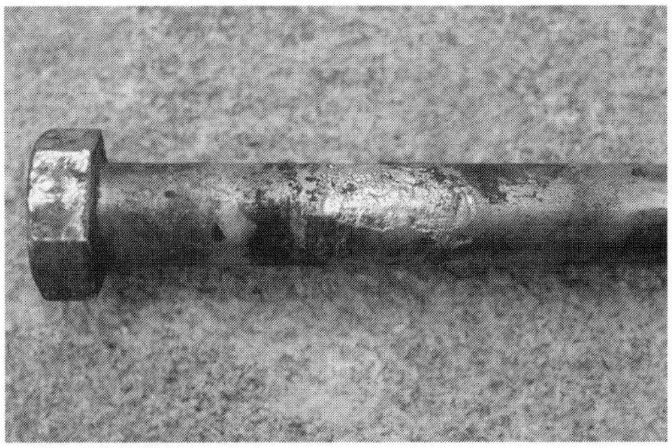

Stainless steel bolt with active galvanic corrosion cell (the shiny metal).

Finally, it is worth noting that the majority of hose clamps that are labeled "all stainless" are, indeed, all stainless, but with a band of 304 stainless steel and a screw of 400-series stainless steel (the 400-series is easy to machine). Unfortunately, a 400-series stainless screw readily corrodes in a salt-laden atmosphere and, in the process, corrodes the band where it is in contact with the screw, which ultimately results in band failure. Although widely used, these hose clamps are not suitable for marine use. Instead, what should be used are "all 300-series stainless" hose clamps (300 series is sometimes known as "18-8") or, better yet, "all 316 stainless" (or any hose clamp from AWAB, a manufacturer that uses only 316 stainless steel). If in doubt about an existing hose clamp, remember that 300-series stainless is not magnetic or only mildly so, whereas 400-series is highly magnetic and can be easily detected with a magnet.

Top: *All-stainless-steel hose clamp freely corroding. The screw is made from 400-series stainless steel.* Left: *400-series stainless steel is highly magnetic.*

Rudders and Skegs

Rudder bearings, tubes, and shaft seals are a reasonably common source of trouble. There are two issues here: having bearings and a rudder-tube construction adequate to absorb the high stresses generated by the rudder; and keeping the rudder free-turning under heavy loads. These are not quite the same, inasmuch as some hulls—particularly lightweight hulls—flex under load, causing even well-mounted rudder stocks to bind. These kinds of problems can be minimized with self-aligning bearings. In any event, if a boat is to be taken offshore, it is important to check both the quality of the rudder installation and its functionality in all conceivable situations.

With wheel-steering, most rudder tubes terminate close to the waterline, necessitating some kind of shaft seal around the rudder stock (similar to the shaft seal on a propeller shaft). The seals are frequently neglected by boatowners and become a source of "mysterious" (and sometimes serious) leaks. Any seal needs to be periodically inspected and maintained—just like the propeller-shaft seal—and should be reasonably accessible in case of trouble at sea.

Although a well-designed spade rudder is the most efficient way to go on a modern boat and results in the "lightest" helm (as a result of part of the rudder being forward of the rudder stock), in the cruising environment we have to ask the same question as we did with the keel: What happens in the event of a serious grounding?

Spade rudder. Excellent performance, but limited strength in a grounding.

This boat hit a reef and was washed over the top. The boat did fine, but the spade rudder was seriously damaged. A skeg-mounted rudder would likely have survived.

Spade-rudder aficionados tell you that this type of rudder can be made as strong as any other—and that the lower end of a skeg is vulnerable to damage, disabling the rudder—whereas a spade rudder can lose its lower end and still function. Perhaps in theory, but spade-rudder stocks on production and semiproduction boats are almost never strong enough to take a serious shock; over the years, I've seen many failed ones (our local boat yard used to have a pile of them) but not a single failed skeg. Ultimately, much of the spade-rudder load is concentrated at the point where the stock enters the hull, as opposed to two or three points on a skeg-mounted rudder. The hull itself will be highly stressed at the point of entry of the spade rudder, as opposed to the more evenly distributed loads generated by a skeg. There is clearly greater potential for trouble, which can be mitigated to some extent by super-high-tech construction (carbon fiber), but the cost puts this outside the reach of most of us.

Some rudders are mounted to a partial skeg, terminating about halfway down the rudder. This provides good support for the rudder, while minimizing the wetted surface area created by the skeg; it also permits the lower part of the rudder to protrude forward of the stock, which helps to establish steering balance (a semibalanced rudder, as opposed to the completely unbalanced rudder with a full skeg, resulting in "heavier" steering), but it does not provide the same support and protection as a full-length skeg. Furthermore, the attachment point halfway down the rudder (at the base of the skeg) can be an open invitation to foul fishing nets and lobster-pot lines at a depth where they are particularly inaccessible.

Partial skeg. The lower rudder bearing is an invitation to foul lines.

Whatever the rudder and skeg configuration, it is essential that the keel has a greater draft than the rudder and/or skeg. This way, in the event of a severe grounding, the keel takes the hit. I've seen contemporary rudders that actually have more draft than the boat's keel; in my opinion, this is absurd!

In the event of a grounding, and if the boat dries out, the keel and rudder must be built strong enough to support the full weight of the boat without damage and in a relatively stable manner. For this to occur, there must be a reasonable surface area on the bottom of the keel (a bulb keel does well here, as in so many other areas), with a flat or nearly flat profile far enough forward and aft of the boat's center of gravity to stop the boat toppling over on its ends if, for example, it is laid up against a jetty.

However, a wide, flat keel is undesirable (some wing keels fall into this category). If the boat runs aground parallel to a steeply sloping shoreline with the tide going out, it will want to lie down on the "downhill" side. This will lay it over far more than if laid down on the "uphill" side and will exacerbate problems such as stowed gear falling around and wet-type batteries leaking. It also makes the boat vulnerable to flooding when the tide comes back in, particularly if any seas are running (for more on running aground and how to deal with it, see chapter 9).

An interesting keel variant: twin bilge keels designed for drying out in tidal waters.

Skegs and Propellers

With a full-depth skeg, the likelihood of fouling lines in the water is minimized if the leading edge of the skeg (as with the keel) has a relatively gentle slope in profile, which allows lines to slide down and under, finally clearing the boat. However, for this to work, the lower rudder bearing (i.e., the heel bearing) must be at the base of the skeg, not partially down (which allows lines to get jammed between the skeg and rudder, from where it is especially difficult to dislodge them).

Even with a full-length skeg with the heel bearing at its base, if the boat has a strut-supported shaft and propeller beneath the hull, lines that work free of the keel are likely to bounce upward and foul the propeller. This is why, on a cruising boat, I prefer a propeller in an aperture, despite the negative impact it has on performance under power. With a modest slope to the keel and skeg and an aperture-mounted propeller, it should be possible to sail through a minefield of lobster pots without concern. Eliminating the strut also removes another piece of hardware that is vulnerable to damage.

Full skeg, but with the lower bearing halfway down. If a line gets trapped between the base of the rudder and the skeg, it will be a devil of a job to clear it. The near-vertical face of the skeg and rudder is also an invitation to snag lines.

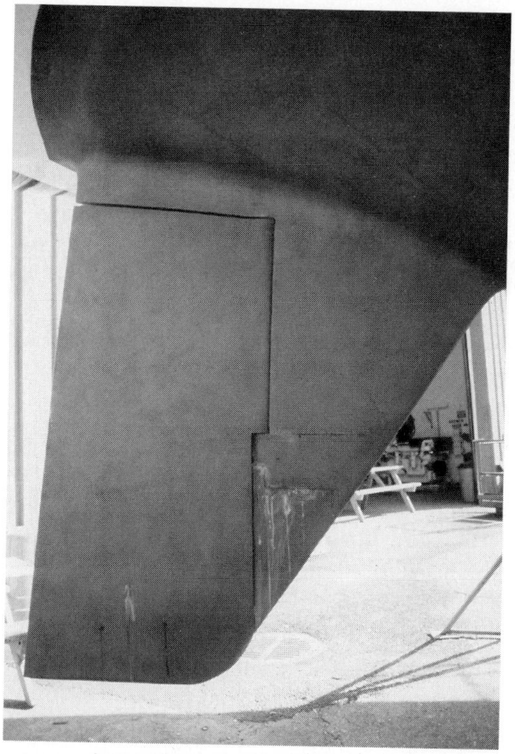

This skeg is angled enough to shed lines, but there is still a risk of something catching between the base of the skeg and the rudder.

Full skeg on Nada, with the heel bearing at the base of the skeg, and the propeller in an aperture—not the most efficient underbody from a speed perspective, but as close to being bulletproof as possible in a cruising environment.

Ideally, the propeller is accessible from the water surface to a swimmer with a face mask and snorkel (it is on our Pacific Seacraft), which obviates the need to dive on the rare occasion when it does get fouled (unfortunately, no propeller on a modern boat in which the beam is carried well aft is this accessible).

If the boat has a propeller strut, pay particular attention to its strength and mounting. A V-shaped strut is much stronger than the common P strut but, of course, creates more drag. A P-shaped strut is frequently fiberglassed in place on the base of the hull. This kind of installation is relatively easy to damage with a sideways shock load, as well as troublesome and expensive to repair. From a cruising perspective, it is better to have a strut that is through-bolted to an accessible, oversized backing block. This spreads the load to a substantial area of the hull, while making inspection and repairs reasonably simple. Some racing boats have the strut set in a reinforced slot in the base of the boat, with the sides of the slot extended upward toward the deck and the strut through-bolted. This provides excellent support while making strut removal and repairs relatively easy.

Bilge Water and Tankage

Traditionally, cruising boats had a relatively narrow beam with a deep hull, resulting in *hull sections* (cross-sectional slices through the boat) that have a characteristic wineglass shape. In contrast, the modern boat is beamier with a canoe body having a flat bottom, producing a U shape. Among other drawbacks, the former shape severely cramps accommodations and minimizes the width of the cabinsole; the latter shape produces great accommodations with a substantial sole.

Bilge-Water Removal

Leaving aside the performance implications of these contrasting hull forms, certain pragmatic matters need to be considered. One is the matter of bilge sumps. With the wineglass section, it is simplicity itself to establish a central sump to which all bilge water drains at all angles of heel and, from there, to pump the water overboard.

Not so on the boat with flat sections. Often there is no designed-in bilge sump at all and, in any case, the moment the boat takes on more than a modest heel, the bilge water surges up the sides of the boat and into wiring harnesses and storage lockers rather than remaining in the bilge. Furthermore, it can be very difficult to

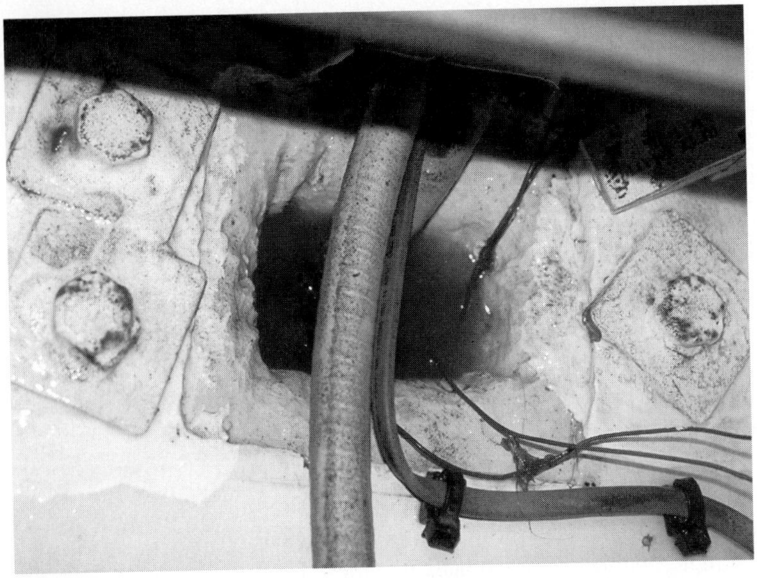

Minimal bilge on a modern, flat-bodied, lightweight production boat. This is still better than some boats that don't have any kind of a bilge sump!

concentrate this water in one location in order to pump it overboard. Several bilge pumps, or multiple *strum boxes* (bilge-water pickups) with a selector valve, may be needed: one on the centerline for static trim and one each to port and starboard for when the boat is heeled.

Another way to approach bilge-water collection on flat-section boats is to bond two low fore-and-aft baffles down the boat on either side of the centerline. Some kind of check valve (a simple flap valve or something more sophisticated) is set into the base of these baffles at appropriate locations, allowing water to flow toward the centerline but not the other way. When the boat is heeled one way, all the water on the windward side flows through the windward check valves into the center channel, but it is blocked from flowing down to the leeward side by the leeward check valves. The water gets concentrated in the center channel, from where it is pumped overboard by the bilge pump. If the boat tacks, the same happens in reverse, clearing any water from the other side of the boat.

A variation on this theme—described to me by Rob Humphreys, a well-known British yacht designer—is to substitute lengths of flexible hose for the check valves, with a float on the end of each hose. The hoses allow bilge water to flow into the central duct, while the floats keep the ends of the hoses above the water level in the duct, thereby preventing any water from flowing out of the hoses on the leeward side.

Many modern boats have a structural grid bonded to the bottom of the hull, forming numerous relatively small compartments. Unfortunately, too often the size of the *limber holes* (drainage holes) in these compartments is woefully inadequate, added to which many times the compartments will drain only on a level keel. Each hull segment needs an adequately sized limber hole that drains to a central bilge sump at normal angles of heel. Even so, irrespective of what is done to concentrate bilge water, one of the side effects of the modern performance-oriented, flat-bottomed hull is the risk of getting bilge water up in the lockers when at sea.

The farther offshore you intend to take a boat and the rougher the conditions that may be encountered, the more the ability to keep the bilges dry should be a matter for concern. It seems to me that, however it is achieved, *any offshore cruising boat needs a bilge sump with the capacity to hold a modest amount of water, and hull sections or drainage that cause bilge water to end up in the sump at all normal angles of heel.* I particularly like the *ventral fin* (the portion of the hull between the keel and the skeg)

Below left: *A technique for bilge-water entrapment on a flat-bottomed boat.* Below right: *Rob Humphreys's method of bilge-water entrapment on a flat-bottomed boat.*

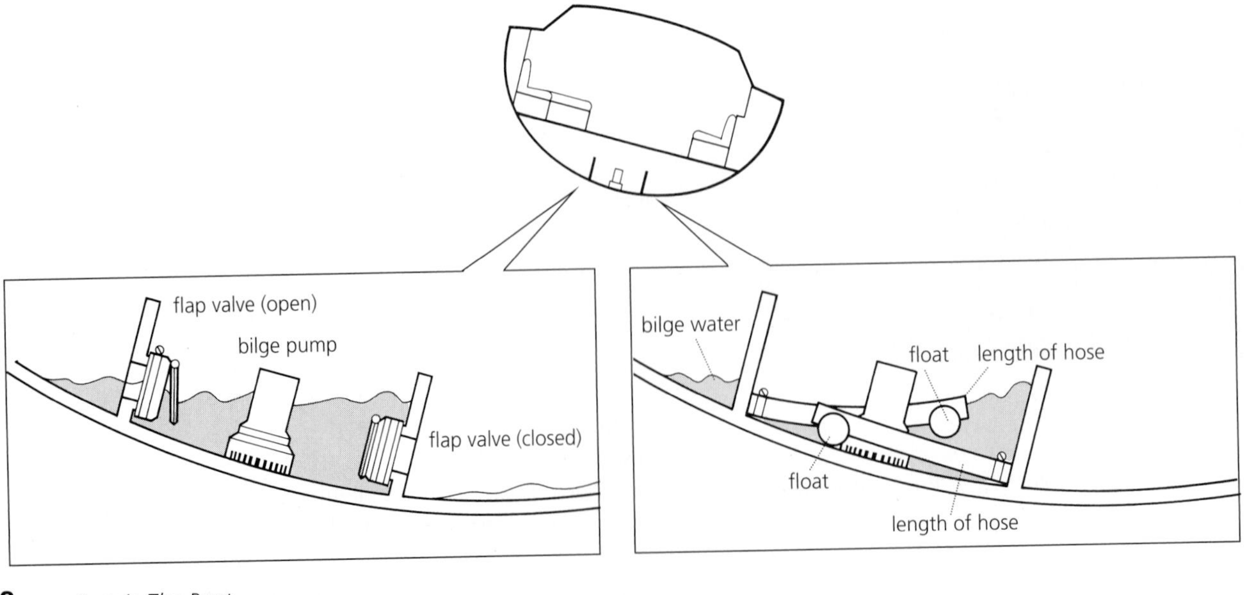

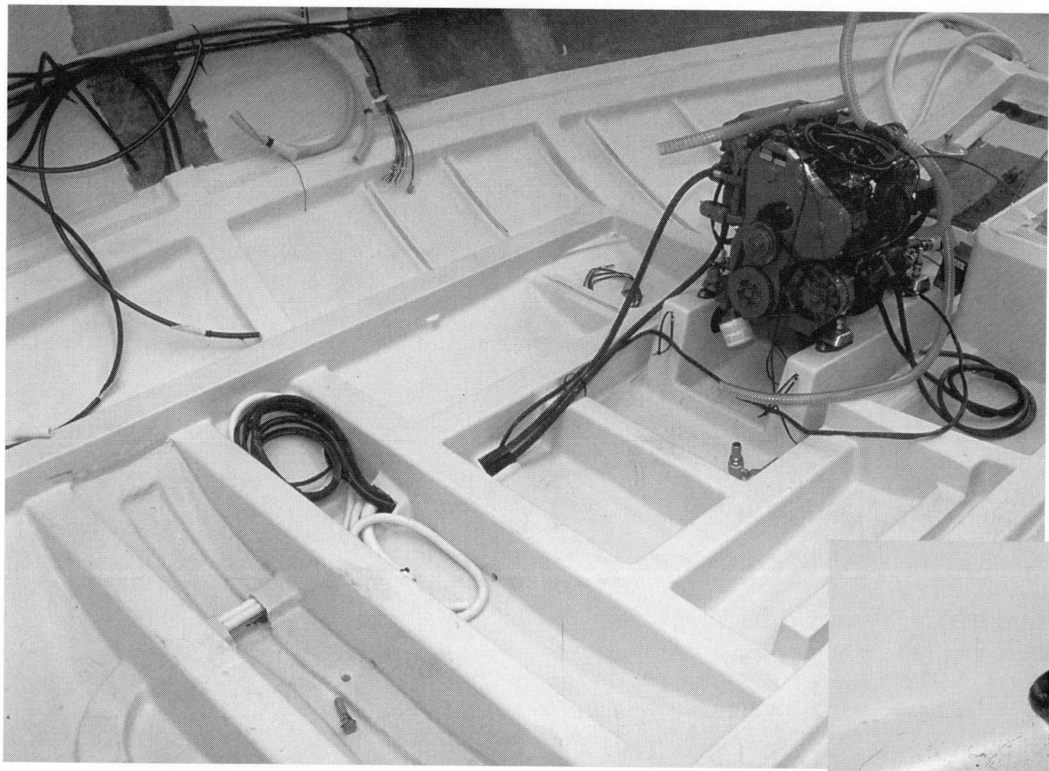

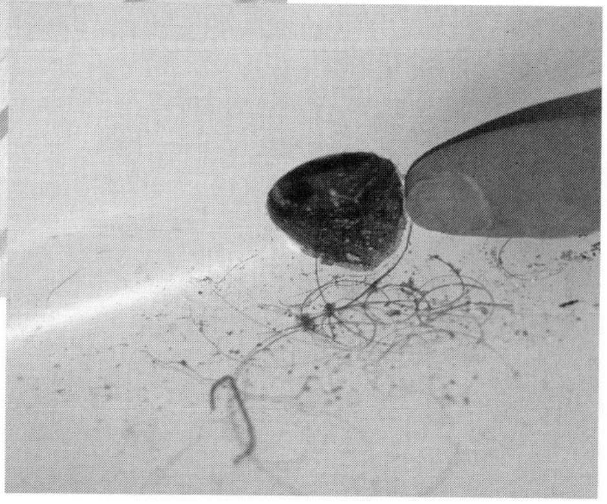

Comprehensive structural grid in a modern boat. (Courtesy Beneteau) Inset: *Small limber hole in the structural grid on a modern, flat-bottomed boat (note the staple for size comparison).*

on the Pacific Seacraft 40. Its primary purpose is to improve directional stability and provide structural reinforcement to the skeg. In the process, it also provides an effective channel to the bilge and, by today's standards, a large sump.

Even with the ventral fin, if for any reason the bilge sump is not pumped down (maybe the pump is out of action), the relatively flat midships sections—driven by the need to increase interior volume to stay competitive at boat shows—will cause water to pool out at the turn of the bilge once the heeling angle exceeds 18 to 20 degrees. Given the size of the sump, a fair amount of water has to be in the boat before this happens. Nevertheless, it is preferable that it does not occur until heeling angles exceed 25 degrees.

In the absence of the ventral fin, it is desirable to have some *rocker* designed into the canoe body; that is, the bottom of the hull, when looked at in profile, curves from both fore and aft down to its deepest section (somewhere amidships). This causes water to puddle out at the low spot, from where it can be pumped overboard. Almost all traditional cruising designs have a fair amount of rocker; many modern boats have little to none (when looked at in profile, the bottom of the boat is more or less flat from well forward to well aft). In addition to making it difficult to concentrate bilge water, the boat without rocker tends to pound in a seaway as its flat bottom smashes down into waves and then stops abruptly. The boat with substantial rocker tends to have a more gentle entry and easier motion.

It goes without saying that any bilge pump, its strainer (or strum box), and its associated level switch should be easily accessible to clear blockages in a crisis, as well as to occasionally check the operation of the float switch. In practice, it often requires a major effort to get to the pump, strainer, and switch (for more on bilge pumps, see chapter 5).

Tankage

In addition to problems with bilge water, wide flat sections have another practical drawback. The area beneath the cabinsole is the ideal place for tankage, which places the weight as low and central as possible—contributing to stability rather than harming it—and puts the tanks in an area that is otherwise somewhat inaccessible and not particularly suitable for stowage because of the risk of saturation with bilge water.

However, the flat sections of contemporary boats result in minimal volume below the sole. If tanks are placed there, they end up being wide and shallow, with the result that the outlet pipe often comes out of the fluid on one tack or the other. It is sometimes necessary to switch from one fuel tank to another every time a boat tacks when motor sailing to windward. In rough conditions, when the security of the boat may depend on the reliability of the engine, if the tanks are partially empty, the engine will periodically suck air whichever tank is used. This is ridiculous! More commonly, because of the lack of space, the tanks are moved up and placed under the saloon settee berths. The weight is now higher and off-center, and the tanks are occupying prime storage space on the boat.

The somewhat deeper sections needed to establish an effective bilge at normal angles of heel result in greater volume beneath the sole, enabling all tankage to be concentrated there. Furthermore, the tanks will function on both tacks.

CONCLUSION

I began this chapter by suggesting that we might be able to determine the fundamental design features that produce an ideal cruising boat. By now, it should be clear that there can be no such accomplishment in the abstract. What is ideal depends very much on the use to which the boat will be put. Given the kinds of choices and compromises that must be made, a boat intended for weekend cruising in essentially protected waters, that will never have to weather a gale, is likely to be very different from a boat intended to voyage offshore with the chance of being caught out in heavy weather.

My focus has been on the offshore end of the spectrum, in which case characteristics such as solid construction, a seakindly motion, ease of handling, a light and balanced helm, the ability to claw off a lee shore, a high limit of positive stability, and a substantial load-carrying capability without a significant loss of performance take precedence over maximizing interior volume and flat-out speed around the buoys.

We can use "the numbers" to provide a broad guide to whether a given boat falls within the general framework of what may be suitable for this kind of cruising. In particular, when looking at "typical" boats in the 35- to 45-foot (10.7–13.7 m) range, I recommend the following:

- a LWL–BWL ratio of 3.00 or higher (using LWL and $B_{max} \times 0.9$)
- a ballast ratio greater than 0.30 (using a realistic half-load displacement number)
- a draft of 6 feet (1.83 m) or less (a cruiser-racer will have a deeper draft, sacrificing some cruising grounds for better performance)
- a displacement–length ratio between 250 and 400 (using a realistic half-load displacement number); for coastal cruising or a cruiser-racer, a lower ratio may be appropriate
- overhangs of 15 to 20 percent of LOH; once again, for coastal cruising or a cruiser-racer, a lower number may be appropriate
- a half angle of entrance of less than 25 degrees (considerably less for a cruiser-racer)
- a sail area–displacement ratio of 15–18 (using a realistic half-load displacement number)
- a waterplane loading that puts the boat on the "comfort" side of Dave Gerr's graph, page 20 (using a realistic half-load displacement number; a cruiser-racer sacrifices some comfort for speed)
- an LPS or AVS greater than 120 degrees (for coastal cruising, this may be as low as 115 degrees; for ocean cruising, 130 or higher)
- a stability ratio greater than 3.0
- an IMS Stability Index Number (if available) greater than 120
- a capsize screening value below 2.0
- a STIX number above 35 for boats up to 40 feet in length, and above 40 for longer boats

In my opinion, we need to add to these numbers the following:

- the ability to carry heavy ground tackle up forward without trimming down by the bow
- a substantial lateral area in keel and rudder
- an external lead ballast keel, preferably with a bulb (to keep the center of effort low with a modest draft)
- a full skeg to mount the rudder

Boat Comparison Worksheet

	BOAT #1	BOAT #2	BOAT #3
Boat Name and Type			
Length of Hull (LOH)			
Waterline Length (LWL)			
Maximum Beam (B_{max})			
Waterline Beam (if not available, use $B_{max} \times 0.9$)			
Waterline Length–Beam Ratio			
Ballast Weight			
Light-Ship Weight (LSW)[1]			
Personal Increment Number (PIN)[2]			
Half-Load Displacement (HDL) (light ship + PIN)			
Ballast Ratio (using half load)			
Displacement–Length Ratio (using HDL)			
Sail Area [(I + J)÷2 + (P + E)÷2]			
Sail Area–Displacement Ratio (using HDL)			
Waterplane Area (WPA = LWL × BWL × 0.7)			
Pounds per Inch Immersion (WPA × 5.33)			
Maximum Allowable Sinkage[3]			
Actual Sinkage (PIN/lb. per inch immersion)			
Limit of Positive Stability (LPS or AVS)[4]			
Capsize Screening Value (based on LSW)			
STIX Number			
Speed–Length Ratio [$8.26/(DLR)^{0.311}$]			
Maximum Speed ($SLR \times \sqrt{LWL}$)			

[1]Determine whether this is the designer's or builder's estimate (if so, treat with skepticism), or is based on actual measurement.
[2]Should not be more than 20 percent of LSW.
[3]0.5 percent (light displacement) to 1 percent (heavy displacement) of LWL.
[4]Determine whether ISO, IMS, or other: the different methodologies produce significantly different results, with the IMS and ISO producing a lower LPS or AVS than other methodologies.

- a reasonably gentle slope in profile to the leading edge of the keel, ballast keel, and skeg
- the ability to take a severe grounding with no more than cosmetic damage
- if possible, a propeller in an aperture
- hull sections that result in a decent bilge, together with space for adequate tankage beneath the cabinsole
- hull rocker to concentrate bilge water in the sump and keep down pounding at sea
- well-engineered construction that is not likely to produce nasty, expensive surprises in ten or twenty years; particular attention needs to be given to preventing osmotic blisters, protecting cores, ensuring a bulletproof hull-to-deck joint, and the proper bonding of bulkheads and other interior structures
- for a world-girdling offshore boat, a watertight bulkhead fore, and also aft if possible, plus collision reinforcement forward

From my "offshore" perspective, a boat with these characteristics fuses the best of traditional design with the best advances developed in the past few decades to produce a well-rounded cruising platform at an "affordable" price. Many excellent boats that reflect these parameters have been and continue to be built, but remember that many more boats are built to fit a formula not really suitable for cruising. It is up to the aspiring sailor to take a close, unemotional look at available boats and to not be swayed by boat-show hype.

It is also important to recognize that my requirements, reflected in the previous numbers, are for a moderately heavy boat intended for long-distance cruising with extensive systems designed to provide a comfortable lifestyle for those onboard. This is just one solution to the cruising equation; others range from the high-performance, light-displacement approach—which is suitable for those who enjoy the simple life and have the discipline to ruthlessly limit their gear and acquisitions—to the heavy-displacement approach with a workboat heritage that is capable of absorbing an extensive payload, but which needs a long bowsprit for light-air sails in order to achieve a satisfactory performance.

For someone whose interest is in sailing in protected waters or coastal cruising without extended offshore passages, with no likelihood of encountering large breaking seas, the design parameters may well be shifted toward another boat. That boat will rely more on form stability than ballast stability (a wider beam with a lower ballast ratio), be lighter (a lower displacement–length ratio), with shorter overhangs and a longer waterline, have a lower limit of positive stability, and combine a canoe body with a fin keel and spade rudder. The boat will have a spacious interior and a lively performance, proving exciting to sail, and will likely be substantially cheaper to buy, but will be increasingly uncomfortable the rougher the conditions.

Finally, there is the matter of aesthetics, which is no small matter indeed, because—when the chips are down—we often are prepared to compromise some of the technical specifications for a boat that warms the heart! For example, I asked Bill Crealock why he did not increase the LWL of the Pacific Seacraft 40, which would be relatively simple to do and would significantly improve (at least, on paper) the numbers (especially the length–beam and the displacement–length ratios). Bill replied: "I wanted to draw a boat that looks graceful. A canoe stern is not a canoe stern unless it has a considerable overhang."

Your ideal boat may be radically different than mine. Nevertheless, I hope I have armed you with enough ideas to enable you to draw it in broad outline, and to find a boat that fits the picture that emerges. In the following chapters, I provide suggestions to help you flesh out the details.

CHAPTER TWO
ON DECK

The gear on a cruising boat must be designed for unexpected loads.

In chapter 1, I established some basic design parameters that need to be considered when thinking about boats for cruising. In this chapter, I take a detailed look at the deck to investigate both necessary and desirable features, starting with the rig. Remember that my focus is on optimizing a boat for worldwide cruising; frequently, a less-demanding perspective requires less-demanding (and significantly cheaper) responses.

RIGS AND RIGGING

Whatever rig is chosen it must enable the boat to live up to its performance potential while remaining well balanced and easy to handle in all conditions and on all points of sail. Generally, the naval architect who designed the boat is going to be the best judge of these issues. The owner, however, should not be shy about providing input!

Rig Options

We've had *ketch*, *sloop*, and *cutter* rigs; other people are aficionados of *yawl* and *schooner* rigs. They can all work well. However, there is little doubt that the *sloop rig* (i.e., single mast and single headsail) is the most efficient and the fastest to windward, not to mention the cheapest (it has the least amount of rigging) and the easiest to use (there are no running backstays or inner forestays to be set up and released); however, as always, there are other considerations on a cruising boat.

The sloop rig results in large sails; as boats get up in size, these can be difficult to handle. The sloop rig also limits sail-shortening options as compared to other rigs. If, as is almost always the case these days, the headsail is on a roller-reefing gear, the only way to shorten sail is to either change it (a major operation) or roll some up. A rolled-up sail sets poorly for windward work. In fact, just when the most control over sail shape is required to minimize sail draft and heeling, we end up with the least control. The sail will probably not be built strongly enough to handle the full range of wind strengths in which it is

Contemporary, relatively light-displacement sloop.

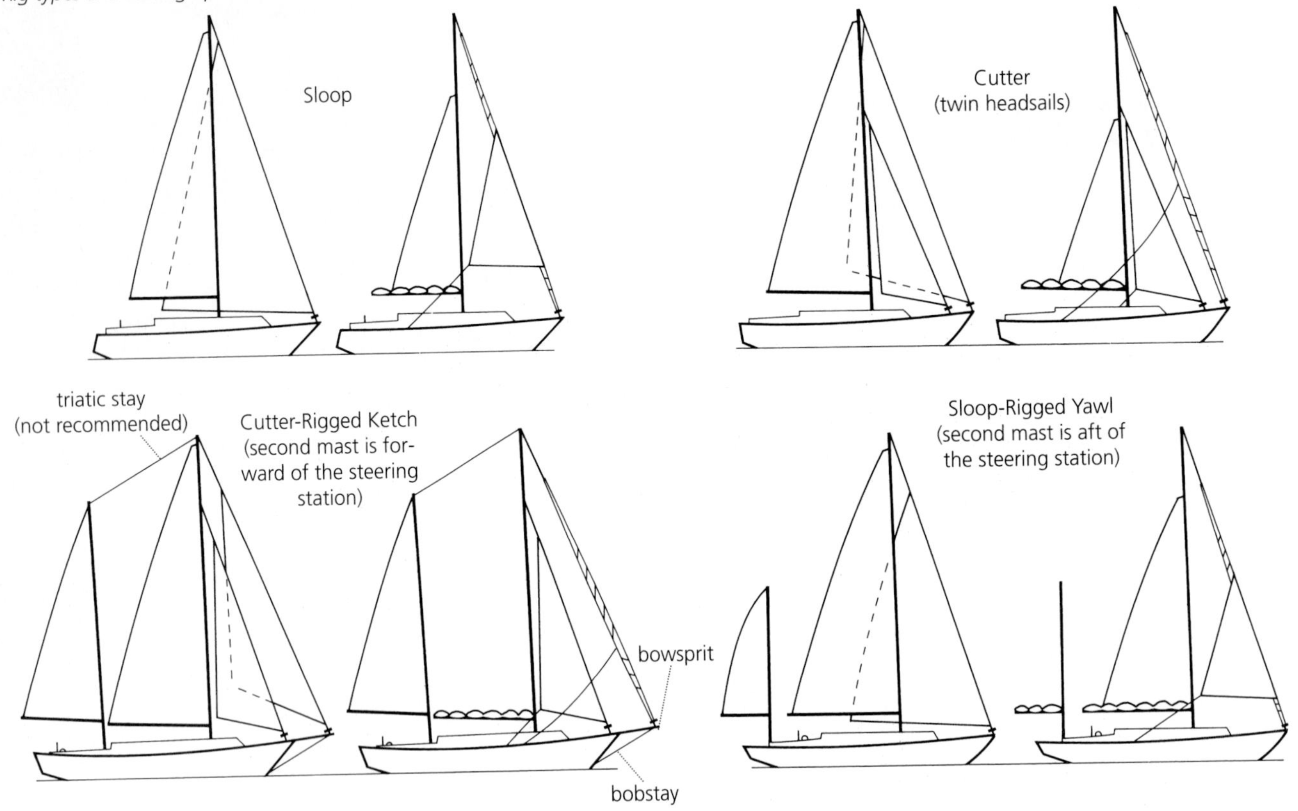

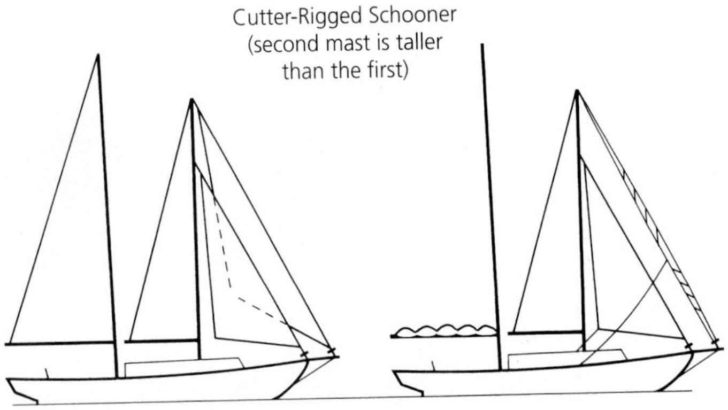

Rig types and reefing options.

Cutter.

likely to be used, which poses a risk of failure at the most inopportune time; if it is built strongly enough, it will probably set poorly in light winds.

Furthermore, as the wind pipes up and sail size is reduced, the center of effort of the headsail moves farther forward, rather than closer, to the center of the boat. If the sail needs attention (e.g., changing sails or problems with a roller reefer), this work has to be accomplished on the most exposed point of the boat.

Cutter Rigs

The modern cutter rig increases the versatility of the sloop rig by adding an inner forestay on which is flown a second foresail (the staysail). As the wind pipes up, the primary headsail can be rolled in (with the same disadvantages as on a sloop); however, at some point, only the smaller area of the staysail is needed. At that time, the headsail is fully rolled up and the center of effort moves inboard toward the mast. The smaller staysail can be built specifically to handle strong winds. If there are problems that require someone going forward to fix them, there is no need to go all the way forward. In fact, problems with the sail are unlikely: staysail sheets are mostly led inboard of shrouds with little potential for them to get fouled, and there is nothing on which the sail itself will chafe.

A well-reefed mainsail and staysail comprise an excellent heavy-weather rig. As conditions worsen, the main can be dropped altogether—a cutter generally sails to windward under staysail alone, whereas a sloop may require some main to be set to counteract a heavily reefed headsail. Cutters tend to behave well when hove-to (see chapter 11) under staysail and reefed main (or trysail). When motor sailing into the wind, the staysail can be carried closer to the wind than a headsail, providing some drive and stabilizing influence.

The principal disadvantages of the cutter are the additional rigging expense (quite modest) and the fact that the rig usually requires some form of intermediate or running backstays to counteract the load imposed by the inner forestay and staysail. We had intermediate backstays on one boat and running backstays on another. Intermediate backstays are convenient inasmuch as they are permanently fixed in place and require no tending, but they do increase the load on a mast (because of the poor angle they make with the mast) and also restrict how far the boom can be let out when running off the wind. Running backstays create more work, but unless the boat is jibed frequently, this does not amount to much.

Depending on the relationship between the headstay and inner forestay, it may be difficult to tack a large headsail with the inner forestay in place. Personally, I think that on a cruising boat, the two stays should be arranged so that this is simply not a problem (it is a matter of getting the inner forestay far enough back). However, if that cannot be achieved, the inner forestay needs to be set up with some kind of quick-release lever.

For serious offshore work, it is worth considering adding a second headstay to the cutter rig, set a little inside the first, perhaps with a roller reefer on both stays. A large, relatively light headsail (i.e., 120 percent or greater) can be set on the outer stay, with a 100 percent heavy-weather jib on the inner stay. With an even heavier and smaller sail on the staysail, the boat will be well set up for all conditions, with an appropriate sail for going to windward in everything from light airs to gale-force winds. It is rarely necessary to use any of these sails partially reefed, with the result that they always set to maximum advantage. On a run, the two headsails can be set at the same time, one on either side of the boat, in the classic "trade-wind" fashion.

The disadvantages to this rig are the added cost and weight (particularly if a roller reefer is used on both headstays), and the likelihood of some loss of performance with the 100 percent sail because of the disturbed airflow created by the other sail when rolled up (this depends to some extent on how close the two stays are). To tack the lightweight headsail (the foremost of the two), it has to be rolled up and then redeployed on the other tack. As long as the roller reefer is properly set up, it should not be much of a task and should take little time.

For all these reasons, I personally like the cutter rig until the sail areas get too large for a short-handed crew to wrestle down in heavy weather (i.e., generally speaking, boats more than 50 feet in length), at which point a ketch rig makes more sense, providing even more versatility—but with increases in weight, complexity, and cost.

Top: *Cutter reefed down. The next step is to roll up the headsail altogether and reef down the main some more. (Patrick Parsons photo, courtesy Harken)* Above: *Ketch. Our old boat at anchor on Lake Izabal, Guatemala.*

Ketch and Yawl Rigs

The addition of a mizzen to a sloop or cutter rig produces still more sail-combination options. This includes an extremely well-balanced heavy-weather sail plan, consisting of the staysail and mizzen (with both reefed in really heavy airs), and a powerful off-the-wind sail plan when a mizzen staysail or spinnaker is set (in addition to the normal cutter headsails). On the debit side, upwind the mizzen is negatively affected by the disturbed air coming off the main.

The mizzenmast on a ketch is a great place to mount all kinds of gear.

On an aft-cockpit boat, the rigging for a mizzen usually forms something of a cocoon around the cockpit, significantly enhancing crew safety. The mizzenmast is a convenient place to put antennas, a radar, a wind generator, and the like; it is also handy for tying on an awning. On the downside, its boom almost certainly gets in the way of a wind vane; the extra mast adds weight and expense.

With a divided rig, the two masts should be stayed independently of one another rather than interconnected with a *triatic* stay (commonly run between the two mastheads). This way, if one mast goes overboard, there is a good chance that the other will stay up. The farther offshore a boat goes, the more attractive this built-in redundancy becomes.

Fractional Rigs

Any of these popular rigs can be set up as a *fractional rig*; that is, the forestay does not go all the way to the top of the mast. A fractional rig results in smaller and, therefore, easier to handle headsails, and affords an opportunity to control the shape of the mainsail (by controlled bending of the mast) to a much greater extent than other rigs. When going upwind in heavy airs, cranking in the backstay not only tightens the headstay, flattening the headsail, but also bends the mast forward in its center sections, flattening the mainsail. The boat sails more upright and faster.

The mast is farther forward with a fractional rig than it is with a masthead rig, resulting in a boat that can be easily handled under mainsail alone in harbors or other restricted waters. The mast also can be rigged so that running backstays are not required (see the next section). Finally, with fewer and smaller headsails, the cost of the sail inventory can be reduced dramatically.

However, fractional rigs can be significantly more difficult than masthead rigs to tune properly, and they require more skill to operate efficiently; in short, they are more work. A cruiser coming from a racing background may find this acceptable in return for a slightly improved performance, but my experience leads me to conclude that they are not an appropriate trade-off for most cruisers.

Swept-Back Spreaders

Most fractional rigs and some masthead rigs employ swept-back spreaders, which are widely seen on the racing circuit. To some extent, these enable the shrouds to play the role of both shrouds and backstays; in fact, on some rigs, it eliminates the backstay altogether. In other cases, swept-back spreaders enable a cutter rig to be installed without intermediate or running backstays. Swept-back spreaders allow a larger headsail to be carried without fouling the shrouds.

The downside to swept-back spreaders is the restriction they place on how far the boom can be let out when running before the wind and the consequent chafe on the mainsail when running off the wind. This doesn't matter on a

Fractional rig with swept-back spreaders.

Off the wind, swept-back spreaders significantly limit the extent to which the boom can be let out.

Nada*'s twin downwind poles, stowed on a track on the forward face of the mast, seen here in the stowed position (hauled up to the top of the track).*

racing boat, because these boats never run dead downwind—they have found that it is faster to jibe from one side of the course line to the other (see chapter 7). On a cruising boat, few of us have the necessary *polar plots* (graphs of boat speed versus wind angle) and computers to work out the optimum sailing angle; in any case, most of us don't want to work this hard! We are mostly content to sacrifice a few tenths of a knot of boat speed for the ease and simplicity of just pointing the boat where we want to go. As a result—notwithstanding their current popularity—I believe swept-back spreaders are a disadvantage in a cruising context.

Downwind Poles

Cruising boats should have at least one downwind (*whisker*) or spinnaker pole (the difference between the two is primarily length and strength: spinnaker poles are longer and are expected to take higher loads, and so are built heavier and stronger). The pole is most conveniently mounted on a track on the face of the mast in such a way that when fully raised, its outboard end can be clipped to either the lifelines or a fitting at the base of the mast. The drawbacks to this arrangement are that it puts the weight relatively high, creates windage, and—in a worst-case scenario—if the mast goes overboard, the pole (a potential jury-rigged mast) goes with it.

1

2

1. *Typically, a pole should extend a little beyond the headstay.*
2. *The poles in action on a downwind run.*

If these issues are of concern, the pole can be stowed in chocks on deck, but it is almost always a toe-stubber. If stowed on deck, it should be positioned well forward so that the rear end simply has to be lifted up to clip it to the mast fitting, instead of maneuvering the entire pole into position. (Remember that this work may have to be done when the boat is rolling vigorously downwind; the less the pole has to be moved around, the better.) The light weight of carbon fiber makes it an ideal material for downwind poles, albeit at a price that is often too high for cruising sailors.

A pole should be of such a length that when mounted to the mast and pulled back against a shroud, the outboard end lines up with the *clew* (the attachment point for the sheets) of the fully extended genoa (which generally means the pole is about 100 percent of the distance from the base of the mast to the base of the forestay). Even better than one pole is two poles mounted to the mast. When sailing downwind, the roller-reefing genoa is set on one pole and another jib or genoa is set on the other. (For more on using downwind poles, see chapter 7.)

Wherever a pole or a sail is likely to chafe on a shroud, it is worthwhile to take the smallest diameter polyvinyl chloride (PVC) tubing that fits over the shroud (found at any hardware store), use a thin blade on a table saw to slit it lengthwise on one side, and clip it over the shroud (marine chandlers sell ready-made shroud rollers).

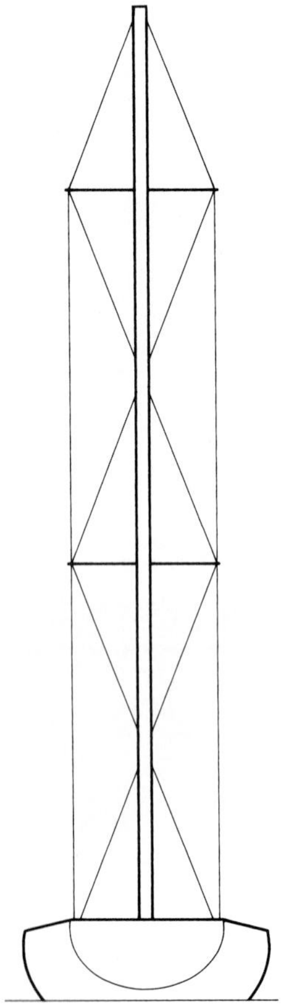

The innovative approach to shrouds used on New Zealand's America's Cup 2000 entry.

Masts, Spreaders, and Shroud Angles

A single mast keeps down weight, which in turn improves the numbers discussed in chapter 1. The use of carbon fiber spars maximizes weight savings, but at a tremendous expense (see the addendum to this chapter).

For an equivalent sail-carrying capability, a keel-stepped mast can be somewhat lighter than a deck-stepped mast. The keel-stepped mast is also more capable of withstanding the failure of a piece of standing rigging. The deck-stepped mast, however, does not obstruct the accommodation spaces, and there is no big hole in the deck through which water can leak (a common problem).

As for aluminum masts, all kinds of extrusions are available, with different trade-offs for cruisers. For example, lighter weight can be achieved through a larger cross section with thinner walls, but this results in increased windage. In general, determining the appropriate extrusion for any boat is a matter for engineers, not the boatowner. The owner needs to ensure that the engineer realizes how the boat will be used and builds in an appropriate safety factor, which is clearly more for an offshore cruiser than it is for a weekend racer.

Weight savings also can be achieved by adding more spreaders and paring down the wall thickness between them. Taken to extremes, this leads to the four- and five-spreader rigs sometimes seen on racing boats, but there is clearly a trade-off between lowering the weight of the mast and increasing the complexity of the rig. In terms of a performance-conscious mid-size cruising boat, the two-spreader rig has found almost universal acceptance; on smaller boats and those less concerned with performance, a single set of spreaders is the norm.

Of interest is a novel idea that was seen on the winning New Zealand boat in the 2000 America's Cup. Shrouds are brought down from the spreader tips to the mast at mid-panel, with the loads transferred through the mast to another shroud attached on the other side of the mast, which is then led down to the next spreader tip or the deck. This has the effect of shortening and stiffening the mast panels, while reducing compressive loads on the spar—I think we will be seeing more of this variant of diamond shrouds.

Spreaders should never extend beyond the beam of a boat. If they do, they will get damaged alongside tall wharves and foul the rigging on other boats when rafting up.

Spreader sockets are a frequent source of problems and failures. The sockets must be designed to spread high loads over a large area of the mast. To minimize drag on the racing circuit, spreaders are given knife-like trailing edges. Unfortunately, this style of spreader is finding its way onto cruising boats where the performance advantages (minimal) are vastly outweighed by the increased likelihood of mainsail damage when the sail is let all the way out off the wind (see my comments on swept-back spreaders, pages 56–57).

In addition to affecting mast weight, the number of spreaders affects the angle that the *shrouds* (the rigging that gives athwartships support to a mast) make to the mast. The greater this angle, the more is the mast support provided for a given compression load on the mast, but the farther out the chainplates end up. Beyond a certain point, this makes it difficult to sheet headsails well inboard, thereby impairing windward performance. By reducing panel lengths in the mast (i.e., putting in more spread-

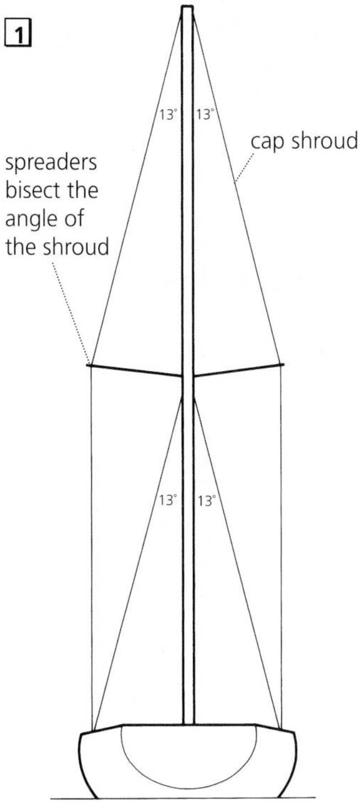

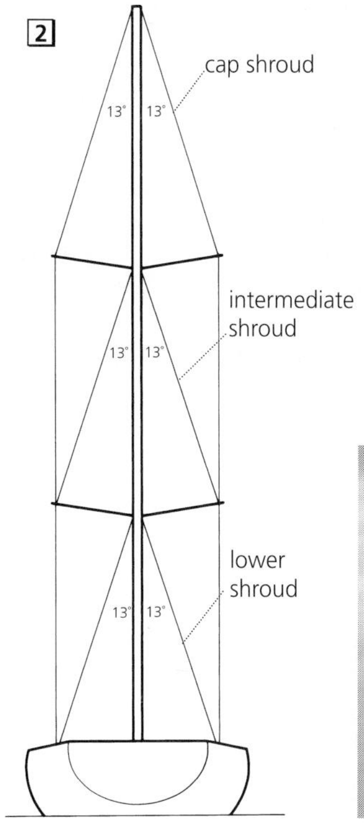

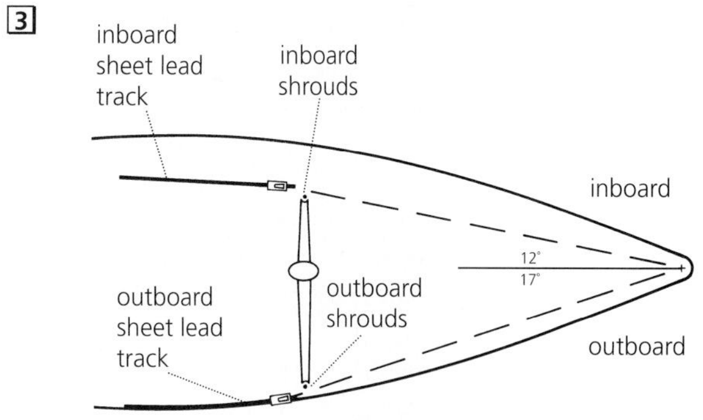

1 and 2. The impact of the number of spreaders on shroud angles, and how far outboard shroud chainplates must go. 3. The effect of inboard and outboard shrouds on headsail sheeting angles. 4. Spreaders should bisect the angle of the shrouds that they support. This boat is asking for trouble.

A neat chafe protector on the base of a radar reflector.

Nada's outboard shrouds limit the extent to which we can sheet the genoa in tight . . . (see next page)

. . . and cause chafe between the shrouds and spreaders, and the sail (just above the tip of the spreader, a patch can be seen that repairs a tear made by the spreader).

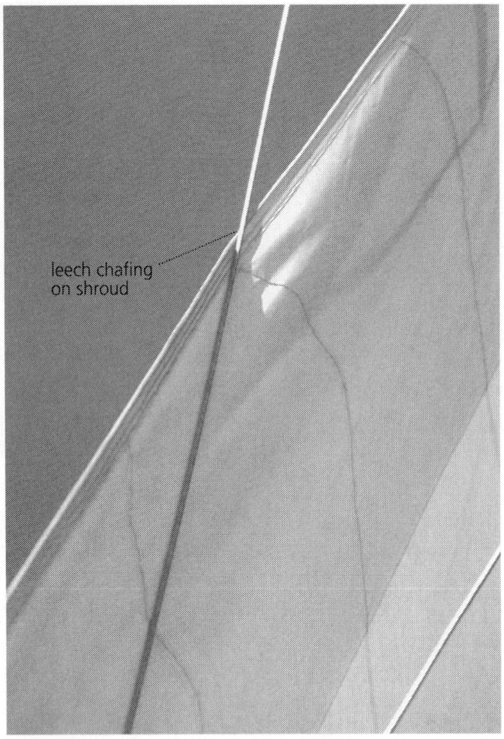

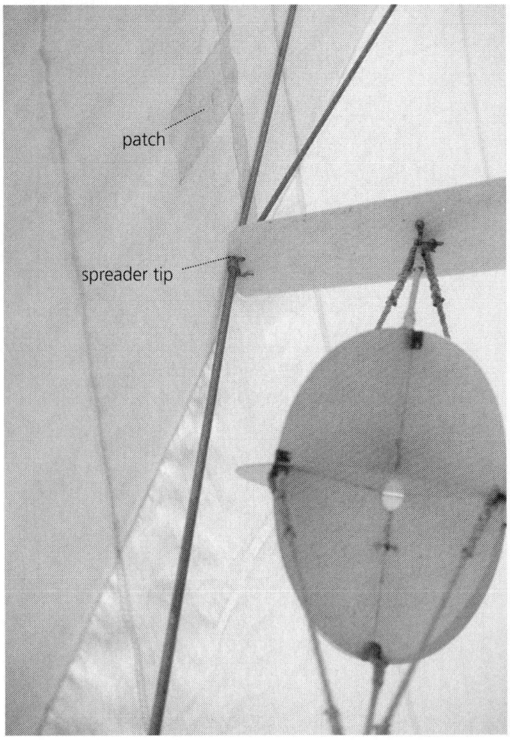

Plastic tubing around the shrouds goes a long way toward minimizing damage from chafe.

ers), the same shroud angle can be maintained with a narrower chainplate base and a tighter *sheeting angle* (the angle between the foot of a headsail and the centerline of the boat). Whatever the installation, spreaders should always bisect the angle of the shroud they are supporting; if they do not, there is a risk of the spreader collapsing under load and the rig coming down.

The shroud angle on a cruising boat should be at least 10 degrees; 13 degrees is recommended by *Yachting Monthly*'s Offshore Yacht Advisory Panel. With a two-spreader rig, this angle can generally be achieved while still bringing the shroud chainplates inboard enough to sheet the headsails down tight. (On a modern, performance-oriented cruising boat, the sheeting angle may be as little as 7½ degrees for headsails and 6 degrees for a staysail; for more on this subject, see chapter 7.)

Our Pacific Seacraft 40 has some rather awkward compromises in regard to shroud and sheeting angles. The cap shrouds (from the top of the mast) and intermediate shrouds (from the upper spreader bases) are brought down to chainplates mounted to the outside of the hull. This maximizes the shroud angles and, therefore, the mast support. The lower shrouds are brought inboard. On either side of the boat, there are two sail tracks for headsail sheeting: one on the caprail, the other on the side deck. The inner track results in a 9- to 10½-degree sheeting angle for windward work; however, it can be used only with a 100 percent or less headsail, because any larger sail fouls the cap and intermediate shrouds and the spreaders. Because the primary headsail is a 120 percent genoa, it has to be partially rolled up in order to sheet it inboard. As a result, the one time that we need optimum sail shape—when hard on the wind—is the one time we have to use the sail partially rolled up, which is when it sets most poorly. The alternative is to take down the 120 percent genoa and replace it with a 100 percent jib, but this defeats the purpose of the roller reefer.

We can resolve this dilemma in a couple of different ways. We can bring the cap and intermediate shrouds inboard, but at the cost of reducing the mast support; I prefer to keep the support. Or we can add a second roller-reefing headsail aft of the present one and mount a 100 percent jib on this, as described previously. We would then use the 100 percent sail (sheeted to the inner sail track) for close-hauled work and heavy weather, and the 120 percent—which I would upgrade to 130 percent—(sheeted to the caprail) as we eased the sheets and in lighter airs. Downwind, we would use both headsails, poled out on either side of the boat.

Unstayed Rigs

Unstayed rigs have been around for a long time but did not come into their own until Garry Hoyt introduced his Freedom cat ketches. At a stroke, this rig eliminates the numerous pieces that comprise a typical set of standing rigging, with their associated failure and chafe points. The freestanding spar is also kinder on the hull (it exerts no compression forces) and more forgiving under sail (the spars bend in a puff, spilling the wind and depowering the sails). More recent variations on the unstayed theme include the AeroRig, which incorporates a conventional-looking headsail and main on a rotating, unstayed mast that has a boom extending both fore and aft of the mast.

Why don't we all have unstayed rigs? First, there is the matter of looks—it just doesn't look right to most traditionalists! Moreover, although unstayed rigs are often more powerful off the wind than a conventional rig, they mostly do not point as high as a conventional rig. Finally, the AeroRig (but not other unstayed rigs) is significantly more expensive than a conventional rig.

Set against this, we have to consider the fact that many cruising sailors, particularly long-distance cruising sailors, go to some trouble not to beat into the wind. In this case, the performance losses to windward may well be a small price to pay for the simplicity, the minimizing of

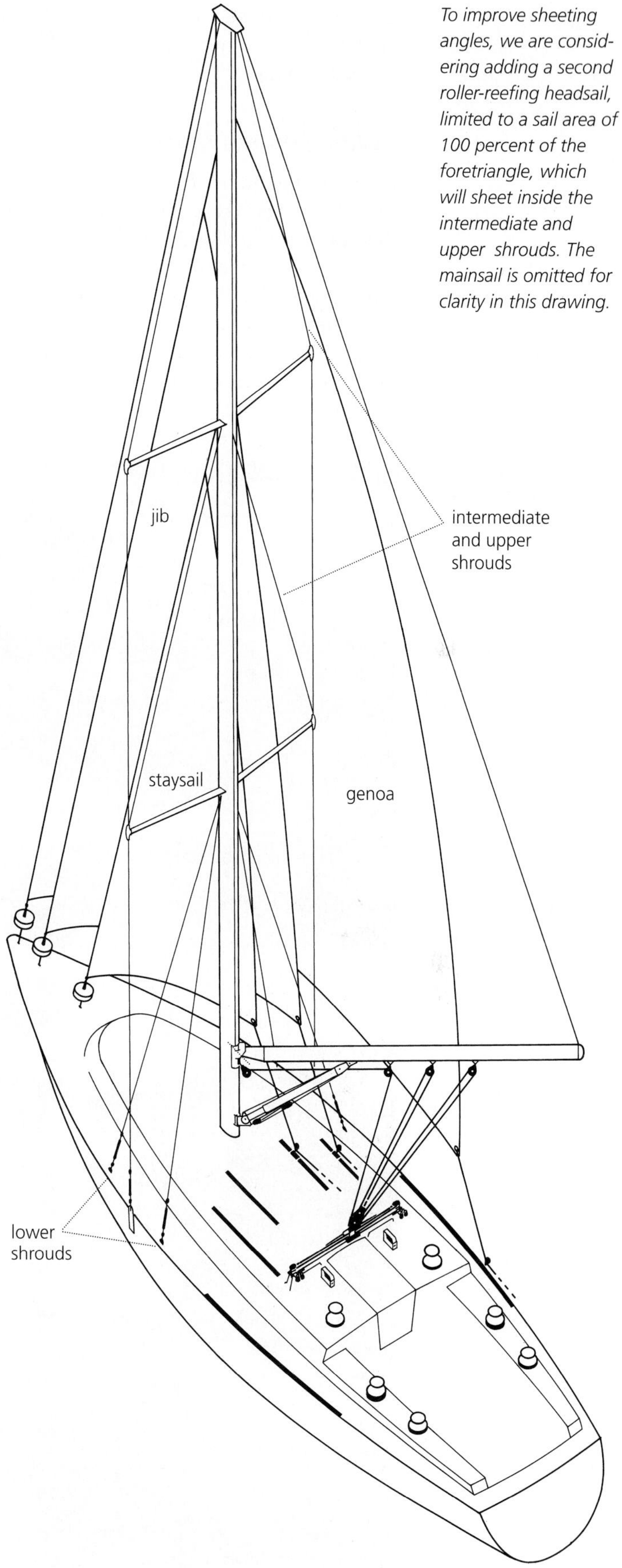

To improve sheeting angles, we are considering adding a second roller-reefing headsail, limited to a sail area of 100 percent of the foretriangle, which will sheet inside the intermediate and upper shrouds. The mainsail is omitted for clarity in this drawing.

failure modes, the lack of sail chafe, the good off-wind performance, and the ease of handling an unstayed rig.

Holding up the Mast

On stayed rigs, standing rigging loads need to be spread over a good area of the hull. In addition, the mast step must be able to take the full compression load of the mast in all conceivable circumstances. The hull structure in way of the mast and chainplates must be such that the loads on the rig do not cause the hull to deform. The more lightweight a boat and the more powerful a rig, the more carefully a boat has to be engineered. If a rig loosens significantly under load, as many do, some part of this equation is not right.

Hull and deck fitting attachments, such as chainplate *tangs*, need to be in perfect alignment with their *stays* (rigging that provides fore and aft support to a mast) or *shrouds* (rigging that provides athwartships support). Any misalignment can result in an unfair load being thrown on the chainplate fasteners and/or the chainplate will flex, ultimately leading to work hardening and failure. Flexing also opens up through-deck seals when present. If moisture wicks in, the deoxygenated environment may lead to crevice corrosion of fasteners and fittings—a common cause of failure. (To forestall failures, a sampling of fasteners should be pulled and inspected at least every ten years).

In use, rigging flexes continuously. Without *toggles* (a kind of universal joint) to absorb the movement, flexing once again leads to work hardening and failure. Forestays with roller-reefing sails flex the most, especially when motoring into head seas with the sails furled. At these times, toggles at the head of the stay are as important as at the foot.

Turnbuckles (rigging screws, bottle screws) come in closed and open versions. Open turnbuckles seem to be less prone to corrosion and

Chainplates need to be ruggedly mounted and in perfect alignment with the shrouds and stays they support, with full toggling of the rigging.

Traditional bronze turnbuckles have a lot to recommend them.

Many turnbuckles today are machined from stainless steel. When adjusted under a load, dirt in the threads or even salt crystals can lead to seizure.

failure. Some turnbuckles are all bronze and some are chrome-plated bronze, but many today are all stainless steel.

Unfortunately, when a stainless steel rigging terminal is screwed into a stainless steel turnbuckle and tensioned, there is a risk of *galling* (a kind of seizure fairly unique to stainless steel). The cause is usually dirt in the threads, which causes friction. Stainless steel is a very poor conductor of heat; therefore, the heat generated is not dissipated. It rapidly builds up to the point at which the surfaces of the metal break down, destroying the threads. Galling is not reversible: the turnbuckle generally has to be cut off.

To avoid galling, it is advisable to use plain or chrome-plated bronze turnbuckles, or stainless turnbuckles with bronze thread inserts. If this advice is ignored, it is important to keep the threads clean and lubricated (with anhydrous lanolin), and to stop screwing a turnbuckle in and out the *second* any undue resistance is felt. Give it a minute to cool internally, dribble in some penetrating fluid, and very slowly try again, working the turnbuckle backward and forward to spread the lubricant over the threads. You may get lucky but, then again, you may not!

Wire Rigging

Shrouds and stays should be assembled from 316 stainless steel wire rope, not the 302 or 304 that is sometimes used. Both 302 and 304 are more prone to corrosion, which is often revealed by telltale rust stains down the rigging.

Most wire rigging is installed with *swage-type terminals* that are attached by cold-molding the metal of the terminal around the wire. All swaging tends to work-harden the metal involved. The use of incorrect swaging pressures and/or the repeated rolling of fittings makes the terminal brittle and prone to premature failure. There are different types of machines for swaging that stress the terminal to a greater or lesser extent. A one-time pass-through hydraulic machine produces the best results; manual boatyard machines (through which the fitting must be passed twice) impose higher stresses with a greater probability of premature failure; and rotary hammers do the most damage.

A swage that is clearly banana-shaped should be replaced (which normally means replacing the entire length of wire rope to which it is attached), as should any swage with hairline cracks or rust stains. When swages are used on the lower ends of rigging, water wicks down into the terminal, causing corrosion and accelerating failure. Swageless terminals (e.g., Norseman

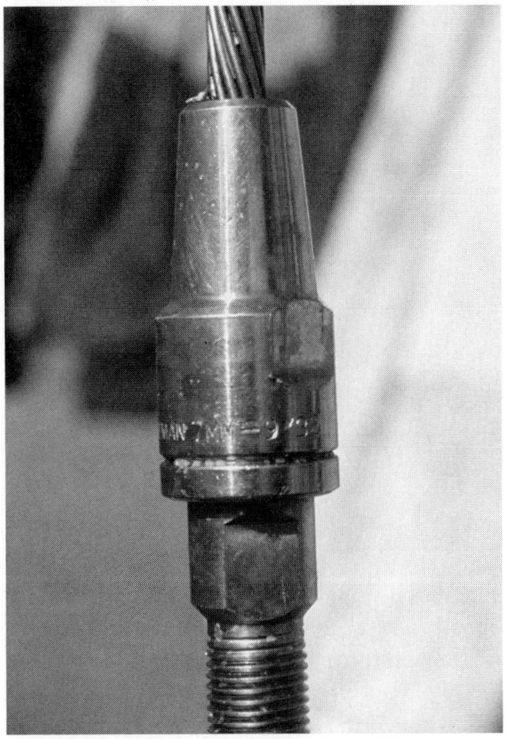

Compression-type terminals, such as this Norseman, are preferable to swage terminals.

and Sta-Lok) are more reliable, in addition to which they can be removed and reinstalled with normal hand tools and without having to replace the wire rope.

Some experienced cruisers heat their swage terminals when the rig is new and then dribble in beeswax or anhydrous lanolin to fill any voids in the terminal to keep moisture out. This practice may well prolong the life of the terminals.

Rod Rigging

Rod rigging has been finding greater acceptance in the cruising world; it has been fitted as standard equipment for many years on Valiants. It has less stretch than and strength equal to wire rope for less weight and windage, but it is more expensive (although the differential has been decreasing). Its greatest perceived drawback is that, whereas wire rope sometimes warns of impending failure by stranding at terminals, rod rigging tends to fail without warning. For this reason, cruising sailors have been wary of it. It is also impossible to carry spare lengths onboard (it cannot be rolled tight enough to stow and needs special tools for installation).

However, rod rigging and its terminals are made from some of the most corrosion-resistant grades of stainless steel. Installed correctly, it should be more reliable than wire rope and, in

Discontinuous rod rigging, utilizing fatigue-indicating fittings (the long, tapered sleeve with a notch in it; the sleeve will break before the fitting fails, providing an early warning of impending trouble). (Courtesy Navtec)

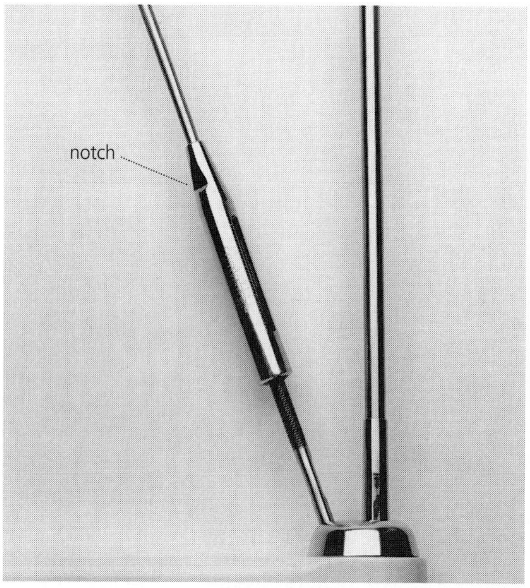

fact, has become significantly more reliable in recent years with improvements in the design of the end fittings (Navtec's new-style end fittings have a predicted life expectancy three times that of the old-style fittings). The keys are (1) to minimize stresses at the end terminals by installing toggles and using end fittings with long, tapered sleeves (this spreads bending stresses over a greater length of the rod), and (2) to use what is known as *discontinuous* rigging; that is, instead of bending cap and intermediate shrouds over the tips of spreaders, the shroud is cut at this point and given two end terminals that are fastened to the spreader.

Adequate toggling of roller reefers, both at deck level and aloft, is essential.

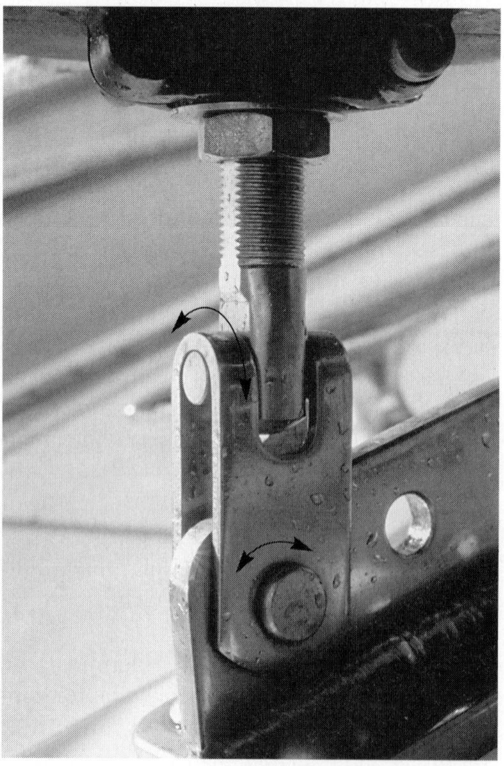

Installed like this, a good case can be made for rod rigging on a performance-conscious cruising boat, especially if all stays and shrouds terminate in eye fittings. Then, in the event of a rod failure, a length of wire with Norseman or Sta-Lok eyes on both ends can be rigged in its place.

Roller-Reefing Foresails

A roller-reefing jib or genoa is almost a foregone conclusion on a modern cruising boat. Roller reefers have been refined to the point that—*assuming proper installation*—they are not only reliable, but also reasonably long-lived. Nevertheless, they add weight aloft, they make it just about impossible to flatten a reefed sail for windward work in heavier airs, they make sail changes—if they become necessary—much more difficult than with a hanked-on sail, and—if they fail—they can be a major embarrassment.

The critical installation points for minimizing the likelihood of problems are as follows:

- ensuring adequate toggling of the headstay
- ensuring that the *halyard* (the line used to hoist a sail) cannot wrap around the headstay when reefing
- providing a fairlead for the reefing line onto the reefing drum
- maintaining a little tension on the line and sail when unfurling and reefing the sail, so that the sail and reefing line both roll up tightly

Halyard wrap is a common problem. It can lead to foil damage, the halyard chafing through, or—in a worst-case scenario—a failure of the stay. To avoid it, the halyard needs to angle away from the stay by at least 10 degrees when the sail is fully hoisted. When this is not possible, the addition of a proprietary halyard stop (supplied with some roller reefers) provides a measure of insurance. If sails of a different size will be used on the same roller reefer, the smaller sails should be fitted with *pendants*—lengths of line or cable at the top and/or bottom of the *luff* (forward edge of the sail) that allow the upper swivel on the roller reefer to hoist to approximately the same position as with the large sails. This maintains a consistent angle between the halyard and the stay.

At the other end of the unit, the reefing line needs to be fed onto the drum at right angles through a fairlead. If this is not done, the

Note that the relationship between the upper swivel on the roller reefer, the halyard, and the halyard sheave virtually eliminates any possibility of the halyard wrapping around the reefing foil.

line is likely to pile up at either the top or the bottom of the drum and then jam. To avoid loose wraps and snarls, tension is required when rolling in and pulling out the line. At times, specifically when the sail is partially reefed in heavy weather, this line is under some serious loads. The blocks used to lead it aft, as well as their mounting bases, must be up to the task.

Finally, for offshore work, a roller reefer should be oversized compared to one intended for day sailing. It is best to buy a proven brand such as Furlex, Harken, Profurl, Reckmann, or Schaefer.

With a cutter rig, it is open to debate as to whether the staysail should also be on a roller reefer. If the boat will be used in situations where a fair amount of tacking is anticipated, and if the headstay and staysail configuration is such as to make it difficult to tack the full genoa without fouling the staysail, a removable inner forestay may be valued over the convenience of a roller reefer. (The two can be combined, but then the entire roller-reefing gear, with the rolled-up sail, has to be detached from the deck and stowed securely out of the way; this is not easy to do.) Also, if the boat is likely to encounter severe storm conditions requiring the use of a separate storm sail on the staysail, hanked-on staysails simplify the necessary sail changes. In most other situations, the convenience of a roller reefer is likely to outweigh any disadvantages.

With our last boat, we originally had a

Above: *A riding turn, locking up the reefing drum, caused by an improper lead angle on the reefing line and inadequate tension when setting the sail.* Left: *This problem was resolved by installing a fairlead that brings the reefing line onto the drum at the correct angle.*

boom (a *club*) on the staysail (a *club-footed* staysail). It made tacking a breeze because it was self-tending, and it also maintained a good sail shape as the sail was eased off the wind. On a broad reach, when conventional staysails lose much of their efficiency, it maintained an optimal shape. Running in stronger winds, the sail could be boomed all the way out, wing and wing with the mainsail. However, the crew was unnerved by the boom flailing around on the foredeck on those occasions when we were head to wind with the sheets eased and it was necessary to go forward. We ended up using the boom to support a birdfeeder at home.

Although I have never used one, I like the look of the Hoyt Jib Boom, which is used on Island Packets of all sizes. I think this device confers the benefits of the old club-footed staysail while minimizing the disadvantages. The Jib Boom is also designed to be used with roller-reefing gear, which the traditional club was not. However, it is generally not available to retrofit existing boats—it has to be ordered with a new boat.

Mainsail

When it comes to the mainsail, a whole raft of ideas has been tried in the past decade in an effort to make sail-handling as simple as with the modern headsail.

In-mast roller reefers have once again been refined to the point where they are fairly reliable, but they keep the weight of the reefed sail high and are expensive (primarily because of the necessarily specialized mast or mast modifications). The mast ends up larger than normal, which disrupts airflow over the sail. The sail cannot be used with horizontal battens (some now use vertical battens), which typically results in a hollow leech, a loss of sail area, and less power (vertical battens overcome this). Sails tend to reef poorly and, if the system jams (it happens), it can be extremely difficult to unjam. On larger sails, expensive, high-tech materials are often necessary in order to get sufficient strength without too much bulk.

Once a sail is partially reefed, there is less control over its shape than with a conventional mainsail (for more on shape control, see chapter 7). This is because the halyard can no longer be used to adjust luff tension. It also will not be possible to reef on a reach or run (something that can often be done with conventional slab reefing—see the following section). However, the ability to reef in small increments does give more control over sail area than with slab reefing.

In summary, there is a cost and performance price associated with in-mast reefing. Nevertheless, a look around any marina or anchorage reveals that an increasing number of people are willing to pay for the ease of using this type of sail.

After an absence of thirty years or more, roller-reefing booms have made a comeback in a new incarnation. The modern boom is easier to reef than the traditional boom, and results in a much better sail shape. Fully battened sails with as much roach as is wanted can be accommodated. The weight of the reefed sail is kept as low as possible. If the gear fails, the sail can be dropped in the conventional manner (i.e., by releasing the halyard). Roller-reefing booms are proving their worth, but are relatively expensive and do require some skill to operate—it is easy to get in a mess with them. Once again, on larger sails, expensive high-tech materials may be necessary to get the necessary sail strength without undue bulk.

The fully battened mainsail is another concept that has been well proven. The battens improve sail shape and, therefore, performance on just about any point of sail, so much so that many fully battened Dacron mainsails set better than high-tech racing mains with short battens. Full-length battens also make sail-handling easier and may well increase the life expectancy of the sail by reducing damage caused by flogging. However, off the wind the sail will chafe where the battens bear on the shrouds—the sail will need additional protection (a patch of Spectra sailcloth—see chapter 10—is the best approach). The cost of a fully battened mainsail is relatively modest compared to in-mast or in-boom reefing, and any problems

Hoyt Jib Boom (Billy Black photo, courtesy Newport R&D)

are likely to be easier to fix. Combined with lazyjacks, the sail can be lowered and stowed with little time and effort. When lowered, the stacked sail will be higher than a traditional main because of all the hardware—mast steps will almost certainly be needed to get up to the halyard and put on a sail cover.

Fully battened mains are growing in size at the expense of headsails, reversing the trend of the 1970s and 1980s, in which headsails got larger and mainsails smaller. From a cruiser's perspective, this is a welcome change, resulting in evenly balanced sails that are easy to handle.

With any of these mainsail options, it is possible to arrange the lines so that all sail-handling functions (short of putting on sail ties and a sail cover) can be accomplished from the security of the cockpit. This is a popular way to go. The drawbacks are the added friction generated by running the lines through the necessary blocks and the mass of lines that end up in the cockpit, with the substantial number of rope clutches needed to keep the lines under control.

Slab (Jiffy) Reefing

In the absence of in-mast reefing or a roller-reefing boom, there's the good old standby of slab (*jiffy*) reefing, which utilizes either a traditional sail with short battens or a fully battened main. I like the economy, simplicity, and reliability of this approach. Reefing can be done from the cockpit or by going forward to the mast. It is especially easy if the boat has a rigid *vang* so that there is no need to set up and take off a *topping lift* when reefing.

Slab reefing from the cockpit often utilizes a single reefing line that is run through a reef *cringle* (a ring sewn or pressed into the sail) on the *leech* (aft edge) of the sail and is then led forward to another cringle in the luff , and then back to the cockpit. To reef, the mainsheet and vang are eased and the topping lift set up (if needed to support the boom), the halyard is eased, and the reefing line is cranked in, pulling down both the leech and the luff of the sail. The halyard is re-tensioned, the topping lift let off (if set), and the vang tensioned. Unfortunately, this approach has several drawbacks:

- There is a fair amount of friction on the reefing line; therefore, good, properly positioned hardware is needed, particularly blocks at the leech and luff cringles rather than simply leading the reefing line through stainless steel rings.

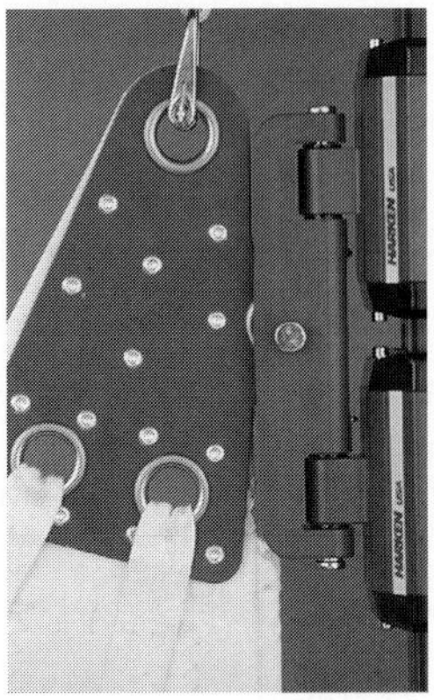

Above left: *Even head-to-wind, a fully battened sail ripples as opposed to the flogging that occurs with a regular mainsail.* Above right: *Harken Battcar hardware. (Courtesy Harken)*

- The load from the leech is passed along to the luff, increasing the stresses at this point.
- There is little control over sail shape because it is not possible to tension the luff and leech independently.
- A lot of line ends up in the cockpit (particularly with second and third reefs).
- The friction in the system often makes it difficult to shake out a reef.

The same approach to reefing can be used—but with separate lines—for the leech and luff. To reef, the halyard is eased, the luff line is hauled down tight, the halyard is re-tensioned, and the leech line is hauled in tight. There are even more lines in the cockpit than with single-line reefing but not as much line length, and with less friction on each line and more control over the process. Most often, tying in a reef is actually faster than with a single-line system. When the reef is no longer needed, it is easier to shake out.

Personally, I prefer to keep the necessary lines out of the cockpit altogether, carrying out the entire operation from the base of the mast—which, although frequently wet, is a reasonably secure location. This requires the halyard winch to be at the mast and the halyard to be stowed

Single-line reefing. The person in the foreground is easing the halyard while the crew member in the background cranks in the reef. No one needs to leave the cockpit.

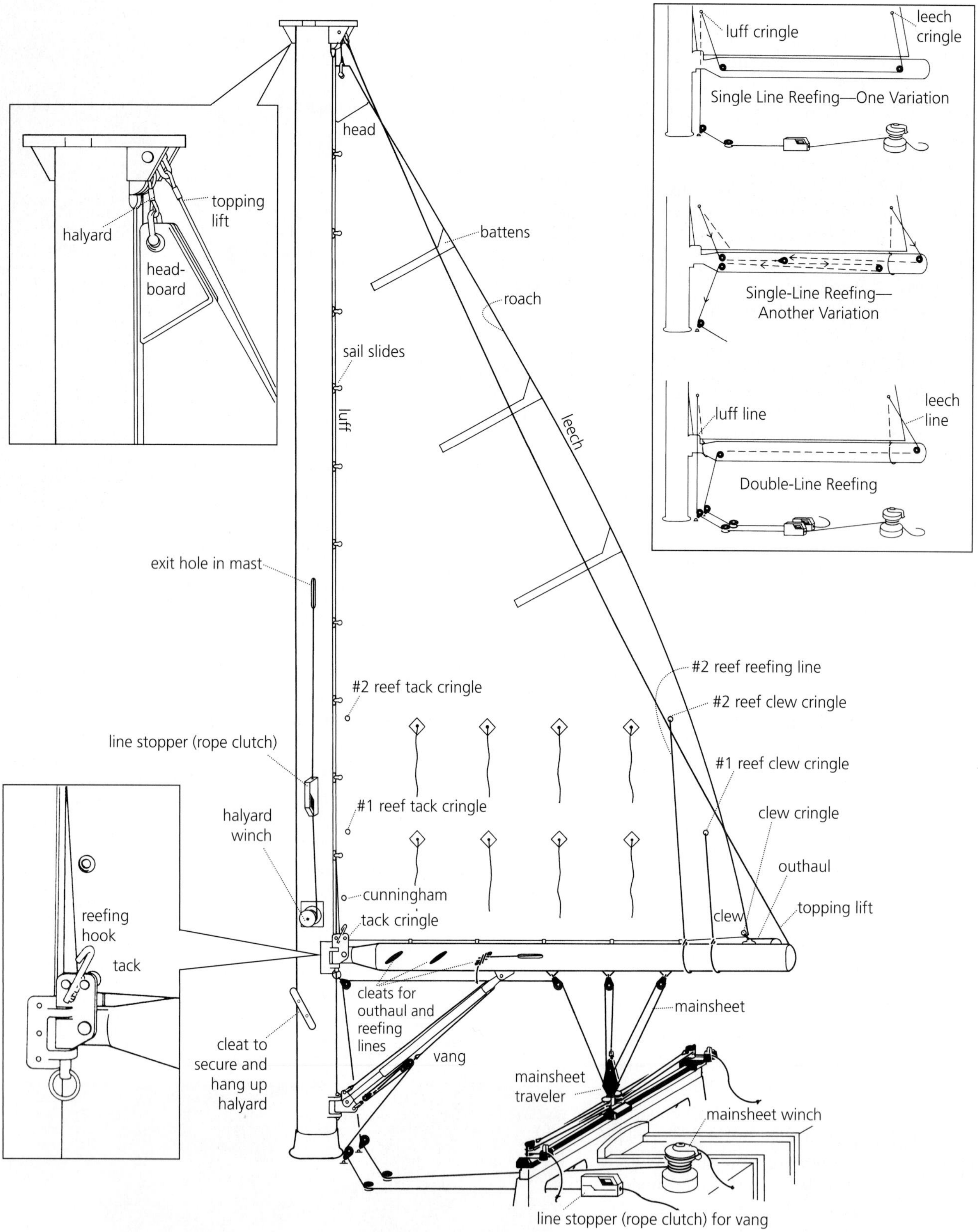

Left: *Mainsail terminology.* Inset upper right: *Cockpit reefing options.*

there. The reefing lines are run through line jammers on the base of the boom to a winch low down on the mast. They are stowed on the boom.

I have found that the line jammers fitted to booms are commonly frustrating. Most have handles with insufficient leverage to release the line under a load. To shake out a reef, the reefing line has to be put back on the winch and tensioned until the jammer can be released. Some jammers are then so poorly designed that they tend to bounce back into the locked posi-

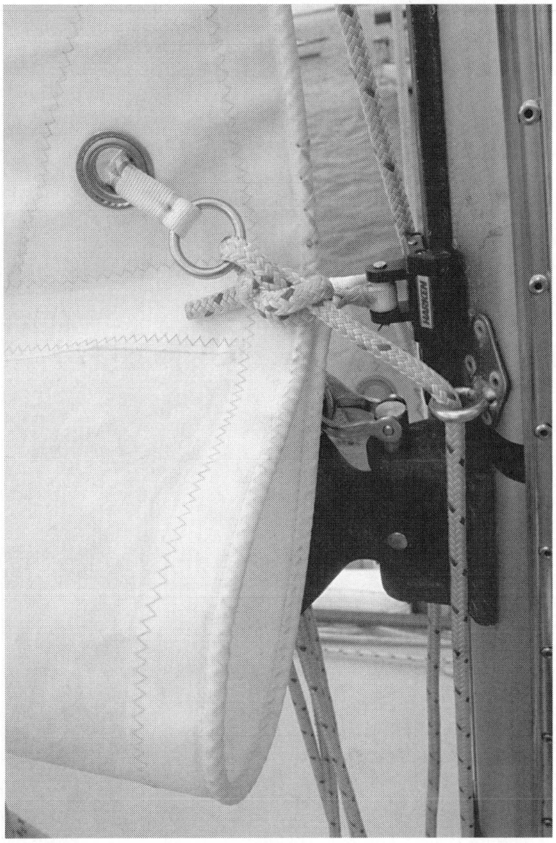

tion as the line is fed out, rather than stay open. Unfortunately, about the only way to determine how well a given jammer will work is to use it, which generally means you already own the boat, so there's not much you can do if you don't like it! However, when looking at a new boom, it is worth finding one on another boat made by the same manufacturer and giving it a workout before making a commitment.

Reefing from the mast enables a reefing hook (*horn*) on the boom to be used in place of the luff *downhaul*. This gets rid of one line and a chafe point. When I'm all done, I'm in the right place to inspect the reef and the set of the sail, and to put in an added chafe-prevention line through the leech cringle if the reef is likely to be left in for any length of time.

Many mainsails utilizing a reefing hook simply have reefing cringles fastened into the luff of the sail at the appropriate points. In theory, the sail is hauled down, the cringle is pulled over the hook, and the halyard is re-tensioned. However, it is often difficult to get the cringle over the hook and to keep it there while re-tensioning the halyard. Furthermore, if it's done incorrectly, there is a risk of tearing the sail. A much better approach is to place a length of heavy webbing through the cringle, and to sew a couple of rings to each end of it so that one hangs down on either side of the sail. It is then simplicity itself to pull one of these *floppy rings* over the hook (as long as it is possible to get the ring over the hook without having to remove any of the bottom sail slides from the mast track; it's hard to believe, but there are some boats on which it is necessary to remove the lower sail slides in order to reef).

Top left: *When all the control lines are led aft to the cockpit, a large number of blocks are necessary at the base of the mast. (Courtesy Pacific Seacraft)*
Top right: *In addition to the mass of line that ends up in the cockpit, one of the disadvantages of cockpit reefing is that the reef tack cringle is not rigidly fastened (as it is with a reefing hook). This makes it more difficult to optimize sail shape.*

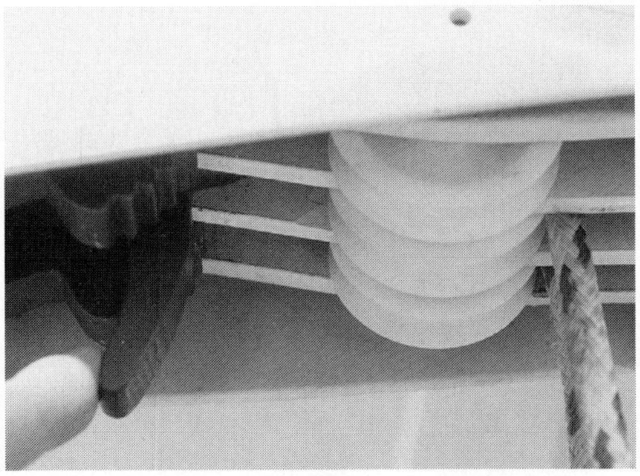

Line jammers on the forward end of a boom. The levers are not long enough to provide the leverage necessary to release a heavily loaded line.

Reefing hook in action—the halyard is eased sufficiently to enable the floppy ring attached to the tack cringle to be pulled over the hook.

Pulling in a reef on Nada *.*

1. Mainsheet and vang are eased from the cockpit. The topping lift is set up if needed (not in this case—the boat has a rigid vang). The halyard is eased and the floppy ring is pulled over the hook. 2. The halyard is re-tensioned. 3. The clew reefing line is pulled in, winched up tight, and locked with the line jammer on the underside of the boom. At this point, the reef is completed—all that remains is to tidy up and stow the lines. 4. The clew line is cleated off and tidied up. 5. The mainsail halyard is tidied up. 6. The slack is taken out of the second reefing line and the line is tidied up (I would prefer to have this line cleated on the same side as the first reef—something on my "to-do" list).

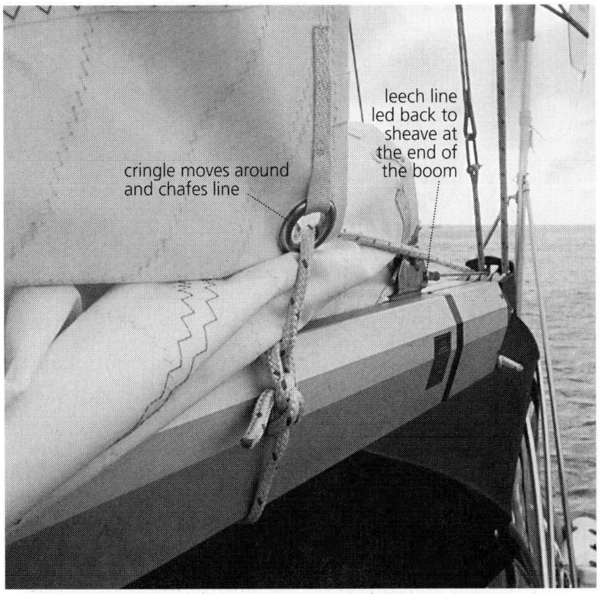

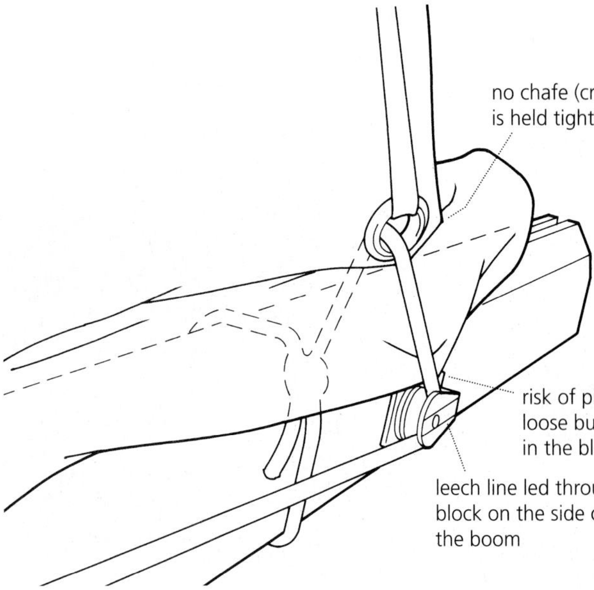

The reefing procedure is as described in the caption (opposite).

Regardless of how slab reefing is set up, what makes no sense at all for sailing shorthanded (as opposed to racing with a large crew) is to have the halyard on the mast and the reefing lines in the cockpit, or else the halyard and leech reefing lines led to the cockpit but with a reefing hook on the boom (both of these arrangements are common). If it is necessary to go forward to release the halyard or to get the luff of the sail over the reefing hook, what's the point of running the other lines aft? Specifically, having the lines aft but still using a reefing hook is simply absurd. Whoever is reefing the sail has to release the halyard, go forward to get the luff onto the hook, and then return to the cockpit to crank up the halyard and the leech line—by this time, the luff has probably come off the hook! In practice, two people are needed to reef: one to hold the luff on the hook and the other to work the lines.

If more than one reef is needed at any time, all should be tied in properly, rather than simply going straight to the second or third. This way there is less likelihood of lines tangling, and the reefs can be shaken out one at a time when the wind eases.

Damage Control

Whatever approach to slab reefing is used, remember that the leech line is vulnerable to chafe where it passes through the leech cringle. The problem arises because the reefing line is generally led back to a sheave on the end of the boom, which results in a run of several feet from the cringle to the sheave. As the sail works, the changing loads cause the cringle to move minimally from side to side, chafing the reefing line.

Chafe can be virtually eliminated (we used the same reefing line on our old boat for fifteen years, through 30,000 miles of cruising and many squalls) by positioning a cheek block on the side of the boom just aft of the reefed position of the cringle; the reefing line is led from there to the sheave on the back of the boom and so forward. This results in the cringle being trapped in such a way that it eliminates side-to-side movement, thereby eliminating chafe. However, it is not easy to establish a fairlead from a block on the side of a boom to the sheaves at the end of it on the typical aluminum boom with internal reefing lines. Even if it can be done, there is a risk of pinching the reefed sail in the block on the side of the boom, damaging the sail.

If this block is not used, it is generally necessary to live with the chafe. It can be minimized by tying in an additional line through the cringle and around the boom once the reef is in place but, of course, you have to go on deck to tie in and take out this line. In addition, the cringle may be difficult to reach over the top of a *bimini* or *dodger* (spray hood), or out over the water if the boom is at all eased—in the latter case, trying to get to it may be dangerous.

Traditionally, after a main is reefed, a series of reef points have been tied in to gather up the reefed portion of the sail (the *bunt*) and prevent it from flapping around. This is now considered to be bad practice. If the leech line chafes through, a tremendous load—for which it is not designed—is transferred to the reef point ahead

Left: *It doesn't matter how tight the clew line is pulled down, with this approach to reefing, there is always potential for the clew ring to move when the sail is loaded, chafing the line.* Right: *Chafe can be virtually eliminated by running the reefing line through a block on the side of the boom. Unfortunately, this cannot be done on most modern booms with internal reefing lines.*

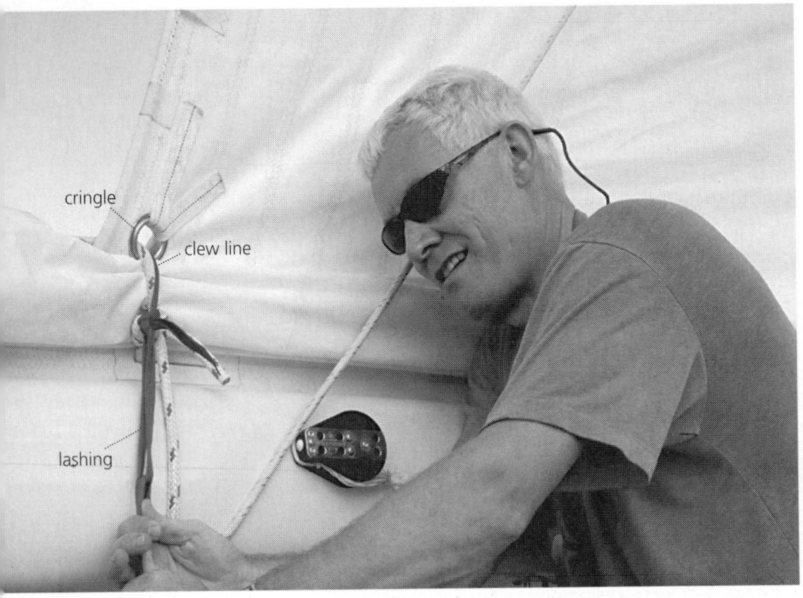

Above: *If a reef is to be left in for any time, it is advisable to supplement the clew line with a lashing through the cringle and around the boom.* Above right: *If reef points are to be tied in, the cringles in the sail through which the various lines pass should be installed by the sailmaker lower down the sail than the tack and leech cringles. This way, if the leech line slips, the reef point next in line will still not take up the load.*

of the leech cringle, very often tearing the sail. The next reefing point then takes up the load and tears, and so on. We never tie in the reefing points and have never found the loose bunt of sail to be a problem—with or without *lazyjacks* (which consist of a couple of lines rigged from the boom to the mast on either side of the sail). If reef points are to be tied in, the cringles in the sail through which the various lines pass should be installed by the sailmaker lower down the sail than the tack and leech cringles. This way, the leech line can slip a bit before the reef point next in line comes under the load.

Many cruising mains have three sets of reef points, which result in a number of reefing lines and the potential for considerable confusion. Furthermore, the third reef is only used in extreme conditions. With the reef in place, the leech of the sail will now be well forward on the boom, while the mainsheet will frequently exert its usual pressure well aft on the boom, which can result in a bent boom.

If the conditions that require a third reef are anticipated, it is preferable to add a separate sail

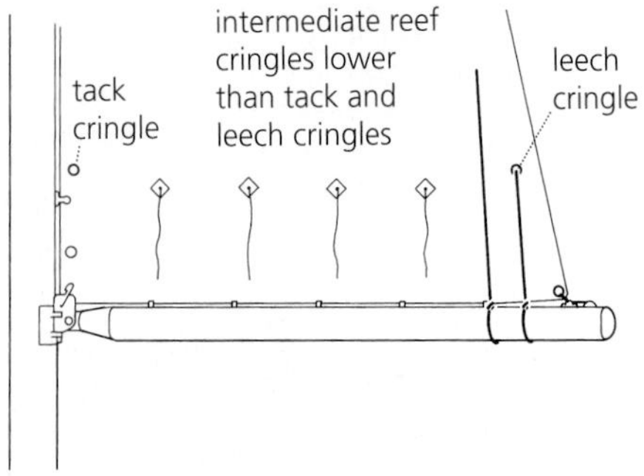

track to the mast and to have a trysail onboard. The track should come down close to the deck so that the sail can be *bent on* (attached to its track) in anticipation of rough conditions and then kept tidily stowed in its bag. The track should be as long as is needed rather than feeding into a gate on the mainsail track, which is likely to lead to snafus at the most inopportune times (for more on trysails, see chapter 11).

Taming the Main and Mainsail Covers

When a mainsail is reefed or put away, in-mast and in-boom reefing provide effective control and then good protection from ultraviolet (UV) radiation for the rolled-up sail. With any kind of slab reefing, when the sail is dropped, a large mass of loose sailcloth will need to be gathered up and covered. The sailcloth is likely to be billowing around all over the deck. Popular methods of restraining it include lazyjacks and some kind of Dutchman or StackPack arrangement.

Lazyjacks keep the loose sail from falling off the boom onto the deck. The sail then has to be tidied up and strapped to the boom with a series of sail ties before putting on a cover. Depending on the height of the boom off the deck and the boom's accessibility (dodgers, biminis, and center cockpits frequently get in the way), this may be easy or something of a chore. If the boom is fairly high, shorter people may be unable to reach to the top of the sail cover where it wraps around the mast; in this case, some kind of step up will be needed to complete the job.

The Dutchman system uses vertical lines hanging from a topping lift and tied off on the boom. On their way down to the boom, these lines are woven back and forth through a series of reinforced eyes in the sail. When the sail is dropped, it naturally concertinas on top of the boom. With the Dutchman system, a conventional sail cover still has to be put on. The StackPack, on the other hand, has integral sail cover panels attached to lazyjacks in such a way that the sail drops between the panels, which are then zipped up.

When a sail is dropped, it will fall all over the deck if it is not restrained in some way.

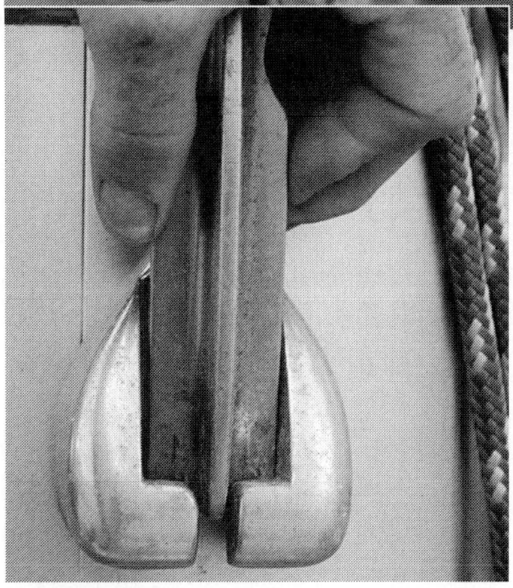

Far left: *Some kind of a step up may be needed to enable the halyard and sail cover to be put on and off.* Above and left: *Details of the folding step seen in the photo far left.*

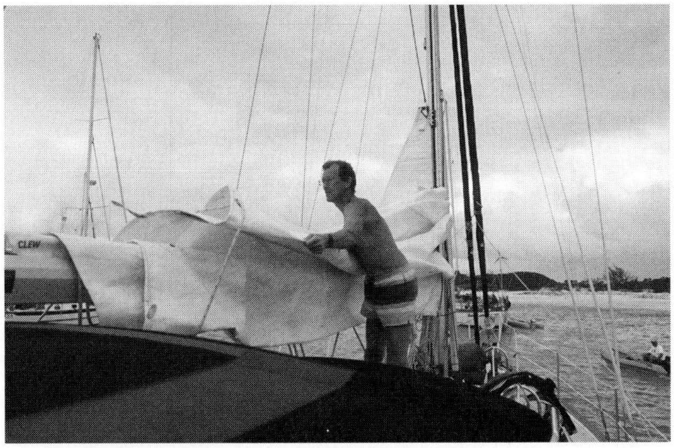

The Dutchman system, which . . .

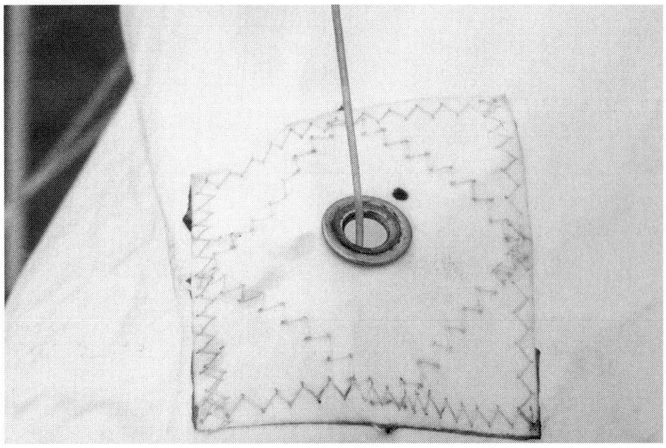

. . . utilizes heavy-duty fishing line led through a series of grommets in the sail to flake the sail down on the boom.

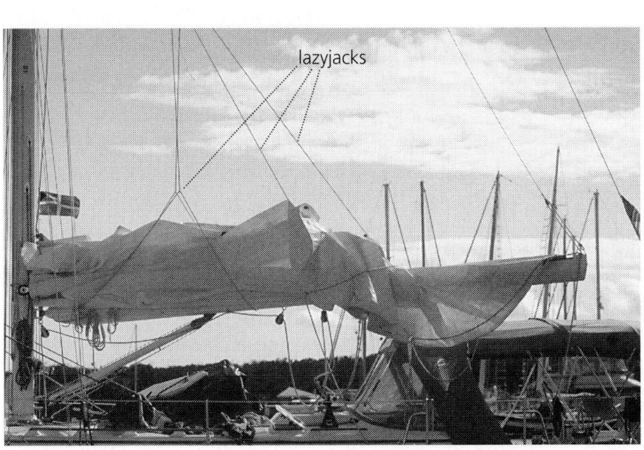

Lazyjacks on Nada.

The StackPack system, which drops the sail into a permanently installed sail cover.

Odds and Ends

Before ending the discussion of rigs and rigging, here is a miscellaneous collection of other ideas:

- Electrical cabling is sometimes run loosely inside masts. It rattles and bangs annoyingly, and may eventually chafe through (at which point it may cause severe stray-current corrosion). It should always be installed in plastic conduit. Conduit can be retroactively installed on masts by laying the mast down horizontally, removing the existing cables, building up the necessary length of conduit outside the mast, putting a generous bead of silicone rubber or polyurethane adhesive on one side of the conduit, sliding the conduit into place with the silicon or polyurethane facing away from the mast wall (so that it does not get rubbed off), and then rolling the conduit over so that the silicon or polyurethane ends up between the mast wall and conduit, gluing the conduit in place. The conduit is then drilled for the necessary exit holes (e.g., spreader lights), after which *fishing wires* are used to pull through *fishing lines*, which are then used to pull the cables back into place.
- Anodized aluminum masts hold up better over time than painted ones, but few mast-builders have the capability to anodize long masts; therefore, most are painted. In either case, it is essential to add corrosion-inhibitor wherever stainless steel components (e.g., rivets and halyard exit plates) contact the aluminum. If this is not done (and it frequently is not—mast-builders are quite lax about this), galvanic corrosion causes the paint or galvanizing to blister around all the components within a couple of years.
- Any fastener put into an aluminum mast needs to be corrosion-inhibited by smearing it with Tef-Gel, Duralac, or a similar substance. It is truly surprising how often this is ignored.
- Keel-stepped masts frequently develop annoying leaks where the mast comes through the deck or housetop. To achieve a good seal, a mast ring should be installed on the deck, with a raised lip at least 1 inch (25 mm) high. After the mast has been positioned in the opening and wedged in place (see Tuning a Rig in chapter 7), a rubber boot is fitted around the mast, over the sealing ring, and hose-clamped in place. With a little help from some silicon caulk, there is no reason why it can't be made 100 percent watertight.
- Mast height and sail area are a function of anticipated wind speeds. Naval architects design to an "average." If a boat will be used almost exclusively in a light wind area (e.g., Maine in the summertime) or a region with relatively strong winds (e.g., San Francisco Bay), something other than the average rig and sail plan may be appropriate. However, always remember that a rig with a large sail area produces a sprightly performance in light winds and can be reefed if necessary in strong winds; whereas, one with a small sail area may be appropriate for strong winds but will leave the boat underpowered in light winds. In either case, if it is intended to transit the U.S. Intracoastal Waterway, mast height should be limited to less than 65 feet (19.8 m) *from the waterline* because this is the minimum height for most of the bridges.
- Mast steps encourage thorough rig inspections. The stirrup type (with a bar over the foot) is preferable inasmuch as feet are less likely to slip off. However, any mast step that does not fold may foul lines, and all require numerous holes to be drilled in the mast while adding weight and windage aloft.
- Any time cruising in reef-strewn waters is contemplated, mast steps or ratlines (or some other means to climb up toward the lower spreaders) are more or less essential for navigating through the coral (for more on ratlines, see chapter 10).
- A rigid vang is well worth having—it eliminates the need for both a topping lift and a boom gallows.
- Mainsheet travelers should be horizontal rather than curved to match the camber of the cabintop. Curved travelers look nice but, as the boom is eased outboard, the sheet tightens, necessitating a change in the sheet tension.
- On a cruising boat, the boom should clear heads in the cockpit *at all times*.
- In my opinion, blocks for running rigging should have plastic or stainless steel *cheek* (side) plates rather than the commonly used anodized aluminum; sooner or later, the aluminum corrodes. Rather than being riveted together, larger blocks should be designed to be disassembled for cleaning.
- The black anodized aluminum tracks commonly used for headsail cars get very

hot under foot, and sooner or later the aluminum corrodes. Polished stainless steel is preferable.

- It is very nice if the genoa cars can be set up so that they are adjustable under load from the cockpit. This generally requires running a line from the car forward through a block and then back to a rope clutch and winch in the cockpit.
- The primary cockpit winches need to be large enough for a small person in strong winds to comfortably sheet in the largest headsail on the boat.
- Lastly, a pet peeve of mine: All cleats on the mast (and many elsewhere) need to be large enough to take not only the two turns needed to cleat off a line, but also (at least on the top end of the cleat) to then comfortably hold another turn that is used to stow the line (as a general rule, the length of a cleat should be at least sixteen times the diameter of the line to be stowed on it). Too often, the horns are barely long enough; in rough weather, the stowed line comes loose and streams back down a side deck or overboard.

A curved mainsheet traveler looks nice but is not as functional as a straight traveler. If the sheet is hauled in tight, it must be adjusted when the boom is eased down the traveler.

Blocks with stainless steel or plastic cheek plates are preferable to anodized aluminum, which inevitably corrodes over time.

Black anodized tracks get very hot underfoot—stainless steel is better. For a Cadillac installation, the car can be given a line on its forward face that is led around a block at the forward end of the track and then back to the cockpit. This enables the car to be adjusted under load from the cockpit—a nice feature for those who like to optimize performance.

COCKPITS AND DECK LAYOUT

The cockpit is the hub of activity on a boat, both at sea and in harbor. As such, it fulfills numerous functions. It requires careful design if it is to operate to best advantage.

Putting a center cockpit on boats less than 45 feet in length sometimes results in high freeboard, a boxy appearance, and the loss of a significant amount of cockpit stowage. In this case, when combined with the ketch rig, it also breaks up the deck spaces to where it is just about impossible to stow a dinghy on deck. Of course, the boat has a rather nice aft cabin.

Center or Aft Cockpit

The most basic question to be settled is whether to have a center or aft cockpit. Center cockpits have grown in popularity over the past couple of decades, particularly since the popularization of the "deck-saloon" concept by Oyster Yachts. The center cockpit puts the cockpit closer to the longitudinal center of motion of the boat and closer to the mast, making it easier to run the lines to the cockpit and to go forward to work the sails if necessary. There is almost always much better visibility forward.

When combined with the deck-saloon concept, the raised sole beneath the deck saloon provides volume for the engine, batteries, tankage, and an AC generator, keeping all this weight low in the boat and close to the longitudinal center of gravity (which reduces pitching in head seas). Above all, the center cockpit enables a substantial aft cabin to be put on a boat, transforming the accommodations.

An aft cabin does not work too well until a boat is large enough to provide reasonable inside access to it down the underside of the cockpit coaming. If this is not possible, the aft cabin will have a forward-facing companionway, which will be exposed to the weather. It will be necessary to transit the cockpit to enter and exit the cabin. If the aft cabin's companionway hatch is opened for light or ventilation, there is no privacy in the cabin. With or without a companionway, aft cabins typically suffer from a lack of ventilation.

The cockpit is the social center of any cruising boat.

The attempt to provide an aft cabin with inside access on a smaller boat leads to excessive freeboard with a high, shallow cockpit that is uncomfortable and unseaworthy, and a raised house on the aft cabin that makes it difficult to work on deck in rough weather. Inevitably, there is always someone who tries to push the design envelope too far.

Hard on the wind, the center cockpit—being that much farther forward than an aft cockpit—tends to catch a lot more spray. Some are notoriously wet. A center cockpit is invariably higher than an aft cockpit, which may put the heads of taller people within range of the

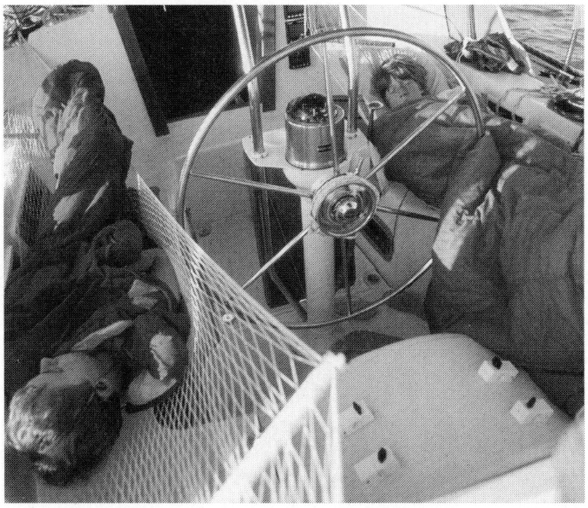

boom—a potentially dangerous situation. On many boats, the cockpit sole is close to the height of the lifelines, with the coamings well above the lifelines. In rough weather, there is a significantly greater chance of getting pitched overboard when entering or leaving the cockpit than on an aft-cockpit boat. The center cockpit complicates steering and makes it difficult to rig the control lines for a wind vane. A center cockpit often has somewhat limited cockpit stowage. It also precludes dinghy stowage between the cockpit and the mast (which is often the optimum location on an aft-cockpit boat).

Then there is the matter of aesthetics. It is difficult to put a center cockpit and aft cabin on a boat that is less than 45 feet (13.7 m) in length without making the boat look boxy. (The same can be said about a pilothouse, the idea of which gets increasingly attractive the older I get.) This is, of course, a very subjective matter. With two growing children, the physical separation in the accommodation spaces provided by an aft cabin is very alluring to us; however, the only boats on which we think it works well and looks good are larger than we are willing to own and maintain. In any case, the children will be cruising full time with us for only a few more years. We settled for an aft cockpit, but this is clearly one of those choices that can be made only in light of your own short- and long-term cruising plans.

Basic Parameters and the Comfort Factor

Above all else, a cockpit has to create a secure, comfortable working space at sea. On the one hand, it has to be large enough to accommodate all usual crew; on the other hand, its volume needs to be limited so that in case it gets filled by a breaking wave, it does not hold an inordinate weight of water.

Regardless of boat size or type, some parameters remain consistent. The lower limit on length should be determined by the need to have the seats long enough for someone to sleep on them (i.e., something more than 6 feet or 1.8 m). The seats need to be straight for at least 6 feet and as parallel to the centerline as possible (so that one end is not higher than the other when the boat is heeled). To make comfortable berths, the seats need to be 20 to 24 inches (500–600 mm) wide.

Cockpit-well width is determined by the need to be able to sit on one seat and comfortably brace your feet on the opposite seat when

Above left: *The lower limit on cockpit length and seat width should be determined by the need to be able to sleep on deck.* Above right: *A particularly spacious and comfortable cockpit. Note the (currently unfashionable) square cockpit corners, which are far more comfortable than fashionably rounded corners.*

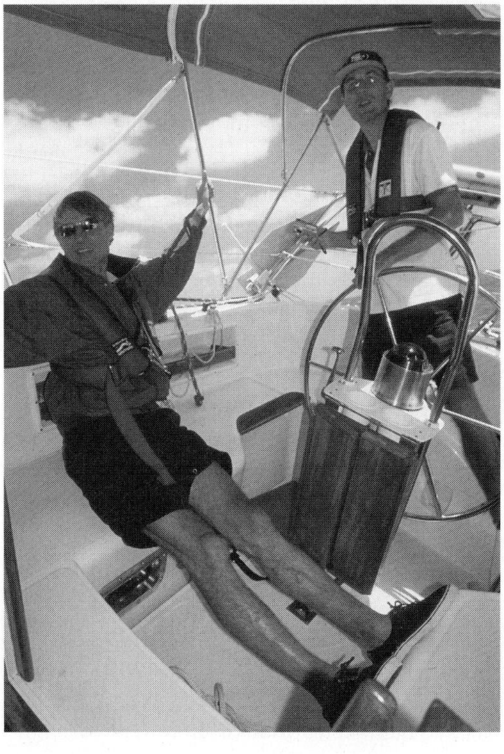

Cockpit seats need to be close enough to brace yourself on the opposite seat.

the boat is well heeled. In practice, 24 inches (600 mm) is about ideal, 30 inches (760 mm) very much the upper limit (to some extent, this depends on the width of the seats: the narrower the seats, the wider the well can be). Cockpits wider than this need some kind of a bracing bar, which will then invariably get in the way when in harbor (maybe it could be made removable).

To be comfortable, seats need to be 15 to 18 inches (380–460 mm) above the cockpit sole (including the depth of any cushions), and with seat backs 15 to 20 inches (380–500 mm) high, angled outboard by 10 to 15 degrees. Ideally, the aft end of the main cabin will also be sufficiently raked to form a comfortable backrest (it rarely is). The cockpit coamings should meet the cabin at right angles, enabling someone to get comfortably wedged in place when stretched out on the seat facing aft. Too often, designers round the corners on modern cockpits. Regardless of how aesthetically pleasing this may be, it is not comfortable!

Because of the pressure to create large aft cabins—which necessitates relatively high, shallow cockpits—very few modern boats meet these parameters. In particular, the seats are closer to the cockpit sole, and the cockpit coamings (i.e., seatbacks) are generally low and more or less vertical, becoming a real pain in the back. Considering the amount of time spent in the cockpit, both at sea and in harbor, this is simply unacceptable on a cruising boat. European boatbuilders generally do a better job than do U.S. boatbuilders of producing comfortable coamings. In particular, they angle the top half of the coaming outboard more than the bottom half, and round the top edge. The coaming is thus shaped to fit the curvature of a back, with no hard spot at the top. It doesn't cost any more to produce comfortable coamings than it does uncomfortable ones—it's about time more boatbuilders got this right. If stuck with uncomfortable coamings, you can add a plywood-backed cushion that extends above the level of the coaming.

My family and I are relatively skinny with skinny backsides. Cockpit cushions are a necessity, despite the fact that they are next to impossible to keep clean and difficult to keep in place at sea. Effective nonskid on the seats, which is essential on a seagoing boat, holds them reasonably well. Velcro strips, with one half glued to the seat, are even better. However, any kind of snap that involves putting a screw into the seat should be avoided. The screws are frequently wet and liable to corrode (even if made of stainless steel), and the screw holes will probably allow moisture into the deck core.

A high cockpit with coamings of a decent height raises the coamings a considerable way off the deck, making it difficult to enter and exit the cockpit. Some kind of a step or lowered section of coaming (or both) is needed. Another factor to be considered relative to high cockpits—with or without decent coamings—is safety in rough weather or when moving in and out of the cockpit. If the boat makes a sudden lurch at the wrong moment, there is a much greater likelihood of being pitched clear over the lifelines (especially with many center cockpits) than with a more traditional cockpit. There needs to be an adequate number of handholds and harness-attachment points.

If a cockpit has the kind of seat-back depth recommended (15–20 in./380–500 mm) and if the coamings are wide enough (12 in./300 mm or more), they become comfortable seats themselves. This is an excellent watchkeeping location in fair weather, especially if it is still possible to comfortably reach the rim of the steering wheel. There is a good line-of-sight up the side deck and a view of the set of the sails.

Coamings should incorporate coaming boxes for stowage of halyards, sheets, binoculars, gloves, winch handles, suntan oil, and all the other miscellanea that invariably end up in the cockpit. On many modern boats, these invaluable lockers are completely absent.

The primary (i.e., headsail) winches are almost always on the coamings. It just so happens that the optimum height for a winch handle to be above the cockpit sole is 40 to 45 inches (1.02–1.14 m), which fits rather nicely the optimum dimensions already outlined (seats 15–18 in./380–460 mm off the sole, coamings 15–20 in./380–500 mm high, and the winch and its handle adding another 10 in./250 mm or so). The coamings almost always need to be angled outboard to provide a fairlead for the headsail sheets up onto the winches. Winches need to be located such that they are both comfortable to work and accessible from the watchkeeping station so that lines can be rapidly cast off when necessary.

Likewise, instruments need to be clearly visible from the watchkeeping station, which needs a clear line-of-sight forward. Remember that on a cruising boat, the watchkeeping station is rarely at the wheel or tiller because the boat is almost always being steered by an autopilot or wind vane. For this reason, on a wheel-steered boat, it is better to mount the sailing instruments above the companionway hatch

Variations on the theme of cockpit line stowage.

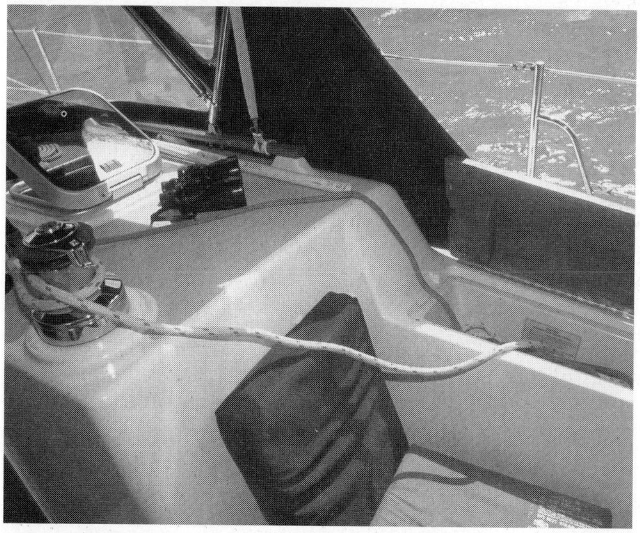

The primary winches should always be accessible from the steering and watch-keeping stations.

Pedestal-mounted instruments: note how it is necessary to refocus to read the instruments and look in the distance, whereas this is not necessary with instruments mounted over the companionway (which, unlike the binnacle-mounted instruments, are also visible from other watchkeeping stations).

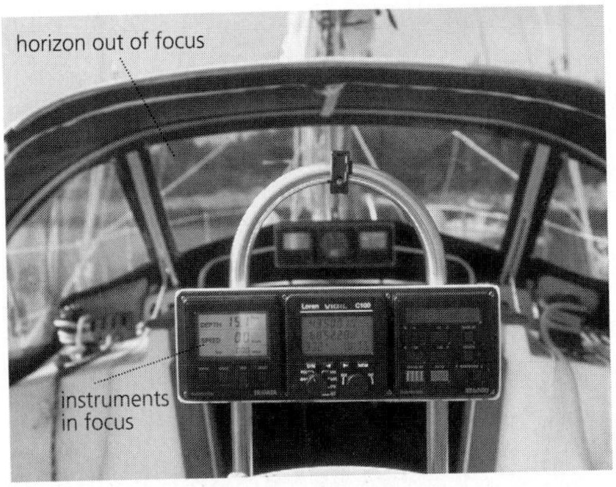

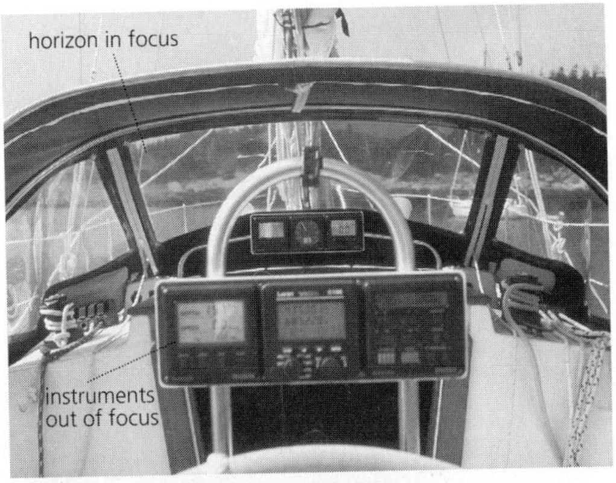

(the best place for all-around visibility) or on the cabin bulkhead (as long as they are not obscured by halyards and reefing lines hanging off the aft end of the cabintop) rather than on the pedestal. Even when wheel-steering, instruments mounted off the pedestal are more convenient (as long as the displays are large enough to read) because of the need to refocus one's vision whenever looking at pedestal-mounted instruments. If instruments are mounted on the pedestal, it is important to ensure that the mounting bracket angles them upward in such a way that they are readily visible; otherwise, it will be necessary to crouch down to read them (as ridiculous as this sounds, it is not uncommon).

The cockpit sole must clearly be high enough for an average person standing at the wheel, sitting on the helmsperson's seat, or operating a tiller to have a clear line-of-sight forward, but also low enough to provide a clear view under the sails. If necessary, the sole can be raised with what I have heard tactfully described as a "runt board"! Almost always, visibility when seated at the helm of an aft cockpit boat is very poor; the addition of a raised seat makes a huge difference. With wheel-steering, a curved helmsperson's seat is preferable to a flat one.

Here's a nifty device—a gimbaled seat! We raised it to give the helmsperson a great view forward. It was particularly nice motoring down the Intracoastal Waterway, but not so useful at sea (because we rarely steer the boat by hand).

The visibility forward is almost always compromised on a sailboat; in this case, both by the genoa to starboard (which completely obstructs the view in this direction) and the gear lashed on deck.

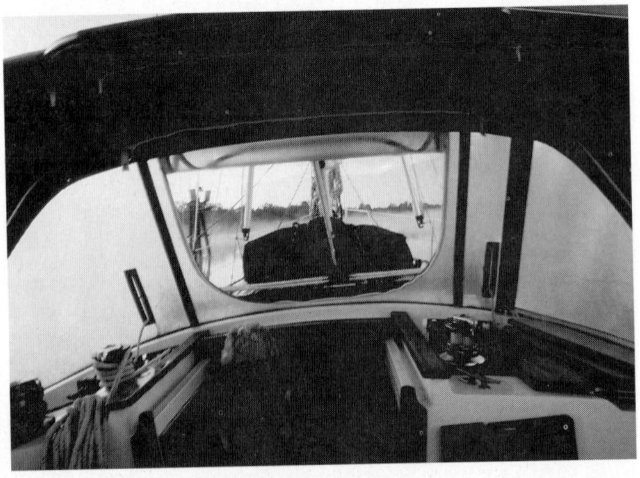

When the clear plastic in the dodger is fogged up, visibility is downright awful. At times like these, the dodger needs to be laid down. To do this, it needs to be easy to get up and down, and must not obstruct the working of the boat when down.

Given that very little watchkeeping is done from behind the wheel or holding the tiller, there needs to be a secure, comfortable location for the watchkeeper, protected from the elements, but still with good all-around visibility. This is not so easy to achieve, especially once a dinghy and maybe a life raft are stowed on deck. Visibility is commonly compromised.

At sea, there needs to be a place to safely stow drinks. In harbor, a table is needed. In the case of wheel-steering with a pedestal, a table is easily attached to the forward face of the pedestal. With tiller-steering, a little more ingenuity is required. On our old boat, we had stainless steel brackets hinged to the top forward and aft faces of the cockpit well. At sea, the brackets hung down in the well. In harbor, they flipped up against stops that prevented them traveling beyond the vertical. The foot-well grate dropped onto the top of the brackets to make a table; it worked like a charm. As an added refinement, the grate was designed so that when the brackets were folded down, the grate could rest squarely on the hinged portions of the brackets at the top of the well. This closed off the well and leveled the entire cockpit into a suitable area for a couple to sleep. Terrie and I spent many nights out there under the stars.

I have a strong dislike of bridge-deck-mounted mainsheet travelers. At best, they always seem to be in the way; at worst, they are a distinct hazard, particularly if the blocks fly across the cockpit in a jibe. The traveler should be moved up onto the cabintop out of the way. If the boom still overhangs the cockpit, it goes without saying that at its lowest point, it should easily clear all heads. It will still be a danger to anyone standing on the seats; therefore, if possible, it should not overhang an aft cockpit at all.

The problem with moving a bridge-deck-mounted mainsheet traveler forward is that it puts the sheet attachment point somewhere in the middle of the boom, while most of the

For longer passages, it is essential to have a comfortable, protected watchkeeping station from which there is a good view forward.

Pedestal-mounted cockpit table.

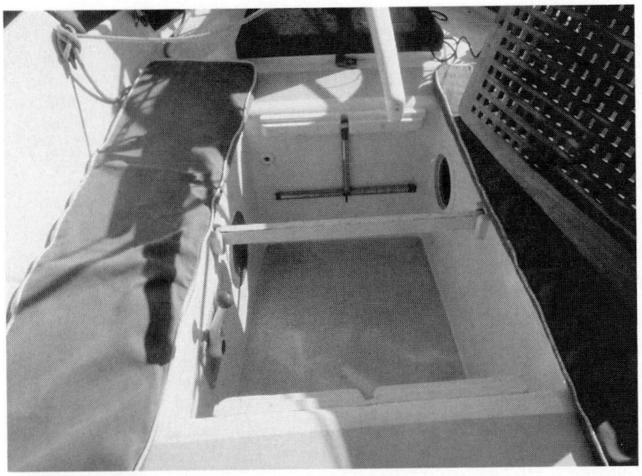

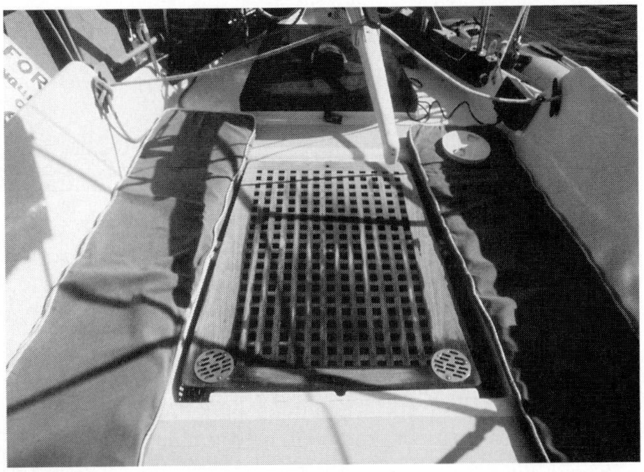

A bar is used in combination with ledges at both ends of the cockpit well to support the grate. The entire cockpit can now be used for sleeping.

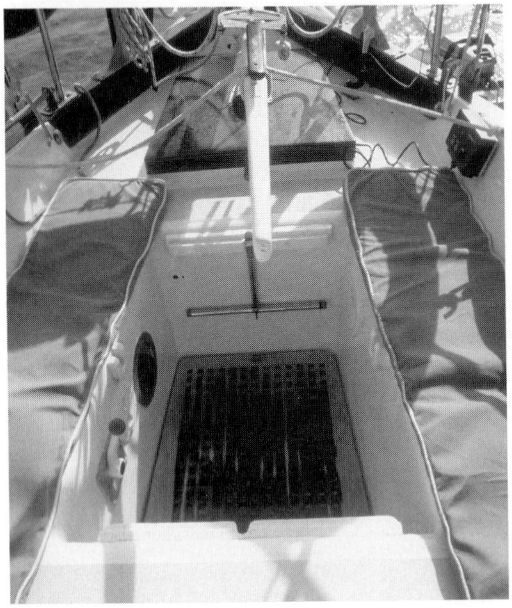

The grate is in the down position.

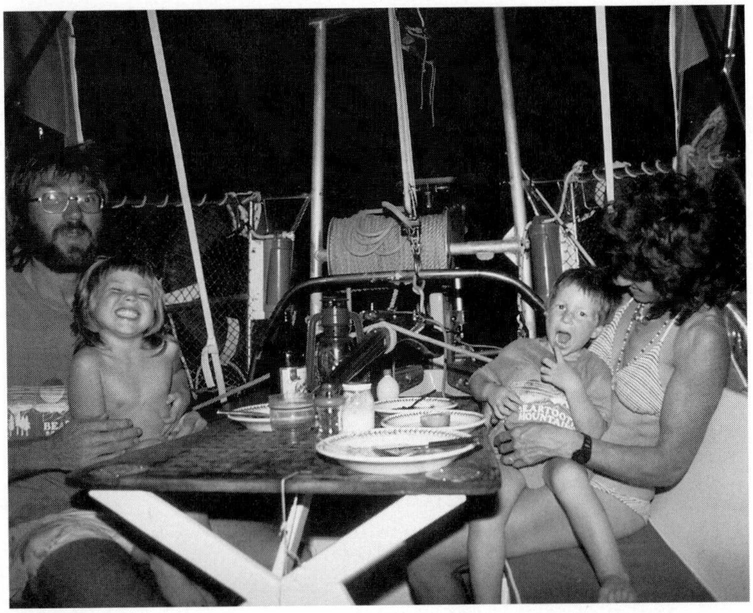

The support bars are hinged up to support the table (this is an earlier version of the table; in the previous two photos, the wooden support bars were replaced with an elegant stainless steel T bar).

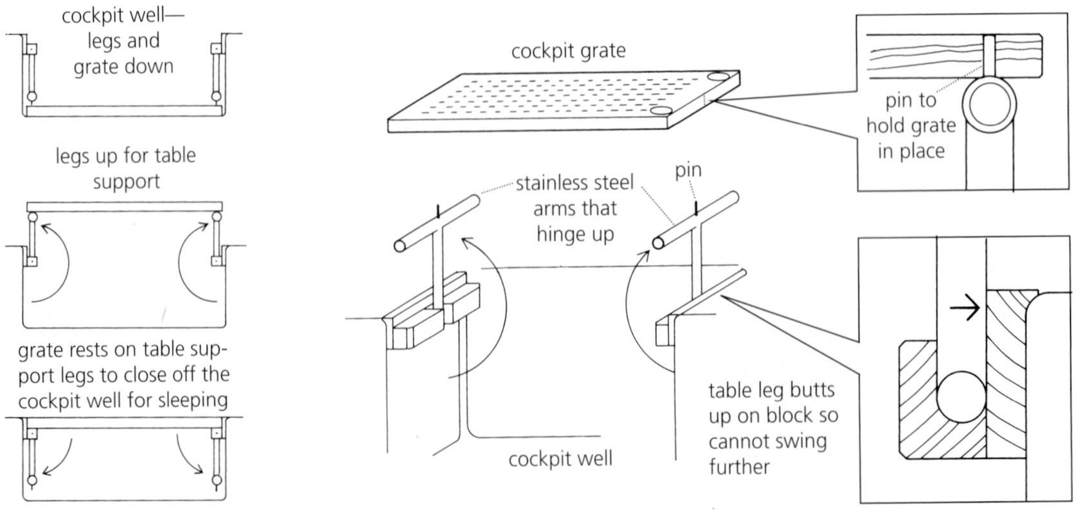

Using the cockpit grate on a tiller-steered boat to level the cockpit for sleeping and to make a table.

upward load is concentrated toward the end of the boom (where the leech of the sail is attached). This can result in a bent boom. The way to spread the loads is with a four- or six-part tackle, with two or three attachment points spread out along the boom. It results in a very long main sheet, but there's not much that can be done about that.

A cockpit accumulates a surprising amount of dirt and debris (e.g., sand, food, hair), so it should be easy to hose down. To clean the grating in our old foot well (the new one doesn't have a grate), we tied a line to it, tossed it overboard, and towed it behind the boat for a while (this also works well for shower grates that accumulate a nasty mess between all the squares, which otherwise is best cleaned out with a toothbrush—not my favorite job).

Steering

The tiller or pedestal tends to dominate a cockpit, particularly on modern boats in which the pedestal is increasingly being turned into a substantial multipurpose command, control, and entertainment center. It ought to go without saying that it should be easy to move around the wheel, but it rarely is. A T-shaped cockpit is best, as long as it does not compromise the use of the cockpit seats for sleeping.

Often with wheel-steering, an unnecessarily large wheel is used. This reduces the effort required to steer and looks fashionable (the bigger, the better); however, with a little more effort,

There is frequently insufficient space to move comfortably around the wheel.

For comfort, the upper rim of the wheel should not be above chest height.

a smaller wheel—which is easier to get around—can be used. The increase in effort may be an acceptable price to pay for greater accessibility. In any case, for comfort at the wheel, its upper rim should not be much above waist height. If a large wheel is used, the lower rim should be set in a slot in the deck to keep it at this level (although this collects all kinds of crud).

Steering loads are light most of the time but, in heavy weather, they rise exponentially. It is difficult to test a steering system at dockside to see if it is adequately built; but clearly, a pedestal must be extremely well-fastened down, with the cockpit sole thoroughly reinforced at that point. On some systems, one way to check this is to vigorously turn the rim of the wheel from side to side a few inches. Depending on the gearing, the rapid reversal of steering loads may put quite a strain on the system, making some cockpit soles flex in a rather unnerving manner. In addition to steering loads, the pedestal must take the force of a heavy person being thrown across the cockpit. The top of the pedestal should incorporate a grab bar or guard, which also must be able to withstand similar impacts.

Most U.S.-built boats with wheel-steering use some variant of cable-steering. To be trouble-free, it must be properly installed, with rugged enough mounting structures to withstand all conceivable stresses (not always the case), and regularly maintained (frequently neglected). In particular, if a cable-steering system uses independently mounted sheaves on either side of the steering quadrant, it is essential to ensure that these sheaves cannot move inboard under any kind of load. If they do, the cable will slacken, which risks it coming off the unloaded sheave (if possible, watch the cables while someone else rocks the wheel, as described previously). The two final sheaves are usually incorporated into one solid fixture; however, if they happen to be mounted independently on either side of the quadrant, a rigid brace should exist or be installed between the structures to which they are fastened. All steering-system components should be bolted (not screwed) in place with substantial backing blocks.

In Europe, wheel-steering is dominated by "rack-and-pinion" pedestal-type units (they should more properly be called *bevel-geared* units), which are just about bulletproof and virtually maintenance-free. Whitlock is the major player in this market, with a proven track record for its Cobra systems, which are available in the United States. In my opinion, rack-and-pinion pedestal steering is the way to go on a cruising boat (the Cobra system comes as standard equipment on Pacific Seacrafts). However, it more or less requires an aft cockpit boat; installation is possible with center cockpits, but it can get quite complex.

Steering quadrants are frequently just clamped around a rudder stock, with a captive key, set in a keyway, to stop the quadrant slipping around the stock. If the quadrant loosens, it can slide down the stock until it parts company with the key, at which point steering control is lost. To prevent this, a quadrant should ideally be through-bolted; at the least, it should have set screws seating in dimples on the stock. As a backup, a hose clamp around the rudder stock, immediately below the quadrant, will keep a loose quadrant from sliding down the stock.

Whatever the steering system, a cruising boat needs an effective emergency tiller; that is, one that can be rapidly and easily installed in difficult circumstances, which will then provide meaningful steering. Too often, it is a struggle to fit the tiller and then, once in place, it has neither the leverage nor the swinging room to control the boat in heavy weather. Few are built strong enough to withstand serious steering loads (the weak link is generally the point at which the tiller slips over the rudder stock).

Engine Controls

With wheel-steering, the engine controls can be mounted on the pedestal where they are readily accessible. The conventional arrangement has the wheel on the aft side of the pedestal, making it necessary to reach through the spokes on larger wheels to operate the controls (with smaller wheels, it is possible to reach around the rim). This is potentially dangerous. Whitlock and others are now manufacturing larger wheels that mount to the forward face of the pedestal, with the spokes bent aft to make the rim accessible so there is no obstruction of the controls. It looks a little odd to my eye, but works fine.

The emergency tiller on Nada*—easy enough to fit, but I doubt it has the leverage to steer the boat in much of a seaway.*

With tiller-steering, the engine controls are usually placed on the side of the cockpit well. Wherever they are located, it is important to be able to operate them while steering the boat and to do so without a loss of visibility. If a single lever control is used (as opposed to separate throttle and transmission controls), it can often be operated by a foot, which increases the range of installation options. Wherever the controls are located, they need to be placed so that they are not likely to get fouled by loose halyards or sheets.

Wind Vanes

Many cruisers augment their steering with wind-vane self-steering. There is no question that the servo-pendulum type is the most effective—I would not consider any other type for offshore work. Of these, the old Aries (now made in Denmark), the Monitor, the Sailomat, and the Windpilot (popular in Europe) are the best known: all work reliably and well on "typical" cruising boats, although with some subtle differences (they do not work well on multihulls, as well as some monohulls moving at speed, because the boat speed changes the apparent wind direction, resulting in undesirable course changes; for more about the apparent wind, see chapter 7).

Servo-pendulum wind vanes develop a tremendous amount of power when a boat is moving at speed and, as a result, require a very sturdy mounting bracket. From a safety perspective, it is essential that all course adjustments can be made from within the security of the cockpit rather than having to hang over the stern. However, it is frequently difficult to run the necessary control lines to a center cockpit. A wind vane must be set up so that it can be disconnected almost instantly if it becomes necessary to recover control of the wheel or tiller. It is also important to be able to easily get the oar out of the water when not in use. The oar itself needs a weak link so that if it fouls something at speed, it will fold or break away rather than rip the entire unit off the back of the boat.

A wind vane needs to be able to control the boat in relatively light apparent winds; otherwise, it is not going to be useful much of the time when going downwind. If the boat will not balance, or has poor directional stability and wants to scoot all over the place, even the best of wind vanes will not do well. A narrow boat or one with a relatively long keel generally performs better with a wind vane than a fin-keeler. As the wind pipes up and the steering loads increase, the vane needs the power to keep going. It should not be necessary to reef down prematurely just to ease the load on the vane, which means the vane must be powerful enough for the job and the boat must be well-enough balanced not to overwhelm it.

To be most effective, wind vanes should be installed on the centerline—which poses a problem for many modern boats with swim steps or a swim ladder in the center of the stern.

Given the relatively high cost of a wind vane and the fact that they are not appropriate for inshore work (if the wind shifts, you may find yourself on the beach), I believe that unless it is intended to do long offshore passages, it is best to invest in a back-up autopilot. For offshore passages, the primary justification for using a wind vane is that it uses no power, as opposed to the typical autopilot that consumes a considerable amount. Furthermore, wind vanes have a fairly good reliability record, which many autopilots do not. *The farther it is intended to travel offshore, the better a wind vane looks.*

If a wind vane is fitted, a gimbaled telltale compass should also be fitted above the skipper's berth. This way, without getting out of bed, the skipper can check the boat's heading, making sure that a wind shift has not moved the vessel off course.

Autopilots

The principal reason for the poor record of autopilots is that many of the cheaper models—particularly the cockpit autopilots—are not built for serious, sustained use. As the wind and waves build, the loads on an autopilot can increase exponentially. A unit that is perfectly adequate for light weekend use gets overwhelmed. Not only will the autopilot be unable

Nada *under wind vane. There is a quick-release pin on the wheel if it becomes necessary to trip the wind vane; the control lines can be untied to get them out of the way when the unit is not in use.*

to steer the boat properly, but it also will be continuously stressed to its limits, resulting in mechanical and electrical failures (destroyed linkages and gears, burned-out motors, and failed electronics components through overheating—all are common). As Randy Morris of Annapolis Marine Electronics told me: "Picture the boat coming down hard off a wave. The autopilot is trying to hold the rudder. If it is undersized, the ram will blow its seals or get bent, or the electronic unit will get overloaded and fry its brains."

At the core of the drive end of most autopilots is a small electric motor. To get the kind of force out of it needed to steer a boat, it is geared down. The more it is geared down, the greater the force it will develop, but the slower its response time will be. From the point of view of steering a boat, the problem is that as conditions worsen, steering loads increase—requiring a powerful autopilot—just when response time needs to decrease if a steady course is to be maintained.

The only way to be sure of accurate helming from an autopilot in all sea states and conditions is to have a large, powerful, fast, and expensive system. If it can cope with the rough times, it will also handle the smooth without a murmur. Ideally, the unit will incorporate a *rate sensor* or *gyro plus* compass that can identify motion that results from wave action (especially in conditions with large, following seas) and does not overcompensate. If going offshore, the bottom line is to buy a unit big enough for bad weather. Otherwise, the crew ends up hand-steering the boat at precisely the time they would rather not steer at all—in fact, they may end up steering all the time if the autopilot fails altogether. Simrad/Robertson autopilots enjoy an enviable reputation among cruising sailors.

When installing an autopilot, it is important to ensure that the electrical cables are adequately sized. Under load, many below-decks autopilots draw 20 amps or more (tiller or wheel-mounted pilots use much less energy, but with a commensurate reduction in power). Inadequate cabling results in voltage drop, loss of power, overheating, and motor burnout.

Ideally, the autopilot on a wheel-steered boat will be installed with its own independent tiller arm on the rudder stock; this provides a redundant steering system in the event that the wheel-steering fails. In practice, the autopilot may be connected to the steering-system quadrant or made an integral part of a cable-steering system. Both the electronics and the drive motor need to be in a cool, dry location with a reasonable air flow.

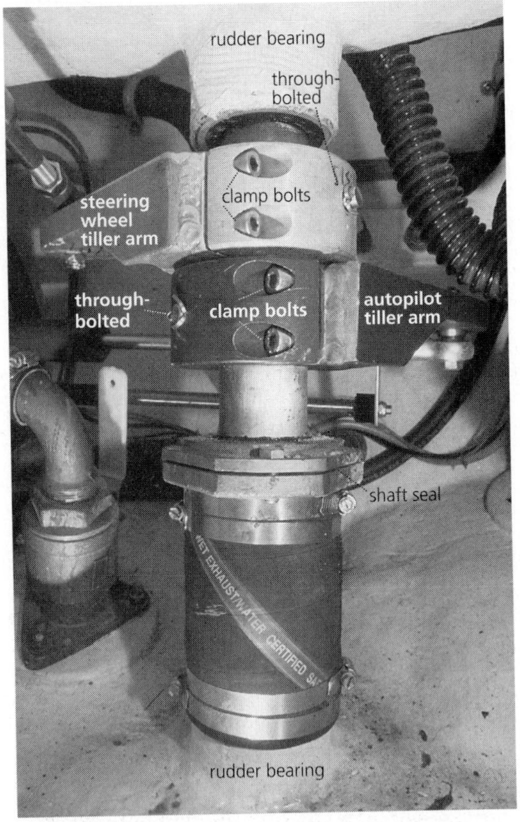

Rudder shaft seal and steering tiller arms. Note the use of separate tiller arms for the Whitlock Cobra system (the upper arm) and the autopilot (the lower arm), resulting in two independent steering systems. Both tiller arms are clamped and also through-bolted for added security. The system has three bearings: the heel bearing (seen in previous photos), a bearing where the shaft enters the hull (at the base of the hose), and a bearing at cockpit level (visible above the upper tiller arm). This is about as bulletproof as you can get. Access is also good.

Autopilots typically consume from 50 to 150 amp-hours a day at 12 volts (for more about electrical systems, see chapter 4). At sea, this is likely to be the biggest single load on a DC system. When navigation lights, navigation electronics, a VHF radio, maybe a radar and an SSB radio, and the boat's normal lighting and DC load are added in, the total load can easily top 200 amp-hours a day—and may go as high as 300 amp-hours. In other words, *the load may be double what it is at anchor.*

Unless the boat has a large solar-panel array and/or a wind generator (with the apparent wind speed high enough to keep it spinning), *a passage of just a day or two results in an energy crunch on most modern boats.* The engine will have to be run for at least an hour a day—in many cases, for two or more—to recharge batteries. Just a few days into their first long-distance cruise, too many boatowners discover that however good their DC system may be on the hook, it is not set up for passagemaking. *This energy crunch, as much as anything else, makes a wind vane such an attractive proposition for offshore cruising*—not to mention that if both an autopilot and a wind vane are fitted, the boat now has redundancy in case one fails (in practice, it almost certainly will be the autopilot).

Dodgers and Biminis

A *dodger* (spray hood) has to be high on the priority list of any cruising sailor, with a *cockpit bimini* not far behind. Together, they make a

A fully enclosed cockpit adds a considerable living area to the boat. The dark color, however, will soak up the sun in hot climates.

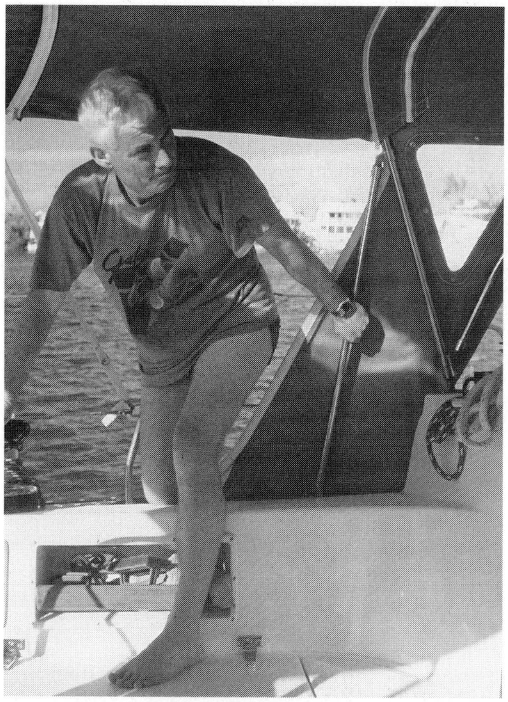

Good access with a rugged frame.

Ventilation is critical.

Too many dodgers obstruct basic boat operations. In this case, the winch handle cannot swing through a full circle, and the line stoppers (rope clutches) are difficult to operate.

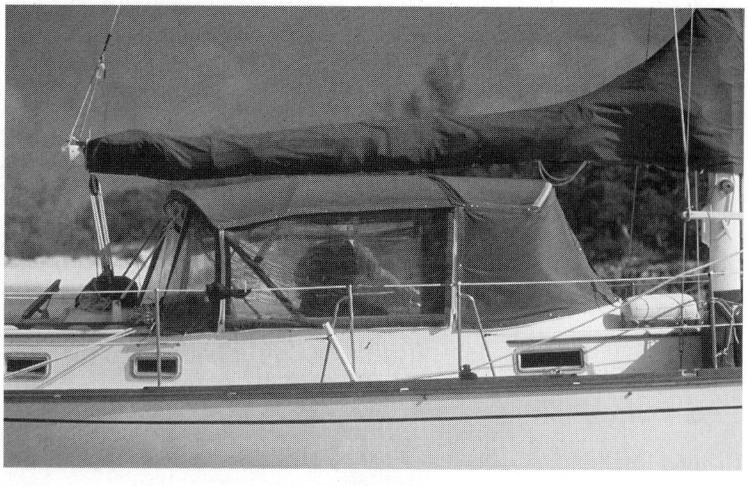

Note the covers on the front of this dodger, which reduce the greenhouse effect and extend the life of the clear plastic (which suffers from UV degradation over time). This is a 40-foot center-cockpit boat that manages to maintain attractive lines—quite an achievement.

Left: *The best visibility is provided with a low dodger over which it is possible to look, but this leaves the helmsperson somewhat exposed to the weather and often results in cramped companionway access.* Above: *The view over the dodger.*

A ridiculous dodger and bimini combination. The plastic window in the dodger is too low for visibility forward . . .

. . . and the slot between the bimini and dodger provides no visibility at all. Either the bimini or the dodger has to be taken down when underway.

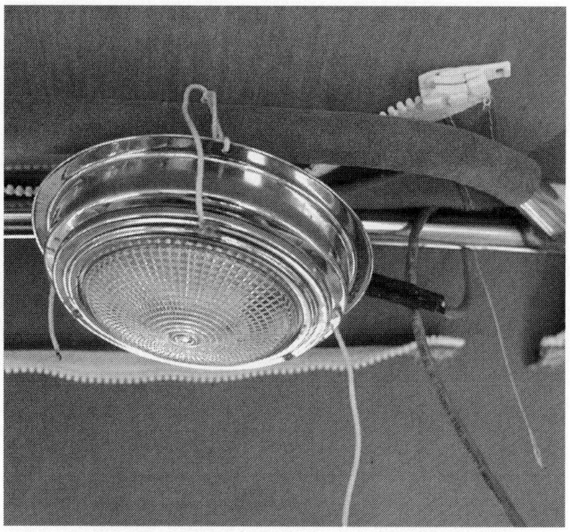

Something that is almost always forgotten is to work a cockpit light into the bimini frame. We also forgot; hence, this lash-up!

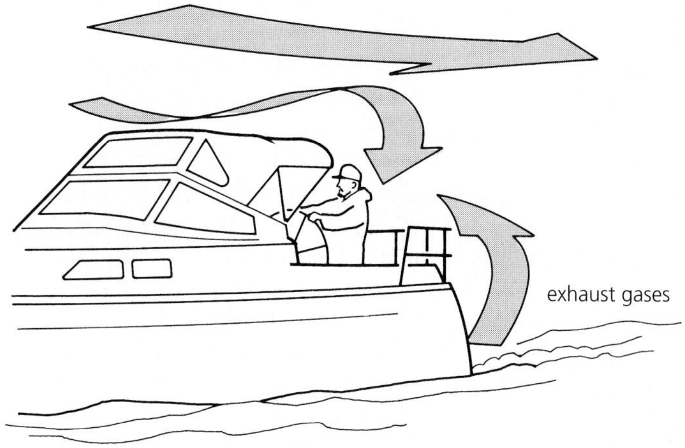

The "station-wagon effect," which can lead to deadly exhaust fumes being sucked into the cockpit. It can be minimized by partially opening a flap in the face of the dodger to ensure an airflow through the dodger. This helps equalize air pressure on both sides of the dodger, thereby stopping the exhaust gases from getting sucked in.

tremendous contribution to onboard comfort, particularly when watchkeeping in foul weather or sailing under a tropical sun. To get the most out of them, they have to be carefully thought out, including the following features:

- standing headroom in the cockpit
- easy entry into and exit from the cockpit, including strategically placed grab bars (rarely fitted), and perhaps zippered overhead sections between the dodger and bimini to open up the point of entry/exit
- sufficient strength to withstand people swinging on and lurching into the support structures, and to stand up to gale-force winds and the impact of wave crests coming aboard
- the framework, when erected or folded down, to be located so that it does not interfere with the working of the boat (e.g., operating rope clutches on the cabintop and cranking winches) and to have some means of tying it down in the face of boarding waves
- a dodger coaming (to which the dodger attaches) that stops water surging across the deck before it gets under the dodger
- both the dodger and the bimini to be designed and cambered so that rainwater is shed outside the cockpit, not inside it
- both the dodger and the bimini to be stretched tight enough and to have sufficient camber to prevent pockets of water forming (as the fabric ages, water drips through if puddles form)
- side curtains to the dodger that fully protect a watchkeeper when beating to windward
- zippered windows in the dodger for visibility and ventilation, with snap-on covers for all windows to protect the plastic from premature aging when the boat is not in use
- windows in the bimini, where needed, to check the set of sails (the windows with zippered or Velcro covers to prevent the cockpit turning into a greenhouse when in harbor)
- the dodger and bimini covers to be attached to their frames in such a way that they can be removed without disassembling any of the framework
- covers for any zippers to make them more or less waterproof, and installed so that water does not drive under them and come through the zippers (basically, the covers should be attached on the forward edges of the zippers and open on their aft edges)
- leather chafe patches to be added wherever a dodger and bimini rub on something else, or wherever they are likely to be grabbed by people

Dodgers are often made lower than biminis so that the helmsperson has good visibility forward over the top of the dodger. This has the advantage of minimizing the surface area of the dodger and, therefore, the probability of damage if hit by a boarding wave (important on an ocean-cruising boat). However, this frequently results in an uncomfortable passage through the companionway and obstruction of winches or rope clutches (line stoppers) on the cabintop. If the space is available, my preference is to build the dodger high enough to provide forward visibility beneath it, and to then link it to the bimini so that together they form a continuous cover over the cockpit. In extreme conditions, it will have to be folded down. The addition of side curtains or screens makes it possible to keep out rain and bugs, and enables the cockpit to be used as another "cabin" when at anchor. A less-complicated approach is to use mosquito netting to make a bag large enough to throw over both the bimini and dodger and drape down to the deck; weight the edges with light stainless steel chain or something similar.

With all dodgers and biminis, it is important to remember the "station-wagon effect" that is created any time the boat is powering into the wind. Unless ventilation flaps in the forward face of the dodger are opened, there will be a slight vacuum behind the dodger, into which the engine exhaust gases may be drawn. At best, this is simply unpleasant; at worst, it can result in carbon monoxide poisoning (for more on this important but neglected subject, see the addendum to chapter 3).

Sunbrella is an excellent fabric to use for dodgers, biminis, and awnings. Some colors come with additional waterproofing (recognizable by its glossy appearance), which is worth having. Even so, in time the fabric will start to leak. It can be resealed with Thompson's Water Seal (used for sealing masonry and wood; available at hardware stores). Dark fabric colors should be avoided because they soak up the heat. Even if the boat has a dark blue or maroon mainsail cover, the urge to make the dodger and bimini the same color should be resisted—however nice they might look from the dock.

Finally, here is a point on fastening dodgers and biminis. Frequently, button-type snaps are used, which have a base that is screwed into the deck or cockpit coaming—this puts numerous holes in the deck core. At the very least, the screws should be well bedded; even so, it has been my experience that the screws are often an inferior grade of stainless steel and soon rust, at which time moisture penetrates the core. Although it is time-consuming, I inject epoxy (with a syringe) into each hole, letting it soak into and penetrate the core, before installing the screws.

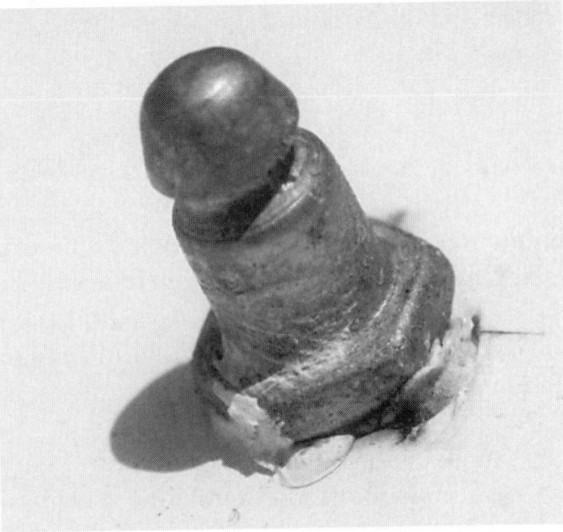

A common way of fastening dodgers and biminis. Note the corrosion around the base of the fastener. Almost always these are simply screwed into a cored deck, with no thought given to protecting the core.

Cockpit Flooding

At sea, if a boat gets *pooped* (a wave breaks over the stern) and the cockpit fills with water, it is of paramount importance that the cockpit drains rapidly. The ideal in this respect is the open stern on many aft-cockpit modern boats, although some kind of a restraint is needed to stop gear and babies from sliding out the back (I've watched some quite expensive stuff go overboard by this route). Even where there is not an open stern, it is often possible to design in a couple of large drains at the aft end of the cockpit that lead through pipes to the transom. In addition to the rapid drainage this provides, it has the advantage of putting the through-hulls just above the waterline. This is preferable to the conventional below-the-waterline arrangement, which means that when the boat is left unattended, there are at least a couple of poten-

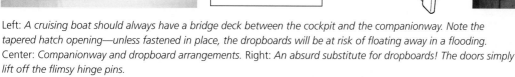

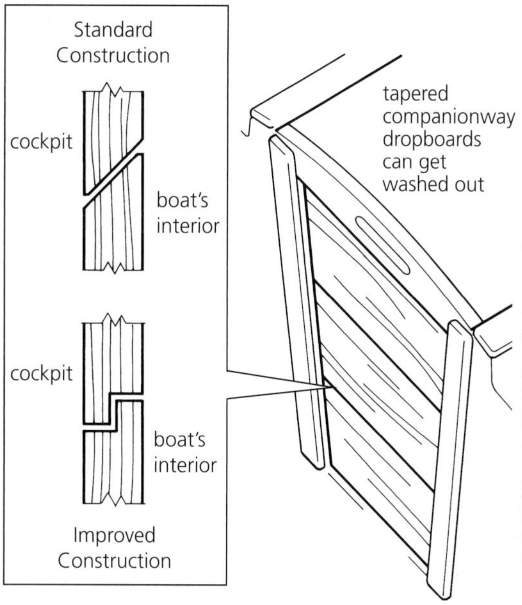

Left: *A cruising boat should always have a bridge deck between the cockpit and the companionway. Note the tapered hatch opening—unless fastened in place, the dropboards will be at risk of floating away in a flooding.* Center: *Companionway and dropboard arrangements.* Right: *An absurd substitute for dropboards! The doors simply lift off the flimsy hinge pins.*

tially boat-sinking seacocks that have to be left open.

The Offshore Racing Council (ORC), an international body that governs offshore racing, requires large-enough drains to empty the entire cockpit—if filled to the coamings—in three minutes. In reality, in the kind of conditions in which the cockpit will fill, the boat will be rolling heavily; much of the water will be shed on the first roll. However, the cockpit well is likely to remain filled; therefore, substantial drains are still needed. If the well takes even a minute to drain, it will seem like a very long time; the larger the drains, the better (again, with some type of screen).

The question should be asked: In the event of a cockpit flooding, where will the water go in the short time that the cockpit is filled to its coamings? Almost invariably, the answer is: Down the companionway hatch! This emphasizes the need to limit—as much as is practicable—the extent to which the companionway opening comes down below the level of the coamings. Ideally, the sill will be higher than the lowest point in the coamings. Too often, especially on smaller boats, the opening extends to the bottom of the foot well, which is not a seaworthy approach on a cruising boat. *The farther offshore a boat is intended to sail, the greater the importance of having a bridge deck between the cockpit well and the companionway hatch.*

Regardless of whether a companionway comes down into the well or down to a bridge deck, it must have at least a minimal sill—the higher the better. If it does not, even small amounts of water running around in the cockpit will flow into the accommodation spaces. However, on boats with bridge decks, the companionway is a popular watchkeeping station that any kind of a sill makes uncomfortable. This can be resolved by hinging the lower dropboard aft onto the deck, creating a seat rather than lift out, or else by having a separate board that sits on the sill to create a seat.

During the course of the 1979 Fastnet race, tapered companionway openings caused a number of boats to lose their companionway dropboards (washboards), and subsequently flood. The boards only had to lift an inch or two to come loose and get washed overboard. It is better to have a straight-sided opening, although this makes it more difficult to get the boards in and out because they have to be taken to the top of the slot (this can be aggravating if they get cockeyed and jam, which they commonly do). In the event that the slot is tapered, there should be some method of securing the boards.

Almost all companionway dropboards are made with a simple beveled edge for the mating surface between the boards. This joint admits a surprising amount of water when hit by a wave. Much better is a rabbeted edge between the boards, so that there is a lip on the inside of the joint.

The companionway should be on the centerline. If not, in the event of a knockdown or jibe on one tack, there is a risk of the companionway becoming submerged and admitting huge amounts of water. One of the factors used when calculating the STIX number (see chapter 1) is the *downflooding angle*; that is, the angle of heel at which hatches, if left open, start to flood the boat. This is a number that we may see published in the future. On a cruising boat, it should be greater than 90 degrees, and preferably above 100 degrees.

Collateral Damage

Some thought has to be given to what will be underwater if the cockpit floods. Commonly, the engine panel is located in the side of the cockpit well. Although these panels are mostly

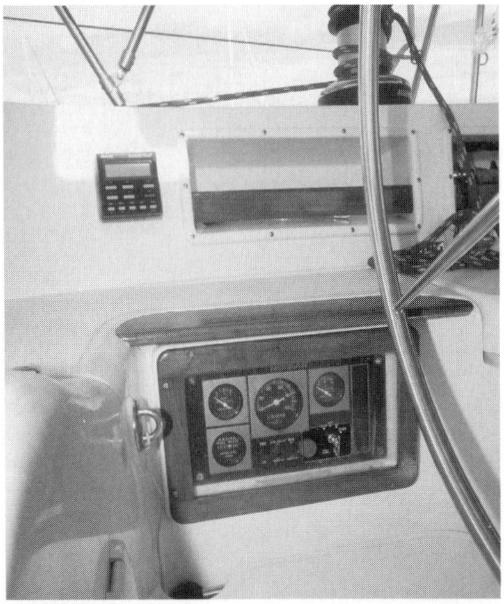

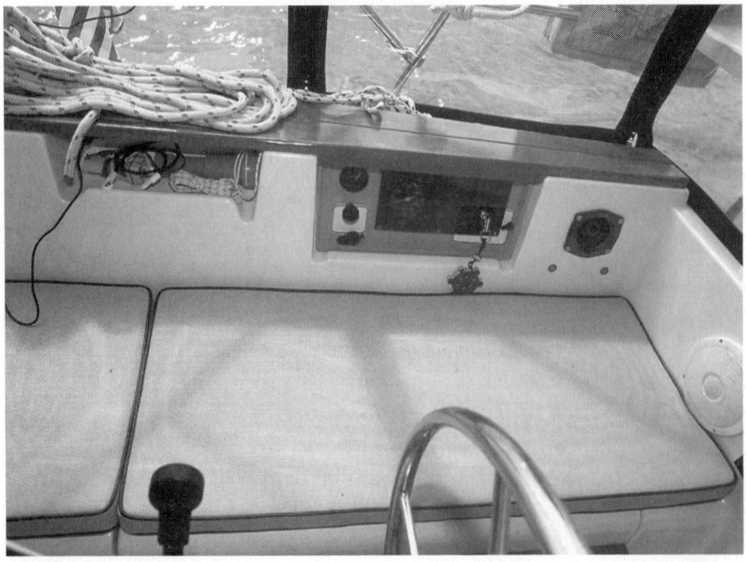

Right: Nada*'s engine panel, in the side of the cockpit well. I should have had it moved at least to the coaming, and preferably to inside the boat.* Below: *A better location for the engine panel.*

"spray-proof," they are not waterproof. When the going gets tough is not the time for the boat's engine electrical circuits to short out.

It is better to have the panel in the coaming rather than in the well, so that it is as high as possible and to provide additional protection by placing it in a recess with a watertight, clear-plastic cover—but this is rarely done. Such an installation also protects the key and switches from being snagged by people and lines, and the panel will not be uncomfortable when leaned against. On our last boat, we placed the panel below decks in the navigation station. The minor inconvenience of having to go below to crank and shut down the engine, in my opinion, was more than compensated for by the fact that after fifteen years, the panel was still as corrosion-free as the day it was installed. (There is no great need to have the gauges in the cockpit; given an engine overheat or low-oil-pressure situation, the alarms would have alerted us.)

Fuel- and water-tank vents are also commonly placed in the cockpit, frequently in the side of the well. This is a terrible place for them, particularly a fuel-tank vent. A small amount of salt water in the freshwater tanks does not amount to much, but in the fuel tank, it can disable the engine. These vents should be placed as high as possible in the coaming, and on the outboard face so that they do not have to be leaned against. Better yet, they should terminate at a suitable place inside the boat (more suggestions are in chapter 5).

Thought needs to be given to drainage at different angles of heel when lesser quantities of water are flying around. Cockpits frequently accumulate puddles in the most aggravating places (e.g., the outside edges of the leeward seat and the foot well), resulting in permanently wet backsides and feet. Some cockpit wells are actually partly below the waterline when well heeled, resulting in back-flooding (this can sometimes be avoided by crossing the hoses from the drains to the through-hulls). Worse are cockpit seats that accumulate water and feed it into a locker. Seats should be designed to drain at up to a 30-degree angle of heel.

Some boats have cockpit coamings that form a water-trapping angle at the point at which they merge with the cabinsides. When the boat is hard on the wind with spray or rain flying about, a pool accumulates on the windward (i.e., high) side between the cabinside and coaming, eventually spilling over into the cockpit. Some Tayanas, for example, end up with a small stream flowing across the bridge deck.

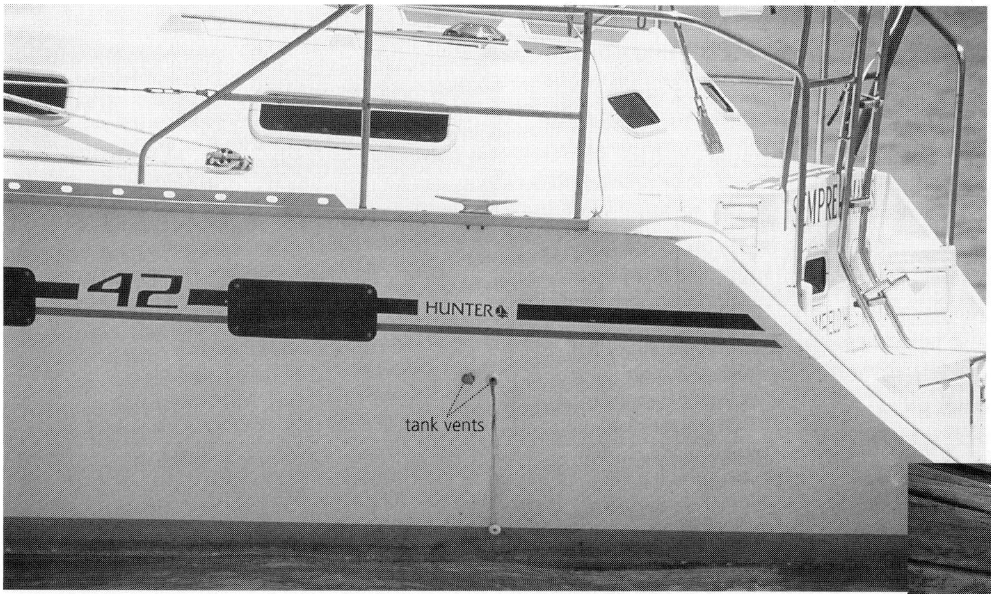

Tank vents in the side of a hull are an open invitation for saltwater contamination of the tank at some point.

The solution to this problem is to put a deck drain in the angle between the cabin and the coaming and to run a hose across to a similar deck drain on the other side of the boat. The water then drains from the windward side to the leeward side, bypassing the cockpit.

To deal with water that gets below, all cockpits need a manual bilge pump that can be operated from the helm station without having to open any lockers. The pump needs to be plumbed to the lowest point of the bilge. Large-capacity diaphragm pumps are, by far, the best in this application (for more on bilge pumps, see chapter 5).

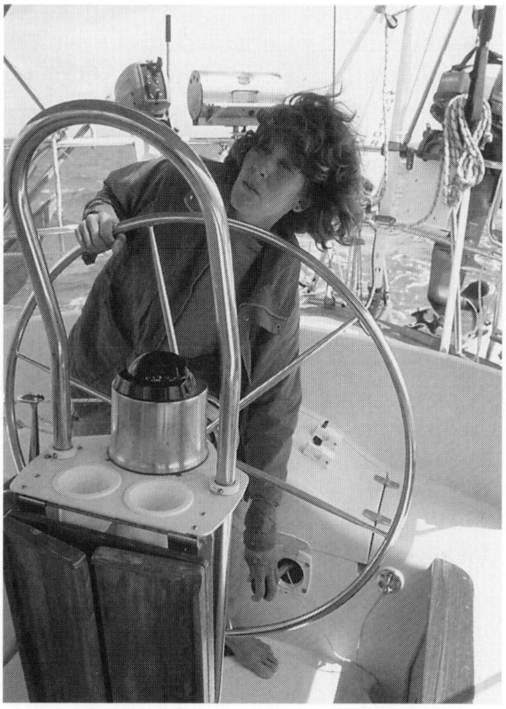

It is important to have a manual bilge pump that is operable from the steering position. In this example the ergonomics could be improved.

Deck Design and Layout

Turning now to the deck itself, two primary concerns that must be addressed are its watertight integrity (i.e., seaworthiness) and the need to make it as safe a working platform as possible.

Seaworthiness

The best way to think about watertight integrity is to imagine the boat caught in breaking seas with solid water sweeping the decks and filling the cockpit. This raises two questions: What might get swept away or stove in, and where might the water come in?

Anything lashed down on deck may get swept away, especially large objects such as a dinghy and a life raft. To minimize the likelihood of this, they will need extra strong *chocks* (mounting blocks) and pad eyes, or other attachment points, through-bolted to the deck with substantial backing blocks. Cowl ventilators are also vulnerable; it should be possible to remove them and fit threaded blanking plugs into the resulting holes.

Windows, hatches, and portholes are vulnerable to being stove in. Interestingly enough, this seems to occur at least as often on the leeward side as the windward side as a result of the boat falling off a wave and crashing down on the leeward side. In severe gales, there are numerous reports of relatively small portholes with solid ⅜-inch-thick glass getting stove in, which should give pause to anyone thinking of going offshore in a boat with large plastic windows!

Depending on how far offshore you intend to cruise, various blanking plugs should be carried for windows and portholes. We have rectangular portholes. We carry pieces of plywood with a bolt through the center that holds a clamping piece a little shorter than the longest dimension of the glass. If the glass gets broken, the blank can be offered up from outside the porthole. The clamping piece slips through the porthole and is then rotated 90 degrees so that it overlaps the frame. The bolt is tightened, holding everything in place. A piece of foam gasketing or rubber between the plywood and porthole makes a completely watertight seal.

Opening portholes always seem to leak after a few years. Given that they provide minimal ventilation when anchored out, I was tempted to have fixed ports on our new boat, but was talked out of it. To minimize aggravation, the external frames should be designed with drains so that when the boat is on an even keel, there is no puddle of standing water in the frame. In addition, a rail should be run around the inside of the cabinside to catch any drips that get through. The rail makes an excellent handhold at exactly the right height for most people to hang onto when the boat is heeled (see chapter 3).

A forehatch will catch the most air if it hinges on its aft edge, but if it is open at sea, a boarding wave will dump a huge amount of water below and may rip it off its hinges. This hatch is reversible, a nice touch.

Hatches

Hatches need to be ruggedly constructed with solid hardware to dog them down tight.

Simply because of their size, hatches are much more difficult than portholes to protect and to seal if broken. It is impractical to carry blanking pieces. Consequently, it is important to ensure that hatches are installed in less vulnerable locations—primarily horizontal surfaces on the cabintop—and to ensure that they are ruggedly built, with solid hardware that enables them to be dogged down tight. Hatch frames should be through-bolted.

To minimize chances of damage, a forecabin hatch should be installed in the cabintop rather than the foredeck. This foremost hatch should hinge on its forward face so that if a wave comes aboard when it is open, it will be knocked closed rather than ripped off. All hatches should be installed as close to the centerline as possible (in the event of a knockdown, an open, off-center hatch can let in a huge amount of water in a very short period—see the note about downflooding angles on page 92).

I like to see aluminum-framed hatches installed on a molded-in, raised base because the base helps deflect water away from the seals. Wooden hatches should have an inner coaming that is higher than the outer coaming on which the hatch sits. That way, any water that makes it under the edge of the hatch will be stopped by the inner coaming. Companionway hatches need a cover into which the hatch slides, with runners designed to exclude water driving up and under the hatch.

Safety on Deck

Perhaps the most important factor for establishing a safe working platform in rough conditions is a boat with an easy motion, which was discussed in chapter 1. In addition, unobstructed access is needed to all work areas (primarily the foredeck for headsail changes and the base of the mast), with excellent nonskid, plenty of rugged handholds, solid stanchions, high lifelines, and a means to fasten oneself to the boat.

I am a fan of wide side decks (up to 24 in./600 mm) sandwiched between solid bulwarks and a raised cabin trunk with through-bolted handrails on its top. The combination of bulwarks and cabin trunk provide a great sense of security when going forward on either the leeward or the windward side. These decks should be unobstructed (inboard shrouds are frequently in the way) and without toe-stubbers (genoa tracks and cars, and poles stored on deck, are the most common offenders); however, this is frequently compromised on modern boats.

If a cabin trunk is not raised sufficiently to put handrails at a reasonable height, it is better to angle in the cabinside quite sharply so that when the boat is heeled it makes a relatively level platform on the windward side. In this case, it will need a nonskid surface.

In addition to providing excellent footing, a bulwark is the ideal place to mount lifeline stanchions. It raises the lifelines an extra inch or two while eliminating all the through-deck fasteners with their associated leaks. A bulwark-mounted stanchion generally withstands a greater force than a deck-mounted one before ripping loose. Given 30-inch (820 mm) stanchions, lifelines can be as high as 34 inches (860 mm), which puts them close to hip height. Never use 20- or 24-inch (500–600 mm) lifelines on an offshore boat—they are little better than trip wires.

The optimum way to mount stanchions. The mounting is extremely strong while also minimizing the chances of deck leaks. It also gets the lifelines an extra inch or two off the deck.

Lifelines should be at least 30 inches high (preferably 34 to 36 inches) as opposed to . . .

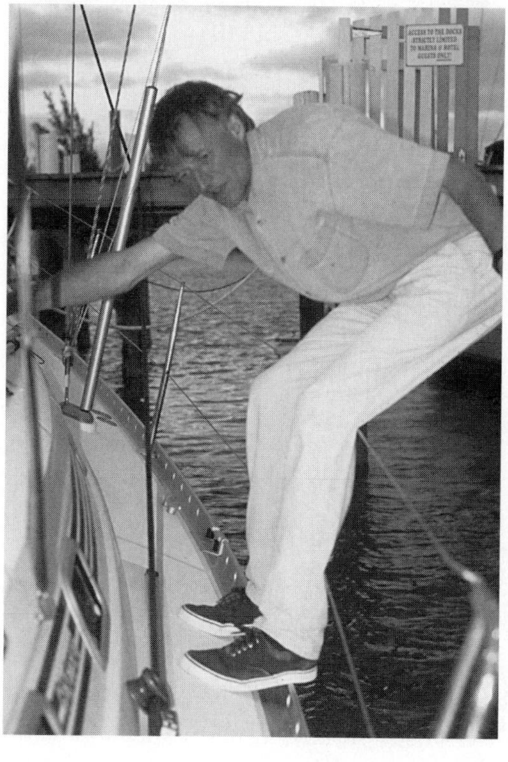

. . . the approximately 24-inch-high lifelines found on many boats.

Safety at sea requires a clear run up the side decks, with good handholds. In this case, the shrouds are somewhat in the way, but the handrails on the high cabintop combined with the bulwarks and relatively high lifelines provide a good sense of security.

The typical stanchion base has four fasteners through the deck. It must have (but often doesn't) a backing plate; without it, a sudden shock load to the stanchion will likely rip it out of the deck. Over time, lesser loads will cause the fasteners to leak. With a backing block, the stanchion base may withstand the shock load, but the stanchion will almost certainly bend at the point where it enters the base.

In the absence of bulwarks, a substantial toerail is a must, not only to provide secure footing and to stop things from going overboard, but also so that the stanchion bases can be fastened through both the deck and the toerail. If the stanchion base is given a relatively deep socket, it helps to absorb some of the loads on the stanchion. In any case, when looking at stanchion mounts, remember that they need to be designed not only to stop people from falling overboard, but also to take the stresses of people using them to push the boat off the dock (no matter how often you try to stop this, it will still be done at some point).

Stanchions with braces are used on either side of a gate. Typically, the braces come up to somewhere around the lower lifeline attachment point. A heavy load on the upper lifeline causes the stanchion to bend just above the brace. These braces should be brought all the way to the tops of their stanchions. The gates themselves need to be close to the widest part of the boat (to minimize the distance from the dock when moored alongside), but also opposite the entry to the cockpit (to make loading of people and supplies easier).

Here's a pretty-looking stanchion base with little strength and a high propensity to create leaks around the fasteners . . .

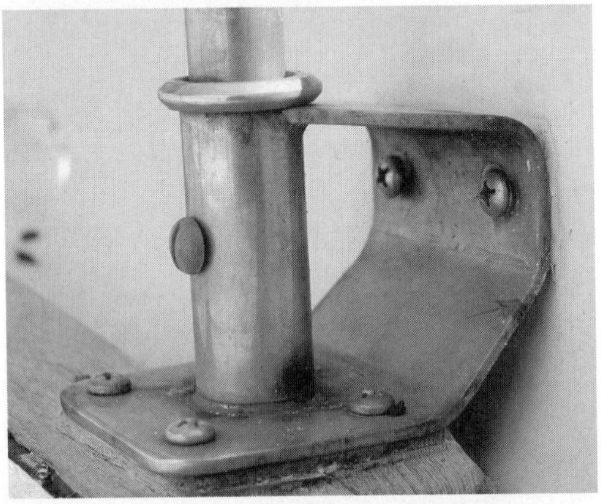

. . . whereas this base is fastened with self-tapping screws, which are certain to suffer from galvanic corrosion and result in deck leaks.

Below: *A solidly bolted base—a stanchion failure is preferable to ripping the base out of the deck.*

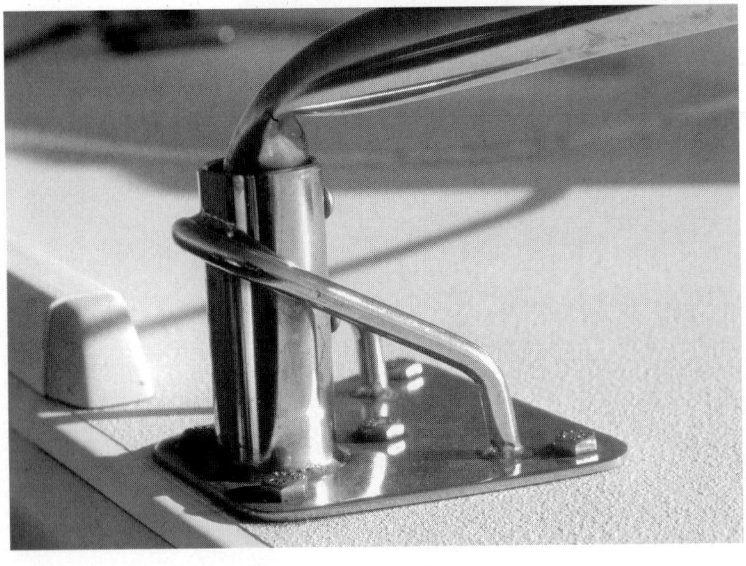

No matter how you try to stop it, sooner or later stanchions will be used for fending off. They need to be able to take this kind of inboard load.

A pitiful gate! The reinforcing strut is completely inadequate to the task, and intersects the stanchion way too low.

A better gate, in which the support frame comes to the top of the gate . . .

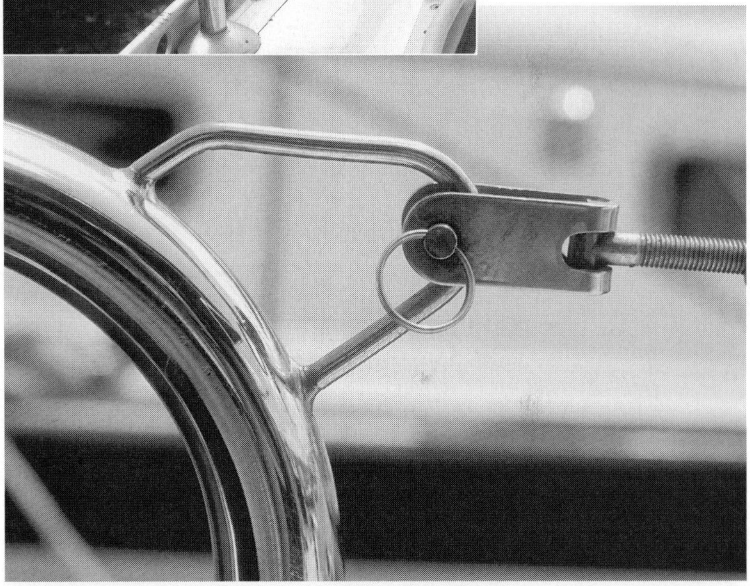

. . . but with a relatively flimsy attachment for the lifelines. The welds will be easily broken.

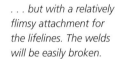

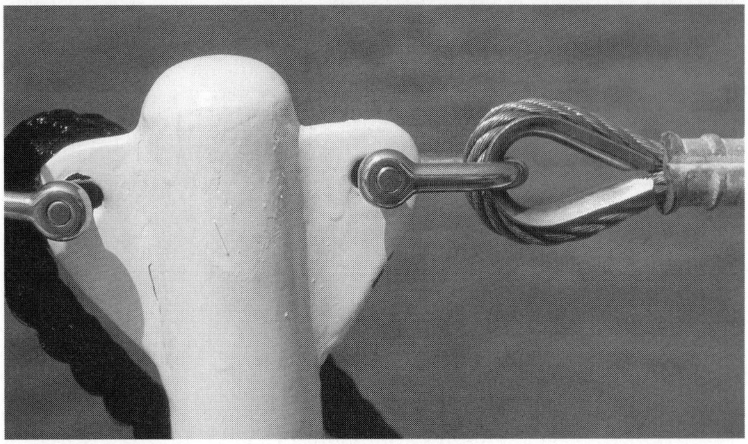

Solid plates welded to the stanchions for lifeline attachment—in this case, on a steel boat—but it can just as easily be done with stainless steel stanchions.

The usual method of attaching lifelines to pulpits (at the bow) and pushpits (at the stern) is to weld a piece of bent stainless steel rod to the pulpit or pushpit. The pin of a forked rigging terminal on the end of the lifeline connects to the rod. Over time, the rod welds are prone to failure. A better approach is to weld solid-metal plates to the pulpit and pushpit, drilling them to take the rigging terminal pin.

Lifeline gates are almost always closed with pelican hooks, some of which are prone to opening accidentally and, therefore, are dangerous. The type that has a spring-loaded pin (like a snap shackle) is better. Most lifeline gates are about 2 feet wide, which is not wide enough to haul a possibly unconscious crew member, who has gone over the side, back onboard. To facilitate rescues, at least one set of lifelines should be attached to their gate stanchion, either with pelican hooks (with the same previous proviso), or else attached with multiple turns of light line that can be cut free in seconds.

Lifelines are often made of plastic-coated 304 stainless steel, which soon starts to rust; only

Pin-type pelican hook—this is unlikely to open accidentally.

Corroding lifeline. Would you put your trust in this wire?

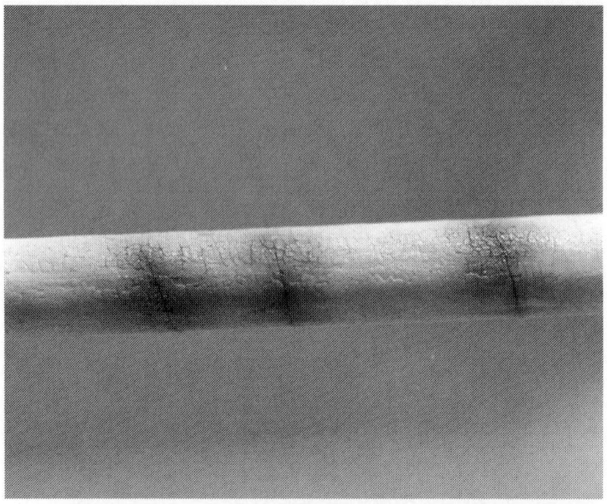

One way to get a plastic-coated lifeline that can be checked for corrosion is to have the lifelines made with uncoated wire and then slip a PVC chafe guard over the top.

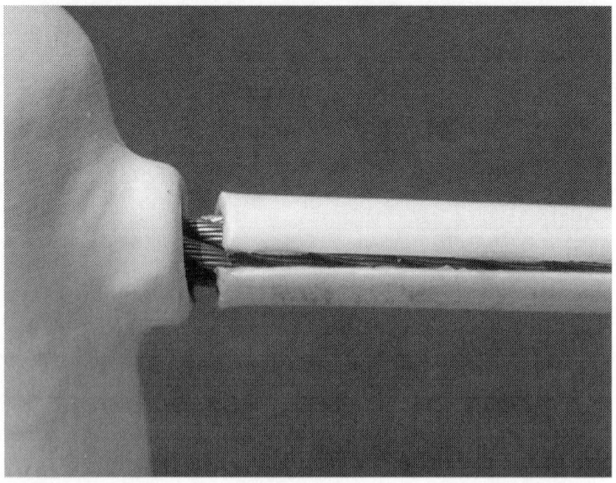

316 stainless steel should be used. Better yet is to leave the plastic off altogether because it traps moisture and promotes corrosion. However, this makes the lifelines hard on the hands (and leaves rust stains on clothing hung up to dry). We compromise by having plastic-coated upper lifelines (for comfort), but omitting the plastic on the lower lifelines where it serves no useful purpose. (As of 1999, the ORC banned plastic-coated lifelines.)

As far as I am concerned, you can keep your teak decks!

Nonskid and Jacklines

When it comes to nonskid, teak is often touted as the ideal material. This may have been so in the old days when a crew was available to keep it clean, but as far as I am concerned, it is not worth the trouble. (For the same reason, I like to eliminate as much exterior teak trim as possible; it requires too much maintenance to keep it looking good.) In any case, in the tropics, teak's relatively dark surface absorbs heat and becomes too hot to walk on with bare feet. This raises another point: dark colors may look great in northern Europe, New England, or on Puget Sound, but white is the only suitable color for hulls and decks in the tropics; if a two-tone deck is wanted, it can be white-white and off-white.

Many molded-in, nonskid patterns on fiberglass hulls get quite slick when wet, and positively treacherous if a little diesel is spilled. Much better traction is provided by finishes in which sand, ground-up shells, or polymer are embedded in the paint; however, these can be quite abrasive and difficult to keep clean. Somewhere in between there is a balance. One thing we have learned the hard way is that if a sand or ground-up-shell finish is used, the paint should be given a gloss finish. Some boatyards like to add a flattening agent to the paint, which improves the nonskid effect but makes it much more difficult to clean.

When going forward in rough weather, the crew should always wear a safety harness and use it. I know this firsthand, having been thrown overboard one night without a harness: I am extremely lucky to be alive to tell the tale. The boat needs to be set up so that it is possible to clip on *before* exiting the companionway (a suitably located pad eye in the cockpit serves this purpose). Once in the cockpit, it should be possible to clip onto *jacklines* (safety lines) from inside the cockpit. The jacklines need to provide an unobstructed run along the side deck or cabintop to all working areas of the boat to avoid unclipping and reclipping to carry out any normal tasks.

Ideally, jacklines will be far enough inboard to prevent a tethered person from being thrown over the side, but the location must still be compatible with the ability to move the length of the boat without having to unclip and reclip. If the shrouds are outboard, this can be achieved by mounting the jacklines on the cabintop and moving forward inside the shrouds. However, if the shrouds are inboard, the jacklines generally have to go outboard of them, which puts them well out on the side decks. If the jacklines are in a location where they will not get stepped on (e.g., the cabintop), stainless steel wire works best. However, if they will end up underfoot—as most do—flat nylon webbing is the most comfortable (the ORC requires stainless steel).

Jacklines need to be accessible from the cockpit, and should allow movement from one end of the boat to the other without having to unclip and reclip.

All pad eyes and other attachment points for jacklines and safety harnesses must be rated for loads of *several thousand pounds* (a 200-pound/90 kg person thrown across a boat or overboard creates a tremendous shock load) and given suitable backing plates. (During the Fastnet race, lives were lost when pad eyes ripped out of decks.)

Finally, here's some miscellaneous safety-related thoughts:

- Before leaving the cockpit, always check the position of the boom, and make sure there is no risk of getting caught in a tack or jibe. If the boat is running before the wind, make sure a preventer is set. Always stay low enough so that if the boom does unexpectedly come your way, it won't hit you.
- Always go forward on the high (windward) side—there's less chance of going overboard, and it keeps you away from the taut (loaded) headsail sheet. When running, watch out for sheets that may go slack and snap taut as the headsail luffs and fills.
- Be especially careful around powered winches and windlasses—they've been responsible for a number of mangled limbs.
- Never put any part of your body between the boat and another hard object (the dock or another boat).
- Guys should not pee overboard! If you must, make sure one arm is firmly wrapped around a shroud or other reliable support.

Stowage

On cruising boats, one of the most difficult problems to resolve is how to stow—in a shipshape manner—all the gear that ends up on the boat. Much of it has to be carried on any boat, regardless of boat size; therefore, the smaller the boat, the greater the problem.

Nada's cockpit locker, which (right) is considerably bigger than it looks. Just about all of the "stuff" in this pile is found on any modern cruising boat, regardless of size.

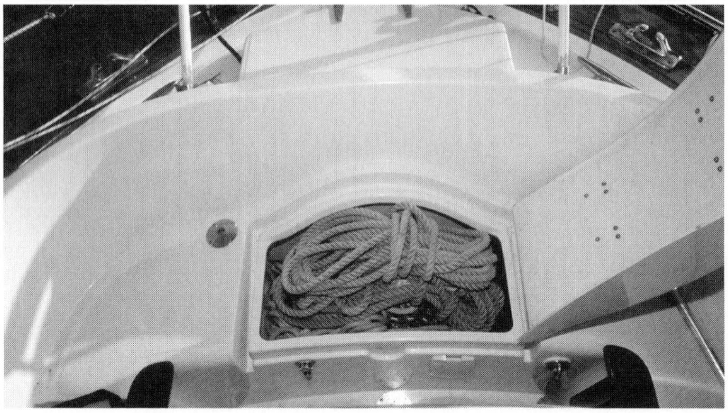

In addition, we have a locker under the helmsperson's seat, for stowage of lines, and . . .

. . . the lazarette locker (below), which normally contains just the propane bottles, but which we had enlarged for stowage of oil, the outboard-motor gas tank, and spare jerricans of gasoline. It has sufficient residual space for a trash bag or two of garbage.

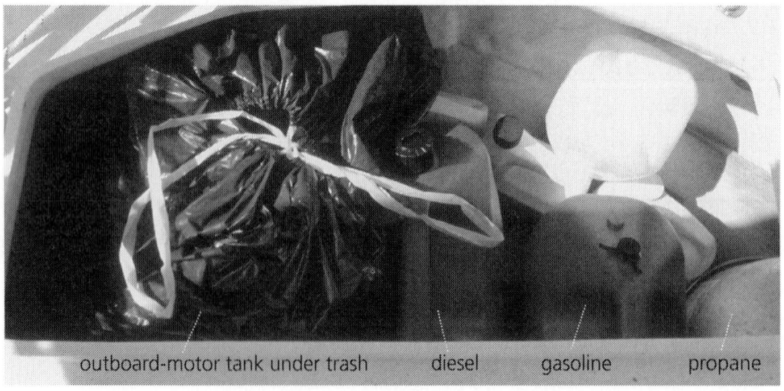

Problems are exacerbated on many center-cockpit boats because a fair amount of the traditional cockpit stowage space is absorbed by the below-decks passageway and accommodations. This is also increasingly the case on contemporary aft-cockpit boats in which the designer has managed to shoehorn a double cabin in and around the underside of the cockpit. This type of cabin looks good at boat shows; however, from a cruising perspective, it is counterproductive to maximize the number of berths at the expense of stowage and functionality.

Cockpit and Deck Locker Design

An older aft-cockpit boat generally has one or two relatively massive lockers under the side seats, a locker under the helmsperson's seat (on wheel-steered boats), and a *lazarette* locker (a locker at the back of the boat). Together, these lockers provide more than enough stowage for most cruisers.

On newer boats, these lockers tend to get removed or filled up before the owner ever stows the first piece of gear. If the boat has a cockpit well that is open to the stern, the lazarette will be eliminated, as it will be with some sugar-scoop sterns and *retrousse* sterns (angled forward from the waterline). (The retrousse stern was developed as a rule-dodger in the racing world because it maximizes sailing length while minimizing deck weight. However, it does so at the expense of valuable stowage space and, therefore, does not make sense on a cruising boat.) In the words of one designer of sugar-scoop sterns, "quite honestly, the usual negative transom only has one advantage for a cruising yacht—the boarding platform." Its continuing popularity is driven more by fashion than reason.

Even on those boats with several lockers, there is a tendency to put more and more fixed equipment in them, limiting the remaining stowage space. Typical items include autopilots, refrigeration condensing units, and inverters—all of which have electrical and electronic components vulnerable to moisture (especially salt-laden moisture). However, they are rarely adequately protected from contact with wet gear or spray when the locker lids are open; they would be better located elsewhere. By the time the boatbuilder has finished adding all the options the boatowner wants, there may not be a lot of remaining room.

Whatever lockers there are should have (although few do) gasketed, watertight lids. The lids need hinges and clamps designed to take the worst the sea can throw at them, installed in such a way that they will not snag lines and bodies. Locker lids are often quite heavy, so it is important to have some means of holding them open (e.g., a gas-filled strut) so that they don't crash down when someone is digging around inside for a buried piece of equipment. I know of one boatyard technician who got trapped in a locker for several hours when the lid blew shut. For a single-hander at sea, this would be a most unpleasant way to die!

Just in case a lid gets ripped off and the locker floods, lockers should be more or less watertight to the interior of the boat. Almost none are; what frequently is found is an enormous pit that is wide open to the boat's interior.

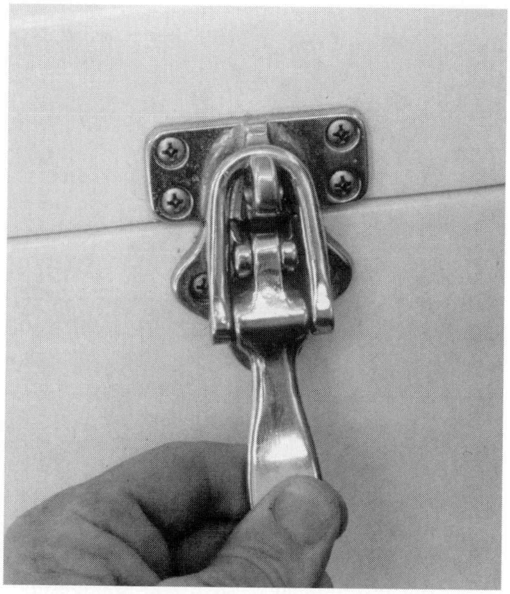

Cockpit lockers need hardware that can stand up to boarding waves.

It is probably also open to the steering gear so that in rough weather, stowed items can shift and foul the mechanism.

If a locker is sealed, it will need a drain, which—if at all possible—should lead back out into the cockpit or overboard rather than into the bilge. This is not possible with deep lockers.

The typical oversized pit is best broken up into smaller spaces by the addition of shelves and dividers. However, it is important to maintain access to seacocks and through-hulls so that in an emergency they can be rapidly closed or plugged. Mesh-type bags with saltwater-resistant zippers (the kind used to stow snorkeling and diving gear) are handy for maintaining control over locker contents.

At this point, rather than make specific suggestions about where to stow gear, it may be more useful to provide a comprehensive list of equipment likely to need stowing, together with some pertinent comments on stowage—and then leave it to the reader to figure out where to put everything relative to any given boat. It makes sense to start with the most difficult items, which are *liquefied petroleum gas* (LPG) cylinders—propane and/or butane—and gasoline tanks.

LPG and Gasoline

LPG requires a locker that is gas-tight to the boat's interior and that has a drain from the base of the locker overboard (for more detailed information on LPG installations, see chapter 5). For cruising, two well-secured 5-gallon (19 L) cylinders need to be carried. (In Europe, smaller cylinder sizes are commonly used; if buying a European boat for world cruising, make sure the propane locker is large enough to hold U.S.-style cylinders.) If a suitable locker cannot be provided, the propane cylinders have to be strapped down on deck. *They should never be stowed in any locker that drains or vents into accommodation spaces.*

Gasoline has almost the same storage requirements as propane; that is, a sealed locker vented from its base. As with LPG, *gasoline should never be stored in any locker that connects with the boat's interior spaces.* Despite the fact that almost all cruisers now use an inflatable for a dinghy (see chapter 10) and, therefore, invariably carry an outboard motor and gasoline, few boats come with any safe place to stow the gasoline other than tying the cans down on deck. This is a ridiculous oversight on the part of boatbuilders.

To deal with this problem, we expanded the propane locker on our Pacific Seacraft 40 to cre-

A neat solution to the stowage of gas cans, which otherwise tend to get tied down on deck.

ate space for the outboard-motor gas tank (a 5 gal./19 L tank) and spare cans of fuel (two 5 gal. cans). This runs contrary to boatbuilding standards developed by the American Boat and Yacht Council (ABYC), which call for a dedicated propane locker, but is preferable to having the cans on deck.

Whereas a few years ago, most of us had a small outboard motor (2–4 hp), today it is common to see 10- to 15-horsepower motors. These are best stowed on a pad clamped to the stern pushpit, although the pushpit may need reinforcing (a 10 hp motor weighs as much as 100 lb./45 kg). Depending on the state of a person's back (I have two slipped discs) and the size of the motor, some type of "crane" may be needed to get the motor on and off.

The Rest of the Stuff

The cruising sailor needs the ability to ferry diesel and water out to the boat. This requires more cans—ideally, two or more 5-gallon (19 L) cans for diesel and the same for water. Despite the fact that diesel is nowhere near as volatile or dangerous as gasoline, it is not advisable to carry it in a locker that is open to the accommodation spaces, although there may be no other choice (other than the usual expedient of tying it down on deck). The water cans, at least one of which should be readily accessible in case it is necessary to abandon ship in a hurry, can be stored in a cockpit locker.

A cruising boat needs several good-size fenders. Often, they end up tied to the lifelines, but this is far from ideal. When hit by a breaking wave, they are likely to cause damage. A cockpit locker is best adapted to take them.

We have already exceeded the storage capacity of many boats that maximize accommodations at the expense of practicality, and there's still some bulky gear to be stowed, including a storm anchor and its rode, maybe a parachute sea anchor or drogue and its associated gear, mooring lines, a shore-power cord and adapters, a water hose, spare rigging (a length of wire rope as long as the longest stay on the boat), lengths of hose (for replacement parts and also for chafe protection on lines), a large funnel (for filling water and fuel tanks from cans), sail covers when at sea, and bags of trash (the longer a voyage, the more trash that will accumulate; almost everyone forgets to allow suitable space for it). I like a relatively small locker (maybe under the helmsperson's

A couple of large fenders are very useful but difficult to stow—we have not found a satisfactory location for them.

This is a more elegant approach to fender stowage, but it restricts visibility and the fenders are vulnerable to boarding waves.

seat) dedicated to the mooring lines so they are nearby when needed. Otherwise, a vertical bulkhead with large hooks serves well.

The boat cushions need to be stored somewhere when leaving the boat. A cruising sailor needs a bucket, sponges, and a deck brush, and will probably be carrying snorkeling gear—maybe even diving gear. Hatchboards need to be put away safely when not installed in the companionway. Life jackets must be in a readily accessible location in case they are needed in a hurry (we have ours on a shelf in our custom-built wet locker, near the companionway; see chapter 3).

And then there's the smaller gear, much of which needs specialized stowage or protection. This includes binoculars, a hand-bearing compass, a flashlight, a spotlight, a foghorn—maybe a fishing pole and tackle—certainly, a couple of winch handles (with at least one extra stored securely below in case they go overboard), some small pieces of line for tying off sails and other odd jobs, probably a couple of snatch blocks and, of course, all the loose lines that have been led back to the cockpit.

Stern Pushpit

On a cruising boat, the stern pushpit gets a lot of use. I've already discussed the outboard motor; there also will be a stern anchor, with its rode. To have the anchor ready to let go at a moment's notice on our old boat, I built a rope spool into the pushpit, but I haven't seen anyone else do this.

An incredibly elaborate custom-made pushpit that includes mounts for a wind generator, solar panels, a radar, various antennas, an outboard motor and crane, a Lifesling, another rescue throw device, a stern anchor, fishing poles, and probably several other things I have missed!

Outboard-motor crane and stowage.

A somewhat less fancy approach: wind generator, outboard motor, barbecue grill, stern anchor, fishing pole, bicycle, a large deck box, and so on.

A sugar-scoop stern makes an excellent boarding platform in calm water, but needs to be supplemented by some other means to get onboard in rough seas. (Courtesy Avon Marine)

A home has to be found for a Lifesling (Crew-Link) or ring buoy and maybe a crew overboard (COB) pole (*Dan buoy*). There may also be a barbecue grill (disassembled and stowed before going to sea, which requires another substantial space). Many of us have a wind vane, solar panels, and a wind generator to squeeze into the same general area. And we still have to be able to board the boat from the water, so we have to find room for a ladder. (The popular sugar-scoop stern makes an excellent boarding platform at anchor—and in advertising literature—but can be lethal if a boat is bouncing up and down in a seaway; there needs to be an additional means of boarding.)

While we're at it, it is worth noting the accumulated weight of all this gear, as well as the various fluids stowed in or near the lazarette: it can easily reach several hundred pounds, placed about as far aft as you can get it. Most likely, the gear will be balanced by a couple of anchors and a good length of chain up forward (more on that later), so the boat will trim out OK; however, the weight is still bound to affect sailing qualities and performance—the lighter the boat, the more significant is the impact.

Sails

With roller-reefing headsails, most of the time the bulkiest sail on the boat—the genoa—is stored on the headstay. This is fine until it has to be taken down in heavy weather and replaced with a smaller sail. Frequently, after it is bagged, the forehatch is not large enough to get it down below and, in any case, no provision has been made to stow it. It has to be hauled back to the cockpit and either stuffed in a cockpit locker (it is unlikely that one is large enough) or dragged through the boat and dumped (maybe wet and dripping) on the forepeak berth.

The tendency today is to see the forehatch simply as a ventilator and escape hatch, and to limit its size to whatever is necessary to get a body through. Our Pacific Seacraft 40 is like this. I tried to get a larger hatch installed, but it would have required expensive tooling changes to the deck mold, so I had to let it go.

Even if the hatch is big enough, nowadays there is rarely a sail bin large enough to take a loosely bagged genoa, let alone an additional 100 percent jib, a storm trysail, and an asymmetric spinnaker and/or lightweight genoa, which comprise the minimum complement of sails for an offshore cruising boat.

Most modern forehatches (ours included) are designed to comply with legal requirements for escape hatches, which is not big enough to serve as a useful sail-bag hatch.

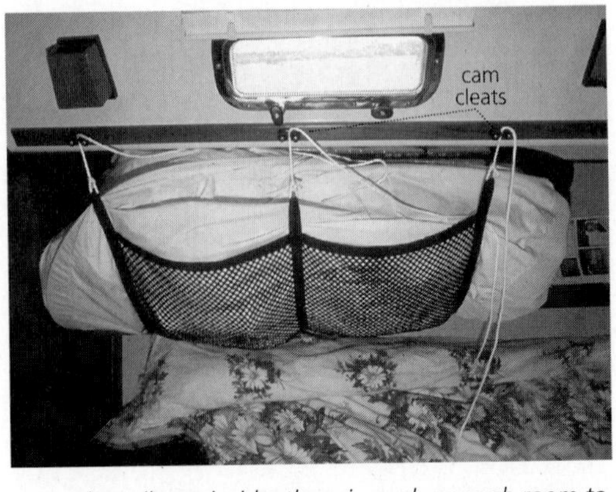

Once the sails are inside, there is rarely enough room to stow them. Here is one solution for an asymmetric spinnaker, with an elegant way to hold it in place.

Dinghies and Life Rafts

This brings us to the dinghy. I have long since come to the conclusion that—faced with the near impossibility of providing onboard dinghy stowage that still allows a boat to be worked in all conditions and that does not interfere with the watchkeeper's line-of-sight—most naval architects simply go into denial and pretend that the boatowner will not have a dinghy.

At about 40 feet (12 m) in boat length, it is generally possible to find room behind or in front of the mast for a rigid dinghy or an inflated inflatable, up to 10 or 11 feet (3–3.4 m) in length, albeit with a significant loss of visibility. Under this boat length, smaller and less useful dinghies have to be carried or else an inflatable has to be partially or fully deflated. In any event, the stowed dinghy should not obstruct any escape hatches (they commonly do), and will have to be lashed down so as not to foul lines. If a life raft is carried, it too has to be worked in somewhere.

Dinghy stowage is almost always a headache. As shown above and right, the best location is generaly on the foredeck.

The mother of all inflatables. Davits are great in harbor, but I would not go to sea with a dinghy hanging off my stern (nor will I tow one). There is no way this dinghy will fit onboard. It will have to be deflated and stowed (which takes a lot of space).

A folding dinghy that can be lashed to the shrouds. The disadvantage is that it will only take a small outboard and, as a result, will not move as fast as an inflatable on a plane.

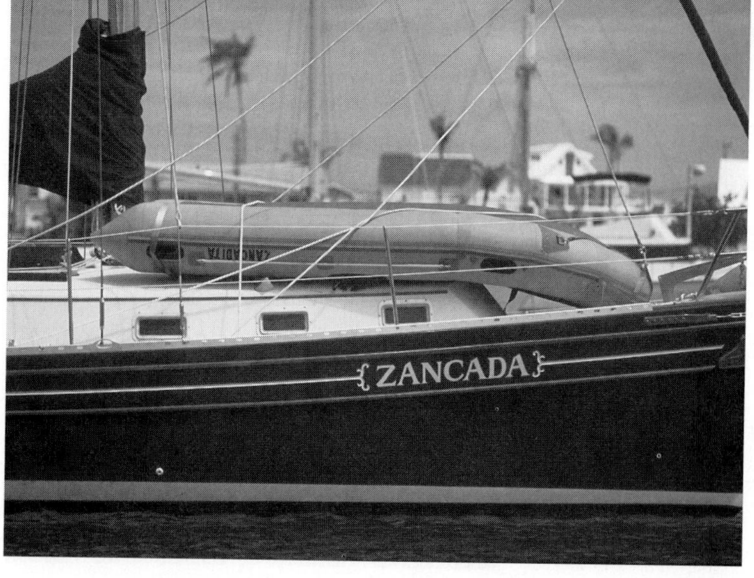

DEALING WITH GROUND TACKLE

If there's one thing that defines the ofshore cruising boat, it is its ground tackle and the means used to handle it. Every once in a while, we are reminded why, such as when sixty boats were caught at Cabo San Lucas in a sudden onshore gale. Eighteen of them were driven up on the beach as a result of parted rodes and hardware tearing loose.

Bow Platform

A properly designed and constructed bow platform is a major component in a serious cruising-boat anchor-handling system. To be effective, it needs to incorporate the following features:

- double bow rollers, so that two anchors can be handled and stowed
- sufficient separation between the two rollers to keep a plough-type or similar anchor (e.g., C.Q.R., Bruce, or Spade; see chapter 9 for more about anchor types) and a fluke-type anchor (e.g., Danforth, West Marine, or Fortress) from fouling one another, regardless of which is launched or retrieved first (almost no bow platforms allow this, which I find exceedingly frustrating)
- sufficient clearance from the bow of the boat to allow the anchors to hang vertically, rotate on their rodes, and swing

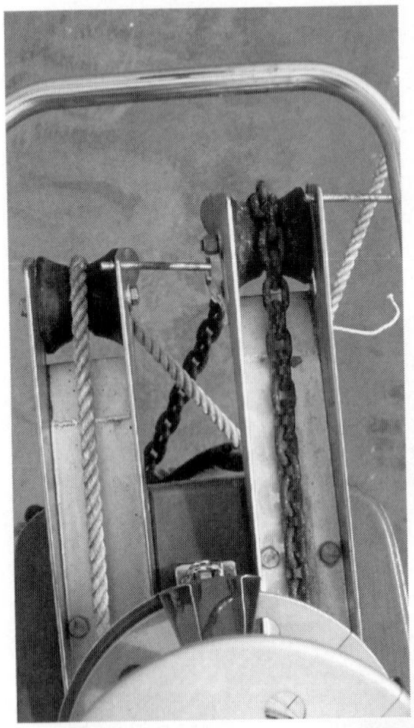

Solid double bow rollers that, nevertheless, still do not allow a Danforth-style anchor to be stowed with a plow-type anchor.

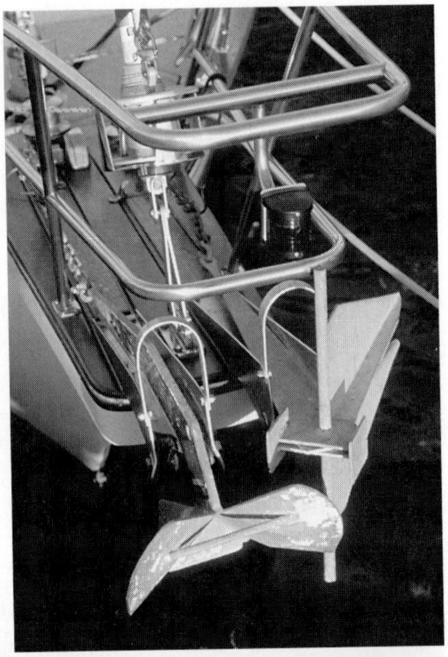

Left: *Sometimes a Danforth-type anchor can be stowed on its side as shown here, but most often the shank is too wide to fit between the cheek plates.*

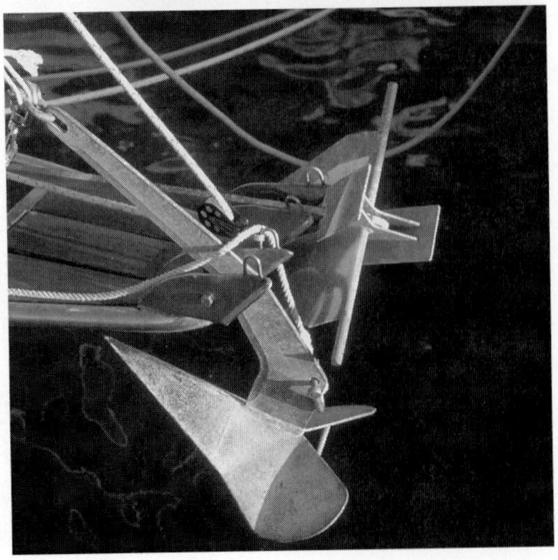

This is more like it, although the two anchors still tend to foul each other when being launched and retrieved.

The only boat on which I have seen it possible to stow a Danforth alongside a plow—and to launch and retrieve either without moving the other—is our old boat, which we built ourselves.

The boat needs either sufficient overhangs or a bow platform that will allow an anchor to swing freely without hitting the topsides.

I guess we will have to build our own bow platform for the new boat because we are currently forced to stow the Danforth-type anchor (in this case, a Fortress) on the pulpit!

about without damaging the topsides (not easy with a plumb stem; it requires the addition of a short bowsprit)

- bow rollers with a minimum diameter of 3 to 4 inches (75–100 mm), with a concave surface to keep the rode in the middle, and constructed of a material that withstands abrasion and severe snubbing loads (bronze is best, although hard to find these days)
- the cheek plates installed close enough to the bow rollers (¼ in./6 mm or less) to prevent a ½-inch (12 mm) nylon rode under tension from jamming between a roller and a cheek plate
- angled cheek plates or welded pipe chafe guards on either side of the bow rollers that provide a fairlead, without chafe, onto the bow rollers at any likely *shearing angle* (the angle the boat forms to its rode as it moves about at anchor; on some lightweight, high-freeboard boats, this can be quite extreme)
- an attachment point for a snatch block that provides a fairlead onto the bow roller from any angle (including astern) to facilitate kedging off after running aground (this attachment point is often overlooked; it is a tough one to achieve, but will be much appreciated if ever needed)
- a *strong* pin through the cheek blocks or some other mechanism to stop the rode from jumping off the roller when the boat is pitching up and down in a short, steep chop (in extreme conditions, this pin will

At times, this anchor will hit the topsides.

With a plumb stem, a boat needs a bow platform for handling ground tackle. (Courtesy Saga Yachts)

A nice bronze roller, but with way too much clearance between it and the cheek plate which, in this case, is a pipe. In general, pipes are much better than plates because they minimize chafe.

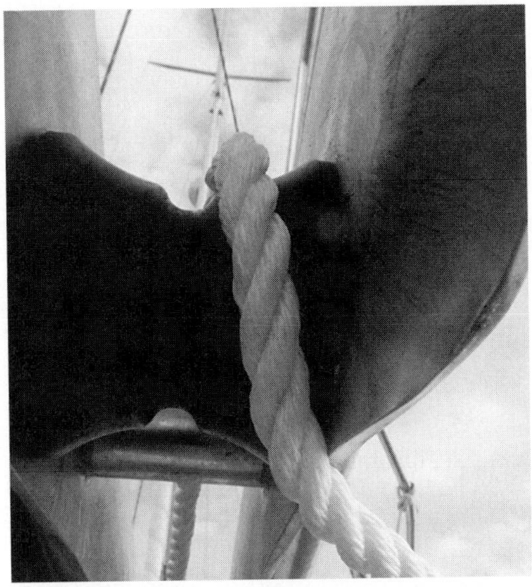

The bow roller on Nada. Despite the flared cheek plate, at times the rode chafes on the edge of the plate—a pipe welded along this edge is an excellent solution.

be subjected to heavy loads; it must be built to take them)

- a mechanism for securing the anchor when at sea (maybe the same pin as described previously; otherwise, permanently attach a short length of line to the anchor shackle and use it to cleat off the anchor)
- an attachment point for the tack line of an asymmetric spinnaker (see chapter 7), so designed that it keeps the sail's tack clear of the bow pulpit and any navigation lights, and allows a fairlead aft for the tack-line

In the past, many bow platforms incorporated a chain stopper or *chain pawl* (a ratchet device that allows the chain to be pulled up but not let out until released). These are useful, although by no means essential, particularly if a powered windlass is fitted.

A beautiful bronze chain stopper from another era.

Below: *Chafe can be minimized with a snatch block, which is also necessary to achieve a fairlead for the rode in some kedging situations, but this requires an appropriately located attachment point for the snatch block.*

Deck Layout

The cruising boat needs several pairs of *hawseholes* (holes in the bulwarks through which mooring and anchoring lines are led) or sturdy chocks (a fitting on the caprail or bulwark that serves the same purpose). These should include a pair up forward (port and starboard), a pair amidships (used for spring lines and maneuvering on and off docks; see chapter 7), and a pair aft (for the stern anchor). In all cases, they must lead to substantial cleats through-bolted to the deck or bulwarks with large backing blocks. In addition to brute strength, the other critical installation feature is to minimize chafe to rodes (see chapter 9 for more on this subject), remembering that when the going gets rough, the rode will be sawing backward and forward through the hawsehole or chock.

The farther a cleat from its hawsehole or fairlead, the greater is the stretch and sag in the rode under changing loads, and the greater is the sawing action. In my opinion, if the boat has substantial enough bulwarks, using the kind of hawsehole that has cleat horns built into it represents the best setup. *This almost completely eliminates chafe* and, short of the bulwark being torn out of the boat or the horns breaking off, the cleat is not going to let go.

Bulwark-mounted cleats do not provide a fairlead from the bow rollers to the cleats, so they need to be backed up with either two more large cleats in line with the bow rollers, or some kind of *samson post* (a strong post mounted through the foredeck) or *bitts* (two strong posts, generally at the base of a bowsprit and designed to absorb its compression loads).

At all times, the locations of hawseholes, fairleads, cleats, and posts relative to a windlass (if fitted) and the forestays must be such that it is possible to handle the ground tackle without getting fouled up in the rigging. If no windlass is fitted, there should be a fairlead to a mast-mounted winch or aft to a cockpit winch for those occasions when the anchor cannot be broken out by hand.

As an anchor comes up, it sometimes brings a significant amount of mud with it. A washdown pump is a great asset. In addition, a low dam can be built across the foredeck aft of the windlass or rode stowage location, and angled so that it drains outboard to a scupper cut in the bulwark or toerail. The dam confines the mess to a small area that is easily flushed with a bucket of water, rather than having mud run all the way aft down the side decks.

The foredeck on Nada*: lots of space to handle ground tackle and plenty of large, well-placed cleats.*

Some kind of an anchor washdown pump is a nice addition to the foredeck.

Anchor Wells

Many modern boats come with an anchor well. This makes for a tidy installation, in which the anchor and rode are completely sealed from the boat's interior, with the anchor-locker bulkhead forming a watertight bulkhead. There's no problem with water flooding down a chain pipe, and any mud on the rode goes out the locker drain rather than through the anchor locker into the bilge. With the lid down, the foredeck is kept clear for any necessary sail-handling activities.

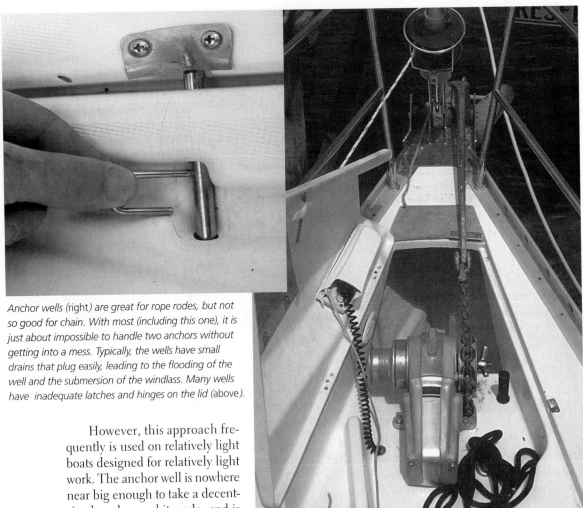

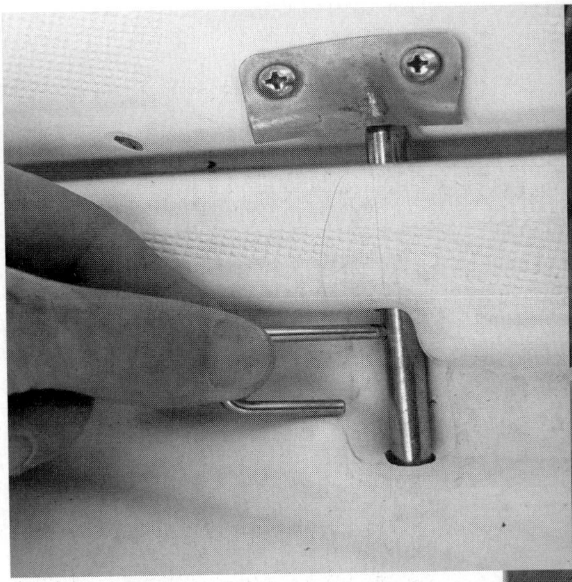

Anchor wells (right) *are great for rope rodes, but not so good for chain. With most (including this one), it is just about impossible to handle two anchors without getting into a mess. Typically, the wells have small drains that plug easily, leading to the flooding of the well and the submersion of the windlass. Many wells have inadequate latches and hinges on the lid* (above).

However, this approach frequently is used on relatively light boats designed for relatively light work. The anchor well is nowhere near big enough to take a decent-sized anchor and its rode, and is generally coupled to a thoroughly inadequate bow roller without a platform. As often as not, the well is set far enough forward to make it difficult to put in a trouble-free windlass installation, which limits the boatowner to hauling anchors by hand.

Even with larger wells and stronger rollers, an anchor well has drawbacks. It is very difficult to handle two anchors (a requisite on a cruising boat) without getting into a tangle—in fact, it is often difficult to handle one anchor and its rode without getting into a tangle!

If it is sturdily constructed (which it needs to be), the lid to the well will be quite heavy. When open, it will be vulnerable to getting fouled or even torn off if solid water is coming over the bow. Many lids have inadequate latches that can get knocked open by boarding waves. If the latch opens or breaks, the lid on a pounding boat may fly open when the boat falls off a wave, leaving it wide open as the boat dives into the next wave. If the well gets flooded, the water adds a considerable weight to the bow of the boat.

Of necessity, the drains to an anchor well are often close to the waterline, causing water to jet into the locker every time the boat dives into a wave. Some boats now have the anchor coming through an open slot in the bow of the boat. Whatever merits this design might have, the slot allows a tremendous amount of water into the anchor well every time the boat dives into a wave. Given the small and inadequate size of most anchor-locker drains, it takes little effort to plug the drains (a gob of mud does it), at which time the well will fill with water.

Despite these drawbacks, an anchor well really shines when it comes to handling rope rodes. A rope rode will not self-stow through a chain pipe so, if combined with a below-decks anchor locker, you end up with the ridiculous sight of someone feeding the rode down the pipe by hand a few inches at a time. With an anchor well, the rode is either tailed as it comes off a windlass or pulled in by hand and simply allowed to free-fall into the locker. The best way to stow a rope rode in these circumstances is to simply feed it in and let it pile up, without trying to coil it. This may look untidy—and make old salts shudder—but it works! If it is coiled, you can be just about certain that when it is let out, one of the loops will grab the rest and take the entire lot in a massive tangle.

Given a boat with no anchor well, we found on our last boat that the easiest way to deal with the pile of rode on deck is to build a stainless steel rope spool and fasten it to the forward face of the cabin trunk. The rode is stowed on the spool by sitting on the cabintop and spinning the spool by hand. Six hundred feet of line can be stored very neatly and compactly. When it comes time to let it out, there is *never* a foul-up.

We solved the problem of handling a rope rode on our old boat by adding a rope spool to the forward face of the cabin. The spool held 600 feet (273 m) of ⅝-inch (16 mm) rode that never got in a tangle.

Perhaps the best approach to rode stowage on an offshore boat is to combine a below-decks chain locker (see the next section) with a relatively shallow anchor well (this keeps the drains well above the waterline) for stowage of a nylon rode. The well will need large drains and a strong lid with adequate hinges and fasteners.

Chain Locker

Chain is heavy; therefore, it needs to be stowed as low and as far aft as possible. However, it does not slide down an inclined surface too well, so the chain pipe should not angle back more than 30 degrees. If this does not get the chain far enough aft, the only way to move it farther is to put the windlass well aft, which may not be desirable for other reasons.

Left to its own devices, chain forms a relatively narrow, cone-shaped mound. Without sufficient height in its locker, it builds up until it plugs the chain pipe or underside of the deck and jams the windlass. The primary anchor-locker design criterion, therefore, is something that is relatively tall, narrow, and straight-sided, without any corners or angles that can trap the chain. This is in contrast to the typical anchor locker formed by bulkheading off the bow of the boat, creating a V-shaped space that gets wider the higher you go and keeps the chain high and far forward (just where it is not wanted).

If the vertical space within a chain locker is limited, as it often is, the need to maximize the stowage space often leads designers to omit a chain pipe and to simply drop the chain through the deck. As the chain piles up, the distance between the top of the cone and the wind-

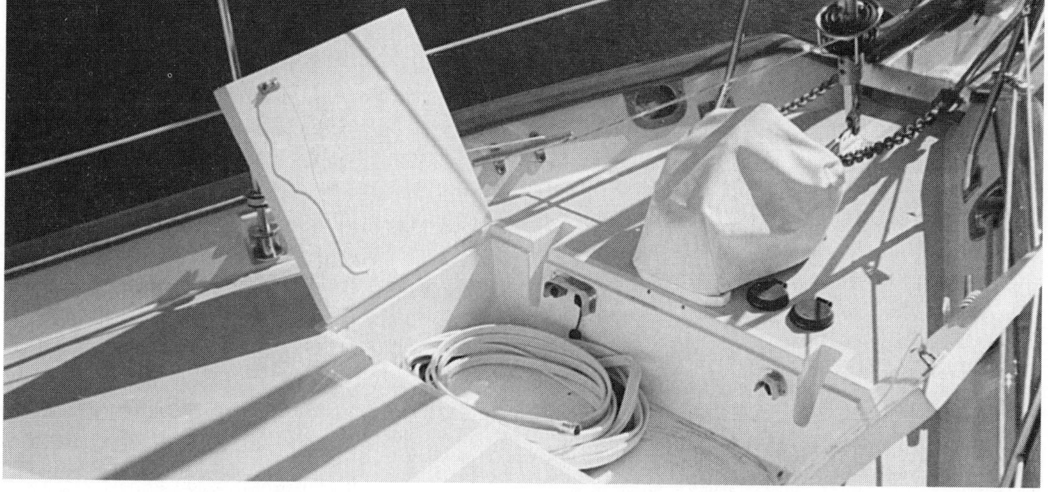

A nice setup, with the chain leading below to a chain locker and an anchor well behind the windlass for stowing a rope rode or other deck gear. (Courtesy Cabo Rico)

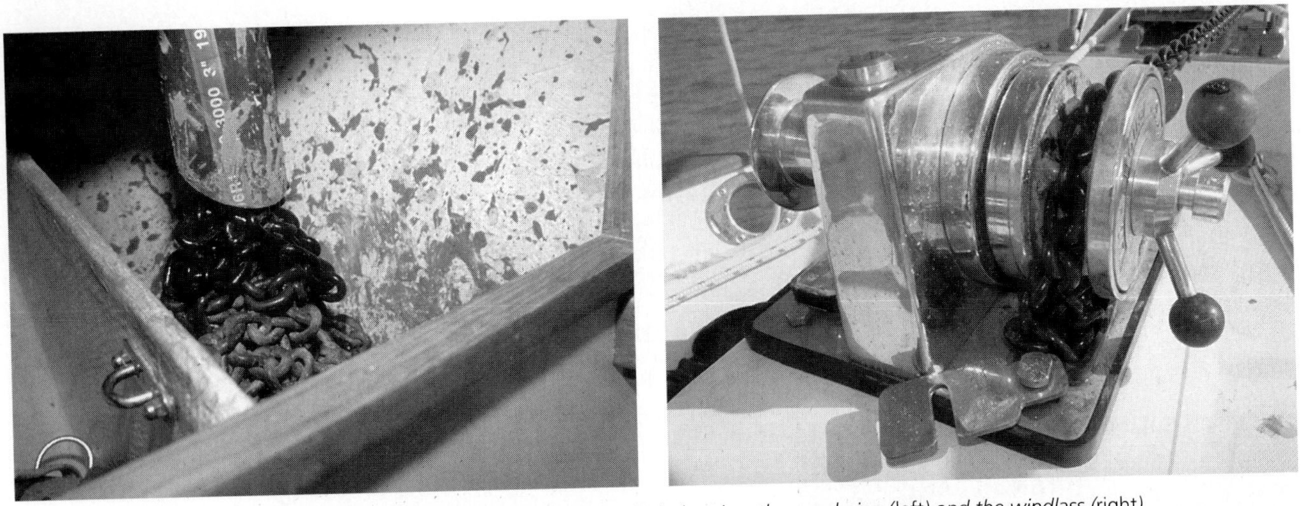

Chain rodes build up steep-sided cones, which then jam the navel pipe (left) *and the windlass* (right).

lass decreases until there is insufficient weight hanging down to keep the chain on the gypsy—a foul-up occurs. Access to this kind of locker is provided via locker doors or a hatch in the forward bulkhead. In heavy weather, some of the water coming through the deck openings may find its way into the forecabin.

A better approach to chain stowage is to establish a locker farther aft and lower in the boat, with a sealed chain pipe leading down to it. This way, any water goes straight to the chain locker and from there to the bilge. In addition, there is a decent vertical drop from the windlass, which helps strip the chain off the gypsy.

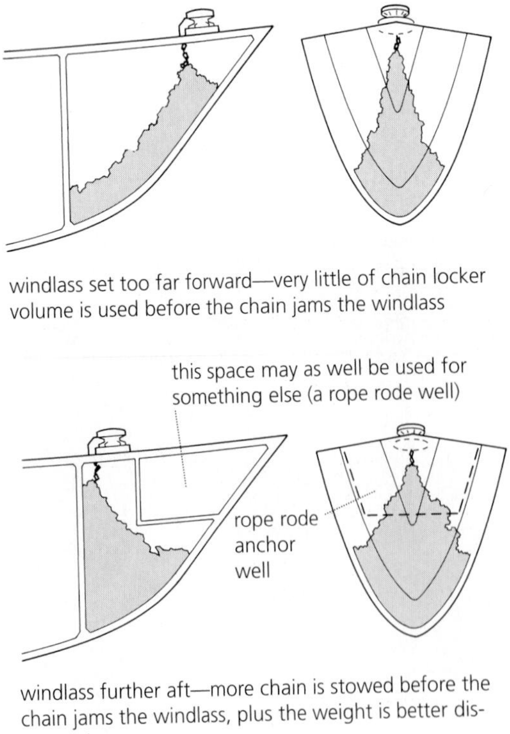

windlass set too far forward—very little of chain locker volume is used before the chain jams the windlass
this space may as well be used for something else (a rope rode well)
rope rode anchor well
windlass further aft—more chain is stowed before the chain jams the windlass, plus the weight is better distributed

To be effective, a chain locker needs to be narrow and deep.

On cruising boats in the 35- to 45-foot (10–14 m) range, the locker should be large enough to take at least 150 feet (46 m) of $\frac{3}{8}$-inch (10 mm) BBB chain; it will need a generous access hatch in its top at some suitable location.

To maximize chain stowage on our old boat, instead of the typical 3- or 4-inch-diameter (75–100 mm) chain pipe, we installed a 10-inch-diameter (250 mm) fiberglass tube, bonded to the underside of the deck and to the top of the chain locker. After the chain locker filled, we could continue to feed chain in until the tube was filled. For access, we had a hatch in the top of the chain locker such that we could reach the underside of the tube, if necessary, to knock down the pile of chain in the locker (thereby creating room for additional chain) or to clear a snag (we never had one).

All chain lockers need a decent-sized drain (*limber pipe* or *limber hole*) down to the bilge (a 3 or 4 in. PVC pipe cut in half and bonded into the bottom of the boat works well), with access from both ends so that blockages can be cleared—on most production boats, limber pipes and holes are much too small. The locker also needs a strong point, with a large U-bolt to which the bitter end (the end that is supposed to stay on the boat) of the rode can be fastened. Chain rodes should be attached with a length of rope long enough to allow the end of the chain to come up on deck. This way, the rode can be cut loose if the anchor has to be abandoned in a hurry.

Windlasses

Once a boat gets much above 30 feet (9 m), the weight of its ground tackle makes a windlass almost essential on a cruising boat. If it can be afforded, a powered windlass (generally, 12- or 24-volt DC) is a wonderful asset. In addition to

Hauling anchors by hand is hard work! A windlass is a great investment for those who use the anchor a fair amount.

A deck (navel) pipe can let in a surprising amount of water. It needs some kind of a stopper, such as this pivoting plate.

the labor savings, if there is any doubt at all about the set of an anchor, it is no trouble to take it back up and try again. On occasion, we have done this as many as seven times.

Windlasses come in horizontal and vertical configurations. With both types, effective trouble-free operation depends on establishing a fairlead from the bow roller to the windlass, and ensuring a freefall from the windlass to the anchor locker. The fall must be adequate to keep the line or chain running smoothly off the drum or gypsy (wildcat). With chain, the gypsy must be precisely matched to the rode; to ensure that it is, the chain is best bought from the windlass manufacturer. The windlass needs a properly positioned stripper to pull the line or chain off.

Although windlasses are not designed to handle snubbing loads, at times it is inevitable that they will. To avoid being torn out of the deck, a windlass needs a very substantial backing block. The deck also may need reinforcing.

Chain pipes can let in a surprising amount of water in heavy weather. They need some kind of a reasonably weatherproof cover that will not be dislodged when solid water comes over the foredeck. The caps supplied with most windlasses keep out much of the water. In seriously heavy weather, the chain or rode needs to be disconnected so that the pipe can be plugged with rags or something similar.

Because we do most of our cruising in regions with a lot of coral, I insist on having an all-chain rode on the primary anchor. In addition to its chafe resistance, chain is also the easiest rode to handle because—when properly set up—it is entirely self-stowing. The drawback is its weight.

For the secondary anchor, we have a $\frac{5}{8}$-inch (16 mm), three-strand nylon rode, but with 15 feet (4.5 m) of chain at the anchor to hold the shank down when setting the anchor. The rope needs to be tailed as it comes off the windlass, which means it piles up on deck because we do not have an anchor well. When we reach the chain, it is necessary to pull it and the anchor in by hand. This can be hard on the back, especially if the anchor is fouled with weeds and mud. This work can be avoided if a fairlead is established to either a mast-mounted winch or a cockpit winch, and the last of the rode is pulled in with it. Long before the chain reaches the winch, the anchor will be stowed on the bow roller.

Using a halyard winch to haul up the chain lead on an anchor with a mostly rope rode. The rope rode has been hauled in until the chain lead reaches the windlass. Now another line has been tied to the chain with a rolling hitch and is being cranked in using a mast-mounted halyard winch.

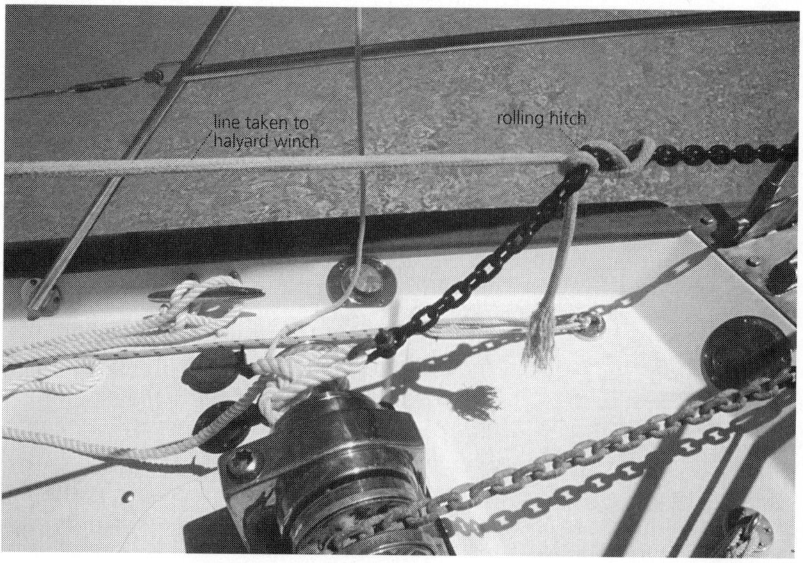

ADDENDUM: CARBON FIBER MASTS

Carbon fiber spars cost about twice as much as comparable aluminum spars, so why would anyone buy carbon fiber? The answer, of course, is weight. When we decided to convert our previous wooden-masted ketch to a cutter rig—solely to reduce weight aloft—we discovered just how dramatic those weight savings can be. The aluminum mast we eventually installed weighed 262 pounds (119 kg; without fittings); the equivalent carbon fiber spar, which we could not afford, was estimated to weigh 113 pounds (51 kg; also without fittings)—just 43 percent of the weight of the aluminum.

To achieve the same reduction in heeling moment that this weight savings represented on our boat, we would need to add between 750 and 1,000 pounds (341–455 kg) of lead to the bottom of our keel. This is typical on a keel boat inasmuch as for a given heeling moment, 1 pound (0.45 kg) aloft has to be counterbalanced by somewhere between 7 and 10 pounds (3.2–4.5 kg) of ballast. Any reduction in weight aloft thus translates into either less heeling or the ability to carry more sail for a given heeling angle. This, in turn, translates into greater power to drive through waves with less pitching.

This all sounds great, and often it is. However, in addition to the cost aspect of carbon fiber, there are other issues that modify this rosy picture to a greater or lesser extent.

The weight most often quoted when comparing carbon fiber to aluminum is the "bare-pole" weight. For aluminum, this is the weight of the extrusion; for carbon fiber, it is likely to be the weight when the pole comes off the tool (either the *male mandrel* or the *female mold*). All the fittings then have to be attached to the spar (e.g., headboxes, spreader brackets), which also can be made of carbon fiber, but only at considerable expense—typically, aluminum or stainless steel is used. The weight added in installing the fittings is likely to be similar to that added to the aluminum extrusion.

Then there are the spreaders, the boom, and the rig. Because of the cost of producing carbon fiber spreaders and booms, it is common to use aluminum, as with an aluminum spar. The rig itself is the same for both carbon fiber and aluminum, with the same weight in the wire or rod and in the terminals. When all of this is added to the spar weight, the savings on the *gross rig weight* are nowhere near as dramatic as those on the bare-pole weight. In other words, although a carbon fiber mast can save as much as 40 percent over the bare-pole weight of an equivalent aluminum spar, the savings on the total rig weight are likely to be 10 to 20 percent, depending on whether carbon spreaders and other fittings are used.

The picture is complicated by the fact that these weight savings are highly dependent on the individual manufacturer and the methodology used to produce the spar. Unlike aluminum masts, which are extruded from the same raw material with predictable engineering properties, carbon fiber spars are hand-constructed from varying grades of carbon fibers, with the result that every single one has slightly different engineering properties.

The higher (stronger) grades of carbon fiber are dramatically more expensive than other grades (up to ten times more expensive). Because even with standard grades of carbon fiber the raw material is approximately one quarter to one third the cost of the finished product, it has a significant impact on the overall cost of a spar. As a result, in practice, most spar manufacturers use *standard modulus* (*T-300*) material or something very similar, rather than more exotic and expensive fibers. However, when it comes to high-performance racing masts—such as those for the America's Cup—*intermediate modulus* (*T-800*) material) is used. It is approximately 20 percent stiffer than T-300, but two and a half to three times as expensive.

Assuming basically the same raw material from one manufacturer to another, there are several different ways in which it can be laminated into the finished product, including layup with a male or female mold, *uni-directional prepreg* or *braided construction*, *vacuum-bag* or *pull-tape debulking*, and vacuum-bag or autoclave curing. Discussing the differences is not appropriate here; the point I want to make is that a carbon spar is significantly a handmade, one-off product, in which quality control is critical. If the engineering or production is in any way messed up, the mast may either end up grossly overweight or come down around the ears of the buyer (or both). Before going to the considerable expense of investing in a carbon fiber spar, it is wise to study the technology and make sure that what you are getting will meet your needs and expectations.

Lightning and Other Survival Issues

The last thing to remember is that carbon is a good electrical conductor, whereas the glue in a carbon fiber laminate is not. If the carbon fibers in a mast were to be fused into an electrically tight connection, the mast—in all likelihood—would be able to conduct to ground (without damage) the high currents of a lightning strike. However, in the event of a strike, any resistance (e.g., caused by the glue) will result in localized heating, which softens or melts the resin and potentially causes irreparable damage to the mast. As a result, all carbon fiber mast manufacturers recommend installing a lightning ground system that meets ABYC standards: essentially a lightning terminal (some type of conductive, pointed device) mounted at least 6 inches above the highest component on the masthead, connected with a #4 AWG (20 mm^2) stranded copper cable to an immersed ground plate that has a surface area of at least 1 square foot (an external keel or a metal hull can be used as the ground plate). (The ground cable is not needed on an aluminum mast and, therefore, constitutes additional weight on the carbon fiber spar; a ½-inch-diameter (12 mm) aluminum rod, insulated where it contacts the mast, will provide an equivalent conductivity with significantly less weight.)

Even with such a lightning-protection system, there is no guarantee that there won't be localized damage due to heating around the base of a lightning terminal and in other areas. Given the small number of carbon fiber masts in use, and the even smaller number of known lightning strikes, there is almost no baseline data with which to assess the impact of such damage.

This raises a more general point. Given the limited experience accumulated with carbon fiber spars, we still do not have a good practical understanding of how the laminates stand up over time in real-life as opposed to laboratory applications. Fatigue is the unknown. In addition, there are other issues. How do you keep an eye on the spar over its lifetime? What are the kinds of maintenance items and warning signs of impending failure to watch for? What happens if you want to move a winch, add another one, or change the position of an exit hole? What will be the effect of a loose shackle or halyard beating against the mast? And so on; only time will tell.

A cruising boat interior has to be both functional and comfortable.

CHAPTER THREE

CRUISING ACCOMMODATIONS

Fusing Functionality at Sea with Comfort on the Hook

"No yacht is comfortable at sea, though some are less uncomfortable than others."

ERIC HISCOCK, *Cruising under Sail*

Boats have changed since Eric Hiscock's day, but the sea hasn't. The acid test of a cruising boat is still its ability to perform safely and to provide a functioning life-support system in difficult and sometimes downright nasty conditions. This sets parameters that have played a large part in determining the hull and rig design and construction criteria discussed in the previous two chapters. It also determines many aspects of interior layout. However, in reality, almost no time will be spent in such conditions. For most of its life, a cruising boat serves as a floating home, at which time it must provide comfort on the hook or at dockside with a minimum of maintenance and aggravation.

Trying to reconcile the demands of these two radically different operating environments is not easy. It inevitably involves compromises, which in turn results in a spectrum of possible choices, ranging from those that prioritize safety and functionality at sea at the expense of comfort on the hook, to those that prioritize comfort on the hook or in the marina at the expense of functionality at sea. A cursory inspection of the boats on display at a boat show demonstrates any number off different approaches to this balancing act.

Given my "offshore" perspective, I approach this spectrum from the conservative (i.e., functionality at sea) end; however, given the time my family and I live aboard (on average, several months of the year), and given my interest in boat systems, I want to make sure that at the end of the day we still have a comfortable home away from home. Others with a more coastal or a cruiser-racer perspective may want to shift the focus somewhat, but should still remember that any boat headed offshore for however limited a period may get caught out in some truly nasty weather and conditions.

The kind of photo you won't see in advertising literature. The question that has to be answered is: Can typical household functions be sustained when heeled 20 to 30 degrees and crashing into waves?

GENERAL CONSIDERATIONS

It is no accident that the most popular interior layout for the "typical" cruising boat up to 40 feet in length has a cabin forward (the forecabin), a saloon in the midships section, a galley and navigation station just forward of the companionway, and a quarter berth or small cabin tucked in alongside the cockpit. The head tends to be either forward of the saloon or aft of the navigation station.

Many contemporary aft-cockpit boats expand the quarter berth to a full cabin; some even squeeze in another head. Center-cockpit boats usually replace the quarter berth with a galley alongside the cockpit and have a spacious aft cabin, probably with its own head. Above 45 feet (14 m) in length, the predominant design is now the deck-saloon configuration popularized by the Oyster line, in which there is a raised saloon with a view forward (for those tall enough to see out), a center cockpit, and a large cabin aft. Nevertheless, the basic layout—tinkered with and refined through countless designs—remains fundamentally the same. What makes it so popular?

Minimizing Motion

First and foremost, the galley and the navigation station—whose associated activities are most affected by motion—are clustered in the midsection of the boat where motion is minimized.

Time-tested, "conventional" layout with all kinds of nice features. Notice, in particular, sinks almost on the centerline; the straight settees parallel to the centerline, which make excellent sea berths; the contoured seat cushions that are comfortable for sitting; excellent fiddle rails; rounded corners; sinks under-mounted to the Corian countertop (easier to clean); and so on. . . . Obviously designed by a sailor! (Courtesy J-Boats)

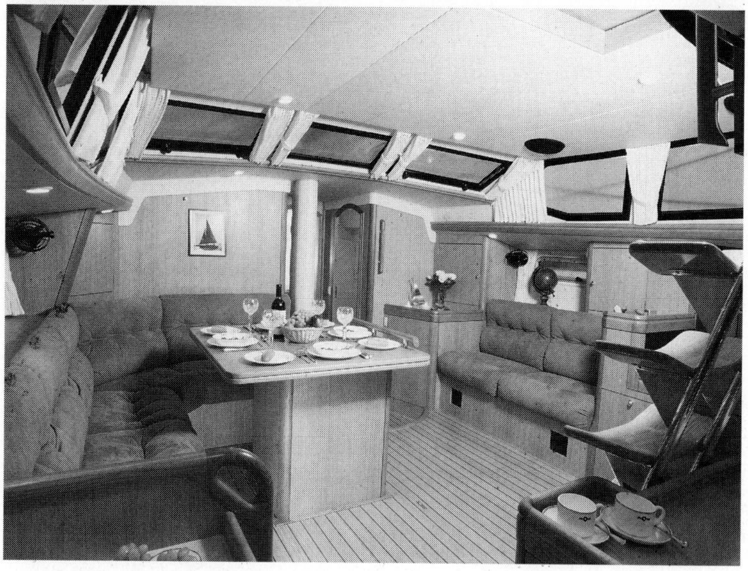

Top: *Oyster deck saloon design.* Above: *Interior of the Oyster deck saloon. (Courtesy Oyster Yachts)*

Placing these two workstations alongside the companionway allows the navigator and the watchkeeper to move in and out of the boat and take care of essential business with the least amount of effort and disruption of anyone resting below. As an added benefit, the galley is strategically placed for food and drinks to be handed up to the cockpit or forward to the saloon. The companionway needs to be designed so that the navigation station, in particular, is protected from spray in all conditions; this can be easily accomplished with a dodger.

But there is no point in having a raised cabintop if you can't see out the portholes!

Below: Large aft cabin squeezed into an aft-cockpit boat—lots of accommodations, but the trade-off is a loss of traditional cockpit stowage space. If the stowage is not needed, this is a very acceptable compromise. (Courtesy Hunter Marine)

Navigation station and galley close by the companionway hatch. (Billy Black photo; courtesy Newport R&D)

With the primary workstations alongside the companionway, if the crew comes below dripping wet, the water can be confined to the smallest possible area, especially if there is a substantial grate and drain beneath the companionway ladder. A self-draining wet locker nearby completes this aspect of the design. However, such a locker is rarely fitted to today's cruising boats; this is one of those items for which a cooperative boatbuilder is needed. We had to make substantial changes to our Pacific Seacraft 40 to work in our locker.

The conventional interior also places the saloon close to the center of motion, creating an excellent environment in which to locate a couple of sea berths.

Next in importance in terms of minimizing motion is the head compartment. It doesn't get used much of the time, so is often given low-priority status by designers; as a result, it is sometimes shunted off to the forecabin. However, the motion can be almost intolerable here and it's almost guaranteed that an already squeamish crew member who needs to use the head will be pushed over the edge. By the time a boat gets up around 40 feet (12 m), there is generally space enough to tuck in a substantial head compartment alongside the companionway or to include

Dripping-wet crew members need to be able to get below and change without causing a problem.

Hunter 410

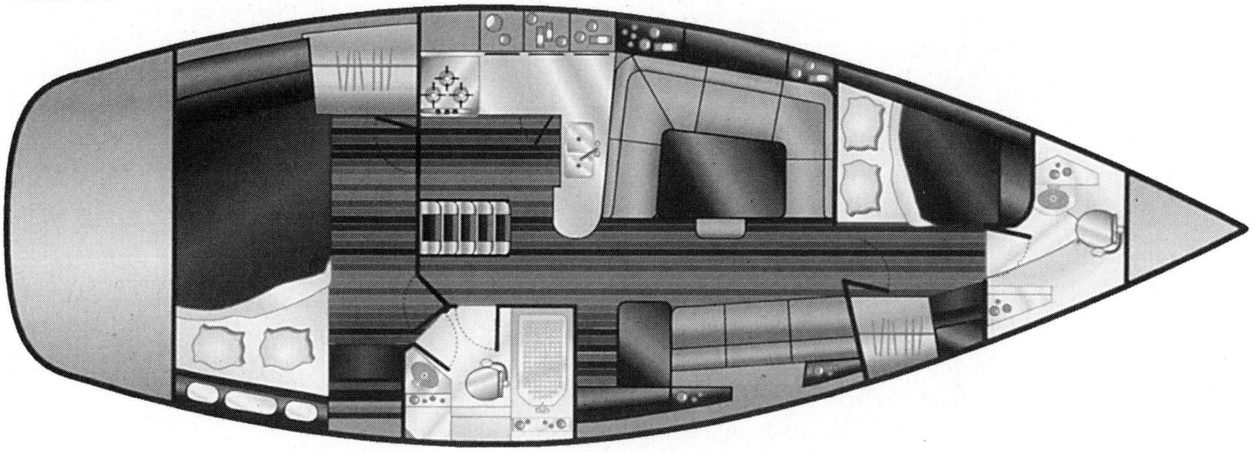

Pacific Seacraft 40

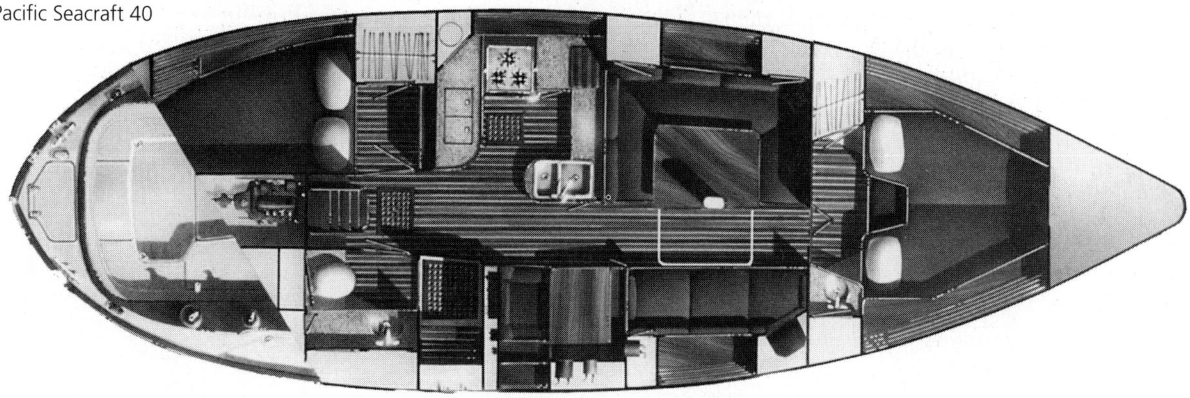

Two superficially similar 40-foot boats but, the closer you look, the more differences you see. The Hunter has a magnificent aft stateroom contrasted to the Pacific Seacraft's cramped quarter berth. For the stateroom, cockpit stowage is sacrificed, along with some of the galley (no counter on the aft side of the stove). The Hunter has a second head up forward, but to find the space for it, it has a smaller navigation station. And so on. Neither is necessarily "better"; they are simply optimized for different markets. (Courtesy Hunter Marine and Pacific Seacraft)

it in an aft-cabin arrangement; either one works well. The aft location also minimizes the tubing runs from the hot-water heater (which is somewhere close to the engine), thereby minimizing the water lost when waiting for hot water to reach the shower.

The aft cabin, whether in the form of a quarter berth or a separate cabin, is also reasonably comfortable and usable at sea. Between it and the sea berths in the saloon, there is sufficient room for the off-duty watch when passagemaking, although sail-handling noises in the cockpit tend to get transmitted down to a quarter berth or aft cabin. Most quarter berths are also located alongside the engine and, as a result, are both hot and noisy when motoring or motor sailing. Ventilation is frequently an issue—I'll discuss this later.

In broad terms, the layout described so far leaves the forecabin as a forward cabin, which can incorporate either a double berth or two singles. It is unlikely to be habitable in rough conditions—the crew will have to camp out in the saloon, quarter berth, or aft cabin—but at least it can serve as a repository for sails. At anchor, the forecabin makes an excellent cabin, situated as it is beneath the forehatch. Even in the tropics, if a wind scoop is mounted over the hatch, the merest whisper of a breeze creates the best ventilated and most comfortable sleeping quarters on the boat, as well as a fair measure of privacy by being out of the way of all below-decks traffic. If an all-chain rode is used for anchoring, the noise of a dragging anchor will be heard clearly from this berth, alerting the crew to the problem.

Crew Size

This conventional layout works extremely well for a couple with occasional guests, and stretches to cover a family of up to four, but it will become increasingly cramped as children reach teenage years. In our case, for example, we have a teenage girl and boy. We thought that with a quarter berth just about large enough to accommodate Terrie and me, we could get the children to share the forecabin. It is big enough, but it is difficult to give them enough privacy (it would be easier if they were the same gender). However, in practice, we have found that one or the other prefers to camp out in the saloon, so we evicted them from the forecabin, which we now use ourselves (it is much more commodious than the quarter berth). We leave them to sort things out themselves. In reality, we would all be a lot more comfortable in a 45-foot (14 m) boat, which provides the length necessary for another small cabin.

In the short term, it would be great to have an extra cabin; however, looking down the road a few years to when we will be cruising without the children, Terrie and I realize that our current boat will be more than big enough for us.

As crew size grows, there is simply no substitute for a bigger boat with more cabins. While it may be possible to pack half a dozen friends into a 40-foot (12 m) boat for a two-week charter (we have had up to nine onboard for ten days)—and have everybody leave the boat still friends—it is quite another scenario to take the same group on the same boat on an extended cruise. It is always useful to be able to convert the saloon table and settee berth into a double berth, and maybe tuck in another guest on the other settee for a short visit, but the longer the voyage, the more is the need for private spaces.

It is also important to remember that the more berths stuffed into a boat, the less stowage space but the greater need. To quote Dave Gerr: "When evaluating boats, keep a sharp eye on the compromises and sacrifices that have been made for additional interior accommodations. All boats and all designs are compromises, but make sure that your boat embodies the kind of trade-offs that match the way you'll use her" (*Nature of Boats*).

Keeping Things in Place

Regardless of its layout, a cruising boat must be designed to keep things in their assigned places. This means that once closed, all cabinets, drawers, and hatches must remain closed, regardless of the angle of heel or the extent to which the boat is pounding.

Cabinet doors commonly have finger latches—the kind of spring-loaded catch that is accessed through a hole in the door. I positively hate these. What happens if the boat makes a sudden lurch just as you poke your finger through the hole to open the door? If ever there was a finger-breaker, this is it. Much to be preferred are button latches (although these need to be spring-loaded to prevent them vibrating open) or any other type of latch that is operated from outside the door (our Pacific Seacraft 40 has nice push-button latches). Just as effective, although not as aesthetically pleasing, are barrel bolts. Cabinet doors should be hinged from the side or base, never from the top (on one tack or the other, the contents will spill out whenever the door is opened).

Drawers are typically held shut by machining an indent into the base of the drawer that fits over a raised rail in the supporting framework. To open the drawer, it is lifted and pulled out. This simple approach is quite effective until a boat starts to pound hard, at which time the G-forces can sometimes lift the drawer. If it is on the windward side, it may fly open and dump

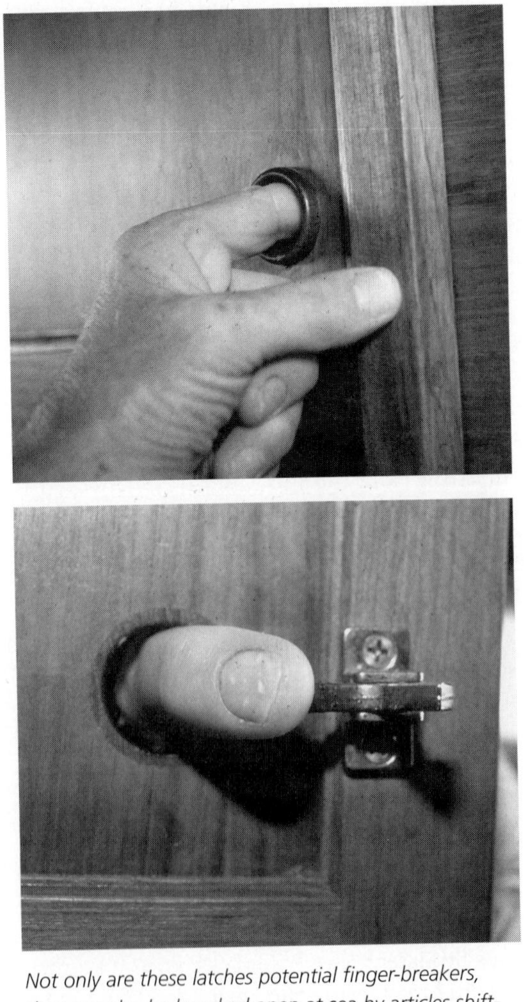

Not only are these latches potential finger-breakers, they can also be knocked open at sea by articles shifting inside the lockers.

A superior cupboard latch.

Single and double drawer pulls. The top drawer, with two drawer pulls, is difficult to open one-handed underway. A single pull in the center of the drawer does not look as elegant, but is more functional.

itself and its contents on the cabinsole. Because of this, drawers opening in an athwartships direction should have back-up barrel bolts or some other means of locking them shut. Accidents are less likely to happen with drawers opening in a fore and aft direction; on these drawers, no additional hardware is necessary.

Many drawers also have finger holes to open them. These are not as bad as on cabinet doors; nevertheless, proper drawer pulls are much nicer. Wider drawers are likely to have two drawer pulls, one on each side. Unfortunately, this often means that two hands are needed to open the drawer, which makes it difficult to open it in rough weather when it is necessary to hang onto the boat with one hand. It is preferable to have a single drawer pull in the center of the drawer.

All locker-access hatches within the boat should be locked in place to prevent them from flying off in a knockdown. In particular, hatches in cabinsoles tend to be heavy and are potentially quite dangerous if the boat gets thrown on its beam ends or rolled beyond this. In addition to the sole hatches, there are numerous locker lids beneath and behind settee berths and in other locations. They are generally not nearly as heavy as sole hatches, although there may be a substantial weight of contents inside the locker itself. On an ocean-voyaging boat, they too should be locked in place. For coastal cruising it is desirable, but rarely done—and, in reality, it is unlikely that conditions will warrant the necessity of fitting locks. (We have none on our boat; if extreme conditions seem possible, we can always use duct tape to hold the lids in place.)

What is not debatable is the need to strap down all heavy items on the boat. Particular attention needs to be given to water and fuel tanks (which are frequently poorly held in place), batteries (which are frequently nowhere near adequately restrained), and stoves (many of which can jump out of their mounts in a knockdown). An often-overlooked item (including on our new boat) is the icebox lid, which is usually heavy. If not secured in place with a hinge, it too needs locking down; there are numerous reports of unsecured icebox lids getting thrown across boats—even a frozen chicken in flight can do significant damage!

For offshore work, all hatches in the cabinsole need to be positively locked down.

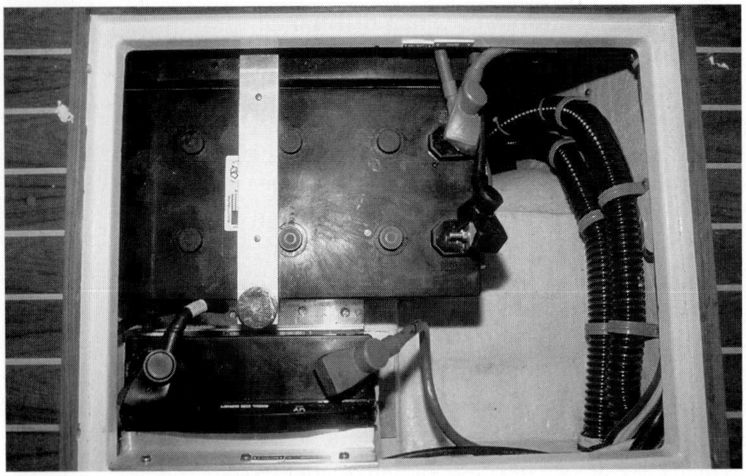

For any kind of work, all heavy items need to be strapped down . . .

. . . whereas this cranking battery is not (and the house battery is also none too well secured).

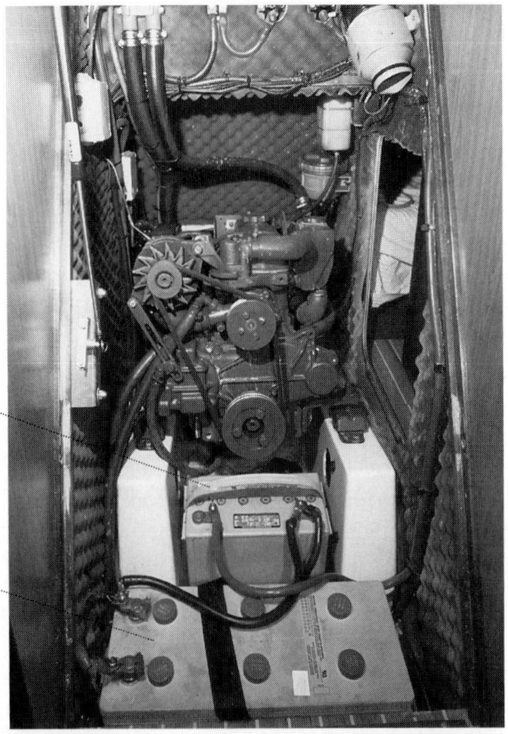

Attractively bull-nosed fiddle rail that is well designed for launching dishware into space!

Then there is the matter of keeping things in place on tables and countertops in less violent conditions. This requires respectable fiddle rails with a minimum height of 1½ inches (38 mm). The fiddle rails should have *vertical inner faces*, as opposed to the nicely rounded bull-nosed upper edges invariably installed by boatbuilders. Although the rounded-off molding looks great at boat shows, it serves as a natural launching pad for any plate lip that slides up onto it.

The one surface on which I don't like a fixed fiddle rail is the saloon table. In practice, the table is rarely usable at sea, with or without a fiddle rail, and the fiddle rail just gets in the way at anchor or in harbor. If fiddles are fitted, I recommend that they be removable.

Fiddle rails on tables and on countertops with square corners make it difficult to clean the surfaces they surround. For this reason, they should incorporate clean-out slots, preferably at the corners, although this allows spills to dribble out. These slots are not appropriate if small items can slide off; for example, pencils and dividers on a chart table.

In addition to the boat's stores and gear, people need to be able to stay in place. To make this possible, a cruising boat needs many strategically located handholds placed so as to naturally lend themselves to being grabbed when the boat is heeled 30 degrees and pounding into short steep seas, or when rolling violently from side to side going downwind. Light boats can have an especially violent motion. If the handholds are not there, something else will get grabbed (and likely broken) or else people will get thrown about the boat.

Unfortunately, on modern boats there seems to be an inverse ratio between the size of the saloon and the number and utility of handholds. We have found the most effective handhold to be a shaped molding around both cabinsides at shoulder height. It also serves as a driprail for portholes and a useful place to stash pencils, cigarette lighters, and reading glasses. Overhead handholds, beloved of boatbuilders, are not the most comfortable to hang onto, especially for children and shorter people for whom they are often completely out of reach: about all they are useful for is hanging up dish towels!

The cabinsole needs to have a reasonably nonskid surface rather than a boat-show high gloss. Some people recommend proper nonskid surfaces, but these are difficult to clean and aesthetically not at all pleasing. We have found a good compromise to be a semigloss or matte

The optimum height for handholds is approximately shoulder height. Overhead handholds are frequently out of reach of shorter crew members.

The companionway ladder needs excellent nonskid, as seen here. Note also the grate at the base of the ladder with a removable pan. It is not large enough to serve as an effective drip pan if crew members come down wet, but it is a nice feature that makes cleaning the boat easier.

polyurethane finish. True, it can get slippery when wet but, given enough handholds, we have had no problems remaining on our feet in the roughest conditions.

However, we have slid down a companionway ladder on a number of occasions. The ladder needs wide treads with effective nonskid—either teak strips set into the treads or Treadmaster inserts (a popular and effective cork-based nonskid material that is glued in place) or something similar.

Many ladders are made near vertical, which means you have to turn around when going below. There are times when this can be annoying, especially when darting in and out of the navigation station. Before buying a boat, I recommend dashing up and down the ladder a few times, preferably when heeled, to get a sense of how it will work out in practice.

Insulation

To a considerable extent, insulation and ventilation are opposite sides of the same coin. Both are essential to maintaining comfortable temperatures inside a boat, as well as keeping the interior dry and minimizing the occurrence of mold and mildew—especially when the boat is laid up for any length of time.

Without insulation, temperatures within a fiberglass or metal boat respond rapidly to the outside temperature—when it is too hot, the boat gets too hot; when it is too cold, the boat is cold. And any time the outside temperature falls below that in the boat, condensation can form on the hull and cabinsides, on the cabintop, and on the frames of metal portlights and hatches. It is not uncommon for people living on an uninsulated boat in a cold climate to find the hull sides covered in moisture, with all metal hatch and porthole frames steadily dripping. (If possible, hatches and metal portholes should be located where they will not drip on the berths and other sensitive areas; the wooden hatches on our old boat never gave us a problem.) Condensation inside lockers leads to the growth of mildew and mold.

Condensation is exacerbated by the use of propane-, alcohol-, and diesel-fueled galley stoves and unvented (i.e., without chimneys) heaters because they put at least a gallon of moisture into the air for every gallon of fuel burned. Condensation can be minimized by good ventilation and the use of "dry" sources of heat (primarily, heaters with vented combustion chambers); even so, this often does not take care of the annoying drips from hatch and porthole rims. Liveaboards will find that a dehumidifier

Top: *Condensation forming on the cabin sides during a late-season sail in Maine with nighttime temperatures moving toward freezing.* Bottom: *All the metal hatch frames on the boat were also dripping steadily.*

A combination of insulated hull sides, wooden hatch frames, and ventilated lockers such as this one made our old boat just about immune to condensation.

solves many problems, but this requires a permanent shore-side hookup, which may create its own problems (see chapter 4). If a dehumidifier is used on an unattended boat, rather than have it drain into the bilge, which then requires the bilge pump to get the water off the boat, it's preferable to have it drain directly overboard through the galley sink or its own dedicated through-hull. What is really needed is an insulated boat—or to move to a warmer climate!

Cored hulls and decks mitigate the worst effects of a lack of insulation, but there is really no substitute for proper insulation if it can be installed. On our old boat, which Terrie and I built ourselves, we glued ¾ inch (19 mm) of foam insulation over the entire hull side from the cabinsole on up (including inside all lockers) and on the cabintop. We then applied the interior paneling over the foam. We also added cane inserts to every locker door on the boat, so that the lockers could "breathe" (cane inserts or louvers should be standard on all cruising boats; doors with solid panels are not acceptable). As a result of these measures, we were able to leave clothes and other personal belongings on the boat in humid Louisiana from one year to the next without fear of mildew or mold. Our new Pacific Seacraft 40, despite its cored hull and deck, is not as good, but is nevertheless better than most production boats that have no insulation at all.

For those faced with a "sweaty" boat that is driving them nuts, the most economical way to deal with the problem is to glue ½-inch (12 mm) or thicker sheets of flexible closed-cell foam to the hull sides and cabintop.

Ventilation

After insulation, the next best defense against condensation, mold, and mildew is excellent ventilation, which is required in hot climates to keep cabin temperatures at tolerable levels.

There is quite a science to ventilation. To work well, the openings on the boat that are bringing air in must be counterbalanced by openings that exhaust it; without this, the airflow stalls out. Crudely speaking, if a hatch, ventilator, or canvas structure (e.g., a dodger) sticks up into the airflow past the boat in such a way that it deflects air downward, it brings air into the boat; if the same device deflects air upward, it creates a low pressure (a partial vacuum) in the boat, sucking air out. Knowing this, the trick is to create the desired airflow through the boat in a variety of different conditions, including at anchor, in a marina, at sea, and when the boat is laid up.

At anchor is the easiest to deal with: not only is the wind coming from a predictable direction (ahead), but also it is usually possible to open numerous hatches and portholes, creating multiple paths for air entry and exit. In terms of their effectiveness, a dodger is likely to be the largest channeler of the airflow, followed (in order of usefulness) by hatches, cowl vents, mushroom vents, and opening portlights.

If the forehatch is hinged on its forward face (as it should be, so that it gets knocked shut at sea by boarding waves, rather than ripped off), with the wind coming from ahead (as it will be most times at anchor), the hatch deflects the airflow upward—thereby creating a low pressure—and sucks air out of the boat. If the boat has a similar hatch in the saloon that opens on its aft edge, it deflects the airflow down into the boat. The net effect so far is to create an airflow down into the saloon and out the forecabin.

However, if a dodger is in place, its likely effect will be to create a low pressure over the

Typical ventilation scenario. The forehatch opens on its aft edge, deflecting any breeze into the boat from where it exits via the companionway hatch. However, for offshore work, I believe a forehatch should open on its forward edge, although this restricts the airflow.

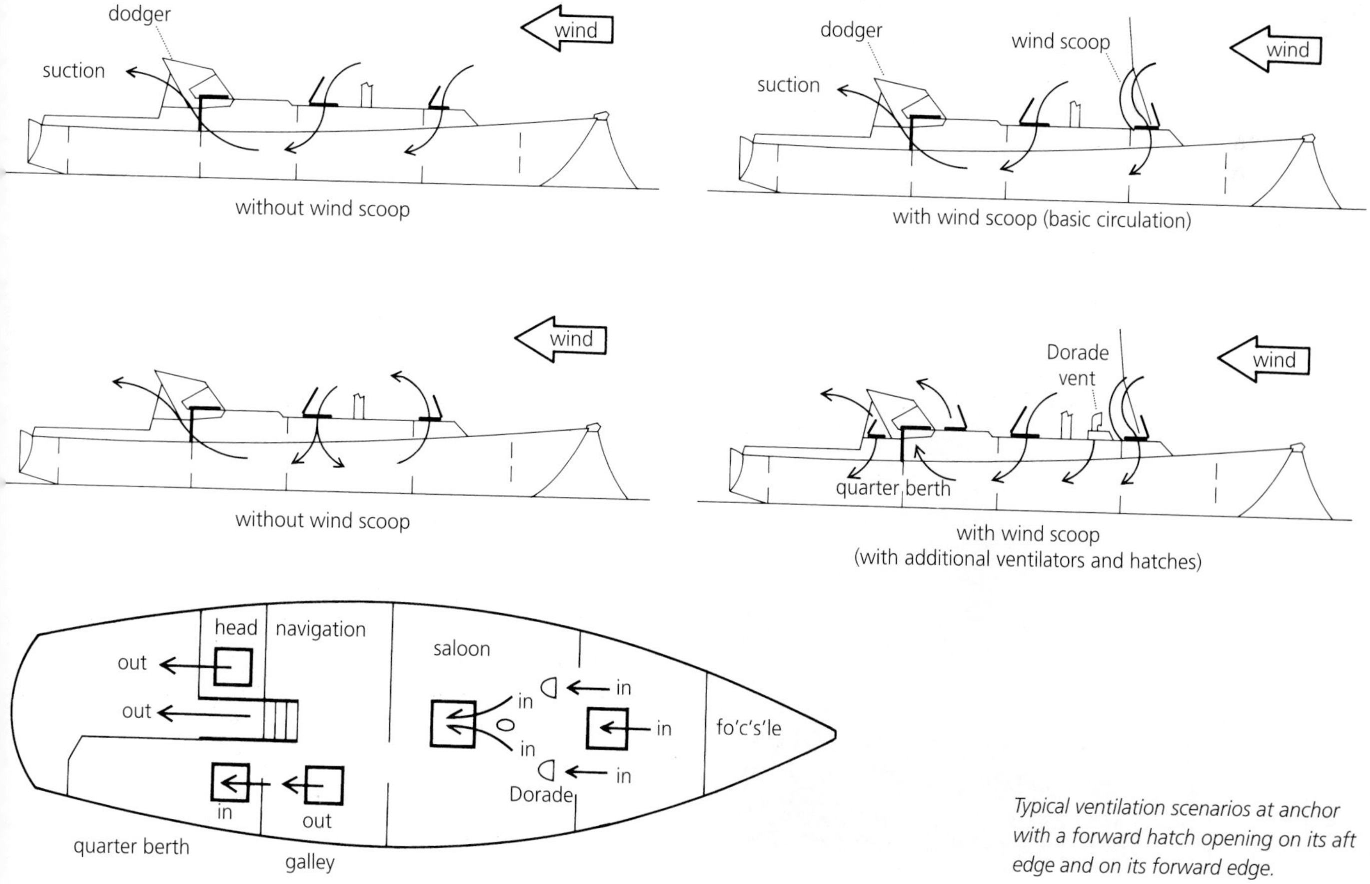

Typical ventilation scenarios at anchor with a forward hatch opening on its aft edge and on its forward edge.

companionway hatch, diverting much of the flow through the saloon hatch aft. Other hatches and ventilators modify this overall picture, depending on whether they are bringing air in or sucking it out. With careful placement of hatches and ventilators, and by turning cowl vents in different directions, it is possible—to a significant extent—to control the direction and force of the airflows through the boat. When determining hatch placement, remember that hatches should not be too far off the centerline (to avoid flooding in a knockdown) and, if possible, there should be no hatches in the foredeck (this risks damage and flooding; at times, green water will sweep over it). This puts the foremost hatch at the forward end of the cabintop.

We almost never use marinas, so we spend the greater part of our boat time anchored out. Because Terrie and I now occupy the forecabin, we are particularly interested in keeping this well ventilated! For safety reasons, we have the hatch hinged on its forward edge, but prefer the airflow to be "in" rather than "out." To achieve this, we use a homemade wind scoop. In even a modest trade-wind breeze, we get a regular blast of air through the hatch, so much so that we frequently have to almost close the hatch to throttle down the airflow.

At first sight, the hatch hinged on its forward edge seems to interfere with airflow, but as long as a wind scoop is in use, the reverse is true; in fact, if there is an option about which way to open a hatch, it is best to do it this way. Rather than being installed inside the hatch opening (as is commonly done), a wind scoop should be wrapped around the exterior of a hatch. This way, the hatch can be closed from inside the boat in inclement weather without having to take the wind scoop down.

A wind scoop maximizes the airflow through a boat. Notice how this wind scoop bells out to maximize the wind-catchment area.

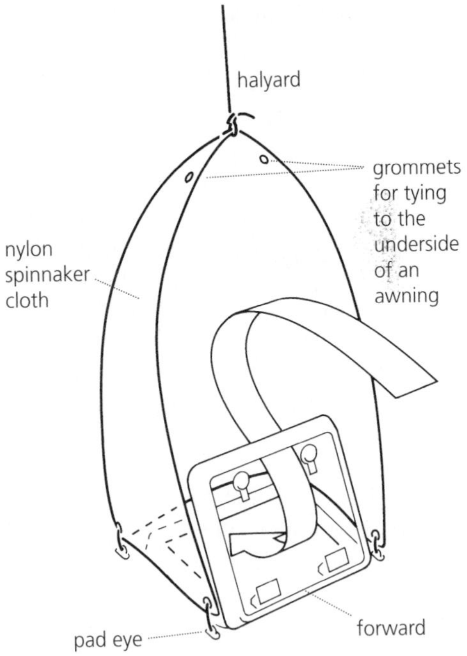

Wind scoop design on Nada. Note that the hatch can be used to throttle the airflow and can be closed without taking down the wind scoop.

Commercial wind scoops are often made multidirectional through a system of internal baffles, but the net effect is to reduce the overall airflow. We prefer to have the scoop operate in only one direction, turning it if necessary. To make this possible, we install four small pad eyes on the deck outside the perimeter of the hatch (don't forget to seal the deck core when putting in the fasteners), and then tie down the corners of the scoop to these pad eyes. To turn the scoop, we untie it and retie it. In terms of shape, all that is needed is a near-triangular piece of cloth that surrounds the hatch on three sides and is held up in its middle (it may need a cross bar to hold it open). If the top edge is held forward when it is hoisted, the sides will balloon out, minimizing the chances of it repeatedly collapsing and refilling (which can be quite noisy) as the boat moves at anchor or the wind shifts. To make our wind scoops, we use lightweight nylon spinnaker cloth, reinforced with nylon webbing around the perimeter, with grommets at each corner.

The breeze from our wind scoop blows through the louvers in the forecabin door into the main saloon. It is augmented by the airflow through the saloon hatch (hinged on its aft edge with no wind scoop) and two mushroom ventilators (we should have Dorade vents—more about them later in this chapter), which keeps the saloon well ventilated. All this air has to go somewhere; in practice, out the companionway,

Our friend Peter Hancock's Kylie, *a 26-foot (7.9 m) Contessa that he has twice taken across the Atlantic, with its wind scoop and awning rigged, making him much more comfortable in the tropics than many other more luxurious boats.*

which is big enough to take it without backing up the airflow. If the galley has its hatch hinged on its forward edge, it too acts as an exhaust, getting the heat out of the kitchen; if the head compartment also has a hatch hinged on its forward edge, it will exhaust odors rather than feed them into the boat and out the companionway.

You may not want the airflows in the same direction on your boat. The point is to understand how they can be manipulated so that you can establish the ventilation that suits your living spaces and boat use. A pilothouse or deck saloon is likely to be especially difficult to keep cool in hot climates because of the substantial area of fixed glass panels almost always found in its forward face. Reflective screens on the inside help minimize heat entry; nevertheless, two or more hatches are almost certain to be needed.

Another space that is hard to ventilate is a quarter berth. We solved this problem by happily sacrificing a cabintop reefing winch and associated rope clutch, replacing them with a hatch. The hatch is inside the dodger, so we designed that section of the dodger so that it zips open and folds back around the perimeter of the hatch, acting as a wind scoop. The hatch opens on its aft edge. Between it and the wind scoop/dodger, it feeds a lot of air into the quarter berth, which then exits out the companionway hatch. In contrast, the typical portlights in the cabinside and in the side of the cockpit well are not much use.

Aft cabins, too, can be hot and airless; the answer is a substantial hatch, opening on its aft edge and combined with a wind scoop. The inflow of air will exit through the companionway.

Opening portlights (of which we have fourteen) contribute almost nothing to the ventilation of a boat when at anchor. Their contribution can be improved with individual wind scoops, which we have seen on other boats from time to time, but we have never felt the need to go to this much trouble and work.

In a marina, where the wind comes from all kinds of directions, it is necessary to be able to turn wind scoops and cowl ventilators toward the wind. This is the one time when opening portlights can contribute significantly to the airflow. Portlights need (although often do not have) an external drain that prevents the accumulation of water on the lower edges. Without this, very often a slug of water enters the cabin when the porthole is opened. However, if the grabrail discussed previously is fitted around the cabinsides, it will catch the water.

All vents, ports, and hatches (including the companionway hatch) require easily installed

To get good ventilation in our quarter berth, we sacrificed a cabintop winch, installed a hatch, and designed the dodger to wrap around the hatch to form a small wind scoop.

Portholes need external drains so they do not hold water on the lower edge of the frame.

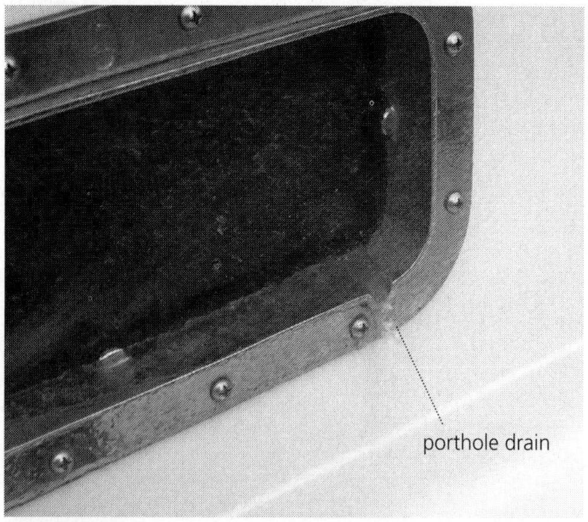

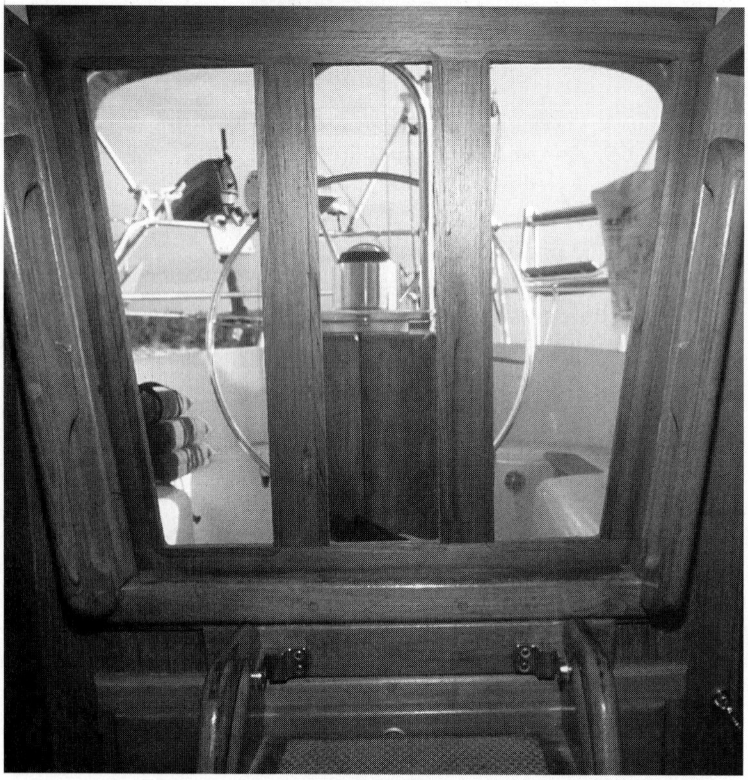

Companionway bug screen—the wooden bars obstruct the airflow, but make the openings too small for an intruder to get through.

bug screens. We have a screen that drops into the companionway in place of the hatchboards. For security reasons, it is ruggedly constructed with divider bars that break up the screened areas into spaces too small for someone to squeeze into the boat. All of the screens, particularly the larger ones, need a designated stowage space where they will be protected from damage when not in use.

Many portlight bug screens are retained by screws that make the installation semipermanent. Given that a screen severely limits the airflow (and also the light), it is preferable to have clip-in screens, which will be used only when needed.

The ventilation scenario presented so far depends on open hatches and wind scoops. Typically, as soon as it starts raining, the hatches must be closed, which means that boats frequently become humid sweat baths in tropical climates in the rainy season. We solved this problem on our old boat by building a full-length awning using Sunbrella (which is more or less waterproof), with attachment points on its underside for the wind scoops. In all but the windiest squalls, the awning kept the rainwater away from the hatches, enabling us to leave the wind scoops in place and the hatches open.

It has taken a certain amount of experimentation to refine our ideas on awnings. There are various contradictory requirements. Given that it is next to impossible to spread the awning wider than the boat, any time the sun is not directly overhead (most of the time, even in the tropics), it is going to shine under one or another edge. The higher the awning is off the deck, the less the deck area that is shaded—but the lower the awning, the more difficult it is for people to move around onboard.

We've tried raising the awning and adding side curtains. However, this made it time-consuming to put up because there had to be a number of lines tying down the base of the side curtains to prevent them from flapping around. After a while, we found we simply weren't bothering with the side curtains. We ended up raising the awning in the center and pulling it down toward the lifelines at the edges to form something resembling an open-sided tent. To move around freely, all we had to do was develop an inward-leaning stoop!

At sea, any awning and the wind scoops will come down and the hatches and portlights will mostly be closed. In rough conditions, two of the three companionway boards—and maybe all three—are likely to be in place and the hatch closed. The ventilation picture is radically different.

At these times, the only effective ventilation is provided by baffled cowl vents, commonly known as Dorade vents. A Dorade vent has a cowl ventilator mounted on the top of a box that is fastened to the deck with drain holes in its base. Offset from the cowl vent is a duct, with a raised lip, into the boat. The idea is that water entering the cowl vent runs out of the box before reaching the lip of the duct, enabling the vent to be kept open in all but the roughest conditions. However, for this to work, the duct must have a substantial lip; ideally, the cowl itself will have a lip on the underside of the box that projects below the top of the duct. This way, it is just about impossible for water entering the cowl to get into the duct. In practice, most cowls

An excellent awning (manufactured by Shadetree of Elberta, Alabama) that has sufficient curvature to enable people to move around on deck, but yet comes down low enough at the sides to create effective shading.

are simply fastened to the top of the box, and many ducts don't have much of a lip—the Dorade ends up being less effective at excluding water than it might be.

In really rough weather, even a Dorade needs closing off, which is accomplished by unscrewing the cowl and replacing it with a deckplate. At these times, the crew will just have to sweat it out down below. Sometimes, in place of the duct into the boat, a regular mushroom vent is fitted, in which case it too can be closed (from inside the boat, which is handy). The downside is that the mushroom vents are commonly installed on the deck and, therefore, are not as effective at deflecting water as a higher duct; they will need to be closed long before the higher duct.

Dorade vents are more or less essential equipment on a well-found cruising boat. Ideally, there will be at least a couple forward and another couple aft. Better yet is one over every berth, in the galley, and in the head. If the forward and aft vents are set up to face in opposite directions—regardless of the direction from

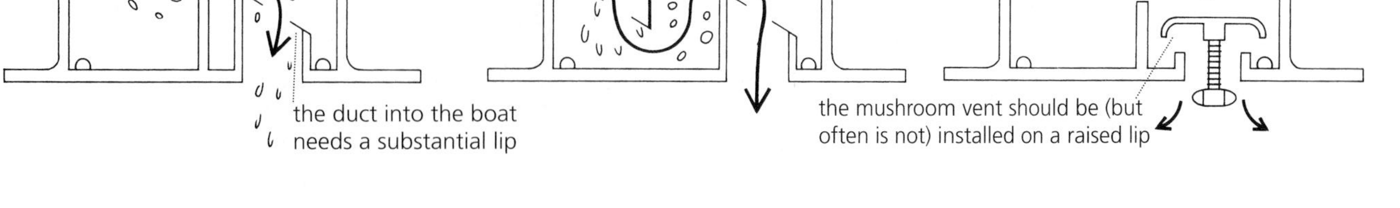

typically, the cowl vent is screwed into the top of the Dorade box; in strong winds, spray can be carried into the boat
the duct into the boat needs a substantial lip
an arrangement such as this will keep all but solid water out of the boat
a mushroom ventilator makes it possible to seal the Dorade vent from inside the boat, but at the expense of increased resistance to air flow when opened
the mushroom vent should be (but often is not) installed on a raised lip

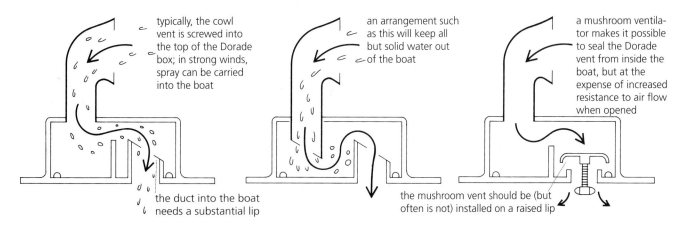

Dorade vents.

This Dorade vent incorporates a mushroom ventilator, which makes it possible to close the vent from inside the boat.

which the wind is coming—there will be a reasonable airflow through the boat.

When a boat is laid up, it will most likely be closed up for security reasons—in other words, the ventilation situation is similar to that of a boat at sea in rough weather. Once again, there is no substitute for Dorade vents: the more the better. There are also vents on the market with solar-powered fans that, in direct sunlight, move a substantial amount of air; these are almost completely effective at excluding rainwater, even in a heavy downpour accompanied by strong winds. If the boat has a dedicated shower stall, a hatch there can be left open. Any rainwater making its way inside is caught by the shower pan, from where it will evaporate over time.

To minimize chances of mold and mildew forming during long periods of non-use, it is worthwhile to get a container of "Calcium Hardness Increaser" (calcium chloride) from a local swimming-pool supply store, and place some of it in several open-topped plastic containers in the boat. The calcium chloride absorbs moisture, reducing the chances of mold and mildew developing. Anything that does form can be cleaned off wood, fiberglass, and plastic surfaces (but not metal and fabrics) with a solution of 2 cups of bleach and 2 tablespoons of trisodium phosphate (TSP) (available at hardware stores) dissolved in 1 gallon of water. Wipe down the affected surfaces, wait a few minutes, and then rinse with freshwater. This is a fairly strong bleach solution, so wear rubber gloves and avoid inhaling the fumes.

Air Conditioning and Heating

Most Americans have come to believe that air conditioning is a necessity in hot, even warm, climates. Nevertheless, it must be given a lot of thought before being installed on a boat. Air conditioning totally transforms the energy requirements of most boats, making a constantly running AC generator (or a permanent shoreside hookup) a necessity. Not only is the financial price tag high, but also the collateral price tag in terms of noise, fuel consumption, exhaust fumes, maintenance, and loss of interior space (in addition to the generator, the ducting requires a surprising amount of room).

We have spent several years cruising in the tropics and have almost never felt the need for air conditioning. The benefits of not having air conditioning far outweigh the few times when we would really have appreciated it. The keys to keeping the boat cool were outlined previously: insulation, ventilation, and anchoring out.

Having said this, I recognize that air conditioning is more or less a necessity for those living aboard for any length of time in a marina environment in hot climates. For these people, it is worth considering a drop-in type of installation (i.e., a stand-alone unit installed in a hatch, the marine equivalent of a household window unit) rather than a permanently installed central unit with ducting. As long as the boat has a shore-power connection, the air conditioner can be run from dockside power. When going cruising, it can be put in storage, eliminating the need for an AC generator with all its attendant drawbacks (including an underrecognized safety hazard; see the addendum to this chapter).

At the other end of the spectrum is heating. Boats used for summertime cruising in higher latitudes and in the tropics year-round do not need heaters. Those seeking to stretch the season in higher latitudes will appreciate a cabin heater. If the boat has propane for cooking (which I highly recommend), a propane heater is almost always the best choice. Otherwise, there are solid- and diesel-fueled options. For more serious heat, various central-heating systems are available, most of them fueled by diesel; the best known are the Espar and

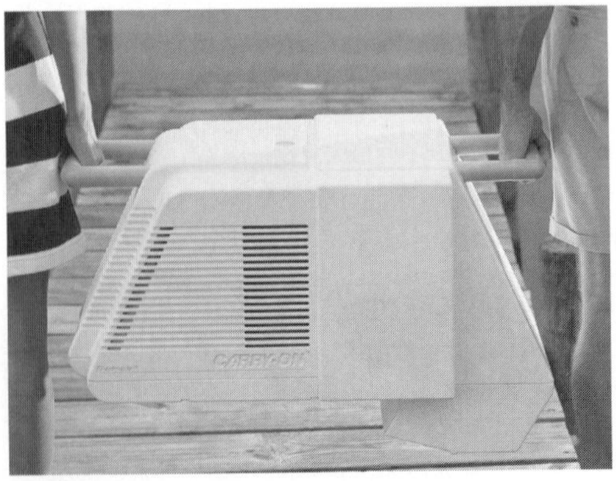

Portable air conditioner from Cruisair. (Courtesy Cruisair)

Webasto heaters. However, these significantly increase boat cost, level of complexity, necessary maintenance, and loss of space (the ducting). Of course, if a reverse-cycle central-air-conditioning unit is installed, it can be used for heat with no additional ducting.

Central heat is another thing that deserves considerable thought before taking the plunge, and also carries with it an underrecognized safety hazard (see the addendum at the end of this chapter).

At this point, let's look at the nitty-gritty of successfully utilizing individual spaces on a cruising boat. Attention to the following kinds of small details is what ultimately makes or breaks a boat.

SPECIFIC SPACES

Navigation Station

As electronic navigation becomes more commonplace, there is a distressing trend to reduce the size of chart tables. In the words of *The Glénans Manual of Sailing*, this "represents a triumph of modern design over common sense," and should be categorically rejected by any cruising sailor, whether coastal or offshore.

The one time the electronics are most likely to go down, forcing a return to paper charts, is when the boat is taking a battering. These are precisely the conditions when a decent-size chart table in a properly designed navigation station is essential. In particular, to plot fixes and carry out other critical tasks, you need both hands free. This means the chart must remain stationary (generally laid up against the back of the chart table or a fiddle rail on the front, rather than sliding around on the saloon table), and you must be able to brace yourself (generally by getting wedged in a seat) without having to hang on with one hand. You will need all the tools of the trade—pencils, dividers, parallel rules, and so on—immediately at hand, which means a dedicated stowage space out of which they will not bounce. You should also have any electronic displays (e.g., Global Positioning System [GPS] and radar) readily visible and radios (e.g., VHF and SSB) nearby. These requirements can be met only with a "proper" navigation station.

What constitutes a "decent-size chart table"? In my opinion, something on the order of 36 inches long by 30 inches deep (910 by 760 mm), or bigger. Unfortunately, there is hardly a boat under 45 feet (14 m) in length that comes close to this (and many above this length that don't); in fact, many designers argue that it is just about impossible to incorporate such a chart table without unduly compromising other aspects of the interior design. I disagree. If necessary, I believe that the key to finding the space is eliminating the conventional

Top: *Good-size chart table. The angle at which it is set up makes it comfortable to use, but restricts it to this one single purpose—an extravagant use of space.* Above: *A more conventional navigation station, tucked in at the base of the companionway on a 40-foot center-cockpit boat. The chart-table lid can be leveled to serve double duty as a work surface when not at sea.* Left: *Excellent "conventional" navigation station: good-size chart table, plenty of stowage, comfortable seat, and near the companionway. (Courtesy Hallberg-Rassy)*

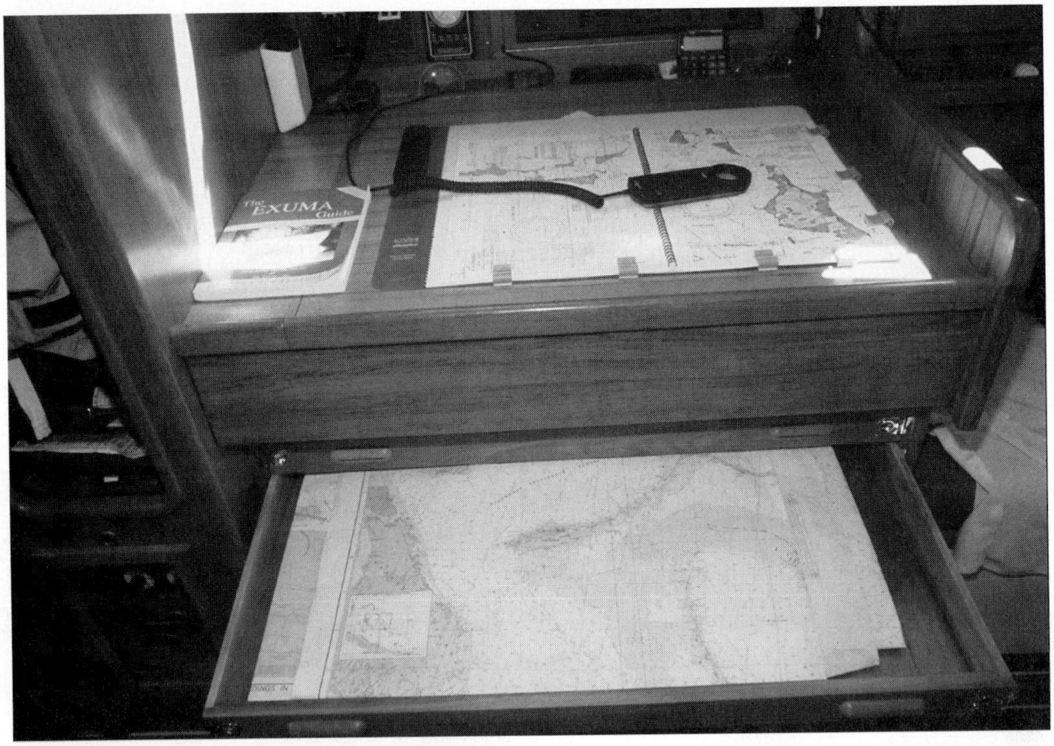
The navigation station on Nada. We sacrificed the navigator's seat for a large chart table (which serves double duty as a great work surface when not underway), fabulous chart stowage, a substantial amount of other stowage, and the wet locker seen on the left-hand side. If you look closely, you can see a narrow trough in the back of the chart table—this is where we store parallel rules, dividers, pencils, and a spare handheld GPS, among various other items. Because charts can slide over the top of the trough, it does not take up any usable chart surface.

Nada's chart table lifts up to reveal a large stowage area that Terrie has purloined for art supplies!

sit-down navigation station—facing fore or aft—and instead having a stand-up chart table with the navigator facing athwartships, wedged between the chart table and a counter in the galley or some other solid structure. We've done this on two boats now, so I know it works.

Such an arrangement has a couple of distinct advantages. First and foremost, the seating area typically absorbs between 20 and 24 inches (500–600 mm) of horizontal space, which can be incorporated into the chart table. Suddenly, a 30-inch (760 mm) table is expanded to more than 50 inches (1.25 m). It is then realistic to take 12 or more of those inches (300 mm), with a few others squeezed from elsewhere, to form a narrow but serviceable wet locker alongside the chart table—and still have a 36-inch (910 mm) or larger chart table. This is how we got our wet locker, which, on our boat, is in fact 15 inches (380 mm) across its face; the chart table is 42 inches wide by 30 inches (1.07 by 0.76 m) deep.

Second, eliminating the seating arrangement at the chart table frees up a tremendous amount of storage space beneath the table. I don't like rolled up charts but, on the other hand, I don't want them with a mass of creases in them. The stand-up chart table allows a series of large, relatively shallow chart drawers to be installed beneath the table; 2 inches (50 mm) is a good depth (each drawer holds more than fifty charts). We have three chart drawers, in addition to a substantial chart and miscellaneous storage area beneath the tabletop itself, which lifts on a hinge. We also have a couple of deeper drawers for larger objects (e.g., camera and computer equipment).

The stand-up chart table is flat rather than the sloped arrangement in most navigation stations, which is a benefit, not a disadvantage. As the displayed-chart area gets larger, you need to be able to bend over the top as you pore over the charts. This is the standard arrangement on large ships. On our boat, the chart table is opposite the galley, and it becomes another substantial work surface when preparing more elaborate meals

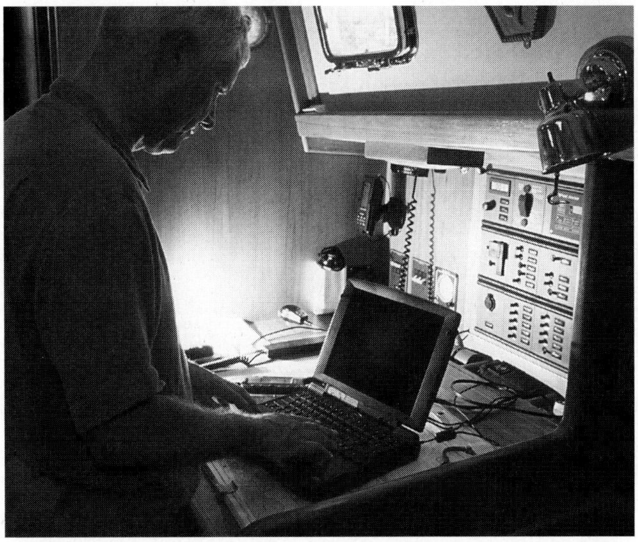

The one disadvantage to this arrangement is that it makes working at the laptop for extended periods uncomfortable—instead, I use the saloon table.

Any modern navigation station needs a significant area of fascia panels, with adequate depth behind them to mount electrical panels and electronics. The backs of all electrical panels need to be readily accessible, and easy to work on. Note the beautiful wiring harness—the only loose wires are ones I installed!

in harbor. The height of the table should be approximately 35 to 36 inches (890–910 mm), including the fiddle rail (if it is higher, it will be difficult to get satisfactorily positioned above the charts). The space between the stand-up table and the structure against which the navigator braces in a seaway (in our case, a galley counter) should be between 21 and 24 inches (530–600 mm), but no more.

The principal disadvantages to the loss of the navigator's seat that results from a stand-up chart table are that it is not comfortable for working on a laptop for any length of time and it also makes life somewhat uncomfortable for those ham-radio aficionados who spend a lot of time on the radio. However, if necessary, both of these operations can be moved to the saloon, where sufficient seating is available.

Whatever the chart-table arrangement, the tabletop needs a modest fiddle rail, which—as with all fiddle rails—needs a vertical interior face. As mentioned previously, stowage is also needed for the "tools of the trade." I like an open box along the back of the chart table with partitions to house pencils, dividers, parallel rules, a hand-bearing compass, a magnifying glass, a flashlight, and other odds and ends; these essential tools are always accessible but do not get thrown about the boat.

A 36-inch (910 mm) or larger chart table results in plenty of fascia space behind it in which to mount electronic equipment and electrical distribution panels. Given the rate at which electronic equipment changes these days, this panel should be designed for easy removal and replacement, which will lower the carpentry bills when modifications are made in the future. In addition, the section of the fascia panel that is devoted to the distribution panels should hinge open such that full access is provided to all the wiring, which facilitates troubleshooting and upgrades.

Careful thought must be given to the placement of gear in the navigation station, particularly radios (which contain magnets) and compasses (which don't like magnets). Ideally, there

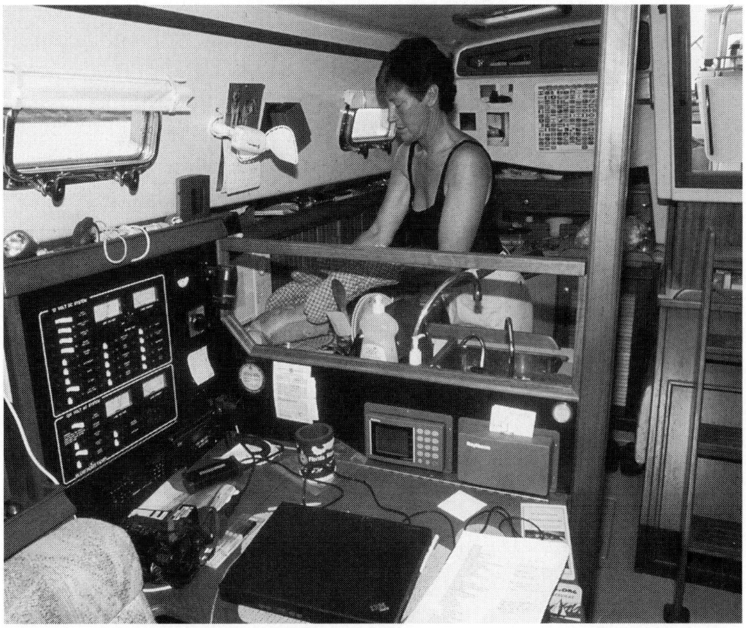

Here's another navigation station approach that can work well. The navigation station is tacked onto the saloon so that the saloon seating does double duty as a navigator's seat (in another variation seen on some boats, the end of the quarter berth provides seating). The owners have added a splashguard (clear plastic) between the galley and navigation station—a very sensible precautionary move.

is also a small bookcase either in the navigation station or immediately adjacent to it for tide tables, light lists, cruising guides, and sight-reduction tables if sextant navigation is practiced. If the bookshelf is aligned athwartships, an upper fiddle (in the middle of the books) will not be required, which makes it easier to get the books in and out; however, if it is aligned fore and aft, the fiddle is necessary.

Nighttime lighting is very important and frequently inadequate. A dim light is essential for protecting night vision but of no use whatsoever if it is not strong enough to properly illuminate a chart (this is frequently the case with the red lights installed in navigation stations), causing the navigator to turn on a flashlight or a regular light. The other aspect of lighting is to contain it, as far as possible, within the navigation station so that at night the navigator does not disturb any crew sleeping on the sea berths in the saloon. Generally speaking, a strategically placed bulkhead or partial bulkhead is necessary to contain the light.

Lastly, of course, the navigation station needs total protection from the weather, regardless of the conditions outside. To ensure this, I believe there should be no opening portlights (we slipped up on this with our new boat) and no overhead hatches.

Stowing Charts

It is almost impossible to stow charts flat and unfolded on a cruising boat; therefore, the choice is to either fold and stow them flat or roll them. I much prefer to fold them. It is exceedingly aggravating in rough weather to have to deal with a chart that has been rolled. You can't hold its edges down with weights because they will get thrown off—and you may be hanging on with one hand, leaving only one hand free to flatten the chart and do your chart work. If charts are rolled, they should be rolled with the chart on the outside (not on the inside, as is typically done); when they are laid out flat, this at least stops the edges from constantly trying to roll into the center.

When folding charts, you want as few creases as possible. It is best to fold them to fit the chart table so that you don't have to add extra creases when you use them. Ideally, the chart table is big enough to handle most charts with a single fold in them (they should be folded with the chart on the outside). In this case, the ideal is to also have chart drawers with the same dimensions under the chart table. Few boats have them, although the space under a lifting chart-table lid is generally the same size. However, this area becomes the repository for all kinds of junk, making it difficult to get charts in and out and to store them without damage. On our old boat, we ended up storing most of our charts under the berth cushions, which worked quite well.

Wet Locker

There was a time when a wet locker was more or less a given on a cruising boat; however, the more interior designers have come to dominate the accommodation spaces, the less importance has been given to the wet locker. On most modern boats below 45 feet (14 m), little more than lip service is given to the concept.

Our Pacific Seacraft 40 is somewhat better. The "base" boat has a sealed fiberglass locker with a drain in the head compartment, but this is barely big enough to stuff in two sets of foul-weather gear. As mentioned previously, we replaced it with a full-length, self-draining locker that is large enough to hold four sets of foul-weather gear (hanging up, not stuffed) with our sea boots; there are also hooks for harnesses. Behind the foul-weather clothing, we have a couple of shelves, one of which holds six life jackets and the other an abandon-ship bag. It is an excellent arrangement that I recommend to anybody.

Whatever the arrangement, decent stowage for all this gear is a frequently overlooked must.

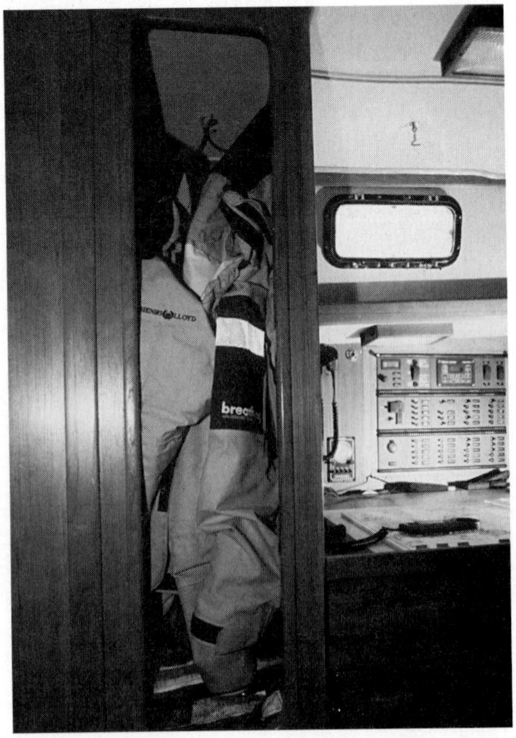

Nada's wet locker.

Galley

The galley is one of the most heavily utilized spaces on a boat, with the most complex functions. As such, it is probably the most difficult space to design, requiring a lot of thought. First and foremost is its location (close to the center of motion), with a shape that enables the cook to brace himself or herself when preparing food, cooking, and cleaning up. This frees up both hands for the work in progress. Of course, the galley should also be next to the locations where food is served (i.e., the saloon and cockpit)—but also out of the way of traffic flow through the boat (set off to one side).

Traditionally, the galley has been to port (and the navigation station to starboard) so that the galley is on the leeward side and, therefore, easier to use when the boat is hove to on the starboard tack (which technically gives the boat the right-of-way in most situations). However, little attention is given to this detail today, and it does not really seem to be of much importance (our current galley is on the starboard side).

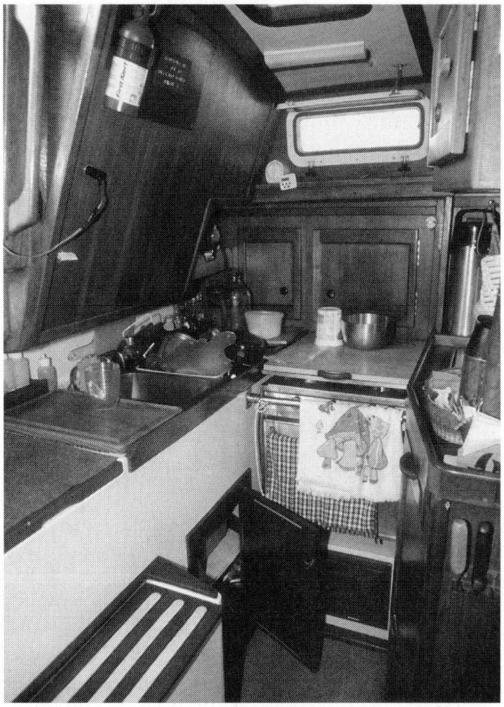

A compact galley on a 40-foot center-cockpit boat (compare it to the previous two galleys). The space absorbed by the aft cabin has to come from somewhere; in this case, it is squeezed out of the galley and other parts of the accommodations. These are the kinds of trade-offs that make choosing a boat for any particular purpose such a challenging and complicated process.

Typically, galleys are L-shaped, U-shaped, G-shaped, or—on center-cockpit boats—set up in a straight line alongside the cockpit. In Europe, it is currently fashionable to place galleys on the hull side opposite the saloon. Regardless of how well this works in calm water, it is a very poor location at sea in rough weather. There is very little support for the cook; it is quite a trek from the galley to the cockpit; at night, galley use thoroughly disturbs anyone using the saloon settees as sea berths; and it is much more difficult to get the cooking heat and odors out of the boat.

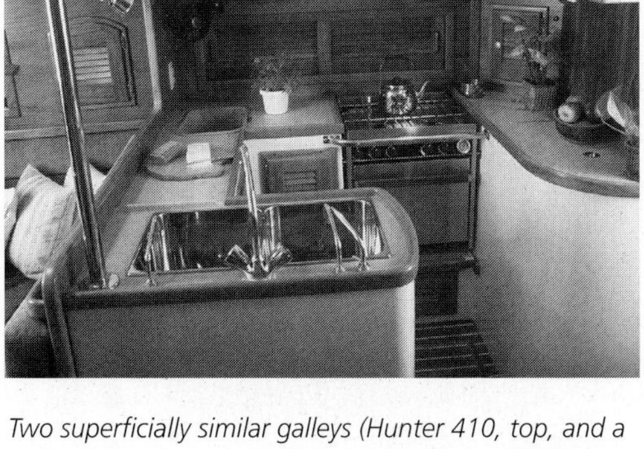

Two superficially similar galleys (Hunter 410, top, and a Pacific Seacraft 40, above) with significant differences. The Hunter is more open, which gives it a more spacious feel but provides significantly less support at sea. In a similar vein, the Hunter has a much lower backsplash between the galley and the saloon. The Pacific Seacraft has its sinks on the centerline; those on the Hunter are well offset. The Pacific Seacraft has more places for the cook to get wedged in when well heeled. The two are optimized for different conditions. (Courtesy Hunter Marine and Pacific Seacraft)

A popular layout in Europe—the galley is opposite the saloon. The center settee provides a fair amount of support to the cook. (Courtesy Bavaria Yachts)

There is no question in my mind that the optimum shape is the wraparound G shape (i.e., a U with the end partially closed off). This puts the maximum possible amount of work surface in range with the minimum amount of movement, and provides the most opportunities to get wedged in. Furthermore, if the stove is installed opposite the opening into the galley, the cook can get supported in a position that is offset from the stove—and out of the firing line if pots get thrown off the stove in rough weather. The sinks should be placed in a section of countertop offset from the stove so that if the boat lurches when someone is washing dishes, he or she will not be thrown into hot pots on the stove.

When cooking, there are times when it is simply not possible to keep "one hand for the boat," in which case any sudden movement can send the cook flying. To prevent this, it is helpful to have a relatively narrow space in front of the stove with a solid support, especially for the feet, on the other side against which the cook can brace himself or herself (this is another reason why the G-shaped galley works so well). Otherwise, a "butt strap" should be installed, and there should always be a safety bar in front of the stove (which is also a convenient place to hang dish towels).

Generally, stoves are on the hull side, which makes them difficult to use when the boat is well heeled (it is difficult to get firmly braced in front of the stove and the cook is in the firing line of flying pots). A good case can be made for placing the stove against an athwartships bulkhead: it is easier to maintain footing in front of the stove, and any sudden lurches throw the cook to one side or the other, but not into the stove. Gimbaling is difficult (but not impossible) with an athwartships mount, but generally is not necessary—even at extreme angles of heel, pots stay in place as long as the stove has good potholders (*fiddle clamps*). Pots cannot be filled to the top and cakes baked in the oven will come out somewhat lopsided, but this is no great problem. We had such an arrangement on our last boat (an extremely tender boat that frequently heeled 30 degrees) and found it to be perfectly satisfactory.

With stoves mounted on the hull side, the gimbals are installed in a fore and aft direction to minimize the chance of flying pots when the boat is heeled. Stoves are frequently installed with cabinets behind them that have insufficient clearance between the stovetop and the cabinet. On one tack, the stove swings under the cabinet, at which time either the pots get knocked off or they jam under the counter. In addition, when the boat is heeled, the stove may obstruct cabinet doors (when well-heeled on starboard tack, we cannot open our front-opening icebox door). Given the compact space of a galley, this may be unavoidable even with careful design.

We've used diesel, kerosene, alcohol, and propane stoves. For ease of use, there's no question in our opinion that a three- or four- burner gimbaled propane stove with a grill and oven is

Ideally, the cook can get wedged in to one side of the stove. Note how the back of the stove is swinging under the cabinet, a common arrangement. If the clearance is inadequate here (as it often is), it is possible for pots to slip under the cabinet and then jam when the stove levels up.

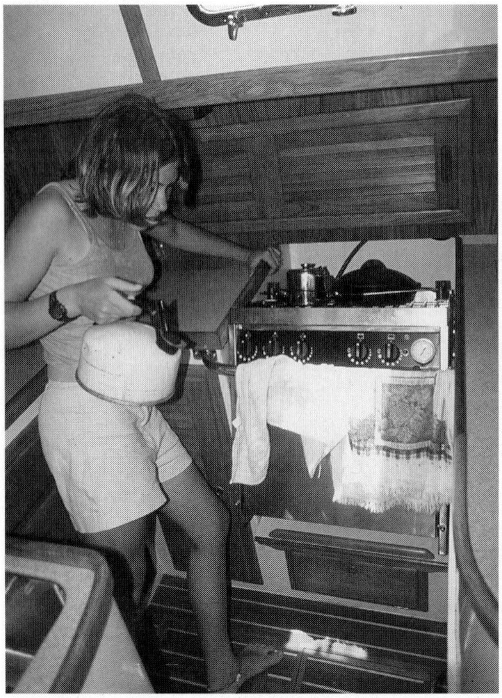

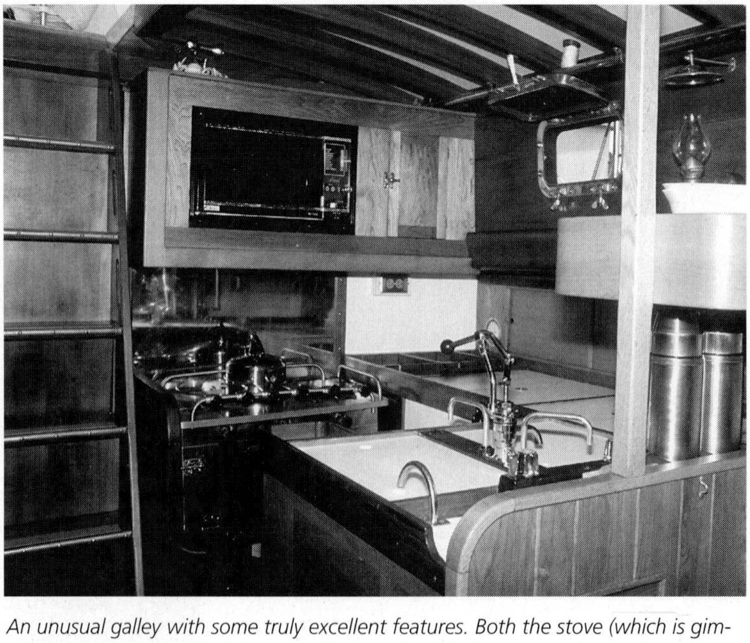

An unusual galley with some truly excellent features. Both the stove (which is gimbaled) and the sinks are mounted athwartships, which is the optimum way to install them. (Courtesy J. E. Paris)

Thought needs to be given to what (if anything) will be obstructed by a gimbaled stove at maximum heel angles. Here, the stove fouls the lower door on the refrigerator.

the way to go. For safety, the installation must include a remotely controlled solenoid at the gas bottles, with the operating switch next to the stove but not behind it—in other words, the switch must be located where it can be accessed without reaching over the top of the stove. (Propane installations are discussed in more detail in chapter 5.)

In addition to the propane stove, the modern cruising boat has a microwave oven run off an inverter. Once considered a luxury, this is nowadays verging on the edge of being "essential" equipment. I highly recommend it, as long as the DC system can support the load (see chapter 4). When the conditions get particularly nasty, we eat lots of baked potatoes and popcorn. When not in use for cooking, the microwave makes a handy breadbox, so the space is not wasted.

A microwave oven should be installed athwartships so that its door opening faces forward or aft. If this is not done, it will be almost impossible to use it without accidents on one tack.

Any stove, especially in the tropics, needs a vent, fan, or opening hatch directly above it to remove unwanted heat from the boat. To act as an extractor when anchored out, a hatch should open on its forward rather than aft edge.

Counter space is always at a premium. For a given area, it is maximized with the G-shaped galley. As a general rule-of-thumb, counters should be 32 to 36 inches high and 18 inches wide (810–910 by 460 mm), and preferably incorporate a 3- by 3-inch (75 by 75 mm) kick space at the base (which makes it more comfortable to stand at the counter). Nowadays, almost all quality boatbuilders use Corian for countertops, which is far superior to either wood or plastic laminates. Better yet is a molded Corian countertop that includes a splash rail at the back, thereby eliminating a joint which, no matter how well sealed, eventually is always penetrated and stained.

Counter space can be increased with a removable lid for the stove, as long as the lid has a secure stowage space that does not interfere with the gimbaling of the stove at any likely angle of heel (the lid generally gets stowed under or behind the stove, where it often gets in the way). Another handy item is a chopping board that fits inside a sink rim so that it does not slide around when in use. The chopping board also needs its own stowage space.

I've seen some incredibly dumb sinks on boats, including round shallow bowls and regular household sinks (i.e., wide and shallow). What is needed is something deep (9 in./230 mm is about right) and just large enough to take a dinner plate or good-sized saucepan. This minimizes both water consumption and spills.

On all modern boats, there will be pressurized cold water and probably pressurized hot water as well. (A hot-water heater is one of those things that used to be considered a luxury, but which is now considered close to essential; I agree.) In addition, there should always be a manual cold-water pump. There is nothing more frustrating than having the electric water pump go down and not being able to get water

A nice chopping block that fits inside the top of the sinks.

out of the tanks. Many boats incorporate a manual saltwater supply in the galley, but I am of two minds about this. Sooner or later, the salt corrodes the sinks and associated fittings (for this reason, chrome-plated, plastic drain fittings are preferable to stainless steel). With adequate tankage, maybe a watermaker, and proper water management, I see no great need for salt water in the galley—we omitted it on our newest boat and haven't missed it.

Dishwashing is greatly simplified with two sinks—one for washing and one for rinsing and/or draining. The sinks need to be close to the centerline to ensure that they are above the waterline and drain properly at any angle of heel. Sinks mounted off the centerline, especially those on the hull side, almost always end up below the waterline and flood when well heeled on one tack. To prevent this, either the seacock must be closed at sea—putting the sinks out of commission—or a diaphragm-type pump (manual or electric) must be added to the discharge (these pumps include check valves that block any back flow). Alternatively, the sinks can be drained to a gray-water tank (see chapter 5). All three approaches have undesirable complications: it is much better to situate the sinks where they can't flood.

Just as with the galley stove, it is easier to maintain your footing in front of the sinks when the boat is well heeled and/or pounding if the sinks are mounted athwartships rather than fore and aft.

Ideally, sinks are installed under the countertop—this makes cleanup that much easier (however, if the sink ever needs to be replaced, it may prove to be a major construction job).

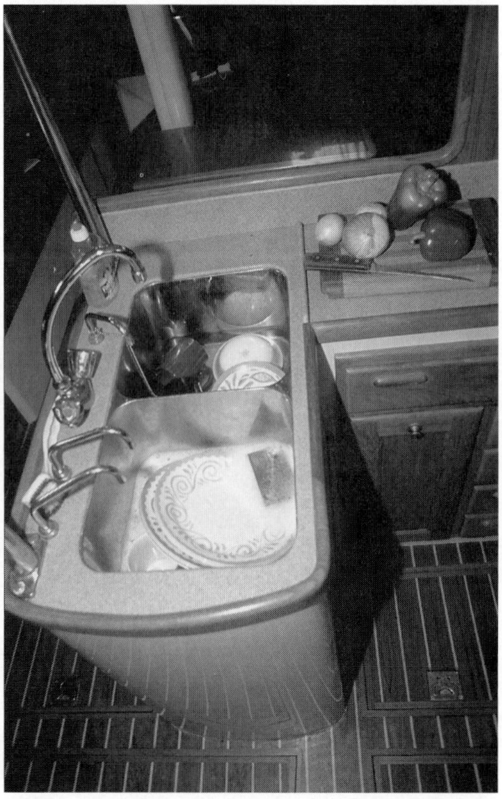

The optimum arrangement for dishwashing is a set of deep double sinks on the centerline, which—if possible—should be mounted athwartships (these are not) because this makes it easier to maintain your footing when heeled.

Drains should not incorporate U-traps (except when a gray-water tank is used), because they cause nasty smells, but they should contain a couple of bends before connecting to a through-hull. If this is not done, when the boat is pounding into head seas, salt water may be driven up the drainpipe, spraying out of the sink drains.

Ideally, the sinks are installed *below* the Corian countertop rather than over the top of it. There is then no lip around the sinks, which makes it much easier to clean up the surrounding area. A sealed fiddle rail should be located between the sink area and the rest of the countertop to keep dishwashing water from migrating to other parts of the galley.

Dishware and cutlery stowage should be readily accessible and within easy reach of the sink. The ideal arrangement is a plate rack suspended over the sinks; wet dishes can drip-dry into the sinks, eliminating the need for towel-drying. However, the rack must be designed so it's not a head-banger on either tack. On our old boat, we also had a self-draining cutlery box that worked well. Another way to store dishware is to mark out the diameters of the plates and bowls on the base of a locker, drill a series of holes, and push in pegs. If plates of a different size are substituted later, it is easy enough to drill another set of holes and move the pegs. Whatever arrangement is used, thought must be given to getting the dishware in and out as easily as possible—you will do it half a dozen times a day. Cups and mugs are best stowed on hooks in a convenient location.

The primary galley stowage is beneath the countertops. The longer the cruises, the more important it becomes to think through storage

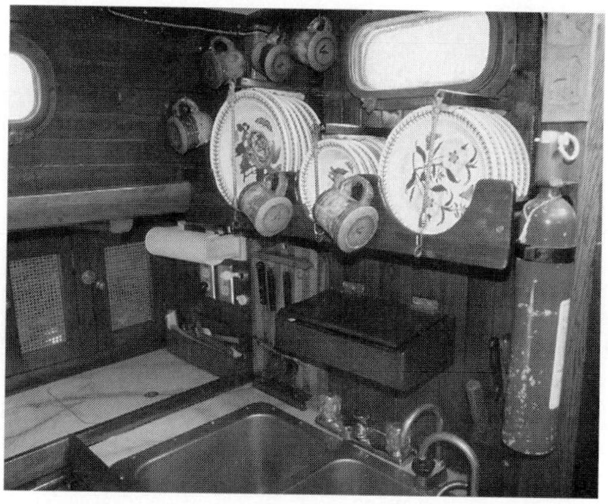

Cutlery (in the box) and dishware stowage above the sinks on our old boat. Despite having china, in 40,000 miles of cruising, we broke just a couple of bowls.

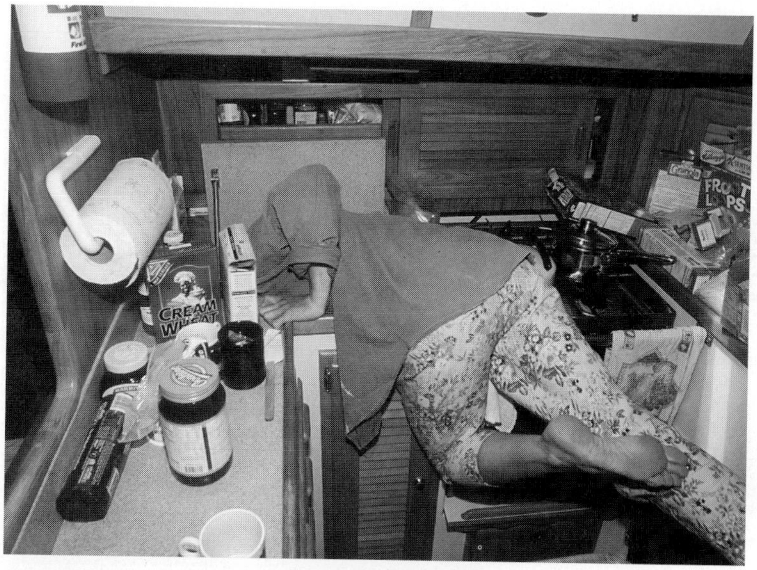

There is almost always some space that is difficult to access! Careful design minimizes these kinds of contortions.

Cutlery stowage on Nada. *This is the drawer with two drawer pulls—it is difficult to open single-handedly, which is annoying in rough conditions.*

A large Thermos flask to be filled with hot water for drinks and packaged soups prior to a passage.

details. Whereas a weekend cruiser can get by with a couple of pots and pans, the long-term voyager will need a range of pots of different sizes, frying pans, cake pans, bread pans, pizza trays, and roasting pans. These take up a lot of space—all need a home. Pots are easier to stow and less likely to get overturned when in use if they have small handles on each side, rather than the typical long one that sticks out.

Most cruisers want a teakettle with a whistle for making instant coffee, tea, or soup. Although not popular with Americans, a pressure cooker is a truly worthwhile investment on a cruising boat: it cooks faster, saves fuel, puts less heat into the cabin, does not spill, can be used for canning, and is an excellent container in which to take hot food in the dinghy if going to a potluck supper. It does, however, use a lot of storage space.

Another substantial item is a trash bin. It has to be accessible and designed so that it stays open by itself (so that, for example, when dumping stuff off a chopping board, you can hold the board with one hand and wipe it clean with the other). It needs to be a suitable size to accommodate a trash bag with a mechanism for holding the bag in place. It should be located so that pieces of food that miss the bag can be easily cleaned up, rather than becoming lodged in inaccessible joiner work and smelling after a few days.

As with so much else associated with galley design, most of the previous discussion is self-evident yet rarely achieved. I have long since concluded that naval architects and boatbuilders never use their galleys!

In terms of the rest of the stowage space, every galley needs a small cabinet or rack for

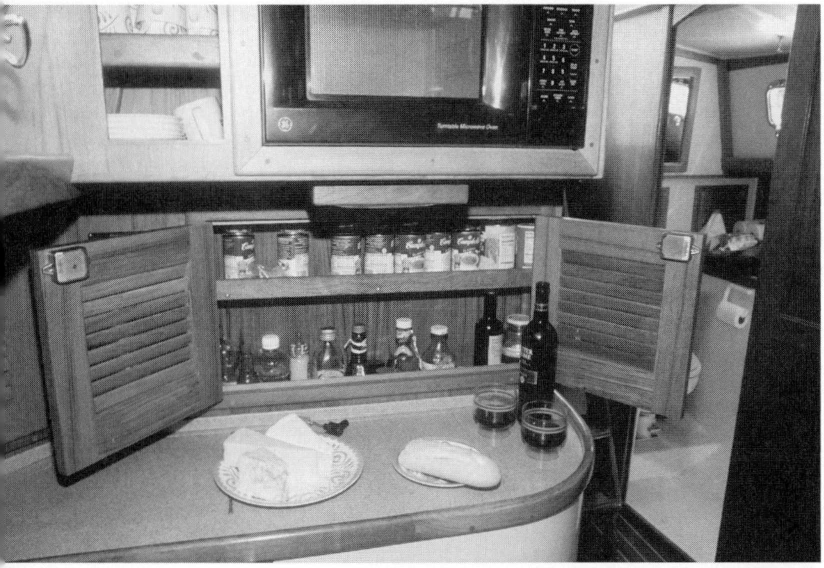

Top: *Spice cupboard.* Right: *Hinged-out trash bin. It would work better if there were some means of keeping it open (it has to be held with one hand) and some way of attaching trash bags. It is these nit-picky details that ultimately determine the functionality of a galley.*

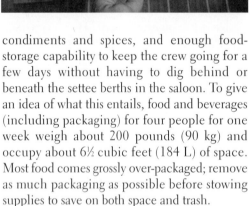

Top: *Under the sink.* Bottom: *Paper towels and toilet paper are bulky items—sometimes difficult to find in foreign ports—which can require a lot of stowage space on longer cruises.*

condiments and spices, and enough food-storage capability to keep the crew going for a few days without having to dig behind or beneath the settee berths in the saloon. To give an idea of what this entails, food and beverages (including packaging) for four people for one week weigh about 200 pounds (90 kg) and occupy about 6½ cubic feet (184 L) of space. Most food comes grossly over-packaged; remove as much packaging as possible before stowing supplies to save on both space and trash.

Storage space is also needed for potholders and dish towels, plastic storage bags, trash bags, cling wrap, and aluminum foil, as well as for cleaning supplies, which are usually stored beneath the sinks near the sink-drain seacock. However, note that in Europe, it is now illegal to put a shelf in any locker containing a seacock; with or without shelves, the seacock must be easily accessible. Mounting space is needed for a paper-towel holder and a fire extinguisher.

Locker doors need to be large enough to allow full access to the locker, which means that shelves must all be fiddled to stop things from falling out when the doors are opened. The shelves should be divided by fiddle rails to reduce the size of individual spaces. This minimizes the distance that objects can slide when the boat is rolling around and the locker is half empty. We fabricate more or less bulletproof stowage for glass jars by cutting up 4- to 6-inch (100–150 mm) lengths of Schedule 20 (i.e., thin wall) PVC sewer vent pipe (3–4 in./75–100 mm in diameter), standing the pieces on end, and gluing them together edge to edge using PVC pipe cement. This forms "honeycombs" of various sizes to fit in the locker; in all our cruising, we have never had a broken jar.

We have found that unrefrigerated fresh fruit and many vegetables are best stored in a small hammock. There is unlikely to be the space in which to swing the hammock in the galley, but there is almost always room above the saloon table, suspended from a couple of small pad eyes. The hammock is easy to reach but not in anyone's way. It is an enticing sight

A small hammock is a great way to store fruit and some vegetables.

when stuffed full of mangoes, pineapples, bananas, and other tropical delights! Potatoes, carrots, cabbages, onions, and other less aesthetically pleasing foodstuffs get relegated to a locker beneath the cabinsole. Although we have not tried them, we are told that the "green" bags now available for long-term storage of fruits and vegetables really do work, delaying the onset of ripening by weeks.

The galley on all but the most spartan boats nowadays includes a refrigerator and freezer. (The systems implications of this are discussed in chapter 4.) It is important that the boxes for the refrigerator and freezer are located somewhere other than up against an engine-room bulkhead. Not only are engines hot when they are running, but also the engine compartment remains hot for hours afterwards, significantly increasing the "heat loading" on any adjacent icebox and, thus, the energy requirements of the system. Iceboxes also should not be adjacent to stoves for the same reason, although the heat loading will be much less than that of an engine compartment.

Neither a refrigerator nor a freezer need be particularly large; I think a 3-cubic-foot (85 L) freezer (after allowing for the space occupied by cold plates) and a 5-cubic-foot (142 L) refrigerator are adequate for all but long-term, long-distance cruising; even then, not much more is needed (a larger freezer volume is handy). This flies in the face of the modern trend, which is to try and replicate the volume of the refrigerator and freezer at home. I'd rather see that space put into insulation, holding down the energy demands of the system.

I've always been an advocate of top-opening boxes to minimize heat entry into the icebox and the consequent energy losses when putting things in and taking them out, but I have come to believe that the added convenience of a properly sealed, front-opening door is more than worth the small energy cost. Our Pacific Seacraft 40 has a shelf midway down both the freezer box and the refrigerator. Both boxes have top-opening lids; the refrigerator also has a front-opening door in its lower half. To access the lower half of the freezer, the upper half has to be unloaded. This is acceptable, inasmuch as access is rarely needed. To access the top of the refrigerator (where we keep mostly fresh produce), the lid is lifted. To access the lower half (where we keep mostly cold drinks), the door is opened. This is a vast improvement over having to unload half the refrigerator every time we want a drink—I would recommend it to anybody, as long as the door is properly insulated and sealed. As mentioned previously, icebox lids should be secured in place so that they will not fly off in a knockdown.

Lighting is particularly important in the galley. It needs to be considered from two per-

Left: *A front-opening door—as long as it is properly insulated and sealed—is a tremendous aid in accessing the lower half of a refrigerator.* Bottom: *Freezer (on the left) and refrigerator boxes. Neither need be too big—it is better to put any unnecessary volume into more insulation.*

spectives: (1) ensuring good visibility over countertops and the stove and into the iceboxes, and (2) ensuring that the galley can be used at night with minimum disruption to anyone sleeping on the sea berths in the saloon. We had Pacific Seacraft extend the bulkhead between the galley and the saloon. Combined with a red light tucked away under the side deck close to the stove, this makes the galley serviceable with minimal disruption to those in the saloon. The bulkhead is also a convenient place on which to mount an instantly accessible fire extinguisher and a paper-towel holder.

Thought should be given to the business of cleaning a galley. Flat, shiny surfaces such as gelcoated fiberglass, Corian, varnished plywood bulkheads, Formica-coated cabinsides, and an easily cleaned cabin liner are recommended. Tightly fitting seams that will not trap dirt or moisture are needed between the various surfaces. I particularly like the combination of Pacific Seacraft's fiberglass liner—which extends from the cabinsole to the countertops and includes the icebox exterior, the stove surround, and all the cabinet bases in a one-piece molding—with its Corian countertops and teak cabinets. The fiberglass is exceptionally easy to clean—including all around the stove, which can be a bear to get at on many boats— while the other surfaces obviate any excessive "plastic" feel.

Following is a series of miscellaneous but useful thoughts on galleys and their contents:

- Melamine, which is almost unbreakable, is the best all-around material for dishes. Melamine dishes can be bought with nonskid inserts on the base; however, the inserts are not microwavable—if a microwave is onboard, it's better to buy dishes without inserts. You can always stop dishes from sliding around by laying a damp dish towel on the countertop.
- Corelle (from Corning) is also nearly indestructible, is microwavable, and has a less plastic feel than Melamine. However, on occasion, it will shatter explosively into thousands of minute, razor-sharp shards that fly all over the boat. We found out the hard way.
- Whatever dishware is bought, bowls should have straight rather than curved sides. Curved ones slide over the top of all but the highest fiddles, launching the bowl into space.
- Cups are inherently unstable and have no place on a boat; instead, flat-bottomed mugs should be used.
- A couple of gimbaled mugholders alongside the stove are great for minimizing spills when making hot drinks in rough weather.
- Cutlery (especially knives) should not have heavy handles. Otherwise, things will be forever falling off plates.
- All cutlery should be made from good quality stainless steel; cheap cutlery will rust.
- Sharp knives are best stowed in a knife block rather than loose in a drawer.
- It is useful to have a "grab box" fastened at the back of a countertop for larger utensils, a corkscrew and bottle opener, a can opener, maybe a flat cheese grater, and miscellaneous junk such as old wine-bottle corks.
- Square plastic containers stow much better than round ones.

Saloon

The saloon on most cruising boats (even quite large ones) serves a dual function: it is not only the entertainment and dining center in port, but often also the most comfortable place to sack out on passage. To fulfill the latter function, certain features are desirable.

Clearly, the settees must be long enough to be used as berths. This means—ideally—6 feet, 6 inches (2 m), although it is possible to get by with a little less. Given a couple of settee berths on a "typical mom-and-pop" cruising boat, it is fair to assume that one of the partners will be under 6 feet (1.8 m) tall, allowing some space to be stolen from one of the berths for another purpose.

For sleeping purposes, settees need to be at least 21 inches wide (excluding any seatback cushions) and preferably 24 inches (530–600 mm). However, they can taper at both ends if hull curvature makes this necessary. To be used for seating, the settees should have dimensions similar to the ideal cockpit seat; that is, the top of the seat cushions should be 15 to 18 inches (380–460 mm) above the cabinsole, the seatbacks should be 15 to 20 inches (380–510 mm) high, and the backs should be angled outboard about 15 degrees. The settee berths on our Pacific Seacraft 40 have vertical seatbacks and, as a result, are uncomfortable; this is one of the few things we would change on our boat. Given the expense of modifying the angle of the seatbacks, we will fit tapered seatback cushions (i.e., wider at the base than at the top) that work just as well.

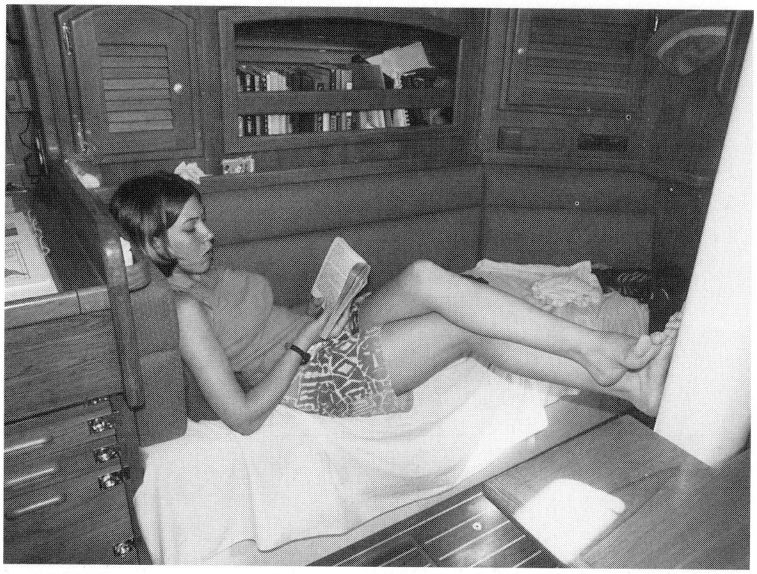

The saloon seating on Nada has vertical seatbacks that are somewhat uncomfortable (above) as opposed to seatbacks angled at 10 to 15 degrees (right).

With an 18-inch (460 mm) seat height, there should be a minimum of 16 inches (410 mm) of legroom in front of the settee. If the height is lowered, more legroom is needed—for example, 20 inches (510 mm) with a 16-inch (410 mm) seat height and 24 inches (600 mm) if the seat is dropped down to 12 inches (300 mm; not desirable). If settees are set under side decks, they need a minimum of 33 inches (840 mm) of headroom above the level of the seat cushions. There should always be at least 6 feet, 2 inches (1.9 m) of headroom under deck beams or the cabin liner in the standing parts of the boat. Speaking for myself, the one thing I cannot tolerate is having to stoop—with two slipped discs, it rapidly gives me a serious backache.

If settees are to be used as sea berths, it is no good having curved seating in the saloon; in fact, anything other than square corners at either end of a settee can result in discomfort when lying down. Something that is not so obvious is that the settees need to be parallel to—or at least more or less so—the centerline of the boat. If not, one end of the settee/berth will be higher on one tack and the other end higher on the other tack, creating problems for anyone trying to sleep. It is ironic that on many contemporary boats, the larger the boat, the more the interior designers are given free reign and the less functional the interior at sea: currently, a number of "cruising" boats more than 40 feet (12 m) in length are being built without a single decent sea berth!

The privacy of crew members camped out in the saloon is enhanced if there are at least partial deck-level bulkheads at the forward ends

It is ironic that with many contemporary designs, boats below 40 feet have compact saloons with plenty of handholds and excellent sea berths (note the straight settees, parallel to the centerline, in the middle photo), whereas . . . above 40 feet, the interior designers are given a freer hand, the spaces open out, the curves start to creep in, and we end up with an interior that is less functional at sea (bottom). (Both photos Courtesy Bavaria Yachts)

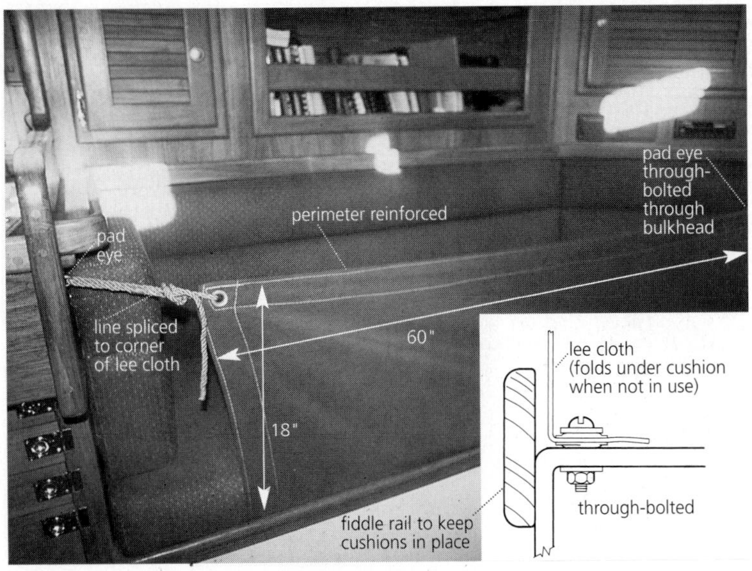

Lee cloths are easier to stow and more comfortable than lee boards.

of the navigation station and galley, shading the saloon from the lighting in those areas. Such bulkheads fly in the face of the tendency to build modern boats with open interiors that look great at boat shows, but are maybe not so functional at sea. More bulkheads and smaller spaces create opportunities for many handholds and minimize the distance a body can be thrown. On the other hand, there is no doubt that the effect can be somewhat claustrophobic by modern standards, and providing adequate ventilation can be difficult.

To be of use as berths when hard on the wind or rolling down wind, the settee berths need *lee cloths* or boards. My preference is for lee cloths because they are more comfortable and easier to stow—they can be fastened along the outside of the berth, under the edge of the cushion, and simply pushed under the cushion when not in use. The attachment needs to be strong and the lee cloth needs a reinforced perimeter. A couple of lines from each of the top corners to pad eyes on adjacent bulkheads is all that is needed to hold them up. In the tropics, lee cloths preferably should be made of an open-mesh or breathable fabric. Dimensions that have worked well for us are given in the photo at left. On those boats where the saloon table drops to form a double berth, it is generally best to treat it as a single at sea, with the leeing cloth/board along the outside of the settee (i.e., in the middle of the double berth).

Cushions are almost always made of foam. For comfort, 4 to 5 inches (100–125 mm) is a desirable thickness, although it is possible to get away with 3 inches (75 mm) where dimensions are tight. There is a substantial difference in quality between foams. Lightweight, low-cost foams dent easily, retain the dents, and do not hold up well. Given the hard usage on a boat, it pays to buy an expensive, high-density foam.

This foam is open-celled; that is, it wicks up moisture like a sponge. In particular, warm bodies on a mattress that is resting on a cool surface cause moisture to condense out in the foam. If the foam is not allowed to breathe, it—and the fabrics around it—soon become mildewed. If the foam is allowed to breathe, the moisture evaporates without doing any harm.

Salt water is altogether different. Once salt is in the foam, it is almost impossible to flush it out. Because salt is *hygroscopic* (moisture-attracting), the cushion remains permanently damp, and mildew is sure to follow. There's not much that can be done about this except replace the foam.

So we have contradictory needs for cushion covers: a watertight fabric to prevent saltwater entry and a breathable fabric to let freshwater evaporate. I suppose the ultimate cover is Gore-Tex, if it can be afforded. More practically, if something fairly watertight is used on the top

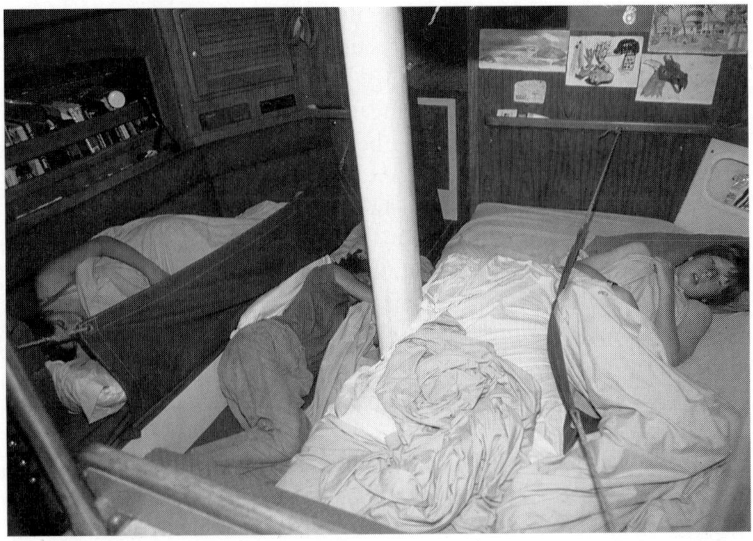

Even on a seakindly boat, in rough weather the fo'c's'le will be just about uninhabitable, so the crew will be driven to camp out in the saloon. Very often, the most comfortable berth is on the saloon floor, padded with the seatback cushions. In this photo, Nada *is heeled 20 degrees and pounding into the seas; nevertheless, some sleep is possible.*

and exposed sides, and something breathable is used on the bottom and hidden sides, and the cushion is allowed to air out (to remove any residual moisture) before the boat is put into storage, the cushions should be fine. Given the likely spills, body oils, and dirty feet with which cushions get contaminated, whatever is used for the top fabric should be tough, stain-resistant, and easily cleaned—not crushed velour, of which Dave Gerr writes: "A particularly nice feature . . . is its ability to retain salt. Once this stuff gets a good dousing of seawater, it's permapickled!" (*Nature of Boats*). Fabrics are coded according to how they can be cleaned. For boat use, the fabric should be classified as "W" or "WS," which means it can be cleaned, or scrubbed if necessary, with water and mild detergents, as opposed to "X" or "S" fabrics, which require more specialized cleaning.

Seat cushions have to be held in place at all likely angles of heel. Horizontal cushions need nothing more than a low fiddle rail around the edge of the settee base. Seatback cushions generally require some form of a snap fastener or Velcro. Whatever is done, it is important to have easy access to any lockers—it is very frustrating if all the cushions have to be removed every time you want to get into a locker.

The saloon table needs to be large enough to comfortably seat the regular crew and a couple of guests; depending on the size of boat, this generally means four to six people. However, this should not be at the expense of blocking the passageway forward, especially if the head compartment is forward of the saloon. An L-shaped settee around two sides of the table, rather than the more common U shape, makes it easier for people to slide in and out of the settee seating, but provides fewer seats for a given space.

The table often has an additional leaf that stretches across the center aisle to a settee berth on the other side. If it can be stowed on the table when not in use without getting in the way (I have seen some fabulously inventive ideas for this), so much the better. If not, secure stowage for the extra leaf must be found—it is a large and relatively heavy chunk of wood that must be properly restrained. We found the perfect spot for ours on the inside face of the settee berth.

Once a boat gets up around 13 feet (4 m) in beam, it is generally possible to work in an offset saloon table with a center seat or settee. This provides a good-sized table and excellent seating without obstructing the passage forward.

Most saloon tables have fiddle rails. These are not needed in harbor, are uncomfortable under the wrists, and trap dirt. If fitted, they should be removable. We don't have any at all and have never missed them. On our last boat, over a period of fifteen years, we progressed through a series of stages from a fully gimbaled table with fiddles to an ungimbaled table without fiddles, so we have experimented with the full range of options!

Sooner or later, someone will be thrown into the table. Both it and its supporting structure must be built to take the shock load. In particular, if the pedestal is not firmly bolted on at both ends, it can get ripped out of the cabinsole or the table can get ripped off of it.

If the saloon settee berth is designed to convert into a double berth, the ideal approach is to have the table drop down, preferably on gas-filled cylinders so that it is easy to put up again. The next-best option is to have the table fold out of the way and have an insert take its place (but then the insert needs stowing when not in use). The worst approach is one in which the table has to be removed and stowed elsewhere.

Top: *When it comes to entertaining, the more space the better! It helps to have the saloon table offset so that it does not obstruct passage through the boat.* Above: *Once the beam gets up around 13 feet (4 m), it is possible to have a center settee without obstructing the passage forward. Note that with all this seating there is not a single sea berth because of the curves! (Courtesy Beneteau USA)*

The modern saloon is also the boat's entertainment center. Dramatic changes have taken place in this area in the last decade, and not all boats have caught up. More and more cruisers have a TV and VCR—and now a DVD—in addition to a tape deck, CD player, and radio. The TV needs a location that makes it comfortable to view. Secure stowage is also needed for videotapes, cassette tapes, and CDs. Just as with navigation and communication electronics, given the rate at which entertainment electronics are changing, it makes sense to install the equipment in an easily removed and replaced fascia panel so that future upgrades will not result in expensive carpentry bills.

The saloon also includes one or more bookcases, which should provide secure stowage for books up to 11 inches high and 8½ inches deep (280 by 215 mm), which is the largest standard U.S. book size—and which will enable you to stow *Boatowner's Mechanical and Electrical Manual* and this book! (Note that A4 size—used in Europe—is 11⅝ in. high by 8¼ in./295 by 210 mm.) Most books, especially paperbacks, fit into a 9-inch-high by 6-inch-deep (230 by 150 mm) shelf. To restrain books, there should be a *low* fiddle at the base of each shelf (if it is too high, the books may jam on the shelf or overhead above before they come out). This is all that is needed on athwartships bookshelves (i.e., those in which the shelves run across the boat).

Bookshelves installed fore and aft (usually along the sides of the saloon) need an additional restraint about halfway up the books. We have used shock (bungee) cord and removable wooden battens. Both work well, although the shock cord can only be run over relatively short spans (up to 2 ft./600 mm)—beyond this, when pounding to windward, the weight of the books on the windward side can overwhelm it and then they all fly out. We completely buried our son one time when he was about six months old! The advantage of shock cord is that it can be held down to extract a book, whereas the batten must be taken out.

Forecabins, Quarter Berths, and Aft Cabins

Forecabins, quarter berths, and aft cabins are primarily sleeping areas on most boats, with less complex functions than other spaces and fewer detailed design considerations. However, it is worth noting the following:

- Any space used regularly for sleeping should have at least one area with standing headroom, not just to give a visual sense of space, but also for the practical reason that it's difficult to dress and undress without it.
- Where berths extend under the cockpit or deck, with limited headroom, it is important to maintain sufficient headroom over the end of the berth to climb in and out without banging your head, and to be able to sit up comfortably in bed to read. Also required is a suitable surface as a backrest and an appropriately located reading light (the lights often are set too low).
- All berths should have fans.
- A double berth needs to be at least 44 inches (1.1 m) wide. It can taper at both the head (to 40 in./1 m) and the foot (to 22 in./560 mm), but anything smaller is

All cabins need at least one area in which there is standing headroom with sufficient space to dress and undress.

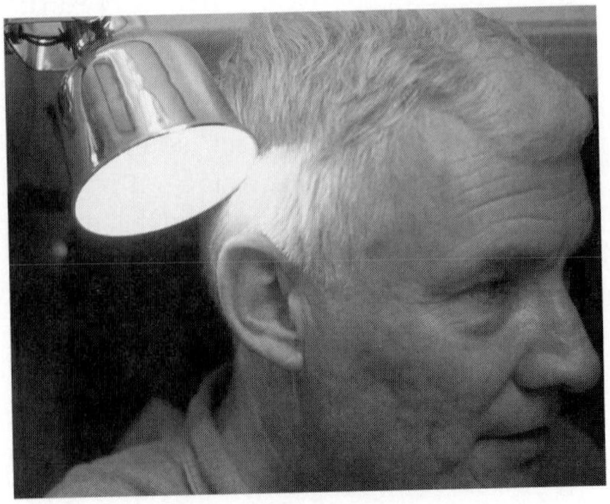

It is quite remarkable how few boats have a comfortable, properly lit spot for reading in bed. This light needs to be raised at least 6 inches (150 mm).

going to get awfully cozy. (Because of its canoe stern, the quarter berth on our Pacific Seacraft 40 is too pinched at the feet to be considered a decent double berth.)

- Sleeping bags are fine for short cruises, but longer-term cruisers will want regular sheets and blankets. It is easier to make beds if you can work around them (i.e., "island"-type berths), but then there is little to stop you from falling out when heeled. For awkward-to-access berth cushions, it may be worthwhile to tailor fitted sheets so that once put on, they stay in place (but then they will only fit that particular berth).
- If storage spaces beneath berths require the cushions to be lifted for access, it is much easier if the cushions are divided up. However, then you may find a hard spot where they join or, worse yet, the cushions may slide apart. Careful placement of the seams, with adequate fiddle rails around the berth, will keep you comfortable.
- There is often a shortage of locker space in a forecabin. This can be remedied by incorporating the largely dead space under the side decks into drop-front cabinets. These are more useful than shelves because most of the volume in these areas is up under the deck where there is the maximum hull flare.

It is also worth commenting on the increasingly popular use of transverse bunks, particularly in aft cabins. These enable unbelievably large double berths to be slipped into many boats, but at the price of being somewhat unusable at sea. When the boat is heeled, it is difficult to sleep lengthwise in the berth (you will slide down in a heap to the lower side); even if you can, every time the boat is tacked, you will need to turn around. These berths should be considered harbor berths.

Head Compartment

There are two schools of thought concerning the head compartment. One is that it gets used for very little time, so it doesn't deserve much space; the other is that the functions performed are important and deserve to be accomplished with a little comfort, so they should be given the necessary space. I must say I subscribe to the latter school. It is one thing to have the toilet double up as a shower seat and to bang your elbows every time you turn around on a one- or two-week cruise once a year; it is quite another to put up with the frustrations this entails over a longer period.

I see no point in adding a second head until boats get well above 45 feet (14 m) in length. The second head adds substantially to the cost and complexity of a boat, as well as the maintenance, while conferring little benefit. In practice, a second head frequently gets used as additional storage space. It is much better to consolidate this space into a single head of a decent size.

With this philosophy in mind, I am a strong believer in a separate shower stall large enough to comfortably shower (at least 26 by 26 in./660 by 660 mm), preferably with a seat sandwiched between bulkheads because then it is much easier to shower at sea (if space is at a premium, the seat can be hinged). When sitting, it is handy to have a handheld showerhead on a hose; at other times, it is nice to have the showerhead rigidly mounted. Several brackets are available that make these dual functions possible, as long as the showerhead has a hose long enough for it to be clipped into the rigid fixture.

In addition to sufficient space, other features that are important are grab handles, a shower pan that drains on both tacks (this generally requires two drains, one at either side of the pan—it is rarely done), and an effective means of closing off the shower stall so that the towels and toilet paper in the head compartment don't get soggy. Nonskid in the shower pan is preferable to a grate, which just gets slimy and is hard to clean. At sea, the shower stall is a convenient dumping ground for wet and soggy clothes, and maybe vomit-soaked towels, when the crew does not feel up to dealing with them.

If the sill of the shower stall is raised (by as much as 10 in./250 mm), the stall also can be used to wash clothes, which is much easier than trying to do laundry in buckets (the cruiser's traditional approach). The raised lip eliminates the likelihood of water migrating out of the shower pan in even the worst conditions at sea. On our last boat, we constructed a raised, contoured shower pan that made a small but comfortable bathtub. It was great for soaking a sore back on those occasions when water was not an issue.

Shower curtains invariably get mildewed. Not much can be done about this other than to fit a rigid door, but they are almost always constructed with glass panels that I consider an unacceptable hazard. If a curtain is used, the rod should be set an inch or so below the cabintop so that it can be used to hang up a damp

Nada has a separate shower stall, large enough to comfortably shower, with a raised sill so that it can do double duty for washing clothes.

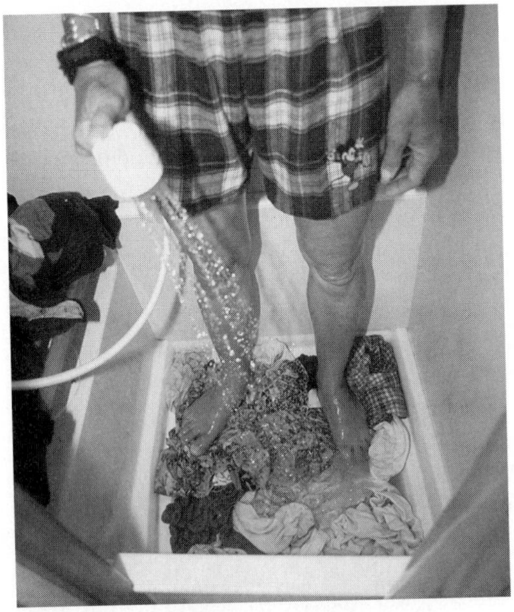

A separate shower stall is a great place to hang wet foul-weather gear, especially if the boat has no foul-weather locker. This only works well if the shower compartment is close to the companionway.

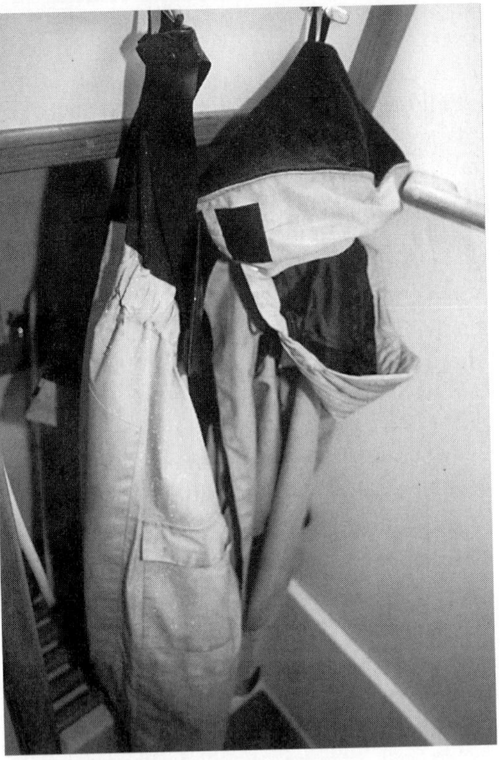

towel (there's never enough towel-hanging space on a boat).

The rest of the head compartment needs to be large enough to put on and take off foul-weather gear (this requires an unobstructed space of approximately 26 by 26 in./660 by 660 mm), but should be no larger—you don't want it to be large enough to bounce around in. Of course, it needs strategically placed handholds. When struggling with clothes, people sometimes lose their balance; therefore, the door to the head compartment and anything else that is likely to be fallen into must be strong enough to take the shocks. The Pacific Seacraft 40 has a beautifully built folding door on which the lock tears loose and the door flies open when anyone crashes into it! Head doors should open inward so that if the boat gets knocked down while someone is in there and gear gets thrown against the door, there is no risk of getting trapped in the compartment.

A toilet should be installed so that when using it, you are facing in a fore and aft direction, sandwiched between adjacent fore and aft bulkheads. This way, you are supported on both tacks. If the toilet is mounted the other way, sooner or later you will get thrown off it with your pants around your ankles! The closer the toilet is to the centerline, the better in terms of minimizing motion. Even so, when someone is sitting on it with the boat well heeled, the seat hinges will be severely stressed and, therefore, need to be built to take the load. (As far as I know, none are. To prevent damage, it is advisable to attach guide blocks that fit inside the toilet-bowl rim to the underside of the seat.)

Ideally, the toilet will be set on a raised dais such that a man can kneel comfortably on the edge of it and be at the right height to urinate into the bowl without mishaps! The dais is an excellent location for a holding tank, which minimizes the tubing runs and associated odors.

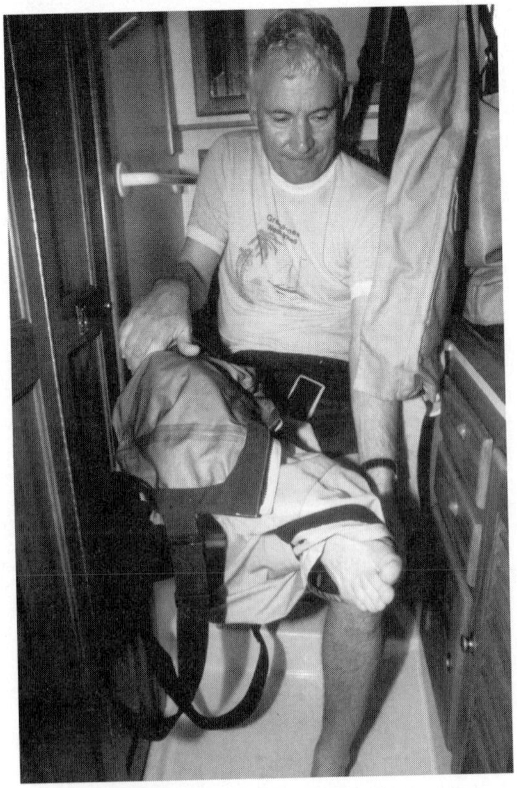

The head compartment needs to be large enough to struggle into and out of foul-weather gear.

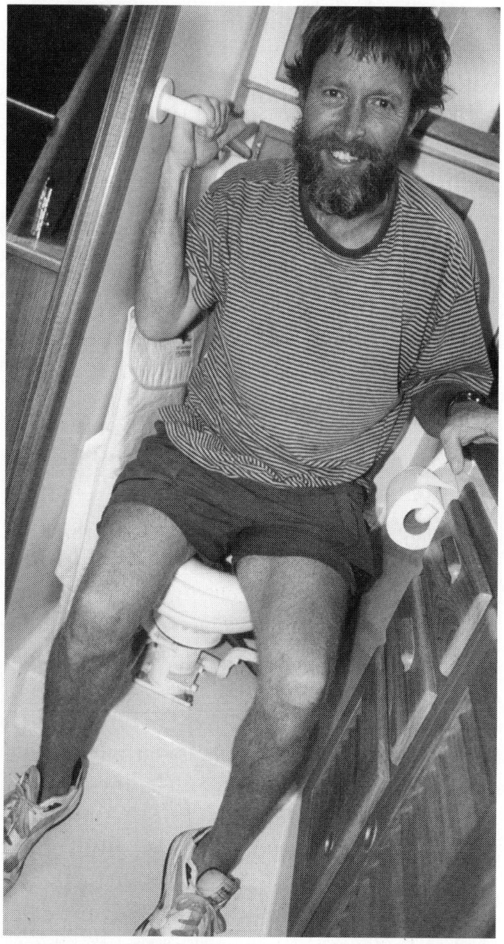

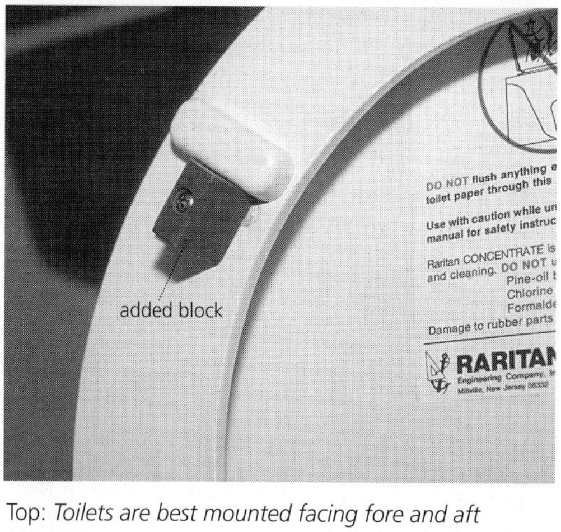

Top: *Toilets are best mounted facing fore and aft between solid bulkheads. I asked my friend Mark to drop his pants to make this shot more authentic, but he declined (I also couldn't get Terrie to pose naked in the shower)!* Bottom: *The hinges on toilet seats are generally inadequate to take the stresses when the boat is well heeled. A toilet installed facing fore and aft minimizes these stresses by providing excellent body support. An additional measure is to install a block on each side of the underside of the toilet seat so that the blocks fit just inside the toilet-bowl rim when the seat is down, stopping the seat from slipping sideways.*

With a little luck, raising the toilet will put the rim of the bowl above the at-rest waterline (if the toilet is on the centerline, the rim will also be above the heeled waterline), eliminating the risk of siphoning the suction water into the toilet and sinking the boat (which has sunk many boats including—almost—our last one).

If the toilet rim is not above the waterline at all angles of heel, either the suction hose must have a vented loop (a siphon break) to prevent flooding the toilet when not in use or the suction line needs a positive shut-off valve next to the toilet. This valve must be closed whenever the toilet is not in use. For added security, both a vented loop and a valve can be installed. A vented loop is also needed on the discharge side of the toilet to prevent back-siphoning. The vented loop invariably emits odors, which can be dealt with by either hiding it in a cabinet that is rarely opened (although the loop must still be accessible for maintenance) or plumbing a hose from the valve on the vented loop to an overboard through-hull. If the latter is done, the through-hull must be above the waterline at all angles of heel; otherwise, it defeats the purpose of the vented loop.

The toilet must be designed and installed so that the entire surrounding area can be readily flushed down and sanitized. By far, the optimum situation is a head compartment constructed from a one-piece fiberglass liner that can be hosed down without damaging any woodwork or other surfaces.

It is very difficult to create a toilet installation that does not work up a fair old smell when the boat is closed up. The odors may then permeate the rest of the boat and prove extremely difficult to eliminate. Following are the keys to minimizing odors:

- Use only the best quality sanitation hose; it is expensive, but worth it.
- Make sure that both ends of all hoses are seated on a correctly sized end fitting and clamped with quality stainless steel hose clamps (for more about hose clamps, see chapter 1).
- Keep the hose runs as short as possible.
- Do not leave standing sewage in the hoses. In particular, if the discharge hose slopes up from the toilet (which it almost always does), keep the section of hose that remains full as short as possible—and always sufficiently flush the toilet to clear it of effluent.
- Provide an excellent means of ventilation that can be left open when the boat is

unattended; for example, a hatch over the shower stall so that any rain that gets in does no harm.

Holding tanks need a good-sized vent (U.S. regulations require a minimum internal diameter of 9/16 in./14 mm; European regulations require 1½ in./38 mm) that has no liquid-trapping U-bends. The tank should have a level indicator to avoid overfilling it. There are many stories of holding tanks on U.S.-built boats (which have the smaller vents) being overfilled, resulting in plugged vents—when the toilets are flushed again, the tanks burst. That's one mess I hope I *never* have to clean up! The other thing that can happen if a vent gets plugged is the tank collapses when pumped out at dockside (SeaLand manufactures a "Tanksaver" vent that, when installed on a tank, prevents the tank from imploding).

On a cruising boat, there should always be a mechanism for pumping out the holding tank at sea. I prefer a manual pump (easier to fix if it goes wrong), but an electric macerator pump also works well. With such a setup, after a spell in a harbor with no pump-out facilities, you can take the boat out to sea and pump and flush the holding tank yourself.

It should be understood that a separation of several feet is required between the head inlet and discharge, with the inlet forward of the discharge. Better yet is to put seawater intakes on one side of the boat and discharges on the other. The inlet needs to be set well down in the hull so that it does not suck air at any angle of heel—it is amazing how many toilets cannot be flushed on one tack or the other!

All hoses on the discharge side of any toilet system must be readily accessible and easy to remove. Over time, they will slowly plug with calcium. Eventually, they will need taking off and either beating on a dock to break up the calcium or replacing. This day can be postponed (maybe indefinitely) by treating the head with a shot of vinegar or dilute muriatic acid every month (both dissolve the calcium), followed by a squirt of baby oil to lubricate the rubber parts in the toilet.

The sink in a head compartment usually ends up set in a counter under the side deck. This has a major drawback: on one tack when the boat is well heeled, the sink will probably be below the waterline. If it discharges directly overboard, as most do, and the seacock on the drain is open, water will flood into the boat. To prevent this, the seacock has to be closed on the relevant tack.

The risk of flooding can be eliminated by adding a diaphragm-type pump to the discharge (electric or manual), but doing so unduly complicates the plumbing. Where possible (it depends on the toilet), I like to plumb the sink discharge into the toilet and use the toilet to pump the waste overboard. The sinks are invariably small, so the volumes of liquid involved are also quite small—a few strokes of the toilet pump are all that is needed. To my mind, the added security is well worth the little bit of effort, plus it gets rid of a below-the-waterline through-hull. Another way to prevent back flooding is to plumb the sink to a gray-water tank (see chapter 5).

A head compartment should include red nighttime lighting so that if whoever is on watch has to use it, it does not destroy his or her night vision.

CONCLUSION

When it comes to cruising-boat accommodations, it is attention to the myriad details such as those described above that distinguish the serious cruising boat from its less well-conceived cousins. At the end of the day, if the details are right, the boat will not only be functional in the most extreme conditions, but also eminently comfortable lying to the hook in a placid anchorage. If a boat can rise to both occasions, the formula truly can be said to be right.

ADDENDUM: CARBON MONOXIDE POISONING

All forms of heating (with the exception of electric heat) and the running of all engines involve the burning of a fuel in which oxygen from the air is converted to carbon dioxide. If the air that is consumed comes from cabin spaces, oxygen levels may be steadily depleted, which in itself is potentially hazardous; if combustion is at all incomplete (as it almost always is), carbon monoxide rather than carbon dioxide is created. Carbon monoxide can be deadly.

Carbon monoxide poisoning is the leading cause of death by poisoning in the United States (I don't have the equivalent statistics for Europe). Boatowners are particularly at risk because of the small volumes of air in a boat; the fact that boats are necessarily tightly sealed (to keep the water out); and within these small, sealed spaces, there are generally several appliances capable of producing carbon monoxide (e.g., the galley stove, the main engine, any AC generator, any nonelectric cabin heater, and a gas-powered water heater).

Carbon monoxide is odorless, colorless, tasteless, and more or less the same weight as air (just a little lighter), causing it to hang around. When present, it is absorbed by the lungs. It enters the bloodstream, reacts with blood hemoglobin to replace critical oxygen molecules, and forms something known as *carboxyhemoglobin (COHb)*. The body is deprived of oxygen.

Carbon monoxide binds to blood hemoglobin far more readily than does oxygen in the air, even if oxygen is available. *The mere presence of carbon monoxide is dangerous, with or without plenty of fresh air.* Once attached to the hemoglobin, carbon monoxide is relatively stable. As a result, very low levels can progressively poison people. As little as 0.2 percent carbon monoxide in the air binds up red blood cells (i.e., forms carboxyhemoglobin) at the rate of 1 percent (of the body's red blood cells) per minute. If the person is working, the rate can double to more than 2 percent per minute. Within 45 minutes, the red blood cells are 75 percent taken up with carbon monoxide, resulting in a lethal concentration. At the other end of the scale, high doses of carbon monoxide can be lethal in a matter of minutes (see table below). If a victim escapes death, there may still be permanent brain damage.

Typically, carbon monoxide poisoning produces a range of symptoms, beginning with watery and itchy eyes and a flushed appearance, and progressing to an inability to think coherently, headaches, drowsiness, nausea, dizziness, fatigue, vomiting, collapse, coma, and death. Many of the early symptoms are similar to those of seasickness, flu, or food poisoning— people suffering from carbon monoxide poisoning frequently fail to recognize the problem. The poisoning creeps up on people; it dulls the senses, causing a failure to recognize the problem, which enables the fatal punch to be delivered. *Seaworthy* magazine (BoatU.S., Alexandria, Virginia) quotes an example of a family of three on a large sailboat with a washing machine and a propane-fueled water heater. The washing machine malfunctioned, causing the water heater to stay lit. The heater consumed the air in the cabin and then produced carbon monoxide. The son fell, tried to get up, and fell again. Hearing the loud thump, the wife got up, was overcome, and collapsed.

Effects of Carbon Monoxide

AMOUNT, IN PPM	SYMPTOMS
200	slight headache within 2 to 3 hours
400	frontal headache within 1 to 2 hours
800	dizziness, nausea, and convulsions within 45 minutes; insensible within 2 hours
1,600	headache, dizziness, and nausea within 20 minutes; death within 60 minutes
3,200	headache, dizziness, and nausea in 5 to 10 minutes; death within 30 minutes
6,400	headache and dizziness in 1 to 2 minutes; death in less than 15 minutes
12,800	death in less than 3 minutes

Data courtesy Fireboy/Xintex

ppm = parts per million carbon monoxide in the atmosphere; 1,000 ppm = 0.1% carbon monoxide in the atmosphere

"My husband saw me go down and thought I had fainted because of seeing our son (whose lip was bleeding). He stepped over me to assist our son and, looking back, he noticed the cat lying beside me. It clicked—I might faint, but not the cat. He picked up the phone and pushed a preprogrammed button to call our neighbors and let them know we were in trouble. He tried to pull us out, but he too was going down." All three were rescued by the local fire department and regained consciousness. What is particularly interesting about this case is that the boat's hatches were wide open with a 10-knot wind blowing outside. The question is: What can be done to prevent such incidents?

All engine exhausts contain carbon monoxide; *gasoline engines produce much higher levels than diesels.* (For this reason, Onan, a major manufacturer of generators, stopped selling gasoline-powered AC generators in the marine market and conducted an extensive advertising campaign warning of the dangers of carbon monoxide poisoning.) Cold, poorly tuned, and overloaded engines produce more carbon monoxide than warm, properly tuned, and load-matched engines. Therefore, the first task to minimize the potential for carbon monoxide formation is to ensure that the engine is properly matched to its task and, as far as possible, will be operated as designed. However, there is always the cruising sailor who uses the engine more for battery-charging at anchor than for propulsion, which results in the engine running long, under-loaded hours below its designed temperature. There is not much that can be done about this, other than to make sure that the carbon monoxide gets out of the boat.

Of particular importance is an exhaust system that is gas-tight to the hull. This requires adequate support and strain relief built into the exhaust system (to absorb engine vibration without failure), the use of galvanically compatible materials (to lessen corrosion—for more on this, see chapter 4), proper marine exhaust hose in wet exhaust systems (see chapter 5), and double-clamping of all hose connections with *all* stainless steel hose clamps (see chapter 1). Each engine on a boat must have its own dedicated exhaust system, with nothing T'ed into this exhaust (with the sole exception of a cooling-water injection line on a water-cooled exhaust).

Regardless of the quality of the initial exhaust installation, *an exhaust system is a regular maintenance item.* Leaking gasoline exhausts on boats are far and above the leading cause of death from carbon monoxide poisoning. At least annually, the entire system should be inspected for any signs of corrosion or leaks. Warning signs include discoloration or stains around joints, water leaks, rusting around the screws on hose clamps, corrosion of the manifold discharge elbow on water-cooled engines, and carbon buildup within the exhaust (which increases the back pressure and the probability of leaks). To check a discharge elbow, the exhaust hose must be removed, which also enables a check to be made for carbon buildup.

When it comes to fuel-burning appliances, which are almost always in the accommodation spaces, certain other protective measures need to be taken. The optimum situation is one in which the appliance has its combustion air ducted in from outside the accommodation spaces, with combustion occurring inside a sealed chamber that exhausts through an external flue. Such an appliance cannot cause oxygen depletion, nor can it emit carbon monoxide directly into accommodation spaces. There are cabin heaters built in this manner (e.g., by Wallas Marin and Ardic, distributed in the U.S. by Scan Marine, of Seattle, Washington), although most are not. The combustion chambers need to be checked as part of a regular maintenance schedule to make sure there is no damage or corrosion. Both inlet and exhaust ducting should be inspected to make sure that it is gas-tight.

The next best option in terms of safety is represented by those appliances that, although they use cabin air for combustion, confine the combustion process to a chamber that is vented via an external flue. In general, as long as there is no back draft down the flue (which is a matter of proper design, although there may be situations in which the airflow off sails causes back-drafting with almost any flue), and as long as the flue is not obstructed (primarily a matter of design; in particular, ensuring that the flue cannot trap water), and even in a situation of oxygen depletion and carbon monoxide formation, the carbon monoxide will be vented outside accommodation spaces. Periodic maintenance includes inspection of the combustion chamber and flue (an improperly vented flue killed tennis star Vitas Gerulaitas).

I say "in general" because the nature of ventilation on boats is such that it is sometimes possible to create a *negative* pressure (with respect to the outside air pressure) inside the boat. This occurs, for example, when the hatches, ventilators, openings, and canvas structures (e.g., dodgers) are lined up with respect to the wind such that air is being sucked out of the cabin rather than driven in (this is not hard to do). In such a situation, any unsealed combustion chamber, whether vented outside the cabin or not, has the potential to feed carbon monoxide into the boat. Over the years, this has been the cause of a number of deaths.

Safety can be enhanced by the addition of an *oxygen-depletion sensor* wired so that it automatically cuts off the fuel supply to an appliance in the event of oxygen depletion. (Oxygen-depletion sensors have been used for years by Force 10, a Canadian stove manufacturer. Its sensors shut down the fuel supply if the oxygen in the combustion air falls below 95 percent of normal.) However, in a situation where carbon monoxide is produced but there is still a good airflow through the cabin, the oxygen-depletion sensor does nothing to protect the occupants.

Then there are all those appliances that not only draw their air from accommodation spaces, but also exhaust the combustion gases into the same atmosphere, including all nonelectric galley stoves and some cabin heaters and water heaters. These appliances are potentially the most lethal of all; boatowners should think long and hard before using them. It is essential to understand that these appliances should (1) *never* be used when unattended or when occupants are sleeping (carbon monoxide is especially dangerous when people are sleeping because victims don't feel any side effects and may simply not wake up); and (2) *only* be used in conjunction with adequate ventilation; specifically, galley stoves should not be used for cabin heat. (This is easier said than done if you have no other source of cabin heat; I confess that we use our stove occasionally, but never unattended and never when sleeping).

This leaves certain potentially lethal situations that cannot be eliminated at the equipment design and installation phases. Examples include running an engine with the boat against a dockside so that the exhaust is deflected back into accommodation spaces, and running the engine when rafted to another boat, with similar results. The operation of AC generators in these situations is of particular concern, especially if run at night when people are sleeping, which is commonly done to keep an air conditioner going. And then there is always our cruising sailor who decides to save the wear and tear on the main engine when battery-charging at anchor by buying an inexpensive portable gasoline generator, which is placed on the foredeck for an hour a day and run with the exhaust blowing down the hatch! These kinds of hazards can be mitigated only through a process of public education and the use of effective carbon monoxide alarms.

Carbon Monoxide Alarms

The design of an effective carbon monoxide alarm is a complicated business. This is because relatively low levels of carbon monoxide over an extended period can be just as lethal as high doses over a short period. Conversely, relatively high levels over a short period are not necessarily harmful. It is not unusual for there to be such relatively high levels from time to time, but for these to rapidly disperse (e.g., when an engine is first cranked at dockside, or a boat in proximity to other boats fires up its engine or generator, with the exhaust drifting across the other boats). If an alarm is designed simply to respond to a given threshold level of carbon monoxide, the threshold must be set at a very low level to protect against long-term low-level contamination. This causes the alarm to be triggered by any short-term rise in carbon monoxide levels, resulting in many nuisance alarms (which almost invariably results in the boat operator disconnecting or bypassing the alarm, effectively making it useless). If, on the other hand, an alarm is set to respond to a higher threshold, it provides no protection against low levels of carbon monoxide contamination sustained over long periods.

An effective carbon monoxide alarm must have the ability to track carbon monoxide levels over time and to monitor in some way the likely impact on carboxyhemoglobin levels. This is a complicated process, particularly because carbon monoxide concentrations, when present, almost certainly are constantly changing. Newer devices incorporate microprocessors that enable them to keep track of time-weighted carbon monoxide concentrations (known as *time-weighted averaging*) and to calculate the corresponding carboxyhemoglobin levels in the blood. This would filter out most nuisance alarms if it were not for the fact that it has proved extremely difficult to find affordable sensors that react solely to carbon monoxide (as opposed to styrene emissions from fiberglass and all kinds of other chemicals commonly found on boats). As a result, carbon monoxide alarms still sometimes falsely alarm.

In addition to sensitivity issues, once many carbon monoxide alarms go off, they may continue to sound for some time, which can be annoying to the boat operator who has already dealt with the carbon monoxide problem. The alarms continue to sound because the internal microprocessor is simulating the carboxyhemoglobin levels in the blood. As discussed previously, once attached to hemoglobin, carbon monoxide is relatively stable. Even if the atmosphere is cleared of all carbon monoxide (or other contaminants), the simulated carboxyhemoglobin levels will reduce only slowly; it may take fifteen or twenty minutes for an alarm to clear.

Newer alarms (in the United States) include a pushbutton that can be used to silence an alarm for up to six minutes, after which—if the device still records dangerous levels of carbon monoxide—it will start alarming again, with no additional override allowed. In combination with the kinds of adjustments to microprocessor logic already mentioned, this should resolve many past problems.

Beyond the manufacturing issues with carbon monoxide detectors, there are installation issues. Ideally, there will be a detector in all sleeping areas. Detectors need to be located away from corners and other dead-air areas that do not experience the natural circulation of air through the boat; on the other hand, they should not be in the airstream from ventilators or air-conditioning ducts that may dilute any concentrations of carbon monoxide in a cabin. In other words, a detector needs to be located somewhere where it receives a representative sample of air. The location must be protected from spray and out of the way of likely physical interference. To minimize nuisance alarms, it should also be at least 5 feet (1.5 m) from any galley stove (particularly alcohol stoves because alcohol is another substance that triggers most alarms). The detector should be at eye level to make it easy to monitor.

The detector should be wired so that any time the boat's batteries are in service (i.e., the battery-isolation switch is "on"), the detector is in service. Some boat manufacturers go a step farther and wire carbon monoxide detectors to the *battery side* of the isolation switch so that they are in continuous service. The one disadvantage to this is the fact that older detectors draw 90 to 240 milliamps at 12 volts, which amounts to a 2- to 6-amp-hour battery drain per day. This may be enough to kill a Group 27 battery (approximately 100-amp-hour capacity) stone dead over a period of a month if the boat is not in use and not plugged into shore power or other charging sources. However, some detectors now draw as little as 60 milliamps, which amounts to less than 1.5 amp-hours a day in continuous use, or 40 amp-hours a month. Given a moderately powerful DC system (see chapter 4), it is practicable to permanently leave these on.

The bottom line is that although carbon monoxide alarms have had something of a bad reputation in the past for nuisance alarming, the latest generation has resolved most of the problems. *IMPORTANT: Carbon monoxide alarms should be standard equipment on any boat with a gasoline engine (including a portable AC generator), any boat that leaves an AC generator (diesel or gasoline) running when crew members are sleeping, and any boat that has a heating system that operates when people are sleeping.* They are recommended on all other cruising boats.

CHAPTER FOUR

ELECTRICAL SYSTEMS

A beautiful panel installation using first-class materials. This should give excellent service for the life of the boat. (Courtesy Saga Marine)

"I have lost all patience with electricity. It requires far too much time to keep an extensive electrical system operating. . . . The most miserable man in the world is the owner of an electrical miscarriage who can't get a drink, flush the head, raise the anchor, hoist the sails, or even see what he is doing because his batteries are flat and he can't start his generator."

BOB GRIFFITH, *Blue Water*

It is in the area of the electrical systems and electrical equipment that the modern cruising sailboat differs most from its forebears. The transformation that has taken place has brought with it a radical improvement in creature comforts and ease of boat handling, but with a high price tag in terms of initial cost, complexity, and—in many cases—frustrating breakdowns.

At the time that Bob Griffith wrote the book quoted previously (1979), most of the defining features of a modern cruising boat's electrical system—deep-cycle batteries, a high-output alternator, a multistep voltage regulator, a systems monitor, a DC to AC inverter, and so on—had been introduced to the marine market but were going through their teething stages, resulting in many "electrical miscarriages." Two decades later, the basic parameters for a powerful and effective electrical system are mostly unchanged, but the technology has improved. When this improved technology is coupled with the vast body of experience accumulated over the years, it is possible to put together reliable, trouble-free systems that would be the envy of any cruising sailor from earlier times.

Nevertheless, there are still numerous electrical miscarriages on cruising boats. In fact, it is probably true to say that among longer-term cruisers, more frustration is caused by electrical

A typical electrical miscarriage resulting from twenty years of add-ons and modifications to what was an inadequate electrical system in the first place! All the usual suspects—undersized bus bars, improperly sized and untinned cables, no labeling of wires, inadequate over-current protection, and corrosion—are present. In addition to the fact that this electrical system functions poorly, it is a fire risk. The owner should bite the bullet, rip it out, and start again. Compare this photo to the one at top.

problems (and more time and money is spent trying to resolve them) than by any other gear and equipment failures. In contrast, I can honestly say that once they were set up correctly (there are often some initial problems), our systems have operated almost flawlessly and with minimal maintenance for years—we get the benefits of modern technology without the drawbacks. This chapter is all about how to establish similarly successful systems.

However, before getting into the nitty-gritty of the systems, I must reiterate that a significant number of the systems that go into modern boats are not necessary for the effective functioning of the boat—they are there simply for comfort and convenience. In what follows, as in chapters 1 through 3, I look at a complex and demanding systems situation—a "maxed-out," "off-the-grid" ocean cruising boat—as a way to bring the picture into focus. Less complex and expensive systems (as well as much lighter!) are appropriate for many coastal cruisers, so it is important to extract from the information presented only what is appropriate to your situation.

And remember, however well installed, with more systems and greater complexity, you will not only have higher cost, but also higher probability of failure and greater maintenance overhead (in terms of both time and money). Without question, there is a point of diminishing returns beyond which fancy systems are no longer worth having. Where this point occurs is different for everyone—it is a function of a boatowner's financial resources, technical skills, and core vision about the cruising life.

I urge all those contemplating cruising to categorize the systems on their wish lists according to those that are essential (e.g., navigation and communication electronics, navigation lights, and a basic complement of cabin lights), those that are highly desirable, and those that are simply luxuries. When considering the systems issues discussed herein, it is an excellent idea to think long and hard about doing without the luxuries and perhaps some of those things that seem highly desirable; it is likely that the trade-off in terms of cruising satisfaction will be much more than the value of what is sacrificed.

Once you have got your priorities sorted out, the single greatest step you can take to ensure trouble-free cruising systems is to implement—prior to leaving the dock—the systems advice provided in this chapter and the next!

A BALANCED SYSTEM

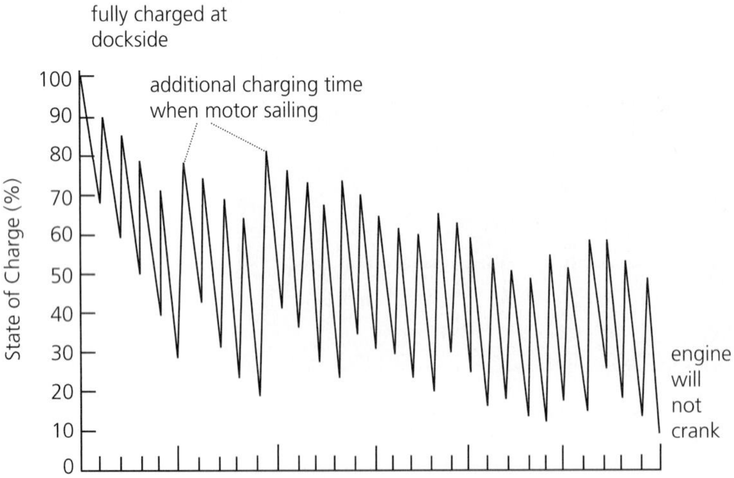

Cruising boats tend to cycle their batteries on a daily basis. If more is pulled out each day than is put back, the batteries slowly go dead. This can take weeks. A boat operator faced with dead batteries typically assumes something just "broke," whereas often there is a systemic imbalance between the discharge and recharge cycles that took this long to make itself evident.

The heart of the systems on most modern cruising boats is the DC system; for several good reasons, it behooves us to keep it functioning. To do this, we absolutely must balance the energy demand and supply. This may sound easy, but getting the power equation right on a cruising boat is one of the more difficult design issues, primarily because there is no single correct formula. I discuss this in great detail in *Boatowner's Mechanical and Electrical Manual*, so it is only summarized herein.

The starting point in understanding the power equation for any boat has to be an analysis of anticipated use, resulting in an *energy audit*. This is accomplished by listing all the energy consumers you want to have onboard (everything from cabin lights to the microwave—if it is to be run off a DC to AC inverter), along with the operating voltage (generally 12 volts DC or 120 volts AC in the U.S., 240 volts AC in Europe) and the energy draw of each one (in *amps* or *watts*), with an estimate of hours of daily use. Using these numbers and a little arithmetic (see the sidebar), it is a simple matter to calculate the boat's 24-hour energy need and to express it in terms of a unit known as *amp-hours* at 12 or 24 volts DC, depending on the boat's DC system. (From here on, I am assuming a 12-volt DC system when I refer to amp-hours because this is the most common.) This is the load side of the power equation.

I am an advocate of DC-based refrigeration on cruising boats (see the section on refrigeration later in this chapter). If DC refrigeration is installed, I like to do a second energy audit based on the seven-day demands of the boat if it is left unattended, but with the refrigerator running (seven days enables extensive forays to be made ashore while the boat is left anchored out). The audit should be taken assuming a worst-case situation; for example, a closed-up

AUDIT ARITHMETIC

Amp-hour loads are calculated as follows:

- If the operating load of DC equipment is given in amps (e.g., a bilge pump with a 5-amp draw), multiply the hours of use in 24 hours by the amperage (e.g., ½ hour × 5 amps = 2.5 amp-hours).
- If the operating load of DC equipment is given in watts, divide the wattage by the system voltage (12 or 24 volts) to get amps, and then continue as in the previous item.
- When looking at AC equipment that will be run off a DC to AC inverter, take the power drain in watts of each appliance and divide this total by 10 or 20 (for a 12- and a 24-volt DC system, respectively) to establish the approximate load, in amps, on the DC system. Multiply this by the hours of use to derive amp-hours.

Daily Energy Requirements (12 Volts) of a Hypothetical Cruising Boat Anchored off a Bahamian Beach

DC EQUIPMENT	RATING (amps)	HOURS OF USE (in 24 hours)	TOTAL LOAD (amp-hours in 24 hours)
6 Lights	1.5 each	2 each = 12	18
1 Refrigeration compressor	5	10	50
Masthead navigation lights	1.5	8	12
2 Fans	1 each	5 each = 10	10
VHF radio, tape deck, etc.	2 total	5 total	10
Total			100 amp-hours

Calculating Inverter Loads

APPLIANCE	WATTS	WATTS ÷ 10 = APPROXIMATE AMPS (at 12 V)	HOURS OF USE	AMP-HOURS (at 12 V)
TV	100	10	2	20
VCR	50	5	2	10
Stereo	50	5	2	10
Coffeemaker	1,000	100	0.2 (12 min.)	20
Toaster	1,200	120	0.1 (6 min.)	12
Microwave	1,200	120	0.3 (18 min.)	36
Blender	300	30	0.2 (12 min.)	6
Vacuum cleaner	800	80	0.1 (6 min.)	8
Hair dryer	1,250	125	0.1 (6 min.)	12.5
Total				134.5

Total Daily Energy Consumption

DC equipment	100 amp-hours	
Inverter	134.5 amp-hours	
Total	234.5 amp-hours	**OUCH!**

Energy Audit Form

EQUIPMENT	AMPERAGE	HOURS OF USE (in 24 hours)	TOTAL LOAD (24 hours)
Refrigeration			
Lights: Deck			
Cockpit			
Navigation			
Anchor			
Aft cabin			
Quarter berth			
Galley			
Navigation station			
Head			
Saloon			
Fo'c's'le			
Guest cabin			
Closets, lockers			
VHF			
SSB			
Autopilot			
Radar			
Misc. navigation			
Entertainment			
Freshwater pump			
Saltwater pump			
Shower pump			
Bilge pump			
Macerator pump			
Gray-water pump			
Engine-room blower			
LPG solenoid			
Windlass			
Watermaker			
DC vacuum cleaner			
Systems monitor			
CO monitor			
LEDs			
Heater			
Inverter standby			
Inverter load (see Inverter Loads Form table next page)			
TOTAL AMP-HOURS (in 24 hours)			

Inverter Loads Form

APPLIANCE	WATTS ÷ 10 (12-Volt DC system)	HOURS OF USE (in 24 hours)	AMP-HOURS (24 hours)
Microwave			
TV			
VCR			
Stereo			
Coffeemaker			
Toaster			
Blender			
Hairdryer			
Vacuum cleaner			
Hot-water heater			
TOTAL AMP-HOURS (insert in Energy Audit Form)			

7-Day Refrigeration Requirement for an Unattended Boat with an Efficient, Well-Insulated Refrigerator and Freezer

Assuming, for example, an estimated daily energy consumption of 56 amp-hours, the 7-day requirement is 56 × 7 = 392 amp-hours.

At the same time, the anchor light may be burning, consuming anywhere from 12 to 24 amp-hours a day.

This comes to a total of 84 to 168 amp-hours a week.

Total: 476–560

Note: the anchor light load can be reduced to around 10 amp-hours with an LED anchor light controlled by a photoelectric cell (see later in this chapter).

boat in the tropics with cabin temperatures at 100°F (38°C) or higher. The audit must include not only the requirements of the refrigeration unit, but also those of any other electrical loads that will come on during the seven days. The most likely of these is an anchor light, but there may also be a bilge pump, a carbon monoxide alarm, and the combined load of various *light-emitting diodes (LEDs)* scattered around the boat. The anchor-light load can be kept to a minimum by wiring it through a photoelectric cell that automatically turns it off in the daytime, or by using an LED cluster light (this is discussed later in this chapter).

Keeping the Load Down

If the DC load comes to more than 200 amp-hours per day, as it commonly does (particularly if air conditioning is wanted), there is a problem. Once the boat unplugs from shore power and goes "off the grid," there is no way it will function without excessive main engine use unless it has an AC generator.

Before concluding that the generator is necessary, the notion of what is considered essential, desirable, and luxurious should be reviewed; perhaps a few lifestyle compromises are preferable to installing and operating a generator. The questions to be asked include the following:

- Is air conditioning really necessary (see the section on ventilation in chapter 3)? If so, then a generator is unavoidable. When it is running, it can be used to charge batteries and run DC equipment, which greatly reduces the necessary "hold-over" capacity of the DC system.
- Can the refrigeration load be reduced? After air conditioning, refrigeration is generally the highest energy consumer on a cruising boat. The icebox is frequently larger than it needs to be and

poorly constructed and insulated. Using some of the unnecessary volume to add extra insulation and tightening up on the construction standards can cut the energy load in half. There is also potential for dramatically reducing energy requirements—albeit at a high cost—by using some of the new high-tech, vacuum-based "super" insulations (see the section on refrigeration later in this chapter).

- At sea, can the autopilot load be reduced? This is generally the largest energy consumer when passagemaking. It can be completely eliminated with a wind vane and/or minimized by the output from a towed water generator.
- Can the lighting load be reduced? Learning to turn off lights when not in use and substituting fluorescent lighting for incandescent lighting often reduces the load by half (lighting is discussed in more detail later in this chapter).
- How about fan usage? Replacing higher-energy fans (such as those manufactured by Guest) with lower-energy units (such as those manufactured by Hella) reduces the load by half.
- Do you really need an electric toilet, or an electric shower pump?
- Do you really need the microwave for anything other than intermittent use when energy is in plentiful supply (e.g., when tied to a dock with shore power or when motor sailing)? If you can limit use to fit available energy supplies, it removes an enormous strain from the DC system.

Battery discharge-recharge cycles on a well-balanced cruising boat.

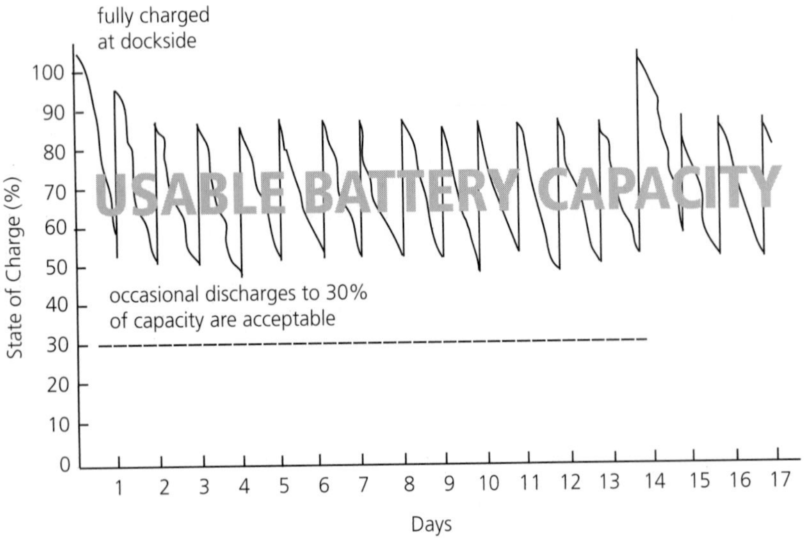

With careful equipment selection and minor lifestyle compromises, it is almost always possible to get the energy consumption on a "typical" cruising boat well below 200 amp-hours a day; it's even possible to get it down to not much more than 100 amp-hours. This brings us within the practical realm of a DC-based system that requires no supplementary AC generator, and which derives most of its necessary energy supplies from routine boat operations (e.g., motoring in and out of anchorages) without additional engine running time devoted solely to recharging batteries. In many ways, this is the ideal for a cruising boat.

The Supply Side

Once the load is established, it is necessary to look at the supply side, beginning with the batteries because they are the limiting factor in the system.

Batteries and Battery Capacity

Batteries in "house" use on boats are typically cycled; that is, repeatedly discharged and recharged. Automotive-type batteries soon fail in this kind of service. A *deep-cycle battery* is needed to withstand the stresses.

There are numerous deep-cycle batteries on the market, including wet-cells (the type that need topping up from time to time), gel-cells (sealed, no-maintenance batteries), and AGMs (absorbed glass mat, another type of sealed battery). The pros and cons of each type can be argued, but all work well as long as only quality batteries are bought (you usually get what you pay for), different battery types are not mixed in use, and the manufacturer's recommended charging regimen is adhered to (this may require special voltage regulators).

Even with a quality deep-cycle battery, battery life is significantly shortened if the battery is repeatedly discharged much below 50 percent of its capacity. At the other end of the spectrum, for reasons inherent in the internal chemistry of batteries, it takes a long time to charge a battery much beyond 75 to 80 percent of its capacity. As a result, cruising-boat batteries are rarely fully charged (the exception is when the boat is plugged into shore power and a battery charger is left on).

If a battery is discharged to 50 percent of its capacity and then recharged to 75 or 80 percent, for practical purposes, only 25 to 30 percent of its capacity is usable on a day-to-day basis. This leads to a rule-of-thumb that the batteries on a cruising boat should have a rated amp-hour capacity of four times the daily load established by the energy audit (amp-hour capacity is given in the battery specifications). However, a battery bank of this size is often not practical because of the space requirements and the weight. This leads to an acceptance of battery banks with a capacity of as little as 2½ times the daily load. However, compared to a larger bank, there will be a significant loss of DC system performance and reduction in battery life.

Let's assume the energy audit produces a daily load of 150 amp-hours. For a DC system, it is desirable to have a battery bank of four times 150, which equals 600 amp-hours. However, the batteries weigh around 400 pounds and occupy 3.5 cubic feet of space (100 L). It may be necessary to settle for a battery bank of as little as 150 times 2.5, which equals 375 amp-hours. Referring back to the seven-day refrigeration and anchor-light load, we hope it isn't more than 60 to 70 percent of the total battery bank capacity (because we don't often leave the boat for seven days, a higher level of discharge than in normal use is acceptable). If it is more than this percentage, attempt to reduce the refrigeration load (discussed later in this chapter) or increase the battery capacity.

At this point, if the size and weight of the necessary batteries are unacceptable, *you need to cut more demand out of the system.* Go back to the beginning and review what is considered essential, desirable, and luxurious. If you try to fudge this, you will create a long-term problem for yourself. If you intend to make long passages, pay particular attention to the load at sea, which, on electrically loaded boats, often exceeds that at anchor.

One Bank

For many years, conventional wisdom held that the best arrangement for batteries in house use on a boat is to have two separate battery banks, alternating between them daily. The two banks may be supplemented with a third battery, reserved solely for engine cranking, or the idle house bank is recharged and held in reserve for that purpose. However, this is not the most efficient way to use batteries.

For a number of reasons explained in *Boatowner's Mechanical and Electrical Manual*, it makes more sense to combine all the house batteries into a single large bank. Likewise, it makes little sense to have a separate battery up forward for the windlass, which should be powered from the house bank. (This may need to be

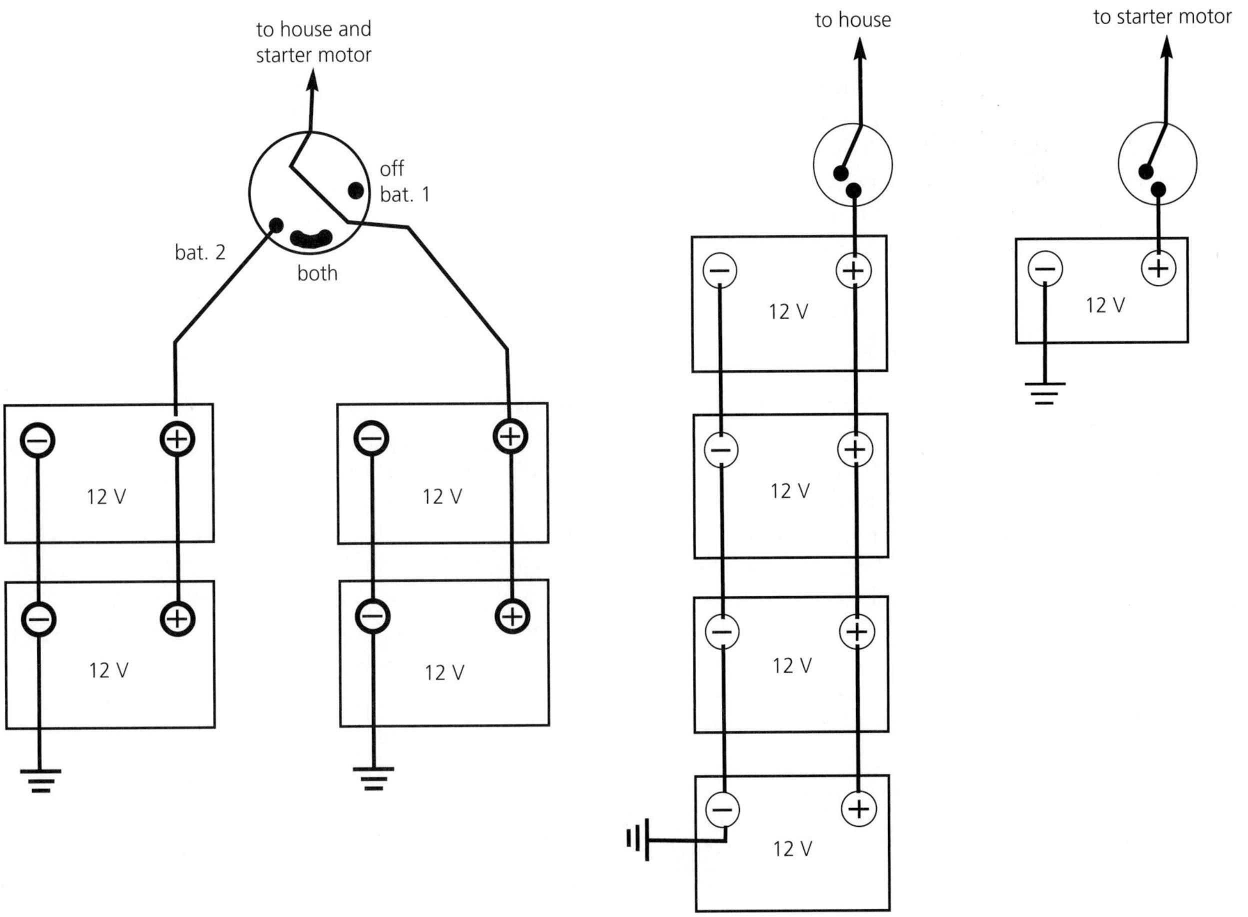

Typical two-bank battery installation versus the preferred single-house-bank approach.

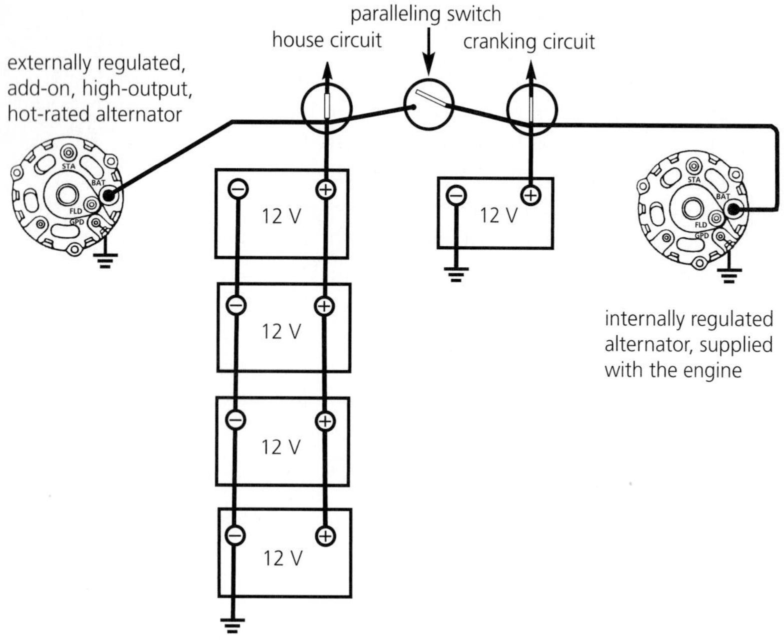

The optimum battery and alternator setup on a cruising boat.

qualified for DC bow thrusters, some of which draw horrendous amounts of current, requiring huge cables if the batteries are not nearby—each situation has to be considered on its own merits.)

To be viable, a single house bank must be combined with an almost bulletproof method of ensuring an ability to crank the engine. Because it must be assumed that at some time the house bank will be discharged to the point at which it cannot crank the boat's engine, *the single house bank must be combined with a separate battery reserved solely for engine cranking, and always kept in a state of full charge*. This is achieved by wiring all the house loads to the house bank and *nothing but the starter motor to the cranking battery;* that way, there is no possibility of accidentally draining the cranking battery in house service. Set up like this, the cranking battery need be no larger than what is needed to crank the engine (see your engine manual). An emergency paralleling switch between the house bank and the cranking battery can be added just in case one is needed as a backup for engine cranking or for house use; however, this function also can be accomplished by keeping a set of jumper cables onboard.

Regardless of how your batteries are currently wired, for optimum DC system performance, consider going to a single house battery bank with an isolated cranking battery.

Charging Batteries

How do we charge a house bank and an isolated cranking battery? The best arrangement, particularly if the boat has substantial DC needs, is to leave the existing alternator and voltage regulator wired to the engine-cranking battery. Then add a second high-output alternator, controlled by a multistep regulator, which is wired to the house bank. This way, the two banks can be charged independently, with the voltage-regulation parameters on each alternator adjusted to provide the most efficient charging regimen for the individual battery banks. (In practice, the existing regulator will probably not be adjustable, but will provide a regimen suitable for a cranking battery; the multistep regulator can be programmed to achieve the maximum state-of-charge for, and life expectancy from, the house batteries.) If either alternator or voltage regulator fails, the emergency battery-paralleling switch or jumper cables can charge both battery banks from the remaining alternator and regulator.

In the kind of dual-alternator system just described, there is no need to touch the battery switches except in the case of fire, or to isolate a failed battery bank, or to shut down the circuits when leaving the boat for long periods. The house and cranking switches are turned on when the boat is first boarded and then left alone until the boat is laid up. That's it. However, if for some reason (most likely accidentally) the house-battery-bank switch is turned off when the engine is running, the high-output alternator may be open-circuited (depending on how it is wired), which usually destroys the diodes in the alternator. To ensure that this does not happen, the installation should automatically shut down the alternator whenever the battery switch is turned off. A special kind of battery switch (readily available) is required that incorporates an *alternator field disconnect switch*; it is important to remember that *the alternator field must be wired through this switch* (see *Boatowner's Mechanical and Electrical Manual*).

What happens in the more typical installation where two or more battery banks must be charged from a single alternator? This requires that the banks be paralleled while charging—so that both are charged—but then isolated when the engine is shut down, preventing the cranking battery from becoming discharged in house service. Traditionally, one of the following two methods has been used to accomplish these objectives:

- A manual switch is used to parallel the batteries when the engine is running and to isolate the cranking battery when the engine is not running.

• Battery isolation diodes are used to provide the same service automatically.

Neither option is ideal. Any kind of switching arrangement is subject to operator error, resulting in one battery bank not being charged or both being discharged. In addition, the act of switching from one bank to another can sometimes result in alternator damage.

Battery isolation diodes are a separate subject. Their principal advantage is that they parallel batteries for charging and isolate them in service without any user interaction; as such, they are "idiot-proof." The major stumbling block is that they create a *voltage drop* in the charging circuit, which frequently plays havoc with voltage-regulation circuits, resulting in perennially undercharged batteries that die prematurely. Historically, battery isolation diodes, installed to guarantee proper charging of more than one battery bank, have been a major cause of premature battery death.

A much better device for concurrently charging more than one battery bank is a voltage-sensitive, heavy-duty *relay* or *solenoid* (commonly known as a *battery combiner*, a name coined by West Marine for its device but which has now become fairly generic), wired between the two battery banks. Any time the combiner senses a rising voltage on any battery bank (caused by a charging device coming online), it parallels the batteries. If the voltage falls (the charging device goes offline), the paralleling circuit is broken. With a combiner, the alternator should be wired to the house batteries because they will need the most charging (this keeps the current flow through the paralleling circuit to a minimum).

If you currently have more than one battery bank that needs to be charged from a single alternator (or other charging device), the best approach is to replace any switches or isolation diodes in the charging circuit with an appropriately rated battery combiner (its amp rating should be at least as great as the maximum output from the most powerful charging device onboard—generally the alternator), with a simple "On/Off" battery-isolation switch for each battery bank.

Alternators

To minimize engine-running time on a cruising boat, we want to be able to recharge house batteries as fast as possible whenever the main engine is running. In practice, there is a limit to how fast a battery can be recharged without suffering damage. Different types of batteries have different limits. Even when heavily discharged, wet-type deep-cycle batteries cannot be charged at a rate that is much above 25 percent of their amp-hour capacity; gel cells take up to 33 percent of rated capacity; and AGMs take up to 40 percent of rated capacity. Regardless of a charger's output capability, as the batteries approach full charge, the maximum charge rates steadily taper down.

What this means is that with a 600 amp-hour battery bank, there is little benefit in having an alternator output higher than 150 amps for wet cells (25 percent of battery capacity), 200 amps for gel cells (33 percent), and 240 amps for AGMs (40 percent). In practice, 150- and 200-amp alternators are widely available; 240 amps is pushing the envelope.

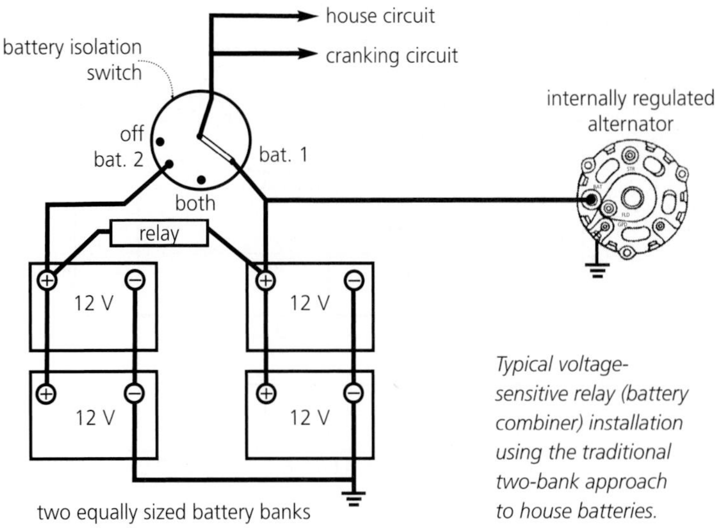

Typical voltage-sensitive relay (battery combiner) installation using the traditional two-bank approach to house batteries.

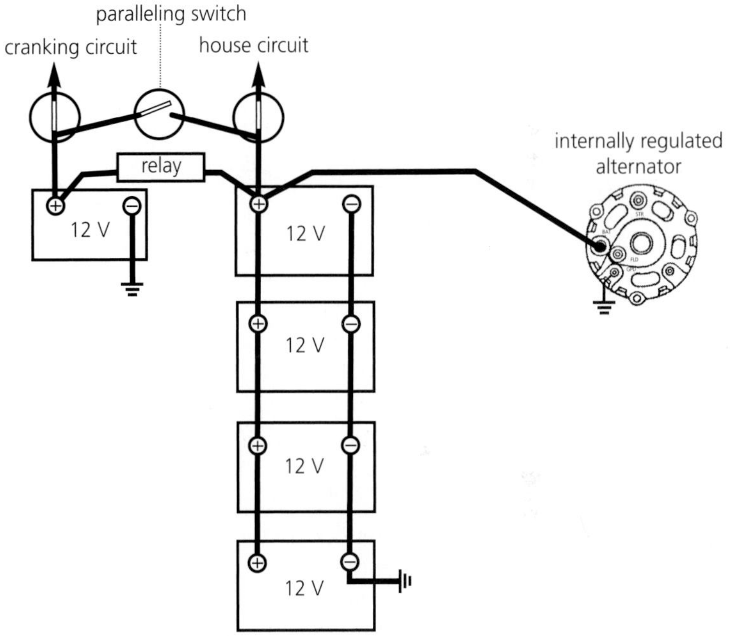

A better approach to battery and voltage-sensitive relay usage.

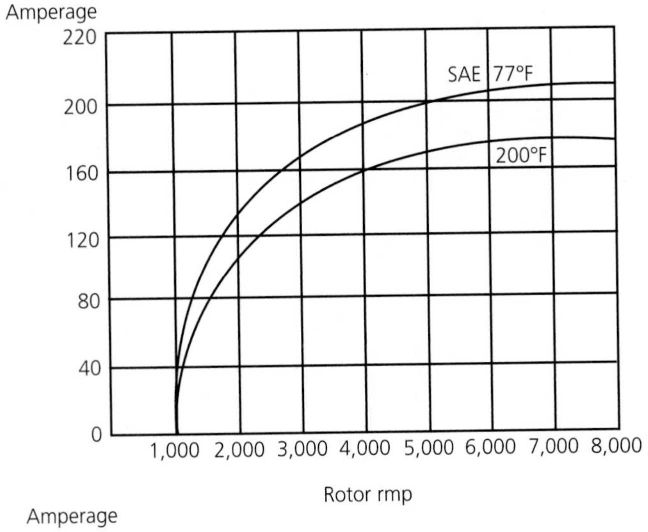

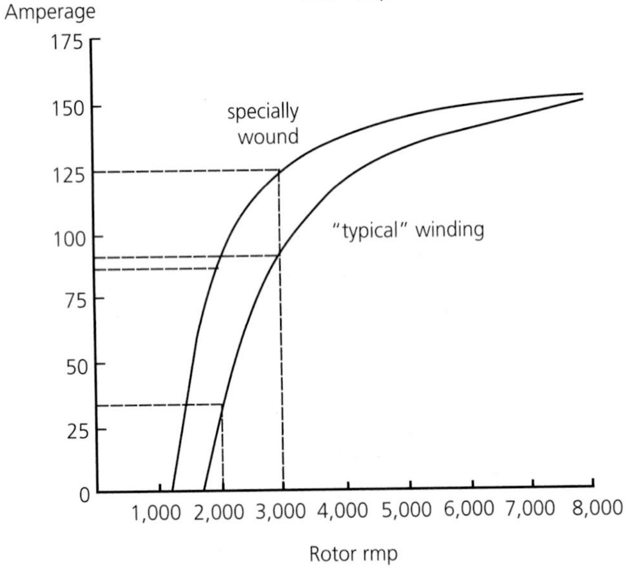

Top: *Cold (SAE) and hot (KKK) alternator output curves.* Bottom: *The effect of different alternator windings on the output curve for two alternators with nominally the same output. Note the dramatic difference at 2,000 rpm (engine idle speed). At higher speeds, the difference starts to level out.*

Alternators are typically rated "cold" (in an ambient temperature of 80°F), but as soon as they warm up—which they do the minute they start producing power or in a hot engine room—the higher ambient air temperature reduces their output, sometimes by as much as 25 percent. Some alternators have a second "hot" rating, which may be at 122°F or 200°F (50°C or 93°C; in the latter case, it is known as a "KKK" rating). The hot ratings are more representative of real-life output than the cold rating.

The manufacturer will have a curve that shows alternator output (amps) as a function of speed of rotation (rpm) and ambient temperature. Some alternators reach full-rated output at much lower speeds than others. The sooner an alternator reaches full output, the more desirable it is in a cruising application because it maximizes effectiveness on those occasions when the engine is idled at anchor solely for battery-charging purposes. For example, Balmar offers a 160-amp alternator that has a higher output until quite high engine speeds than its 200-amp alternator—in many cruising situations, the 160-amp alternator is not only cheaper, but is also a better performer.

If a second alternator is added to the boat's engine, it usually can be mounted opposite the first; however, if this is not possible because of space or other considerations, it can be mounted "backwards" on a bracket on the front of the engine (make sure the alternator has a *bidirectional fan* or it will burn up). A high-output alternator can add a significant load to an engine (up to 7 horsepower per 100 amps of output); therefore, any mounting bracket must be very solidly constructed. An additional pulley wheel is needed on the end of the engine's crankshaft to drive the alternator. Only high-quality drive belts will take the load (I always recommend Gates' Green Stripe or the equivalent).

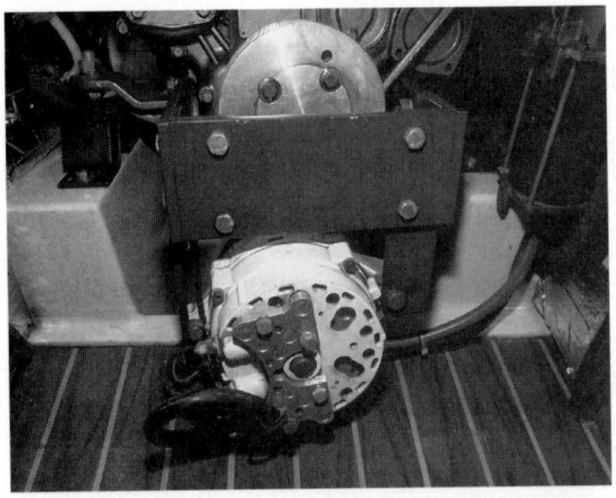

Top: *A second alternator, mounted to a bracket on the front of the engine. Note how rugged the bracket needs to be.* Above: *A neat way to adjust belt tension on a high-output alternator. (Courtesy Statpower)*

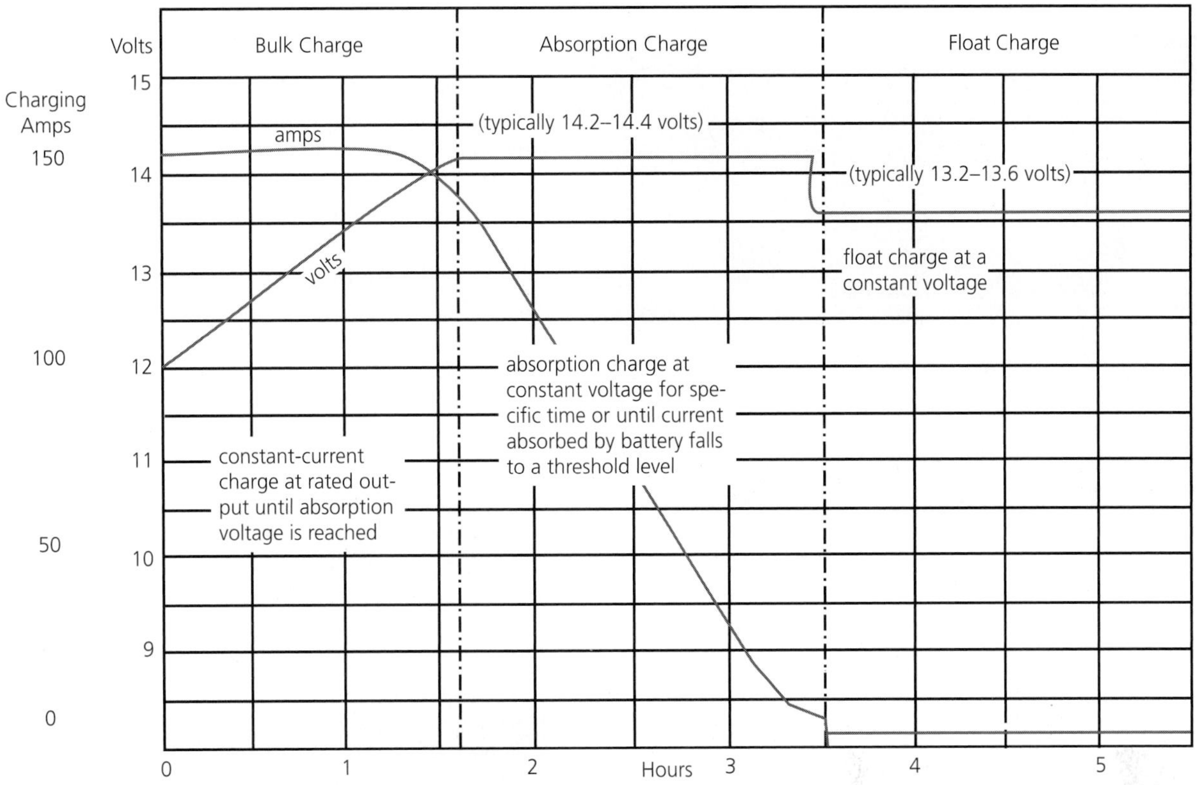

Voltage and amperage curves for a 150-amp (KKK-rated) alternator controlled by a multistep regulator, charging a 50% discharged 450 amp-hour battery bank.

To increase charging capability in the more common single-alternator installation, the alternator that comes with the engine will likely have to be replaced with an appropriately sized high-output alternator wired to the house bank of batteries. A battery combiner wired between the house bank and the cranking battery keeps the cranking battery charged without compromising its isolation.

The bottom line is that to minimize charging times, the boat needs an alternator with a hot-rated output in amps *at typical charging rpms* at least 25 percent (preferably 33 percent) of the amp-hour rating of all the batteries it is charging. Without this, it is extremely difficult to keep the batteries charged in a cruising environment.

Voltage Regulation and DC Monitors

A properly sized alternator is only one piece of the charging puzzle; just as important is the voltage-regulation program. No matter the capability of the alternator, its potential is largely wasted unless it is regulated to optimum effect.

The standard voltage regulator installed inside the alternator that comes with most engines is optimized for charging cranking batteries, but is very poorly set up for charging batteries that are regularly cycled in house applications. When used on house batteries, the net effect is to unnecessarily prolong charging times (by a substantial factor), while also contributing to premature battery death.

Optimizing voltage regulation on cruising boats is complicated. The idea is to force-feed the batteries with the maximum charging current they can absorb without pushing this process to the point at which the batteries are damaged. This requires a sophisticated multistep voltage regulator, such as those manufactured by Ample Technologies, Balmar, Xantrex/Heart Interface, TWC, and Sterling.

In the ideal two-alternator installation described previously, the alternator that came with the engine will be internally regulated, with a voltage-regulation program adequate for taking care of the engine-cranking battery; it can be left alone. The add-on high-output alternator should be externally regulated (most are), in which case it can be controlled by one of the multistep regulators. The regulator must be fine-tuned to match its charging characteristics to the type of battery being charged (the house bank). The instructions that come with the regulator will explain how to do this.

In a single-alternator installation, the high-output alternator that replaces the original engine-mounted alternator will be controlled by a multistep regulator, with the charging regimen fine-tuned to suit the house batteries.

A *multistep voltage regulator does more to improve the health of the DC system on a typical cruising boat than any other device on the market*. The improved charging regimen often extends the life of the batteries, with the result that the regulator may be one of the few things

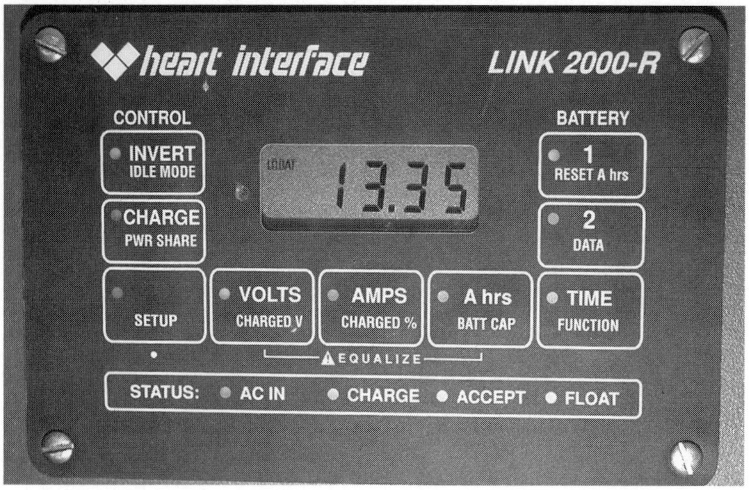

Sophisticated DC system's monitoring device.

on the boat that almost pays for itself! Of all the equipment available to the contemporary cruising sailor, this is one of the single most important pieces.

When using a high-output alternator and multistep voltage regulator, it can be a very thin line that separates force-feeding the batteries from doing damage. To walk this line, as well as to manage the DC system to best advantage, precise monitoring and control of the system is needed, which is accomplished in the fine-tuning of the regulator. Although it is not strictly necessary, for those of us who like to keep an eye on these things thereafter, it helps to have an accurate systems-monitoring device onboard. This is best bought as part of an integrated package from the voltage-regulator manufacturer. My favorites are those from Ample Technologies (the Energy Monitor) and Xantrex/Heart Interface (the E-Meter for simple systems or two E-Meters for more complicated systems; the Link 2000 can be used for sophisticated systems).

Supplementary Sources of Power

No matter how powerful an alternator and how well regulated it may be, battery chemistry is such that it is just about impossible to replace the daily drain on a house battery bank in less than an hour to an hour-and-a-half of engine running time. This is often longer than the engine is used for propulsive purposes, with the result that the engine gets used solely for battery charging when at anchor—something we want to avoid both to reduce wear and tear on the engine and to preserve the tranquility of the cruising lifestyle.

Engine-running time for battery charging alone can be significantly reduced—and sometimes eliminated altogether—through the judicious use of solar panels and/or a wind generator. (Other less common but very effective approaches at sea are a towed water generator and an alternator driven by a freewheeling propeller or by its own small propeller and shaft.) The choice of what to use somewhat depends on the chosen cruising grounds. The Gulf of Maine in the summer, for example, is notorious for light winds. A wind generator may prove to be a poor investment, whereas a couple of properly located 75-watt solar panels may crank out as much as 50 amp-hours a day in sunny conditions. When it comes to the Caribbean,

Top: *In a typical trade wind, a wind generator can supply a good part of the energy needs of an energy-conscious boat.* Above: *Solar panels generally can only supply supplemental energy, but when the array gets up to this size, it can supply a good part of the total energy requirement. The problem is keeping the panels facing the sun!*

the solar panels will do as well as in Maine—maybe even a little better—but will be far eclipsed in terms of output by a good-sized wind generator that may produce more than 100 amp-hours a day in the trade winds.

On many cruising boats, the combination of a minimum amount of engine-running time supplemented by alternative energy sources is enough to sustain the DC system for extended periods. However, with this type of regimen, the batteries almost certainly will never be fully recharged—they are, in effect, cycled daily from around 80 percent of full charge down to maybe 50 percent and back up again to 80 percent. This situation carries with it the risk of long-term battery damage through a process known as *sulfation*. To prevent sulfation, the batteries periodically need to be brought to a state of full charge, either by running the engine for several hours (ideally, when motor sailing so the engine does not have to be run solely for battery charging) or by plugging a battery charger into shore power when it is available.

The batteries also must be fully charged periodically when a boat is not in use because all batteries slowly discharge when left idle; if left alone, they eventually suffer irreparable damage through sulfation. Wet cells discharge considerably faster than gel cells or AGMs and, therefore, are at greater risk.

If shore power is available, the obvious choice for maintaining batteries in a charged state seems to be a battery charger, but I don't like to leave our boat plugged in for extended periods because there is a risk of corrosion that comes with a shore-power connection (discussed later in this chapter). So, after fully charging our batteries with either the alternator or a battery charger, we use solar panels to keep the batteries in a state of full charge when we are not on our boat. If no others are installed, a couple of small 5-watt solar panels are generally adequate for this task. If larger panels have already been installed to supplement the engine-driven alternator while cruising, these do nicely but will need their own voltage regulator to avoid overcharging the batteries when there is no load on the system. Ample Technologies, Trace Engineering (now Xantrex), West Marine, and others make excellent multistep regulators for solar panels.

Nada's 12-watt solar panel contributes next to nothing to our daily energy needs when cruising, but is adequate to keep the batteries fully charged when the boat is not in use.

Defining the Limits

The previous discussion comprises the basic building blocks of a successful DC system on a modern electrically loaded cruising boat. If properly sized and put together, it really is possible to enjoy—with a minimum of maintenance and inconvenience—many of the comforts that we have come to take for granted. However, there are very real limits as to how far this process can be taken.

If we assume a single-engine boat, it is rarely practical to install more than two alternators—the one that comes with the engine plus an add-on. High-output alternators up to 200-amps output (hot-rated) are commonly available at an "affordable" price; above this, they get extremely expensive. Multistep regulators are also widely available to control alternator outputs up to 200 amps; above this, the *field current* demand of the alternator (the energy that kicks the alternator into life) may be more than the regulator can tolerate. A 200-amp alternator is ideally sized for charging a 600- to 800-amp-hour battery bank. This is good for up to a 200-amp-hour-a-day load, as long as adequate time is set aside for recharging. This defines the practical limits of current technology.

The core configuration outlined—up to an 800-amp-hour battery bank with up to a 200-amp alternator and an appropriate multistep regulator—was fairly well established as a realistic goal by the early 1980s and has remained remarkably consistent ever since. What has changed over time is the ability of battery and component manufacturers and equipment installers to bring the pieces together into reliable, trouble-free, user-friendly systems. Combined with the tendency of boatowners to fit the latest "gadgets," this has led to ever more powerful DC systems becoming the mainstream cruising norm.

Our new Pacific Seacraft 40 is a good

example of the "state of the art" in cruising-boat DC systems. We replaced the standard 60-amp engine-mounted Yanmar alternator with an 80-amp Yanmar alternator. This charges our 100-amp-hour cranking battery, for which it is grossly oversized; the surplus capacity serves as a backup to the main alternator. We have a second 200-amp alternator (Balmar) mounted on a custom bracket (Stuart Marine) and fastened to the front of the engine. This charges a 675-amp-hour house battery bank (Lifeline AGMs). The 80-amp alternator is internally regulated. The 200-amp alternator is controlled by a multistep regulator linked to a sophisticated DC systems monitor (Link 2000R from Xantrex/Heart Interface). This core system is supplemented by a wind generator (Air Marine) and a couple of solar panels (Siemens). We have all the energy we need to run the boat, including a refrigerator and freezer, lights, an electric windlass, and a 2,500-watt DC to AC inverter that powers a microwave and, on occasion, the AC hot water heater (which is one hell of a DC draw—130 amps—so we only run it off the DC system when we have plenty of energy). We enjoy a wonderful lifestyle when cruising—far more comfortable than anything in the old days—but, in the final analysis, we can still sail the boat and do fine without it if it all fails.

It is possible to create significantly more powerful systems—some of the Dashews' boats, I believe, have 2,000-amp-hour battery banks with appropriately sized alternators—but it becomes quite involved and expensive. It is necessary to design and install brackets to mount at least two high-output alternators, each of which needs an output of well over 200 amps. This probably entails separately mounted and cooled rectifiers (a key component of an alternator) and specially configured multistep regulators; these kinds of esoteric systems are beyond the scope of this book.

Looking down the road, there are technical advances in the pipeline that may lessen the loads on DC systems, including vacuum-based insulations that dramatically reduce the heat load (and thus the energy requirements) of refrigeration systems and LED cluster lights that dramatically reduce the energy requirements for some lighting. Battery and alternator technology is also constantly improving. It is conceivable that in a few years, we may see the reversal of the trend to try and fit ever more powerful DC systems to boats, but I have a hunch that most boatowners will always find a way to use any "surplus" energy!

Miscellaneous DC Systems Issues

Before moving on, here are some miscellaneous DC systems issues that need to be incorporated into the big picture (and are covered in more detail in *Boatowner's Mechanical and Electrical Manual*).

- The kind of battery banks under consideration are large and heavy; ours occupies several cubic feet and weighs hundreds of pounds. The batteries need secure stowage low in the boat to keep the center of gravity down, but high enough to not get flooded with bilge water. If upgrading a battery bank, consider the weight implications for the boat's trim (and for the performance parameters discussed in chapter 1).
- Batteries perform best in a cool environment and will be harmed by high temperatures, so they should not be in the engine compartment. However, it is desirable to keep the high-current circuits as short as possible; therefore, the cranking battery should be close to the starter motor and the house batteries close to any high-output alternator and an inverter (if fitted).
- Wet-type batteries must be accessible for maintenance.
- All batteries must be in well-ventilated battery compartments because all can occasionally give off explosive hydrogen gas. This includes gel-cell and AGM batteries that occasionally get buried in unvented lockers. In certain circumstances, this can result in an explosion!
- Battery types should never be mixed in use and, ideally, not mixed when

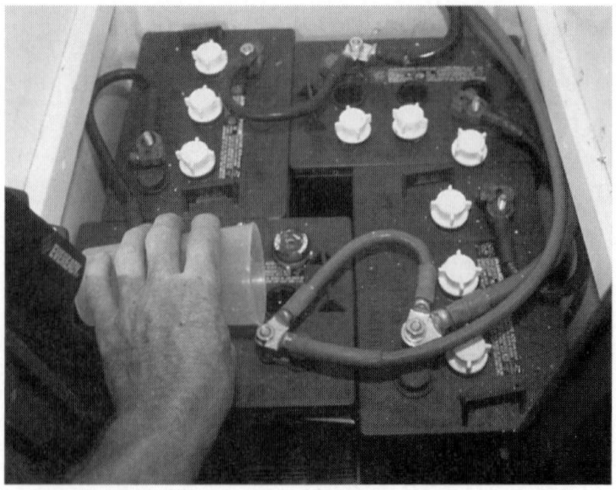

Wet-type batteries must be readily accessible for maintenance. Note that these are not fastened down—a serious oversight.

SUMMARIZING TABLE FOR SIZING A DC SYSTEM*

Total 24-hour DC System Load (From Energy Audit Form, page 158)

Total 24-hour DC System Load	

Alternative Energy Sources (AES)

Alternative energy sources, like solar panels and wind generators, produce amp-hours each day that replace the amp-hours drawn out of batteries by DC loads. Like DC loads, you need to estimate the amount of current (amps) and amount of time (hours) that the devices will be generating power. In general, you should underestimate the output of those devices because it is very difficult to anticipate the number of hours of sunshine or the average speed of the wind.

DEVICE	AMPS	HOURS	AH/DAY
Solar, average			
Wind Generator, average			
Water Generator, average			
AES AH/Day			

AES = alternative energy sources

Net Energy Consumption, AH/Day

Subtract AES line from Total 24-hour DC System Load to find out how much energy must be made up using other sources.

Total 24-Hour DC System Load AH/Day	
Subtract AES AH/Day	
Net Energy Consumption, AH/Day	

Recommended Battery Capacity

Your need for battery capacity is determined by how much energy you use daily and how deeply you want to discharge your batteries (the recommendation is to not discharge below 50 percent of capacity and to assume that recharges will typically not be above 80 percent of capacity, thereby limiting the daily cycle to 30 percent of capacity). For example, with a 200-amp-hour-a-day load, using 30 percent of battery capacity, the recommended battery capacity is 200 divided by 0.30, which equals 667 AH.

Net Energy Consumption AH/Day	
Range of Battery Use in Typical Conditions (e.g., 0.30)	
Battery Capacity Needed (amp-hours)	

*Adapted from a table, courtesy West Marine

Alternator Output, Amps

The alternator is the primary method of recharging your batteries. Base the output on how much it produces at typical engine rpm, not on its maximum output. Ideally, the hot-rated output at changing rpms will be 25 to 33 percent of the battery capacity determined previously.

Alternator Output at Typical Charging rpms	

Charge Efficiency Factor (CEF)

Batteries are not 100 percent efficient when they are recharged. Flooded (wet) batteries, in good condition, are about 85 percent efficient; gel batteries are about 95 percent efficient.

Enter 85% for Flooded; 95% for Gel Batteries	

Minimum Time to Charge

If an alternator is sized as suggested (i.e., an amp rating that is 25 to 33 percent of battery amp-hour capacity), the batteries will be unable to accept its full output when they are around 60 percent charged. Above this charge level, the *Charge Acceptance Rate (CAR)* steadily tapers off, prolonging charge times.

To calculate the minimum time to charge, divide the Net Energy Consumption Per Day by the alternator output, then multiply this by the CEF (0.85 or 0.95). For example, if you need to recharge 200 AH, your alternator puts out 150 amps, and you have flooded batteries, it will take a minimum of 200 divided by 150 times 0.85, which equals 1.57 hours. In reality, your batteries will not be able to accept full alternator output much after the first thirty minutes; *the real-life charge time is significantly longer—generally 1½ to 2 times longer.*

Net Energy Consumption, AH/Day	
Alternator Output at Typical Charging rpms: 85% for Flooded; 95% for Gel Batteries	
Minimum Time to Recharge (multiply by 1.5 or 2 for more realistic number)	

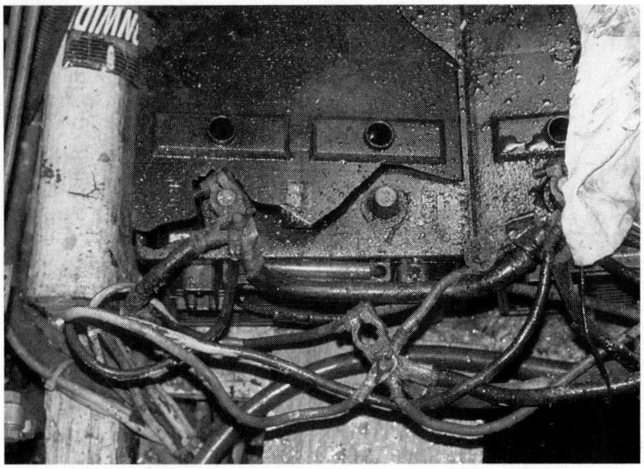

Battery explosion caused by overcharging. All battery boxes need excellent ventilation.

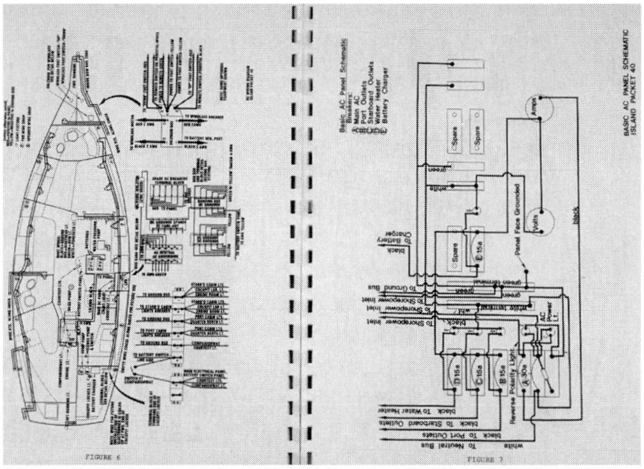

Few boat manufacturers produce this kind of essential documentation.

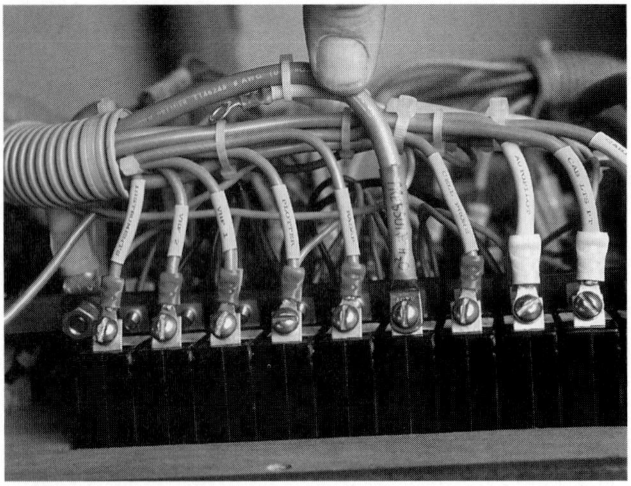

Beautiful electrical installation.

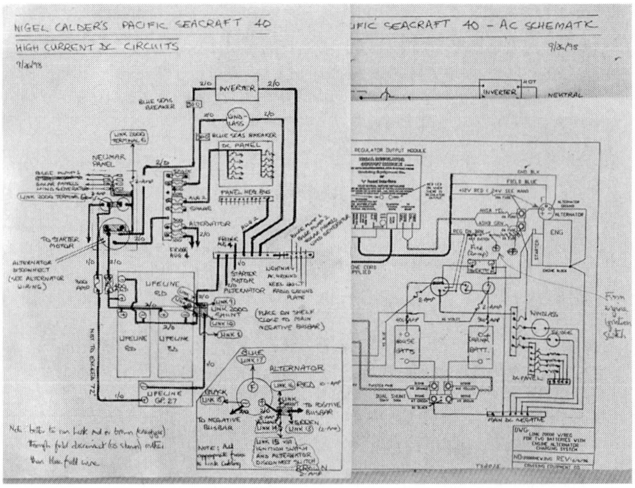

Making a wiring diagram for your boat is one of the best ways to learn about the electrical system; these are my drawings for Nada.

recharging (although this is often difficult to avoid). It is preferable that all batteries on the boat be the same type, from the same manufacturer, and the same age.

- All electrical installations should use *tinned, oil-resistant, multistranded copper cable*, preferably with a 105°C temperature rating. Pay particular attention to this on European-built boats, which often have poorer-quality electrical installations than U.S.-built boats. In the United States, the cable should comply with a standard known as *UL-1426 BC5W2* (if this is not stamped on the insulation, the cable does not comply).
- Electric cables should be sized for a 3 percent voltage drop in most applications, and certainly no more than a 10 percent voltage drop.
- If possible, all terminals should be sealed with heat shrink.
- All cables should be labeled at both ends.
- A boat should have a comprehensive wiring diagram; making one is an excellent way to learn about a boat's electrical system.

DC TO AC INVERTERS

Over the last couple of decades, *DC to AC inverters* (which convert battery power to mains power) have come of age. These enable all kinds of handy household gadgets to be used onboard without the noise, weight, space requirements, exhaust fumes, and expense of a generator. What a boon this has been for many cruising sailors! Few recent innovations have had such far-reaching potential to improve shipboard living standards.

But there is a downside. As many boatowners have found to their cost, an inverter can be a mixed blessing. It is an unfortunate fact of life that many of the luxuries we like the best (e.g., ice cubes in the cocktails) are high-energy consumers. Unless an inverter is properly matched to onboard energy sources, it can drain the DC system to the point at which it starts a chain reaction of failures. To avoid such disappointments, an inverter must be properly sized and matched to available energy sources, and properly installed.

Sizing an Inverter

An inverter must be sized for both the highest AC load it is to carry and for the DC system that is to power it. On the AC side, load calculations are simple. List all the appliances you expect to use with their power drain in watts (found on a label attached to the equipment or in the manufacturer's bulletin; the Inverter Loads Form table on page 159 gives some common examples). Now determine which appliances are likely to be used simultaneously to discover *the maximum AC demand at any given time*. The inverter must be sized to match or exceed this demand. Although many appliances momentarily draw several times their running load when they first kick on, if the inverter is sized as outlined, it should have an adequate *surge* capability to meet any temporary demand.

Some inverters produce AC output as what is called a *modified sine wave*, others as a *pure sine wave*. The former is generally cheaper and with a lower *idle drain* (the power consumed when an inverter is turned "on" but not in use), but is also heavier and bulkier. It works well on most loads, but may cause lines on a TV screen, reduce the efficiency of a microwave, and not work at all with some specialized loads (such as laser printers, some medical equipment, and many breadmakers); for these loads, a pure sine wave inverter may be needed.

On the DC side, the interest is not so much in the peak demand as in the total drain on batteries between full charges, calculated as already described (see An Energy Audit at the beginning of this chapter).

You are likely to be a little stunned by the projected amp-hour drain on your batteries that an energy audit reveals, especially if you have been blithely planning to use the microwave and other powerful AC appliances. You will have discovered the limiting factor for most inverter-based systems: not the ability of the inverter to power the AC appliances, but rather the ability of the DC system to power the inverter.

Recharging the Batteries

Whatever is pulled out of the batteries must be replaced. Given the ability of even a moderately sized inverter to rapidly deplete a battery bank (unless inverter use is sandwiched between extended periods of battery-charging), some form of high-capacity fast-charging, as described previously, is essential for the survival of the DC system.

Many inverters can be used "backwards" to charge a battery. In fact, several incorporate multistep battery-charging capabilities as powerful as any battery charger on the market; a 2,000-watt inverter may have a 100-amp or more charging capability at 12 volts, controlled by a sophisticated multistage regulation program

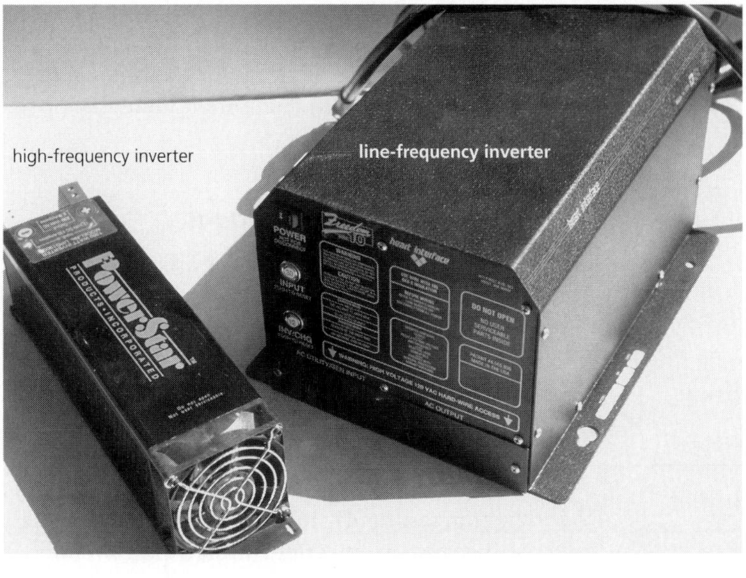

A 1,000-watt high-frequency inverter versus a line-frequency inverter. Note the difference in size (there's also a weight difference). However, the line-frequency inverter can be used as a battery charger, whereas the high-frequency inverter cannot (some can); there are other subtle differences that affect choices.

designed to recharge batteries at the fastest safe rate. A weekend cruiser can use this charger at dockside during the week to replace the battery's weekend drain. Other inverters, however, have no battery-charging capability. Without such a battery-charging option, a high-capacity (and relatively expensive) battery charger may be required for battery-charging.

Once a boat moves away from the dockside for longer periods, the principal means of recharging the batteries is almost always the boat's main engine and alternator. However, there is little point in transferring the AC load to the DC system if the engine then has to be run long hours to recharge the batteries; it makes more sense to buy an AC generator in the first place. If battery-charging hours are to be kept to a minimum, the engine-driven alternator almost certainly needs upgrading to a high-output unit with its own multistep regulator (as described previously).

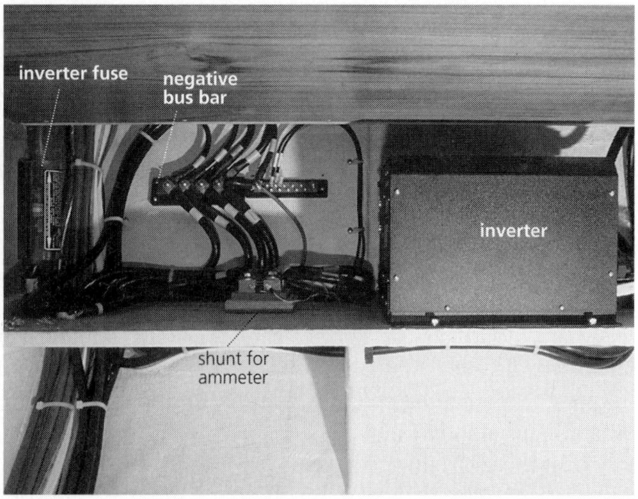

Nada's inverter installation, on a shelf behind our chart drawers. This puts it in a totally dry, well-ventilated environment close to the batteries. Access is somewhat restricted (the chart drawers need to be removed), but this is of little concern. Note also the ship's common ground point (negative bus bar) alongside, which is physically at some distance from the main positive bus bar (to eliminate any chance of shorts between these powerful bus bars). The inverter positive supply is fused (on the left-hand side in the photo). The fuse is covered to protect against shorts—it would have been better to put the fuse below the shelf to get better physical separation from the negative bus bar.

What this all boils down to is the fact that the enticing prospect of constantly available AC power onboard without the need for a generator is a real one, but only in a limited sense—and even then, not one that can be met by simply wiring an inverter to the ship's batteries. As with any additional DC load—particularly such a potentially heavy load—it is necessary to look at the boat's overall power equation and take the necessary steps to keep it in balance.

Without such a holistic approach, an inverter is likely to become a "cancer" that destroys key components of the DC system; with such an approach, one truly can enjoy many of the comforts of home, as long as the inverter is properly installed to ensure trouble-free operation.

DC and AC Installations

When it comes to installing an inverter, one of the more difficult decisions is where to put it, with three potentially contradictory factors at work. First, the inverter should be as close as possible to its batteries (to minimize the lengths of the DC cables; see the following section). Second, it needs to be in a cool area with a good airflow over the unit (i.e., not in the engine compartment). Keeping it cool is necessary because an inverter's overall performance is linked to its temperature; elevated temperatures lead to accelerated electronic-component failure. Third, it must be kept dry and protected from spray or condensation because an inverter is a complex electronic device, incorporating different metals. If moisture is added, we have all the ingredients—water, DC electricity, and dissimilar metals—for destructive galvanic and stray-current corrosion.

The best location is likely in a locker inside the main cabin, alongside the battery compartment. However, an inverter often is stuck in a cockpit locker, where it is at risk of saltwater penetration—a near certain recipe for failure. Whatever locker is used, it needs to be given adequate ventilation to ensure a free flow of air over the inverter. To assist the cooling process, the inverter should also have a temperature-activated fan (not all do), especially if it is intended to sail south into warmer parts, such as the Caribbean or Mediterranean.

If the chosen location is not readily accessible, it is well worth investing in a remote monitoring and control panel (an option with most inverters). Although the *standby drain* (i.e., the drain on the DC system when the inverter is turned "on" but not actually in use) of most modern inverters is quite low, it nevertheless adds up to a significant amount during a twenty-four-hour period. With the remote panel, it is easy to turn the inverter off when it is not needed.

DC Installation

Because of the very high loads that an inverter can impose on a DC system, its DC cables have to be large and short to minimize power-robbing voltage drops in them. In typical circumstances, inverter cables should not exceed 10 feet in length; even with this short distance, a 2,500-watt inverter needs cables of approximately 2/0 gauge (70 mm^2) or larger (about as big as your thumb).

To keep cables as short as possible, inverters are commonly wired directly to the batteries that power them. However, if such a connection is made without a fuse or circuit breaker, and if a short circuit develops in the cables, a dead short will be created across the batteries. *This almost always starts a fire*. It is essential to fit a fuse or circuit breaker as close as possible to the positive terminal of the battery (see Over-Current Protection and High-Current Circuits on the next page). A 2,500-watt inverter needs a fuse or circuit breaker on the order of 250 amps; as a general rule on a 12-volt system, the fuse should have a rating in amps of approximately 10 percent of the rating in watts of the inverter.

Finally, many inverters have a *sleep mode*, in which the inverter's AC output is reduced to a very low level (typically around 9 V) when there is no load on it. As soon as an AC appliance is turned on, the inverter jumps to full output. Given that AC and DC wiring are commonly mixed up on boats, it is easy for someone working on a boat's electrical system to make a quick check for AC voltage, misinterpret the 9 volts AC produced by an inverter in its sleep mode as some anomaly, assume that the AC circuits are in fact depowered, and then go to work without isolating the inverter. If an AC circuit is bridged, the inverter jumps to full output—quite possibly electrocuting the troubleshooter. Unfortunately, I believe it is only a matter of time before someone gets killed in this way.

To deal with this problem—although it is rarely done—I consider it essential to fit an isolation switch or breaker in the DC positive feed to all inverters so that the inverter can be fully disabled before any circuits are worked on. A 2,500-watt, 12-volt inverter needs a switch or circuit breaker with a *continuous* current rating of 250 amps or more.

AC Installation

AC power can be lethal. *Whenever wiring or troubleshooting an inverter, any shore-power cord must be disconnected, any generator shut down, and the inverter disconnected from its DC source.* If in doubt, call a licensed marine electrician.

Three-hundred-amp inverter and windlass breakers.

Under no circumstances must it be possible to bring an inverter and another source of AC power online at the same time. Instant and catastrophic damage is likely to occur to the inverter. To avoid such a possibility, a couple of different wiring options are commonly used. The first routes all the boat's AC inputs (the shore-power supply, any AC generator, and the inverter) through a selector switch that only allows one AC source at a time to be connected to the boat's circuits. The second uses an automatic transfer switch inside the inverter; the shore-power input (and any AC generator output) is routed through the inverter, which senses whenever another source of AC power comes online, automatically switching itself off.

Sometimes boats with an inverter have loads that are too heavy for the inverter to handle (e.g., an electric stove or water heater) or that should not be fed from the inverter (e.g., a battery charger; if a battery charger is powered by an inverter, we get into a loop in which the inverter is feeding the battery charger, which is charging the batteries supplying the inverter, with power losses at every stage of the process). In this case, a subsidiary AC distribution panel is needed for the inverter-based loads, with the noninverter loads tied into the main panel in such a way that they cannot be fed by the inverter.

Finally, for safety reasons beyond the scope of this book, when an inverter is supplying AC power to the boat's circuits, the neutral and ground sides of the inverter's AC output should be internally connected—but when the inverter is switched out of the AC circuits, this connection should be broken. Inverters designed for the marine market do this automatically; some designed for other markets do not. If you are contemplating a nonmarine model, check this feature before your purchase.

OVER-CURRENT PROTECTION AND HIGH-CURRENT CIRCUITS

Occasionally, I teach a week-long course titled Marine Electrics and Mechanics. I have a few stunts and gimmicks designed to hold the attention of my students. The most exciting moment comes when I create a dead short across a 12-volt battery, using a length of 12-gauge (3 mm^2) cable. The moment I throw the switch on the circuit, the cable vaporizes, filling the entire room with a cloud of noxious smoke and forcing us to hastily evacuate the premises!

I am not suggesting that you try this experiment, but I bet many people reading this have already unintentionally set up the same test apparatus on their own boats—or had it set up by someone else. It is done by wiring one or more pieces of equipment directly to the boat's batteries without installing a fuse or circuit breaker at the battery positive connection. *Every single one of these unfused or unbreakered connections is a cable meltdown waiting to happen.* All it takes to set things in motion is a short to ground (earth), such as may occur if the insulation gets damaged or a terminal comes adrift and contacts any grounded object.

Unfortunately, the plethora of electrical circuits on modern boats, compared to those of even a few years ago, has greatly increased the likelihood of unprotected circuits. Worse yet are older boats that have been upgraded by tacking on additional circuits rather than by rewiring the boat. Worst of all are often boats on which the owners have done the wiring!

The net result is that, nowadays, *electrical shorts are probably the number-one cause of fires on boats*. So, be warned: if you or anyone else adds any circuits to your boat, make sure they are properly protected! Better yet, compile a complete wiring diagram for the boat and ensure that all existing circuits are properly protected. It is amazing how many boats come from boatbuilders with one or more unprotected or inadequately protected circuits.

This leaves us with two questions: What size fuse or circuit breaker should be used on a given circuit, and what is the best practical method for ensuring that all circuits are properly protected?

Below: *The consequences of a "dead" short.* Bottom: *One mechanism for a "dead" short.*

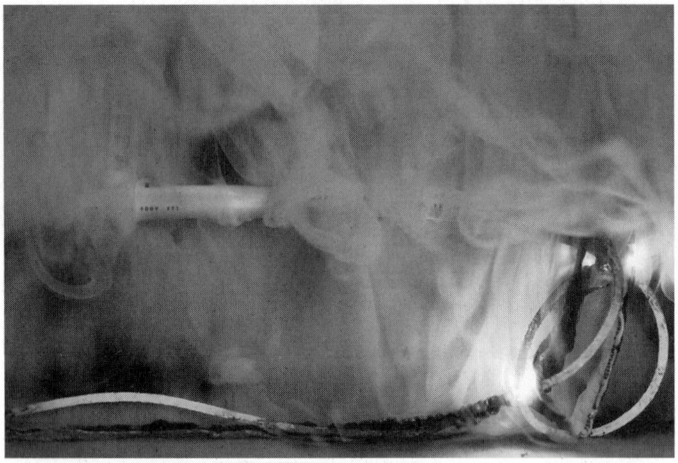

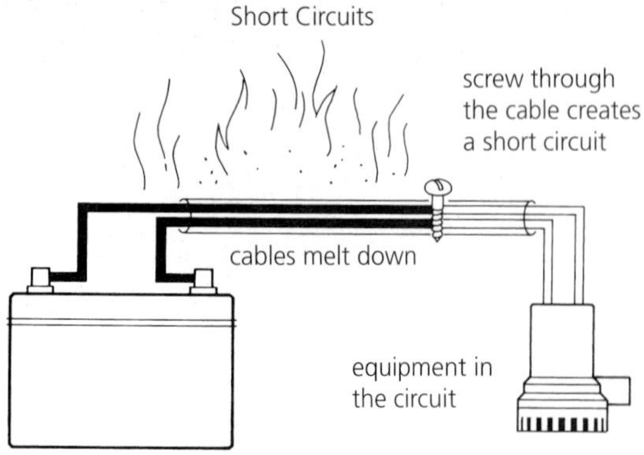

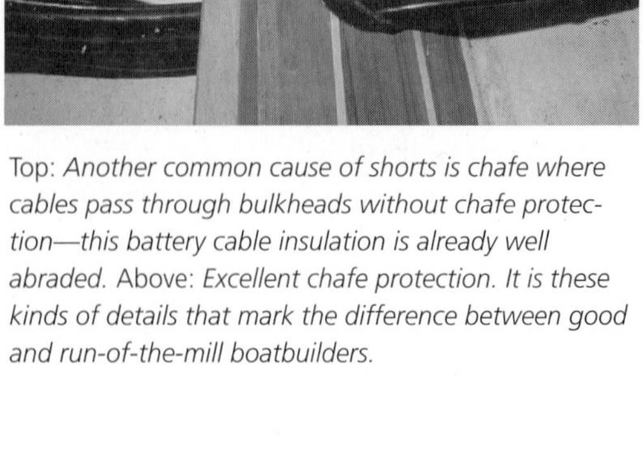

Top: *Another common cause of shorts is chafe where cables pass through bulkheads without chafe protection—this battery cable insulation is already well abraded.* Above: *Excellent chafe protection. It is these kinds of details that mark the difference between good and run-of-the-mill boatbuilders.*

What Size Fuse or Circuit Breaker?

There is a popular misconception that fuses and circuit breakers (*over-current devices*) should be sized according to the current rating (i.e., amperage) of the equipment on a circuit. This is a misunderstanding of the purpose of the over-current device, which is to prevent the wiring in the circuit from melting down in the event of a short circuit. Because the most heat in any circuit is generated by the section of wiring with the highest resistance (the smallest wire), an over-current device is sized to protect the smallest wire in any given circuit. The current-carrying capability of this wire and, therefore, the rating of the over-current device, is found in tables in books such as *Boatowner's Mechanical and Electrical Manual.*

For example, if a GPS, which draws minimal current, is hooked into a circuit wired with 12-gauge (3 mm^2) cable, the over-current device should be rated to protect the wire—not the GPS—from meltdown. Something on the order of a 20-amp fuse or breaker will do fine (note that if poor-quality cable is used, as on many European-built boats, this current rating will be lower). Separate protection (generally a fuse, probably as low as 1 amp) is needed for the GPS or any other equipment on the circuit.

Having said this, if a circuit breaker in a distribution panel protects a circuit to a single load, and the protection required by the load is less than that required by the cables, the breaker can always be sized to protect the load, down to about 5 amps, which is typically the smallest breaker available. On the other hand, if the same approach is used on a breaker that protects several circuits, its sizing is a little more complex. There are two factors to consider: the total load of all the electrical equipment to be served by the breaker; and the current-carrying capability of the *smallest* wire being protected. The breaker must be sized according to the *lower* of the total load or current-carrying capability of the smallest conductor.

Finally, if a breaker feeds another subsidiary panel or fuse block, and if all the conductors from the panel or fuse block to individual appliances are protected by their own breakers or fuses, the only conductor that the first breaker has to protect is the feeder cable to the subsidiary panel. In this case, the breaker is rated according to the lower of the total load on the subsidiary panel or the current-carrying capability of the conductor to the feeder panel.

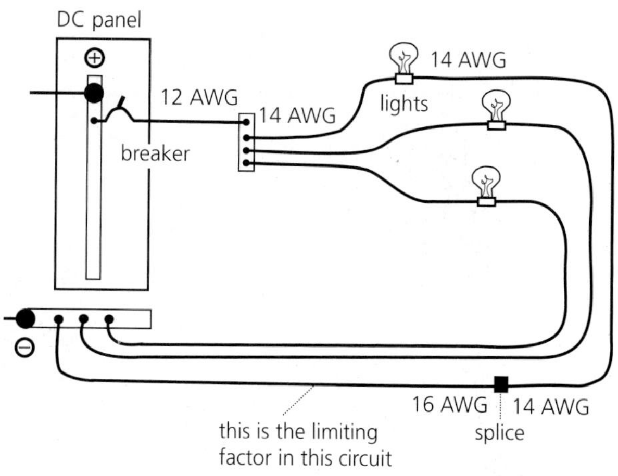

Cable Size	Ampacity Outside Engine Spaces
12 AWG	45
14 AWG	35
16 AWG	25

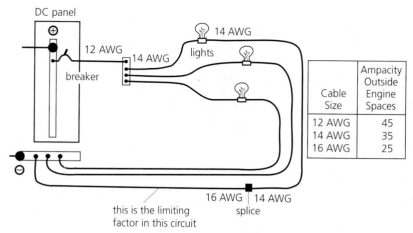

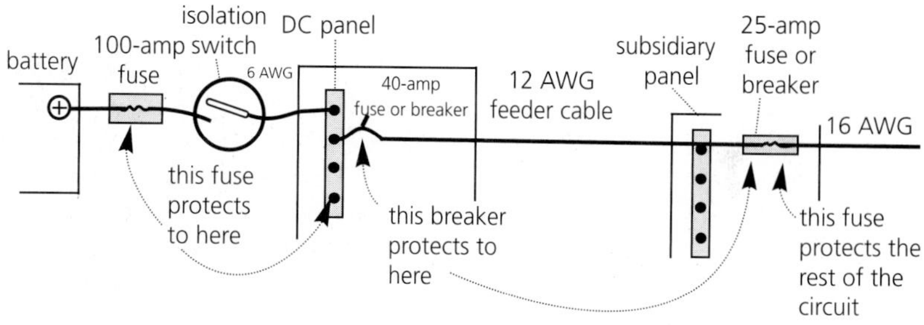

Top: *The smallest cable in a circuit determines the over-current protection.* Above: *Over-current protection of feeder cables and subsidiary circuits.*

High-Current Circuits

Historically, high-current circuits (100 amps and up) have been the most difficult to protect simply because of the lack of affordable over-current protection devices—but this is no longer the case. Relatively cheap (and compact) breakers rated up to 150 amps are now widely available, with cheap (and compact) fuses up to 800 amps. There is simply no excuse for not protecting all high-current circuits, including the cranking circuit.

However, these circuits have large cables that are awkward to handle. The neatest way to deal with them, and provide the necessary protection, is to run a single heavy cable—typically 2/0 gauge (70 mm^2) from the positive post on the house batteries to a battery-isolation switch. The cable is fused as close to the battery as possible, with an appropriately sized fuse (2/0 gauge generally has a current-carrying capability of 300 to 400 amps, depending on the quality of the cable). The isolation switch must have a continuous current rating *at least as high* as the fuse (otherwise, the switch—not the fuse—becomes the weak link).

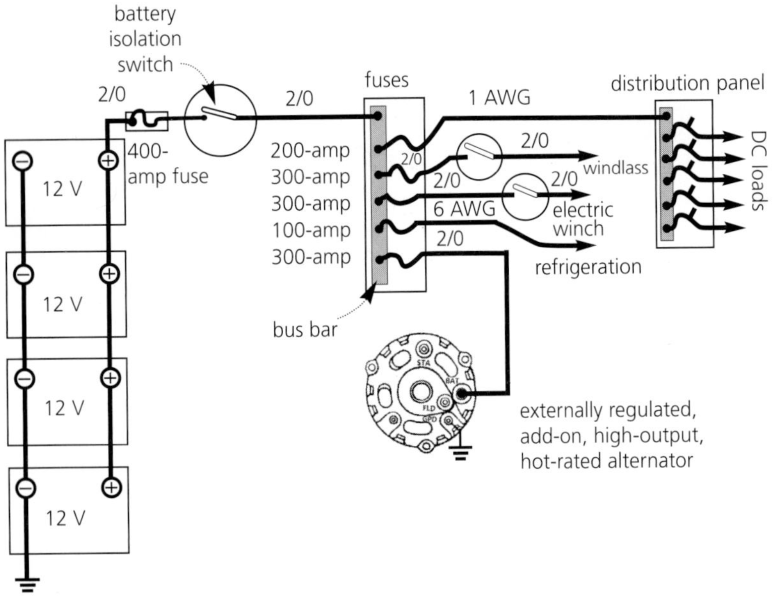

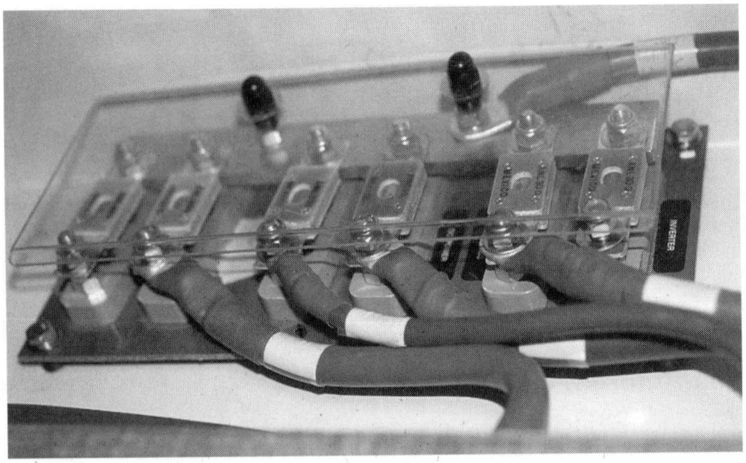

Top: *Basic battery cabling and high-current bus bar for a boat with several high-current DC circuits.* Above: Nada*'s high-current bus bar, which is connected to the isolation switch by a short length of cable (see it coming into the bus bar at top right). The high-current circuits are all tapped off this bus bar, via appropriately rated fuses, at left.*

Another cable (the same size as the first) is run from the isolation switch to a high-current *bus bar,* which is a heavy metal plate drilled and tapped to take a series of bolts. The cable from the isolation switch is bolted onto the bus bar. The bus bar is mounted on a *phenolic*—a plastic—base plate with another series of bolts set up parallel to the bolts in the bus bar. Fuses are bolted in place between the bus bar and the electrically isolated bolts. Now the boat's various high-current circuits (typically a windlass, a high-output alternator, the DC panel, and maybe sail-reefing devices) can be attached to the isolated bolts. The various fuses are sized according to the current-carrying capability of the cables bolted to them.

For example, a windlass may need a 2/0 (70 mm^2) cable with a 250-amp fuse; a distribution panel typically has cables of around 4 gauge (20 mm^2), protected with a fuse of around 100 amps. From the distribution panel, the rest of the boat's circuits are protected with fuses or circuit breakers appropriately rated for the size of the cables in the various circuits.

If the boat has an isolated cranking battery (as recommended previously), there should be an in-line fuse close to the battery in the cable to the starter motor. To prevent this fuse from blowing under a heavy cranking load (e.g., in cold weather), it should be a *slow-blow fuse,* rated at 150 percent of the *ampacity* (the amps rating) of the cranking cables. (Even overrated like this, the fuse still protects against a meltdown if the starter motor or its cables short out.) If the boat has two battery banks, alternated in use, with the cranking circuit coming off whatever bank is in service, the two banks will be wired to a "1, 2, Both, Off" switch, with fuses at the batteries in the two feeder cables.

Nada*'s battery switches, with excellent access to all the cables and terminals.*

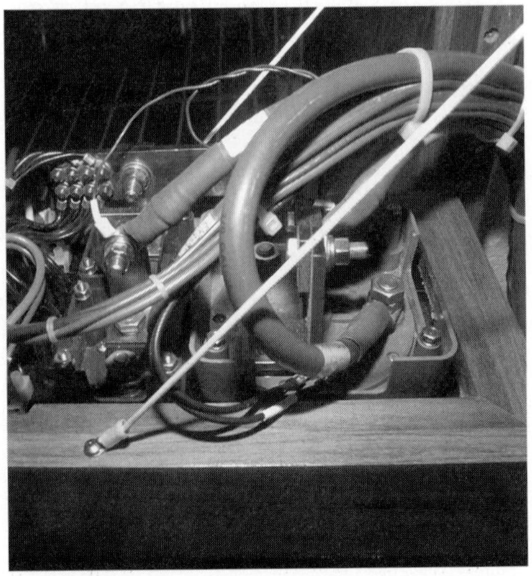

The output of the switch will go to the high-current bus bar; the cranking circuit will simply be another of the fused circuits coming off the bus bar, with its fuse rated as described previously.

Circuits That Bypass the Isolation Switch

This still leaves some circuits that need to bypass the isolation switch so that they can be left "on" when the rest of the boat is shut down. These circuits typically include a bilge pump and any charging devices left on when the boat is not in use (e.g., solar panels, maybe a wind generator, and the inverter if it also doubles as a battery charger); there may also be a carbon monoxide or propane alarm and DC systems monitoring devices. All except the inverter are wired to a separate auxiliary bus bar that is fed by a fused cable tied into the *battery* side of the isolation switch. In turn, each circuit is fused at the bus bar. Given the heavy cable likely to be associated with the inverter, it is best wired directly to the terminal on the switch and provided with its own fuse as close to the switch as possible.

The net result of such an approach is that every circuit on the boat will be fully over-current-protected at its source. However, wired as suggested, the circuits that bypass the battery switch are fused but not switched (in other words, they can never be turned off). I like it this way because it prevents the bilge pump and other key circuits from getting accidentally turned off. Others prefer a switch or circuit breaker in this circuit. (If a circuit breaker is used, it's preferable to use the push-button type, not the switch type—this minimizes the risk of accidentally tripping the breaker.)

Check Your Own Boat

As the electrical load on a boat increases, so does the complexity of electrical circuits and the potential for short circuits and electrical fires. It is more important than ever to wire all circuits with proper over-current protection—yet this is so often omitted. Take a close look at all the cables attached to your battery positive posts; if you find any that are unfused, take immediate steps to correct the situation. It will be time and money well spent.

You should also check the current rating of any high-current bus bars because these too, if overloaded, can get hot and start a fire. Brass often is used as the base material and then maybe tin-, nickel-, or chrome-plated. It is a little-known fact that brass has only 28 percent of the electrical conductivity of copper; therefore, large bus bars are needed to carry high currents. It is preferable to use tin- or nickel-plated copper, which also does not corrode like brass.

Stainless steel bolts and washers are almost universally used in marine bus bars. Stainless has only 3 percent of the electrical conductivity of copper—in other words, it is a poor conductor.

Circuits that need to be left on when all else is isolated are tapped off the battery side of the main house switch, via an appropriately rated fuse. (On Nada, this is all built into the top of the switch panel; refer to the photo bottom left on the opposite page).

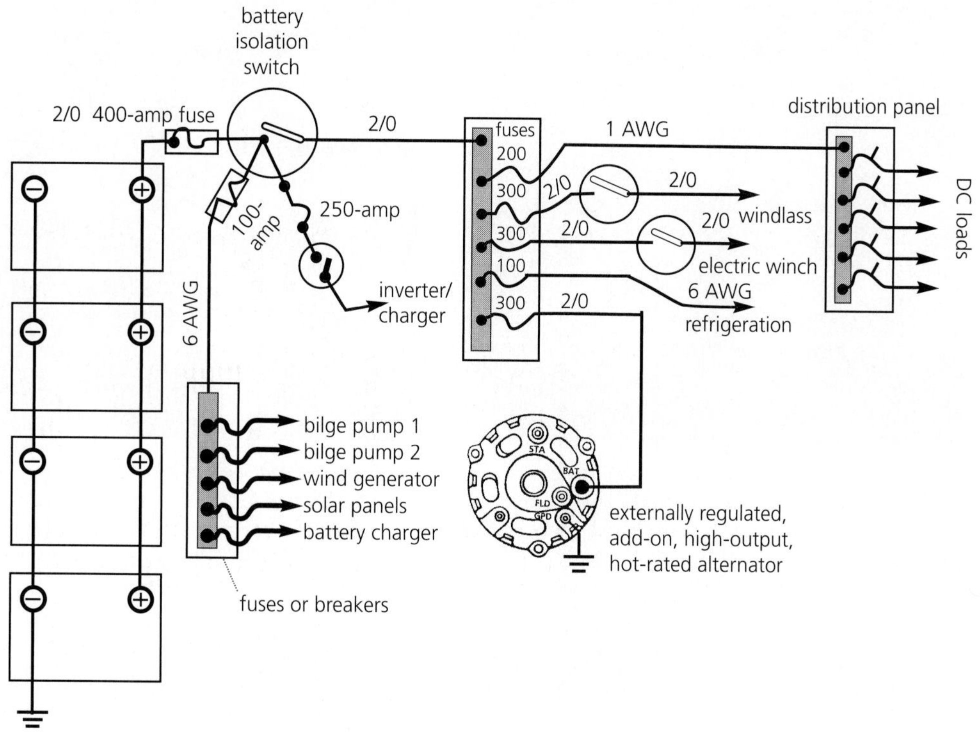

Cables bolted to a battery post. Bolted connections are preferable to the more common cable clamp, but it is not advisable to stack high-current circuits on a battery post. A very small resistance can create enough heat to melt the battery post and/or start a fire. It is also almost certain that these cables are not properly over-current protected.

Any cable terminal bolted down with a stainless steel bolt must be in direct contact with the bus bar to which it is bolted. If a stainless steel washer is allowed to come between a cable terminal and the bus bar (which is not that uncommon), the washer puts a relatively high resistance in the circuit. This resistance not only seriously impairs the performance of the equipment in the circuit, but also creates a lot of heat—more than enough in many high-current circuits to start a fire. Because there is no short circuit and, therefore, no excessively high-current flows, a fuse or circuit breaker does not protect against this kind of a fire. I have seen several fires that originated this way.

Finally, if a terminal is only loosely attached to a bus bar (or anything else, for that matter), it tends to arc whenever current flows (i.e., the equipment is turned on). The higher the current flow, the more powerful is the arc and the greater is the risk of starting a fire. Once again, a fuse does nothing to protect against this kind of fault. *Every connection in a high-current circuit must be well fastened, preferably with a Nylok nut or a similar fastener that will not vibrate loose.* High-output alternators need special attention given the inherent vibration in the installation. I have seen several fires started by output cables working loose. The cable attachment to the alternator should be designed to support the cable so that the cable's weight is not hanging from the terminal. The nut attaching the cable to the alternator must be vibration-proof (i.e., Nylok or locking washer).

A fire at sea can be a truly terrifying experience. Smoke billowing out of the companionway hatch is not the way to find out that your boat is improperly wired!

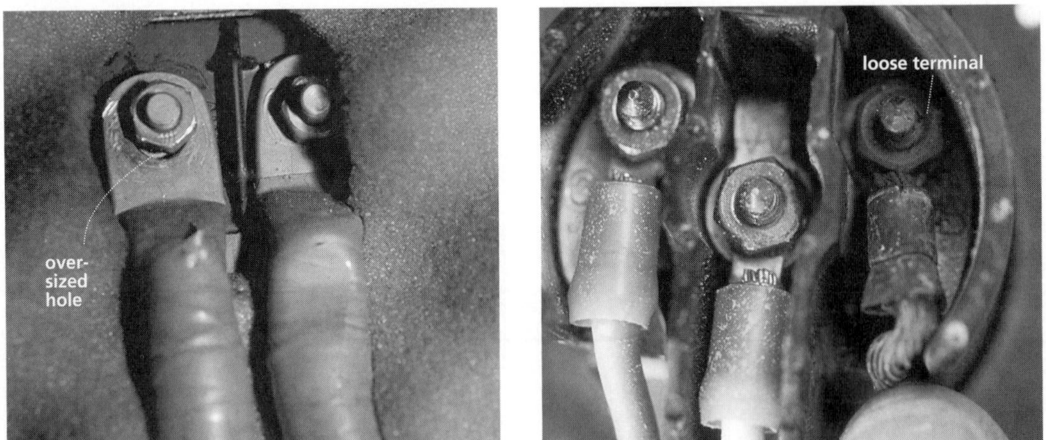

Left: *Note the oversized hole in the cable terminal and the loose nut on this windlass installation. The cable has been arcing and, in doing so, has melted the surrounding foam. Here's a fire waiting to start regardless of whether the circuit is properly over-current-protected (it was not).* Right: *In this case, a loose terminal on a shore-power inlet did start a fire.*

LOW-ENERGY REFRIGERATION

It is my experience that few systems on cruising boats cause more trouble than refrigeration systems. This is particularly the case for boats moving into warmer climates such as the Caribbean or the Mediterranean. This is most unfortunate for a couple of reasons: first, because most of us have come to consider refrigeration a necessity rather than a luxury, and second, because the warmer the climate, the more of a necessity it becomes!

Over the years, I have experimented with several different engine-driven and DC refrigeration systems, and have gradually refined my thinking on the subject. Boats that have regular access to a shore-power cord (i.e., not "off the grid" for more than a few days at a time) find that a small, constantly cycling (like your refrigerator at home) DC unit is both adequate and economical (e.g., Adler Barbour's Cold Machine or the Frigoboat and Isotherm units popular in Europe).

For cruising boats that are off the grid for longer periods, I recommend heavy-duty *holding-plate DC refrigeration* (as long as the boat has a powerful DC system, described previously), although it significantly increases complexity and cost. These systems run just once or twice a day, freezing the contents of a cold plate, which then acts like a super-cooled block of ice to keep down the temperature in the box until the next time the unit is run. However, there are two exceptions to this recommendation:

- a boat with a regularly operating AC generator: it might just as well have AC refrigeration (which is much cheaper to install)
- an off-the-grid boat with an undersized DC system and no regular source of AC power: it is best with engine-driven refrigeration

This choice of DC refrigeration is based on two considerations: efficiency and versatility.

Efficiency

At first, it seems irrational to claim efficiency as a benefit of DC refrigeration. The key component in a refrigeration system is the compressor, which has to be driven by some kind of motor. When it comes to DC refrigeration, the process goes something like this: an engine drives an alternator (up to a 50 percent energy loss), which charges a battery (an approximate 10 to 15 percent energy loss), which is used to power a DC motor (an approximate 15 percent energy loss), which in turn is used to spin the compressor. Some efficiency!

Engine-driven refrigeration. (Courtesy Sea Frost)

In fact, the DC-driven compressor could just as easily have been spun by the engine in the first place (i.e., engine-driven refrigeration), eliminating all those intermediary energy losses. Engine-driven refrigeration has been a popular choice among cruisers and charter-fleet operators for many years. It is less complex, considerably cheaper, and more effective than holding-plate DC refrigeration.

To see how a holding-plate DC system, in many circumstances, can be more efficient than an engine-driven system, we have to delve a little deeper into the workings of a refrigeration system. The cold plates that both systems use contain a special solution that freezes at controlled temperatures. This solution is frozen when the engine is running or the DC unit is operating. After the engine or DC system is shut down, the solution slowly thaws, holding down the temperature in the icebox (in thawing, the solution "soaks up" heat that infiltrates the icebox).

Given the substantial engine horsepower available to most engine-driven systems, it seems that a large compressor could be used to rapidly freeze a cold plate, quickly producing the desired refrigeration effect. However, we must consider the following rather obscure but highly significant fact: the limiting factor in the rate at which all but the largest cold plates can be pulled down is the rate at which heat can be pulled out of the cold plate, *not* the refrigerating capability of the compressor doing the work.

What does this mean in practice? It means that no matter how powerful the compressor, the cold plates in the system will take their own sweet time to freeze. In warm climates, this typically amounts to well over an hour a day—in some cases, two to three hours. With an engine-driven system, the engine must be running all this time. However, if DC refrigeration is used, despite the energy losses inherent in the process, it is often possible for an alternator to replace the twenty-four-hour refrigeration drain on the batteries in less time—*maybe thirty minutes to an hour*—than it would take an engine-driven system to pull down the cold plates. In other words, even though the DC system is substantially less efficient than an engine-driven system (from a narrow refrigeration point of view), engine-running time—the one factor we are trying to minimize on a cruising boat—ends up being less with the DC system than with the engine-driven system.

The key factor is to have a charging system and battery bank that have the ability to produce and store the energy needed to pull down the cold plates in less time than the cold plates in fact can be pulled down. This generally requires the high-output alternator, multistep voltage regulator, large battery bank, and carefully designed DC system described previously. If this system is backed up with supplemental energy sources, such as solar panels and a wind generator, at times it may be possible to refrigerate without any engine-running time at all. Given such a DC system—in the overall context of boat use—the DC refrigeration system becomes more efficient than the engine-driven system (albeit at a sometimes horrendous purchase price).

Cold plate—the limiting factor in the rate of heat removal from many refrigeration systems. (Courtesy Glacier Bay)

Versatility

This brings us to the second significant advantage of DC refrigeration (both constant-cycling and cold-plate units): its versatility.

Whenever a boat is at dockside, regardless of whether shore power is available, the engine must still be run to operate an engine-driven refrigeration system. With DC refrigeration, if the boat can be plugged into shore power, the refrigeration unit can be run via a battery charger; no engine-running time is required. Some engine-driven systems include a secondary AC- or DC-powered circuit so that they too can be used at dockside without running the engine. However, the second circuit results in a reduction in the rate at which the cold plates can be pulled down when in the engine-drive mode, lengthening the time it takes to refrigerate—at the one time when the system needs to be at its most efficient. The secondary AC or DC system also substantially increases the cost. These are lousy trade-offs.

Then there is the matter of shore leave. One of the reasons my family and I go cruising is to explore foreign lands and cultures. We like to occasionally leave our boat anchored out and unattended to travel inland. With engine-driven refrigeration, food in the refrigerator and freezer will soon spoil unless someone is around to run the engine on a daily basis. With DC refrigeration and a control mechanism that allows the unit to be cycled "on" and "off" with a thermostat, the refrigeration unit will keep up with the heat infiltration into the icebox until the batteries are dead. As discussed previously, I try to design DC systems that will support the refrigeration load for at least seven days.

Insulate, Insulate, Insulate

Achieving adequate icebox insulation is very often the most difficult part of establishing this seven-day refrigeration capability.

Most of us with production sailboats are fairly well stuck with the iceboxes that come with the boats; even our new Pacific Seacraft 40 gave us little flexibility in this respect. It has a

The icebox insulation on Nada *is as good as most production boats but, at 4 inches, is not adequate for a freezer on a cruising boat.*

comprehensive molded-fiberglass cabin module that includes the surround for the icebox. Prior to installation in the hull, the module is popped off its mold and turned upside down. The icebox liner—a separate molding—is then bonded into the cabin module to the underside of what will be a galley countertop. The space between the icebox liner and the cabin module is filled with poured-in foam; then the cabin module is turned right side up and dropped into the hull. At a later time, an inch or so of Styrofoam insulation is glued to the underside of the counter, inside the icebox, to insulate its top.

If done correctly, this method of construction eliminates voids in the insulation, and the result is at least as good as almost any other production boat on the market. However, given the relative sizes of the cabin module and icebox liner, the foam thickness is limited to no more than 4 inches (100 mm), and significantly less in some places. In my opinion, this is just about adequate for a refrigerator but inadequate for the freezer on a cruising boat. Over time, even the poured-in foam will absorb moisture, further reducing its insulating properties. The Styrofoam under the countertop is inadequate from any perspective.

Changing the physical dimensions of this icebox to allow more insulation to be poured in would be very costly. So what can people in these and similar situations do?

Vacuum-Based "Super" Insulation

Experience gained over many years has shown that the refrigerator icebox on a cruising boat should have insulation equal to at least R-20; a freezer icebox should have insulation equal to at least R-30. This translates to approximately 4 inches (100 mm) of closed-cell foam on the refrigerator and 6 inches (150 mm) on the freezer. However, as noted previously, over time there will be a slow deterioration in the insulation, in addition to which this amount of foam takes up a lot of room (4 in./100 mm of foam around a 6.5 cubic ft./184 L refrigerator icebox occupies about 10 cubic ft./283 L).

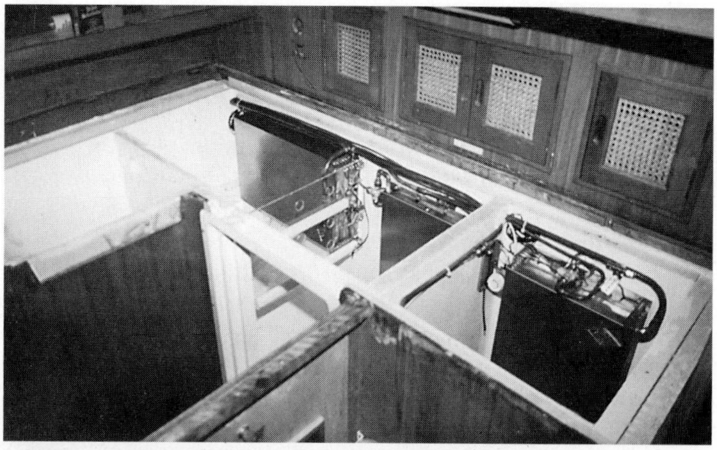

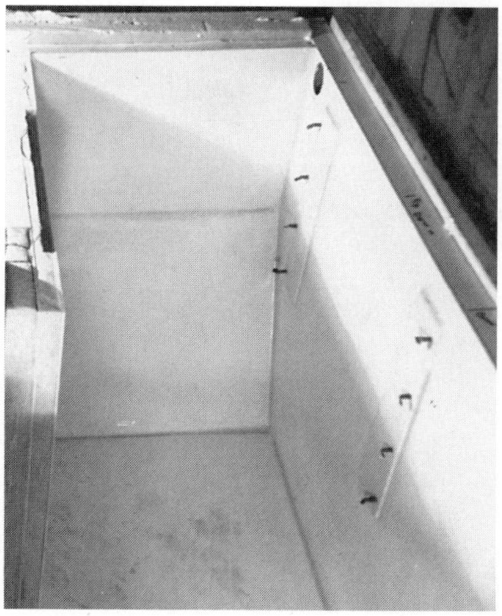

"Super"-insulation panels being installed (below left and below) *. . . with a nicely constructed icebox lid* (bottom)*. (Courtesy Glacier Bay)*

In recent years, several attempts have been made to produce "super" insulations that will not only have a vastly higher "R" number than conventional insulation (so that 1 in./25 mm exceeds the insulating properties of even 6 in./150 mm of conventional foam), but also will not deteriorate over time. The most promising are based on vacuum technology, with several companies now supplying vacuum-based super-insulation panels for the marine market.

The panels use a variety of different materials and construction methods, which affects not only the initial R value (i.e., the effectiveness), but also (1) the likelihood of them losing their vacuum and, therefore, their insulation value over time; and (2) the ultimate insulation value if the vacuum is lost altogether. Almost all of the panels on the market will deteriorate over time, although the rate of degradation is in dispute. Depending on whom you talk to, it ranges from the relatively insignificant (fifty-plus years before the insulation value is affected) to a total loss of super-insulation properties *in less than a year*.

Super insulation is very attractive to cruising sailors, either in new construction (as in our case) or as a retrofit to an older, problematic icebox. However, given the inherent risk in using a new technology, we deemed it prudent to bed the super insulation we used (Barrier-20 from Glacier Bay; the aerogel-based Barrier Ultra-R—their latest product—was not available when we built our boat) in conventional foam. If the super insulation fails, we still have insulation that is as good as Pacific Seacraft's conventional icebox.

Unfortunately, it was cost-prohibitive to use super insulation in the top of our icebox, so we substituted 2 inches (50 mm) of Styrofoam blueboard for Pacific Seacraft's 1 inch (25 mm) of regular Styrofoam. This solution is less than ideal, but suffices.

If we were building today, I would use the Barrier Ultra-R, not just because of its increased R value (2½ times as great as Barrier-20), but also because the nature of the new technology represented by this product is such that if the vacuum fails, the panel still has an ultimate R value considerably higher than that of conventional foam. With a product like this, there is no way you can lose . . . as long as you can afford the not inconsiderable price tag. (For a useful discussion of super insulation, consult Glacier Bay's Web site at www.Glacierbay.com, remembering that this company is just one of an increasing number in this field.)

A well-constructed and sealed small front-opening door at the base of the refrigerator icebox greatly improves access.

Testing the seal on an icebox door.

For those who are stuck with an existing icebox that is a poor performer, it may be possible to install a layer of super insulation on the inside of the icebox. Even if only three sides and the bottom can be covered, or even just parts of the sides and bottom (it may be too difficult to deal with the side on which the cold plate is mounted), it will have significant benefits. The key is to remember to adequately protect the super-insulation panels—if they get punctured, the loss of vacuum will render them ineffective. In some cases, if there are no voids in the insulation, the panels can be mounted on the external cabinetry that surrounds the icebox. On our old boat, we also added a 1-inch-thick (25 mm) hinged insulation panel with a surface of Formica to the top of our icebox. To access the icebox, we simply lifted the panel and locked it up with a barrel bolt. It worked well without being the least bit inconvenient.

And then there are the seals on icebox lids and doors and the drain: all need to be carefully inspected to make sure that they are not a source of heat infiltration. I have always been an opponent of front-opening boxes because the door allows cold air to spill out every time it is opened, but I have been persuaded that the actual energy loss is not that great and have been seduced by the convenience on our new boat. The key is to ensure that the door is as well insulated as the rest of the box and that no air can leak around the seals. Our door is super insulated, with excellent seals.

Enhancing Performance

These types of measures reduce the *heat load* of an icebox to the minimum practicable level. The next task is to make the refrigeration unit as efficient as possible, so that it consumes the minimum amount of energy necessary to keep the icebox cold.

The most popular DC refrigeration units are small, air-cooled machines. They are relatively cheap, easy to install, and work well for weekend and coastal cruising if batteries can be recharged at dockside or during relatively frequent periods of engine operation. However, once a boat moves away from its shore-power connection and engine-running time is reduced, these units can really knock the stuffing out of a battery bank, particularly if the boat sails into warmer climates. The rising air temperature substantially reduces the efficiency of an air-cooled unit at the same time as the heat load of the icebox goes up: all the variables are moving in the wrong direction!

DC refrigeration systems vary as widely in energy consumption as they do in cost. However, it is fair to say that of the many steps that can be taken to improve the efficiency of a DC unit, two are particularly significant: install a water-cooled condensing unit (an option with many units); and use a much larger motor and refrigeration compressor, the practical option being ½-horsepower (⅓ kW) units or even larger. These units are produced by most of the leading manufacturers.

Whereas the compressor on a small, air-cooled unit draws 6 or 7 amps when it is running, the ½-horsepower (⅓ kW) compressor draws up to 40 amps. However, the small unit may end up running just about full time in the tropics (and still do a poor job of refrigerating), whereas the ½-horsepower (⅓ kW) unit will likely run for just an hour or two. The net result is better refrigeration with a much-reduced overall battery drain. Battery drain will be further minimized if the refrigeration unit is so configured that it comes on and "tops up" the cold plates any time the engine is running. Of the ½-horsepower (⅓ kW) DC units, tests show the Glacier Bay to be the most efficient—hence, our preference for it.

Cold Plates (Holding Plates)

The cold plates also play an important role in both refrigeration efficiency and effectiveness. There are two issues here: one concerning construction, the other the kind of solution used in the plate. Cold plates contain a long tube (the *evaporator coil*) through which refrigerant is passed. The coil is immersed in some kind of solution. When the refrigeration unit is running, the refrigerant pulls down the temperature of the coil, which freezes the solution. After the unit is shut down, the solution thaws out, keeping the icebox cold.

The greater the surface area of the evaporator coil is for a given cold plate size and the closer together is the spacing of the coils, the faster and more efficiently the cold plate can be frozen down. Of all the cold-plate manufacturers, Glacier Bay currently packs the most surface area into its plates with the narrowest spacing.

As for the solution inside the plates, many manufacturers use an antifreeze mixture. When you cool an antifreeze solution, it reaches a certain temperature at which it starts to freeze. To freeze it some more, its temperature must be lowered some more—in other words, to freeze the entire solution, there must be a progressive lowering of the temperature. The lower the temperature has to go to continue the freezing

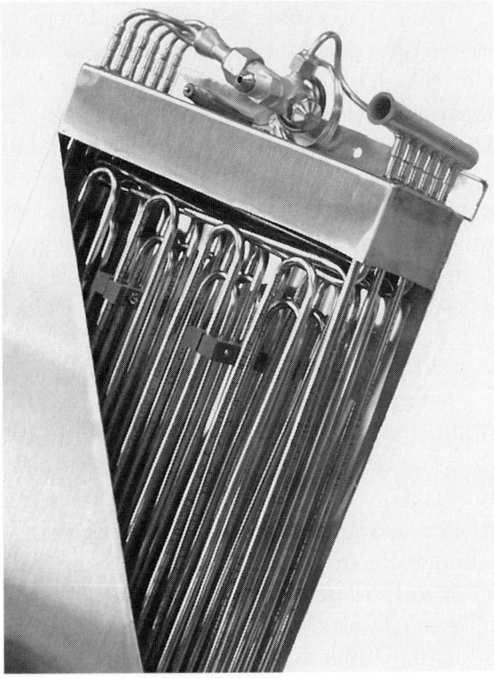

Spider Coil inside a Glacier Bay cold plate: the most efficient—but also the most expensive—on the market.

process, the less efficient is the system. In addition, if plates containing such a solution are used in a refrigerator icebox, fresh produce tends to freeze toward the end of the refrigeration cycle.

Much to be preferred are plates that contain what is known as a *eutectic solution*, which freezes at a specific temperature—for example, water freezes at 32°F (0°C). For effective cold-plate refrigeration, solutions that freeze around 26°F (–3°C) are desirable in a refrigerator box and 0°F (–18°C) in a freezer box. Not only will plates with true eutectic solutions freeze down more efficiently than those containing antifreeze solutions, but they will also maintain a much more consistent temperature in the icebox in which they are mounted.

If a boat has both a freezer and a refrigerator, it will be much easier to maintain consistent temperatures in the two boxes if the respective cold plates are individually controlled rather than mounted in a common circuit. Individual control is also preferable to using any kind of a "spill-over" arrangement between the freezer and the refrigerator.

Cold plates come in stock sizes. Custom sizes can be manufactured, but tend to be expensive. So, when having an icebox built or modified or when adding a cold-plate refrigeration system to an icebox, it is a good idea to make sure that any plates will fit through the icebox openings before getting too involved (it is surprising how often this is forgotten until it's too late). It should be understood that the plates need to be removable to service the system; however, it is not unheard of for boatbuilders to put them in before bonding on an icebox lid that prevents them from being removed!

Installation

Whatever refrigeration unit and cold plates are used, they need careful installation, which will make or break the long-term functionality of many systems. Two aspects are critical: ensuring leak-free joints in the refrigeration tubing; and properly sealing the holes that must be cut through the icebox insulation to accommodate the refrigerant tubing (if using superinsulation panels, make sure you don't drill through them!). The latter requirement is often not given enough attention. If there is any kind of a space around the refrigerant tubing, air can penetrate. Moisture then condenses on the tubing and drains into the insulation. Over the course of months and years, the insulation becomes saturated and its effectiveness is destroyed. The unhappy boatowner will conclude that the refrigeration unit is no longer working properly (after all, it used to run far less and do a better job), whereas the real problem is degraded insulation—which is very difficult and expensive to fix.

The installer forgot to seal these refrigeration tubes where they pass through the icebox wall. To make matters worse, they were brought in at the bottom of the box. Not only is this a huge energy leak, but also moisture condensing on the tubes is dripping into the foam and saturating it.

Suction lines (the larger of the lines that run between the refrigeration unit and the cold plates) "sweat" when the unit is in operation. They need to be wrapped with tightly fitting and well-sealed insulation to avoid energy losses and annoying drips and puddles inside the lockers through which they run.

User-Friendly Iceboxes

Finally, the ergonomics of icebox design need to be discussed—something that seems to be ignored on many boats. Often, the icebox is a deep pit with a couple of shelves that must be removed (together with all their contents) to access the bottom of the box. Once the shelves are out, only tall people can actually reach the bottom of the box without disappearing into it headfirst. Access is sometimes made even more difficult by tucking iceboxes into spaces that place the lids well back from the edges of countertops. The following rules-of-thumb should be observed:

- Icebox lids should be close to the edge of the countertop in which they are placed.
- It should not be necessary to unload the top of a refrigerator box to access the bottom. If the icebox does not have a front-opening door at the bottom, shelves can be designed to slide backward and forward or from side to side. If this is not possible, any shelves should at least be designed so they can be lifted out without having to unload their contents.
- Because it doesn't have to be done very often, it *is* acceptable to have to unload the top of a freezer to reach the bottom.
- The bottoms of both refrigerator and freezer iceboxes should be accessible to a person with an "average" reach.
- These measures also make it reasonably easy to clean the iceboxes, especially if the refrigerator has a drain at its low point. However, it is important to seal the drain so that it does not become a source of heat gain. The drain should lead to a container, or pump into the galley sink, but not to the bilge (it causes smells). Freezer boxes do not need (and should not have) drains.
- The galley lighting should illuminate the insides of the iceboxes, which usually requires a light specifically located above them.

Effective Refrigeration

With attention given to these kinds of details, it is possible to have easy-to-use iceboxes and effective refrigeration on a cruising boat, without the system destroying the equanimity of those onboard. Without this attention to detail, the boatowner may become one of the many frustrated cruisers who provide a meal ticket to refrigeration mechanics in far-flung corners of the world.

LOW-ENERGY LIGHTING

A few years ago, I was inspecting a new offering from a well-known cruising boatbuilder. I told the builder I really liked the boat, but felt that the DC systems were not adequate for today's cruising lifestyle. He responded: "Nigel, the owners have just got to learn to turn the f . . . ing lights off!"

Lighting is another heavy DC load on many boats—more of a load than most people realize. Conservation in this area pays significant dividends; therefore, the first thing, of course, is to learn to turn the lights off (something at which Americans don't seem to be too good). Beyond that, nothing reduces the load more than using fluorescent or LED lighting as the primary lighting in place of the typical incandescent dome and reading lights.

Fluorescent Lights

The choice of fluorescent lighting on a cruising boat is an obvious one (except for boats going into high latitudes—conventional fluorescents do not work well in low-temperature environments). According to GE, manufacturer of both fluorescent and incandescent lamps, fluorescent lamps typically produce about 72 *lumens* (a measure of light output) per watt of energy consumed (some highly efficient fluorescents produce 100 lumens per watt of energy consumed), whereas incandescent lights typically produce about 17.5 lumens per watt. In other words, fluorescent lights are approximately four times more efficient than incandescent lights. Or, put another way, an entire cabin can be lit with a 26-watt fluorescent light that

Fluorescent lights are far more efficient than dome lights.

produces about 1,700 lumens; whereas, for the same power consumption, only about 400 lumens of light output is produced by an incandescent dome or reading light.

Fluorescent lights have another benefit to cruisers such as ourselves who spend most of their time in tropical climates: they produce considerably less heat than incandescent lights. Finally, *on paper*, they have a much greater life expectancy than incandescent lamps—20,000 hours on average (over two years continuous use), as opposed to between 750 and 1,000 hours for incandescent lamps. *In practice*, they rarely achieve this life expectancy because it is based on a stable voltage (12.6 V) and temperature (70°F/21°C), with the light left on all the time.

On a boat, voltages may be below 11.0 volts (when the batteries are down and if there is significant voltage drop in the wiring) or above 14.4 volts (when charging with a multistep regulator). In both cases, the life expectancy of just about all kinds of lights is significantly reduced. The other thing that really shortens the life expectancy of a conventional fluorescent light is constantly turning it on and off (for this reason, it is often a good idea to use an incandescent light in the head compartment, even on an energy-conscious boat).

Once a fluorescent light starts to act up (it is slow to come on, it flickers, or there is a purple flash at the end of the tube when coming on) or the ends of the tube (or tubes, as in a dual-fixture unit) are substantially blackened, the tube(s) should be replaced right away rather than waiting for total failure. This helps protect the much more expensive and harder to replace *ballast unit* that powers the tube. Although 8-, 13-, and 26-watt (single- and dual-tube) units are the most common fluorescent lights on boats, 15- or 30-watt units—which use a larger-diameter 15-watt tube—are more efficient and less prone to failure.

On boats, fluorescent lights are generally run from the DC system. Even so, DC fluorescent lights use regular AC fluorescent tubes. To generate the necessary AC power, the ballast unit contains a small DC to AC inverter, which switches the incoming DC current (from the boat's batteries) from negative to positive at a very high rate to generate the necessary AC output. Unfortunately, this high-frequency switching often generates *radio frequency interference* (RFI). Specially "screened" fluorescent lights are needed to minimize the RFI, especially if the light unit is close to a navigation station or anywhere else where there may be sensitive electronics. Because the marine environment is a high-humidity environment, these units should also have special humidity protection.

Many fluorescent lights marketed for boats have come out of the recreational-vehicle market (the best known of which in the U.S. are manufactured by Thin-Lite). These lights are economical, generally work well, and use tubes that can be found at just about any hardware store, but are often not RFI-suppressed or humidity-protected. Currently, the Cadillacs of the marine market are manufactured by Alpenglow in the U.S., using compact fluorescent technology with RFI and humidity protection, and Resolux (a German company; IMTRA–New Bedford, Massachusetts, imports these lights into the U.S.). They are not cheap, but they are extremely nice!

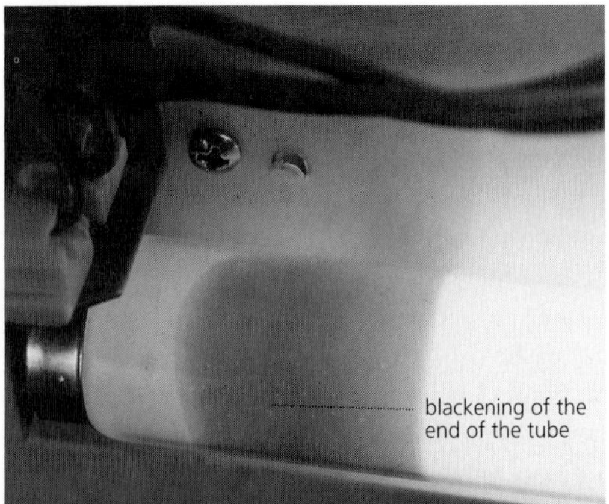

When the end of a fluorescent tube looks like this, it is time to replace it before it damages the more expensive and more difficult to replace ballast unit.

Cold Cathode Fluorescent Lights

Conventional fluorescents rely on an electric current to heat a filament in the end of the tubes—the *cathode*—to a high temperature. The cathode degrades every time the lamp is lit, and slowly burns out (the most common mechanism for tube failure). The thin filament is also susceptible to damage from shocks and vibration. As the cathode ages, the tube gets more difficult to light up, which stresses the ballast unit and leads to ballast failure.

Recently, we have seen the introduction of a new technology—*cold cathode fluorescents* (CCF)—that not only utilizes a more substantial cathode than a conventional fluorescent, but also activates the cathode through an electronic process instead of heating it. The net result, according to Mark Matousek, General Manager of Taylorbrite (a manufacturer), is efficiency similar to a traditional fluorescent, but with less sensitivity to voltage fluctuations, shocks, and vibration. (The Taylorbrite units are Marine UL-listed, which includes shock, vibration, moisture, and RFI testing; they are waterproof and ignition-proof.) The nature of the electronic ballast is such that the units can be dimmed (something that can't be done with most fluorescents). In addition, Mark reports that the life expectancy of CCFs is not affected when frequently switched on for short periods. Given these properties, they have a significantly longer predicted life span than a traditional fluorescent, which looks like a great set of characteristics. It remains to be seen how the lights work out in practice in the marine environment (they've been on the market since mid-2000).

One issue of concern to long-distance cruisers is the fact that CCFs require specialized tubes that are not widely available. If this lighting is installed on a cruising boat, it is advisable to stock up on a few spares.

LED Lighting

LED cluster lights have been on the market since early 2000. This is a new technology that holds great promise for energy conservation, but not quite in the way that many people believe.

LEDs are typically red and green. For years, getting white light out of an LED "has been the Holy Grail of the LED industry," says Rob Hoffman of Deep Creek Design (a manufacturer of LED lighting). A Japanese company, Nichia, is dominant in this technology, although there is reputed to be competition on the way. Nichia developed an LED bulb that uses a blue LED to excite a phosphor coating inside the bulb to produce a near-white light (it has a bluish tinge).

In operation, LEDs consume miniscule amounts of energy, but also produce miniscule amounts of light. Given the low light output of an LED, several have to be clustered together to get any significant output. Even then, they are nowhere near as efficient as fluorescents, currently producing at best about 15 to 20 lumens per watt of energy consumed (as opposed to 72+ lumens for fluorescents). This means it is likely to be a long time before we see LED lights supplanting fluorescents or even incandescents for general lighting purposes. However, LEDs do have an application where low-level, highly focused task lighting is required (e.g., nighttime lighting in a navigation station, some reading lights, and lighting of instrument panels).

Despite the low lumen output, light from an LED can be highly visable. This makes LEDs particularly useful in situations where visibility rather than illumination is the primary purpose, particularly navigation and anchor lights. The benefits are especially noticeable for red and green navigation lights because red and green LEDs can be used with a clear lens, which utilizes the full 15- to 20-lumens-per-watt output of the LEDs, rather than putting a colored lens in front of an incandescent bulb, with the lens reducing the light output to between 1 and 5 lumens per watt. The same applies to red nighttime lighting inside the boat (and also to traffic lights, in which a 10-watt LED cluster can replace a 100-watt light bulb!).

For a given energy consumption, visibility can be further increased by pulsing LEDs on and off at a high frequency (too high for the human eye to detect; what is seen is a steady light) that reduces the duty cycle to around 50 percent, doubling the theoretical life of the LED while cutting the energy consumption in half. The net result is that with differently colored LEDs, chip-based technology, and the clustering of several LEDs, it is possible to create navigation and anchor lights that meet the U.S. Coast Guard (USCG) 2- and 3-mile visibility requirements—at a fraction of the energy consumption of an equivalent incandescent or halogen light.

Other benefits accruing from LED technology are an insensitivity to voltage fluctuations, high resistance to shocks, and an extremely long life. This long life expectancy makes it reasonable to think of placing LEDs in totally sealed and, therefore, waterproofed housings (essentially, the entire fixture is replaced if the light fails).

However, it is important to remember that life-expectancy numbers are derived in laboratory conditions. Even in the laboratory, white LEDs have a life expectancy of fifty thousand hours, as opposed to a hundred thousand hours for other colors. Furthermore, well before the LEDs reach the end of their life cycle, there is a significant loss of light output, such that Taylorbrite only rates its white LED units for ten thousand hours. Remember too that this is just the rated life of the LEDs themselves; there is also the "driver" unit, which powers the LEDs and is made by the light manufacturer, not the LED manufacturer. Some of these drivers (e.g., Deep Creek Design's "Pulse Width Modulated" unit) are electronically quite complex. The drivers have their own life expectancy, which may turn out to be the limiting factor in the life of the light. In other words, there are several unknowns that cannot be resolved in the laboratory.

In summary, LED lights are still expensive, have decidedly limited light outputs, and—to a considerable extent—have an unknown life expectancy in the marine environment. Nevertheless, the technology is exciting and definitely worth watching. We have a prototype LED anchor light with a built-in photoelectric cell (it turns itself off in the daytime) from Deep Creek Design (www.deepcreekdesign.com). It fits a standard bulb socket, puts out a fairly good light, and draws only 0.05 to 0.10 amps at 12 volts, but costs more than $100. Deep Creek Design advertises a life expectancy of a hundred thousand hours; we'll see how it holds up over time.

First-generation LED cluster light for an anchor light. It consumes very little energy and has a built-in photoelectric cell to automatically turn it off during the day—two great features.

Halogen Lights

Halogen lights, sometimes known as "quartz halogen," are a refinement of a regular incandescent bulb. As with other incandescents, there is a tungsten filament that is heated to give off light. In the halogen lamp, the filament is mounted inside a crystal ("quartz") case that is filled with pressurized halogen gas. As the lamp burns, particles of tungsten are thrown off the filament. In a regular incandescent lamp, this eventually leads to lamp burnout; in a halogen lamp, the tungsten combines with the halogen vapor and then gets redeposited on the filament. This has several beneficial effects: the filaments can be raised to a temperature higher than normal without loss of life span, resulting in a higher light output for the same power consumption; the lamps last longer than regular incandescent lamps; and there is no blackening of the bulb over the life of the lamp, resulting in minimal light loss as the lamp ages.

The extent to which halogen lamps are more efficient than regular incandescents is quite variable and often not as significant as many boatowners believe. At the low end, the improvement may be only 25 percent; at the high end, it may be as much as 200 percent. Halogens are certainly no match for fluorescents, although the nature of the bulbs is such that the light can be highly focused, making them excellent reading lamps, added to which the light output is extremely "white," rendering most objects in their natural colors.

The drawbacks to halogen lamps include the high cost relative to regular incandescents, the significant amount of heat produced by the lamps (hot spots on the bulbs can go as high as 1,230°F/665°C), and the sensitivity of the bulbs to over-voltage. At 13.8 volts (the lowest likely voltage-regulator setting on an alternator or battery charger), life expectancy of a nominal 12-volt bulb is reduced to just 30 percent of rated life; at 14.4 volts, it is below one fifth of rated life. We found out the hard way, blowing our halogen masthead tricolor light three times in three extended cruises. Given a replacement cost of $14 and the difficulty of replacing the lamp (many halogen bulbs are a fiddle to get in and out), I changed the masthead unit to one using regular incandescent bulbs (subsequently changed for the LED cluster light). Incandescents don't last a whole lot longer, but they are easier to replace and a lot cheaper.

Note, however, that the latest generation of xenon bulbs are less sensitive to voltage, create less heat, last up to two times as long as standard halogens, and appear to combine the benefits of halogens with increased cost effectiveness in comparison to incandescents. Here's another technology worth watching.

AC SYSTEMS

The AC system on most cruising boats (even those with AC generators and inverters) is generally quite simple. Essentially, there is likely to be just a half-dozen circuits: a microwave, a hot-water heater, and various AC outlets scattered around the boat. To these may be added air conditioning, an AC watermaker, AC refrigeration, a dive compressor, and so on; however, they simply increase the number of circuits rather than complicate the overall picture.

Regarding a shore-power connection, the choice (in the United States) is between a 30- and a 50-amp inlet (in Europe, it is commonly 16 amps or less). Without air conditioning, a single 30-amp inlet is almost always adequate. If air conditioning is installed, a single 50-amp inlet generally handles the boat's entire AC load; however, I recommend separating out the air conditioner and having two independent 30-amp inlets—one running the air conditioner and the other the rest of the boat's AC circuits.

Although the two independent 30-amp circuits create a modest increase in complexity over a single 50-amp inlet, there are two good reasons for this approach: (1) cost, weight, and ease of use—30-amp shore-power cords are well under half the price, half the weight, and half the bulk of same-length 50-amp cords; and (2) flexibility—with three or four adapters, a 30-amp cord can be plugged in just about anywhere. These adapters are also much cheaper than adapters for 50-amp cords. For times when only one 30-amp inlet is available, the boat's AC selector switch can be configured to line up one of the inlets with all the boat's AC circuits. The shore-power cord cannot support all the loads at once, but at least the boatowner can determine which ones to use.

In Europe, the standard voltage is 240 volts instead of 120 volts as in the United States. Given an appliance of a specific wattage, the amperage drawn will be two times as high in the United States as it is in Europe (hence the 16-amp shoreside supply in Europe). The corollary to this is that the wiring must be twice as large, which means that unless a European boat has been specifically built for the U.S. market, it may not be safe to plug its AC circuits into 120 volts—the cables may be dangerously undersized. A qualified marine electrician should be consulted before making such a move.

Safety

AC power kills; therefore, it is essential that AC installations are up to "code." In particular, it should be impossible to access any bare terminals without the use of tools. This means that all junction boxes should have screwed-on—not snap-on—covers, and that any distribution panel that contains AC circuits should have at least one screw that needs to be undone to open it. (This is not the case with many distribution panels, which are mostly held shut with spring-loaded catches.) These are fairly obvious safety considerations designed to keep children out of harm's way.

With just three or four adapters, a U.S.-style 30-amp shore-power cord can be plugged into just about any U.S. outlet.

All AC circuits need proper over-current protection, as with DC circuits. One circuit that is commonly neglected is the feeder cable from the shore-power inlet to the AC panel; it should have a breaker as close to the inlet as possible. In any event, various boatbuilding standards mandate that it should have a breaker within 10 feet of the inlet (if the cable run to the panel is less than 10 feet, the main breaker in the panel will suffice).

Whenever plugging into or unplugging from shore power, the breaker on the shore-power outlet should first be turned off. To plug in, make the connection on the boat first; to unplug, break the connection at the shore-power outlet first. These are commonsense precautions that ensure that a cord dropped in the water is not live and will not electrocute anybody.

As soon as a boat is plugged in, the polarity needs to be checked to ensure that it is not reversed (see *Boatowner's Mechanical and Electrical Manual*). If the boat does not have a reverse-polarity indicator or alarm, it should not be plugged in until there is a way to check the polarity (the exception being a boat with an isolation transformer).

When a boat is plugged in, the connections at both ends of the shore-power cord are problematic. In a house, all circuits have bolted connections right up to the wall outlets, at which point plugs are used. The nature of a shore-power cord is such that it has plugs at both ends. Connections using plugs are not as reliable as bolted connections. If either plug makes a poor fit or has corroded pins or sockets, resistance will be created, which then creates heat—the greater the current flow, the more heat. The resistance may also result in arcing. In both cases (heat and arcing), the end result may be a fire for which the various over-current devices in the circuit provide no protection. The higher the current flow, the greater is the probability of a fire. These kinds of fires are not that uncommon, particularly with AC-loaded boats, so be warned and pay close attention to the condition of shore-power cords and inlets: *replace any that have corroded, pitted, or blackened pins or sockets.*

When a boat is plugged into shore power, the power source is the dock. The nature of electricity is such that "leaks" attempt to return to their source. This means that if for any reason AC equipment on the boat develops a dangerous electrical fault, the *fault current* will be looking for a conductive path back to the dock. Many electrical appliances have not just two wires (the "hot" and "neutral"), but also a third (the "ground" or "earth") that is connected to the case of the appliance. In typical circumstances, the ground wire does nothing, but if the hot wire shorts to the appliance case (making the equipment potentially dangerous to touch), the ground wire will safely conduct the fault current back to shore.

If the ground wire does not have a low-resistance path to shore, any short to an appliance case will seek another path, generally from the boat to the water and then through the water. Anybody on the boat or swimming in the water can become part of the path, running the risk of being electrocuted. To prevent this, *any shore-power connection must have a low-resistance connection to the shore-side ground*. Ideally, the AC distribution panel has a *ground-continuity test light* that enables the connection to be checked. If it does not, every time the boat is plugged into a new shore-power outlet, boatowners are well advised to have it checked or learn how to check it themselves (see *Boatowner's Mechanical and Electrical Manual*).

There are also times when AC appliances short into DC circuits. At some point, a boat's DC circuits almost always have a connection to the water, through either the engine block and propeller shaft, or a ground plate, or a through-hull—or all three. If the DC system is not wired back to the AC ground, AC leakage current is likely to be fed into the water, with potentially lethal results. For this reason, on boats with an AC shore-power connection *there should always be (but frequently is not) a connection between the DC and the AC ground* (the exception, once again, being a boat with an isolation transformer). The connection allows AC leakage currents into DC circuits to find their way back to the AC ground and, from there, down the shore-power cord back to where they belong. This AC-to-DC ground connection should also be checked as a matter of basic safety.

Additional security against AC shorts is provided by using a *ground fault circuit interrupter* (GFCI), also known as a *residual current circuit breaker* (RCCB). This is a special kind of a breaker that is tripped by very small leaks to ground. Ideally, all AC outlets on a boat will be GFCI-protected; at the very least, outlets in the galley and head should be protected. In the United States, the trip limit is set at 5 mA (milliamps); in Europe it is 30 mA. If importing a European boat into the United States, the lower limit should be used.

Corrosion

Unfortunately, if a boat with a shore-power cord is properly and safely wired, including the

U.S.-style GFCI-protected outlet. To test, push the red button. To reset, push the black.

ground connection back ashore and a connection from the AC ground to the DC ground, *every time the shore-power cord is plugged in, there is a risk of corrosion of any underwater metal fittings connected to the DC ground*—primarily the propeller and propeller shaft, and any bonded through-hulls. This is because the various ground connections lead from the underwater metal back ashore. When another boat plugs into shore power, its underwater metal will be similarly connected, and the two boats are effectively wired together through the AC ground wire.

When different metals (the underwater hardware on the two boats) are put in an electrically conductive solution (in this case, seawater) and wired together (the ground wires), in effect, a giant battery is created. A small voltage and current results; this is of no concern. What is of concern is that the voltage and current are created by the dissolution of one of the metals! This is known as *galvanic corrosion*.

Breaking the ground circuit back ashore by disconnecting the ground wire breaks the circuit that causes the galvanic corrosion, but only at the expense of voiding protection against potential electrocution for those onboard and in the surrounding water. However, the circuit can be safely broken by installing either an isolation transformer or a *galvanic isolator* in the ground wire. (A galvanic isolator is a device that blocks low-level galvanic—that is, corrosion-producing—voltages and currents, but passes higher-level AC voltages and currents.)

Galvanic isolators vary significantly in quality. Whatever is used should have a *continuous-current rating* equal to the rating of the shore-power cord (e.g., 16, 30, or 50 amps) and should also incorporate a *capacitor* (see *Boatowner's Mechanical and Electrical Manual* for an explanation). An even more effective way to block galvanic corrosion is with an *isolation transformer*, but these are bulky, heavy, and expensive and, therefore, rarely fitted. However, for boats cruising overseas, they can be set up to enable the boat to plug into different shoreside voltages (for more information, consult *Boatowner's Mechanical and Electrical Manual*).

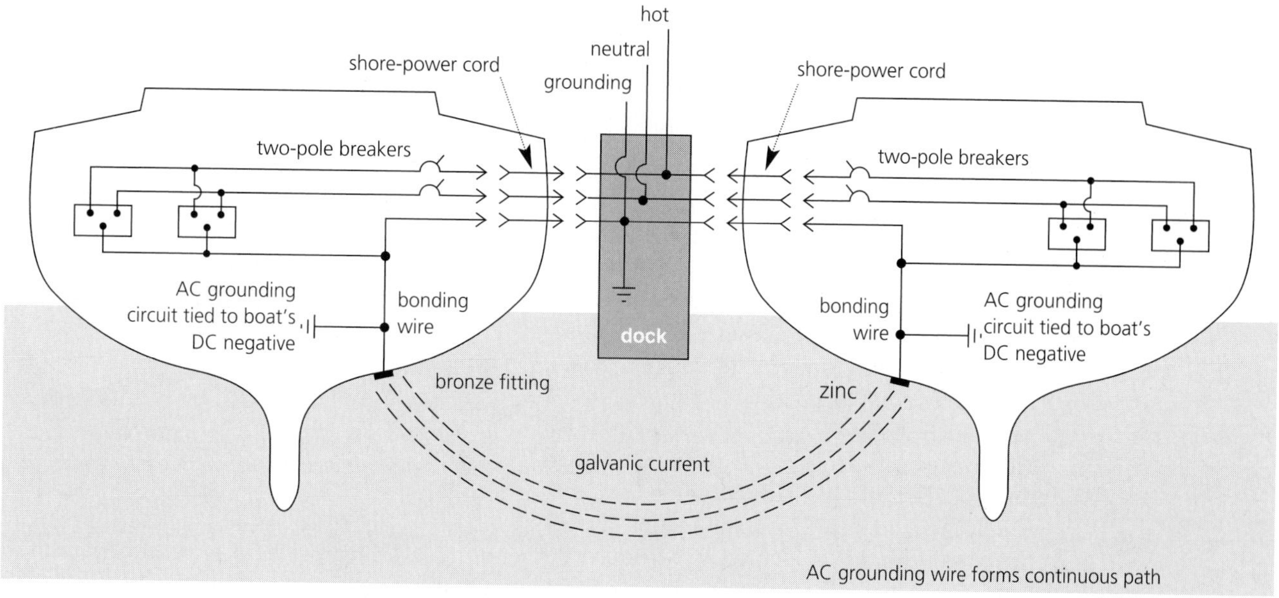

Dockside outlets wired to main panel and grounded on shore.

If two shore-power inlets are fitted, two galvanic isolators or isolation transformers are needed. Remember that a ship-to-shore cable TV hookup or telephone connection almost always bypasses and, therefore, voids the galvanic isolation provided by either of the devices. The TV and telephone need their own galvanic protection.

Ultimately, the best way to block galvanic currents is to not plug in to shore power or to minimize the time that a boat is plugged in. It is for this reason that we have a couple of solar panels to keep our batteries charged when we are not on the boat. At dockside, we plug in for a limited time to charge the batteries and then we unplug. When we leave the boat, we unplug. We *never* leave the boat plugged in when we are away from it.

Miscellaneous AC Systems Comments

Before moving on, the following miscellaneous points need to be mentioned:

- Marine AC systems have quirks that differentiate them from household AC systems. Only marine electricians should work on them. Furthermore, unless boatowners know what they are doing, they should stay out of the AC circuits (primarily for safety reasons).
- Although the neutral wire in a household AC circuit is connected to the grounding (earth) wire at the main panel box, the neutral is never grounded on a boat (if you don't know why, you shouldn't be messing around with the wiring).
- Household AC wiring has a single solid-copper strand prone to vibration failure on boats. Marine AC wiring should use the same tinned, multistrand, oil-resistant UL-1426 BC5W2 cables (or equivalent) that I previously recommended for DC wiring (many European boats use solid-stranded cable).
- The AC distribution panel should include a permanently connected polarity indicator that lights up in a case of reverse polarity (the exception is a boat with an isolation transformer).
- Any time a shore-power connection has reverse polarity or lacks ground continuity, it should be disconnected until the problem is resolved (which may mean rewiring the marina).
- It must *never* be possible to connect two separate AC sources (e.g., shore power and an onboard AC generator) to the same circuit at the same time—expensive damage will result. To prevent this, all AC sources should come to a selector switch that lines up one at a time with the boat's circuits.

BONDING, ZINC ANODES, AND LIGHTNING PROTECTION

Corrosion brought onboard by the shore-power cord is not the only source of galvanic corrosion on boats. If the boat itself has immersed metal objects that are wired together or otherwise in electrical contact (e.g., the physical contact of a bronze propeller with its stainless steel propeller shaft), any differences in the composition of the metals is likely to lead to galvanic corrosion.

The best way to stop this corrosion is to keep the various metal masses electrically isolated. This is why, for example, it is generally a bad idea to *bond* together (i.e., connect with a wire) otherwise isolated bronze through-hulls. However, some metals cannot be isolated (e.g., the propeller and its shaft) and some are deliberately interconnected for other reasons, such as the prevention of stray-current corrosion and protection against lightning strikes.

Stray-Current Corrosion and Bonding

Stray-current corrosion is relatively uncommon but can be quite devastating if it occurs. In

A stainless steel ball valve mounted to a bronze through-hull and elbow with a bronze tailpiece, something I have seen on a number of European boats in recent years, along with nickel-plated brass seacocks. I can't help thinking both of these are an invitation for galvanic corrosion.

worst-case scenarios, it can wipe out underwater hardware in days—even hours. It occurs when an immersed metal object becomes a conduit for DC current (AC does not cause corrosion), feeding the current into the water. An example is a through-hull against which a positive DC wire has been rubbing until the insulation breaks down, allowing battery current to flow through the fitting.

Just as with AC currents, this current seeks a path back to its source—in this case, the battery. The most likely path is through the water to the propeller, then up the propeller shaft, and through the engine block to the negative battery cable attached to the engine. Any metal that feeds a current into the water (in this case, the through-hull) will be corroded; the metal receiving the current—the propeller—will be OK. The higher the current, the greater is the rate of corrosion.

In addition to assuring the integrity of all circuits on a boat, the most effective way to prevent stray-current corrosion is to have a connection (a *bonding cable*) from underwater metal fittings directly back to battery negative. If a stray current occurs, it will follow the path of least resistance back to the battery, which is the wire rather than the water.

The problem with this approach is that in wiring underwater metal objects back to battery negative, all these objects are simultaneously wired together, thereby establishing the prerequisite for galvanic corrosion! This is why it is better not to bond electrically isolated bronze through-hulls—just be sure no current-carrying DC wires are lying against them.

For those objects that are bonded, protection can be provided against galvanic corrosion by also wiring an immersed *sacrificial zinc anode* into the circuit. The zinc is fastened to the outside of the boat and then wired inside the boat into the bonding circuit. Zinc is galvanically more active than any typical boatbuilding metal; that is, it corrodes before any other metal. In doing so, it protects all the other metals wired in the same circuit. However, zinc does nothing to protect against stray-current corrosion; the only protection is proper wiring of all onboard circuits (to eliminate sources of stray currents), with bonding as a backup.

Over time, zincs are consumed by galvanic activity. To be effective, they should always be replaced when they are about half gone (if you wait any longer, their effectiveness is reduced).

To be effective, a zinc anode must have a good electrical contact with the metal it is protecting (through either attachment, as in this case, or an interconnecting cable). This collar has eroded to the point where it is loose. It will do little good.

Lightning Protection

Bonding is done not just for protection against stray-current corrosion, but also for protection against lightning strikes. In the case of lightning, it is not just immersed metal, but also all major metal objects that should be wired together. If a boat gets hit by lightning, any metal mass can get charged up with a very high voltage. If the metal objects are bonded together, the bonding cable holds everything at a common voltage and provides a path for the strike to run to ground through an attached ground plate (an external keel or some other immersed metal). Without bonding, there may be massive voltage differences between metal objects, with the potential for "side flashes" to leap from one surface to another, injuring or killing people in the process and wreaking havoc on the boat and its equipment.

To ground a direct lightning strike, the bonding system needs cables of a certain size (4 gauge/20 mm^2 for the primary grounding cable from the masthead to the ground plate, and 6 gauge/13 mm^2 for peripheral cables to chainplates, metal water tanks, the engine, and so on; an aluminum mast is an adequate conductor, substituting for the primary grounding cable in this part of the circuit) and a ground plate with an equivalent area (electrically speaking) of at least 1 square foot (0.1 sq. m) of copper. Such a ground plane can be achieved by attaching a copper plate to the bottom of the boat, but it is more commonly established by making a connection to a keel bolt on an external keel.

Where there is no external keel, reliance is often placed on the combined surface area of an accumulation of bonded objects (e.g., through-

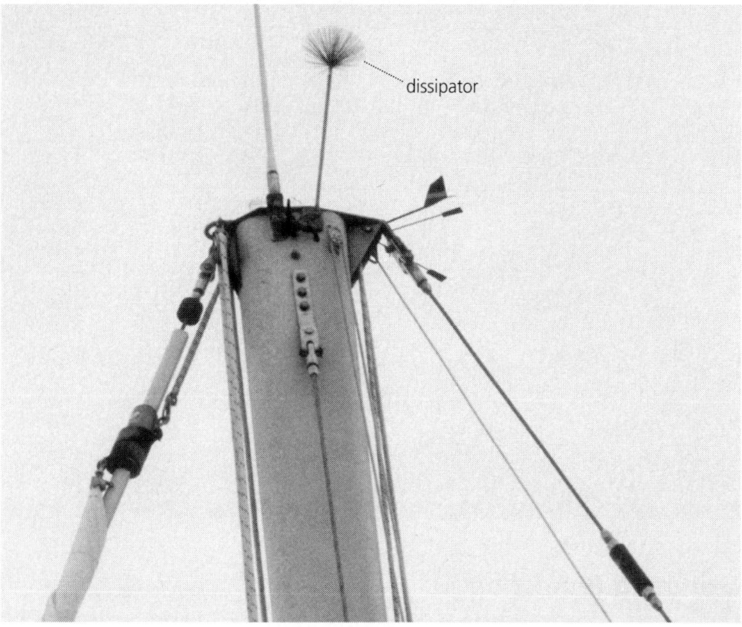

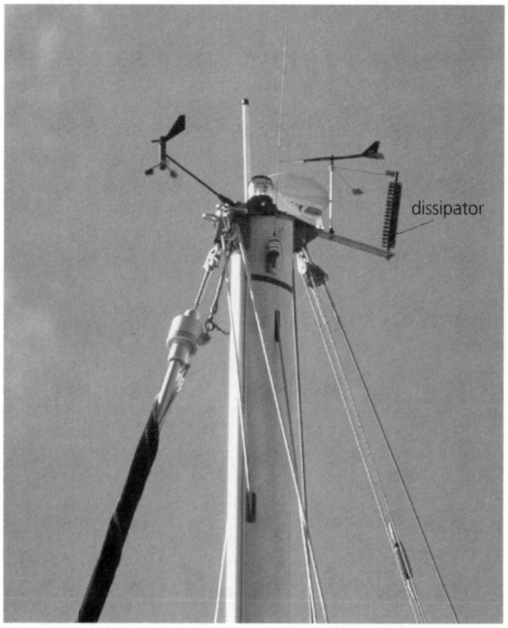

Lightning protection. Two variations on a "lightning dissipator." There is considerable discussion about whether they are effective. What is not *in doubt is that the boat should also be properly grounded to a lightning grounding plate.*

hulls and the engine, which is connected to the propeller and its shaft) rather than installing a proper ground plate. The problem with this approach is that these are often resistive paths to ground (e.g., the oil in an engine obstructs the path to ground through the crankshaft to the propeller shaft). Resistance means heat: the more current, the greater is the heat. In direct lightning strikes, there are many instances of bearings melting down in engines, and through-hulls melting out of fiberglass hulls. With internal ballast, an external metal plate almost always has to be attached to the hull and wired to the bonding system to achieve an effective ground.

To ensure that the crew comes through in one piece during a lightning storm, no one should go on deck unless necessary. If on deck, do not hold onto any metal objects (e.g., the wheel or rigging) and be especially careful not to act as a potential conductive path between two different metal objects (e.g., by hanging onto the wheel and the backstay at the same time, or a shroud and the mast). Given these measures and a proper ground plane, the boat and its crew will likely come through just fine in a major strike; however, the electronics probably won't—the forces involved are just too great to be fully tamed. Unfortunately, that's life!

Bonding, galvanic corrosion, stray-current corrosion, and lightning protection cause more confusion among boatowners and boatbuilders than just about any other matter related to boat electrical systems. This section just scratches the surface of the subject; for a more detailed discussion, see *Boatowner's Mechanical and Electrical Manual*.

CONCLUSION

It is the functioning (successful or otherwise) of the electrical systems that makes or breaks most contemporary cruising boats. In this chapter, I described the broad precepts that should govern electrical systems on cruising boats, with specific advice on key components and some important safety considerations. If this general information is combined with the specific applications and installation advice provided in books such as *Boatowner's Mechanical and Electrical Manual*, you should, with a little luck, end up with a dependable and trouble-free electrical system. It can be done!

CHAPTER FIVE

THE REST OF THE SYSTEMS

Good systems access is important on a cruising boat.

"Certainly the cruises most worth reading about, and therefore most worth doing, are those which were undertaken by yachts without engines . . . "

ERIC HISCOCK, *Cruising under Sail*

In this chapter, we look at the rest of the systems on a cruising boat—the engine and associated systems, many aspects of plumbing, and propane installations—focusing on matters of importance to cruising sailors that are commonly overlooked. I make some observations about key factors to consider when making choices about equipment for your boat.

ENGINE AND PROPELLER

Notwithstanding Eric Hiscock, who wrote the words quoted above in 1949, the power of engines installed in sailboats and the hours of use that they get have been steadily increasing in tandem over the years. It seems today as if cruising sailors are actually motoring or motor sailing for close to half the time they are at sea. In the past, these long hours of engine-running time frequently resulted in numerous engine-related problems, but nowadays the modern marine diesel engine is incredibly reliable as long as it is properly matched to its tasks, properly installed (specifically, the cooling and exhaust systems), and given clean fuel to burn. So let's look at these factors.

Nowadays, boats seem to spend up to half their time at sea under power.

How Big an Engine?

Relative to matching an engine to its tasks, the first question that has to be resolved is: "How big an engine do we need?"

In 1949, a sailboat "auxiliary" was considered truly an auxiliary—primarily for maneuvering in calm water—and as such, ½ horsepower (⅓ kW) per long ton of boat displacement was considered adequate. Today, the engine is often expected to power auxiliary equipment at the same time as it drives the boat at its "hull speed"—as a ballpark figure, 4 horsepower (3 kW) or more are required per long ton (1,016 kg) of displacement. In fact, without getting into detailed calculations, you can figure on 1 horsepower per 500 pounds of boat displacement (approximately 1 kW per 300 kg) for a "typical" cruising boat and skip to the end of this section!

To calculate horsepower requirements in detail, I turn to one of my trusted reference books—worthy of any nautical bookshelf—*The Propeller Handbook* by Dave Gerr, who kindly gave me permission to quote from it extensively (note that 1 hp = 0.75 kW; 1 kW = 1.34 hp). Dave adapted various formulas to produce an engine-sizing procedure that at first sight looks rather complicated, but is, in fact, a breeze to follow. The last math I did was in the British equivalent of junior high school, thirty-six years ago—if I can handle the numbers, you can too! I will go through the principal steps relative to our new *Nada* to illustrate the process for any boat.

The underlying assumption to these calculations is that the boat is to be driven at its maximum potential speed. As discussed in chapter 1, as a boat approaches its maximum speed potential, wave-making drag rises exponentially. This means that if we set ourselves a somewhat lower speed target, there is a substantial drop in the horsepower requirements. In other words, as in the preceding chapters, I am looking at the most demanding situation; in less demanding situations, it may be appropriate to substantially scale back the calculated horsepower requirements.

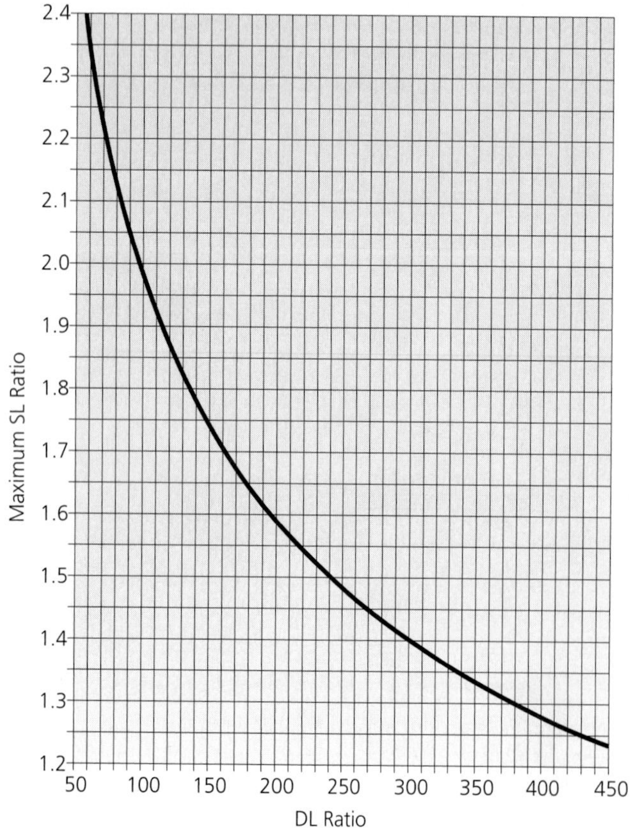

Speed–length ratio as a function of the displacement–length ratio. Enter the graph with the DLR on the bottom, and read off the SLR at the side. (Illustration by Kim Downing © Sail Publications from data supplied by Dave Gerr)

Step 1

The first step in the horsepower-estimation process is to calculate the boat's displacement–length ratio (DLR). As we saw in chapter 1, the relevant formula is

$$DLR = \frac{displacement\ (lb.) \div 2240}{(0.01 \times LWL)^3}$$

where:

LWL = waterline length (in ft.)

In our case:

Displacement = 24,280 lb. (light local sailing)

Displacement ÷ 2,240 = 10.84

LWL = 31.25

$(0.01 \times LWL)^3 = 0.0305$

Therefore, the DLR = 10.84 ÷ 0.0305 = 355

Note that for the purposes of this exercise, I used the manufacturer's displacement number because it is readily available. For greater precision, I should have estimated the actual displacement when equipped and loaded for cruising, the half-load displacement, as described in chapter 1.

Step 2

Based on much experience, Dave developed his own formula for using the displacement–length ratio (DLR) to determine the speed–length ratio (SLR) (see chapter 1). This formula is

$$SLR = \frac{8.26}{DLR^{0.311}}$$

I don't have a scientific calculator—and wouldn't know how to use it if I did—so this math gets a little beyond me. Fortunately, Dave produced a graph from this formula (reproduced at left) that is much easier to use. It gives our speed–length ratio as 1.33.

Step 3

The third step is to determine the boat's hull speed (see chapter 1), which is more or less the maximum speed at which a displacement hull (e.g., a sailboat) can be moved. The formula is

$$hull\ speed\ (in\ knots) = SLR \times \sqrt{LWL}$$

In our case,

$SLR = 1.33$

$LWL = 31.25$

$\sqrt{LWL} = 5.59$

Therefore, $hull\ speed = 1.33 \times 5.59 = 7.43\ knots$

Step 4

The fourth step is to use a rather complicated formula to determine the horsepower needed to move the boat at hull speed. The formula is

$$shp = \frac{HLD \times SLR^3}{1{,}213}$$

where:

shp = *shaft horsepower (explained below)*

HLD = *half-load displacement (in lb.)*

SLR = *the speed–length ratio*

Again, the math is a little complex, but Dave produced another graph from this formula, which is simplicity itself to use (see below). Using the math, with published displacement in place of HLD, I calculated that to drive our boat at hull speed, we need 47 horsepower. From the graph, I determined that we need 1 horsepower for every 525 pounds of boat weight. In other words, we need

$$24{,}280 \div 525 = 46.25\ hp$$

This is fairly close to the calculated figure; clearly, the graph works!

The number that has just been calculated refers to something known as *shaft horsepower* (shp), which is the actual power delivered to the propeller. It is always lower than the engine's rated horsepower (commonly known as *brake horsepower* [bhp], or simply hp). In general, most marine transmissions absorb about 5 percent of the engine's bhp, so the required shp should be divided by 0.95 to determine bhp. Looking at our boat, we have

$$47 \div 0.95 = 49.47\ hp$$

Step 5

The fifth step is to factor in auxiliary loads that the engine manufacturer has not considered; the two most common are a high-output alternator and a refrigeration compressor. Alternators absorb about 5 horsepower for every 100 amps output, but rarely run at full output for long. As a ballpark figure based on "typical" outputs, I add about 2.5 to 3.5 horsepower for alternators from 100 to 200 amps, and 2 horsepower for a refrigeration compressor. We don't have a compressor, but we do have a 200-amp alternator, so I rounded the required engine horsepower up to 53 horsepower.

Step 6

The sixth step is to fudge things! For several reasons (reliability, reputation, and the fact that this is Pacific Seacraft's standard engine), I wanted a 50-horsepower Yanmar 4JH2E naturally aspirated diesel engine. But I had to recognize that by the time we factored in transmission losses, which bring the theoretical shp down to

$$50 \times 0.95 = 47.5\ hp$$

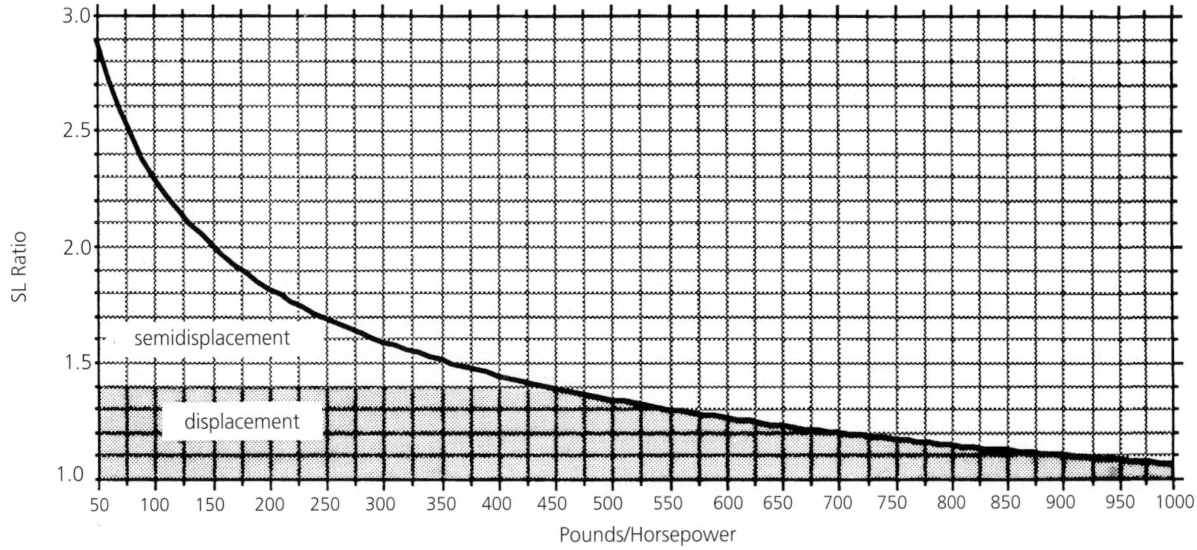

Horsepower requirements as a function of the speed–length ratio and displacement. Enter the graph with the SLR at the side, and read off the lb/hp at the bottom. (Courtesy Dave Gerr; reprinted from The Propeller Handbook*)*

and the high-output alternator (which knocks off approximately another 3.5 horsepower), this engine would at times be down to a maximum of 44 shaft horsepower (shp). Would this be enough for our purposes?

Working the numbers backward, I calculated that this means we would have

$$\frac{24{,}280}{44} = 550\ lb.\ per\ hp$$

Dave's graph indicates that this will give us a speed–length ratio of 1.3. This in turn gives a boat speed of

$$1.3 \times \sqrt{LWL} = 1.3 \times 5.59 = 7.3\ knots$$

This is more than adequate for our purposes. The formulas used for calculating this speed are based on the assumption that the boat will be moving at its hull speed. Because of the way wave-making drag increases exponentially around hull speed, at slower speeds the reduction in drag is actually greater than accounted for in the formula, so we can expect the boat to perform better than predicted by these formulas. (In practice, it does: in calm water with a clean hull, we get 8 knots at full engine speed.)

Next, we had to find a propeller to match this engine.

UNDERSTANDING ENGINE CURVES

Looking at the graph of "Output Measured at the Propeller Shaft" for the Yanmar 4JH2E, we see curves with and without a marine gear. The one without the gear represents brake horsepower; the one with the gear gives us the theoretical shaft horsepower. From this must be deducted additional small losses for the packing gland, stern bearing, and any intermediate bearings—and bigger losses if a high-output alternator or refrigeration compressor is driven from the engine—to give us real-life shaft horsepower.

Many engine manufacturers simply give the rated horsepower of the engine (i.e., the top curve). Derating this by 5 percent and then deducting for a high-output alternator and refrigeration compressor approximates real-life shaft horsepower.

The propeller-power curve (which is not always given) represents the power requirement of a "typical" three-bladed propeller at different engine rpms. Unfortunately, propeller design is such that a fixed-pitch propeller cannot be made to absorb energy at the same rate that an engine produces it. In fact, the engine-output curve and the propeller-power curve can only be matched at one point. Maximum engine output (i.e., shaft horsepower) should be chosen as this match point. If a propeller has a power curve that crosses the engine curve below full engine speed, the propeller will fully load the engine at this speed and overload it at higher speeds. The engine will "bog down" and fail to reach its maximum speed. If, on the other hand, a propeller has a power curve that never crosses the engine curve, the engine will go to full rpm, but its full power will never be used and boat performance will be commensurably reduced.

At anything other than full power, the propeller absorbs considerably less power than the engine is capable of producing—this is unavoidable. It does not mean, however, that the engine is particularly inefficient in terms of its fuel consumption; the engine's governor will simply cut back the fuel flow to whatever is necessary to produce the horsepower that the propeller absorbs at a given speed of rotation.

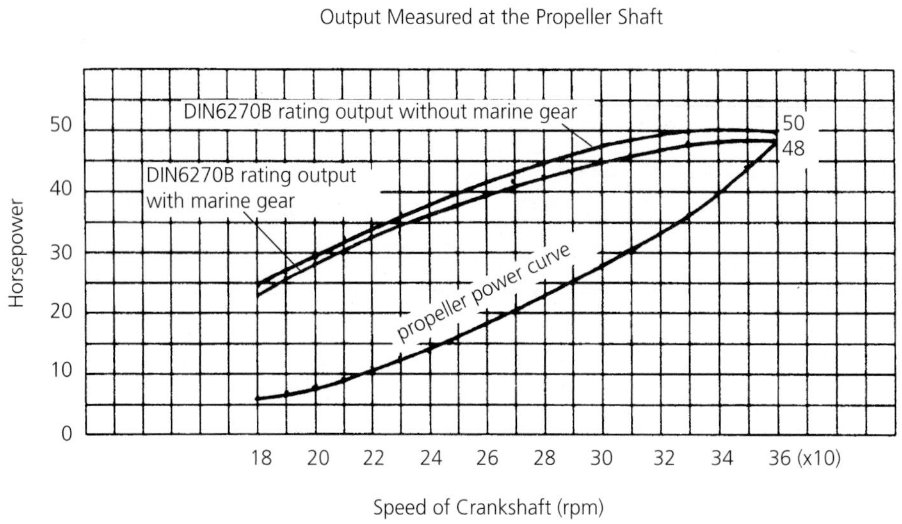

Output curve for the Yanmar 4JH2E. The top curve is without a transmission attached, the middle curve is with a transmission attached, and the lower curve represents the horsepower absorbed by a "typical" three-bladed propeller. (Courtesy Yanmar)

Propeller Sizing

Propeller sizing is both a science and an art; that is, after the science has been completed, a certain amount of intuition needs to be factored into the equation. I found this out the hard way. When we re-engined and re-propped on our old boat, the propeller manufacturer made the calculations and came up with a propeller size, which I ran past several experts for a second opinion. Some said it looked fine; some said they felt we would be overpropped. After we were all done, we duly found out that we were, indeed, somewhat overpropped, so the prop had to come off and be reworked.

As a result of this experience, I made my own calculations using charts, formulas, and tables developed by Dave Gerr and published in both *Propeller Handbook* and *The Nature of Boats*. These indicated that our propeller was oversized, so I probably should have worked the numbers in the first place. The exercise is worth printing (this time, using our new boat), inasmuch as it demonstrates a process for those interested in calculating a ballpark figure for a propeller for their own boat, and it may help to understand problems with an existing prop. However, it should always be remembered that propeller sizing is quite complex; therefore, expert advice should also be sought.

Step 1

The first step is to understand a couple of technical terms: *pitch* and *slip*. To understand them, we can compare a propeller to a wood screw (although this comparison is not technically accurate). The propeller can be considered to slice its way through the water in much the same way that a screw penetrates wood. In theory, the more extreme the angle at which the blades cut the water, the farther the propeller will move at each complete revolution. This theoretical distance is known as pitch. If a propeller were 100 percent effective and if it had, for example, a 12-inch (300 mm) pitch, it would move its boat forward 12 inches for each revolution it made. Of course, it doesn't do this. The amount by which it fails to achieve this theoretical result is known as slip. If the boat moves forward 9 inches (230 mm), there is 25 percent slip.

Turning now to our new *Nada*: she is a moderately-heavy-displacement (24,280 lb.) cutter with a hull speed of approximately 7.5 knots. However, to use the Yanmar engine, we decided to settle for a speed under power of 7.3 knots. One knot equals 101.3 feet (30.9 m) per minute; therefore, at 7.3 knots, *Nada* travels 739.5 feet (225 m) per minute:

$$101.3 \times 7.3 = 739.5 \text{ ft.}$$

The first thing we want to know is what pitch propeller is needed to produce this speed.

The chosen Yanmar has a maximum rated speed of 3,600 rpm and a reduction gear ratio of 2.62:1 (3.06:1 in reverse). At full engine speed, the shaft rotates at

$$3{,}600 \div 2.62 = 1{,}374 \text{ rpm}$$

We could use this number for determining pitch, but to provide a little cushion for adverse conditions, we want the boat to reach rated speed at 95 percent of rated engine speed; that is, a shaft speed of

$$1{,}374 \times 0.95 = 1{,}305 \text{ rpm}$$

(Referring to the engine-horsepower curves, you see that the engine is up to its maximum rated horsepower at around 95 percent of maximum speed; this is quite common.)

Without slip, if the propeller is turning at 1,305 rpm, a pitch of

$$739.5 \div 1{,}305 = 0.56 \text{ feet} = 6.8 \text{ in.}$$

will produce a boat speed of 7.3 knots. So far, so good, but now we get to the tricky part. To what extent will *Nada*'s moderately heavy displacement and associated wetted surface area induce slip? Various tables provide a guide, but at the end of the day, there is no substitute for experience when making this judgment call. Better still is a direct comparison with the performance of sister ships.

Based on my reading of several textbooks, 40 to 45 percent seemed a reasonable amount to factor in for slip, which means the propeller is assumed to be 55 to 60 percent effective at full speed. Let's split the difference at 57.5 percent. The theoretical 6.8-inch pitch was increased to a real-world pitch of

$$6.8 \div 0.575 = 11.8 \text{ in. (rounded up to 12 in.)}$$

Step 2

The second step is to answer the question: "What diameter should this propeller be?"

Larger-diameter propellers are more efficient than smaller-diameter ones, but obviously there is a limiting factor in terms of the size of *aperture* available; that is, the clearance beneath the hull. *Nada* has a 23-inch (580 mm) aperture. It is desirable to maintain 10 to 15 percent of this (i.e., 2.30–3.45 in./60–90 mm) as clearance between the tips of the propeller blades and the boat (to reduce turbulence). Given that *Nada*'s propeller is mounted in an aperture, this clearance is needed at both the top and bottom of the aperture, leaving us with a maximum propeller diameter of

$$23 - 4.6 = 18.4 \ in.$$

Would this size propeller be too big for the engine to handle (overpropped) or too small to absorb the engine's full output (underpropped)?

Dave Gerr has developed a formula and a nomograph that show the relationship among maximum shaft speed, shaft horsepower (i.e., the actual horsepower delivered to the propeller), and propeller diameter (in inches). The formula is as follows:

$$D = 632.7 \times shp^{0.2} \div rpm^{0.6}$$

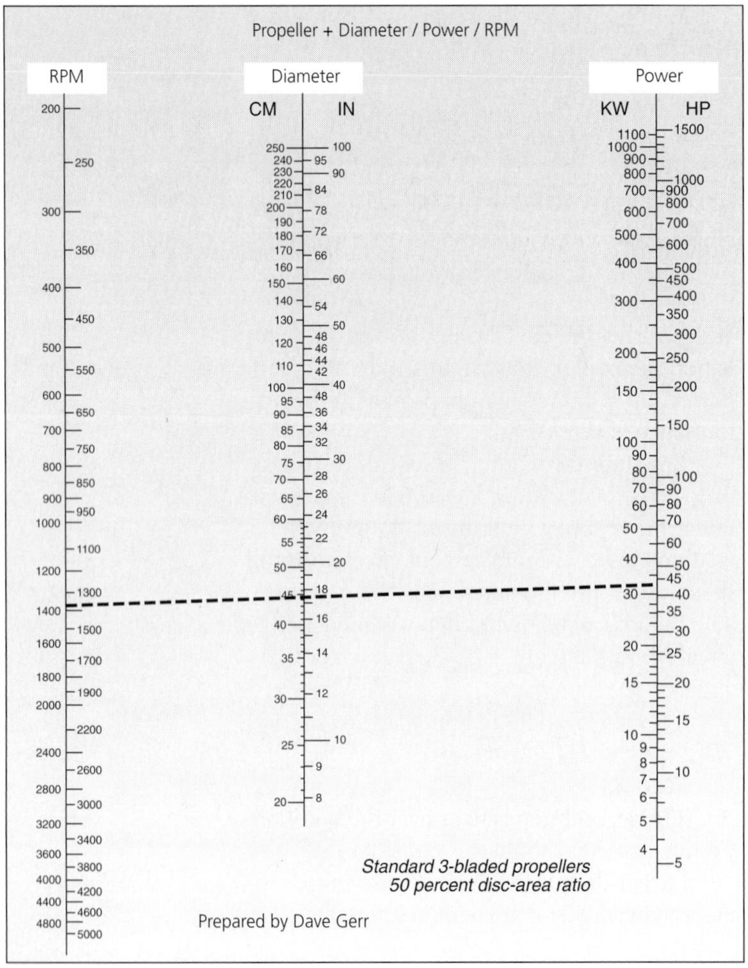

Nomograph indicating shaft speed, propeller diameter, and engine shaft horsepower. (Illustration by Kim Downing © Sail Publications from data supplied by Dave Gerr)

where

D = propeller diameter (in inches)

shp = shaft horsepower at the propeller

rpm = maximum shaft revolutions per minute at the propeller

This is a little complicated! The nomograph (reprinted from *Sail Magazine*) is much easier to use.

We already know our maximum shaft speed (1,374 rpm). The engine is rated at 50 horsepower, but with the loss in the transmission (approximately 5 percent), we have a maximum shaft-horsepower rating of 50 × 0.95 = 47.5 horsepower. Our high-output alternator is frequently running at near full output, absorbing up to 7 horsepower, so I decided to average its draw at 3.5 horsepower. Considering these factors, as we have already seen, I chose to downgrade the shaft-horsepower rating to 44 horsepower as the basis for determining propeller diameter.

If we enter Dave's nomograph with a shaft speed of 1,374 rpm and a shaft horsepower of 44, it indicates using a 17.7-inch-diameter propeller; 18 inches (460 mm) is close enough (this is not rocket science), so we end up with an 18-inch diameter times a 12-inch (300 mm) pitch propeller.

If the recommended diameter is too large for the aperture, a lower gear ratio is needed on the transmission (typically, engine manufacturers offer a choice of two or three different transmission ratios). This raises the shaft speed, which results in a smaller-diameter propeller. If the recommended propeller is considerably smaller than the aperture can accommodate, it is desirable to use a higher gear ratio; this lowers the shaft speed and results in a larger-diameter (more efficient) propeller.

Step 3

The third step is to calculate blade area, which determines *blade loading*—the amount of thrust developed by each square inch of the blades. The higher the engine output and the lower the blade area, the higher is the blade loading. Above a certain point, this blade loading results in *cavitation*, which in turn may damage the propeller. In other words, blade loading must be kept below a certain level.

Calculations of blade loading can become quite complex; fortunately, Dave has developed another formula and a graph that enable fair estimates to be made quite easily. The formula, as follows, determines the blade area (in square inches) needed to absorb the energy produced by the engine:

$$100 \times shp \div hull\ speed \times \sqrt{hull\ speed}$$

Looking at Nada, *we have the following statistics:*

$shp = 44$

$top\ speed = 7.3\ knots$

$\sqrt{top\ speed} = 2.7\ knots$

Therefore, blade area $= 100 \times 44 \div 7.3 \times 2.7 = 223\ sq.\ in.$

Looking at Dave's graph of blade area against propeller diameter, we see that *Nada* falls between a three- and a four-bladed propeller. Three-bladed propellers are widely available and relatively cheap, so this is what we used. We installed the propeller (18-in./460 mm diameter times 12-in./300 mm pitch) knowing that at full engine speed, there is likely to be a certain amount of cavitation. This is not a problem in typical use because we rarely use the engine above 80 percent of rated rpm.

So how did these calculations work out in practice? With a clean bottom, *Nada* does 7 knots at 3,000 rpm and tops out at 8 knots in calm water, which is somewhat better than expected.

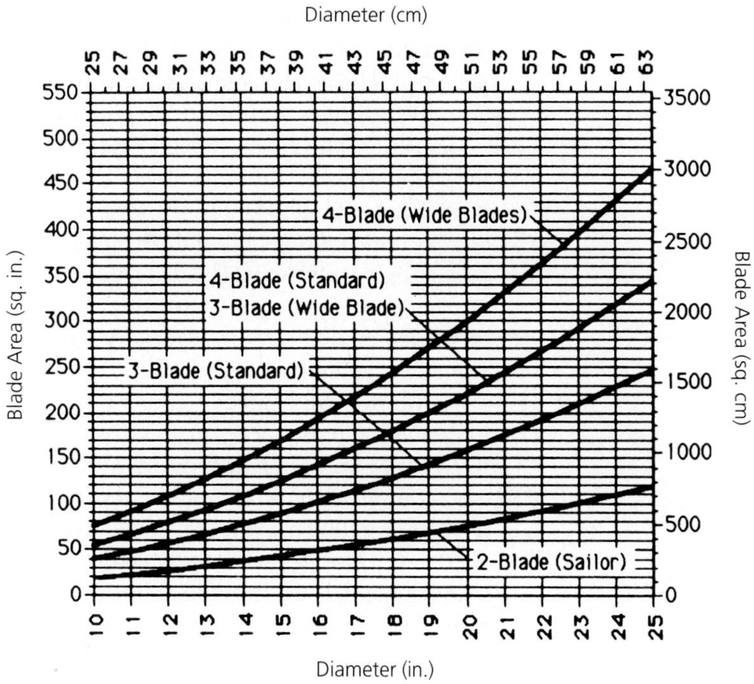

Blade areas of propellers as a function of diameter. (Courtesy Dave Gerr; reprinted from The Propeller Handbook)

Propeller Matters

At one time, almost all cruising boats had fixed-blade propellers, although the odd performance-conscious boat sported a folding propeller. In the past few decades, this picture has been radically transformed with the advent of all kinds of feathering propellers and adaptations of folding propellers. Most of them greatly reduce drag when under sail, so it is ironic to see their proliferation at a time when less and less time is spent under sail! Depending on the type of propeller, the improved performance under sail may or may not carry a penalty when under power.

Unless racing is of paramount importance,

USEFUL NUMBERS AND FORMULAS FOR SIZING PROPELLERS

1 knot = 101.3 ft. per minute

Shaft speed for determining pitch = maximum engine speed × 0.95 ÷ reduction gear ratio

"Pitch without slip" (in inches) = 101.3 × hull speed × 12 ÷ shaft speed for determining pitch (multiply by 25.4 to convert to mm)

Typical auxiliary sailboat "propeller effectiveness" as a fraction of pitch without slip:

- Three-bladed propeller: 0.5–0.6
- Fixed two-bladed propeller: 0.35–0.45
- Folding two-bladed propeller: 0.1–0.35

"Real-world pitch" = pitch without slip/propeller effectiveness

Minimum propeller tip clearance = 10 to 15 percent of propeller diameter

Shaft horsepower for determining propeller diameter = (rated horsepower × 0.95) minus auxiliary loads that do not come with the engine (the most significant are high-output alternators and refrigeration compressors)

Formula for determining propeller diameter (in inches):

$D = 632.7 \times shp^{0.2} \div rpm^{0.6}$

where

D = propeller diameter (in inches)

shp = shaft horsepower at the propeller

rpm = maximum shaft rpm at the propeller

(Note: It is much easier to use the nomograph based on this formula in *The Nature of Boats* than it is to make this calculation.)

blade area (in sq. in.) = $100 \times shp \div hull\ speed \times \sqrt{hull\ speed}$

the starting point for selecting one of these propellers should still be a determination of the propeller's pitch, diameter, and blade area (as already described), which maximizes the performance under power. Then, if the propeller can be made to line up with the water in a streamlined manner when under sail, so much the better.

As a general rule-of-thumb, the folding propellers, especially the two-bladed type, offer the least drag under sail but have the worst performance under power, especially when in reverse. The feathering propellers (e.g., Max-Prop, Martec, and Luke) create a little more drag under sail, but perform about as well as a fixed-blade propeller in forward, and almost always perform considerably better than the fixed propeller in reverse. The Brunston Autoprop, a unique variable-pitch propeller, has a little more drag under sail than the feathering propellers, but a significantly improved performance under power throughout a boat's speed range.

There is something to suit every taste and pocketbook. My only comment is that at some point, the propeller may get damaged. The farther offshore it is intended to cruise, the more important it is that it can be easily removed for repairs and replaced—if necessary—with a locally acquired fixed-blade propeller. Some of the feathering propellers require more disassembly to get on and off than others. Some also require the propeller shaft to be modified (which makes it difficult to retrofit a fixed-blade propeller); others fit onto a standard propeller shaft.

If a standard fixed-pitch propeller is installed, the boat will want to spin the propeller shaft when under sail, causing an annoying noise and creating unnecessary wear in the (cutlass) bearing and the transmission. With some transmissions, the propeller shaft can be braked by putting the transmission in gear (reverse is recommended); with others, a separate shaft brake will need to be fitted.

Note that on some boats the propeller cannot be taken off or put back on without removing the rudder—a highly undesirable feature on a cruising boat. The same often also applies to propeller shafts.

Avoiding Entangling Lines

As discussed in chapter 1, the propellers on boats with propeller shafts that simply protrude from the bottom of the boat and on those with shafts supported by a strut are more likely to foul fishing nets and lobster-pot warps than those that are mounted in an aperture. At times, this can put the boat in jeopardy. To deal with such situations, various devices on the market can cut through fouled lines, thereby freeing the boat; the most effective seems to be the Spurs line cutter.

I have been on boats where we have been extremely grateful for the efficient way in which a line cutter disposed of entangling warps; nevertheless, I have qualms about their use. Every time a lobsterman's pot line is cut in Maine, he loses $60. In third-world countries, the line cutter literally may be taking food off a poor family's table. I believe that those of us who use boats for recreation have a duty to respect those who make their livelihood from the sea, which means—first and foremost—trying to avoid entanglement; then, if entangled, trying to extricate ourselves without damage to the net or pot warp. The line

Left: *Spurs line cutter. (Courtesy Spurs Marine Manufacturing)* Right: *Line cutter in action.*

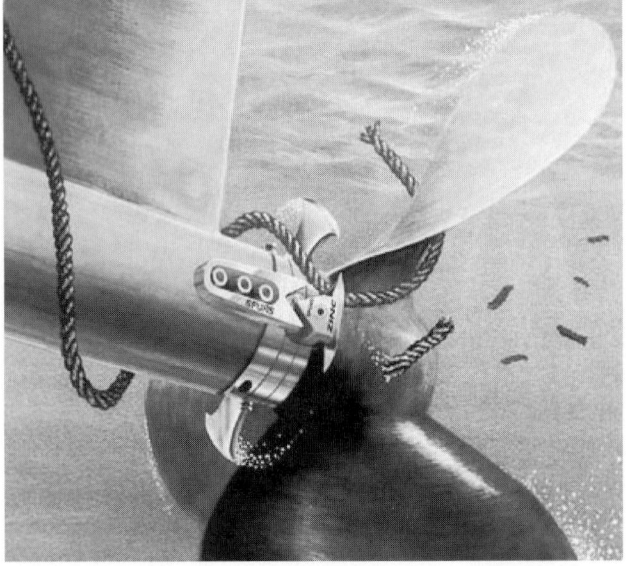

cutter makes the latter impossible; better to have an aperture-mounted propeller and try to avoid entanglement in the first place!

Keeping the Propeller in the Boat

It sounds stupid, but every year I hear of cases where the prop-shaft coupling fails and the propeller pulls the shaft out the back of the boat, leaving a big hole through which water floods in at a terrifying rate (more about flooding later).

In most cases of shaft loss, the propeller shaft is held in its coupling with set screws that work loose. If this (common) method of attachment is used, it is essential to ensure that the set screws seat in a good-sized dimple in the propeller shaft, and that after being done up tightly, they are locked off so that they cannot possibly vibrate loose. The most effective method of locking the screws is to drill a small hole through each screwhead and then tie them together with stainless steel or Monel locking wire. However, rather than use set screws in couplings, I prefer to drill right through the coupling and shaft, and add a through-bolt held in place with a Nylok nut. This method is almost foolproof.

A measure of security can be provided by putting a hose clamp around the propeller shaft just forward of the shaft seal. If the shaft comes loose, the hose clamp keeps the shaft in the boat. However, with certain high-speed shafts, the clamp may cause sufficient imbalance to create vibration. It may be possible to remedy this by using two hose clamps with counterposed screws. If not, the clamps will have to be left off.

The coupling bolts themselves also can work loose on occasion. In this case, at least the shaft does not leave the boat (the coupling half still attached to the shaft prevents it). Once again, coupling bolts need to be locked off (with lock washers, Nyloc nuts, or locking wire).

Propeller-shaft retaining screw properly locked off with seizing wire (they frequently are not).

After launching, mechanical seals should be pulled back to allow the seal to flood.

Shaft-seal failures also let in a lot of water over time. In fact, dripping stuffing boxes are a major source of sinkings of unattended boats. I discuss shaft seals in detail in *Boatowner's Mechanical and Electrical Manual*; suffice it to say here that the key to an effective installation is proper engine alignment. Beyond this, I am a fan of the "drip-free" mechanical seals, of which my two favorites are the PSS and the John Crane (Halyard) seal. Given a well-aligned engine, they really are drip-free (our bilge pump does not kick on from one week to the next).

If a mechanical seal is fitted and the boat is hauled, it is important to remember to pull back the seal until water squirts into the boat when the boat is re-launched. If the seal is not lubricated in this way, it may burn up—which is when you discover the real drawback of these seals: the propeller shaft has to be withdrawn from its coupling to install a new seal. Meanwhile, unless the boat has been hauled, a lot of water will likely be coming in the boat.

Peripheral Systems

Given the reliability of modern diesel engines, it is more likely to be the peripheral systems that cause problems. The three most troublesome are the cooling system, various parts of the exhaust system, and the fuel system. The cruising sailor can avoid most problems through a combination of proper installation and proactive maintenance.

Cooling Systems

All modern marine diesel engines have heat exchangers. Raw water (seawater) is pumped through one side, freshwater is circulated through the other side. The raw water is sucked out of the sea by a raw-water pump, driven through the heat exchanger, and then usually dumped into the exhaust and pushed overboard by the exhaust gases. The freshwater is recirculated through the engine, the same as cooling water on an automobile.

Freshwater circuits almost never cause trouble as long as antifreeze is added and periodically changed (every couple of years; the antifreeze has corrosion inhibitors that "wear out") and the water-pump belt is kept in good condition. Raw-water circuits are another matter: they are susceptible to blockages, pump failures, and corrosion. If the raw water fails, the engine will overheat—in some cases, the exhaust system will melt down (see the next section).

To forestall problems on the raw-water side:

- Check that the raw-water inlet remains under water at all angles of heel (this also applies to the raw-water inlets for refrigeration systems, air-conditioning units, and toilets). It is hard to believe, but boatbuilders still sometimes set the through-hulls too high, with the result that the raw-water pump sucks air on one tack, leading to pump failure and engine overheating.
- Make sure that there is a good-sized, readily accessible, see-through raw-water strainer.
- Renew the raw-water pump impeller before a long voyage and at least every couple of years thereafter (the engine manual tells you how). Impellers can get destroyed for various reasons, so at least one spare should always be carried onboard, and you should know how to change it (which may be more difficult than you think if the pump is inaccessible, as it sometimes is).

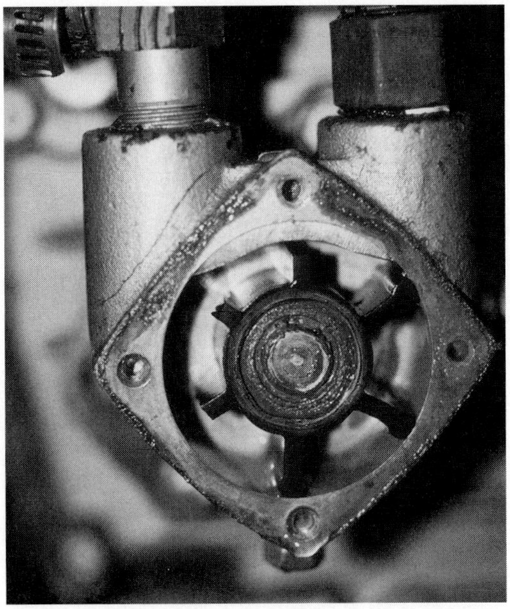

Damaged raw-water pump impeller. As is often the case, the engine was still running fine (most engines have excess cooling capacity in normal circumstances). This kind of damage is only found through regular inspections.

Accessible raw-water strainer. The top is just above the waterline so that it can be opened and cleaned without closing the seacock.

- Make sure the heat exchanger has a sacrificial zinc anode. Without one, corrosion is likely to occur on the raw-water side as a result of the mix of different metals and the presence of salt water—which provide the ingredients for galvanic interaction, exacerbated by engine heat. Most marine diesel engines have at least one *zinc pencil anode* in the heat exchanger and maybe more. These function just the same as zinc anodes on a hull (see chapter 4). Pencil zincs are a regular maintenance item; they should be replaced by the time they are *half gone*, not when there is nothing left. Failure to change them in time may result in expensive damage, including the complete disabling of the engine. Some engines don't have raw-water zincs. Most of these are at risk of corrosion and should have zincs retrofitted, but on a few—notably some Yanmars—the manufacturer claims that the engines are built of galvanically compatible metals and don't need zincs. In any case, all engines and heat exchangers should be checked for zincs; if not present, investigate further to see if they are advisable.

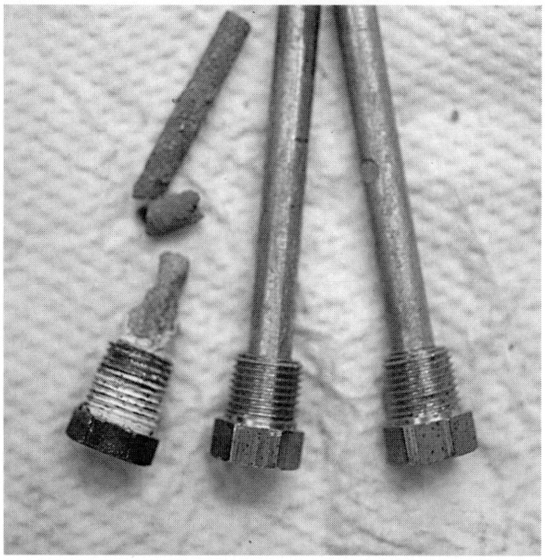

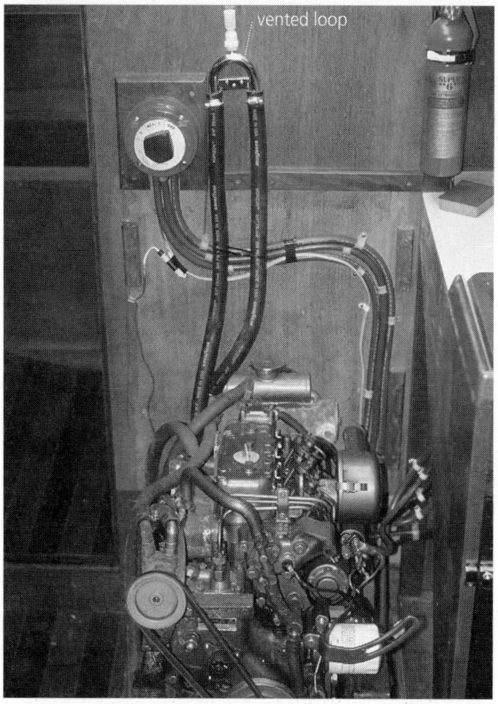

Top: *A common sight—the engine raw-water injection line is plumbed directly from the heat exchanger to the exhaust manifold. There is a risk of flooding the engine with salt water.* Left: *The problem was corrected by installing a vented loop well above the waterline.*

Top: *The zinc in this heat exchanger is almost all gone and is virtually worthless. The heat exchanger is at risk of galvanic corrosion.* Above: *New and old zinc pencil anodes. The old one is at the point where it should be replaced (about half gone).*

Exhaust Systems

Years ago, it was not uncommon for marine engines to be damaged or destroyed as a result of salt water siphoning into or backing up the exhaust. It is still not uncommon, particularly when boats go offshore. The increase in hydrostatic pressure that occurs in the cooling and exhaust systems when larger-than-normal seas move past the boat reveals longstanding deficiencies that have, until then, remained hidden. Although it is inexcusable for engine installers to continue to put in exhausts incorrectly, they do. If flooding is to be avoided, a cruising sailor needs to ensure that the boat has a "proper" exhaust installation before going to sea.

I provide a detailed explanation of this subject in *Boatowner's Mechanical and Electrical Manual*; following is a summary of the key features of a proper exhaust system:

- With a conventional water-lift-type exhaust system, the raw-water injection line, which runs from the heat exchanger into the exhaust, must be looped well above the waterline (at all angles of heel), and must have a siphon break installed at the top of the loop (many boats don't). If your boat does not have this hose loop and siphon break, they need to be installed.

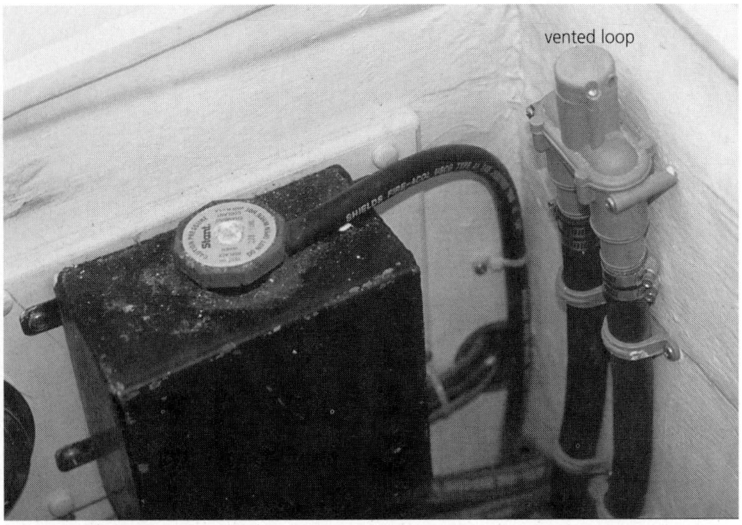

The vented loop needs to be accessible for maintenance (i.e., periodic flushing).

- A traditional rubber-flap type of siphon break tends to plug up with salt crystals. This can render the siphon break inoperative and/or cause the raw-water cooling system to spray salt water over the engine and its electrical harness. These valves need to be removed and flushed regularly in freshwater.
- A better type of valve is a *vacuum breaker* from Scot Ardox (Fort Lauderdale, Florida). It operates on the same principle, but instead of the rubber flap, it contains a spring-loaded valve designed to be less prone to fouling. However, it too needs occasional flushing.
- Better yet is to remove the valve element altogether, and instead attach a small length of hose that is vented via a through-hull into the cockpit or overboard (above the waterline at all angles of heel). This way, there is no valve to leak or plug.
- From the siphon break, the cooling-water injection line will drop down to an injection point into the exhaust. To keep water out of the engine, the injection point should be at least 4 inches (100 mm) below the level of the exhaust manifold. The injection nipple must point down the exhaust line, away from the manifold.
- The elbow in which the injection nipple is found combines very hot exhaust gases, high exhaust velocity, a curve in the exhaust pipe, and salt water; it is a potent corrosion troublemaker. If an elbow is fabricated (rather than cast in one piece as most now are), it needs to be welded rather than braised, with all the components (including the welding rods) of a similar metal. Once a year, the water injection hose and exhaust hose should be broken loose from any elbow to inspect the injection nipple (this is a likely location for scale and debris from the engine to form a plug) and the inside of the elbow (a likely location for corrosion).

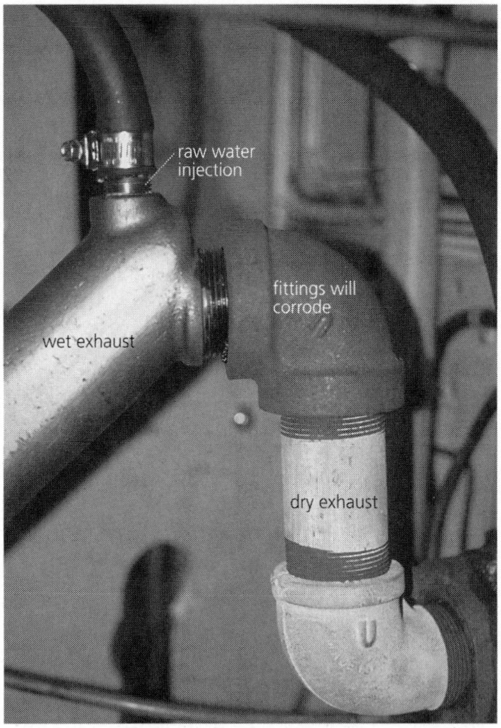

Raw-water injection elbow. The length of dry exhaust formed by the galvanized fittings needs to be insulated. These fittings are also a recipe for trouble—over time, they will corrode.

- *From the injection point, the exhaust should drop another 8 inches (200 mm) or more into a water-lift-type silencer.* Here the water gathers in the base of a cylinder until it blocks the exhaust discharge pipe, at which time the exhaust gas pressure drives the water up and out of the final section of the exhaust.
- The water-catchment chamber in the silencer must have a volume *at least as great as the volume of the upward-sloping section of the exhaust hose leaving the silencer*. Then, when the engine is shut down, even if the exhaust is full of water and even if it all drains back into the silencer, it will still not back-flood the engine.
- Water-lift silencers are best made of fire-resistant fiberglass or plastic, not metal (which invariably corrodes, unless Monel or another highly corrosion-

resistant alloy is used). Many plastic water-lift silencers (including the popular Vetus silencers) melt down if the cooling-water flow is lost for any length of time. There should be (but rarely is) an alarm that signals loss of flow—either a flow meter in the water circuit or a temperature probe in the exhaust. Both are readily available.

- If an exhaust melts down, it raises the specter of carbon monoxide poisoning. The same is true of any exhaust-joint leaks. To minimize the chance of this happening, U.S. and European standards require hose connections to be double clamped using all 300-series stainless steel hose clamps (see chapter 1). Better yet for clamping an exhaust is a *T-bolt clamp*, but it needs a stainless steel fastener (rather than carbon steel, which are sometimes found).
- To avoid water being driven up the exhaust by following waves or wakes, the exhaust hose from the silencer must be looped up inside the boat *well above the waterline* before dropping down to the exhaust through-hull.
- If an engine is proving difficult to start and is repeatedly cranked, the raw-water pump moves water into the exhaust at every cranking attempt. Because it takes the pressure of the exhaust gases to lift the water up and out of the exhaust pipe, this water will not be driven out until the engine fires. Eventually, enough water can be pumped into an exhaust to flood the engine: *a water-lift silencer needs draining after several unsuccessful cranking attempts*. Unfortunately, drains are not always fitted and, even when they are, they may be inaccessible.

Not all boats can meet the physical requirements of an exhaust installation as described here. The most common problem is inadequate space below the engine to provide the necessary drop from the exhaust manifold into the water-lift silencer. This is easily circumvented by adding a riser to the exhaust—that is, a raised loop of exhaust pipe (preferably with a water-cooled jacket) that provides enough height for a proper water-cooled installation (refer to the photo above).

Even with adequate space below an engine, there is another difficulty that may arise: the creation of excessive back pressure in the exhaust. The higher the water must be lifted from the

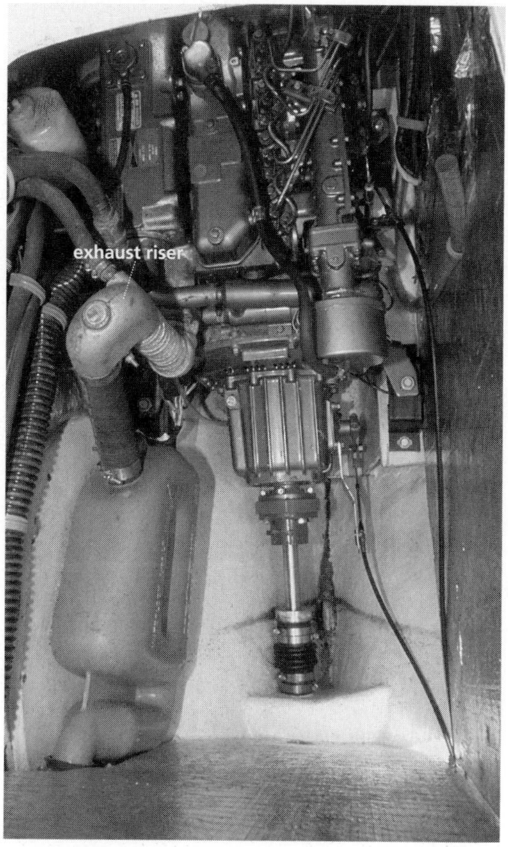

Properly insulated exhaust riser. Note the excellent access to the exhaust, the transmission, and the shaft seal. The plastic water-lift silencer (the popular Vetus model) is not fire-retardant—it will melt down if the raw-water flow is lost for any length of time. The exhaust hose is fastened with single hose clamps, whereas the standards call for double clamping—at least these clamps are the T-bolt type.

water-lift silencer to the top of the exhaust pipe, the greater is the back pressure in the system. A little back pressure is highly beneficial in damping exhaust noise, but any significant pressure impairs engine performance. Turbocharged engines are particularly sensitive to back pressure. As a general rule-of-thumb, the vertical water lift on a nonturbocharged (i.e., naturally aspirated) engine should not exceed 40 inches (1 m); on a turbocharged engine, it should not exceed 20 inches (500 mm). A riser may be needed to raise the whole exhaust system and thereby reduce the vertical lift.

Keeping the Fuel Clean

Turning now to the fuel system, it should be emphasized that the various components in a diesel engine's fuel system are machined to incredibly precise and miniscule clearances that simply do not tolerate contaminants. Given this fact, the cavalier attitude of many cruisers toward their fuel system constantly boggles my mind, especially because of all the engine problems that afflict cruising sailors, those caused by dirty fuel are the easiest to avoid—and potentially the most expensive if not avoided.

As always, prevention—keeping contaminants out of the fuel—is better than a cure—removing contaminants from the fuel. Whenever possible, fuel should be taken on from a fuel

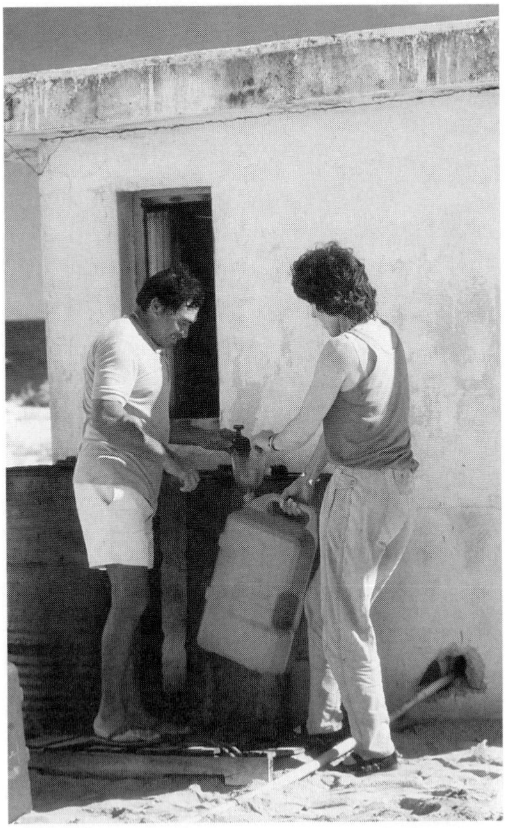

It is inevitable when cruising that once in a while fuel will be taken on from dubious sources. Here we bum some diesel from a Mexican lighthouse-keeper.

dock that has a good reputation for filtering its fuel. However, this is not always possible.

A variety of screened funnels on the market (Baja funnels are the best known) can be used to take out the worst sediments when refueling, but it is often difficult to throttle down the flow from the fuel pump to the rate at which the fuel moves through the funnel, which leads to spills. On dozens of occasions, we have been driven to simply dumping fuel of an unknown quality into our tanks.

To ensure the cleanliness of our fuel, on both our old and new boats, we plumbed a fuel sampling/draining line to about ⅛ inch (3 mm) off the bottom of the lowest point of the fuel tank. The fuel suction line (the one to the engine) is set a little farther off the bottom of the tank (to avoid sucking up sediment). As a result, the sampling line is lower than the suction line. The sampling line is connected to either a hand pump (the old boat) or a small electric fuel pump (the new boat). The pump discharge is run through a shutoff valve into a milk jug or jam jar.

After we have taken on fuel, we always sit at the dock for a few minutes or pull off, drop the anchor, and shut the motor down. If we have been unlucky enough to take on a batch of seriously contaminated fuel (it has happened twice in fifteen years), the worst of the contaminants will start to settle out. After ten minutes or so, we pump a sample from the base of the tank into the milk jug or jam jar and hold it up to the light. If it shows contamination (water, sediment, or algae), we know we will fire up the engine at our peril. We are faced with pumping down the tank and disposing of the contaminated fuel—not a pleasant task, but preferable to rebuilding the engine.

These measures are not a substitute for recommended routine maintenance on the primary and secondary fuel filters. These filters are still essential to pick up lesser levels of contaminants. Mostly, however, we find that the filter elements come out almost spotlessly clean because we have caught the greater part of any contamination with the sampling pump.

The sampling pump has other significant benefits for cruisers. Over time, all fuel tanks tend to accumulate some sediment and water (from condensation inside the tank). The water then provides the necessary conditions for algae to grow (the algae live and breed at the interface of the diesel and water). Water, sediment, and algae build up unbeknown to the boatowner until the engine is fired up in rough weather, at which time everything gets stirred up, the crud gets sucked into the filters, and the engine dies through fuel starvation caused by plugged filters. If the boatowner is really unlucky, the suction pressure generated by the engine fuel pump may collapse the filters, allowing all the muck into the fuel-injection system. This can cause enough damage to make a new engine the cheapest way to fix the problem.

A fuel-sampling pump eliminates these risks. Any water or sediment in the tank gets sucked out every time a sample is taken, resulting in an almost spotlessly clean tank. Having

Nada's fuel-sampling system. The pump is plumbed to a low spot in the tank.

seen numerous cruisers disabled as a result of dirty fuel, *I cannot emphasize enough the benefits of these simple preventive measures, and I recommend them to all cruising sailors regardless of their cruising grounds.*

Living with an Engine

Engines vibrate, get hot, and make a lot of noise. Failing to tame these unpleasant characteristics can impinge quite severely on the quality of life sought on a cruising boat.

Most often, little can be done about vibration, other than ensuring that the engine is accurately aligned. If vibration is still at nuisance levels, changing the composition of the rubber in the engine feet, stiffening engine beds, and other measures may help, but these are beyond the scope of this book. Better yet is to soft-mount the engine and install an Aquadrive or similar constant-velocity joint in the propeller shaft; however, this is quite expensive and requires a certain amount of space in which to mount the unit. Nevertheless, the results can be quite dramatic.

Insulation is the key to noise reduction and keeping heat out of living spaces (particularly quarter berths when they are fitted alongside engine compartments). As for noise insulation, there is no substitute for *lead sandwich foams,* in which a layer of lead is bonded between a couple of layers of foam. This kind of insulation is expensive and relatively heavy, but it is extremely effective: the thicker the better.

However, just as the insulation on an icebox is voided if a lid or door is left open, so too sound insulation is ineffective if there are any holes or cracks through which sound waves can pass. The insulation, particularly its seams, must tightly seal the compartment, including around all cables and hoses. This makes life a little difficult because a diesel engine requires a substantial supply of fresh air for combustion. The minimum air vent size, in square inches, can be estimated by dividing 3.3 into the horsepower rating (e.g., $50 \div 3.3 = 15$ square inches for our 50 hp Yanmar; to find the vent size in square centimeters, multiply the horsepower by 2, e.g., $50 \times 2 = 100$ sq. cm). Thought has to be given to how to duct in this air with the least impact on the insulation—maybe from cockpit lockers or through the bilges.

Good insulation, of course, also traps heat, which is undesirable not just because of its impact on living spaces (the engine room remains hot long after the engine is shut down, slowly feeding its heat into the rest of the boat), but also because it lowers the efficiency of the engine. Although it is rarely done with diesel engines, sometimes it is worth installing an engine-room blower specifically to get rid of as much of the heat as possible. The question is: Should it blow in or should it suck out?

Engine alignment is one of those things that should be checked from time to time, although it is routinely ignored (including by us!).

If it blows in, it slightly pressurizes the engine compartment. This improves the engine's performance, but may blow the hot air (and any carbon monoxide) out into accommodation spaces—definitely to be avoided. If the blower sucks out, the hot air can be directed away from accommodation spaces. However, in this case, there must be a sufficient surface area of inlet-air ducting to ensure that only minimal negative pressure is created in the engine compartment by the blower; otherwise, engine performance will be impaired. On balance, I would have it suck out, with the blower wired to the ignition switch so that it runs whenever the engine is operating—but also wired to a manual override so that it can be kept running for a while after the engine is shut down.

Access for Maintenance

Very often, the better an engine is insulated, the more difficult it is to access. To combine effective insulation with excellent access takes careful construction, more engine compartment space than most naval architects and boatbuilders are willing to provide, and attention to detail. Nevertheless, it can be done (our Pacific Seacraft 40 is quite good in this respect, although the insulation could be tighter).

Regarding maintenance purposes, there are some real screwups on the market, including boats in which

- The stuffing box cannot be serviced without removing the engine from the boat.

The engine is mounted too close to the stuffing box,—the packing cannot be replaced without removing the shaft coupling! As a result, the packing has not been serviced, the stuffing box is leaking like a sieve, the salt water has sprayed all over the back of the engine room and rusted numerous components, and it is just a matter of luck that the boat hasn't sunk.

Sooner or later, the starter motor will have to come out. On many boats (not this one), it is an extremely difficult operation.

Excellent access, especially to the fuel filters.

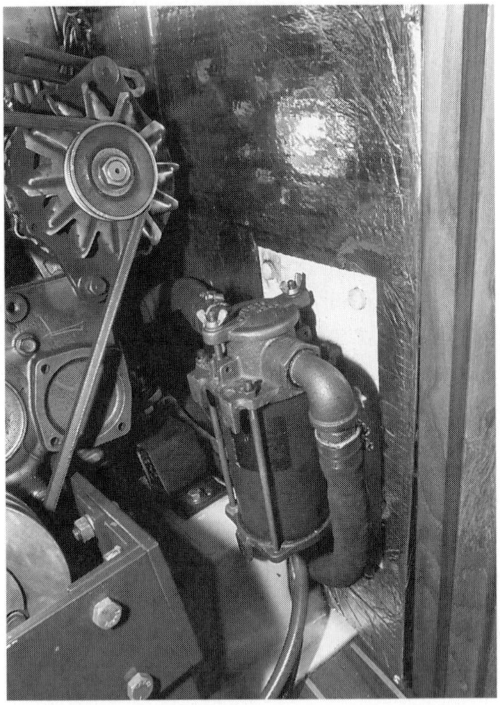
Excellent access to the raw-water strainer.

- The propeller and/or propeller shaft cannot be withdrawn from the boat without dropping the rudder or removing the engine.
- The starter motor cannot be removed without cutting up structural bulkheads.
- The water-pump impeller cannot be changed without taking the starter motor off.
- And so on; the list of egregious insults to boatowners is actually quite long.

The more it is intended to cruise a boat, the more important it is to have decent access to all the service points. As a general rule, the amount and quality of maintenance are in direct proportion to the ease of access. Specifically, access for the following tasks must be considered:

- changing all belts
- tensioning alternator belts
- draining the primary fuel-filter bowl

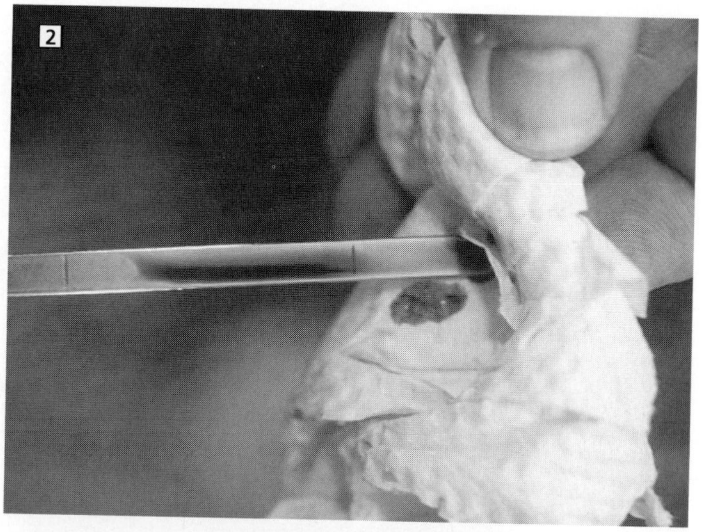

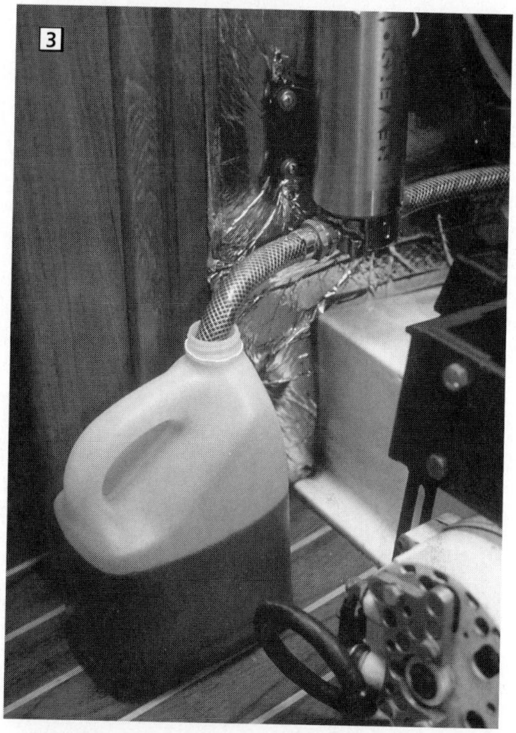

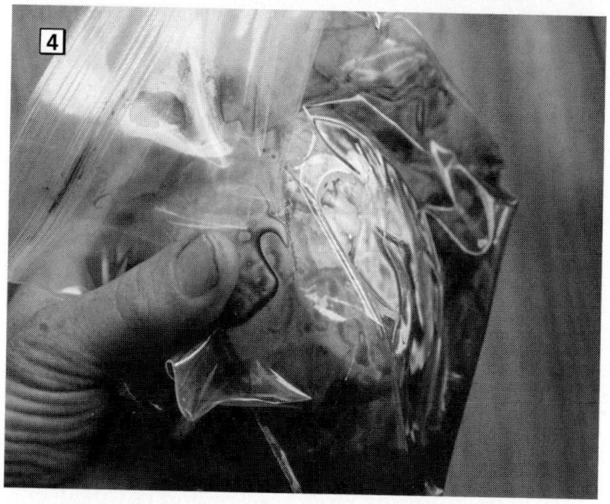

1, 2. *Checking and changing the oil on* Nada. 3. *Note the oil-change pump and the use of a plastic storage bag . . .* 4. *to contain the mess when removing the filter (diapers also work well). I would like to have the filter remotely mounted and hanging down (rather than mounted horizontally on the engine)—it would be even easier to change, with no mess.* 5. *Adding oil.*

Nada's filter service station. The fuel-tank vent also comes in here. We place a milk jug under it when refueling, as shown in this photo. This eliminates all possibilities of overboard spills.

- changing all filters (fuel and oil): as designed, to change the primary fuel filter on our Pacific Seacraft 40, the cockpit sole had to be taken up. The one time the filter is likely to plug is in rough weather (when the tank is stirred up), which is the one time you don't want a great big hole in the cockpit sole (we moved the filter)
- checking the dipstick and pumping out the engine oil
- pumping out the transmission oil (this is tough on many boats)
- bleeding the fuel system and injectors
- checking and cleaning the engine and other raw-water filters
- changing the raw-water pump impeller
- replacing zinc pencil anodes in the heat exchanger and elsewhere
- cleaning the raw-water side of the heat exchanger
- cleaning the vented loop on the raw-water injection line into the exhaust
- checking the exhaust elbow and injection nipple
- draining water from the block and heat exchanger when winterizing
- checking the coolant overflow bottle
- accessing the engine feet to set the alignment (another tough one on many boats)
- setting valve clearances, pulling injectors, and other "top-end" work
- removing the starter motor
- adjusting and lubricating the engine and transmission controls
- inspecting and adjusting the shaft seal

On a couple of boats with which I have been involved (including our new Pacific Seacraft 40), I designed a "filter service station" that is external to the engine room and readily accessible. The service station is a fiberglass- or Formica-lined compartment in which are set the primary fuel filter, a remotely mounted oil filter, an oil-change pump, and the fuel-tank sampling pump. There is space to insert a 1-gallon milk jug (or similar container) under the discharge hoses from the oil-change pump and the fuel-tank sampling pump. Changing filters and oil and sampling the fuel tank are a breeze, with any spills contained in the liner and easily wiped up. I recommend this approach to anyone.

Rather than have the fuel-tank vents go overboard, where there is a risk of both spills and water ingress in certain conditions, I also placed them in the filter station, running them into the milk jug. This results in a diesel odor for a short while after refueling, but it soon dissipates. I consider this a small trade-off for protection from potential oil-spill lawsuits and the total protection of the fuel tank from saltwater contamination (saltwater ingress into fuel tanks via tank vents is not uncommon). However, it needs to be noted that this violates ABYC standards, and in any event should *never* be done with gasoline tanks.

Finally, before leaving the subject of engine access, let's give some thought to retrieving dropped tools, catching oil and water spills when servicing the engine, and cleaning the engine itself. The key here is a smooth, one-piece engine bed and pan (preferably gel-coated fiberglass) designed so that it contains all likely spills. The engine clearance needs to be such that it is possible to reach comfortably to all corners of the pan (too often, this is not possible). Oh, and let's paint the engine compartment white and install some lighting so we can see what we're doing!

Remarkably, our Pacific Seacraft 40 meets just about all of these parameters—which goes to show that it can be done. It is one of the reasons I like it so much.

FUEL AND WATER TANKS

Fuel- and water-tank failures are all too common on boats, especially boats more than ten years old. Failures frequently are compounded by the fact that the tanks cannot be removed without tearing the boat apart. To avoid extremely frustrating and expensive problems, tank construction and installation need to be carefully considered.

Copper and brass fittings should never be screwed directly into aluminum (as shown here).

Metal Tanks

I discuss tank materials and construction in detail in *Boatowner's Mechanical and Electrical Manual*. Following is a summary of the key points, looking first at metal tanks:

- Metal tanks should be avoided if at all possible, especially in damp areas of the boat. Both aluminum and stainless will corrode, and frequently do.
- If aluminum is used, it should not be in contact with any copper fittings (commonly used in plumbing systems). Even a copper penny sitting on top of a damp tank eventually eats a hole in it.
- If stainless steel is used, it should be at least the corrosion-resistant 316L or 317L (the "L" is important for welding) and not 304 (which is commonly used). Even 316L and 317L will corrode; better yet are high-molybdenum alloys and Monel, but they are generally considered prohibitively expensive.
- To avoid trapping moisture, all tank bearers should be separated from tank surfaces by a nonmetallic, non-moisture-absorbent, nonabrasive material such as neoprene, Teflon, or high-density plastic.
- Tanks must be installed to allow drainage of water from the tank's surfaces.
- Tanks should be installed above any likely bilge-water level and out of the "splash zone."
- The preferred method of installing metal tanks is to use flanges on the tank or welded on tabs so that no part of the tank itself is in contact with any mounting surface. That way, moisture will not be trapped against any tank surfaces, and any corrosion that does occur will likely be concentrated under the flanges or

A penny fell on this aluminum tank, initiating galvanic corrosion that eventually ate clean through the tank.

Given unfavorable conditions, most grades of stainless steel used in boat tanks will also corrode, some worse than others.

tabs and will not threaten the integrity of the tank itself. For this approach to work, the flanges or tabs and any associated welds must clearly be strong enough to withstand all stresses to which the tank will be subjected.

- *All metal tanks must be removable without destroying the fabric of the boat.*

Plastic Tanks

Plastic (i.e., fiberglass and polyethylene) is generally a better material choice for tanks. We built in fiberglass tanks in our old boat. However, such tanks are labor-intensive (and, therefore, costly to produce), they require a very rigid hull (flexing and wracking may crack the tanks), and—if they fail—they can be expensive to fix (primarily because access may require ripping the boat apart). For these reasons, boatbuilders rarely install integral fiberglass tanks, although *this is my preferred option where feasible* (it makes the best use of available space and gets the weight down as low as possible).

What about independently mounted fiberglass tanks? As far as I know, there are no production builders of such tanks: each must be custom-fabricated. If properly constructed and installed, the tanks can be expected to last the life of a boat. However, they are also labor-intensive to produce, making them time- and cost-prohibitive. There also may be legal problems if the tanks are used for fuel storage (especially gasoline; the tanks must pass certain tests).

Polyethylene is the other commonly available "plastic" for tank construction. It is amazingly tough and durable. Best of all, of course, is the fact that in common with all plastics, polyethylene is immune to corrosion.

Polyethylene comes in two forms: *linear* and *cross-linked*. Linear polyethylene is not suitable for fuel tanks (hydrocarbons eventually cause it to crack) but is commonly used for water tanks and holding tanks. Cross-linked polyethylene (XLPE) makes an excellent fuel-tank material, although it is not acceptable for use on potable water systems.

Both linear and cross-linked polyethylene generally have UV inhibitors added to the mix, which just about eliminates problems with age-hardening (which was an issue years ago). As a result, this material should last the life of a boat as long as the tanks are properly manufactured. Two processes are used:

- Welding: quality is all over the map—there are numerous cases of welded seams bursting at sea.
- *Rotomolding*: produces a seamless tank—this is the preferred method of construction *as long as the tank has a sturdy wall thickness.*

The failures that do occur on rotomolded tanks are mostly around the fittings for water and holding tanks (i.e., linear polyethylene tanks, not cross-linked), typically as a result of the following:

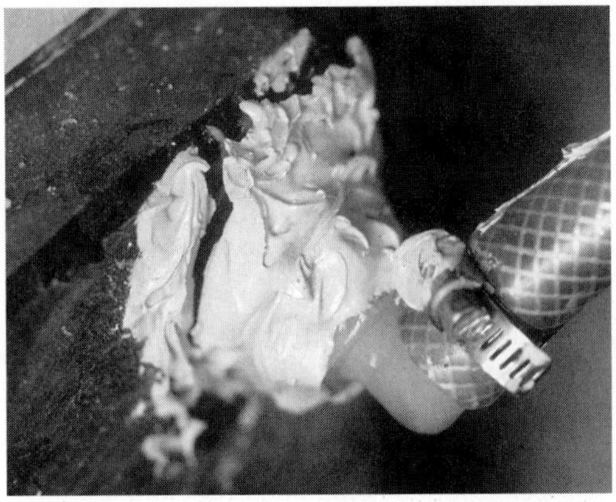

The most common failure with polyethylene tanks is broken fittings. They need to be well protected against being knocked.

Below left: *Custom-made fiberglass fuel tank. (Courtesy Cabo Rico)* Below right: *The tank bonded into the hull—here's a tank that will last the life of the boat. (Courtesy Cabo Rico)*

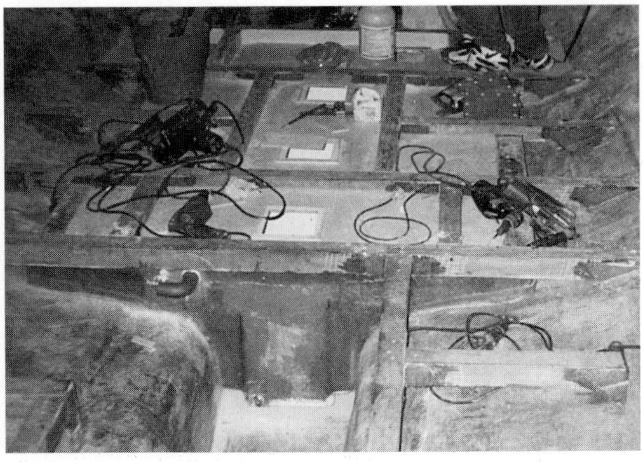

- improper installation of hose barbs and lines (too much torque when screwing in threaded components; failure to add a flexible section in attached piping; or inadequate support of hoses and piping)
- improper stowage of gear
- someone accidentally stepping on the fitting while working on the boat

As for installation of polyethylene tanks, the rules differ from those that apply to metal tanks:

- The bottom of a tank must be fully supported, with a surface shaped to match that of the tank, and with neoprene padding between the tank and other contact points.
- Whatever method is used to restrain the tank, it must not create chafing, cutting, or abrasion.
- A fuel tank must be given room to "grow." When filled with gasoline or diesel, during the first month or so of use, an XLPE tank expands in all directions by about 2 percent (approximately ¼ in./6 mm per foot). After this expansion, it stabilizes, regardless of whether it is full of fuel. Nylon webbing works well as a retainer because it is impervious to corrosion and it stretches enough to accommodate the growth of a tank.
- Once the tank is secured, all connections need to be made with well-supported, flexible lines.

A good-quality, heavy-wall (i.e., ruggedly constructed), properly installed, and suitably protected polyethylene tank can be fitted and just about forgotten. The one drawback to polyethylene is that if there is not a stock tank to fit an application, the cost of developing a mold is prohibitive. In contrast, one-off production is—of course—one area where metal shines. Nevertheless, there are now literally hundreds of different shapes and sizes of polyethylene tanks that can be bought off the shelf. If necessary, the interior spaces can be modified during the design stage of a boat to accept a stock tank, which seems preferable to using a custom-built metal tank that may fail before the boat reaches the end of its life.

Our New Boat

The stock Pacific Seacraft 40 comes with two molded-in fiberglass water tanks, an aluminum water tank, and an aluminum fuel tank.

Nada's custom-made fiberglass fuel tank is impervious to corrosion. Nevertheless, if necessary, it still can be taken out of the boat through this hatch without disassembling any joinerwork.

The fiberglass tanks are great; the aluminum I would not accept. Unfortunately, the spaces did not lend themselves to stock polyethylene tanks. So Pacific Seacraft agreed to build a one-off fiberglass tank to replace one tank; for the other (which is usually the fuel tank), I had to settle for stainless steel—we'll see how it does. I did switch the fuel from the stainless tank to the custom fiberglass tank so that if and when the stainless fails, we will only lose one of three water tanks rather than our fuel tank.

All the tanks on a Pacific Seacraft 40 are fully accessible and removable without tearing the boat apart, which is just as it should be. (For additional practical considerations concerning tanks, see the later section on plumbing.)

Freshwater Systems

The most basic freshwater question is: How much should you carry? The answer varies from boat to boat. I figure a crew of four being moderately careful will use 40 gallons (150 L) or more a week, which is approximately 1.5 gallons (5.6 L) per person per day. (Contrast this to Hiscock's estimate of half a gallon per person per day: we are all getting soft!) With this in mind, I like to set a target for an offshore boat of approximately 160 gallons (600 L); the boat should have this whether or not there is a watermaker. This is a conservative approach that assumes the watermaker will break down at some point—four weeks away from a potential water source. Obviously, for coastal cruising, with its greater opportunities for resupply, this number can be lower.

The freshwater should be kept in at least two tanks; that way, if one fails or gets polluted, there is a backup. Of course, this won't help much if the backup is empty, so part of water management when offshore should be to use half of one tank and then switch to the other, so that neither is completely depleted.

We have successfully used the Hart Tank Tender for keeping track of water-tank levels (and diesel and holding tanks); there are other similar devices. A small air pump is used to force air down a tube into the tank being measured. The resistance to pumping varies according to the depth of liquid in the tank. A gauge registers the resistance, which is then converted into a volume. The device works exceptionally well on tall tanks that have a significant change in fluid level with a small change in volume, but it is not much use on wide shallow tanks in which fluid levels change slowly in response to volume changes (also, when the boat heels, the meter gives a totally false reading). With the latter type of tank, more conventional measurement devices (electrical, mechanical, or sight) are needed, although none works well when heeled.

Water tanks frequently end up under berths. If so, they need to be well baffled to mitigate the annoying sloshing noises they will make. They also need to be extremely well secured. A 60-gallon (227 L) tank full of water weighs 500 pounds (226 kg). Depending on the tank's location, it will develop considerable G-forces when the boat is pounding, constantly working away at its mounting brackets. Too many tanks rely primarily on gravity to stay in place—if the boat gets knocked down, there is a serious risk of the tank coming loose.

A desirable feature of the installation is to have a defined low spot in the tank from which the water is withdrawn, so that the water pump will not suck air on one tack or the other until the tank is empty. Just as with a fuel tank, the suction line should be inserted from the top of the tank to minimize the chance of leaks. All tanks need inspection hatches large enough to accommodate getting inside to clean out the interior; if there are baffles, it should be possible to stick a hose under them to flush out all sections.

Some people like all kinds of filters on their freshwater system. We have never had one, and have almost never treated the tanks with bleach or any other chemical. So far (I suppose I should knock on wood), we have not had any problems. Sometimes on the old boat we left water in the tanks for more than a year and it was still sweet. I believe this was because we had totally *opaque tanks* and totally *opaque plumbing* (stainless steel rather than the more common slightly translucent plastic). Without light, there can be no mold, algae, and slime. If it is necessary to treat a tank, 1 teaspoon of American household bleach (± 5 percent sodium hypochlorite, e.g., Clorox; similar "pure" bleaches are hard to find in Europe) for every 10 gallons (40 L) of water will kill most noxious substances without leaving too strong a taste (as long as the water sits for a while before use; see chapter 12).

However, chlorinated water left in stainless steel tanks may corrode the tank, although the chlorine tends to break down quite quickly, especially if the tank is in any way opened up. Chlorinated water also damages the membranes in watermakers, so it is essential to ensure that it cannot get to any watermaker (e.g., when back-flushing the membrane).

The one freshwater failure we have had—along with many other cruisers—is the freshwater pump; sooner or later, they all act up. Most often, it is the pressure switch that gives out; therefore, whatever pump is used should have an easily replaced switch (not all do). Beyond this, if the boat also has a saltwater washdown pump, it is well worth using the same make and model of pump as on the freshwater system with the same hose fittings, and placing it next to the freshwater pump. This way, if the freshwater system fails, the saltwater pump can be pressed into service.

I like to have the freshwater pump mounted in a location that makes it audible every time it kicks on. The advantage of being able to hear it outweighs the minor inconven-

Stainless steel water tank with fittings for the fill and vent hoses, a watermaker, and a tank gauge. The filter is for the watermaker.

ience of the intermittent low-level noise. We can tell if a faucet is dripping or a tank has run dry. Better yet, if the pump runs for more than a few seconds when guests are onboard, Terrie and I start to fidget, and then cough loudly, and then bang on the bulkheads . . . our visitors get the message fast!

There may be times when water has to be hauled from shore in the dinghy and then poured into the tanks via a funnel. To make this possible, the tank fills need to be located so that a decent-sized funnel can be put into them. Generally, this means locating the fill fittings away from stanchions and high bulwarks. (The other way to put in water without spilling any is to siphon it from the can into the tank.)

On a long-distance cruising boat, it is well worth trying to set the decks up as a water-catchment area. This requires some type of low bulwark or continuous toerail to channel the water aft and a tank fill more or less at the low point in a side deck. If the tank fill is just a little above the low point, any sediment that comes off the decks tends to settle out at the low point, and only clean water will flow into the tank. We had a setup like this on our old boat. In a good squall, we first gave the deck a quick scrub to clean off any salt and dirt, and then plugged the scuppers. The water would form a puddle and build up until it spilled into the now-open tank fill. Sometimes we got as much as 100 gallons (400 L) in one squall. We found this approach far superior to using an awning for rainwater collection.

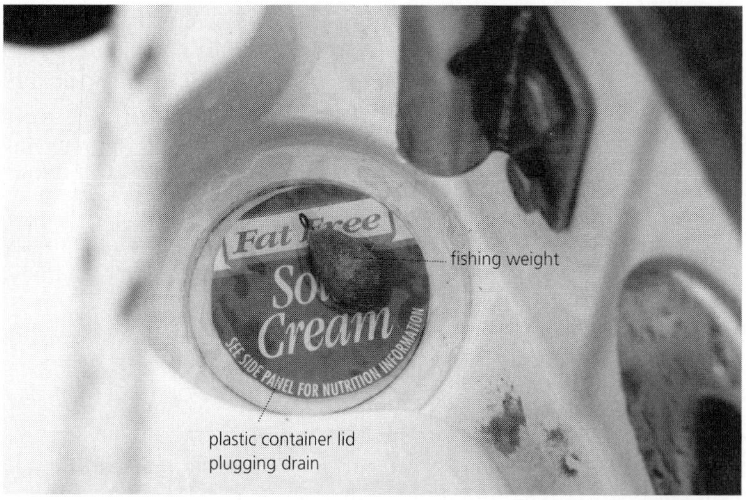

We plug our deck drains with a piece of plastic kept in place by a fishing weight, and then run rainwater straight into a freshwater tank.

Deck fill fittings need to be located so that a good-size funnel fits in without obstruction. Another couple of inches clearance between the bulwark and the deck would be helpful here.

If the tank fill is set well up the side deck, a significant amount of rainwater runoff can still be channeled into it by placing rolled-up towels across the deck just aft of it. The towels create a reasonably effective dam.

Watermakers

Watermakers are becoming increasingly popular. I have heard it argued that with a watermaker, you can cut down your tankage with consequent savings on weight and space. But what happens if the watermaker fails? *There is no substitute for having sufficient water onboard to see you through all emergencies.* The longer the passages that will be made, the more water should be carried.

Within this framework, a watermaker can play a definite (and expensive) role in the water equation. It can free you from most constraints on water consumption, allowing you a more extravagant lifestyle. It can completely free you from dependence on shore-side facilities and from the necessity of collecting rainwater. When operated at sea, a watermaker guarantees you a safe water supply; however, harbor water must be treated with discretion.

This latter point needs elaboration. Many watermakers come with relatively lightweight pre-filters, which cannot handle significant amounts of oil and other contaminants. Dirty harbor conditions require large commercial pre-filters with an *effective* oil-water separation capability. Harbor water is also likely to be contaminated with fecal matter and other pollutants. While an *undamaged* watermaker membrane filters out most bacteria, some can still pass through, as can a number of the smaller viruses—a damaged membrane, of course, lets anything through. When using a watermaker in suspect water, you need to have some means of sterilizing the water to make it safe for drinking.

When a watermaker moves from salt to brackish water or freshwater, other problems can arise. Without salt, the flow rate through the membrane increases dramatically, while the quality of the finished product decreases (some silt particles are small enough to pass through any filter or membrane). Membranes become plugged; pumps and motors are overworked and may burn out. If you are anticipating sustained operation in brackish water or freshwater, you need to fit a special membrane. For temporary use, reduce the operating pressure on the watermaker to a level at which its output is the same as in salt water (normal pressure is approximately 800 psi/56 kg/cm^2; you may need to drop this to as low as 400 psi/28 kg/cm^2).

Twelve-volt DC water maker (the popular PUR type).

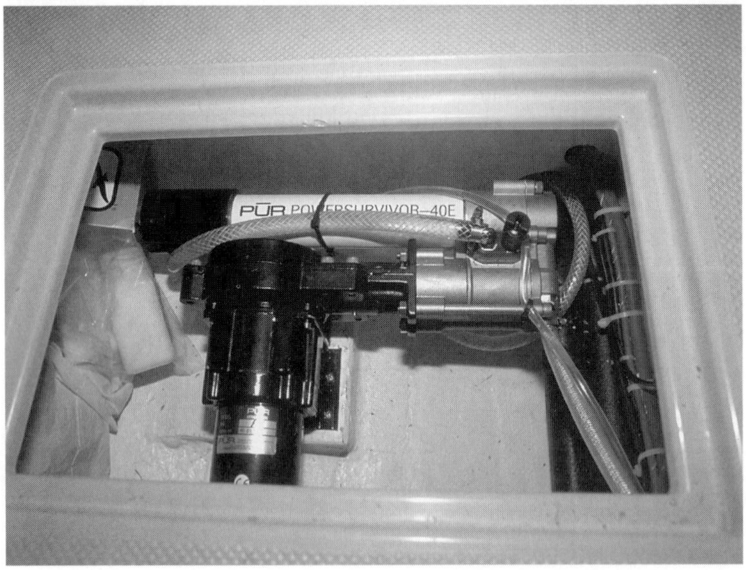

Watermakers are power-hungry. If you plan to use one on a regular basis, carefully factor this into your overall power equation. If you have engine-driven refrigeration, you will probably want an engine-driven watermaker, but you must take care to match this to the operating characteristics of your engine during refrigerating and watermaking hours. Watermaker pumps need to be run at a near constant speed to maintain the correct system pressure. The watermaker's capacity needs to be large enough to meet your water requirements in your normal refrigerating (i.e., engine-running) time. If you have an intermittently operated AC generator, an AC watermaker is probably the best bet, with sufficient capacity to do its job in the regular generating hours.

DC watermaking is only feasible at lower levels of output. The popular PUR DC watermakers take 3 amp-hours at 12 volts to produce a gallon of water; 10 gallons (40 L) a day comes to 30 or more amp-hours—a significant load on most cruising boats. Spectra watermakers make a remarkable gallon per amp-hour (I am tempted to try one of them).

The other side of the watermaker picture is the required maintenance. If it is not to be used for a few days, the membrane needs backflushing and "pickling," and whenever the boat is laid up, it needs pickling. These jobs have to be added to what is already a long list on the modern cruising boat.

In summary, I am of two minds as to whether the extra water is worth the expense, energy consumption, and maintenance, but I know that I am increasingly in the minority position regarding this matter.

BILGE PUMPS

It is time now to consider some other aspects of plumbing a cruising boat, starting with that most essential component: the bilge pump. A bilge pump has two separate functions: to remove small amounts of water from the boat—such as from a dripping shaft seal—on a routine basis; and to help remove large amounts of water in a catastrophic event, such as when heavy seas get below, a through-hull fails, or the hull is damaged. A pump capable of dealing with large amounts of water will always be capable of dealing with small amounts, so let's look at the second function first.

Here's a fine mess. The stuffing box has seized to the propeller shaft. The hose is oversized for the stuffing box and held with a single hose clamp that is rusting. When the shaft is turned, it may just rip the stuffing box out of the hose; if not, the hose clamp will ultimately fail. Either way, the bilge pump will be working hard!

Flooding Rates and Pumping Capacities

The table below, adapted from an old U.S. Navy salvage manual, assumes an open hole in the bottom of a boat (e.g., the through-hull fell out or the boat was holed in a collision) and shows how much water will enter in one minute.

These flow rates are scary! Out of curiosity, I did some kitchen-sink experiments at home, replicating a 1-inch hole in a hull. The results confirmed the decidedly catastrophic-looking numbers in the Navy handbook. When I compared these flooding rates to published bilge-pump flow rates, I concluded that once a hole gets up to around 2 inches (50 mm) in diameter (the kind of hole you could get if a through-hull fails, or if the boat hits the sharp end of a submerged piece of timber or the corner of a container), the predicted flow rate with even a minimal head pressure will exceed the rated capacity of any popular bilge pump. This is a sobering thought: in other words, no popular bilge pump can keep up with anything other than minor below-the-waterline damage.

Note that I refer to the *rated* capacity of pumps. The reality, unfortunately, is that installed bilge pumps almost never produce their rated flow; in fact, the

Kitchen-sink flow-rate experiments. The results came surprisingly close to the numbers in the U.S. Navy Salvors Handbook*!*

Flooding Rates (gpm)* of Various Size Openings at Various Depths

DEPTH OF HOLE (ft.)	DIAMETER OPENING IN HULL (in.)							
	1	1.5	2	2.5	3	3.5	4	6
1	20	44	79	123	177	241	314	707
2	28	62	111	174	250	340	444	1,000
3	34	77	136	213	306	417	544	1,224
4	39	88	157	245	353	481	628	1,414
5	44	99	176	274	395	538	702	1,581
6	48	108	192	301	433	589	770	1,731
7	52	117	208	325	468	636	831	1,870
8	56	125	222	347	500	680	889	1,999
9	59	133	236	368	530	722	942	2,121
10	62	140	248	388	559	761	993	2,235

*gpm in U.S. gallons (1 gal. = 3.785 L)

Source: Adapted from Naval Sea Systems command, *U.S. Navy Salvors Handbook.*

majority don't even come close, so the picture is much worse than it first appears. Almost all bilge pumps are the immersed-centrifugal type. In *Boatowner's Mechanical and Electrical Manual*, I outline a procedure for calculating the real-life rather than rated performance of these pumps, and then look at a "typical" installation using a relatively large (3,000 gallons per hour [gph]/11,355 L/h) submersible pump as an example. It turns out that this pump almost never produces even half its rated output and, at times (especially if the boat's batteries are a little low and the boat is heeled), pumps as little as 700 gph (2,650 L/h), which is under 25 percent of rated output.

There are other pump types that do not show this dramatic loss of performance, specifically electric diaphragm pumps and flexible impeller pumps. The latter, however, are not suitable for bilge-pumping applications because they burn up if run dry and they are also vulnerable to damage from solids entrained in the bilge water. Electric diaphragm pumps do get used as bilge pumps (Pacific Seacraft uses them), but I don't like them because even small particles lodged in their valves can disable them and, in any case, they have a low flow rate. Although the real-life performance approximates the rated performance, the total volume of water moved will still be considerably less than that moved by a good-sized centrifugal pump operating at just 25 percent of capacity. Therefore, despite their limitations, in my opinion the centrifugal pumps are the best of the bunch.

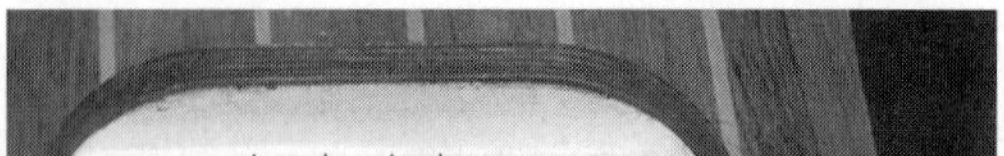
connections low in the bilge are vulnerable to getting wet
minimal bilge sump
flat bottom—bilge water will migrate to the boat's lockers when the boat is heeled

Although rated at 2,000 gph (7,570 L/h), this bilge pump will be lucky to do half that in this installation. Note also the switch connections, barely above the bilge-water level, in an area where they are certain to get splashed. This leads to stray-current corrosion, which will disable the wiring and render the pump out of commission.

A 3,000 gph (11,355 L/h) pump good for about 1,500 gph (5,678 L/h) in this installation, placed in a decent bilge sump. All wiring connections are well above any likely water level. Although the hose is corrugated on its outer face, it is smooth on the inside.

Improving Performance: Hoses and Check Valves

So what can be done to improve the performance of centrifugal pumps? The primary reason why they perform so poorly is that the pumps are rated in a totally unrealistic environment that includes no discharge piping and no back pressure on the system. As soon as the resistance created by a discharge hose—and the resistance caused by the need to actually lift the water up and out of a boat—are factored in, the pump's output dives. This cumulative resistance is known as *head pressure*.

The single greatest improvement in the performance of a centrifugal pump comes from reducing the head pressure. Given that the vertical lift component is more or less fixed by the physical dimensions of a boat, the only component of head pressure that can be readily reduced is that which is created by the piping run. There is a clear need to use a hose no smaller than the pump's outlet, to keep the hose run as short and as direct as possible, and to avoid any additional resistance such as that imposed by check valves or dirty suction filters. The discharge hose must maintain a steady rise at all angles of heel up to its through-hull or vented loop. Otherwise, every time the pump stops, the low spots will trap water. When the pump restarts, the trapped water may act as a plug, "air-locking" the pump and effectively stalling it out.

To minimize friction, hoses should have a smooth interior wall. Many of the most popular bilge pumps on the market have a 1⅛-inch outside diameter discharge nipple. As far as I know, the only hoses manufactured to fit this size nipple are corrugated hoses, some of which have a smooth internal bore but many of which do not. Internal corrugations in a hose wall *significantly* increase the head pressure created by a given length of hose and, therefore, should be avoided. In any case, such hoses are often extremely thin-walled and, as a result, are easily damaged—not the kind of stuff I want on my boat in such an important application. When pump nipple sizes get above 1⅛ inches (29 mm), any high-quality, smooth-bore hose can be used.

Check valves are another problem in bilge-pumping applications. Sailboats in particular are liable to have a centralized bilge sump. The shortest path overboard for bilge water is to the side of the vessel; however, when well heeled on one tack or the other, any discharge fitting may be under water. This creates the potential for water to siphon back into the boat, which has resulted in many floodings, including on our old boat. The response is often to fit a check valve in the line (we had one); however, not only do check valves create a resistance equal to that of many feet of pipe or hose, they also are prone to both plugging (in which case the pump is inoperative) and getting jammed in the open position (in which case they will not stop water from siphoning into the boat).

If a check valve is installed, it is advantageous to mount the pump on a small pedestal. Heavier sediments then settle out below the level of the pump, from where they can be periodically cleaned out manually. Even so, if at all possible, a check valve should be avoided like the plague—if it cannot be avoided, it should be a type that can be easily disassembled. It must be in a readily accessible position so that it can be serviced when necessary.

A better approach to siphon prevention is to dispense with the check valve, raise the discharge hose from the pump above the highest possible heeled waterline level, and fit a siphon break at the top of the loop. The extra static head has to be factored into any bilge-pump flow-rate calculations, but it will be substantially less than the head pressure created by a check valve. The extent to which the hose must be raised above the waterline can be minimized by discharging it overboard on the centerline at the stern (rather than over the side), but this may result in unacceptably long hose runs.

Improving Performance: Electrical Considerations

The second greatest improvement in bilge-pumping performance comes from wiring a pump with cables sized to minimize voltage drop. Typically, there is a relatively long cable run from the distribution panel or battery to a bilge pump. For a given size of cable, the longer the cable run, the greater is the cumulative voltage drop. Frequently, the cables are not sized to take this into consideration, and voltage drop

wiring
connections

Left: *This looks like a clean installation until you realize the wiring connections may get splashed, which leads to corrosion and failure.* Below: *The effect of wiring a bilge pump switch in the negative side of the circuit: the pump will still work, but there may be devastating stray-current corrosion.*

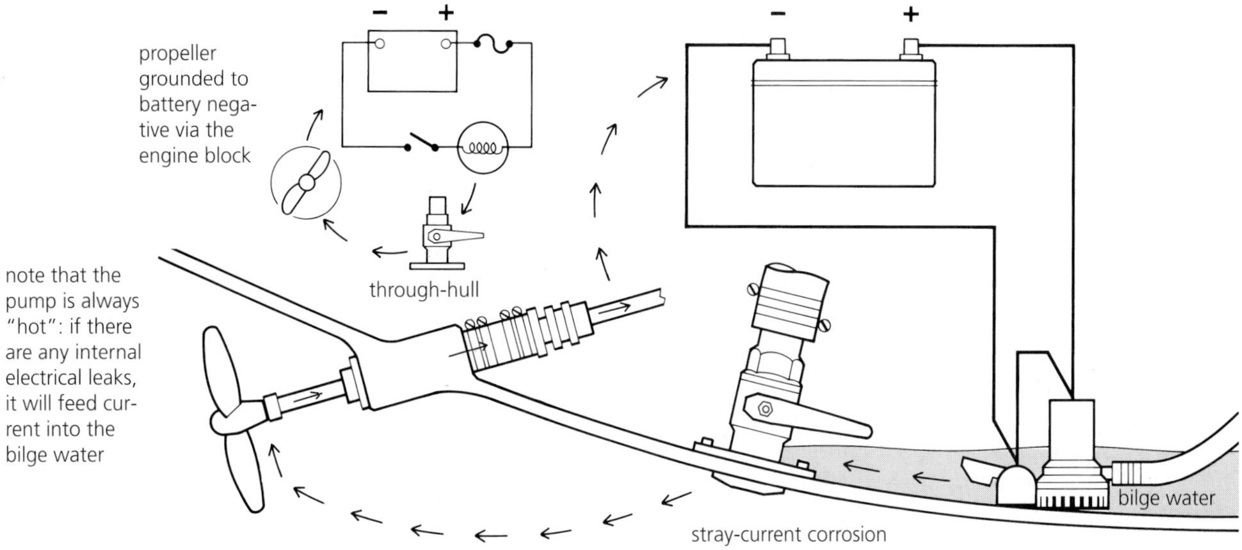
propeller grounded to battery negative via the engine block
–
+
–
+
note that the pump is always "hot": if there are any internal electrical leaks, it will feed current into the bilge water
through-hull
bilge water
stray-current corrosion

ends up at around 10 percent or even higher. What this means is that, given a battery voltage of 12.0 volts (not uncommon), the pump will only be seeing 10.8 volts, which results in a drop in the pump's rated output by as much as 20 percent. (For more about voltage drop and wiring sizes, see *Boatowner's Mechanical and Electrical Manual.*)

Although it is sometimes considered acceptable to wire pumps with cables that result in a 10 percent voltage drop, pump performance will be significantly improved by using cables that result in a 3 percent voltage drop. Given the inhospitable environment in a bilge, tinned cable is preferred over plain copper, and all connections should be sealed with glue-type heat-shrink tubing to make them as waterproof as possible.

Something often overlooked by do-it-yourself installers when wiring a pump is the importance of ensuring that the pump switch is installed in the *positive* feed to the pump. The pump itself works as well with the switch in the negative side of the circuit as it does in the positive side. However, if the switch gets installed in the negative side, the bilge pump and, more importantly, any metal through-hulls below the level of the bilge water may suffer from potentially devastating stray-current corrosion.

Even if a switch is installed correctly, stray-current corrosion will destroy the electrical connections inside the switch and disable the switch if water penetrates the seals. Its operation should always be checked by lifting the float before leaving a boat (if the float isn't accessible, it needs to be made accessible).

Over-Current Protection and Locked Rotors

Another electrical issue that has to be addressed is over-current protection. As with all other circuits on a boat, a bilge-pump circuit should be protected at its source. My preference is for a fuse rather than a breaker because it creates less of an opportunity to accidentally turn off the bilge pump when leaving the boat. The fuse should have a rating that does not exceed the current-carrying capability (the ampacity) of the smallest cables in the circuit (usually the cables that come attached to the pump or its float switch).

Properly sized, the fuse will prevent the pump wiring from melting down in the event of a serious short circuit. However, with centrifugal bilge pumps, there is always the risk of a piece of debris jamming the pump impeller, creating what is called a *locked rotor state*. Given a locked rotor, the current draw of a pump rises dramatically, but not necessarily enough to blow the fuse. The pump may then get hot enough to start a fire. This is especially likely to happen if the wiring to the pump is undersized: the cumulative resistance of the undersized cables may be enough to limit the current flow on the circuit to a level at which the fuse will not blow. Using a lower rated fuse is not the way to handle this problem because it may result in nuisance blowing; upgrade the cabling instead. Then, given a locked rotor, the cables will pass a current flow that is high enough to blow the fuse, shutting down the circuit.

Float Switches

A mechanism is required to turn a pump on and off. There is much to be said for making it a manual switch because it forces one to regularly check the state of the bilge; however, in practice, the boating public demands an automatic switch that is generally backed up with a manual override.

The most common switch is a float switch, but there are also switches operated by air pressure and at least three forms of electronic switch. The variety of switches is testimony to the fact that no one type is universally satisfactory in bilge-pumping applications.

The popular float switches are prone to a number of failures, the most obvious of which is trash jamming the hinge so that the switch is either locked "on" or "off." If the boat is unattended and has any kind of leak, it is likely to sink regardless of which way the switch is jammed—even if it is on, sooner or later the battery will die, at which point it might as well be off. Most switches have optional covers that filter out the worst debris: *this type should always be installed.* Beyond this, there are various electrical modes of failure. Many of the switches are built with lightweight electrical components that have a bad habit of burning out. *Any switch needs to have a continuous current rating (amperage) at least equal to the amps rating of the pump to which it is attached, and preferably a substantially higher rating.*

The best float switches currently on the market are the Ultimate switches manufactured by Ultra Safety Systems (Riviera Beach, Florida) or the equivalent. Instead of a hinged float, these switches have a float riding on a vertical shaft inside a plastic tube with holes that allow water in and out. The switch is at the top of the tube, above normal water levels, and enclosed in a watertight housing. It is triggered magnetically any time the float rises up the

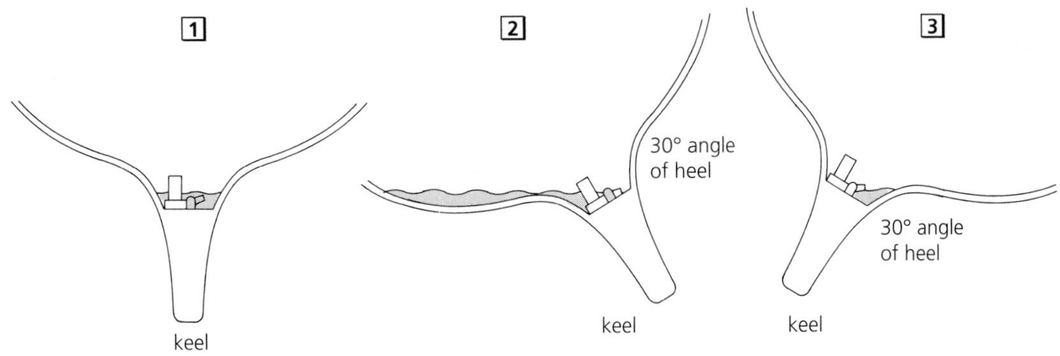

Effect of an off-center bilge-pump float switch. 1. On an even keel, the pump works fine. 2. When heeled one way, the pump does not come on until after bilge water has escaped the bilge and flooded a locker. 3. When heeled the other way, the pump stays on after it has sucked the bilge dry.

tube. Not only are these switches fairly immune to fouling, they are also ruggedly built from an electrical point of view.

Switch Location

The location of a switch relative to its pump is important. If a switch is mounted in a position where it is laterally offset from the pump intake, when the boat is heeled on one tack the switch will not respond until considerably more water is in the bilge than is needed for a level-state response. On the other tack, there is a very real danger that the switch will stay energized after the pump has sucked itself dry, causing the pump to run continuously and creating a heavy drain on the batteries and a risk of pump failure. To minimize these problems, a float switch should always be mounted as close to its pump as possible and in the same fore-and-aft plane. In practice, many switches are simply clipped into the base of the pump; in this case, it is essential to ensure that the switch is aligned fore and aft: if it is set to one side, the pump will definitely run dry on one tack or the other.

The nature of a float switch is such that the change in water level between switching on and turning off is only an inch or two. Even if a switch is mounted in the same fore-and-aft plane as its pump, when the boat is pounding into a head sea or rolling from side to side, the action of a small amount of water surging backward and forward in the bilge can flick the switch on and off until eventually something fails (the wiring, the switch points, the hinge on the switch, or the motor). This situation also creates an unnecessary drain on the batteries.

A similar but even more annoying condition occurs when the bilge pump and switch are installed in a deep, narrow sump, with a moderately long discharge hose from the pump to the overboard through-hull. Every time the pump is shut down, the water in the hose flows back down into the bilge, raising the level of the bilge water—sometimes to the point at which the pump kicks back on. The pump keeps on cycling until the battery is dead. I know of no practical way to deal with this, other than using a different type of switch (the Ultimate switches come with a series of operating differentials from as little as ¾ in. up to 2½ in./20–60 mm; greater differentials, up to 1 or 2 ft./300–600 mm, are available as special-order items).

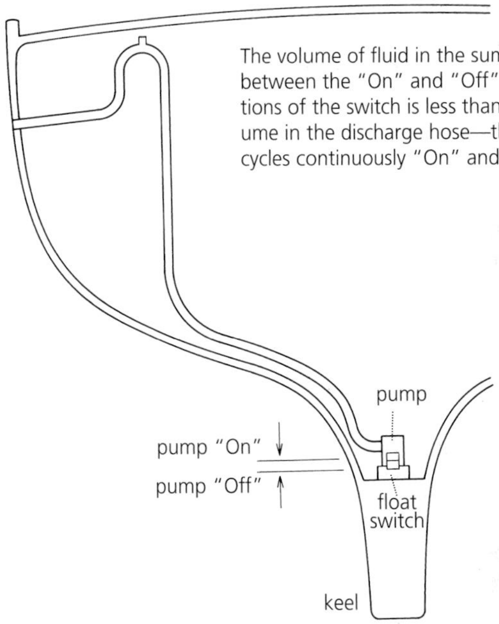

Bilge pump cycling as a result of installation in a deep, narrow sump.

Other Switches

These types of difficulties have led to the development of other kinds of switches, including switches operated by air pressure and electronic switches. These switches solve some problems but introduce new ones of their own.

In recent years, we have seen the introduction of an electronic switch that tracks fluid levels through the current draw of the bilge-pump

LEAVING A BOAT UNATTENDED

I have read somewhere that more boats sink on their moorings or in their slips than at sea. It certainly seems quite plausible. Over an extended period, a slow drip from a stuffing box will allow large amounts of water into a boat. If the battery is not regularly charged, this will cause the bilge pump to flatten the battery until the pump no longer operates and the boat goes down. Even with adequate provisions for battery charging, there are several ways that the bilge pump can be put out of action, including a failed level switch, a jammed pump impeller, and a failed electrical circuit (e.g., corrosion in a fuse holder causing the fuse to overheat and blow).

When leaving a boat unattended, it is foolhardy to place undue reliance on the bilge pump. Instead, the ingress of water into the boat should be stopped, primarily by ensuring that the propeller and rudder shaft seals are not leaking. If seals cannot be made drip-free, there is a problem that needs attention (in the case of a propeller shaft seal, it may be an engine-alignment problem rather than a seal problem). All but cockpit-drain seacocks should be routinely closed. The bilges should be flushed, pumped dry, and cleaned of all debris. The bilge-pump wiring circuit needs a close inspection for any signs of corrosion or damage. The bilge-pump switch should be activated to ensure that it and the pump are still operational. There also must be some way of keeping the batteries charged, particularly wet-type batteries, which—in hot climates—discharge to the point of being useless in just a few months.

Finally, it is worth considering the addition of a high-level alarm circuit to the bilge-pump circuit. This can take the form of a separate level switch or sensor mounted above the regular level switch or sensor, or—with some of the electronic switches—a built-in timer that activates a secondary alarm circuit if the pump remains on for more than a set period (e.g., five minutes). Depending on the complexity of the system and the current-carrying capability of the alarm circuit, it may be possible to wire a secondary back-up pump into the circuit. If the boat is kept in a marina or another public place, it is advisable to also include an external alarm light or bell.

motor. The sensing unit and switch are built into the pump itself. There is either a timer that turns the pump on at preset intervals (every two and a half minutes in one popular unit) or an internal float switch. If there is water in the bilge, the pump has to work harder than if there is no water, in which case the motor's current draw will be higher than in the no-load situation. The sensing unit measures the current draw to determine whether to keep the pump running. Once it senses a no-load draw, it shuts down the pump.

These "automatic" bilge pumps have certain obvious advantages. Because the sensing unit and switch are built into the pump itself, there is no need for any external switching device. That makes installation simpler and immediately solves all problems with offset switches and fluctuating (i.e., surging) water levels. The principal disadvantage is that on the type with a timer, the pump is cycling on and off repeatedly whether or not there is a leak into the bilge (every two and a half minutes is 24 times an hour, 576 times a day, 4,032 times a week, 17,472 times a month, and 209,664 times a year). This is bound to accelerate pump and switch wear, and imposes an unnecessary drain on the batteries (albeit a small one: for a 12-volt, 1,100 gph pump, the manufacturer claims a 0.25 amp-hour drain per day). A less obvious problem—but perhaps more serious—with these "automatic" pumps is that if the pump impeller develops an increased resistance to movement (e.g., pet hair wrapped around the impeller or some other obstruction), the sensor will "interpret" it as water in the bilge and keep the pump running constantly. It won't take long to flatten a battery. On balance, I believe a good-quality float switch (e.g., Ultimate) is the best way to go.

Keeping Dry Below Decks

In terms of a bilge-pump installation, I recommend the following:

- Use the largest centrifugal pump that can be accommodated.
- Use an Ultimate or equivalent float switch.
- Position switches so that they work properly at all conceivable angles of heel.
- Make sure the pump discharge is siphon-proof.
- Keep all hoses as short and as straight as possible.
- Use the largest-diameter hose feasible on the discharge side.
- Size the wiring and switches for a 3 percent voltage drop at the maximum current rating of the pump.
- Make sure the switch is on the positive side of the circuit.
- Properly fuse the circuit.
- Keep all electrical connections above the highest water level.
- *Make sure the pump and switch are readily accessible for cleaning and mainte-*

nance (it is quite absurd to find them buried under cabinetry and other obstructions, as is so often the case).

At least one manual bilge pump should be operable from the helm station (U.S. Sailing recommends two on a cruising boat). Beyond this, it is important to understand the potential weaknesses of a given installation so you do not become overreliant on it. Fundamental aspects of housekeeping and seamanship must still be stressed. The bilge must be kept clean, objects properly stowed, and—above all—it should be part of the ship's routine to check the bilge on every watch. Even so, in the event of a serious flooding situation, the bilge pump cannot keep up. If the leak is not fixed, the boat is going down.

Regarding damage control during serious leaks, it is worth mentioning the Ericson Safety Pump, which is a centrifugal pump that mounts around the propeller shaft on a boat (it takes a lot of space). Even the smallest size has a phenomenal pumping capacity that will certainly keep up with the loss of a through-hull, and maybe even a larger hole in the hull.

THROUGH-HULLS, SEACOCKS, AND HOSES

The inability of even a large bilge pump to keep up with the inflow from even a relatively small below-the-waterline hole points up the need to ensure that all through-hull, seacock, and hose installations on a boat are first class. Unfortunately, many are not.

Fundamentally, any through-hull should be as dependable at keeping water out of the boat as the hull in which it is installed. Clearly, even the best hoses installed on a through-hull do not meet this criterion, which is why various standards-writing groups require the installation of a seacock on any through-hull below the waterline *at any angle of heel* (not just the *at-rest* waterline). This way, if the hose fails, the seacock can be closed to stop the influx of water. However, I don't think I have ever seen a boat that complies with this requirement (ours included—our exhaust through-hull has no seacock). Nevertheless, it is a good starting point when looking at any boat.

Another fine mess. An oversized hose clamped down with a rusting hose clamp. If the clamp fails, the boat is likely to go to the bottom.

Quality Through-Hulls and Seacocks

The quality (and suitability) of through-hulls and seacocks is all over the map. The following features are important:

- Gate and globe valves (the type that are operated by handwheels requiring multiple turns to open and close; they are commonly found on boats) *should not be used* because they are easily obstructed by marine growth, the valve stems are easily sheared, and it is not possible to tell if they are open or closed by simply looking at them.
- All valves should have a lever-type handle that operates through 90 degrees; this way, you can see immediately if the valve is opened or closed.
- Metal components must be cast from high-quality bronze (silicon bronze or Everdur, but not man-

Seacocks should turn through 90 degrees, as these do, so that it is always possible to tell at a glance whether they are open or closed.

ganese bronze because it has a high zinc content that is prone to galvanic corrosion). Because it is impossible for most of us to tell what alloy has been used, *it is important to buy only name-brand fittings from reputable chandlers* (not the local hardware store). In the past few years I have seen numerous nickel-plated brass seacocks on European boats—these are an invitation to galvanic corrosion (brass has a very high zinc content).

- Any fasteners used to retain a bronze seacock must be of the same or a better quality bronze. If they are not, galvanic corrosion is likely to eat up the fasteners.
- Plastic through-hulls and seacocks should be made from fiberglass-reinforced, UV-inhibited nylons, acetals, and polybutylene terephthalate (PBTs). The best known of these products are the Marelon fittings manufactured by Forespar.
- PVC, chlorinated polyvinyl chloride (CPVC), and acrylonitrile butadiene styrene (ABS), *which all may be found in through-hull fittings*, should not be used. Over time, they are likely to be weakened by UV degradation; embrittlement with age; the inability to withstand temperature extremes; and inadequate resistance to shock, fatigue, and abrasion. *It is important to buy only name-brand fittings from reputable chandlers* (not the local hardware store).
- The best guarantee of through-hull and seacock quality is a label that reads "*Marine* UL Listed," which means the fitting has passed rigorous tests and inspections. Personally, I would not have a non-UL-Listed below-the-waterline fitting on my boat. (Although UL is a U.S.-based testing agency, UL-Listed marine products are widely available in Europe.)

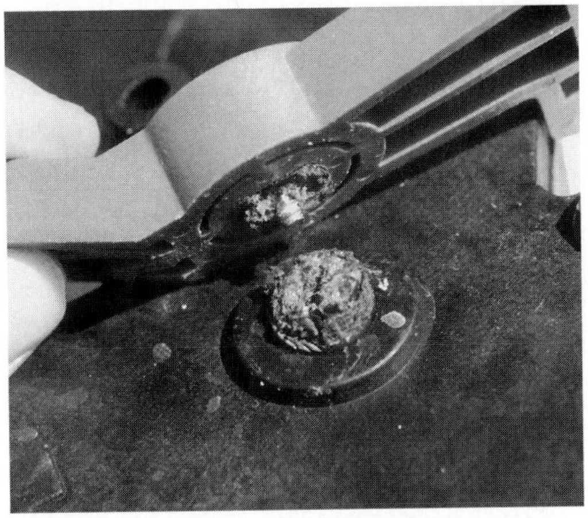

The single-most common failure point on plastic seacocks and valves is the handle breaking off, as on this (almost-new) toilet Y-valve.

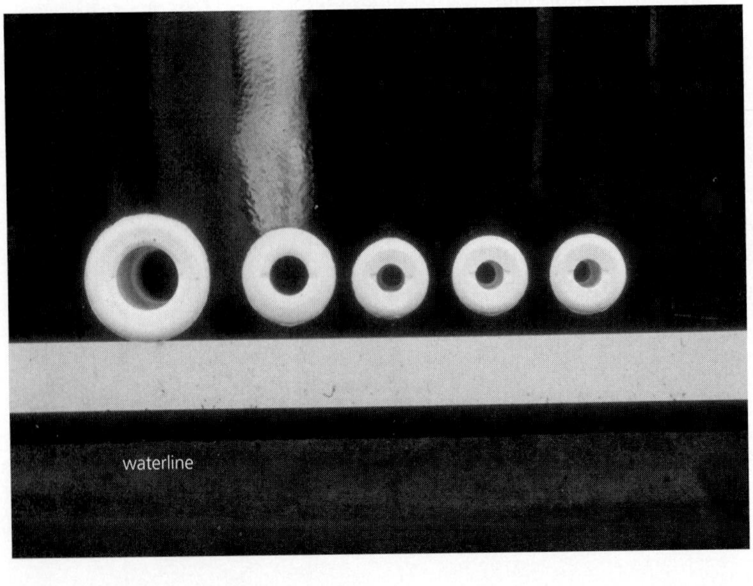

A not-uncommon sight: a line of non-UL-listed plastic through-hulls just above the waterline. A failure of just one will jeopardize the boat.

The corrosion problems associated with metal through-hulls and seacocks make plastic an attractive alternative. Plastic fittings are totally noncorrosive and require no corrosion-prevention strategies, in addition to which they are lighter, frequently easier (and, therefore, cheaper) to install, and mostly cheaper to buy in the first place. Of course, there are drawbacks—including reduced physical strength when compared to metal, less abrasion resistance, susceptibility to damage from UV degradation and chemicals, a limited ability to tolerate temperature extremes (especially fire), embrittlement with age, and—above all—a tendency for the handles to fail.

One manufacturer told me that handles only break when valves freeze up from a lack of lubrication and use (all seacocks—both metal and plastic—should be "exercised" at least once or twice a season). This is probably true. Given this lack of maintenance, the explanation continues, the handle—as the weak link—is protecting the valve from being overstressed. I personally find this ridiculous. If I have a failed hose with water flooding into my boat, it's going to be small consolation when the handle breaks off the seacock to know that the broken handle is protecting the valve from damage! It is significant that most manufacturers have enhanced their handles over the years; even so, I still get nervous around a tight plastic seacock (as opposed to the old tapered bronze ones that a good whack with a hammer loosened up).

Installation

Even if a product is UL-listed, it is not guaranteed to be installed correctly or safely. Key issues to consider are protecting the hull in way of the fitting, maintaining watertight integrity at all times, providing adequate fastening, making sure that the fitting can withstand the impact of stowed gear crashing into it, and ensuring that it is physically strong enough to be stood on.

Particularly in fiberglass hulls, through-hulls and seacocks need some kind of a backing block, faired to the shape of the hull, and providing a level surface on its inboard side on which to seat the retaining nut or seacock. This helps spread to a larger area of the hull the inevitable shocks, stresses, and vibrations experienced by the fitting. Clearly, the through-hull needs to be bedded or bonded in place in such a way that it will not develop leaks over time. This is most essential in cored hulls, where even a small leak can do extensive and expensive damage to the core (see chapter 1).

Plastic seacocks are invariably held in place by the through-hull fitting, with maybe some additional bonding inside the hull. With the integrity of the installation riding solely on the through-hull, it is essential to have a properly qualified through-hull (preferably UL-listed; fiber-reinforced at a minimum) that is not vulnerable to external damage (e.g., being broken off if the boat bangs against a dock or piling), and that is properly installed with the seacock or retaining nut bedded to a backing block.

The last installation requirement—which would be too obvious to state if it were not for the fact that it is routinely ignored— is to *make sure that all seacocks are readily accessible.* A seacock is nothing more than an insurance policy designed to protect against the failure of the hose attached to it. If the hose does fail, the seacock won't do any good—and might just as well not have been there in the first place—if the operator can't access it to close it! Accessibility is also necessary for maintenance and to drain the seacock when winterizing the boat (when installing a seacock, make sure the drain is on the lower side).

Seacocks need to be readily accessible, as is the case here with the raw-water inlet to our engine and refrigeration unit, and the raw-water filter for the refrigeration unit.

Installation of a transducer. Note the fairing blocks both inside and outside to create a level mounting surface and (if this were a through-hull or seacock) spread any accidental load (e.g., being hit by gear or trodden on). Note also the generous amounts of bedding compound.

Keeping Down the Numbers

At the end of the day, the fewer seacocks, the better I like it. Too many boatbuilders sprinkle them all over the hull: it is not uncommon to find a dozen below the waterline. This is simply not necessary; for example, with a little thought, it is often possible to use a single large through-hull and seacock feeding a manifold of some kind to supply all the saltwater needs on the boat: the engine raw-water circuit, galley sink, toilet(s), refrigeration condenser, saltwater washdown, maybe an air-conditioning condenser, perhaps a watermaker, and so on.

However, if a common raw-water inlet is used, instead of using a single large filter between the seacock and the manifold, it is important to independently filter the supply to the engine and—preferably—that to any centrifugal pumps (often used for refrigeration and air conditioning). If this is not done and two or more systems are fed from a common filter, a plugged filter may result in one system sucking back through the other, with a loss of flow and damage. The same can happen even with independent filters if the water inlet screen on the hull gets blocked; however, this is a risk that I find acceptable to reduce the number of holes in the hull. If this risk is considered unacceptable, centrifugal pumps must be given independent seacocks.

Everything but the engine raw-water supply should be independently valved at the raw-water manifold. This is so individual circuits can be shut down in the event of a hose failure or for maintenance without having to shut the main seacock, which necessitates the engine being shut down. If the engine raw-water supply needs to be shut down for any reason, the main seacock has to be closed, which shuts down everything else until the main seacock is reopened—this should be no big deal. In addition to the raw-water seacock, the toilet(s) needs a discharge, as does the galley sink and maybe the head compartment sink(s) (these can be plumbed into the toilet; see chapter 3). Showers are something of a problem: they can discharge above the waterline, but this leaves unsightly stains; they can be T'ed into the head discharge at the seacock, but if the valves in the shower discharge pump leak back, it lets odors and even effluent (although not likely) into the shower compartment. Depending on how determined you are to minimize through-hulls and seacocks, they may need their own.

Another approach worth considering is to plumb all the sinks and showers to a common gray-water tank (a dedicated holding tank) containing a float switch that operates a macerator pump discharging overboard. This results in a single through-hull for all gray-water systems, and builds in a level of environmental protection that may be required in some cruising grounds in the future. It also eliminates all problems with galley and head sinks back-flooding when the boat is well heeled. On the negative side, it introduces another level of complexity to the boat's systems. If the macerator pump or its float switch fails, it will be almost impossible to get the gray water out of the boat (for this reason, I recommend backing up the macerator pump with a manual diaphragm pump).

On our old boat, in addition to the cockpit drains, we had just three below-the-waterline seacocks: a common raw-water intake, the head discharge, and the galley-sink drain. The head-compartment sink drained into the toilet; the shower discharged through the toilet through-hull. All three seacocks were readily accessible—I thought nothing of closing them every time we left the boat for more than an hour or two. The new boat has cockpit drains plus nine seacocks, of which four could have been eliminated (I slipped up).

Hoses

Over the years, I have been amazed at how little attention sailors pay to the hoses in their boats—I have been as guilty of this as anybody. When Terrie and I built our old boat, I bought the various hoses for the boat—cockpit drains, engine raw-water circuit, toilet and bilge-pump hoses—primarily on the basis of price rather than quality, only to be brought up against reality with a shock soon after the boat was launched. I spilled some acetone in the cockpit and it ran down the cockpit drains. All of a sudden, water was flooding into the boat. The acetone had eaten straight through the cheap spiral-reinforced PVC "cockpit drain hose" that I

Two different hoses. Heavy-duty polyester-reinforced rubber on the left; heavy-duty vinyl on the right. I much prefer the former.

had installed. I was quite badly shaken. By nightfall, I had those drains plumbed with heavy-duty hoses, which—although not impervious to acetone—at least stood some chance of resisting a spill. I also took all of the acetone off the boat.

Then there was the time the raw-water screen for the engine cooling water got blocked. The raw-water pump put a vacuum on the raw-water suction hose, collapsing the hose and causing the engine to overheat. Out went the cheap heater hose that had come from the local automotive parts store and in went a quality, wire-reinforced (noncollapsing) hose. Some months later, I was standing in front of the engine when another hose on the raw-water circuit blew, giving me a hot saltwater bath—the *same* cheap hose. This time I replaced all of it.

And so on. One way or another, over the years I was forced to upgrade most of the hoses on the boat. It was a frustrating and expensive way to learn that hoses are a rather specialized field and that on a boat, where hoses are essential to keeping the boat functional and afloat, there is no substitute for a quality product specifically designed for a given purpose.

Basic Hose Requirements

Keep in mind the following requirements when considering hoses and hose applications on a cruising boat:

- Exhaust hose requires a heavy-duty, fabric-reinforced construction. Until recently, there were no standards governing these hoses, but quality hose was invariably labeled "Type Certified Marine Exhaust Hose" or something similar. In the United States, the Society of Automotive Engineers (SAE) now has a standard (SAE J2006) for marine exhaust hose. The standard requires that the hose be able to withstand a total loss of cooling water for two minutes with the engine running at full power, and still not suffer a loss of integrity—a very tough test. Any hose that meets the J2006 standard (it is written on the hose itself) can be counted on to give good service (J2006 hose is now sold worldwide).
- Exhaust hose comes with or without wire reinforcement. In the former case, it is known as *hardwall*; in the latter, *softwall*. Most manufacturers recommend that hose runs longer than four to six times the inside diameter of the hose (most exhaust hoses), or those with relatively tight curves, be wire-reinforced for added support. The objective is to prevent the hose kinking on bends, sagging on long horizontal runs, and panting (pulsing) from the constant pressure changes that occur in an exhaust. If a hose is adequately supported and if tight bends are avoided, the reinforcement can be avoided; however, the support is critical. The hose should never span open spaces or be hung from deck beams because the panting will cause chafe at the supports or hangers. If necessary, the hose should be given a bed to sit on.
- Below the waterline, including on engine raw-water circuits, I believe in using heavy-duty, fabric-reinforced hose (often made to comply with SAE J2006).

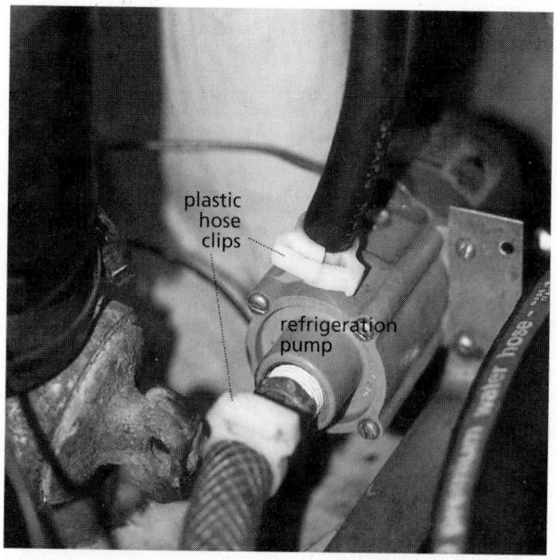

Another potential boat-sinker. This refrigeration pump is well below the waterline. The hoses are held on the pump with cheap plastic clips that will work-harden and crack with age.

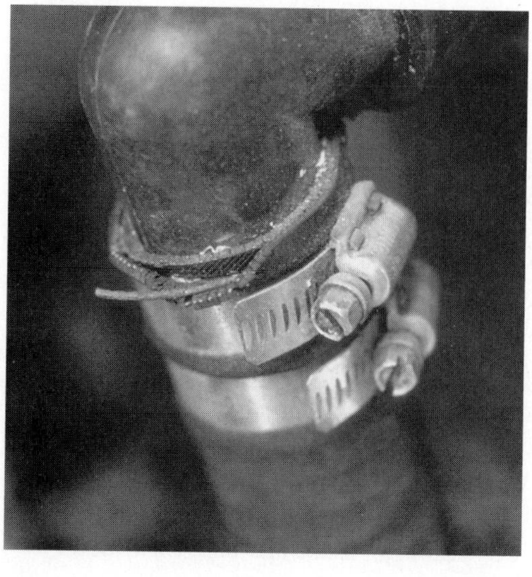

The biggest problem with hardwall hose is that the reinforcing wire spiral is almost always spring steel and, as such, rusts in the marine environment, encouraging delamination of the hose.

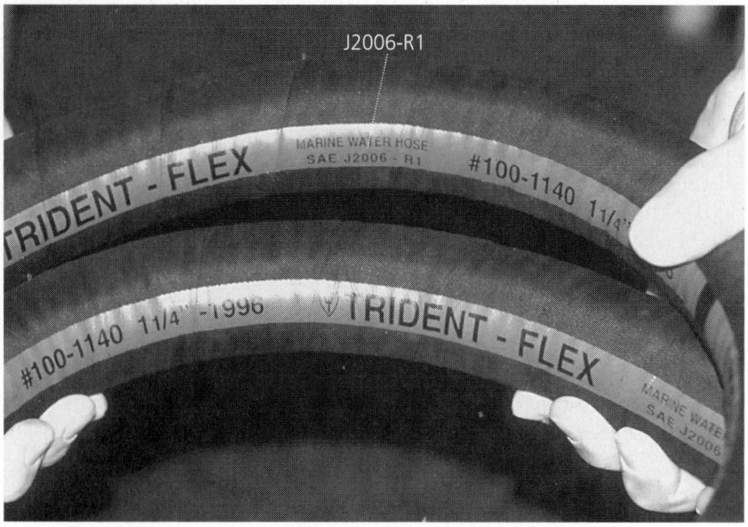

Good hose is always clearly labeled. In terms of exhaust hose, the label to look for is "SAE J2006—R1."

It should also be used for cockpit drains, sink drains, toilet suction lines, and associated applications. Instead, what is often found is some variant of a flexible, reinforced, thin-wall rubber or PVC hose, which even the manufacturer or wholesaler may label as "not recommended for below-the-waterline use." Remember that anything attached to a through-hull is an extension of the hull; its integrity should be as close as possible to that of the hull.

- Toilet discharge hoses require special attention. Even some heavy-duty hoses are minutely porous and, in time, will emit foul odors (to test, rub a clean rag up and down the hose jacket and then sniff the rag). Special impermeable hoses are required (usually labeled "Sanitation Hose"), and only the best (and most expensive!) should be used.
- When installing sanitation hoses, low spots that retain effluent should be avoided. If they are unavoidable, the toilet should be flushed sufficiently after each use to clear all the effluent out of the line (however, this may fill the holding tank too fast . . .).
- Whatever hose is used for sanitation purposes, it should have a smooth wall on the inside, which minimizes the chance of clogging. Even so, over time, the inside of the hose will slowly plug up with calcium deposits. As noted in chapter 3, at some point it will be necessary to either remove the hose and beat it on the dock to break the calcium loose or replace the hose. In my opinion, if a hose is not built rugged enough to take a beating, it is not suitable for the job!
- Fuel hoses, particularly on gasoline engines, are the only hoses on a boat for which the construction must, *by law*—both in the United States and Europe—comply with certain standards. These are based on the fire resistance of a hose and its permeability. In the United States, fire resistance is determined by something known as the *2-½-minute burn test* (similar tests apply in Europe). Hoses that pass the most stringent test are classified as Type A; hoses with slightly less fire resistance are classified as Type B. As for permeability, hoses that pass the most stringent test are classified as Class 1; those with somewhat higher permeation are classified as Class 2. We end up with four classes of hose referenced in the USCG regulations: USCG Type A1, USCG Type A2, USCG Type B1, and USCG Type B2.
- The regulations state that for inboard gasoline engines and inboard/outboards, any hose used for a fuel line must be classified as Type A1. Vent or fill lines have to be Type A1 or A2. Similar standards are in place for diesel fuel lines, except that the fill and vent lines can be Type B1 or B2.

Safety First

The manufacturing of hoses is a worldwide cottage industry, with factories scattered all the way from the Asian Pacific to Turkey, Italy, and the United States. Almost none of the handful of wholesalers or retailers of marine hoses in Europe or the United States actually make their own hoses. Some really awful hose occasionally makes its way into the marketplace. What this means is that the boatowner is very dependent

More good hose, beautifully installed to eliminate any possibility of chafe. The fuel-tank vent hose (left) complies with USCG Type A1; the other hose complies with J2006.

on the wholesaler or retailer when buying hose. To ensure that only quality hose is bought, it is best to buy from a recognized dealer and to ensure that the hose is manufactured to recognized standards (the UL, SAE, USCG, or ISO standard is printed on the hose jacket).

No matter how carefully hoses are selected and installed, there is always the unforeseeable failure. For example, friends of ours got a rat aboard. The first they knew of it was when one night it chewed through the flexible connection to their propane galley stove. Fortunately, being safety-conscious cruisers, they always close the tank valve after using the stove; otherwise, the rat might have killed them. Once they had come face to face with the beast and realized what was going on, they had the foresight to close their seacocks, which was just as well because before they finally cornered it and bludgeoned it to death, it took a bite out of half the hoses on the boat!

Our friends were able to close their seacocks because they had been regularly maintained. This is in contrast to so many boatowners who leave crucial seacocks open from one season to another, and who never inspect their hoses and hose clamps. After a year or two, the valves become frozen in place and the hose clamps are covered in rust. The boat is an accident waiting to happen—any kind of a below-the-waterline hose failure, for any reason whatsoever, has the potential to sink the boat. These days, even with all high-quality hoses and hose clamps on our boat, they still get at least an annual checkup. In addition, we never leave the boat for long without closing the seacocks. We've had enough scares in the past to never ever again take these things for granted.

PROPANE INSTALLATIONS

Propane (liquefied petroleum gas, or LPG) is the fuel of choice for cooking on most cruising boats, and with good reason: it is clean, easy to use, easy to obtain worldwide (although sometimes butane is substituted), and cheap. It is also potentially explosive. In the past, there have been enough instances of boats being blown up to cause substantial concern, but nowadays—with a proper installation—this is rare. However, just recently I heard of two explosions (one of which caused fatalities); both occurred as a result of improper installations. Therefore, it behooves the cruising sailor to make sure that any installation is "up to code," paying particular attention to the following:

- *Compartment requirements.* Gas bottles, both in use and in storage, must be kept well secured in compartments that are sealed from all machinery and living spaces, and vented overboard. LPG compartments need to be vented from the base, with a minimum ½-inch (13 mm) inside-diameter (ID) vent (preferably 1 in./25 mm), which slopes continuously downward so that no water can form a U-trap, and which exits the hull above the waterline at all angles of heel. All gas vents must exit well clear of engine exhausts, ventilators, and air intakes. Gas cylinders must be secured in an upright position (unless specifically designed to be stored horizontally)—if LPG bottles tip over, liquid rather than gas comes out, with potentially dangerous results.

Details of a "proper" propane installation.

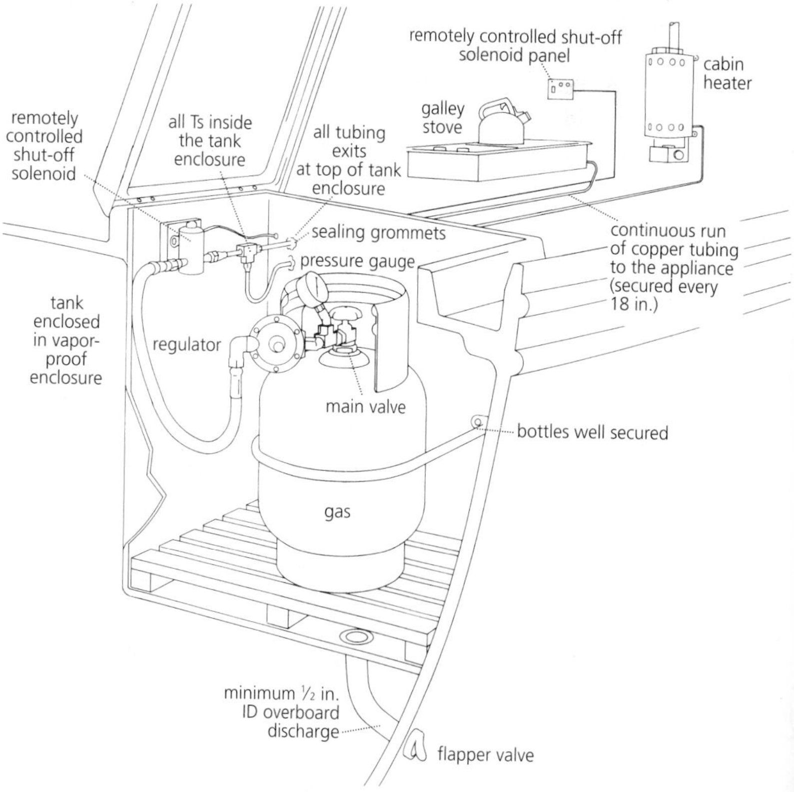

Below: *Neat propane installation in a side deck locker. However, water sluicing down the side deck pours into the locker and out of its drain—in time, the salt will corrode the regulator and other fittings.* Bottom: *Detail of the previous installation. It's a bit of a tight fit, with potential chafe points on the gas hose that have been protected with duct tape. The remotely controlled shut-down solenoid is on the low-pressure side of the regulator. These are old-style U.S. gas bottles.*

- *The pressure gauge.* A pressure gauge is required immediately downstream of the main cylinder valve and before the *gas regulator* (the valve that reduces cylinder pressure to operating pressure). The gauge then will be measuring cylinder pressure—a 300 psi (20 bar) gauge is needed on LPG installations (3,000 psi with compressed natural gas [CNG]). The gauge is an essential leak-testing tool (see Periodic Testing later in this section).
- *The step-down regulator.* Regulators should be installed with the vent port facing down so that water cannot collect in the vent and enter the system. Different gases (propane, butane, and CNG) are regulated to different pressures. Some regulators corrode quite rapidly in a marine environment. When buying a regulator, make sure it comes from a supplier used to dealing with boats.
- *The master shut-off valve.* Somewhere there should be a normally closed, solenoid-operated, master shut-off valve wired to a remote switch close to the galley stove. The remote switch makes it possible to close off the cylinder without having to get at it anytime the appliance is not in use. This switch should have a light to indicate when the solenoid is open. The cylinder valve should still be closed manually when leaving the boat. However, tripping the battery-isolation switch closes the master shut-off valve and provides a fair measure of safety for those who forget to close the cylinder valve manually.
- *T fittings.* If more than one appliance is to be run from one gas cylinder, the necessary Ts should be fitted after the solenoid but still inside the gas-bottle compartment. For LPG systems, unbroken (i.e., without fittings) soft copper tubing (type K or L) or LPG hose is run to each appliance (hose must be *specifically approved* for this purpose). The only connections in the system outside the gas-bottle compartment are those at either end of the flexible hose that leads to a gimbaled stove. Copper tubing is not acceptable with CNG unless it is tinned on the inside. Special hose is generally used, with permanently attached end fittings (i.e., no flares).
- *Securing tubing runs.* Any tubing run must be securely fastened at least every 18 inches (460 mm). Tubing needs to be protected from abrasion, flexing, pinching, and knocks where equipment may bounce around in lockers. Where tubing passes through bulkheads or decks, the holes should be sealed.
- *Periodic testing.* The system should be tested at least every two weeks, as follows:

  1. Close all appliance valves.
  2. Open the cylinder valve and master solenoid valve.
  3. Observe the pressure on the cylinder gauge and let it stabilize. Make a note of the pressure.
  4. Close the cylinder valve, but not the solenoid valve, and wait fifteen minutes.
  5. Check the cylinder gauge. If the pressure has fallen at all, there is a leak somewhere.

Never use a flame for leak testing! Mix a 50–50 solution of dishwashing liquid and water; brush it liberally onto all connections between the cylinder valve and the appliance. Any leak

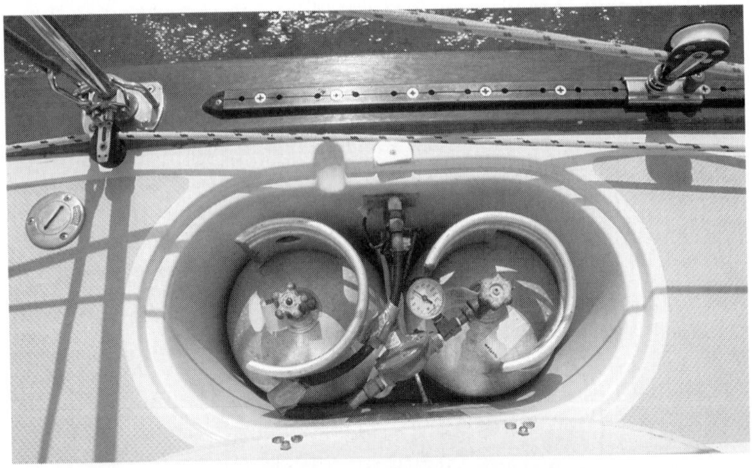

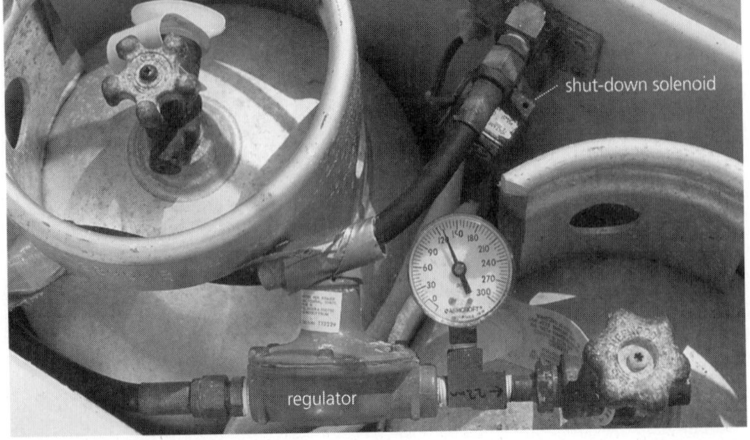

will cause the solution to form a mass of tiny bubbles. However, never use detergents that contain ammonia for leak testing (check the detergent label); in a matter of months, ammonia can cause brass fittings to develop cracks and leaks.

Solenoid Valves and Tubing Sizes

For years, the most popular remotely controlled solenoid valve in the United States was one sold by Marinetics. It installs on the downstream (low-pressure) side of the regulator. It has ¼-inch (6 mm) ports for plumbing in tubing. Unfortunately, once galley stoves get up to a size where they have two or three burners plus an oven and maybe a grill, this port size is too restrictive to allow all the burners to be used at once. I have come across a number of cruisers who think they have a stove problem, whereas all they have is an undersized valve.

There are other ¼-inch (6 mm) solenoid valves (e.g., supplied by Trident) that can be installed on the upstream (high-pressure) side of the regulator where they will not cause a problem. On most modern boats, this is the way to go. If a downstream solenoid is used, it is best to use one with ⅜-inch (10 mm) ports. Either way, solenoids have a relatively high failure rate, putting the LPG system out of commission. For this reason, it is desirable to have a manual override built into the solenoid (Fueltrol makes such a solenoid).

Even if the solenoid is properly sized, a restrictive tubing or hose run can still choke down the supply to a stove or heater. As a rule of thumb, if the tubing run is shorter than 20 feet, ¼-inch (6 mm) tubing is generally adequate; however, longer than 20 feet, ⅜-inch (10 mm) tubing should be used on a stove with more than two burners plus an oven. If in doubt, use ⅜-inch tubing. Connections at the regulator end and the appliance should be made with flare fittings (compression fittings are not acceptable).

The Problem of Refills When Cruising

CNG is virtually unobtainable outside the United States and is not always easy to find there. If for no other reason than this, it is not suitable as a fuel on a cruising boat (also, it is considerably more expensive per British thermal unit [Btu] of output than LPG).

As for LPG, there is no worldwide standardization of gas usage, gas cylinders, or gas valves and fittings, which causes problems for cruising sailors, but they are not insurmountable. Propane is the predominant LPG in the United States, the Caribbean Islands, Australia, New Zealand, and Scandinavia; butane in the United Kingdom, the Mediterranean, and many tropical countries (including Brazil, Venezuela, and many South Pacific islands).

Although LPG devices work on both propane and butane, propane cannot be stored in a butane cylinder—propane has much higher cylinder pressures that will blow the safety valve on a butane cylinder. Butane, however, can be stored in a propane cylinder; therefore, for worldwide cruising, start out with propane cylinders (all U.S. cylinders are propane cylinders).

There are numerous different threads and fittings (both male and female) on LPG cylinders and two ways to deal with them when overseas (a cautious sailor would follow both approaches):

- Connect the boat's gas regulator to its gas cylinder using fittings that will take LPG-approved high-pressure hose (ordinary hose will *not* do because LPG attacks rubber and similar materials). Then, if the gas cylinder cannot be refilled, an appropriate cylinder can be bought with a discharge fitting that accepts a hose, and the hose simply can be connected to this fitting.
- Obtain an adapter that enables the onboard cylinder to be hooked to a length of LPG-approved high-pressure hose; when in a foreign country, find a suitable adapter that can be fitted to the other end of this hose to allow the cylinder to be refilled.

In some countries (particularly Europe), it is not possible to get anything other than locally approved cylinders refilled, in which case new cylinders must be bought or rented. A U.S. propane fitting will fit a U.K. propane cylinder, although in reality, the threads are marginally smaller so this is not recommended; a U.K. propane fitting will not fit a U.S. cylinder.

When refilling cylinders, it is essential that they are not refilled beyond 80 percent of their capacity (70 percent in hot climates). The reason for this is that if a cylinder is completely filled with liquid and the ambient temperature rises, the expanding liquid can generate enough pressure to rupture the cylinder. Another problem with overfilled cylinders is that they increase the possibility of liquid carryover into

New-style U.S. gas-bottle fittings—recommended for all new construction and retrofits.

the regulator and the low-pressure lines to the appliances, which can result in a dangerous seventy-fold increase in pressure on this side of the system (even if it does no other damage, it can destroy the thermostat on a thermostatically controlled oven).

Many cylinders (in the United States and Europe) are so designed that once they are 80 percent full, they begin to vent; however, others do not have this important safety device. Every cylinder should be stamped with both its *tare weight* (empty weight) and *net fill weight* (the weight of gas it is designed to hold). A full cylinder can be weighed; if its weight exceeds the tare weight plus the net fill weight, it is overcharged—some of the contents should be carefully vented.

In the United States, a new-style cylinder was introduced in the late 1990s that cannot be overfilled. It also accepts a new-style, hand-tightened connector that makes changing cylinders much easier than in the past. In addition to the fact that these cylinders are more convenient to use than the old-style ones, in a few years it will not be possible to get the old ones refilled, so cruisers should make sure they have the new ones.

A final note: U.S. LPG cylinders are typically painted white or are bare aluminum. No cylinder should ever be painted a dark color: in direct sunlight, a cylinder could absorb enough heat to burst. In some states, it is illegal to paint a cylinder anything other than its original color.

MAKING EQUIPMENT CHOICES

I want to finish this chapter with some thoughts on equipment purchases. The range of choices facing boatowners today can be quite bewildering. To narrow the range, I commonly apply certain "benchmarks" to weed out inappropriate gear (for cruising), as follows:

- Has the equipment been well tested? In the course of my work, I see a lot of neat new equipment. Invariably, the manufacturer claims that it has been bench-tested to a trillion cycles and the average time before failure is at least a billion years. Soon after being put into service, the first failures start to appear, leading to product modifications and improvements. This happens because the marine environment is incredibly harsh and complex, and simply can't be adequately simulated. The only basis for asserting that a product will truly hold up is prolonged real-life testing. I don't want to be the guinea pig. As a rule of thumb, for offshore work, I don't buy equipment until it has been proven for at least five years. This puts me somewhat behind the technological curve, but we have reliable systems. If there are two similar products from different companies, one of which has been proven and one not, I go for the one that I know works in practice; for example, Whitlock and Edson rack-and-pinion pedestal steering. At the time we bought our boat, Whitlock's system had been proven over twenty-five years, whereas Edson's was relatively new. There was no question as to which I wanted.
- Will the company be around when you need it? The marine market is a tough one, with relatively low-volume sales and high marketing overheads. A lot of people and companies come up with a bright idea and think they will make a killing. Regardless of how good the product is, they find it takes a lot of money and effort to create a market. Many companies fail before they get there, in which case there is no continuing product support. In general, I apply the five-year rule. For example, when Glacier Bay hit the refrigeration scene, I immediately recognized that this was an excellent product, but had my doubts about whether the company had the capitalization and staying power to tough it out in this competitive market. I personally would not have used its products at that stage of development. Today, I do not hesitate to recommend Glacier Bay.

- What is the manufacturer's or supplier's reputation with respect to backup and return policies? Some people ship out replacement parts Federal Express with no questions asked; for others, the customer is almost always wrong. I know who is going to get my business!
- How international is the company or the equipment? This is of particular concern to people buying boats that have been built overseas or who are planning on doing long-distance cruising. If I am buying a French-built boat for use in the United States, I want to know that all the equipment installed in that boat is readily repairable or replaceable in the United States—or even works in the United States (a 220-volt European AC generator will not be much use to me; also, many European boats use circuit breakers and other electrical components that are not easy to find outside Europe). If something fails out in the boonies, I want to know that I can either get it fixed locally or get what I need to fix it.
- How much maintenance does the equipment require, how easy is this to do, and what does the maintenance cost? Looking at wheel-steering systems again, when building a new wheel-steered boat, boatowners have a choice between some type of cable-operated system or rack-and-pinion pedestal steering. The latter is a little more expensive up front, but is just about bulletproof, is virtually maintenance-free, and has almost no associated operating cost. This is why we have rack and pinion on our new boat (Whitlock's Cobra system).
- How easy will the equipment be to replace if and when it fails? A good example of this is a metal fuel tank more or less built into a boat. If the tank cannot be made accessible, it is worth going to considerable trouble to use polyethylene or fiberglass in its place.
- What is the lifetime cost versus the benefit of the equipment? Some equipment (e.g., a DC to AC inverter) is not unduly expensive up front, once bought has no further associated cost, and provides a substantial return in terms of creature comforts or other benefits. Other equipment (e.g., a watermaker) is relatively expensive up front and has a significant ownership cost (filters, pickling agents, replacement membranes, and pump parts); as a result, it has a substantial lifetime cost (most people would be horrified if they knew how much they actually paid per gallon of output from a watermaker). This is why we still don't have a watermaker, despite the fact that we would love to have the water.
- How much studying is required before using the equipment? It seems that to operate most modern boats, you've got to spend a couple of days reading various manuals. I hate this—I like to get on a boat and go. So I have a natural dislike of any equipment that cannot be operated intuitively. I will choose a piece of equipment that is simple to use over another that may be technically a little better but is more complex. For example, the Link 2000 from Heart Interface may not be the best systems monitor on the market (I suspect that the Ample Technologies products are technologically superior), but it is simplicity itself to use: if I want to read the house battery bank voltage, I press "Battery 1" and "Volts"; if I want amperage, I press "Amps." This is the kind of stuff my manuals-challenged mind can handle and this is why we have a Link 2000 on our boat.
- Regarding electronics, the extent to which the equipment can be integrated with existing equipment is often important. There also may be significant installation issues. For example, SSB needs an excellent ground for effective transmission and radar can be quite complex to install (numerous cables to be hooked up). It may prove worthwhile to buy some equipment from a local dealer who can supply technical backup rather than from a discount catalog that advertises a lower price.

What Spares to Carry?

What spares should be carried for this equipment? Of course, this depends on how far offshore it is intended to sail, how self-sufficient the boat needs to be, and your personal level of paranoia. Over the past couple of decades, as more of our western Caribbean cruising grounds have come within the range of Federal Express and other hotshot delivery services, I have steadily lightened up on the spares I carry.

When deciding what to carry, it helps to remember the following criteria:

- essential versus nonessential (i.e., spares that are necessary to keep the boat sailing rather than to maintain luxury systems)
- likely to fail or be needed versus not likely to fail or be needed
- difficult to get versus easy to get
- light, small, and cheap versus heavy, large, and expensive

Something that scores 4 out of 4 or 3 out of 4 should probably be onboard—but 2 out of 4 or less, forget it! Parts that hit 3 or 4 out of 4 include the following:

- all engine and alternator belts
- raw-water pump impeller
- zinc pencil anodes
- fuel and oil filters (with the wrenches necessary to get them on and off) and engine and transmission oil
- pressure switch for the freshwater pump
- spare winch handle or two
- springs and pawls for the winches
- electrical cables, terminals, heat shrink, and tools
- good-quality digital multimeter with a clamp-on DC ammeter
- light bulbs and fuses
- basic mechanic's toolkit
- collection of stainless steel fasteners
- collection of hose clamps
- collection of shackles, snap shackles, and snatch blocks
- various lubricants and corrosion inhibitors (e.g., Vaseline, Tef-Gel, Boeshield, and Teflon-based grease)
- tube (or more) of bedding compound (3M's 5200, polysulfide, or silicon)
- some odds and ends of plywood and fiberglass cloth, with two-part epoxy glue
- basic sail-repair kit (see chapter 10)
- a bosun's chair
- duct tape, plastic electrical tape, and Teflon tape
- repair kit for an inflatable dinghy
- watermaker biocide if a watermaker is onboard
- a spare halyard and sheet, long enough to replace the longest halyard and sheet onboard

For offshore work, I would personally add to this list at least the following:

- spare alternator and voltage regulator (essential and hard to get, but not likely to fail and not particularly cheap; nevertheless, so vital to the functioning of a modern boat that spares should always be carried)
- toilet-rebuild kit
- length of wire rope together with fittings (Norseman or Sta-Lok) that enable the longest stay or shroud on the boat to be replaced
- cable cutters robust enough to enable the rig to be cut away in a hurry if necessary (there are some very nice, compact, hydraulic cable cutters on the market)
- spare steering cable on a boat with cable steering
- spare membrane for any watermaker

As for tools (in addition to the obvious wrenches, sockets, screwdrivers, and pliers), a set of Allen wrenches, adjustable pliers for breaking loose hoses from hose barbs, two pairs of Vise-Grips, a good-size ball-peen hammer with a set of punches, a couple of metal files, a hacksaw, and an electric drill with a set of drill bits should always be onboard. WD-40 or some other penetrating oil is essential.

This is not a particularly long list, nor one that is terribly expensive, bulky to stow, or heavy. Other than these items, I believe it depends on your personal level of paranoia. If you think, for example, that you can't live without the refrigerator, you may need to carry a spare condenser water pump, a gauge set, refrigerant, and a vacuum pump. I decided I'd rather take my chances—fix it when I get home if necessary—and keep that locker clear for something else—most likely, the family will fill it with flotsam, jetsam, and shells!

Finally, if a boat is an older one with well-used equipment—particularly the engine—it may be necessary to considerably increase the spare-parts inventory to include injectors, gasket sets, injector pipes, a lift pump, and so on, but this can only be determined in light of a specific boat and specific cruising plans.

Regardless of what spares are carried, it is important to put together a manual for the boat that lists all the equipment onboard with model and serial numbers, the manufacturer, and contact information (address, telephone and fax numbers, e-mail, and Web site). This greatly expedites the supply process if parts are needed.

CHAPTER SIX

ACQUISITION STRATEGIES

However clichéd this image may be, this is ultimately what it is all about!

"Some modern ocean racers, and the cruising boats derived from them, are dangerous to their crews."

OLIN STEPHENS IN *Desirable and Undesirable Characteristics of Offshore Yachts*

"Every boatowner needs a reasonable understanding of his or her own requirements, a deep concern about safety, and a willingness to buck trends to find the boat that meets these requirements and provides safety for the inevitable difficult and testing situation."

OLIN STEPHENS IN *Desirable and Undesirable Characteristics of Offshore Yachts*

"Never rely on a yacht built to a Rating Rule as a guarantee for seaworthiness. For when speed is the main criteria, seaworthiness passes largely into the hands of the crew. Seaworthiness in cruising terms must be firmly in the design and construction of the yacht."

DAVID THOMAS IN *The Complete Offshore Yacht*

"Life goes by fast, and you only get one shot at it. It makes sense to make your dreams happen sooner, rather than later."

JOHN NEAL, NOTABLE SAILOR AND EDUCATOR

In the previous chapters, I tried to provide enough information for you to be able to define the key features of a boat that will fit your intended cruising style, and to understand many of the crucial systems issues that underlie a safe and functional contemporary cruising boat. Now let's assume you are in the market for this boat. In this chapter, we look at some of the issues that need to be considered to find the boat of your dreams at an affordable price.

DEFINING PRIORITIES

When looking for a boat, it is important to not unduly limit your choices up front. Unless your heart is set on a particular boat and nothing else will do, it is a mistake to focus on a narrow range of boats: it unnecessarily circumscribes your options and maybe cuts you off from an incredible deal.

In 2000, *Yachting Monthly* took three "old gaffers" (hundred-year-old boats) and three modern fiberglass boats of a similar length, and test-sailed them against one another. They were surprised by the results. The modern boats outperformed the gaffers to windward, sailing closer to the wind and faster, but on other points of sail the gaffers kept up and sometimes did better. In heavier conditions, the gaffers were far more comfortable and "reassuring to sail," and outsailed the modern boats. Where they lost out was in terms of maneuverability and the accommodations. The editors concluded: "A century of cruising yacht evolution has not improved the breed to the extent we had thought. What we have gained in some areas, we have lost in others." (Aug. 2000) The moral of this story is to be open-minded when looking for a boat.

Perhaps the best approach is to make a list of characteristics you would like to see in your boat, subdivide them into essential and desirable characteristics, and then maybe subdivide the essential characteristics into those that are inherent in the boat itself (e.g., the keel configuration) and those that can be added following the purchase (e.g., certain systems). Now you can start looking at boats that fit these criteria. Using this approach, you are likely to find some boats that you would otherwise have overlooked. For example, my list of essential characteristics (in no particular order) that are inherent in the boat itself includes the following:

- proven blue-water construction
- the ability to take a severe grounding with nothing more than cosmetic damage

Our old boat up on an uncharted coral head. A nasty shock at the time, but no damage was done to the boat.

Note the functional navigation station and galley by the companionway, excellent sea berths in the saloon parallel to the centerline, good handholds, and so on. (Courtesy Hallberg Rassy)

- reasonable upwind performance
- a reasonably balanced helm
- seakindly motion
- directional stability
- a design that can be single-handed
- a safe and comfortable cockpit
- an interior that is functional at sea and comfortable on the hook
- adequate load-carrying capability for long-distance cruising
- accessibility and serviceability for the boat's systems
- compliance, or near compliance, with the numbers outlined in chapter 1

I simply am not going to consider boats that do not meet these criteria; even so, this gives me a broad framework with which to start my search. I also have a budget, which rules out many otherwise highly desirable boats. This budget is a total project budget so, when looking at any potential boat, I always have to add to the purchase cost whatever is necessary to get the boat up to my personal cruising standards (more about this later). These standards include certain essential requirements that are not inherent in the boat itself, such as the following:

- a decent set of sails
- deck gear (e.g., winches) that will make it easy for one person to handle the sails
- adequate, easily handled ground tackle
- an engine in good running condition
- adequate fuel and water tankage in tanks that are in good condition
- a decent-size chart table

- a family-size galley with hot and cold water and effective refrigeration
- a family-size head compartment
- comfortable sea berths
- etc., etc.

Depending on the initial price paid for a boat, all of these can be added following purchase. In extreme cases, if the purchase price is low enough, bulkheads can be ripped out, the interior completely reworked, a new engine and all new systems installed, and so on.

What Size Boat?

Early in the decision-making process, a boat buyer has to roughly determine how big a boat is needed to fulfill his or her cruising dreams. The two extreme opinions frequently expressed on this subject are "the smallest that will enable me to do what I want to do" and "the largest that can be afforded." In practice, it is often found that the largest that can be afforded is not quite big enough to do what is wanted; therefore, expectations have to be scaled back a little! Let's look at this in more detail.

A small boat generally costs less to buy. It will most likely be lighter than a larger boat and, therefore, require a smaller sail plan and lighter equipment (e.g., winches and ground tackle). The boat will probably be significantly less complex than a larger boat; it will be easy to sail short-handed. Because of its simplicity and the little time it takes to get underway, it may see more use than a larger boat. The boat will probably have a relatively shoal draft that opens up all kinds of cruising grounds closed to larger boats. Not only will it and its gear be easier to handle, it will also be cheaper to maintain and repair. Mooring, docking, haul-out, and bottom-job expenses will be considerably less (all of these costs are based strictly on length). In summary, a small, well-found boat can make an excellent cruising boat, especially for coastal cruises of a week or two when a few sacrifices of creature comforts are easily taken in stride. The overall cost of ownership will be relatively low considering the pleasure derived.

As the cruising range and the time spent onboard increases, the added comforts of a larger, more complex boat are greatly appreciated. There are other significant benefits: all else being equal, a larger boat is stiffer and has a more comfortable motion; with its longer waterline, it will be faster. That added speed provides an opportunity to outrun foul weather. If foul weather is encountered, a larger boat is inherently safer. However, it will be disproportionately more costly to buy and own (cost seems to increase exponentially with length) and it will require significantly more maintenance. Taken to extremes, cruisers can become slaves to their boats and systems, at which point the reason for cruising in the first place seems to be called into question.

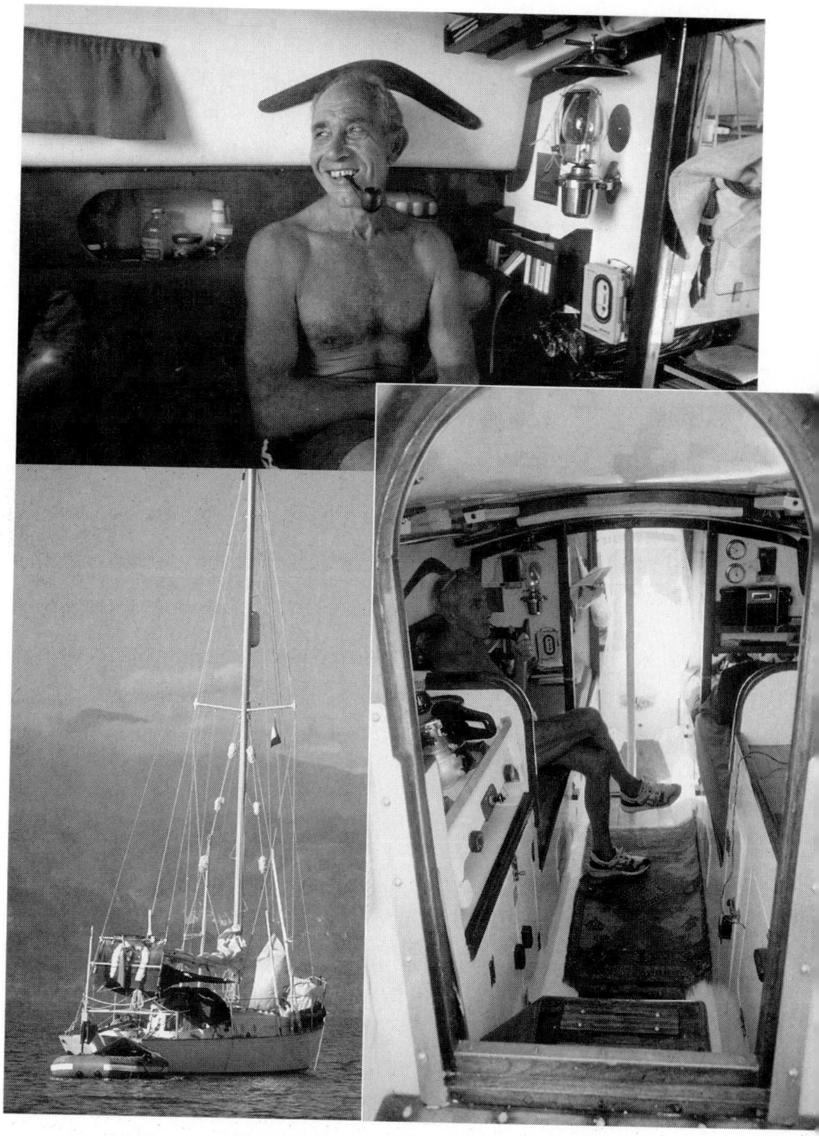

Our old friend Peter Hancock cruised very happily for years in his Contessa 26 Kylie, *which he progressively simplified until he was without an engine and had a bucket for a toilet.*

In contrast, our Nada *has an excellent diesel engine and most of the comforts of home.*

Steve and Linda Dashew have an interesting perspective on the big-boat approach that runs counter to some of what I have just written. Their concept is that if you take the cruising systems associated with a couple who wish to cruise in comfort—the freshwater systems, refrigeration, galley stove, head—and put these in a 60-, 70-, or even 80-foot boat (18, 21, 24 m) instead of, say, a 40-foot boat (12 m), there need be no increase in complexity. In fact, the space that can be devoted to the systems side of the boat will render the equipment easier to install (lowering construction costs) and easier to maintain (likely decreasing maintenance costs).

Given the length of the boat, it is now possible to design spectacular accommodations for a couple but in a boat that is quite narrow. If the construction weight is kept down, the total boat weight need not be much heavier than a much smaller boat, in which case the rig, rig-handling gear, ground tackle, and so on need not be that much heavier. Overall cost need not be that much higher. The boat itself will then be no more difficult to handle, but will end up with a spectacular length–beam ratio, a very low displacement–length ratio, a high speed–length ratio, and so on, resulting in a greatly enhanced performance.

Chuck Paine has taken the same concept in a rather more mainstream form and applied it to his Bermuda Series boats. It is an alluring concept, but the bottom line is that both the Dashews' and Paine's boats are still out of reach price-wise for the majority of cruising sailors. When you get to the size of boat typically developed by the Dashews, the cost of ownership will be relatively high just because so many features (e.g., bottom jobs and dockage fees) are based on length. In addition, I have some concerns about my ability to handle a boat of that size shorthanded in adverse conditions. For example, the primary anchor will weigh up to 100 pounds (45 kg). Let's say we have it out with 100 feet of chain. If the windlass fails, I am not physically capable of hauling in the anchor by hand—the envelope is being pushed just a little too far.

Perhaps the best size formula is to go for the largest boat that can be comfortably handled by the regular crew—and single-handed when necessary—in the worst conditions likely to be encountered. The single-handed part is important—there may come a day when your partner is out of action and you have to go it alone. When following this approach, the farther offshore it is intended to sail, the more important it is to base the assessment on the assumption that at some point the boat will have to be handled without the benefit of powered-sail reefing and anchoring devices.

It is for a mix of reasons such as these that most cruising couples have settled on an "ideal" boat length from 35 to 45 feet (10.6–13.7 m). Our 40-foot (12 m) Pacific Seacraft falls right in the middle of this range. It gives us quite spacious accommodations for two people, with more locker and storage space than we need,

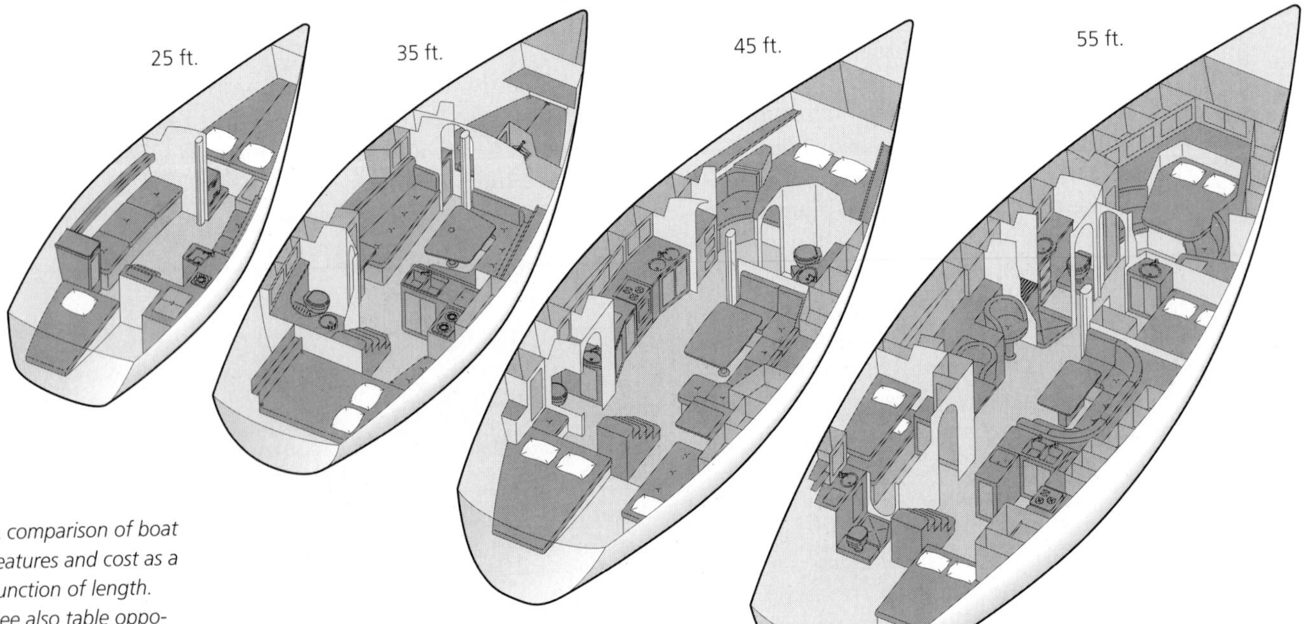

A comparison of boat features and cost as a function of length. See also table opposite. (Illustration courtesy Sail *magazine and Kim Dowling)*

Boat Size and Cost Comparisons

Boat length	25.0 ft.	35.0 ft.	45.0 ft.	55.0 ft.
LWL at 0.8 LOA	20.0 ft.	28.0 ft.	36.0 ft.	44.0 ft.
Beam	8.5 ft.	11.5 ft.	14.0 ft.	15.5 ft.
Length–beam ratio	2.94	3.04	3.21	3.55
Displacement–length ratio	301	244	230	220
Displacement[1]	5,400 lb.	12,000 lb.	24,000 lb.	42,000 lb.
Cabin area[2]	120 sq. ft.	240 sq. ft.	360 sq. ft.	480 sq. ft.
Stowage volume[3]	120 cu. ft.	360 cu. ft.	720 cu. ft.	1,200 cu. ft.
Berths (singles, doubles)	3, 1	2, 2	2, 2	2, 3
Heads, separate shower	1, 0	1, 0	2, 0	2, 1
Tankage[4] (fuel, water)	18, 36 gal.	40, 80 gal.	80, 160 gal.	140, 280 gal.
Engine size[5]	14 hp	30 hp	60 hp	105 hp
Battery bank(s)[6]	200 ah	300 ah	450 ah	675 ah
Sail area–displacement ratio	17.15	18.31	19.23	19.86
Sail area (main + genoa)[7]	330 sq. ft.	600 sq. ft.	1,000 sq. ft.	1,500 sq. ft.
Mainsail area	132 sq. ft.	240 sq. ft.	400 sq. ft.	600 sq. ft.
Genoa area (130%)	198 sq. ft.	360 sq. ft.	600 sq. ft.	900 sq. ft.
Primary winch rating[8]	16	40	53	66
U.S. Dollars per Pound[9]	10	11	12	13
Price	54,000	132,000	288,000	546,000
Electronics & Gear	5,400	13,200	28,800	54,600
Sail Costs (main + genoa)	1,819	4,972	7,899	11,935
Basic Aquisition Cost	$61,219	$150,172	$324,699	$612,535
Finance Charges per Year	5,400	11,388	24,420	46,560
Insurance	404	801	1,445	3,025
Berthage	1,375	1,925	2,475	3,025
Haulout/Storage	531	1,050	1,575	2,131
Maintenance	540	1,320	2,880	5,460
Annual Cost[9]	$8,250	$16,484	$32,795	$60,201

Notes:
[1]Displacements are averages of published values for stock cruising boats.
[2]Cabin area varies in proportion to length × beam.
[3]Stowage volume is space available for stowage and optional systems; actual usable stowage volumes can be significantly less than those given.
[4]Tankage proportional to displacement.
[5]Engines sized at 2.5 hp per 1000 lb.
[6]Battery capacity increases by 50% for every 10 feet in length.
[7]Mainsail–genoa split at 40% and 60%.
[8]Primary winches sized using Harken catalog.
[9]All costs are in U.S. dollars; sterling prices are broadly sim-

but gets tight with four people on anything other than an occasional basis. It gives us all the galley we want and an excellent head compartment, including a separate shower stall. We have all the systems I like, regardless of boat size, with everything reasonably accessible. The boat is easily handled by two people and can be single-handed without difficulty, even if the systems go down. I would like to sail faster (who wouldn't), but can consistently make 150-mile days, which is not bad. At 40 feet, slip rent, haulout fees, and bottom jobs are not too expensive. All in all, for us it represents a good set of compromises.

The Test Sail

It's remarkable how many people buy boats without test sailing them! The more serious you are about cruising, and the longer the cruises you intend to take, the more important it is to know if a boat has any vices under sail. Once you have narrowed your choices, you should attempt to test sail or charter the boat that interests you or a sister ship, or, if you are contemplating building a custom boat, a similar boat from the same designer.

To be of optimum use, a test sail requires a couple of hours in a breeze strong enough to require a reef, and with enough wave action to

BETH LEONARD'S EXPERIENCE

Beth Leonard and her partner, Evans Starzinger, circumnavigated in *Silk*, a Shannon 37—a somewhat "traditionally" styled, moderately-heavy-displacement cruising boat. From that experience came her book, *The Voyager's Handbook* (International Marine and Adlard Coles Nautical, 1998). Subsequently, she and Evans sold the Shannon and bought a custom-built 47-foot (14.3 m) sloop (*Hawk*) with more "contemporary" lines. After a few months of cruising in the new boat, she summarized her thoughts on the change in "Moving on Up" in *Sail* magazine (Aug. 2000), from which I quote:

A bigger boat costs more—it's more expensive to buy, to dock, to cruise, to maintain . . . but we gained stability, speed, and space. We've averaged 175 nautical miles per day on *Hawk* compared to 135 on *Silk*.

Our increased speed actually benefits us most where we least expected it, by increasing our range during daylight hours. We can now sail some 30 percent farther between ports during the day, which has greatly reduced the need to sail at night.

The biggest overall benefit has been a radical increase in our self-sufficiency [as a result of dramatically increased tankage and stowage]. We have effectively doubled our cruising time away from "civilization."

In conditions where *Hawk* will happily keep sailing, we would have heaved-to on *Silk*. *Hawk*'s stability and her ability to sail well to windward keep us sailing in a lot of conditions where she's far happier than we are. However, the increased stability, resulting in more rapid motion, corresponds more to increased seasickness than to increased safety.

Though *Hawk* is much more stable than *Silk*, and therefore much "safer" in extreme conditions, *Silk* was much more forgiving. If we misjudged a squall and didn't get the chute off in time, we could wrestle the sock down over it and manhandle the spinnaker to the deck. If we wrapped the jib during a jibe, we could unwrap it by hand in light air and with a winch in windy conditions. But brute force gets us nowhere aboard *Hawk*. She requires much greater forethought, because the forces she generates quickly become unmanageable and dangerous. . . . *Silk* offered the perfect learning environment while we made every mistake in the book; *Hawk* demands all the skills we've acquired to sail safely and efficiently.

Bigger winches won't carry a bigger, heavier sail bag to the bow; won't wrestle a larger, weightier anchor out of a locker; won't flake and tie down an oversized, ill-mannered mainsail; and won't claw down and secure a furling sail if the furler breaks . . . *Hawk* requires greater fitness than *Silk* . . . but . . . no matter how fit we are, we still have to rely on mechanical aids to handle the forces generated by *Hawk*'s sails and anchors.

All of this equipment costs money, but more than that, it reduces our reaction time when trying to control a sail and decreases our independence and our options.

I'm about 5 feet, 4 inches [1.6 m] tall, and on *Hawk* everything seems to be just one size too large for me. . . . While things initially felt large on *Silk*, I was physically able to hold a coiled line in my hand, reach the top of both booms, carry a sail without dragging it. I've been surprised at how frustrating I find it to always be wishing I were 2 inches [5 cm] taller. Unlike on *Silk*, I have to depend on Evans to flake the mainsail and put on the sail cover.

I used to daysail with my parents aboard their 25-foot [7.6 m] Bristol Corsair. We'd dump ice in the cooler, whip the sail cover off, and be sailing in less than half an hour. When we returned from sailing, we'd throw the sail cover back on the boat, toss our duffel bags in the car, and be on our way. . . . A larger boat means more effort to get off the dock, more time to tidy up, and more money to keep up. . . . A bigger boat will almost guarantee that you spend less time under sail and more time at the dock. In our experience, the happiest crews sail the smallest, simplest boats, whether up and down the Chesapeake, around the Great Lakes, or across the Pacific.

test the boat's motion in uncomfortable seas. Ideally, the wind will be blowing at, or at least gusting up to, 15 knots or more. When the boat is put hard on the wind, this should result in an apparent wind of 20 knots or more (see chapter 7 for more on apparent wind), the point at which most boats require their first reef. In any event, you will get a good idea of how she goes to windward. If the wind is gusty, you will also get a good idea of how tender she is—does she stand up to it, or does she roll over—and how much work she is going to be to sail in these kinds of conditions (will you have to be constantly easing and tightening the sheets, or tying in and untying reefs, to keep her on her feet?).

You want the wind to be strong enough so that you can set sufficient sail area to overpress the boat. This is when she will really start to show her vices in terms of how she handles. In particular, these are the conditions in which any tendency to develop excessive weather helm, or for the rudder to stall out, will show up. I have been on boats that are as nimble as can be, and light on the helm, in 15 knots apparent, but which, when hit with a 20-knot gust, round up uncontrollably with absolutely nothing the helmsperson can do to prevent this other than letting fly the sheets. It is extremely disconcerting to find the boat is suddenly completely out of control!

You will want to carry out all common maneuvers such as tacking and jibing, reefing and unreefing, close and broad reaching, and heaving-to, to see how she handles, how easy it is to work the boat, whether the winches are properly sited and large enough, and so on. Does she have directional stability or is she skittish? How balanced is the helm? If you are forced to single-hand without an autopilot or wind vane, will you be able to let go of the wheel or tiller to perform necessary tasks? Turn on the autopilot and check the cockpit for comfortable and protected watchkeeping stations on both tacks.

Put her hard on the wind with as uncomfortable a motion as the seas will permit, and then go below and see how the galley, the saloon, and the head function. Check for sea berths. Do the same with the boat on a run, rolling from side to side. Tack her back and forth: if she doesn't come around nimbly, when the conditions get really nasty you may have real problems getting her head through the wind. Finally, drop the sails and try her under power, both at sea with some wave action, and also maneuvering at the dock.

Given suitable test conditions, in the space of a couple of hours you can get a pretty good idea of whether or not a boat will live up to your expectations.

From start (above) to finish (below) took six years of hard work!

To Build or Not to Build

Once a boat's basic parameters have been defined, you will often find that there is not a stock boat out there that fits the parameters. If you are going for a new boat, a decision has to be made about building the boat yourself, having a custom boat built to meet those parameters, having a production boat customized (i.e., semicustom), or taking a production boat and modifying it yourself. The alternative is to buy a boat in the secondhand market and customize it.

Home-Building

Home-building peaked in popularity in the 1970s and 1980s, and since then has been steadily on the decline. There are good reasons for this. Home-builders typically massively underestimate the time, complexity, and cost involved in building a boat. Of the minority of projects that get completed (a majority get abandoned), most take five to ten years and go several hundred percent over budget.

The home-builder needs a broad range of skills, from cabinet making to marine electrician, but is almost always lacking in some area. As a result, home-built boats are frequently deficient in some important respect. Even when not so (there are some gorgeous, state-of-the-art home-built boats), they tend to incorporate the builder's idiosyncrasies. The net result is that they have a low resale value.

If none of this deters you from home-building, a couple of things can be done to speed up the building process and hold down costs. When building a fiberglass hull, it is simply not worthwhile to construct the necessary mold for a single hull: it is better to buy a hull from a builder and work from there. This almost certainly proves cheaper, and shaves as much as two years off the project time. However, the same is not necessarily true of a deck. Whereas hulls are relatively cheap to buy (often less than 10 percent of the total project cost), deck molds tend to be complex; as a result, decks are proportionately more expensive. Quite significant savings can be made by home-building a deck, but at the expense of a massive amount of work—much of which can be quite unpleasant (to get the external finish we wanted, Terrie and I spent a month grinding on the deck of our old boat, which we built in the early 1980s).

As for the purchase of supplies, it is more or less imperative to establish some kind of marine corporation in order to open wholesale accounts with suppliers. The typical retail markup in the marine industry is from 80 to 100 percent (i.e., the retailer buys at half the retail price), although on some products—notably electronics—the markup is not this high. Given the equipment that goes into a modern boat and that it is several times more costly than the hull and deck, any savings gained by putting your own labor into the home-building project will be lost by the higher cost of purchasing supplies (unless you can get the full original equipment manufacturer—OEM—or wholesale discount).

At the beginning of our project, I opened a wholesale account with a large marine retailer in Seattle, Washington (Doc Freeman's) and bought everything through it. We were building in Louisiana, so I had to factor freight charges into the cost, but they averaged less than the sales tax we would have had to pay if we bought locally. This arrangement worked out extremely well.

Our boat took six years to build (I had estimated two) despite the fact that I spent twenty-six weeks a year working on it full time (I had a job on oil-production platforms in the Gulf of Mexico doing seven days on and seven days off, which gave me a lot of free time). The project went 100 percent over budget. However, one reason why it went so much over budget was because it took so long—it gave me more time to earn money, which enabled us to put in fancier systems. This is one of the hidden benefits of home-building: not much money has to be put in up front. With careful planning, the major costs (i.e., engine, sails, rig, and systems) can be deferred until close to the end of the project, at which time you can go for whatever you can afford. We never had to go into debt over that boat.

We enjoyed the building process and had a wonderful time cruising in our boat for fifteen years—but we are the exceptions. Most home-built projects fall apart long before they are finished, causing nothing but anguish to the builder.

Custom-Building

What about hiring someone else to build the boat? This, too, is almost as fraught with pitfalls as home-building. I have been involved with one or two projects (as a consultant) in which there have been significant frustrations, delays, and cost overruns. I have also seen the opposite situation in which the owners thoroughly enjoyed their involvement in the design and construction process, and loved the boat when it was finished.

Clearly, the major advantage to custom boatbuilding is that you can get exactly what you want. However, for this to work, you have to know exactly what you want—not just in general terms, but in very precise detail. Otherwise, you get what the yacht designer or the boatbuilder thinks you want, which may turn out to be something quite different. Given the complexity of modern boats, you also may get some unpleasant surprises (e.g., an engine raw-water seacock that comes out of the water when the boat is heeled on one tack or the other). It is going to be at least partly up to you to check the nitty-gritty of every detail on the boat. I am sticking my neck out by saying that it is not until people have owned a couple of boats and done some extensive cruising that they have clear enough ideas and the depth of experience to make a custom project worthwhile.

Your ideas have to be translated into a format that can be interpreted by a boatbuilder and that produce the desired results. Just about any competent yacht designer can produce a set of lines plans, laminate schedules (if the boat is fiberglass), and rig and interior plans. This enables the hull and interior to be manufactured and the boat to be rigged. Too many architects leave it at that, leaving the tankage, batteries, systems, and so on to be installed according to the boatbuilder's "custom and practice." Given the importance of the systems on a modern boat, this is simply not adequate.

To be successful, a custom design should include just about every detail of the boat, down to the placement of all major components, the location of plumbing and wiring runs, the size of cables, the type of hoses to be used, the positioning of through-hulls and seacocks, and myriad other details (including, for example, the density and thickness of the foam to be used in cushions, the fabric used to cover them, and a thousand other small details). Deciding these details up front should ensure that everything fits, as well as whether these are the best locations for use and serviceability. It gives the owner the opportunity to review absolutely every aspect of the design before the building process begins. It is expensive—a typical architect's design fee runs at least 8 percent of the total project cost, which is $80,000 on a million-dollar boat—but it may well be the best money spent on the project.

If this approach is not adopted, all kinds of nasty (and expensive-to-fix) surprises can derail the smooth flow of the project. For example, I was called in on the systems side of two projects only to discover that the space allotted to the iceboxes was inadequate for the necessary insulation. Rectifying something like this once the boat is under construction can make an extra few thousand on the architect's fee look like chicken feed.

As for the economics of custom boatbuilding, the picture is all over the map. Typically, a custom boat costs up to twice as much as a similar production boat, but this need not be the case. It is true that the production boatbuilder benefits from being able to amortize the cost of the design fees, the mold (if one has to be built), and other setup costs over a production run. The production builder also finds that it takes maybe as few as half the hours to build the third and successive boats in a production run as it does to build the first (there is a steep learning curve). On the other hand, the production boatbuilder has to include 15 to 20 percent off the top as the dealer's commission and has to have a marketing budget (maybe 10 percent)—right there is an approximate 25 to 30 percent savings for a custom project. If you add to this the fact that on larger custom projects it is possible to shop the world for a boatbuilder, thereby taking advantage of exchange-rate fluctuations, it is sometimes possible to get as much and maybe more custom boat for the money; however, this doesn't happen too often.

Building overseas has its own associated costs. Who is going to supervise the project and how will this person be paid? What happens if the boatbuilder does not perform as promised or runs into financial problems? The rate of bankruptcies among boatbuilders is high. Depending on how far along your project is, you may have handed over up to two thirds of the cost of your boat before it is anywhere near ready for delivery. If the boatbuilder goes under, you risk losing all of it.

To what standards will the boat be built and the systems installed? In the United States, you can, for example, simply specify that the systems installations are to be "as per ABYC"; in Europe, the relevant standards are written by the ISO. But what about Thailand or Taiwan or New Zealand?

You will want to visit the boatbuilder several times during the project: Has this cost been factored in? The boat should be commissioned and sea-trialed before it is accepted, but who will do that, who will pay for it, and if problems arise, how will they be resolved? After commissioning, unless you intend to sail the boat away, it must be decommissioned in order to ship it, and then it will have to be recommissioned on arrival at its destination; this is another substantial cost. Of course, there will be a significant freight charge.

In summary, a one-off custom boat, especially one built overseas, has many hidden costs and pitfalls built into it. These can be avoided—unfortunately, it takes more experience and attention to detail than some owners can muster, with unhappy results.

Semicustom

What about semicustom? The big advantage here is that you will be dealing with a known commodity. Unless yours is No. 1 in the production run, the manufacturer will already have had feedback and time to iron out any obvious wrinkles (that incorrectly located seacock should have been found and moved!). You also will also be able to see a sister ship before commencing the project and work out all the changes that you want to make. Even so, for the process to work well, certain things are still important, as follows:

- You need to be clear about what you want. Just as with custom boatbuilding, change orders are not only expensive, but also disruptive of the rhythm of the whole project.
- The boat needs to have a well-established reputation as the kind of boat you want. Furthermore, it should have been in production *with the same company* for some time—it is not uncommon for a boat name to outlast more than one company. The boat may have built a reputation

with one manufacturer, but when you become interested, it is being built by another company that does not have the same high standards.

- The company needs to have a reputation for consistently high standards. The loss of a few key people from a production facility can dramatically impact production standards, but is unlikely to do so if the manufacturer has an overall culture of excellence.
- The company needs to be truly willing to work with you in implementing the changes you want to make. One of the determining factors in our choice of a Pacific Seacraft was my gut feeling that I could work with the folks there on some quite substantial changes without raising any hackles. This turned out to be the case—the entire experience was extremely positive.
- The company needs to be solvent. You will be depositing a substantial chunk of change and then making further payments as work progresses. As the boat nears completion, you will have largely paid for it. If the builder goes belly-up at this point, you will be caught in the middle of a very messy situation.

At the end of the day, semicustom boats can still be as expensive as some similar custom projects. This is partly because the customizing disrupts the boatbuilder's routine, which disproportionately drives up the labor time and associated overhead, and partly because if the manufacturer has a dealer network, every change you make and every piece of gear you add has built into it the 15 to 20 percent that goes to the dealer. However, you know up front almost exactly what you are getting for your money, what it will cost, and usually when it will be delivered. You may need to add 10 percent or more over and above the purchase price for commissioning costs (depending on how much you intend to load up the boat).

A Production Boat

The last new-boat approach is to buy a stock production boat and customize it yourself. The benefit is that it is likely to get you into a new boat for less money than any other approach. The downside, of course, is that you are somewhat limited in what you can do to customize the boat. You also have to factor in from 15 to 40 percent of the purchase price for commissioning and customizing costs.

The quality of the hardware and systems installations vary enormously from one manufacturer to another. It really is important to see that both the equipment fitted to a boat you are thinking of buying and the way it is fitted are appropriate to how you intend to use the boat. An inexpensive boat up front, with poor quality hardware and systems, and deficient installations, is an expensive boat in the long run—with a low resale value when you finally get fed up with trying to keep it operating and decide to sell it.

When considering the purchase of a production boat, be sure to look at overseas boatbuilders. Depending on what the exchange rates are at the time you buy, it may be possible, for example, for an American to buy "cheaply" in Europe or vice versa. This works best if the boatbuilder has a dealer in your country; otherwise, you have to go overseas to collect and commission the boat (or have it shipped sight unseen), which adds an entirely new level of complexity and expense to the project.

Commissioning Costs

Commissioning is a substantial part of the cost of *any* new boat. It is important to get a clear idea of what is included in the boat's purchase price and, more importantly, what is not. It may be that by the time the features not included are factored in, the boat turns out to be substantially more expensive than a similar boat from another builder that comes more fully fitted. The Pacific Seacraft 40 comes with thousands of dollars worth of deck hardware and winches—a more complete inventory than on most comparable boats. All of it is top of the line—there is a reason why the base price is so high!

Before committing to a boat, it is an excellent idea to ask for a full inventory of what comes with it, including who makes it and what model it is (to get a good idea of real value); then list what you want over and above this. The "extra" equipment can be priced from a West Marine, BoatU.S., Sowester, or other catalog, enabling a total boat cost to be derived—with a sense of the quality of what is already installed as original equipment. The trucking and launching costs, maybe the cost of a bottom job (sometimes done by the boatbuilder, sometimes not), rigging costs, and sea-trial costs can easily add thousands more dollars.

Following is a list of features often not included in the cost of a "base" boat, most of which will be found on a contemporary cruising boat:

Electronics are rarely included in the base price of a boat. Here, the navigation station has plenty of fascia panel space, waiting for the owner to spend money! (Courtesy Beneteau)

- sails
- sailing instruments (speed/depth)
- VHF and SSB radios, radar, and autopilot
- satellite-based communications
- entertainment equipment
- ground tackle, including a windlass, anchors, and rodes
- saltwater washdown pump
- extra and/or larger winches to make the boat easier to handle
- spinnaker or reaching poles and associated tackle
- roller-reefing gear
- upgrade from a fixed propeller to a feathering propeller
- dodger and bimini
- Dorade vents
- awning and wind scoops
- necessary DC-systems upgrade (larger battery bank, high-output alternator, systems monitor)
- DC to AC inverter
- refrigeration (or maybe a necessary upgrade)
- fans
- upgrade from incandescent lights to fluorescent
- microwave
- galvanic isolator on the shore-power inlet
- solar panels and/or a wind generator

Refrigeration is generally another add-on.

- dinghy
- dinghy chocks and/or davits
- outboard motor
- place to mount the outboard motor and a crane to get it on and off
- barbecue grill
- safety gear (life jackets, harnesses, foghorn and bell, flares, life ring, Lifesling or Crew-Saver, COB pole, searchlight, and first-aid kit)
- emergency position-indicating radio beacon (EPIRB)
- life raft
- jacklines
- boarding ladder
- second LPG bottle
- fenders and dock lines
- cockpit cushions
- cockpit table
- locks on all hatches in the cabinsole
- lee cloths
- spare winch handles, shackles, snap shackles, snatch blocks, blocks, and so on
- engine spares
- foul-weather gear
- all the kitchen "stuff" (dishes, cutlery, pots and pans)
- bedding
- and so on

Taken together, this can (and often does) amount to *tens of thousands of dollars* before the first person has set foot on the boat. It all has to be factored into the overall cost equation.

Once the boat is bought, ownership costs are relatively low for the first year or two (primarily haul-out, winter-storage, and bottom-job costs), but will then slowly start to creep up as the boat requires more maintenance and the replacement of parts. In very broad terms—and leaving out slip rent or mooring costs—for the first five years, ownership costs are likely to average around 2 percent of the purchase price; thereafter, they will creep up toward 5 percent and maybe more. Five percent will not be spent every year, but sooner or later there will be some big-ticket items (e.g., sails, engine) that result in a 5 percent average. Of course, the boat can be sold before those expenses come due, but then its depreciated sale price will reflect the fact that the next owner is going to have to spend the money.

An owner willing to spend an average of 10 percent of the purchase price on maintenance can keep the boat in an "as-new" condition and updated to remain "state of the art."

USED-BOAT MARKET

Boats are like automobiles—they depreciate substantially as soon as they leave the lot, creating some excellent buying opportunities. Furthermore, new-boat owners typically sink thousands of additional dollars into the boat as soon as it is bought, buying many of the items on the previous list. This frequently makes an almost-new boat an even better deal than it first appears to be. So why even think of buying a new boat?

First, of course, is the thrill associated with buying anything new! It is also possible to get exactly what you want, as opposed to buying someone else's concept. More than this, however, boats age remarkably fast. By buying new, it is possible to stave off many maintenance hassles and expenses for a few years.

There are at least a couple of reasons why boats age so fast: the marine environment is an incredibly harsh one; and cruising-boat technology is constantly being improved, and with it the public perception of what are "minimum" comfort levels on boats. The result is that by the time a boat is ten years old, the systems are mostly either worn out or obsolete. Furthermore, they cannot be fixed by tinkering; to bring a ten-year-old boat up to contemporary cruising standards, it is not unusual to have to gut it, including ripping out the entire wiring harness and starting from scratch on the electrical systems. This can be phenomenally expensive—it is not difficult to drop $50,000 into a boat, and this is doing all the work yourself (note that sterling costs are broadly similar, despite the exchange rate differential).

What this means is that the good value often associated with a well-equipped, almost-new boat can rapidly diminish. Unless the boat has been exceptionally well maintained, no matter how loaded it may be, the systems may be more trouble than they are worth after just a few years.

I have a friend who bought a nicely constructed ten-year-old boat loaded with equipment for a "steal"—a mere $100,000. He proudly showed me the two air conditioners, the refrigerator and freezer, the watermaker, and numerous other pieces of gear. The boat probably cost $600,000 to build and equip and was still in good shape, so on the surface, it really did look like a steal. However, all I could see was the way the equipment had been stuffed into lockers all over the boat, its inaccessibility, the messy wiring harness, numerous areas of incipient corrosion, and so on. What my friend had bought could just as easily turn out to be a long-term nightmare into which he constantly pours money and time in an attempt to fix faulty systems without ever getting on top of them. There may even be problems that are insurmountable at just about any cost, such as a core that isn't properly sealed and/or has delaminated from the skins.

This raises another point, which is that some boats are designed to be troublemakers before they even leave the boatyard. They are not worth touching with the proverbial barge pole at any price. This is because the systems have not been properly thought out or installed (or both). There will be constant problems that ultimately will be resolved only by gutting the boat and starting again—a step which, for good reason, few owners are willing to take.

In other words, the "loaded" boat from five to fifteen years old needs to be carefully considered before any money is put down. Then we get into still older boats in which the systems are clearly shot (or were never there in the first place). These boats may still have a sound hull, deck, and rig and a decent accommodation plan. They frequently sell for very cheap prices, especially if they have suffered cosmetically. For many people, especially those willing to do their own work and those who have a grasp of systems and installations, a boat like this can provide a relatively affordable way of realizing a cruising dream. As long as the sweat equity is discounted and the work has been neatly executed, it might even be possible to go cruising and subsequently sell the boat for whatever has been put into it (but don't count on it).

Refurbishing an Older Sailboat

What are some of the costs likely to be faced with a fixer-upper? First, let me reiterate that if the boat is basically seaworthy, perhaps the best course of action is to enjoy it and not fix it up at all! This almost certainly proves to be the most economical way to go cruising.

If you are hell-bent on fixing up the boat, the "big-ticket" items are the DC system and associated equipment, the engine, the sails, and the rig. The DC system needs the most careful consideration because it is almost certainly not adequate to support a contemporary cruising lifestyle and will have to be completely upgraded—in many cases, replacing the entire wiring harness. In addition to the huge amount of work this entails, and the fact that accessing wiring may require cutting into some of the boat's cabinet work, it is not difficult to spend thousands of dollars on batteries, alternators, a systems monitor, distribution panels (panelboards), cables, and so on. Throw a wind generator and a solar panel into the mix, and the total cost is likely to be more than that of a new engine.

This is not to say the engine will be cheap, because it won't be. A marine diesel engine,

When refurbishing an older boat to contemporary standards, it is often best to rip out the old systems and start again from scratch.

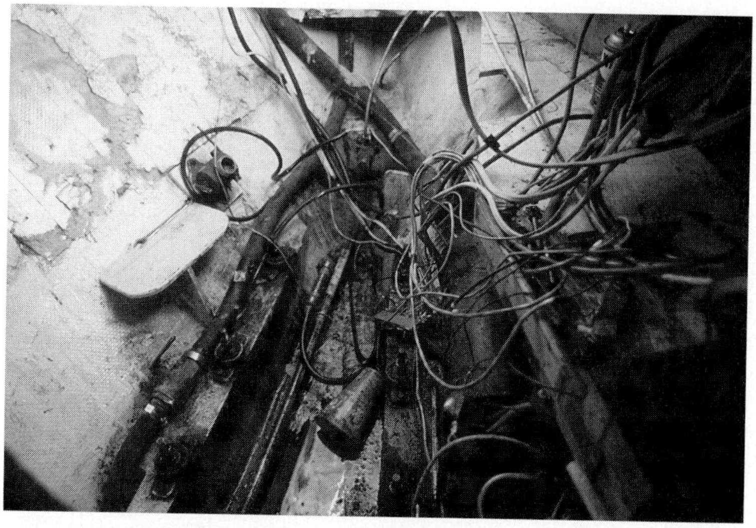

Repowering generally ends up being a bigger job than was anticipated.

without installation, is as expensive as a brand-new small car. Installation adds appreciably to the cost because, invariably, ancillary components will also need replacing (e.g., exhaust systems and rubber mounting feet). The final tab on a midsize cruiser is generally somewhere between $14,000 and $24,000.

Older sails, even if in apparently sound condition, will have lost their shape and will not set as well as they once did, especially upwind. If the boat is to go offshore, there is always a question mark hanging over them: When will they fail and when should they be renewed? Unfortunately, to replace them is likely to add up to as much as the cost of another engine.

Deciding what to do with the rig is an even more difficult judgment call. Ultimately, the flexing of stays and shrouds leads to a fatigue failure of the wire or rod—that is, if the end fittings don't give out first. A failure can bring down the entire rig. In addition to the inconvenience of a mast failure, the cost of replacing one is another thing that runs about the same as a new engine. It is worth proactively spending quite a lot of money to keep the mast onboard.

At what point do you rerig? This boat left it a little late!

From a conservative standpoint, the standing rigging should be replaced about every ten years. If I were upgrading an older sailboat to engage in long-distance cruising, I would be conservative—but the cost will be thousands of dollars. For coastal cruising, like most people, I would keep a close eye on an older rig and not replace anything until there is some evidence of impending failure (e.g., broken wire strands, incipient corrosion of terminals); unfortunately, there are few signs of impending failure with rod rigging.

Something often overlooked is the chainplates, which are invariably made of stainless steel and almost always pass through the deck. Over time, moisture works its way into this anaerobic (oxygen-deprived) environment and corrosion of most stainless steels will start. Ultimately, the plate may fail. There is really no way to check on the condition of chainplates without removing them, so this is another task to be done on an older boat. Depending on the installation, removing chainplates can be from relatively easy to monstrously difficult.

So far, we may have spent as much as it would take to buy four new engines for the boat and we are still far from done! The refrigeration system is likely to be another major expense (in addition to which the icebox will probably need to be rebuilt, which in turn may well require ripping out a lot of joinerwork). If the boat has an alcohol or kerosene stove, it will most likely want upgrading to LPG, which in turn requires construction of a dedicated gas locker.

All the pumps will be suspect (freshwater, bilge, and toilet). The electronics will mostly be history. The fire extinguishers, flares, and other safety equipment will have exceeded their expiration dates. The dodger, bimini, awning, and sail covers may be on their last legs (ten years is a good lifespan, especially if used in the tropics). And then there are the cosmetics: cushion covers, paint and varnish, and an exterior hull and deck paint job. Together, these things can easily add up to the equivalent of another engine.

In summary, refurbishing an older boat to contemporary standards can be extraordinarily expensive, on top of which it will probably involve thousands of hours of labor. When it comes to selling the boat—no matter how good its condition—it is unlikely to fetch much above its "book" value; in other words, you will never recover what is put into the boat unless you bought it extremely cheaply in the first place. However, if you can get it cheaply enough and you have the time and necessary skills to fix it

Two different approaches to retrofitting an LPG stove. One is to add a deck box for the cylinders (below), the other to add an off-the-shelf, sealed LPG locker to a cockpit locker (bottom).

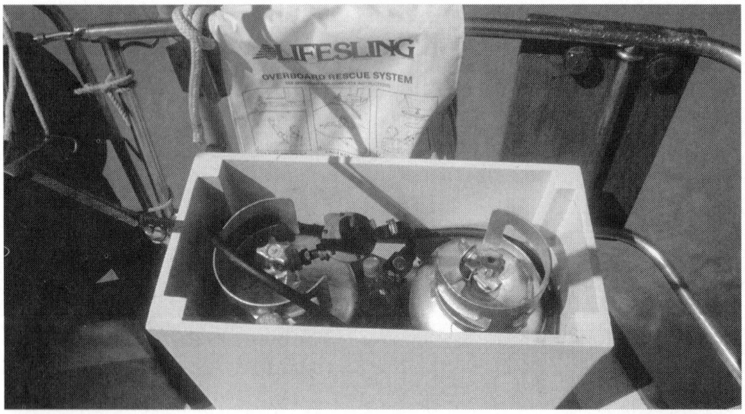

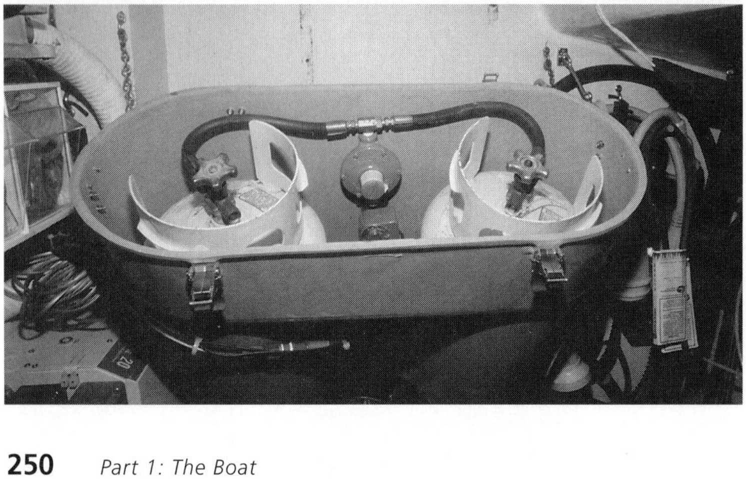

A paint job adds another major expense.

up, you can end up with far more boat for the dollar than any other way. You will also acquire an excellent knowledge of both the boat and its systems. But, quite clearly, it is not worth investing this kind of time and money in just any old boat. So what kinds of boats should be looked at for refurbishment?

What to Refurbish?

In my opinion, the most important factor is the reputation of any given boat. There are lots of boats out there that have time and time again proved themselves to be an excellent cruising platform: older Pearsons, Masons, Tartans, Valiants, Pacific Seacrafts, Bowmans, Rivals, Vancouvers—the list is relatively long. There are also various excellent sources, such as *Practical Sailor*, *Yachting Monthly* (in the U.K.), and *Cruising World* magazines, from which to garner informed opinions of these and other boats when drawing up your own shortlist.

Many boats have a particular problem associated with that boat. For example, it might be the deck-stepped mast of the Pearson 30 on a cored deck, leading to structural problems as a result of compression of the core. Or the notorious problems Valiant had in the early 1980s with fire-retardant resin, which led to terrible hull blistering. Once your shortlist is compiled, it is worth tracking down this kind of information so that when inspecting one of these boats, you know to look for specific problems.

An excellent way to get to know the problems associated with any boat is to track down an owners' bulletin board or message exchange on the Internet: owners write about their troubles and seek advice on how to deal with them. Other owners respond: "Oh, yes, we've all had that problem; here's what you do. . . ." You can join in yourself and ask for an opinion of the boat—you'll generally get quite frank reviews and all kinds of information that the boatbuilder would rather not share with the public!

Old Racing Boats

When looking at older boats for cruising, you should be especially wary of any built to a rating rule. A rating rule, such as the old CCA rule, is a formula that looks at speed-producing and -reducing factors (e.g., LWL, beam, keel depth, ballast ratio, sail area) and attempts to level the playing field between different boats by establishing the dimensions of an "ideal" boat. It then penalizes speed-producing factors that go beyond the formula. The formula invariably is based on certain fixed measurement points.

As soon as a rule is propagated, talented yacht designers are looking for "loopholes"—modifications that can be made to a boat to increase its speed without incurring a penalty, or that increase speed disproportionately to the penalty incurred. The opposite also can be true: there may be modifications that actually impair performance and decrease speed but, in doing so, gain a disproportionate decrease in a

There are many older boats that make lovely, seaworthy cruising boats, but frequently not with the interior volume and accommodations offered by modern boats.

penalty. The bottom line is that none of the characteristics important to a cruising sailor—absolute speed, seakindly motion, controllability, and so on—are driving the process, with the result that some remarkable aberrations (from a cruising perspective) are created. However stupid or unseaworthy, anything that decreases a boat's penalty disproportionately more than it decreases its speed is worthwhile from the racing perspective. Olin Stephens recounts a race that was won in the 1960s (much to his disgust) through the deliberate addition of a heavy steel deck and engine to one of his designs, giving the boat an improved rating out of proportion to the resulting loss of stability and speed.

These kinds of rule-beating distortions were not as pronounced decades ago when racing in the United States was dominated by the CCA rules. These rules tended to encourage boats with long overhangs, wide (for those days) beam, and low ballast–displacement ratios. This style of boat can be seen in many anchorages and, to some extent, is still considered the epitome of graceful lines. From a cruising perspective, it was one of the least obnoxious rules. However, during the CCA era, in the United Kingdom racing was dominated by the Royal Ocean Racing Club (RORC) rules, which encouraged narrow, deep-ballasted boats that sailed to windward well but were wet and had limited (in many cases, lousy) space for accommodations—a poor combination of features in a cruising boat.

It was found that boats built to the CCA and RORC rules could not compete equitably against each other. This led to the development of a unified International Offshore Rule (IOR) in the 1960s. The IOR rule rapidly became a powerful influence on both racing and cruising boat designs. Among other things, it penalized deep, heavy ballast, which led to beamier boats and finally to "a large rig on a rather light hull, with a stability so limited that the typical boat must carry a big crew on the weather rail to keep it on its feet. Some smaller IOR boats may not be comfortable or even safe in heavy weather" (Olin Stephens, one of the architects of the rule, writing in *Desirable and Undesirable Characteristics of Offshore Yachts*).

The typical IOR boat has a flat underbody, a wide beam providing substantial form stability, a relatively low ballast ratio, a very small narrow fin keel and spade rudder, and little buoyancy in the bow (from above, these boats are diamond-shaped). This results in an unpleasant motion. Chuck Paine, writing in *The Complete Offshore Yacht*, had this to say: "Research conducted many years ago with the object of developing the ideal shape for bell and gong buoys, where it is desirable to produce the maximum rolling motion with the minimum wave input, produced a shape not unlike that of the present-day IOR racer!"

When hard-pressed, IOR boats tend to trim down by the bow, the rudder comes out of the water, and the boats broach uncontrollably. Once they lose speed, the minimal fin keel and spade rudder provide little resistance to making leeway. On the interior, there are substantial accommodation spaces (because of the wide beam) but little storage below the cabinsole for water, fuel, and the like (because of the flat shallow hull).

This was a quite awful design trend from the point of view of cruising sailors. Many IOR-influenced "cruising" boats and "cruiser-racers" built in the past few decades are not only too lightly constructed for serious offshore work, but also are unstable, temperamental, and downright hard to handle. What a miserable combination of features.

It took the Fastnet disaster in 1979 and the death of fifteen sailors to finally drive home some of the absurdities of this rule. A lot of soul-searching on the part of the rules committees eventually led to the adoption of a new rule—the *International Measurement System* (IMS). It places greater emphasis on less extreme design features and has resulted in many boats that can be adapted to make an excellent fast cruising boat; however, such boats are still likely to be less desirable for cruising than a purpose-built boat that ignores the rating rules. To give one example, long waterlines are advantageous under the IMS rules. As a result, to get the most speed out of a given length, designers invariably have a vertical stem. This reduces the reserve buoyancy forward that is necessary to support heavy ground tackle (the racer doesn't care) and is likely to produce a wet boat.

The net result is that when looking at a boat with a racing pedigree, particularly one from the 1970s and 1980s, with a view to refurbishing it for cruising, it is important to see to what extent it was built to a rating rule, and to what extent this resulted in undesirable qualities from a cruising perspective. At all times, there have always been sensible boats built with little or no lip service to any rule other than the precepts of sound design, so there is absolutely no need to saddle yourself with a boat with unpleasant characteristics or unsafe construction and features.

Finally, in recent decades, increasingly

more boats—both racing and cruising—have been built utilizing comprehensive internal liners and modules. All the deck fittings often are installed before the deck goes on the boat, and many of the interior fittings may be installed in the liner before it goes in; then the pieces are put together. This frequently leads to many fasteners for hardware—as well as parts of the wiring harness and the plumbing—being completely inaccessible. Trying to renovate and upgrade a boat like that is a challenging proposition!

A Survey

Before committing to an older boat, you should always get a professional survey. In fact, even when buying a new boat, you should pay to have it surveyed before it leaves the factory—you would be surprised at some of the things surveyors find.

Unfortunately, in the United States, there is no official licensing body for marine surveyors; anyone can hang out a shingle and hustle work. As a result, there are some quite awful surveyors out there. However, two professional associations—the National Association of Marine Surveyors (NAMS) (800-822-6267) and the Society of Accredited Marine Surveyors (SAMS) (800-344-9077)—have certain entrance requirements that result in surveyors a cut above the average; in the United States you should always hire a NAMS or SAMS accredited surveyor. Beyond this, it is a matter of checking a surveyor's reputation relative to the kind of boat you are thinking of buying—it is no good hiring someone who specializes in lobster boats to look at an old CCA racer.

A surveyor is relatively expensive; starting fees are approximately $400 a survey. However, a surveyor often finds one or two problems that have to be fixed before the boat is purchased or that result in a reduction in price. In both cases, the money saved is frequently more than the cost of the survey, added to which you now have reasonable assurance that you are not buying a "pig in a poke."

I say "reasonable assurance" because a competent surveyor usually does a good job of picking up hull and rig deficiencies, but many are not too versed on the minutiae of electrical systems and engines, which as we have seen, comprise a significant (and ever increasing) part of the overall cost of a boat. It is sometimes necessary to hire a separate expert to do a systems and engine audit, which then doubles the survey cost.

Hull, Deck, and Rig

Before spending this kind of money on surveys, I want to be fairly confident that the boat is basically in good shape and that the survey is not likely to lead to a change of heart, resulting in me being out of pocket for the cost of the survey. I would do my own preliminary survey, for which the boat will need to be hauled. Following are some of the "big-ticket" items for which I would be looking:

- If the keel is external, a secure keel-to-hull joint (some minor cracking around the joint is normal, but this should be nothing more than hairline). I look for evidence of damage to the hull at the aft end of the keel (where the keel will be levered up into the hull in a grounding). Hulls with deep fin keels are more likely to have suffered damage than hulls with substantial fiberglass keel stubs to which is fastened a lead keel with a broad cross-sectional area at the root. I want to see adequate structural support for the keel inside the boat, with plates under keel-bolt nuts to spread loads. There should be no signs of loose nuts and bolts, which indicate movement of the keel or compression of the support structure, or corrosion.
- Rudders suffer from a number of problems. After tying off the wheel or tiller, they should be firmly grasped and forced from side to side to see if there is excessive play in the bearings (there should be just about none). They need to be turned from lock to lock to see if there is any binding. The rudder tube

Look for cracks around the root of the keel, especially on boats with fin keels.

should be inspected for signs of cracking where it is bonded into the hull. The rudder likely has been laid up in two halves around a stainless steel stock to which a web was first welded. The seam between the two rudder halves should be closely inspected for signs of separation or "weeping" (cores commonly become saturated, cracking the rudder open). Rust stains may be indicative of a corroded web, necessitating a new rudder.

- Steering-gear failures are not uncommon. If possible, have someone rock the wheel or tiller aggressively from side to side while you watch for flexing and play in the various components of the system. All sheaves and other components need to be very rigidly mounted. Cables should develop no more than minimal slack on the unloaded side of the system. Cables and sheaves should be inspected for signs of wear.
- The (cutlass) bearing typically is seriously worn. There should be no more than minimal play between it and the propeller shaft (to test it, grab the propeller and rock it from side to side).
- The hull and deck need to be solid and well laid-up. They should be tapped with a plastic-headed hammer or something similar; listen for a crisp sound. A dull thud may indicate delamination or moisture saturation. I also try to flex any large, flat panels in and out, and then jump up and down on the deck to see if it flexes. If it does, I have serious misgivings about its ability to stand up to boarding waves.
- A cored hull and deck need especially close attention. If the core has become saturated or delaminated, the boat is unlikely to be worth any further attention.
- Any signs of osmotic blistering should raise a red flag because the cost of a cure can be so high. Sometimes incipient blistering is revealed by miniscule amounts of weeping for a day or two after haulout; therefore, closely inspect the hull after the surface has had time to dry off. If the boat has already had blisters and was properly repaired with no signs of a recurrence, it most likely is OK.
- The hull should be "sighted" from a small distance at different angles looking for any "hard" spots, which are indicative of excessive stresses around bulkheads and other structural elements.

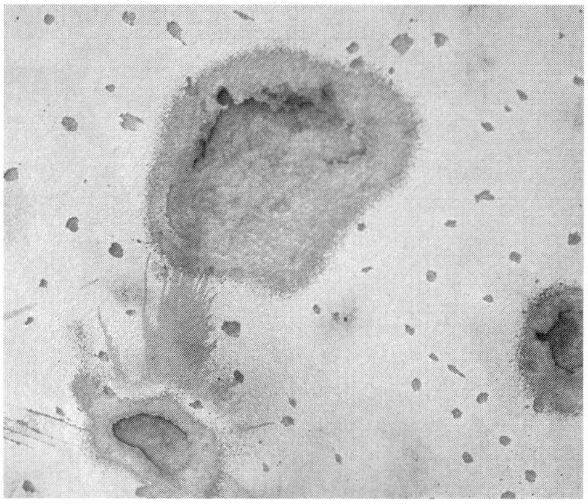

What initially looked like minor blistering in the gel coat (relatively cheap and easy to fix, with no worrisome implication for the fiberglass layup) turned out—after sandblasting—to have penetrated the fiberglass in several areas (much more expensive to fix).

- Decks commonly have tight curves from which stress cracks radiate as the boat ages. Superficial cracks will polish out, but any that have depth to them have structural implications (if nothing else, they will admit moisture to the layup).
- The stemhead fitting needs to be inspected to see if it is adequate to handle cruising ground tackle. Stanchion bases should be inspected for signs of stress and for deck leaks. Lifelines should be inspected for damaged turnbuckles and signs of corrosion under the plastic covers.
- Bulkheads need to be continuously bonded in place, with 4 to 6 inches of fiberglass tabbing on the bulkhead, all the way around (sometimes bulkheads are not bonded to the deck or at their base; when the boat is hard-pressed, they will flex). The tabbing should be inspected wherever possible to make sure that it is more than just a single layer of glass mat and that it is still well glued to the plywood of the bulkhead. On boats with flat bilges, pay particular attention to the base of bulkheads because there is a good chance that this area got wet and the bulkhead has rotted. Wherever furniture contacts the hull, it too should be bonded in place.
- Plywood should be marine grade rather than the exterior grade commonly used—the latter is prone to rotting out from the interior.

- Every available inch of the hull-to-deck joint should be inspected. For offshore work, there needs to be a significant mating surface between the hull and deck—sealed with polyurethane or polysulfide—and mechanically fastened with stainless steel bolts (not self-tapping screws, which are susceptible to crevice corrosion and failure).
- All deck hardware needs backing plates. If they can't be observed because of an interior cabin liner, this in itself indicates a problem—how will anything be replaced if it becomes necessary?
- All seacocks need to be inspected and opened and closed. Bronze seacocks should be checked for hairline cracks, corrosion, and green or pink tinges (signs of galvanic corrosion). Plastic seacocks should preferably be marine UL-listed or at least Marelon. If they have been neglected, you likely cannot turn the valve—the handle will break off first!
- The cockpit should be reviewed for strength (does the sole flex?), size (is it appropriate for offshore work?), comfort, drains, the risk of water pouring in through the companionway into the boat (is there a bridge deck to stop this?), and whether lockers are adequately closed and sealed.
- Winches should be spun to see that they are free-turning and that the pawls are operating (if not, the winch may just need cleaning—or it may have significant internal corrosion).
- Every terminal on the rig needs inspecting for signs of cracking or corrosion. The same goes for all welds on chainplates and other fixtures supporting the rig. Close attention should be given to chainplates and chainplate bolts where they pass through the deck or hull.
- The sails are one of the big-ticket items on the boat. Give them a good lookover for chafe, seam damage, and any signs of damage to or loss of fabric strength.
- If the mast is keel-stepped, inspect the mast step and the base of the mast for corrosion and signs of damage to the step (e.g., compressed floors, loose fasteners).
- All fuel and water tanks should be closely inspected for signs of damage and/or corrosion and to see if the tanks can be removed without tearing the boat apart.

Engine

A knowledgeable person can always disguise some engine problems sufficiently to fool even an expert; nevertheless, in most circumstances, it is possible to get a fair idea of the state of an engine without major disassembly or expense. Following are some of the checks I like to make:

- *Cleanliness*. The cleanliness of the engine is an important indicator of the caliber of maintenance it has received. There is a good chance that if the owner has taken pride in its appearance, he or she has also taken care of maintenance.
- *Maintenance Records*. These records should note, at the least, every oil and filter change, all fuel-filter changes, and any other work undertaken, with the engine hours at which the work was done. If the engine has no hour meter or the hours are not noted, it is likely that the maintenance was not done on schedule.
- *Fuel System*. Contaminated fuel is one of the principal sources of marine diesel-engine breakdowns, so I want to know that the fuel system has been kept rigorously and scrupulously clean. A useful check of the general state of the fuel system can be made by pumping a small sample of fuel from the lowest spot in the fuel tank into a jam jar and allowing it to settle. If it is seriously contaminated with

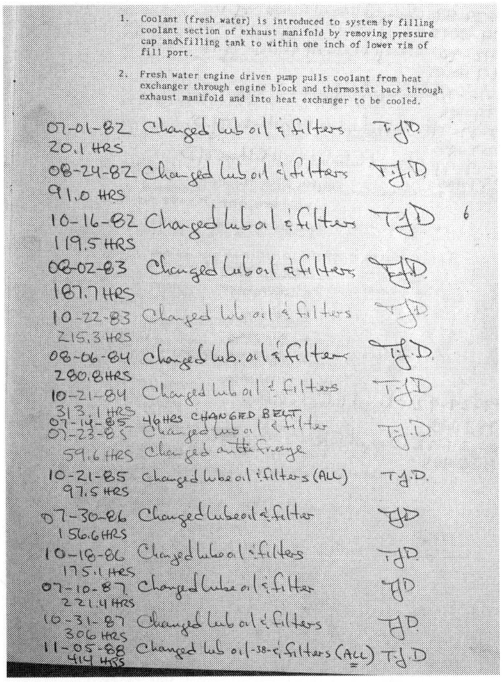

1. Coolant (fresh water) is introduced to system by filling coolant section of exhaust manifold by removing pressure cap and filling tank to within one inch of lower rim of fill port.

2. Fresh water engine driven pump pulls coolant from heat exchanger through engine block and thermostat back through exhaust manifold and into heat exchanger to be cooled.

07-01-82 Changed lub oil & filters T.J.D.
20.1 HRS
08-24-82 Changed lub oil & filters T.J.D.
91.0 HRS
10-16-82 Changed lub oil & filters T.J.D. 6
119.5 HRS
08-02-83 Changed lub oil & filters T.J.D.
187.7 HRS
10-22-83 Changed lub oil & filters T.J.D.
215.3 HRS
08-06-84 Changed lub. oil & filter T.J.D.
280.8 HRS
10-21-84 Changed lub oil & filters T.J.D.
313.1 HRS
07-14-85 46 HRS CHANGED BELT
07-23-85 Changed lub oil & filter T.J.D.
59.6 HRS Changed antifreeze
10-21-85 Changed lube oil & filters (ALL) T.J.D.
97.5 HRS
07-30-86 Changed lube oil & filter TJD
156.6 HRS
10-18-86 Changed lube oil & filters TJD
175.1 HRS
07-10-87 Changed lube oil & filter TJD
221.4 HRS
10-31-87 Changed lub oil & filters TJD
306 HRS
11-05-88 Changed lub oil -38- & filters (ALL) T.J.D
414 HRS

Some type of log is the best indication of attention to routine maintenance.

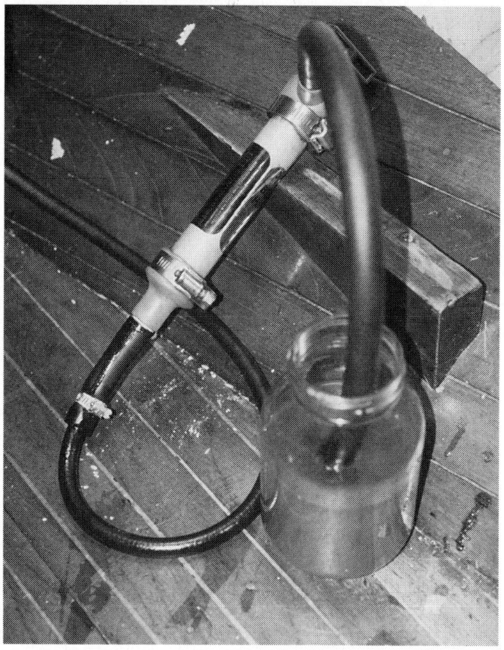

I like to check the state of a fuel tank by pumping a sample from the lowest spot.

Wiping my finger around the underside of a valve cover. A heavy black sludge in here indicates poor oil-change procedures.

either dirt or water, the entire fuel system is suspect. Depending on how extensive a survey I wish to make, I might open up both filters to gauge the extent of any fuel contamination.

- *Clean Oil*. As for the oil, a visual inspection generally does not reveal much. Because soot is a normal byproduct of diesel-engine operation (unless the oil has just been changed), it will be black—this is of no concern. However, if oil-change procedures have been neglected, the oil is likely to be intensely black and thicker than normal. I remove the oil filler cap and wipe my finger around the underside of the valve cover; a black sludge indicates poor oil-change procedures.
- *Water in the Crankcase*. The other thing that sometimes shows up is oil with a creamy color and texture. In this case, there is water in the oil, which may have been produced by condensation (because water is a normal byproduct of the combustion process) or may have an external source (the cooling or exhaust systems). If the water has come from the cooling system rather than condensation, there is likely to be a blown head gasket, a cracked cylinder head, or a corroded cylinder liner. If the water also contains antifreeze, the antifreeze will react with the engine oil to form a varnish that bonds to bearing and cylinder surfaces and is extremely hard to remove. Water in the oil is generally bad news!
- *Cooling System*. If the heat exchanger is not protected with sacrificial zinc anodes, it may have corrosion damage. Heat exchangers are expensive, so I want to know that the zincs have been properly maintained. It is a simple matter to close the raw-water (engine intake) seacock and unscrew a zinc—it should be no more than half eaten away. If it is entirely gone, as is so often the case, the heat exchanger is suspect.
- *Exhaust Hose*. This should be removed from the exhaust elbow to check for corrosion inside the elbow and excessive carbon in the exhaust pipe (it should be

Remove the exhaust hose from the water-lift muffler. The exhaust should be clean (with maybe just a surface coating of carbon). Any kind of a carbon buildup here indicates poor operating practices that have probably resulted in a carbon buildup in cylinders and on valves, necessitating an expensive overhaul.

basically clean). Exhaust carbon is an indicator of poor operating practices that have potentially fouled the valves and piston rings, thereby shortening engine life.

- *Engine Feet.* Spilled diesel softens flexible engine feet and insulation on the wiring harness, which may entail expensive replacements. I give these a close inspection.
- *Compression and Ignition.* So far, I haven't even turned the engine over! It's time to crank it and see what kind of story it has to tell. A diesel engine needs good compression to start. The normal wear of cylinder walls and piston rings as it ages slowly reduces compression. Over *thousands* of hours of run time, this results in a starting problem, which is one indicator of aging. Compression also can be lost—causing starting problems—through repeated operation at low loads and temperatures. This accelerates cylinder and ring wear and causes other problems, sometimes after just a *few hundred* hours of engine operation. It follows that *the number of hours of use on an auxiliary sailboat engine is not a useful indicator of its internal state of affairs.* What is of greater significance is whether the engine still retains effective compression levels; this we can roughly gauge from its willingness to fire when first cranked.
- *Cold-Start Test.* The compression levels necessary for ignition purposes are directly related to engine and ambient air temperatures; the colder these are, the higher the compression levels must be. Consequently, *to gauge compression levels without a compression tester, the engine should be cranked when cold.* Unless there is a good reason for an engine to have been run before an inspection (e.g., the need to bring a boat to the dock for boarding), I am immediately suspicious when confronted with an already warm engine (is the owner trying to hide a compression problem?). Given a cold engine, even if it has preheat devices, it is worth trying to start it without them. If it fires right up, the compression is excellent. If it does not fire, the cold-start devices can be activated, after which the motor should crank right away. If it does not, it probably has a compression problem (except in extremely cold weather—there has to be some balance between the ambient temperature and the ease of starting).
- *Running Tests.* Let's assume the engine fired up on the first attempt—the compression looks good. I immediately check the overboard raw-water discharge and the exhaust smoke. Whitish smoke during warm-up is probably nothing more than water vapor, but also may be unburned diesel, signaling a compression problem—with a water-cooled exhaust, it is hard to tell the difference. Blue smoke comes from engine oil that has found its way into the combustion chamber—a little is normal on startup until the pistons and rings warm and seat fully; however, if it continues, there is probably a compression problem. Black smoke comes from unburned fuel—at high engine loadings, it may be the result of an obstruction in the air inlet (particularly the filter) or the exhaust. At low loads, it is more likely to be caused by fuel-injection problems—the injection pump or injectors need servicing, which is another expensive proposition.

Remaining Systems

If the boat has a high-capacity DC system, I want to check that the alternator and voltage regulator are working, which should be easy if there is also a systems monitor. The batteries also should be tested; unfortunately, it is not that easy to do. As much of the wiring harness as possible, including the back of the panel, should be inspected—not only to see if suitable cabling has been used (i.e., UL-1426 BC5W2 or equivalent), but also to get a sense of the quality of the installation. If this is a mess, as it commonly is, you may be faced with ripping it all out.

Surveyors typically do a poor job of checking out wiring harnesses. If you understand cable sizing procedures, over-current protection issues, and so on, you will probably do as good or better a job of going through the circuits than a surveyor. If an inverter and microwave are onboard, both can be checked by boiling a cup of water in the microwave. Any refrigeration system needs to be operated and the thickness and effectiveness of icebox insulation gauged (by trying to get a sense of how often the refrigeration system runs and how much energy it consumes). Then there are the pumps, lights, fans, and so on, all of which should be operated.

Beyond this, utilizing the questionnaire that follows will enable numerous small details of boat design and construction to be checked out. If the boat passes muster, it is

Checking the charging voltage at the battery (ignore the minus sign—I have the meter leads the wrong way around). This is way too low. The batteries will be seriously undercharged and almost certainly need replacing.

time to call in the professionals and see what they can dig up!

Go Sailing as Soon as Possible!

Once you have acquired a boat, you should focus on the structural issues—and those that are essential to the safe conduct of the vessel—before getting into the systems and cosmetics. Unless you have already cruised extensively and have very clear ideas about the boat and its systems, my advice is to deal with the basic matters as quickly as possible, get the boat into a functional shape, and go cruising for a while. You will then be in a position to determine what other modifications and systems you want on the basis of real-life experience; your conclusions may be quite different from those you might have come to through pondering these issues at dockside.

CRUISING-BOAT QUESTIONNAIRE AND CHECKLIST OF DESIRABLE FEATURES

The following questionnaire is provided as a means of focusing attention on both the big-picture issues and the minutiae that have to be right when considering the suitability of a boat for cruising purposes. The questions are explained in chapters 1 through 5.

To go through this entire questionnaire relative to any boat could easily take days (maybe weeks)! For those who are really serious about finding the "right" boat, the way I envision this questionnaire being used is first, there will be some narrowing down of choices, maybe using some of the readily available parameters in chapter 1 and other general criteria described in that chapter (summarized in sections 1–6 of the questionnaire). Once the choices are narrowed down to maybe three or four boats, you can start using the very detailed questions in the rest of the questionnaire as a kind of checklist, choosing those questions applicable to the kind of boat you are looking for and putting your own spin on them. The purpose of listing everything in such detail is to enable you to cover all the bases and not overlook some small item that may come back to haunt you (e.g., a raw-water seacock that comes out of the water on one tack or the other!).†

†The questions are numbered to make it easier for you to write your answers on sheets of paper.

I have to say that in our own boat search, we probably used no more than half of these questions—but that was before I wrote this book; a number that we didn't use are now on the list because I wish I had thought of them at the time! Remember, you will *never* find a boat that provides satisfactory answers to all the questions (even if you have a boat custom-built).

Only you can decide which are the more important questions, thereby determining the kind of compromises that will set your boat apart from all others.

As a partial illustration of this questionnaire, I have used a concept design (it has not been built) developed by Jay Paris and *Sail* magazine. The design is based on a definition of an "ideal" offshore cruising boat that emerged from the answers to a questionnaire submitted to members of the U.K.-based Ocean Cruising Club (OCC). The design embodies many of the ideas that I developed in the preceding chapters. Remember that the focus is very much that of a world-girdling cruising boat; the concept needs to be significantly modified for coastal cruising. (My thanks to Jay, Steve Davis, and *Sail* magazine for permission to use this material.)

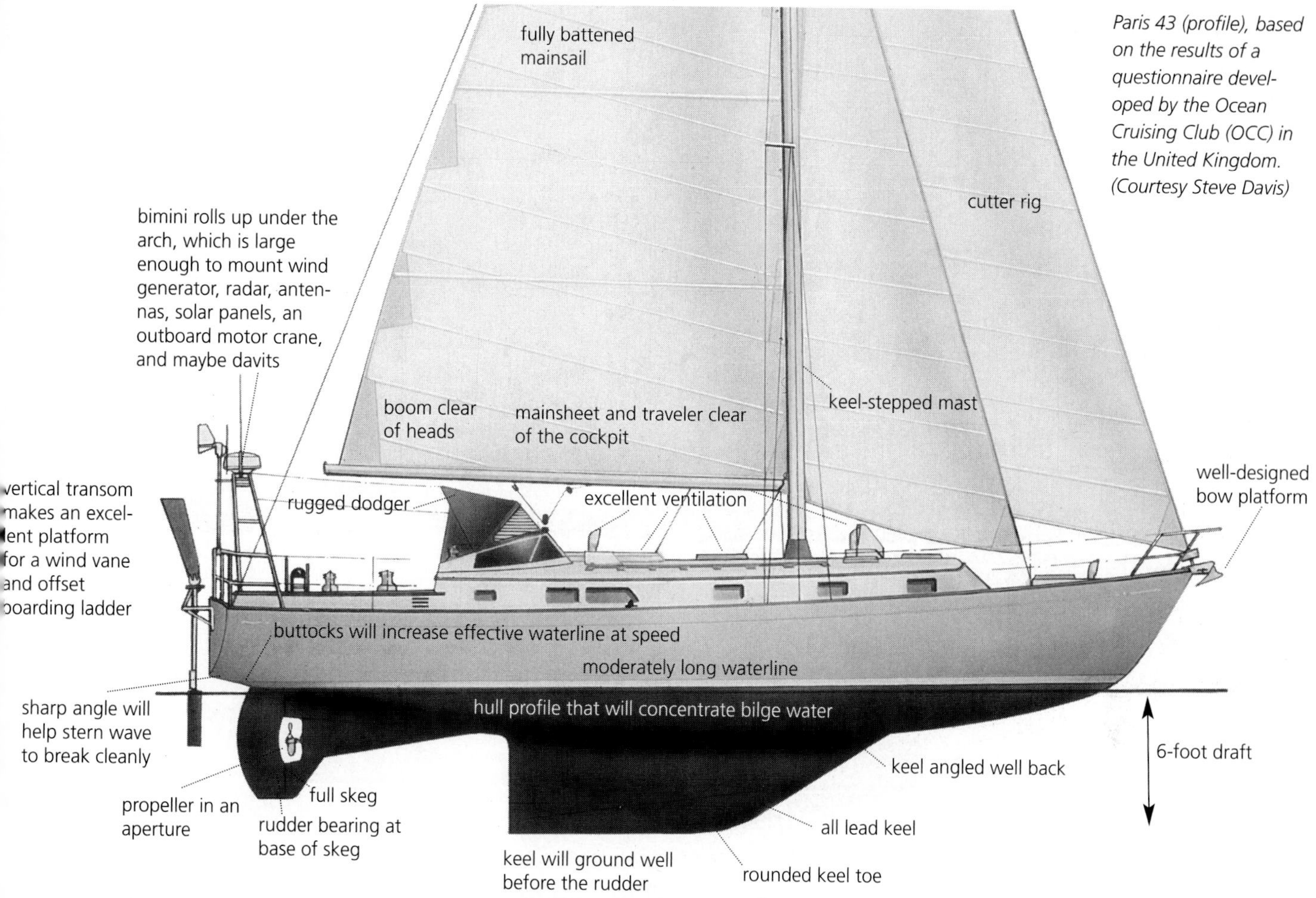

Paris 43 (profile), based on the results of a questionnaire developed by the Ocean Cruising Club (OCC) in the United Kingdom. (Courtesy Steve Davis)

Paris 43 Specifications and Performance Parameters

Length overall (LOA)/length of hull (LOH)	43.00 ft. (13.10 m)
Waterline length (LWL)	36.00 ft. (10.96 m)
Maximum beam (B_{max})	12.50 ft. (3.81 m)
Beam on waterline (BWL)	11.50 ft. (3.50 m)
Draft	6.00 ft. (1.8 m)
LWL/BWL	3.13
Waterplane area	275 sq. ft. (25.55 sq. m)
Pounds per inch immersion (LPI)	1,465 lb. (666 kg)
Ballast	11,200 lb. (5,091 kg)
Displacement—half-load condition	27,000 lb. (12,273 kg)
Displacement—light ship (LSW)	23,220 lb. (10,555 kg)
Ballast–displacement ratio (BDR, using half-load displacement)	0.41
Displacement–length ratio (DLR, using half-load displacement)	258
Sail area (SA)	945 sq. ft. (87.79 sq. m)
Foretriangle $17 \times 55.25 \div 2 =$	470 ft.^{2} (43.66 m^2)
Main $19.50 \times 48.75 \div 2 =$	475 ft.^{2} (44.13 m^2)
Sail area–displacement ratio (SADR, using half-load displacement)	16.77
Fuel capacity	120 gal. U.S. (454 L)
Water capacity	180 gal. U.S. (681 L)
LPG capacity	40 lb. (18 kg)
Horsepower at 3,000/2,000 rpm	50 hp/20 hp
Propeller	18 in. (460 mm)
Speed: maximum/cruise	8.3 knots/ 7.0 knots
Range at cruise speed	102 hr., 714 nm

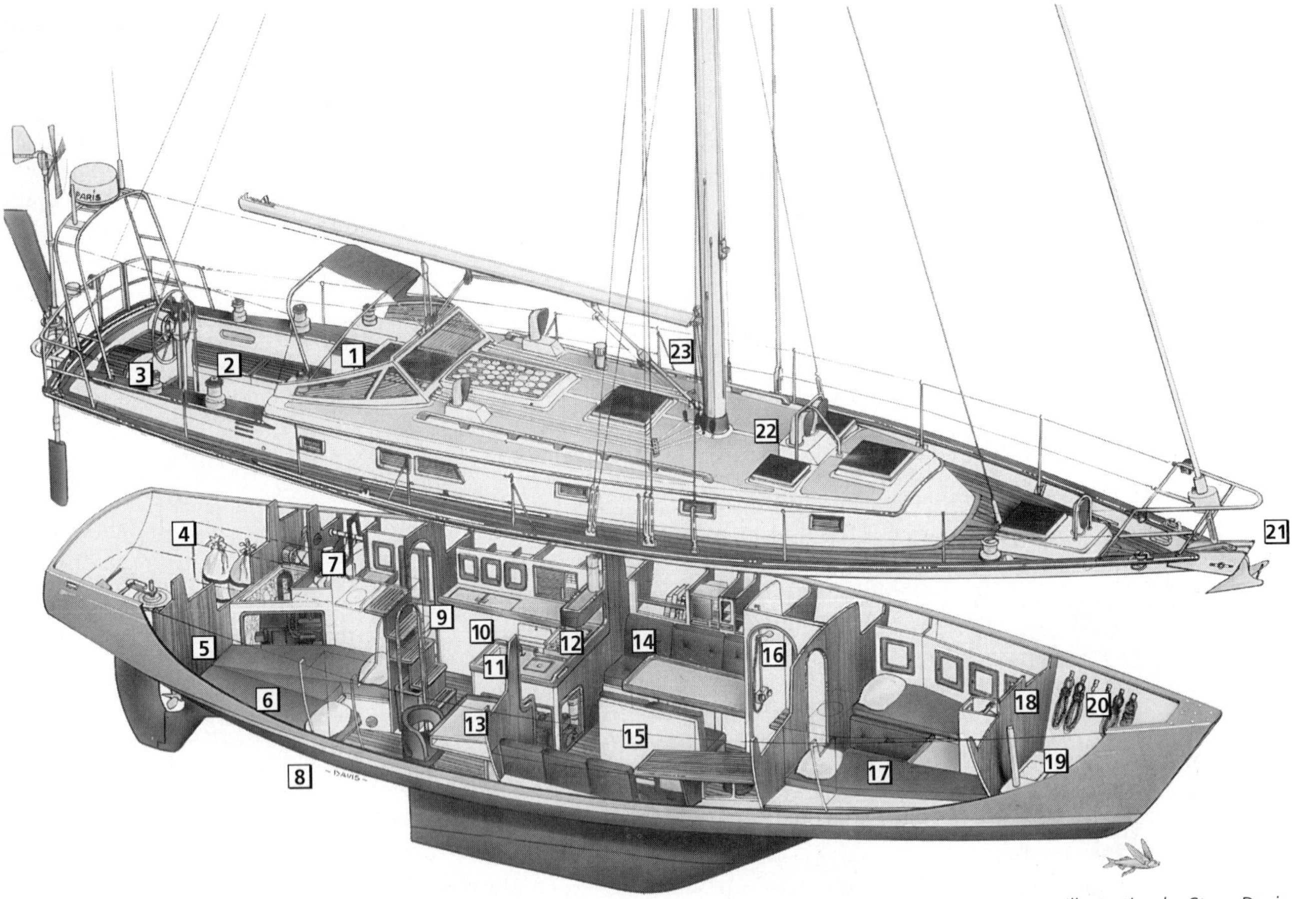

Illustration by Steve Davis

Paris 43 Features

1. Protected watchkeeping stations with good visibility
2. Cockpit seats, parallel to the centerline, long enough to sleep on, with sealed lockers beneath that drain to the cockpit well
3. Room to move around the wheel
4. Sealed lockers for LPG and gasoline stowage
5. Watertight bulkhead
6. V-berths at sea, with lee cloths, that convert to a double at anchor
7. Large wet locker with ducted hot air from the engine compartment
8. Tankage low and on the centerline
9. Toilet faces aft with good support on both sides
10. G-shaped galley, alongside companionway, with plenty of support
11. Athwartships-mounted sinks on the centerline
12. Athwartships-mounted gimbaled stove
13. Large chart table alongside companionway
14. All saloon berths parallel to the centerline, with lee cloths, designed to make excellent sea berths
15. Additional tankage low and on the centerline
16. Independent shower stall with high sill for clothes washing
17. Forecabin far enough aft for the berths to be usable at sea except in really rough conditions, with the berths almost parallel to the centerline; the port berth converts to a double at anchor
18. Watertight bulkhead
19. Deep, narrow chain locker low in the boat and well aft
20. Large forepeak with access from deck for stowage of ground tackle and sails
21. Bow rollers that will accommodate plough-type and Danforth-type anchors side by side
22. Excellent ventilation provided by opening hatches and Dorade vents
23. Rigid vang

CHAPTER 1

Note: For comparison purposes, to make meaningful use of those formulas using displacement, it is important to make a reasonably accurate estimate of half-load payload, with the kind of options, gear, and equipment you will have onboard. The easiest way to do this is to estimate your half-load payload in abstraction from any particular boat, but including everything you expect to put on whatever boat you buy (referred to in chapter 1 as your Personal Increment Number [PIN]), and to then add this to the light-ship weight (or LCC) of boats of interest (with some adjustment for what comes as standard equipment in the light-ship weight package; see chapter 1). If necessary, use a separate sheet of paper to answer these questions.

1. Numbers, Formulas, and Specifications

1.1 LOA (ft.):

1.2 LOH (ft.):

1.3 LWL (ft.):

1.4 B_{max} (ft.):

1.5 BWL (ft.):

1.6 Draft (ft.):

1.7 Mast Height (Note: Under 65 ft., including antennas, is necessary for the U.S. Intracoastal Waterway):

1.8 Displacement (LSW or LCC, lb.):

1.9 Displacement (HLD with all cruising options and tankage; i.e., LSW or LCC plus PIN, lb.):

1.10 Displacement volume in cubic feet (HLD ÷ 64):

1.11 Ballast (lb.):

1.12 Sail Area—main (sq. ft.):

1.13 Sail Area—100 percent foretriangle (sq. ft.):

1.14 Sail Area (main plus 100 percent foretriangle):

1.15 Length–Beam Ratio (LWL ÷ 0.9 × B_{max}):

1.16 Ballast Ratio (ballast ÷ HLD):

1.17 Displacement–Length Ratio $\frac{(HLD \div 2{,}240)}{(0.01 \times LWL)^3}$:

1.18 Speed–Length Ratio ($8.26 \div DLR^{0.311}$)

1.19 Maximum Speed ($SLR \times \sqrt{LWL}$)

1.20 Waterplane Area (LWL × BWL × 0.70, sq. ft.):

1.21 Pounds Per Inch of Immersion (waterplane area × 5.33):

1.22 1 Percent of Waterline Length (in.):

1.23 Maximum Half-Load PIN: lower of (1 percent of LWL × Pounds Per Inch of Immersion) or (20% of LSW):

1.24 Sail Area–Displacement Ratio [$SA \div (HLD)^{2/3}$]:

1.25 Point of Maximum Stability:

1.26 Limit of Positive Stability (LPS; AVS):

1.27 Stability Ratio:

1.28 Stability Index (IMS):

1.29 Capsize Screening Value ($\frac{B_{max}}{\sqrt[3]{\text{displacement volume}}}$):

1.30 STIX Number:

1.31 Fuel Capacity:

1.32 Water Capacity:

1.33 Engine Make, Model, and Horsepower:

1.34 AC Generator Make, Model, and Horsepower:

2. Hull Construction

2.1 Does the hull have a ten-year blister-free warranty?

2.2 Is the principal resin orthophthalic, isophthalic, or vinylester?

2.3 Is there at least a vinylester or epoxy barrier coat?

2.4 Is there a bonded-in ground plane?

2.5 Is there cored construction?

Below the waterline?

Above the waterline?

If so, is the core fully sealed wherever it is penetrated and, if so, how?

Is the external skin adequate to withstand impact and abrasion in a grounding?

2.6 What is the method of deck construction?

How is the deck core sealed in way of through-deck fasteners?

Does all deck hardware have accessible backing blocks?

Describe the hull-to-deck joint:

2.7 Does the hull have adequate structural reinforcement for offshore work?

3. Keel

3.1	What type of keel (e.g., bulb, wing)?
	Is the keel made of lead?
	Is the keel internal or external?
	If external, what is the keel bolt material?
	Are keel bolts accessible?
	Are keel bolts replaceable?
	What is the keel sweep-back angle?
	Is the keel toe rounded?
3.2	Will the hull absorb severe grounding stresses without hull or keel damage?

4. Skeg and Rudder

4.1	What is the rudder configuration (spade, half skeg, full skeg)?
4.2	If full skeg, is the lower rudder bearing at the base of the skeg?
4.3	Will the keel hit the bottom before the skeg and/or rudder?
4.4	Will the skeg and/or rudder absorb severe grounding stresses?
4.5	How is the rudder shaft sealed?
4.6	Is the shaft seal readily accessible?

5. Strut

5.1	Does the boat have a propeller strut?
	Is this a P or V strut?
	How is this strut mounted?
	Are the fasteners accessible?
5.2	Is the propeller accessible from the surface of the water with a face mask and snorkel?

6. Hull Sections

6.1	Is there an effective central sump?
6.2	At what angle of heel will the bilge no longer contain bilge water?
6.3	If the hull construction includes an interior grid, do all compartments have adequate drainage to the bilge at all normal angles of heel?
6.4	Where are the fuel and water tanks?
6.5	Are they usable on both tacks?

CHAPTER 2

7. The Rig

7.1	Rig type (e.g., sloop, cutter, ketch, fractional)?
7.2	Deck-stepped or keel-stepped mast?
	If keel-stepped, is there a sealing ring on deck of adequate height to properly seal the aperture?
7.3	Are the spreaders swept back?
7.4	Do the spreader sockets spread loads over a large area?
7.5	Rod or wire rigging?
	If wire, is it 304 stainless steel or 316 (should be 316)?
7.6	Shroud angles (should be at least 10 degrees, preferably 13)?
7.7	Standing rigging terminal type (e.g., swaged, Norseman; Sta-Lok or Norseman preferred)?
	Full toggling?
	Are the chainplates properly aligned with their stays and shrouds?
	Do the turnbuckles (i.e., bottle screws) have stainless steel or bronze threads (bronze preferred)?
7.8	List the sails (name, size, fabric, and weight):
7.9	Foresail reefing type?
	Is it fully toggled at top and bottom?
	Will it prevent halyard wrap?
	Is there a fairlead for the reefing line onto the reefing drum?
7.10	Are the foresails sheeted inboard or outboard?
7.11	Can the full foresail be sheeted in tight without fouling the spreaders or shrouds?
7.12	Sheeting angles:
	Headsail?
	Staysail (if fitted)?

7.13 Describe the mainsail reefing system:

Can the mainsail be reefed by one person working from a single location?

7.14 Describe the mainsail traveler:

7.15 Describe the vang (rigid is preferred):

7.16 Can a preventer be easily rigged and controlled from the cockpit?

7.17 Describe downwind, reaching, and spinnaker pole arrangements (on-mast stowage is preferred):

7.18 Describe sail-handling layout, winches, line-stoppers (rope clutches), etc.:

7.19 Is there a separate trysail track (and trysail)?

7.20 Can the main halyard shackle and the top of the boom be reached for halyard attachment and removal, and putting on the sail cover?

7.21 Are there mast steps or ratlines?

8. Cockpit

8.1 Center cockpit or aft cockpit?

If center, is there reasonable access over the coamings?

Can you exit/enter in rough weather without risk of being thrown over the lifelines?

8.2 Is the boom well clear of heads in the cockpit?

8.3 Is the mainsheet traveler and sheet out of the way?

8.4 Is the companionway sill set well above the cockpit sole?

8.5 Can the dropboards (washboards) be locked in place?

8.6 How is the cockpit drained?

How long will a completely flooded cockpit take to drain?

Will the leeward side of the seats and the cockpit footwell drain when heeled?

8.7 Does the windward sidedeck dump water into the cockpit?

8.8 Are the cockpit seats long enough and wide enough to sleep on?

8.9 Are the cockpit seats close enough to brace oneself on the opposite seat?

8.10 Are the cockpit coamings high enough and angled outboard enough to be comfortable as seatbacks?

8.11 Are the tops of the coamings comfortable to sit on?

8.12 Are the primary winches readily accessible from the wheel and when "sacked out"?

Can the primaries be cranked comfortably?

Do the sheets make a fairlead onto the winches?

8.13 Do the coamings incorporate boxes for lines, winch handles, and miscellaneous stowage?

8.14 Steering manufacturer/type (e.g., Whitlock Cobra)?

8.15 Is there good visibility both from the wheel or tiller and when "sacked out"?

8.16 Is there good access around the wheel?

8.17 Is the top of the wheel a comfortable height (a little above waist height)?

8.18 Are the steering-system components accessible?

Are all components bolted in place with backing blocks and adequately braced?

Is the steering system protected from stowed objects falling into it?

Is the cockpit sole adequately reinforced?

8.19 Emergency steering accessibility?

Is the emergency tiller easy to install?

Does it have the leverage, swinging room, and strength to steer the boat in heavy seas?

8.20 Is there an autopilot?

If so, what make and type?

Does it have the power to handle heavy weather?

8.21 Is there a wind vane?

If so, what make and type?

Does it have the power to handle light winds and heavy weather?

8.22 Is there a cockpit table?

8.23 What about drinkholders?

8.24 Cockpit cushions?

8.25 Are the cockpit locker lids sealed?

How and where do the cockpit lockers drain?

8.26 Are the engine controls readily accessible from the wheel or tiller without having to bend down?

Are they in a position where they won't foul sheets and lines?

8.27 Is the engine panel set above likely cockpit-flooding levels?

8.28 Are fuel-tank vents well clear of possible flooding and well above the heeled waterline?

8.29 Are cockpit instruments visible from both the helm and the "sacked-out" position?

8.30 If the instruments are mounted on the binnacle, can they be read when standing at the wheel without crouching down?

8.31 Is there a manual bilge pump accessible from the helm?

9. Dodgers and Biminis

9.1 Is there standing headroom?

9.2 Is there easy entry and exit from the cockpit?

9.3 Do the dodger and bimini have the strength to resist gales, boarding waves, and being swung on?

9.4 Can the covers be removed without frame disassembly?

9.5 Will the frames and covers fold down in such a way as to not obstruct boat operations?

9.6 Is the base of the dodger attached to a coaming molded into the deck (to keep water out)?

9.7 Is there good visibility both when standing at the wheel or tiller and sitting?

9.8 Is there good protection for the normal watchkeeping station?

9.9 Do the dodger and bimini shed water outside the cockpit?

9.10 Are there removable covers for all windows?

9.11 Are the dodger and bimini waterproof (including seams and zippers)?

9.12 Can side and aft screens be added?

9.13 Can the forward face of the dodger be opened for ventilation?

9.14 Can the winches and rope clutches be operated without fouling the dodger and bimini (either up or down)?

10. Stowage

10.1 Is there a sealed, vented locker for two 5-gallon (19 L) LPG bottles?

10.2 Is there a sealed, vented locker for outboard motor tanks and fuel?

10.3 Is there stowage for outboard motors?

10.4 Is there a crane to get the outboard motors on and off?

10.5 How will a dinghy be stowed?

What size dinghy?

How do you get the dinghy on and off?

Are there davits?

10.6 Is there a life raft and how is it stowed?

10.7 What about a Lifesling or Crew-Saver and COB pole?

10.8 Is there stowage for:

Diesel cans?

Water cans?

Large funnel?

Fenders?

Dock lines and spare lines?

Shore-power cord and adapters?

Water hose?

Spare length of rigging?

Sail covers when at sea?

Sails?

Life jackets?

Hatchboards when not in use?

Fishing tackle?

Snorkeling (and diving) gear?

Dive compressor?

Binoculars, flashlight, hand-bearing compass, spotlight, foghorn, snatch blocks?

Stern anchor and rode?

Spare anchors and rodes?

Boat hook?

Deck brush and sponges?

Buckets?

10.9	Is there a suitable location to mount the following?
	Wind vane?
	Wind generator?
	Solar panels?
	Boarding ladder?
10.10	Is there stowage protected from all contact with salt water for:
	Refrigeration condensing unit?
	Autopilot electronics?
	Inverter?
	Watermaker?
	AC generator?

11. Deck Design and Layout

11.1	Will the portholes, windows, and hatches withstand boarding waves?
	Are hatches close to the centerline?
	If the hatches are open, what is the down-flooding angle (it should be a minimum of 90 degrees, preferably a minimum of 100)?
11.2	Is there adequate nonskid on the side decks and cabintop?
11.3	Is there a clear run forward along the side decks?
	Are the headsail reefing lines, sheets, cars, and tracks out of the way?
	Are there hand/footholds all the way forward?
11.4	Are jacklines accessible from the cockpit with access forward without unclipping?
	Are the jackline–pad eye mountings strong enough to take shock loads?
11.5	Are the lifelines a minimum of 30 inches (760 mm) high (higher is better)?
	How are the stanchions mounted? Consider strength/leaks:
	Are the gates in line with the cockpit to make loading of supplies easier?
	Is the freeboard low enough to make boarding and unloading supplies from a dinghy relatively easy?
	Do the side supports (braces) to gate stanchions come to the top of the stanchions?
	Are the lifeline attachment points formed from drilled metal plates rather than bent rod?
	Are the lifelines made from 316 stainless steel?
11.6	Is there a double bow roller?
	Will it take a Danforth-type anchor alongside a plough-type anchor?
	With the boat pitching, can the anchors be launched and retrieved without fouling each other?
	With the boat pitching, can the anchors hang from the bow roller and rotate without hitting the topsides?
	Are there angled cheek plates or welded pipes on either side of the bow rollers to provide a fairlead?
	Are the cheek plates close enough to the bow rollers to prevent rodes from jamming?
	Is there a method for securing the anchors at sea?
11.7	Are there large, well-mounted cleats in line with the bow rollers?
	Are there additional cleats in line with the bow chocks/hawseholes?
	Are there midships and stern cleats with appropriate chafing protection on the bulwarks and toerail?
11.8	Is all deck hardware backed with accessible metal plates?
11.9	What is the windlass type?
11.10	Is there a dam behind the windlass to contain mud?
11.11	Is there a saltwater washdown pump?
11.12	How is a rope rode stowed?
11.13	Will a chain rode fully self-stow?

CHAPTER 3

12. Basic Layout Below

12.1	Are the navigation station and galley close to the center of motion?
12.2	Are the head and saloon reasonably close to the center of motion?
12.3	Is there a wet locker or head compartment close to the companionway?
12.4	Are there comfortable sea berths for the entire crew close to the center of motion?
12.5	Is there a dedicated berth and stowage space for all long-term crew members?

13. Keeping Things in Place

13.1	How are cabinet doors and lockers kept closed (no finger latches)?
13.2	How are drawers kept closed?
13.3	Are hatches in the cabinsole locked down?
13.4	Is the icebox lid locked down?
13.5	Are the batteries, tanks, and stove adequately locked down?
13.6	Are fiddle rails high enough and vertical enough?
	Do fiddle rails have clean-out slots?
13.7	Are there adequate handholds inside the boat at all angles of heel?
	Are they reachable by shorter people?
13.8	Are the treads on the companionway ladder sufficiently nonskid?
	Can you safely dash up and down the ladder, backwards and forwards, in rough weather?

14. Insulation and Ventilation

14.1	Are the hull sides and cabintop insulated?
14.2	If metal-framed portholes and hatches are used, will they drip on berths?
14.3	Is there a driprail/grabrail beneath the portholes?
14.4	Do the portholes have effective external drains?
14.5	Are there louvers or cane inserts in all locker doors?
14.6	How many hatches are there, and where?
	Is there a hatch in the foredeck?
	Does the forward hatch hinge open on its forward edge (it should)?
	Is there a hatch in the head (over the shower compartment)?
	Does it hinge open on its forward edge (it should)?
	Is there a hatch over the galley stove?
	Does it hinge open on its forward edge (it should)?
	Do all other hatches hinge open on their aft edge?
	Can the hatches be left open in a rain squall without admitting rain?
	Is there provision for adding wind scoops?
	Can the hatches be closed with the wind scoops in place?
	Will the wind scoops work under an awning?
14.7	Are there opening portlights for cross ventilation in marinas?
14.8	Is there adequate ventilation of a deck saloon or pilot-house?
14.9	Are there Dorade vents for ventilation in rough weather and when the boat is unattended?
	What are the locations of Dorade vents?
14.10	Is an aft cabin adequately ventilated?
14.11	Is a quarter berth adequately ventilated?
14.12	Are there easy-to-fit-and-store bug screens for all hatches and portholes?

15. Air Conditioning and Heating

15.1	Will the boat require an air conditioner?
	If so, does it have the necessary shore-power connection?
	Is there space for an AC generator?
	If central AC is used, where will the unit and ducting go?
15.2	Will the boat require a heater?
	If so, will it be a stand-alone unit or central heat?
	Where will a stand-alone unit go?
	If central heat, where and what about the ducting?
15.3	Is there a carbon monoxide detector (there should be)?

16. Navigation Station

16.1	Is the navigation station readily accessible from the companionway?
	Is it completely protected from spray?
16.2	Is there a minimum 36- × 30-inch (910 × 760 mm) chart table?
	Is there accessible stowage for charts?
	Is there stowage for dividers, parallel rules, pencils, a pencil sharpener, etc.?
	Is there stowage for light lists, cruising guides, almanacs, etc.?
	Is there stowage for a flashlight, a hand-bearing compass, and miscellaneous odds and ends?

Is there stowage for flares, a bell, and a foghorn?

16.3 Are the backs of the distribution panels easy to access?

16.4 Is there a replaceable fascia panel large enough for electronics?

16.5 Is there nighttime lighting powerful enough to enable charts to be read?

Can the navigation station be used at night without disturbing the off-watch crew?

17. Wet Locker

17.1 Is it close to the companionway?

17.2 Is it large enough to hold four sets of foul-weather gear plus sea boots?

17.3 Is it watertight with a drain to the bilge?

17.4 What about stowage for life jackets, an abandon-ship bag, harnesses, and safety lines?

18. Galley

18.1 Is it close to both the cockpit and the saloon?

18.2 Is it out of the way of through-ship traffic?

18.3 Does it have an enclosed shape that offers good support when heeled and in rough conditions?

18.4 Is the stove gimbaled?

Can it swing freely?

Will the stove obstruct other lockers when the boat is heeled?

Will pots on the stovetop clear surrounding lockers when the stove swings?

18.5 Can the cook keep to one side of the stove?

18.6 Are there sufficient bracing surfaces to free up both hands for the stove?

18.7 Is there a grab bar in front of the stove?

18.8 Is there a hatch or vent over the stove?

18.9 What is the stove fuel (LPG is preferred)?

If LPG, is there a remotely controlled shut-off valve?

Is the shut-off accessible without reaching over the stove?

18.10 Is there a microwave?

If so, is it mounted so that its door faces fore or aft?

18.11 Is the dishwashing location offset from the stove?

18.12 What is the countertop material (Corian is best)?

Are the sinks set below the countertop?

Does the countertop have a molded-in backsplash?

Is the sink counter sealed with a fiddle rail from the rest of the counter?

18.13 Are there two sinks or one?

What is the sink size?

Do the sinks drain on both tacks and at all angles of heel without at any time going below the waterline (they should)?

Are the sink drains offset to prevent spraying when pounding?

Do the sinks have U-traps (not advisable, except when they drain to a gray-water tank)?

18.14 Are all seacocks readily accessible?

18.15 Is there a backup manual water pump?

18.16 Is there appropriate dedicated stowage for dishes, cutlery, mugs, and glasses?

18.17 What about pots; a pressure cooker; frying, baking, pizza, and bread pans; a teakettle?

18.18 Is there an accessible trash can with a mechanism for holding a bin liner in place?

18.19 Is there a condiments-and-spice rack or locker?

18.20 Is shelving adequately fiddled?

18.21 Are locker doors large enough to make shelves readily accessible?

18.22 Is there a paper-towel holder and fire extinguisher?

18.23 Is there stowage for:

Potholders and dish towels?

Plastic storage bags, trash bags, aluminum foil, cling wrap, etc.?

Cleaning supplies?

Paper towels?

18.24 Food stowage for:

Vegetables?

Fruit?

6½ cubic feet (184 L) of canned and packaged goods (four people for one week)?

18.25 Is there a chopping board that won't slide around?

18.26 Is the galley easy to clean (especially around the stove and sinks)?

18.27 Is the galley well lit (especially under countertops, over the stove and sinks, and over the icebox openings)?

18.28 Can the galley be used at night without disturbing the off-watch crew?

18.29 Consider the following icebox questions (systems implications are considered later):

Are the boxes easy to get into?

Can you get to the bottom of the boxes without having to unload everything?

Can you reach to the bottom of the boxes?

Can you see inside the boxes?

Are the boxes easy to clean?

Is there a front-opening door?

19. Saloon

19.1 Is there adequate headroom throughout?

19.2 Can the settee berths be used as sea berths?

Long enough?

Wide enough?

Straight enough?

Parallel to centerline?

19.3 Do the settees provide comfortable seating?

Seat height ± 18 inches (460 mm) (with cushions)?

Seat depth 21 to 24 inches (530–600 mm)?

Seatback ± 18 inches (460 mm) high, angled outboard 15 degrees?

19.4 Do the sea berths have lee cloths?

19.5 How thick is the seat-cushion foam?

Is it high quality/high density?

Are the cushion covers made of a suitable material?

Are the covers designed to prevent condensation/mildew?

Will the cushions stay in place at all angles of heel?

Are they nevertheless easy to remove to get at lockers?

19.6 Is it possible to sit down to a meal without blocking traffic through the boat?

19.7 If the table has a removable leaf, does it have a secure stowage place?

19.8 Does the table have fiddle rails?

If so, are they removable?

19.9 If the table doubles as a berth, is it easy to put up and down?

19.10 Is the table strong enough and mounted securely enough for heavy shock loads?

19.11 Is there a replaceable fascia for mounting entertainment equipment (i.e., TV, VCR, CDs, DVDs)?

19.12 Is there adequate customized stowage for:

Books (are the shelves properly fiddled)?

Videos, CDs, DVDs, and cassette tapes?

Wine and liquor?

20. Cabins

20.1 Is there standing headroom for dressing and undressing?

20.2 Is there adequate headroom to climb in and out of bed?

20.3 Are the berths usable when heeled and when rolling from side to side?

20.4 Is there adequate headroom and back support to read comfortably in bed?

Is there adequate lighting suitably located for reading in bed?

Is there a place to put books, reading glasses, etc.?

20.5 Is there a fan for every berth?

20.6 Are there lee cloths where appropriate?

20.7 Is there sufficient closet space?

20.8 How easy is it to make the bed?

20.9 How easy is it to access lockers under the bed?

20.10 Is there insulation from engine noise and heat, cockpit noise, and boat traffic?

20.11 Is there adequate ventilation?

21. Head Compartment

21.1 Is there a separate shower stall large enough to comfortably shower (26 × 26 in./660 × 660 mm)?

Are there grab handles and a seat in the shower stall?

Will the pan drain on both tacks?

Does the pan have a raised sill?

Can the showerhead be handheld as well as mounted on a bulkhead fixture?

Is there a place to put soap, shampoo, etc.?

21.2 Is the head compartment large enough to put on and take off foul-weather gear?

21.3 Does the door open inward (it should)?

Is it strong enough to withstand being fallen against?

21.4 Are there adequate handholds?

21.5 Does the toilet face fore and aft with solid bracing on both sides?

21.6 Can the toilet surround be hosed down?

21.7 If the toilet rim is below the waterline at any angle of heel, is there a siphon break and valve on the suction line?

Is there a siphon break on the toilet discharge?

Is the suction through-hull forward of the discharge or on the other side of the hull?

Are both through-hulls immersed at all angles of heel?

21.8 Is the toilet plumbed with high-quality sanitation hose?

Are all hose ends and hoses accessible and easy to remove?

21.9 Does the holding tank have a level indicator?

21.10 Is there a mechanism for pumping out the holding tank at sea?

21.11 Will the sink be below the waterline at some angle of heel?

If so, consider discharging it into the toilet?

21.12 Are all through-hulls readily accessible?

21.13 Is there nighttime lighting so the watchkeeper will not lose night vision?

CHAPTER 4

22. Refrigeration

22.1 Icebox volumes:

22.2 Interior surface areas:

22.3 Insulation type and thickness:

22.4 Heat influx (refrigerator box)?

22.5 Heat influx (freezer box)?

22.6 Super insulation?

Estimated heat influx with super insulation:

22.7 Are the iceboxes up against the engine-room bulkhead (they should not be)?

22.8 Do the icebox doors and lids have double seals?

22.9 Is any drain sealed with a valve or U-trap?

Heat Influx Per Square Foot of Interior Box Surface Per 24 Hours Using Foam Insulation

INSULATION THICKNESS, in. (cm)	APPROXIMATE "R" VALUE	REFRIGERATOR BOX (Btu)	FREEZER BOX (Btu)
2 (5)	10	150	280
3 (7.5)	15	120	225
4 (10)	20	100	185
5 (12.5)	25	90	170
6 (15)	30	80	160

Note: 1 kilowatt (kW) = 3,413 Btu's.

22.10 Refrigeration unit (manufacturer and model)?

22.11 Cold plates (refrigerator—Btu capacity and estimated hold-over time)?

22.12 Cold plates (freezer—Btu capacity and estimated hold-over time)?

22.13 Do the cold plates contain a true eutectic solution (they should)?

22.14 DC powered, estimated DC load (amp-hours)?

Will the refrigeration unit operate automatically whenever the engine is running?

22.15 Can the cold plates be gotten in and out of the icebox without tearing it apart?

23. Seven-Day Load

23.1 Will the refrigeration unit operate when the boat is anchored out and left unattended?

23.2 If so, seven-day refrigeration load:

+ Miscellaneous seven-day load:

Total seven-day load:

24. DC System Components

24.1 What is the total daily DC energy drain in amp-hours?

24.2 What is the seven-day refrigeration load (if applicable)?

24.3 House battery capacity (it should be up to four times the daily load and a minimum of 120 percent of the seven-day load)?

24.4 One or two house banks (one is preferable)?

Are the house batteries quality deep-cycle batteries (they should be)?

Does the windlass have its own battery (it should not)?

Are all the batteries the same type and from the same manufacturer?

Are the batteries in a cool environment?

Are the batteries secured in a vented battery box/ compartment?

Are wet-type batteries readily accessible for maintenance?

24.5 Is there a dedicated, isolated cranking battery?

Engine-cranking battery capacity (CCA as specified in engine manual)?

24.6 Alternator hot rating (it should be 25 to 40 percent of the total house-bank capacity)?

One or two alternators?

Alternator model(s)?

24.7 Multistep regulator model?

Are the voltage regulation parameters matched to the batteries?

24.8 Systems monitor model?

24.9 Battery paralleling (manual, diodes, or battery combiner; if diodes, consider removal)?

24.10 Wind generator?

24.11 Solar panels?

24.12 Voltage regulation for wind generator and solar panels?

24.13 Is a DC to AC inverter correctly sized (it should be based on the maximum continuous AC load)?

Is an inverter easy to turn off?

Is the DC side over-current-protected?

Is there an isolation switch in the DC side (a breaker serves this purpose)?

24.14 Is DC lighting primarily fluorescent?

24.15 Are fans a low-energy type?

25. DC Panel

25.1 Check which of the following are installed:

- ❑ Voltmeter?
- ❑ Ammeter?
- ❑ Systems monitor?
- ❑ Bilge-pump(s) panel?
- ❑ Main breaker? (specify amps)
- ❑ Circuit breakers (specify amps)?
- ❑ Tricolor?
- ❑ Running lights?
- ❑ Bow light?
- ❑ Anchor light?
- ❑ Strobe?
- ❑ Compass light?
- ❑ Spreader lights?
- ❑ Autopilot?
- ❑ SSB?
- ❑ Radar?
- ❑ VHF?
- ❑ Cell phone?
- ❑ Weatherfax?
- ❑ Spotlight?

❑ Navigation 1?	❑ Navigation 2?
❑ Cabin lights port?	❑ Cabin lights starboard?
❑ Engine-room lights?	❑ Engine-room blower?
❑ Fans?	❑ Entertainment?
❑ Stereo?	❑ DC outlets?
❑ Freshwater?	❑ Saltwater washdown?
❑ Shower pump-out?	❑ Macerator?
❑ Oil-change pump?	❑ Fuel-sampling pump?
❑ LPG?	❑ Refrigerator?
❑ Panel lights?	❑ Watermaker?
❑ Heater?	❑ Other?
❑ Other?	

25.2 Are there separate breakers/switches for the windlass and inverter?

26. Circuit Specifications

26.1 Are circuits wired for a 3 percent voltage drop?

26.2 Is tinned, oil-resistant, multistranded UL-1426 BC5W2 (or equivalent) cable used throughout?

26.3 Are terminals plated copper?

26.4 Are terminals heat-shrink sealed and labeled?

26.5 Are cables adequately supported (at least every 18 in./460 mm)?

26.6 Are cables protected against chafe where they pass through bulkheads?

26.7 Are all circuits properly over-current-protected?

26.8 Is there a comprehensive wiring diagram?

27. AC System

27.1 Will there be air conditioning?

If so, an AC generator is needed—make and model; volt and amp ratings?

27.2 AC inlets (in the U.S., one or two 30-amp, or one 50-amp)?

If there are two 30-amp inlets, when only one shore-power feed is available, will the selector switch allow all the ship's circuits to be fed from this single inlet?

27.3 Is there an appropriate shore-power cord, in good condition, with locking end fittings?

27.4 Are there adapters onboard for different shore-side outlets?

27.5 Is the cable run from the shore-power inlet to the AC panel more than 10 feet?

If so, is there a breaker near the inlet?

27.6 Is there a galvanic isolator or isolation transformer?

27.7 Make and model?

27.8 Will all the AC circuits also be powered by the inverter?

If so, put the inverter in series with the shore-power inlet:

If there are noninverter AC loads, establish a separate inverter subpanel:

27.9 Is the AC system properly grounded back ashore and to the DC system?

Check that the neutral is not connected to ground onboard:

27.10 Are all AC circuits fully over-current-protected?

27.11 Is there a whole-boat GFCI (RCCB) or, alternatively, GFCIs (RCCBs) in the head and galley?

27.12 Is tinned, oil-resistant, multistranded UL-1426 BC5W2 (or equivalent) cable used throughout?

27.13 Are all AC connections made inside protected enclosures that require tools for access?

27.14 Is there physical separation between AC and DC circuits?

27.15 Are all cables adequately supported and protected against chafe?

27.16 Is there a comprehensive wiring diagram?

28. AC Panel

28.1 Check which of the following are installed:

❑ Voltmeter?	❑ Ammeter?
❑ Frequency meter?	❑ Ground-continuity test?
❑ Reverse-polarity indicator/alarm?	❑ Ship/shore/generator selector switch?
❑ Circuit breakers (specify amps, and include if on separate inverter bus bar)?	❑ Microwave?
❑ Water heater?	❑ Outlets port?
❑ Outlets starboard?	❑ Engine-room outlets?

- ❑ Battery charger?
- ❑ Inverter?
- ❑ Watermaker?
- ❑ Refrigeration?
- ❑ Air conditioning?
- ❑ Dive compressor?
- ❑ Washer/dryer?
- ❑ Trash compactor?
- ❑ Ice machine?
- ❑ Other?
- ❑ Other?

29. Bonding and Lightning Protection

29.1 Are isolated bronze through-hulls bonded (they should not be in most cases)?

29.2 Ensure cathodic protection for bonded underwater metal fittings:

29.3 Are the mast, chainplates, engine, and other large metal objects bonded as per ABYC for lightning protection?

29.4 Is there an adequate ground plane for the lightning protection system?

CHAPTER 5

30. Engine and Propeller

30.1 What horsepower for propulsive purposes?

30.2 What horsepower for auxiliary systems?

Alternator(s)?

Refrigeration?

Watermaker?

Dive compressor?

30.3 Engine choice?

30.4 Propeller pitch, diameter, and blade area?

30.5 Propeller choice?

30.6 Can the propeller be changed relatively easily in the water?

30.7 If it is a fixed-pitch propeller, does the boat need a propeller shaft brake and, if so, is it fitted?

30.8 Does the raw-water circuit have zincs?

If so, where?

If not, does it need them?

30.9 Is there a vented loop on the raw-water injection line?

30.10 Does the exhaust system conform to the minimum specifications necessary to keep water out?

30.11 Are all exhaust-hose connections double-clamped?

30.12 Are the clamps all 300 series stainless steel (including the screws)?

30.13 If the water-lift muffler is not fire-retardant, is there a high-temperature or low-flow alarm?

30.14 Is the water-injection elbow cast in one piece (if not, consider the corrosion potential)?

30.15 Is there a fuel-tank sampling pump?

30.16 Are the fuel filters readily accessible, including in rough weather?

30.17 Is the engine compartment adequately noise-insulated?

30.18 Is there a sufficient airflow for combustion purposes?

30.19 Will the heat create problems in accommodation spaces?

30.20 Can the following be readily accessed?

All belts?

Alternator-tensioning device?

All filters (fuel and oil)?

Dipstick, including for pumping out oil?

Transmission for pumping out oil?

Any zincs?

Heat exchanger for cleaning?

Raw-water pump impeller?

Raw-water injection-line vented loop?

Exhaust-injection elbow?

Block and heat exchanger drains (for winterizing)?

Coolant overflow bottle?

Engine feet for setting alignment?

Top end for setting valve clearances, pulling injectors, etc.?

Starter motor and solenoid?

Engine and transmission controls?

Shaft seal?

	Engine pan for cleaning spills and retrieving tools?
30.21	Is the engine room well lit?
30.22	Is the propeller coupling adequately secured to its shaft (check dimples, torquing, and locking)?
	Is there a back-up hose clamp on the propeller shaft?
30.23	Is any hose on a flexible shaft seal in first-class condition?
	Are the hose clamps tight and all 300 series stainless steel?
30.24	Can the propeller and propeller shaft be pulled without removing the rudder?

31. Bilge Pumps

31.1	Is there a central sump to which all compartments drain at all angles of heel?
	If not, is there provision for pumping-out spaces where water will accumulate?
31.2	Are the necessary limber holes in place and large enough to be effective?
31.3	What type/capacity is the electric bilge pump (diaphragm/centrifugal)?
	If diaphragm, does it have a suitable filter in a readily accessible location?
31.4	If centrifugal:
	Is it readily accessible?
	Have the implications of low voltage and back pressure been factored into the estimated real-life output?
	Will the pump and its circuit safely handle a locked rotor state?
31.5	What type is the level switch?
	Is it adequately protected against likely failure modes (e.g., trash and oil)?
	Is the relationship among sump, switch, and discharge hose such that the pump will not short-cycle?
31.6	Is the pump discharge through-hull above the waterline at all angles of heel?
	If not, is the hose looped above the waterline at all angles of heel and fitted with a vented loop?
31.7	Does the discharge line have a check valve (if so, find a way to get rid of it)?
31.8	Is the bilge-pump and switch wiring fully protected from moisture and corrosion?
31.9	If it does corrode, can it cause stray-current corrosion of any through-hulls?
31.10	Is the pump wired so that it will operate when the boat is unattended?
31.11	Is this circuit properly over-current-protected?
31.12	Is there a back-up high-water alarm?
31.13	Is there a manual bilge pump operable from the helm?
	If so, what type/capacity?

32. Through-Hulls and Seacocks

32.1	Are all through-hulls and seacocks UL-listed?
32.2	Are all seacocks readily accessible even with gear stowed?
32.3	Are all through-hulls appropriately located in the hull for their purpose?
32.4	Has an attempt been made to minimize the number of through-hulls?
32.5	Are all seacocks easily winterized (including having the drains installed on the low side—amazingly, boatbuilders often forget this)?
32.6	Do all hoses connected to below-the-heeled waterline through-hulls meet the requirements of J2006 or similar standards?
32.7	Are all hoses clamped with all 300-series stainless steel clamps?

33. Plumbing

33.1	Is there more than one freshwater tank (there should be)?
33.2	Is there adequate tankage for the boat's intended use?
33.3	Are the tanks made of noncorrosive materials?
	Are they adequately baffled?
	Are they adequately secured?
	Can they be removed without tearing the boat apart?
	Can they be used on both tacks without sucking air?

	Are the tank vents located so that no salt water can enter at any angle of heel or when pooped?
33.4	How are tank levels tracked? Is this relatively easy to do?
33.5	Is the freshwater pump readily accessible?
	Is the pressure switch easy to replace?
33.6	Is there a manual freshwater pump in the galley?

34. LPG

34.1	Is the LPG installation up to ABYC standards?
34.2	Are LPG cylinders in a sealed locker vented overboard from its base?
	Are the cylinders adequately secured against movement?
	Are they new-style cylinders (if not, plan on replacing them)?
	Are all fittings and connections—except the final connection to appliances—inside the locker?
	Is there a pressure gauge?
	Is there a remotely controlled solenoid shut-down valve, operated from the galley?
	Can this solenoid be manually overridden if it fails?
	Is the solenoid large enough not to restrict gas flow when all appliances are lit?
34.3	Are all tubing runs secured at least every 18 inches (460 mm)?

PART 2
CRUISING SKILLS

Barreling along on a reach—a sailor's dream come true. (Courtesy Harken)

CHAPTER SEVEN

BOAT HANDLING UNDER POWER AND SAIL

So far, we have determined the kind of boat in which we wish to go cruising, and have put the systems we want into shipshape order. It is time to use the boat! In this chapter, we look at maneuvering and making way under both power and sail, starting with power.

MANEUVERING UNDER POWER

It is easy to drive a boat under power in open water—it is a lot like driving a car except that, if the boat has a tiller, the boat turns the opposite way that the tiller is pushed.

Typically, novice sailors have a tendency to oversteer, particularly when trying to hold a compass course. This results in a zigzag track through the water. The primary reason for this is the momentum developed by a boat as it turns, which causes it to keep turning after the wheel or tiller is centered. To avoid oversteering, the helmsperson should come out of the turn just a little before the boat has come around to the desired new track. Most people steer a more consistent course if they can steer to a fixed feature ashore. However, attention also must be given to the compass in case the boat is being set to one side or the other of its intended track (in which case, the compass course steadily changes even though the boat is still being steered for the same mark).

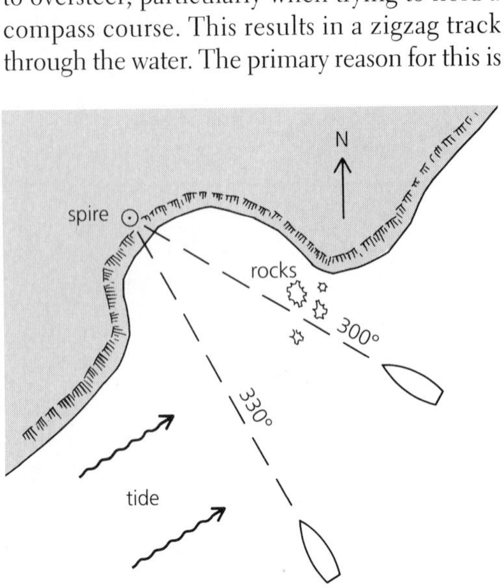

Steering to a fixed object ashore. It is important to monitor the compass to see if the boat is being set down by the tide.

It doesn't take long to get the hang of open-water helming. Difficulties come in close quarters and at slow speeds. Probably more accidents happen, more tempers become frayed, and more egos are bruised getting on and off docks and in and out of slips than in any other aspect of boating (anchoring is a close second; see chapter 9). As boating becomes ever more popular and marinas ever more crowded, the potential for getting into trouble increases. So let's look in some detail at this aspect of maneuvering under power.

Close Quarters Maneuvering under Power

The first thing to remember is that it is difficult to make generalizations. The amount of windage, the shape of the underbody, the relationship of the propeller to the keel and rudder, and so on all significantly impact how a boat handles. The slower the boat speed, the bigger the impact because as boat speed declines, the flow of water over the rudder diminishes, steering power (*steerageway*) is lost, and factors other than the rudder angle dominate the maneuvering picture.

It is at this time that a phenomenon known as *prop walk* becomes significant. On most cruising boats, the propeller turns in a *right-handed* direction; that is, looked at from astern when in forward gear, the propeller turns clockwise (a *left-handed* propeller turns counterclockwise). In reverse, the right-handed propeller turns counterclockwise (the left-handed propeller turns clockwise). An easy way to determine the direction of rotation of any propeller is to put the boat in forward and see which way the propeller shaft and its coupling are turning.

When a propeller is turning—in addition to its normal forward or backward force—it exerts a small sideways force. In forward gear, *a right-handed propeller tends to kick the stern to starboard; in reverse, it kicks it to port.* A left-handed propeller has the opposite effect.

The sideways kick is most pronounced when a boat is stationary and the engine is first put in gear, especially if the propeller is given a burst of power. In general, the greater the inertia of the boat and the stronger the burst of power, the more is the sideways kick. It is almost always more noticeable in reverse than it is in forward.

This picture must be qualified by the effect that the stream of water generated by the propeller has on the rudder. Assuming that the propeller is more or less in line with the rudder (which it is on almost all cruising boats), in forward gear the propeller drives a relatively strong flow of water (*prop wash*) past the rudder; however, in reverse, the flow of water sucked into the propeller past the rudder is relatively diffuse and weak. What this means is that in forward gear, the direction in which the rudder deflects the prop wash generally has more influence on how the boat turns than the prop walk; in reverse, the latter is true until the boat picks up enough speed (*sternway*) to produce a relatively fast water flow past the rudder.

Let's put these pieces together in terms of turning a boat in tight quarters. We'll assume that the boat has a single engine and propeller mounted more or less on the centerline, driving a right-handed propeller (the most common arrangement). The boat is dead in the water. The rudder is turned to starboard (right rudder) and a burst of power is applied in forward. The prop walk tends to kick the stern to starboard, but will be overwhelmed by the effect of the prop wash on the rudder, which will move the stern to port. If the boat is allowed to gather steerageway, the right turn is accentuated by the additional flow of water over the rudder.

With or without way on, if a burst of power is applied in reverse, the prop walk moves the

Below: *Right-handed and left-handed propellers.* Bottom: *Turning a boat with a right-handed propeller in tight quarters.*

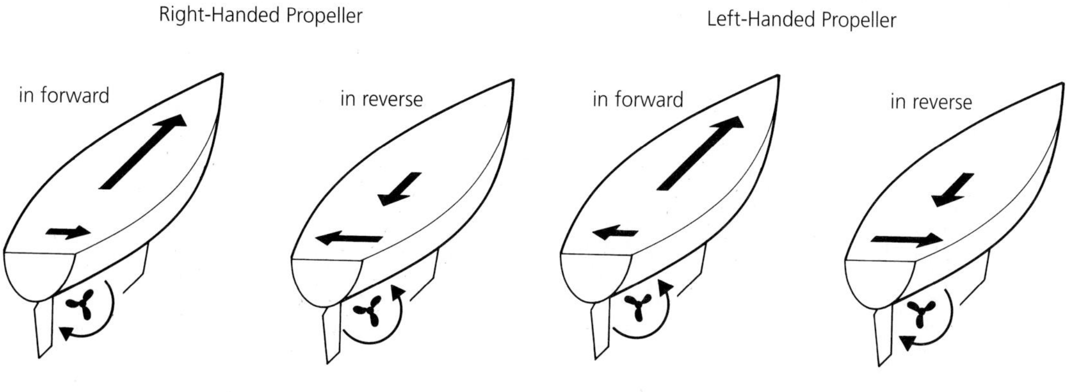

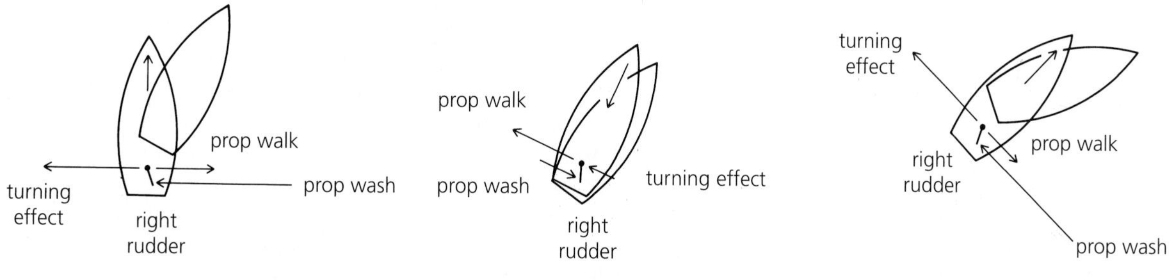

1. Power applied in forward.

2. Power applied in reverse.

3. Power applied in forward.

stern to port, accentuating the right turn. As long as the boat does not gather sternway, the rudder position has little to no effect; therefore, the rudder might as well be kept to starboard, particularly if the boat still has any forward motion. However, if the boat begins to gather sternway, creating a reverse flow over the rudder, the rudder should be put hard over to port. In practice, before this happens, the boat should be given another burst in forward, then in reverse, and so on. In other words, hard right rudder is maintained while the boat is given alternate bursts of forward and reverse, utilizing the stern prop walk to achieve a turn in not much more than the boat's own length.

The same type of approach can be used to turn the boat to port; however, this time when in reverse, the prop walk of the right-handed propeller tends to cancel out the port turn imparted when in forward. It is likely to take many more gear shifts to turn the boat. The key to success is to use aggressive bursts of power so that the boat gains turning momentum when in forward, but with little actual forward movement. With a left-handed propeller, the same considerations apply but in reverse. The boat turns more efficiently to port.

In summary, as forward momentum is lost, a boat becomes increasingly less responsive to the rudder and potentially more unmanageable. Where there is adequate room, maintaining boat speed is often the key to maintaining control, but when it comes to tight-quarters, slow-speed maneuvering, it is essential to have a feel for any given boat. In particular, it is important to know that with a right-handed propeller, in the absence of other influences, the boat turns more easily to starboard than to port, and with a left-handed propeller, to port rather than to starboard.

Turning in Wind

Wind always complicates a turn, sometimes assisting, and sometimes causing trouble. If the wind is from ahead, irrespective of a right-handed, or left-handed, propeller, you can turn

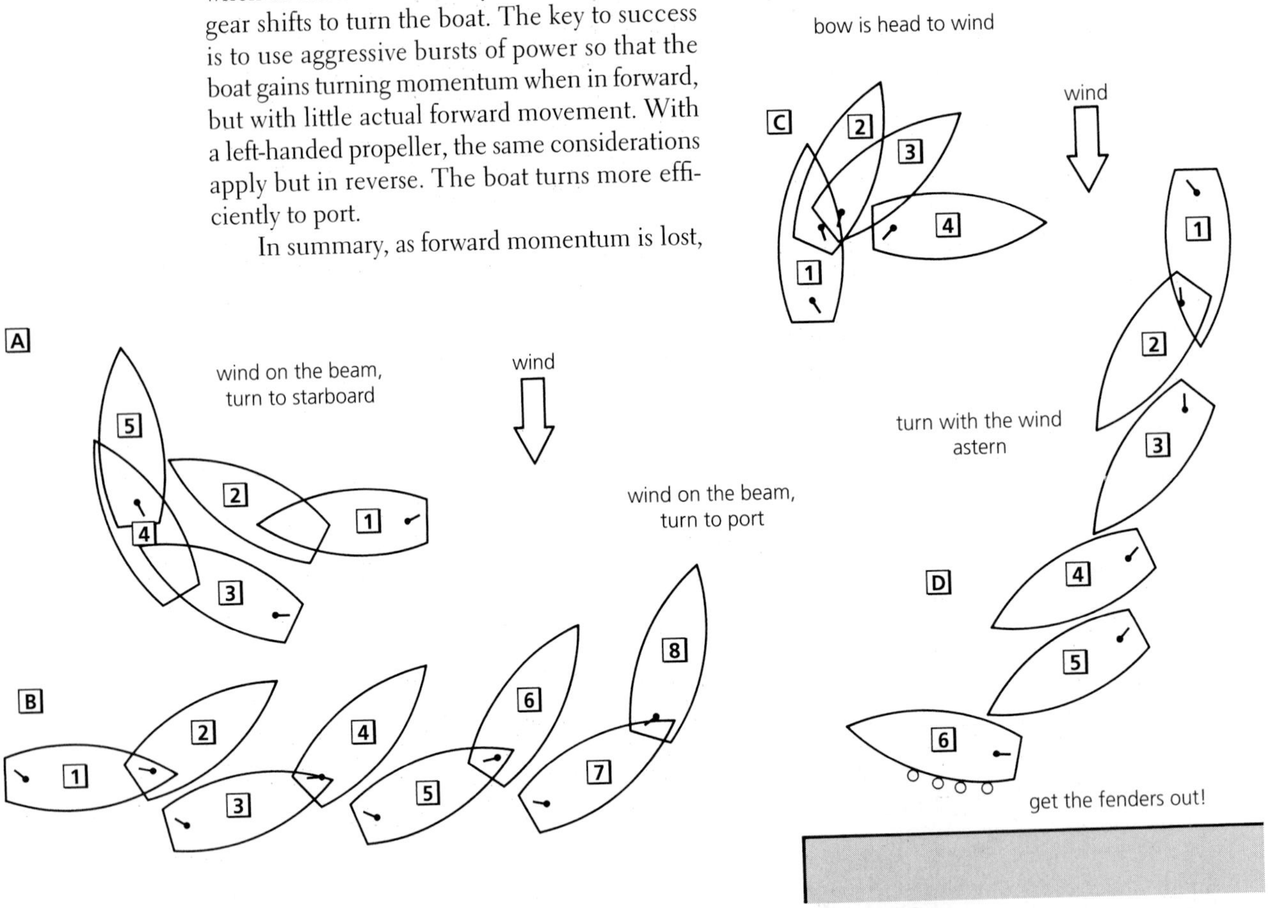

Turning a boat with a right-handed propeller in tight quarters in windy conditions. A. Wind on the beam, turn to starboard. When the boat is in reverse, the beneficial prop walk will tend to cancel out the effect of the wind blowing the bow off, so the boat slips sideways (2–3). B. Wind on the beam, turn to port. When the boat is in reverse (2–3, 4–5, and 6–7), the combined effect of the negative prop walk and the wind will undo much of the turning effect imparted in forward. C. Turn with the bow head to wind. The easiest turn, either to port or starboard, because the wind will assist by blowing the bow off. D. Turn with the wind astern. The hardest turn. The boat is likely to make a lot of leeway. Any time reverse is used, the wind will stall out, and maybe undo, much of the turn made so far (2–3 and 4–5). If you run out of maneuvering room when more or less broadside to the wind, you had better check all forward or reverse momentum and grab the fenders!

to port or starboard and the wind will help to blow the boat around.

If the wind is on the beam, it is almost always advisable to turn into the wind, rather than away from it. With a right-handed propeller, the easiest turn is to starboard: a strong burst in forward with hard right rudder should get the boat head to wind, after which the wind will blow the head off to complete the turn. If a turn to port is made, any time the boat is put into reverse, the prop walk will tend to cancel the turn at the same time as the wind blows the head off—even more than the turn to starboard, you need to give the boat a powerful burst in forward to get the bow through the wind, at which point the wind will once again complete the turn. Once a boat is head to wind, any turn is easy because the wind will be blowing the bow off to increase the turning force.

Where people really get into trouble is making a turn in tight quarters with the wind from astern. Any time steerageway is lost, the wind will counteract the turn, blowing the bow back off down wind, causing the boat to crab steadily sideways into trouble. It is essential to have enough maneuvering room to drive the bow all the way around in forward until it is up into the wind. If this can't be done, the boat should be backed up (see right) until enough maneuvering room has been gained. In the event that a turn is attempted with the wind astern and fails, once the boat has stalled out, if you no longer have maneuvering room you will pretty much lose control of the situation to the wind. You may be able to regain control by backing up into the wind. If not, it's time to check all forward motion (to minimize the boat's momentum and the damage it can do to itself and others), grab the fenders, and cushion the point of impact with whatever it blows into.

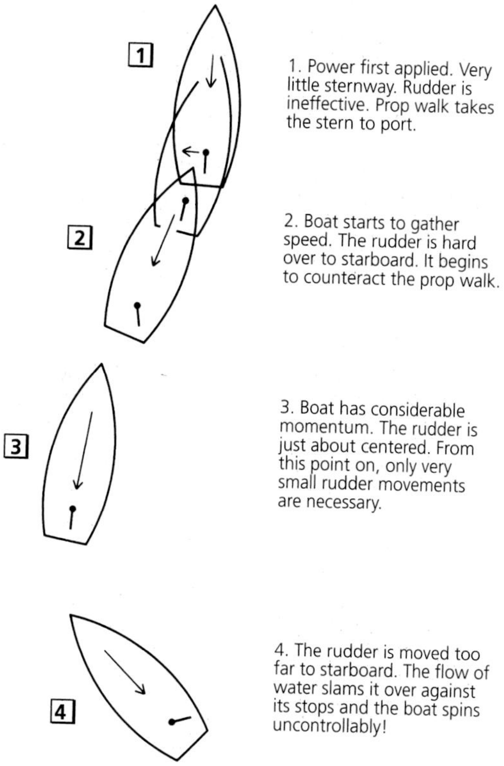

1
1. Power first applied. Very little sternway. Rudder is ineffective. Prop walk takes the stern to port.
2
2. Boat starts to gather speed. The rudder is hard over to starboard. It begins to counteract the prop walk.
3
3. Boat has considerable momentum. The rudder is just about centered. From this point on, only very small rudder movements are necessary.
4
4. The rudder is moved too far to starboard. The flow of water slams it over against its stops and the boat spins uncontrollably!

Backing up under power, in this case with a right-handed propeller.

Going Astern

One of the more difficult maneuvers in any single-engine boat such as a sailboat is to power any distance in reverse, particularly in a crosswind. (The ideal situation is a wind from astern, which automatically tends to line the boat up with the wind, with the bow lying downwind.). With any new boat, it is a good idea to practice backing up in a clear space before getting into a tight-quarters situation. With a little experience, it will be found that it is a rare boat that cannot be controlled.

Initially, the prop walk tends to kick the stern off to port or starboard. *The only way to regain steerageway is to get up sufficient speed to establish a substantial water flow over the rudder.* While the boat is gathering speed, radical rudder movements are needed to have any steering effect at all—generally, the rudder is put all the way over to port or starboard. However, as soon as the boat begins to pick up steerageway, the rudder needs to be centered, with *very small rudder movements* used to change course—any kind of radical movement throws the stern over and generally results in an immediate loss of control. If control is lost, it is usually best to give the boat a strong burst in forward, use this to regain control and put the boat back on its intended heading, and then go back into reverse and try again.

When looking over the stern, it is often difficult to get a sense of how a boat is responding to a given rudder movement, which leads to oversteering, at which point control is lost. The trick is to keep glancing forward. You can immediately see the direction in which the bow is swinging and how fast it is swinging, and you will know whether to apply a little more or a little less rudder action.

Remember, *hard rudder movements at speed must be avoided*. The minute the rudder starts to move off the centerline, the flow of water over it will exert a greatly magnified pressure that could whip the tiller out of your hand or spin the wheel, resulting in the rudder slamming savagely into its stops and quite possibly doing some expensive damage.

With a tiller-steered boat, there is never any question about the rudder's position; with a wheel-steered boat, it is not so obvious, which makes it particularly difficult to steer when backing up. When the rudder is amidships, the top of the wheel should always be marked in some way (a piece of line woven in a Turk's head is the traditional mark). However, given that most wheels have two or more full turns from lock to lock, until the boat has picked up speed and gained some steerageway and the helmsperson has gotten a feel for the situation, there is still lots of room for confusion.

Docking (Mooring) Lines

Now that we have a sense of how to drive the boat, let's look at specific docking and mooring maneuvers, starting with dock lines.

First, some terminology: three sets of lines (sometimes called *warps*) may be used for securing a boat—*bow* and *stern lines*, *breast lines*, and *spring lines* (subdivided into *bow*, *midships*, and *stern* spring lines). Bow lines are led from the bow in a *forward* direction, stern lines from the stern in an *aft* direction. A bow spring line is led from the bow in an *aft* direction; a stern spring line from the stern in a *forward* direction. Springs are also sometimes led fore and aft from amidships. Breast lines are short lines led directly ashore (i.e., more or less at right angles to the centerline of the boat) at the bow and stern.

Dock Line Choices

Although braided polyester is sometimes used for mooring lines, my preference is for double-braided or three-strand nylon—primarily because it has significant stretch, which helps to absorb shocks (polyester stretches up to 5 percent under a load of 15 percent of its breaking strength; nylon stretches around 15 percent at 15 percent of breaking strength). Nylon is also substantially cheaper, with the three-strand cheaper than double-braided. Even cheaper is polypropylene, which is sometimes used for mooring lines; however, it is not suitable because it is seriously weakened by UV rays in sunlight, in addition to which it is unpleasant to handle (for more about lines, see chapter 10).

All three-strand nylons look pretty much the same (as do double-braided); nevertheless, there are significant variations in quality from one manufacturer to another. In particular, nylon is hygroscopic (i.e., absorbs moisture), which reduces its strength by up to 11 percent and lowers its abrasion resistance. Better-quality nylon lines are given a water-repellant treatment that limits strength loss when wet to around 5 percent, while also improving abrasion resistance and handling characteristics. It pays to buy good line.

To work as a shock absorber, a nylon mooring line must be matched to its boat. It is no good putting ⅝-inch (16 mm) line on a lightweight 20-foot (6 m) boat. In general, ½-inch (12 mm) line is fine for cruising boats up to about 40 feet (12 m) in length, with ⅝-inch (16 mm) line on boats up to 50 feet (15 m), and ¾-inch (19 mm) line on larger boats—a good rule of thumb is ⅛-inch (3 mm) line diameter for every 9 feet (3 m) of boat length. Mooring lines should be at least as long as the boat and up to twice the length. If they are any shorter, they will not be adequate for some situations; if they are any longer, they will become hard to handle. A cruising boat should have at least four mooring lines (a bow and stern line, and two springs) and preferably six (or, at least, a couple more lengths of general-purpose line nearby). It is useful but by no means necessary to have a good-sized loop (about a foot in length) spliced into one end of each line. In any case, unspliced ends should be *whipped* to prevent the strands from unraveling (see chapter 10).

Mooring line terminology.

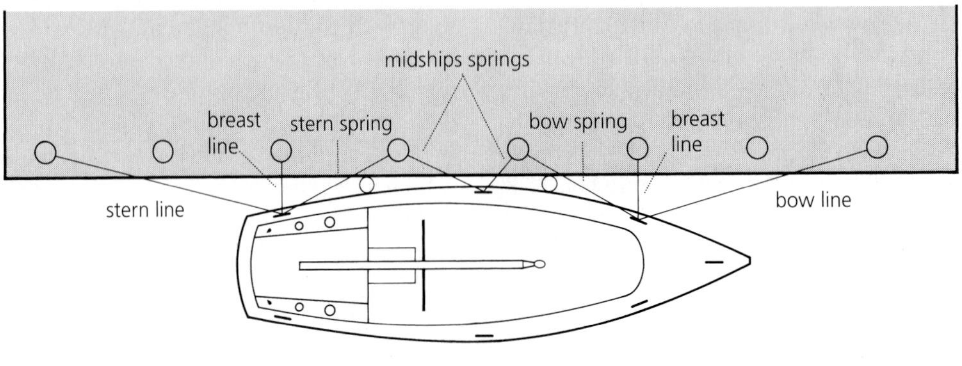

Handling Dock Lines

It is often necessary to toss a mooring line from the boat to someone ashore. Many times this simply results in a tangle of line falling in the water. While the line is being retrieved, the skipper—who no longer has any way on—loses control of the boat and confusion ensues!

The secret to successfully throwing a line is to attach one end to the boat; bring the other end out through a chock, fairlead, or hawsehole and back over the lifelines; and then coil the line in the hand you don't use for writing (i.e., the left hand if right-handed; the right hand if left-handed). It is essential to ensure that the line is brought over the rail so that it will not foul stanchions, biminis, and other parts of the boat once it is thrown and secured ashore.

Mooring lines are always coiled clockwise

Tossing a mooring line without getting in a tangle. 1. *The line is cleated off. Make sure it is brought outside the lifelines!* 2. *The line is coiled and then divided between both hands.* 3 & 4. *Stand at about a 60° angle to the dock and throw the line (now coiled inside the lifelines) across the front of your body more or less horizontally.* 5. *Follow through with the lines in the other hand (I hope you remembered to cleat the end off before you started this process!).*

using moderately large loops. Assuming the forearm of the hand that is holding the line is more or less at right angles to your body, at about stomach height, the loops should hang down to around your knees. If the hand that is making the loops (rather than holding them) is fully stretched out each time a new loop is gathered in, an excellent loop size results.

As each loop is made, the line—which is held between the thumb and forefinger of the hand making the loops—is given a twist by rolling the wrist in toward the body. This should result in the loops hanging down cleanly from the other hand. Sometimes they try to take on a figure-eight shape, in which case the line needs to be given more of a twist as it is gathered in. If this still doesn't remove the figures eights, the line needs to be given a good shake as it is gathered in—this works the excess tension that is causing the problem down to and out of the end of the line. Once a line has been coiled correctly, it proves easier thereafter.

After the line has been coiled into one hand, three or four loops are taken in the other hand (the throwing hand), the body is placed at about a 60-degree angle to the dock, and the line is thrown vigorously across the front of the body in a near horizontal direction. If you stand facing the dock, there is a good chance you will simply throw the line up in the air with it falling down in the water. With a good near-horizontal throw, the momentum imparted to the first few loops of line strips the rest of the line from the other hand—but only if you remember to let go of it, which is done by opening the palm of the hand and holding it flat. If not, the line stops with a jerk and falls into the water. If this happens, no matter what kind of chaos is developing onboard, you need to take the time to coil it up properly before making another throwing attempt—if you don't, it will fall into the water again! A little practice in the privacy of your backyard is not a bad idea before getting into the sometimes stressful situation of real-life docking.

Fenders

In addition to mooring lines, the other essential component of a docking system is the *fenders*. Sooner or later, a cruising boat is going to come alongside a beat-up dock in less-than-ideal conditions resulting in a fair amount of boat movement. Without substantial fenders, the boat will suffer damage. Then there are times when the boat is tied up between two other boats, so fenders are required on both sides. To deal with these situations, a cruising boat should carry at least four fenders, despite the stowage problems they create. *The fenders should have eyes at both ends* (or a hole through the center) so they can be hung horizontally when the boat is laying up against a piling. Even so, it is very difficult to stop the fender from rolling out, leaving the boat banging on the piling. For this kind of situation, a *fender*

Fender with eyes at both ends—more useful than a fender with an eye at just one end.

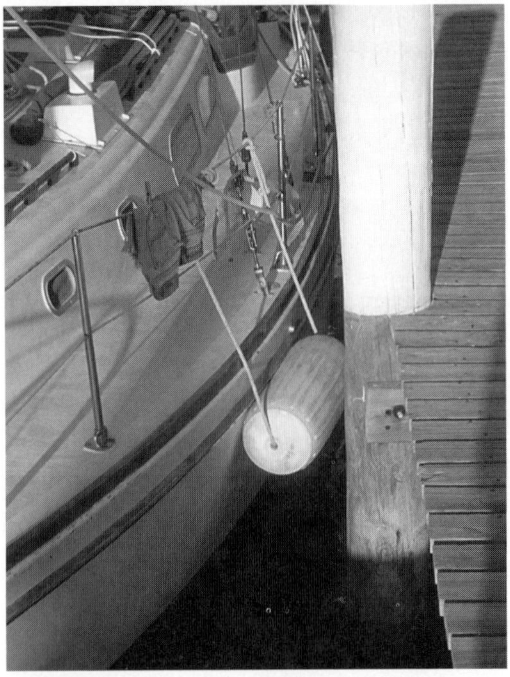

Fender with a hole through the middle (this serves the same purpose as eyes).

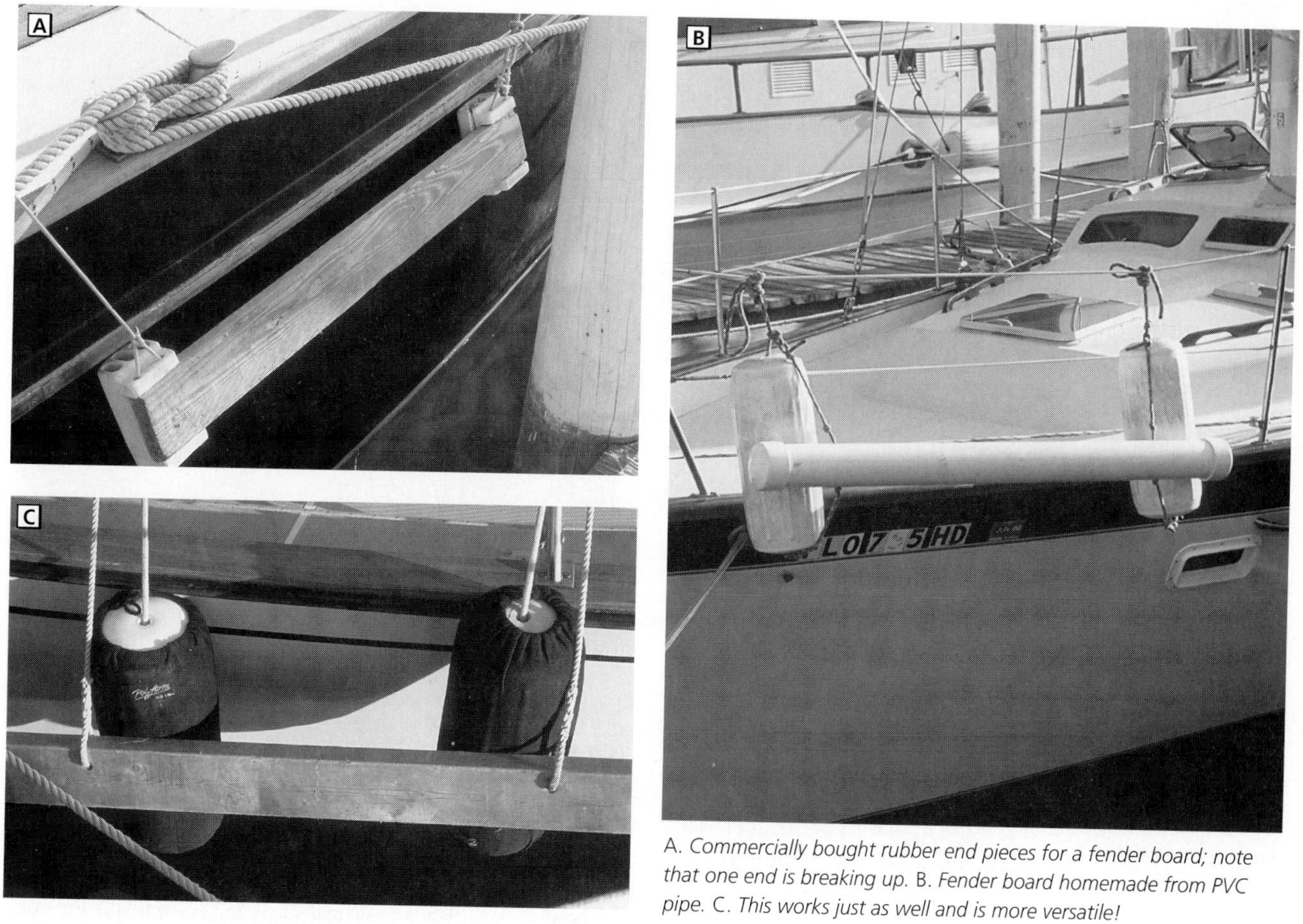

A. *Commercially bought rubber end pieces for a fender board; note that one end is breaking up.* B. *Fender board homemade from PVC pipe.* C. *This works just as well and is more versatile!*

board is the answer, although it is even more difficult to stow because of its length. A cheap and easy way to make a fender board is to add a couple of fender-board guards (around $20 from marine catalogs) to a length of two-by-four (50 × 100 mm) lumber. Even cheaper and easier is to just carry the board and hang it outboard of a couple of fenders.

Fenders and fender boards should not be secured to lifelines (although sometimes it is unavoidable)—the stresses may lead to premature lifeline failure. The best option is strategically placed cleats; next best (and most likely) is the base of stanchions.

Docking Situations

It is useful to distinguish docking techniques—the art of bringing a boat alongside or leaving from a straight dock or pier—from techniques required to get a boat in and out of a slip.

Coming Alongside

In a situation with no wind or current, given a right-handed propeller, the phenomenon of prop walk generally makes it easier to dock with the port side to the dock (with a left-handed prop, a starboard-side approach is easier). The approach is made at a fairly sharp angle to the dock, the rudder is put hard over as the bow closes the dock, and then a burst of power is applied in reverse to stop the boat. The turning momentum generated by the rudder, coupled with the prop walk in reverse, should bring the stern neatly onto the dock as all motion is lost.

If the dock has to be approached on the "wrong" side (i.e., starboard side to with a right-handed propeller; port side to with a left-handed propeller), the approach should be made at a shallower angle. The boat is likely to come to a stop with the stern still off the dock. If the rudder is put over to the outboard side (i.e., port side if the starboard side is to the dock) and the engine is given a sharp burst of power in forward, the prop wash over the rudder will drive the stern in while imparting minimal forward motion. Alternatively, if an aft spring line can be gotten ashore (from the stern of the boat to a point on the dock farther forward), going astern on the spring line will swing the stern in.

If the dock is a long one with no one on it, you can come in at a much shallower angle than normal and ease alongside. However, the shorter

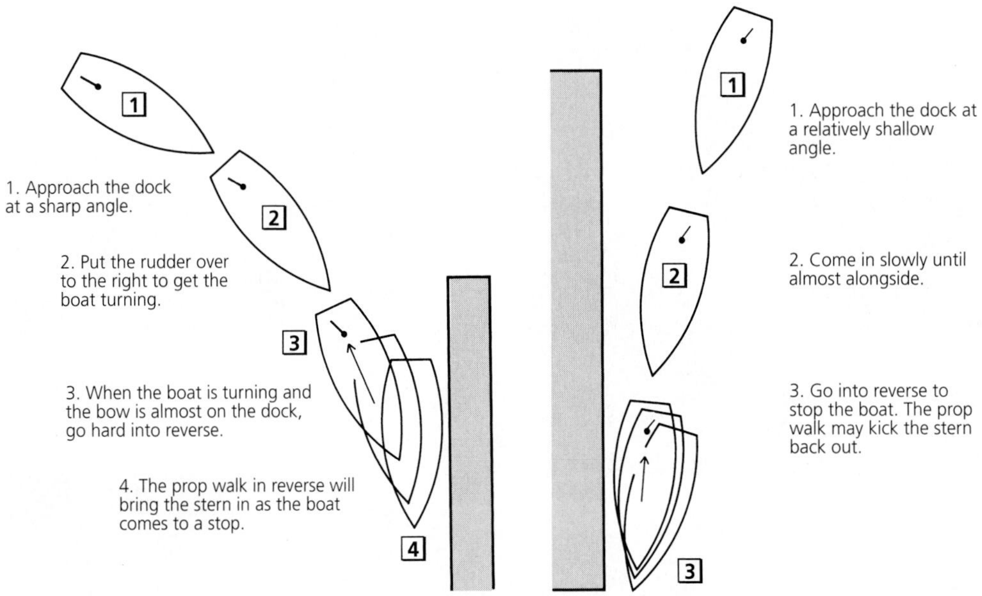

1. Approach the dock at a sharp angle.
2. Put the rudder over to the right to get the boat turning.
3. When the boat is turning and the bow is almost on the dock, go hard into reverse.
4. The prop walk in reverse will bring the stern in as the boat comes to a stop.
1. Approach the dock at a relatively shallow angle.
2. Come in slowly until almost alongside.
3. Go into reverse to stop the boat. The prop walk may kick the stern back out.

Left: *Bringing a boat with a right-handed propeller port side onto a dock (no wind or current).* Right: *Bringing a boat with a right-handed propeller starboard side onto a dock (no wind or current).*

the space in which it is necessary to dock, the sharper the approach angle must be and the more forceful the rudder and throttle action.

If the final turn as the dock is approached is made too soon, the stern may come onto the dock, but the bow will drift out and confusion will ensue. If the turn is made too late, the bow will either hit or scrape the dock. Clearly, it is necessary to have a feel for how a boat turns, which can be gained only through practice and experience—a fin-keeled boat with spade rudder behaves in an entirely different manner than a long-keeled boat with an attached rudder.

Do's and don'ts of braking a boat with dock lines.

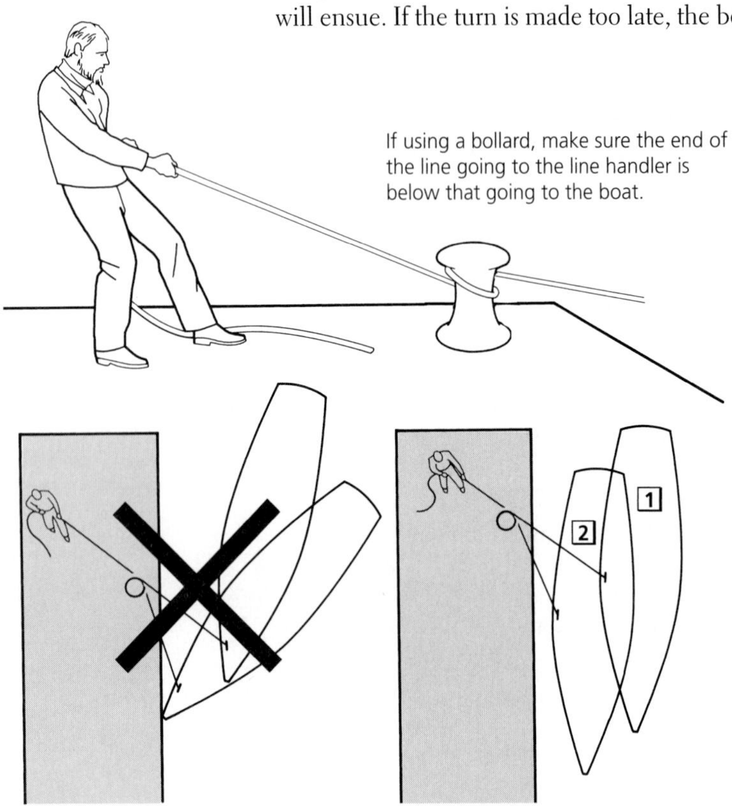

If using a bollard, make sure the end of the line going to the line handler is below that going to the boat.
1
2

Do NOT brake a boat with a bow line!

Braking from amidships or farther astern will swing the whole boat into the dock.

Because most of us have a natural inclination to be a little cautious, we are likely to turn too soon. *Assuming the boat is properly snubbed up*, there should be no problems as long as the person in the bow has a long-enough dock line and a good throwing arm, and as long as there is someone ashore or someone can be gotten ashore from the stern to receive it.

However, snubbing up is the point at which many nicely executed docking maneuvers start to go awry. First, if a line is put around a *bollard* (rather than a cleat or a tall piling), a half hitch needs to be made so that the end of the line held by the person on shore is below the line going to the boat. If this is not done, the line is likely to pop off the bollard. Second, if the boat has any forward motion, *it should not be braked with the bow line*—this simply swings the bow into the dock and the stern out. If the boat has to be braked with a dock line, it needs to be braked from an attachment point *amidships or farther aft*—this causes the entire boat to be swung into the dock, more or less parallel to the dock. Ideally, the line handlers will not brake the boat at all—the skipper will do it with the engine. Then the bow and stern lines will be used to bring the boat up against the dock. Third, if the lines are used as brakes, tension should be applied gradually to minimize shock loads, so

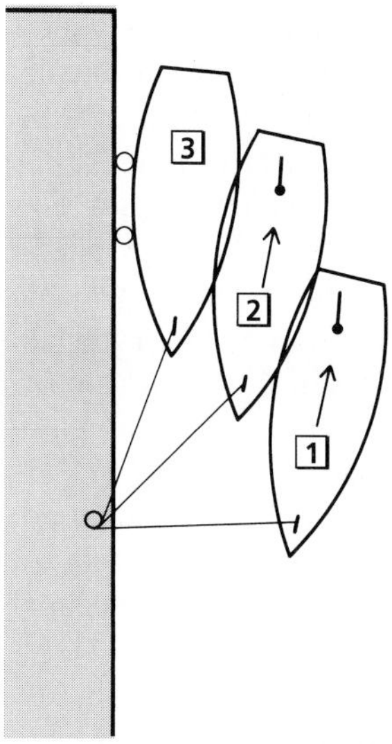

Going astern on a bow line to bring a boat alongside a dock.

there is time to see whether the desired effect is being achieved rather than creating problems.

In the event that only the bow line got ashore and the boat is still well off the dock, going gently in reverse with the bow line cleated off brings the boat alongside.

So far, we're assuming no wind and current. In the event of either, more control will be maintained if the boat is docked head to wind or head to current (whichever has the most effect), regardless of whether this results in the optimum port-side or starboard-side approach. Because of the relatively large wetted surface area of sailboats, if the wind is blowing against the current, the current usually has the greater effect—the boat should be docked head to current. The current actually increases the controllability and maneuverability of the boat by increasing the speed of the water flow over the rudder at any given boat speed. In fact, it is often possible to get a boat to "crab" sideways with complete control, with no forward or backward movement at all. Trying to dock with the current behind the boat has the opposite effect: the water flow over the rudder is reduced, resulting in a loss of control.

When docking into a current or wind, the key docking line is the bow line. Once it is secured, it doesn't really matter where the stern ends up—the wind or current causes the boat to fall back on the bow line, and then the stern drifts into the dock. The reverse is true if the wind or current are from astern—the key line to secure is the stern line. Once this is done, the boat tends to sort itself out.

When the wind is blowing off the dock with any force (i.e., docking to windward), the substantial amount of windage on most sailboats can make it quite difficult to get laid alongside. This is where knowledge of the boat and a competent skipper are particularly important. The dock needs to be approached at the maximum safe speed and at a sharp angle. At the last safe moment, the rudder is thrown over as the engine is put in reverse and given a burst of power. The boat will turn rapidly with its momentum carrying it upwind toward the dock. Between this and the prop walk bringing the stern in, it should come alongside. Clearly, good line-handling is also essential—the window for getting the lines ashore and secured is likely to be quite short. If only one end of the boat gets secured, it may be necessary to cast off and repeat the maneuver.

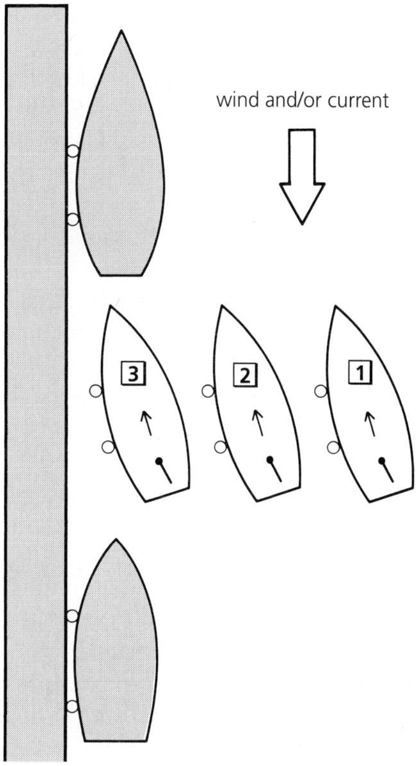

Using the wind or current to "crab" sideways. Motoring slowly forward with just enough speed to counteract the wind and/or current.

When the wind is blowing onto the dock with any strength, it is difficult to avoid being driven into the dock. Docking in this situation should be avoided if at all possible. If the boat must be brought alongside, there are two ways to handle the situation, as follows:

- Bring the boat to a standstill parallel to the dock and allow the wind to blow it on, cushioning the contact with fenders. This approach is fraught with potential problems. Once the boat is stopped, the skipper no longer has any control. The farther off the dock, the more sideways momentum that will build up; at the same time, on most boats the head will be blown off downwind, coming into the dock first. If the situation starts to get out of control, the skipper should not attempt to power out of trouble forward because this drives the stern of the boat into the dock as the boat comes around. Instead, the boat should be brought off in reverse.

- Drop a *breast anchor* some way off the dock and use it to control the drift onto the dock. If the anchor is dropped over the bow, the stern can be eased onto the dock (see Mediterranean Moor section later in this chapter); if the anchor is sheeted amidships, the boat can be brought in side on (see chapter 9).

If there is any kind of a surge running, the breast anchor will be needed to stop the boat pounding against the dock. Because it is much easier to deploy the anchor on the way in rather than rowing it out once tied up, the second approach is the preferred one.

Securing the Boat

If a boat has to be moved once it is alongside a dock, it should be pulled along by a longish line attached at the end opposite to the direction in which it is being moved (i.e., at the stern if being pulled forward, and forward if being pulled aft). As the boat moves, the tendency is for the other end to swing out from the dock. A second person can use a relatively short breast line to hold the boat in (but not actually pull it along)—it moves along quite nicely without banging along the dockside.

When in the desired location—in the simplest of docking situations—the boat is held with just bow and stern lines, which is adequate in most situations. If there is a tidal rise and fall, it is important to either adjust the lines as necessary or ensure that they are long enough to absorb the full tidal range.

Given the slack that is necessary to absorb tidal changes, if there is any kind of a surge, a boat can move around quite a lot when secured like this, ranging up and down the dock. This is where spring lines come in: a bow spring (led aft) pulls the boat up short if it tries to move forward; the stern spring (led forward) prevents it from moving aft. The net effect is to hold the boat stationary and parallel to the dock. If the spring lines are reasonably long, they will absorb significant tidal changes without adjustment.

Midships springs (led forward and aft from amidships) also stop surging, but allow the bow and stern to swing in and out. Even with bow and stern springs, a crosswind blowing off the dock still causes the boat to sit farther out than desired. In this case, bow and stern breast lines (short lines led directly ashore at right angles to the dock) hold the boat in and prevent the bow and stern from swinging, but need constant tending if there is much of a tide.

If lines are attached to bollards on which other lines are already in place, the loop in the new line should be fed up through the loop in the one already there, and then dropped over the bollard. This way, either line can be

Below: *Pulling a boat along a dock.* Bottom: *Recommended docking lines in most situations.*

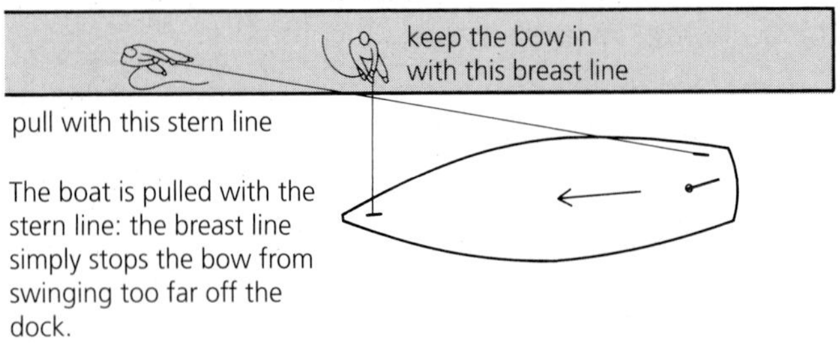

keep the bow in
with this breast line
pull with this stern line
The boat is pulled with the stern line: the breast line simply stops the bow from swinging too far off the dock.

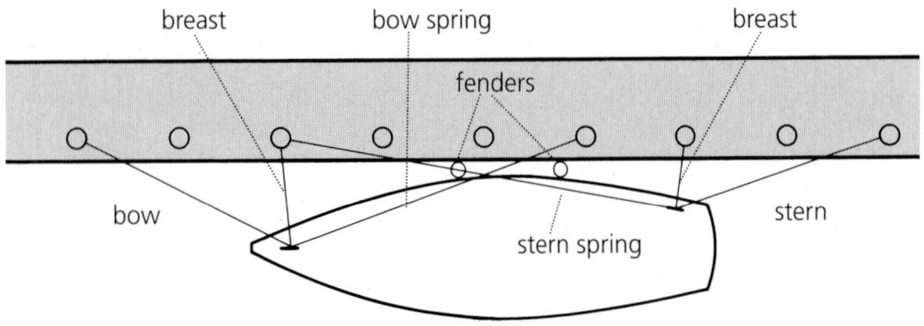

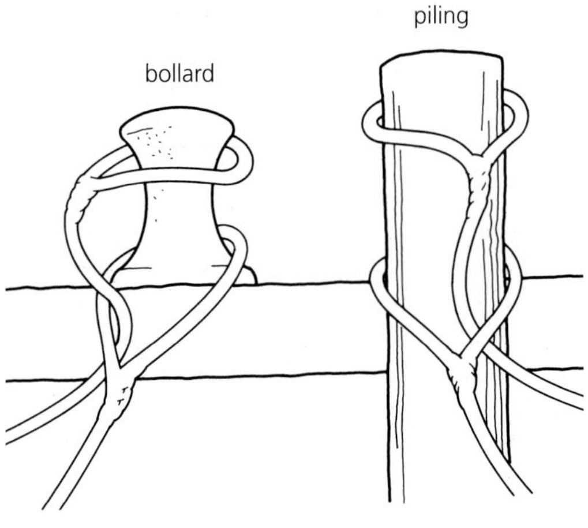

The "polite" way to put a mooring line onto a bollard or piling that already has other lines on it.

removed without disturbing the other. If your lines do not have spliced loops, the best way to form a loop is with a bowline (see chapter 10).

Getting under Way

When getting under way, first check that all shore-power cords and hoses have been disconnected and stowed. This sounds obvious, but we have been known to leave a dock at night still plugged in, ripping the shore-power cord in half!

The natural tendency when leaving a dock is to do it forward—we do it all the time. However, given that a boat tends to turn around some point more or less amidships, when the rudder is first put over, the stern swings in as the bow swings out, causing the stern to scrape along the dock as the boat continues to turn. Attempts to get the stern clear of the dock lead to the bow swinging back in. With any kind of wind blowing onto the dock, it is easy to get into quite a pickle—we've done it lots of times! When leaving in this manner, it is essential to give both the bow and stern a good push out from the dock to establish the necessary swinging room for the stern. Alternatively, take in all the lines except a stern spring line and then back down gently on this. The stern swings in (you need a fender to cushion it against the dockside) and the bow out. When the bow is clear of other boats, a straight burst of power in forward brings the boat off.

The recommended way to leave a dock is stern first. If the stern can be pushed out, in most circumstances, a good burst of power straight astern provides the necessary clearance from the dock to then maneuver in either forward or reverse.

However, with a strong wind blowing onto the dock, it may not prove possible to push the stern far enough out to get the necessary maneuvering room. This is where the forward spring line is worth its weight in gold. The other lines are cast off, the boat is brought slowly forward until the spring line is taut, and then gentle power is applied in forward with the rudder set to steer the boat off the dock. The deflected prop wash swings the stern of the boat out and away from the dock. The bow will want to crunch on the dock, so a fender is needed at this point. The stern can be pushed out as far as is desired. The engine is then put in reverse. The boat is backed up into the wind and away from the dock.

To make any maneuver with spring lines as trouble-free as possible, the spring line should be run from the relevant cleat on the boat; around the bollard, cleat, or piling ashore; and back to the boat where it is secured. Then, once the boat starts to clear the dock, one end of the spring is *slipped* (undone) at the boat and dragged around the attachment point ashore to be pulled aboard from the other end. To avoid tangling the line in the propeller, *if the line goes in the water, the engine should be put in neutral until it is recovered.*

Rafting Up

A variant of coming alongside a dock is *rafting up*; that is, one boat is brought alongside another. The same principles apply, with the caveat that even small mistakes can cause quite expensive damage as stanchions and masts grapple with one another. With two sailboats, it is critical to ensure that the masts are staggered so that if the boats roll, the rigging does not tan-

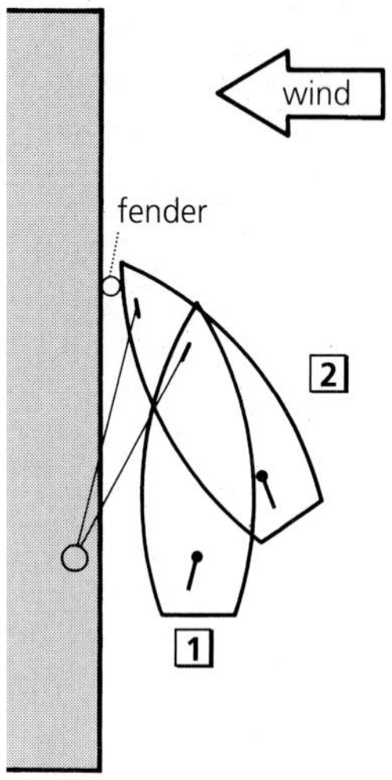

Using a forward spring line to get off a dock.

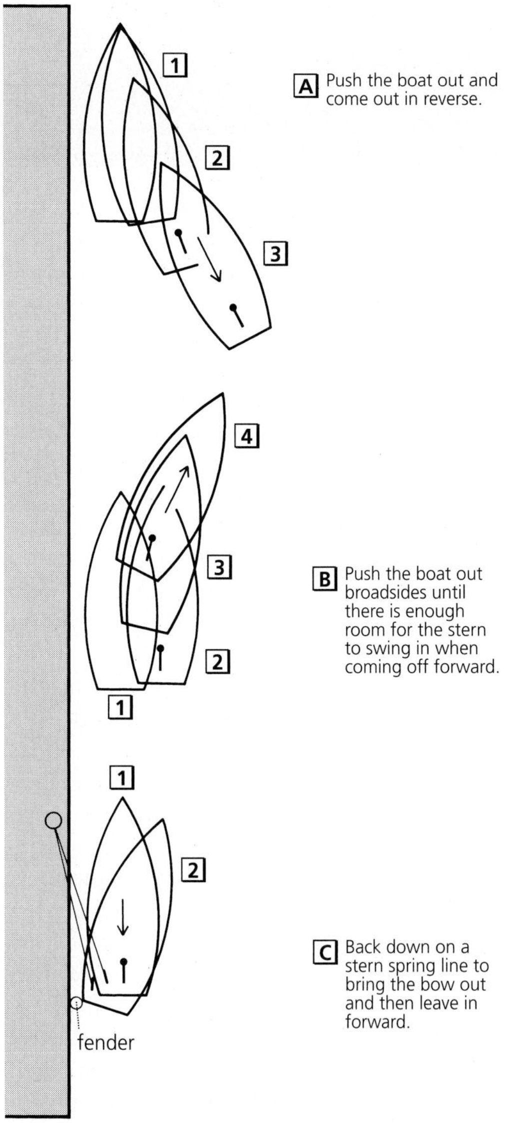

1
2
3
A Push the boat out and come out in reverse.
4
3
2
1
B Push the boat out broadsides until there is enough room for the stern to swing in when coming off forward.
1
2
C Back down on a stern spring line to bring the bow out and then leave in forward.
fender

Methods of getting off a dock.

Rafting up. Large fenders and plenty of spring lines are needed, together with staggered masts and rigging.

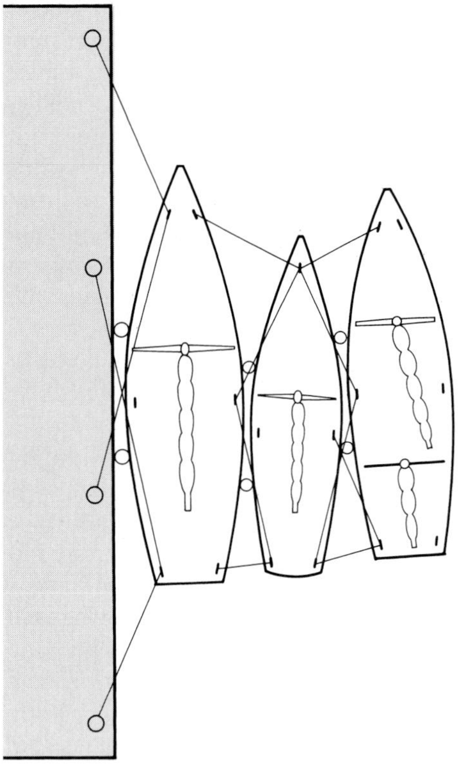

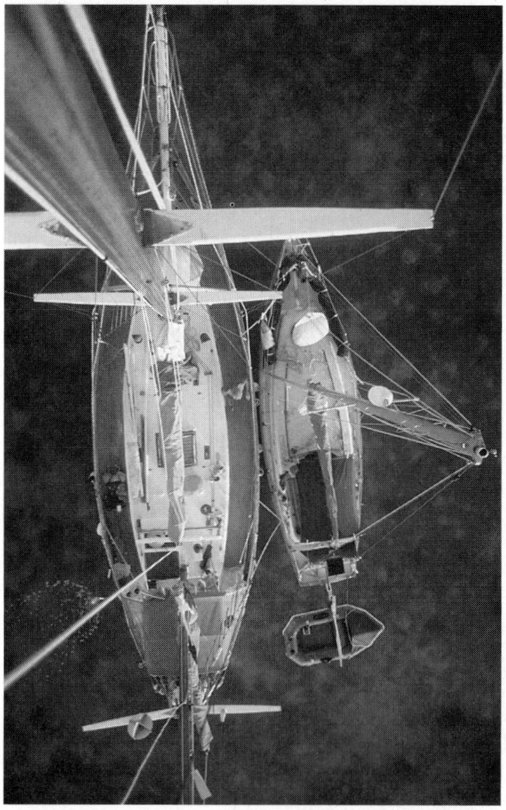

gle. To ensure that the boats do not surge back and forth relative to one another, bow and stern breast lines have to be supplemented with springs—the idea is to make an "X" between the boats from the bow of one to the stern of the other and vice versa. Excellent fenders also are needed. Even so, to avoid damage if any kind of a wave action develops, the boats should immediately be disengaged and separately docked or anchored.

Mediterranean Moor

A *Mediterranean moor* is necessary when limited dock space forces boats to tie stern to or bow on. In theory, it is quite simple: the boat is brought to a position well off the dock, the anchor is dropped, the boat is backed down onto the dock, and then held in place between the taut anchor rode and a couple of lines led from the stern quarters to the dockside.

Of course, once the boat has stopped, it loses steerageway—backing down can be a real headache. To minimize problems and foul-ups, all lines and fenders should be gotten ready before starting the maneuver, with the anchor hung over the bow ready to let go. Before the anchor is dropped, the boat should be swung around until it is lined up with the berthing slot on the dock. The anchor is then let go and paid out at the same time the skipper gives a good burst in reverse to get the boat moving back to the dock with some semblance of control. If the boat starts to swing off course, vigorous use of the rudder with a short, hard burst in forward should straighten it out, at which point the backing down is continued.

A little tension on the anchor rode helps to set the anchor and, in some circumstances, may help keep the boat aligned; in other circumstances, however, it inhibits maneuverability. In any case, with an onshore wind or a crosswind, it is a good idea to make sure the anchor is properly set before getting too close to the dock. With an offshore wind, the anchor is not so important at this time and, if necessary, always can be recovered later and reset using the dinghy. When the boat approaches the dock, it is braked by a burst in forward, the stern lines are gotten ashore (windward line first), and then the anchor rode is tensioned. With a two-person crew and no help ashore to tend lines, the skipper has to drive the boat and throw the stern lines; the crew drops the anchor, pays out the rode (making sure there is enough slack for the stern to reach the dock), and then comes aft as the dock is approached to hop off the boat and catch the stern lines. Meanwhile, the bow may be drifting off, but as long as the anchor is well set, it can always be recovered later by tightening the anchor rode.

Things can get really hairy with a crosscurrent or crosswind. The anchor will likely have to be dropped upcurrent or upwind (whichever has the most effect) of the slot on the dock to allow for the diagonal path the boat takes on backing down. When backing between other boats, there is no substitute for extra hands and fenders. Once the boat is secured, a second anchor may be needed—set in the other diagonal direction to hold the boat in place when the tide and/or wind changes. With any kind of a Mediterranean moor, it is preferable to have all-chain rodes on the anchors so the rodes will be well submerged at all times and not fouled by other boats. At the least, the anchors need a substantial chain lead (see chapter 9).

Stern lines are typically fairly short, providing minimal cushion for tidal changes. Their length is increased if they are crossed behind the boat; that is, the line attached to the port quarter is led across to the dock bollard on the starboard side and vice versa. When leaving, the lines should be looped around the bollards ashore with both ends brought back onboard, enabling them to be slipped without having to get off the boat.

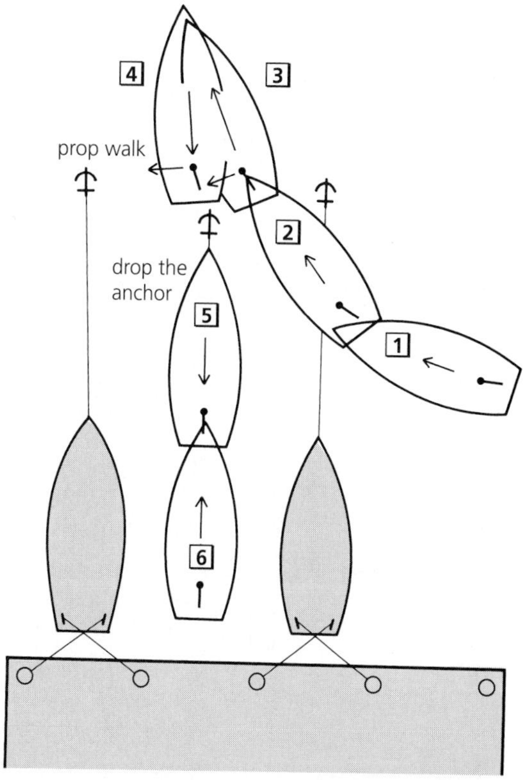

1, 2, 3. The boat is swung into line with its berth, moving slowly forward.

4. A burst in reverse, combined with reverse prop walk, stops the boat and completes the lining up maneuver.

5. The anchor is let go as the boat backs up.

6. The anchor is gently snubbed up to set it and the boat given a burst in forward to bring it to a stop.

The Mediterranean moor.

Mediterranean moor in the Bahamas to fit more boats into a crowded space—the anchors are dropped on the other side of the inlet and the sterns tied off to trees ashore.

1. The slip is passed up and the boat turned so as to enter the slip with a turn to starboard (right-handed propeller).

2, 3. The boat is brought in slowly and turned toward the slip.

4. A burst in reverse utilizes the prop walk to complete the lining up process.

5. As the slip is entered a couple of lines amidships are set up to be thrown over the outermost pilings.

6. The midships lines are slipped over the outer pilings and paid out as the boat is stopped with a burst in reverse. The rest of the lines are secured.

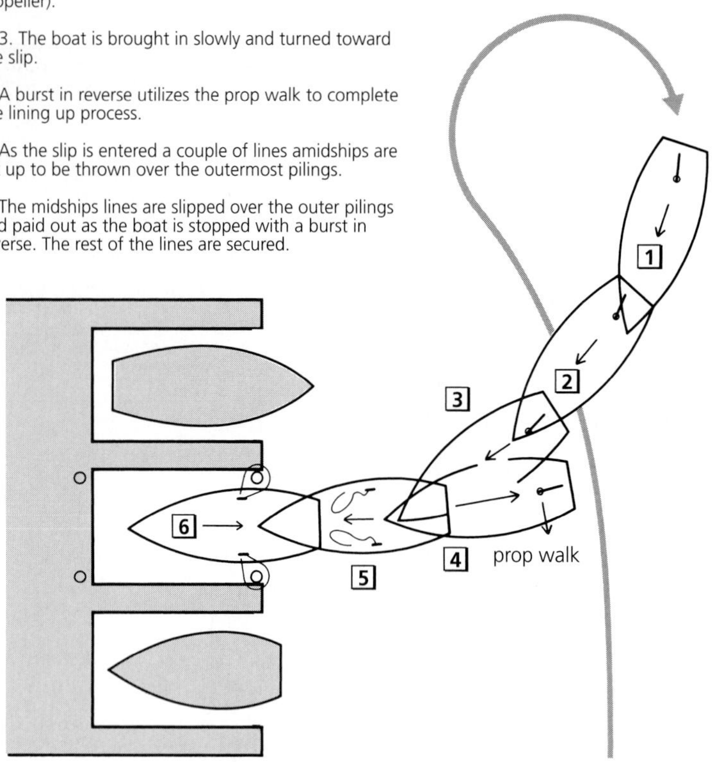

Maneuvering into a slip, bow first (right-handed propeller).

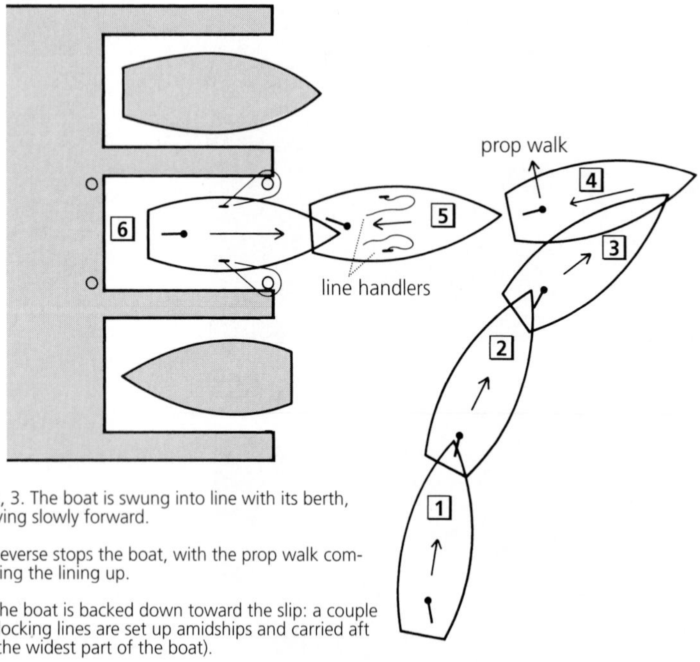

1, 2, 3. The boat is swung into line with its berth, moving slowly forward.

4. Reverse stops the boat, with the prop walk completing the lining up.

5. The boat is backed down toward the slip: a couple of docking lines are set up amidships and carried aft (to the widest part of the boat).

6. As the boat passes the outermost pilings, the midships lines are slipped over the pilings and paid out. If possible, a crew member scrambles ashore to take the stern lines. The boat is braked by a burst in forward.

Maneuvering into a slip, stern first.

Getting in and out of Slips

Getting in and out of slips is often significantly trickier than coming alongside a dock. Even in calm conditions, it takes a good understanding of how the boat behaves and a fair amount of skill. Sooner or later, we all mess up. As long as the boat is not moving at any great speed, it is usually only our dignity that suffers.

Getting In

Typically, the approach channel to a slip is not broad enough to be able to make a wide turn and come straight into the slip. The boat has to be worked around until it is lined up with the slip, and then motored in. With adverse winds or currents, it is easy to lose control. If the boat has to be backed in, things are just that much more difficult. In the following discussion, I assume the boat is going in forward; reverse is almost the same—it just requires more skill.

The first thing is to understand in which direction the boat turns best (e.g., when going forward, a boat with a right-handed propeller turns best to starboard) and to try and approach the slip so the boat is turned in that direction to enter. This may necessitate passing up the slip, doing a complete turn, and coming back to the slip from the opposite direction.

The turn is begun before the slip is reached to allow for the inevitable sideways drift that occurs. The key is to get some turning momentum going, and then work the boat around by repeated applications of forward and reverse, with short bursts of power (described previously). The boat should be fairly well lined up before entering the slip—any attempt to complete the turn while going in is likely to throw the bow or stern into a piling, at which point the boat will bounce off and your nicely executed maneuver will start to unravel. If it looks like this is going to happen, it is better to stop the boat, grab the nearest piling, and manhandle the boat into the slip. It may be a little undignified, but it beats doing damage.

Assuming a clean entrance is made, in many cases the outermost pilings are less than a boat length away from the dock at the head of the slip. If the pilings are to be used to snub up the boat, a line has to be gotten around them from the bow or from amidships as the boat comes by. Lines should be progressively snubbed so as to brake the boat gently and not produce any sudden changes of direction. It is better, in fact, if the boat is braked under power and the lines are held in reserve for insurance purposes.

Once the bow is on the dock, the bow lines are taken ashore and secured. If the engine is now put in slow reverse, it will hold the boat off the dock while the rest of the lines are put in place, after which the engine can be shut down.

Securing the Boat

The boat needs port and starboard bow lines, taken as far up the dock as is reasonably possible to increase their length. This is to accommodate changing water levels (unless, of course, the dock is a floating one, in which case there is nothing to worry about). Port and starboard spring lines are then led back from the bow to the after pilings or to cleats on any pontoons alongside the boat. The length of these lines is adjusted to keep the bow of the boat off the dock at any state of the tide. Finally, breast lines are added from the boat to the rear pilings, as far aft as possible (which, in many cases, may be not much more than amidships). These lines keep the stern of the boat from weaving around in the slip.

Any line around a piling is best put on in a loop, with both ends brought back onboard, rather than using an eye splice or a loop tied in with a bowline. It is easier to get the line onto the piling (the line is formed into a big loop and flipped over the top of the piling as the boat passes by on its way into the slip) and easier to get it off (by slipping one end and dragging it around the piling).

Getting Out

If there is a wide channel outside the slip, you can simply power out and then make a turn. If not, a sharp turn needs to be made on the way out. If possible, the boat should be turned in the direction in which it turns best.

Let's assume a boat with a right-handed propeller is backing out of a slip. In reverse, the prop walk causes the boat to back down to port. As it turns, the stern moves to port and the bow to starboard. The bow will need swinging room to clear the pilings as it comes out of the slip. Although most books tell you to pull the boat over to the starboard side of the slip before backing up, I prefer to get it to the port side. Once the widest part of the beam has passed the outer piling, I start to give the boat left (port) rudder. Between the effect of the minimal water flow over the rudder and the prop walk, the stern starts to swing to port and the bow to starboard. It is important to make sure that the rate of turn is such that the bow does not whack the outer piling on its way out. Once the bow is past the piling, full left rudder is

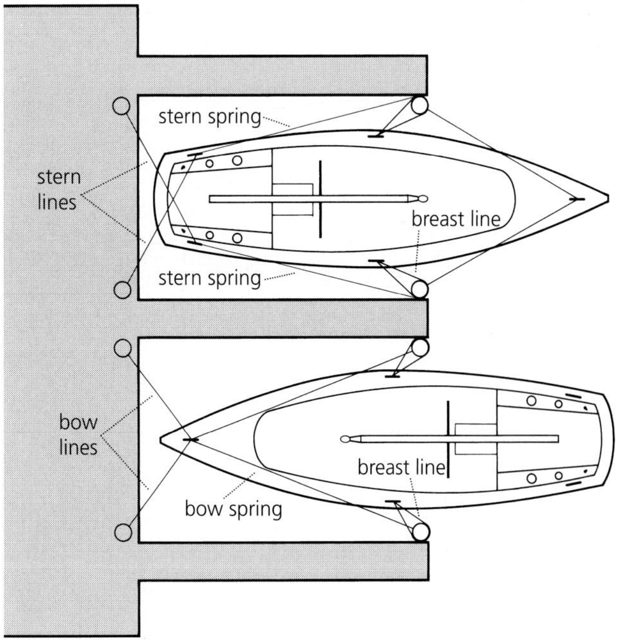

Securing a boat in a finger slip.

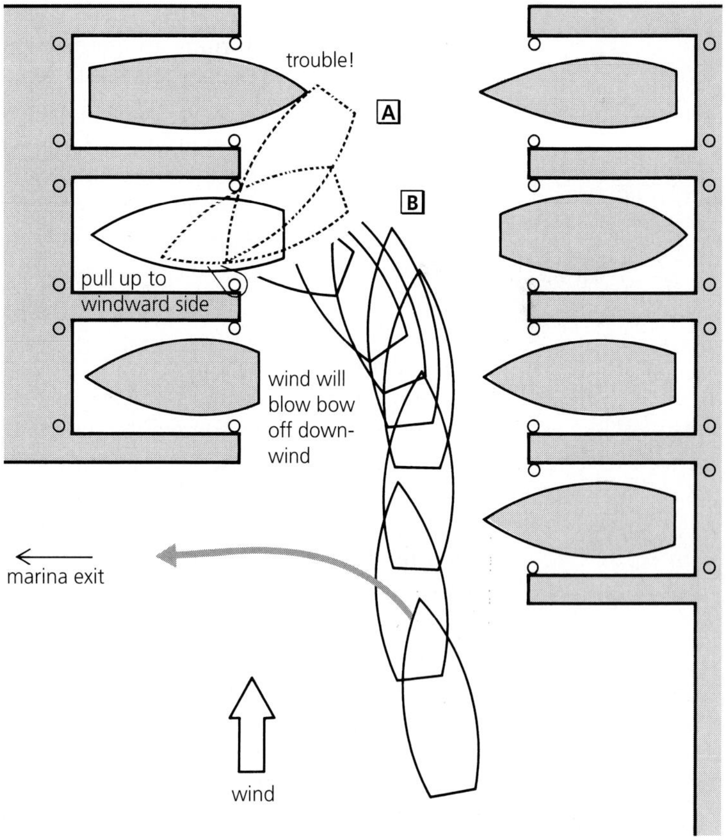

Getting out of a slip with a crosswind. A. If the exit path lies upwind, with the slip broadside to the wind, an attempt to turn the bow into the wind while backing out of the slip may get you into trouble. B. Instead of trying to get the bow into the wind from the slip, where you have very little maneuverability, let the wind blow the bow off and back up until you have both maneuvering room and sufficient speed for steerageway.

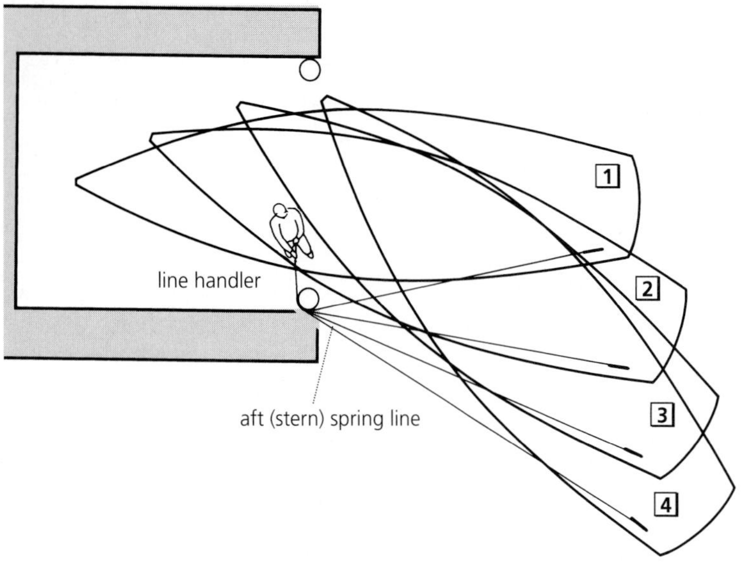

Using a stern spring line to turn a boat as it comes out of a slip.

applied, accelerating the rate of turn. A burst in forward with full right rudder should then be all that is needed to line the boat up with the exit channel at right angles to the slip, completing the maneuver.

However, many times a crosswind or crosscurrent messes up the maneuver, making it difficult to get the boat turning and/or driving it into the pilings. To stay out of trouble, sometimes all that is needed is to have a crew member flip a line around the piling on the windward side of the slip and then hold the boat up to this piling as the boat comes out of the slip (walking forward along the deck to maintain station opposite the piling as the boat moves backward). When the bow reaches the piling, one end of the line is let go and it is dragged onboard from the other end.

To get the boat turning as it leaves the slip, a spring line can be rigged from the stern to the piling around which the boat will turn. This line is paid out as the boat backs up until the widest part of the beam is past the piling, and then the line is gently tensioned. It has the effect of swinging the stern around and in toward the dock. The rate of turn must be kept down until the bow has cleared the piling on the other side of the slip, after which the stern can be brought around quite aggressively. As soon as the bow is pointing down the channel, the spring line is given some slack, the rudder is centered, and the engine is given enough of a burst to brake the boat's reverse movement. *The engine is then put in neutral while one end of the spring line is slipped and the line is recovered.* As soon as the line is out of the water, the boat is motored clear of the slip.

Picking up and Leaving a Mooring

To pick up a mooring, it is approached from downwind or downcurrent, depending on which has the greatest effect on the boat. If the mooring is close to other moorings, you just need to see which way nearby boats are lying and come onto the mooring at more or less the same angle. Rather than approaching the buoy head on, I like to keep it off the side of the bow on which I want to pick it up. This keeps the mooring in view a little longer than if coming head on, and avoids accidentally getting it on the wrong side of the boat.

As the boat gets closer, the mooring buoy enters the "dead zone" under the bow where it is no longer visible. The most difficult part in picking it up is judging where it lies and when to put the motor in reverse to kill the boat's forward motion. If the mooring is approached with it off the bow, a turn toward it at the last minute as the boat is stopped lays it up against the side of the boat and makes it reasonably easy to grab. It helps to have a bow person giving directions but, just as with anchoring, agreed-upon hand signals are better than voices, which often can't be heard over the motor and leads to confusion, anger, and perceived humiliation.

The person picking up the mooring cannot give hand signals and operate a boat hook at the same time, but this should not be a problem. There is no need to deploy the boat hook until the mooring buoy is within range. Once it is in range, it needs to be hooked or grabbed in such a way that the mooring line can be brought onboard through a fairlead or over the bow roller without fouling stanchions or other parts of the boat. As soon as the pickup buoy has been grabbed, the helmsperson needs to ensure that the boat is dead in the water, and can then go forward to help secure the boat.

If the maneuver goes awry, it is generally best to let go of the mooring line (if someone has a hold on it) and simply come around and try again. It's really no big deal, even if an entire fleet of spectators is watching: we all do it from time to time.

When leaving a mooring, ladders, fenders, and so on are first brought aboard, the boat is checked for any trailing lines, and the dinghy painter is shortened (if the dinghy is being towed) to where it cannot be sucked into the propeller. The mooring is dropped and the boat is either allowed to drift with the wind or tide or backed down until the buoy and any associated pickup buoy are well clear of the bow; this avoids nasty tangles.

SAILING SKILLS

So far, we have done everything under power. It's time we raised the sails—that is, after all, what sailing is all about!

A Little Theory (of Sorts!)

To sail a boat well, I believe it helps to have a mental picture of how the wind is imparting motion to the boat. I have read various treatises on fluid mechanics and similar topics, and can't pretend to understand them. It's not really the science that concerns me; I just want a mental picture—even one that is not technically correct—that helps me trim my sails to best effect.

In this picture, air is considered more or less incompressible. It is also considered to flow in relatively straight lines in typical circumstances. A sail is set up so that its leading edge lines up with the airflow and its trailing edge is pulled back in a gentle curve into the airflow. The airflow (the wind) separates as it hits the leading edge of the sail and then reforms as it leaves the trailing edge. For various highly complicated reasons, the airflow over the leeward (forward) side of the sail is faster than on the windward (aft) side.

For some reason that I have never understood, but which was established by Bernoulli a long time ago, if airflow accelerates, pressure is reduced (in other words, a partial vacuum is formed). It is this vacuum on the forward face of the sail that sucks the boat forward (I can hear the fluid-mechanics people out there sobbing; sorry, folks!). This entire effect only works, of course, as long as the sail can be set up to part the wind flow. As the wind moves aft of the beam, it is no longer possible—at which point, the sails simply obstruct the airflow and the boat gets pushed along by the wind.

To achieve the maximum possible vacuum effect, a sail must present a curved surface to the wind and must be held at just the right angle (*angle of attack*). The maximum force developed by the sail is more or less at right angles to the surface of the sail at its point of maximum curvature (*draft* or *camber*). In principle, the more of a curve the airflow on the leeward side of the sail can be induced to follow, the faster it will have to accelerate and the greater the vacuum that will be created. Beyond a certain point, however, the airflow starts to separate from the after part of the sail, resulting in a *stall zone*, which reduces the sail's effectiveness. Sails are built and trimmed to maximize the vacuum effect and, in so doing, use it to impart forward motion to the boat. Let's see how this pans out on different points of sail.

Going to Windward

Assuming a boat is lying head to wind, when a sail is first hoisted with the sheets loose, the sail will simply flap like a flag in the breeze. If the head of the boat is moved away from the wind and the sheet is tightened, the leech will be pulled out of line with the airflow, causing that part of the sail to fill with wind and stop flapping. The forward part of the sail will still be lined up with the wind and will still be flapping (*luffing*).

Increasing sheet tension pulls the entire sail out of line with the airflow until luffing ceases. At this point, the sail is in the region of its critical (most efficient or optimum) angle of attack. After this, further tensioning of the sheet drags the leech of the sail around some more, increasing curvature but causing the airflow over the aft part of the sail to separate from the sail and stall out, thereby reducing the sail's effectiveness (the sail is *oversheeted*).

While luffing provides obvious visual signs of *undersheeting*, there are, unfortunately, no such obvious visual *(continued on page 299)*

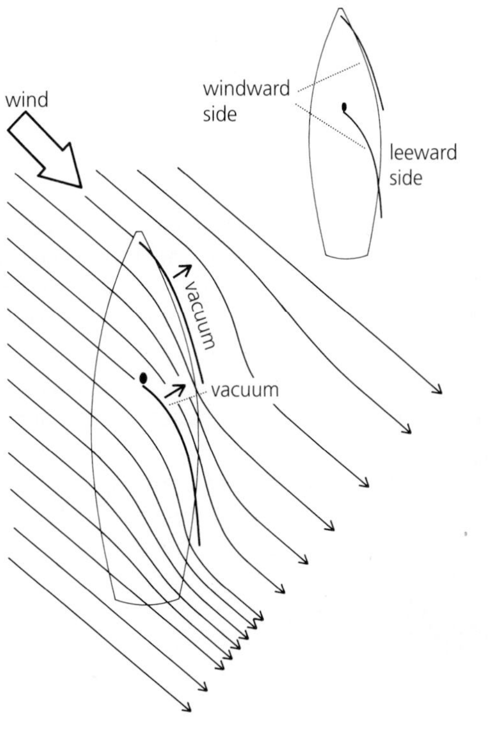

An imaginary picture of the airflow past properly trimmed sails.

RAISING AND LOWERING A MAINSAIL

Before raising or lowering the sail, close any hatches and the companionway hatch. When you are concentrating on handling the sail, it's too easy to step through an open hatch!

Most of the time, the sail will be stowed on the boom; however, if it has been removed, the first thing is to reinstall it. It has either slides or a boltrope along its foot, which are fed into a slot in the boom or onto a track, starting at the mast end and dragging the sail aft until the clew cringle (the ring at the lower back corner of the sail) can be attached to the *outhaul fitting* on the end of the boom (on most modern boats, it consists of a car riding on a short track). The outhaul is left loose for the time being. The tack cringle (the ring in the lower forward corner of the sail; is attached to the boom's *gooseneck* (the swivel fitting that holds the boom on the mast; refer to the drawing on page 68 for a list of these terms).

The boom must now be supported either with a topping lift or a rigid vang (either of which holds it up when the sail is not up). The mainsheet is loosened as well as the vang, if it is the nonrigid type (if this is not done, it will likely prove impossible to get the last bit of the sail up). The boat must be more or less head-to-wind so that the sail does not fill as it is raised (if it does, you will never get it up, and you may damage it). The crew is warned to keep out of the way of the boom, which may swing wildly from side to side during sail-hoisting.

The halyard (the line used to hoist the sail) is shackled to the sail's *headboard*. Just as with the foot, the forward edge of the sail (the luff) has a series of slides or a boltrope, which are fed into a slot on the mast or onto a track. The sail is raised by the halyard. With most sails, it should not be necessary to use a winch to raise the sail. If things jam up, either the slides need lubricating (a non-staining Teflon grease works well) or something else is hung up; for example, maybe you are trying to raise the sail off the wind, causing the battens to foul the shrouds, or one of the reefing lines is partially hauled in and either cleated off or hung up. However, with large sails, as more of the sail goes up, the weight of the sail and the friction in the slides or boltrope may make it necessary to get a little help from the halyard winch to get the last bit of sail up. If any reefs were tied in the last time the sail was used, they may need to be shaken out at this time.

Hoisting the mainsail.

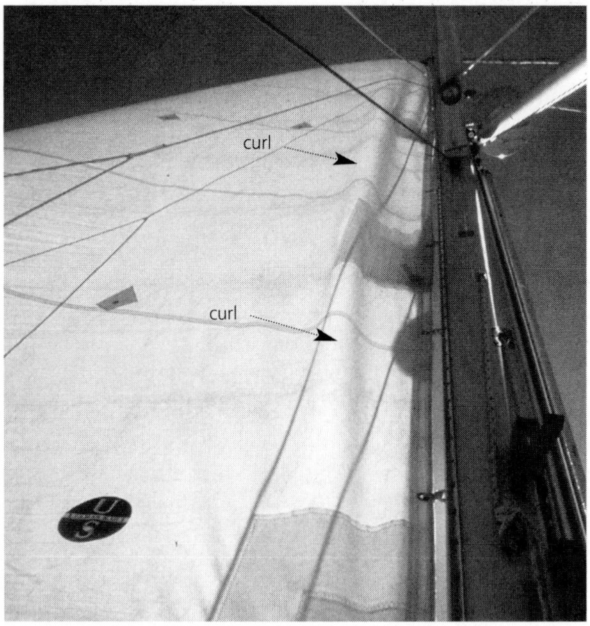

Luff tension curls.

Now it is time to tension the various lines: the stronger the wind speed, the more the tension. The halyard is put on its winch and generally cranked up until the sail is stretched to the point at which it starts to form a couple of vertical ripples (*tension curls*) from top to bottom just aft of the luff. The outhaul is tensioned until similar tension curls start to appear just above the foot of the sail. On some boats, a *cunningham* (a line led through a cringle a couple of feet up from the tack cringle) is tightened to tension the lower part of the luff of the sail.

The various lines need to be cleated off and tidied up before the headsail is raised. To cleat off a halyard, a turn is made around the cleat and then a figure eight is formed, incorporating a half hitch in the second part. The two most common mistakes in cleating off a line are leading the line onto the wrong side of the cleat and putting the half hitch on the wrong way. Taken together, under load these errors tend to cause the line to jam. (When cleating sheets, as opposed to halyards, it may be advisable to leave off the half hitch and, instead, add another full turn around the cleat. This ensures that the sheet does not bind up and, therefore, can be cast off in a hurry if necessary.) If the cleat and line are properly sized, there should be enough of the top horn of the cleat sticking up to take another turn of the line, which is used to hang the line up (see the next paragraph).

Braided halyards are coiled a little differently than dock lines inasmuch as the twist is not imparted to each loop as the line is gathered in. This results in the line hanging in a figure-eight fashion, which minimizes the chances of kinks forming in the line when the halyard is

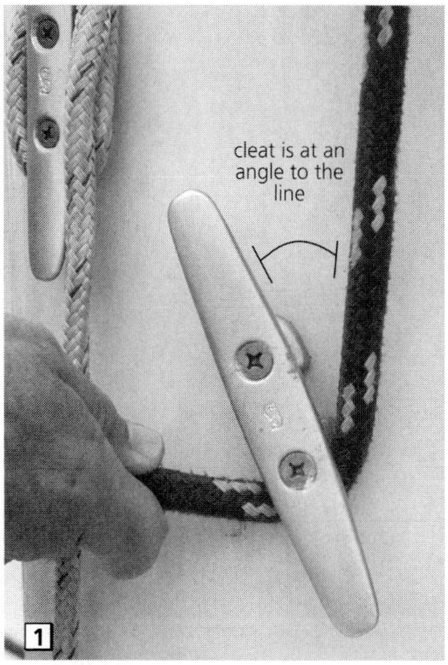

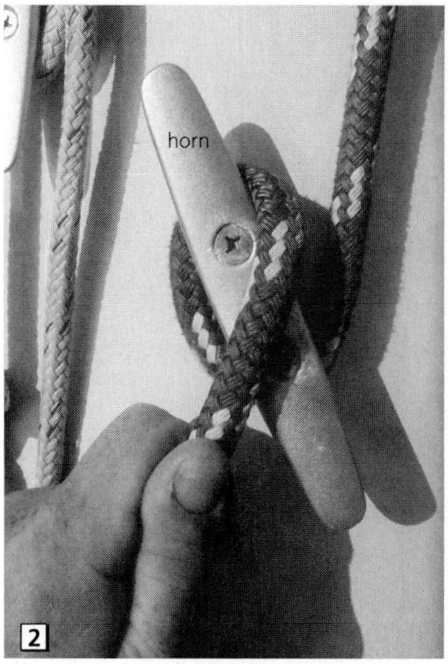

The proper way to cleat off a line. 1. The line is brought onto the cleat so that it is not laid up alongside the cleat. 2. A turn is taken under the top horn . . . 3. and then across the cleat and under the lower horn . . . 4. and back across the cleat, under the top horn, and through itself to form a figure eight.

let loose and the sail is dropped. If the first loop is made starting about a foot or so from the cleat on which the halyard is to be stowed, when all the halyard has been gathered in, you can reach through the center of the loops, grasp the remaining foot or so of line, pull it through the loops, give it a twist, and then hook it back over the top of the loops onto the cleat. This stows the halyard neatly on the mast, although too often in rough weather, it will fall off the cleat and stream aft down the deck or overboard. This problem would be almost eliminated if cleat-builders made the horns just a little longer or boatbuilders installed oversized cleats. In any case, if the loop of line used to stow the halyard is grasped on either side of the cleat, it can be worked down behind the cleated line, which more or less locks it in place.

To reef or lower a mainsail, the boat should be reasonably close to the wind. If not, the battens will wrap around the shrouds, the sail will hang up, and something is likely to get damaged. With the boat on the wind, if the mainsheet is eased and the halyard let go, most times the sail flaps itself down; however, before releasing the halyard, the topping lift has to be set up on those boats that don't have a rigid vang. If this is not done, the boom will drop on the heads of those in the cockpit (for more about reefing procedures, see chapter 2). Lazyjacks, Dutchmen, or similar devices help contain the sail as it comes down (see chapter 2); without them, it will tumble on deck.

To stow a mainsail on its boom, it is best to start at the rear end, tugging the *leech* (the aft end of the sail) aft as it is gathered in. This keeps the battens in line with the boom and avoids damage. Most people like to *flake* a sail down; that is, fold it in a series of zigzags over the boom so that it hangs down on both sides of the boom. However, some people like to grab the leech a few feet above the foot, pull this out sideways, stuff the rest of the sail into the loose "bag" that is formed, and then roll the remainder of the sail into and onto the boom, where it is held in place with sail ties. We've done it both ways and found that both work fine. However, Mylar and Kevlar sails are best rolled from the head of the sail (which requires the luff of the sail to be slid out of the mast slot or track) to help prevent cracking of the material (see chapter 10).

For long-term towage, the halyard should be disconnected, attached somewhere where it does not chafe against the mast and spreaders, and tensioned. For short-term stowage, I leave it attached, but pull down a loop of halyard from the head of the sail that I hook under a winch or cleat, after which I tension the halyard. This pulls the head of the sail down tightly on top of the stowed sail, ensuring that it does not come loose and flap around.

(continued)

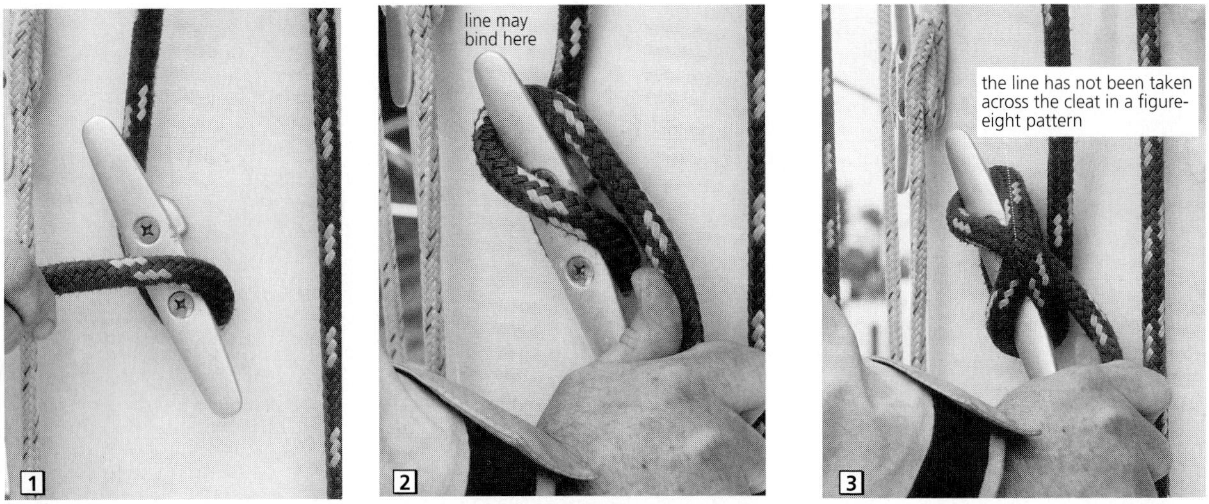
line may bind here
the line has not been taken across the cleat in a figure-eight pattern
1
2
3

Common mistakes when cleating off a line. 1, 2. *The line is brought onto the cleat on the wrong side. The ensuing knot is likely to bind up under a load.* 3. *The line is not taken across the cleat on the last wrap around the horn. The knot may bind under tension.*

1
2
3
4
5
6

Coiling and hanging up a halyard. 1. *The line is coiled, allowing each loop to form a figure eight.* 2. *Reach through the center of the coil and grab the line a little beyond where it comes off the cleat . . .* 3. *and pull a loop through the coil . . .* 4. *and then twist the loop one or two full turns . . .* 5. *before hooking it back over the cleat.* 6. *If the loop is dragged down until it has worked its way behind the top loop on the cleat, there is a good chance that it will not come loose, even in rough weather.*

*This mainsheet looks very neat (*left*), but coiling it this way is working twists into the line that do this (*middle*) at the other end! Right: The proper way to coil a braided halyard.*

With the wind piping up, it is important to have all lines properly stowed and secured.

To stow a mainsail neatly on its boom, start at the aft end and tug it backward as you fold it down and tie it off.

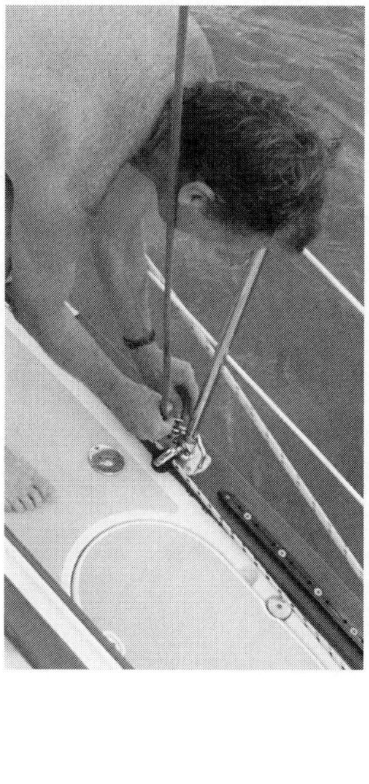

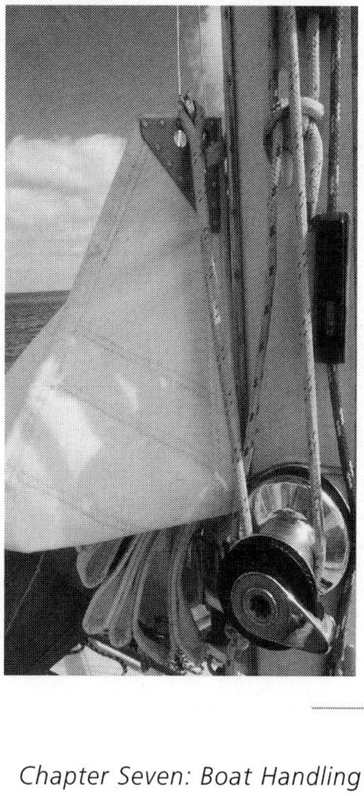

*For long-term stowage, it is better to remove the halyard from the mainsail and put it where it will not bang against the mast (*left and middle*). For short-term stowage, I simply loop it under a winch or cleat and pull it tight (*right*)—this keeps the head of the sail from riding up the track.*

RAISING AND LOWERING HEADSAILS, AND OPERATING A ROLLER REEFER

Before doing any sail-handling chores on the foredeck, close any open hatches! To raise a hanked-on headsail, the sheets are first attached to the clew cringle, using a bowline (see chapter 10) with an approximate 6-inch tail to prevent it working undone when the sail is flogging. It is unwise to use snap shackles for this job because any time the sail is flogging, they pose a hazard to life and limb; they also may open up or fail under heavy loads. The sheets are run through their respective sheet leads to the cockpit, where they are given a figure-eight knot to make sure they don't pull back out. The tack cringle is fastened to the stemhead. The sail is clipped on using either piston-style hanks or Wichard hanks (which can be put on and off with one hand leaving the other free to hang on in rough weather). Make sure the hanks all clip on from the same side—if any are reversed, the sail is twisted. The halyard is attached to the headboard, the boat is brought more or less head to wind, and the sail is hoisted. As with the main, halyard tension is related to wind strength; in general, a couple of tension curls should be starting to form just aft of the luff of the sail.

To drop a hanked-on sail, the boat is brought more or less head to wind, the sheets are eased until the sail flaps, and the halyard is let go. It helps to have someone grab the clew of the sail, pulling it inboard as the sail comes down, and generally gathering up the sailcloth so that it does not blow overboard and get dragged under the boat. The sail can then be tied off (*gasketed*) to get it firmly under control before taking the hanks off the headstay.

Raising and lowering a roller-reefed headsail is similar except that even with various pre-feeder devices, it is nowhere near as easy to feed the sail's luff rope or tape into the slot on a roller reefer as it is to clip hanks around a headstay. It generally takes two people to get a sail up. When a roller-reefed sail is lowered, it slides out of the luff groove in the roller reefer, leaving the entire sail billowing around on the foredeck with a much greater chance of going overboard than the hanked-on sail—again, two people are recommended.

Once a sail has been raised, when rolling it up on the roller reefer, a little tension must be maintained on the sheets. This ensures that the sail rolls tightly around its foil, minimizing windage and the likelihood of sail damage. Once the sail is in, a couple of extra turns wrap the sheets around it to hold everything in place. The reefing line is then locked off and the sheets gently tensioned to keep everything held snugly. To protect against damage from sunlight, the sail will have a UV cover down one side of its leech. It does not do a damn bit of good if the sail is rolled up with the UV cover on the inside (it happens)!

When unrolling a roller-reefed sail, it is essential to maintain a little pressure on the reefing line so that the line rolls cleanly and tightly onto the reefing drum. If this is not done, the line is likely to wad up on the reefing drum, making it difficult to roll the sail back in. In some instances, the line forms a riding turn and totally jams the drum. If it jams with the sail partially furled, it will not be possible to get the sail in, let it out, or get it down until the problem is fixed, which can be extremely unpleasant if the wind is kicking up.

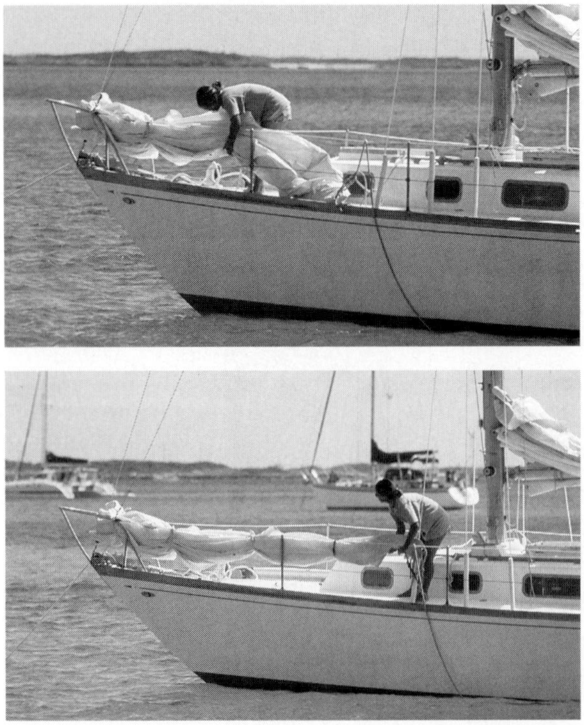

To gasket off a headsail, start at the forward end and work aft.

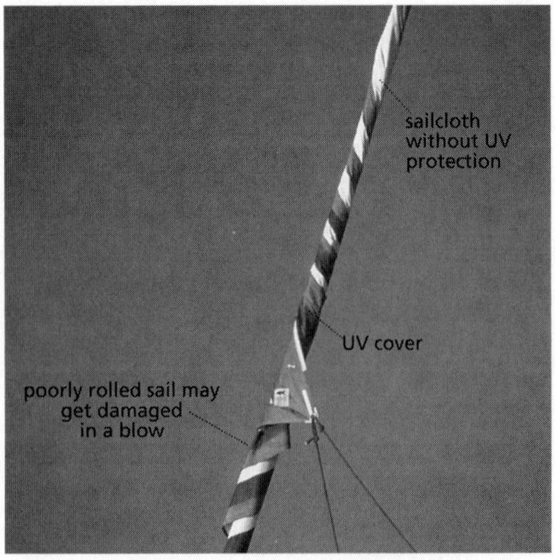

This poorly rolled sail is likely to result in sail damage in a blow. In addition, the UV cover (the dark cloth) is not fully protecting the sailcloth, which will deteriorate relatively rapidly in the sun.

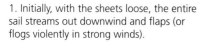

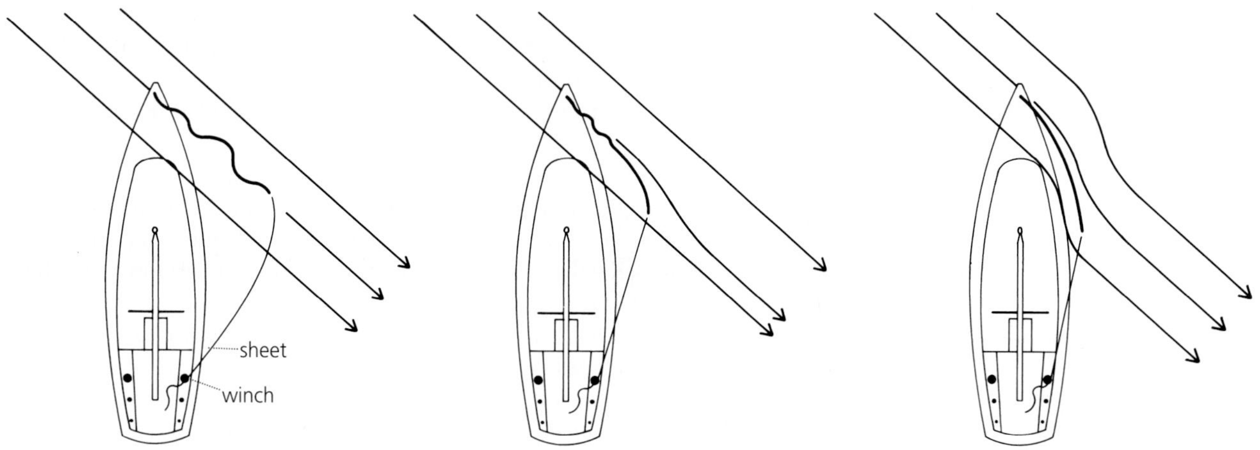

1. Initially, with the sheets loose, the entire sail streams out downwind and flaps (or flogs violently in strong winds).

2. Hauling in the sheet pulls the aft end of the sail out of line with the wind which stops the aft end flapping—the forward section still flaps (it is "luffing").

3. Further sheet tension stops the forward section of sail from luffing.

Trimming a headsail.

(continued from page 293) clues to oversheeting. The easiest way to check that the sails are not oversheeted is to occasionally bring the boat a little closer to the wind. The sail should almost immediately start to luff over its full length, in which case bearing away a degree or two puts it back at the critical angle of attack.

The closer it is desired to sail to the wind, the farther inboard the sails must be sheeted to keep them from luffing (hence, the inboard headsail tracks on many boats). On most modern cruising boats, the headsail tracks are set up so that a jib or genoa can be sheeted to within 7 to 10 degrees of the centerline of the boat (the *sheeting angle*); a staysail within 6 to 8 degrees of the centerline; and the main to any angle by a combination of dragging the traveler up and down its track and adjusting sheet tension.

The farther inboard sheets are brought, the more the force developed by the sails becomes a sideways (heeling) force, and the less it becomes a forward force. As long as the boat can be kept moving forward, the leeway caused by this sideways force is kept down by the *lift* generated by the keel and rudder. However, if the boat is driven too close to the wind, it will begin to stall and leeway will rise dramatically—the exercise becomes self-defeating. It is common for novice sailors to drive a boat too close to the wind, killing boat speed and increasing leeway.

How close is too close is affected by a number of factors including boat design (e.g., half angle of entry, hull shape), wind strength, sea state, and skill of the people sailing the boat. In light winds, it is often necessary to ease the sheets and fall off the wind a degree or two to maintain enough boat speed to counteract leeway. This has the added benefit of the boat's speed contributing to the apparent wind speed, which often results in a significant increase in boat speed (which in turn raises the apparent wind speed). As the wind picks up, a boat can be sailed at its closest to the wind; however, when the wind really kicks up and the seas start to build, the waves may cause the boat to stall out—again, it will be necessary to fall off the wind a few degrees to keep up boat speed.

Using Telltales

These are the basics of trimming sails when going to windward. From here, we get into all kinds of refinements that maximize performance, the adjustment of which adds greatly to the challenge and fun of sailing. In fact, on no other point of sail do small adjustments in sail trim have such a big effect on the boat's performance. In making these adjustments, it helps to have a series of *telltales*—brightly colored lengths of ribbon (polyester and mohair are better than wool because they are moisture-resistant)—fastened to both sides of a headsail, about a foot aft of the luff. There should be at least three sets: one near the base of the sail, one about halfway up, and one near the head. On a mainsail, telltales are attached to the trailing edge (leech) of the sail.

From the helm, the telltales on the aft (windward) side of a headsail are directly visible; those on the forward side are visible through the sail. When a sail is correctly trimmed, all the telltales on both sides of the sail will be streaming aft almost horizontally. If the sail is improperly trimmed, one or more of the telltales will be fluttering around in some other direction.

The beginning point of trimming a headsail is to sheet it in until at least one pair of telltales is streaming aft correctly. One or more of the other pairs is usually still fluttering around. There are two reasons for this:

- Depending on the angle the sheet makes with the foot of the sail, the tension applied to different parts of the sail will vary. If the sheet is led well aft on the boat, it makes a relatively shallow angle with the foot of the sail, which stretches this part of the sail out tight, but puts less tension on the head of the sail, allowing it to sag off to leeward (a phenomenon known as *twist*). Moving the sheet lead forward puts less tension on the foot of the sail (allowing it to belly out and increasing its draft or camber), but increases the tension at the head of the sail (reducing twist).
- Going to windward, the boat's forward motion has the effect of bringing the *apparent wind* (i.e., the wind actually experienced by the boat) forward of the true wind. The slower the true wind and the faster the boat, the more is this effect—which is why it sometimes seems that no matter what direction we sail, we end up going to windward. This effect is complicated by the fact that wind speed increases with height above the water. Given that the wind at the masthead is stronger than that at deck height, the extent to which the boat's speed moves the apparent wind forward is less in the upper part of the sail than it is in the lower part, which means the critical angle of attack of the sail will vary along its entire length.

Using a sheet lead position to control twist in a headsail.

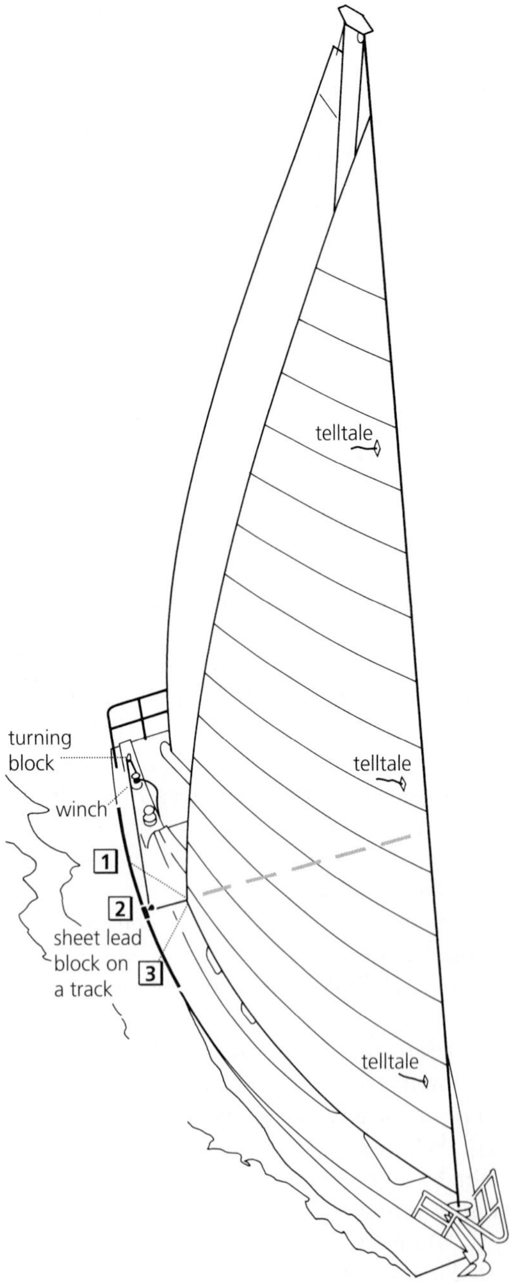

Position 1. Foot pulled tight, head would sag off (twist).

Position 2. Head and foot evenly tensioned.

Position 3. Head of sail pulled tight, foot would be loose (no twist).

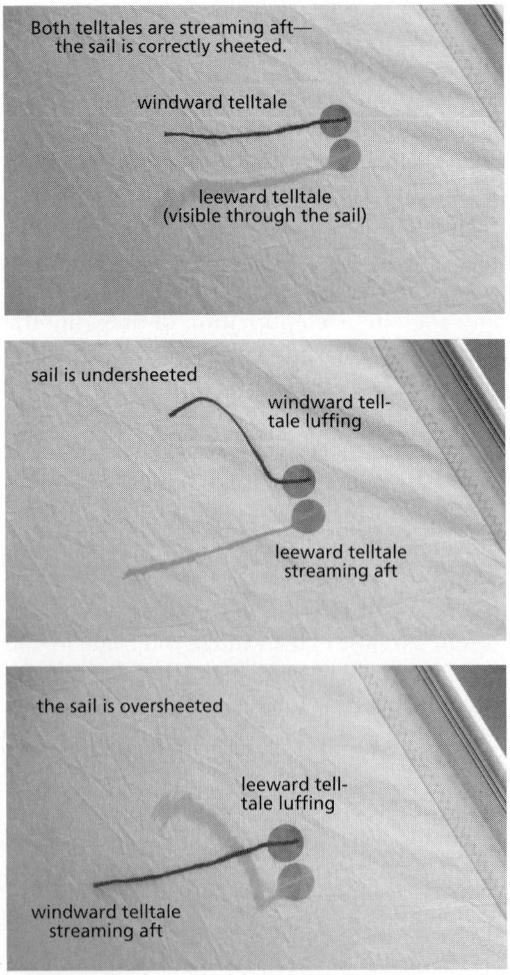

Using telltales to determine proper sheeting angles.

To get all the telltales to luff uniformly, sheet leads must be adjusted so that the amount of twist in a sail is appropriate for both the wind speed and how close the boat is being sailed to the wind. This is largely a matter of trial and error. Nowadays, almost all boats have sheet lead blocks mounted on tracks. The blocks are relatively simple to move backward and forward, although the tension on the sheet usually has to be eased each time an adjustment is made, and then the sheet has to be cranked back in (some boats have sheet leads that can be adjusted under load—these are real Cadillacs). It is amazing the difference that a few inches in lead-block positioning can make on sail trim.

To determine a starting point for sheet lead positions, draw an imaginary line from the center of the luff down through the clew to deck level; this is approximately where the sheet lead block should be.

If any part of a jib or genoa is undersheeted, the windward telltales (those on the aft side of the sail) in that area tend to flutter up and down. If the telltales at the bottom of the sail are streaming aft correctly, but those at the top are not, the sheet lead needs to be brought forward to tighten the upper part of the sail (remove twist). If the telltales at the top are setting correctly and those at the bottom are fluttering, the sheet lead needs to be moved aft (increase twist). In general, it is better to have the sheet lead too far aft rather than too far forward.

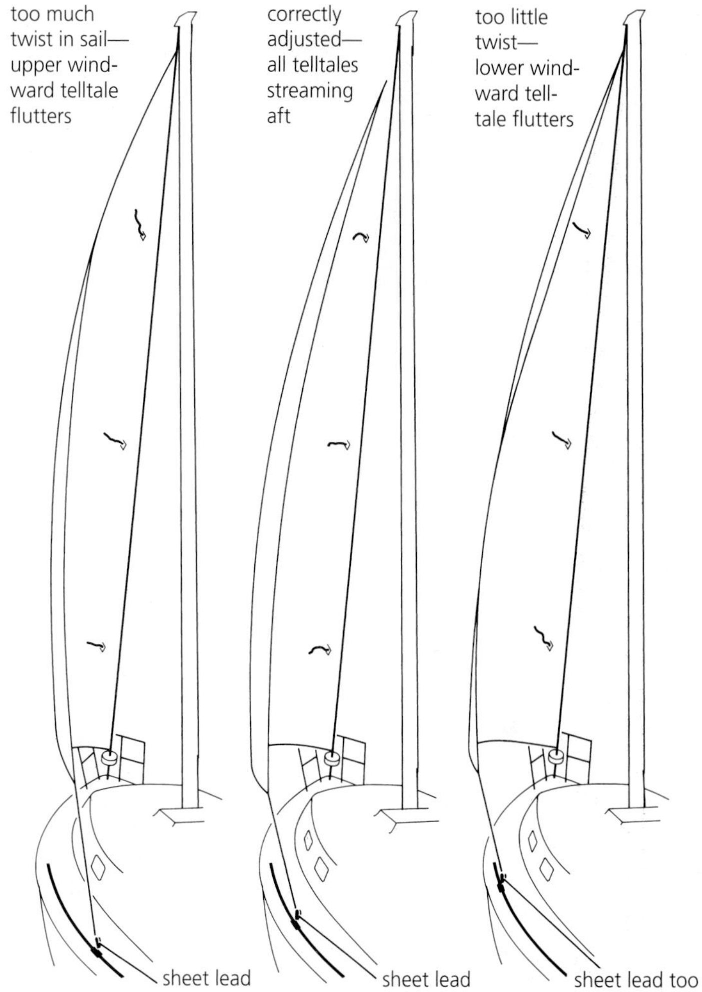

The effect of sheet-lead positions on twist and sail trim.

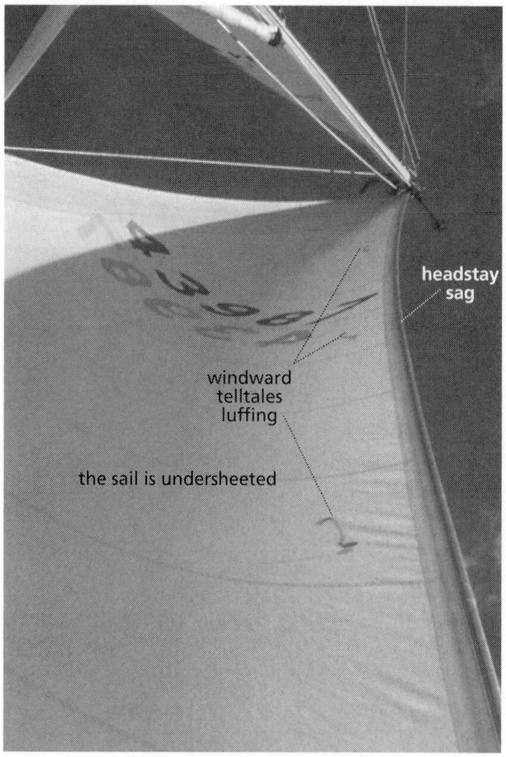

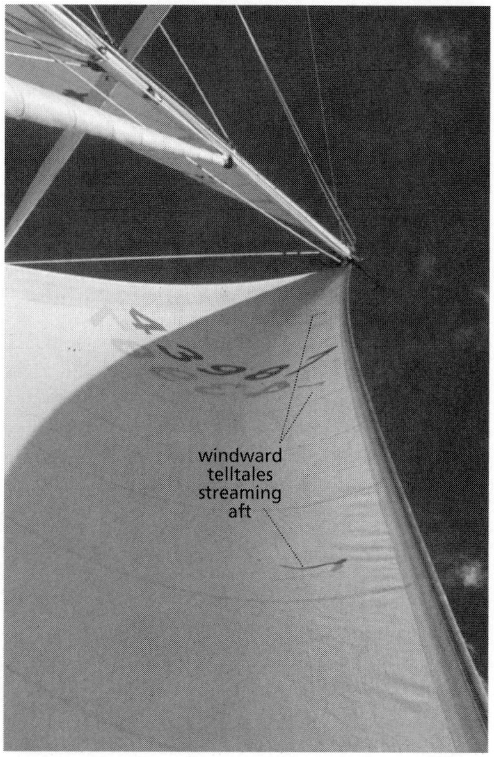

There is too much sag in this headstay! In the photo far left, all three windward telltales are luffing—the sheet needs to be tightened or the boat sailed a little farther off the wind. In the next photo, all telltales are flying aft—the sheet is nicely trimmed.

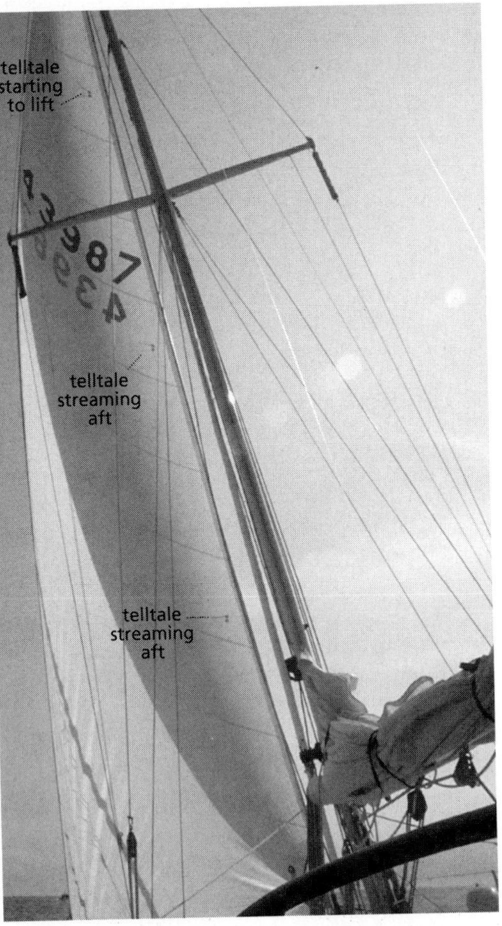

Mainsail telltales. In the top photo, the telltale is just lifting to windward—the sail could benefit from being moved a tad to windward. In the lower photo, it is just falling off to leeward—the sail could benefit from being eased out a tad.

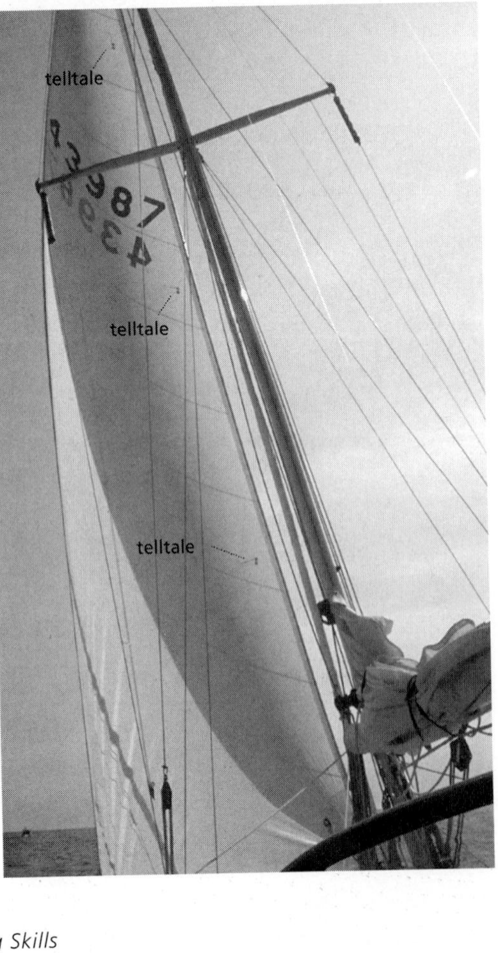

In the top photo, the telltales are looking good, although the upper windward one is just starting to lift. In the bottom photo, the upper windward one is lifting, but the rest are OK. There is still a little too much twist in this sail—the sheet lead block needs to be moved forward.

On the other hand, if the sail is oversheeted in any area, the leeward telltales (those on the forward side of the sail) tend to hang down or flutter. If the lower ones are streaming aft correctly while those at the top are not, the sheet leads need to be moved aft to put more twist in the sail. If the upper ones are streaming aft but the lower ones are not, the sheet leads need to be moved forward to put more draft in the lower part of the sail.

On a mainsail, the telltales are on the trailing edge of the sail. Going to windward, the traveler should be used to put the boom more or less on the centerline of the boat (the traveler car needs to be a little up to windward of the centerline to do this). As with a headsail, the sheet should be trimmed until the sail has just stopped luffing (or perhaps is luffing slightly as a result of turbulence created by the mast or backwinding from the headsail). At this point, the telltales should be streaming aft in the same direction as the sail. If they aren't, it is time to do some experimenting, making a couple of different adjustments. The amount of twist in the sail can be increased by pulling the mainsheet traveler up to windward on its track, while easing the sheet and vang. It can be reduced by easing the traveler down on its track while tightening the sheet and vang. In general, if the telltales fall off to leeward, the main is sheeted in too tight; if they flutter around, it is not sheeted tight enough. Again, if they react differently, there is too little or too much twist in the sail.

Larger sails generally have *leech lines*; that is, lines sewn into the leech of the sail, the tension of which can be adjusted from the foot of the sail. If the sail adjustments described previously produce a leech that flutters, the leech line needs to be tightened just enough to stop the flutter. If the leech cups up to windward, the leech line needs to be loosened to just before the point of flutter.

Adjusting Draft

Going to windward, the headsail should be trimmed first, and then the main trimmed just enough to stop it being back-winded (i.e., to stop it luffing). The main should be trimmed so that the twist in its leech matches that in the headsail. Once the sails are trimmed, if the boat is brought a few degrees into the wind, both sails should luff along their entire length at the same time. When properly trimmed, most boats show an appreciable acceleration as they settle down with their sails at the critical (optimum) angle of attack. The boat is said to be *in the groove*. It is a tremendously satisfying feeling to get a boat into this happy state of affairs, and an exceedingly frustrating one to be continually tweaking sheets and sheet leads, and still not achieving it (which sometimes happens).

As wind strengths increase, the point of maximum curvature (the camber) in sails tends to be blown aft. Because the force developed by a sail is just about at right angles to this point of maximum curvature, the sail develops a stronger sideways thrust with less forward drive—the boat heels more and slows down. To counteract this, the camber needs to be brought forward again. Initially, this is done by tightening the luff of the sail (cranking up on the halyard or using various downhauls, such as a cunningham, to pull down on the base of the luff). This stretches the forward part of the sail tight and pulls the camber forward. On a mainsail, tightening the outhaul also helps to move the draft forward in the lower part of the sail.

Another way to reduce draft in headsails and pull the camber forward is to keep headstays as tight as possible, minimizing sag. To minimize the draft in a mainsail, bend is pulled into a mast so that its midsection curves forward. Both can be achieved by tightening the backstay (hence,

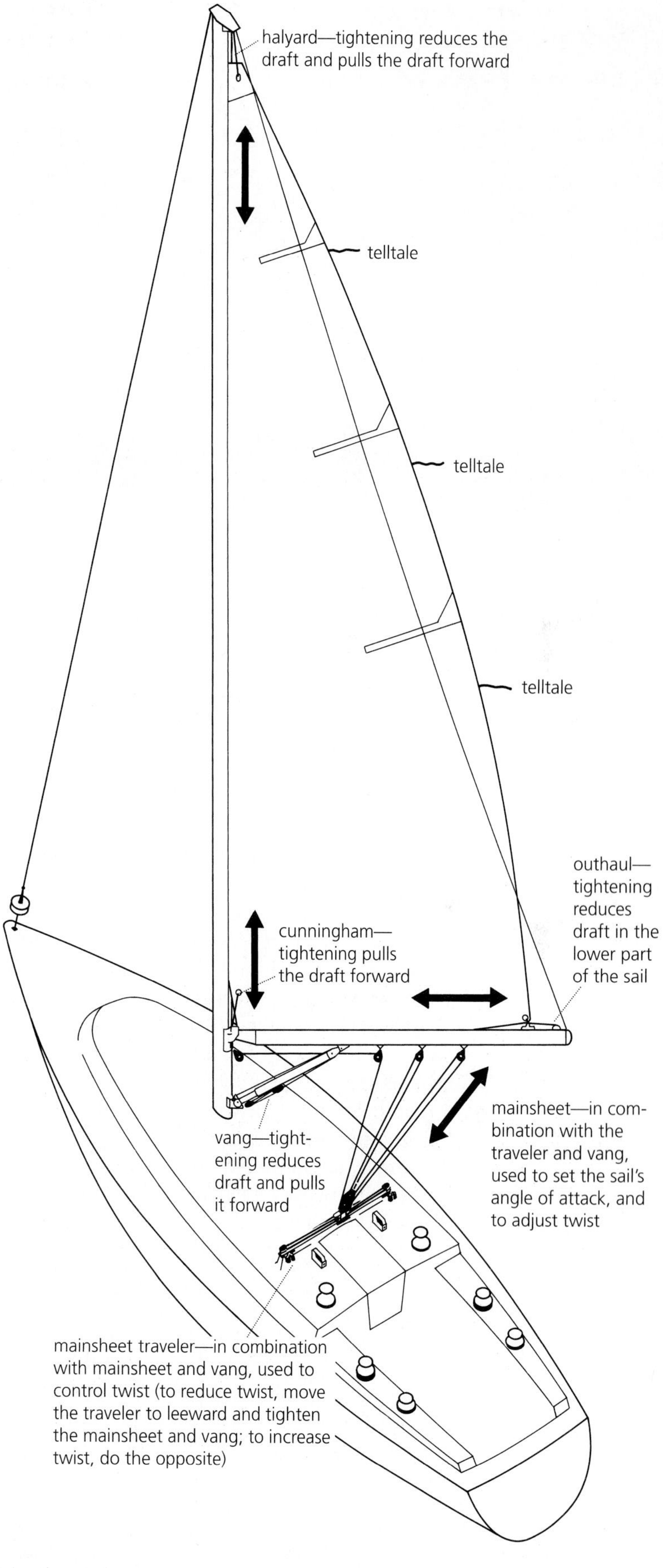

halyard—tightening reduces the draft and pulls the draft forward
telltale
telltale
telltale
outhaul—tightening reduces draft in the lower part of the sail
cunningham—tightening pulls the draft forward
mainsheet—in combination with the traveler and vang, used to set the sail's angle of attack, and to adjust twist
vang—tightening reduces draft and pulls it forward
mainsheet traveler—in combination with mainsheet and vang, used to control twist (to reduce twist, move the traveler to leeward and tighten the mainsheet and vang; to increase twist, do the opposite)

Mainsail controls.

The padded foam luff on this roller-reefing headsail will help to flatten the sail when it is partially rolled up. (Courtesy Harken)

the use of various backstay adjusters on many boats), although the degree to which backstay tension and mast bend can be increased varies substantially among boat designs.

Easing the sheets also reduces draft, but at the expense of causing sails, which are cut with considerable camber, to luff. As wind speed continues to increase, headsails can be changed for smaller sails built with less camber (flatter cut); however, nowadays, the sail tends to be partially rolled up—which, unfortunately, often increases the camber. Various devices can minimize this, including foam luffs and reefing devices that take a roll in the center of the sail before the head and foot are brought in. Slab-reefed mainsails are generally built flatter in their upper portions so that as they are progressively reefed down, they exhibit increasingly less camber.

In any event, for any given angle of attack, the flatter a sail is cut and sheeted, the farther outboard it can be eased without luffing. This maximizes the forward component of the sail's thrust and minimizes the heeling component. Heeling momentum can be further reduced by increasing the twist in the sail, which allows the upper portions that contribute the most to heeling to luff and lose power. In strong winds, when the boat is starting to be overpressed, the sails are correctly trimmed when the upper portions of both the headsail and the mainsail luff at the same time, a little before the lower portions. In stronger gusts, the boat can be allowed to round up some, which spills more of the wind from the sails.

On almost all boats, if draft is not controlled and heeling is allowed to become excessive, the boat develops a strong *weather helm* (a tendency to round up into the wind), which significantly impairs performance. Weather helm makes a boat difficult to handle and slows the boat down because of the increased resistance created by the excessive rudder angle needed to counteract it. Reefing down (especially reefing the mainsail) generally makes the boat more comfortable and easier to handle with no loss of speed, and sometimes with a gain in speed (weather helm is discussed in more detail later in this chapter).

Tacking

If the wind is coming over the starboard side of the boat (the right side when looking forward) and the boom is out to port (the left side when looking forward), the boat is said to be on *starboard tack*. When the wind is coming over the port side with the boom out to starboard, the boat is on *port tack*.

Tacking (coming about) is the act of bringing the boat from close hauled on one tack to close hauled on the other, passing through the eye of the wind, rather than running off downwind on one "tack" and then turning back up into the wind on the other. (This is known as *wearing ship* and is rarely practiced because it loses a lot of ground and involves a potentially hazardous *jibe*—described in the following section). Tacking requires sufficient momentum to carry the boat through the maneuver. The required momentum varies according to circumstances and boat type; however, in almost all cases, more momentum is needed as the wind and waves build.

With insufficient momentum, if a boat gets hit by a wave or gust of wind at the wrong moment, its bow may be knocked off at the same time as almost all forward motion ceases. Steerageway is lost as the headsail refills (on the same tack as before). The pressure of the wind in the headsail spins the boat farther off the wind, with little the helmsperson can do to control the situation until the boat builds up sufficient speed to restore steerageway. In these circumstances, the headsail sheets should be loosened to increase the forward drive of the headsail and to reduce the extent to which the bow gets blown downwind. As the boat regains momentum, it can be brought back onto the wind, hardening in the sheets as it comes around.

In light and heavy weather, it often pays to bear away a few degrees before tacking simply to build up speed and momentum. Regardless of weather conditions and assuming the boat is moving fast enough, the basic tacking procedure is as follows:

1. The helmsperson warns the crew that the maneuver is about to take place by calling out, "Ready about." A check is made to see that the windward sheet on the headsail is accessible, unobstructed, and ready to go on its winch, with the winch handle nearby. A similar check is made to ensure that when the leeward sheet is let go, it is not going to tangle or foul anything. If the boat has running backstays, what will become the windward runner can be set up.
2. The helmsperson calls out, "Lee oh" or "Hard alee" as he or she puts down the helm so that the boat swings up into the wind. It is important not to make too radical a helm movement—this causes the rudder to stall, killing the boat's speed. In the early part of the tack, the sails are still drawing and the boat should be, to some extent, "sailed around."
3. It is at this time that many crew members let fly the headsail sheets too soon, enthusiastically dragging the headsail across the boat with the other sheet, causing the headsail to get back-winded on the windward side. This stalls out the turn. Headsails should be kept sheeted on the leeward side until they start to back-wind because the act of turning the boat moves the apparent wind aft so that the headsail keeps drawing through the first part of the turn, driving the boat around. Also, the initial back-winding on the leeward side (which is now becoming the windward side) helps maintain the speed of the turn.
4. Just after the sail starts to back-wind, the sheet is let go. The helm may now be put over somewhat more aggressively to speed up the rate of turn. The sail should be allowed to blow across the boat. Again, an enthusiastic crew member may try to drag it across with the other sheet, which often ends up with something getting fouled (typically, the clew gets caught in the inner forestay on a cutter or in the shrouds). Left to its own devices, the sail usually comes through quite cleanly, even on a cutter.
5. Once the sail has come across, it needs to be sheeted home *by hand* on the new tack *as fast and as hard as possible*. At this time, there should be just one turn on the winch to minimize friction. As *soon as the sheet starts to go tight*, second and third turns are thrown on (and maybe fourth or fifth), and then the winch handle is used to do any final trimming. With proper timing and coordination, it is possible to get even large headsails almost sheeted home without the use of the winch handle. On a shorthanded cutter, the headsail is sheeted home first, then the staysail.
6. Meanwhile, the helmsperson needs to be coming out of the turn a little before it is completed. If not, the boat is likely to be oversteered. If oversteered, the headsail is then sheeted too tight for the boat's heading, and excessive heeling forces and continuing turning momentum is generated. If this happens, it may be necessary to ease the headsail sheets until the boat picks up speed and the helmsperson regains control. In any event, if the boat has more or less stalled out during the tack, the headsails should not be sheeted in too tight until speed and steerageway have been regained.

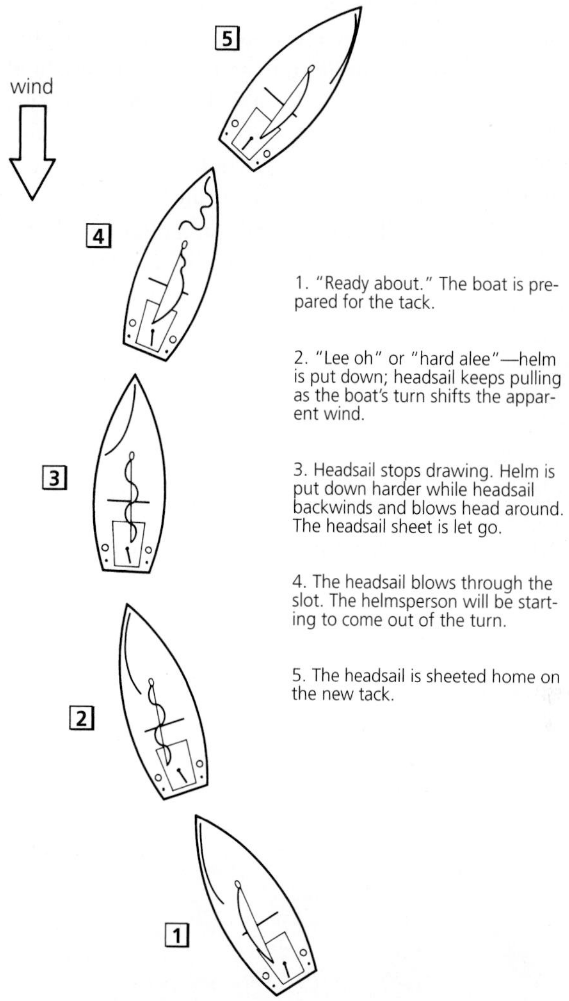

wind
5
4
3
2
1
1. "Ready about." The boat is prepared for the tack.
2. "Lee oh" or "hard alee"—helm is put down; headsail keeps pulling as the boat's turn shifts the apparent wind.
3. Headsail stops drawing. Helm is put down harder while headsail backwinds and blows head around. The headsail sheet is let go.
4. The headsail blows through the slot. The helmsperson will be starting to come out of the turn.
5. The headsail is sheeted home on the new tack.

Tacking.

Right: *Close reaching to broad reaching.* Below: *Contemporary boat (1, 2) moving nicely on a reach. Note that the leeches of the two sails are more or less parallel, as they should be; however, the upper half of the main (3) has too much twist, is falling off to leeward, and is contributing no drive. This is probably just as well because the boat is hard-pressed in the gusts, at which time the bow is digging in, the stern is lifting, and the top of the rudder is starting to come out of the water. The boat is trying to round up and is becoming harder to handle; it is time to reef down.*

Reaching

As soon as a boat moves off the wind a little and is in a position to ease its sheets, it is said to be *reaching*. While still close to the wind, it is *close reaching*; as the wind moves on the beam, it is *beam reaching*; and as the wind moves aft of the beam, it is *broad reaching*.

Trimming sails on a close reach is almost the same as trimming them when close hauled; that is, the sheets are hardened until the luff stops fluttering, with the sheet lead blocks, mainsail traveler, and vang all adjusted so that twist is properly controlled and the telltales stream aft in unison. However, the sails should be given more draft (camber) to increase their pulling power, which is accomplished by easing halyards, cunninghams, and outhauls. The effect of increasing the draft is to bring the sails

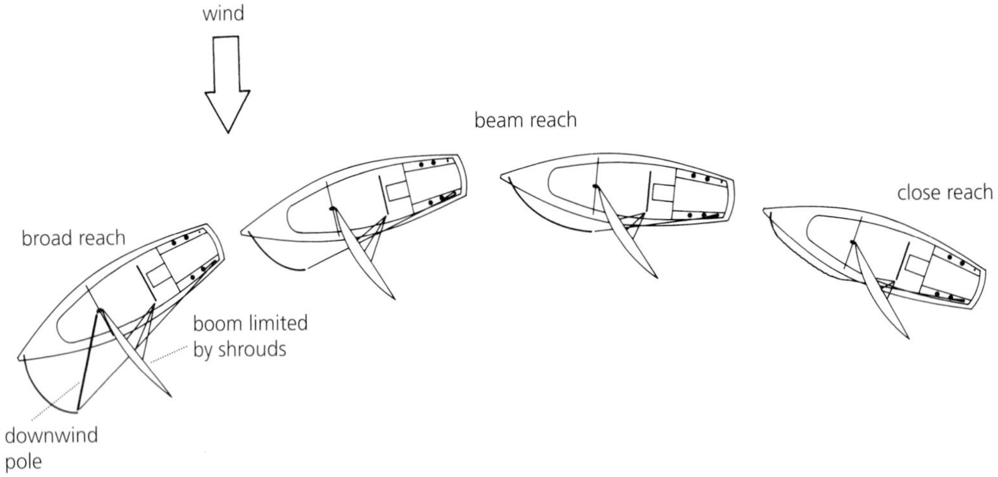

closer to a luff; as a result, the sheets cannot be eased as much as might be expected.

As a boat moves farther off the wind, the sheets are increasingly eased. The force generated by the sail is more in a forward direction and less sideways. Boat speed picks up while heeling diminishes. In theory, a beam reach is the fastest point of sail, but this is only the case as long as there is sufficient wind to get the boat up to its hull speed or higher. With lesser winds, a close reach is often faster because the boat's forward motion contributes to the apparent-wind speed, raising the wind speed flowing over the sails.

On any kind of reach, the faster the boat's speed relative to the true wind speed, the farther forward is the apparent wind. To get the most out of a boat in lighter winds, the sails need to be constantly trimmed to take account of changes in boat speed and the changing apparent-wind angle. As the wind increases in strength, the apparent wind changes less and, in any event, it is easier to sail the boat to its full potential. With a strong wind, there is little skill in getting just about any boat up to its nominal hull speed on a reach, and many can be made to go considerably faster.

However, as the wind and boat speed increases, a boat is likely to prove more difficult to handle. Specifically, weather helm rises markedly on most boats. It becomes necessary to reef down to maintain control. Prior to this, however, it may be possible to restore helm balance by tightening the halyard on the headsail and easing the mainsheet until the main is being sailed on the edge of a luff. Putting more twist into the main until its upper sections start to luff also helps depower it, reducing weather helm.

Running before the Wind

A boat is considered to be *running before the wind* when the wind is coming from astern to somewhere around 40 degrees either side of astern. As the wind moves well aft of the beam, it pushes rather than sucks the boat forward. Sail trim tends to be less finicky. The boat's speed lessens the apparent wind so that there is just a gentle breeze blowing across the decks. There is little or no heeling, the boat makes little or no leeway, it moves with the waves rather than bashing into them, and—in general—everything is rather comfortable and relaxed.

At times, this can lead to complacency. If it becomes necessary to round up, it may suddenly be discovered that there is a near gale out there and the boat is seriously over-canvassed. For example, a boat barreling downwind at 7 or 8 knots under full canvas in a 20-knot wind will experience an apparent wind of 12 or 13 knots. However, if that same boat comes onto the wind at a boat speed of 6 knots, the apparent wind will jump to 26 knots—twice what it was a couple of minutes before. Some hasty reefing down will be needed.

On a downwind run, the idea is to put as much sail area as possible, at as near a right angle as possible, to the flow of the wind. The mainsail is let out until the boom almost bears against the shrouds, the halyard and outhaul are eased to add draft, and the vang is tightened to stop the boom from lifting. The danger in this configuration is that if the wind gets around the backside of the mainsail and suddenly throws the boom over to the other side of the boat, it can have enough force to do considerable damage (up to and including bringing down the mast). This is known as an *accidental jibe*—rather than deliberately jibing the sail in a controlled manner.

The closer a boat is sailed to dead downwind, the greater the chances of an accidental jibe, especially in following seas because they will set the boat rolling from side to side. To avoid a jibe, it is normal to keep the wind at least a few degrees off the stern. In addition, the mainsheet should have a stopper knot that brings the boom up short before it hits the

Swept-back spreaders are a liability on a run.

shrouds. This breaks some of the force of an accidental jibe, although quite possibly inflicting expensive damage on the mainsheet traveler. On a downwind run—from a performance point of view—the position of the mainsheet traveler is irrelevant (the vang is doing all the work in controlling twist), so the traveler may as well be centered—its control lines also help absorb some of the shock in a jibe.

If there is any likelihood of an accidental jibe, a *preventer* should be rigged on the boom. In its simplest form, it is a line taken from the boom down to an attachment point on the caprail and tensioned so that the boom cannot move aft. A better approach is to rig the line through a block on the rail or a hawsehole forward, and then bring it back to a cleat in the cockpit. A second line is rigged in a similar manner on the other side of the boat. In a controlled jibe, the one preventer is let off and the other is hauled in. The cleats need to be extremely strong—the loads on them can be enormous.

Whatever is done, *a preventer should always be attached in some way to the mainsheet block attachment shackle or bale rather than to the boom itself*. This way, if the mainsheet is cranked in without remembering to loosen the preventer, the two lines simply pull against one another, whereas if the preventer is fastened to the boom, the boom may get bent. If the mainsheet is attached to the end of the boom, the attachment point for a preventer may be well out over the water on a run. Rather than lean overboard to reach it, a couple of short lengths of line can be permanently attached and run forward to a cleat on the boom. When preventers are needed, they can be attached to these lengths of line.

A preventer should be rigged to the mainsheet block and not to the boom. This way, if the boom is accidentally sheeted in without easing the preventer, the boom will not get bent.

There are various proprietary anti-jibe devices (boom brakes and locks) on the market that, to some extent, substitute for preventers. These devices consist of a line lead from one caprail to the other through a device attached to the boom. Different devices either have a lock or can be set up to induce a high degree of

"Dutchman" boom brake. (Courtesy Martin Van Breems)

The Scott Boomlock in action. The device acts as both a lock and a brake. (Courtesy Scott Boomlock)

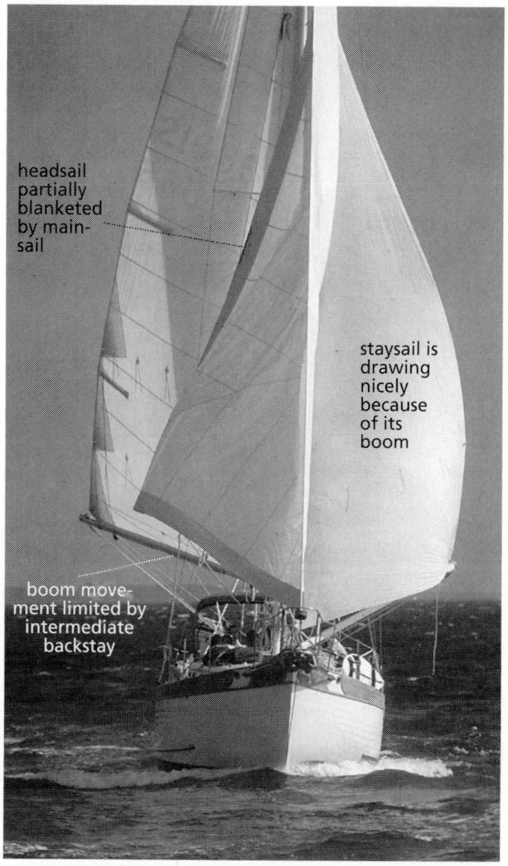
headsail partially blanketed by main-sail
staysail is drawing nicely because of its boom
boom move-ment limited by intermediate backstay

Running dead before the wind, this cutter has a couple of disadvantages. First, the rig has intermediate permanently attached backstays that limit the extent to which the boom can be let out. Second, there is no pole for the genoa, which—as a result—is collapsing and filling, contributing little drive while it wears out the sail. Note that the club-footed staysail is drawing nicely because the club is acting as a pole, booming it out.

Nada *running wing and wing with the genoa poled out and drawing nicely.*

resistance to movement of the line. In the event of a jibe, the type of device that locks the line acts just like a preventer; the type that imparts resistance keeps the rate of the boom moving down to a speed at which damage is not done.

Anti-jibe devices work, but the leeward line generally cannot be set up tight enough to keep the boom from slatting back and forth when the boat rolls in light winds—the movement is restricted, but not stopped. It may be necessary to add a preventer (in which case, the anti-jibe device is serving little purpose). The two lines led to the caprails also make it impossible to move up and down the side decks when wearing a safety harness and safety line without unclipping the safety line halfway down the side deck, and then reconnecting it on the other side of the control lines. Of course, there is also the expense of another piece of gear.

To execute a controlled jibe with or without an anti-jibe device, the boat is put on a dead downwind course and kept more or less on it until the jibe is completed. If the boat has running backstays and either is set up, it is eased. The vang is hauled in tight to control mainsail twist and keep the boom from riding up in the air at any time. If this is not done, the boom may foul the backstay—a situation that for some reason is known as a *Chinese jibe*. The mainsheet traveler is centered (if not already), the loaded preventer is eased (or the anti-jibe device is released), and the mainsheet is hauled in until the boom is on the centerline. As soon as the boom has come across to the other side and the sail has filled with wind (the boom can be helped over by changing course a few degrees to bring the wind onto its other side), the mainsheet is eased until the boom is all the way out—at which time the other preventer is set up or the anti-jibe device is locked.

To keep a jibe under control without an anti-jibe device, the two preventers should be eased and tightened in concert with the main sheet. This way, even if the wind throws the boom over unexpectedly in either direction, the boom cannot travel far before it is brought up short, which limits the momentum it can build up.

When running before the wind, if the headsail is set on the same side as the mainsail, it will be blanketed by the main and simply flap around. In this case, it pays to put a reef or two in the main or to take the main down altogether. If the boat is almost dead before the wind, the headsail often can be poled out on the side opposite the main (*running wing and wing*). However, if any kind of a sea is running, it requires a fair amount of concentration on the part of the helmsperson to avoid the wind periodically collapsing the headsail. The greater

Pole-end arrangements, clipped into the clew of a sail (no pole lift or foreguy required) and clipped around the sheet (pole lift and foreguy required).

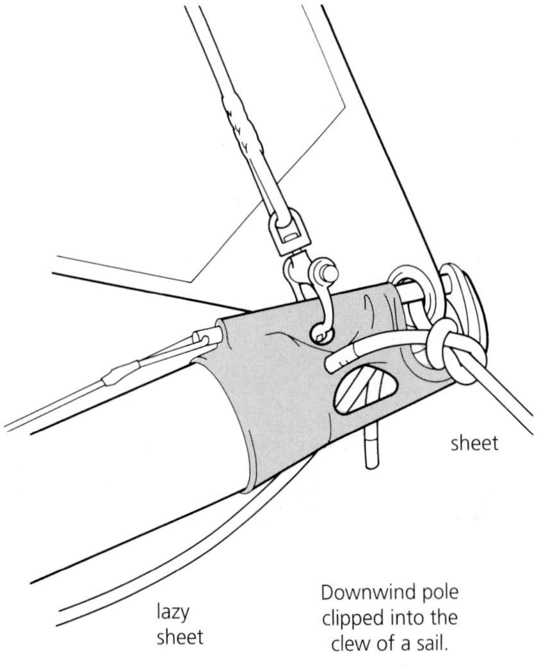

Downwind pole clipped into the clew of a sail.

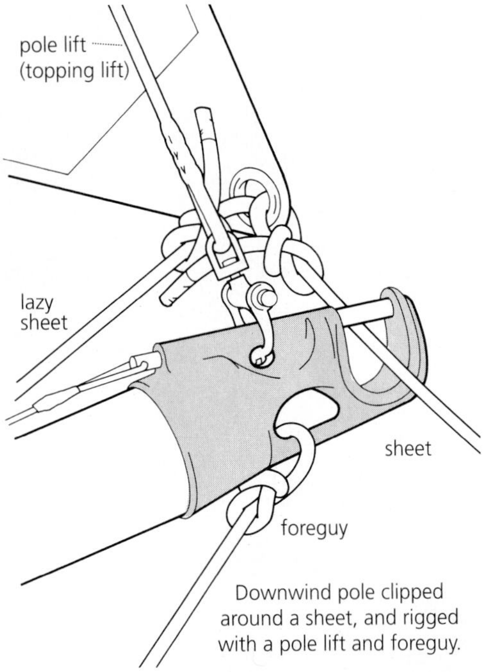

Downwind pole clipped around a sheet, and rigged with a pole lift and foreguy.

danger is that, in trying to keep the headsail filled, the helmsperson brings the wind across the stern and accidentally jibes the mainsail.

The easiest way to set a pole to hold out a headsail is to clip the pole's outboard end into the clew of the sail. This can be done if the sail is cut low enough for a crew member to reach the clew (most cruising sails are not cut this low) or if the sail is hanked on (in which case, the halyard can be eased enough to put the clew in reach and then re-hoist the sail). Otherwise, the pole is clipped over the sheet, but it will need a *pole lift* (topping lift) to raise its outboard end to the height of the clew, and a foreguy to keep it from being dragged back into and bent around the shrouds.

The pole lift is rigged from the outboard end or middle of the pole through a block on the forward face of the mast and down to a cleat. The foreguy is rigged from the tip of the pole through a block or hawsehole near the bow of the boat and back to a convenient cleat. The pole itself should always be horizontal; if not, the compression loads sometimes generated by a sail tend to drive it up or down the mast and may buckle it. Nowadays, most poles are fitted to a car that rides on a track up and down the face of the mast.

In practice, modern racing boats do not run wing and wing—it has been found that they get to where they are going faster if they "tack" downwind (i.e., run with the wind far enough over the stern quarter to keep the mainsail from blanketing the headsail, allowing this sail to draw properly). The boat is periodically jibed onto the other "tack" to keep moving in the desired direction. Many cruisers, ourselves included, find this to be too much hard work: we prefer to point the boat at a downwind destination, run wing and wing if that is what is needed, and suffer the slight performance penalty!

Double Headsails

Another way to run before the wind is with the classic "trade-wind" rig, which utilizes two headsails, poled out on either side of the boat. The main is generally dropped or sheeted amidships to lessen the boat's rolling (which can be quite atrocious at times). If the wind is over one or another quarter, the two sails can be set with a single pole (the sail on the windward side has the pole). The idea is to set the pole(s) up at right angles to the wind so that the sails catch as much of the wind as possible. To be most effective, the pole length should be somewhere between 100 and 110 percent of the distance from the base of the mast to the base of the forestay (known to sailmakers as the *"J" length*).

It is not necessary to have two headstays for this rig. On a typical modern cruising boat that has a roller-reefing headsail, the roller-reefed sail is set and then a second genoa is hoisted, fastened at just its tack, head, and clew. Because sail shape is not important in these conditions, the second sail can be made of a material that does not hold its shape too well (e.g., nylon).

We carry a 130 percent nylon genoa that is a joy to handle because of its light weight. We

Wing and Wing

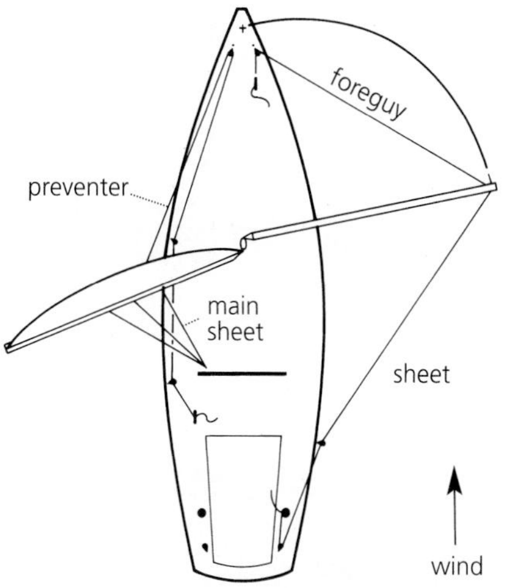

Two Headsails Poled Out

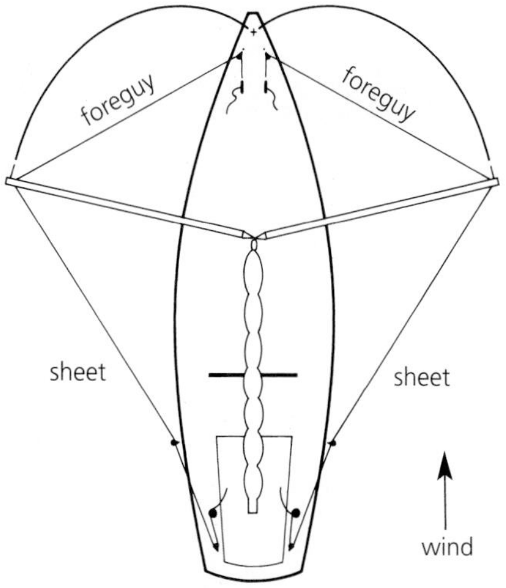

Two Headsails with Single Pole Used to Pole out First Sail and Boom Used for Second. Main is Reefed or Furled.

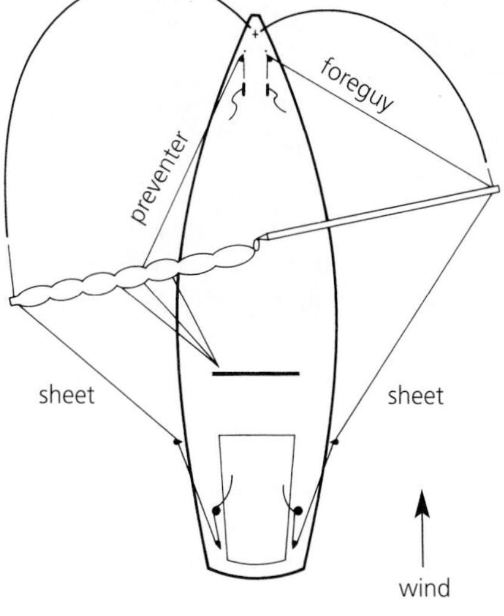

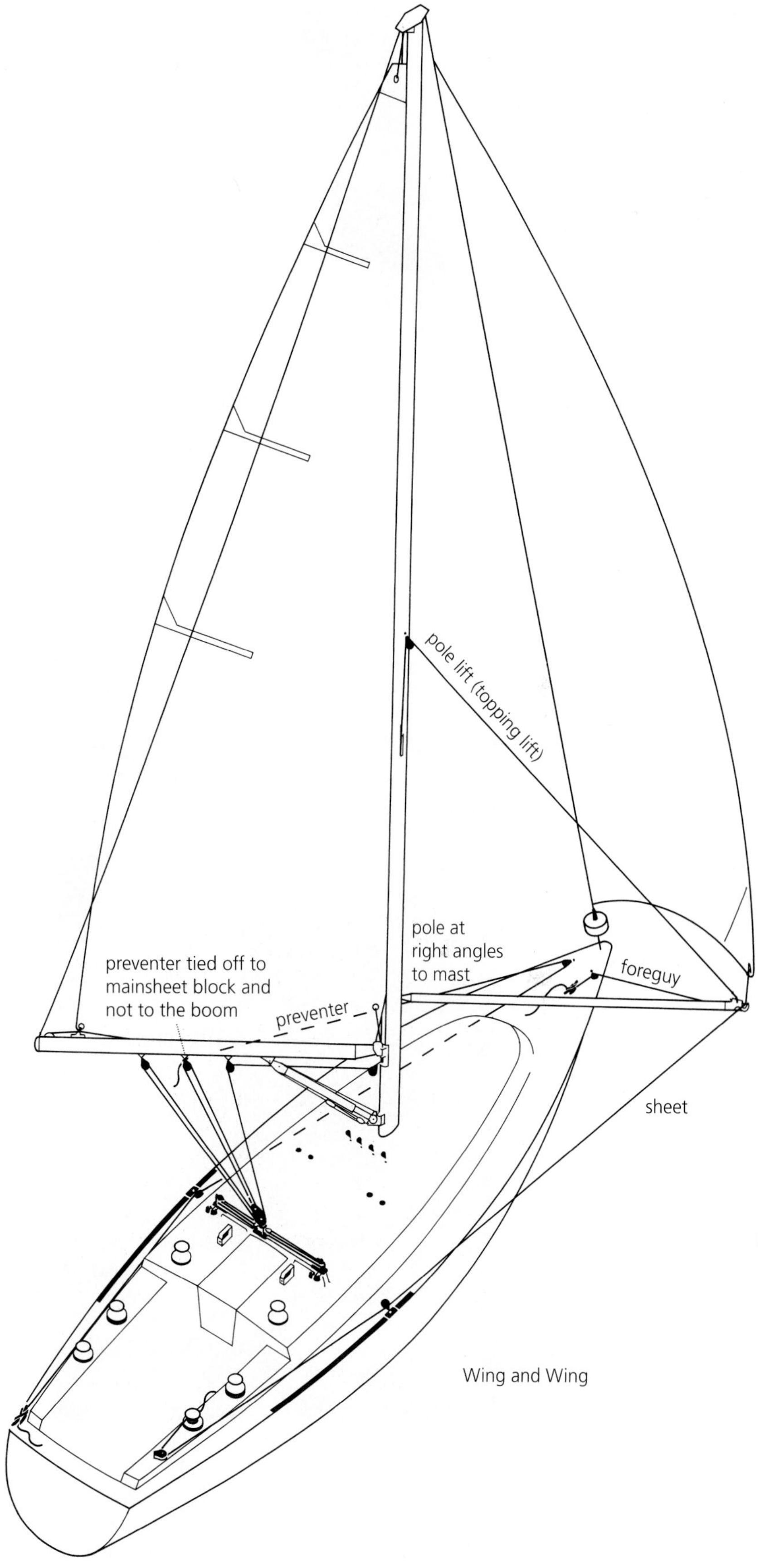

Wing and Wing

Downwind rigs in the absence of a spinnaker or asymmetric spinnaker.

Right and below left: Nada *running with twin poled-out headsails both with and without the mainsail. Dropping the main has little effect on the speed because when it is up, it significantly blankets and depowers one of the headsails.* Below right: *Our second lightweight (nylon) genoa is flown loose, simply attached at the foot, head, and clew. The tack line (at the foot) is subject to chafe as currently set up—it needs to be modified.*

have two poles stowed on the mast, each with its own topping lift (pole lift). To set two headsails, we first pole our roller-reefed genoa out on one side of the boat, clipping the pole around the sheet. We add a foreguy from the tip of the pole to a cleat forward, which is used to keep the pole from being dragged back into the shrouds. The second genoa is then fastened at its tack, given a sheet that is led aft and hoisted using a spare halyard. The second pole is clipped around its sheet and rigged the same way as the first pole. (If a boat only has one pole, the mainsail can be dropped, the boom pulled way out with a preventer, and the sheet of the second sail led through a block on the end of the boom, which now acts as a second pole.)

This rig takes but a few minutes to set up, is almost self-tending once up, never gets out of control, and is easy to take down (lifting the inboard end of the pole brings the sheet inboard, spilling most of the wind out of the sail). However, it is nowhere near as versatile as a spinnaker (it cannot be used with the wind forward of a very broad reach) and has significantly less driving power. Furthermore, as mentioned previously, these rigs sometimes set the boat to rolling abominably, primarily because the two headsails are almost the same size and, therefore, well balanced, which allows the passing waves to roll the boat from side to side. Increasing the size of one headsail or decreasing the other produces an imbalance that helps dampen the roll.

Spinnakers

There used to be two types of cruisers: those who focused on performance and who flew spinnakers, most of whom had relatively light and fast boats that did not venture too far from home; and those who were concerned with comfort and ease of handling, who did not fly spinnakers, and who had relatively heavy-displacement boats that they would take anywhere. To some extent, this is still true—I don't think we have ever seen a boat flying a spinnaker in those parts of the world that we typically cruise. However, the distinction is blurring as sailors of all stripes get more involved with the technology of getting the best out of their boat at the same time as the development of "cruising spinnakers" has reduced the handling and control problems associated with full-blown spinnakers.

The truth of the matter is, unless your chosen cruising grounds are the high latitudes, more time is likely to be spent in light airs than heavy airs. While it is easy to reef down sails to deal with the heavy stuff, the typical overloaded cruising boat is seriously under-canvassed in the light stuff. Light-air sails do more to improve overall performance than just about anything else.

Nevertheless, the full-blown spinnaker is a somewhat temperamental beast that rightfully intimidates short-handed cruising sailors. It requires a fair amount of rigging, which translates into a lot of work to set it and douse it. Once up, it also has the potential to overwhelm the boat and get the boat and crew into a whole lot of trouble. Its more recent derivative—the "cruising spinnaker" or "gennaker"—is a pussycat by comparison, but still delivers many of the same benefits. I discuss both in the following paragraphs.

Spinnakers used to be mostly *cross cut*; that is, with horizontal panels of sailcloth stitched together. However, stretching of the upper panels on a reach spoils the sail's shape. Today's spinnakers have a *radial head* (vertical panels at the top, with the lower half cross-cut) or a *tri-radial* construction (also known as *tri-star*): all the panels are lined up with the main load direction, resulting in a complicated, expensive sail, but with minimal stretch.

A traditional spinnaker is a symmetrical sail that has a head and two clews. There is no tack or, more properly, depending on which way the sail is set, one of the clews functions as a tack and the other as a clew, with the roles reversing if the boat jibes; I refer to them as the tack and the clew. At any given time, the edge of the sail leading from the tack to the head is the luff, and the edge leading from the clew to the head is the leech. These, too, reverse in a jibe.

The spinnaker is raised on a halyard that allows the sail to blow out in front of the boat. Sheets are attached to the clews. The sheet that is to windward, and which is taking the place of the tack fitting on a headsail, is known as the *guy*; the sheet that is to leeward, and which functions as a normal sheet, is known as the *sheet*. If the boat jibes, the sheet that is now to windward becomes the guy and the one that is now to leeward becomes the sheet (in other words, their names reverse).

A pole is used to hold the tack up to windward, out from the mast, so that the sail can fill with air. This pole has a topping lift or pole lift, as mentioned previously, and will need a *downhaul* (or foreguy) to control the height of the tack. The pole should always be set up with the open end of its jaw facing upward so that it can be dropped down and away from the line it is supporting.

To launch a spinnaker, the pole is set up at right angles to the mast and swung forward until it rests against the forestay. The guy is fed from the cockpit around a turning block at the stern of the boat, taken outside all the rigging, passed through the end of the pole, and attached to the tack of the sail. The sheet is fed around another turning block on the other side of the stern, taken outside of all the rigging, and attached to the clew. The halyard is attached to the headboard. It helps immensely in keeping the sail under control to have some kind of a sock and *squeezer* or *snuffer* that slides down over the sail and keeps it from opening until all is ready, the most popular of which is manufactured by

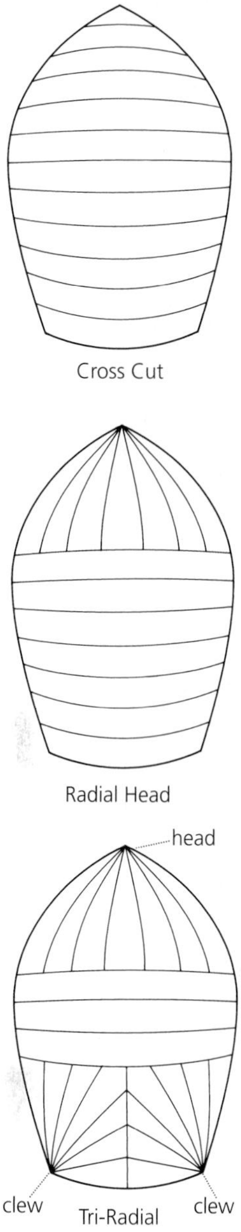

Spinnaker types.

Spinnaker ready to hoist.

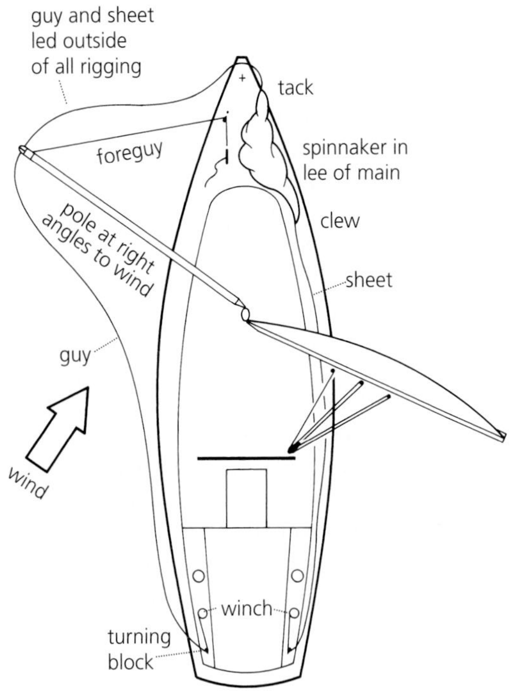

ATN, Fort Lauderdale, Florida. In this case, when the guy and sheet are attached, it is important to make sure that the control lines for the snuffer are inboard of them.

It is easiest to hoist a spinnaker when on a broad reach, and to do it in the "wind shadow" of a headsail or the mainsail. The sail is raised on its halyard and the guy is tensioned until the tack and pole are pulled around *at right angles to the apparent wind.* It is important to tension the foreguy; if it is not done, the pole will fly up in the air when the spinnaker opens. The sock and squeezer are hoisted to the top of the sail using a second halyard and a block built into the sail. As the squeezer goes up, the sail is free to open, filling from the bottom upwards. The sheet is cranked home to trim the sail.

The curvature of a spinnaker is such that if it is set up properly, the airflow curves around the luff of the sail and adheres to at least a portion of the sail before the additional curvature causes separation to occur. What this means is that the spinnaker does not just block the airflow as other sails do when going downwind, it also develops lift on its forward face in the same manner that sails do when going to windward. To do this—just as with a headsail—once the guy and pole have been set up so that the luff is at right angles to the apparent wind, the sheet is tensioned to produce the merest hint of a wrinkle or crease along the luff of the sail. If the sheet is any tighter, the sail is oversheeted; if it is eased any further, the sail will start to collapse.

Although the guy and sheets are commonly led to a turning block aft, performance will be improved with adjustable sheet leads. When reaching in light winds, the sheet lead is moved forward; in medium winds, it is moved aft. In heavy airs, a spinnaker can be "choked down" by moving the sheet lead forward and lowering the pole somewhat. Another way to adjust sheet leads is with a *Barber hauler*—a light snatch block with a pigtail (pennant) attached. The block is placed around the spinnaker sheet and the pigtail is used to haul the sheet down to the rail wherever desired.

Every time the wind changes, the guy needs to be adjusted to keep the pole at right angles to the apparent wind and the sheet adjusted to keep the luff just fluttering. It is also important to keep the foot of the spinnaker horizontal, *regardless of the angle of heel of the boat.* This is accomplished primarily by adjusting the height of the pole using the pole lift and downhaul, remembering to also raise or lower the inboard end of the pole so that the pole remains horizontal. If the pole height is correct, the luff fluttering occurs about two thirds of the way up the sail (on the *shoulder*). If the flutter is low down, the pole is set too high and the entire sail is in danger of collapsing; if the flutter is high, the pole is too low.

Set up like this, a spinnaker can be flown on everything from a fairly close reach to a dead run. If it becomes necessary to jibe the pole, it has to be unclipped from the guy, raised at its mast end until it can be swung across the boat behind the headstay (and inner forestay on a cutter), and then set up on the sheet on the other side (which now becomes the guy). It may be necessary to unclip or re-run some of the control lines. If necessary to maintain control, the spinnaker should be doused, the main jibed, the pole moved and set up again, and then the spinnaker re-hoisted.

If a boat has two poles, it can be set up with two guys and two sheets. The pole on what is the windward side is set up as usual on its guy, which will be tensioned; the sheet on this side will be loose (no tension). The pole on the leeward side is stowed on the mast; the sheet on this side will be tensioned while the guy is left loose. Prior to the jibe, the sheet will be eased enough to set the leeward pole in place around its guy with the guy still loose. During the jibe, the guy in use (windward side) is released with its place taken by the sheet that was not in use. This allows the pole that was in use to be unclipped from the

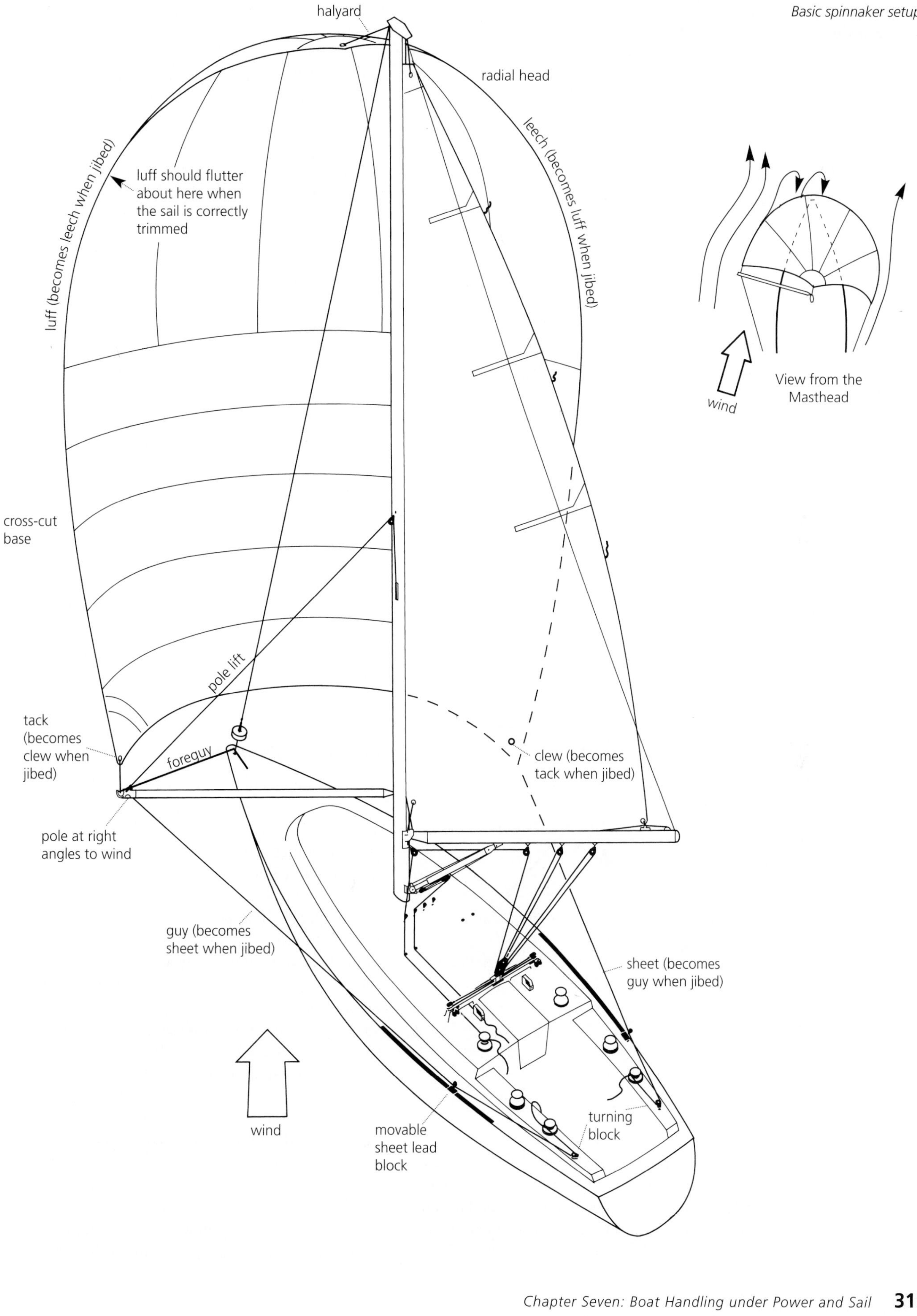
halyard
radial head
leech (becomes luff when jibed)
luff (becomes leech when jibed)
luff should flutter about here when the sail is correctly trimmed
cross-cut base
pole lift
tack (becomes clew when jibed)
foreguy
clew (becomes tack when jibed)
pole at right angles to wind
guy (becomes sheet when jibed)
sheet (becomes guy when jibed)
wind
movable sheet lead block
turning block
wind
View from the Masthead

Basic spinnaker setup.

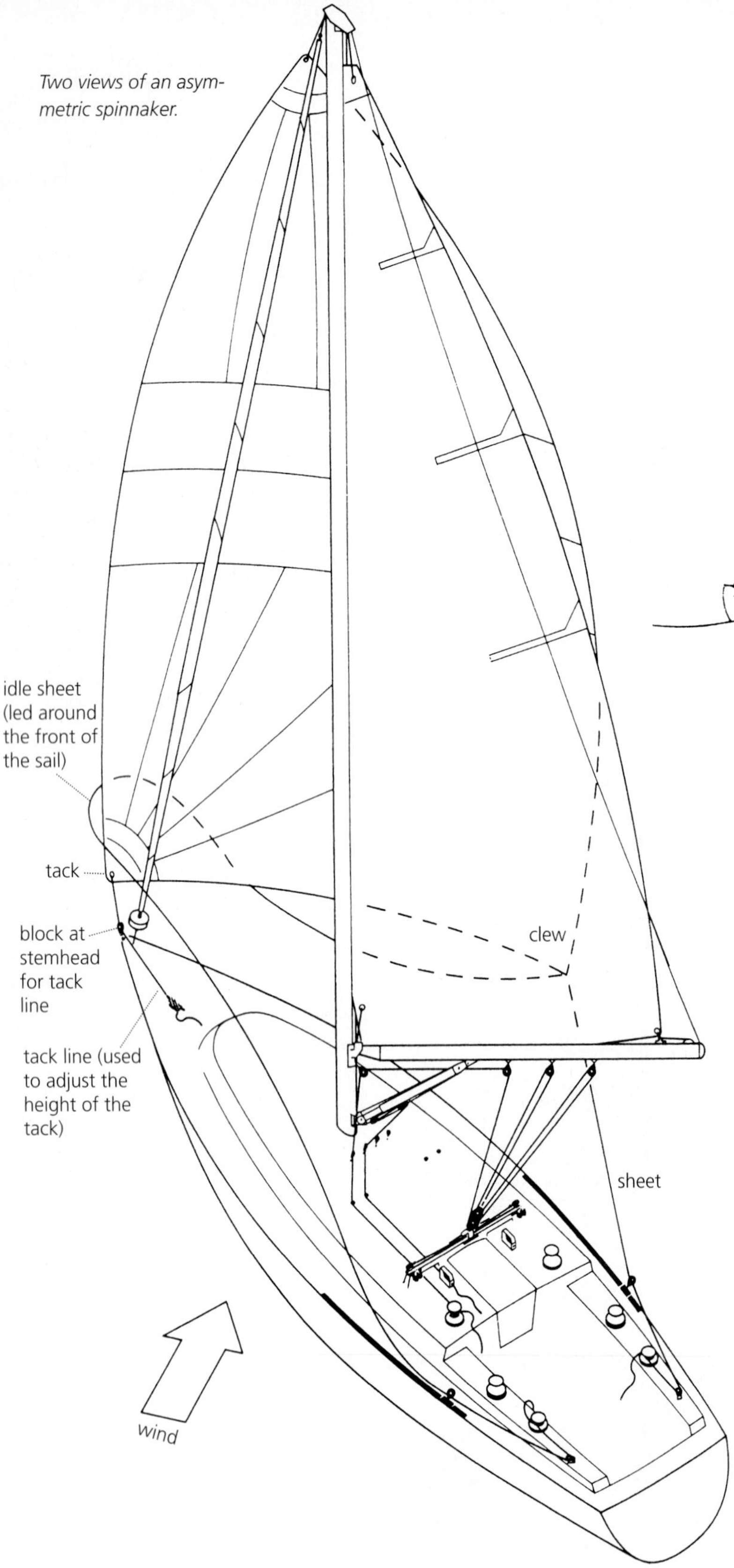

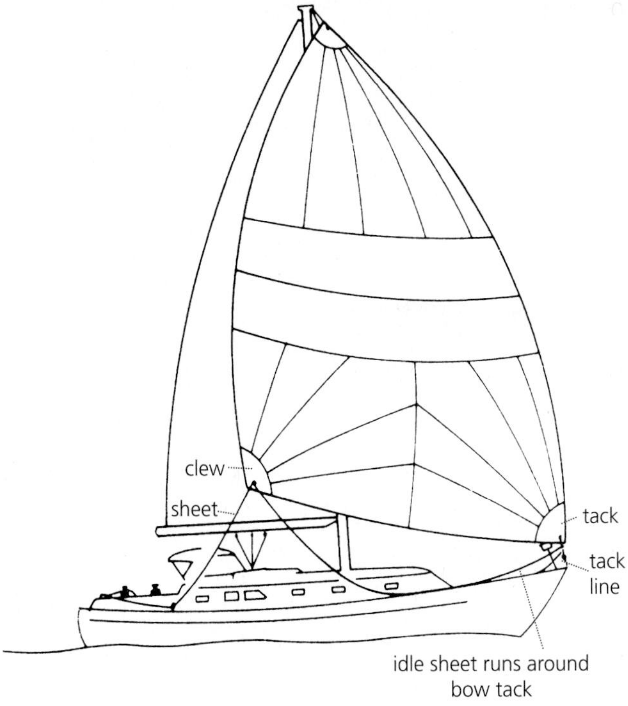

Two views of an asymmetric spinnaker.

guy, raised up the mast, and stowed. At the same time, the sheet that was in use (leeward side) is released and replaced with the guy that has now been set up. At this time, the jibe is essentially complete, other than trimming the various lines.

A spinnaker is taken down by easing the guy, hauling in on the sheet, and immediately pulling the snuffer and sock down. The sail is then gathered up on deck as the halyard is let out. It helps if this is all done behind the mainsail so that the operation is blanketed from the wind.

Cruising Spinnakers

If all this sounds like a lot of work, it is! A cruising spinnaker (*asymmetric spinnaker*) makes life a lot easier, but at the expense of less versatility and sometimes a loss of performance. The cruising spinnaker is an asymmetrical sail; that is, its shape is not balanced. This results in a defined luff and leech. The sail has a tack fitting that is secured to a line run through a block at the bow of the boat and either cleated off or run back to the cockpit, from where it can be adjusted (the latter is preferred). The clew is controlled by the sheet and run back to the cockpit through a snatch block or lead block on the rail and a turning block as far aft as possible. A second sheet runs around the headstay to the other side of the boat (just as with a regular headsail). The sail is treated much as an oversized genoa that is held in place by its halyard, tack line, and sheet (there are no other attachment points). The sail does not require a pole.

As with regular spinnakers, a cruising spinnaker can be built using a sock and squeezer or

Asymmetric spinnaker on a cruising boat. Unlike a racing boat, there is no retractable carbon fiber bowsprit for the tack line, so this is fastened to the stemhead, with the sail attached around the roller-reefing headsail using a special strap. The sail is kept under control with a snuffer, which is raised to the masthead on an internal halyard.

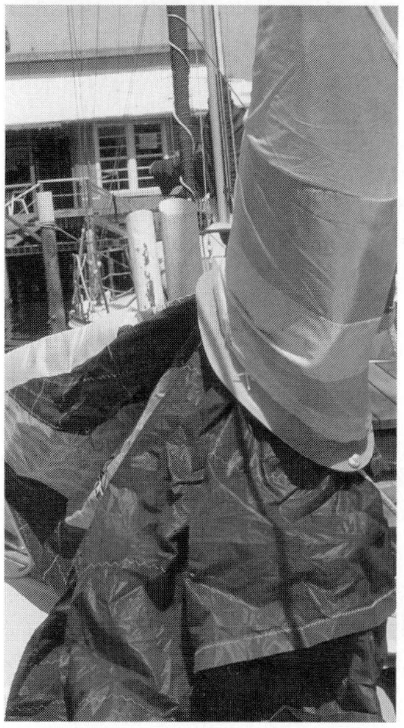

snuffer, which makes setting and retrieving it reasonably simple. The tack is fastened to its tack line; the sheets are attached to the clew and brought aft outside all rigging; the halyard is brought outside and in front of the headstay and attached to the headboard; the sail is hoisted in its sock and tensioned with the halyard and tack line (which should put the sail 3 to 4 feet off the deck); and then the snuffer and sock are raised to the top of the sail, allowing the sail to fill with air from the bottom up. The sheet is gently tensioned as the sock goes up. The less sag there is in the sail and sock, the easier the sock will go up. The major concern in all of this is to keep the sail out of the water as it goes up (and comes down). Once up, the sail is sheeted home.

The tack line and leeward sheet are adjusted to allow the sail to fly as free as possible while keeping its foot more or less horizontal. Over-trimming of the sail is the most common problem—the sheet should always be eased enough to maintain a little luff flutter (in essence, the sail is trimmed the same way as a genoa). When reaching, the halyard and tack line are tightened to pull the camber forward and put the tack at about the height of the bow pulpit; when running, they are eased (the tack can be allowed to rise 4 to 6 feet off the deck).

Set like this, a cruising spinnaker can be used without a pole on all points of sail from a reach (apparent wind around 50 degrees) to a very broad reach (around 140 degrees apparent), at which point the *dirty air* coming off the mainsail will interfere with the spinnaker. A bowsprit significantly enhances performance by getting the sail well forward of the main (hence, the retractable bowsprits now fashionable on many racing boats and their cruising derivatives). The bowsprit also allows a much larger sail to be set and simplifies handling during a jibe because the sail is well away from the forestay.

Instead of sailing dead downwind, boats are jibed from one "tack" to the other. However, if so desired, a cruising spinnaker can be rigged with sheets and guys and the tack poled out like a regular spinnaker to go dead downwind. Alternatively, the boat can be sailed wing and wing, with the clew of the spinnaker poled out as with a genoa, except that a longer pole is desirable (a telescoping pole).

A cruising spinnaker is generally jibed by letting go the one sheet, allowing the sail to blow out downwind ahead of the forestay, and then hauling it around the stay and sheeting it home with the other sheet. In other words, the sail swings around ahead of the forestay rather than coming across the boat inside the forestay, which minimizes the chances of it catching on something and getting damaged. However, given a bowsprit long enough, the sail can be jibed by pulling the clew between the sail's luff and the forestay (i.e., in the same manner as other headsails). To tack through the wind with a cruising spinnaker, the sail has to be dropped and reset on the new tack, or the boat run off downwind, jibed, and brought up onto the wind on the new tack.

Weather Helm and Lee Helm

As the various sailing techniques described so far are practiced and refined, it will be found that very few boats have a balanced helm on all points of sail. Most have some weather helm (a tendency to round up into the wind if the wheel or tiller is let go); a few exhibit *lee helm* (a tendency to fall off the wind if the wheel or tiller is let go). Slight weather helm is desirable and, in fact, is generally designed into a boat's sailing characteristics, for the following reasons:

- The gentle pressure it creates on the helm "gives life to the tiller" (Hiscock, *Cruising under Sail*), making it easier to get a sense of how the boat is sailing.
- The rudder develops a side force acting to weather that assists the keel in counteracting leeway.
- In an emergency in which the helm is abandoned (in the worst case, falling overboard when single-handing), the boat will round up into the wind and stall out. In less extreme circumstances (e.g., being hit by a squall), the boat tends to round up into the wind, spilling the wind out of its sails—thereby easing the pressure on them—and letting the boat recover if it has been knocked down.

Lee helm of any kind is undesirable; in fact, it can be downright dangerous. If the wheel or tiller is let go, the boat falls off the wind, continuing to sail. If the wind is forward of the beam, the pressure in the sails increases, potentially overwhelming the boat; if the wind is aft of the beam, there is a risk of an uncontrolled jibe. Fortunately, lee helm is rare, so it is not discussed further herein.

Excessive weather helm, on the other hand, is common. What is at issue is a lack of balance among the headsails, the mainsail (and mizzen, if fitted), and the underwater profile of the boat. Crudely speaking, the pressure of the wind in a mainsail causes a boat to pivot around the mast into the wind; the pressure of the wind in the headsails causes the boat to be blown away from the wind, pivoting in the opposite direction. If the boat is perfectly balanced and on an even keel, these two forces cancel each other out. If the mast is set too far forward, the main has little pivoting effect, resulting in lee helm (the headsails are the predominant pivoting force); if the mast is set well aft, the main exerts tremendous leverage, overwhelming the pivoting force of the headsails and resulting in weather helm.

Typically, weather helm increases with increasing wind pressure in the sails and with increasing angles of heel, especially if the underwater profile becomes increasingly asymmetrical (as it usually does). Weather helm is generally exacerbated if the boat is "trimmed down by the bow" (not floating on her designed fore-and-aft lines as a result of too much weight forward, generally from heavy ground tackle). In other words, as the wind strengthens, weather helm becomes more pronounced if the sails are not progressively reefed. On many boats, weather helm can build up to the point where it overwhelms a wind vane or autopilot, even making the boat completely unmanageable when hand-steered.

What to do in cases of excessive weather helm? First, make sure the rig is set up tightly, specifically the headstay, and that halyards are tight. This has the effect of moving the *center of effort* of both the main and headsail forward, increasing the pivoting force of the headsail and reducing that of the main. If weather helm still persists, even in moderate wind conditions, check the fore-and-aft trim. Next, move the mast forward by loosening the backstay and tightening the headstay. In some instances, it also may be possible to shift the mast step forward or shift the mast on its mast step.

As wind strength builds, make every effort to keep sails as flat as possible, the draft (camber) well forward, and the boat on as even a keel as possible. Essentially, this means cranking up on halyards, cunninghams, outhauls, and vangs, while easing sheets. A boom should be as far as possible down its traveler. If necessary, sails (specifically, the mainsail) can be given extra twist so that they start to luff in their upper regions, spilling the wind and thereby easing the heeling forces experienced by the boat. The main can be further depowered by sailing it constantly with a slight luff.

Once it becomes necessary to start reefing down, reefing the main does the most to reduce weather helm. However, this should not be taken to extremes, such as dropping the mainsail altogether while still keeping up the full genoa. To sail to best advantage, most boats require the headsails and main to be balanced; therefore, before a second reef is taken in the main, the headsail should be partially reefed.

If these measures fail to solve the weather-helm problem, a solution will not be easy. What is needed is to shift the center of effort of the sails forward, which can be done in the following ways:

- recutting the main to have a flatter shape, particularly in its upper portion
- replacing Dacron (Terylene) halyards with lower-stretch halyards (see chapter 10)
- shortening the boom and removing sail area from the leech of the mainsail
- moving the entire mast forward (which is likely to have significant structural implications for the boat)
- adding (or lengthening) a bowsprit

At one time or another, we've done all of them. The bills were horrendous!

Motor Sailing

Motor sailing is a tactic that is most commonly adopted when trying to make progress to windward in heavy weather and unpleasant seas. Typically, the conditions are such that beating to windward under sail alone is uncomfortable, with the boat making little progress; trying to power straight into the seas is generally even less comfortable and produces no improvement in speed made good to windward. Motor sailing enables better progress to be made with a reduced sail area, which translates into reduced heeling and, in most cases, greater comfort.

The most efficient way to motor sail is almost always with the headsail (genoa or jib) dropped or rolled up and the main sheeted hard in, with the mainsheet traveler centered or even pulled a little to windward. This enables the boat to point several degrees higher than it can under sail alone, but yet still get significant lift out of the main. In addition, the sail helps reduce the motion. On a cutter, the staysail—sheeted hard in—also can often provide some useful drive and steadying action.

TUNING A RIG

Regardless of sea states and weather conditions, for a boat to be sailed to best effect, its rig must be properly tuned. The prerequisite for tuning a rig on a sailboat is a solid platform for the rig—that is, a well-built and properly engineered boat. Without this, all efforts are doomed to failure. Given such a platform, basic rig tuning is a straightforward business that just about any owner can undertake (I'm talking about typical cruising rigs, not fancy racing rigs). The idea is to keep the mast centered in the boat, vertical (except for maybe a degree or two of rake aft), and supported in such a way that the head neither flops off to leeward when the boat is hard-pressed nor does the mast itself buckle out of column.

Preparatory Measurements

Getting the masthead centered in the boat is the first order of business. If starting from scratch with an unknown boat, the *mast step* (on a deck-stepped mast) or the *partners* (the aperture in the deck for a keel-stepped mast) should be measured to make sure it is centered athwartships in the boat (this is by no means guaranteed). Then the shroud chainplates should be checked to make sure that counterposed port and starboard plates are equidistant from the mast, equidistant from the bow of the boat, and protruding the same distance above the deck (again, by no means guaranteed). The next step is to measure the cap shrouds to make sure they are exactly equal in length (this assumes the mast is off the boat; if it isn't, see the next section).

If the shrouds are not the same length and the aforementioned port and starboard measurements are equal, before stepping the mast, the rigging screws (*turnbuckles* in the U.S.; *bottle screws* in the U.K.) need adjusting to produce shrouds of equal length. The same is then done with any other shrouds, as well as the backstays if the boat has twin backstays (in which case, the backstay chainplates also need to be checked for equidistant placement from the mast).

Static Tuning

I look first at masthead rigs and then fractional rigs.

Masthead Rig

Almost all cruising boats have masthead rigs; that is, the forestay comes to the top of the mast, as opposed to a fractional rig, on which the forestay is attached below the masthead. After the mast is stepped on a masthead rig, it is loosely tensioned (by hand) using the forestay, the backstay(s), and the cap shrouds. If the shrouds have been equalized in length (as described previously), and as long as the same number of turns in the same direction are made to the rigging screws on the cap shrouds (and the backstays, if twin backstays are used), simple geometry shows that the masthead will be centered athwartships above the mast step.

If it has not been possible to check the shroud lengths with the mast off the boat, or there is some disparity in chainplate placement, I have recommended in the past using a halyard to check the athwartships centering of the mast. The halyard is cleated off in such a way that it just touches the caprail at right angles to the base of the mast on one side of the boat. It is then taken across the boat to the other caprail, which it should just touch. (This requires a halyard that comes off a sheave centered in the masthead.) However, I've come to the conclusion that even a shift of several inches at the masthead produces a minimal change in halyard length that would be hard to distinguish from stretch. I think I do better by simply maneuvering the boat into a position where I can eyeball the athwartships mast trim from the dock. If the boat is trimmed so that it is level in the water (the finicky ones can use a spirit level on the cabinsole), it is usually possible to detect even tiny mast deviations from the vertical.

While eyeballing the athwartships trim, the cap shrouds should also be inspected to make sure that where they pass over the (upper) spreaders, the angle the shrouds make with the spreaders is the same on the top and bottom sides. This rule is frequently violated. A spreader is designed to take a compression load straight into the mast. The more the top and bottom shroud angles differ, the greater is the bending moment on the spreader, and the more likely it is to fail (either by buckling or as a result of its tip sliding up or down the shroud).

With the masthead centered athwartships, the rest of the shrouds are lightly tensioned, while eyeballing the mast to make sure it is not pulled out of column. This can be accurately double-checked by sighting up the mast track (with the mainsail slides removed); any sideways curvature is immediately apparent. If the boat has intermediate shrouds, it is important to ensure that the angles the shrouds make with their spreaders are equal on the top and bottom sides of the spreaders.

Next, the boat needs to be maneuvered so that it is lying alongside the dock. The fore-and-aft rake (if any) is established by tensioning the forestay and backstay(s), while eyeballing the rig from the dock. If the boat is leveled fore and aft in the water (using the waterline as a gauge or a spirit level on the cabinsole), a weight hung from the mainsail halyard will act as a plumb bob for those who want accurate measurements. Rake should not exceed 1 percent of the mast height (e.g., 6 in./150 mm on a 50 ft./15 m mast) except on fractional rigs, which often have significant mast bend or rake.

The forestay, backstay(s), and cap shrouds can now be tightened to close to their final tension. For most of us, this is somewhat of a guessing game. You can buy various tension gauges and look up in tables the breaking strain of different cable sizes—and do all of this scientifically—but I have to confess that I generally just tweak the cables to see that they are taut and that they all flex about the same amount under the same kind of tweaking load.

A rather more scientific approach to tensioning rigging is to measure *exactly* 6 feet, 6 inches (2 m) up from the top of the rigging screw after a shroud or stay has first been tensioned by hand, and to put a piece of tape around the wire at this point. Stainless steel wire rope stretches approximately 0.04 inch (1 mm) over a 6-foot, 6-inch (2 m) length when loaded to 5 percent of its breaking strength. Given that it is desirable to preload cap shrouds by 15 to 25 percent of their breaking strength, they should be tightened until each cable has stretched by ⅛ to ²⁄₁₀ inch (3–5 mm) over the

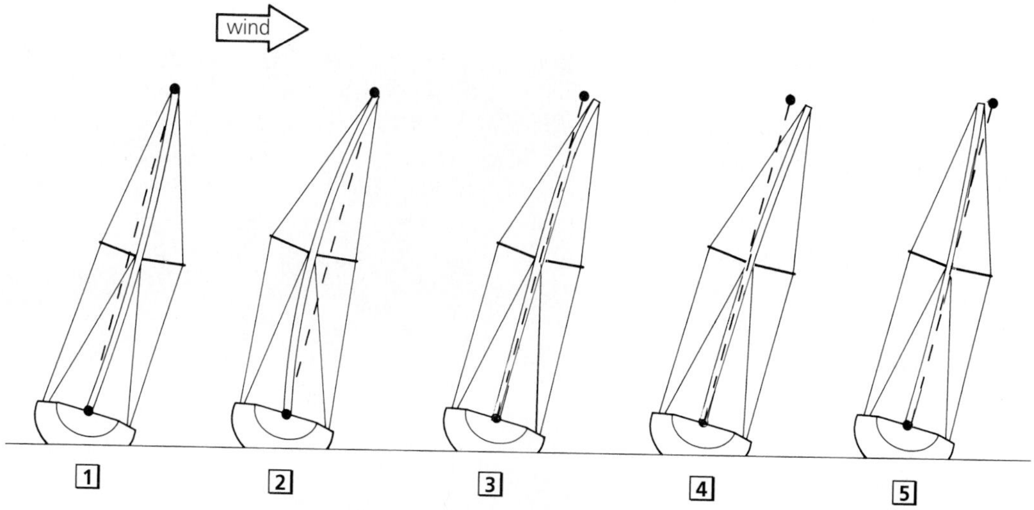

Tuning faults with single spreaders:

1. Windward lowers too loose.

2. Windward lowers too tight

3. Cap shrouds slack.

4. All shrouds too slack.

5. All shrouds too tight.

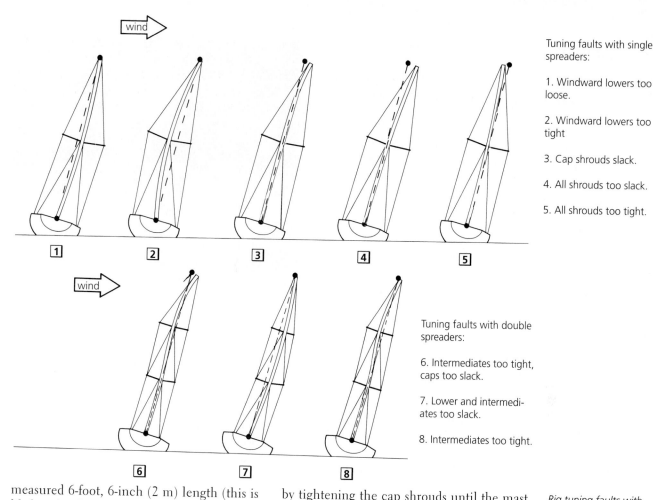

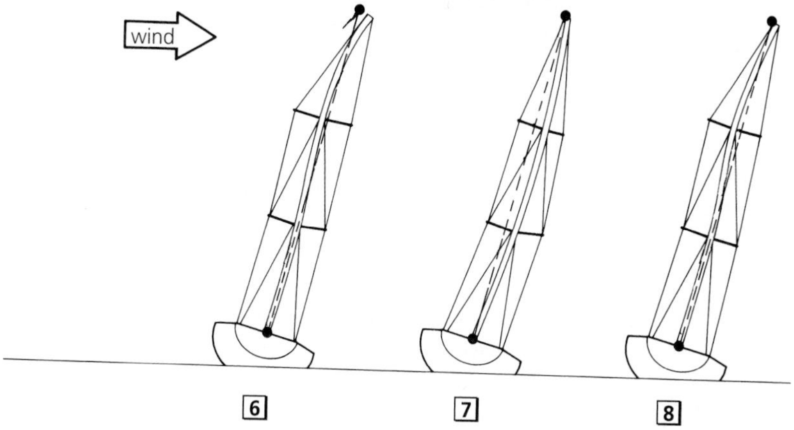

Tuning faults with double spreaders:

6. Intermediates too tight, caps too slack.

7. Lower and intermediates too slack.

8. Intermediates too tight.

Rig tuning faults with single- and double-spreader rigs.

measured 6-foot, 6-inch (2 m) length (this is likely to be about two full turns on the rigging screw, after it can be tightened no more by hand). The forestay and backstay are given at least as much tension (± 25 percent of breaking strength).

If the boat has an inner forestay, it is generally desirable to induce a small bend aft in the head of the mast, which is accomplished primarily by tightening the inner forestay and the backstay(s). The degree of bend can be eyeballed from dockside or by sighting up the side of the mast. Finally, the lower (and intermediate, if fitted) shrouds are tightened, making equal adjustments to counterposed shrouds, and then sighting up the mast track after each pair of adjustments to see that the mast is still in column. Intermediate shrouds are not tensioned quite as much as cap shrouds; lower shrouds are tensioned about the same as cap shrouds.

Fractional Rig

A fractional rig is treated a little differently than a masthead rig. On most, the spreaders are swept back, bringing the cap shrouds aft of the mast. The cap shrouds provide most of the forestay tension (rather than the backstay). At the same time, pre-bend is forced into the mast by tightening the cap shrouds until the mast bends forward in the middle. The lower shrouds are used to control the amount of pre-bend. When sailing, the backstay is used to control the mainsail shape with additional mast bend.

The rig is set up by tightening the cap shrouds and forestay at the same time, generally to higher loadings than are used on a masthead rig. Then, intermediate shrouds (if present) and the lower shrouds are tensioned to keep the mast centered athwartships and to control the mast bend. Finally, the backstay (if present) is tensioned.

Dynamic Tuning at Sea

That's basically all there is to it. With keel-stepped masts, wedges (*chocking*) are installed at the partners. Wood can be used on wood spars, but hard rubber is always used on aluminum: one pad in front and one to the rear. The total thickness of the pads should be 120 to 125 percent of the total gap between the mast and partners. The total length of the pads should add up to 30 to 40 percent of the total circumference of the mast. No pads are placed at the mast sides. The pads are easier to slip in if they are soaked in dishwashing liquid. If the aft pads are put in place first, a line *(continued on page 323)*

GOING ALOFT

Having been at a masthead for several hours at a time on more than one occasion, let me tell you that comfort (or, at the least, minimizing discomfort) is a prime consideration. I would advise sailboat owners to get one of those deep-sided canvas bosun's chairs with lots of pockets all the way around. Just one point: The pockets tend to sag and do not retain tools securely—it is worth putting Velcro tape on the larger pockets to close them off.

Safety

- Do *not* hook a bosun's chair to a snap shackle on the halyard. Use a screw shackle or a bowline.
- Do *not* use a wire halyard with a rope tail. If this must be done, first check the rope-to-wire splice *very closely*.
- Do *not* use a winch directly below the mast to go aloft—any tool dropped will land on the winch operator who will probably let go of the rope tail, and down you will come. Rig a block and take the line to a cockpit winch.
- Do *not* use electric winches—it is all too easy for the winch operator to run the bosun's chair up into the head box and tear the halyard loose from the bosun's chair.
- *Do* set up another external halyard or taut line so that you have something to hang onto and help pull yourself up. In the event of a riding turn on the winch (which can create quite a dangerous situation as it is unwrapped), you can take the weight off the hoisting line.
- *Do* place a safety line or strap around the mast as you go aloft. Should the hoisting line fail or come loose, the safety strap will hold you. It will have to be undone and reset at each spreader.
- *Do* tie off once up. This is a most basic safety precaution. It also frees up both hands for working. A good strong belt will be more comfortable than a piece of line. Once up, have the winch operator *cleat off the hoisting line* even if using a self-tailing winch.

This person has no safety line (I've done it myself lots of times!). If the halyard lets go, he's a goner . . .

Never trust a snap shackle on a bosun's chair when going aloft—always tie a bowline.

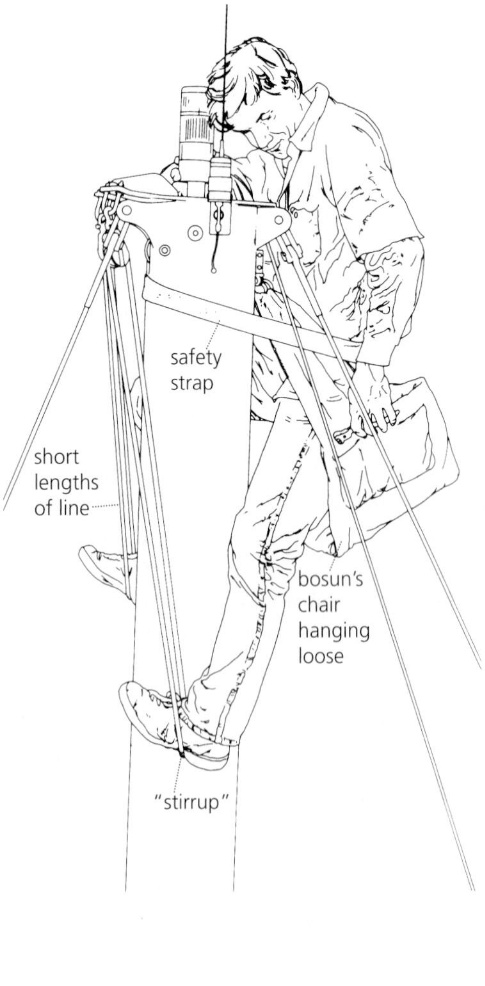

The most difficult work aloft is repairing things *on top of* the mast—for example, masthead lights. The bosun's chair most likely will not get you high enough. I take up a couple of short lengths of line and hang "stirrups" from the masthead, one higher than the other, such that the lower one puts my chest at masthead level (with a straight leg), and the other (about a foot higher) allows me to push myself up a little more if necessary. I stay in the bosun's chair so that if I slip it will hold me, and strap myself off as high as possible. It's still a pretty nerve-racking business. Do you have any better method?

Single-handers who have to go aloft need to rig a three- or four-part tackle from a halyard, hauling one half of the tackle to the masthead and leaving the other half at deck level. (This requires a line that is three or four times as long as the mast is high; nylon should not be used because its stretch will cause the bosun's chair to bounce around.) The bosun's chair is attached to the lower half of the tackle. It is then possible for someone to haul himself or herself to the masthead. It helps considerably if the lower half of the tackle incorporates a jam cleat, although this alone should never be relied on to tie off the bosun's chair once up at the masthead.

Our friend Peter checking his masthead light. The steps enable him to get up above the masthead (which can't be done with a bosun's chair). Note his safety harness—it would be better if he clipped it on!

(continued from page 321) can be run from a cockpit winch around the front of the mast and back to another winch. Cranking in the line pulls the mast aft, compressing the aft wedges and allowing the forward pads to be slipped in place.

An alternative to chocking is Spartite (and similar products)—a two-part solution that sets to a hard, rubber-like consistency. After the static tuning is completed at dockside, the mast aperture is sealed from below and greased with Vaseline (so that the Spartite does not adhere to it), and then the solution is poured in, forming a near-watertight seal. Any time the mast is removed, the ring of Spartite comes out with it.

To test a rig tune, the boat is taken out in a stiff breeze (Force 4–5, 10–20 knots) and put hard on the wind on both tacks. At about a 20-degree angle of heel, the lee shrouds on a masthead rig should lose tension but should not be slack. (On a fractional rig, the shrouds should never go loose.) If the shrouds are loose, the slack is taken up on the rigging screws, adjusting counterposed (port and starboard) shrouds equally, until the slackness is gone. (Remember that a rigging screw should only be tightened when it is on the leeward side. If an attempt is made to adjust it under tension, it may seize up.)

Sighting up the mast track reveals whether the mast is remaining in column. In fact, the masthead will probably sag off slightly to leeward. If the sag looks excessive, the cap shrouds should be tightened a little (tightening port and starboard shrouds equally). If the masthead is centered in the boat but the mast is out of column (the center section curves to windward or leeward), it can be pulled back into column using the intermediate (if fitted) and lower shrouds. However, if the dockside work was done correctly, this should not be necessary.

Sighting up the mast from the side reveals whether it is bending aft or forward or not at all. Under sailing loads, the headstay tension will likely take out most of any aft bend induced in the head of the mast by the static tuning, but the mast should not be curving forward. If it is, the backstay(s) needs tightening.

At this point, the rig is adequately tensioned for cruising purposes. Of course, it should be rechecked at regular intervals, especially if the rig is new (wire rope stretches somewhat when first put in service). If it will not hold its tension in stronger winds but it regains tension when the load is taken off, most likely the hull is flexing; nothing can be done to the rig to resolve this problem. Even worse, if the rig repeatedly slackens up and no amount of adjustment of the rigging screws restores tension for long, the hull is likely to be permanently deforming. In either case, it is time to call in the professionals.

Check the leeward rig tension in about 20 knots of wind when heeled about 20 degrees—the shrouds should be just slack.

Fog on the Mississippi River makes for stressful piloting.

CHAPTER EIGHT

PILOTING, NAVIGATION, AND THE RULES OF THE ROAD

Traditionally, piloting has been that set of techniques used to fix the location of a boat when it is relatively close to land; navigation has been the set of techniques used on the high seas, specifically celestial navigation, using a sextant. With the advent of various forms of electronic navigation, this neat distinction has completely broken down. Today, almost everybody has at least one GPS onboard, and almost nobody knows celestial navigation.

Speaking for myself, I carry a sextant, and at one time I knew how to use it; however, it has been twelve years since I took a sight and reduced it, and right now I wouldn't be able to save my life! I carry a celestial navigation primer onboard in the hope that if the situation were ever so desperate that I needed a sight, I could relearn how to do it fairly quickly—but this is probably wishful thinking. In all honesty, our sextant would probably be more useful as a mantelpiece decoration than it is tucked away in a locker on the boat.

Along with the majority of contemporary cruisers, this cavalier attitude toward our sextant makes us overly dependent on electronics. This does not bother me in coastal waters—where I prefer the challenge of traditional piloting over electronic navigation and only use the GPS as a backup—but on long passages, it clearly makes us vulnerable to electrical or electronics failures and to a government shutdown of the GPS system.

I provide a measure of insurance by ensuring that we have as bulletproof an electrical system as possible (see chapter 4), by carrying redundant GPSs (we have at least three "cheapies" onboard), and by putting a couple of the handheld GPSs in the oven during thunderstorms. (My theory is that if we get a direct lightning strike, whatever happens to the rest of the electronics, the oven—consisting as it does of a metal box—will protect the GPSs. As I write this, I realize it would make more sense to simply keep one in a metal tin as a backup!) On passage, we log the GPS position every hour so that if our system fails, we have an accurate fix from which to start plotting our "dead reckoning" (explained later in this chapter). If we do have a midocean GPS failure, I should have enough time to relearn how to use the sextant.

With this in mind, in what follows I do not attempt to provide a comprehensive course in navigation. My objective is to describe the knowledge base and techniques that have worked well for us, and which have taken us safely through more than 40,000 miles of often challenging cruising. I completely ignore celestial navigation and presuppose a functioning GPS for position-fixing on offshore passages; however, I do this with a strong emphasis on many traditional piloting skills.

I believe that a mastery of these skills is essential to a safe cruising lifestyle and to the development of an "intuitive" feel for where you are when in coastal waters. If you cruise long enough, there will be inevitable moments of stress when it is necessary to make rapid navigational judgments based on a sense of where you are, which cannot—for one reason or another—be backed up at that moment with a precise fix.

Our most extreme example of such a situation occurred on the coast of Cuba, in boisterous conditions. We were suddenly confronted with an uncharted reef at a time when we were negotiating numerous areas of patch reef. I had to make an immediate decision about which way to turn. We had an electronic chart plotter with a GPS fix that simply did not fit my picture of the situation—a picture derived through the chart plotter and close, careful piloting. It is the only time I have overridden the GPS, refusing to believe it. It left me soft in the knees—but it also took us and our boat out of danger. On this occasion, the GPS was temporarily more than a half-mile out (the only time we have seen such errors).

This is, indeed, a rather extreme example. In reality, many more accidents occur because people feel sure they know where they are and follow their intuition rather than their instruments than the other way around. Nevertheless, the point remains valid—there is a need, over time, to develop piloting skills to the level where, in difficult circumstances, you can maintain an accurate sense of where you are when conditions do not allow you to secure and plot a fix. In moments of crisis, this "sixth sense" may make the difference between bringing the boat and the crew safely through and hitting the rocks. Let's look at some of the skills necessary for developing such a sixth sense.

The skipper thought he was in the right place, but missed the channel by 50 yards.

PAPER CHARTS

The most basic prerequisite to all forms of navigation and piloting is the ability to read a paper chart (even if, in typical circumstances, your navigation is all done electronically).

Paper charts are created by hydrographic offices around the world. In the United States, the National Oceanic and Atmospheric Administration (NOAA) is in charge of charts of U.S. coastal waters, and the National Imagery and Mapping Agency (NIMA) (formerly the Defense Mapping Agency Hydrographic/Topographic Center [DMAHTC]) is in charge of U.S.-produced charts of overseas regions. The overseas charts are developed using a combination of data acquired directly by NIMA (through its own surveys) and data supplied by other hydrographic offices (the most famous of which is the British Admiralty).

Most industrialized nations have their own hydrographic offices, as do even some third-world countries (e.g., Cuba, which has an outstanding hydrographic office and excellent charts of its own country—considerably better than any NIMA or British Admiralty charts). Although there are subtle differences among hydrographic offices (particularly in terms of coloration—British Admiralty charts are especially good-looking; as hydrographic offices move from the current limitations of ink-based lithographic printing to colored plotters we are likely to see changes in this area), fundamentally all use the same agreed-upon basic techniques, conventions, symbols, and standards of accuracy in chart-making (as set down by the International Hydrographic Organization/IHO).

To take full advantage of any chart, a navigator must have some understanding of how it is constructed and must know the conventions and symbols used to depict specific features.

Chart Construction

Two projections are commonly used for making charts: Mercator and gnomonic.

Mercator Projections

The fundamental problem that a chart has to overcome is how to accurately display (project) a spherical surface (the surface of the world) on a flat piece of paper. In practice, it cannot be done. To preserve one value (e.g., the correct relationship of length to breadth at any given point or the accurate depiction of angles), another must be sacrificed (in this example, consistent measurement of distance).

All coastal and inshore charts use a projection known as the *Mercator projection*. It is based on the idea of wrapping a cylinder around a globe, projecting the image of the globe onto the inner wall of the cylinder, and then cutting the cylinder up one side and laying the image out flat. The net result is that instead of converging at the north and south poles, lines of longitude (those that run north and south between the poles, also known as *meridians*) become equally spaced parallel lines (there is no convergence toward the poles).

Mercator projection.

map is projected from the earth onto the cylinder, with greatest distortion at the poles

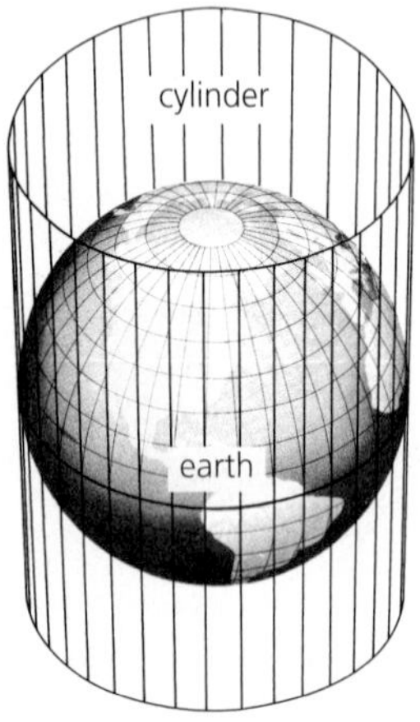

In real life, the farther north or south you go from the equator, the closer together are the lines of longitude as they move toward convergence at the poles. This means that the distance on the ground covered by a degree of longitude steadily diminishes until it reduces to zero at the poles. With a Mercator projection, however, the distance between the lines of longitude remains constant—in other words, the farther the distance from the equator, the greater the distortion.

Something similar is happening with lines of latitude (*parallels*). In real life, all are equally spaced, with the result that the distance on the ground covered by a degree of latitude is the same at any point on the surface of the earth (with minor exceptions, due to the fact that the earth is not perfectly spherical). With a Mercator projection, however, the farther north or south the distance is from the equator, the farther apart are the lines of latitude. At any given point on a Mercator projection, this distortion in the distance between the lines of latitude is equal to the distortion in the distance between the lines of longitude. Therefore, the chart preserves the correct relationship of length to breadth and the correct angular relationship between lines of latitude and longitude, but at the expense of losing any consistent measurement of distance. On a map of the world, Greenland comes out the same size as Africa, which is actually fourteen times bigger.

If a chart covers a relatively small area (confusingly known as a *large-scale chart*), the distortion of distance with a Mercator projection is minimal; however, where large areas are covered (a *small-scale chart*), it becomes significant. At a continental scale (e.g., a map of the entire United States), the distortion is quite substantial.

Given that a degree of latitude covers the same distance anywhere on the surface of the earth, latitude scales (those shown up the sides of a chart) are always used for measuring distances on Mercator charts. However, given that the Mercator projection causes the latitude scale to change with changes in latitude, *the part of the latitude scale alongside (i.e., east or west of) the points being measured is always used when measuring the distance between two points on a chart.*

One minute of latitude is equal to 1 nautical mile (by definition); 1 nautical mile is equal

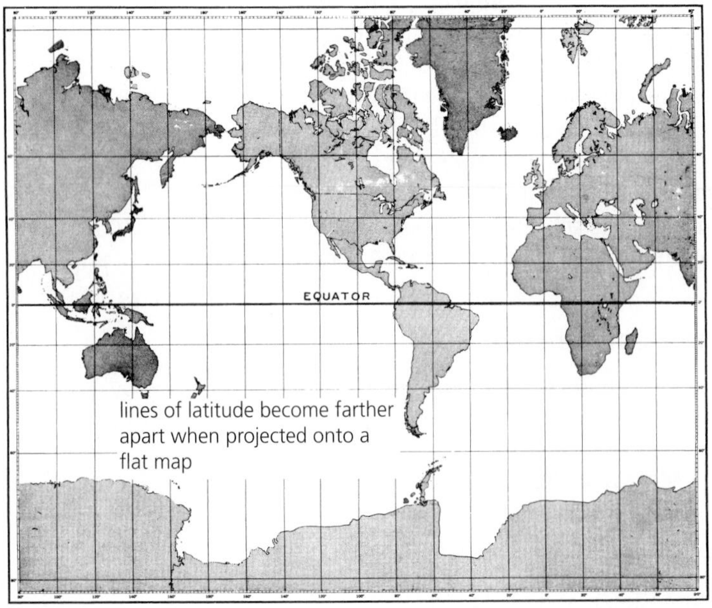

EQUATOR
lines of latitude become farther apart when projected onto a flat map

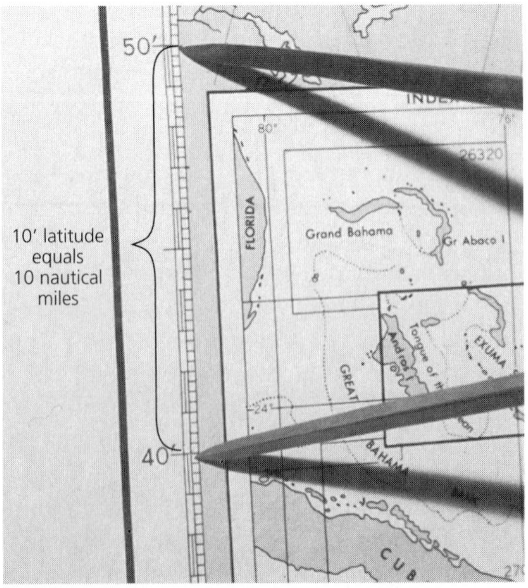

Distances on a Mercator chart are always measured from the adjacent latitude scale.

to approximately 2,000 yards. This greatly simplifies the arithmetic involved in any distance calculations. For example, a tenth of 1 nautical mile is 200 yards; one hundredth (two decimal places) is 20 yards; one thousandth (three decimal places, commonly displayed on GPSs—although none are anywhere near this accurate without significant corrections) is 2 yards (this is discussed further later in this chapter).

Historically, minutes of latitude have always been divided into sixty seconds of latitude (not tenths), but since the advent of electronic navigation, it has become customary to use decimal minutes on small-scale charts. However, many older charts and large-scale charts still have latitude scales subdivided into seconds (not tenths). When using electronic equipment in combination with paper charts, *it is essential to ensure that the electronics are programmed to the same units used for plotting on the chart.*

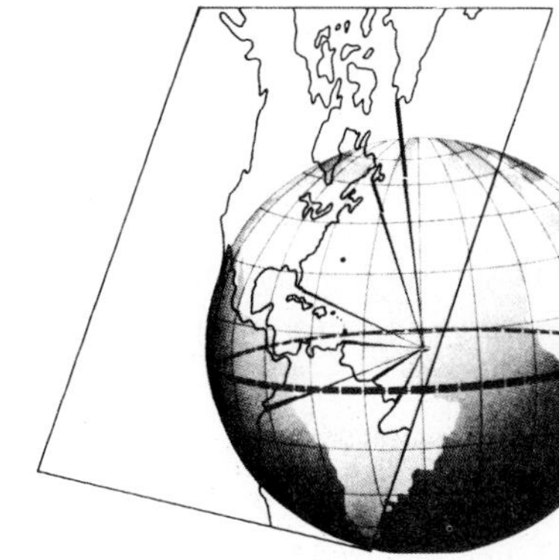

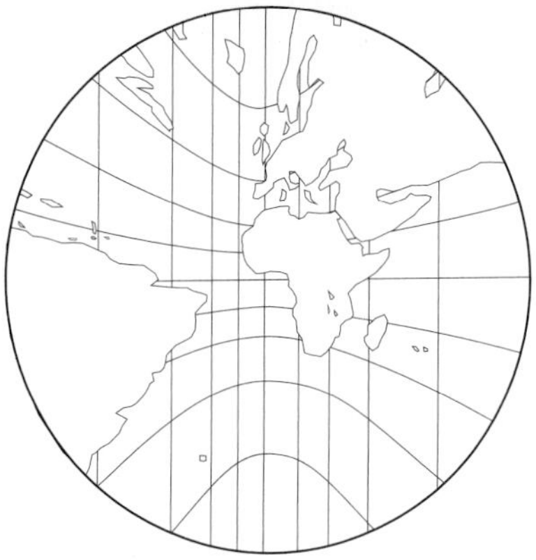

Left: *An oblique gnomonic projection. Imagine a light at the center of the globe, projecting outward.* Below: *Gnomonic projection.*

Gnomonic Projections

Coastal sailors are unlikely to see anything other than Mercator charts. However, these are not necessarily the best for ocean passages, not just because of scale distortions, but also because it is difficult to plot the shortest distance between two points. At first glance, this seems a little absurd—after all, everybody knows the shortest distance between two points is a straight line. However, this is often not the case with a Mercator projection.

Because latitude and longitude lines form a grid on a Mercator chart with the lines intersecting one another at right angles, a straight line drawn on a Mercator chart crosses all lines of latitude and longitude at a constant angle. However, if we think of a globe and connect a couple of points (say, New York and London) by stretching a piece of string between them, the line formed by the string (the shortest distance between the two points) actually crosses the lines of latitude and longitude at changing angles (it forms part of a "great" circle that has its center at the center of the earth). If we record the points at which these lines are crossed and then plot these positions on the Mercator chart, we end up with a curved line.

Therefore, for transoceanic planning purposes, a different type of chart is used. This employs something known as a *gnomonic projection*, which results in lines of longitude appearing as straight lines and lines of latitude appearing as curved lines. The benefit of this projection is that the shortest distance between two points is always a straight line. For navigational purposes, the points at which the lines of latitude and longitude are crossed are transferred to a Mercator chart (described previously) and then connected to determine a course to be steered, which gradually changes during the passage.

This changing course—the shortest distance between two points—is known as a *great-circle route*. The distance saved over the course described by drawing a straight line on a Mercator chart—known as a *rhumb-line course*—is insignificant on short passages but may be quite significant on longer passages, particularly

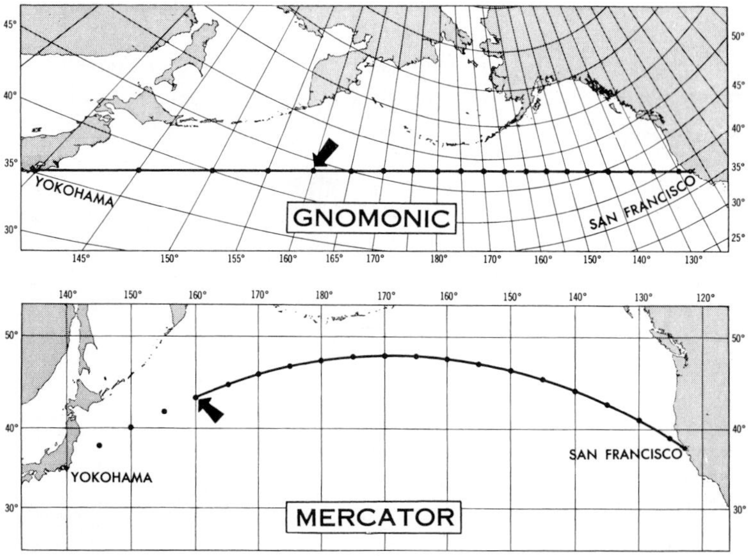

Great-circle course as plotted on gnomonic and Mercator charts.

east–west passages in higher latitudes; on north–south passages, the rhumb-line and great-circle routes are identical. However, the farther a course diverges from due north or due south and the longer the passage, the greater is the difference between the rhumb line and the great circle—and, therefore, the greater the benefit in using a gnomonic projection to calculate the great-circle route.

Chart Terminology and Symbols

The type of projection used to make a chart is written in the small print under its title, along with other important information. For example, on my NOAA chart for Penobscot Bay, Maine (United States), the small print reads:

> *PENOBSCOT BAY*
> *Mercator Projection*
> *Scale 1:40,000 at Lat. 44° 08´*
> *North American Datum of 1983*
> *(World Geodetic System 1984)*
> *SOUNDINGS IN FEET*
> *AT MEAN LOWER LOW WATER*

The scale is given at just one latitude, which is at the midpoint of the coverage of the chart. To the north and south of this point, there is increasing distortion; however, given the relatively large scale of the chart (1:40,000, which means the chart covers a relatively small area but provides a considerable amount of detail), the distortion is not measurable on this chart. The reference to the *North American Datum* used to make this chart is a key piece of information when it comes to electronic navigation (more about that shortly). Finally, *soundings* (depths) are measured in feet "at mean lower low water," which is the *chart sounding datum* for this chart.

Depths (soundings) on a chart have to be measured from a defined surface level (the chart sounding datum). At different times, hydrographic offices have used different surface levels, including mean low water (MLW) (the average of all low tides compiled over a period of years) and mean lower low water (MLLW) (a number used in areas with two daily tides, one of which is lower than the other; an average is taken of the lower of the two). The British Admiralty formerly used low water ordinary springs (LWOS)—a number computed from averaging low-water springs over many years—but now uses lowest astronomical tides (LAT, the "lowest tidal level that can be predicted to occur under average meteorological conditions and under any combination of astronomical conditions").

Chart title for Penobscot Bay, Maine.

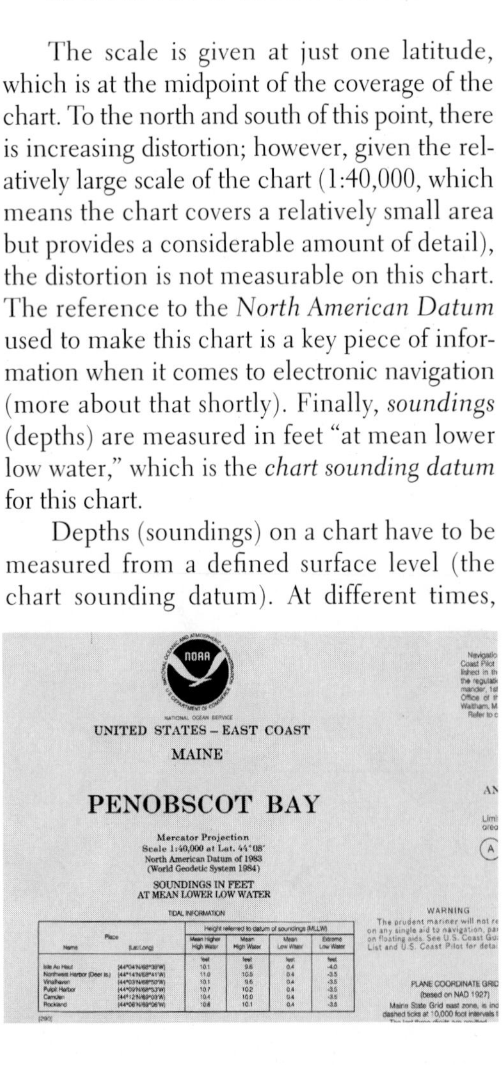

None of these points are the same! All of them are fairly conservative; that is, most of the time, low tides are not actually as low as is assumed in making the chart (even at low tide, there is a greater depth of water than is shown on the chart). However, with all these points, *there will be times when low tides are lower than those assumed when making the chart—sometimes by as much as several feet.* In other words, *charted depths exceed actual depths for a short period.* When navigating in "skinny" waters close to low tide, it is important to establish the chart sounding datum and to reference it to local tide tables to establish whether there really is adequate water to avoid running aground.

Depths on the chart are given as depths below the chart's sounding datum (e.g., MLLW). On all but U.S. charts, these depths are now given in meters, although older British Admiralty charts may be based on feet or on fathoms and feet. Most (but not all) U.S. charts are still in feet and are likely to stay that way since the metrification program has stalled in recent years. *When using a chart, first check the units used for depth.*

Points of equal depth may be connected by a line (a *depth contour* or *bathymetric line*). Typically, all depths at or less than a certain depth contour (e.g., 6 ft./1.83 m on large-scale U.S. charts) are colored to highlight shoal water. A variety of symbols (mostly crosses and stars) is used to denote hazards, especially rocks. A cross indicates a rock awash or almost awash at low water; a dotted line around it indicates the danger area. A depth (at the chart's sounding datum) over the top of permanently submerged rocks and reefs may or may not be given. Depending on the extent of the tide, hazards will occur in the *intertidal zone*; that is, the area exposed at low tide but covered at high tide (it may be colored; it is green on U.S. charts). Rocks and other features in the intertidal zone

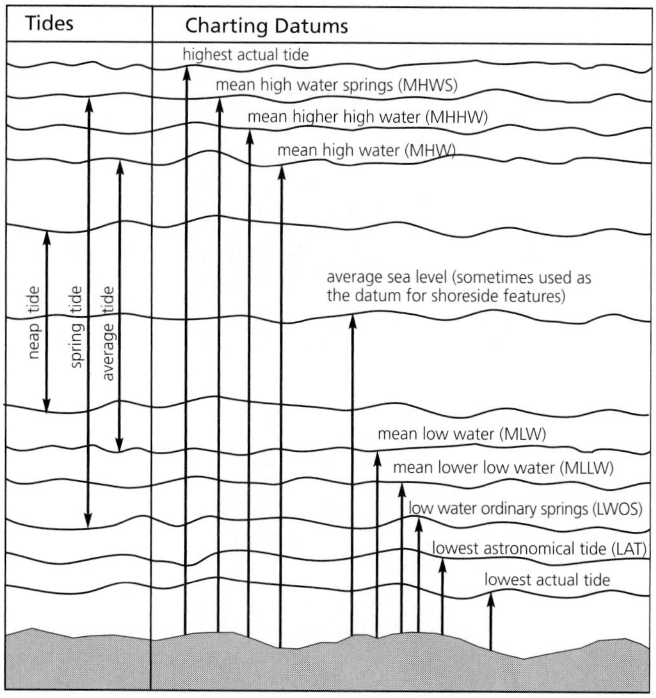

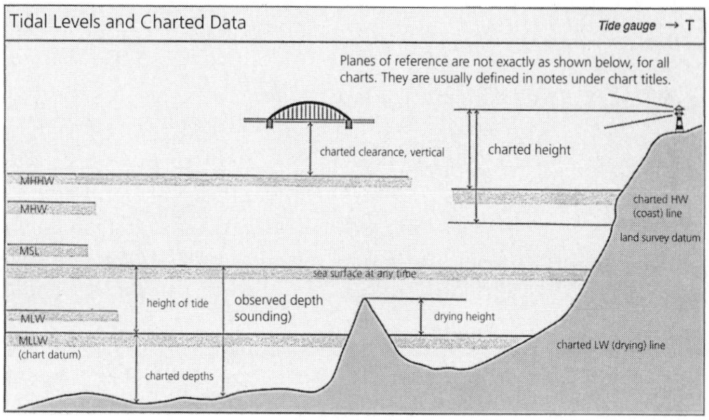

Left: *Charting datums for depths, shorelines, and heights above sea level. Various height, high-water, and depth datums in use around the world.* Above: *Typical chart datums used on American charts. (From Chart #1, courtesy NOAA/NIMA)*

may be given a *drying height*, which is the height that is exposed when the water level goes down to the level of the chart's sounding datum. Drying heights are underlined.

Then there are features that are permanently above the mean high water (MHW) mark, which is an average high-water level (sometimes high water is higher, sometimes lower). This may be replaced by some other high-water datum, such as mean high water springs (MHWS). Again, there are variations among hydrographic offices as well as variations in the same office over time. The high-water datum is used to define the coastline; generally, features above it (land) are colored. Ashore, the chart shows contour lines with some spot heights, which are generally referenced to the high-water datum (e.g., MHW), but not always.

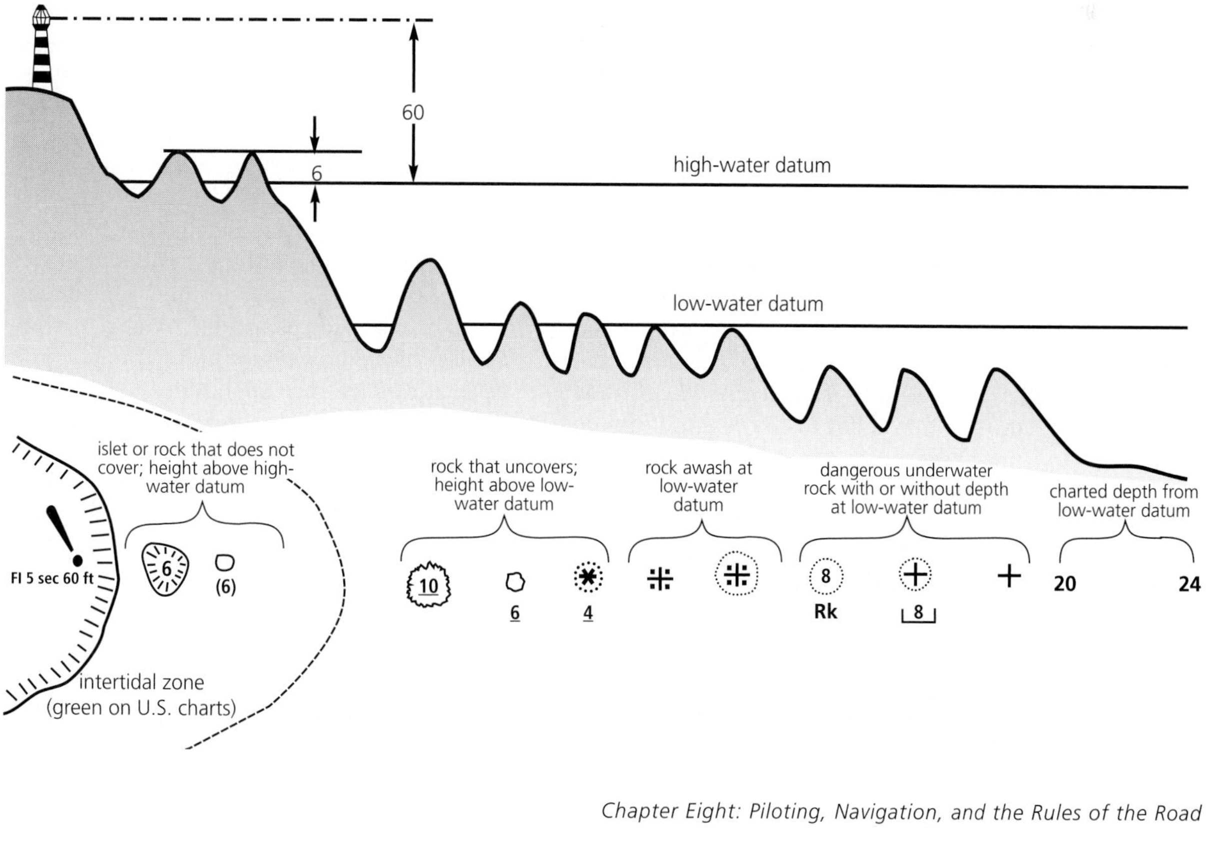

Common charting conventions for water depths, rocks, islets, and so on.

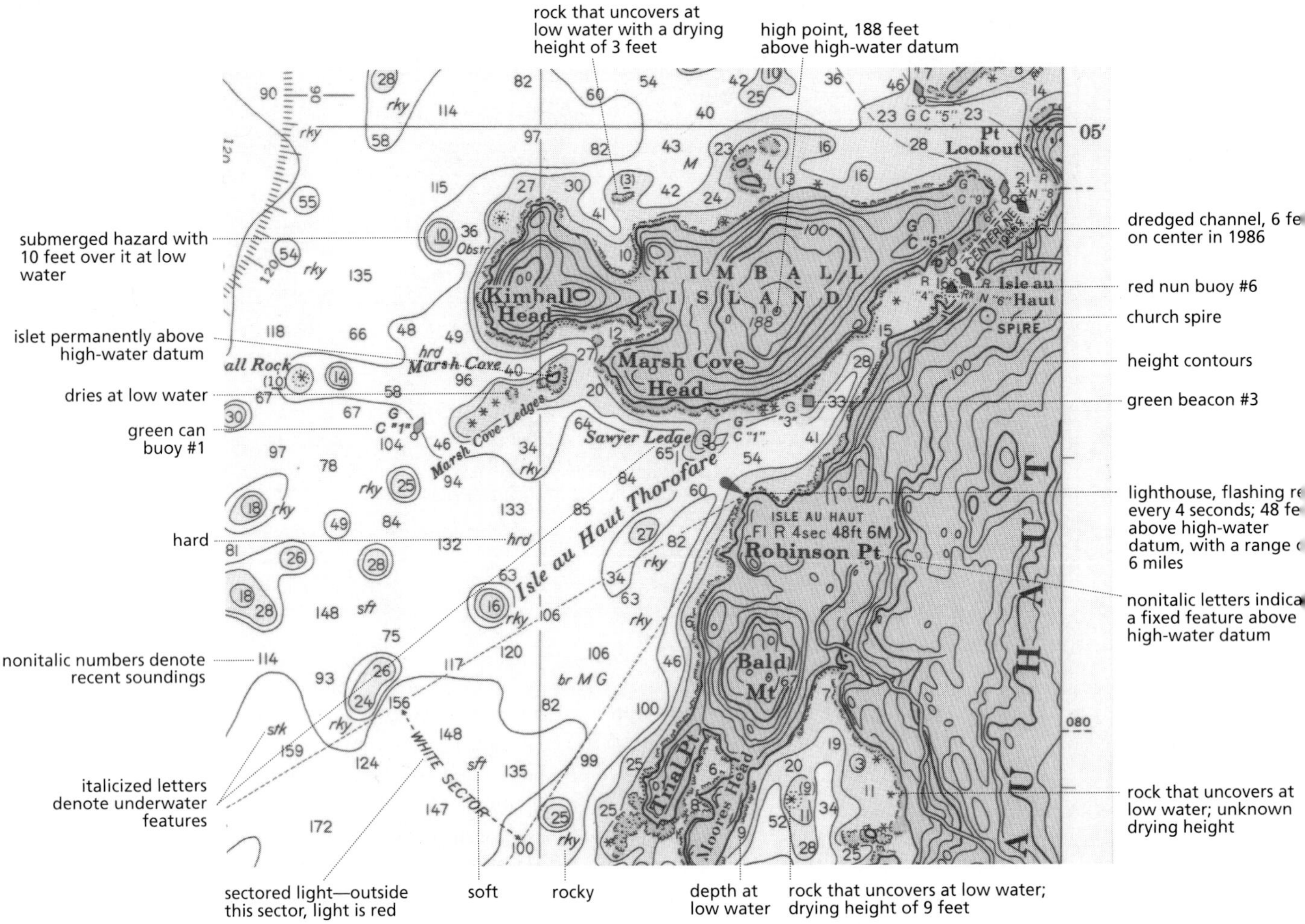

Common charting conventions (Isle au Haut, Maine) and bottom descriptions.

Another datum may be used, such as *average sea level* (the average level of the sea surface over a long period—usually, 18.6 years—or the average level that would exist in the absence of tides). I know this is confusing; unfortunately, it's the way things are. Somewhere on the chart, it says what datum is being used for heights above sea level.

Again, it is important to check the units being used (feet or meters). Man-made features that are useful for navigation may be shown (e.g., tall chimneys and radio towers). Whichever datum is used for measuring heights above sea level (e.g., MHW), it is rarely the same as that used for measuring depths (the sounding datum)—they differ by the extent of the tidal range in the area.

The margins of dredged channels are shown with dotted lines. The minimum dredged depth (*controlling depth*), with the date on which the channel was last dredged, are given. The date is important—there may have been significant shoaling since the last dredging. The width of the dredged channel also may be given.

The nature of the ocean bottom (sand, mud, shells) is frequently recorded through the use of various abbreviations (for more on this, see chapter 9). Different symbols are used to denote rocky or sandy shorelines, cliffs, dunes, marshes, mangroves, and so on. Bridges with navigational significance are shown, with information about the width of any navigational channel (e.g., "HOR CL 26 FT"—horizontal closed width of 26 feet); the height of the bridge when closed (e.g., "VERT CL 3 FT"—vertical closed height of 3 feet at the high-water datum; when the tide is out, there is a considerably greater clearance); whether the bridge opens; and if so, what kind of a bridge it is (e.g., a swing bridge). Height restrictions when the bridge is open also are given, if applicable.

Navigational aids—lighthouses, beacons, buoys, and so on—are shown, each with its own symbol. Buoys, for example, are often designated by a diamond with a small circle attached at one end (there may be different symbology for large buoys and on some electronic charts). The circle represents the circle that the buoy describes as it swings around its anchor. The diamond is colored to indicate the color of the buoy. Letters indicate the shape ("C" for can and "N" for nun on U.S. charts). Numbers indicate the buoy's number. The range, color, and flash characteristic of any light also are noted.

In summary, there is a vast amount of infor- mation displayed on a chart in an extremely condensed and abbreviated manner (more than I can possibly outline herein). Everything on the chart has significance, even whether labels or soundings are printed with roman or nonitalic or *italicized* letters and numbers (roman or nonitalic letters denote fixed features above the high-water datum; *italicized* letters denote underwater or floating features; roman or nonitalic numbers denote recent soundings; and *italicized* numbers denote old soundings that may not be as accurate). All of this is summarized (for U.S. charts) in Chart #1, which is actually a booklet available from chart agencies (and on line at *http://chartmaker.ncd.noaa.gov/*; click on Chart #1). Other hydrographic offices have similar publications (in the U.K., the British Admiralty produces Chart #5011, Symbols and Abbreviations Used on Admiralty Charts).

Even after decades of cruising and using charts, I still don't recognize numerous obscure symbols sometimes used on charts. However, I do have a good grasp of the basics: depths, features, land forms, buoys, lights, and so on; this is an essential prerequisite to any form of piloting. Studying a booklet like NOAA's Chart #1 (or the Admiralty's chart #5011) is an excellent way to spend a long winter's evening dreaming about next year's cruising. Better yet is combining this exercise with a close study of charts of the area you intend to cruise, perusing them for symbols you don't recognize, and then looking them up on Chart #1 (U.K. Chart #5011).

Chart Corrections

Although much navigational information remains unchanged over long periods (e.g., the location and depth of rocks), it is surprising how much can change. Hydrographic offices are constantly updating their databases to include these changes. Every time a chart is reprinted, it is brought up to date. Some hydrographic offices (e.g., the British Admiralty, the Canadians, and the Cubans) then require their chart agents to maintain databases of changes subsequent to the chart printing and to bring the chart fully up to date at the time of sale to the public. Other hydrographic offices (e.g., NOAA and NIMA) require no further corrections beyond the date of printing. (In 2000 NOAA initiated an experimental print on demand service that enables charts to be corrected up to the moment of purchase.)

In any event, it is up to the consumer to find out when the chart was last corrected and to keep it corrected from that date on. All hydrographic offices make available regular bulletins (*Notices to Mariners*), with charts listed by number and details of any recent changes to the chart.

In the United States, *Notices to Mariners* are supplemented with *Local Notices to Mariners*, which are specifically aimed at small-boat sailors and can be obtained free from the USCG or downloaded from the Internet at *www.navcen.uscg.mil/lnm/* (go to section IV, Chart Corrections). There are also summaries that detail all changes to charts since the last printing. For example, *Summary of Corrections* is available from NIMA in five volumes. The relevant information is also available at *www.pollux.nss.nima.mil/untm* (go to Query the Database and click on the relevant item; e.g., Chart Corrections.) Finally, NOAA and NIMA have lists of when charts were last printed (*Dates of Latest Editions*, free from NOAA and NIMA quarterly; call 800-638-8972).

With this kind of information, it is possible to keep a chart fully updated and corrected. With old U.S. charts that have not been corrected for some time, the procedure is to start with *Dates of Latest Editions* to see if the chart is the latest printing; if not, it should be replaced. (However, Ken Olum has compiled lists of chart corrections that go back beyond the most recent printings; his Web site is at *www.Cosmos2.phy.tufts.edu/~kdo/charts/*.) Given an up-to-date printing, the *Summary of Corrections* for the relevant region should be consulted to find corrections that will bring the chart more or less up to date (or use the Web site given previously). Then you can work backward from the latest *Local Notices to Mariners* to the date at which the *Summary of Corrections* stops. However, the *Summary of Corrections* only logs information of interest to deep-draft vessels; for all corrections relevant to a chart, you have to work your way backward through all the *Local Notices to Mariners*.

In the United Kingdom, since January 2001 the British Admiralty has been posting its *Notices to Mariners* at *www.hydro.gov.uk/* (click on Notices to Mariners); during 2001 it expected to post historical data going back as far as 1996.

In practice, few people outside major shipping lines keep their charts updated (it can be quite a chore). In our case, given the hundreds of charts that we have from half a dozen different hydrographic offices, it is simply impractical.

And given the cost of charts these days, few of us buy new printings or editions of our old charts. When Terrie and I crossed the North Sea in 1971, we were using a chart dating from before World War II. This is a little extreme and definitely ill advised; none of the lights and buoys off the coast of Europe matched those shown on the chart, which is hardly surprising. Nevertheless, I still regularly use twenty-year-old uncorrected charts for crossing the Gulf of Mexico.

Each of us has to judge about how much time and money we are prepared to put into maintaining an updated set of charts. Large-scale charts, especially those covering areas where there may have been changes with navigational significance (e.g., lots of new construction, maybe a devastating hurricane), clearly require more attention than small-scale charts for offshore use. Beyond this, we need to be cognizant of the age of our charts and when they were last updated, and factor it into our navigational practices (e.g., don't place undue reliance on an old chart in conditions of poor visibility).

Finally, for those sailors using electronic charts, remember that the ability to correct them varies widely according to the method by which they were produced and who produced them. In practice, many charts cannot be corrected, particularly the cheaper ones used in cockpit chart plotters. "High-end" charts issued by hydrographic offices may be easier to correct than paper charts (downloading corrections from the Internet), which is often overlooked when considering electronic charting.

Other Nautical Publications

Charts can be supplemented with a host of additional publications. Among the most useful are updated light lists (which include detailed information on all lighthouses, lighted buoys, lighted beacons, and radio beacons) and tide tables (essential where there is any substantial tidal rise and fall, but also extremely useful in areas with little tide but interesting cruising in shoal waters, such as the Gulf of Mexico and the Caribbean). In popular cruising areas such as Europe, the Caribbean, and the East Coast of the United States, all this information, along with much other useful information, is included in compendiums such as *Reed's Nautical Almanac* (Macmillan *Reeds* in the U.K.).

There are cruising guides and similar publications that provide a mass of detailed information on a given area. We always buy all available guides to any area we intend to cruise—the information is cheap at the price. However, we use these guides with a degree of caution—the information is privately collected and processed with varying degrees of skill and quality control; it is not unusual to find mistakes (including the odd one in my own guides)!

BUOYAGE SYSTEMS AND LIGHTHOUSES

Unfortunately, there are two different systems of buoyage in use worldwide, which is, nevertheless, an improvement on the twenty-six or more systems in use up to 1982. In the United States, Canada, and much of the Caribbean, the system used is known as the International Association of Lighthouse Authorities (IALA) Region B system; in Europe, it is the IALA Region A system. Elsewhere in the world, either system may be used, with the colonial history of an area having a significant impact on the choice made.

Lateral and Cardinal Marks

Both systems employ *lateral* and *cardinal marks*. A lateral mark defines the edge of a safe channel; a cardinal mark defines safe water by reference to the points of the compass.

Lateral Marks

Lateral buoys and other marks are painted red or green (in the past, many green marks were black—some still are). IALA Region B (used in the Americas) employs the "Red, Right, Returning" principle; that is, *when approaching from seaward*, the red marks are on the right-hand (starboard) side of the vessel; the green marks are on the left-hand (port) side of the vessel. *IALA Region A (Europe) uses the exact opposite convention!*

Both IALA Regions B and A further define lateral marks by using nun (cone-shaped) buoys on the starboard side of the channel and cans (square-topped) on the port side. Nun buoys and other starboard-side markers (e.g., beacons) may be further identified with triangular topmarks; can buoys and other port-side markers may have

IALA MARITME BOUYAGE SYSTEM

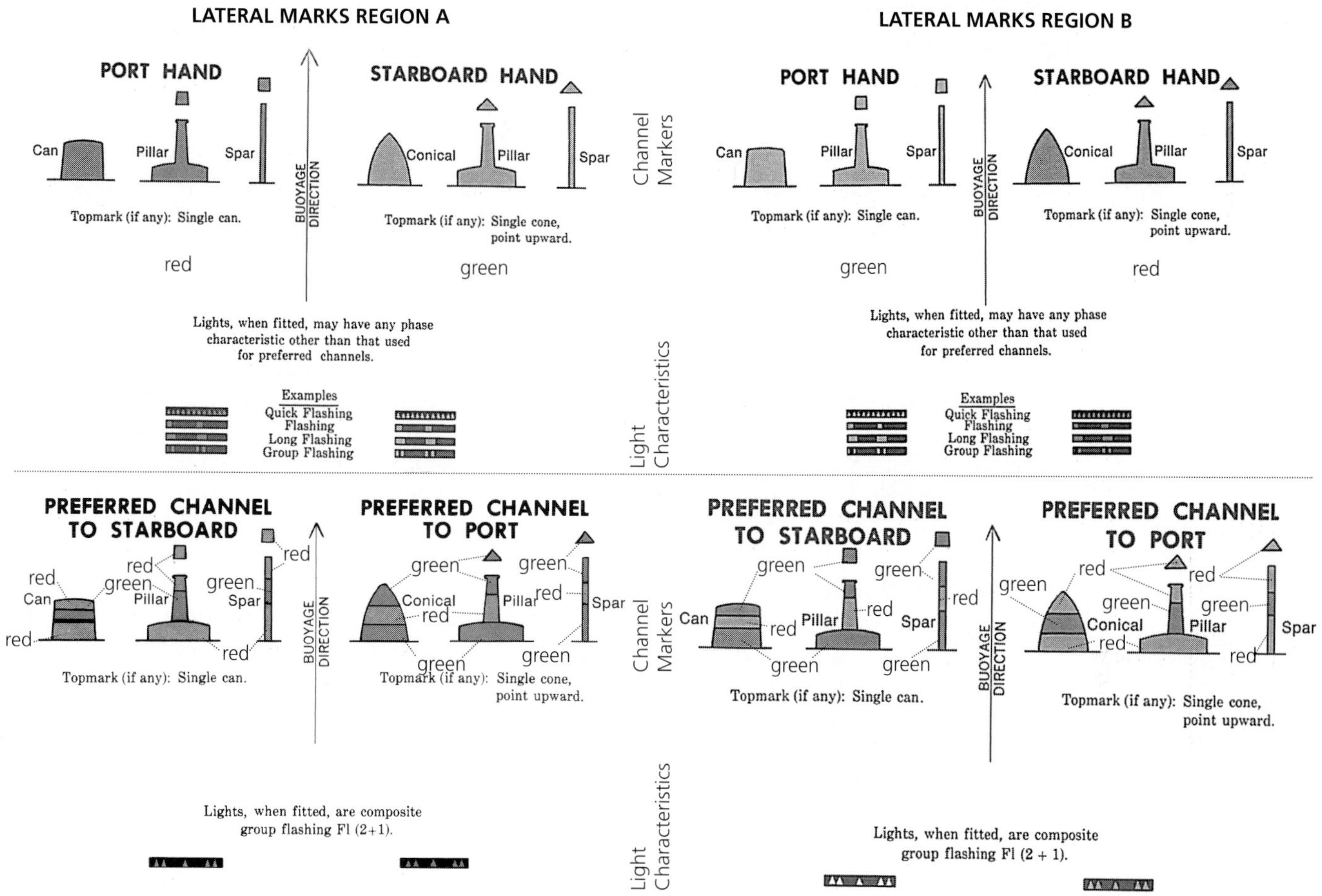

IALA System lateral marks for Regions A and B.

square topmarks. In all cases, the topmarks use the same color coding as the buoys (red to starboard, green to port for IALA Region B; green to starboard, red to port for IALA Region A). If the buoys carry lights, these too are the same color as the buoy. All buoys are numbered, starting from seaward: red buoys have even numbers, green buoys have odd numbers (in other words, even and odd numbers are on opposite sides of the channel in the two different systems).

Buoys with light or sound signals tend to be flat-topped—that is, they resemble a can—regardless of whether they are starboard- or port-side buoys.

Midchannel marks have red and green horizontal stripes. In IALA Region B, if the top band is red and a buoy is nun-shaped, the preferred channel is to treat it as a red-nun buoy (leave it to starboard when going up-channel). If the top band is green and a buoy is can-shaped, the preferred channel is to leave it to port. In IALA Region A, the colors reverse (also, if the top band is red, the buoy will be can-shaped; if it is green, the buoy will be nun-shaped).

With both systems, buoys with red and black horizontal bands, surmounted by two balls, are anchored on top of isolated dangers; spherical and other buoys with red and white vertical stripes are "safe-water" marks that can be passed on any side. They are generally used offshore to indicate approaches to a channel. When lit, red and white buoys have white lights.

Cardinal Marks

The same conventions for cardinal marks are used in IALA Regions B and A. However, cardinal marks are little used in North America; they are more widely used in Europe.

The idea of the cardinal system is to set up a buoy or mark in such a way as to indicate on which side a hazard can be safely passed. A southern cardinal mark is set to the south of a hazard and must be passed to its south. A northern cardinal mark is set to the north of a hazard and must be passed to its north—and so on.

Cardinal marks are distinguished both by coloration (yellow and black horizontal bands) and by a pair of triangular topmarks, one on top of the other. A northern cardinal mark has a black band above a yellow band, with both triangular topmarks pointing upward (to the "north"). A southern cardinal mark has the yellow band above the black, with both topmarks pointing down (to the "south"). An eastern cardinal mark has black bands at the top and bottom, with yellow in between; the top topmark points upward, the bottom down (together, they form a diamond). Finally, a western cardinal mark has yellow bands at the top and bottom, with black in between; the two topmarks point in toward one another. In all cases, the two topmarks point toward the location of the black band(s), which helps to remember the banding on the marks (e.g., the northern mark has the topmarks pointing upward, so the black band is on top; the western mark has the topmarks pointing in toward one another, so the black band is in the middle; and so on).

U.S. Intracoastal Waterway

In addition to the IALA Regions B and A, modified buoyage systems may be employed for specific bodies of water (e.g., the U.S. western rivers). Of these, the most important for U.S. sailors is that used on the Intracoastal Waterway (ICW), which stretches from Maine in the northeast, south along the Atlantic seaboard, around Florida, and west around the Gulf of Mexico to Texas.

The IALA Region B system is used on the ICW with the modification that it is assumed that the "Red, Right, Returning" rule (i.e., the concept of approaching from seaward) is applied from north to south along the Atlantic coast and from east to west along the Gulf of Mexico coastline. The various marks often have some part colored yellow, which differentiates them from the rest of the IALA System B. If headed south along the Atlantic coast, red marks are to starboard and green to port; if headed north, the opposite applies. Yellow triangles go with red marks, yellow squares with green marks, and yellow bars simply mean the ICW.

The ICW frequently intersects and utilizes stretches of water (e.g., river estuaries) that are governed by the standard IALA Region B rules. If such a stretch of water is approached from seaward from the south, those stretches that come under the standard IALA Region B rules

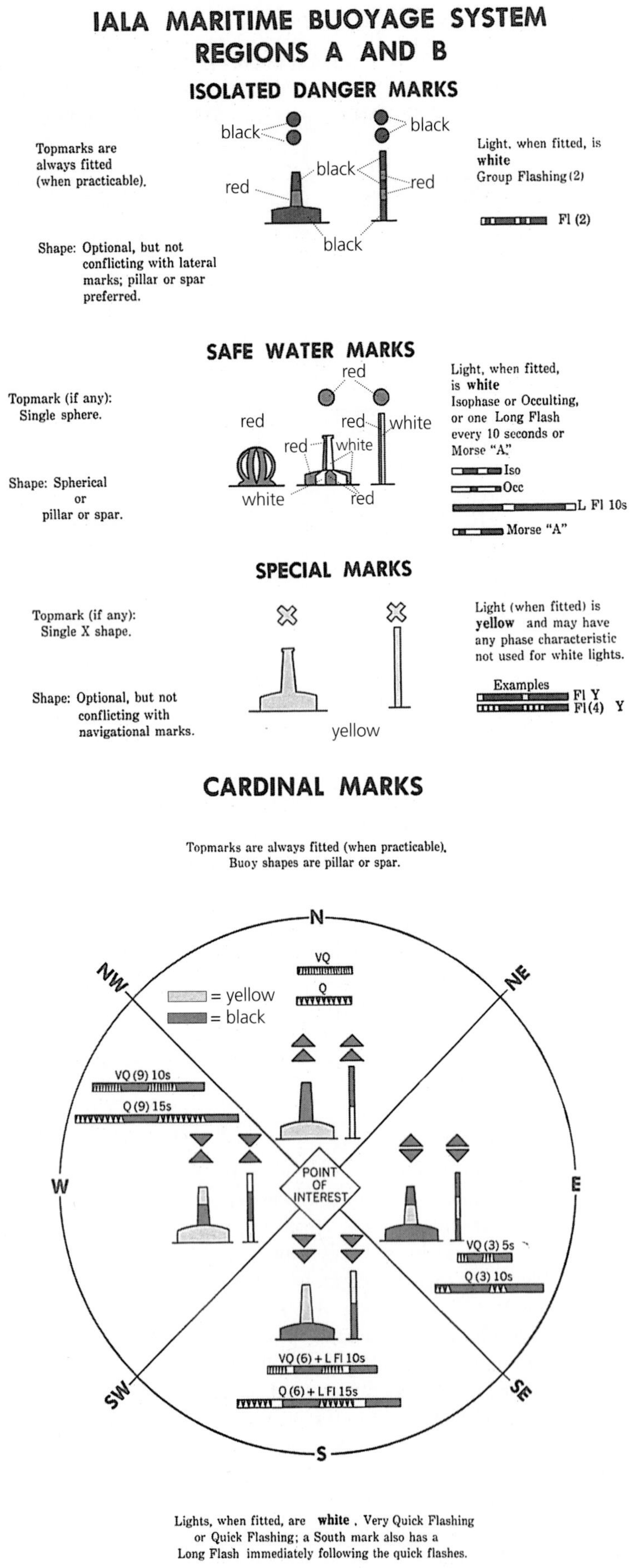

IALA Systems designations for isolated danger, safe-water, special marks, and cardinal marks for regions A & B.

will have the red and green markers on the opposite sides to those stretches governed by the ICW rules. Failure to appreciate at which point the switch occurs from one system to the other will rapidly put you aground. We found this out one year when coming into Fort Lauderdale, Florida, from seaward and then heading north up the ICW—we left the first red waterway mark to starboard and promptly got stuck.

Lighted Marks

At night, the color and shape of marks cannot be seen; therefore, various lighting conventions are used to help in identification. As mentioned previously, red lateral marks have red lights, green lateral marks have green lights, and red and green midchannel marks have a color appropriate to the preferred channel. Red and black isolated hazard buoys and red and white safe-water buoys have white lights. In addition, various flash characteristics are used to impart further information including the following:

- Flashing [Fl]: the light comes on for a single flash at regular intervals. The "on" time is always less than the "off" time. The light flashes fewer than fifty times a minute.
- Quick Flash [Q]: the light flashes "on" and "off" rapidly (at least fifty times a minute).
- Group Flashing [e.g., Fl (2)]: a specified group of flashes (e.g., two) is repeated at regular intervals.
- Composite Group Flashing [e.g., Fl (2+1)]: a group flash in which the flashes within the group are not evenly separated (in this case, there are two flashes, with a third following after a pause longer than that between the first two).
- Morse Code A [Mo(A)]: flashes of different duration are used to form the Morse Code signal for the letter "A" (i.e., a "dot" and a "dash").
- Isophase [Iso]: a light with equal duration of light and dark [also known as "Equal Interval" (E Int)].
- Occulting [Oc]: a light in which the "on" period is longer than the "off" period.

There are more permutations than this, but these cover the majority of applications. Flashing red or green lights (Fl) are used only on red or green marks, thereby serving to mark the sides of channels (lateral marks). Quick-flashing red or green lights (Q) are used to emphasize the need for special caution, such as at tight turns or narrow spots in the channel. Composite-group red and green flashing lights [e.g., Fl (2+1)] are used on red and green marks at channel junctions where it is safe to pass on either side, with the color of the light indicating the preferred channel.

Group-flashing white lights [e.g., Fl (2)] are used on isolated danger marks (red and black horizontal bands, surmounted by two balls). White Morse A lights [Mo(A)] are used on red and white safe-channel buoys.

In all cases, the printed light description on a chart gives not only the light characteris-

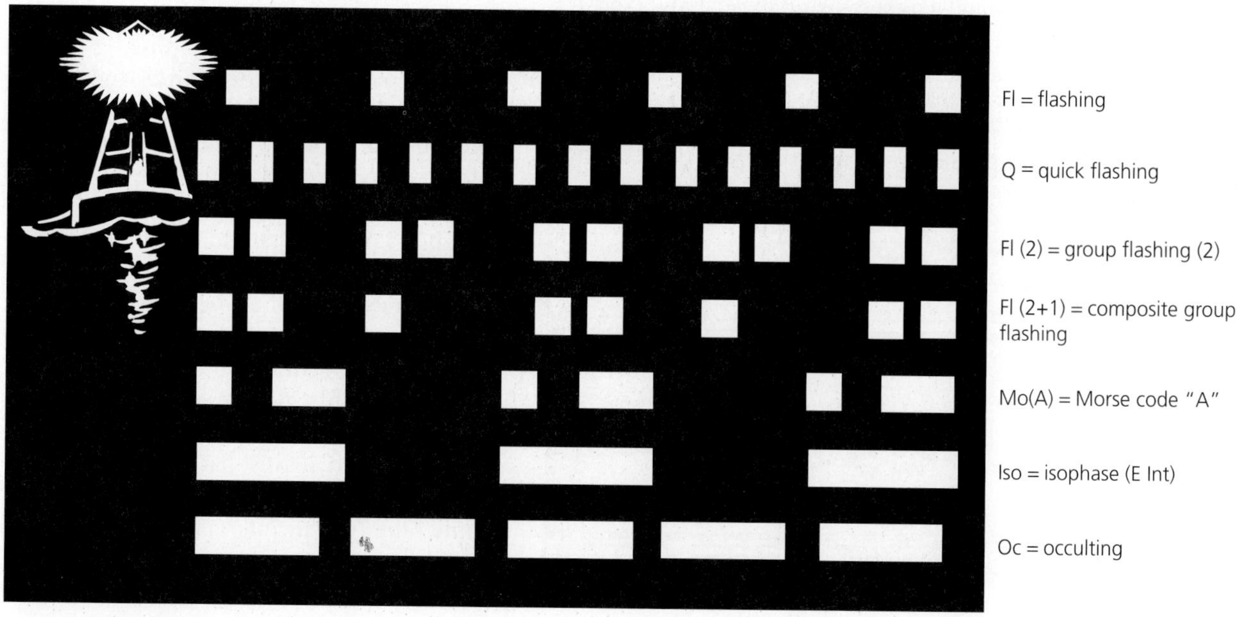

Light characteristics of channel markers.

Light Characteristics of Channel Markers (IALA Region B—for Region A, the reds and greens reverse)

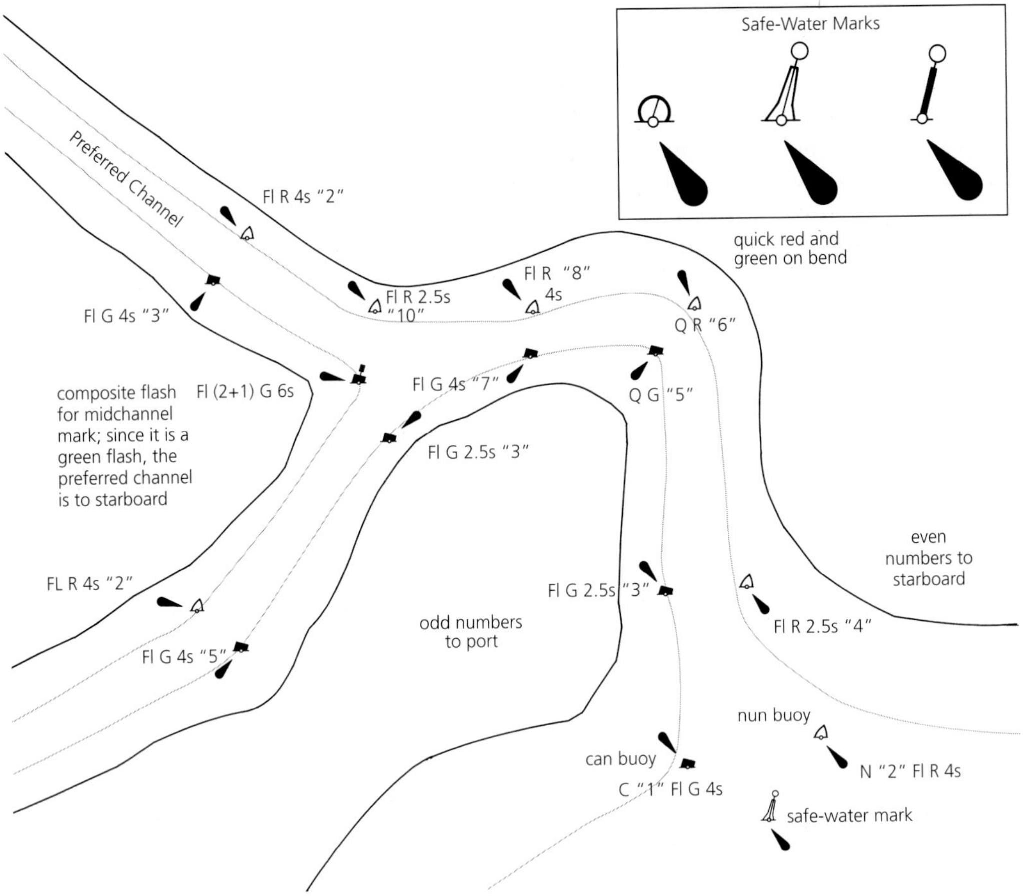

tic and its color if it is other than white, but also the total time (in seconds) for one complete cycle of the light (known as its *period*). For example, "Fl (2+1) G 6s" describes a green light (G) that has a composite-group flash consisting of two flashes followed by another single flash [Fl (2+1)], with the entire cycle of light and darkness taking six seconds before it is repeated (6s). The fact that it is a composite-group flash tells us it is a (lateral) midchannel mark; the fact that it is green in the IALA Region B tells us the preferred channel when approaching from seaward is to starboard (i.e., leave it to port). All this information is derived from such a little label!

Range markers and range lights. (American Practical Navigator, *courtesy DMA)*

Ranges and Leading Lights

Ranges (transits) and leading lights consist of a pair of markers and/or lights, one behind the other, that must be lined up to safely negotiate a confined channel. The aft one is always higher than the forward one. They make extremely precise piloting possible, although it is important to check the chart to determine to which part of a channel they apply. For example, the range may be set up on the bank of a river at a bend; if you approach too closely, you will run into the riverbank.

Range lights may be any color and any flash pattern. The primary concern is to make them stand out against background lighting. Most are white with an *isophase* rear light (same time "on" as "off") and a flashing front light.

Lighthouses

Lighthouses utilize flash patterns similar to buoys, although some may be considerably more complex. The big difference is the range at which the light can be seen, which is a function of both the height of the light and its power. Both are given in the light description on a chart. For example, consider the Cuckolds light approaching Boothbay Harbor, Maine (U.S.): "Gp Fl (2) 6 sec 59 ft 12M HORN." This is a light that flashes twice every six seconds, that is at a height of 59 feet above the chart's high-water datum (in this example, MHW), and that can be seen at a distance of 12 miles. It also has a foghorn. If the height of the light is given in meters, a lowercase "m" is used (e.g., 18 m) to differentiate it from miles, which is indicated by an uppercase "M."

Although this explanation seems clear enough, we may have to qualify the picture in two ways: whether the light is actually high enough to be seen at 12 miles and, even if it is, whether it is really powerful enough to be seen at this distance.

Height determines a light's *geographic range*; that is, the maximum distance at which it can theoretically be seen, limited only by the curvature of the earth. The geographic range assumes that the light is powerful enough to be seen from this distance. It also presupposes a certain height above the horizon of the eye of the observer. *Until 1972, the range of lights given on charts was the geographic range, with the assumption that the observer had a height of eye of 15 feet (the deck of a small ship).*

Luminous range defines the distance at which a light can be seen in a specific set of atmospheric conditions, determined solely by the intensity of light and ignoring its geographic range. This can be further refined to *nominal range*, which is the luminous range when the "meteorological visibility" is 10 nautical miles (a good definition of "meteorological visibility" can be found in the glossary to *American Practical Navigator*, universally known as *Bowditch*; see also Hubbard, page 363). Since 1972, most hydrographic offices (including NOAA and NIMA/DMAHTC) have given the nominal range of lights on charts, not the geographic range.

The actual range of visibility of a light in clear conditions is the lower of the geographic range and the luminous or nominal range. To compute geographic range, we need to know not just the height of the light (h1), but also the

Light characteristics of lighthouses.

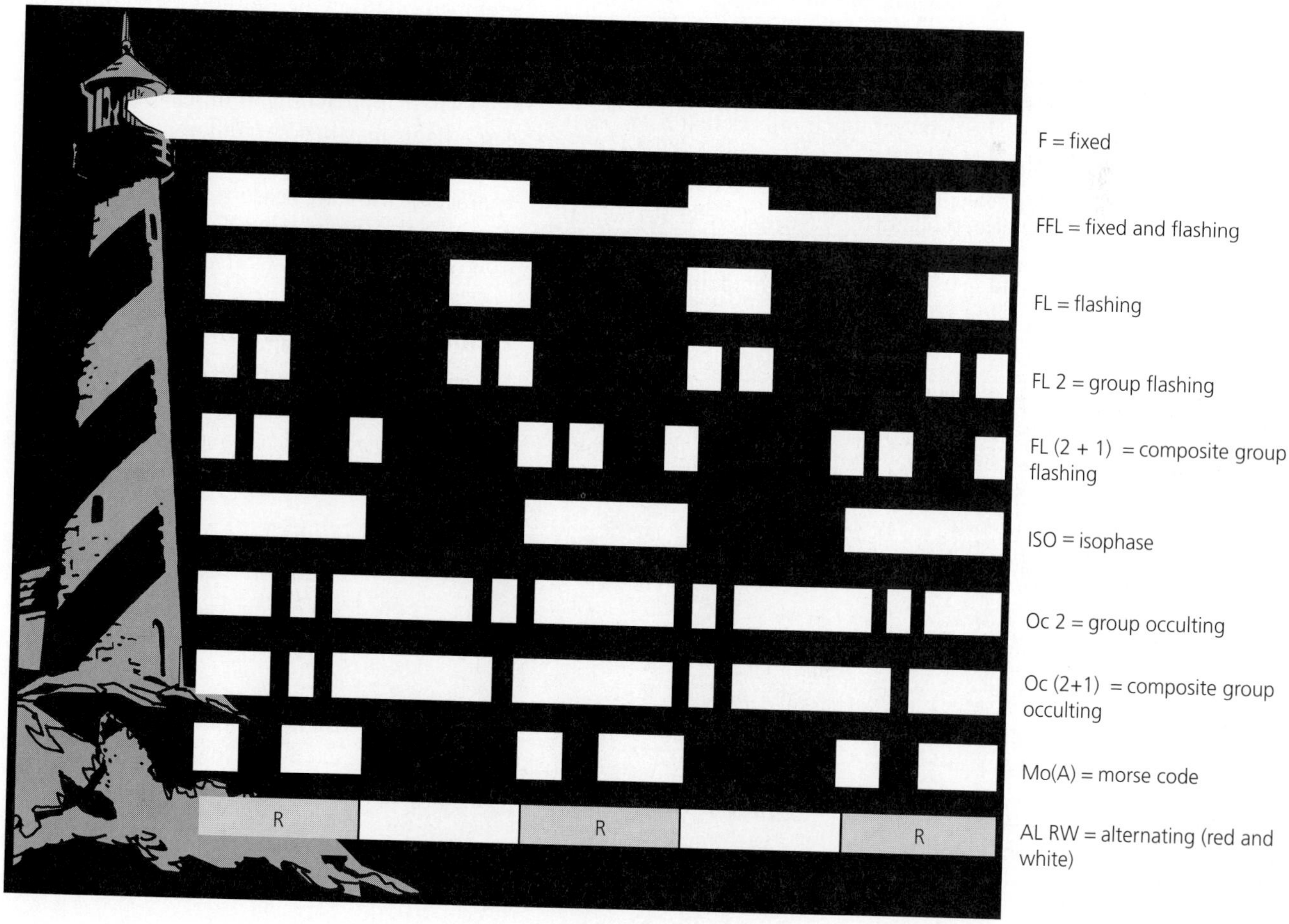

height of eye of the observer (h2). The range (in nautical miles) is then computed as follows:

$$d = 1.17 \times (\sqrt{h1} + \sqrt{h2})$$

where

d = visible distance in nautical miles

h1 = height of light in feet

h2 = height of observer in feet

If h1 and h2 are in meters, use 2.12 as the multiplier to keep the result in nautical miles.

Using the Cuckolds light, and assuming a height of eye of 9 feet (about right from the cockpit of most cruising boats), we have the following equation:

$$d = 1.17 \times (7.68 + 3) = 12.5 \text{ miles}$$

In this case, the geographic range (12.5 miles) from our small boat is almost the same as the nominal range (12 miles). On a clear night, we should be able to pick out the light almost as soon as it comes over our horizon. Of course, if visibility is reduced, we will not see the light at this distance.

Geographic range also can be looked up in a table showing the distance of visibility of objects at sea (see opposite page). The light's height and the height of eye of the observer are looked up separately (not added together), and then the two visibility numbers that have been extracted from the table are added together.

Looking at the table for the Cuckolds light, the nearest height to 59 feet (h1) is 60 feet, which gives a geographic range of 9.1 miles; the nearest height to 9 feet (h2, the height of the observer) is 10 feet, which gives a range of 3.7 miles.

$$d \text{ (geographic range)} = 9.1 + 3.7 = 12.8 \text{ miles}$$

This is a little on the high side because both height numbers have been rounded up.

Finally, we need to note that the height of the Cuckolds light given on the chart is calculated from the chart's high-water datum, which is MHW. On other charts, it may be calculated from another datum—this must be checked in the small print. In any event, at most states of the tide, the height of the light above sea level is greater than its charted height, and the geographic range is commensurably increased (e.g., at low tide with a 10 ft. tide, the light will be 69 ft. above the water level, extending its geographic range to 13.2 miles—which is somewhat above its nominal range; in this case, the nominal range is the limiting factor).

In practice, in many cases the nominal (charted) range of a major lighthouse substantially exceeds its geographic range when viewed from a small boat—in other words, the light will not come into view (come over the horizon) until well after the chart tells us it is visible. Its *loom* (the glow it makes in the sky) may be visible long before the light is over the horizon, especially on a night with low-lying clouds (the light reflects off the underside of the clouds). It is not unusual to be able to pick out the loom of a powerful light from 20 or 30 miles away.

Some lights only shine over a particular sector, which will be shown on the chart. The sector may simply be defined by a couple of lines on the chart or defined in degrees. In the latter case, each line is given its bearing as measured when approaching from seaward. In other cases, lights may be given different colored sectors (e.g., red for danger, green for a safe approach), with any bearings on the sectors displayed as they are measured when approaching from seaward.

Picking out Navigation Marks

When it comes to identifying navigation marks (and reading numbers off them) during both the day and the night, there is no substitute for a good pair of binoculars. The most useful are 7 × 50

Computing geographic range.

Using the table and interpolating for the nearest numbers, we have

1. the visible range with 10-foot height of eye = 3.7 nm

2. the range of a 60-foot light is 9.1 nm

Total = 3.7 + 9.1 = 12.8 nm

This is a little on the high side because we have rounded up both the height of eye and the height of the light.

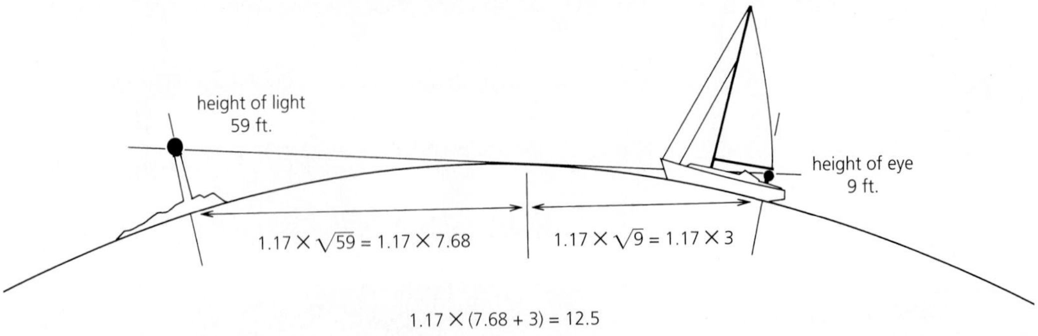

binoculars; that is, the magnification is seven times and the diameter of the *objective lens* (the front lens, which gathers the light) is 50 mm.

In theory, higher levels of magnification enable more distant objects to be seen, but at the expense of the *field of view*; that is, the width of the horizon covered, typically given as X feet at 1,000 meters (e.g., Fujinon marine binoculars have an outstanding 425 ft. at 1,000 m). The greater the field of view, the easier it is to find objects and to keep them in view. On a moving platform such as a boat, higher magnification with little field of view makes it extremely difficult to find and keep in view small objects such as distant buoys. However, some high-end binoculars incorporate *image stabilization* (IS) technology that automatically compensates for movement to produce a sharp image. To some extent, this makes it practical to use higher levels of magnification (e.g., Canon 10 × 30 IS binoculars combine IS technology with a respectable field of view of 314 ft. at 1,000 m).

The size of the objective lens is also important. With all other factors being equal, the bigger the lens is, the more light will enter the binoculars and the brighter the image will be. (Of course, all other factors are not equal.) The quality of the optics and specialized lens coatings to minimize light losses are also important. Light loss is expressed as a percentage of available light getting through to the eye (*transmission efficiency*, which varies from 70 percent at the low end to near 100 percent). An excellent compromise between brightness and size and weight are the 50 mm lenses (relatively large for binoculars) commonly found on marine binoculars.

Geographic Range Table

HEIGHT Feet	Meters	DISTANCE, nm
5	1.5	2.6
10	3.0	3.7
15	4.6	4.5
20	6.1	5.2
25	7.6	5.9
30	9.1	6.4
35	10.7	6.9
40	12.2	7.4
45	13.7	7.8
50	15.2	8.3
55	16.8	8.7
60	18.3	9.1
65	19.8	9.4
70	21.3	9.8
75	22.9	10.1
80	24.4	10.5
85	25.9	10.8
90	27.4	11.1
95	29.0	11.4
100	30.5	11.7
110	33.5	12.3
120	36.6	12.8
130	39.6	13.3
140	42.7	13.8
150	45.7	14.3
200	61.0	16.5
250	76.2	18.5
300	91.4	20.3
350	106.7	21.9
400	121.9	23.4
450	137.2	24.8
500	152.4	26.2
550	167.6	27.4
600	182.9	28.7
650	198.1	29.8
700	213.4	31
800	243.8	33.1
900	274.3	35.1
1,000	304.8	37

Note: nm = nautical miles. Courtesy Navigator Publishing

Binoculars are essential on a boat.

Beyond this, binoculars should be waterproof and, preferably, should float if dropped overboard. An excellent feature often incorporated is a compass.

For night work, a good quality nightscope enables you literally to see in the dark—but at a staggering price! A considerably cheaper option is a powerful spotlight. However, it should have a much longer lead than what is provided by the manufacturer so that it can be held over the side before turning it on. If this is not done first, its beam is likely to get reflected back from rigging and other fixtures, dazzling the user rather than illuminating the horizon. Even better is a waterproof DC outlet up near the bow, in addition to the standard one near the cockpit, so that someone in the bow can use the spotlight free of all onboard obstructions. Once a spotlight has been used, it takes some time to reestablish your night vision, so it should not be turned on unless necessary.

COMPASSES AND PLOTTING

In addition to understanding charts and recognizing navigation marks, at the core of all piloting are an understanding of compasses and compass courses and an ability to determine and plot positions, courses, and distances.

Compass Basics

Regardless of whether a boat has a full complement of navigational electronics or none at all, the ship's compass is the single most important tool onboard. As everyone knows, a compass responds to the earth's magnetic field, indicating *magnetic north* (M), not *true north* (T). The difference between true and magnetic north, which varies widely over the surface of the earth, is known as *magnetic variation*. If magnetic north is to the east of true north, we have east variation; if it is to the west, then west variation. The variation is shown on all charts by displaying a magnetic compass rose inside one that shows true north (which is aligned with the lines of longitude on the chart).

Variation changes over time, often by as much as six or more minutes a year. Usually this has little significance, but it can become significant when using old charts. The rate of change is shown at the center of the magnetic compass rose, with the year to which the displayed magnetic variation applies. Locally, for example, I am still using a 1988 chart. Magnetic variation in 1988 was 17 degrees 30′ W. The rate of change is given as Annual Decrease 1′. In other words, in the year 2000, the magnetic variation was 12′ less; that is, 17 degrees 18′W. This change is too small to be of any significance in small-boat navigation. However, if for argument's sake, the annual change was 10′ (not unusual in some parts of the world), the total change would be 120′; that is, 2 degrees, which reduces the variation to 15 degrees 30′—a significant change.

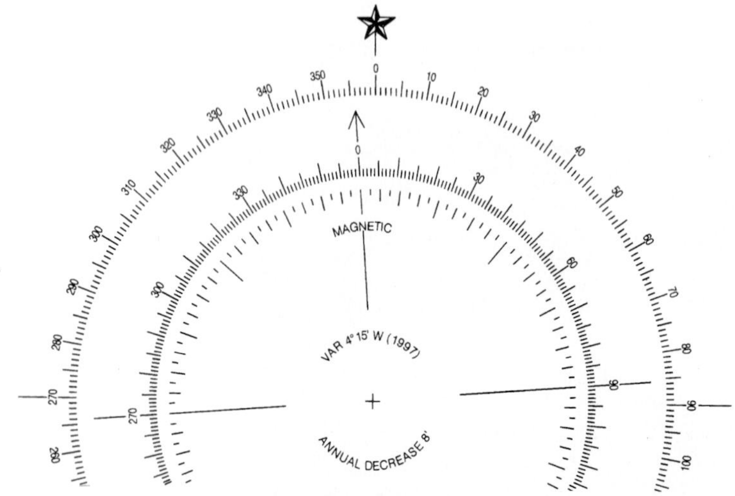

Compass rose giving variation and annual change.

In addition to global magnetic influences, a compass is subject to nearby magnetic influences, such as may be caused by large hunks of metal (e.g., an engine), loudspeakers, and instruments and gauges. These can cause the compass reading to deviate from magnetic north, with the amount of *deviation* varying according to the heading and degree of heel of the boat. Just as with magnetic variation, deviation is given as east or west.

A boat's heading, therefore, can be described in terms of its relationship to (i.e., angle from) true north (T), magnetic north (M), and compass north (C). Only if deviation is zero will magnetic north and compass north be the same; at any other time, compass north is a function of magnetic north and deviation. If both are operating in the same direction (e.g., both easterly), they will be added together to determine what is known as *compass error* (the angular difference between compass north and true north). Conversely, if both have opposite signs (one is east and the other west), they are subtracted to derive compass error.

It is frequently necessary to convert true headings into compass headings and vice versa. All kinds of mnemonics and other memory devices have been suggested to help remember the process. I like the approach in *Bowditch*, which suggests thinking of true headings as the most "correct" and compass as the least "correct." Going from compass to true is "correcting," and from true to compass is "uncorrecting." With this in mind, remember that

> *when correcting, add easterly errors and subtract westerly errors*
>
> *when uncorrecting, subtract easterly errors and add westerly errors*

In other words, if deviation is easterly, when going from a compass course (C) to a magnetic course (M), add the deviation. If variation is easterly, when going from a magnetic course (M) to a true course (T), add the variation. When going the other way (from true north to magnetic or from magnetic to compass), subtract easterly variation and deviation. Everything reverses for westerly variation and deviation: that is, subtract when going from compass to magnetic or from magnetic to true; add when going from true to magnetic or from magnetic to compass.

I can never remember those rules! In practice, I always look at the compass roses on the chart and simply compare a true and magnetic heading to see if I should be adding or subtracting the variation going from one to the other. I also try to adjust my compass so that deviation is close to zero (see the following section) and I don't have to worry about deviation. On a typical cruise, the variation may slowly change during its course, but it rarely changes its sign (from east to west or vice versa). Once true and magnetic bearings have been converted into one another a couple of times, there will be no problem in remembering the relevant procedure.

Compass Installation and Adjustment

To function as a reliable navigational instrument, a ship's compass must be set up so that its *lubber line* (the line across the rim of the compass) lines up exactly with the fore-and-aft line of the boat.

The location of a compass should be at

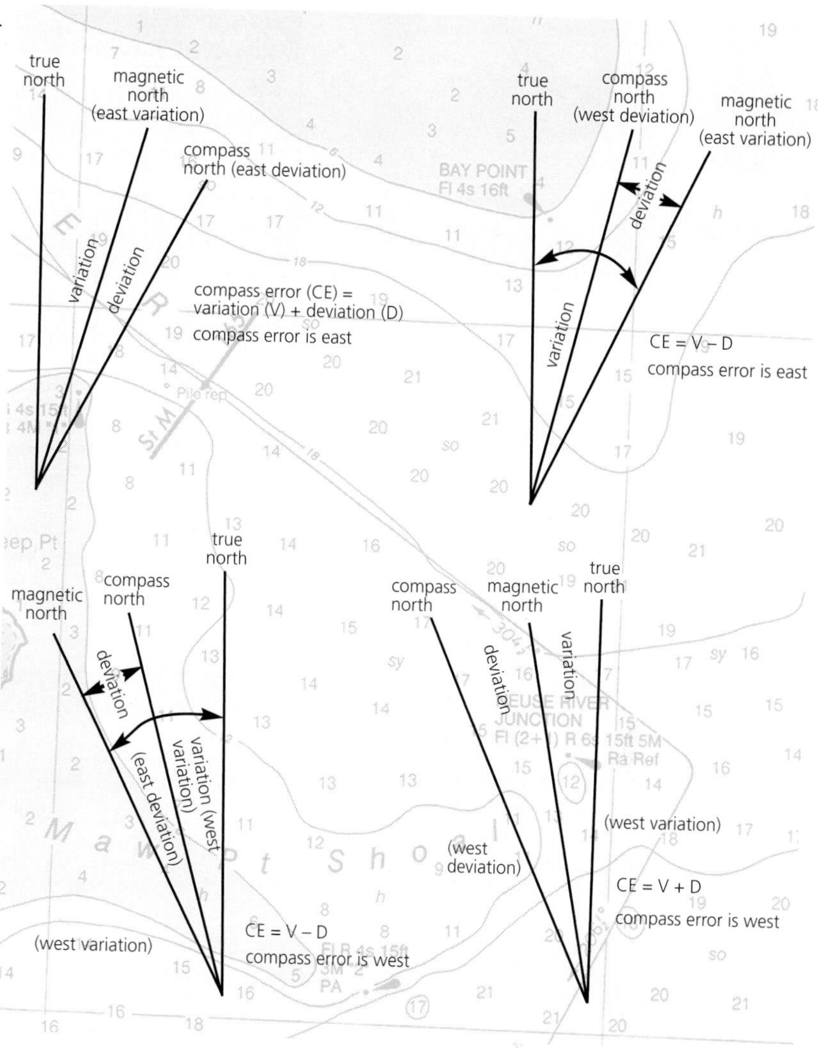

True, magnetic, and compass north; variation and deviation.

least 2 feet (0.6 m) from potential magnetic influences (3 ft./1 m is better, but not always practicable on a small boat). When thinking about magnetic influences, remember that DC current flowing through electrical cables creates a magnetic field, with the field proportional to the current flow. Twisting the positive and negative cables in any given circuit around each other eliminates this magnetic field. If electrical cables cannot be kept away from the compass (e.g., the cables to the compass light), they should be installed with twisted pairs. I also like to put a dedicated switch in the compass-light circuit so that I can turn it off without having to turn off any other circuits.

Modern compasses invariably have plastic domes that craze if exposed to sunlight for long periods; therefore, wherever it goes, the compass should have a cover for when it is not being used.

Following installation, a compass must be fine-tuned to either eliminate deviation or establish the deviation on all points of sail so that it can be taken into account when using the com-

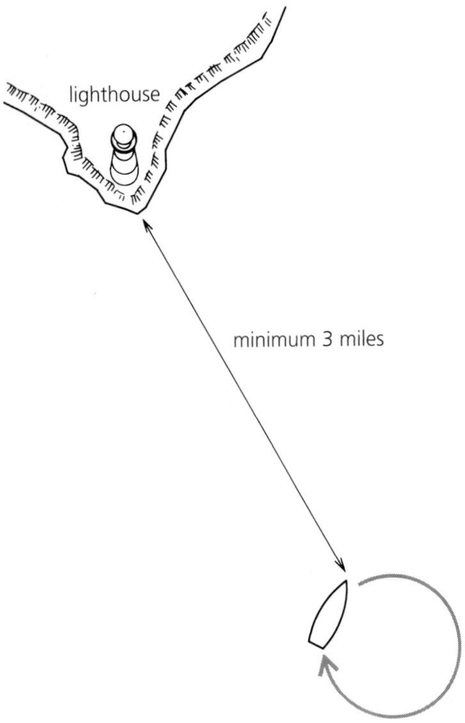

Boat is motored around in a tight circle while measuring the bearing to the lighthouse with a hand-bearing compass. The bearing should remain constant. If so, the boat is steered *by the hand-bearing compass* on headings of 000 M, 045 M, 090 M, etc., noting the boat's compass heading on each heading. The difference between the magnetic and compass headings is the deviation on that particular heading.

Deviation

Magnetic Heading	7° W	6° W	5° W	4° W	3° W	2° W	1° W	0°	1° E	2° E	3° E	4° E	5° E	6° E	7° E
000°										X					
045°								X							
090°							X								
135°								X							
180°										X					
225°										X					
270°										X					
315°								X							

Simple Deviation Table

MAGNETIC HEADING	BOAT'S COMPASS	DEVIATION
000	358	2°E
045	045	0
090	091	1°W
135	135	0
180	178	2°E
225	223	2°E
270	268	2°E
315	315	0

Measuring and logging deviation.

pass. This process of eliminating or determining deviation is known as *swinging the compass*. It should be repeated periodically to ensure that the compass is still reading within known parameters.

Professional compass adjusters employ fairly elaborate procedures to determine deviation. In practice, the following simple approach is fine in most situations. It requires a good hand-bearing compass (a "hockey-puck" type or, better yet, a KVH DataScope or a pair of binoculars with a built-in compass). The boat is taken out on a calm day with no tidal flow or current and motored around in a tight circle at least 3 miles from a prominent feature (e.g., a radio tower or lighthouse). While this is being done, the hand-bearing compass is trained on the feature. The bearing should remain constant. If it does not, the hand-bearing compass is being affected by deviation; another onboard location should be tried.

Once a deviation-free spot has been found for the hand-bearing compass, the boat is steered on eight hand-bearing compass headings, 45 degrees apart (000 M, 045 M, 090 M, 135 M, 180 M, 225 M, 270 M, and 315 M) to compare the boat's compass readings to the hand-bearing compass. Any difference is deviation in the boat's compass. If the boat's compass reads less than the hand-bearing compass, deviation is easterly; if it reads more than the hand-bearing compass, deviation is westerly. The results can be plotted on a graph to produce a simple deviation card. If so desired, more headings can be incorporated (a professional compass adjuster probably checks the deviation every 15 degrees; that is, on twenty-four headings in all).

Most permanently mounted compasses have built-in compensating magnets that are adjusted with a *nonmagnetic* (this is very important) screwdriver. If deviation is more than a degree or two on either an east or west heading or a north or south heading, the following procedure should be employed. First put the boat on an easterly or westerly heading (using the hand-bearing compass) and then turn the east-west compensating screw (the one in a fore-and-aft alignment) until half the deviation has been removed from the ship's compass. (This takes three people: one to operate the hand-bearing compass, one to steer the boat, and one to adjust the compass.) Turn the screw first one way and then the other to find out which way reduces the deviation. Now put the boat on the reciprocal course and remove half the remaining deviation. Continue until the deviation is as close to gone as you can get it. Then repeat the procedure on north and south headings using the north-south compensating screw (it is in an athwartships alignment). On most modern fiberglass boats, deviation can be almost eliminated; steel boats can be problematic and may require the services of a professional compass adjuster.

If deviation remains high on any point of sail, check for unnoticed magnetic influences in the vicinity of the compass. Once a compass has been swung and corrected, remember that all kinds of things can throw it for a loop. For example, consider the typical binnacle-mounted compass with a drinkholder attached to the binnacle; if someone pops a flashlight in the drinkholder, it may knock the compass way off. It is a good idea to periodically make a quick check of the compass with a hand-bearing compass (however, the hand-bearing compass itself may be thrown off by metal jewelry, metal eyeglass rims, and so on).

Transferring Bearings to and from a Chart

Almost all piloting operations involve plotting bearing and course lines on a chart. Maybe we want to figure the course to steer from point A to point B. Or we know we are sailing on a particular heading from point A and want to know where we will end up. Or we are looking at a known point, have a bearing to it, and want to transfer this information to the chart. We end up with two basic charting operations: taking a given line on the chart and finding a way to measure its bearing; and taking a bearing from a given point and using it to draw a line on the chart.

When performing such plotting activities, we have a choice of plotting bearings relative to true north or magnetic north. For several good reasons, commercial ships use true north; small-boat navigators tend to work with magnetic north (much of the time, it obviates the need to convert bearings to and from true and magnetic

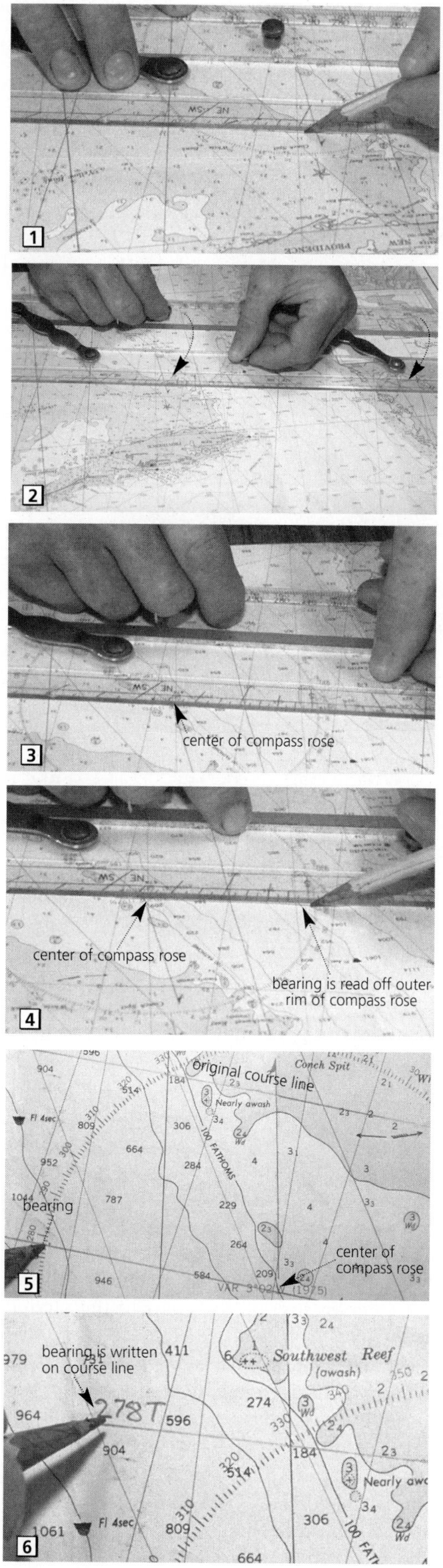

Transferring a bearing from a course line to a compass. 1. The course line is drawn on the chart. 2. The parallel rules are "walked" to the nearest compass rose. 3. The parallel rules are set up on the center of the compass rose. 4. The bearing is read off . . . 5. from the edge of the compass rose. 6. The bearing is transferred to the course line.

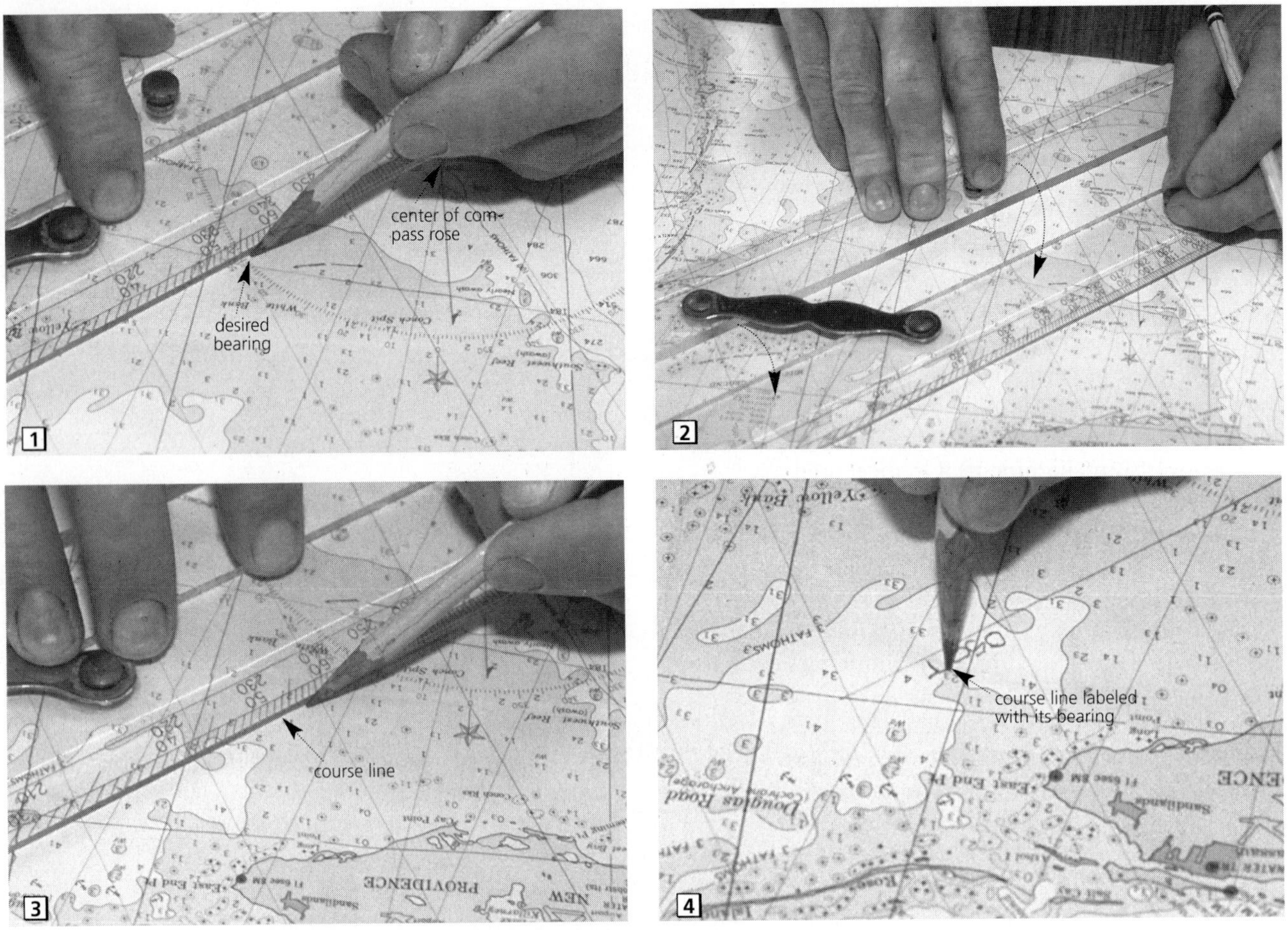

Transferring a bearing from a compass to the chart. 1. The parallel rules are set up to the appropriate bearing on the compass rose. 2. The parallel rules are "walked" to the desired location on the chart. 3. The course line is drawn in . . . 4. and labeled with the bearing.

north). For reasons that will become clear shortly, I prefer to work in true north. Whatever is done, all bearing lines should be clearly marked with the bearing, including the suffix "T" or "M" to indicate whether it is a true or magnetic bearing.

Let's assume we have drawn a course line between two points and wish to determine its bearing so that we can give this information to the helmsperson. The easiest way to measure the bearing is with a set of *parallel rules*, which are two plastic rulers connected by a pair of straps so that the rulers can be moved apart and brought back together while at all times remaining parallel to one another. The edge of the first ruler is laid alongside the course line and the second ruler is hinged outward toward the nearest compass rose on the chart. If the second ruler doesn't make it to the compass rose, it is held down and the first is moved in alongside it. The first is then held down and the second once again hinged outward toward the compass rose. In this way, the parallel rulers are "walked" across the chart to the compass rose until the edge of one ruler can be set on the tiny cross in the center of the compass rose, at which time the bearing of the course line can be read on the rim of either the magnetic compass rose (the inner one) or the true compass rose (the outer one). The appropriate bearing is written alongside the course line; *be sure to note whether it is magnetic or true*.

Transferring a bearing line from the compass rose to any point on the chart is the reverse of this procedure. First, one edge of the parallel rules is set across the compass rose to read the appropriate bearing on either the magnetic or true rose, and then the parallel rules are "walked" to the desired spot on the chart. The bearing line is penciled in and annotated with the bearing—*make sure to note whether it is magnetic or true*.

The problem with this approach is that very often on a cruising boat, the chart has to be folded to fit on the chart table and ends up with no compass rose visible. How to measure bearings? The answer is ridiculously simple. Buy a set of parallel rules that has degrees (from 0 to 360) marked out around the perimeter (what West Marine and others call "deluxe" parallel rules). These have a mark for south ("S") in the center of one edge.

To measure the bearing of a line drawn on the chart, set the parallel rules alongside the line,

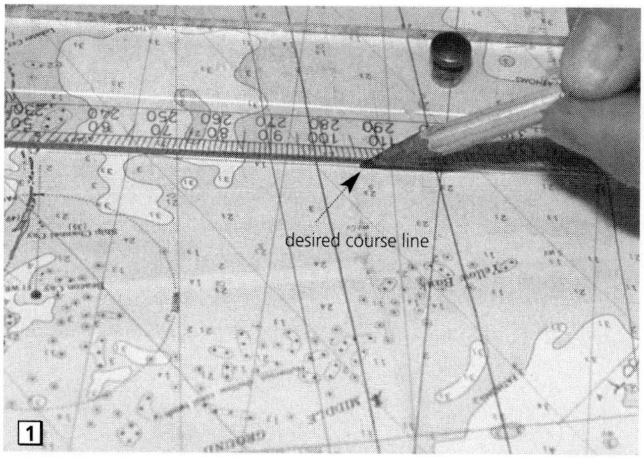

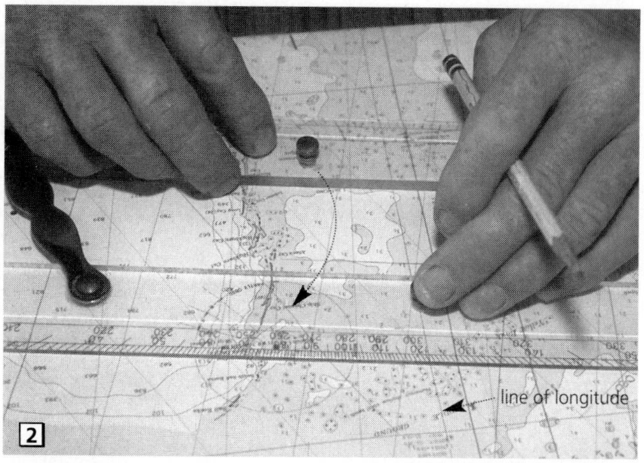

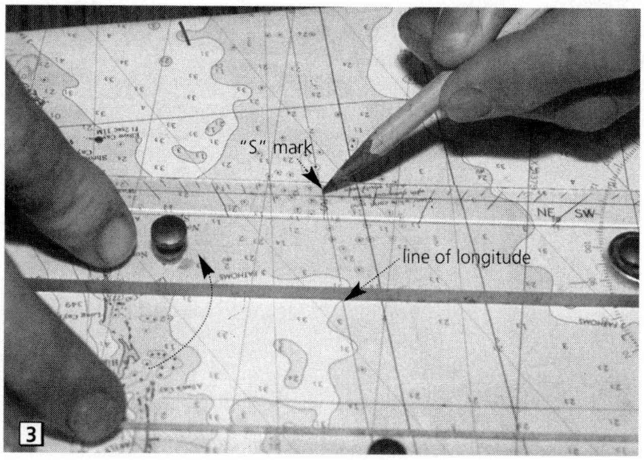

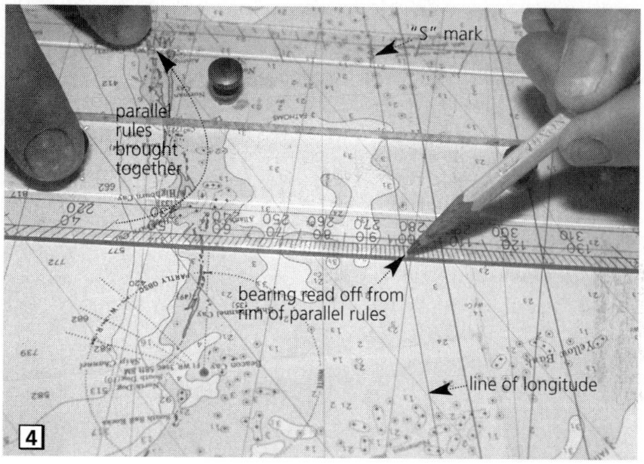

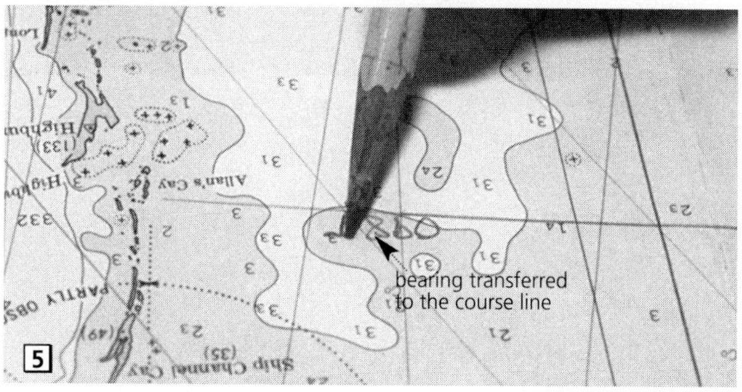

Using lines of longitude to measure bearings. 1. The parallel rules are set up on the course line. 2. The parallel rules are "walked" to the nearest line of longitude until . . . 3. the S mark is on the line of longitude. 4. The parallel rules are closed up (keeping the S mark on the line of longitude), and the bearing is read off where the line of longitude crosses the other side of the parallel rules. 5. The bearing is marked on the course line.

with the "S" mark on the south side of the rules, and then walk the rulers across the chart until the S mark is on a line of longitude. Bring the two rulers together. The degree marking on the upper ruler that is crossed by the line of longitude is the *true* bearing of the line. That's it! If so desired, this bearing can now be converted to a magnetic bearing by applying the relevant variation (obtained from the compass rose).

To go the other way (i.e., transferring a bearing line to some point on the chart), set the parallel rules across a line of longitude. With the S mark on the line and the rulers closed up, rotate the rules until the desired degree marking is also on the line of longitude. Then walk the rulers across to the desired location on the chart—again, that's it! If it is desired to plot a magnetic bearing, it has to be converted to a true bearing before starting the procedure.

In a cramped navigation station, or when using chart kits with spiral bindings, often when walking parallel rules across a chart they foul some obstruction. In this case, a couple of right-angle triangles may prove easier to use. These are specially made for the purpose, with degrees from 0 to 360 marked out around the perimeter, and a handle or knob to move them around. To measure the bearing of a line on the chart, set the hypotenuse of one triangle alongside the line, hold this triangle in place, and then slide the hypotenuse of the other triangle along the first until the S mark on the

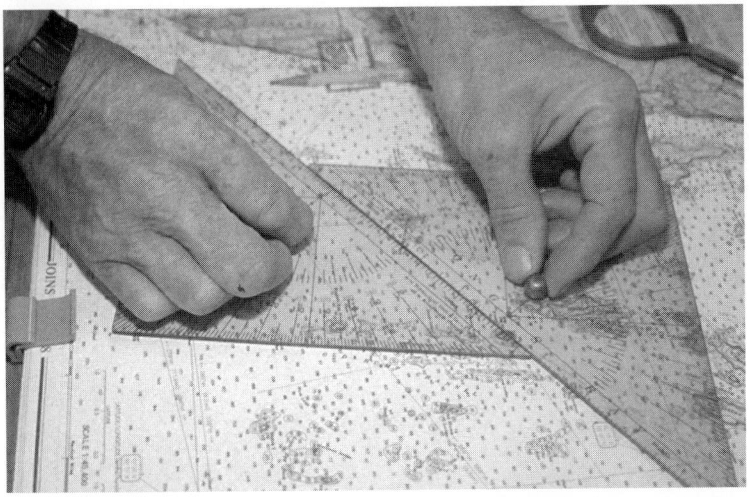

Using triangles to transfer bearings to and from a chart. In this case, one triangle is set up on a course line. The other is slid up it until its S mark is on a line of longitude, at which point the bearing for the course line is read off where the line of longitude crosses the other side of the triangle.

second crosses a line of longitude, at which time you can read the bearing off from the other side of this triangle. Alternatively, place a side of the second triangle against a side of the first such that the two hypotenuses are parallel to one another, and slide the sides up or down the chart. If the second triangle doesn't cross a line of longitude, hold it in place, set the first back against it, and then slide the first farther across the chart until a line of longitude is found.

To go the other way (transferring a bearing to some point on the chart), set one triangle across a line of longitude. With the S mark on the line, rotate the triangle until the desired degree marking is also on the line. Set the second triangle up against the first such that the two hypotenuses are parallel to one another, and then progressively slide them across to the desired location on the chart. Use one or other hypotenuse to mark the bearing line on the chart.

Plotting Positions

The parallel rules are also used to plot positions on a chart or to work out the latitude and longitude of some point. When plotting a position, the parallel rules are set up to cross the latitude scale at one side or another of the chart, with one edge of the rules alongside (parallel to) a line of latitude. The rules are walked up or down the latitude scale until one ruler intersects the desired latitude. The other ruler is swung across the chart until it closes back up with the first. Now the first ruler can be swung across the chart until it closes with the second, walking sideways across the chart in the process. As long as the two rulers are always brought together before moving either one, they will walk directly east or west, transferring the desired latitude across the chart.

When the rules are in the approximate

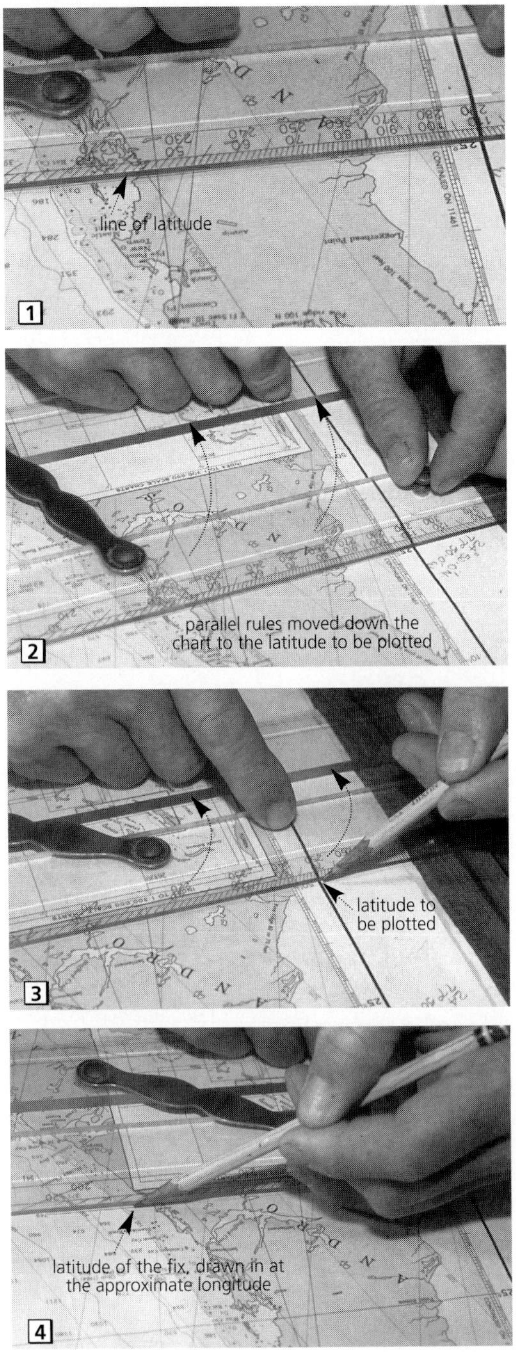

Using parallel rules to plot a fix on a chart. 1. *The parallel rules are set up along a line of latitude close to the latitude that is to be plotted . . .* 2. *"walked" to the latitude . . .* 3. *that is to be plotted and then . . .* 4. *"walked" across the chart to the approximate desired longitude, where a line is drawn on the chart to represent the latitude of the fix.*

vicinity of the desired longitude, I hold them in place (in calm conditions) while I use a pair of dividers to pick up the exact longitude at the top or bottom of the chart, measuring from the nearest longitude line. The dividers are then set alongside the top of the parallel rules, with one arm on the relevant longitude line. The point

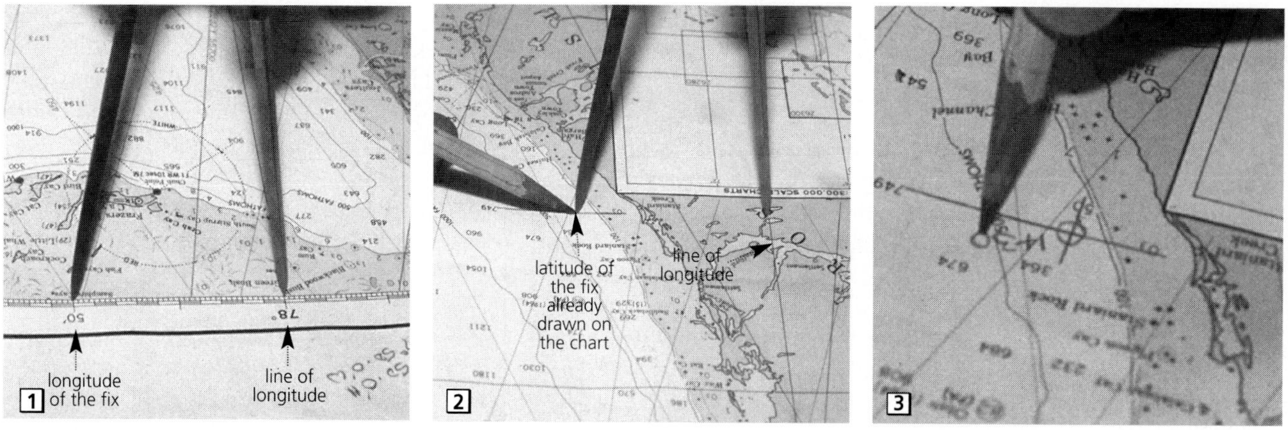

Using dividers to plot longitudes on a chart. 1. The longitude of the fix is picked off at the top or bottom of the chart with a pair of dividers, working from the nearest longitude line. 2. The dividers are moved to the desired latitude, with one leg on the line of longitude and . . . 3. a cross is put on the line of latitude to mark the "fix" (the circle around the fix denotes that it is a nonelectronic fix; the time is always written alongside it).

at which the other arm rests on the top of the parallel rules is the position to be plotted.

In rough weather, it may not be so easy to keep the parallel rules in place while measuring the longitude. In this case, I draw a line across the top of the parallel rules, long enough to be sure it intercepts the desired longitude, and set the rules aside. I determine the longitude position as described previously (the parallel rules could be used, but the dividers are easier to handle). The point at which the relevant divider arm intersects the latitude line I have drawn is the position to be plotted.

For this kind of work, one-handed dividers cannot be surpassed—I would not have any others onboard. These have curved arms so that when they are squeezed together at the top, the points open out. The points can be brought back together by squeezing together the lower halves of the arms. They truly are one-handed.

Determining the latitude and longitude of any given position on the chart is accomplished with the dividers by spreading the points to measure from the location to the nearest line of latitude, transferring that measurement to the latitude scales at the sides of the chart, and then employing the same technique to pick up the longitude reading. Alternatively, the parallel rules can be set up on a line of latitude or longitude, opened out until one edge intersects the position, and then walked to the margins of the chart to get a latitude or longitude reading.

Sometimes, however, the chart is folded in such a way that no margins are showing (i.e., the latitude and longitude divisions are not accessible). In this case, before folding the chart, either ink in the relevant subdivisions on lines of latitude and longitude in areas of the chart that will be visible or copy the latitude and longitude scales onto a piece of light cardboard and keep it handy. In the latter case, remember that for a given chart scale (e.g., 1:40,000), the latitude scale is constant from one chart to another (the same piece of cardboard can be used). However, *the longitude scale varies with latitude*, with the distance covered by a minute of longitude steadily decreasing the farther north or

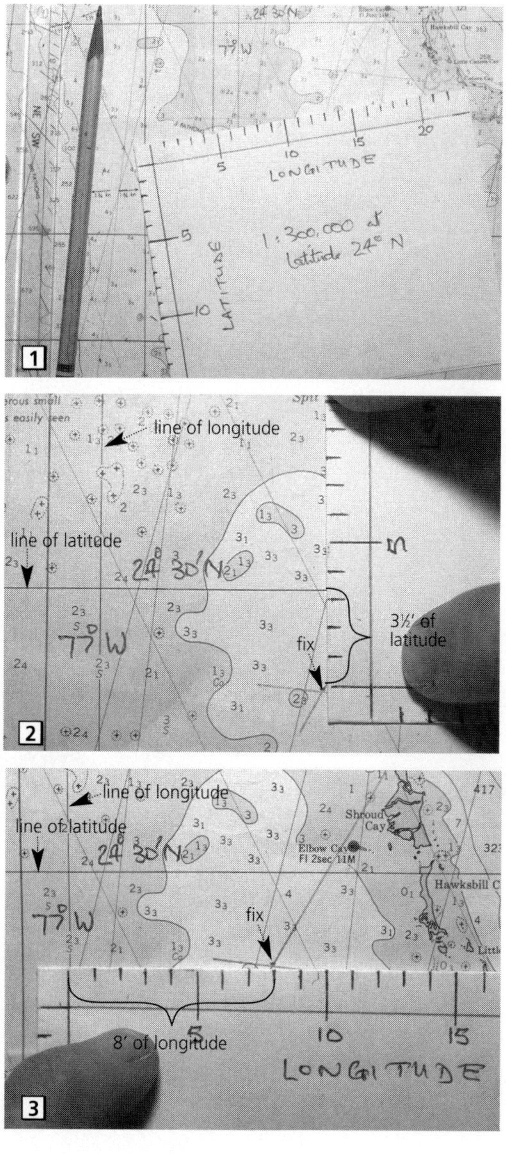

Using a piece of cardboard for interpolating latitudes and longitudes. 1. The cardboard is marked with latitude and longitude scales appropriate to the chart scale and its latitude. 2. The line of latitude closest to the fix is used to read off the latitude of the fix (in this case, 24 degrees 30 minutes N minus 3.5 minutes equals 24 degrees 26.5 minutes N). 3. The line of longitude closest to the fix is used to read off the longitude of the fix (in this case, 77 degrees W minus 8 minutes equals 76 degrees 52 minutes W).

south you go from the equator (this reflects the convergence of longitude lines at the north and south poles).

Measuring Distance

Distance is measured with the dividers. For short distances, the dividers are simply opened to span the distance and then taken to the latitude scales *alongside the distance being measured* to get the measurement. Longer distances are measured by opening the dividers to a measured distance on the latitude scale (e.g., 5 miles), walking them up the relevant course line, rotating the dividers around first one point and then the other—totaling the cumulative distance as each new move is made. Invariably, as the end of the line is neared, the final span is less than that to which the dividers are set. The arms of the dividers are brought together to match the span, which is then transferred to the latitude scales to get an appropriate measurement. This measurement is added to the running total to produce a final figure.

In addition to parallel rules, triangles, and one-handed dividers, there are all kinds of other plotting tools available to the navigator, including one- and two-arm protractors, rolling parallel rules, course plotters, and so on. At different times, I have tried them all. In my opinion, they are simply not needed and just clutter up the chart table. In fact, a deluxe set of parallel rules and a pair of one-handed dividers have met all of our plotting needs over the years and through many plotting-intensive cruises.

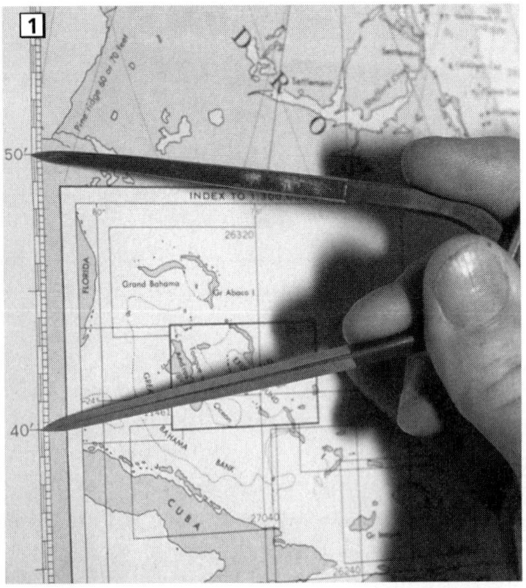

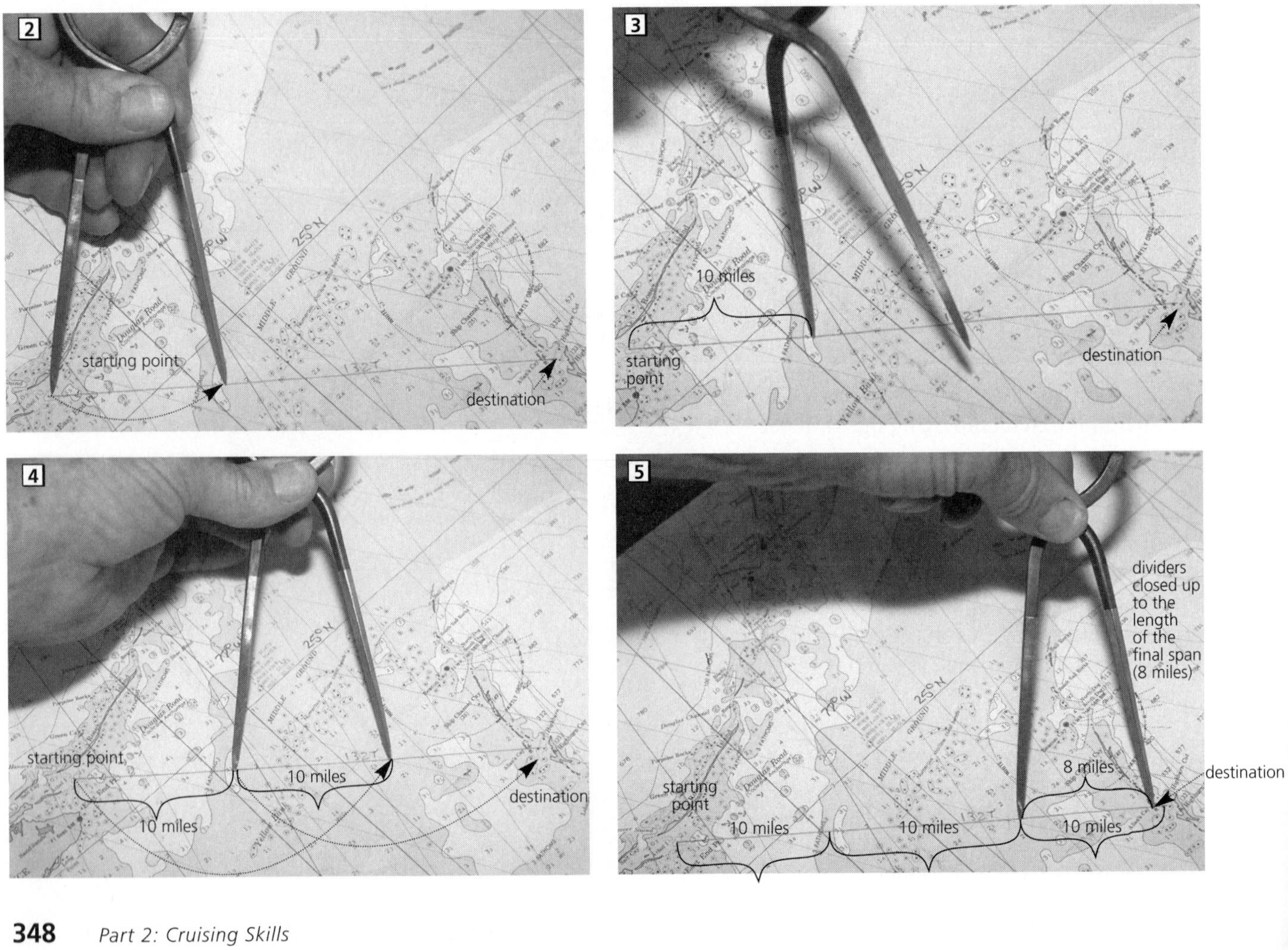

Measuring distances with a pair of dividers. 1. The dividers are opened to an appropriate distance (in this case, 10 minutes = 10 miles) on the adjacent latitude scale. 2. The dividers are . . . 3. "walked" along the course line . . . 4. tallying the distance. 5. The final length is less than 10 miles; the dividers are set to the distance and taken back to the latitude scale to see how much it is.

BASIC PILOTING

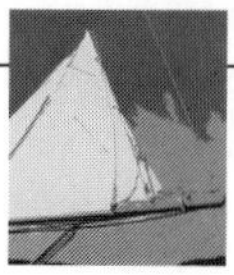

The most basic piloting technique is known as *dead reckoning* (DR), which provides a crude approximation of the boat's position. The next step up in position-fixing sophistication is an *estimated position* (EP). And then we have *fixes,* which accurately establish the boat's position.

Dead Reckoning

DR is not needed on a boat with functioning navigational electronics (with one qualifier explained later in this section), but it is a basic skill that should be understood in case all the electronics go down. DR simply entails starting from a known position and then plotting the course steered (the boat's *heading*) and the distance covered to arrive at a DR position. The heading can be plotted as a compass heading (C), but is more typically plotted as a magnetic heading (M) (the compass is corrected for deviation) or a true heading (T) (the compass is corrected for both deviation and magnetic variation).

Distance is read off the boat's *log* (any device used to measure distance run). Nowadays, almost all boats have an electronic knotmeter consisting of a paddlewheel that spins at a speed proportional to the boat's speed. It gives a constant readout of the boat's speed, from which distance run is derived and displayed on the log. A knotmeter-log is not much use unless it is properly calibrated (the procedure is described in the manual that comes with the knotmeter). Calibration should be repeated occasionally because even if the knotmeter is accurately calibrated, its operation is easily messed up (e.g., marine growth on the paddlewheel or fouling with seaweed).

Other forms of speed-distance measurement include (1) *pitot tubes,* in which a tube faces forward into the flow of water beneath the hull so that the faster the boat travels, the greater is the pressure in the tube (this pressure is converted to a speed reading, from which distance is also derived); and (2) the traditional towed-impeller knotmeter-log, in which an impeller is towed behind the boat—the faster the boat moves, the faster the impeller spins (this is used to drive the knotmeter-log). At the time of this writing, electronic transducers—which avoid all problems associated with paddlewheels and pitot tubes and which are reputed to be exceedingly accurate—are making their debut appearance. They hold great promise for the future.

Of course, distance run can always be derived from a GPS and other modern electronics. On long passages, we used to always carry a towed knotmeter-log as a backup to the boat's knotmeter-log, but in recent years I have not done so, believing that the three GPSs onboard provide adequate insurance. If all else fails, I have a good sense of our speed through the water simply based on the kind of waves the boat is making (e.g., when the stern wave is at the aft quarter, we are close to hull speed; that is, moving at 7+ knots). This method can be used to estimate distance run.

The distance in any given time is measured off along the plotted heading (which is given a single arrowhead pointing in the direction of travel) to derive the DR position (which is marked on the chart by a dot within a semicircle). If the boat's heading is changed, a new heading line is begun, starting from an updated DR position on the old heading line. If at any time an accurate fix is obtained, the DR plot is restarted from this fix (this fix often puts the boat in a different position than the one derived from the existing DR plot). And so on. *If headed toward restricted waters, even when using electronic navigation, it is an excellent idea to pro-*

Basic DR plot.

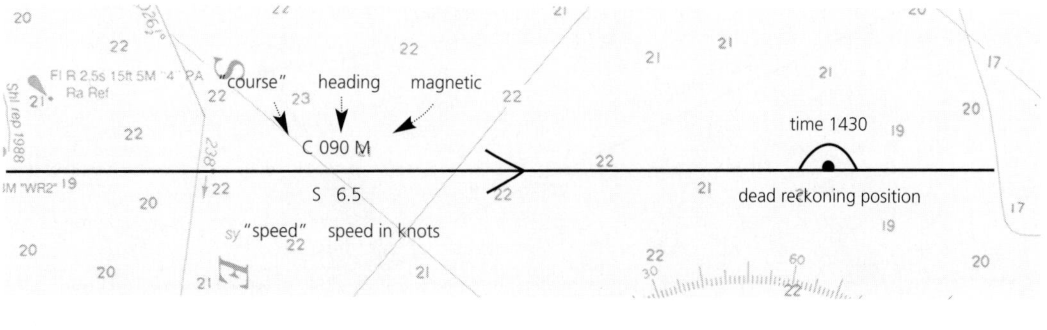

ject the boat's DR position an hour or two ahead. Doing so may alert you to impending danger and, in fact, may be the only practical use of a DR plot on a boat in which the navigational electronics are functioning and thereby providing regular fixes.

DR takes no account of leeway, tides, currents, or any other factors that might set the boat to one side or another of its plotted heading, or that might slow it down or speed it up. The longer a boat runs on DR, the more in error the DR position is likely to be.

Estimated Positions, and Set and Drift

An EP considers the factors likely to be setting the boat away from its DR position—it is a DR position corrected for leeway and current.

Leeway is defined by Bowditch and other authorities as the difference between a boat's heading (course steered) and the *course sailed, assuming there are no tidal or other current influences*. This is generally different from the actual *course over the ground* (COG), which includes tidal and other influences. The COG is rarely a straight line, which leads to another term, the *course made good* (CMG), sometimes referred to as the *track made good* (TMG). This is the direct line from a point of origin to a destination (if the COG is a straight line, it is the same as the CMG); in practice, the two get used interchangeably.

All sailing boats make leeway; the closer the boat is sailing to windward and the rougher the conditions, the more the leeway is likely to be. On an upwind slog in a fast boat, it may be less than 5 degrees; on a heavy-displacement boat with poor upwind performance, it may be well over 10 degrees. Going downwind, it will be negligible in all boats. Leeway can be gauged by looking astern at the angle between the boat's heading and its wake.

When plotting the boat's heading (course steered) on a chart, the estimated leeway can be added to or subtracted from (whichever is appropriate) the course steered. This bearing is plotted in place of the actual course steered (a short arrow showing the heading before adjustment for leeway also may be included for reference purposes). The adjusted heading gives the course sailed, taking into account no tidal or other current influences. It must now be further adjusted for these influences.

If accurate fixes can be obtained, the easiest way to determine tide and current influences is to plot the course sailed over a specific period (an hour works well) and to then plot a fix, which will be offset from the latest position derived from the course sailed by the effects of tidal and other currents. The bearing from the position derived from the course sailed to the fix

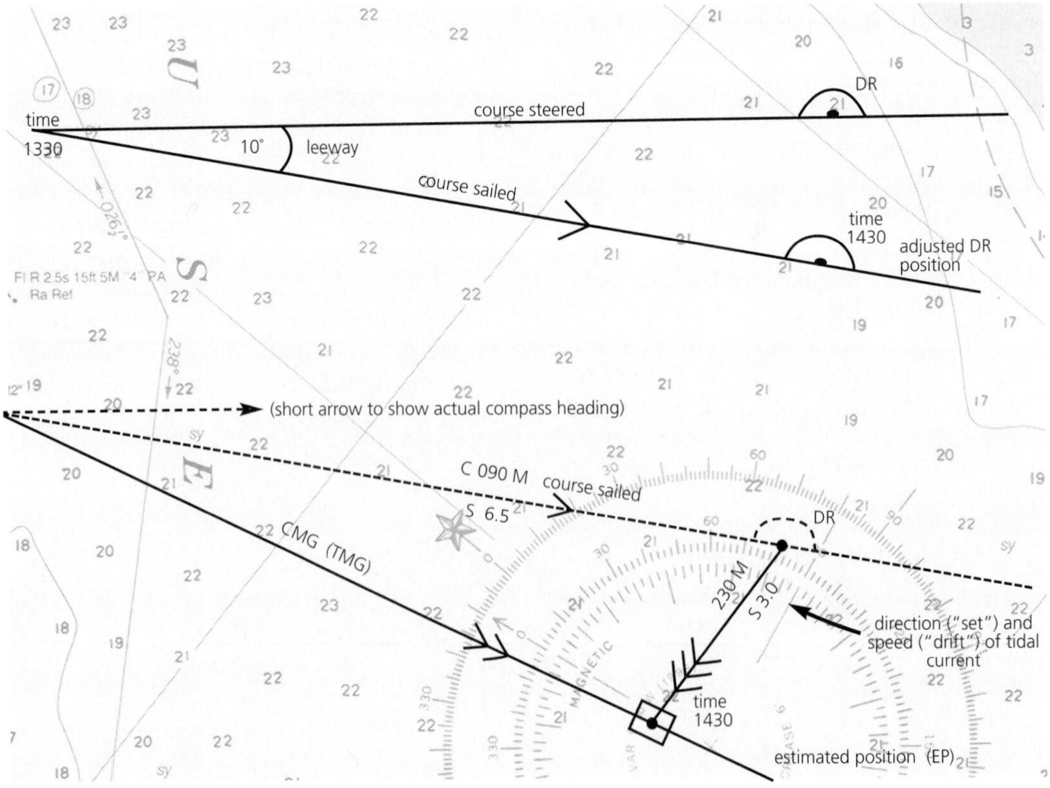

Top: *Course sailed adds an estimate for leeway.* Bottom: *Course sailed adjusted for set and drift to produce a course made good (CMG) or track made good (TMG) and an estimated position (EP).*

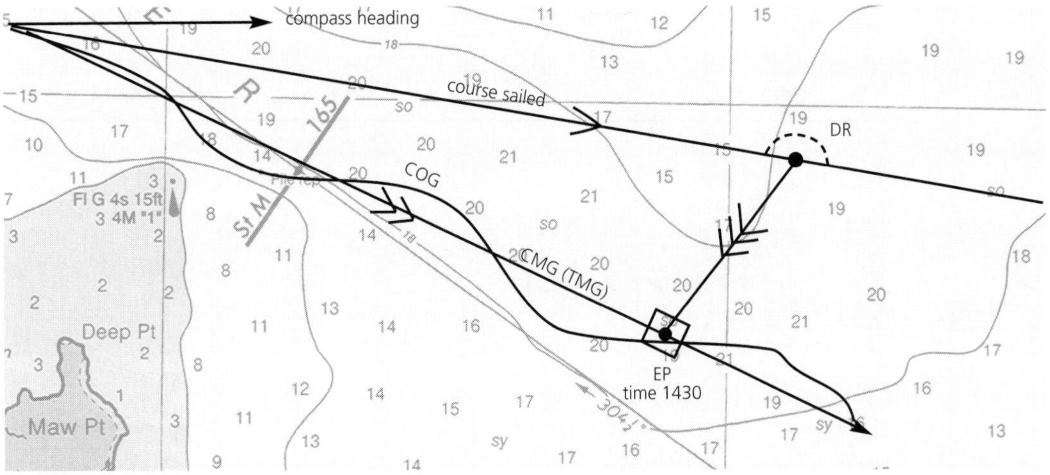

The course made good (CMG) or track made good (TMG) is a straight line from the point of origin to the boat's present position. The course over the ground (COG) may be different.

is known as *set*—it gives the direction in which the boat is being set by the tide and/or current (in other words, *set* is the direction toward which a current is flowing). The distance between the course sailed position and the fix represents the speed of this tide and/or current, and is referred to as *drift*. In other words, drift is the speed (in knots) of a current. To calculate drift, the distance between the course sailed position and the fix is divided by the number of hours over which this difference developed.

A line drawn from the boat's starting point to a fix shows the CMG (TMG). This is denoted with double arrowheads pointing in the direction of travel. The distance represented by this line, divided by the number of hours it took to cover this distance, gives the *speed made good* (SMG), also sometimes called the *speed over the ground* (SOG), rather than the speed through the water displayed on the boat's knotmeter.

Even in the electronic age, using the course sailed (derived from DR but adjusted for leeway) plus a fix to calculate set and drift can be useful. More than once when crossing the Gulf of Mexico, we have been caught in massive eddies of the Gulf Stream. I use a combination of the course sailed and GPS fixes to determine set and drift, and from this attempt to determine the overall nature of the eddy so that we can position ourselves on the favorable side. (Getting it right can make a huge difference in passage times; some of those eddies are 100 miles in diameter and rotate at up to 4 knots.)

The more conventional use of set and drift is to go from a DR to an EP in the absence of electronic and other fixes. Given a plotted course sailed (DR adjusted for leeway), if we can estimate set and drift from tide tables and other information, we then can adjust our course sailed position to get the EP. We do this by taking our latest course sailed position and then drawing a line from it on a bearing that represents set and with a length that represents drift over the relevant period. The end point of this line is our latest EP (which should be cross-checked with any other available information, particularly depth soundings). If we subsequently get a fix, the process is restarted from it, just as with a DR plot. An EP is denoted by a dot with a square box around it. In a situation of frequent course changes (e.g., tacking to windward), we do not have to calculate set and drift at each course change. Instead, the cumulative set and drift can be applied at each hour—or even after several hours if in unobstructed waters—to derive a new EP.

A similar technique is used to determine which course to steer to counteract tidal and other influences. We first draw a line from where we are to where we want to go (the desired CMG). From tide tables (see the following section) and other sources, we estimate the proba-

Adjusting the course sailed for multiple changes in set and drift.

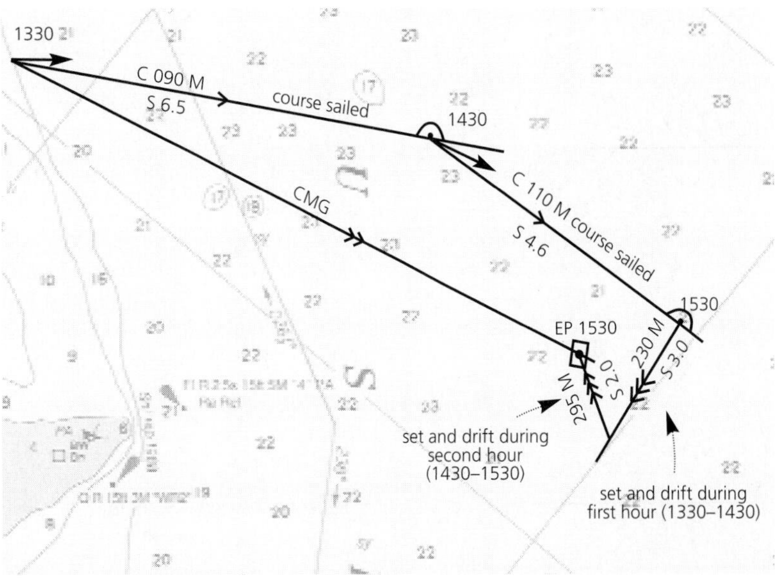

A vector plot used to determine a course to steer to counteract tidal currents. Bearing to destination: 090 M Boat's speed: 6.5 knots Set and drift: 230 M at 3.0 knots.

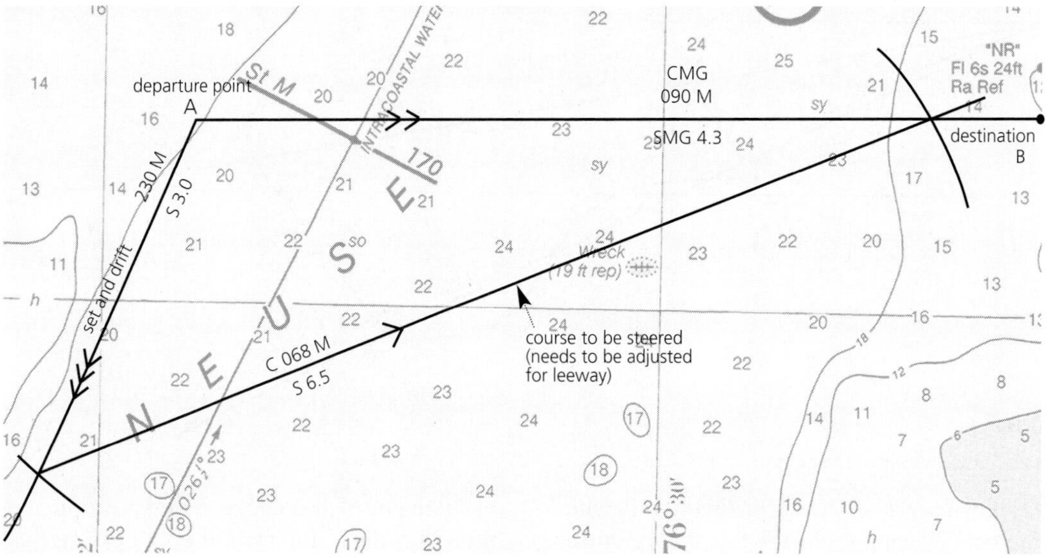

ble set and drift over an hour (or multiples of an hour). We plot this with a second line drawn *from our starting point*, on a bearing equal to the anticipated set and with a length representative of the anticipated drift (e.g., an anticipated drift of 1 knot over an hour results in a line 1 mile long). We set our dividers to a length *equal to the distance we expect to travel in the period used to determine the set and drift* (usually an hour). We place one end of the dividers on the end of the set and drift line, and swing the dividers until they cross the desired CMG line, marking the line at this point. We draw a line from the end of the set and drift line to the marked point on the CMG line. This new line, *adjusted for leeway*, represents the course that must be steered to achieve the desired CMG. This kind of a plot is known as a *vector plot*.

In a situation where tidal currents change in strength and direction over time, you can estimate the set and drift at different states of the tide and then draw these in from your starting point, adding each successive line to the end of the last. The dividers are then set to span the total distance that will be sailed during the period covered by all these set and drift lines.

Note how the use of multiple tide and current sets to predetermine a course to steer may in this case put the boat on the rocks!

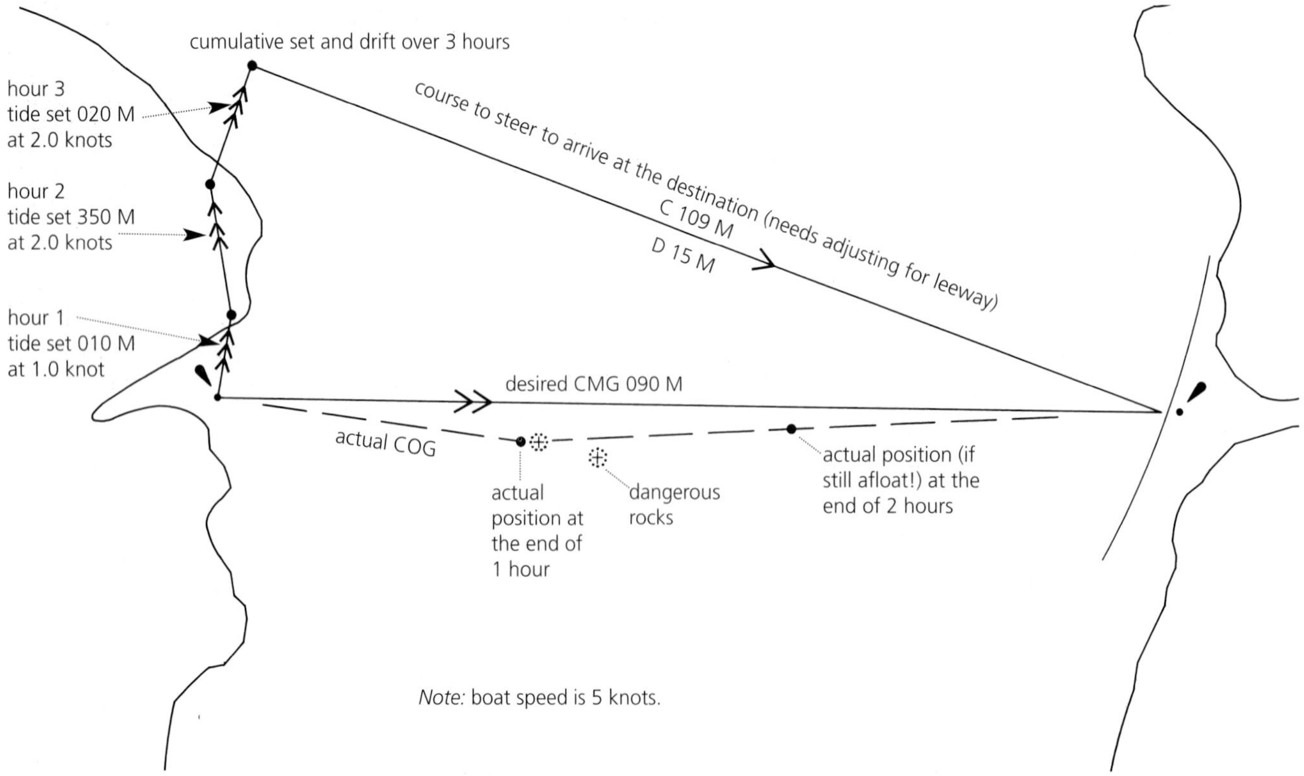

The dividers are swung from the end of the last set and drift line to the desired CMG line. The new line drawn between these two points gives a course to steer (to be adjusted for leeway), which results in the various tidal influences canceling out and places the boat at the desired destination. However, during the course of the passage, at various times the boat may deviate significantly from the plotted CMG—if there are any nearby hazards, the course steered may have to be modified to clear them.

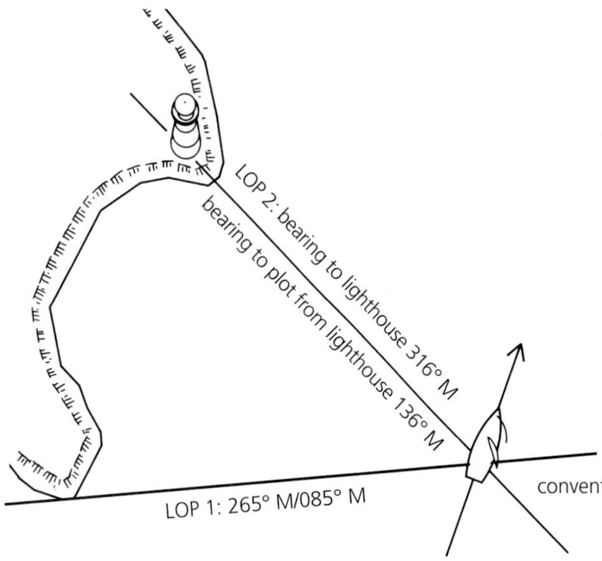

Using a hand-bearing compass to get a fix.

Fixes

Fixes are known positions. Nowadays, they are generally supplied by navigational electronics (primarily GPS), but several other techniques are available to the navigator, some of which should be learned and practiced in case the electronics go down. The most common and the easiest to apply involve the use of a hand-bearing compass.

Hand-bearing compasses vary enormously in accuracy and ease of use. I strongly recommend buying a good one, such as the hockey-puck type (around $100 in the U.S.) or, better yet, a KVH DataScope (a jewel of an instrument) or a quality pair of binoculars with a built-in compass. In my opinion, such a compass is not an option; it is a basic piece of a navigator's kit—along with the deluxe parallel rules and the one-handed dividers mentioned previously. These three items together are all that need to be added to a chart and a pencil for coastal navigation.

When a hand-bearing compass is used to derive the bearing of some object, it must be remembered that this bearing is from the boat to the object. When plotting this bearing, however, you will be working from the depiction of the object on the chart back to the boat's position; that is, the reciprocal of the bearing that was taken. The reciprocal is found by adding 180 degrees if the bearing is below 180 degrees, and subtracting 180 degrees if it is above 180 degrees. It also must be remembered that the bearing will be a magnetic one, and must be either corrected to true before plotting or plotted using the magnetic compass rose on the chart.

When this bearing is plotted, the resultant line forms a *line of position* (LOP). At the time the bearing was taken, the boat must have been somewhere on this LOP (of course, the boat may have moved in the time it took to plot the LOP). If two bearings are taken of two objects, two LOPs will result. If the two are taken at the same time, the LOPs will cross one another. The point at which they intersect is the boat's position (a fix); just as with an EP, it should be cross-checked from habit with any other available information, particularly depth soundings. Conventional fixes (as opposed to electronic fixes) are denoted by a dot with a circle around it and annotated with the time of the fix. If three LOPs are derived at the same time, in theory they too will intersect at a common point (the fix); however, in practice, they form a triangle. The boat is presumed to be somewhere inside this triangle.

The following factors affect the accuracy of fixes obtained through LOPs:

- If the LOPs cross at a shallow angle, a small error in a bearing will produce a significant position error. LOPs that cross at or near right angles are the most accurate; those that cross at less than 60 degrees are suspect.
- If the bearings are taken on distant objects, a small error will also produce a significant position error. LOPs derived from nearby objects are better than those derived from distant objects.

Crossed LOPs are the single-most useful conventional piloting tool for fixing a boat's position in coastal waters. LOPs can be taken from any visible object that can be identified on the chart—the obvious, such as buoys and lighthouses, and the not-so-obvious, such as the side of an otherwise nondescript headland or island.

Sometimes, at any given time only one suitable object is in sight from which to derive a LOP. In this case, the LOP (LOP 1) is taken

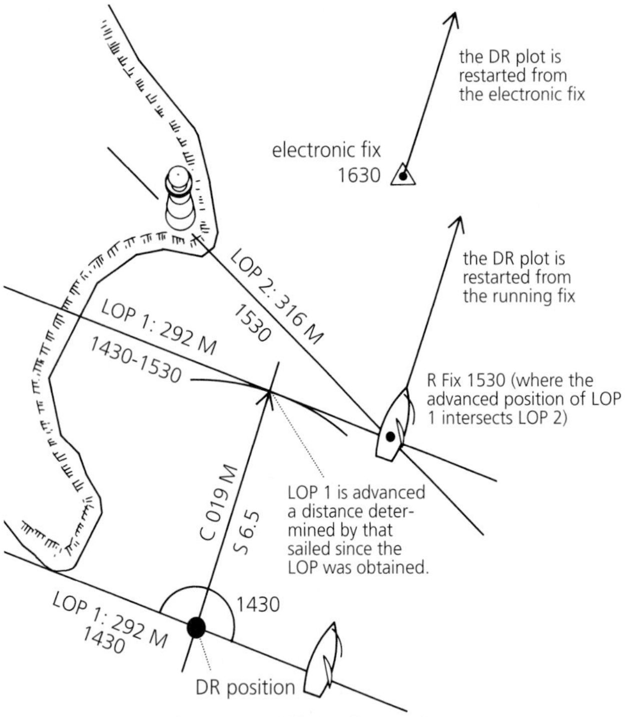

Variation 1 (using two different features)

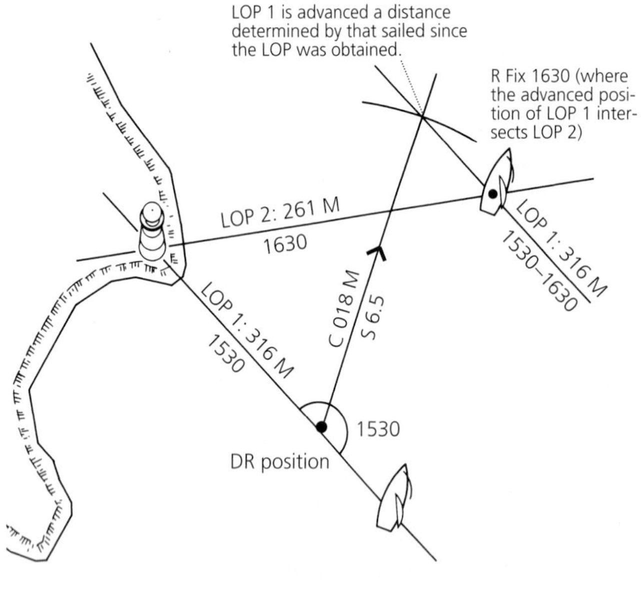

Variation 2 (using the same feature)

Two variations on a running fix: using two different objects and using the same object twice.

and plotted, and then the DR plot is restarted from *any point* on LOP 1. A little later, another feature may enable a second LOP (LOP 2) to be plotted (or perhaps LOP 2 can be plotted from the original feature). LOP 1 is brought forward, using parallel rules, and drawn in (parallel to its original location, but at a distance from it determined by the distance run since the time of the sighting for LOP 1). The boat is presumed to be at the point where this *advanced* LOP 1 now crosses LOP 2. This is known as a *running fix*, which is clearly not as accurate as a fix; nevertheless, it can be a useful navigational tool.

A single LOP also can be used at times with a depth sounding to fix a boat's position. For example, if the boat is approaching a lighthouse with a shoaling bottom, a bearing taken on the lighthouse establishes a LOP; the boat must be somewhere on this line. The precise location of the boat can be established by noting when a particular depth contour is crossed (e.g., 20 ft.). However, the accuracy of this technique depends on the accuracy of the depth sounder. (Is it properly calibrated? Is it measuring the actual depth, or the depth below the keel?) In waters with a significant tidal rise and fall, at anything other than low tide, 20-foot depths are found farther inshore than charted. In other words, to determine when the charted 20-foot contour is crossed, the tide height must be added to the charted 20 feet.

Plotting Conventions

The various plotting techniques described to date are likely to result in a fair number of pencil lines and other marks on a chart. It is essential that the navigator and anyone else using the chart understand what all these mean, which ones are dependable (fixes), which ones are guesstimates (EPs), and so on. This level of clarity is achieved by using and sticking to recognized plotting conventions, such as the following (many of which have already been used):

- A boat's heading (course steered), or the course sailed (course steered adjusted for leeway) is denoted by a line with a single arrowhead somewhere along its length. The course may be written in along the line with the prefix "C" (for course). This is followed by the relevant bearing, which in turn is followed by the appropriate letter indicating whether the bearing is a compass bearing (C), a magnetic bearing (M), or a true bearing (T). Professional navigators use only true bearings (e.g., C 093 T). The speed of the boat (in knots) may be written on the other side of the line with the prefix "S" for "speed" (e.g., S 7.4), or maybe the distance run between fixes with the prefix "D" for "distance" (e.g., D 7.4). If the bearing and speed are not entered on the chart, they should be recorded in a logbook.

- Any line denoting current set and drift is given three arrowheads somewhere along its length. It too may be annotated with its bearing and speed.
- Any line denoting the boat's CMG (also known as TMG) is given two arrowheads somewhere along its length.
- A DR position is indicated by a dot with a semicircle around it.
- An EP is denoted by a dot with a square around it.
- A fix derived by conventional means is denoted by a dot with a circle around it.
- A fix derived electronically is denoted by a dot with a triangle around it.
- All fixes should be labeled with the time at which they were obtained, using the twenty-four-hour clock notation (e.g., 4:30 P.M. is 1630). To avoid confusion, these labels should be set at an angle to any lines. Fixes do not require additional notation except for a running fix, which should be labeled "R Fix" to indicate that its reliability may be questionable.
- A fix should be plotted (or logged) every hour on the hour. (At sea, when we are not in confined waters, we log GPS fixes every hour in the logbook and not on the chart to avoid cluttering it up. If the electronics fail, we can transfer this fix to the chart and start our DR/EP plot from this position.)
- All LOPs should be labeled with the bearing and the time at which they were taken (e.g., 089 T 1725). If a LOP is advanced (for a running fix), it should be relabeled with its bearing and the original time at which it was taken, with the time at which it was advanced (e.g., 089 T 1725–1845).

Tides, Tidal Currents, and Currents

In many parts of the world, tides are a major navigational consideration, perhaps the single most important consideration (e.g., the Bay of Fundy with its 40-foot tides). In other parts of the world, tides are quite minor (e.g., much of the Bahamas and the Caribbean) but are nevertheless significant (when navigating one of the wide shallow banks in the Bahamas, 12 in. one way or the other can make a big difference). Tides almost always have to be considered.

Tides are the "periodic motion of the waters of the sea due to changes in the attractive forces of the moon and sun upon the rotating earth" (Bowditch, 1995). We need to distinguish the vertical rise and fall of water (*tide*) from any horizontal movement that also may occur (*tidal current* or *tidal stream*). Tidal currents *flood* (rising tide) and *ebb* (falling tide).

The moon has approximately twice the influence as the sun on tides. When the two act in concert (during new and full moons), tides are above average (both in how high and how low they go); these are *spring tides*. When the influence of the moon and sun offset each other (the moon is in its first and third quarters, it is "half full"), tides are below average; these are *neap tides*.

The *lunar day* is twenty-four hours and fifty minutes. All else being equal, there are two high tides and two low tides every twenty-four hours (*semidiurnal*), with the times occurring fifty minutes later each successive day. One of these tides is frequently greater than the other (hence, we have the MLLW level used in many chart-sounding datums). In many parts of the world, this pattern is upset by a combination of factors: there may be only one high and low tide a day (*diurnal*; for example, the Gulf of Mexico) or tides may be irregular (*irregular semidiurnal* and *irregular diurnal*).

The times of high and low tide and the changes in water depth are given in tide tables. When using these tables, it is important to first check the time standard employed—it may be *Zone Time* (e.g., Eastern Standard Time/EST on the East Coast of the U.S. or Greenwich Mean Time/GMT in the U.K.), which may have to be adjusted for Daylight Savings Time (Summer Time in the U.K.). The changes in water depth have to be referenced to some type of datum, which will be the same as that used for the charts of the same area (the chart-sounding datum). In other words, the depth shown is above that shown on local charts (or below—in some instances, a low tide is below the chart-sounding datum).

Tides are computed for selected locations around the coast (*reference stations*). Other nearby locations (*subordinate stations*) are keyed to the reference stations in terms of *tidal differences*, which include the difference in times of high or low water and the amount by which the high and low tides differ from the reference station. Sometimes a ratio is given, which is a multiplier that is applied to the tidal heights at the reference station to derive those at the subordinate station (e.g., Lubec, Maine, might be given a multiplier of 1.7 relative to Portland, Maine; that is, if Portland has a 10 ft. tide, Lubec will have a 17 ft. tide: 10 × 1.7). Various computer programs are available that

Nantucket, Massachusetts, 2001

Times and Heights of High and Low Waters

January							
	Time	Height			Time	Height	
	h m	ft	cm		h m	ft	cm
1	0441	2.8	85	16	0534	3.5	107
M	1019	0.7	21	Tu	1122	0.0	0
	1647	3.0	91		1800	3.1	94
	2250	0.3	9	◑	2340	0.0	0
2	0526	2.9	88	17	0631	3.5	107
Tu	1112	0.6	18	W	1228	0.1	3
	1738	2.9	88		1904	2.9	88
◐	2334	0.4	12				
3	0611	3.0	91	18	0036	0.2	6
W	1207	0.5	15	Th	0727	3.6	110
	1831	2.8	85		1332	0.1	3
					2008	2.7	82
4	0020	0.4	12	19	0130	0.3	9
Th	0658	3.2	98	F	0822	3.5	107
	1303	0.4	12		1432	0.1	3
	1926	2.7	82		2110	2.6	79
5	0107	0.4	12	20	0223	0.4	12
F	0746	3.4	104	Sa	0914	3.5	107
	1358	0.2	6		1526	0.1	3
	2022	2.7	82		2207	2.6	79
6	0156	0.4	12	21	0313	0.5	15
Sa	0835	3.6	110	Su	1003	3.5	107
	1452	±0.1	±3		1615	0.1	3
	2119	2.7	82		2256	2.5	76
7	0247	0.3	9	22	0359	0.5	15
Su	0926	3.8	116	M	1046	3.5	107
	1545	±0.3	±9		1659	0.1	3
	2214	2.7	82		2337	2.5	76

February							
	Time	Height			Time	Height	
	h m	ft	cm		h m	ft	cm
1	0530	3.1	94	16	0006	0.3	9
Th	1132	0.3	9	F	0653	3.4	104
	1759	2.6	79		1305	0.1	3
◐	2338	0.4	12		1941	2.6	79
2	0618	3.3	101	17	0101	0.4	12
F	1229	0.1	3	Sa	0749	3.4	104
	1855	2.6	79		1404	0.1	3
					2041	2.5	76
3	0029	0.4	12	18	0156	0.5	15
Sa	0710	3.5	107	Su	0843	3.3	101
	1327	0.0	0		1459	0.2	6
	1954	2.5	76		2136	2.5	76
4	0123	0.3	9	19	0247	0.5	15
Su	0805	3.6	110	M	0934	3.3	101
	1425	±0.2	±6		1548	0.2	6
	2053	2.6	79		2222	2.5	76
5	0219	0.2	6	20	0335	0.5	15
M	0902	3.8	116	Tu	1019	3.3	101
	1521	±0.3	±9		1631	0.2	6
	2151	2.7	82		2303	2.5	76
6	0316	0.0	0	21	0420	0.5	15
Tu	0959	4.0	122	W	1101	3.3	101
	1616	±0.5	±15		1711	0.2	6
	2248	2.8	85		2339	2.5	76
7	0413	±0.1	±3	22	0503	0.4	12
W	1057	4.1	125	Th	1141	3.3	101
	1708	±0.6	±18		1747	0.2	6
	2343	3.0	91				

March							
	Time	Height			Time	Height	
	h m	ft	cm		h m	ft	cm
1	0407	3.2	98	16	0521	3.4	104
Th	1008	0.1	3	F	1132	0.0	0
	1641	2.7	82		1809	2.6	79
	2214	0.3	9	◑	2333	0.5	15
2	0454	3.3	101	17	0615	3.3	101
F	1103	0.0	0	Sa	1231	0.1	3
	1735	2.6	79		1907	2.5	76
◐	2304	0.4	12				
3	0546	3.4	104	18	0030	0.6	18
Sa	1201	0.0	0	Su	0711	3.2	98
	1832	2.5	76		1329	0.2	6
					2002	2.5	76
4	0000	0.3	9	19	0126	0.6	18
Su	0642	3.5	107	M	0806	3.2	98
	1301	±0.1	±3		1424	0.3	9
	1931	2.5	76		2054	2.5	76
5	0059	0.3	9	20	0219	0.6	18
M	0742	3.6	110	Tu	0858	3.2	98
	1401	±0.2	±6		1512	0.3	9
	2032	2.6	79		2140	2.5	76
6	0200	0.1	3	21	0309	0.5	15
Tu	0843	3.8	116	W	0946	3.2	98
	1458	±0.3	±9		1555	0.3	9
	2131	2.8	85		2221	2.6	79
7	0300	0.0	0	22	0355	0.4	12
W	0944	3.9	119	Th	1030	3.2	98
	1553	±0.4	±12		1634	0.3	9
	2228	3.0	91		2300	2.7	82

A portion of a tide table.

make the calculations and produce tide predictions for just about any point on the coasts of the United States, Europe, and other regions of the world.

For semidiurnal tides (two highs and lows a day), the approximate state of the tide can be gauged at any given time using the Rule of Twelfths. This says that in the first hour after high or low tide, the water falls or rises by one twelfth of the total tide; in the second and fifth hours, it is two twelfths; and in the third and fourth hours, it is three twelfths. This is an extremely handy rule when navigating in "skinny" tidal waters. All you need to know to use it is the time of the next high or low tide, the approximate range of the tide, and the time of day at which you want to know the water depth. It also can be used to give a good idea of how rapidly the water depth is going to change (e.g., in a region with 12 ft. tides, during the third and fourth hours, the water depth will change by 3 ft. per hour).

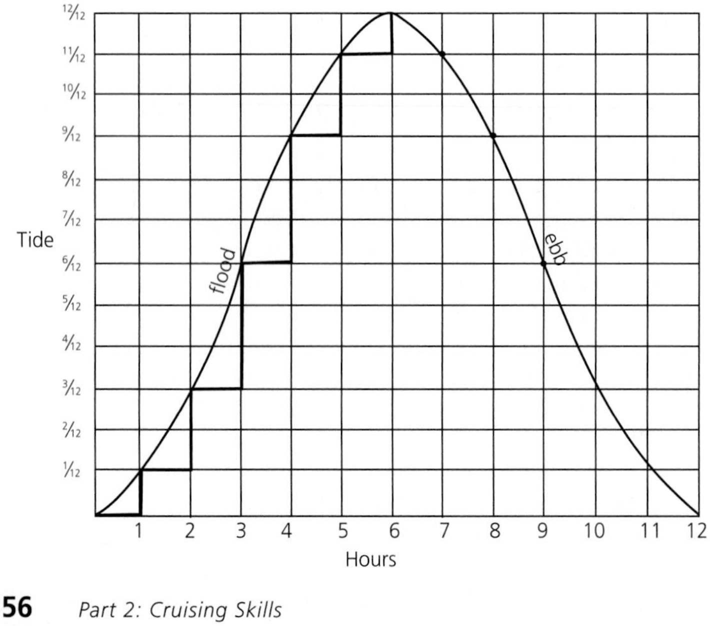

The Rule of Twelfths (semidiurnal tide with no unusual features).

Tidal currents result from the ebb and flow of tides, and reverse with the flow of water. However, where there are physical restrictions of one type or another (e.g., a narrow channel at the head of a wide bay), the tidal current may not be in sync with times of high and low water. At high tide, for example, the current may continue flowing through a restriction until the falling tide neutralizes the differences in water level on either side of the restriction. This can result in offsets between times of high and low water, and times of *slack water* (no tidal current) of up to several hours.

It does not take a large *tidal range* (the difference between low and high tide) to create strong tidal currents; conversely, a large tidal range does not necessarily create a strong current. These things have as much to do with topography as they do with tidal range. There are plenty of 3-knot tidal currents in the Bahamas and around the coast of Cuba—some as high as 7 knots—in areas with a tidal range of 2 feet or less. In general, tidal currents tend to flow along a coastline rather than setting into and off the shoreline. Clearly, when coastal cruising, it pays to learn about these differences

Cape Cod Canal (RR. Bridge), Massachusetts, 2001

F±Flood, Dir. 070° True E±Ebb, Dir. 250° True

January

Day	Slack (h m)	Maximum (h m)	Maximum (knots)
1 M	0155	0443	3.8E
	0737	1030	3.6F
	1350	1701	4.0E
	2000	2303	3.8F
2 Tu	0242	0533	3.8E
	0828	1121	3.5F
	1444	1752	3.9E
◐	2051	2354	3.7F
3 W	0333	0625	3.8E
	0923	1217	3.5F
	1543	1847	3.9E
	2146		
4 Th		0048	3.7F
	0425	0719	3.9E
	1020	1317	3.6F
	1646	1943	3.9E
	2243		
5 F		0145	3.8F
	0518	0814	4.0E
	1118	1417	3.8F
	1747	2040	4.0E
	2341		
6 Sa		0242	3.9F
	0609	0907	4.2E
	1214	1516	4.0F
	1845	2135	4.2E
7 Su	0037	0338	4.0F
	0659	1000	4.5E
	1308	1612	4.3F

Day	Slack (h m)	Maximum (h m)	Maximum (knots)
16 Tu	0238	0524	4.4E
	0834	1134	4.1F
	1454	1748	4.4E
◑	2101		
17 W		0009	4.2F
	0336	0622	4.3E
	0936	1240	3.9F
	1559	1848	4.2E
	2202		
18 Th		0114	4.0F
	0434	0721	4.2E
	1039	1351	3.9F
	1705	1949	4.0E
	2304		
19 F		0220	3.9F
	0531	0820	4.1E
	1141	1501	3.9F
	1808	2050	3.9E
20 Sa	0005	0322	3.8F
	0625	0916	4.2E
	1238	1602	4.0F
	1906	2146	3.9E
21 Su	0100	0417	3.8F
	0716	1008	4.2E
	1330	1654	4.1F
	1959	2238	4.0E
22 M	0150	0504	3.8F
	0802	1055	4.3E
	1416	1738	4.1F

February

Day	Slack (h m)	Maximum (h m)	Maximum (knots)
1 Th	0242	0545	3.9E
	0838	1136	3.7F
	1502	1810	3.9E
◐	2104		
2 F		0004	3.7F
	0334	0639	3.9E
	0936	1235	3.7F
	1607	1908	3.9E
	2203		
3 Sa		0103	3.7F
	0432	0737	4.0E
	1039	1340	3.8F
	1715	2008	3.9E
	2307		
4 Su		0206	3.7F
	0532	0836	4.2E
	1142	1447	4.0F
	1821	2109	4.1E
5 M	0010	0309	3.9F
	0631	0933	4.4E
	1243	1551	4.2F
	1921	2207	4.3E
6 Tu	0110	0410	4.1F
	0726	1029	4.7E
	1340	1649	4.5F
	2017	2302	4.5E
7 W	0206	0506	4.3F
	0819	1122	4.9E
	1434	1743	4.8F

Day	Slack (h m)	Maximum (h m)	Maximum (knots)
16 F		0033	3.8F
	0356	0645	4.1E
	1003	1314	3.7F
	1637	1917	3.8E
	2231		
17 Sa		0141	3.6F
	0456	0745	4.0E
	1107	1430	3.7F
	1742	2019	3.7E
	2335		
18 Su		0251	3.5F
	0554	0844	4.0E
	1208	1538	3.8F
	1842	2119	3.7E
19 M	0034	0353	3.5F
	0649	0940	4.0E
	1303	1633	3.9F
	1935	2213	3.8E
20 Tu	0126	0443	3.7F
	0738	1030	4.2E
	1352	1717	4.0F
	2022	2300	3.9E
21 W	0212	0524	3.8F
	0823	1116	4.3E
	1434	1754	4.1F
	2104	2343	4.1E
22 Th	0252	0559	3.9F
	0904	1157	4.4E
	1513	1826	4.2F

March

Day	Slack (h m)	Maximum (h m)	Maximum (knots)
1 Th	0114	0421	4.2E
	0713	1012	4.0F
	1336	1646	4.1E
	1939	2237	3.9F
2 F	0159	0511	4.1E
	0804	1104	3.9F
	1433	1739	4.0E
◐	2032	2330	3.8F
3 Sa	0252	0606	4.0E
	0903	1205	3.8F
	1541	1839	3.9E
	2134		
4 Su		0031	3.6F
	0355	0706	4.1E
	1008	1313	3.9F
	1653	1943	3.9E
	2242		
5 M		0139	3.7F
	0503	0809	4.2E
	1117	1425	4.0F
	1802	2047	4.0E
	2350		
6 Tu		0249	3.8F
	0608	0911	4.4E
	1223	1533	4.3F
	1904	2148	4.2E
7 W	0053	0354	4.1F
	0709	1010	4.7E
	1322	1634	4.5F

Day	Slack (h m)	Maximum (h m)	Maximum (knots)
16 F	0219	0512	4.2E
	0824	1129	3.9F
	1502	1744	3.9E
◑	2053	2351	3.6F
17 Sa	0316	0608	4.0E
	0924	1234	3.7F
	1607	1843	3.6E
	2156		
18 Su		0057	3.3F
	0418	0708	3.8E
	1028	1350	3.6F
	1711	1946	3.5E
	2301		
19 M		0212	3.3F
	0520	0809	3.8E
	1132	1502	3.6F
	1812	2047	3.6E
20 Tu	0003	0320	3.4F
	0618	0908	3.9E
	1230	1600	3.8F
	1904	2142	3.7E
21 W	0057	0413	3.5F
	0710	1000	4.1E
	1320	1645	3.9F
	1951	2230	3.9E
22 Th	0143	0455	3.8F
	0756	1047	4.2E
	1404	1722	4.1F

A portion of a tidal-current table.

and take advantage of the current wherever possible.

The strength, timing, and direction of tidal currents is given in *Tidal Current Tables*, using a system of reference stations and constants and differences for subordinate stations, similar to those used for tide tables. These tables, which are available in print and computerized form, are also available in chart form for some localities (not many). The charts display tidal-current data graphically, usually coming in a set of twelve that shows tidal set and drift (i.e., direction and speed) for each hour from one high tide through to the next.

Ocean currents are different from tidal currents in that they tend to flow in the same direction at all times. Some are both strong and remarkably consistent (e.g., the Gulf Stream) and are ignored at the navigator's peril; others are far less dependable. The strength with which a current flows is affected by meteorological and tidal factors; at times, even the strongest and most consistent may be temporarily reversed. The average set and drift of major currents is shown on the relevant charts and various other route-planning charts (e.g., those contained in *Ocean Passages of the World*, published by the British Admiralty).

Keeping a Logbook

A logbook is an essential component in the piloting process, even with fully electronic navigation. It does not have to be anything elaborate; it doesn't even have to be a book as such—many times, I have used a scratch pad. Its primary purpose is to maintain an up-to-date record of the voyage.

The kind of information needed depends on the kind of piloting or navigation being undertaken. In its simplest form, it might be nothing more than an hourly log of the GPS reading, which is all we record much of the time during open-water passages such as Gulf of Mexico crossings (we tend to be a little casual about log records). The log should also include basic weather information, including barometric pressure, wind speed, and wind direction (see chapter 11). With such a log, if the GPS goes down, a DR plot can be started from the last known fix. Of course, it is extremely helpful in developing an EP if the electronics also have been used to gauge leeway, set, and drift.

Sample logbook entry.

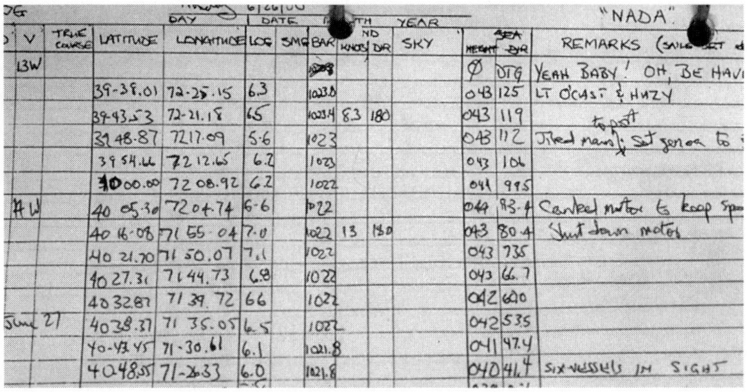

When using more traditional piloting methods, it is customary to make hourly entries (using local time but in 2400-hour notation) of at least the time, the log reading (the cumulative distance covered since the log was last reset), the course being steered (the boat's heading, noting whether it is C, M, or T), and weather information. If the course steered deviates from the planned course or the course asked for, this also might be noted. This is the minimum information needed to work up a DR plot; it is supplemented with records of any course changes; fixes; estimates (or known quantities) of leeway, set, and drift; and other pertinent information (e.g., tidal information) for working up an EP. If fixes or EPs are plotted on the chart, they should be noted in the log (e.g., "1645: fix plotted," or "1645: fix on chart"). There is also a column for comments or remarks, such as "weighed anchor from . . . at 1530," "set the main and genoa," "put #1 reef in the main," "cranked the engine," "shut down the engine."

When plotting courses, LOPs, and fixes directly on a chart, much of the logbook information will duplicate what has been plotted. Nevertheless, the purists argue that the written log should contain the same information. I am strictly pragmatic—if the information is on the chart, I am not particularly concerned about whether it goes in the logbook, especially if I am operating short-handed in difficult conditions. Nevertheless, maintaining some sort of an hourly plot or entry is important for the following reasons:

- to have a recent update from which to start a DR plot if necessary
- to ensure that whoever is on watch is awake, alert, and paying attention to the boat's navigation
- in the unlikely event that whoever is on watch goes over the side undetected, to give the rest of the crew some clue as to when it happened and an idea of where to start searching

In some countries, such as France, the maintenance of an up-to-date log is a legal requirement. Beyond the information already discussed, some people like to record different amounts of detail about a passage. For example, "heavy going motor sailing to windward; Terrie and the children seasick" or "glorious sunset, followed by a green flash." However, it might be better to record this descriptive material—which is not strictly related to navigational considerations—in another personal log. I regret that I tend to record too few personal details; it is fun to read old logbooks and reminisce about past voyages.

Expanding the Piloting Repertoire

The various piloting techniques described so far serve to fix and plot positions, estimate set and drift, and set the course to steer in most circumstances. They can be augmented with any number of additional techniques; however, in practice we use very few. The most useful are described in the following sections.

Ranges (Transits)

A range consists of any two distinct objects that can be lined up, one in front of the other. Ranges are tremendously useful in piloting inasmuch as they provide an extremely accurate bearing and, moreover, one from which the slightest deviation (e.g., the effects of tidal set) becomes instantly obvious. This is why ranges are commonly established to guide boats through narrow channels. Beyond this, any kind

An unusual range at Hope Town in the Bahamas: not the guy on the seat, but the two triangles on the poles to the left. The triangles have to be lined up to keep in center channel. Note, however, that aiming for the center of the road has the same effect, and is much easier to pick out from farther offshore, illustrating that just about anything can be used for a range as long as it is accurate and unambiguous.

of temporary range that can be observed (e.g., two buoys in line) is useful for determining the effects of leeway and tidal set on a boat's course.

Properly selected, a range is both unambiguous and precise. Furthermore, the use of a range does not require any bearings to be taken—the two objects are either in line or not. For this reason, *a range is a far more useful navigational tool than a bearing line on some object*, particularly in rough weather when it is difficult to take accurate bearings with a hand-bearing compass. (In these kinds of conditions, the KVH DataScope really shines—it averages readings over time with the result that, even perched on the spreaders with the compass swinging wildly, I have been able to get bearings to within ± 1 or 2 degrees of accuracy.)

Any two unambiguous objects can be used for a range. For example, two headlands, or a buoy and a lighthouse (the buoy will have its own swinging circle—the closer the buoy is approached, the less accurate the range), a prominent house and a radio tower, the edges of two islands and so on. However, bear in mind a few caveats:

- The closer together the front and back objects in the range, the more distance you have to move off the range line before any deviation from the range becomes readily apparent (i.e., the less precise is the range).
- The farther you are from the front part of the range, the more distance you have to move off the range line before any deviation from the range becomes readily apparent (again, the less precise is the range).
- Conversely, the farther apart the two halves of the range and the closer you are to the front of the range, the more precise it is.

These caveats must be considered when determining the suitability of a range for a specific function (e.g., passing through a narrow reef entry). Even so, when writing my cruising guides, I am constantly on the lookout for objects that will make clearly identifiable ranges, especially when defining reef entries and narrow channels—quite simply, *there is no other piloting tool that has anywhere near the same utility*. Similarly, when cruising in restricted or complicated waters, I first "cruise" the charts with parallel rules in hand, looking for potential ranges that help define safe and dangerous waters or assist in complicated piloting.

Ranges are just as useful used backward as forward. In that case, you simply keep glancing over the stern and steer the boat to keep the two halves of the range in line.

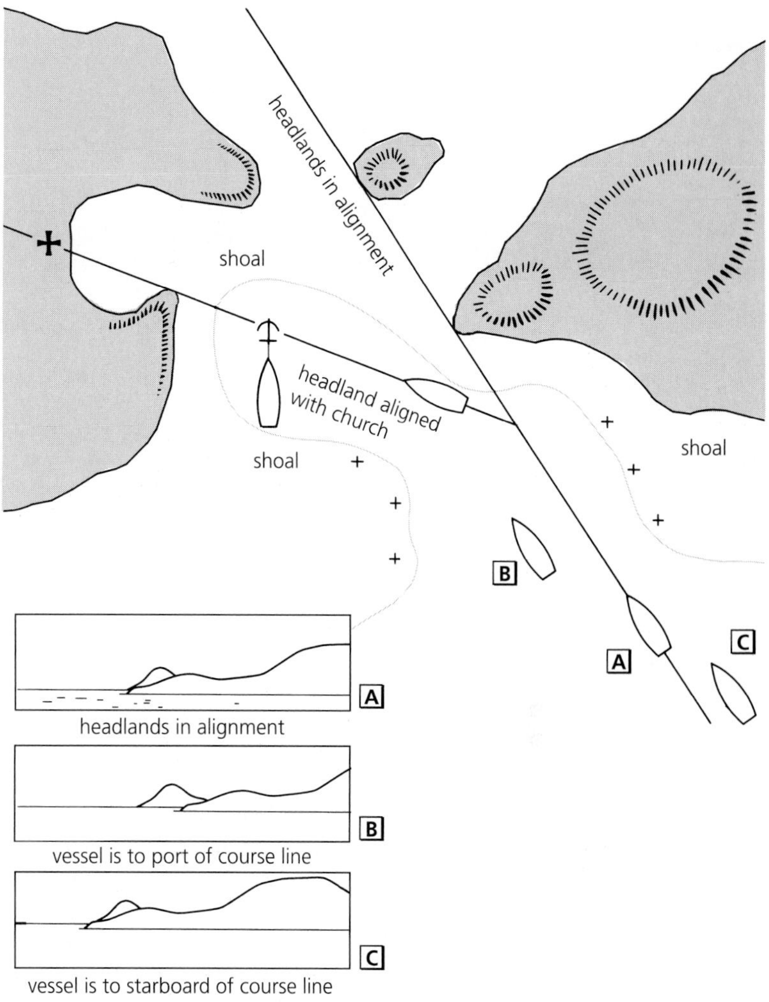

Using "unofficial" ranges for a tricky harbor entrance.

Safe and Dangerous Bearings

Here's another extremely useful "trick" that I frequently employ. Let's say we are sailing along a coastline with dangerous off-lying reefs or shoals. In the distance is a distinct headland or maybe a lighthouse or some other clearly identifiable feature that can be located on the chart. I draw a line on the chart from this feature to just clear the danger zone, and then measure the bearing along that line to the feature. On one side of this bearing line we are in safe water; on the other, we are in peril. Periodically, we make sure we are on the safe side of the line by either turning the boat's head to point at the feature (if we are headed toward it) and taking a reading off the main compass; or measuring the bearing to the feature with a hand-bearing compass. Regular bearings enable us to see if leeway or any current is setting us down toward the danger zone; if so, we can take appropriate defensive action.

Safe and dangerous bearings.

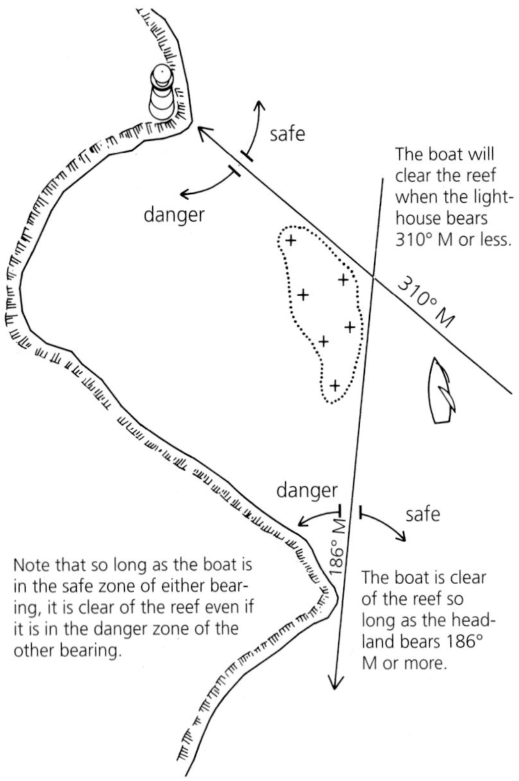

safe
danger
The boat will clear the reef when the lighthouse bears 310° M or less.
310° M
danger
safe
186° M
Note that so long as the boat is in the safe zone of either bearing, it is clear of the reef even if it is in the danger zone of the other bearing.
The boat is clear of the reef so long as the headland bears 186° M or more.

Ranges are even better for defining a danger zone for the reasons discussed previously: they are very precise, any deviation from the range is immediately apparent, and there is no need to take bearings. In this situation, the range or any danger bearing is not the course line for the boat. If the range comes in line or we end up on the bearing, this is a warning that we are moving into danger—it is time to change course into safer waters.

Sometimes we may want to establish more than one danger bearing; for example, one from a prominent headland behind us and one from a headland ahead, which between them defines the outer edges of an isolated reef patch. In this case, it is quite possible to be inside the danger area of one or another bearing, but as long as we are in the safe area defined by either one of them, we will be OK.

In restricted and complicated waters, danger bearings are another of those things I routinely go "cruising" for on the chart before setting sail. They also can be used as easily backward as forward.

Doubling the angle on the bow.

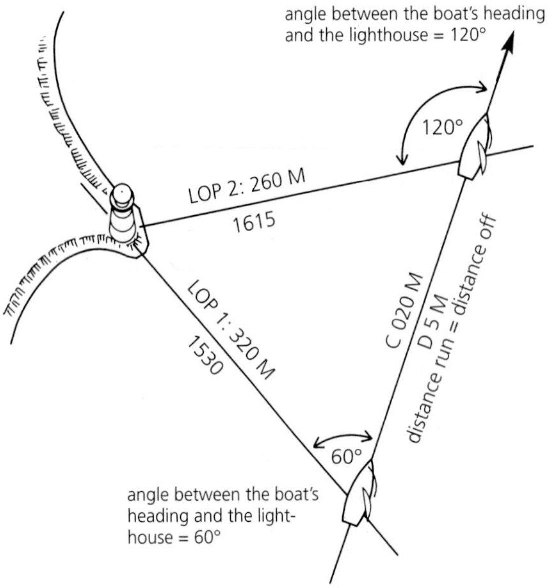

angle between the boat's heading and the lighthouse = 120°
120°
LOP 2: 260 M
1615
LOP 1: 320 M
1530
C 020 M
D 5 M
distance run = distance off
60°
angle between the boat's heading and the lighthouse = 60°

Doubling the Angle on the Bow

Doubling the angle on the bow is a useful technique for determining your distance off the coast. It involves measuring the relative angle between the boat and some object ashore. It is calculated by noting the boat's heading, taking a bearing of the object, and then calculating the difference between the two bearings (e.g., the boat's heading is 335 M and the object bears 305 M; the difference—the *relative angle*—is 30 degrees). The current log reading is jotted down (e.g., 28.7 miles). The boat remains on the same heading while a watch is maintained on the object until the relative bearing has doubled (in this case, to 60 degrees; the object will be bearing 335 M – 60 = 275 M). Another log reading is taken (e.g., 32.4 miles). The distance traveled between the bearings (in this case, 32.4 miles – 28.7 miles = 4.7 miles) is equal to the distance from the object at the time of the second observation, *assuming no tidal set or leeway*.

At the time of the second observation, we have both an LOP (the bearing to the object) and a distance off, which together give us a fix. However, this fix is subject to leeway and tidal-set errors, inaccuracies in the log, and so on, and should be treated with caution. In addition to these errors, which are inherent in the process, it is not always easy to get bearings accurate enough to achieve much reliability with this technique, particularly when fine (i.e., narrow) relative angles are used. The best results are likely to be achieved with the first relative angle around 45 degrees and the second around 90 degrees (i.e., the object is abeam); however, in this case, the distance off is not known until you are abreast of the object, which in some cases may not be soon enough.

Finally, here's a nifty little trick that has its uses on occasion. If you measure the time it takes for the bearing of an object ashore (that is more or less abeam) to change by the same amount as the boat's speed (e.g., if the boat is doing 7 knots, the bearing changes by 7 degrees), the time (in minutes) equals the distance off (e.g., 2 minutes 40 seconds = 2⅔ miles). The object has to be almost abeam for this to work.

The Rule of Sixty

The Rule of Sixty is a useful bit of navigational miscellanea. It derives from the fact that if you draw two lines emanating from the same point with just a 1-degree angle between them, after a distance of 60 miles, they will be 1 mile apart. I use this all the time to make quick mental calculations when crossing the Gulf of Mexico, which just happens to be 600 miles across from our old home base in Mandeville, Louisiana, to Isla Mujeres at the tip of the Yucatán Peninsula in Mexico.

Let's say we clear the Rigolets Channel at the mouth of Lake Ponchartrain, Louisiana, and head out into the Gulf of Mexico. Our rhumbline course is 165T, but the wind is heading us and we can only lay 180T. We are 15 degrees off course. Over 60 miles, every degree equals 1 mile; over 600 miles, every degree equals 10 miles—therefore, 15 degrees equals 150 miles. Ouch! We had better hope for a favorable wind shift.

Bringing this down to a local scale, if I am being set 15 degrees, I know that over 60 miles every degree equals 1 mile; therefore, 15 degrees equals 15 miles. Over 1 mile every degree equals $\frac{1}{60}$ of a mile, so 15 degrees equals $\frac{15}{60}$ equals ¼ of a mile set per mile sailed.

This kind of simple mathematics works in many ways. Let's say we are approaching a lighthouse at night with a nominal range of 20 miles. It's a clear night and our geographic range exceeds 20 miles, so as soon as we pick up the light, we know we really are approximately 20 miles off. We want to clear by a mile the headland on which the light sits: 20 miles is ⅓ of 60, so every change in heading of 1 degree gives us a clearance of ⅓ of a mile; we must change course by 3 degrees. In other words, if the distance A of an object ahead is known and it is desired to pass B miles from it, the course must be altered by (60 ÷ A × B) degrees.

Following are two somewhat different derivations based on time:

Time (in minutes) required to cover 1 mile at a given speed = (60 ÷ speed)

$\frac{1}{10}$ speed = distance traveled in 6 minutes; multiples of 6 minutes can be used to calculate distance or speed (e.g., distance traveled in 36 minutes = $\frac{6}{10}$ speed)

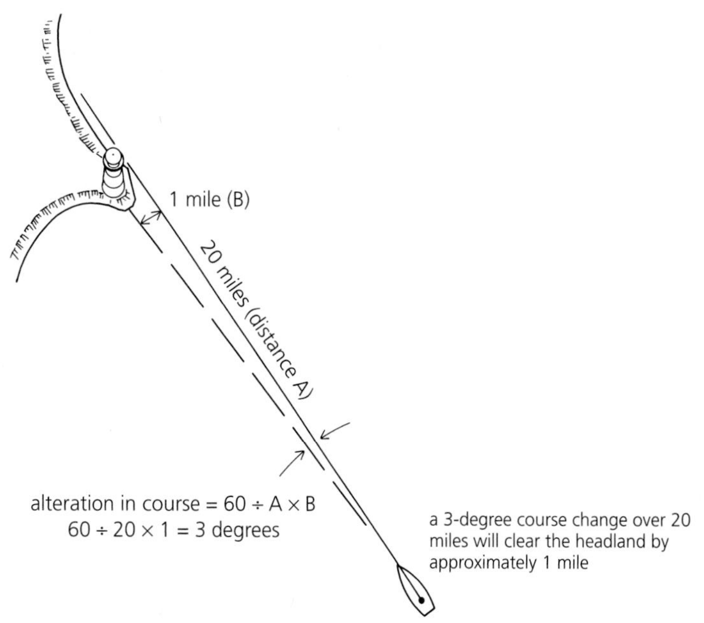

1 mile (B)
20 miles (distance A)
alteration in course = 60 ÷ A × B
60 ÷ 20 × 1 = 3 degrees
a 3-degree course change over 20 miles will clear the headland by approximately 1 mile

Using the Rule of Sixty.

This is all quite rough, but at times it may be the best that can be done.

Sailing Strategies Dead to Windward

Despite our best intentions, we seem to spend an undue amount of time going to windward. The question then is: How can we get this over with as quickly as possible? Clearly, if we are in restricted waters, or we anticipate a wind shift, or there are tidal or other currents, these factors must play a significant part in the navigational equation. However, in the absence of these factors, some general principles can be established, based on sound mathematical considerations (which I do not explain):

- If the destination is dead to windward, you should tack whenever you get to the boundaries of a cone established by drawing lines 20 degrees or so either side of the direct course to the destination. In other words, don't make a long tack off to one or another side of the direct course. For longer passages, draw a line dead downwind from the destination, put parallel lines at appropriate distances on either side of this line to establish an upwind corridor, and tack whenever at the boundary of the corridor.
- If the destination is not dead to windward, choose the most favorable tack until it is dead to windward, and then proceed as described previously (this results in sailing the longest leg first).
- If the wind shifts so that the favorable tack becomes the unfavorable tack, come about onto the favorable tack.

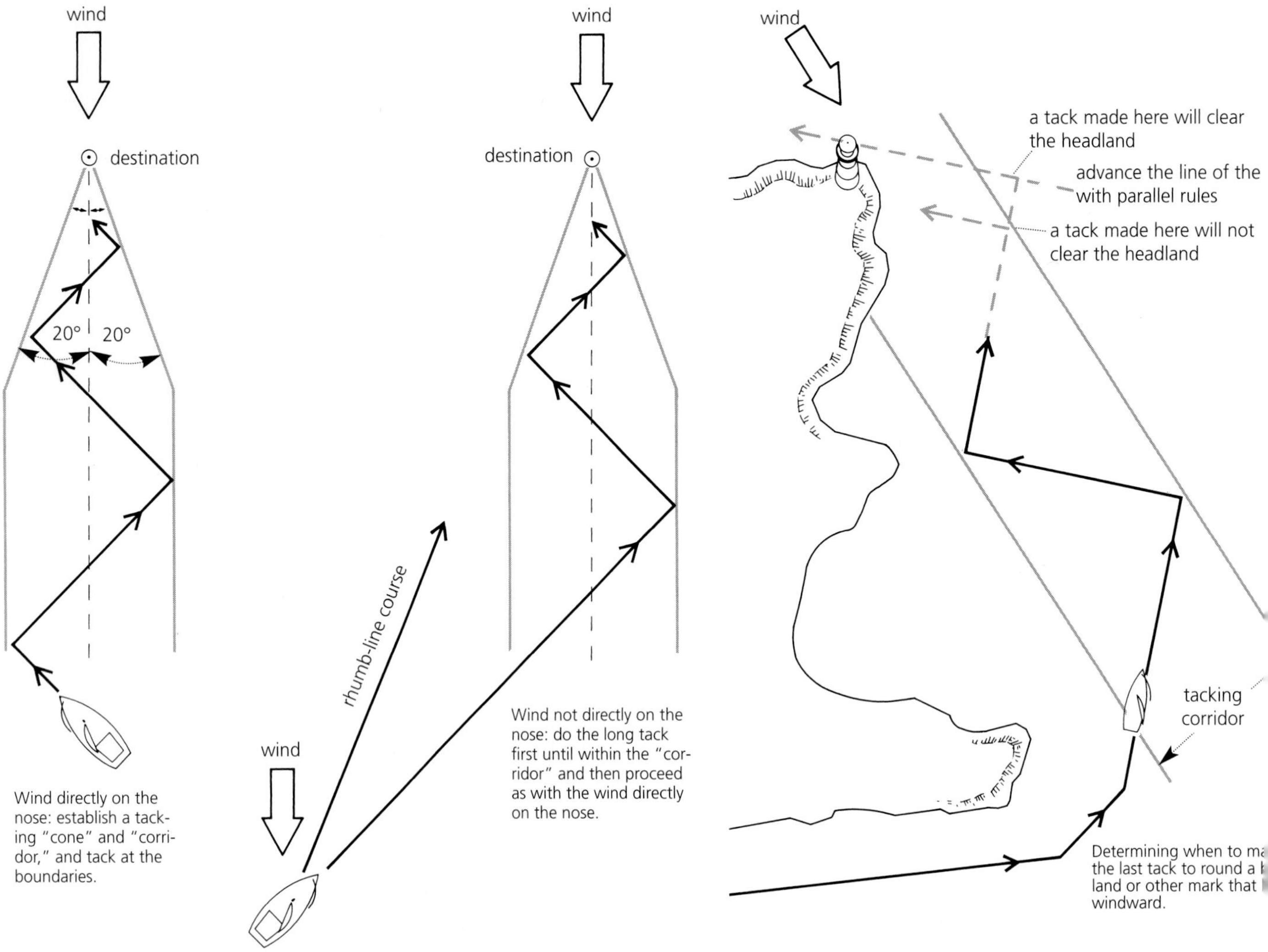
wind
destination
20°
20°
Wind directly on the nose: establish a tacking "cone" and "corridor," and tack at the boundaries.
wind
destination
rhumb-line course
wind
Wind not directly on the nose: do the long tack first until within the "corridor" and then proceed as with the wind directly on the nose.
wind
a tack made here will clear the headland
advance the line of the
with parallel rules
a tack made here will not clear the headland
tacking corridor
Determining when to
the last tack to round a
land or other mark that
windward.

Strategies for determining when to tack when going to windward.

- If a wind shift can be predicted with some certainty, keep to that side of the course from which the wind is expected to come.
- The greater the wind shift is expected to be, the less you should move away from the direct course.

These tactics will have you tacking through ever-shorter tacks as you approach your destination. Obviously, at some point it becomes impractical to stay within the "cone" described by a line 20 degrees to either side of the direct course. At this time, you will have to start tacking outside the cone.

If you are using a GPS to navigate along an upwind corridor and your destination is entered as a waypoint, the *Cross Track Error* (XTE) function can be used to determine when to tack. For example, if you set the boundaries of the corridor 2 miles either side of the direct course line, once you are in the corridor, it is time to tack whenever the Cross Track Error reads 2 miles. Once you get within the final cone leading up to the destination, note the bearing from the waypoint of each boundary line forming the cone, and then tack whenever the Bearing to Waypoint function on the GPS reads one of these bearings.

Finally, when tacking up to round a headland or mark, use parallel rules to advance the line of the tack you will be on when you round the headland, and then make the last tack when you reach this line.

Complex Situations, Fog, and Coral

Coastal piloting is generally more challenging than offshore navigation. Frequently, a shorthanded vessel gets into a situation where there are numerous potential hazards to be negotiated and decision after decision that must be made quite rapidly, often in an environment where the boat is crashing around and any kind of chart work is difficult to do. Even if the boat has GPS, the requirements of handling the boat, or the conditions, or the need to make a rapid

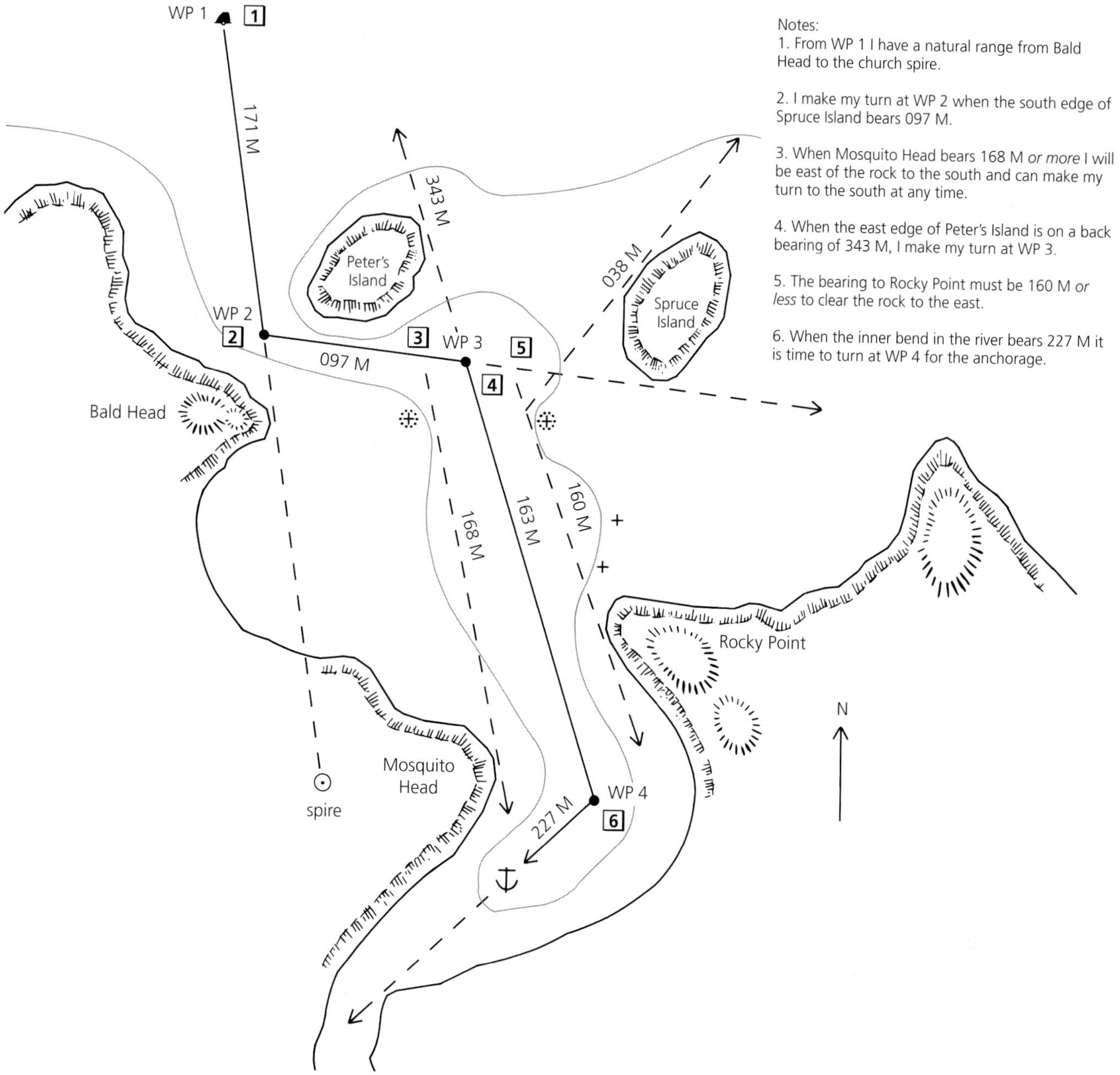
WP 1
1
171 M
343 M
Peter's Island
WP 2
2
097 M
3
WP 3
5
4
038 M
Spruce Island
Bald Head
168 M
163 M
160 M
Rocky Point
N
Mosquito Head
spire
WP 4
6
227 M
Notes:
1. From WP 1 I have a natural range from Bald Head to the church spire.
2. I make my turn at WP 2 when the south edge of Spruce Island bears 097 M.
3. When Mosquito Head bears 168 M *or more* I will be east of the rock to the south and can make my turn to the south at any time.
4. When the east edge of Peter's Island is on a back bearing of 343 M, I make my turn at WP 3.
5. The bearing to Rocky Point must be 160 M *or less* to clear the rock to the east.
6. When the inner bend in the river bears 227 M it is time to turn at WP 4 for the anchorage.

Hand-prepared quick-reference chart for tricky navigation.

judgment may simply not permit the time needed to plot a fix.

In these circumstances, the key to maintaining your equanimity and to ensuring the safety of the boat and its crew is to be well prepared. Specifically, I like to develop a sketch chart of the area to be navigated ahead of time that I can keep in the cockpit (often inside a plastic storage bag) regardless of the weather and conditions. I note on this chart those features that are critical to the piloting process, including waypoints that I have programmed into my electronics, clearly recognizable shoreside features, aids to navigation, ranges and danger bearings derived from the chart, those points at which I intend to change course together with my course lines (each of which will be given its bearing), and any other information that helps me safely pilot the boat—even if I am unable to get to the chart table to plot our progress.

At these times, I have learned to sail defensively, including not sailing downwind into trouble (I have twice come close to wrecking a boat through ignoring this basic common sense), keeping an anchor ready to let go (on one of those two occasions, it was only the rapid deployment of a stern anchor that kept us off the rocks), and having the engine ready to fire up if necessary (the engine was working on that occasion, but we had no reverse).

If the piloting involves a landfall on a relatively featureless coastline, and I am at all

Making landfall on a featureless coast.

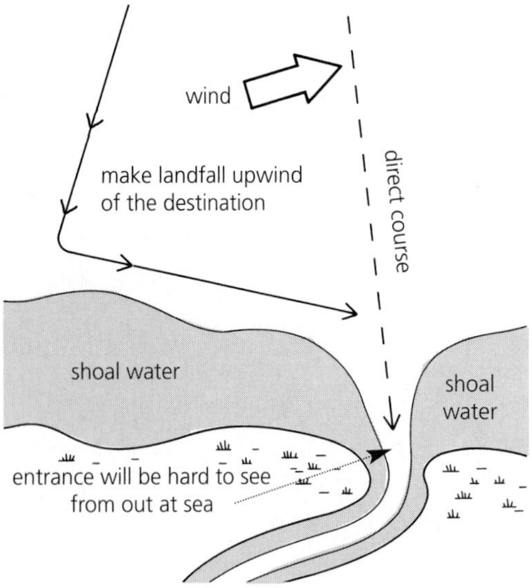

uncertain of my position, *I always set a course to one side of the desired landfall* (preferably upwind). This way, when I reach the coast, if I can't immediately recognize the features I need to fix my position, I at least know which way to turn (which I would not know if I tried to make my landfall dead on, but then missed the location for some reason).

On longer passages that involve an open-water segment, it is almost always preferable to sail overnight and make landfall around dawn. This way, if there are any lighted aids to navigation (particularly lighthouses), they will be easy to pick up and will help with the approaches. However, any coastal piloting in tricky waters will be done in daylight. A dawn arrival also means that in the event of unforeseen delays, there are still several hours of daylight to get safely tucked up in an anchorage.

Many beginning sailors have an unreasonable fear of night sailing, which is quite unwarranted provided there are no shipping lanes, unmarked buoys, or other hazards that may not be seen in the dark (e.g., lobster pots along the coast of Maine). In fact, where there are lighted aids to navigation, they are frequently easier to pick out at night than during the day, so even relatively complex coastal piloting can be simpler in the dark. However, because it is easier to get disoriented at night, it is important to maintain a constantly updated plot on your chart. In addition, you really need to be able to recognize ships by their lights and figure out which way they are going. (This is discussed below in Rules of the Road.)

For the inexperienced, the best way to gain confidence in night sailing is to pick a familiar area on a clear night with benign conditions—and just get out there and do it.

Fog

Fog and other conditions of very low visibility are something altogether different. It doesn't matter how sophisticated the electronics and how accurately the boat's position is known, I don't know anyone who is comfortable in fog, particularly if there is no radar onboard. There is good reason for this. If you can't see other people, they can't see you: the risk of collision is greatly magnified.

Fog is generally accompanied by little wind, in which case the engine is likely to be running. You should reduce speed because the engine noise will mask the sound of foghorns and approaching boats; therefore, a lookout needs to be posted in the bow of the boat (a cold and miserable job). In addition, your engine should be shut down every few minutes to enable the sounds of any other traffic to be heard.

You should get out of shipping lanes. My preference is to get into water shallow enough that any large vessel will run aground before it can hit me! Ideally, it will be possible to creep into a protected anchorage and wait for the fog to lift.

Given the lack of visible features in fog, a GPS or another form of electronic navigation is worth its weight in gold. However, *you should not get yourself into any situation from which it will be difficult to extricate the boat if the electronics go down.*

In the absence of electronics, it is essential to maintain a carefully updated DR and EP plot, supplemented by close attention to depth

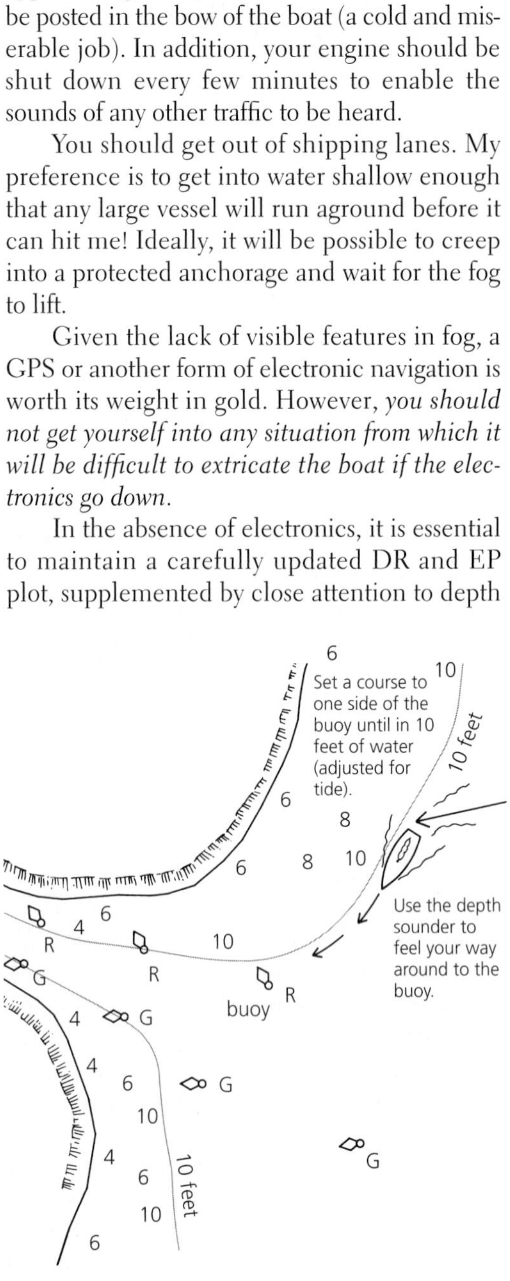

A strategy for using a depth contour to find a harbor entrance.

A precise fix enables you to confirm your position and increase your confidence in finding the next mark.

soundings (one of the few navigational inputs unaffected by fog). You may be able to use depths more creatively than usual. For example, when looking for a channel-entry buoy on a coastline with gradually shoaling depths, aim to one side of the buoy until you are in its charted depth (adjusted for the state of the tide), and then follow that depth contour until the buoy is found.

Another technique for position-fixing based on soundings is to maintain a constant heading while jotting on a piece of paper a series of soundings in a straight line. The distance between the soundings should be based on the scale of the chart you are using for plotting purposes. (It is easiest to plot at regular distances as defined by the boat's log; for example, every quarter mile.) Based on the approximate idea of where you are and the heading you are on, maneuver the piece of paper around the chart of this area and line it up with the boat's heading—with any luck, you will see a close correlation between charted depths and those on the paper, which gives you a reasonable fix. (This works particularly well if the bottom has well-defined changes in depth.)

Navigating in Coral

Navigating in coral poses special challenges (and delights) all its own. Coral reefs frequently sit atop plateaus that emerge quite suddenly from great depths (and, therefore, are not detected by a depth sounder until the boat is almost on the reef) and that have little if any land mass above sea level (and, therefore, little or nothing is visible above the horizon). When you consider the fact that many coral-strewn waters are poorly charted, it becomes obvious why so many boats are lost on reefs in the Pacific and the Caribbean.

When approaching a reef for the first time, *it is essential to place no reliance on electronic navigation*, to make any approach in good light, and to maintain a bow watch as the region of the reef is approached. Once in the vicinity of a reef, piloting is mostly an eyeball affair, using all the techniques outlined so far.

Coral does not grow where sediment is present; therefore, almost always the water around reefs is clear, sometimes astonishingly so. In the right light conditions, it is easy to pick out coral patches and reefs; however, in the wrong light conditions, nothing can be seen.

The higher you can get, the easier it is to navigate through coral.

*The same view without (*left*) and with (*right*) polarized sunglasses. Note how the coral and shallow water "pop out" with the polarized glasses.*

*The same view with polarized sunglasses: without cloud (*left*); with partial cloud—note how difficult it is to differentiate between the cloud and the coral (*middle*); and with full cloud cover—the coral is almost indistinguishable (*right*).*

"Right light" means that the sun is well above the horizon—preferably behind the boat or overhead, but certainly not ahead (this creates a glare that obscures visibility). There are then two key ingredients to choosing a path through coral: a perch as high as possible on the boat (standing on the bow pulpit may be the best you can do but, ideally, there are ratlines or mast steps to the lower spreaders); and a pair of high-quality polarized sunglasses, *which is absolutely essential*.

With polarized sunglasses, it doesn't take long to get your eyes "tuned in." Pretty soon you can distinguish sand bottoms from turtle-grass and coral, and estimate with a surprising degree of accuracy (down to inches) the depth of the water. That is, as long as the sun is still in the right position and not obscured by clouds. The minute the sun becomes obscured, it will be almost impossible to pick out coral, even if it is almost breaking the surface of the water. It is time to anchor and wait for better conditions.

What this means is that when picking your way through a substantial amount of coral, you need to make sure the sky is clear and that you have adequate light conditions to see you through to a safe anchorage. You also should have in mind secure locations in which to hole up if conditions unexpectedly deteriorate. We have more than once been forced to anchor for the night in the midst of a veritable coral maze because we ran out of the light conditions needed to finish picking our way through.

ELECTRONIC NAVIGATION

The piloting techniques outlined so far are, in essence, an irreducible minimum for a coastal or offshore cruiser, *regardless of the extent of the electronics onboard*. There are at least three reasons for this:

- If the electronics go down, this is what you will have to fall back on.
- It is not uncommon for operators of electronic equipment to enter incorrect data into the equipment (the classic example is incorrect waypoints). Without some type of independent check on the electronics, the boat may well get into trouble (wrongly entered waypoints cause many accidents).
- Even if the electronics are functioning perfectly, there are times when you will need to fall back on these techniques. When involved in close-quarters piloting, particularly in difficult conditions and when sailing short-handed, there is frequently no time to plot GPS positions; in any case, you may not be able to leave the cockpit to plot the positions. Of course, this can be accomplished electronically with a chart plotter or computer, but invariably they have relatively small screens that provide little "peripheral vision." If the scale is large enough to provide inshore detail, the area covered will be quite small; if the area covered is enlarged to give peripheral vision, there won't be the needed detail for inshore work. *When the chips are down, all the electronics in the world are not as useful as an appropriate range or danger bearing.* They cannot substitute for the confidence that comes from having what I call an "intuitive" sense of position, derived from familiarity with basic piloting techniques.

Besides which, piloting with traditional techniques is fun! After we returned from our last four-month cruise to Mexico and Belize, I realized (somewhat to my surprise) that I had not programmed a single waypoint into our GPSs; in fact, I had not even turned them on for days at a time. This is not because I am any kind of a purist; it is simply that, once in the region, I found that traditional piloting techniques were more useful than GPS, and rarely needed to be supplemented with GPS fixes. However, when I wanted the level of precision and the degree of confidence provided by the GPS, I was, of course, delighted to have it. In this day and age, I would not go to sea without at least one GPS.

Chart and GPS Datums

As with any other navigational tool, in using GPS it is extremely important to understand the limits of its accuracy. In the past, it was common to read about *selective availability* (SA): errors deliberately programmed into the civilian GPS signal by the U.S. Defense Department. This meant that 95 percent of the time, the displayed latitude and longitude could be in error by as much as 100 meters; the other 5 percent of the time, the error could be considerably greater (e.g., our error on the coast of Cuba). These errors could be significantly reduced with *Differential GPS* (DGPS), which provided (and still does) *continuous* accuracy (no wild cards) of between 4 and 20 meters.

SA is now history, giving a system accuracy (without DGPS) of better than 30 meters (in theory, to within 12 meters 95 percent of the time), and we now have the *Wide Area Augmentation System* (WAAS), which, for those units that have it and in those areas where it is operable, has a design accuracy of 7 meters but in fact is mostly below 3 meters. In April 2001, WAAS coverage was available along the entire North American coastline, while a European system (European geostationary overlay system—EGNOS) was on the way, and a Japanese system (MSAS) was under development.

Despite ever-expanding WAAS-compatible coverage, it is important to remember that the U.S. Defense Department can reinstate SA to any level of error without warning. It is even more important to realize that, with or without SA, DGPS, or WAAS, *there may be substantial plotting errors when GPS-derived positions are plotted on charts*. At issue are complex questions concerning the shape of the world and how it is modeled for map and chart-making purposes.

As GPS increasingly supplants traditional navigational tools, it becomes more important for sailors to have a firm grasp of its limitations. This was brought home on another occasion in Cuba when I discovered a half-mile difference between our actual position and the GPS position when plotted on a recently published large-scale (detailed) British Admiralty chart of

Chart of Santiago Harbor, Cuba. Note: 1. Satellite-derived positions based on WGS72 (the forerunner of WGS84) must be adjusted 0.57 minutes southward (more than a ½ mile!) to fit the chart, while . . . 2. to agree with the local Cuban charts (based on NAD27), positions read from this chart must be moved 0.53 minute northward. It is not clear what datum has been used to produce this chart.

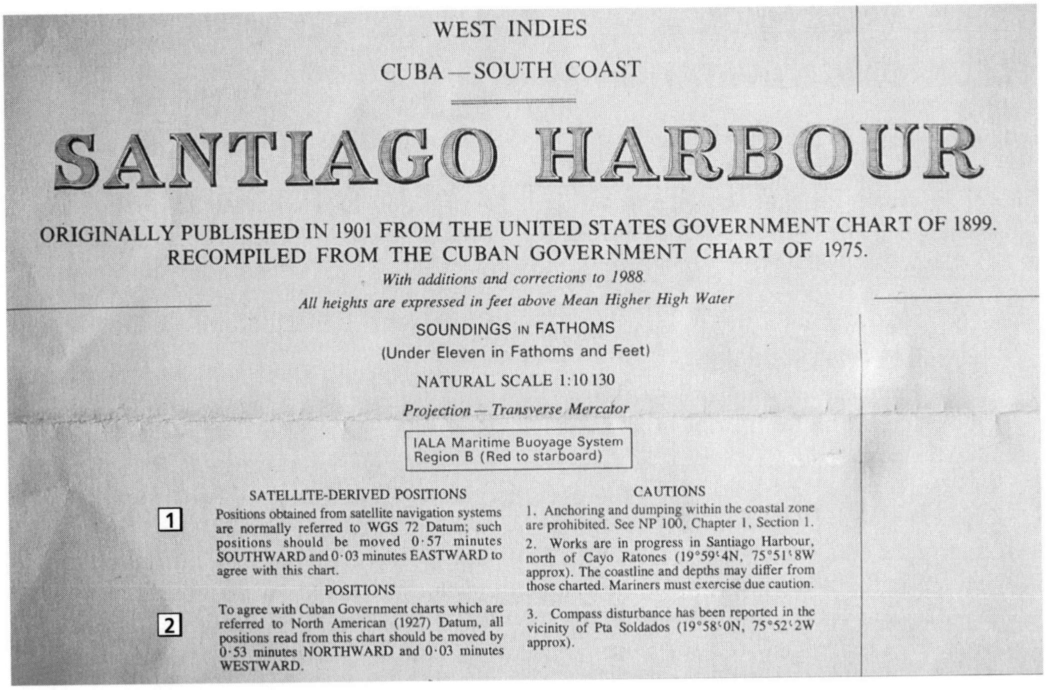

WEST INDIES

CUBA—SOUTH COAST

SANTIAGO HARBOUR

ORIGINALLY PUBLISHED IN 1901 FROM THE UNITED STATES GOVERNMENT CHART OF 1899.
RECOMPILED FROM THE CUBAN GOVERNMENT CHART OF 1975.

With additions and corrections to 1988.

All heights are expressed in feet above Mean Higher High Water

SOUNDINGS IN FATHOMS

(Under Eleven in Fathoms and Feet)

NATURAL SCALE 1:10 130

Projection—Transverse Mercator

IALA Maritime Buoyage System
Region B (Red to starboard)

SATELLITE-DERIVED POSITIONS

1 Positions obtained from satellite navigation systems are normally referred to WGS 72 Datum; such positions should be moved 0·57 minutes SOUTHWARD and 0·03 minutes EASTWARD to agree with this chart.

POSITIONS

2 To agree with Cuban Government charts which are referred to North American (1927) Datum, all positions read from this chart should be moved by 0·53 minutes NORTHWARD and 0·03 minutes WESTWARD.

CAUTIONS

1. Anchoring and dumping within the coastal zone are prohibited. See NP 100, Chapter 1, Section 1.

2. Works are in progress in Santiago Harbour, north of Cayo Ratones (19°59′4N, 75°51′8W approx). The coastline and depths may differ from those charted. Mariners must exercise due caution.

3. Compass disturbance has been reported in the vicinity of Pta Soldados (19°58′0N, 75°52′2W approx).

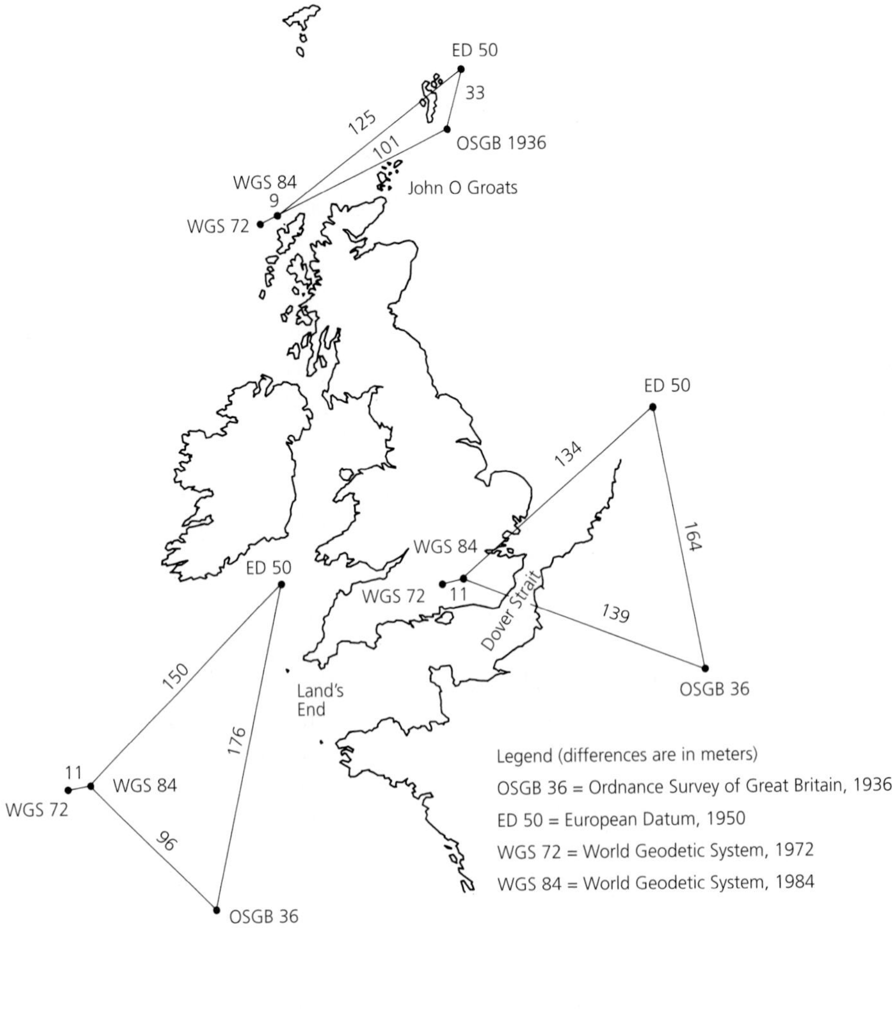

Position differences (in meters) relative to astronomical positions that result from using different datums at three different points around the British Isles. Note, in particular, the 130+ m shift in the Dover Straits, an exceedingly congested area with narrow, clearly defined shipping lanes.

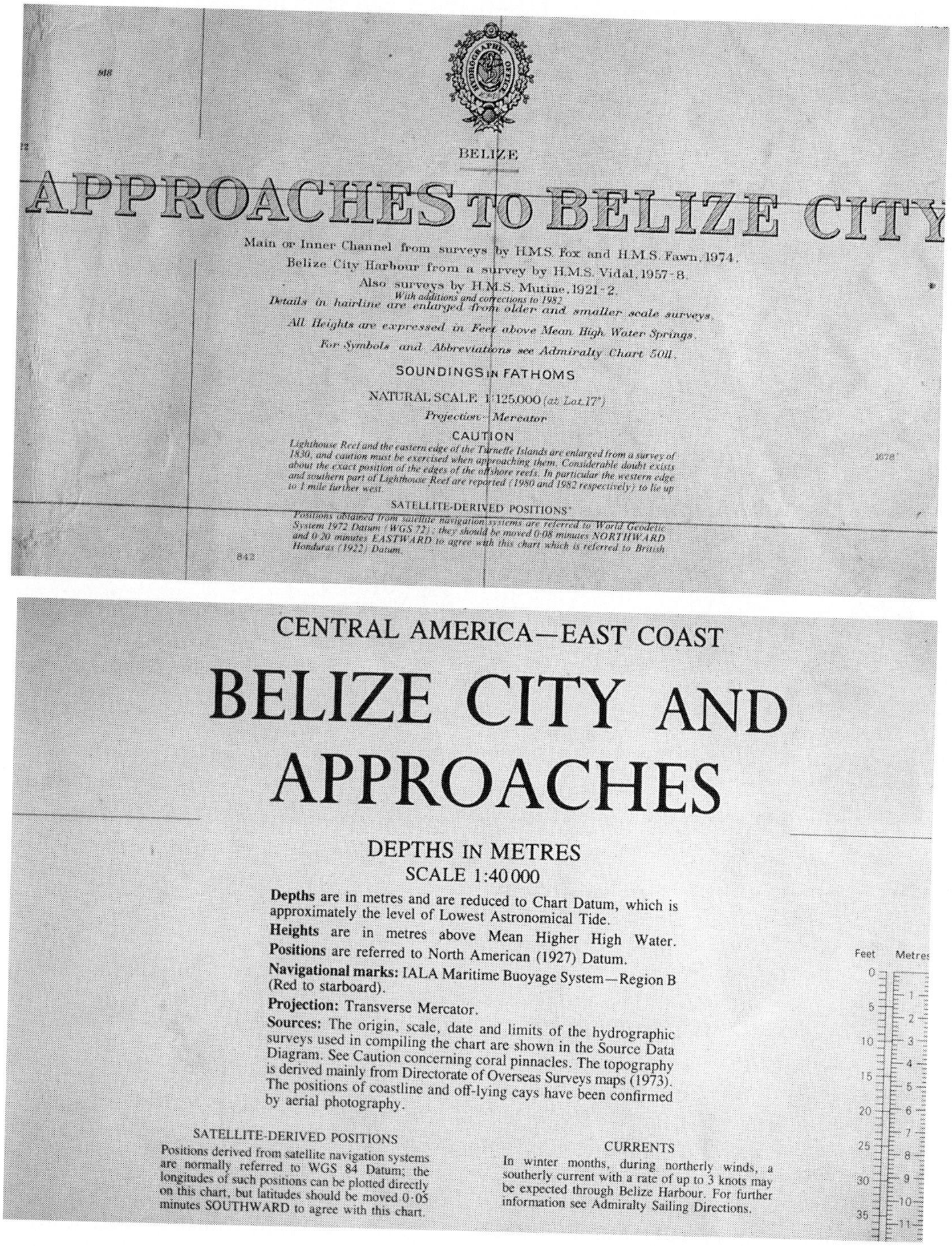

Two different datums. A. My old Belize charts are referenced to British Honduras datum of 1922 (see the small print under "Satellite Derived Positions" . . . B. while the next edition of charts is made to NAD27 (see the small print under Depths in Meters). Future editions will likely be made to WGS84: three different datums in about twenty years!

Santiago de Cuba. What was going on? The chart was based on a model of the world—a datum—that was different than the model used by the GPS in making its calculations. Neither model was wrong; they were just different.

This brings up an essential point when using a GPS: *it must be set to the same datum that has been used to make the chart on which the GPS positions are being plotted.* The default datum on all recently manufactured GPSs is something known as the *World Geodetic System 1984* (WGS84). Older North American charts are all based on a datum known as the *North American Datum of 1927* (NAD27); more recent charts have all been converted to the *North American Datum of 1983* (NAD83).

In North American waters there are no differences between NAD 83 and WGS 84. The discrepancies between WGS84 and NAD27 on the East Coast are quite small (a maximum of 30 meters) but on the West Coast can be as high as 100 meters. Differences between NAD27 and WGS84 in the Caribbean can be greater. In Europe, differences between WGS84 and local chart datums can be more than 100 meters; in the western Pacific they can be as much as 900

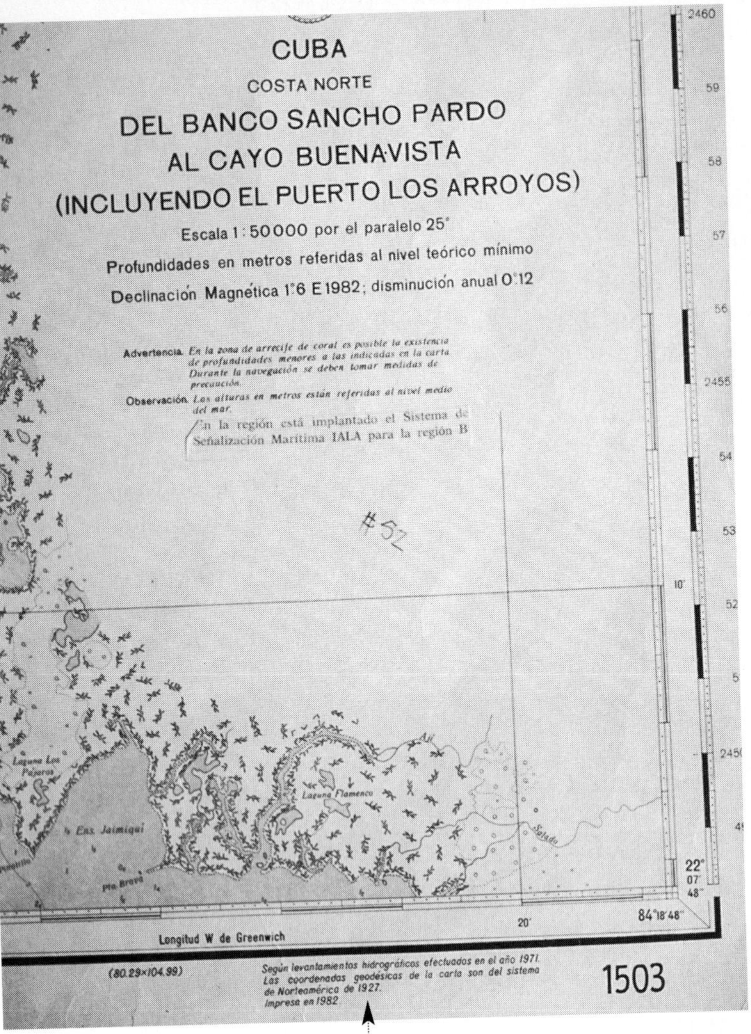

How about this Cuban survey: what's the datum? If you look closely, you can see it buried in the small print in the lower right-hand corner of the survey.

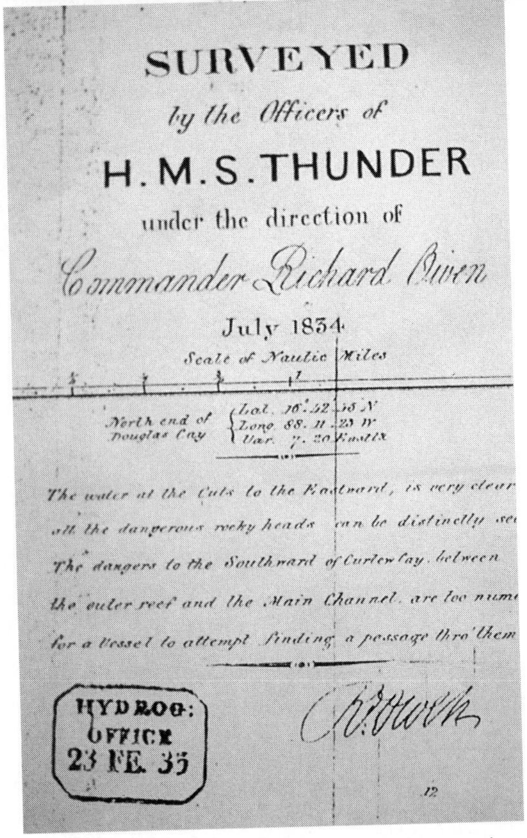

The original Belize surveys (which I still use because they show the most inshore details) were made to no particular datum and cannot be used with any form of electronic navigation. *Note the hydrographic office date stamp in the lower left corner—that is 23 February 1835, not 1935!*

meters. I repeat, to avoid a navigational error, a *GPS must always be set to the same datum that has been used to make the chart on which the GPS positions are being plotted.* In some remote areas (notably in the Pacific Ocean), the charts do not have a datum that is recognized by any GPS unit, *in which case the GPS unit cannot be relied upon for navigation.* (For an explanation of these datum issues, see the addendum to this chapter.)

Once the correct datum has been established, it is important to remember that GPS, particularly if differentially or WAAS corrected, *is a more accurate positioning system than was used to fix the soundings and details on most charts.* In other words, "the mariner can now navigate with greater accuracy than could the hydrographic surveyor who collected the chart source data" (Bowditch).

In the past, the required positioning accuracies when making charts were largely based on the practical limitations of draftsmanship at a given scale. The thinnest line that can be drawn is around 0.2 mm (0.0078 in.). On a 1:5,000 chart (large-scale harbor chart), this 0.2 mm represents 3.3 feet (1 m): $0.2 \times 5{,}000 = 1{,}000$ nm. At a scale of 1:80,000 (U.S. coastal charts), 0.2 mm represents 53 feet (16 m) on the ground.

Even for the most position-sensitive data, surveyors saw little need to exceed the levels of accuracy inherent in the scale at which a survey was being plotted. Because of limitations in marine surveying technologies, much of the time they couldn't come anywhere close to even these levels of accuracy, and even where they could, they often made judgment calls as to the level of accuracy required by different features (e.g., a deep-water depth sounding in the open ocean might be deemed to require less precision than a dangerous rock in an otherwise navigable area).

The net result is that at chart scales of 1:20,000 and greater, even an off-the-shelf, basic GPS may well position a boat with greater accuracy than was used to survey *any* of the data displayed on the chart. A differentially or WAAS-corrected GPS will almost certainly have positioning errors several times less than those of even the most accurately plotted data on the chart. Problems may be compounded by the fact that electronic chartmakers sometimes use data collected for small-scale surveys (in which positioning errors may be relatively high) on larger-scale electronic charts (for which the user tends to presuppose a high level of accuracy). If you're picking your way down a narrow channel using GPS, the chart and GPS positions could easily show you in midchannel when you are hard aground!

In many parts of the world, chart accuracy doesn't even come close to the standard mentioned above. For example, much of Belize has not been resurveyed since 1841. Although the positions of land masses, islands, and some reefs have been corrected in recent years to WGS84 using satellite imagery, *many of the charted reef patches and soundings are still based on highly inaccurate surveys by today's standards* (but they were a marvel in their own time). Reliance on GPS for navigation will surely put you on a reef sooner or later; therefore, in addition to checking the datum on a chart, it is important to check the age of the survey data and to make some estimate of its reliability.

Using Published Waypoints with GPS

More and more people are using Chart Kits or similar packaged paper charts on which various course lines and waypoints have been marked. At the same time, interfaced electronics in which a GPS unit is connected to an autopilot are becoming widespread. There is an increasing tendency for people to develop a route by programming the GPS unit with the waypoints given on the charts, and then sailing under autopilot with the autopilot governed by the GPS. This is great until you realize that if two boats are coming toward each other under autopilot using the same waypoints, given the accuracy of GPS there is a good probability that they will run into each other! The other thing that may happen is, if you aren't paying attention you may hit a buoy or some other aid to navigation you're using as a waypoint.

The ease of navigating and sailing with preprogrammed waypoints is likely to lure people into a false sense of security. I would recommend that, if using published waypoints, and if there is sufficient searoom, an offset be added to the waypoints to put you to one side of the track published on the chart. This will keep you out of the path of those running down the published track. In spite of such precautions, it is, of course, incumbent on you to keep a good watch at all times.

Electronic Charting

As more laptops and built-in computers appear on boats, the options facing navigators expand at the same exponential rate as the power and memory of modern computers.

A state-of-the-art navigation station has electronic representation of paper charts indistinguishable from the originals, with "point-and-click navigation." This includes real-time depiction of the boat's position; range and bearing to preprogrammed waypoints; SOG and speed made good (SMG; the speed toward a waypoint; it will be the same as SOG if the boat sails directly to the waypoint, but will be different if the boat follows anything other than a direct course); TMG; XTE (the deviation from the direct track toward a waypoint); tide and current predictions for any place in the world; set and drift of currents; a memorized record of the boat's track; and interfaces with all other onboard electronics, including the autopilot, for fully automated helming. The GPS has a crew overboard (COB) button that can be hit to store the boat's position immediately if someone goes over the side.

A satellite and/or SSB interface provides Weatherfax information and even real-time satellite weather imagery. The system will have Internet access and e-mail send and receive capabilities.

It is quite impossible to keep up with these kinds of developments in this type of book (for one thing, in the time it takes to publish it, computer hardware and software will have evolved through at least another generation). However, some broad generalizations can be made:

Two types of electronic chart are widely available: a *raster-based chart*, which is an "elec-

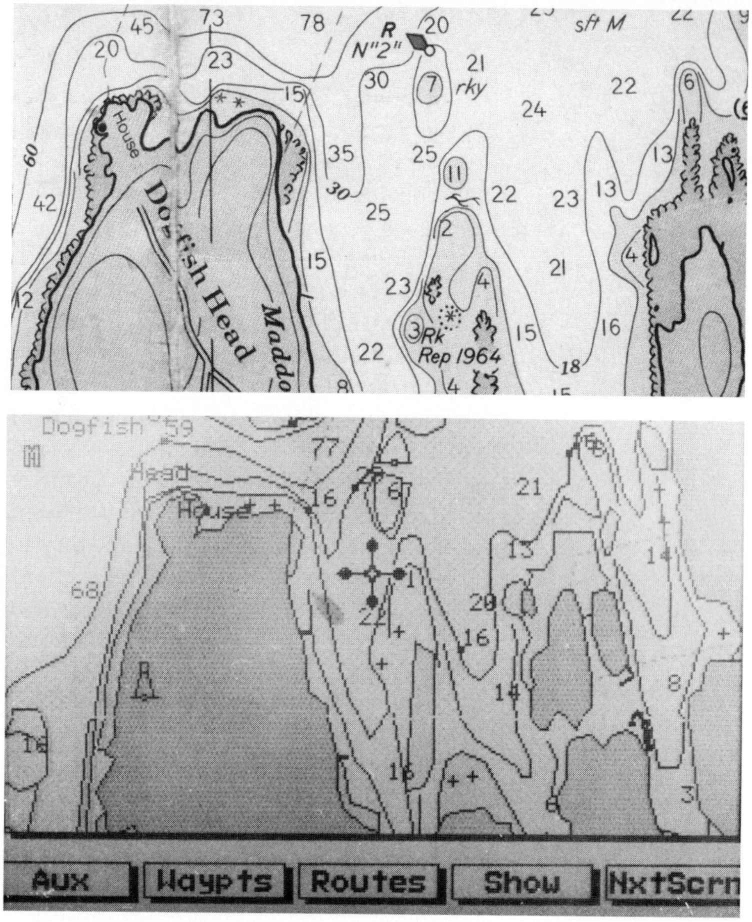

Contrast the detail on this paper chart (top), *which would be replicated on a raster chart, with the simplified vector version presented by this chart plotter* (above).

tronic photograph" of a paper chart that captures all its detail in Technicolor glory; and a *vector-based chart*, which is created by painstakingly copying the details of a paper chart and referencing every piece of information to a latitude and longitude grid. Depending on how much detail is captured on a vector-based chart, it may provide anything from a full representation (indistinguishable from a raster-based chart) to a thoroughly "stripped-out" version (no color, just the outline of any landforms and primary aids to navigation, with some spot soundings). Raster-based charts are much cheaper to produce, but require huge amounts of computer memory to store and operate, and they are not as versatile in use as vector-based charts. Several hydrographic offices have already converted their entire chart inventory into raster-based charts because of the ease of production. Vectorizing is lagging way behind; depending on where you intend to cruise, raster-based charts may be the only electronic way to go if you want inshore detail.

In terms of hardware, the choices are between dedicated chart plotters, laptops, and desktop computers. Chart plotters are by far the cheapest, but have small screens (no "peripheral vision"), limited memory (and, therefore, can use only vector charts, many of which are substantially stripped out, although we are currently seeing exponential rises in memory to the point at which some chart plotters will soon handle raster charts), and are often difficult to read in sunlight. However, chart plotters are generally fully marinized and so can be used in the cockpit, which makes them tremendously useful at times.

Modern laptops have the memory and computing capabilities to use both raster and vector charts and any software on the market. Being portable, they can be used for voyage-planning at home. Their screens are much larger than on a chart plotter, but are smaller than most desktop computers. They take up little room onboard; however, if they are adapted for GPS, Weatherfax, and Internet functions, they can end up with a spaghetti-like collection of wires connected to various peripherals. Unless marinized, laptops are vulnerable in the marine environment, especially when used in the cockpit.

Desktop computers have rarely been installed on cruising boats, but the trend is changing. They have much to recommend them: a clean installation, generally the greatest (and fastest) computing power and memory, and a large-enough screen to display significant chart areas at a large scale. However, the upfront cost is high and the computer will need to be marinized (particularly the hard drive, which must be mounted on a shockproof chassis). Unless a cockpit repeater (expensive) is installed, the computer's use will be limited to the navigation station.

Computers operate on DC power. However, unless specifically customized for a boat (as is a chart plotter), they come set up to run on AC. Unless the boat has a constantly running AC generator, a DC to AC inverter is needed to operate the computer. This creates a significant drain on the boat's DC system (considerably more than a chart plotter or a computer reconfigured to run directly from the DC system).

If the power goes down, you will soon find that no form of electronic charting is a substitute for carrying paper charts and understanding basic piloting skills (as well as having a decent navigation station in which to use them).

Finally, note that *the very versatility of electronic charts makes it possible to use them in all kinds of ways for which the original chart was never designed, and which can rapidly get you into trouble.* For example, electronic charts can be zoomed in and out to smaller and larger scales; this is an excellent feature, but it means that the chart can be zoomed in to a larger scale than justified by the accuracy with which the chart was made. You can enlarge a 50-yard-wide channel until it fills your whole screen and the GPS can situate you smack in the middle of it, but if the image has come from a 1:80,000 chart with a defined accuracy of ± (1½ × 80) = 120 meters, you could just as easily be 100 yards outside the channel on either side!

Yeoman Chart Plotters

An intermediate technology that I particularly like is represented by the Yeoman chart plotter. This references a paper chart (any paper chart, including my old 1830s British Admiralty surveys of Belize) to an electronic grid embedded in a plastic plotting board, and then enables most electronic charting functions to be carried out via the medium of a movable, hockey-puck-type device. In my opinion, it combines most of the benefits of paper charts with the technical wizardry of electronic navigation. If the electronics go down, you still have the chart.

Radar Navigation

Radar is a tremendously useful tool, particularly when visibility is poor (especially at night and in fog) but—as with all other tools—to use it safely and effectively, its limitations must be understood.

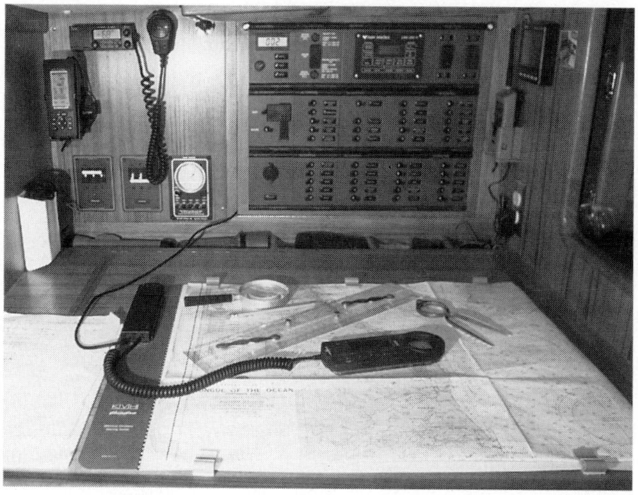

Above left: *Yeoman plotter installed in our navigation station. The unit is wired to a handheld GPS* (upper left) *with an external antenna. It is relatively simple to move it to the cockpit.* Above right: *An even more portable (and weather-resistant) version of the Yeoman plotter is this Sport version.*

Radar measures both the direction (the relative bearing) and the distance of stationary and moving objects. However, although distance measurements are quite precise, bearings are somewhat "fuzzy"—it is not safe to assume an accuracy of better than ± 5 degrees (in general, the larger the *radome*—the component that transmits the radar signal—the more accurate the bearing, but the more power the unit will consume). Even distance measurements have to be treated with some caution, inasmuch as you need to be certain that the radar is "seeing" what you think it is seeing. With large ships and other highly reflective objects, there is generally no question, but there frequently can be a considerable degree of ambiguity.

A radar, for example, may not see a gently sloping beach (or mud flats or a marsh), but it most likely will see a sand dune behind the beach (especially if it is covered in vegetation) or a row of houses. Similarly, it may not see a fringing coral reef or the lagoon behind it, but it will see the island inside the lagoon if it is covered in coconut trees. If the operator mistakes what is displayed on the radar screen for the water's edge, there is a good chance of the boat running aground.

Even if a shoreline is quite distinct and would usually show up clearly on radar, it may in fact be over the radar's horizon, which is dependent on the height of the antenna. The visible range can be calculated as with lighthouses, that is,

$$d = 1.17 \times (\sqrt{h1} + \sqrt{h2})$$

where

d = distance

h1 = height of the object

h2 = height of the radar antenna

Consider a low-lying cliff, over the radar's horizon, with a wide plateau behind it and then higher ground beyond; the radar will show an image that resembles the shoreline, but which, in fact, will be the higher ground inland.

For one reason or another, when looking at a coastline, the image on the screen frequently does not look much like the picture on the chart. It is extremely important that the operator does not superimpose his or her own presuppositions on the radar image: if there is any question about what is being seen, it must be frankly acknowledged that the picture is not clear, and other input should be sought for clarification. Confusion is often compounded by the fact that the radar is usually in a *heads-up* configuration; that is, the image is arranged around the boat's heading (which points to the top of the screen) rather than the *north-up* arrangement of the chart. Every time the boat changes its heading, the displayed objects rotate by the same amount around the radar screen (some radars can be set to operate in a north-up mode, which then more nearly re-creates the chart image).

If a radar is interfaced with a chartplotter, to help clarify things the chart image can be superimposed on the radar, or vice versa, but this generally introduces too much clutter or confusion to be useful. However, a target can be taken off the radar and transferred to the chartplotter to see what it is. This is useful not only for identifying a shoreline but also to determine, for example, if an object at sea is another vessel or a buoy or other aid to navigation.

As for objects at sea, angular metal things (e.g., ships, most buoys) provide an excellent *return* (i.e., stand out clearly on the screen); however, rounded wood and fiberglass things (e.g., most pleasure boats and many fishing

MISCELLANEOUS THOUGHTS ON BOAT ELECTRONICS

- Distinguish *interfaced* units from *integrated*. Interfaced are connected with wires. The individual units should stand alone (a failure of one will not bring down the others) but will share information and "talk" to each other. Integrated units use a common processor and normally come in one box. A failure of one component may shut down the system. "Daisy-chained" units are independent units, which might be mistaken for interfaced, but which in fact are integrated in a manner in which a failure can cause multiple displays to crash.
- The more dependent you are on electronic navigation, the more important it is to have independent, redundant systems (even if interfaced to talk to one another) so that a failure of one will not bring down the others.
- Nowadays, given that most units talk to one another, generally the only reason to buy all your electronics from one manufacturer is aesthetics. Given the rate at which things change, at different times different manufacturers are stronger in one product than another. Often the best system is one in which units from more than one manufacturer are mixed.
- Some chartplotters can share information with computers, which enables a laptop to be used at home to establish waypoints, routes, and so on, and then download or upload them to the chartplotter on the boat, while others can't.
- Given the rate at which computers and software evolve, it is probably better to spend your money replacing a cheap computer every few years than to invest in an expensive waterproof computer that you will then be unwilling to upgrade.
- Touch screens are hard to use when a boat is bouncing around, especially if it is a small screen with small menus and buttons.
- LCD screens are flat and easy to mount in a cockpit but provide poor viewing from the side; CRT screens are deep and often not easy to mount in a cockpit, but they provide excellent viewing from the side.
- Windows-based navigation systems can lock up at the most inopportune time, just like the PC at home!

boats around the world) do not. A strong return from one object may completely mask a weak return from another one nearby. Small vessels rising and falling on large waves come and go on the screen, as will any vessel if your boat is rolling wildly with the antenna pointing alternately at the sky and the nearby sea surface.

With these thoughts in mind, we can look at radar's tremendous strengths from the point of view of a small-boat sailor. Probably the greatest strength is its ability to warn of approaching ships, thereby assisting in collision avoidance. Depending on the height of the antenna and the power of the unit, a radar can easily detect ships at 12 miles. Even if a ship is on a head-on collision course with a combined speed of both vessels at 40 knots, the 12-mile range provides eighteen minutes of advance warning. (Scary, huh! The world's first high-speed container ships, with a designed cruising speed of 40 knots, are currently under construction.) Radars include a *guard zone* that can be programmed to sound an alarm whenever something is detected inside the zone. This is a tremendous boon on a short-handed vessel where watchkeeping may not be as good as is desirable.

All modern radars include a *variable range marker* (VRM) and an *electronic bearing line* (EBL) that can be deployed to give the range

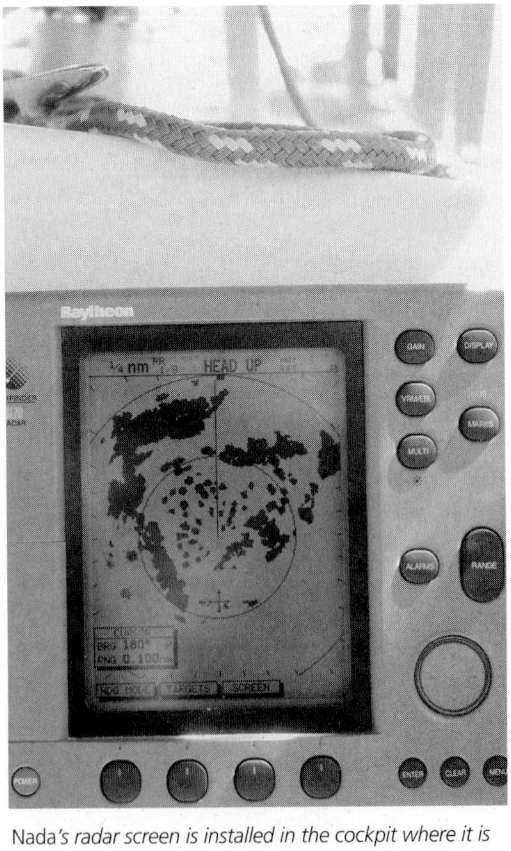

Nada's radar screen is installed in the cockpit where it is clearly visible from the helm and watchkeeping positions. It is more useful here than in the navigation station.

A radar may not see . . .

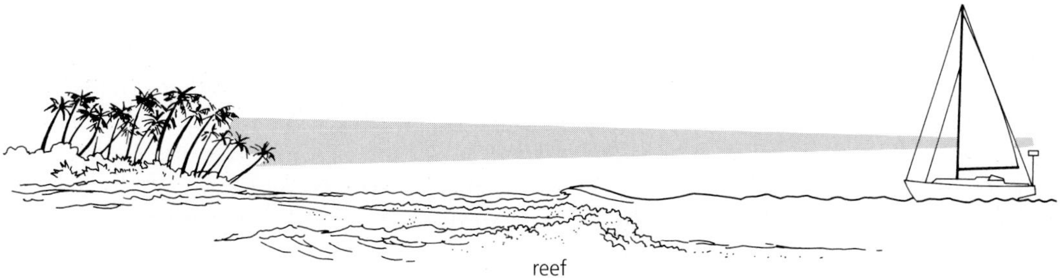

1 a fringing barrier reef

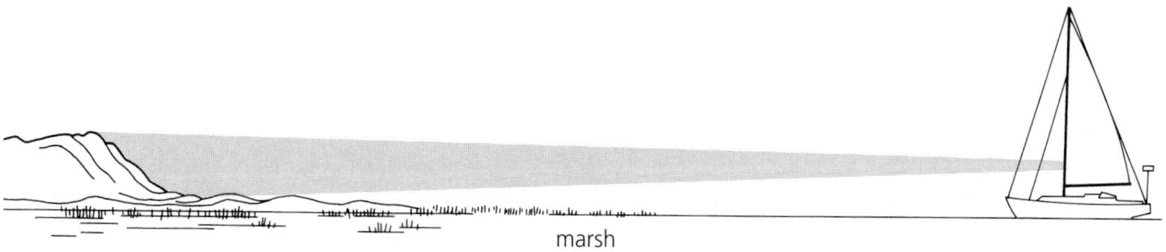

2 low-lying sand dunes or marsh

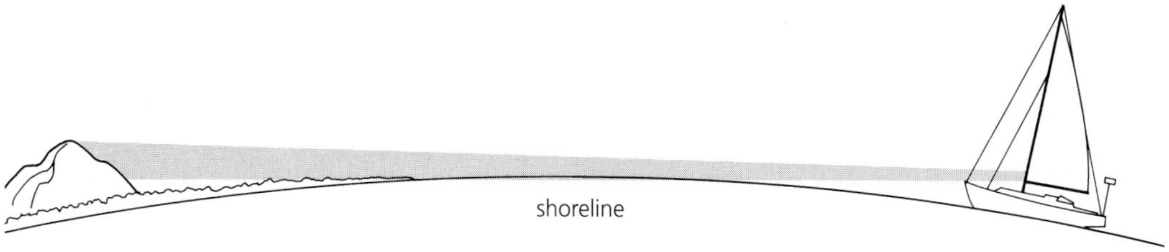

3 a shoreline over its horizon

and relative bearing of an approaching ship. To determine whether a ship is on a collision course, this bearing is monitored over time, either by writing it down or marking the ship's changing position on the radar screen with a grease pencil to establish a *relative motion line* (RML). If the bearing does not change, the ship is on a collision course (the grease marks on the screen also line up in a straight line pointed at the center of the screen). It is time to get on the radio and/or take avoidance action.

The radar is also a powerful position-fixing tool when in radar range of known objects (you must be certain that you know what is returning the radar image). The most accurate methodology involves getting the range of two known objects, setting a pair of compasses to the appropriate distance for each, and then drawing a circle on the chart around each object at its range. The boat's position is at the crossing point of the two circles, which is known as a crossed *circle of position* (COP). If possible, its accuracy should be corroborated with a third COP taken from another known object.

A less accurate position can be determined by taking the range and bearing of a single known object. In this case, the bearing (which, if the radar is in the normal heads-up mode, is a relative bearing between the object and the ship) is converted to a magnetic or true bearing, and then plotted on the chart as an LOP (if the radar is in north-up mode, the bearing is already a magnetic bearing). The range from the object is measured along the LOP to get a fix. However, given the somewhat inaccurate nature of radar bearings, this is not as reliable as crossed COPs. Accuracy is improved if a good-quality hand-bearing compass can be used to measure the bearing for the LOP rather than the radar; however, the object must be in view.

To convert a relative bearing to magnetic or true, the relative bearing is added to the ship's heading to give a compass heading (C), which is then corrected for deviation and variation as usual. When the two bearings are added, if the total comes to more than 360 degrees, simply subtract 360 degrees before making the corrections. For example, for a relative bearing of 075 degrees with the boat heading 335 C, the total bearing is 335 + 075 = 410 degrees. The com-

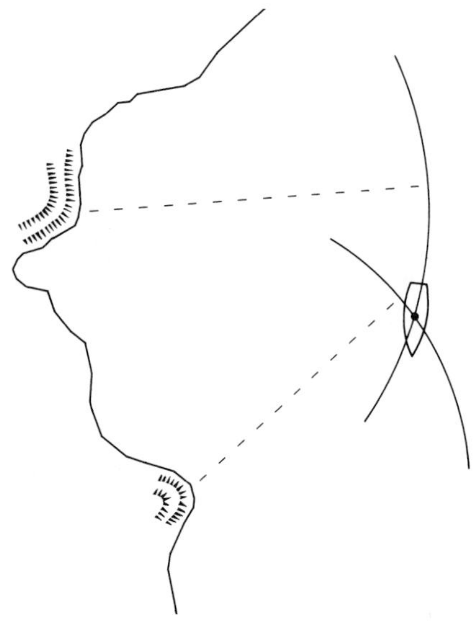

Position-fixing with radar-derived COPs—here a couple of radar-distinct rocky headlands.

pass bearing of the object is 410 – 360 = 050 C. This compass bearing now has to be corrected for deviation, if any, to get a magnetic bearing (M), and then corrected for variation if it is to be plotted as a true bearing (T).

Any fix should be double-checked for accuracy by reference to the depth sounder and the soundings on the chart. Bowditch has this to say: "When a disparity exists between the charted depth at the fix and the recorded sounding, the navigator should assume that the disparity has been caused by fix inaccuracy. . . . When there is consistent disparity (over a number of fixes), the navigator should assume that he or she does not know the ship's position with sufficient accuracy to proceed safely."

In addition to collision avoidance and position fixing, we have found that another particularly useful function of a radar is its ability to keep us in center channel when passing through a canal on a dark night; for example, the "Ditch" (the Intracoastal Waterway in the U.S.) or the Mississippi Gulf Outlet Canal between New Orleans and the Gulf of Mexico.

As noted above, many radars can be interfaced with onboard electronics and even chart plotters. This enables your boat's position, course, and speed to be displayed on the radar screen and the course of a target vessel to be shown in relative or true degrees. It may be possible to show your boat's position on an electronic chart, overlaid with the radar image. In short, the capabilities may be far beyond the basics outlined herein. Any operator is well advised to make a thorough study of the manual.

Finally, the Inland Navigational Rules (see the next section) require that there be someone onboard who knows how to use a radar if there is one, and also require that it be used day and night. In practice, most sailboats are not going to keep the radar on all the time; it is too big a drain on the DC system (generally, at least 2 to 3 amps). Nevertheless, I point out this requirement simply because the courts have upheld the rule when confronted with accidents that could have been prevented by proper use of an available radar. If you have one, you should know how to use it and use it when prudence warrants it.

RULES OF THE ROAD

For U.S. waters, rules of the road for boats are derived from two sources: the International Regulations for Preventing Collisions at Sea (better known as COLREGS) and the Inland Navigational Rules. The line of demarcation between the two is marked (in magenta) on coastal charts. In many U.S. states, the line is placed at the mouth of rivers and large bays; in others (notably New England, the lower Florida Keys, and Puget Sound), the international regulations apply inshore as well as offshore and, therefore, there is no line of demarcation. Outside the United States, the COLREGS apply almost everywhere.

In practice, the two sets of rules are very similar. The principal difference is in the manner in which nearby vessels are alerted to each other's maneuvers. The inland rules require that a prior warning be given and the maneuver assented to before it is made; the international rules require that the maneuvering signal be given during the course of the maneuver; there is no assent process. Boats longer than 39 feet (12 m) are required by law to have a copy of the regulations onboard. In the U.S., the full set of rules can be obtained from marine bookstores or via online ordering from the Government Printing Office (GPO) at *http://orders.access.gpo.gov/sudocs/sale/prf/prf.html* (in the query box enter "COLREGS"—and allow four to six weeks for delivery).

Basic Rules

Clearly, the primary purpose of the COLREGS is to prevent collisions. To this end, there are certain general requirements that could be considered common sense: to exercise "good seamanship"; to "pay due regard" to special circumstances that might necessitate a departure from the rules (e.g., if another boat is not complying with the rules); to maintain a constant lookout; and to "proceed at a safe speed so that the vessel can take proper and effective action to avoid collision and be stopped within a distance appropriate to the prevailing circumstances and conditions."

As discussed previously, a risk of collision exists any time the relative bearing between two vessels does not change. Beyond this, the rules state, "if there is any doubt (as to whether a risk of collision exists), such risk shall be deemed to exist."

In the event of a risk of collision, the rules generally define one vessel as the *stand-on vessel* (formerly the *privileged* vessel). This boat must maintain its course and speed except when the other boat, the *give-way vessel* (formerly the *burdened* vessel) doesn't get out of the way. Sometimes both boats are give-way vessels; for example, when two powerboats are heading straight for each other in open water.

The give-way boat should always make a substantial enough course change (generally 20 degrees or more) for it to be clearly evident to the stand-on vessel. A turn is usually made to starboard, but not if it takes the boat into the path of the other vessel or creates other hazards. In the absence of other considerations:

- A sailboat on port tack (the wind is coming over the port side and the boom is off to starboard) gives way to a sailboat on starboard tack (the wind is coming over the starboard side and the boom is off to port). See A on page 378.
- When on the same tack, a sailboat to windward gives way to a sailboat to leeward. See B.
- A sailboat under power (including one motor sailing) gives way to a sailboat under sail.
- Sailboats give way to fishing boats engaged in fishing.
- Powerboats give way to sailboats.
- In narrow channels, boats stay as close to the starboard side of the channel as is practicable.
- In narrow channels and traffic-separation zones where large boats are constrained in their maneuverability or by draft, small boats (both sail and power) give way to large boats.
- Moving boats give way to stopped boats.
- All overtaking boats give way to those being overtaken. See C.

Rules of the Road.

A risk of collision exists any time the relative bearing between two boats is unchanging.

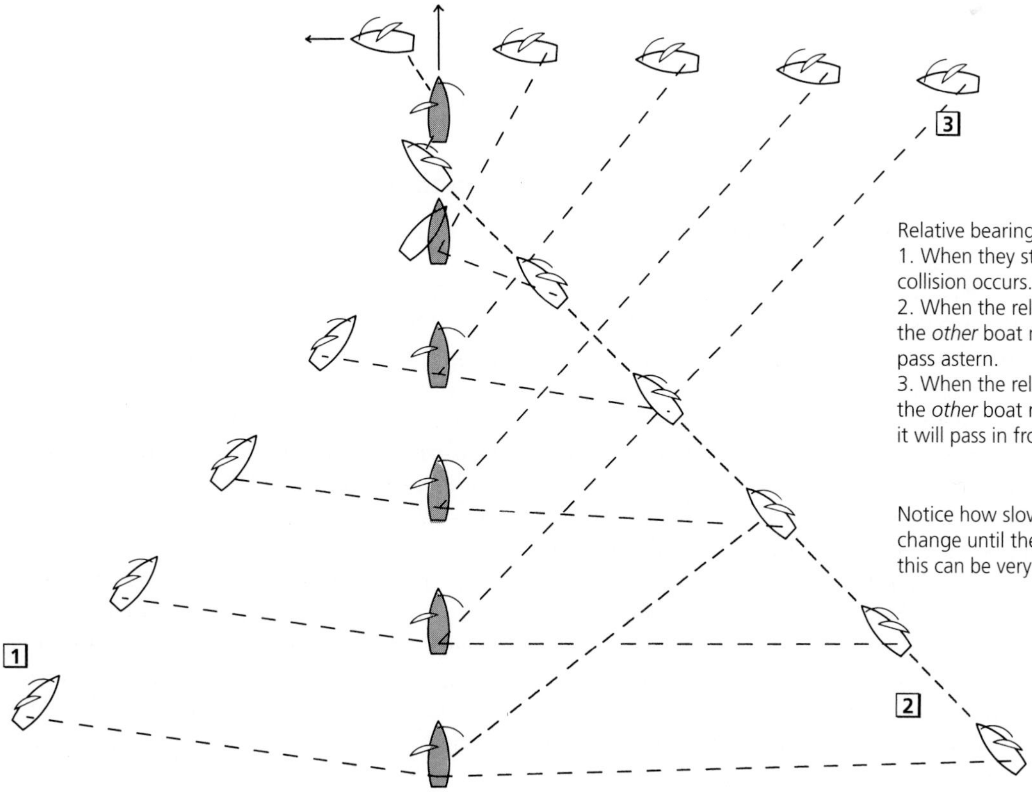

Relative bearings:
1. When they stay the same, a collision occurs.
2. When the relative bearing of the *other* boat moves *aft*, it will pass astern.
3. When the relative bearing of the *other* boat moves *forward*, it will pass in front.

Notice how slowly the relative bearings change until the boats get quite close—this can be very disconcerting in real life!

Rules of the Road. A. A sailboat on port tack gives way to one on starboard. B. When both are on the same tack, a sailboat to windward gives way to one to leeward. C. An overtaking boat always gives way to one being overtaken.

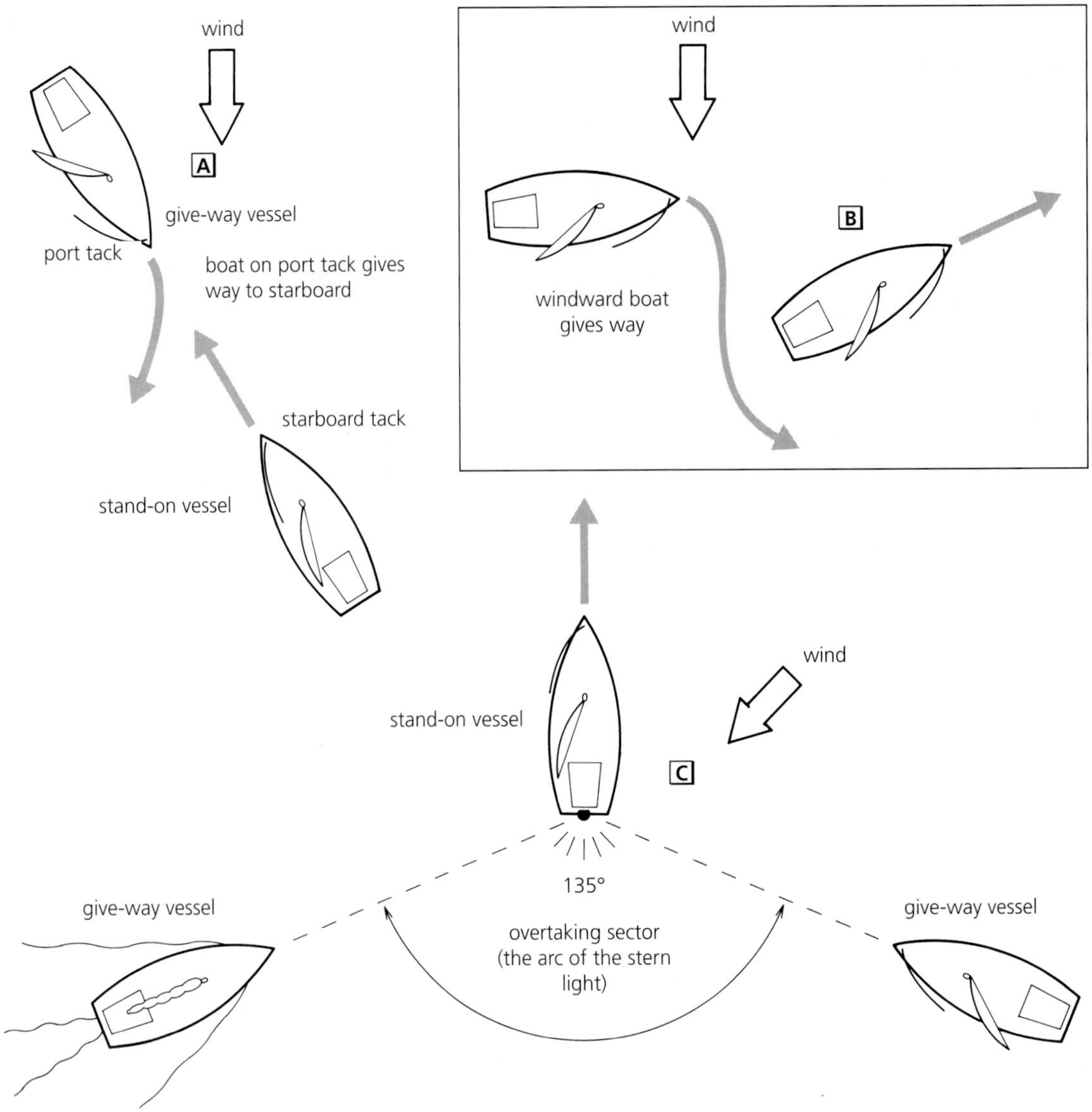

Overtaking is defined in terms of the arc of a vessel's sternlight (explained later in this section). If you are approaching another vessel and are within this arc (67½ degrees either side of the stern), you are deemed to be overtaking. If you are unsure about whether this is the case, you must assume it is.

Of course, these rules are all well and good as long as the other boat is playing by the same rules; however, this is not always the case. For example, motoring down the lower reaches of the Mississippi River one night, trying to keep to the starboard side of the channel, we encountered numerous boats coming up in the other direction on both sides of the channel. At one point, we were faced with a potential collision. We turned to starboard, as prescribed by the rules, to get even farther out of the main channel. The advancing boat—a Gulf of Mexico oilfield crew boat, many of which are skippered by "cowboys" who pay little attention to the Rules of the Road—turned to port and left us no room to maneuver. We headed for the bank and ran into a submerged pile of rocks, which was at least preferable to a collision.

Sound (and Light) Signals

Boats under 39 feet (12 m) in length are not required to have a whistle or bell onboard, but must be able to make "an efficient sound signal." On boats more than 39 feet (12 m) in length, a whistle and bell are required, and more than 328 feet (100 m), a gong is also mandated. The rules call for a *real* bell and gong to be carried (not just an electronic means of making these sounds). On boats from 39 to 66 feet (12—20 m) in length, the mouth of the bell must be at least 7.9 inches (200 mm) wide and the striker must weigh at least 3 percent of the weight of the bell! In the U.S., to make yourself legal, even if you never use it, buy an approved bell; it is something the USCG checks during inspections. Whistles or similar sound-making devices on boats under 66 feet (20 m) must be audible for a half mile. Most electric horns and air-powered horns with replaceable canisters fulfill these requirements.

Both the inland rules and COLREGS use the same sound signals, but with some subtle differences. Under COLREGS, one short blast means "I am altering my course to starboard." Under the inland rules, it means "I intend to leave you on my starboard side." In other words, under the inland rules there may not actually be a change in course, *but the signal must still be made* "when power-driven vessels are in sight of one another and meeting or crossing at a distance within half a mile of each other." Under both rules, three short blasts means "I am operating astern propulsion," and five short blasts is the danger signal. The inland rules require that these signals be given to indicate an *intent* that cannot actually be carried out until the same signal is repeated by the other vessel to show *assent*, whereas the COLREGS (with one exception explained later in this section) say you can continue with your maneuver, but must give the appropriate sound signal at the same time; no assent is required. At night, the sound signals are supplemented with similar light flashes (one flash for a turn to starboard, two for port, three for backing down, and five for the danger signal).

Overtaking

Under the inland regulations, no powerboat (or sailboat under power) should overtake another without a prescribed exchange of signals. Sailboats under sail are not required to give signals at any time except in fog (see the next section); powerboats can dispense with the signals if the boats involved can agree on a specific maneuver over the radio. The overtaking vessel sounds one short whistle blast if it intends to overtake to starboard of the other vessel, and two short whistle blasts if it intends to overtake to port (supplemented with one or two short flashes, as appropriate, on a light at night). The vessel being overtaken gives assent by repeating the signal; disagreement is shown with five short blasts (both signals are supplemented by light flashes at night). When there is disagreement, both vessels stop until it is resolved.

Turning

Under COLREGS, *in narrow channels* the single or double (starboard or port) short blasts described previously are both preceded by two long blasts. The assent signal (from the other vessel) consists of a long blast followed by a short blast followed by a long blast followed by a short blast. The dissent signal is five short blasts. *This is the only time COLREGS requires the intent/assent approach.*

In inland waters, the same intent/assent procedure as for overtaking is mandated when making turns and other maneuvers; under COLREGS, a vessel simply makes its maneuver, giving the appropriate sound signal in the process (one blast for turning to port, two to starboard, and three when backing down, with no requirement for an assent signal before the maneuver is made).

In inland waters, a vessel approaching a blind turn in a river or canal sounds one long blast. Any vessel approaching from the other side responds with the same signal.

Meeting Head On

With both the inland regulations and COLREGS, the basic procedure when powerboats meet head on (including sailboats under power or motor sailing) is to pass port to port, and to make a turn to starboard if necessary to accomplish this. However, if both boats are already set to pass clear of each other starboard to starboard, then both should maintain speed and course. In inland waters, if powerboats are within a half-mile of one another and any turns are made, the same intent/assent procedure should be used as described previously. Under COLREGS, it is only necessary to give the appropriate sound signal if a turn is made or when backing down.

Crossing

With both the inland regulations and COLREGS, in a crossing situation involving powerboats, *the vessel that has the other one on its starboard side is the give-way vessel and must keep out of the way*. The starboard side is defined from dead ahead to 22½ degrees abaft the beam (the same arc as a sidelight; explained later in this section), at which point you get into the overtaking sector (explained previously).

If the give-way vessel has to maneuver, in inland waters it goes through the same intent/assent procedure as with other maneuvers; under COLREGS, it simply gives the appropriate signal as it makes the maneuver. With sailboats, as discussed previously, the boat on port tack gives way to the boat on starboard tack; if both are on the same tack, the one to windward gives way. However, if there is uncertainty as to what tack the other boat is on, a boat on port tack gives way to a boat to windward (i.e., the boat to windward is presumed to be on starboard tack).

Bridges

The signal for requesting a bridge to be opened (in the absence of VHF contact) is one

Overtaking, meeting, and crossing situations (see also top, next page), with sound signals.

Overtaking Signals

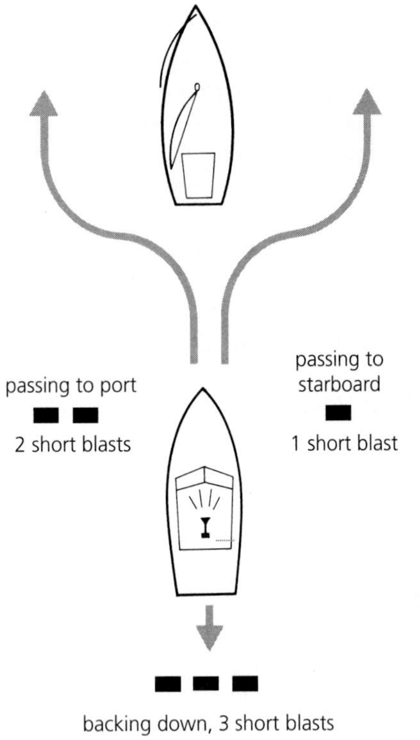

COLREGS: the overtaking boat gives the signal as it makes the maneuver.

Inland regulations: the vessel being overtaken must assent by repeating the signal. Dissent is indicated by 5 short blasts.

Overtaking in a *Narrow* Channel (the only time COLREGS requires the assent signal)

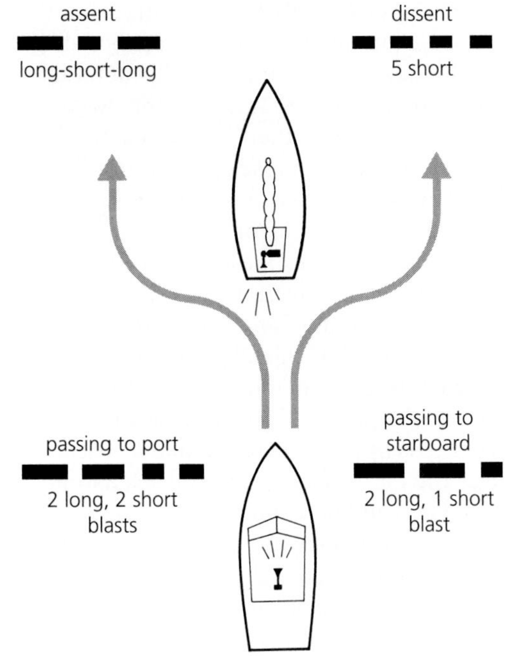

COLREGS: 1. Overtaking vessel gives 2 long blasts followed by the appropriate maneuvering signal. 2. Vessel being overtaken indicates assent a long-short-long blast, or dissent by 5 short blasts.

Inland Regulations: 1. Overtaking vessel gives 2 short blasts to indicate it will pass to port. 2. Vessel being overtaken indicates assent by repeating the signal or dissent by 5 short blasts.

Meeting

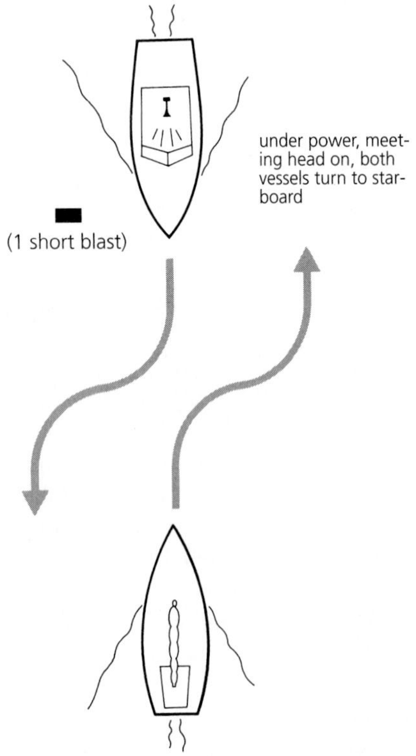

Crossing

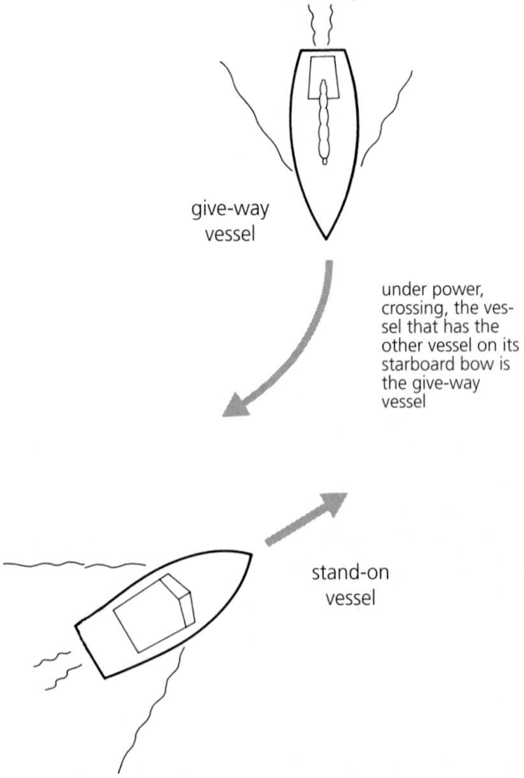

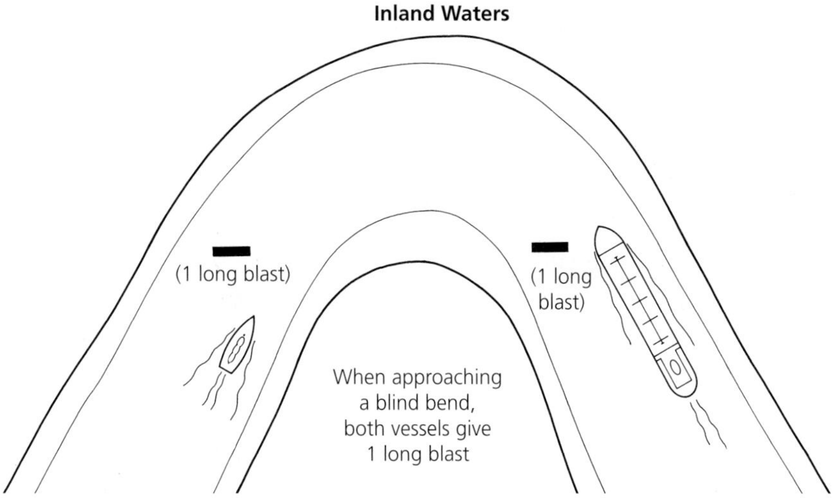

long blast followed by a short blast. The bridgetender responds with the same signal if the bridge is to be opened immediately and with five short blasts if there will be a delay.

Fog Signals

In fog and restricted visibility, remember the COLREGS requirement that a boat be operated at a "safe speed" such that the boat "can take proper and effective action to avoid collision and be stopped within a distance appropriate to the prevailing circumstances and conditions." If a radar is onboard, *it must be used.* If it is not used and you are involved in an accident with a boat without radar, your radar will weigh heavily against you. A watch must be maintained at all times.

Underway, the following signals must be made at intervals of two minutes or less:

- powerboats: one long blast
- sailboats, fishing boats, vessels engaged in pushing or towing, and boats not under command or restricted in their ability to maneuver: one long blast followed by two short blasts (this puts a sailboat in the same category as a supertanker in restricted waters!)
- vessels being towed: one long blast followed by three short blasts to be sounded, when possible, immediately after the signal given by the towing vessel
- powerboats that are underway, but have stopped: two long blasts

In practice, the puny signals from a sailboat are usually inaudible to most powerboats, and the boat itself may be nearly invisible on a ship's radar. It behooves the sailboat operator to keep out of recognized shipping lanes, to take it slowly, to put a watch on the bow (away from the noise of any onboard engine), to keep an ear cocked for the foghorns on other vessels, and to assume if a foghorn is heard that the other vessel quite likely has no idea of your existence.

An anchored boat (or one that is aground) under 39 feet (12 m) merely has to make "some efficient sound signal" at intervals of two minutes or less. From 39 to 328 feet (12–100 m) in boat length, an anchored boat must ring a bell

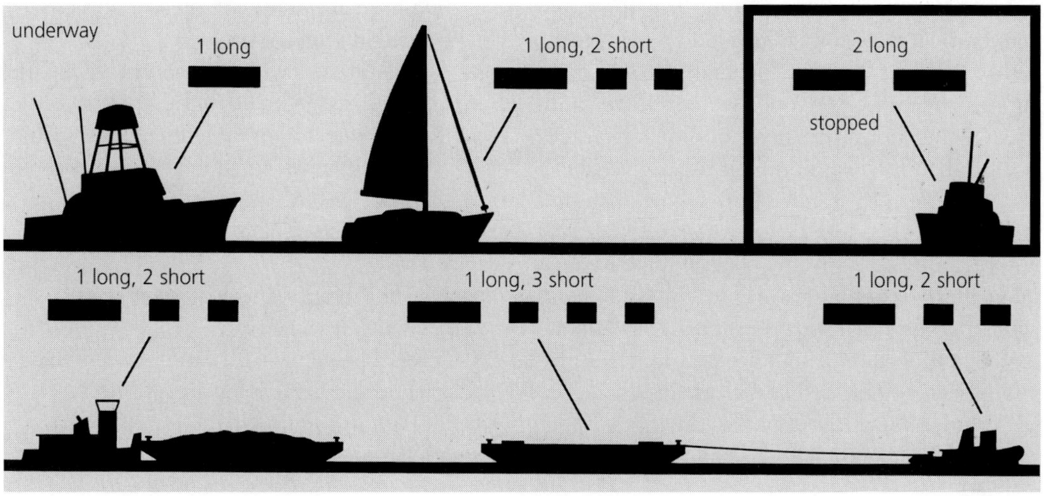

Fog signals, to be given at least every two minutes.

rapidly up forward for five seconds every minute; a boat over 328 feet (100 m) adds a gong aft. In addition, a short-long-short fog signal may be sounded at regular intervals. A vessel under 328 feet (100 m) that is aground sounds three distinct bell strokes, followed by ringing of the bell rapidly for five seconds every minute; a boat over 328 feet (100 m) in length adds a gong aft. In addition, a short-short-long-short, short-short-long, or short-short-short-long signal may be sounded at regular intervals.

Navigation Lights

Navigation lights are the last piece of the basic piloting and navigation picture. If you are contemplating night passages, it is important to learn the significance of all the basic light patterns, and, ideally, the more esoteric ones (I confess that after decades of night passages, I still have to reach for a reference chart once in a while). It is only by understanding these lights that you can figure out in what direction a ship is moving or whether, for example, a tug has a near-invisible barge on a half-mile-long tow. We almost ran between an oceangoing tug and its tow one stormy night in the middle of the Gulf of Mexico; it was a terrifying experience. I don't think they ever knew we were there. Had we been dismasted by the cable or run down by the barge, I doubt they would have noticed.

Under both COLREGS and inland regulations, sailboats and powerboats with a maximum speed of less than 7 knots that are less than 23 feet (7 m) in length need only show an all-around white light (e.g., a flashlight). Powerboats less than 23 feet with a maximum speed of more than 7 knots require the all-around white light to be supplemented with sidelights. Note that this applies to just about any inflatable with an outboard motor that is capable of planing; this rule is frequently violated. Over 23 feet, the basic requirement is to show a red light to port, a green light to starboard, and a white light astern. These lights all have clearly defined sectors: the red and green lights show from the centerline forward to a little abaft the beam on their respective sides; the white stern light shows from a little abaft the beam on both sides all the way aft. To impart information about specific boats and their activities, these basic lights are supplemented by a white masthead light (*the steaming light*) or bow lights (which have a sector equal to the combined sector of the red and green lights) and a variety of other colored and flashing lights. The principal arrangements are as follows:

- Sailboats over 23 feet (7 m) *under sail*: red and green bow lights and a stern light. Typically, the red and green lights are on the bow pulpit in a single fixture; the stern light is on the stern pulpit. However, the bow lights may be mounted as separate fixtures, either on the pulpit or on the sides of the cabintop (the latter is preferred; the combined lights on the pulpit are notorious for getting corroded and failing or else getting damaged by sails). The stern light should be mounted so that it does not reflect off the stern pulpit (the reflection makes it difficult to see anything behind you). Sometimes all three lights are combined in a masthead tricolor fixture (on sailboats under 66 ft./20 m in length).
- Powerboats (including sailboats under power) to 164 feet (50 m) in length: the three basic lights (red and green bow lights and stern light) are supplemented with a white steaming light, which has an arc equal to the total arc of the red and green lights and is mounted above them; that is, any time either the red or green is in sight, you will see a white light above it.
- Ships more than 164 feet (50 m) in length have two steaming lights—one at the bow and one toward the stern—both with an arc equal to the total arc of the red and green lights. The bow light is always lower than the stern light. *This is the single most useful tool for determining the direction of a ship at night*: when you draw an imaginary line from the higher light to the lower light, it shows you the direction of travel of the ship relative to your boat. If the horizontal distance between the two lights increases, the ship is turning away from you; if the distance decreases, it is turning toward you. If the two lights are in line (one above the other), the ship is coming directly at you.
- All vessels use a white all-around light at the masthead as an anchor light. Ships more than 164 feet (50 m) in length use two white all-around lights (with the aft one lower than the forward one). Ships over 328 feet (100 m) must also illuminate their decks.

Now for those tugboats and barges:

- A vessel being towed astern (total length of towline and barge is less than 657 ft./200 m): in addition to the normal red and green bow lights and *(continued page 386)*

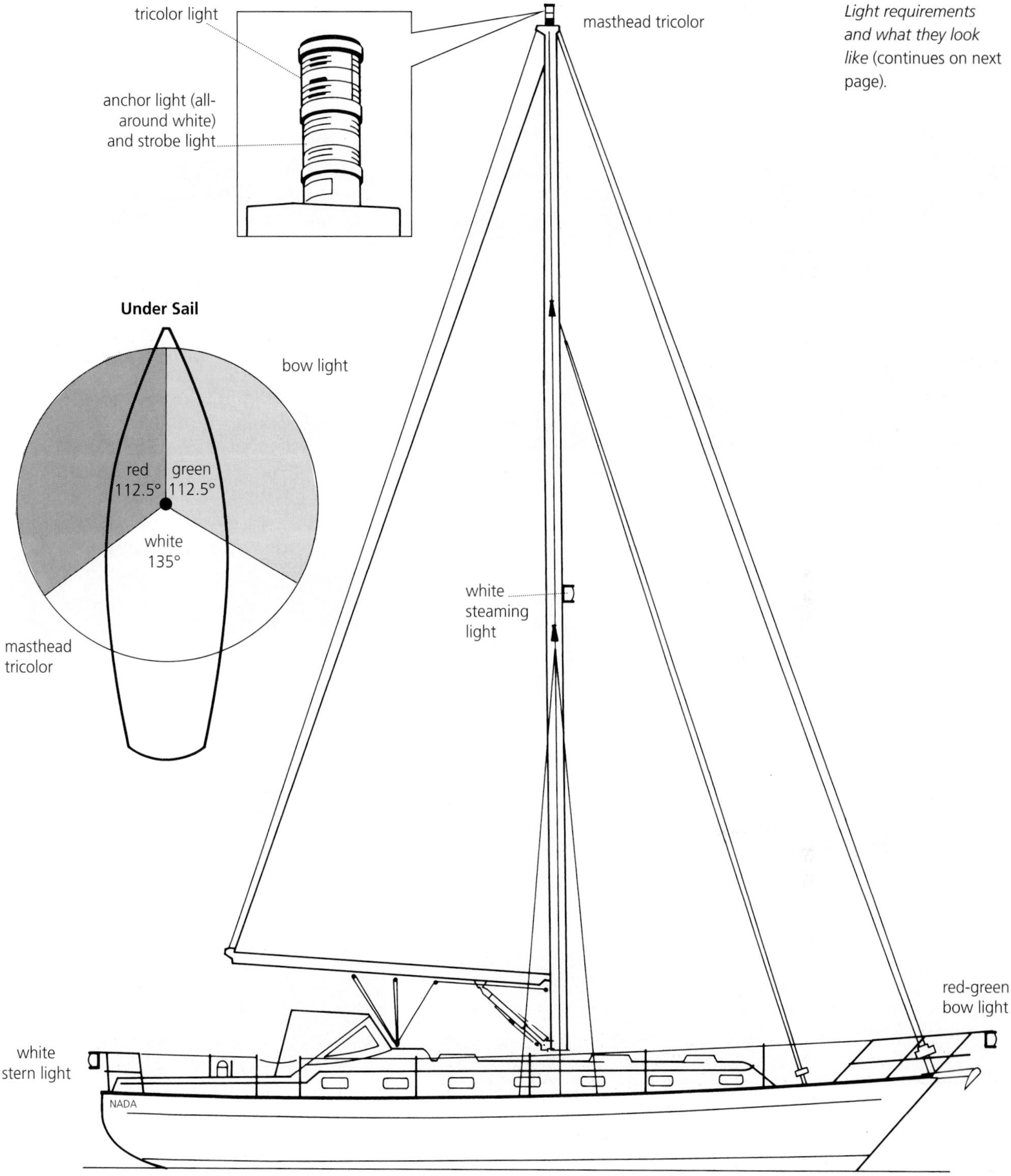

Light requirements and what they look like (continues on next page).

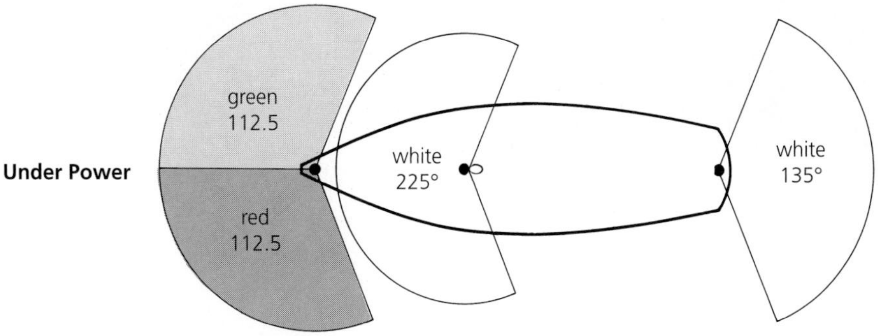

Note: The steaming light is on a separate switch. This way, if the tricolor goes out, we can use the bow and stern light under sail as a backup.

Light requirements and what they look like (continued).

Lights for Power-Driven Vessels Under Way

starboard side view bow stern

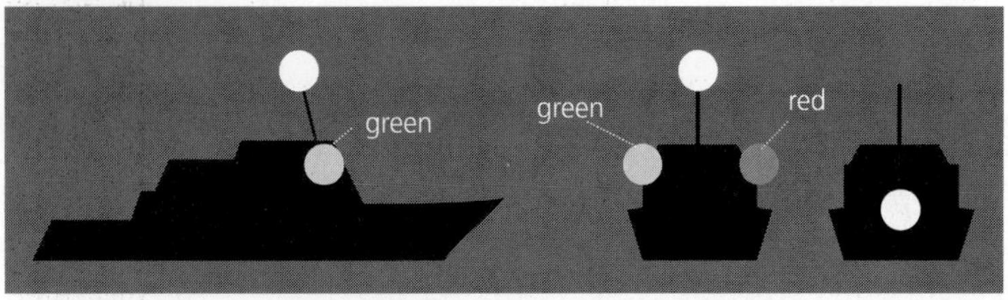

Under 164 ft. (50 m), masthead light, sidelights, and sternlight.

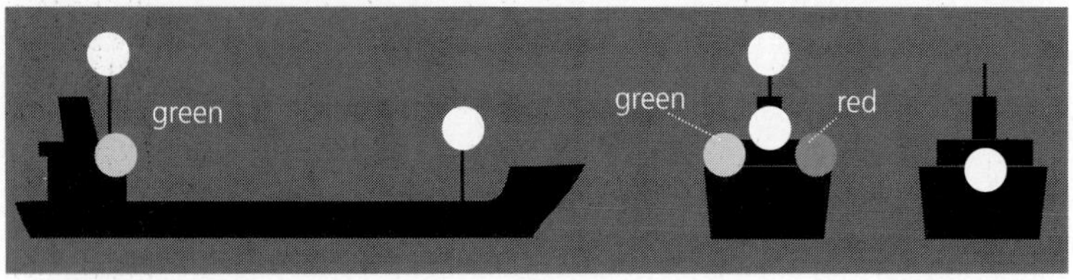

Over 164 ft. (50 m).

Lights When Towing

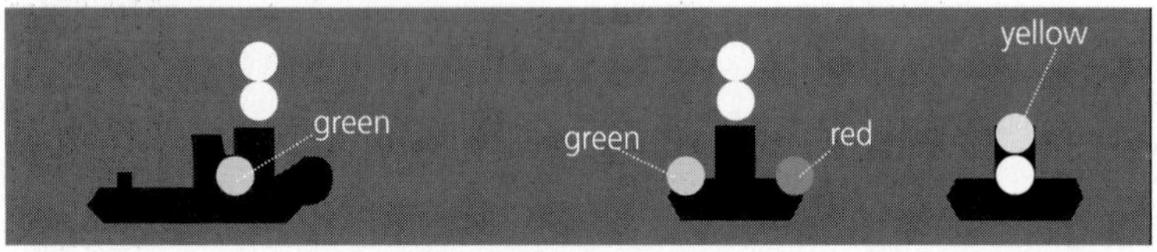

Under 164 ft. (50 m), two white steaming lights and towing light aft (yellow over white).

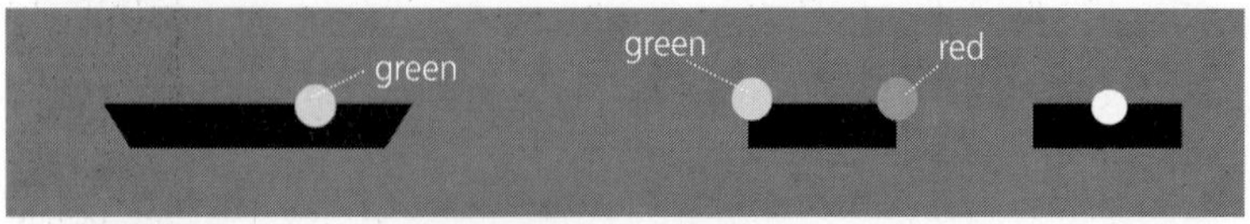

Vessel being towed shows sidelights and sternlight.

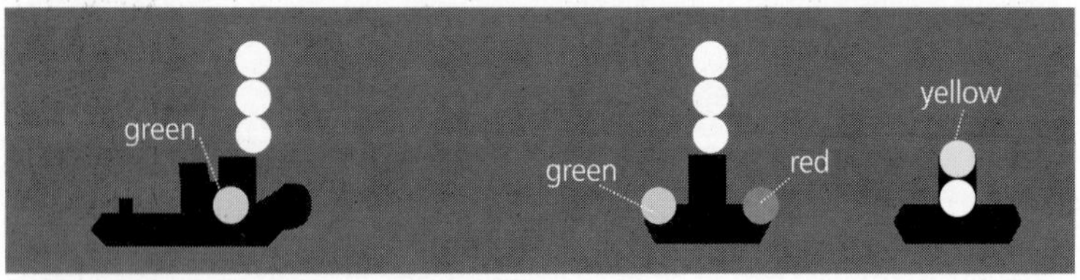

If tow is over 657 ft. (200 m), three steaming lights.

Lights When Pushing

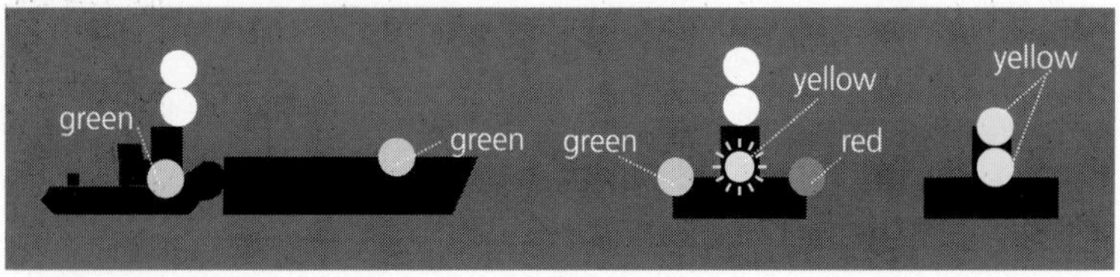

In inland waters only, the lights are as shown, with the yellow bow light flashing. In international waters, there is no yellow bow light, and the two yellow stern lights are replaced by a white stern light.

Deciphering Lights at Night

If you see this at night . . .

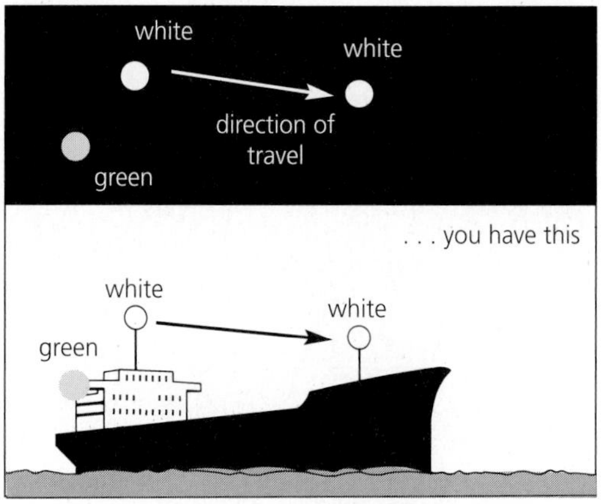

If you see this at night . . .

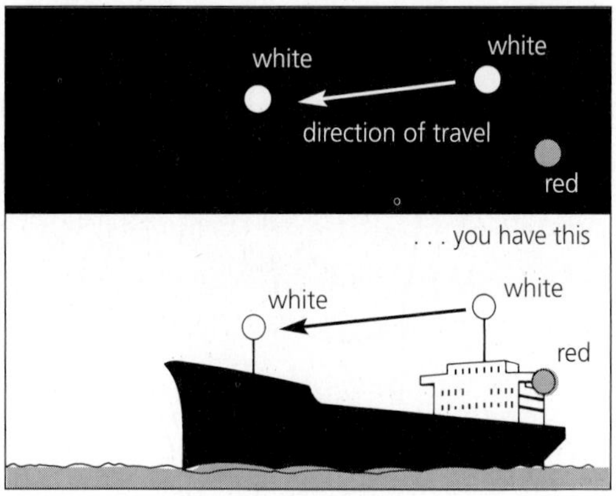

If the two white lights are aligned . . .

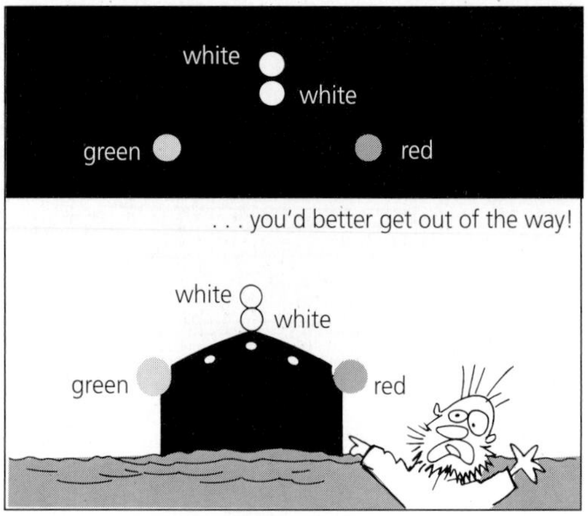

Some Special Lights

Fishing Vessels. Note: A fishing vessel whose gear extends more than 492.5 ft. (150 m) may show a white light in the direction of the gear.

starboard side view bow stern

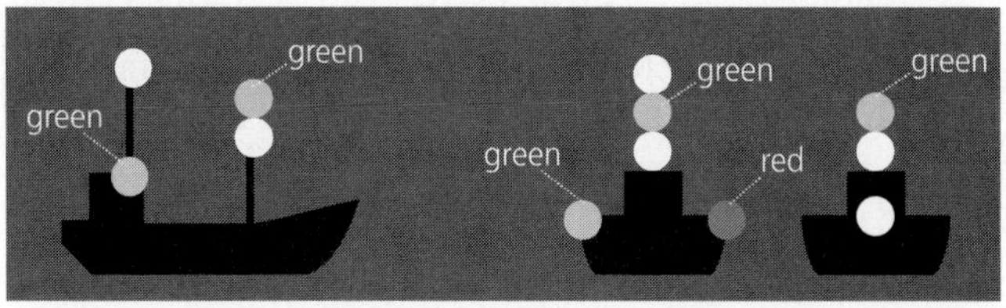

Trawling vessel under 164 ft. (50 m) shows all-round green over white lights (not shown); vessels over 164 ft. show additional white steaming light over green (as shown).

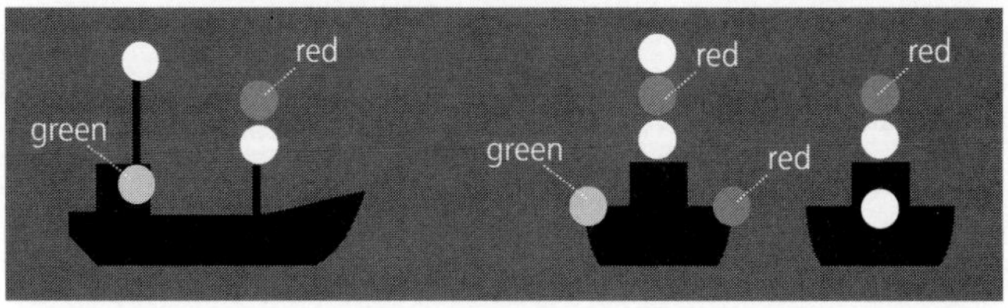

Other fishing vessels (not trawling) under 164 ft. (50 m) show all-round red over white lights (not shown); vessels over 164 ft. show additional white steaming light (as shown).

Pilot Vessels on Duty and Underway

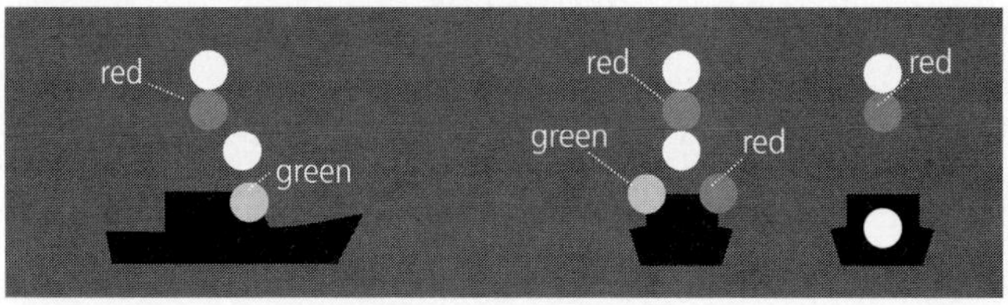

Show all-round white over red vertical lights plus normal anchor or navigation lights.

Vessels over 164 ft. (50 m) Constrained by Draft

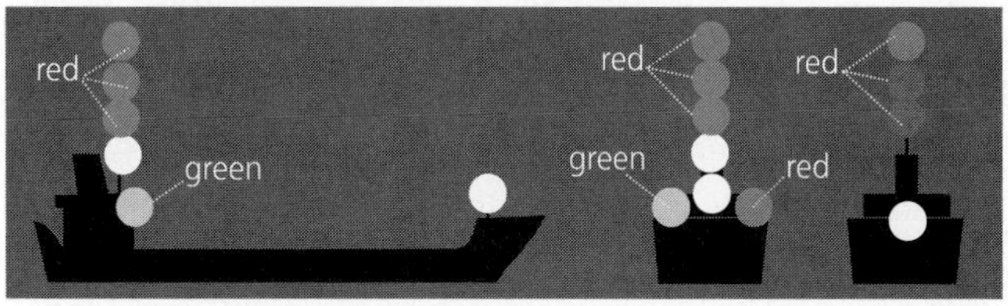

Vessels constrained by draft (eg. a vessel confined to the center of a channel) show three vertical all-round red lights as well as normal navigation lights.

Vessels Not Under Command (eg. with mechanical or steering break-down) and Not Underway

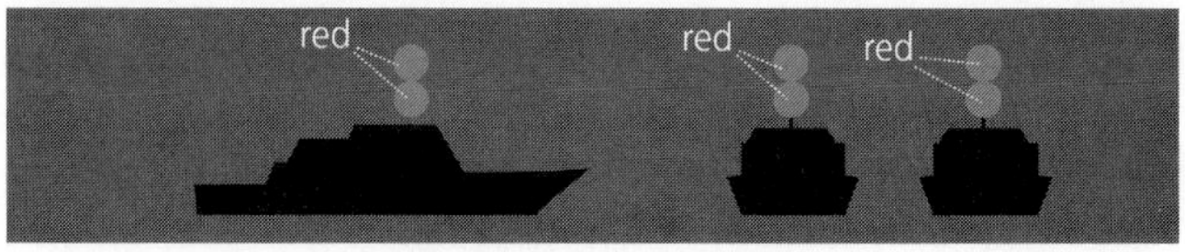

Two clearly visible all-round red lights. Note: although it is unlikely that a vessel not under command would be using her engines, she would, if making way, show navigation lights as well as NUC lights.

(continued from page 382) a stern light, the tugboat will have two steaming lights—one vertically above the other and a yellow stern light above the white stern light. The barge will have the typical bow and stern lights, with no steaming light (i.e., the same lights as a sailboat under sail—always look around to see if these lights are preceded by tugboat lights!).

- A vessel being towed astern (total length of towline and barge is more than 657 ft./200 m): in addition to the typical red and green bow lights and a stern light, the tugboat will have three steaming lights in a vertical line, plus the additional yellow stern light. The barge(s) will have the usual bow and stern lights, with no steaming light (i.e., the same lights as a sailboat under sail, which can be very confusing in the case of a long tow; that is what nearly got us into trouble in the Gulf of Mexico).
- A vessel being pushed ahead: in addition to the typical red and green bow lights and a stern light, the pushing vessel shows two or three steaming lights (depending on length), with the lights vertically above each other (the same lights as a towing vessel); the vessel being pushed has typical red and green bow lights but no stern light. If more than one vessel is being pushed, only the forward one has lights; in inland waters it will also have a flashing yellow light on the centerline, while the pushing boat will have two yellow stern lights instead of the white stern light.

Then there are some special lights:

- Fishing boats (trawling): the steaming light is replaced by a green all-around light above a white all-around light; when underway, typical bow and stern lights are added. As with other ships, boats more than 164 feet (50 m) in length are also required to have an aft steaming light, higher than the green and white lights forward.
- Fishing boats (other than trawling): the steaming light is replaced by a red all-around light above a white all-around light; when underway, typical bow and stern lights are added.
- A pilot boat shows the same lights as a fishing boat underway, except that the white all-around light is above the red one; that is, there will be a white all-around light above a red all-around light, with typical bow and stern lights.
- A vessel restricted in its ability to maneuver shows red-white-red all-around lights in a vertical line; underway, the typical bow, stern, and masthead lights are added.
- A vessel constrained by its draft in international waters may show three red all-around lights in a vertical line in addition to the typical masthead, side, and stern lights.
- A boat aground may show two all-around red lights in a vertical line below its anchor light.
- A vessel not under command and not underway shows the two red all-around lights without the anchor light.
- Many sailboats include a white strobe light at the masthead. It is there to draw attention to the boat in times of distress or if another vessel does not seem aware of your existence and is coming perilously close. It has no official function, but I would not be without one.

IN PERSPECTIVE

When I began writing this chapter, I thought it would be one of the shortest in the book. My idea was to jot down those navigational and piloting techniques that we have found adequate to get us through our cruising—a sort of irreducible minimum. Now that the chapter is finished, it is the longest in the book. There is not only a lot of detail to absorb, but also a large number of mind-numbing acronyms. Unfortunately, to engage in coastal and offshore cruising, most of it does need to be learned.

But I also want to put this in perspective. With GPS during the past ten years, I have worked up almost no DRs or EPs, and have done no more than a handful of vector analyses. I do use LOPs and crossed bearings from a hand-bearing compass all the time; however, beyond this, most of my chart work consists of laying off course lines and then using the GPS to follow them and to plot positions. It's not particularly arduous and it uses few of the techniques outlined.

However, in all honesty, I can say that if I need any of the techniques described, I do know how to use them. I believe that you too, for your safety and mine, should know at least as much!

ADDENDUM: ONE PERSON'S ELLIPSOID IS ANOTHER PERSON'S SHIPWRECK—A BRIEF ODYSSEY THROUGH THE HISTORY OF MAP AND CHART MAKING

Map and chart making essentially began with Eratosthenes, a Greek who lived in Alexandria, Egypt, in the third century B.C. In his time, the idea that the earth was a sphere was already popular in certain intellectual circles, and the concepts of latitude and longitude as a reference system for determining positions on this sphere had been born. The question was: How big is the sphere? Eratosthenes had heard of a dug well at Syene (present-day Aswan), down which the sun shone directly to the bottom at midday on midsummer's day, which meant the sun had to be directly overhead. He knew that at the same time, on the same day, his sundial in Alexandria cast a shadow that extended at an angle of 7.2 degrees from the sundial; that is, the arc of the shadow was $\frac{1}{50}$th of a full circle ($360 \div 7.2 = 50$).

Eratosthenes believed that Syene was due south of Alexandria (he was wrong) and, after talking to camel drivers, concluded that the distance between the two was 5,000 *stadia*. Using basic trigonometry, he postulated that because the angular difference between the arc of the shadow at Alexandria and that at Syene (no shadow) was one fiftieth of a circle, the circumference of the earth must be fifty times the distance between the two places; that is, 250,000 *stadia*. Because we don't now know the exact length of a stadia, we don't know how accurate he was, but most scholars think a stadia was about 607 feet (185 m), which means he was close.

This methodology for determining the size and even the shape of the world—that is, astronomical observations coupled to a measured baseline and some trigonometry—remained the fundamental underpinning for map and chart making right up to the space age. In fact, it was not until the sixteenth century A.D. that there were any advances in map-making techniques at all! These occurred largely as a result of steady improvements in the equipment and methods used for making precise astronomical observations and for measuring distances and changes in elevation on the ground.

By the seventeenth century, it was possible to make sufficiently accurate astronomical observations and distance measurements to discover that in one part of the world a degree of latitude as measured astronomically (i.e., with reference to the stars) does not cover the same distance on the ground as it does in another part of the world. If the world were a perfect sphere, this would be an impossibility. The world could not be spherical! A tremendous scientific debate erupted, with the primary protagonists the French and the British.

Newton versus the Cassini Family

In France, on orders from the king who needed accurate maps to govern his country and tax his people, first Picard and then the Cassini family had taken on the task of mapping the country. In keeping with Eratosthenes's time-honored methodology and its contemporary advancements, surveyors combined astronomical observations and a measured baseline with a process of triangulation.

It is interesting to see how this survey work proceeded because the French methods reflect a norm for both cartographic and inshore hydrographic surveys that remained unchanged until recent decades. The baseline commenced in Paris at a point determined by some exceedingly

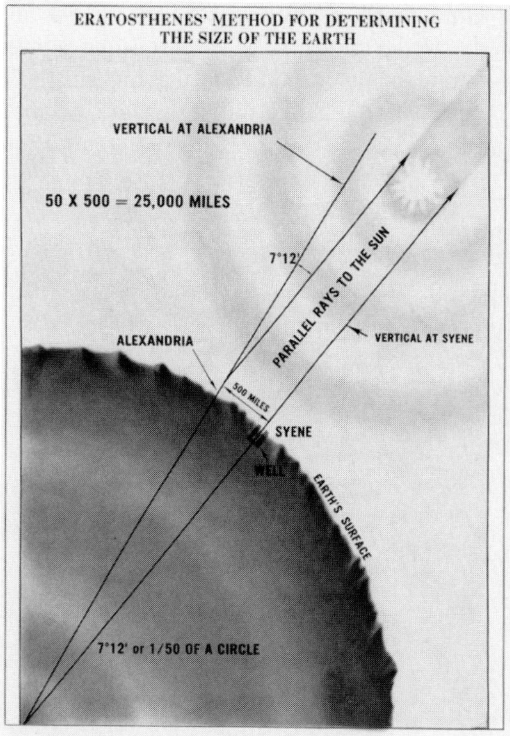

Eratosthenes does a little trigonometry . . . (Courtesy DMA)

precise astronomical observations that required heavy, bulky, and expensive equipment as well as multiple observations by highly trained observers over a considerable period. From Paris, carefully calibrated wooden rods were used to accurately measure distances due north and south. The surveyors also measured changes in vertical elevation to be able to discount the effects of them on the horizontal distances covered. In this way, a very precise log of horizontal distances was maintained. The process was slow and painstaking, and took years to complete.

Once a baseline had been established north and south of Paris, angular measurements were taken from both ends to a third position. Knowing the length of the baseline and the two angles, simple trigonometry established the distances to the third point without having to make field measurements. The sides of the triangle thus established were now used as fresh baselines to extend the survey, again without having to make actual distance measurements in the field. When the English Channel and the Mediterranean Sea were reached, fresh astronomical observations established the length of the arcs from Paris to the north and Paris to the south in degrees of latitude. The measured baselines plus the process of triangulation gave the horizontal distances on the ground.

After the results were in and tabulated, the Cassini family announced to the world: "Et, voilà! A degree of latitude between Paris and Dunkirk is longer than one between Paris and the Mediterranean. The earth must be pointed toward the poles and flattened at the equator."

"Now hang on a minute," said England's Sir Isaac Newton, who meanwhile had been perfecting his theory of gravity, "you've got it the wrong way around." Using various pendulum devices, the British demonstrated that gravity is less at the equator (the pendulum swung fractionally slower) than it is toward the poles. They postulated that the reason for this must be that the equator is farther from the center of the earth than the poles. In other words, the earth must be flattened at the poles and elongated at the equator, in which case the French were guilty of sloppy survey work!

National pride was at stake. The French Academy of Sciences decided to settle the dispute once and for all. Two expeditions were dispatched: one as far north as it was practical to go, which was the Arctic Circle in Lapland on the northern shores of the Baltic Sea; the other was as close to the equator as possible, in Peru. These expeditions were instructed to measure the precise horizontal distance of a substantial north–south arc of latitude at their respective locations.

The Lapland expedition spent seventeen months (April 1736 to August 1737) hacking its way through thick forests; working its way up and down mountainsides; establishing triangulation points; making astronomical observations; and braving hunger, wolves, hordes of mosquitoes, and the incredibly harsh winter. It was cold enough to freeze lips and tongues to the rims of silver brandy goblets so that the skin came away with the goblet; later, the brandy froze solid in its bottles! By the time the Lapland expedition returned home—even without the results of the Peruvian expedition—it was known that Newton

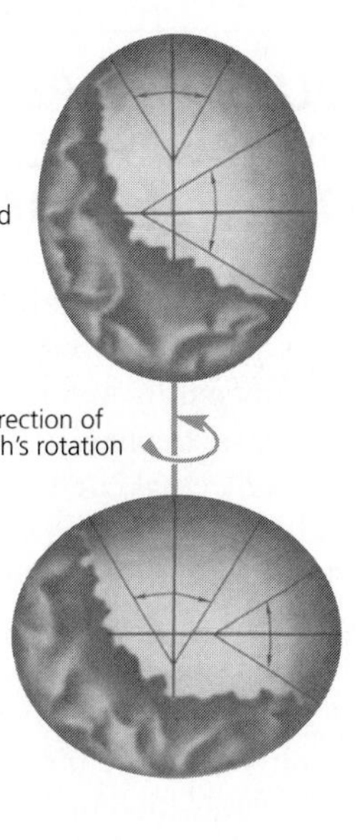

Newton versus the Cassinis. (Courtesy DMA)

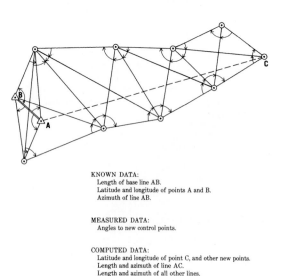

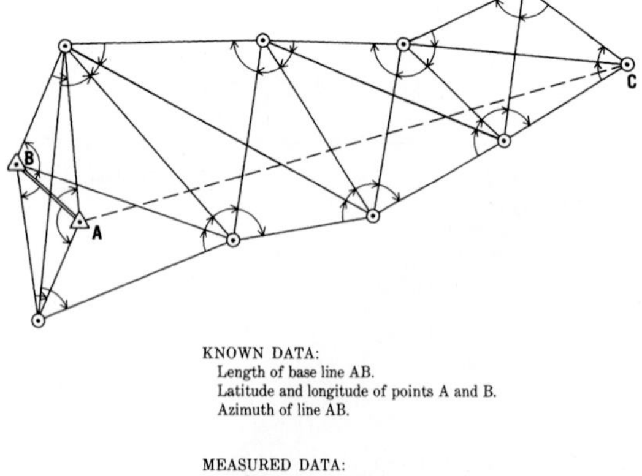

B
A
C
KNOWN DATA:
Length of base line AB.
Latitude and longitude of points A and B.
Azimuth of line AB.
MEASURED DATA:
Angles to new control points.
COMPUTED DATA:
Latitude and longitude of point C, and other new points.
Length and azimuth of line AC.
Length and azimuth of all other lines.

A simple triangulation net. (Courtesy DMA)

was correct. Voltaire, the French poet and dramatist, commented that this survey had "flattened the earth and the Cassinis."

It was to be another six years (1743) before the remnants of the Peruvian expedition limped back to Paris to finally and incontrovertibly corroborate the results. Voltaire had the last word. "You have found by prolonged toil," he remarked, "what Newton found without even leaving his home!" Ever since, gravity measurements have been central in determining the shape of the world.

From Sphere to Ellipsoid

How to model this nonspherical world? This was more than an academic question. To make maps, national surveyors now universally used an astronomically determined starting point and a measured baseline, working away from the beginning point by the process of triangulation. This methodology was adopted because the complexity, expense, and time involved in obtaining precise astronomical fixes made it impractical to get them on a regular basis.

As the surveyors progressed farther afield, if the mapped latitudes and longitudes were to be kept in sync with the occasional astronomical observations (i.e., "real-life" latitudes and longitudes), there had to be a model showing the relationship between the distance on the ground and latitude and longitude, and indicating how this relationship changed as the surveyors moved away from their astronomically determined starting point. This model had to be such that with available trigonometrical and computational methods, the mapmakers could adjust their data to accurately calculate changing latitudes and longitudes over substantial distances—in other words, the model had to be mathematically predictable.

The model that was adopted, and which is used to this day even with satellite-based mapmaking and navigation, is an *ellipsoid* (also called a *spheroid*). In essence, an ellipsoid is nothing more than a flattened sphere, characterized by two measurements: its radius at the equator and the degree of flattening at the poles. Clearly, the key questions become: What is this radius, and what is the degree of flattening?

During the nineteenth century, the continents were first accurately mapped based on this concept of the world as an ellipsoid. For each of the great surveys, preliminary work extending over years used astronomical observations and measured baselines to establish the key dimensions of the ellipsoid that was to underlie the survey. In the United Kingdom, a *geodesist* (a person who does this kind of research) named Sir George Airy developed an ellipsoid (known as Airy 1830) that became the basis for an incredibly detailed survey of the British Isles. His ellipsoid is still used to this day.

Using this ellipsoid, the surveyors commenced at a precisely determined astronomical point on Salisbury Plain, measured a baseline, and triangulated their way across the British Isles. The accuracy of the survey work and the ellipsoid was such that when western Ireland was reached decades later, and the original baseline was checked by computation from the Irish baseline 350 miles away, the two values differed by only 5 inches!

Another British geodesist, Alexander Clarke, came to the United States and was instrumental in developing the ellipsoid that has underlain the mapping of North America. It is known as the Clarke 1866 ellipsoid, and was the basis of map- and chart-making on the North American continent until the advent of satellite-derived ellipsoids. Later, Clarke developed an ellipsoid for mapping France and Africa (Clarke 1880).

Using the Clarke 1866 ellipsoid, and commencing at a single astronomically derived point and a measured baseline at the Meades Ranch in Osborne County, Kansas, the American surveyors from the U.S. Coast and Geodetic Survey (now the National Geodetic Survey) fanned out, establishing triangulation points and mapping the entire continent as they went. This combination of an underlying ellipsoid, a specific astronomically determined starting point, and a measured baseline is known as a *Geodetic Datum*; in this case, it is now known as the North American Datum of 1927 (NAD27). Such is the accuracy of the NAD27 surveys and the correlation of the Clarke 1866 ellipsoid with the real world that at the margins of the survey (the northeast and northwest United States—those areas in the lower forty-eight states farthest from the starting point), the discrepancies between mapped latitudes and longitudes and astronomically derived latitudes and longitudes are no more than 130 to 165 feet (40–50 meters).

From Ellipsoid to Geoid

By the end of the nineteenth century, numerous ellipsoids were in use, all of them differing slightly from one another. This raised another interesting question: Surely they couldn't all be correct, or could they?

GEOID-ELLIPSOID RELATIONSHIPS

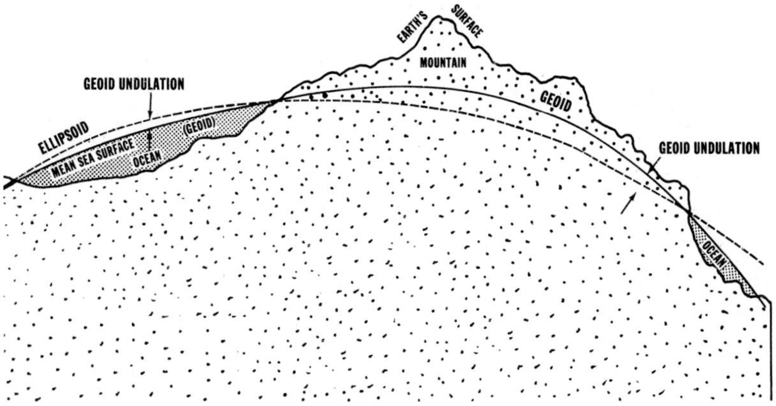

Spheres, ellipsoids, and geoids. (Courtesy DMA)

The answer lies in a more sophisticated understanding of our planet. The individual ellipsoids closely model the shape of the world in the areas in which the surveys were conducted, producing a close correlation between mapped positions and astronomically derived positions even at the margins of the survey. Although these ellipsoids are based on very accurate measurements over large areas of land, they are still only small areas of the world. When extrapolated to the globe as a whole, the ellipsoids produce increasingly serious discrepancies between ellipsoid-derived latitudes and longitudes and astronomically derived positions. Geodesists realized that not only is the world not a sphere, but it is also not an ellipsoid. In fact, it does not have a geometrically uniform shape at all, but rather numerous irregular humps and hollows!

Another concept was needed to deal with this shape. It is the *geoid*, which is defined as the real shape of the surface of the world if we discount all elevations above sea level. In other words, if we were to bulldoze the mountains and valleys to sea level, we would end up with the geoid. This is, in effect, the two-dimensional world as surveyed by mapmakers because the vertical element in the earth's topography is discounted when measuring baselines and other distances—these are all painstakingly reduced to the horizontal, using sea level as the base elevation. Whereas an ellipsoid is a mathematically defined regular surface, the geoid is a very irregular (mathematically unpredictable) shape. Regardless of the ellipsoid used to model the world, at different times the surface of the geoid will be above or below that of the ellipsoid, a phenomenon known as *geoid undulation*.

If we take two positions on an ellipsoid and define them in terms of latitude and longitude, the distance between them can be mathematically determined. However, no such relationship holds with the geoid. If the geoid undulates above the ellipsoid, the horizontal distance between the two points is greater than the corresponding distance on the ellipsoid; if the geoid undulates below the ellipsoid, the horizontal distance is less.

Astronomically derived positions are real-life points on the surface of the earth that have been determined relative to observable celestial phenomena. As such, they are referenced to the mathematically unpredictable geoid, as opposed to mapmakers' positions that are mostly derived from some mathematical model (i.e., an ellipsoid) of the world. Because of the mathematically unpredictable nature of the geoid, *there is no mathematical relationship between astronomically determined positions and positions determined by reference to an ellipsoid.* The only way to correlate the two is either through

Illustrations (grossly exaggerated!) of how the best-fit datum in one region of the world can still not be a best fit elsewhere. (Adapted from drawings; courtesy DMA)

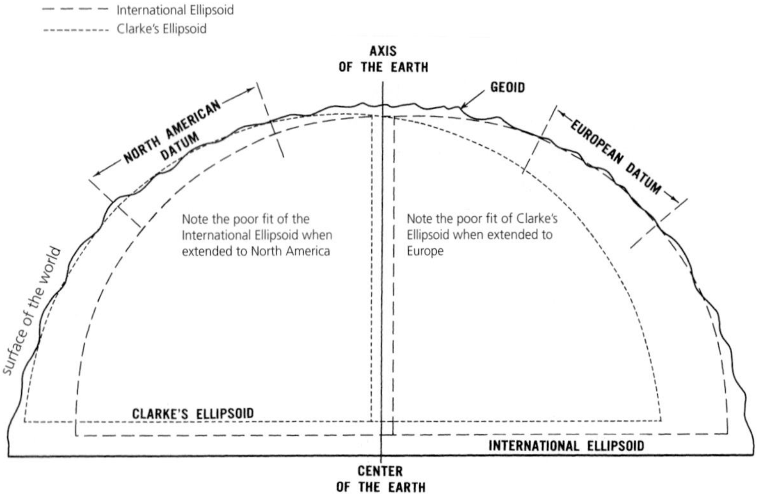

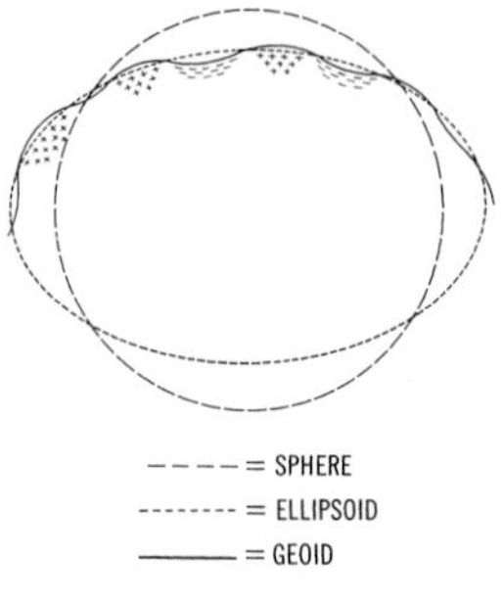

POTENTIAL SURFACES

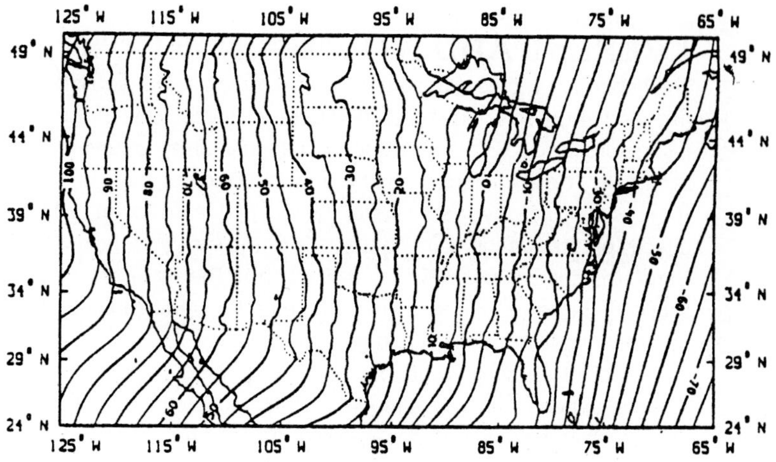

Longitude datum shifts (in meters) in the United States between NAD27 and NAD83 (WGS84). (Courtesy C-Map)

individual measurements or by modeling the geoid and ellipsoid and measuring the offsets.

What this means is that there can be no ellipsoid that produces a precise correlation between ellipsoid-derived latitudes and longitudes and those derived astronomically. This is why we currently have more than twenty different ellipsoids in use around the world, each of which forms the basis for a different map datum, and none of which are compatible. In their own areas, these ellipsoids and datums create a "best fit" between latitudes and longitudes derived from the ellipsoid and those derived astronomically (those referenced to the geoid). However, when expanded to worldwide coverage, latitudes and longitudes based on these ellipsoids exhibit increasingly large discrepancies from those derived astronomically.

A New Age

Geodesists have long tried to resolve these problems. Back in the eighteenth century, British and French surveyors coordinated the lighting of flares on both sides of the English Channel so that they could establish triangulation data that would enable the national surveys to be brought into sync. More recently in North America, sightings were made off aircraft to tie surveys of Greenland, Cuba, and other outlying areas into the NAD27 grid. But until the satellite age, it was not possible to bridge the distances between continents in a way that would enable the inevitable discontinuities in mapmaking from one continent to another to be eliminated.

Today all this has changed. Satellites and space-age technology (e.g., electro-optical distance-measuring devices) have finally unified the globe from a surveyor's perspective. In the past four decades, an incredible mass of geodetic data has become available from all parts of the world. On this basis, a succession of World Geodetic Systems (WGS) were developed (e.g., WGS66, WGS72), culminating in WGS84, which now has worldwide acceptance.

WGS84 is another ellipsoid; however, this one was developed as a best fit with the geoid ("real-life" sea-level world) as a whole, as opposed to having a best fit with just one specific region of the geoid. The irony in this is that given the irregularities in the geoid, the divergence between WGS84 and the geoid is actually greater in many areas than the divergence between older ellipsoids and the geoid. For example, in North America, the difference between the Clarke 1866 ellipsoid and the geoid is generally less than 33 feet (10 m), whereas with WGS84, it is at least 49 feet (15 m) and often 100 to 115 feet (30–35 m. However, on a *worldwide* scale, WGS84 makes a better fit than Clarke 1866. What this means is that the difference between map-derived and astronomically derived latitudes and longitudes is greater on a WGS84-based map than it is on a NAD27 map!

However, almost no one uses astronomically derived position-fixing anymore because, with the advent first of Transit (NavSat) and then GPS and GLONASS (the Russian equivalent of GPS), after 2,500 years we have finally broken the umbilical cord that tied our mapmaking to the stars. In the new age, we have our own artificial stars (satellites) and satellite-based survey techniques that directly relate surveyed positions to the WGS84 ellipsoid. Whereas astronomically determined latitudes and longitudes are "absolute"—in the sense that every "real-life" point on the globe has a fixed, unchanging, astronomical latitude and longitude—ellipsoid-derived latitudes and longitudes are only absolute relative to a particular ellipsoid, which makes them relative in relation to the geoid. A change in ellipsoidal assumptions will alter the latitude and longitude of "real-life" points on the globe.

At first sight, this seems to make it impossible to have precise position fixes. But with a little more thought, it is seen that this "relativity" of ellipsoid-derived latitudes and longitudes is irrelevant as long as the equipment used to derive a latitude and a longitude bases calculations on the same ellipsoid as the map or chart on which the position is plotted. If the maps and charts are made to a particular set of assumptions, and the position-fixing equipment operates on the same set of assumptions, the results will be precise fixes—in some cases, incredibly precise fixes: down to centimeter accuracy at a continental scale!

EVEREST AND MOUNTAIN ROOTS

The geodesist who developed the ellipsoid for India and who led the mapping effort was none other than George Everest. One of the techniques used to ensure accuracy in triangulation-type surveys is to eventually "close the loop"—that is, return to the starting point of the survey. If the survey is accurate, the mapped return point will fall directly on the starting point. In the case of the survey of the Himalayas, there was a 985-foot (300 m) error. The surveyors were shocked; the reputation and honor of the British Empire and its technicians were at stake. What had gone wrong?

Much of the survey work had been done in mountainous terrain. It had long been known that mountains had a distorting effect on gravity—that a plumb bob, for example, instead of hanging vertical to the center of the earth, would be attracted fractionally to one side. The surveyors had used plumb bobs for leveling their instruments during the process of measuring vertical elevations. They had built in an offset for the gravitational effects of the mountains. This offset was based on the then-current assumption that the earth's crust floats uniformly on the underlying magma and that, therefore, mountains must be less dense than the material of valley bottoms and the oceans (otherwise, the added weight of the mountains would cause them to sink into the magma).

To explain the unsatisfactory results of the Indian survey, it was postulated that mountains are, in fact, denser than had been previously thought, and that the added weight is counterbalanced by a "root" pushing into the magma. This produced different gravity-offset calculations that, when factored into the Indian survey, enabled the loop to be closed. This theory sparked an intense scientific debate at the time, but now the concept of mountains with roots is universally accepted.

The rub comes if someone is navigating with electronic equipment that is not operating on the same set of assumptions as those used to make a given map or chart. In this case, at bottom line, a match is being attempted between two different ellipsoids. In the case of WGS84 and Clarke 1866 (NAD27), the resulting position error may be as much as 328 feet (100 m) in the conterminous United States; in the case of the United Kingdom's Ordnance Survey, it is also around 328 feet (100 m); for charts based on the 1950 European Datum (also used in the U.K.), it may be up to 493 feet (150 m); and, in the case of the Tokyo datum, used in much of the Far East, it may be as much as 2,955 feet (900 m).

Nautical Peculiarities

Finally, there are all those nautical surveys made without reference to any ellipsoid at all. Coastal surveys were traditionally made by setting up triangulation points on shore and continuing the land-based process of triangulation out to sea. Farther from shore, ships with high bridges and sometimes buoys on a short scope (so that they did not move around) were used to provide fixed visual markers. Later, radar, Loran, and Decca extended the range of the triangulation process. These surveys were all tied into the shore-based ellipsoid and map datum (e.g., NAD27 in North America). However, once the surveyors moved beyond the range of the shore-based triangulation system, there was no way to tie the surveys into any ellipsoid or shore-based datum. The necessarily precise astronomical and baseline measurements simply could not be made from the moving platform of a ship.

For transoceanic surveys, this inability to tie into a given ellipsoid or datum was immaterial because precise position-fixing was not necessary. Mariners navigating the oceans could not fix their position with any degree of precision using a sextant and other traditional means of celestial navigation.

Problems have always arisen, however, in relation to charts of remote islands, rocks, and other navigational features. Unable to establish a relationship to any ellipsoid or chart datum, the surveyors had to establish a local astronomically determined position, and then conduct a survey working away from this point using traditional methods of triangulation. Apart from the fact that the astronomically derived starting points are often seriously in error (sometimes by miles—the British Admiralty tells me the worst discrepancy on its charts, which is in the South Pacific, is 7 miles), there are frequently surveying errors on these older charts (imprecisely measured angles between features or poorly calculated distances). Surveys made using *open traverses* (starting from a given point and working away from it) as opposed to those made using *closed traverses* (working around in

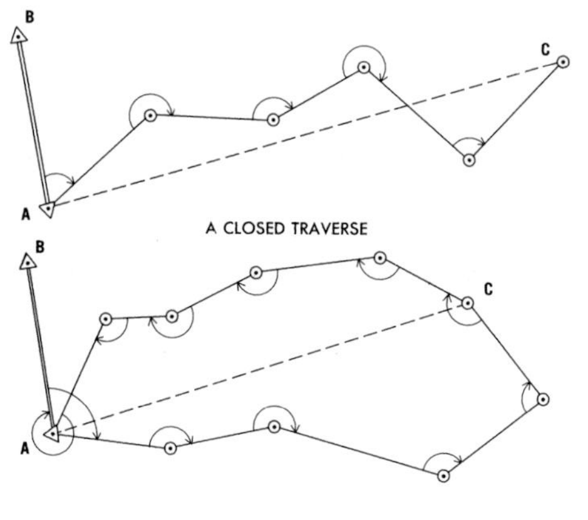

Open and closed traverses. (Courtesy DMA)

a circle back to the starting point) are likely to have the greatest errors. If the closed traverse doesn't close, the surveyors have some sense of the extent of the error and, to some degree, can correct the entire survey.

These survey methods result in charts that cannot be tied into any ellipsoid or datum and that are unreliable relative to all forms of celestial navigation. Nevertheless, prior to the satellite age, once a landfall was made, these surveys were also often adequate for mariners because navigation was by traditional methods using bearings from identified points of land, changes in depth, and so on—all of which are unrelated to latitudes and longitudes.

With the advent of satellite-based navigation systems, mariners have been able to precisely locate themselves anywhere in the world in terms of latitude and longitude. What few of them realize is that this position is with reference to a particular ellipsoid (for GPS, it is WGS84), which may differ markedly from the underlying ellipsoid or datum of the chart they are using. Other than confusing the navigator and providing a false sense of confidence, it serves little purpose to know exactly where you are (latitude and longitude) relative to WGS84 if the chart you are using is based on an ellipsoid and datum that result in the lines of latitude and longitude running through substantially different real-world locations. The half-mile difference between our actual position and our plotted position we experienced in Cuba is an example of the type of differences that can arise when satellite-based navigation equipment is operating on a different datum than the chart datum. Neither the GPS nor the chart was "wrong"; in fact, the chart is a very good one. The two were simply referencing latitude and longitude to a different set of assumptions.

GPS HEIGHT DISPLAYS

GPS provides a three-dimensional position; that is, a vertical readout as well as the two-dimensional latitude and longitude readout. But the vertical figure, particularly on cheaper and older GPS units, is often considerably in "error." Navigators are especially likely to notice this because a boat at sea is by definition at sea level (or, at least, fairly close to it), whereas the GPS may be giving the height of the vessel as plus 300 feet or minus 150 feet, or whatever. Given the supposed incredible accuracy of a GPS, it is not unreasonable to wonder how the vertical readout can be so far off.

To understand this issue, we have to distinguish between the three different surfaces referred to in this addendum: the ellipsoid, which is the reference point for all GPS fixes; the geoid, which is the sea-level surface of the world; and the topographical surface, which—when ashore—is almost always above that of the geoid (and is expressed in terms of feet or meters above sea level). The GPS is providing height *relative to the ellipsoid* (referred to as *ellipsoidal height*); what we usually want to know is height *relative to the geoid*. However, because the geoid undulates in a mathematically unpredictable fashion, there is no mathematical relationship between the ellipsoid and the geoid—in other words, the GPS cannot simply be programmed with an algorithm to convert heights relative to the ellipsoid into heights relative to the geoid. Global differences between the geoid and the WGS84 ellipsoid range from as much as +256 feet (+78 m) in the region of Papua New Guinea to –338 feet (–103 m) in the Indian Ocean off India and Sri Lanka.

Some GPSs simply display height relative to the ellipsoid and leave it at that. This does not provide useful information for most of us. Other units, however, incorporate one of a series of computerized models of the geoid that have been developed by the National Geodetic Survey and the DMA. With such a model, for any given position in the world, the GPS can measure the offset between the ellipsoid and the geoid, apply it as a correction to the displayed height, and produce a vertical readout that is now referenced to the geoid. Clearly, the accuracy of the resulting readout is directly related to the degree of sophistication and the accuracy of the model being used. More sophisticated models require more GPS memory. In general, the older and cheaper a GPS, the less adequate is the model of the geoid and the poorer is the fit between displayed altitudes and actual topographic altitude (discrepancies of 33–66 ft./10–20 m are common).

Avoiding Reefs

This is where the GPS becomes potentially quite dangerous. Unless a GPS receiver is operating on the same datum as that underpinning the chart being used for navigation, the GPS "fix" may result in considerable navigational errors. If the GPS cannot be reset to match the chart datum, or the lines of latitude and longitude on the chart cannot be shifted to match the GPS datum, *the GPS must be treated as an unreliable navigational tool.*

A few years ago, in the course of one boating season, two yachts hit the reefs off the coast of Belize. Both were a total loss. In both cases, the skippers were using satellite navigation and old charts based on surveys of no known datum. Both skippers knew precisely where they were (in terms of latitude and longitude); when plotted, these positions had them well clear of the reefs. Nevertheless, they struck. Losing a boat is a hard way to learn about ellipsoids, chart datums, and the limitations of satellite navigation.

Anchoring skills are essential to successful cruising.

CHAPTER NINE

ANCHORING, RUNNING AGROUND, AND KEDGING OFF

Anchoring proficiency is essential on a cruising boat. Setting an anchor is generally not that difficult, but it is one of those tasks that requires teamwork between the person on the foredeck and the person at the helm in a situation in which voice communication is generally not possible because of noise from the engine and other sources. There is sufficient potential for a screw-up and a meltdown, especially if the maneuver starts to go awry in a crowded anchorage! As a result, for many cruising couples, anchoring can be one of the more stressful components of the cruising life. In this chapter, we see how we can eliminate some of the stress, starting with a discussion of appropriate ground tackle.

GROUND TACKLE

It doesn't matter how good your anchoring routine is; if your ground tackle is not appropriate for the boat or the conditions, sooner or later it will let you down. The most basic requirement is to match the strength of the ground tackle to the boat and its likely cruising grounds.

Calculating the Load

The loads on ground tackle are a function of the following factors:

- the windage of a boat
- the extent to which the boat *shears* (i.e., weaves) around at anchor (the more it swings out of line with the wind, the greater is the windage)
- the impact of any current on the boat
- the boat's weight
- the sea state in which the tackle is deployed
- the extent to which the ground tackle cushions shock loads (the two key factors are *scope*—the relationship of rode length to water depth—and the material from which the rode is made—chain or nylon line)

The number of variables involved makes load calculations incredibly complicated. In typical circumstances, the most significant factor, especially at higher wind speeds, is windage. The load resulting from windage increases with the square of the wind speed; that is, if the wind speed doubles, the wind-induced load increases *four* times.

By making certain assumptions that relate windage to boat length and beam, the wind load at different wind speeds can be readily calculated for "generic" boat lengths and beams. These numbers can then be adjusted on the assumption that a boat at anchor may shear away from the wind, from one side to another, by as much as 30 degrees. Some assumptions also can be made relating boat size and beam to immersed volume and the maximum likely impact of tidal streams and currents on the anchoring load (as you can see, this is getting a little complicated).

Next, we introduce some waves—this is where the situation starts to get really complex. As a boat pitches up and down, it can impart shock loads—snatching or jerking loads—to an anchor rode, well in excess of the wind- and current-generated loads. However, if the boat is anchored with lots of scope (more about this later) and if the rode has some elasticity (through the use of a nylon rode or *snubber*—also discussed later), there is rarely if ever a true shock load; that is, a nearly *instantaneous* application of load, such as when a roped climber falls off a cliff and is suddenly brought up short by the rope. The one exception might be a fouled anchor or rode in which the rode is hauled in until it is up and down, and then wave action is used to try to break out the anchor, without success. Short of this, any wave action increases the loading to a point somewhere on a curve that runs from the wind load without waves to the maximum load that could be imposed by an instantaneous shock.

At different times, different people and organizations have attempted to quantify all these factors and derive some numbers for the likely loads on ground tackle and its associated hardware. The most widely known and used reference is a table published by the American Boat and Yacht Council (ABYC) that shows the design loads for sizing deck hardware resulting from the effects of wind, current, and wave action. These loads have been calculated for four different wind speeds: 15, 30, 42, and 60 knots. From this table, I derived the Design Loads for Ground Tackle Systems table below.

Snubbing loads, such as these imparted by a surge through this anchorage, dramatically increase the loads on ground tackle.

This is a conservative table with substantial built-in safety margins; that is, in most circumstances, *it considerably overstates the loads that will be experienced by the ground tackle and deck hardware*. If windage alone were used to calculate loads, the numbers would be approximately 25 percent of those in this table. Consequently, if this table is used to size ground tackle, it will provide a significant margin for dealing with dynamic (surge) loads and other complicating factors.

The table is entered with a boat's length or beam, using whichever gives the highest numbers, and then move across horizontally to find the potential loads at different wind speeds. A weekend sailor who never goes to sea if strong winds are forecast will need very different ground tackle than an around-the-world cruiser who may, at some point, be faced with violent winds and

Design Loads for Ground Tackle Systems

BOAT LENGTH (LOA), feet (m)	BOAT BEAM (B_{max}), feet (m)		LOAD ON TACKLE AND HARDWARE, pounds (kg)			
	SAIL	POWER	15 KNOTS	30 KNOTS	42 KNOTS	60 KNOTS
10 (3.0)	4 (1.2)	5 (1.5)	40 (20)	160 (75)	320 (145)	640 (290)
15 (4.6)	5 (1.5)	6 (1.8)	60 (30)	250 (115)	500 (230)	1,000 (455)
20 (6.1)	7 (2.1)	8 (2.4)	90 (40)	360 (165)	720 (330)	1,440 (655)
25 (7.6)	8 (2.4)	9 (2.7)	125 (60)	490 (225)	980 (445)	1,960 (890)
30 (9.1)	9 (2.7)	11 (3.4)	175 (80)	700 (320)	1,400 (635)	2,800 (1,275)
35 (10.7)	10 (3.0)	13 (4.0)	225 (100)	900 (410)	1,800 (820)	3,600 (1,640)
40 (12.2)	11 (3.4)	14 (4.3)	300 (135)	1,200 (545)	2,400 (1,090)	4,800 (2,180)
50 (15.2)	13 (4.0)	16 (4.9)	400 (180)	1,600 (730)	3,200 (1,450)	6,400 (2,910)
60 (18.3)	15 (4.6)	18 (5.5)	500 (230)	2,000 (910)	4,000 (1,820)	8,000 (3,640)

Metric measures are approximate; weights are rounded to the nearest 5 kg.
Adapted from a table, courtesy ABYC.

seas at anchor. Clearly, the ground tackle and associated fittings must be matched to the intended use and area of operation. Nevertheless, no boat should have its ground tackle sized according to the 15-knot column. However, a day sailor who never strays far from home might use the 30-knot column. A cruising sailor, whether coastal or offshore, should use the 42-knot column. In the case of a long-distance cruising boat, this column should serve as a *minimum* starting point; a more conservative approach is to take the potential loads at 60 knots.

Matching the Components

Having determined the kinds of loads we might see, we need to size anchor rodes and shackles to meet those loads, making sure that all the components in the ground-tackle system are matched to one another. Unfortunately, at this point, we step into a minefield, but we can start to negotiate a path through it with another table developed by the ABYC, Working Load Limits for Anchor Rodes.

On the surface, if we have a rope or chain rode, we simply make sure the *working load limits* (WLL) of the various pieces are matched, and are at least as high as the number we extracted from the Design Loads for Ground Tackle Systems table. But let's consider our own 40-foot Pacific Seacraft, for which we would like an anchor for up to 42-knot wind speeds, using a rope or chain rode. The first table tells us that at 42 knots, we should anticipate loads of up to 2,400 pounds (1,090 kg) (at 60 knots, these loads increase to 4,800 pounds/2,180 kg). The second table tells us that we can use either ⅜-inch (10 mm) Proof Coil (BBB) chain (also known as grade 30) or ¼-inch (6 mm) High-Test (grade 40), with a 7⁄16-inch (11 mm) shackle. We will need 1-inch (24 mm) nylon line.

What's wrong with this picture? First, no one in their right mind will use a 1-inch nylon rode—⅝ inch (16 mm) is more likely, possibly ¾ inch (18 mm). Second, ¼-inch (6 mm) High-Test chain has an inside diameter (inside link width) of 0.4 inch (10 mm), and a 7⁄16-inch (11 mm) shackle has a pin diameter of ½ inch (12 mm)—the pin won't fit. How do we reconcile this?

First, note that the table below gives WLLs, not breaking strengths. The WLL is defined as a percentage of breaking strength. However, different WLLs are used for the different components in the ground-tackle system, reflecting the different properties of those components (e.g., nylon rope rather than chain), but also reflecting other considerations not necessarily related to functionality in an anchoring system (e.g., legal considerations and use in other applications). For example:

- Nylon rope may be given a WLL of anywhere from 5 to 25 percent of its breaking strength, depending on the application. The numbers used in the ABYC table come from the Cordage Institute (an industry-wide organization in the U.S.), which is using an extremely conservative WLL of about 10 percent of *minimum tensile strength* of generic

Working Load Limits for Anchor Rodes

NOMINAL SIZE (CHAIN)/ DIAMETER (ROPE), inches (mm)	WORKING LOAD LIMIT (WLL), pounds (kg)				
	NYLON		GALVANIZED CHAIN		
	3-STRAND	DOUBLE BRAID	PROOF COIL (BBB)	HIGH-TEST	ANCHOR SHACKLES
¼ (6)	186 (85)	208 (94)	1,300 (590)	2,600 (1,180)	1,000 (450)
5⁄16 (8)	287 (130)	326 (148)	1,900 (865)	3,900 (1,770)	1,500 (675)
⅜ (10)	405 (184)	463 (210)	2,650 (1,205)	5,400 (2,455)	2,000 (910)
7⁄16 (11)	550 (250)	—	3,500 (1,590)	7,200 (3,275)	3,000 (1,365)
½ (12)	709 (321)	816 (370)	4,500 (2,045)	9,200 (4,170)	4,000 (1,820)
⅝ (16)	1,114 (505)	1,275 (578)	6,900 (3,140)	11,500 (5,220)	6,500 (2,950)
¾ (18)	1,598 (725)	1,813 (822)	10,600 (4,820)	16,200 (7,350)	9,500 (4,310)
⅞ (22)	2,160 (980)	2,063 (936)	12,800 (5,800)	—	12,000 (5,440)
1 (24)	2,795 (1,260)	3,153 (1,430)	13,950 (6,330)	—	15,000 (6,800)

Metric measures are approximate.
Adapted from a table, courtesy ABYC. Note that Proof Coil and BBB chain are not the same, but for the purposes of matching the components in a system, are close enough to be considered the same. However, they will not fit on the same wildcat (gypsy)—this must be matched to the chain.

nylon rope. Minimum tensile strength is generally between 80 and 90 percent of the average breaking strength of a rope; in other words, 10 percent of minimum tensile strength is just 8 to 9 percent of average breaking strength. Furthermore, the generic nylon rope used to calculate these numbers has a breaking strength below that of most nylon rope sold for anchoring applications, further lowering the WLL number.

- Proof Coil and BBB chain have a WLL that is 25 percent of their breaking strength.
- High-Test chain has a WLL that is one third of its breaking strength.
- Shackles are commonly given a WLL of 20 percent of their breaking strength (reflecting the fact that they also may be used in lifting applications with wire rope, which in turn has a WLL of 20 percent of its breaking strength).

I am sticking my neck out here and proposing that, in practice, it is reasonable to assume a WLL of 25 percent of minimum tensile strength for nylon rode (i.e., 20–22½ percent of average breaking strength), or 20 percent of average breaking strength (if average breaking strength is the only number available); and a common WLL of 25 percent of breaking strength for Proof Coil, BBB, and High-Test chain, and also anchor shackles. In my modified table (following), I show no nylon line sizes below ⅜ inch (10 mm) because rodes smaller than this are uncomfortable to handle, and because their strength is disproportionately affected by the kind of damage that can be expected in use. Two other key pieces of information in the ground-tackle puzzle are included in the table: the inside diameter of chain links and the diameter of shackle pins. The following Modified Working Load Limits for Anchor Rodes table has chain and pin diameters—in inches and millimeters—after the WLLs.

Now the different pieces start to fit together somewhat better. For the 2,400-pound (1,090 kg) load on our Pacific Seacraft 40, we can still use ⅜-inch (10 mm) Proof Coil or BBB chain

Modified *Working Load Limits for Anchor Rodes* (use at your own risk)

NOMINAL SIZE (CHAIN)/ DIAMETER (ROPE), inches (mm)	MODIFIED WORKING LOAD LIMIT, pounds (kg)				
	NYLON ROPE* pounds (kg)		GALVANIZED CHAIN/CHAIN LINK ID, pounds/inches (kg/mm)		SHACKLES (WELDLESS; DROP-FORGED), pounds/inches (kg/mm)
	3-STRAND BRAID	DOUBLE BRAID	PROOF COIL (BBB)	HIGH-TEST	
¼ (6)	—	—	1,300/0.43 (590/11)	1,950/0.40 (890/10)	1,250/5⁄16 (570/8)
5⁄16 (8)	—	—	1,900/0.50 (865/13)	2,925/0.48 (1,330/12)	1,875/⅜ (850/10)
⅜ (10)	880 (400)	980 (445)	2,650/0.62 (1,205/16)	4,050/0.57 (1,840/14)	2,500/7⁄16 (1,140/11)
7⁄16 (11)	1,180 (540)	1,320 (600)	3,500/0.75 (1,590/19)	5,400/0.65 (2,455/17)	3,750/½(1,705/13)
½ (12)	1,500 (680)	1,700 (775)	4,500/0.81 (2,045/21)	6,900/0.74 (3,140/19)	5,000/⅝ (2,275/16)
9⁄16 (14)	1,880 (855)	—	5,500/0.84 (2,500/21)	—	—
⅝ (16)	2,440 (1,110)	2,700 (1,230)	6,900/1.01 (3,140/26)	8,625/0.82 (3,920/21)	8,125/¾ (3,695/19)
¾ (18)	3,340 (1,520)	3,880 (1,765)	10,600/1.10 (4,820/28)	12,150/1.02 (5,520/26)	11,875/⅞ (5,400/22)
⅞ (22)	4,700 (2,140)	—	—	—	15,000/1 (6,820/25)
1 (24)	5,880 (2,675)	6,800 (3,090)	—	—	18,750/1⅛ (8,520/29)

*The modified nylon rope WLLs are based on high-quality nylon rope (New England Ropes); they need to be downgraded for lower-quality rope.

(WLL of 2,650 lb./1,205 kg), but compared to the previous table we have to go up a size to 5/16 inch (8 mm) for the High-Test chain (*modified* WLL of 2,925 lb./1,330 kg). This High-Test chain has an inside diameter of 0.48 inch (12 mm), which will accept the 7/16-inch pin (0.4375 in./11 mm) of a 3/8-inch (10 mm) shackle (*modified* WLL of 2,500 lb./1,140 kg). The shackle is the weak link. To be on the safe side, I prefer to use the next-size-up shackle (7/16 in./11 mm, with a *modified* WLL of 3,750 lb./1,705 kg), but it won't fit the High-Test chain (the shackle has a 1/2 in./13 mm pin).

Although I might be tempted to use a stainless steel shackle because it has a much higher WLL for the same size as a galvanized anchor shackle, it would be a mistake. Typically, stainless steel shackles are rated at up to 50 percent of breaking strength, so the extra strength may be illusory and, in fact, *the shackle may be weaker.* In addition, the stainless steel may cause galvanic corrosion with the chain. The way to use a larger shackle is to have the chain manufacturer weld in an oversized link at the end(s) of the chain (which is commonly done) before the chain is purchased. If you already have the chain without this link and if you are using High-Test chain, you should use the largest galvanized shackle that fits—and recognize that this is likely to be the weak link in the system. *Any shackle used in a ground-tackle system should be specifically manufactured for this purpose and stamped with its WLL; all other shackles are suspect.* The pin on any shackle must always be *seized* (tied off) to prevent it from working loose in use.

Using my modified table, if I decide to have a combined rope-chain rode, for day-to-day anchoring, I use 5/8-inch (16 mm) three-strand nylon, which fits nicely with a WLL of 2,440 pounds (1,110 kg). On an ocean-voyaging boat, for true storm conditions and bearing in mind the risk of abrasion as the boat surges around its anchor, I would carry a 300-foot (91 m) length of 3/4-inch (18 mm) line with a WLL of 3,340 pounds (1,520 kg). If I decided to cruise in high latitudes where I might be anchoring in 60-knot winds, the anticipated ground-tackle load increases to 4,800 pounds (2,180 kg). This can be met with 1/2-inch (12 mm) Proof Coil or BBB chain (with a WLL of 4,500 lb./2,045 kg, both are a little undersized) or 7/16-inch (11 mm) High-Test chain (WLL of 5,400 lb./2,455 kg), connected with a 1/2-inch (12 mm) shackle (WLL of 5,000 lb./2,275 kg), which has a pin size of 0.625 inch (16 mm) (fitting the 0.65-inch link or 17 mm width of the High-Test chain). The table indicates that I should use a 7/8-inch (22 mm) three-strand nylon rode, but I would use the 3/4-inch (18 mm)—knowing that I had reduced my safety margin—simply because the 7/8-inch (22 mm) would be extremely heavy and bulky to handle. I know that doesn't sound like a good reason to use the smaller size line, but at some point pragmatism has to win out over theory!

Some Caveats Regarding Nylon Line

Remember that the numbers given in my modified table are based on new rope from a quality manufacturer. This rope is made from fibers manufactured by AlliedSignal that not only have a high tensile strength to start with, but also have been treated with a marine overlay finish (MOF; Allied calls its product SeaGard). The MOF significantly reduces strength loss when wet (nylon normally suffers an approximate 10 percent strength loss when wet) and damage from abrasion. Other rope may not have as high initial strength or as good performance in service.

When a boat is bucking up and down wildly in a rough anchorage, the combined effect of any *catenary* in the anchor rode and the inherent stretch of a nylon rode significantly cushions the load. Given that the ABYC Design Loads Table (see the table on page 395) was

Below left: *Stainless steel shackles are not recommended in an anchoring system.* Middle: *Note the WLL of 1 ton stamped on this galvanized shackle; all shackles for use in an anchoring system should be similarly marked.* Below right: *Finally, all shackles need to be seized with stainless steel or Monel seizing wire.*

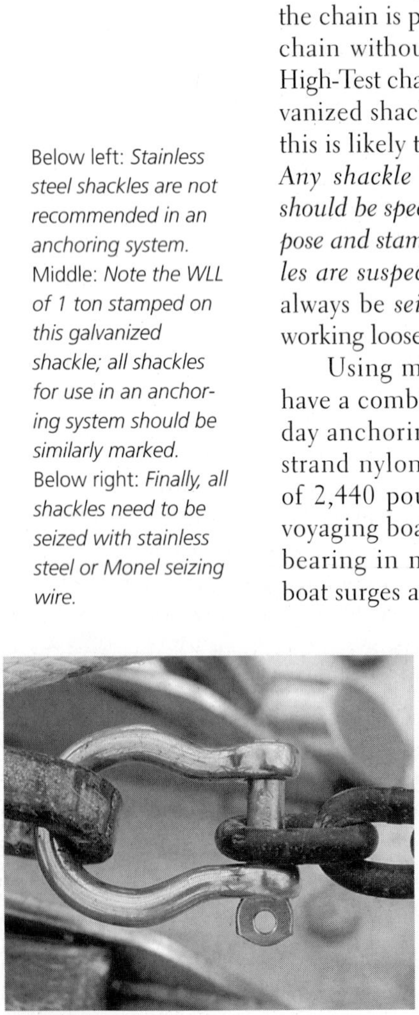

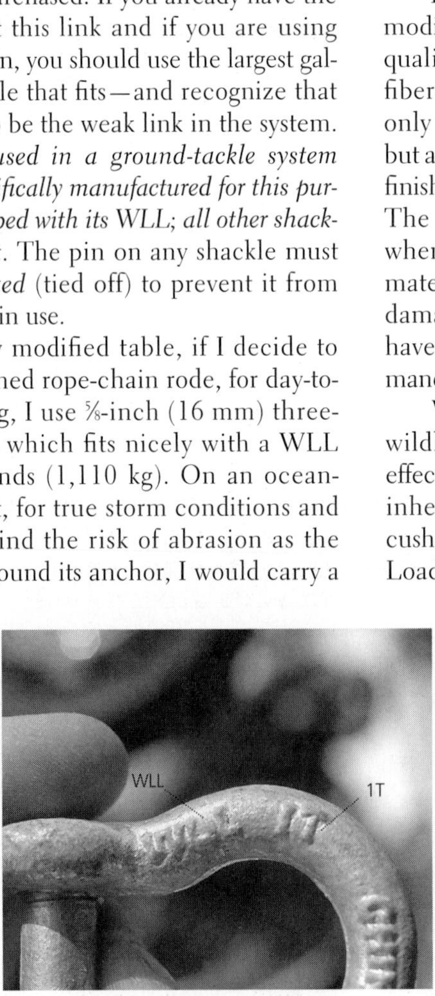

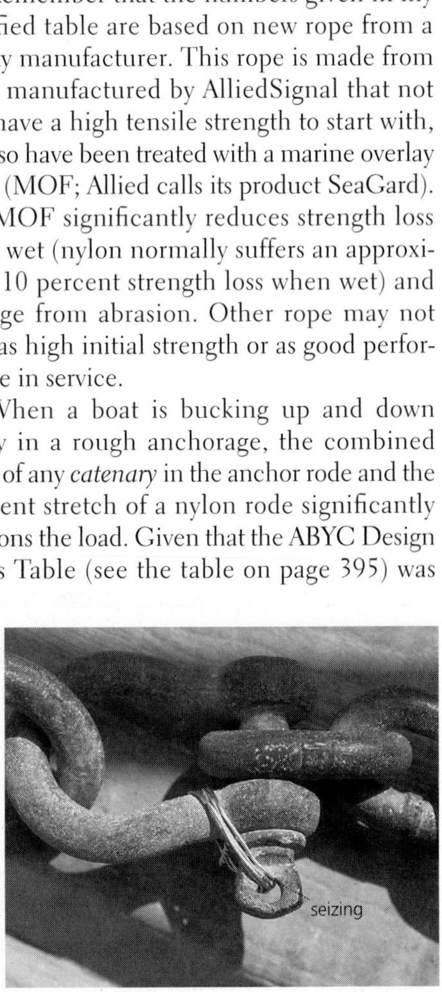

Shock-loading of an anchor rode. If the rode parts, the boat will be on the rocks before anyone has time to react.

developed *considering these kinds of dynamic loads*, it seems reasonable to assume that the ground tackle at any given wind speed (e.g., 30, 42, or 60 knots) will not be subjected to greater dynamic loads than those in the table. However, if ground tackle is sized using my table, and if at any time it seems likely that it has been severely shock-loaded (e.g., a failed attempt to use substantial wave action to break out an anchor), the WLLs in the table on page 396 may be exceeded—in which case, *the line should never again be trusted*.

If you are caught out in a rough anchorage, the simple act of letting out more rode (i.e., increasing scope) not only significantly increases the holding power of your anchor, but also significantly reduces the shock loading on the rode. If yours is a boat that tends to shear around at anchor, the shearing will significantly increase the wind load. Setting a small riding sail on the backstay both reduces the load and makes the boat lie more comfortably at anchor.

What happens if periodically the loads on a nylon rode go above 25 percent of minimum tensile strength? This is a gray area in which it is difficult to get hard and fast data. However, the Oil Companies International Marine Forum (OCIMF) developed data on nylon rodes that are used to moor oil tankers to single-point moorings. The rodes were progressively stressed (i.e., not shock-loaded) to 50 percent of breaking strength for a thousand cycles, then 60 percent of breaking strength for another thousand cycles, then 70 percent of breaking strength, and so on until failure occurred; most failed at the 60 percent loading level. Clearly, any rode sized using 25 percent of the WLL as I suggest has a safety margin built in. However, it is also clear that at some point between this and 60 percent of breaking strength, some type of permanent damage (however minimal) is occurring at each load cycle, which ultimately leads to failure. The industry specialists that I have talked to seem to think that this point occurs at around 30 percent of minimum tensile strength.

If any nylon line under load breaks, *it can spring back (snapback) with enough force to break limbs and tear eyes out of their sockets*. Always exercise extreme caution when in the vicinity of a highly loaded anchor line (or towing line).

Chain Rodes

We spend much time in tropical waters where there is a lot of coral. Although we go to some trouble not to anchor in coral, chafe is still one of the principal hazards. For this reason, our primary rode is all chain. Chain has other advantages: *given a windlass and a properly designed anchor locker* (see chapter 2), it is the easiest rode to handle; its weight causes it to hang down in a catenary, which acts as something of a shock absorber; its weight also holds the shank of an anchor down and, in so doing, helps the anchor to set and increases its holding power; and most of the time, much of the chain lies on the bottom where its friction increases holding power.

Chain has its drawbacks, the two most significant being cost and weight (not just the cost of the chain, but also the cost of the windlass needed to handle it). Chain itself is approximately four times the cost of an equivalent

A riding sail. This sail is somewhat on the small side and, as a result, is not very effective. Two or three times the surface area is better.

nylon rode. However, the high cost can be mitigated over a longer life span, assuming that the galvanizing does not need redoing too often. We used the same chain for twenty years on our old boat, during which time it was regalvanized twice. We sold the chain, still in good condition, with the boat.

As for weight, it ends up in the bow of the boat where it can significantly impair performance. The impact can be minimized by using High-Test chain in place of the more common Proof Coil or BBB (both known as grade 30; they use the same wire size, but the BBB has a shorter link length and is stronger—it is preferred). In general, given any particular Proof Coil or BBB size, the next size High Test down has about the same breaking strength and costs about the same, but weighs one third less. For example, 3/8-inch (10 mm) BBB costs the same as 5/16-inch (8 mm) High Test and has close to the same breaking strength (11,000 vs. 11,600 lb./5,000 vs. 5,320 kg), but it weighs 1.70 pounds per foot (2.54 kg/m) versus 1.09 pounds per foot (1.63 kg/m). On a 150-foot (46 m) rode, the High Test results in a weight savings of 92 pounds (42 kg). Furthermore, it takes up significantly less room; therefore, more of it self-stows before it piles up and jams the chain pipe.

Higher grades of chain (e.g., grades 70 and 80) are commensurably stronger than the High Test (grade 40), yielding even greater weight savings for a given breaking strength—but at a higher cost. In addition, these grades are not widely available through marine stores, and there are problems matching shackle-pin sizes to the chain.

Many people like to use a swivel fitting to connect a chain rode to an anchor, believing that this keeps the rode from twisting. The swivels are often the weak link in the system and, in any case, in our experience it is not needed (we have never used one, and have anchored thousands of times without the rode twisting up). If a swivel is used, on no account should it be connected directly to the anchor: if the boat swings, it puts an unfair sideways load on the swivel for which it is not designed. To provide full articulation, there should always be a shackle between the swivel and the anchor.

Once the wind kicks up or wave action builds, the snubbing action of a boat regularly takes the catenary out of a chain rode, transmitting shock loads to the chain's attachment point on the boat. If it is the windlass, damage is likely. We sheared the main shaft on the windlass on our old boat the first time we used it when we got hit at anchor by a sudden 45-knot squall. A chain rode needs a snubber (a length of nylon rode) to absorb any shock loads. After the anchor is set, one end of the snubber is tied to the chain with a rolling hitch (see chapter 10); the other end is cleated off on deck. Then, 2 or 3 extra feet of chain are fed out and left to hang loose so that the entire load on the rode is transmitted to the boat via the snubber.

Nylon rode is always used for a snubber. It should be sized the same way as a regular rode for a 30- or 42-knot wind (depending on the conditions in which it is likely to be used). There is no point in oversizing a snubber—this simply negates much of its shock-absorbing capabilities. The length need be no more than 20 to 30 feet.

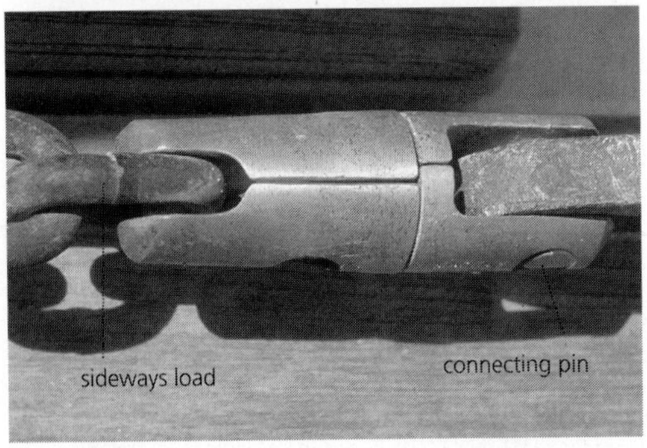

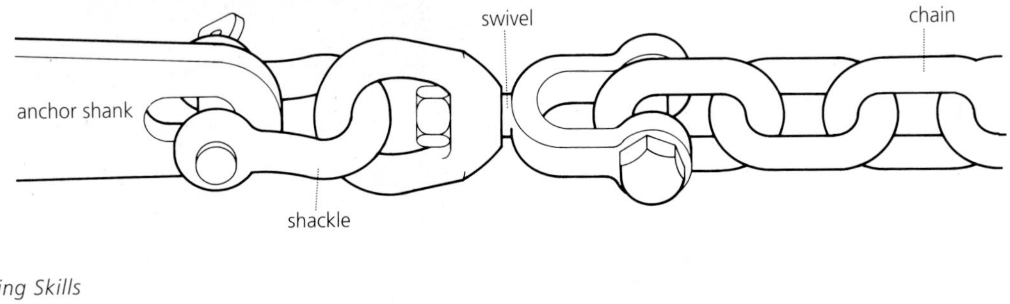

The way this swivel (top) and the chain-to-anchor link (middle) are installed, any sideways load on the anchor risks shearing the connecting pin at the anchor. Bottom: *The proper way to install a swivel.*

Snubber in use.

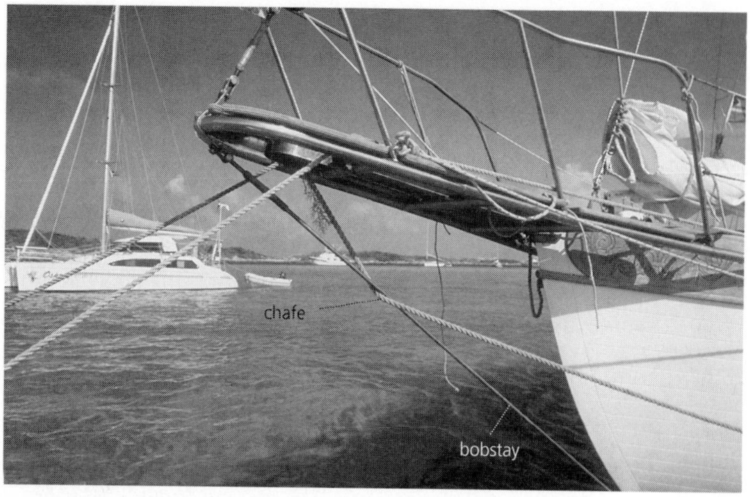

A bobstay is a common chafe point on anchor rodes.

On some boats with an anchor platform, and all boats with a bowsprit, a bobstay runs down to the bow of the boat. Very often, the anchor rollers are set well back from the tip of the bobstay. As the boat moves around at anchor, the snubbing line may chafe on the bobstay. This can be partially mitigated by slitting a length of PVC pipe and slipping it over the bobstay. Better yet is to bring the snubbing line onboard through a fairlead set just back from the bow. This causes the boat to lay just off the wind, helping to stop it from shearing around, thereby keeping the rode away from the bobstay.

Another approach is to incorporate an attachment point in the lower bobstay fitting (the one on the hull) and attach a length of nylon line to it, which is kept lashed to the bow pulpit. With both rope and chain rodes, once the anchor is set, this line can be attached to the rode with a rolling hitch, and then a little more rode can be let out until the load is being taken on the bobstay fitting. This gets the pull away from the bobstay, right down at the waterline (the optimum location); the disadvantage is that if it becomes necessary to let out more rode, you first have to take some up to bring the snubbing line onboard and undo the hitch.

If the snubbing line parts, the windlass will be subjected to a sudden shock load that may break the shaft or simply cause the chain to jump up on the wildcat and start running out. Once a chain starts to do this, it frequently will not reseat itself. *It is essential to have at least one more line of defense against loosing all the chain.* A very strong attachment point for the bitter end of the chain is obviously needed, but *it would be better to have an additional chain stopper on deck or to place a loop of chain around a samson post or cleat.* If all the chain runs out and the boat comes up short on the chain's bitter-end attachment, an enormous shock load may rip the attachment out of the boat, resulting in the loss of the anchor, the chain, and maybe the boat.

A snubbing line attached at the waterline keeps the pull on the anchor rode as low as possible and eliminates chafe on the bobstay.

If this is the last line of defense on this boat for the anchor chain, it is not likely to do much good if hit by a sudden shock load!

A chain rode should be attached to the boat with a length of nylon line long enough for the line to come on deck and be cut in an emergency.

The bitter end of the chain frequently is shackled to a U-bolt in the chain locker: *it should not be*. What is needed is to attach the chain to the U-bolt with a length of nylon rode long enough to allow all the chain to come up on deck. This way, if it is ever necessary to cut the anchor loose in a hurry, it can be done in seconds with a sharp knife or even an axe.

Rope Rodes

On a boat without a windlass, a rope rode is much easier to handle than chain. Nylon is the only choice for rope rodes because of its tremendous strength, its ability to stretch and absorb loads, its resistance to environmental insults, and the fact that it sinks in water and so is less likely to foul the boat and/or propeller than, for example, polypropylene. The choice is between three-strand and double-braided nylon. The former is cheaper, has the most stretch, and is easier to splice; the latter is a little stronger, is softer on the hands, is easier to coil, and will not *hockle* (kink; see chapter 10). Take your pick!

Chafe is the enemy of all nylon snubbers and rodes. To minimize the chances of chafe in the water, anchors should be given a substantial chain lead so that the nylon does not drag across the bottom every time the boat swings at anchor (in any case, a chain lead is needed to hold the anchor's shank down and help it set). Ideally, the chain lead will be at least as long as the boat. A modest load on the line then keeps the entire rode clear of the bottom. In reality, a chain lead of from 8 to 20 feet is more common, but a boat-length lead still works well in most cases. Problems arise when a boat swings and the rode fouls a rock or coral head; unfortunately, little can be done to protect against that.

On deck, chafe is mitigated by providing chafe guards at all points of contact between a nylon rode or snubber and the boat (other than the cleat to which either is fastened). Traditionally, chafe protection has been provided by wrapping a piece of cloth around the rode and tying it on. *In all but an extreme blow* (discussed later in this section), a more effective approach is to use a length of hose, which can be fed onto a snubber in one piece but will need to be slit down one side if it is to be slipped over a rode once the desired amount has been let out. Either way, the hose needs to be securely tied in place; it helps to have holes, through which a lashing can be run, at both ends. In a prolonged blow, the chafe protection needs regular inspection.

As mentioned previously, on some boats with bow platforms or bowsprits, a rope rode chafes on the bobstay in certain circumstances. One way to prevent this is to use a snubber attached to an eye at the lower end of the bobstay (as described previously). Another way is to have an attachment point for a snatch block at the end of the platform or bowsprit and to run the rode through it. The snatch block holds the rode well away from the bobstay.

When it comes to an extreme blow, research by the Massachusetts Institute of Technology and BoatU.S. regarding nylon mooring pendants that failed during Hurricanes Bob and Gloria suggests that a primary cause of failure is heat generated in the pendants as they stretch and contract over the relatively tight bend that occurs where a pendant (or rode or snubber) comes over a bow roller or chock. The failed rodes all had melted strands in the *interior* of the lines (the heat was generated by the fibers working—stretching and contracting—rather than by chafe). The researchers speculated that *the heat buildup is exacerbated when a hose is used for chafe protection* because the hose traps the heat, while also preventing cooling from wind and wind-driven spray.

This raises an interesting idea: in extreme conditions, *it is almost certainly preferable to add a polyester (Dacron or Terylene) snubber to a nylon rode*. The snubber is put on just as with a chain rode; that is, once the anchor is set and the correct amount of rode is paid out, the poly-

Top: *Chafe is the enemy of nylon rodes.* Above: *Chafe can be substantially eliminated with the judicious use of hose.*

A combination of failed rodes and dragged moorings put these boats on the beach during Hurricane Floyd.

ester snubber is attached to the rode with a rolling hitch and cleated off onboard, and then more rode is paid out so that the polyester is bringing the anchoring load onboard. Where the snubber comes onboard, the polyester is protected against chafe with a length of hose. The nylon rode up to the snubber provides the necessary shock absorption for the boat; the polyester, because of its low stretch, will not suffer from the same heat buildup and melting problems.

Because polyester stretches very little, only a few additional inches of nylon rode should be paid out after the snubber has been put in place. This way, if the polyester snubber breaks, the boat will not build up any momentum before the nylon rode takes up the load, which minimizes any shock loading to the rode.

The same thinking can be applied to the nylon snubber on a chain rode; that is, it is an excellent idea to splice in or tie on a length of polyester to run from the onboard cleat to a little beyond the snubber's exit point from the boat, and to then use the requisite length of nylon from that point on.

Finally, it is worth repeating the point made in chapter 2 that the best kind of cleat for minimizing chafe is that which incorporates a couple of horns into the inboard side of a hawsehole through a bulwark. Because there is no distance between the cleat and the exit point from the boat, there is no way for a line to develop more than absolutely minimal movement between its attachment point and the exit point. Friction and heat are minimized.

Attaching Rope to Chain

It seems apparent that the easiest way to attach a rope rode to chain is to simply tie it to the end of the chain! However, if the sizing procedure recommended previously has been used, the rode may be a tight fit in Proof Coil or BBB chain and almost impossible to get through High-Test chain. The answer, then, is to add a shackle to the end of the chain and tie the rode through it. Remember that *any time a shackle is used anywhere in a ground-tackle system, the pin should be seized*—also known as *moused*, for some reason—*so that it cannot work loose*. If the installation is semipermanent, I use stainless steel or Monel seizing wire (available from West Marine and others); otherwise, heavy-duty waxed nylon sailmaker's thread works well.

The two knots that are used for attaching a rode are a fisherman's bend and a bowline (for more about knots, see chapter 10). If a bowline is used, two turns should be taken around the shackle to spread the loads. If the attachment is anything other than temporary, the bitter end of the rode should be seized with light line to the standing part on both knots.

Any kind of a knot weakens the rode and concentrates the load at one or two points. Loads are more uniformly spread if the rode is eye-spliced (see chapter 10) around a thimble, which is then attached to the chain with a shackle. Typically, open-ended galvanized thimbles are used; however, under a load the rode stretches and the thimble compresses, resulting in the rode working its way off the thimble. To minimize the chance of this happening, the rode should be tightly seized both around the base of the thimble and just below the thimble (at the *throat* of the splice). Better yet is a thimble with the ends welded shut, especially if it includes a couple of loops through which the line is passed so that it cannot come off, regardless of how much the rode may stretch and loosen.

The problem with all these approaches is that the knot, shackle, and/or thimble will not pass through a rope-chain wildcat on a windlass. This problem is solved with a rope-to-chain splice, greatly simplifying anchor retrieval with a mixed rope-chain rode. However, remember that static testing on freshly made splices by New England Ropes revealed that the splice has about 85 percent of the strength of the rope. Over time, as the rode works against the chain, friction will degrade the rode; therefore, the strength of the splice can be expected to deteriorate further. The rode also holds moisture

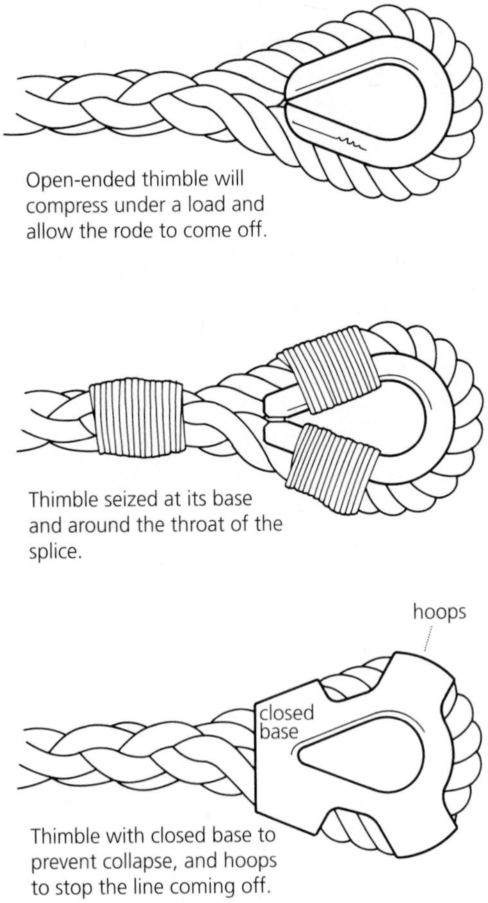

Open-ended thimble will compress under a load and allow the rode to come off.
Thimble seized at its base and around the throat of the splice.
hoops
closed base
Thimble with closed base to prevent collapse, and hoops to stop the line coming off.

Open-ended thimbles do not work well in rodes. Much better are closed thimbles, or at least a thimble well seized in place.

against the chain link, promoting rust, which causes the rode to rot. *If the splice is not the weak link in the ground tackle to start with (it probably is), it is likely to become the weak link over time.* Therefore, any such splices should be regularly checked and perhaps cut off and redone every few years. I would not use such a splice on my primary (bower) anchor.

How Much Rode?

How much rode should a boat carry? This is clearly a function of use and cruising grounds. Someone sailing in the relatively shallow Chesapeake Bay needs much less rode than a world-girdling cruiser who at some time is likely to be anchoring in 60 feet of water or more.

The general rule when anchoring is that with chain, the length of the rode (its scope) should be five times the distance *from the bow of the boat to the seabed at the highest anticipated tide level*. With nylon, the ratio is 7:1. In extreme conditions, these ratios may be increased to 7:1 and 10:1, respectively. Another

MAKING A ROPE-TO-CHAIN SPLICE

These instructions for making a rope-to-chain splice are adapted from instructions by New England Ropes and Simpson Lawrence:

1. With whipping twine or tape, seize the rope ten turns down the lay (about 12 in./300 mm from the rope's end) and unlay the three strands. Fuse the ends of each strand with a cigarette lighter or lighted match to stop them from unraveling.
2. Earl Hinz suggests slipping a short length of large-diameter (larger than the rope) heat-shrink tubing through the chain (*Ocean Navigator*, no. 93, Sept.–Oct. 1998). However, there may not be enough room to do this when using High-Test chain. The heat shrink should be about two rope diameters in length.
3. Pass one strand through the chain-end link (and heat-shrink tubing) from one side and the other two from the other side.
4. Pull the strands up tight and apply heat to the heat-shrink (if used).
5. Remove the seizing and make at least three tucks of a standard back splice with all three strands (see chapter 10). Five tucks would be better—in extreme conditions the splice may slip with fewer.
6. Use a hot knife to pare down the three strands by one third and then put in a couple more tucks.

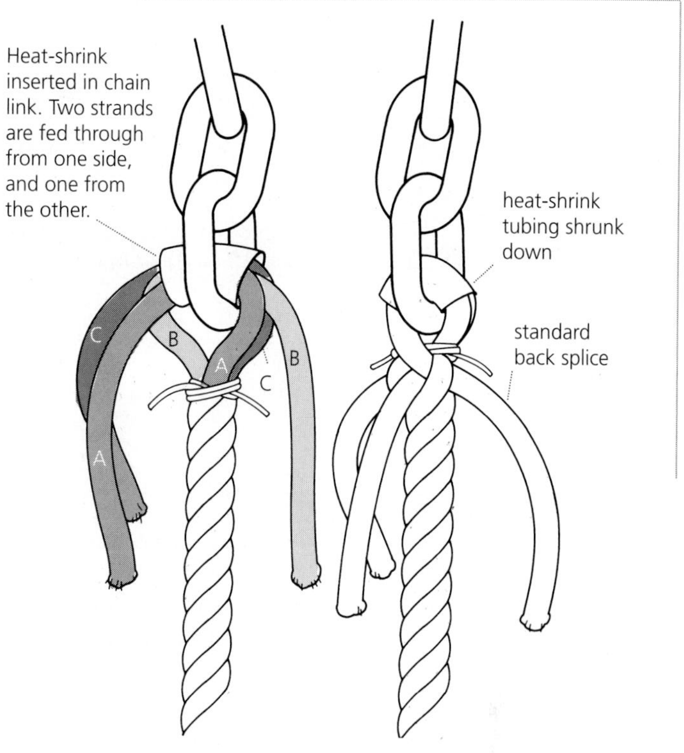
Heat-shrink inserted in chain link. Two strands are fed through from one side, and one from the other.
heat-shrink tubing shrunk down
standard back splice
A
B
C
A
B
C
A
Rope-to-chain splice.

7. Pare the strands down by another third and put in a final two tucks.
8. Cut away the remaining tails and roll the splice underfoot to smooth it out.

rule of thumb is a minimum 3:1 scope in a force 3 wind (7–10 knots), 5:1 in a force 5 (17–21 knots), 7:1 in a force 7 (28–33 knots), etc.

What neither of these rules of thumb recognizes is that when using an *all-chain rode* (as opposed to a mixed chain-rope rode, or a rope rode), the deeper the water, proportionately the less rode is needed because to a significant extent it is the total weight of chain that matters, rather than the ratio of chain to water depth. What is at issue here is the angle the anchor shank makes with the sea bed. Maximum holding power is obtained if the shank is parallel to the seabed (0 degrees); most anchors break out if this angle goes to 10 degrees.

With a chain rode, the weight of the chain creates a catenary in which the chain closest to the anchor generally rests on the bottom, holding the anchor shank at 0 degrees to the bottom. The wind and other forces on the boat act to straighten the chain. At some loading, this results in the shank starting to lift off the bottom. The more the chain that is let out, the greater its weight, and the stronger the force required to lift the shank. This is more a function of chain weight than water depth. Hence the need to let out proportionately less chain (lower ratio of rode length to water depth) in deeper water.

Given the crowding in many anchorages today, and the frequent pressure to anchor on short scope, it is useful to have a relatively more scientific sense of how much scope to let out than that provided by the general rules of thumb. The graph on the next page gives an approximate sense of the necessary ratio of rode length to water depth, using an all-chain rode, at different wind speeds. It shows a minimum value (anchor shank lifted sufficiently for the anchor to be liable to drag or break out), and a preferred value (shank close to 0 degrees to the bottom).

Whatever method is used to determine rode length, two key pieces of information are commonly ignored: the height above the water of the bow of the boat, and the effect of the tide. Let's assume that the depth sounder is reading the actual depth (not the depth under the keel—if this is the case, the boat's draft must also be factored into the equation). We have 15 feet of water; the bow is 4 feet above the water. We are at mid-tide in an area with a 10-foot tide. If

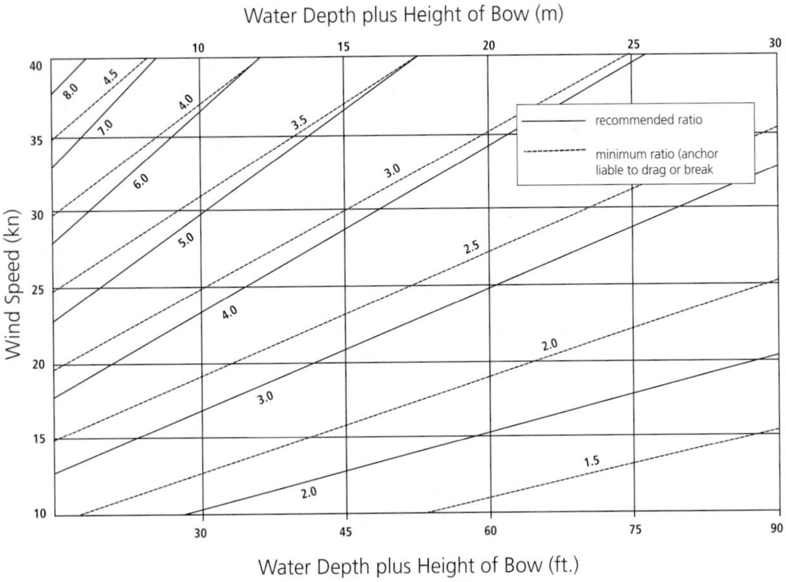

Ratio of rode length to depth, as a function of wind speed and depth (using an all-chain rode).

using an all-chain rode and the 5:1 rule of thumb, in normal circumstances, we need to let out 5 (15 + 4 + 5) = 120 feet of chain; with a nylon rode and the 7:1 rule of thumb, this increases to 168 feet. In extreme conditions, we might need as much as 168 feet of chain (7:1 rule of thumb) or 240 feet of nylon (10:1 rule of thumb).

With this in mind, you can pick an appropriate amount of rode for your intended cruising grounds. For cruising the Caribbean, the Bahamas, and the East Coast of the United States, on a 40-foot (12 m) boat I like to carry a primary all-chain rode of at least 150 feet (46 m) (⅜ in./10 mm BBB or 5⁄16 in./8 mm High-Test), with a couple of secondary ⅝-inch (16 mm) nylon rodes of 300 feet (90 m) each (attached to 15 ft./4.6 m chain "leaders"). We then have 600 feet (180 m) of ½-inch (12 mm) nylon as a backup. For world-girdling cruising, the chain rode should be up to 300 feet (90 m) in length.

Using tie-wraps to mark a chain.

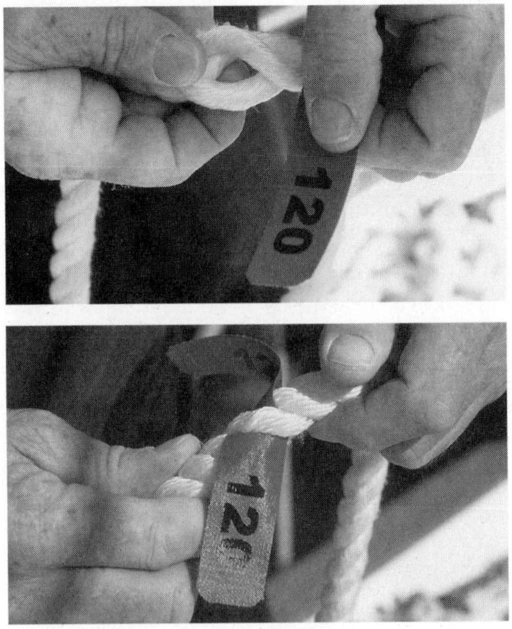

Installing rode markers in a nylon rode.

These rodes need marking in some way so you can tell how much is being let out both during the day and at night. However, too many markers can be confusing: every 25 feet (7.5 m) is

Calculating how much rode to let out.

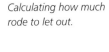

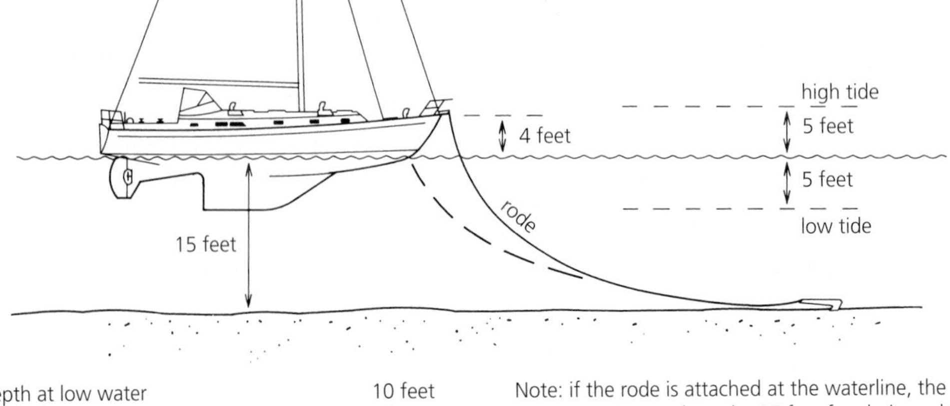

depth at low water	10 feet
tidal range	10 feet
height of anchor roller above the water	+ 4 feet
TOTAL	24 feet
all chain rode (5 × total)	120 feet
nylon rode (7 × total)	168 feet

Note: if the rode is attached at the waterline, the rode requirement goes down by 25 feet for chain and 35 feet for nylon.

probably adequate; every 10 feet (3 m) is likely to be overkill. With chain, we have tried different painted color schemes but it soon wears off. Lately, we have been using colored wire ties. These too break off in time but are easy to replace. What is needed is some easy-to-remember scheme, such as 1 red = 25 feet (7.5 m); 2 red = 50 feet (15.0 m); 3 red = 75 feet (22.5 m); 1 white = 100 feet (30 m); and so on. Changing the color periodically is useful; if you lose track of what is going on or a couple of ties are missing, the color change puts you back in the ballpark.

Cable ties also can be used on nylon rode. Better yet are plastic rode markers that are slipped through the strands (available from West Marine and others). These are highly visible and numbered.

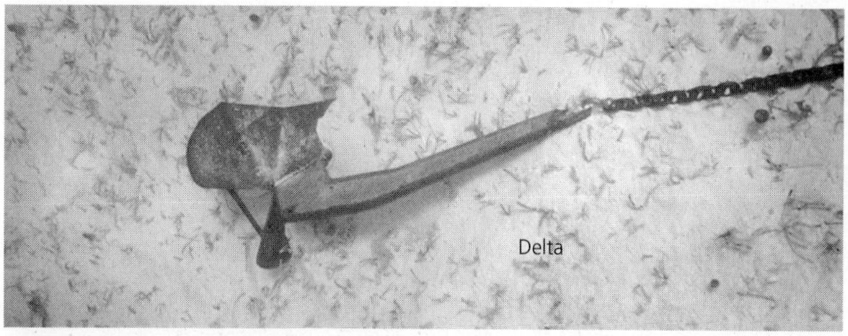

Delta and C.Q.R. anchors about to set. Note the weed fouling the C.Q.R.—it will have little effect on the anchor, whereas if it got wrapped up in the flukes of a Danforth-type anchor, it might impair the set.

Anchor Choices

Having settled on our rode, we now have to attach an anchor to it. This is a minefield if ever there was one! The best I can do is offer some general comments and recommendations about anchor types and suitable weights, and then leave it to the reader to decide.

Anchors can be divided into three broad groups: *plough-type*, *Danforth-type*, and *hooking-type anchors*:

- Plough-type and related anchors include the C.Q.R. and its derivatives, the Delta, the Bruce, the Spade, and the Max.
- Danforth-type anchors (pivoting fluke) include the original Danforth anchors and their derivatives (including West Marine variations and the Fortress).
- A hooking-type anchor in this context refers primarily to the fisherman type, particularly the Luke three-piece yachtsman.

Manufacturers can produce all kinds of tests to show that their anchor is the best. Unfortunately, these tests are really only valid for the particular sea bottom in which the test was conducted, and for that particular boat, with that particular rode, and in that particular sea state and set of weather conditions. The reality is that just about any anchor will set and hold well in sand or heavy mud (*set* defines the ability to dig into the bottom; *holding power* defines the load that can be withstood before the anchor comes loose or breaks). What is of more significance is the ability to set and hold in marginal bottoms: weed, turtlegrass, soft mud, thin sand over rock, coral rubble, and so on. There is no scientific way to gauge either setting ability or holding power in these kinds of bottoms.

Ultimately, the effectiveness of different anchors must be gauged through practical experience. Here's what we have found (this is in the realm of personal opinion and preferences):

- I used to consider the C.Q.R. the best all-around anchor, but now think the Delta is better because it sets faster in more bottoms and is easier to launch. It holds just as well and possibly better. Both share a number of favorable characteristics: the ability to set in a number of different bottoms, the ability to reset if the anchor breaks loose, a low risk of being fouled by the rode if the boat swings around its anchor, and the fact that they self-stow at the stemhead when using a windlass. However, they barely work at all in situations where there is a thin layer of sand over smooth rock or soft mud, and they don't penetrate turtlegrass and weeds very well (the Delta does better than the C.Q.R.).
- The Bruce shares most of these features. However, it does not hold as well in sand and mud bottoms and can get fouled by

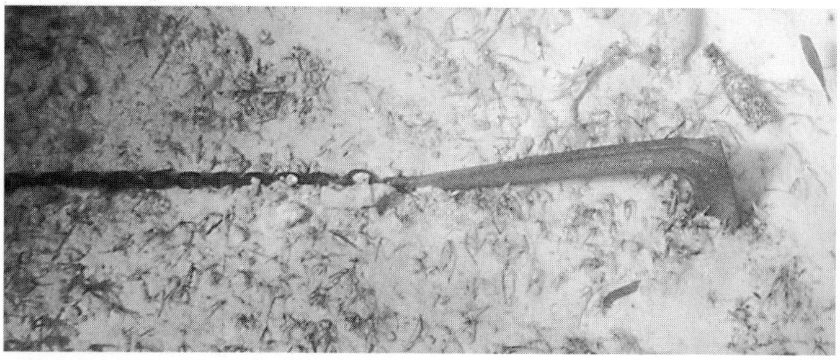

Bruce anchor digging in.

Left: *This Bruce anchor has been only partially set. The boat is swinging around in an arc. With plough-type anchors, this is not a problem; however, with Danforth-type anchors, if the chain snags the flukes, it may trip the anchor and prevent it from resetting.* Right: *Danforth about to dig into sand. If this was a hard bottom, the anchor would rise up on the tips of its points and then roll over, refusing to set.*

grass, but it does set better in foul bottoms (e.g., in coral rubble, it lies on its side and hooks around anything available). It engages the seabed quickly in most conditions but has somewhat limited holding power when it fouls something. When using a Bruce, I recommend an anchor one size heavier than a C.Q.R. or Delta.

- The Max sets extremely well in many bottoms, but the angle that the shank makes with the flukes for different bottoms has to be adjusted (by undoing a bolt and putting it through a different bolt hole). Frankly, I find this ridiculous in an anchor: who wants to do this on a heaving deck, and how do you decide which hole to use in a strange anchorage? In other words, the anchor can be a pain to use. It can also be a pain to stow, depending on the angle at which the shank is set and how it relates to the bow roller.
- The Spade anchor is receiving rave reviews from those who have used it and has scored first in a series of recent anchor tests. Its design places 50 percent of its weight in its tip, with a shape that optimizes its ability to dig in. By all accounts it digs in faster and holds better in more bottoms than any other anchor on the market. If the boat swings, there is little risk of the rode fouling it or the anchor breaking out. It stows well at the stemhead and is easy to launch. It can also be broken down for stowage. We'll have one quite soon!
- The Danforth (on which the West Marine and similar anchors are modeled) has been the anchor to beat for sixty years as far as the pivoting-fluke type is concerned. All pivoting-fluke anchors share the same general advantage: an ability to set in a wide range of bottoms, including better performance than a plough-type in thin sand over smooth rock (the anchor drags until it has built up a mound of sand, but the hold is still quite tenuous), with truly excellent holding power for their weight once set. However, they perform poorly in grass, rocks, coral rubble, and hard clay; they have a limited ability to reset if the anchor comes loose; there is a risk of the rode fouling the flukes if the boat swings over the anchor; and, although a single anchor self-stows at many stemheads (by no means all), it is almost impossible to get this type of anchor to self-stow alongside any other. With two anchors, the anchor generally has to be manhandled over the bow pulpit and stowed in custom chocks.
- The Fortress (a pivoting fluke variant) has impressive setting and holding powers, and is a joy to handle compared to other anchors of this type because of its light weight. However, the downside to the light weight is that the anchor "hydroplanes" very easily. If the boat has any way on when the anchor is lowered over the side, the anchor may never make it to the bottom. If the anchor comes loose in a squall, it may sail around rather than dig back in. Because of its light weight, a Fortress is the easiest anchor to row out and set from a dinghy, which makes it particularly handy as a kedging anchor if you run aground.
- We carry a 55-pound bronze Luke three-piece fisherman/yachtsman (which is easy to stow when taken apart) as an anchor of last resort. Because of its relatively small fluke area, it does not have the holding power of the other anchors in many bottoms; on the other hand, it will penetrate some bottoms the others will not touch (e.g., a heavy vegetative mat) and is the best in rock. It is a pain to handle (it is heavy and awkward; it will not self-stow at the stemhead and must be maneuvered over the lifelines), but on the few occasions when it was the only thing that stopped us dragging, we were delighted to have it onboard.

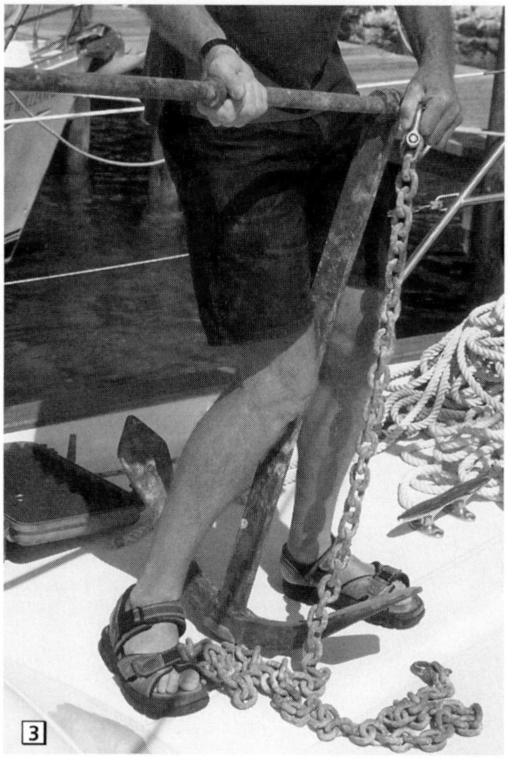

Three-piece 55-pound Luke-style bronze fisherman/yachtsman anchor being assembled. This anchor is our ace in the hole.

- I have not had an opportunity to test, nor have I any first-hand reports on, the Bulwagga anchor, which has received favorable comments from cruisers who have used it and done extremely well in recent anchor tests.
- Cheap knock-offs of (expensive) name-brand anchors sometimes perform very poorly when compared to the original. Buyer beware!

For local cruising, the anchor type should be based on what has been proven to work locally. One anchor should be adequate. For coastal cruising, I recommend a plough-type as the primary anchor (the Delta is my first choice at present, until I have tested a Spade), supplemented by a Danforth-type anchor for those bottoms in which the plough-type will not set. In other words, at least two different anchor types should be carried. For extended cruising, I strongly recommend the plough-type as the primary anchor, supplemented by a Danforth-type that should be stowed at or near the stemhead, ready to launch on short notice, with at least one other anchor as a backup (in case of the loss of an anchor), with a Luke fisherman/yachtsman anchor held in reserve. At least one of the anchors should be stowed on the stern pulpit, also ready to let go on short notice.

In any anchorage that is new to us, we first try to set a plough-type anchor; if it fails to set, we try again. Only after a few failures do we resort to our Danforth-type anchor because once a plough-type anchor is well set, it almost never comes loose, which means we can sleep easy. In contrast, the Danforth-type anchor can come loose and not reset. We have only twice ended up on the beach—both times because the Danforth let go and didn't reset. On other occasions, we have taken off through an anchorage in a squall when either the Danforth or the Fortress let loose and failed to reset. These things rarely happen with plough-type anchors.

In addition to design features, the other key to setting ability and holding power is, quite simply, weight. All else being equal, the heavier an anchor, the more chance it has of penetrating a difficult bottom and the less likelihood of it dragging—but, of course, the more expense, the more weight, and the greater handling difficulties if you do not have a windlass or the windlass breaks down.

Again, the type of cruising you intend to do significantly affects the weight of the anchors you carry. The one thing you can be sure of is that if you get caught out on a lee shore in a blow with undersized anchors, you will wish you had something bigger! Steve and Linda Dashew, whose focus is very much on world cruising, recommend a 66-pound Bruce for 35- to 45-foot boats and a 110-pound Bruce for 45- to 55-foot boats. Without a doubt, this is considerably more

Approximate Minimum Anchor Sizes for Coastal Cruising

BOAT LENGTH feet (m)	ANCHOR TYPE AND MODEL NUMBER (or weight, in pounds)								
	C.Q.R.	DELTA	BRUCE	SPADE	DANFORTH DEEPSET	DANFORTH HI-TENSILE	WEST MARINE TRADITIONAL	WEST MARINE PERFORMANCE	FORTRESS
20–25 (6–7.5)	25	14	16	60	1,200	12H	TRAD-8	PERF-12	FX-7
25–30 (7.5–9.0)	25	22	22	80	1,800	20H	TRAD-13	PERF-12	FX-11
30–35 (9.0–10.5)	35	22	33	80	1,800	20H	TRAD-22	PERF-20	FX-16
35–40 (10.5–12.0)	35	35	44	100	3,000	35H	TRAD-40	PERF-35	FX-23
40–45 (12.0–13.5)	45	44	44	100	3,000	35H	TRAD-40	PERF-35	FX-23
45–50 (13.5–15.0)	60	55	66	100	4,000	60H	—	PERF-70	FX-37

anchor than most people (ourselves included) carry, but it will provide a high degree of anchoring confidence if it can be managed.

The Approximate Minimum Anchor Sizes for Coastal Cruising table, based loosely on manufacturers' recommendations, is a rough guide for coastal cruisers. *Offshore cruisers will want to carry heavier anchors* (at least one size larger).

ANCHORING

It is time to use this ground tackle! The first thing is to pick an appropriate location in which to anchor.

The primary requirement for an anchorage is that it provides protection from the waves and, to a lesser extent, the wind. The chart and/or a local cruising guide can be checked for bays in the lee of a headland or on the leeward side of an island. In tropical waters, a section of reef to windward may be all that is needed. However, sometimes the nature of a coastline is such that waves hook around islands and headlands, and enter what looks to be a protected anchorage broadside to the wind—or even dead against it.

What looks like a cozy anchorage may have problems . . .

Once a potential anchorage has been located, the following questions need to be answered:

- How good is the holding? What will happen if you drag? We have been in lovely anchorages with excellent protection but with lousy holding and rocks or reef all

A. The wind-driven swells will hook around the headland and catch the boat broadside, making it roll heavily.

B. The anchorage is wide open to the W and NW—a wind shift will make it untenable.

C. If evacuation is necessary in the night in rough conditions, it will be easy to get disoriented and hit the reef!

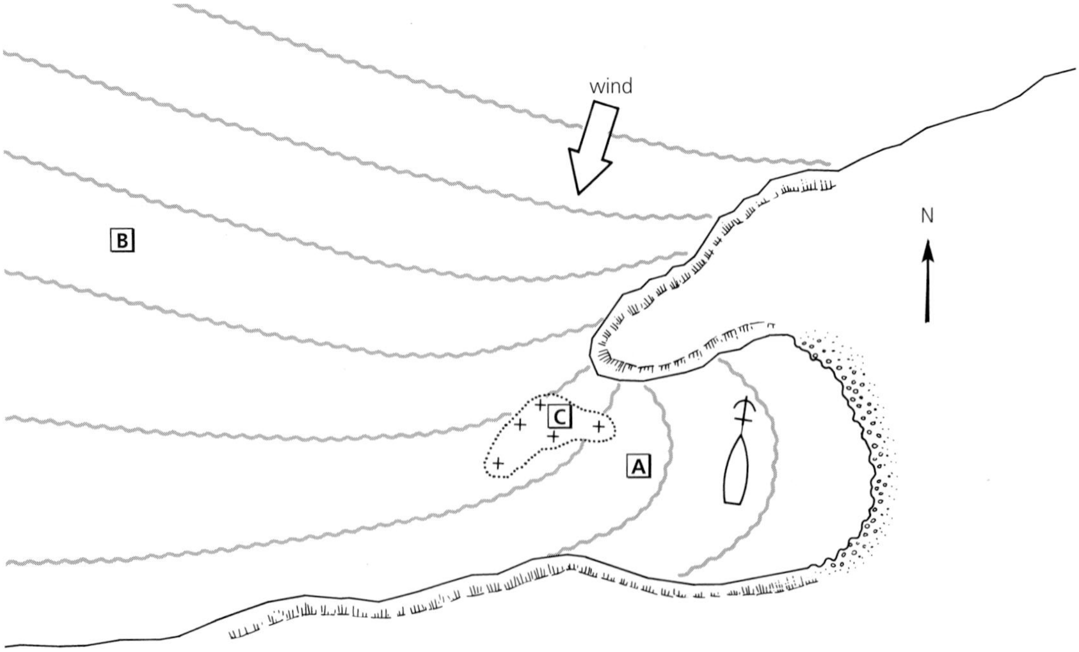

NATURE OF THE SEABED

Types of Seabed

S	Sand
M	Mud
Cy; Cl	Clay
Si	Silt
St	Stones
G	Gravel
P	Pebbles
Cb	Cobbles
R; Rk; rky	Rock; Rocky
Co	Coral and Coralline algae
Sh	Shells
S/M	Two layers, eg. sand over mud
Wd	Weed (including kelp)
Kelp	Kelp, Seaweed

Sandwaves . . . Mobile bottom (sand waves)

Spring . . . Freshwater springs in seabed

Types of Seabed, Intertidal Areas

Gravel . . . Area with stones, gravel, or shingle

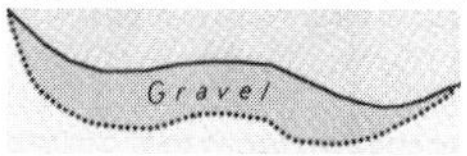

. . . Small area with stones or gravel

Rock . . . Rocky area, which covers and uncovers

Coral . . . Coral reef, which covers and uncovers

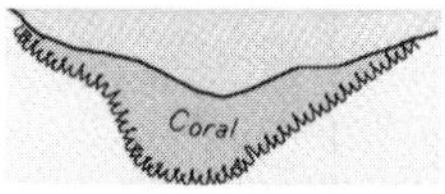

Qualifying Terms

f; fne	fine (only used in relation to sand)
m	medium (only used in relation to sand)
c; crs	coarse (only used in relation to sand)
bk; brk	broken
sy; stk	sticky
so; sft	soft
stf	stiff
Vol	volcanic
Ca	calcareous
h; hrd	hard

Supplementary National Abbreviations (used on U.S. charts)

Grd	Ground
Oz	Ooze
Ml	Marl
Sn	Shingle
Blds	Boulders
Ck	Chalk
Qz	Quartz
Sch	Schist
Co Hd	Coral head
Mds	Madrepores
Vol Ash	Volcanic ash
La	Lava
Pm	Pumice
T	Tufa
Sc	Scoriae
Cn	Cinders
Mn	Manganese
Oys	Oysters
Ms	Mussels
Spg	Sponge
K	Kelp
Grs	Grass
Stg	Sea-tangle
Spi	Spicules
Fr	Foraminifera
Gl	Globigerina
Di	Diatoms
Rd	Radiolaria
Pt	Pteropods
Po	Polyzoa
Cir	Cirripedia
Fu	Fucus
Ma	Mattes
sml	Small
lrg	Large
rt	Rotten
str	Streaky
spk	Speckled
gty	Gritty
dec	Decayed
fly	Flinty
glac	Glacial
ten	Tenacious
wh	White
bl; bk	Black
vi	Violet
bu	Blue
gn	Green
yl	Yellow
or	Orange
rd	Red
br	Brown
ch	Chocolate
gy	Gray
lt	Light
dk	Dark
vard	Varied
unev	Uneven

around. It is simply not possible to relax, go ashore, or sleep with any peace of mind.

- What will be the effect of any tidal streams and/or current? You may end up broadside to the waves, in which case even a slight swell can set a boat to rolling uncomfortably.
- What is the water depth? It may be that an inordinate amount of scope is needed.
- How does the depth change in any given direction? If you are anchoring on the edge of a shelf, and the anchor gets dragged off the shelf, you may find you have totally inadequate scope.
- If there are other boats in the anchorage, is there adequate swinging room to lay out an appropriate amount of scope for the depth?
- If the wind shifts, will the necessary scope put the boat at risk of fouling any hazards or other boats? Often in crowded anchorages, everyone anchors on short scopes—which is all well and good until the wind pipes up or changes direction, at which point there may be chaos.
- More to the point, if the wind shifts, will it put the boat uncomfortably close to a potentially dangerous lee shore?
- And if the wind shifts, what kind of fetch will the waves now have? If it is more than a few hundred yards and the wind kicks up, a substantial chop will rapidly build.
- How easy is it to get in and out? In particular, if it becomes necessary to bail out at night, will there be adequate navigational marks to do so? As with so many other piloting matters, some kind of clearly visible range delineating safe water in and out is the ideal situation.
- Even if it is relatively easy to get out, will this leave you with a clear run to safety, or will there be other navigational hazards difficult to negotiate in the dark?
- And, finally, here are some miscellaneous considerations. If this is a buggy anchorage, are you far enough offshore to get away from the bugs? On the other hand, are you farther than you want to be in terms of taking the dinghy ashore? If there is a lot of local boat traffic, are you in an area where you will be constantly bothered by the wakes of passing boats?

Anchoring Routine

Assuming that you are comfortable with the answers to these questions, a typical anchoring routine (under power) goes something like this:

- On the approach to the anchorage, you should crank the engine and lower or furl the sails, but leave them ready to hoist in case of engine failure. We ran out of diesel one time as we entered English Harbour, Antigua, when it was crowded with boats for race week. If we had not been able to immediately rehoist the sails, we would have been in trouble.
- If the dinghy is being towed, *you need to shorten the painter to the point that it cannot be sucked into the propeller when in reverse.*
- The foredeck is cleared for action and any hatches are closed.
- You make a pass through the anchorage, looking for a likely spot to drop the anchor, and then circle slowly around, checking the depths at the limit of your projected swinging circle to ensure that there are no unpleasant surprises. If the anchorage is crowded but with one clear spot, be especially careful—there is probably a rock or shoal in the middle of it!
- While circling, look at how any other boats are lying (e.g., to the wind or to a tidal stream or current, or maybe a little of both) and attempt to gauge their likely turning circles. Those on moorings will have a tighter turning circle than those anchored, and any boat with two anchors set will turn differently to any boat lying to a single anchor.
- The hardest situation to gauge is one in which the wind is blowing against the tide. Anchored boats may all be lined up with the wind, making you think that their rodes are stretched out in front of them—whereas, the current may have carried the boats upwind so that the rodes are in fact streaming aft. In such a situation, it is common to misjudge the point at which to drop your anchor. Only after it is down will it become apparent that it is in the wrong place! It will have to be retrieved and reset.
- Having chosen a likely spot, you approach slowly with one person in the bow and another driving the boat (I handle the ground tackle; Terrie takes the helm). If the anchor is stowed at the stemhead and the boat has a windlass, the chain is eased out to get the anchor hanging down so that it will be easy to launch. On other boats, it may be necessary to lay the anchor and rode out on

the deck to ensure that it will run out freely without a tangle.

- Voice communication will be difficult because the person in the cockpit is unlikely to be able to hear the person in the bow above the noise of the engine. Terrie and I have an agreed-upon set of hand signals for communicating—I point to port or starboard to indicate a turn, forward to come on, and backward to reverse. I wiggle my forefinger in the air to indicate speed up, I wiggle it down toward the deck to indicate slow down, and I put my hand up in the stop sign for neutral. I run my hand across my throat to ask her to shut the engine down.
- Terrie brings the boat upwind (or upcurrent, if this is having a greater impact on nearby boats) toward the chosen spot. In a crowded anchorage, we come almost under the stern of the boat behind which we intend to anchor; we fall back from there once the anchor is down.
- I give the sign to fall back. Terrie goes into reverse until all forward motion is lost. She calls out the depth so that I know how much rode to let go. I lower the anchor to the bottom with just enough rode to get it there. If the anchor and rode are laid out on deck, I pitch the anchor overboard, *making sure that I am not standing in the bight of the rode* (i.e., inside any coil).
- We either back down *slowly* or else sit in neutral and allow the wind to blow the boat's head off, as I continue to pay out

Above: *Hand signals used on* Nada *when anchoring.* Below: *The basic anchoring routine.*

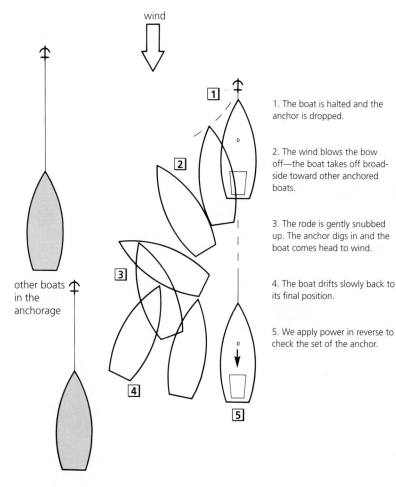

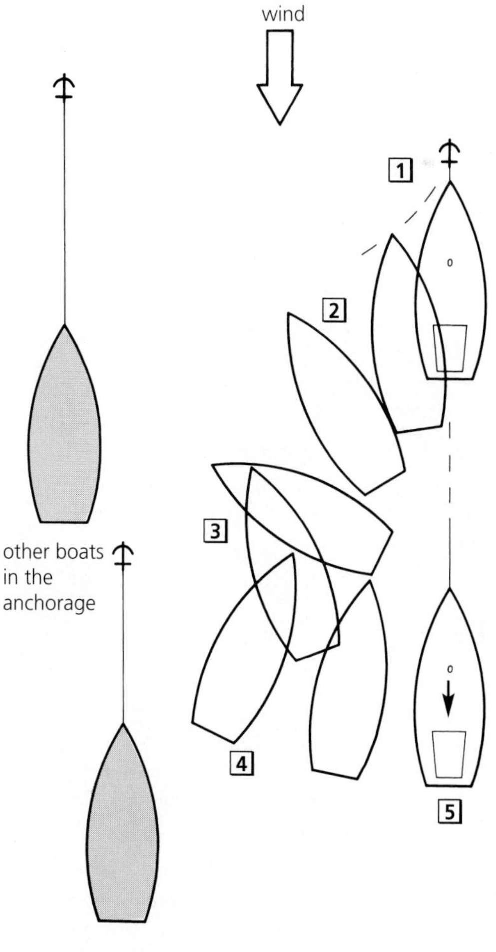

1. The boat is halted and the anchor is dropped.
2. The wind blows the bow off—the boat takes off broadside toward other anchored boats.
3. The rode is gently snubbed up. The anchor digs in and the boat comes head to wind.
4. The boat drifts slowly back to its final position.
5. We apply power in reverse to check the set of the anchor.

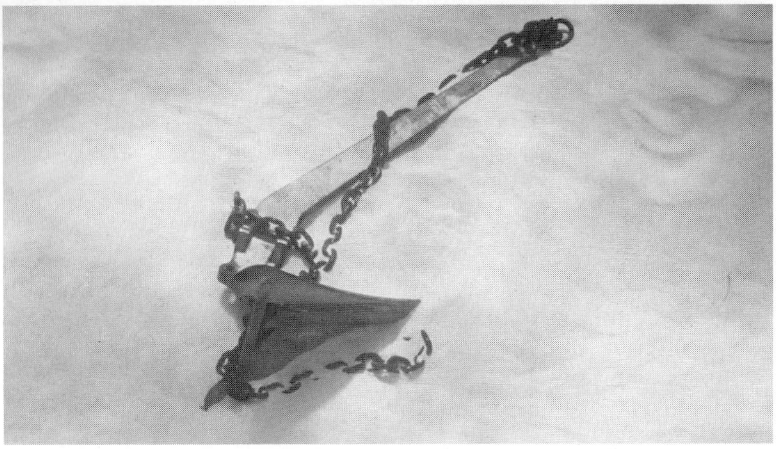

If the anchor rode is let out in a hurry, it may pile up on the anchor and foul it (especially a Danforth-type anchor).

rode *at the same rate as the boat reverses or drifts*. This ensures that there will be no pile-up on the bottom that might foul the anchor. If we are allowing the wind to blow us off, the boat's head will come around broadside to the wind, and the boat will take off at a tangent. It may also be doing the same in reverse; this is normal.

- With chain, when we have about 3:1 scope out, and with nylon at around 5:1, I *gently* snub up on the rode, using the clutch on the windlass for the chain or the warping drum or a cleat for nylon. The idea is to ease the anchor's flukes into the bottom as the rode continues to pay out, now under a little tension.
- At a scope of 4:1 or 5:1 with chain and 6:1 or 7:1 with nylon, I snub the rode up properly, stopping any more from running out. Assuming that the anchor has taken a bite, the boat's head will almost immediately swing into the wind.
- Once we have settled down, Terrie gradually increases the speed in reverse to something more than two thirds the rated engine speed (approximately 2,500 rpm on an engine rated to 3,500 rpm) to thoroughly dig in the anchor and test its set. While this is happening, I keep a hand or foot on the rode.
- If the anchor is dragging, the rode will alternately tighten and slacken; if it is dragging on rocks or some other hard bottom, it will transmit irregular vibrations up the rode. At the first sign of dragging, I give Terrie the signal for neutral, pay out a slug of rode (maybe 10 or 15 feet), and then gently snub up again in the hope of teasing the anchor into the bottom. If this fails and if we have lots of dragging room, we may continue to pull the anchor around for a while, paying out some more rode as we go, to see if it will take a bite. If room is restricted, Terrie goes ahead, we recover the anchor (explained later in this section), and we start again—but not before bringing the anchor to the surface to make sure that its flukes are not fouled. If repeated attempts fail to set the anchor in warm shallow water, we snorkel down and do it by hand.
- Assuming that the anchor takes a hold, we check the set by finding a range (e.g., the mast of another boat in line with a tree ashore or a house in line with a tree) and watch this while Terrie maintains the engine speed. If the two objects remain in line, the set is good. I give the

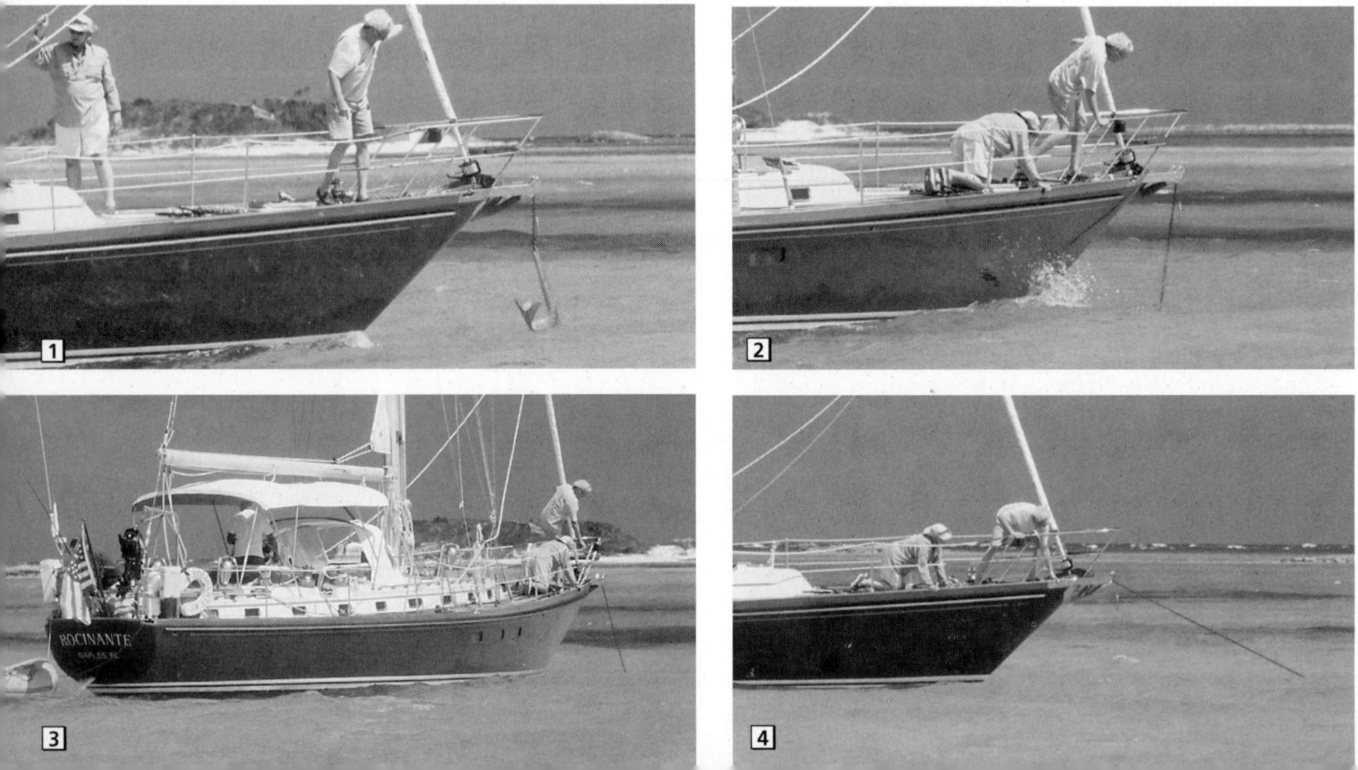

The anchoring routine. 1. The skipper approaches the chosen spot. The foredeck crew has the anchor ready to let go. 2. The boat comes to a stop and the anchor is launched. 3. The wind blows the boat off sideways as the anchor rode is paid out. 4. The rode is snubbed up and the engine put in reverse. The foredeck crew is feeling the rode to see if the anchor is dragging.

Sometimes it is necessary to snorkel down and set an anchor by hand. Just make sure you don't get tangled in the rode!

signal to shut down. The boat then surges forward as the load is taken off the rode, before coming back to its final position.

- If we are lying to a chain rode, I now put on the snubber, pay out some chain, and take a turn with the loose chain around a cleat in case the snubber breaks. If we are lying to a nylon rode, I add some chafing gear, if appropriate.
- If this is not an officially designated anchorage, it may be necessary to hoist into the rigging an appropriate anchoring daymark (the COLREGS require a black ball; this rule is almost never enforced in the Americas but frequently is in Europe).
- The final task is to brew a cup of tea and sit in the cockpit while I drink it. This is a ritual that I have imposed on the children to curb their eagerness to get ashore. It gives me time to observe how we are lying relative to other boats, to check a few more ranges to ensure that we really are not dragging, and to get comfortable with the situation. If it turns out, for example, that I have miscalculated the turning circles of other boats and we are too close to someone else, we will have to pull up the anchor and start again. *The iron rule in anchoring is: First come, first serve.*
- If everything looks fine and we are in a relatively shallow tropical anchorage, before going ashore, one of us will snorkel down to check the set of the anchor.

The same procedure can be used by a singlehander, except that it might prove useful to run the anchor rode through the bow roller, bring it back over the lifelines, attach the anchor, and then haul the anchor aft (outside all rigging) to the cockpit so that it can be launched from there.

In calm, clear water, a viewing bucket (with a glass bottom) does just as well as snorkeling down to check the set of an anchor.

Occasionally, you will enter an anchorage with a foul bottom in which the anchor may snag something and prove very difficult to retrieve. At such times, it pays to rig a *trip line*, which is a line from the head (crown) of the anchor, equal to the water depth at high tide, with a float attached to it. If the anchor gets fouled, heaving on the trip line almost always breaks it loose.

If a trip line is used, it is attached to the anchor and then thrown out, with its buoy, immediately before the anchor is let go. To avoid a tangle, you must ensure that the trip line has a fairlead through the bow roller and not around a stanchion.

Some people routinely use trip lines. We almost never do, considering them more trouble than they are worth most of the time. In practice, we have never had an anchor we could not retrieve without a trip line, although we have struggled mightily on a couple of occasions and wished we had one. (On the one occasion our rode abraded through and we lost the anchor, if we had had a trip line, we could have recovered the anchor.) In a crowded anchorage, it is sometimes worth adding a trip line and float simply to indicate anchor location so other cruisers do not foul the rode when anchoring.

Setting and Retrieving an Anchor under Sail

Although it is rarely done today, there may be times when it is necessary to set or retrieve an anchor under sail. Even when it is not necessary, there is a distinct satisfaction associated with completing a passage without cranking the engine.

Anchors can be set both sailing to windward (the more normal approach) and when sailing downwind. Going to windward, as the chosen spot is approached, the headsail is normally dropped or rolled up and the final approach is made under main alone (the exception is a boat that simply cannot be controlled under main alone). A boat length or so away from the spot at which the anchor is to be dropped, the mainsheet is let go and the boat is turned up into the wind. When the boat comes to a stop, the anchor is let go. The boat will drift back with the wind, allowing the rode to be paid out and then snubbed up.

Unless the wind is really blowing, under sail, it is almost impossible to test the set of an anchor dropped in this manner—you just have to hope it got a good bite. For this reason, it is often better to set the anchor when on a reach or sailing downwind. In an uncrowded anchorage, the reach is easier (it gives more control over the boat); however, in a crowded anchorage, other boats are likely to be in the way, making it necessary to sail downwind through them. In this case, the boat is brought upwind of the anchoring spot, then the mainsail is dropped and gotten out of the way. The boat is sailed downwind at about 2 knots (to maintain steerageway) over the chosen spot. The anchor is let go and *the rode paid out rapidly* (you don't want it to snub up at this time). Meanwhile, the headsail is dropped or rolled up to slow down the boat (if on a reach, the sheets are simply let go).

Once the required amount of rode is out, the rode is snubbed up. At the same time, the rudder is put over to turn the boat toward the side on which the rode is lying (if the rode is streaming aft on the port side, the boat is turned to port). This is done to ensure that the keel, propeller, and rudder swing clear of the rode as it comes tight. The boat's residual motion puts a substantial load on the anchor, hopefully digging it hard into the bottom (in which case, the boat will suddenly turn hard to windward).

Setting an anchor under sail. 1. The approach is made with the jib dropped and the anchor ready to let go; as the chosen spot is reached, the main is allowed to luff. 2. The anchor is dropped and the main backed (by forcing the boom over) to generate sternway. 3. The wind blows the boat off sideways. 4. The rode is snubbed up. 5. The main is dropped while someone snorkels down to check the set of the anchor.

Anchoring under sail: the downwind set.

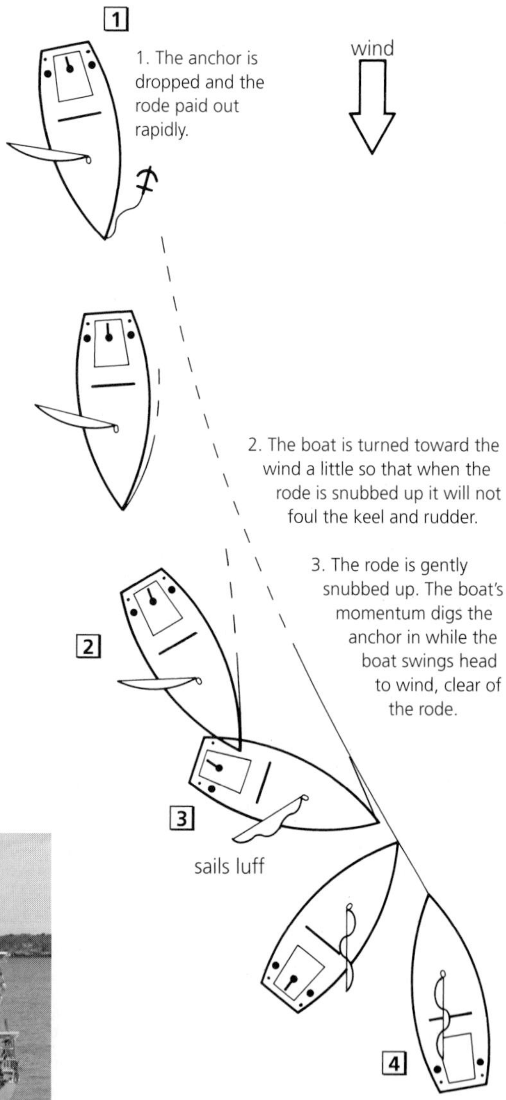

1
1. The anchor is dropped and the rode paid out rapidly.
wind
2. The boat is turned toward the wind a little so that when the rode is snubbed up it will not foul the keel and rudder.
3. The rode is gently snubbed up. The boat's momentum digs the anchor in while the boat swings head to wind, clear of the rode.
2
3
sails luff
4

Regardless of whether the anchor is set to windward, on a reach, or downwind, if it drags there is almost always ample time to reset the sails, sail back over it, recover it, and try again.

Once anchored, if there is no current, the boat will lie more or less to the wind, although many modern lightweight, high-freeboard vessels with minimal wetted surface area shear around (weave from side to side) to a considerable extent. If there is any current, the boat may lie to the current or to any point between the wind and current.

When it comes time to sail out an anchor, the tactics are determined by how the boat is lying relative to the wind. If the boat is lying head to wind and there is sufficient room in the anchorage to maneuver, the mainsail and headsail can be set, leaving the sheets loose. It is best to use a jib rather than a genoa up forward—or at least to keep a genoa partially rolled up—because it will be necessary to tack the headsail a number of times; this makes it easier to handle the sail.

The headsail is *backed* (sheeted to the windward side or held up into the wind). This causes the bow of the boat to be blown off in the opposite direction. Once the bow has been blown off sufficiently for the sails to draw, the headsail is sheeted on the other side and the mainsail sheet is tightened to get the boat sailing. As the boat starts to move, the anchor rode will go slack—it should be hauled in as fast as possible. As soon as no more rode can be pulled in, it should be cleated off. The boat will come up hard on the rode, which causes the bow to swing onto the other tack, at which time the sails are tacked. The anchor rode will slacken once again—enabling more to be pulled in—and then tighten, causing the boat to return to the previous tack. And so on, until the anchor breaks loose, at which time the remaining rode is brought in as the boat sails clear.

If for some reason (e.g., restricted maneuvering room, a lee shore) it is necessary to sail off the anchor on a particular tack, a somewhat different approach is used. First, the main is set with its sheets loose. Then, the anchor rode is shortened until it is about up and down. Finally, the jib is set and backed to get the boat on the appropriate tack. The rode is hauled in and the anchor broken out as the sails begin to fill on this tack. However, sometimes the anchor is difficult to break free, causing the boat to round up onto the wrong tack. In this case, the sheets must be let go and some rode paid out to ensure that the anchor remains set, while the boat is gotten back into position for another attempt.

All of this presupposes that the boat is lying more or less head to wind. If, on the other hand, a current is holding it with the wind aft of the beam, the anchor will need to be broken free before the sails are raised. Once free, if there is sufficient room, the boat can be run off downwind under the headsail and then brought up into the wind to get the main up. If maneuvering room is restricted, it may be necessary to get the main up first to drive the boat around into the wind.

Setting More than One Anchor

It is not uncommon to set two anchors. Following are several good reasons:

- because the holding is poor
- because a big blow is expected
- to hold the boat off a hazard if the wind shifts
- to keep the boat more or less in one spot
- to hold the boat into a chop in a wind-over-tide situation
- simply for peace of mind at night

Where the holding is poor or a big blow is expected, the anchors should be set fairly close to one another (except when a major wind shift is expected, in which case the second anchor should be set in the direction the wind is expected to come from—when doing this, think about which way the boat will swing so the rodes don't get crossed). The most holding power will be achieved by setting the two anchors in line, but if they are set independently in this manner and the boat drags, the nearer one may foul the other's rode. To avoid problems, one anchor can be shackled to the crown of the other at the end of a length of chain so that they both end up on the same rode. This improves the holding power like no other technique, but it makes the anchors awkward to deploy and the first anchor overboard (the one that is attached to the crown of the other anchor) difficult to retrieve (a trip line and float on the first anchor are helpful in getting it back onboard). Because of the problems associated in deploying anchors in this way, we have never done it and have never seen it done! I suppose if faced with a hurricane, we might do it.

Assuming that each anchor is set on its own rode, I like to place them about 30 degrees apart. The first is set in the usual manner, and then the boat is motored forward at the appropriate angle until alongside the first anchor, at which point the second is let go. This is easier

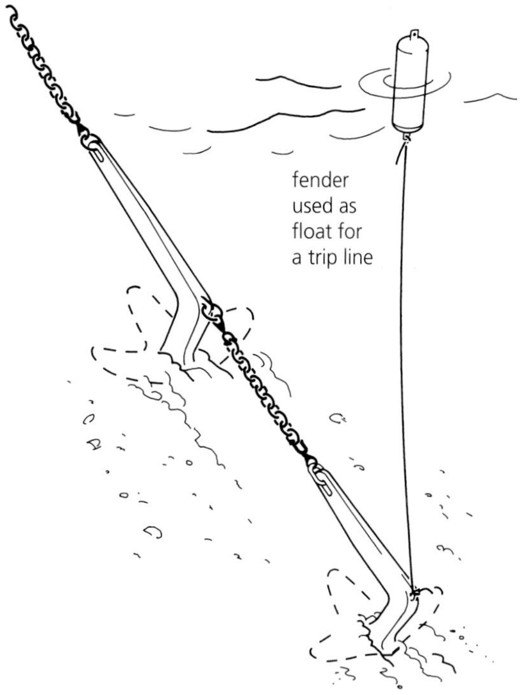

Setting two anchors in line, with the first shackled to the crown of the second.

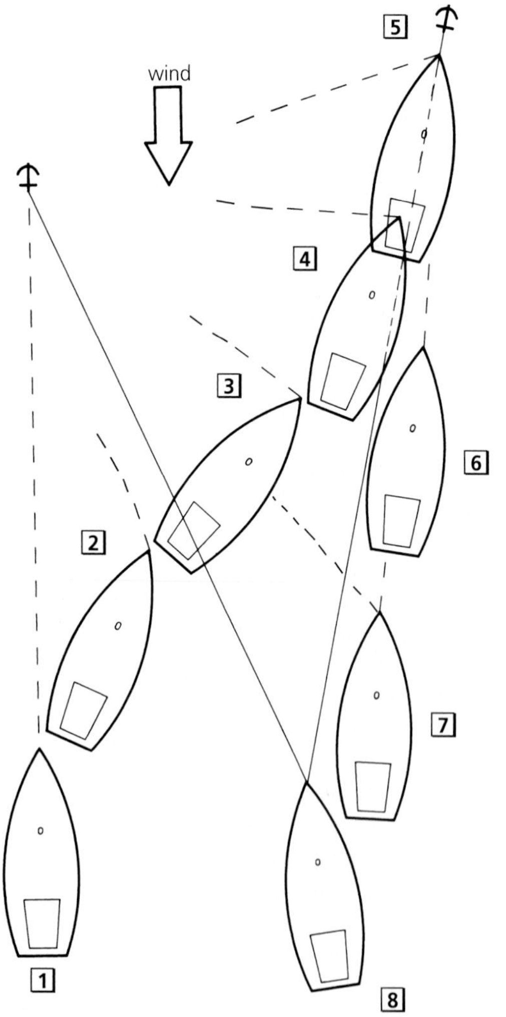

Setting two anchors separately.

1. The first anchor is dropped and set as usual. The rode is cleated off.

2–4. The boat is motored forward, taking up the slack on the first rode.

5. The boat is brought a little ahead of the first anchor (to provide dragging room for the second anchor) and the second anchor dropped.

6–7. The rode is paid out on both anchors. At 7 the second is gently snubbed up and then set.

8. The boat comes to rest between the two anchors.

said than done because it is difficult to judge just where that first anchor is! If you go too far, you risk dislodging the first from its set; if you don't go far enough, you end up with too little scope on the second.

I like to use a rope rode on the first anchor (with a length of chain at the anchor) and our chain (primary) rode on the second anchor. As we motor forward to drop the second anchor, I leave the first rode cleated off but pull in the slack by hand and let it pile up on deck, maintaining a little tension on the line. At some point, the rode stops coming in and I have to start letting it out again. I know now that I am more or less alongside the first anchor. Furthermore, by maintaining a little tension on the first rode while motoring forward, I ensure that we do not foul it in the propeller.

We keep going forward a little more, letting out the rode to the first anchor to give ourselves some dragging room with the second anchor, and then come to a stop and drop the second anchor. As we fall back, I let the rode to the first anchor run back out, snubbing up the second anchor before the first rode comes taut. This way, I can ensure that the second anchor is also well set.

It may be that we are anchored off a beach close enough inshore that if the wind shifts, we are going to end up on the beach. In this case, the second anchor will be set in such a way as to hold us off the beach if necessary. This may be well out to one side or it may be dead astern.

There are times when I am a little unsure about the set of our anchor, but we have lots of dragging room. Very often, rather than go to the trouble of setting a second anchor, I simply drop the second to the bottom off the bow and then lay out on the side deck whatever nylon rode is needed to give it adequate scope, with maybe a half turn around a cleat so that it does not all slide overboard under its own weight. If we drag in the night, this rode is pulled overboard. Once it is all out, the line goes taut and (hopefully) sets the anchor. When using this approach with a chain rode, the anchor should be lowered to the bottom and then an appropriate amount of chain dumped in a pile *a few feet behind the anchor* (this is important to avoid fouling the anchor with the chain).

A Bahamian Moor

When the second anchor is set astern with both rodes coming back over the bow, this is known as a *Bahamian moor* (it gets this name because with both rodes tightened, it significantly limits a boat's turning circle, enabling

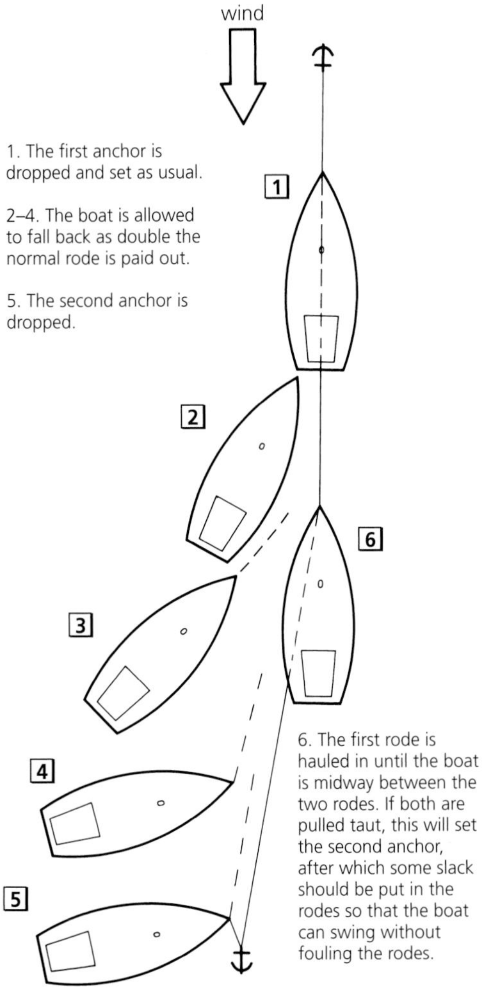

wind
1. The first anchor is dropped and set as usual.
2–4. The boat is allowed to fall back as double the normal rode is paid out.
5. The second anchor is dropped.
1
2
3
4
5
6
6. The first rode is hauled in until the boat is midway between the two rodes. If both are pulled taut, this will set the second anchor, after which some slack should be put in the rodes so that the boat can swing without fouling the rodes.

A Bahamian moor.

more boats to safely anchor in crowded Bahamian anchorages). The other place a Bahamian moor is very useful is when anchoring in an estuary with a strong tidal stream. When the current reverses, the Bahamian moor will stop the boat from swinging into the bank or out into the channel.

There are two ways to execute a Bahamian moor. The first is to drop the first anchor and then continue forward, paying out at least double the necessary scope, to drop the second anchor. The boat is then allowed to fall back to a position midway between the anchors. Tightening the rodes will set both anchors, but thereafter, enough slack should be put in the system to allow the stern rode to hang down below the keel, propeller, and rudder. The second approach (see illustration above) is to drop the first anchor and make sure it is set, and then fall back at least double the necessary scope to drop the second anchor. The first rode is tightened until the boat is positioned midway between the two anchors, at which time tightening the rodes will set the second anchor.

Although we commonly use both methods, I prefer the second approach for the following reasons:

- I can make sure the first anchor is well set before deploying the second.
- There is no chance of fouling the first anchor's rode as you fall back to set the second.

Whatever is done, if the anchorage has a reversing current or tidal stream, it is important to recognize that individual boats respond differently to the change in current. Those with long keels and low freeboard turn first as the current gets a hold on their underbodies; those with fin keels and high freeboard tend to be held in place by the wind. At times, the boats will be lying in completely different directions. If they are anchored too close to one another, they will collide.

With a reversing current, different boats will turn at different times. Note how all four of these boats are lying in different directions . . . which sometimes causes boats to swing into each other!

When the current reverses, sometimes the slack rode fouls the keel, as happened here with Nada, *holding us broadside to the other boats. You would not expect our keel to do this; however, we had a mass of barnacles on the bottom of the keel—from where we had run aground and rubbed off the bottom paint—and the rode fouled on these.*

When using nylon rodes in a reversing stream, with certain keel and rudder types (especially fin keels and spade rudders), there is a risk of fouling one of the rodes as the boat swings through 180 degrees. In this case, it is advisable to lower a weight down the rode that is streaming aft so that this rode is held down. Such a weight is known as a *kellett*; the line on which it is lowered is a *sentinel*. The use of a kellett with a nylon rode also improves the holding power of most anchors.

Another way two anchors might be set is to pitch the second off the stern (rather than streaming both rodes over the bow). This way, the boat cannot swing and foul a rode. The same two approaches used for a Bahamian moor can be used. A variation on the stern-anchor theme, commonly used in some steeply shelving West Indian anchorages, is to pitch an anchor over the stern when approaching the beach and then take a line from the bow to a palm tree ashore. The stern rode is then tightened to keep the boat off the beach.

Wind over Waves and Docking Anchors

Occasionally, a boat will lie head to wind with the waves on the beam—even a modest swell will set many boats to rolling uncomfortably. In theory, it should be possible to set a stern anchor so that it pulls the boat into alignment with the waves (and out of alignment with the wind). In practice, it is extremely difficult to do this, and it greatly increases the wind loading on both rodes. We've tried it a number of times, but with rare success. Furthermore, assuming that both anchors set well, if there is any kind of a wind blowing, it can be quite a

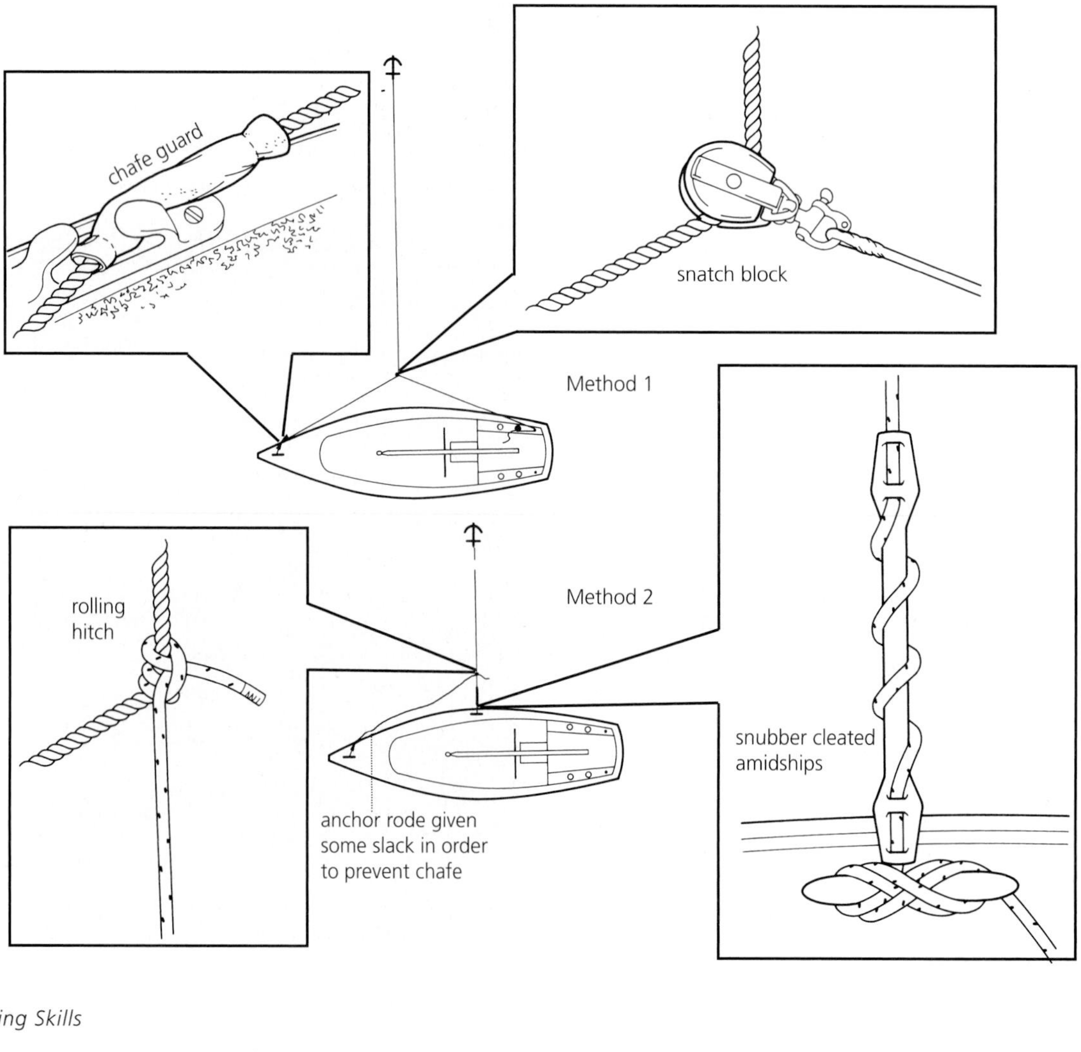

Techniques for getting a boat to lie broadside to an anchor.

business to get the first anchor back onboard against the broadsides pressure of the wind. Once the first anchor is up, the boat will lie head to wind (or stern to, depending on which anchor is still out), which makes it easier to get the second anchor up.

A better way to swing the bow out of the wind and into offset waves is to set an anchor as usual (off the bow), attach a spring line to the rode (use a rolling hitch), then bring this line aft to a cockpit winch, let out more rode, and crank in on the winch (this is known as *springing the anchor*). This effectively forms a bridle. The angle at which the boat lies can be altered by paying out the anchor rode and cranking in or letting out the line on the winch. However, it is essential to ensure that the rode and spring lines both have a fairlead (chafe-free); if not, one or the other will chafe through in short order. If the wind gets up and you are worried about lying beam to it, the spring line can be let out until the boat once again lies head to wind. Anchor retrieval is much easier than with an anchor set over the stern.

If rode chafe is a problem, a snubber should be attached to the rode (in addition to the spring line) and cleated off up forward. A little more rode is now let out so that the snubber is taking the load off the rode, eliminating chafe at the bow. When it comes to taking in the anchor, the spring line will probably have to be cast off from the boat and then recovered at the bow as it comes in with the rode.

The last anchoring scenario is setting an anchor to hold a boat off a dock when the wind and/or waves are driving onto the dock. The easiest way to do this is to drop an anchor off the bow when well out, to snub it up and set it, and then to ease the stern onto the dock by slowly letting out the rode. This maintains excellent control at all times. If the anchor fails to set, you have time to come into the wind and/or waves to recover the anchor and get clear before you get into trouble.

If you need to come alongside the dock broadside, a breast anchor will have to be set to hold you off. The easiest way to do this is to set an anchor off the bow and spring it as described above.

Setting an Anchor from a Dinghy

Sometimes it is not convenient to use the boat to set a second anchor. In this case, it has to be taken out in the dinghy. With a nylon rode, if someone feeds the rode overboard, it is possible to drag it out with the dinghy (especially when using an outboard motor rather than rowing).

Above: *Setting an anchor with a nylon rode from a dinghy—the rode is being dragged out behind the dinghy.*

Left: *Setting an anchor with a substantial chain rode from a dinghy.* 1–2. *It is important to lower the chain into the dinghy and to pay it out from there.* 3. *It is also important to make sure the chain and anchor are lying on the same side of the dinghy before pitching the anchor overboard.*

However, with a chain rode, this is not possible—the rode needs to be loaded in the dinghy with the anchor and paid out as you move away from the boat (this is also an easier way to handle a nylon rode).

The anchor should be rowed to well beyond the point at which you want it to set. Inevitably, when it is thrown overboard from the dinghy, the weight of the rode carries it some way back toward the boat. In addition, you need to give it whatever dragging room is necessary to get a good set, which is achieved by returning to the boat and hauling in the rode until it is tight.

When rowing out a chain rode in a deep anchorage, extreme care must be exercised. As more of the rode goes over the side, there will be a tremendous weight of chain hanging down. This may start uncontrollably dragging the rest of the chain over the side until it snatches forcefully at the anchor. This happened to me in an 80-foot-deep anchorage. When the last of the chain ran out, it jerked our 45-pound C.Q.R. across the dinghy, impaling the side of the dinghy with the anchor's point. The combined weight of chain and anchor capsized the dinghy and left it lying on its side half submerged. If it weren't for the dinghy's considerable amount of built-in flotation, it would have taken the dinghy to the bottom!

Retrieving (Weighing) an Anchor

Anchor retrieval is typically quite straightforward. However, whoever is on the tiller or wheel will not be able to see which way the rode is lying, so it helps to have someone in the bow giving hand signals. Terrie and I simply point in the direction the rode is lying, moving our hand down to point at the water as the boat comes up over the anchor. The retrieval process goes something like this:

The foredeck crew must direct the skipper via hand signals when retrieving an anchor.

- If the dinghy is being towed astern, we shorten its painter so it can't foul the propeller. If the forehatch is open, we close it to clear the decks for action. Generally, we raise the main before getting underway. If not, we at least remove the sail cover so that it can be hoisted on short notice.
- One of us motors slowly forward while the other either stands on the windlass button to retrieve a chain rode or hauls in the slack on a nylon rode, periodically pointing in the direction of the remaining rode. It is important not to overrun the rode, particularly a nylon rode, because then it might foul the keel, propeller, or rudder. If necessary, the motor is periodically put in neutral to slow the pace.
- When the rode is more or less up and down, we put the motor in neutral. If it is a nylon rode we are retrieving, we take a couple of turns around the warping drum on the windlass (or a sturdy cleat if there is no windlass). Before breaking the anchor out, we tidy up any rode on the foredeck (on our old boat, we rolled the nylon rode onto our rope spool).
- We motor the boat slowly forward against the direction in which the anchor was set. This usually breaks it loose, at which point we put the engine in neutral while we recover the remaining rode and the anchor. The head of the boat will slowly blow off downwind, causing the anchor to stream out away from the boat so that it does not foul the topsides as it breaks the surface of the water.

Frequently, a chain rode comes up extremely muddy. It's nice to have a washdown pump to hose it down as it comes up to the bow roller. Otherwise, most mud is dislodged before the chain breaks the surface of the water if you periodically stamp up and down on the length of chain between the bow roller and the windlass, causing the chain to jump up and down. If the chain comes out of the water still muddy, drop the muddy section back down to the waterline and repeat the process. Whatever residual mud ends up on deck should be sluiced down with a bucket of water before it has a chance to dry (if you have the anchor dams recommended in chapter 2, the mess will be confined to the immediate foredeck).

Frequently on small boats or with Danforth-type anchors, once the anchor has broken the surface of the water, it must be hauled over the lifelines and stowed on deck. It helps to have a

If a Danforth-type anchor has to be hauled over the lifelines, it is best to attach a length of line to the anchor shackle. This can be grabbed and used to get the anchor aboard.

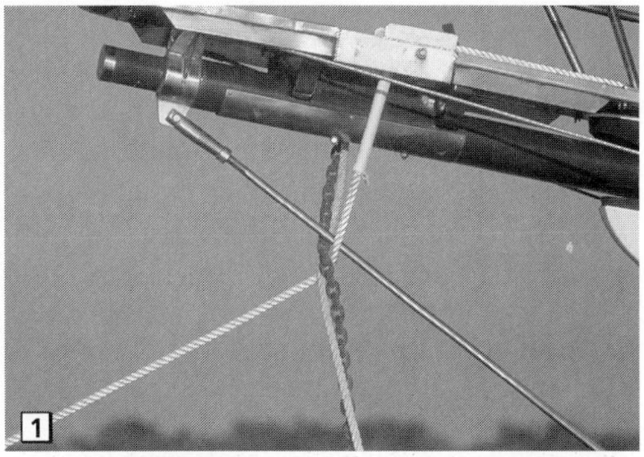

Twisted rodes and one way to unravel them.

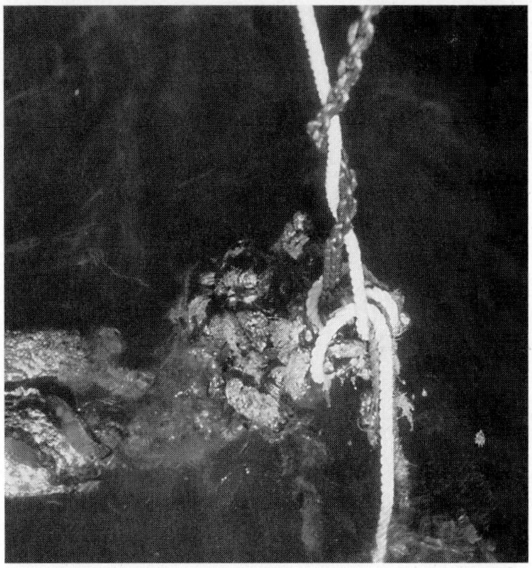

The worst tangle we ever got into. With two anchors set, we swung in circles all night at the same time as we snagged a mass of old lobster pots. We undid the bitter end of the rope rode to sort out the mess.

length of line (3 ft./1 m) spliced to the anchor shackle (at the top of the shank). Bring the anchor to the bow roller in the usual manner, reach over the bow pulpit to grab this line, and then ease off on the rode and pull the anchor up and over the pulpit with the line. Even if the anchor is stowed on the bow roller, this line is useful, inasmuch as it can be brought back to a cleat and used to secure the anchor so that the anchor doesn't work its way overboard at sea.

If we have two anchors set, we bring in the most awkward one first; in our case, it is the one with a nylon rode. We get it stowed and its rode tidied away before bringing in the second anchor. On a boat without a windlass, the heaviest anchor might be the most awkward. When anchored to a Bahamian moor, ease out the rode on the anchor that is taking the load until the boat is over the other anchor, which is then recovered. After this, motor forward to recover the other anchor.

Sometimes when lying to two anchors, the

boat will turn through a circle and twist the rodes together. It usually is possible to sort this out by loosening one rode to the point that the other slides up through it. However, as soon as the anchor being retrieved breaks loose, the boat will start to fall back on the other anchor and rode. Continue paying out the slack rode to keep it loose until the anchor that is being raised has been brought to the stemhead and disengaged from the other rode. After this, the slack rode is snubbed up and retrieved as usual.

If the situation starts to get out of control after the first anchor has broken loose, snub up the slack rode, let it go tight around the other anchor rode, get the boat back under control, motor forward to put some slack back in the rode, and then continue working the first anchor through the slack rode. If you get in too much of a mess, you can always undo the bitter end of the anchor rode being retrieved, and then unravel the rodes by hand.

What if an anchor doesn't break loose? Letting a little rode back out and then motoring around in a circle with the rode under tension often does the trick. Other times, the anchor has hooked another anchor chain, in which case the anchor has to be hauled to the surface and the other chain lifted off (taking care not to break the other anchor loose). On one occasion, we hooked into a 600-pound anchor that had broken loose from a ferryboat in a hurricane (the ferry was blown ashore and destroyed). We could not get disengaged. However, by assisting the windlass with the halyard winches, we got the ferryboat anchor to the surface. We powered into shallow water where we set the ferryboat anchor back on the bottom and then we were able to jump in and disengage our own.

If an anchor won't break loose and there is any wave action, the rode can be brought to the up-and-down position and then tightened as the bow drops into the trough of a wave. The next wave crest should jerk the anchor loose. However, if the anchor fails to move, you sometimes impart tremendous shock loads to the ground tackle, the bow roller, the windlass (if in use), and the associated hardware. Don't forget the caveats already mentioned.

What if the anchor is truly fouled? If a trip line was rigged, it will almost always get it out. If not, snorkel down to check out the problem—you may be able to physically pry the anchor loose. If this is not possible, place a weighted loop around the rode (a short length of chain with the ends shackled together works well, or a length of heavy-duty nylon line with a weight attached), attach a sturdy line to it, and slide the loop down the rode. The idea is to jiggle the loop over the shank of the anchor, down to the crown, so that it can be used as a trip line. It helps if the rode is reasonably up and down, and under some tension to keep it straight (shorten the rode and then put the engine in slow reverse). It also helps if the trip line is taken out in the dinghy beyond the anchor so that the angle of pull is as advantageous as possible for working the weighted loop over the anchor's shank.

Once the trip line is in place, the boat is brought to a position beyond the anchor (it may be necessary to buoy the anchor rode and cast it loose) so that the trip line can be hauled in, dragging the anchor out by its crown.

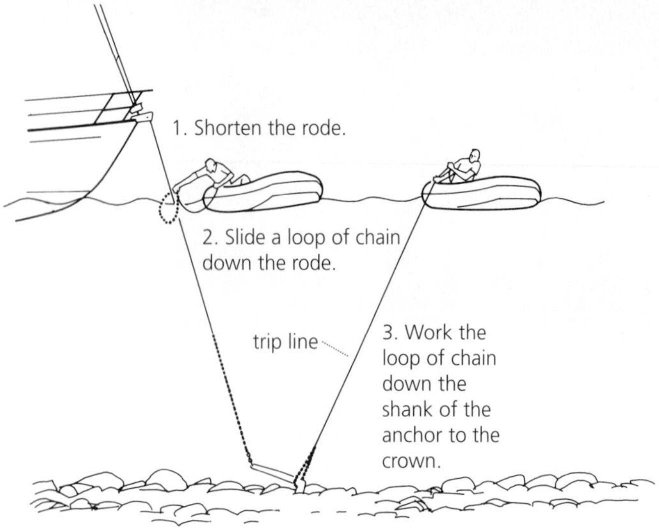

1. Shorten the rode.
2. Slide a loop of chain down the rode.
trip line
3. Work the loop of chain down the shank of the anchor to the crown.

Top: *Retrieving a fouled anchor with the dinghy. The rode is followed by hand (in this case, under another rode) until the anchor can be retrieved with a direct upward pull.* Bottom: *Working a trip line over a fouled anchor.*

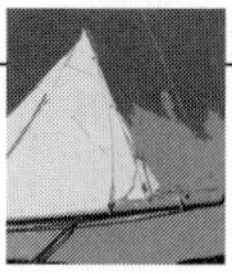

RUNNING AGROUND AND KEDGING OFF

Some people seem to think that running aground is a tremendous indignity. We tend to think that if we don't run aground at least periodically, we are likely to be missing some excellent gunkholing possibilities. However, we only adopt this somewhat cavalier attitude in nonthreatening situations (primarily, no wind and waves, and minimal tide).

If you run aground on a hard bottom, it will be immediately apparent—there will be a series of hard knocks. On a soft bottom, the boat may just lose speed—it may take a moment to realize what is happening. Either way, it is worth looking at the situation from the following four perspectives:

- running aground under sail
- running aground on a rising tide
- running aground on a falling tide
- running aground in tideless waters

Hard aground on the south coast of Cuba with a squall approaching—not a comfortable situation. Luckily, these are protected waters.

Running Aground under Sail

If you are close hauled or close reaching, tack immediately, leaving the headsail sheeted on the old tack. If the boat's head can be brought through the wind, the headsail will back, driving the head around and causing the boat to heel, which will decrease its draft (except with a wing keel). With any luck, you will sail straight off.

On any other point of sail (i.e., a reach or a run), it is almost always best to let go the sheets and get the sails down as quickly as possible. Make a quick check for any trailing lines, shorten the dinghy painter if the dinghy is being towed astern, and then crank the engine and give it full reverse. With any luck, the boat will back off.

If you are still stuck, keep the engine in reverse while the crew rushes rhythmically from one side of the boat to the other, setting it rolling from side to side. Even on our old, heavy, long-keeled double-ender, we could set the boat rolling significantly by leaning far out

On a reach, if you ground, the sails are likely to keep driving you farther on—let them fly.

over one set of lifelines amidships, and then all rushing across to the other side and doing the same. Sometimes the combined effect of this with the reverse prop wash being driven under the keel is enough to break the grip of soft bottoms and get the boat moving.

If the boat has a regular keel (not a wing keel or twin-bilge keels), you can swing the boom out until it comes up against the shrouds, tie it off in this position, and then have the crew work its way as far outboard as possible. This heels most boats quite considerably, hopefully lessening the draft enough to power off. This does not work with wing keels and twin-bilge keels (the draft actually increases with heeling).

If these measures fail, you had better throttle back the engine before you suck a load of sand and/or silt into the cooling system and cause it to overheat. It is time to try one or more of the techniques outlined in the following sections.

Running Aground on a Rising Tide

If you have run aground in tidal waters, the big question is: Is the tide coming in or going out? If it is coming in, it is just a matter of waiting for it to lift you off. However, if the wind and waves are driving you farther aground, it is imperative to launch the dinghy and row out a kedge anchor as soon as possible. Put the anchor and its rode in the dinghy, row it well beyond the point at which you want the anchor to set, pitch the anchor and rode overboard, and then return to the boat to crank in the rode until it is taut.

It is almost always best to set a kedging anchor at least off at right angles to the boat and maybe more or less behind it so that you can drag the boat's head around toward the deeper water; then pull the boat off forward when the opportunity arises. However, to be able to do this, *the rode must make a fairlead onto its bow roller not only when the anchor is first set (i.e., with the rode streaming aft in many cases), but also at whatever changing angles occur as the boat's head comes around.* Almost invariably, with standard bow rollers and cheek blocks, the rode will either chafe terribly or ride up around the forward stanchion on the bow pulpit, threatening to wreck the pulpit as load is applied. In this case, a strategically placed snatch block may provide the necessary fairlead or it may be necessary to bring the rode aboard at some other point. It pays to think about this before a crisis develops!

A kedge anchor should always be set on a *very long rode*, which gives it some dragging room in which to set and ensures that as the boat comes off and the rode shortens, there is still adequate scope to maintain this set and keep the anchor from breaking out.

The children checking the depths with a pole (top) and setting a kedging anchor (above).

If the boat has a fin keel with a narrow, highly loaded, root and/or a spade rudder, think about the kind of stresses that may be created when kedging; it is quite possible to do substantial damage. Likewise, think about what is going on with a wing keel—heeling the boat initially *increases* its draft rather than reducing it.

The sails are set to heel the grounded boat. They need to be sheeted in for the most effect.

When considering your options, don't forget that the most powerful winch on a boat is often the cockpit genoa-sheet winch, not the windlass. The best course of action may be to lay out a stern anchor, bringing the rode onboard through a stern fairlead to a cockpit winch. Alternatively, once the windlass is loaded up, use a running hitch to attach a line to the rode somewhere forward of the windlass; then take this line to a winch and crank in on it to assist the windlass.

Whatever you do, don't stand on an electric windlass button once the windlass starts to stall. As a windlass approaches its stalling point, its current draw rises dramatically (I have measured more than 400 amps on a 12-volt windlass). There is considerable likelihood of burning up the windlass motor, in addition to which its electric cables are almost certainly not rated for anywhere near stalling amperages and, therefore, may overheat or even catch fire!

Remember that a well-tensioned rode is a potentially dangerous beast. The most likely point at which it will break is where it comes aboard; therefore, figure its maximum snapback range if it breaks at that point and attempt to keep everyone out of range.

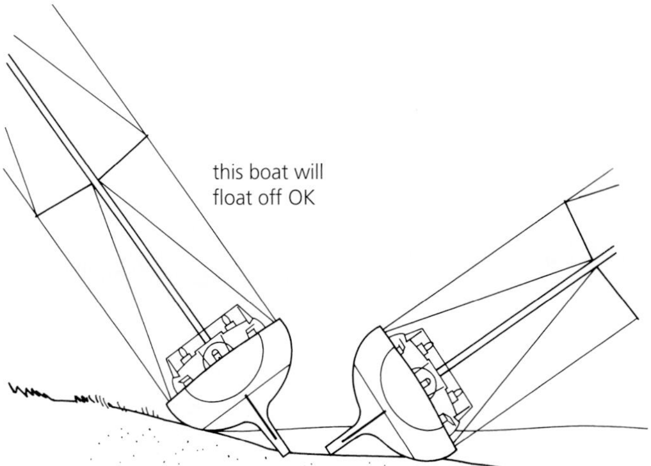
this boat will float off OK
this boat will flood when the tide comes back in
make sure the boat lies down on the "high" side if aground on a shelving coastline

Running Aground on a Falling Tide

If you run aground on a falling tide, you may have just a few minutes to get off, using any of the methods already suggested. If these methods fail, you have to wait for the next tide. If the tide range is more than a few feet and you run aground at much above low tide, you will probably dry out. There is much that needs attention, as follows:

- First make sure that the boat leans toward the side on which the bottom slopes upward. If the boat goes down the other way, it will lie at an extreme angle of heel and may flood when the tide comes back in.
- If necessary to make sure that the boat goes down the right way, set the boom over this side of the boat and have the crew hang from it to provide the necessary heeling.
- If this fails, set an anchor off to the side on which you want the boat to go down, bring its rode up to the end of the main halyard, and tie the halyard to it. Now tighten the halyard; this pulls the boat down by the masthead, exerting tremendous leverage. Unfortunately, unless there is a spinnaker halyard on a block that rotates at the masthead, the halyard will be coming off the masthead sheave at an angle for which the sheave was never designed, which may damage the sheave and/or the halyard. The likelihood of damage can be minimized by putting a snatch block on the end of the halyard, running the anchor rode through it and then to a cockpit winch. Leave the rode loose while the snatch block is hauled to the masthead, cleat off the halyard, and then crank in on the anchor rode. This way, the halyard remains stationary during the winching operation and, as a result, is not dragged through the masthead under load at an unfair angle. If a boat has a fractional rig, there may be no shrouds providing lateral support to the masthead. In this case, it may be advisable to use the genoa halyard for pulling down by the masthead.

If aground on a falling tide and unable to get off, it is essential to see that the boat lies down on the "high" side, not the "low" side.

In the Intracoastal Waterway. These three boats were playing follow the leader and all ran aground (it doesn't always pay to trust someone else's navigation)! There is no wave action, so no danger. Once they got over the initial shock, I hope they laughed as much as we did when we passed by!

the anchor is much too close to the boat—it simply pulled out of the bottom

Above left: *Pulling a boat down by the masthead. This effort was ineffective because the anchor was set way too close to the boat.* Above right: *Wing-keeled boat aground on a reef. It was pulled down by the masthead until the side decks were submerged. The wings bent up and the boat was jerked off with no other damage. Note the masthead bending on this fractional rig. We had some concerns that we would buckle the mast at the cap shrouds, but the situation was desperate enough to take the risk. (Courtesy Heidi Rabel)*

- Pump the bilge before the boat heels significantly so that the bilge water won't flood lockers.
- Cook a meal and then close the propane-cylinder valves. The reason for this is that at an extreme angle of heel, it is possible that liquid propane will enter the propane lines, which is potentially quite dangerous.
- Check that the batteries are properly secured. If you have wet cells, you may need to remove them and keep them more or less upright to prevent the acid from leaking out.
- If the boat goes way over, the engine may start leaking oil out the dipstick tube or some other orifice—keep an eye on it and plug leaks as necessary. Fuel- and water-tank vents also may leak—give special attention to the fuel-tank vents.
- As the boat approaches the point at which it will come to rest on the turn of the bilge, check for sharp rocks or an uneven bottom that may result in point loading. If necessary, use locker lids and even bagged sails to cushion the load.
- Wing keels can be somewhat of a problem. The boat may try to stay upright, which is potentially very dangerous—it may subsequently crash over on its side when the tide is out. It should be pulled over, even at the risk of damaging the keel. If it is left upright, be sure to lash sturdy legs to it on both sides. A couple of spinnaker poles or, if only one pole is available, a pole and the boom (take the mainsail off and disconnect the boom from the mast at the gooseneck) will do the job. If the bottom is soft, lash locker lids or something similar to the base of the poles to spread the loads. Then rig lines from near the base of the poles forward and aft so that the poles cannot

Below: *One approach to pulling a boat down by the masthead.*

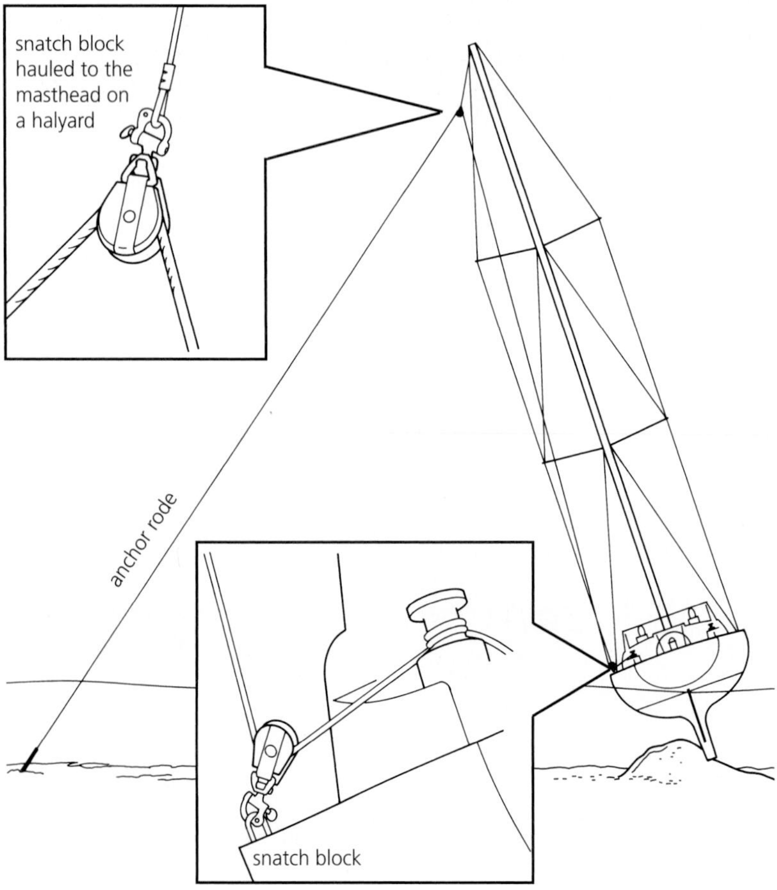

When drying out alongside a wharf or dock, make sure the boat is extremely well secured, because if it falls once the tide is out, considerable damage may occur.

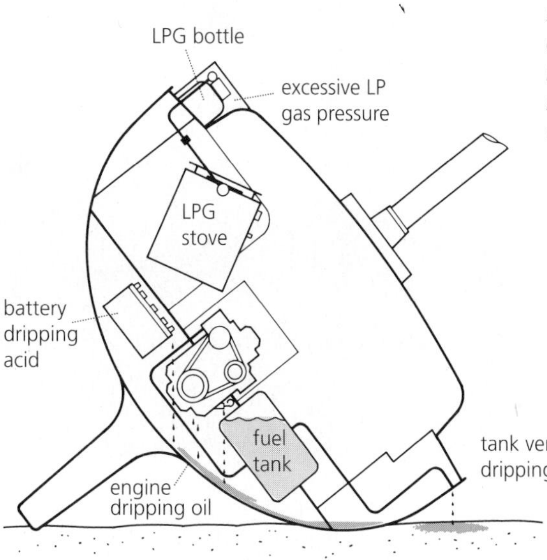

If the boat will reach extreme angles of heel, think about the kinds of things that will spill.

hinge backward or forward. Do everything you can to keep the boat as vertical as possible—this minimizes the load on the supports. For example, set out a couple of anchors (one on each side) connected to halyards so that you can use the leverage of the mast to keep the boat in position.

- Finally, either row out a kedge anchor as far off into deep water as your rode length allows before the tide goes out or walk an anchor out when the tide is down (if the bottom is soft, you will want to row it out before the tide goes out). Check its set by winching the rode taut.

If a boat goes aground at high water on a spring tide and you fail to get off on the next tide, you may be stuck for a couple of weeks. Make every effort to ensure that this does not happen by pumping tanks, taking heavy gear off the boat, and maybe even hiring a local backhoe operator to come in at low tide to dig a canal into deeper water, and/or lining up a powerful towboat. However, in the latter case, consider the salvage implications, which are discussed later in this chapter.

It may be possible to keep a boat upright, especially one with a long keel, with a couple of timbers. Note the fore-and-aft lines from the base of the leg to keep the leg in place. As long as the boat remains vertical, almost all of the weight is on the keel. However, if it starts to tip (e.g., a leg digs into the bottom), the weight on one leg will rapidly build up: the boat is likely to keep on rolling, with potentially catastrophic results. Supporting a boat like this needs considerable thought and planning.

Running Aground in Tideless Waters

If the wind and waves are driving you farther on, the first priority is to get a kedge anchor set. If there is no possibility of setting the kedge to seaward (e.g., you are being driven onto a reef with extremely deep water immediately offshore),

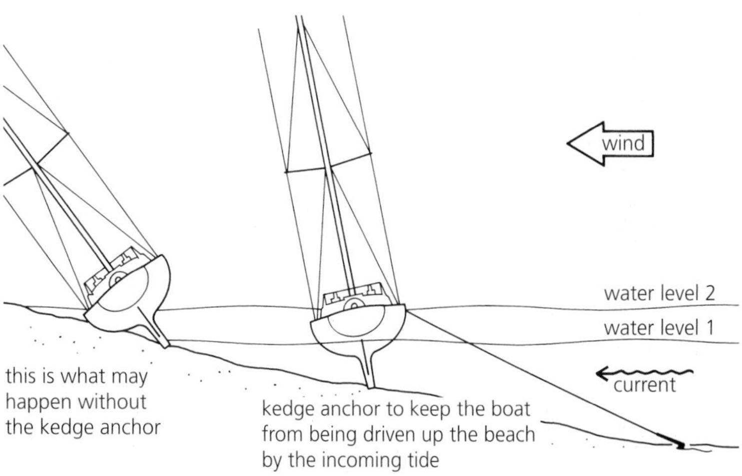

It is important to set a kedge anchor out to sea so that as the tide comes in, the boat is not driven farther ashore.

The leverage of the boom can be used to heel a boat.

your best option may be to drag the boat farther onto the reef to minimize the pounding it is taking. Later, when things have calmed down, you can figure out how to get it back off!

Once the boat is stable, in tideless waters you have time to think, to find out where the deeper water lies, and to develop a strategy for getting off. It might be a good idea to launch the dinghy and paddle around, using an oar to determine where deeper water lies and the best direction in which to get off.

All of the methods described so far for heeling a boat and reducing its draft can be tried. On occasion, to induce heeling we have set our boom over the side, lashed it in place, set up the topping lift, and hung all kinds of heavy objects from its end (including the dinghy, suspended with a cat's cradle of rigging and pumped partially full of water).

Using an anchor to pull the boat down by the masthead is also extremely effective. The farther off the anchor can be set and the lower the masthead can be pulled, the more horizontal the pull that will be exerted, which also helps drag the boat off sideways. On one occasion when we truly impaled ourselves on a spoil bank, we got a powerful shrimp boat to pull us off by the masthead. Before we started to move, our boat rolled over until the portholes in the cabinsides were going under.

If the boat's head can be pulled around until the wind is at least abeam—and preferably forward of the beam—the sails can be set and oversheeted to impart both heeling and drive in the desired direction.

If nothing you do gets you off, it is time to think about a tow.

Towing and Salvage

If you are stuck hard enough to need a tow to get off, you are going to need a fairly powerful tow. If so, it needs to be set up with some care, remembering the following points:

- There must be a fairlead for the towline at any towing angle (see the previous comments about kedge anchors).
- The load needs to be spread over strong-enough structures. With a keel-stepped mast, a line around the mast itself provides the strongest attachment point on the boat (don't do this with a deck-stepped mast; you may bring it down). Alternatively, make up a bridle taken to a couple of heavy cleats and/or a windlass or samson post.
- If the towline attachment points are set back from the bow, you will need a snatch block or some other arrangement at the bow to stop the rode from jumping off the bow roller and exerting its load on the bow pulpit stanchion. Furthermore, *if the pull comes from any point aft of the bow when being towed, the boat will shear violently from side to side, with the risk of rolling itself under at speed.*
- When in tidal waters, and when the boat is not being beaten to death, be patient. Wait until near high tide before commencing the tow so that you put the least strain possible on the boat.
- Before getting a tow, make sure the towboat operator understands the maximum safe speed (hull speed or less) at which you can be safely towed. After we were run down in the North Sea, the ship that hit us took us in tow at way above hull speed for our little vessel and just about shook the boat to pieces.
- Maintain communication with the towboat through an agreed-upon VHF channel (we had no radio when we

Getting a tow has its own perils. To some extent, you are putting the fate of your boat in the hands of an unknown skipper. Here we get a tow from a Cuban fishing boat.

were towed and, therefore, had no way to get the ship to slow down). If there is no radio, agree on a set of hand signals.

- If towing in any seas, adjust the length of the towline so that the two boats are on the same part of different waves at the same time (e.g., both on wave crests at the same time). This reduces the tendency to surf up the back of the towboat in following seas, and minimizes shock loads as the towline sags and tightens in head seas. A drogue (see chapter 11) or some other drag device behind the towed boat will help keep it in line and stop it from surging forward. Even so, in heavy seas the towline will still alternately sag and then come out of the water, with substantial changes in the loading. To smooth out the load, it is a good idea to shackle into it a length of anchor chain, with the anchor also included if substantial seas are running.
- Stay well away from the towline; if it parts, it is going to snap back with ferocious force. I have a friend who had his forehead opened up by a towline; he just missed losing an eye. When I was working on the oil rigs, one of the rigs had an over-tensioned anchor cable that parted; it literally cut two men in half at the waist. Be warned!
- An axe or sharp knife should be kept handy in case it is necessary to cut loose in a hurry. Do this as close to the attachment point as possible to minimize the snapback from the length of line left on the boat.

Finally, let's take a brief look at salvage, which is a complicated business covered by its own body of law (I am no admiralty lawyer, so treat the following remarks with caution). In general, a towing or salvaging boat is entitled to fair compensation; if your boat would otherwise have been lost, this may amount to full salvage rights, although typically awards run 1 to 10 percent of the value of the property saved. Beyond this, I believe it is true that:

- If you attract another boat's attention by the use of distress signals, you strengthen any salvage claim. If, on the other hand, you reach agreement with a towboat (commercial or otherwise) that you are not in peril but are requesting assistance to avoid inconvenience, you weaken any salvage claim.
- In U.S. waters, if you are in a situation that you believe to be life-threatening, call the USCG; in the U.K., call the lifeboat. If it agrees that the situation is life-threatening, it will render assistance itself, in which case salvage is not an issue. If it does not agree, it will likely provide the names of towboat operators (i.e., salvors) in your area.
- If you call a salvor for assistance and the salvor responds, he or she has the right to

Aground on a reef at high tide, this skipper was lucky to save his boat. His wing keel was truly jammed in the coral. As I mentioned in chapter 1, I do not like wing keels on a cruising boat.

bill you for time and services even if no service is performed.

- Most towboat companies ask you to sign a salvage contract that specifies hourly charges (including the time to get to you) and maybe a premium for a "hard grounding." Be sure to read the small print. If you are not in a salvage situation, ask for a simple towing form; if it is not forthcoming, call the USCG and ask for the name of another towing company.
- Salvage cannot be forced on you; you must consent.
- Make sure that you have an agreement regarding payment for services rendered (preferably before witnesses) prior to starting the operation. A verbal agreement counts as an agreement.
- Note in the boat's log such things as the location of the grounding, the weather conditions and sea state, when and who you called for assistance, the time that any assistance was rendered, what you agreed, who did what with which equipment, when you were freed, and when the towboat left. This information may be vital in settling any subsequent disputes.
- As soon as you reach a harbor, notify your insurance company.
- Finally, bear in mind that if you intentionally abandon your boat, it becomes fair game for any salvor.

If you are unlucky enough to be faced with a salvage claim, the amount of any settlement will depend on factors such as the value of your boat and its equipment; the extent to which the boat was in peril and, therefore, the potential damage or loss if you were not towed off; the value of the towboat and the degree of peril to it and its crew; the skill and effort of the towboat crew; and whether the towboat is generally on call for salvage operations (this worsens your case) or is used for other purposes and just happened to be in the area at the time (this strengthens your case).

CHAPTER TEN

THE DITTY BAG

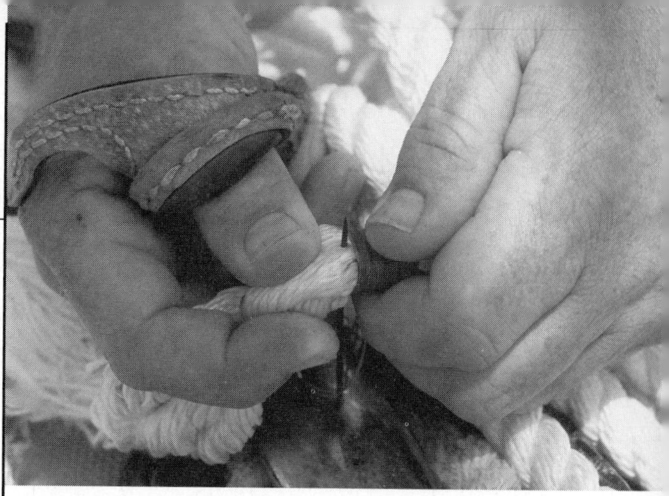

Even a modern sailor needs some traditional skills.

This chapter is a grab bag of miscellaneous yet important information. If there's a theme that unites the contents, it's the incredible way that modern technology has influenced every aspect of boating, from ropes to sails to dinghies to foul-weather gear to safety-related equipment.

MODERN ROPES

A rope is a rope until it gets onboard a boat and is put to use, at which point it becomes a *line*. At one time, ropes (cordage) were all made of natural fibers and all made about the same way (every seaport had its *rope walk*, where ropes were made). The primary distinction between ropes was size (measured in inches of circumference). Today, natural-fiber rope is almost never seen. We have all kinds of synthetic fibers and combinations of fibers—some of them quite exotic—and several different methods are commonly used to assemble them into finished rope. Rope sizes are now specified in terms of diameter (inches or millimeters).

A Look at Construction

A fiber or filament is the base material in a rope. Modern synthetic fibers come in continuous lengths. The fibers are twisted or spun into yarns; yarns are *reeved* into strands; and strands are twisted, braided, or plaited into ropes. Strength, stretch, and other properties are a function of the material used in construction and the way in which the rope is put together. The principal materials in use today are as follows:

- Nylon (polyamide) is not only strong, but also has high stretch capabilities, giving it the ability to absorb and dissipate the dynamic loads experienced in anchoring, mooring, and towing. Three-strand nylon stretches up to 20 percent at a load of 25 percent of its breaking strength; double-braided nylon stretches around 10 percent at the same load. Nylon has a specific gravity of 1.14, which means it sinks in water. If untreated, it absorbs up to 6 percent of its weight in water, with a resulting loss of strength of 10 percent or more. It resists UV degradation and many other environmental insults, and ages well; however, it is more vulnerable to chafe than polyester, the other widely used fiber.
- Polyester, commonly known under various trade names such as Dacron and

Terylene, has strength similar to nylon but with considerably less stretch at not much more cost, which makes it useful for running rigging applications where stretch needs to be minimized. It is a little heavier than nylon, with a specific gravity of 1.38, but it is more or less impervious to water. It too has excellent tolerance for environmental insults and wears well (we used the same Dacron halyards on our old boat for twenty years, and sold them in reasonable condition with the boat).

- Polypropylene has something over half the strength of nylon and polyester with stretch capabilities not far short of nylon. It is light (specific gravity of 0.91) and impervious to water; as a result, it floats in water, which makes it useful for ski tow ropes. However, it is uncomfortable to handle, does not hold knots well, is easily abraded, and suffers badly from UV degradation. Although it is commonly used for the grab ropes and painters on inflatable dinghies, sooner or later it gives out. *Polypropylene has no place on cruising boats.*
- Kevlar (aramid fiber) is several times as strong as nylon and polyester with one tenth the stretch of nylon and one fifth that of polyester. This makes Kevlar an obvious choice for low-stretch applications such as halyards. However, the fibers absorb twice as much water as nylon, are susceptible to UV degradation, and do not take a bend well, such as what occurs when being hauled around a sheave (sheaves should have a diameter of up to twenty-four times that of the rope, although this is rarely achieved). Therefore, the fibers are typically encased in an outer braid of polyester for extra protection. Nevertheless, life expectancy is nowhere near that of polyester. In addition, Kevlar is approximately eight to ten times the price. There has to be a significant performance issue to justify Kevlar-based lines on a cruising boat.
- Technora, a modified aramid, takes a bend much better than Kevlar and, therefore, can be used with conventional sheaves with a diameter of eight times the rope diameter—but it still suffers from UV degradation.
- Spectra and Dyneema (*high modulus polyethylene*, HMPE) are even stronger than Kevlar with similar very low stretch properties at significantly less weight and zero water absorption. They have excellent resistance to abrasion, chemicals, and UV degradation. This is clearly a wonderful set of properties; however, Spectra and Dyneema will stretch permanently over time under sustained loads (*creep*) or deform and ultimately fail, which Kevlar will not do. Unfortunately, they are approximately fifteen times the price of nylon and polyester! As with Kevlar and Technora, Spectra and Dyneema are commonly used as a core material inside a braided polyester sheath. Given their price, they are unlikely to be found on a cruising boat.
- Vectran (*liquid crystal polymer*, LCP) combines the best qualities of aramids and HMPE: incredible strength, very low stretch, a greater tolerance for bending than the other exotic fibers, no water absorption, and no creep under load; however, it is even more expensive than the HMPEs! It is the preferred choice for high-end racers, but beyond the means of the rest of us.

On most cruising boats, nylon and polyester are the only two materials in widespread use. The exotic fibers may find their way into halyards on cruiser-racers and into one or two other very specific applications (e.g., internal sheets on multipart vangs); however, in general, the high cost and lower life expectancy make them cost-prohibitive.

Nylon and polyester fibers can be assembled in a variety of different ways, as follows:

- In three-strand rope, the fibers are twisted into yarns, the yarns are combined into strands, and three strands are then twisted together to form the rope. The twisting is hard on the fibers, resulting in a lower strength for a given rope size than with other construction methods. Furthermore, three-strand ropes are highly susceptible to kinking and *hockling* (a situation in which the strands separate out and knot up), making it sometimes awkward to handle and stow. The ABS estimates that 25 to 30 percent of rope damage on ships is attributable to hockling. The U.S. Navy estimates that a hockle reduces a rope's strength by 30 percent. Despite these drawbacks, three-strand construction does have its bene-

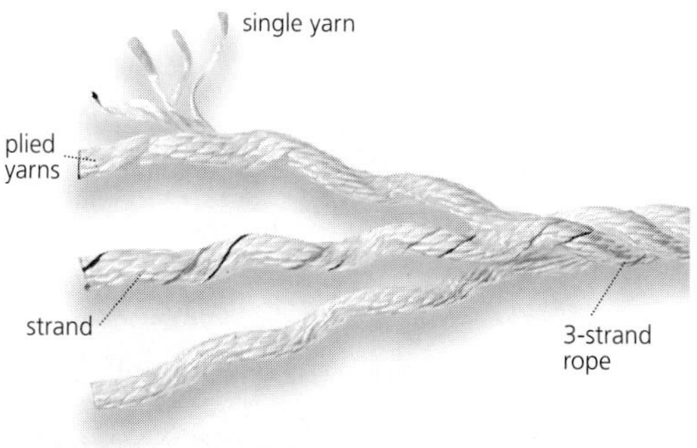

Top: *Three-strand rope construction. (Courtesy New England Ropes).* Above: *Minor* (left) *and severe* (right) *hockling. The former can be worked back into the lay of the rope without damage; the latter is impossible to fully restore—some degree of permanent damage has occurred.*

fits: it provides the greatest amount of stretch in a given line (beneficial in anchoring and mooring), it is easy to splice, and it is cheaper than any other approach.

- Single braid is the basic unit of construction in braided ropes. The yarns are twisted into strands, with half the strands twisted in one direction and the other half in the other direction. The two halves are then braided together in groups of two. The resultant rope is strong, has relatively low stretch, is highly resistant to kinking, cannot be hockled, is comfortable to handle, and is easily spliced.
- Double braid consists of two ropes in one—an inner core of single braid—which usually takes most of the load—encased in a braided sheath that protects the core from abrasion and UV degradation. The inner and outer braids may both be manufactured from the same fibers (e.g., polyester), but sometimes different fibers are used to produce ropes with different properties.
- Parallel core takes advantage of the fact that modern fibers can be produced in continuous lengths (as opposed to natural fibers). In a parallel-core rope, the fibers in the core are laid out more or less in a straight line, which maximizes the strength of the rope and minimizes the stretch. They are then protected with a braided cover. Kevlar and Spectra commonly are used for the core and polyester for the cover. These ropes are excellent when loaded in a straight line but, if pulled over pulleys or sheaves, the core yarns may bunch up. They are the most difficult of all synthetic lines to splice.

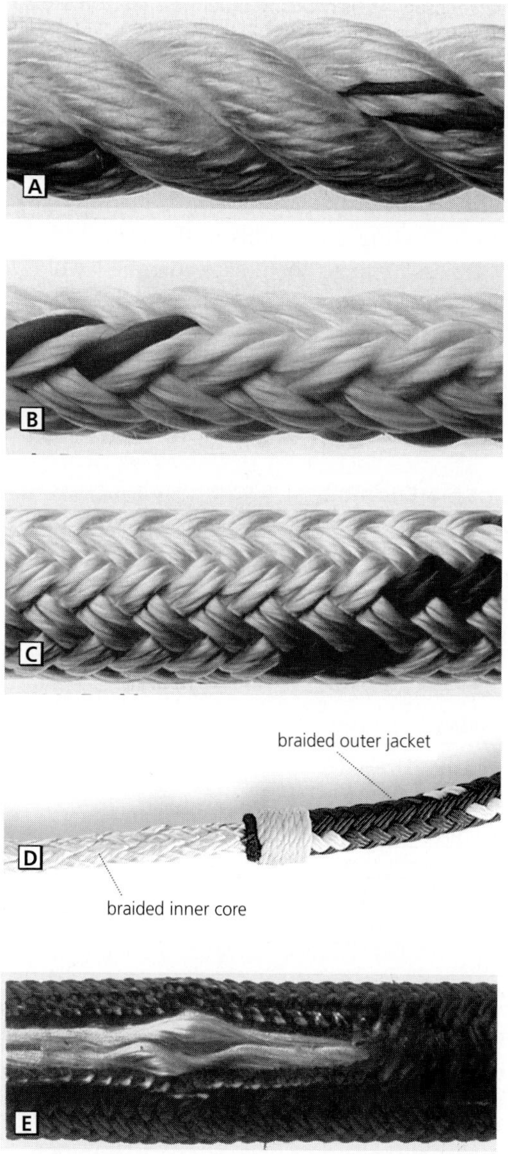

Different kinds of synthetic rope. A. *Three-strand nylon.* B. *Single braid (hollow in the center); rarely found on boats.* C. *Double braid, which essentially consists of two braided ropes, one inside the other.* D. *Double-braid construction.* E. *Parallel core, in which the inner fibers are laid parallel to one another, instead of being twisted or braided. (A–C, E, Courtesy Yale Cordage; D courtesy New England Ropes.)*

Line Selection Guide

The bigger your budget, the more complex is the line-selection process. For most of us, however, it is simplified by the fact that we either cannot afford or are not prepared to shell out for the exotic fibers—we end up with nylon and polyester in a variety of different construction patterns.

The table below, adapted from a table supplied by New England Ropes, is a guide for the cruising sailor and cruiser-racer.

Caring for Ropes

If rope is bought on a spool, it should be removed by setting the spool up to spin and then pulling the rope off. If it is taken off any other way, it is likely to kink and, in the case of three-strand rope, hockle. If it is bought in a coil, assuming it was coiled properly in the first place, it is best to pull it out from the inside of the coil (this minimizes the likelihood of tangles). If a line does develop kinks, it can often be straightened out and made to behave by towing it behind the boat for twenty or thirty minutes, after which it should be turned end for end and towed for another twenty or thirty minutes. Hockles have to be worked out by hand—carefully twisting the strands in the rope and the rope itself—to get them back into the lay of the rope; the rope will still have suffered some permanent loss of strength if it has been put under a load before this is done.

As discussed in chapter 7, if a line is to be coiled with one end fastened in place (e.g., a halyard after the sail has been raised and the line cleated off), the coil is always begun from the *fastened* end working down to the loose end. Because of a natural, built-in twist, all three-strand rope is coiled clockwise. Single and double braids can be coiled either way, but it is just as well to get in the habit of doing everything clockwise. Three-strand line should end up in a neat coil (no figures of eight) unless it is specifically laid out on deck and coiled in a figure-eight pattern (known as *flaking* or *faking down*). Braided line should be coiled in a figure-eight fashion (it will naturally do this). These figure eights should *not* be worked out to create a neat

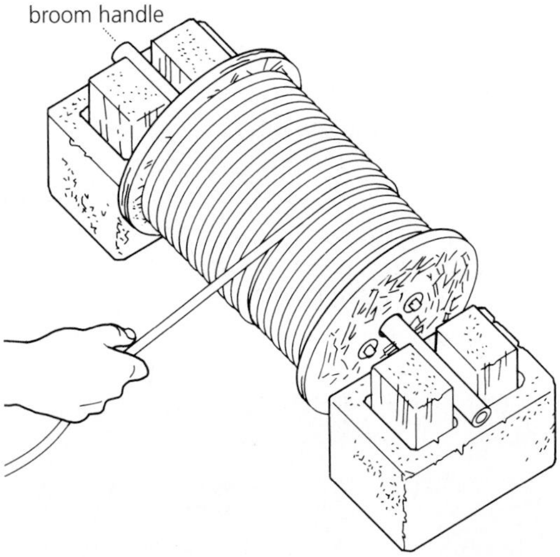

The proper way to remove rope from a spool. Run a pipe through the spool and set it up on a couple of blocks, then pull the line off.

Line Selection Guide

1 = poor; 2 = fair; 3 = good; 4 = very good; 5 = excellent; * = excellent, but at very high cost; — = inappropriate expense

FUNCTION	SINGLE-BRAID POLYESTER	DOUBLE-BRAID POLYESTER, CORE, AND COVER	PARALLEL-CORED POLYESTER, CORE, AND COVER	PARALLEL-CORED HMPE, POLYPRO-PYLENE COVER	DOUBLE-BRAID HMPE, POLYESTER COVER	DOUBLE-BRAID ARAMID, POLYESTER COVER	DOUBLE-BRAID LCP, POLYESTER COVER
Main/Genoa Halyards	1	3	5	2	4	5	5
Mainsheet	5	5	2	1	5	4	4*
Genoa Sheets	5	5	4	2	5	5	4*
Reefing Lines	3	5	4	1	5	1	4*
Spinnaker Halyards	1	4	5	2	5	4*	4*
Spinnaker Sheets	3	4	5	4	5	—	—
Afterguys	1	3	5	2	5	4*	4*
Light-Air Sheets	2	3	3	5	4*	—	—
Foreguy and Pole Lift	3	5	4	4	4*	—	—
Asymmetric Tack	3	4	4	3	5	4*	4*
Vang	3	5	3	2	4*	—	—
Running Backstay Tails	1	3	4	1	5	5	5

coil; if so, the line tends to kink when it is let back out.

When stowing line to be stored in a locker, instead of coiling the final length, it should be wrapped around the center of the coil three or four times, leaving a tail of a couple of feet. Reach through the coiled line, grab the tail about halfway along its length, and pull a loop through the coiled line. Drop this loop over the top of the coiled line and then pull the tail tight. This keeps the line neatly bundled.

Any kind of abrasion is tough on rope. Cleats, chocks, bitts, sheaves, winch drums, blocks, and any other surface over which a line is dragged need to be smooth, free of burrs and rust, and well rounded. Sheaves especially must be free-running—the heat generated by dragging a synthetic line over a frozen sheave can melt fibers, resulting in irreversible damage.

Another kind of damage occurs when a sheave is undersized for the line being run over it—the line is forced through an excessively tight radius, which results in fiber breakage. In general, sheaves for braided lines should have a diameter at least eight times that of the line run over them; for aramids, the ratio is anywhere from 15:1 to 24:1. Braided polyester lines require rounded grooves in a sheave, with the grooves being at least 10 percent wider than the rope diameter to avoid pinching and damaging the line; aramids require flatter grooves.

Rope should not be dragged over dirty surfaces or the ground—grit can work its way into the core of the rope, cutting the inner fibers. Washing lines with freshwater from a garden hose and then allowing them to air dry removes much of this grit. Mild detergents also can be used, but strong detergents may wash some of the lubricating agents out of a rope, accelerating wear. Bleach can chemically damage a rope.

Although most synthetic rope is highly resistant to chemical damage, some chemicals found on and around boats will damage some fibers; it is best to keep lines away from all chemicals. Nylon, for some reason, is rapidly damaged by contact with rust in a salt environment. Rope-to-chain splices are particularly vulnerable and should be regularly inspected.

The breaking strength and tensile strength of ropes is determined at 70°F (21°C). At higher temperatures, strength is lower until the melting point is reached, at which time strength is zero. Polypropylene melts at 330°F (165°C), but permanent damage is done above 150°F (66°C). Polyester and nylon both melt around 460°F (238°C), with permanent damage occurring above 350°F (176°C). Aramid fibers melt at 800°F (426°C) or higher, and suffer permanent damage above 400°F (204°C). HMPE melts at less than 300°F (149°C), and is permanently damaged at temperatures above 150°F (66°C). For all of these materials, the temperature at which permanent damage occurs is typically found around exhaust systems and, in the case of HMPE, can even occur in a closed-up locker near an engine room in hot weather or in the trunk of a dark-colored automobile sitting in the sun.

Synthetic lines should never be *surged* (allowed to slip while the drum is turning) on a winch or windlass; this can rapidly build up enough heat to melt fibers.

All synthetic ropes experience some degradation in sunlight, with polypropylene and some of the exotic fibers (e.g., aramids and HMPE) being the worst affected. When not in use, lines should be put away and not left on deck.

In short, lines need to be stored clean, dry, away from excessive heat, out of direct sunlight, and (if possible) in a well-ventilated space.

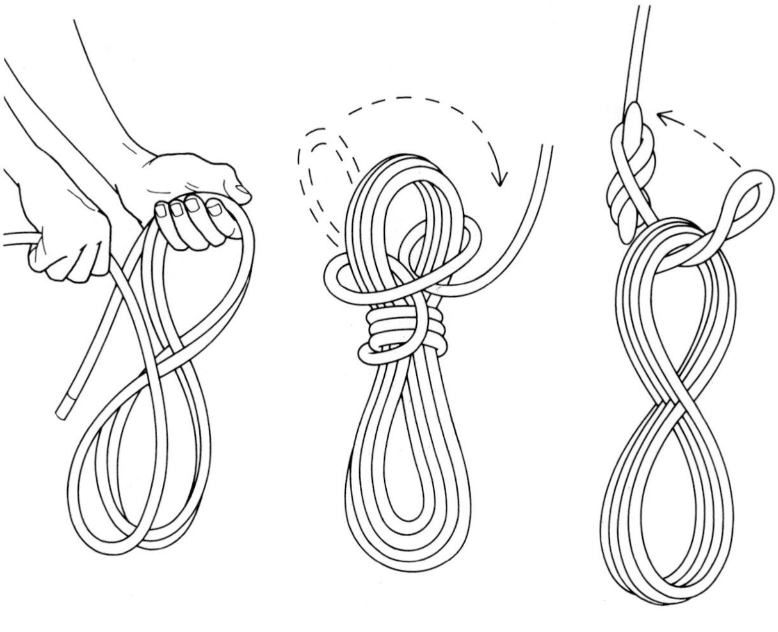

Coiling, stowing, and hanging up braided lines.

MARLINESPIKE SEAMANSHIP

A *marlinespike* is a pointed spike used to open the lay of stranded ropes to enable one strand to be tucked through others when splicing the rope. The term *marlinespike seamanship* has become associated with all those aspects of boat-handling related to ropes, including knots, splices, coiling, and stowing lines. Although the necessary range of knowledge associated with marlinespike seamanship is vastly smaller on a modern boat than it was on a square-rigger, it is still an important part of the cruiser's repertoire of skills.

Knots

Before looking at knots, let's get the basic terminology straight. Once a length of rope comes onboard a boat, it is a line. In the old days, the inboard end of an anchor rode was attached to a couple of upright posts in the foredeck—the *bitts*—so this end of the rode became known as the *bitter end*. I use the term to apply to the loose end of any line that comes out of a knot; the part of the line that leads away from the knot I call the *standing part*. Any loop in a line is known as a *bight*.

The modern sailor needs to know only a handful of knots, but each is important and has a specific role to play. Quite honestly, I can't remember all of those described herein and must consult a book to refresh my memory on the odd occasion when I need a constrictor knot or have to put an eye splice in a line—but I still get by just fine! The key knots are as follows.

The *figure-eight knot* is used as a *stopper knot* in the ends of sheets and halyards. It prevents the line from running out through a block or sheave. To make the knot, the bitter end of the line is brought across the standing part to make a loop, slipped under the standing part, and tucked back through the loop.

Knot terminology.

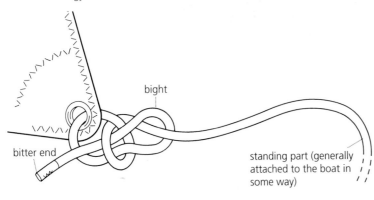

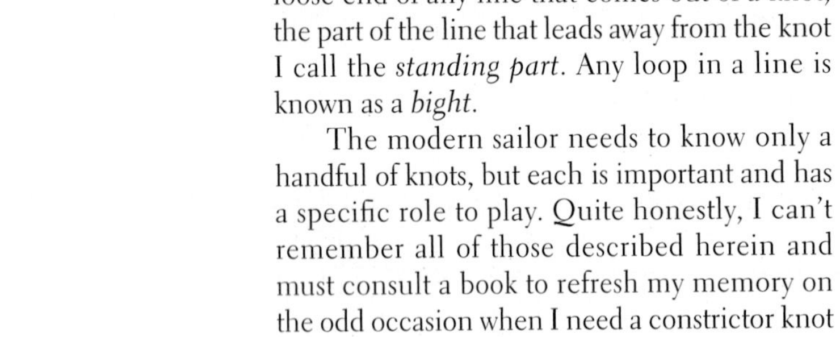

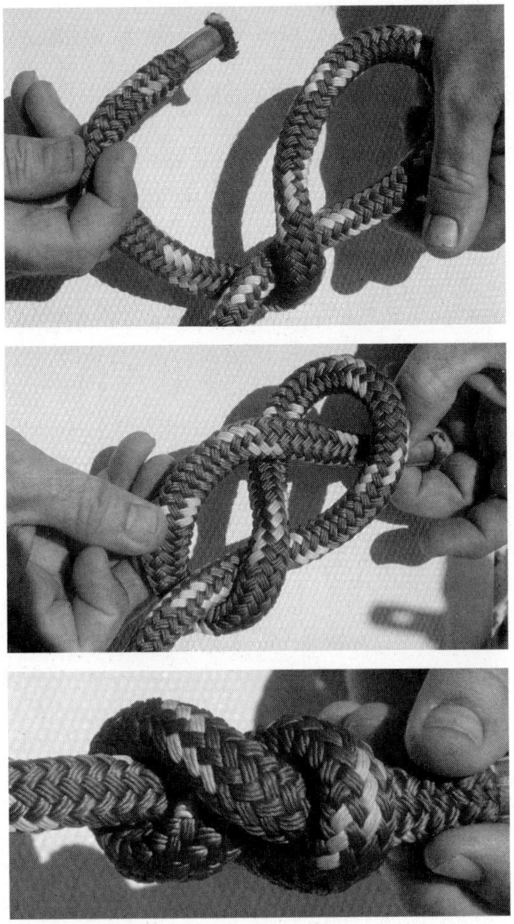

Figure-eight knot.

The *bowline* is used to attach sheets to clews, to put a loop in the end of a line, and in many other applications where a secure loop is required that is nevertheless easy to untie regardless of the load that has been applied to it. There are many different ways to tie a bowline, and various memory mnemonics to remember how to do it; I've used the following to teach my children: Pass the bitter end of the line through the clew of a sail or whatever (depending on the application). Make a small loop in the standing part of the line with the section of line running toward the bitter end *on top* of the loop. Feed the bitter end of the line up through the loop ("the rabbit is coming out of its hole"). Take the bitter end *under* the standing part of the line and bring it back around to the top of the loop ("the rabbit is going around the tree"). Feed the bitter end back through the loop ("the rabbit is going back in its hole") in such a way that the bitter end is now lying on the *inside* of the loop. Pull everything tight. A common mistake is to make the initial loop with the section of line running toward the bitter end on the bottom of the

Bowline. 1. In this example, an anchor rode is being attached with a bowline. The first step is to run the line through the anchor shackle twice. Then a loop is formed in the standing part of the line, with the bitter end on top of the loop. The bitter end is brought up through this loop. 2. After coming up through the loop, the bitter end is passed under the standing part of the line . . . 3. and then fed back down through the loop. Note how the bitter end has ended up inside the noose formed in the line. 4. The knot is cinched up. 5. If, after coming up through the loop, the bitter end is taken across to the other side of the standing part of the line before passing it under the standing part, we end up with this knot. Note how the bitter end has ended up outside the noose formed in the line. This knot may not hold as well as a proper bowline. Lower right: *Toward the end of step 1, a common mistake is to have the bitter end of the line come off the bottom end of the loop—the knot simply will not work.*

loop—the knot won't work at all. Another mistake is to bring the bitter end *across the top of the standing part* of the line before "going around the tree," which then brings the bitter end down through the loop ("going back in the hole") on the wrong side of the loop. This results in a bowline variant, which may not hold as well as a regular bowline on slick synthetic lines.

The *reef knot* (square knot; see next page) is used primarily for tying in reef points on a sail; for securing sail ties; and sometimes for tying two lines together (although the sheet bend is generally much better for this—explained later in this chapter). There will be two bitter ends; one is laid over the other to make a loop and then passed through the loop ("right over left"). The two ends are now laid over one another again to form a second loop, and one bitter end is passed through the loop ("left over right"). There are two ways to do this: the wrong way, which results in a "granny knot" that will both slip and jam, and the right way. The key to success is to make sure that the same bitter end is on top of the loop when both halves of the knot are tied. This results in the bitter ends emerging from both sides of the knot alongside the standing parts. When putting on sail ties, the bitter end is not pulled all the way through the loop on the second part of the knot. This leaves a bow. Tugging sharply on the bitter end releases the knot.

The *clove hitch* (see pages 440–41) is used to tie a mooring line to a piling. The bitter end of the line is run around the post twice. On the first pass, it is brought under the standing part; on the second pass, it comes over the standing part and back through itself. Alternatively, a loop is made in the line with the bitter end *on the bottom*. This is dropped over the piling. A second loop is made the same as the first with the bitter once again *on the bottom*. This is dropped over the first loop and pulled tight. Failure to make the second loop in the same way as the first results in a *cow hitch* (see below). Under a variable load, both a clove hitch and a cow hitch will slip; to prevent this, a couple of half hitches can be added.

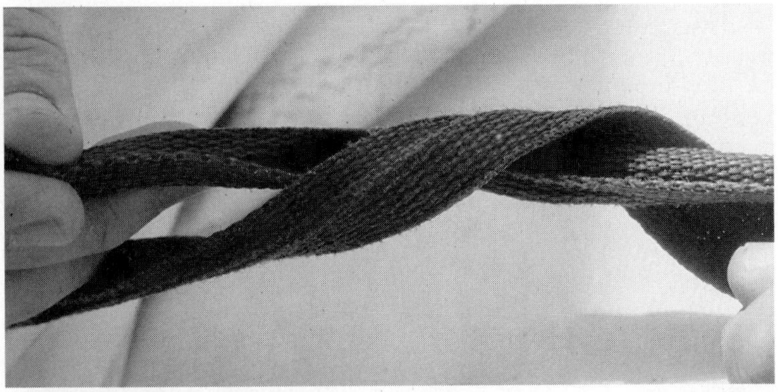

*Reef (square) knot (*above and below*). Note how the standing part and bitter end emerge from the knot alongside one another; if they don't, you have tied a granny knot!*

Reef knot: the bitter ends emerge alongside the standing parts.

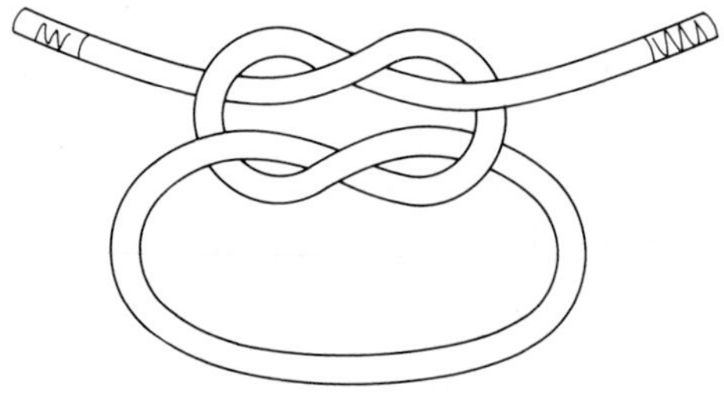

Granny knot: the bitter ends emerge on the other side of the loops to the standing parts.

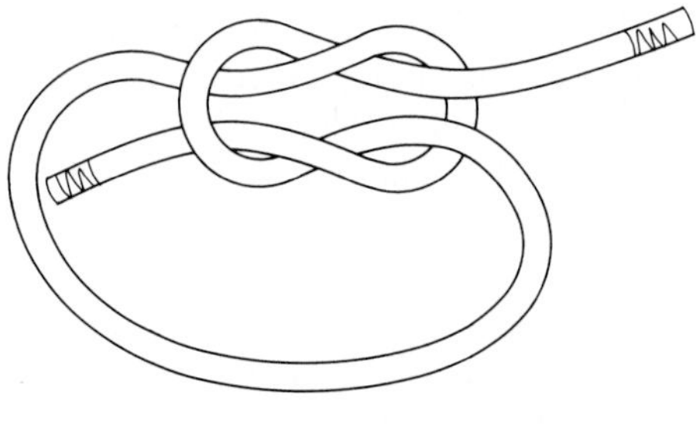

"Fool's" reef knot: this looks like a reef knot—the ends emerge alongside the standing parts—but note that the bitter ends are on opposite sides of the standing parts (one is inside the loop and one outside). The knot will slip under a load.

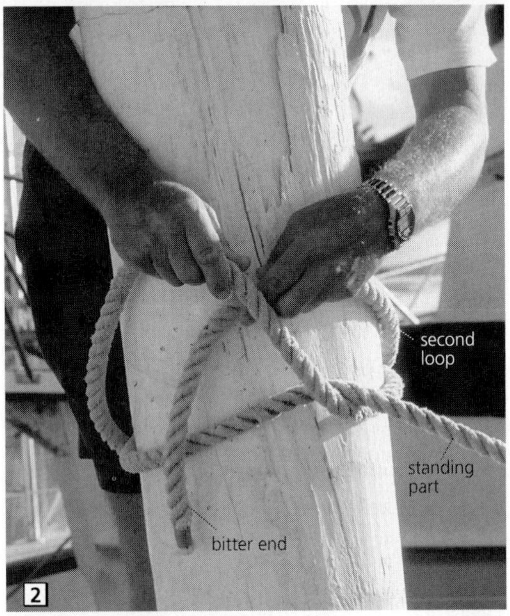

Clove hitch, method 1. 1. The bitter end is run around the piling and under the standing part. 2. The bitter end is run around a second time—this time on top of the standing part—and then slipped under the loop that is formed. 3. The knot is cinched up. A half hitch or two should be added (see the round turns and half hitches in the photos on page 442).

Clove hitch, method 2. 1. A loop is formed in the line, with the bitter end on the bottom, and dropped over the piling. A second loop is made the same way, again with the bitter end on the bottom . . . 2. and dropped over the piling. 3. The knot is cinched up. A half hitch or two should be added.

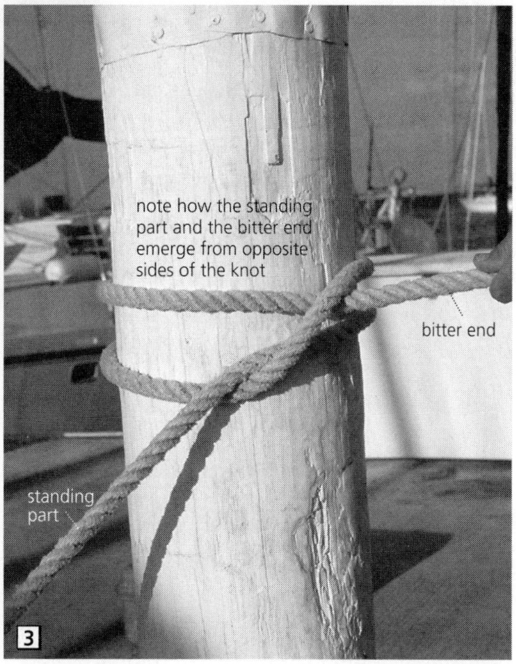

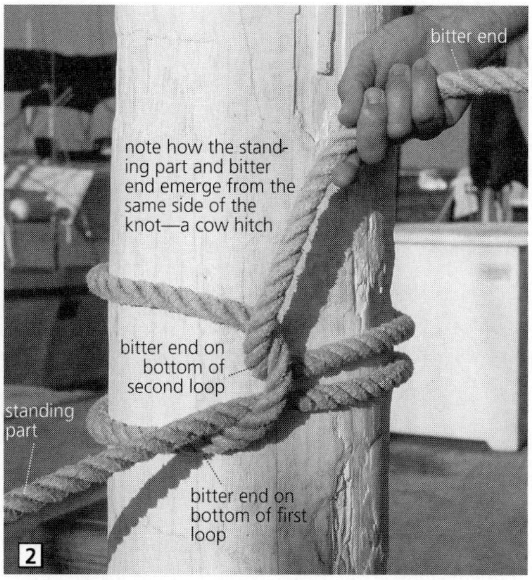

Clove hitch, incorrect method. 1. The first loop has been put on the piling as before (bitter end on the bottom, etc.). The second loop is gotten ready. The bitter end is on top. Although the bitter end can be gotten onto the bottom by flipping the loop over as it is dropped onto the piling, the result is . . . 2. a cow hitch!

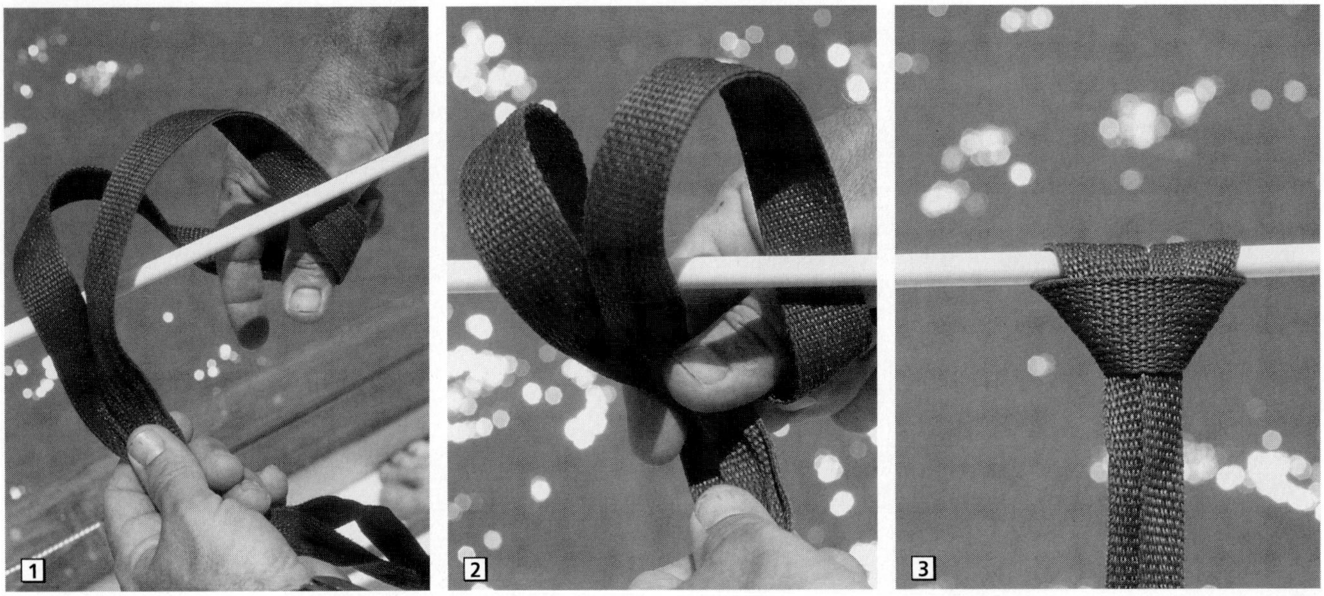

Cow hitch. 1. A cow hitch is generally used for stowing short lengths of line (small stuff) on lifelines and at other convenient locations. The line is doubled up and laid over the lifeline. 2. The rest of the line is then dragged through the loop so formed . . . 3. and given a quick tug to tighten it up.

The *cow hitch* is used for hanging sail ties and other short lengths of line (known as *small stuff*) from the lifelines. The small stuff is folded in half. The loop formed is hooked over the lifelines and both bitter ends are pulled through.

A *half hitch* is made by running a line around a post or a lifeline, or passing the line through a grommet, and so on, and then bringing the bitter end of the line around the standing part and feeding the bitter end through the loop so formed. To make two or more half hitches, this is repeated, always running the bitter end around the standing part in the same direction. When tying a dinghy to a piling or post, a clove hitch with two half hitches is very secure. Alternatively, simply run the bitter end twice around the piling without passing it back through itself at any point (a *round turn*) and add a couple of half hitches.

The *rolling hitch* has already been discussed a number of times in connection with attaching a snubber to an anchor line. It is also used when attaching any line to another loaded line; for example, if you get a *riding turn* on a winch that jams up the sheet to a sail, you can attach another line to the sheet with a rolling hitch, then take this second line to a second winch and crank it in—this takes the load off the first winch and enables the sheet to be freed. Another use is for attaching a line to a spar of any kind, which is not common these days. The rolling hitch is made by wrapping the bitter end

Round turns and half hitches. 1. The line is run around the piling twice without running it under or through itself in any way (two round turns). 2. The bitter end is taken over the standing part and then under and through the loop formed (first half hitch). 3. The bitter end is taken around the standing part a second time, going around in the same direction as before, and passed through the loop formed (second half hitch). A common mistake is to reverse the direction in which the bitter end goes around the standing part on the second hitch, resulting in a cow hitch rather than two half hitches.

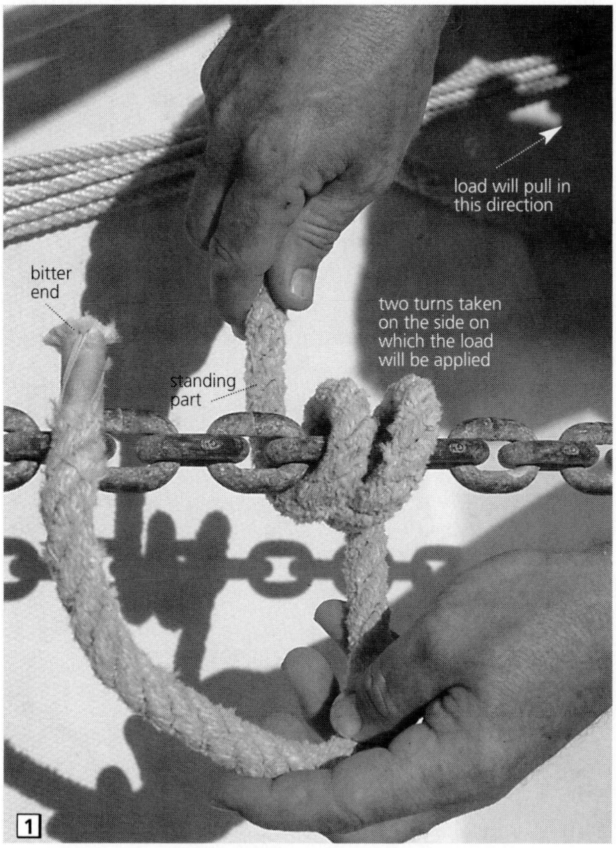

of the line twice around the line to which it is being attached—making the turns *on the same side in which the line will be loaded up*—and then making a third turn on the *other* side of the standing part, tucking the bitter end through this turn. When made this way, the knot will not bind up. However, if the first two turns are made on the unloaded side of the knot and the last turn is made on the loaded side, the knot can roll over the bitter end, bind it up, and make it difficult to undo.

The *trucker's hitch* (see pages 444–45) is a very useful knot for making a temporary loop that will not bind up under a load in the middle of a line. Its primary application is in lashing down dinghies. A line is tied off at one end and then thrown over the dinghy. A trucker's hitch is added in the middle. The bitter end is passed under a handrail or through a pad eye, fed back through the loop formed by the trucker's hitch, and then pulled back down to the handrail or pad eye and lashed off (a couple of half hitches). This arrangement provides a 2:1 purchase that enables the lashing to be pulled tight. To make the trucker's hitch, form a loop with the bitter end on top. Repeat it so the two loops are on top of one another. Grasp the line at the intermediate point between the first and second loops, pull a small bight out sideways, and bring it back over the top of the bitter end. Feed the bight down through the top loop, out between the top and bottom loops, over the top of the first (bottom loop), and around it to come back through the middle of both loops. Pull the bight tight to produce a loop hanging down from the knot.

The *sheet bend* (or becket hitch; see pages 445–46) is used to tie two lines together, even if they are different sizes or textures (e.g., synthetic and natural). It is also used to attach a line to a spliced eye in the end of another line. It is, in fact, a bowline made with two lines and, as such, it can be made in exactly the same way. Just as with a bowline, a loop is made in one line (the thinner line, if they vary in diameter) with the bitter end on top. The bitter end of the second line is fed up through the loop ("the rabbit comes out of the hole"), under and around the standing part of the first line ("the rabbit goes around the tree"), and then back through the hole ("the rabbit goes back in the hole"). Just as with the bowline, it is important that "the rabbit goes around the tree" in the right direction. For additional security, the two bitter ends sticking out of the knot can be given a half hitch or two around the standing parts. If the knot is to stay in place for some time, the bitter ends should be *seized* to the standing parts with whipping twine (explained later in this chapter).

Rolling hitch. 1. The bitter end is wrapped around the chain (or spar, or whatever) twice on the same side as that from which the pull on the standing part will be coming. 2. The bitter end is passed under the standing part and then back around the chain on the other side, going around in the same direction as before, and back through itself. 3. The knot is cinched up.

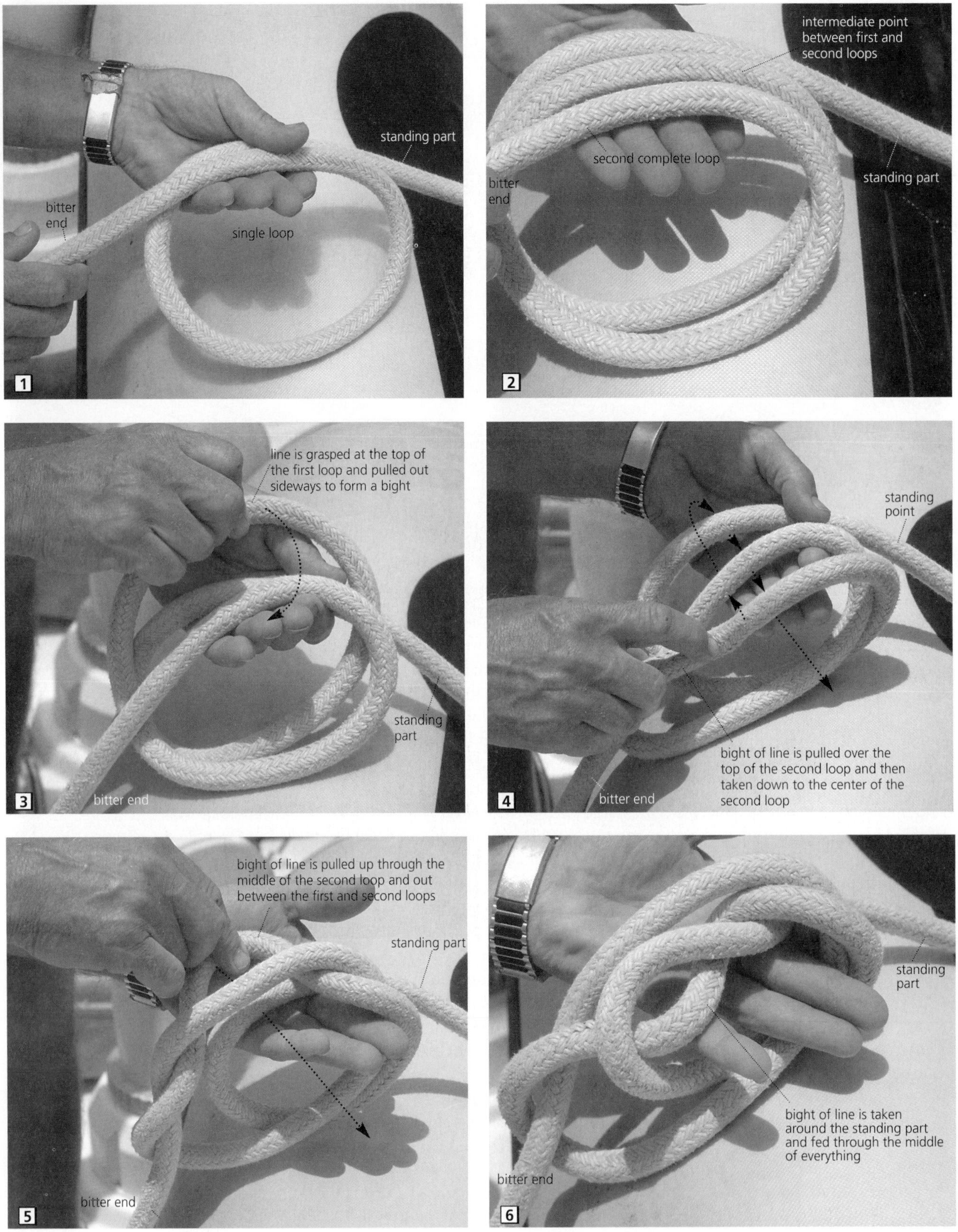

Trucker's hitch. 1. A loop is made in the line. 2. A second identical loop is laid on top of the first. 3. The line is grasped at the intermediate point between the first and second loops and pulled sideways a little to form a bight. 4. The bight of line is taken over the top of the top loop . . . 5. down through the middle and out between the top and bottom loop . . . 6. and then around the top of the bottom loop and back up through the middle of everything . . .

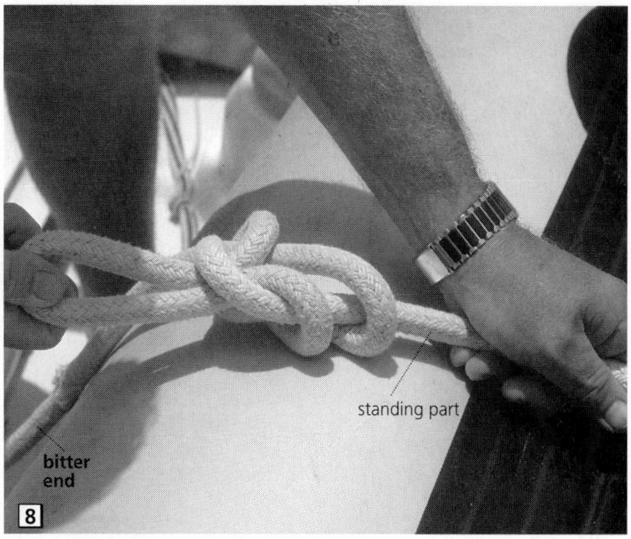

7. . . . and pulled out. 8. The knot is cinched up tight. 9. The bitter end of the line is taken under a handrail or through a pad eye or some other attachment point, run back through the trucker's hitch, and cinched up tight. This gives a 2:1 purchase. 10. The line is tied off with a couple of half hitches (just one is shown; the second is about to be put in).

Sheet bend, method 1 (similar to a bowline).

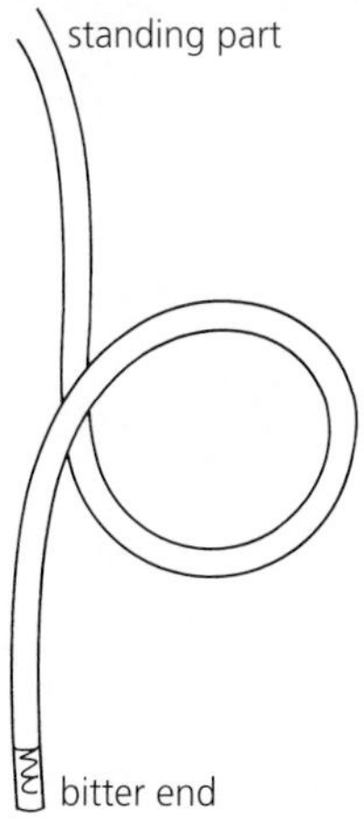

A loop is formed in one line with the bitter end on top.

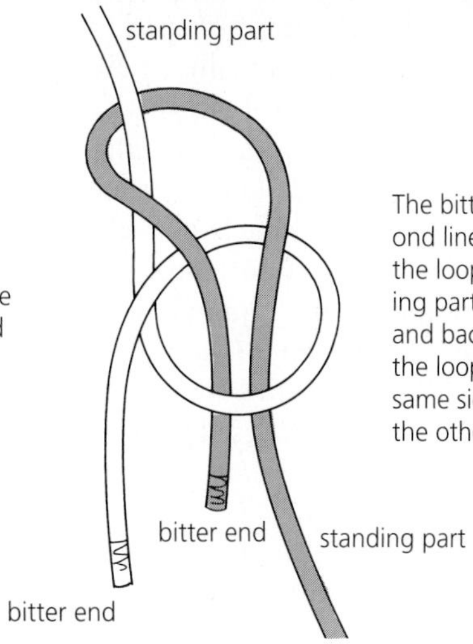

The bitter end of the second line is fed up through the loop under the standing part of the first line, and back down through the loop to emerge on the same side of the knot as the other bitter end.

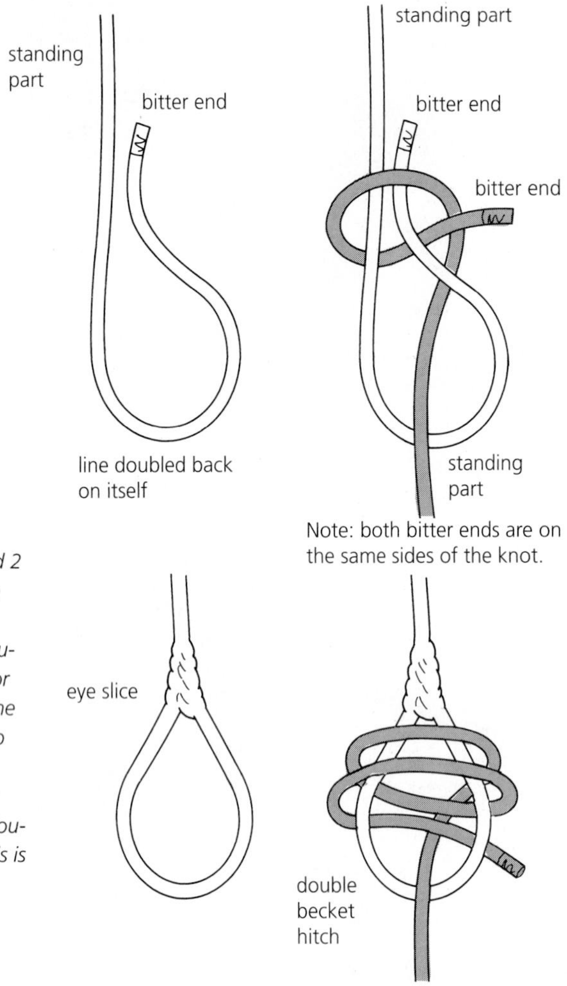

Sheet bend, method 2 (above), and double becket hitch (right). The larger line is doubled back on itself or has a spliced eye. The smaller line is fed up through the loop, around it, and back under itself. For a double becket hitch, this is repeated.

Another popular way to make this knot is to take a line with an eye splice or double one line (the thicker one, if they vary in diameter) back on itself to form a loop. The bitter end of the other line is fed through the loop, around the standing part of the line with the eye or loop, and then back under itself. To improve the holding power of this knot, the bitter end should be taken around the eye a second time, and again tucked under the standing part of its line (a *double becket hitch*). This knot jams up tight under a load and will not slip, yet remains easy to undo once the load is removed. As noted, for added security, the bitter end(s) can be seized off. When a sheet bend or double becket hitch is used without an eye splice in one of the lines, the second line should be taken around the first in such a way that once the knot is completed, the two bitter ends come out the same side of the knot (rather than opposite sides of the knot).

The *anchor bend* (fisherman's bend) is used for temporarily attaching an anchor rode to an anchor (for longer-term attachment, an eye splice and shackle should be used). The bitter end of the rode is looped loosely through

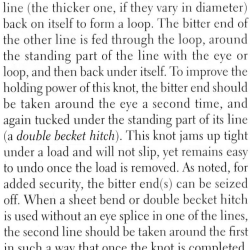

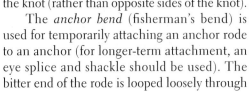

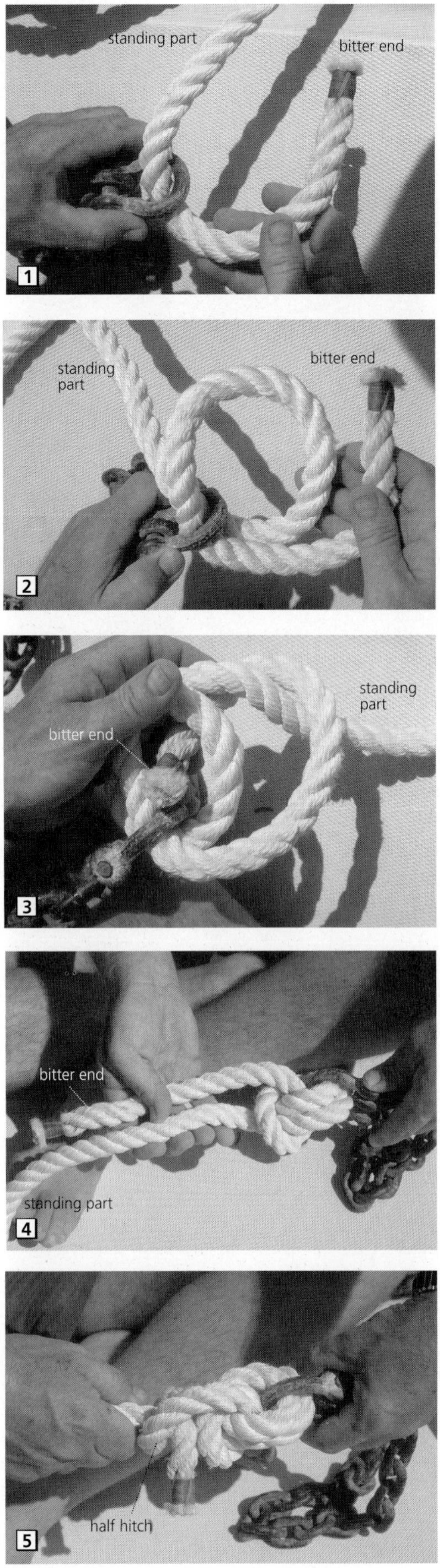

Far right: *Anchor (fisherman's) bend. 1. The bitter end is run through the anchor shackle keeping the loop reasonably loose . . . 2. and then run through the shackle a second time. 3.The bitter end is taken back over the standing part of the line and through the center of the two loops on the shackle. 4. The knot is cinched up . . . 5. and reinforced with a half hitch. (It is a good idea to seize the bitter end to the standing part, except that in this case the bitter end is not long enough!)*

Constrictor knot. 1. *The standing part of the twine is held between the thumb and second finger with the forefinger pointing up. The bitter end of the twine is taken around the line and over the forefinger.* 2. *The bitter end is taken back under the line and up inside the standing part.* 3. *Now the bitter end is fed back through the loop it has formed with the standing part, and through the loop on the forefinger.* 4. *The knot is cinched up.* 5. *A close-up of the knot.*

a shackle twice and then brought across the top of the standing part of the rode and tucked through the two loops. The knot is pulled up tight and a half hitch or two is added around the standing part to finish it off. For added security, the bitter end should be seized back to the standing part.

The *constrictor knot* is used to tie off the end of a piece of twine that is being used for a seizing or whipping (explained later in this chapter). With the standing part of the twine held between the thumb and second finger of the left hand, lay the bitter end over the line to which it is being seized. Bring the bitter end of the twine under the line to the right of the standing part of the twine. Point the forefinger of your left hand into the air and flip the bitter end of the twine over it and back over the line. Bring the bitter end of the twine up to the left of the standing part, over the top of the standing part, and back under the standing part to form a simple *overhand knot* (the first half of a reef knot). Finally, feed the bitter end of the twine out through the slot occupied by your forefinger; withdraw your finger and pull the knot tight.

Eye Splices

All knots weaken the lines in which they are tied, sometimes quite considerably, whereas splices generally retain up to 90 percent of the strength of the rope. The table at right gives some ballpark strength-loss figures for common knots.

Traditionally, rope had a stranded construction, which made it relatively easy to splice. Today, most lines found on a boat have a braided construction that requires a completely different technique. Nevertheless, stranded rope is still commonly used for anchor rodes and many mooring lines, so it is just as well to know how to put in a splice if necessary.

An eye splice is begun by unlaying the rope strands about six to ten turns and then putting a temporary seizing around the rope (e.g., electrician's, rigging, or masking tape or a constrictor knot). With synthetic rope, it is a good idea to fuse the ends of the strands together to stop them unraveling during the splicing process. I use a cigarette lighter to melt the ends, and then wipe them with a paper towel to get a reasonably tapered finish with no big globs of hardened plastic. Melted line is extremely hot and sticks to the skin, causing nasty burns—take care not to drip any on yourself, and make sure that you have a thick-enough wad of paper towel for the melted plastic not to burn you through it.

The line is formed into whatever size loop is wanted, with the unlayed strands placed such that (B) lies across the standing part of the line with (A) and (C) on either side, as shown

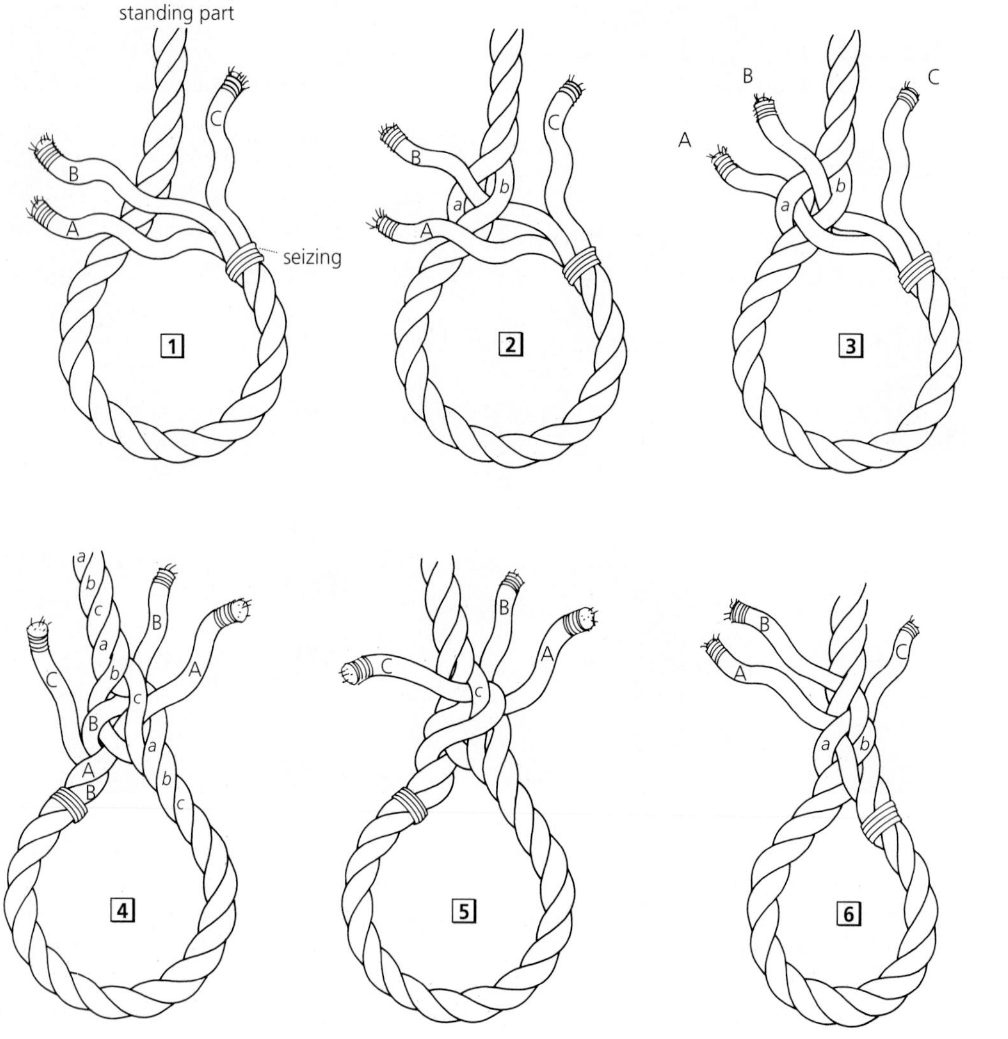

Eye splice. 1. *The bitter end is unlayed six to ten turns and then temporarily seized off. The three strands are laid out against the standing part.* 2. *The standing part is twisted to unlay the rope, and strand B tucked through (under strand* b*).* 3. *Strand A is brought over strand* b *and tucked under strand* a. 4. *The splice is flipped over. Strand C is brought in alongside the point at which strand* A *emerges from the splice, and then . . .* 5. *tucked back under strand* c. 6. *The strands are snugged up, and then each in turn is taken over the next one up the standing part of the line, under the one above that, and so on until the splice is completed.*

Strength Loss of Common Knots

KNOT, BEND, OR HITCH	REDUCTION IN LINE STRENGTH (percent)
bowline	25–30
reef knot	50–60
two half hitches	30–40
sheet bend	40–50
anchor bend:	
through a shackle (tight knot radius)	35–45
around a post (wide knot radius)	10–20

on page 448. The ultimate size of the loop is determined by the point at which the first tuck with B is made back into the standing part. If this is an eye splice around a thimble, the first tuck needs to be such that it will draw the loop up tightly around the thimble. It may help to tape the line to the thimble during the task.

The line is twisted back against its lay at the point where the first tuck is to be made. This opens up the strands. *The center strand (B) is always tucked first*, going from right to left against the lay of the rope, and passing under the center strand (*b*). Now strand A is brought over the top of *b* and tucked under *a* (the next strand up the standing part—A goes in alongside where B comes out), once again going from right to left. So far, so good; the next step is where beginners go wrong.

The line is flipped over. Strand C is brought over *c* more or less alongside the point at which A emerges from the lay of the rope, and then hooked back and tucked under *c*, once again going from right to left (strand C goes in alongside where A comes out).

At this point, the line is flipped back over and the three strands are gently tugged tight. All three strands should be coming out of the rope at approximately the same point along its length and about 120 degrees apart. A second row of tucks is made, starting with B, taking it over the next strand up the standing part (which will be *a*), and tucking it under the one above that (*c*). The other strands are treated the same, going over the next strand up the standing part and under the one above that. With natural fibers, three rounds of tucks are adequate; with synthetic line, which is more slippery, up to six should be put in. A neater splice will be made if the strands are progressively tapered with a knife after the first three or more tucks have been made (lines that will be heavily loaded need five tucks before tapering). Finally, excess strands are cut off, and the splice is rolled underfoot to smooth it out.

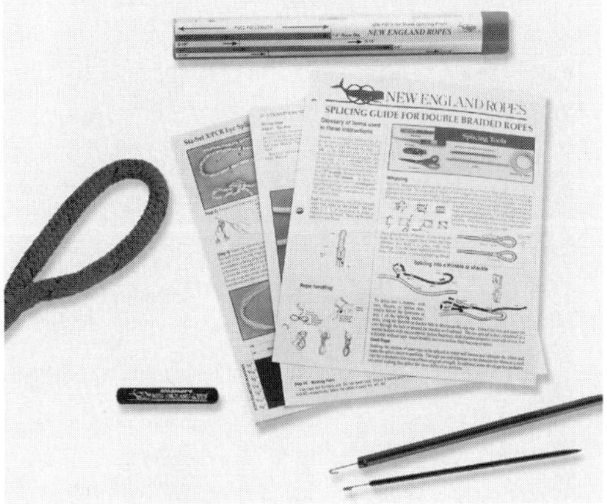

Kit for splicing synthetic lines. (Courtesy New England Ropes)

Braided Eye Splice

A special tool (a customized *fid*) is needed to make an eye splice in braided lines, and is available as part of a kit from New England Ropes and other manufacturers. It comes with detailed instructions for splicing different kinds of braided lines, so they are not repeated here.

Rope-to-Wire Splice

Rope-to-wire splices are sometimes found on halyards, but are not common given today's low-stretch synthetic lines. A rope-to-wire splice is best done by a professional rigger; therefore, it is not discussed herein.

Seizings and Whippings

Seizings and *whippings* are now made with heavy-duty waxed polyester (Dacron or Terylene) thread. A seizing is a lashing used to hold two ropes side by side or at the throat (base) of an eye splice. Whipping is the traditional way of keeping the end of a line from fraying or unraveling but may also be used to seize the throat of a splice.

A *plain whipping* is made by laying a long loop (bight) of whipping twine along the end of a line or at the base of a splice (in which case the loop lies up the standing part away from the eye or thimble), and then wrapping the twine

Plain whipping on the end of a line. 1. If necessary, a constrictor knot or something similar is used to keep the line from unraveling. A bight of twine is laid out along the line. If this were the throat of an eye splice, the bight would be away from the eye. 2. Starting from the end opposite the bight, the twine is wrapped tightly around the line until . . . 3. the whipping is at least as long as the diameter of the line. The standing part of the line is cut and the end of it . . . 4. is slipped through the bight that was originally formed, and the line at the other end of the bight is pulled . . . 5. to drag the bight and with it, the standing part . . . 6. into the center of the whipping.

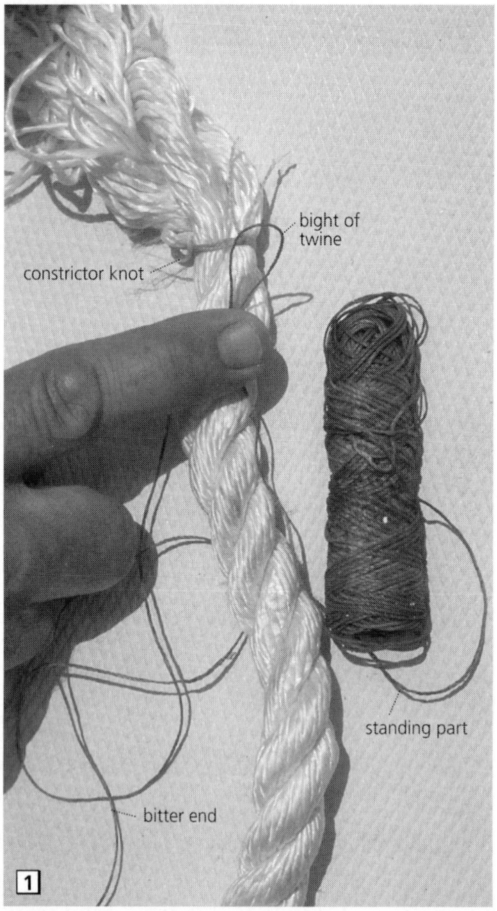

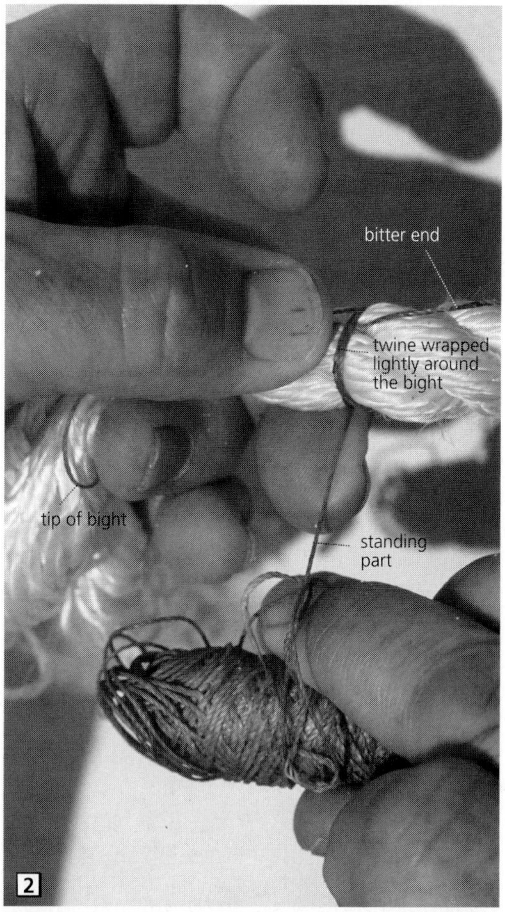

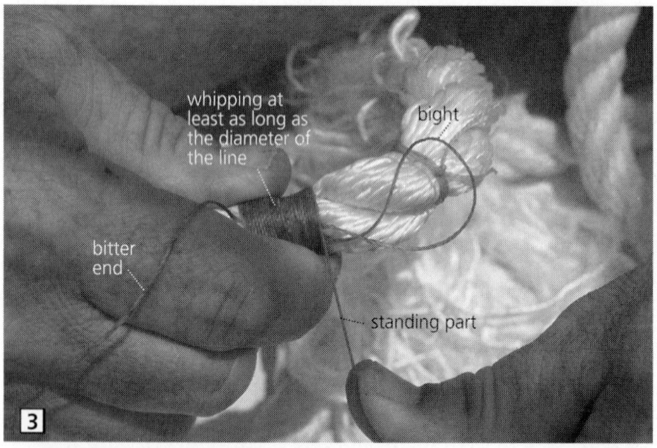

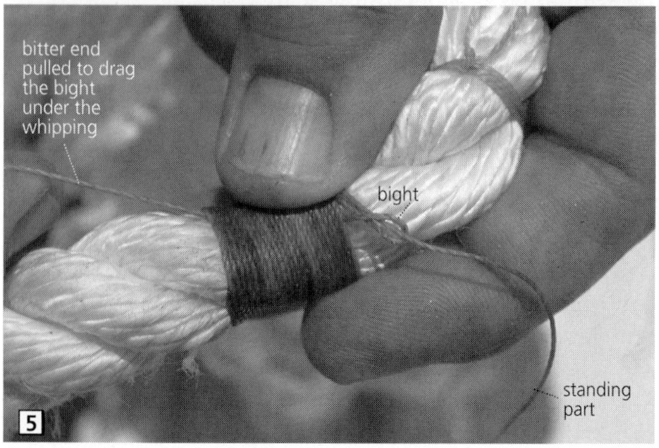

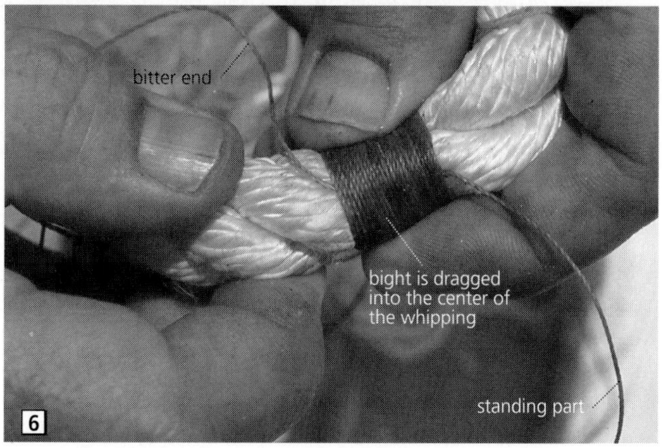

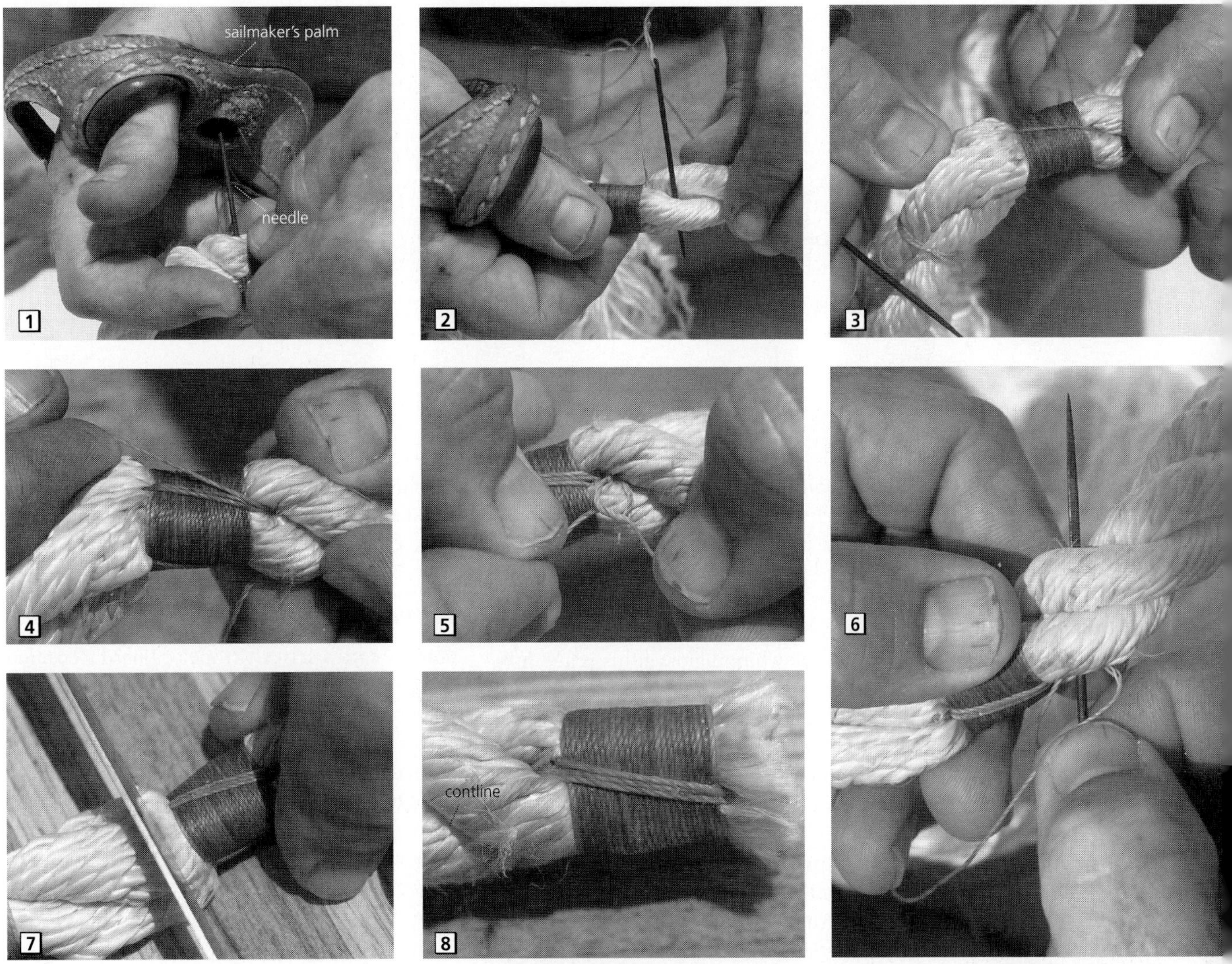

tightly around the line. Start a little way away from the loop, leaving the bitter end of the twine sticking out, and work along the standing part of the line toward the loop. After a dozen or more wraps, the twine is cut, leaving a tail of a couple of inches; the tail is poked through what remains of the original loop. The other end of the whipping twine (the original bitter end) is tugged on to drag the tail into the whipping, which leaves a tail sticking out both ends; the tails are then cut off.

A plain whipping may work loose over time. Greater security is achieved by using a *sailmaker's whipping*.

This requires a needle and a *sailmaker's palm*, which is a heavy leather pad that fits the palm of a hand and is used to push the needle through tough material. To begin with, either a plain whipping is made, leaving a long tail on either end; or the needle is threaded with a length of twine, pushed through the line (leaving a tail of a couple of inches), and wrapped tightly around the line to form a plain whipping,

Sailmaker's whipping. 1. *A whipping is made as before, but leaving a long tail at one end and a shorter tail at the other. The long tail is put on a needle and either driven sideways through a strand, using a sailmaker's palm . . .* 2. *or the rope is unlayed and the needle is slipped between the strands.* 3. *The tail is brought down to the other end of the whipping and again driven through the next strand, or slipped under it, and taken back to the original end.* 4. *This is continued until two or three threads have been laid down the whipping at three or four points on its circumference.* 5. *The two tails are then either tied together (using a square knot) to lock them off . . .* 6. *or stitched back into the line a couple of times and buried so that they will not work loose.* 7. *The end of the line is trimmed off.* 8. *With three-strand rope, the whipping is laid in down the contline, whereas . . .* 9. *with braided rope, it is laid in parallel to the run of the rope.*

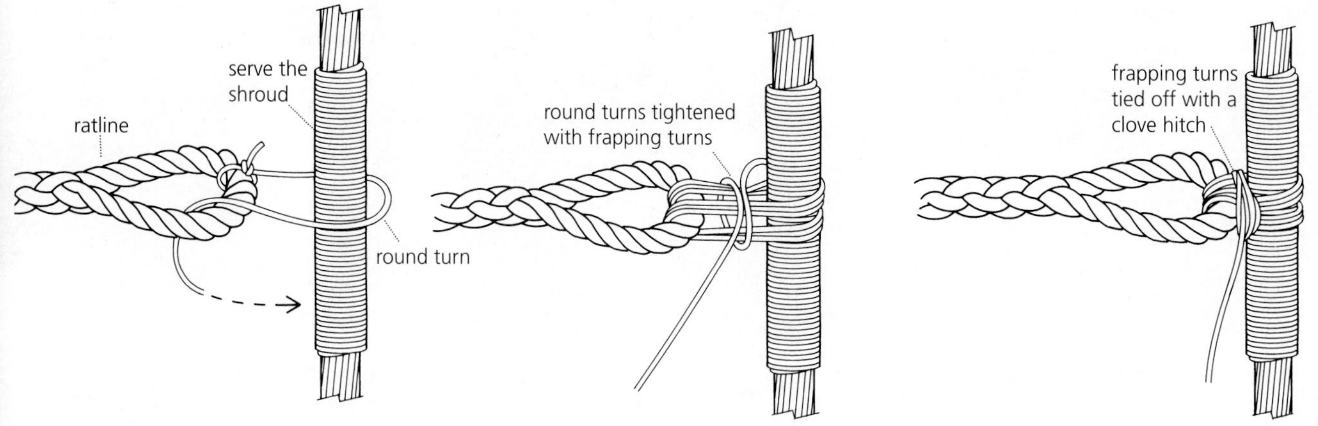

Seizing a rope ratline to a shroud.

at which point the needle is pushed back through the line. In either case, one end of the twine is now brought back over the top of the whipping down to the other end of it. The needle is either pushed through the line under the whipping to bring the twine back up out the other end of the whipping or, if this is too difficult, pushed sideways through the line to emerge one quarter or one third of the way around the line's perimeter. The twine is taken over the top of the whipping again, and then back through the line under the whipping (or sideways), and so on.

With three-strand rope, the twine is brought over the top of the whipping along the *contline* (the hollow between the strands)—that is, at a diagonal—and the needle is then driven through a strand parallel to the run of the line to emerge in the next contline. With braided rope, the twine is brought over the top of the whipping parallel to the run of the line, and then the needle is driven back through the line, or sideways. A sailmaker's whipping is finished off by stitching the ends back into the line, or by tying a square knot in the two ends and trimming the tails.

One way of making board ratlines.

1. Drill the board for the shrouds.

2. Slit the board lengthwise.

3. Apply a liberal bead of epoxy.

4. Fasten the two halves of the board tightly around the shrouds.

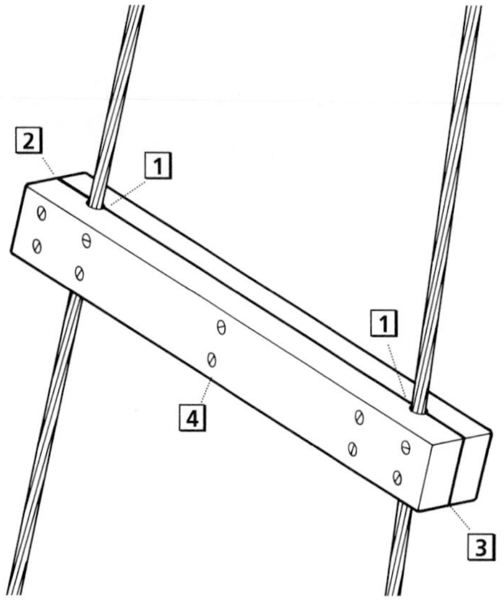

Ratlines

Ratlines are a series of rope or board steps tied between adjacent shrouds. They can be installed only on boats that have fore and aft lower shrouds. Even then, the fore and aft spread of the shrouds at their base may be too wide to make ratlines feasible. However, it may be possible to rig the lower ratlines between the aft lower shroud and the cap shroud, and then between the two lower shrouds once enough height has been gained to bring the shrouds close enough to make this practical.

Ratlines are a tremendous boon to anyone navigating around coral reefs. Just a few feet of extra height greatly improves the visibility down into the water immediately ahead. On occasion, I have gone as high as the lower spreaders and sat up there—one time for six hours—while we picked our way through a veritable labyrinth of coral.

The traditional way to make a ratline is to splice an eye into both ends of a length of line that is then seized to the shrouds. Half-inch (12 mm) three-strand works well; ⅝-inch (16 mm) is more comfortable underfoot, but it gets difficult to splice in the eyes at both ends as the distance between the shrouds decreases.

When ratlines are seized to stainless steel rigging, they tend to slip. One way to stop this is to *serve* the rigging (wrap it in whipping twine) wherever a ratline will be tied on. This is accomplished by placing a constrictor knot (described previously) in one end of a 3-foot length of whipping twine, pulling the knot as tight as possible, cutting the bitter end down to about a ½ inch, and then wrapping the twine tightly around the shroud, laying in the bitter end, and making sure that each turn lies tightly against the preceding one. After an inch or so, several loose wraps are made, feeding the end of the line back through them, and then tightening everything up and cutting off the remaining tail of line.

To seize a ratline to this serving, a length of whipping twine is tied to the spliced eye in the end of the ratline, and then simply wrapped around the shroud and through the eye in a series of round turns (i.e., no figure eights or anything fancy). The seizing is finished with a series of *frapping turns*— turns taken around the seizing between the shroud and the ratline—to tighten the seizing. Finally, two or three half hitches are added and the ends are trimmed off.

Rope ratlines are uncomfortable under bare feet. A more comfortable approach is to drill a board at both ends with a hole the same diameter as the shrouds and at the correct spacing and angle to match the shrouds. Then slit the board lengthwise on the vertical axis using a band saw. The two halves are screwed back together around the shrouds, with a good bead of epoxy in the seam and around the shrouds. The loss of material from the saw cut causes the holes for the shrouds to be a little undersized; this enables the two halves of the ratline to be drawn up tightly enough around the shrouds to keep them from slipping in use.

Left and below: *Board ratlines. Note how the lower ratline has been taken to a cap shroud, to reduce the span. The ratlines are lashed in place and held with cable ("bulldog") clamps, which works but leaves a lot of protruding fasteners that may chafe sails.*

SAILS

Sail technology is constantly evolving, both in terms of materials and design and construction. Despite this, from a cruising perspective, everything has been fairly stable for many years, and it appears that it will remain that way for some time—not because the new technologies are not exciting, but rather because the price tag generally outweighs the benefits. Here I discuss materials, construction, maintenance, and repairs.

Materials and Construction

For two thousand years, sails were made of flax and cotton; then, in the 1950s, came nylon and polyester (more specifically, Dacron—DuPont's version of polyester). Compared to cotton, nylon and Dacron are much stronger and have excellent resistance to chemicals, mildew, mold, and other environmental insults. Nylon, of course, stretches and, therefore, is only of use where sail shape is not critical. It also absorbs water, which causes a significant loss of strength. Polyester stretches much less than nylon and absorbs very little water. It makes an excellent general-purpose sailcloth.

It took a while to adapt the new polyester fibers to sailmaking, but by the 1960s, the process was fairly well established. Special tight weaves result in extremely dense fabrics; variations in the *warp* and *weft* threads (those that run along and across the cloth) control stretch properties; and various heat and surface treatments stabilize the finished fabric, minimize its porosity, and minimize the stretch across the *bias* (the diagonal across the warp and weft).

Polyester makes strong, stable sails that hold their shape well, are dependable, tolerant of abuse, easy to handle, if reasonably cared for have a long service life, and can be repaired just about anywhere in the world. The price is excellent when compared to the alternatives.

However, polyester does stretch, particularly on the bias. This stretch can be reduced by innovative weaves and construction techniques (see below), but ultimately it means that the sail will only hold its optimum shape over a relatively narrow range of wind speeds. Unfortunately, most cruising boats have a small sail inventory, so individual sails have to be able to handle a broad range of conditions. The net result is that polyester sails frequently are operating beyond the limits of their optimized wind speeds, resulting in a loss of performance. Over time, they lose their shape, and performance suffers even more.

Better performance calls for more sails and/or materials that stretch less. The past couple of decades have seen a number of new low-stretch fabrics utilizing the same materials found in modern ropes. The most significant are:

- Mylar is a form of polyester that is melted and extruded as a film. It is then laminated to another fabric (generally regular polyester cloth). Mylar-polyester laminates significantly reduce stretch over polyester at a relatively modest 10 percent increase in cost. However, Mylar is more sensitive to UV degradation, tears more easily, and is easily damaged when a sail flogs. If a sail is given too much halyard tension, it is permanently deformed. The most durable laminates sandwich a film of Mylar between two layers of polyester. Properly cared for, these sails have a life expectancy not much shorter than that of regular sailcloth.
- Kevlar-Mylar fabrics have Kevlar fibers (aramid) laminated to a film of Mylar. For a given weight, Kevlar is eight times stronger than polyester (but at ten times the cost), while the Kevlar-Mylar laminate is five times stronger than polyester. Kevlar-Mylar has tremendous stretch resistance, but is easily damaged when a sail flogs and through creasing and flexing. It also breaks under shock loads. These sails generally have a working life of approximately two seasons.
- Spectra-Mylar, in which Spectra (HMPE) fibers are laminated to a film of Mylar, is even stronger and lighter than Kevlar (and even more expensive). It is less sensitive to flogging, but will creep (permanently deform) under sustained heavy loads, resulting in a loss of sail shape.

Ultimately, the cost and reduced life expectancy of these modern fabrics rules them out for most cruisers, with the possible exception of Mylar-polyester laminates (particularly on a cruiser-racer and on larger boats with big sails where the loads are such that high-tech fabrics may be the only way to get the necessary strength without making sails almost impossibly heavy for a short-handed crew to handle). However, many of the construction techniques developed on the racing circuit have some application in cruising.

Modern sailmakers determine the loads on a sail for any given wind speed, as well as the direction in which these loads are exerted, in a computerized *stress map*. The computer also calculates optimized sail shapes for any given boat. It is then possible to enter the physical properties of any particular fabric, which might include its *yield strength* (the load point at which it is permanently deformed) and stretch characteristics along the warp and weft, as well as on the bias. The computer can work out the optimum way in which to build the sail with the given sailcloth (which way to cut and sew the panels), and how heavy the sailcloth must be in different areas of the sail to make sure it does not exceed its yield point in the designed wind range. Lastly, the computer can determine precisely how each panel must be cut to achieve the desired sail shape, sending the relevant cutting instructions to a computerized cutting table. However, people still must glue and sew the pieces together!

Taken to its extremes, this process results in the incredible sails seen on the high-end racing circuit, some of which have up to ninety individual panels radiating out from the primary stress points (the head, the clew, and the tack—a tri-radial sail). The cruising sailor is not going to want to pay for anywhere near this level of sophistication, but may find an affordable middle ground that yields significant performance benefits somewhere between this and the traditional *cross-cut sail* (in which all the seams run parallel to the foot of the sail).

It is clear that even at the relatively low-tech cruising end of the sailmaking spectrum, sail lofts have the ability to customize sails for any given boat, considering criteria such as the overall sail inventory that will be carried (and, therefore, the wind ranges that any given sail must withstand), the planned cruising grounds (and, therefore, the likely wind speeds), the kinds of sail-tweaking devices onboard (e.g., the extent to which the mast can be bent), and the stresses on the sail. With this information, the optimum construction pattern, cloth types, and cloth weights can be determined.

Regardless of the level of sophistication, the end result for a cruising boat must be "strong, durable, and easy to handle. It should stand up to flogging and moderate overloading and should last for many seasons. Performance is important in such a sail, but the ability to hold shape is more important. . . . Tightly woven Dacron with a moderately soft finish is generally the material of choice" (Tom Whidden, president of North Sails and author of *The Art and Science of Sails*).

Tom Neal, well-known world cruiser and educator, has this to say: "Sails are among the most important equipment on an offshore cruising boat and the last thing you want to fail, yet their selection and care are often left to last in terms of outfitting and budgetary priorities. It is essential to realize that the quality of sails you start out with will directly affect how much time and money you'll spend on repair and replacement once you're actually cruising" (*Offshore Cruising Companion*).

The following points should be considered:

- Only high-quality Dacron should be used. Note that there are numerous fabric styles (e.g., high aspect, low aspect, and balanced Dacron), including some hybrids with other materials in the weave (e.g., Pentex, a high-strength polyester variant), producing a stronger sailcloth. It is important to find a sailmaker who takes the time to optimize the cloth selection for your application.
- Seams should be wide and triple-stitched with UV-protected thread.
- Patches should be added at all likely chafe points, with leather used at high-chafe areas such as corners, headboards, and reef cringles. Pay particular attention to the points at which batten pockets will bear on shrouds when running downwind.
- Stainless steel or bronze should be used for pressed rings rather than aluminum with stainless steel rings (the aluminum will suffer from galvanic corrosion).
- Sail slides should be sewn on with webbing, not fastened with plastic or stainless steel shackles.
- All high-load areas, such as tacks and clews, will need multiple layers of sailcloth, reinforced with nylon webbing.

An absolute minimum inventory for a coastal cruiser includes an all-weather mainsail and roller-reefing genoa, which will be a #1 or #2 in light wind areas, and a #2 or #3 in heavier wind areas (a #1 genoa has an area that is approximately 150 percent of the boat's foretriangle; a #2 is around 130 percent of the fore-

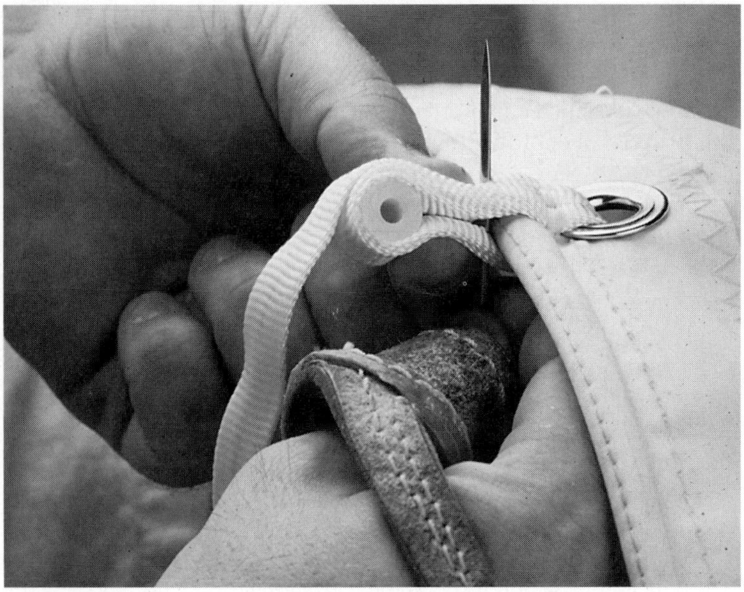

Sail slides should be attached with webbing and sewn rather than attached with shackles. (Courtesy Harken)

triangle; a #3 is 100 percent or less; a #4 is smaller still). The main will need two sets of reef points (three on larger mains). Both sails, when reefed down, will have to handle the strongest winds encountered. The genoa will need a foam luff or some other arrangement that enables it to set reasonably well to windward even when heavily reefed.

The next step up is to add a second, smaller headsail. Then consider an asymmetric spinnaker for light-air conditions. If you are contemplating extended offshore passages, a set of heavy-weather sails is needed: a #4 genoa or storm jib on a sloop or a heavy staysail on a cutter, and a trysail set on its own track. This inventory is adequate to cruise around the world.

Maintenance and Repairs

Modern sails require very little maintenance. However, the nature of the materials used in sailcloth dictates that certain situations be avoided wherever possible, including the following:

- *Use above the designed wind speed.* Once the yield strength is exceeded, permanent deformation occurs. When you buy a sail, find out its limits by asking the sailmaker for its maximum wind speed when fully deployed and when reefed. In use, avoid over-tensioning the halyard. When not in use, ease the halyard on a roller reefing sail and the outhaul on a mainsail.
- *Flogging and creasing.* The high-tech fabrics, in particular, are rapidly damaged by flogging and even by the chattering of a leech. These sails will also be damaged if folded or creased in any way—they should always be rolled after use and stowed in a sausage, which is not practical on most cruising boats. Polyester is not so sensitive, but severe flogging causes it to suffer from a loss of its surface treatment, which then reduces its ability to hold its shape. The fabric is quite tolerant of creases; nevertheless, it should not be repeatedly folded at the same points.

In a high wind, this poorly furled sail will flog, damaging the sailcloth and chafing the stitching.

- *Chafe.* At some time, all sails suffer from chafe, whether it is a genoa rubbing on a bow pulpit or a spreader tip, or the main up against the shrouds when running downwind. The stitching is especially vulnerable to damage because modern sailcloths are too hard to allow the stitches to embed themselves in the fabric. Consequently, the stitches sit on the surface and are first to be abraded. Various seam treatments are available to give the stitches a measure of protection—these should be specified when a sail is ordered. In addition, all likely chafe points are best protected with a sacrificial patch. Batten pockets can be further strengthened by sewing on a strip of sacrificial nylon webbing or even Spectra sailcloth wherever

This batten was improperly installed and, as a result, has punched clean through the batten pocket.

they bear against the spreaders when running downwind. Beyond this, care should be taken to tape up all pins and protrusions on deck that might snag a sail, especially a billowing spinnaker.

- *Exposure to sunlight.* Tests have shown that almost all sailcloth, including polyester, loses 40 percent or more of its strength if subjected to three months of tropical sunlight. Clearly, sails should be kept out of the sun whenever they are not in use. The keys are to ensure that UV strips on roller-reefing headsails are in good condition and to cover a mainsail as soon as it is taken down.
- *Stowing in wet, salty, and high-temperature areas.* Moisture itself is generally not damaging to modern fabrics, but salt can be. However, moisture leads to mildew and mold that, while generally not damaging, are unsightly. Laminated sails can be particularly vulnerable to mildew, especially when the outer laminate is impervious to moisture, because water can wick in between the laminate layers and then can't escape. At the end of the season, sails should be hosed down with freshwater, perhaps cleaned with a mild soap (e.g., dishwashing liquid) and a regular bathroom mildew remover (if necessary), dried by laying them out on a lawn, and then rolled up into a long sausage for storage (particularly high-tech fabrics). The storage location should be cool and dry. Note that Spectra laminates can be permanently damaged at 150°F (65°C), so they should not be left in the trunk of a dark automobile in sunlight or up against a light bulb in a locker.

Sails should be carefully inspected at least annually for signs of damage. One way to do this—if they can't be spread out on a lawn—is to slowly pull them over the boom, checking for damaged stitching and chafe. Sail slides on the main also need close scrutiny, especially those at the headboard because they come under a tremendous load.

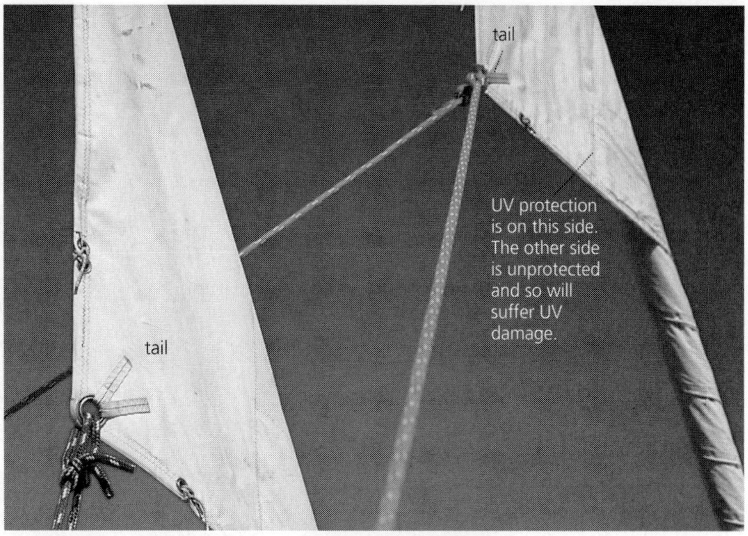
tail
tail
UV protection is on this side. The other side is unprotected and so will suffer UV damage.

mainsail halyard
SCHAEFER
the headboard cut through this strap twice
mainsail headboard

Above: *Because the UV protection is only on one side of a furling sail, every time you see tails like this, you know the sun is going to work on the other side!* Left: *Headboard slides and their attachments need close inspection from time to time. This slide failed twice in short order. It was repaired by filing down the edge of the aluminum headboard where the webbing bends around it, and by beefing up the webbing.*

Repairs

A boat that is headed offshore needs the ability to make at least rudimentary sail repairs. This requires scissors, a sailmaker's palm, needles (keep them in an oil-soaked rag to prevent rusting), polyester thread (Dacron or Terylene), awls (or sturdy push pins, to stake out a sail somewhere ashore), and some bits of sailcloth of the same weight and type as the sails. The palm, needles, and thread can

Rudimentary sail repair kit: Dacron thread, Velcro, needles, twine, needle-sharpening stone, sailmaker's palm, cigarette lighter, self-adhesive Dacron tape, nylon webbing, and some scraps of sailcloth.

be purchased in a kit from marine stores or catalogs; the local sailmaker can supply scraps of sailcloth. It helps also to have double-sided tape and/or self-adhesive cloth—it holds up surprisingly well even without stitching and is easier to work with when stitching—and a can of spray adhesive (such as 3M's Super 77) for cloth without adhesive. In a pinch, duct tape can be used for many temporary repairs. A DC-operated hot knife or a soldering iron with a hot-knife attachment is great for cutting sailcloth and for sealing the edges of tears and patches. Otherwise, the edges can be sealed with a cigarette lighter. Spare hardware should include sail slides, hanks (if the boat has hanked-on sails), and maybe a couple of grommets.

Any area to be repaired needs to be clean, free of salt (rinse with freshwater, or, better yet, alcohol), dry, and laid out on a flat surface. If a tear is to be stitched up, the thread is always used doubled. A simple round stitch will suffice, although a sailmaker probably uses a herringbone stitch. For the herringbone, a knot is put in the end of the thread. The needle is brought *up* through one side of the tear and *down* through the other side. The needle then comes up through the tear itself to the right of the stitch just put in, over the top of the stitch, back down through the tear, and then up through the fabric again—a little to the left to start a second stitch. Five or six stitches are made in every inch.

For patches, 3-ounce (85 g) self-adhesive cloth is the most versatile. For heavier repairs, it can be layered, with each additional layer overlapping the last. Before applying any, make sure the sail is flat with any torn edges properly lined up. After applying a patch, if possible heat

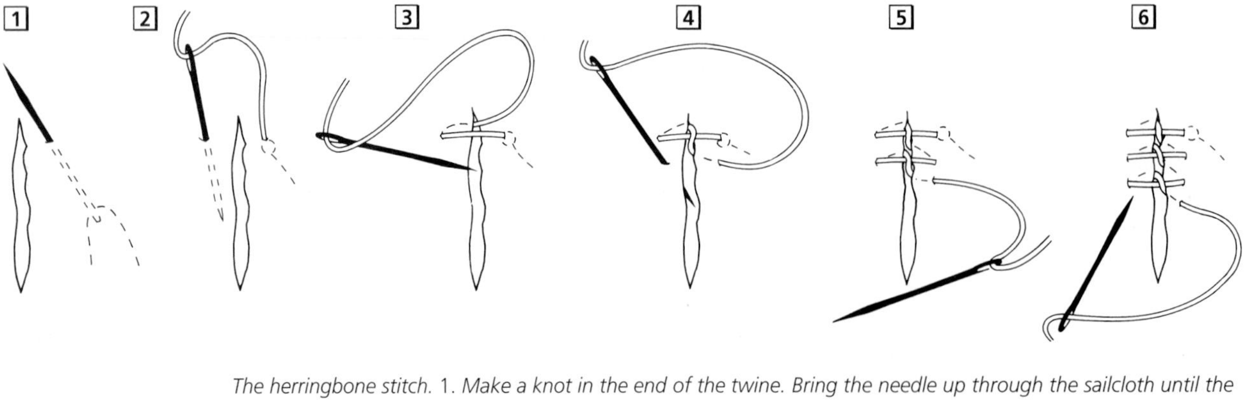

The herringbone stitch. 1. Make a knot in the end of the twine. Bring the needle up through the sailcloth until the knot snugs up. 2. Bring the needle across the tear and push it back through the cloth. 3. Bring the needle up through the tear on one side of the stitch, over the top of the stitch, push it back down through the tear, and . . . 4. bring it back up alongside the first stitch to start again. 5–6. And so on . . .

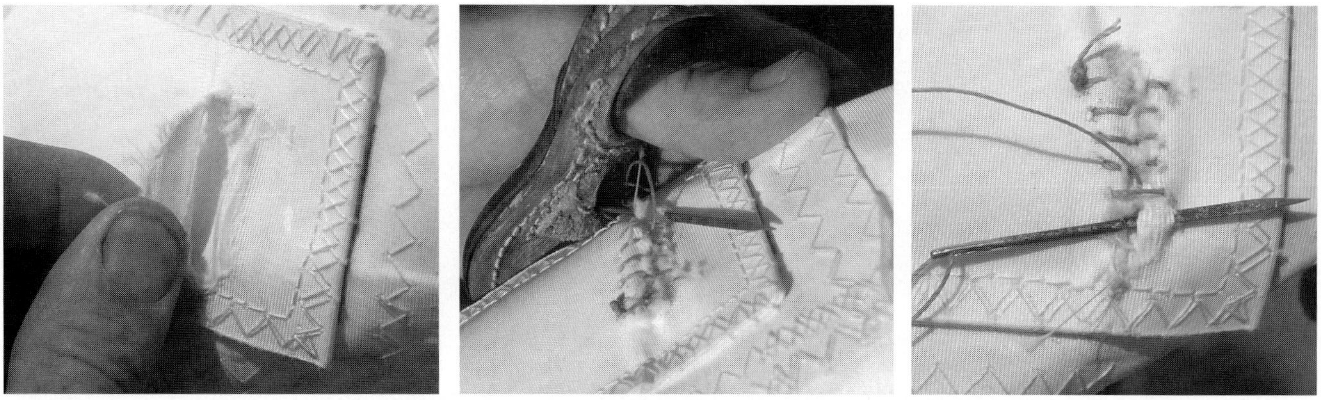

A crude repair, using a herringbone stitch, of the damaged batten pocket shown earlier. Given the multiple layers of heavy sailcloth, which we were unable to stitch through with our limited equipment, this was the best we could do as a temporary repair. It held until the end of the cruise.

it (with a hair dryer) or leave it in the sun to help the glue bond better.

Any patch should be several times the diameter of a hole and extend 2 or 3 inches beyond the ends and on either side of a tear. There should be a patch for both sides of the sail. If stitching is added, a simple zigzag stitch is used, running around the perimeter of the two halves of the patch, again using five or six stitches to the inch.

DINGHIES

The cruising-boat dinghy probably has to satisfy more contradictory requirements than any other piece of gear onboard. It has to be large enough and stable enough to handle the full crew and a load of groceries; for this, it needs a flat bottom and a minimum length of 8 feet (10–11 ft./3.0–3.4 m is better). It has to be seaworthy enough to enable an anchor to be rowed out against gale-force winds and a steep chop, preferably remaining dry in the process; for this, it needs a reasonably fine entry and underbody. It has to be rugged enough to be run repeatedly up beaches, over rocks, and into the occasional coral head; for this, it needs a solid keel and sacrificial runners. It needs excellent buoyancy so that it will not sink in the event of a swamping. It needs to be fast enough to not unduly restrict the options of those onboard. It needs all these features and many more, but yet it still has to be light enough for a short-handed crew to get it on and off the boat, even in rough weather. Once on the boat, it needs to be compact enough to stow on deck without compromising either the working of the boat or the visibility from the cockpit. And, of course, it must represent good value for the money invested.

Hard versus Inflatable

The most fundamental choice is between a hard dinghy and an inflatable. A hard dinghy is less stable than an inflatable, has a lower load-carrying capability, generally lacks adequate buoyancy, is difficult to get into and out of when diving and snorkeling, is much slower than an inflatable with an outboard motor, is relatively heavy, can be difficult to get on and off a boat, and can be awkward to stow. However, a decent rowing dinghy is incomparably better under oar power than an inflatable, is far less likely to get damaged running up on a beach, and is generally not only cheaper than an inflatable with an outboard, but also longer-lived. If it gets seriously damaged, a hard dinghy is easier to repair. We once put a 6-inch (150 mm) hole in a dinghy way up a jungle river in Guatemala; we

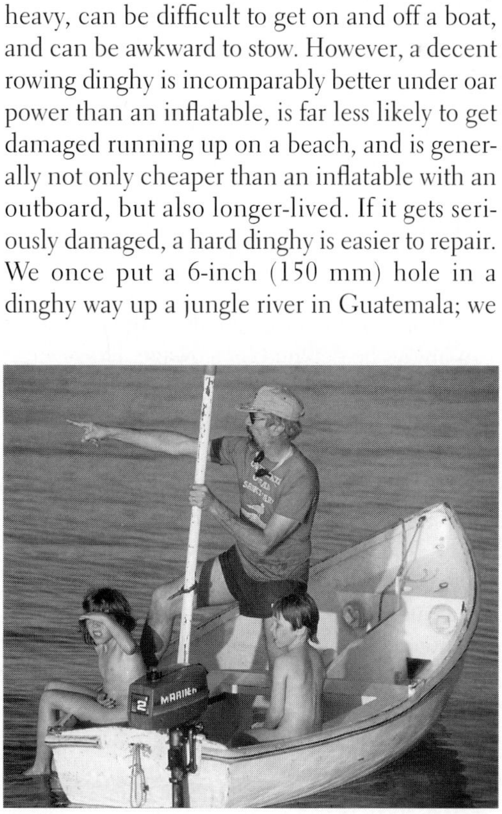

Hard dinghies like this one that Terrie and I built row beautifully and, if converted to sail (as this one can be), do so very nicely. However, they are limited in their load-carrying capability and speed and not as stable as an inflatable. Note the watertight storage tubes in the bow, which is foamed in (as is the stern) to make the dinghy unsinkable.

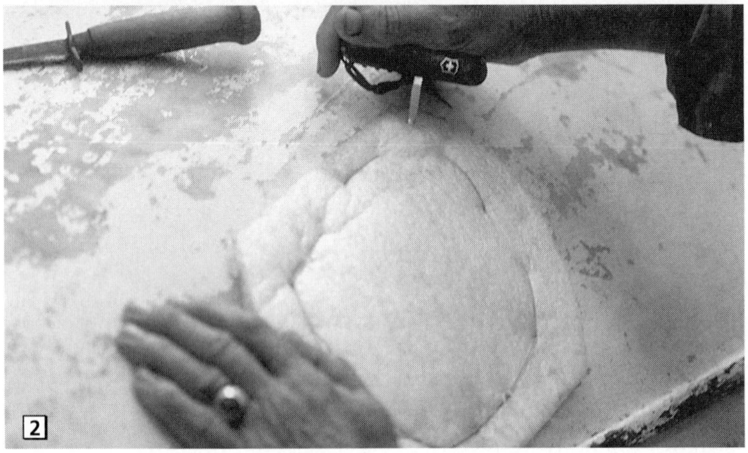

1. *A submerged log punched a fist-size hole in the dinghy way up a jungle river in Guatemala, miles from anywhere* 2. *We temporarily patched it by stitching on the lining from a cockpit cushion. You can't do this with an inflatable!*

temporarily "fixed" it by drilling a series of holes with a pocketknife around the periphery of the damaged area and then "stitching" on the lining from a cockpit cushion—you can't do that with an inflatable!

A traditional inflatable has phenomenal stability and load-carrying capability for its size, is an incomparable dive and snorkeling platform, has tremendous innate buoyancy, will easily move at 10+ knots with a big-enough outboard, is generally much easier to get on and off a boat (it can be dragged up with a halyard without risk of damage to either the dinghy or the boat), and can always be deflated for stowage. However, it won't row worth a damn in serious conditions; is highly vulnerable to damage if run onto a beach, rocks, or coral; and is quite an investment ($3,000+ for an inflatable with an outboard big enough to get it to plane). It may not hold up for more than four or five years. The outboard motor is one more piece of heavy gear that needs to be lugged aboard, stowed somewhere, and maintained. It requires fuel that needs specialized stowage (a locker sealed to the boat's interior and vented overboard from its base).

It may well be that the new wave of rotomolded polyethylene boats will combine many of the best features of hard and inflatable

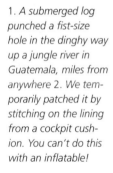

An inflatable has phenomenal load-carrying capability and stability (top and 2nd photo*). An inflatable makes an excellent dive platform (*3rd photo; *courtesy Avon Marine)—and can always be deflated for stowage. This, in fact, is Tinker's folding rigid inflatable that compresses into a package no bigger than most nonrigid inflatables (*bottom*).*

dinghies. Polyethylene is tough, long-lived, virtually indestructible, and inexpensive. This is a technology worth watching.

Inflatable Options

In the past decade or so, we have seen all kinds of variations on the inflatable theme. These include inflatable keels—which improve tracking, make a boat a little easier to row (it is still not easy), and help to get a boat to plane—and several different approaches to rigid floors such as interlocking plywood or aluminum boards, roll-up floors, and inflatable floors. Then there are *rigid inflatable boats* (RIBs), which combine a fiberglass hull with the buoyancy tubes of an inflatable.

Wooden floors (and transoms, for that matter) are heavy, klutzy, often a pain to assemble, and invariably delaminate in short order when used hard. Aluminum floors tend to be lighter but, in time, suffer from corrosion and are no easier to assemble. The roll-up and inflatable floors are unquestionably preferable—they provide just as much rigidity as a solid floor, yet roll up with the boat and, therefore, are less trouble when assembling or stowing the boat. They are much lighter than rigid floors. Their life expectancy is the same as the rest of the boat.

However, all of these approaches to floors suffer from a fundamental problem—the part of the boat that hits the beach or any other obstruction is still a highly vulnerable flexible membrane. RIBs, on the other hand, have a hull that is just as durable as any other rigid hull on the market. Furthermore, in an emergency, this hull is much easier to row than a traditional inflatable (although still not as easy as a rowing dinghy). The downside is that the inflatable is now much more difficult to stow (the best that can be done is to deflate the tubes), and—of course—it costs more and generally (but not always) weighs more. Nevertheless, if space can be found to stow a RIB and a means found to get it on and off the boat, and if the price is acceptable, it is unquestionably the best dinghy compromise for most cruisers.

Finally, there is the foldaway RIB manufactured by Tinker (in the United Kingdom). As far as I know, it is the only foldaway RIB. It has three hinged floor sections, with the tubes attached to the perimeter. The floor pieces fold inside each other to make a package no larger than most traditional inflatables. Blowing up the tubes opens out the floors and locks them in place to form a true RIB. The only drawbacks are that the dinghy is relatively small and narrow, which limits its load-carrying capability, and—as with other Tinkers—it has less buoyancy in the bow than most inflatables, making it wet when going into a chop. It can be purchased with an optional sailing rig (daggerboard, tiller, rig, and sails), and also has an optional inflatable canopy for conversion to a life raft—a really clever piece of design.

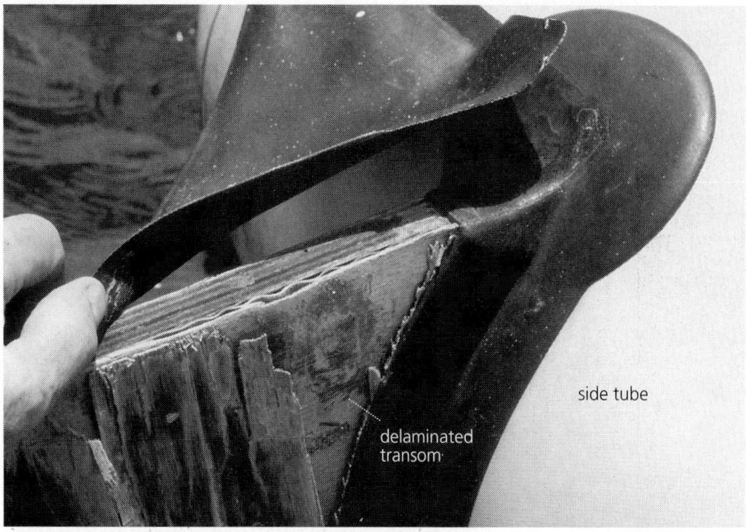

Sooner or later, wooden floors and transoms always delaminate.

PVC versus Hypalon

The single greatest factor affecting the life expectancy of all inflatables (including RIBs) and, therefore, the cost over time is the material from which the tubes are made. There are two fundamental choices: fabrics coated with a synthetic rubber known as Hypalon, manufactured under license from DuPont, and variants of PVC.

All cheaper inflatables are made from PVC; in the tropics, they have a life expectancy of as little as four years (actually, many fail sooner, but almost invariably because of poor construction rather than poor materials). All

The Tinker folding rigid inflatable in action (as far as I know, the only inflatable that can be sailed; it will even go to windward—just!). It is fun to sail, but as with most of the Tinker inflatables, it has a relatively fine bow that tends to make it a little wet.

high-end inflatables are made from Hypalon, which has an indefinite life expectancy (it eventually wears out from abrasion, but does not fail through degradation). There are many twenty-year-old Avons still providing good service.

PVC in its normal state is rigid; plastic pipes are made from it. It is extremely stable and long-lived. However, to use it in fabrics, a *plasticizer* has to be added to make it flexible, along with other substances that improve resistance to UV degradation. This process of mixing up the various ingredients is known as *compounding*. The resulting compound is applied in liquid form to a base fabric—which may be nylon, polyester, or an aramid—to create the PVC fabric. Different cloth weights and weaves may be used, which affects—among other factors—the stretch and tear properties of the finished fabric.

Unfortunately, the plasticizers used to make PVC fabrics slowly leach out of the fabric, which is evidenced by a sticky surface. The fabric itself becomes both porous and stiffer, ultimately failing from porosity or cracking (incidentally, this is why PVC-based sanitation hose smells over time: the plasticizers needed to make it flexible also make it minutely porous). The rate of leaching is accelerated by the UV in sunlight, as well as by contact with oil, gasoline, and other hydrocarbons. Although some PVC-based fabrics are better than others—a function of different compounds, base materials, and construction techniques—eventually, they all suffer from leaching. The underlying fabric, to which the PVC has been applied, also may suffer a progressive loss of tensile strength.

Below: *Leaching plasticizers have made this PVC dinghy sticky (hence the shoe marks).* Bottom: *As the plasticizer leaches out of PVC, it loosens the glue bond with various fittings that start to come loose.*

In contrast, Hypalon-coated fabrics are incredibly stable. Although Hypalon immersed in oil swells by up to 25 percent of its volume, it does not fail. In fact, in a dinghy application, there is essentially no chemical-failure mechanism, which protects the underlying fabric, resulting in insignificant loss of tensile strength over time. The fabric ultimately wears out from abrasion, but even in this respect it performs significantly better than PVC. If necessary, it can be recoated (i.e., repainted) with liquid Hypalon, something that cannot be done with PVC.

Following are other significant differences between PVC and Hypalon:

- PVC can be machine welded ("thermobonded"), whereas Hypalon must be glued. Welding greatly speeds up the production process (it is the only way to do volume production), which helps hold down costs, but it makes repairs more difficult. Gluing adds both cost and another variable—if not done properly, glued seams can fail.
- Leaching of the plasticizers eventually lifts patches off many PVC dinghies, whereas a properly made repair to Hypalon is—for all intents and purposes—permanent.
- PVC-based fabrics generally have less resistance to abrasion and considerably less tear resistance, both initially and over time.

Much of the PVC and Hypalon fabric used in dinghy construction worldwide comes from a couple of French manufacturers, who offer a number of different combinations of fabric weights and laminations. Depending on what is used by a dinghy manufacturer, there are significant differences in the quality and durability of the base materials used to build the dinghy. These materials are then assembled with varying degrees of quality control. At one time or another, most of the major dinghy producers have put out some particularly awful products!

Where does this leave the cruising sailor? Despite the sometimes considerable price difference between Hypalon and PVC, it is my opinion that over time, *Hypalon always represents better value for the money*—the serious cruiser should not look at anything else. Within

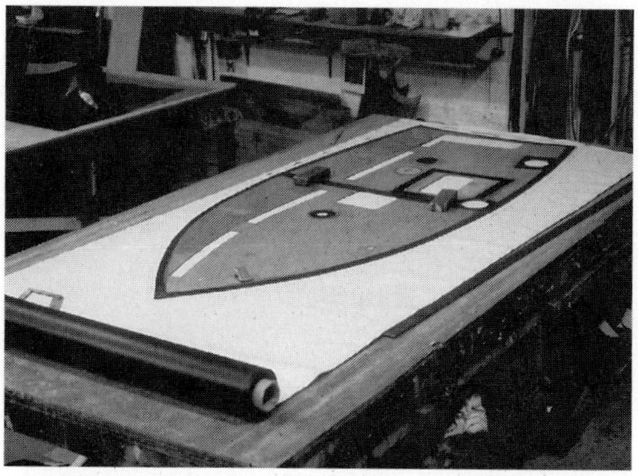

Inflatable dinghies are cut out of a roll of material, using patterns and—to a greater or lesser extent (more so with glued dinghies than welded)—assembled by hand. For a quality dinghy, in addition to using Hypalon, it is essential to have effective quality control in the production process.

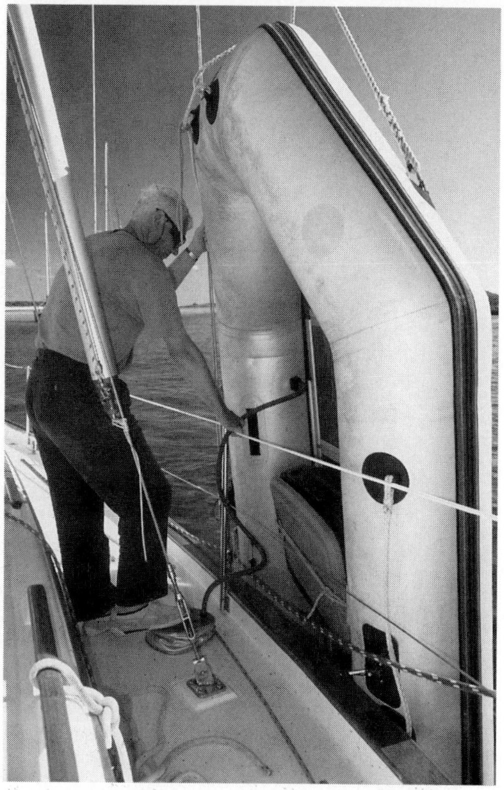

When deck space is limited, a dinghy can be hung over the side and inflated.

the family of Hypalon dinghy builders, most use the same basic fabric, although there may be differences in cloth weights and laminations—it is worth checking.

Avon, with its ten-year warranty, has an enviable reputation for quality. However, in recent years, Avon shifted into the mass-market PVC dinghy business and has been acquired by Zodiac; it remains to be seen if these changes will have any impact on its quality-control standards.

Other Inflatable Considerations

Perhaps the most important consideration with an inflatable is to buy the longest one you can stow on board—both load-carrying capability and performance under power increase dramatically with an increase in length. Beyond this:

- The more chambers, the more trouble an inflatable is to inflate, but the greater the insurance against swamping if one chamber springs a leak or ruptures. If you don't carry a life raft (as we don't), the inflatable may have to serve duty in a catastrophe. Three chambers—one on each side and one up forward—is a good setup.
- Good-sized valves and a decent pump significantly speed up the inflation rate.
- If there is no room to inflate a dinghy on deck, hang it over the side by its painter from a halyard and blow it up in this position.
- Do not blow up a single chamber hard—you may end up blowing out the internal separator between it and the next (uninflated) chamber. With three chambers, blow the sides up first to moderate firmness, then blow up the bow hard, which will also pressurize the sides and equalize the pressure in all three chambers.
- Do not blow up a dinghy and then leave it in bright sunlight—the added pressure generated by the sun's heat may blow out a seam.
- Never clean a PVC dinghy with gasoline or other strong solvents—it will accelerate the rate at which the plasticizers leach out.
- Many dinghy-inflation pumps can be used in reverse. When deflating a dinghy, the pump can be used to suck out the last of the air, making it easier to stow.
- When storing a deflated dinghy, make sure it is dry. Dust a PVC dinghy with French chalk or talcum powder to stop the surfaces from sticking to one another. Store it in a cool, dry place.
- The single most important factor in prolonging the life of a PVC dinghy is to make a cover for the tubes, and to keep the cover in place at all times when the dinghy is in use.

Getting a Dinghy on and off a Boat

Non-RIB inflatable dinghies are easy to get on and off a boat. Attach a halyard to the towing eye and simply hoist the dinghy in the air, for-

Non-RIB inflatables are easy to get on and off a boat—they can simply be dragged up the side with a halyard and rolled over to stow on deck.

Davits are a great way to stow a dinghy at anchor, but I am not comfortable going to sea with a dinghy hanging off the stern.

ward end uppermost, until it clears the lifelines. The fabric floor will bounce up and down the side of the boat and the lifelines without doing any damage. The dinghy can be set down on deck either way up, wherever desired. I have no problem getting our 11-foot dinghy on and off single-handed—although in a strong wind, it does tend to blow around!

RIBs and hard dinghies are another matter because of the potential to do damage to both the topsides and the dinghy. The easiest way to handle such a dinghy is with davits at the stern of the boat. However, this puts a significant amount of weight at the stern, adds appreciably to windage, can make docking difficult (especially if the dinghy extends beyond the width of the stern), makes it just about impossible to fit a self-steering wind vane, and—of course—adds significant expense. I am also not comfortable with a dinghy hanging off the stern in rough weather.

If the dinghy has to be stowed onboard, some type of derrick will be needed to get it on deck. The only two likely stowage locations are in front of and behind the mast. For stowage forward, a spinnaker or downwind pole makes hoisting easy; stowage aft of the mast is more of a problem.

For stowage forward of the mast, the spinnaker pole is rigged with a suitable block and tackle from its tip. Depending on the weight of the dinghy, the tackle will have between four and six *parts* (i.e., the number of lines running between the two blocks). The inboard end of the pole is set low on the mast so that raising and lowering its outboard end (with the pole's topping lift) moves the pole's tip toward and away from the mast. If the dinghy is in the water, the pole is swung outboard and the topping lift is let out until the tip of the pole is centered over the dinghy, which is then hauled up with the block and tackle. Once the dinghy is up to the top of the lifelines, it can be swung inboard. Pulling in the topping lift raises the tip of the spinnaker pole to position the dinghy over its stowage location, at which point it is lowered into place. Taking the dinghy off is a reversal of this procedure.

Stowage aft of the mast is not nearly as easy. If the tip of the boom can be raised and lowered with the topping lift in the same way as a spinnaker pole, the process is easy—but this is generally not possible. Another way to achieve the same result is to add a spinnaker pole fitting to the aft side of the mast so that the pole can be used on this side of the mast. The main halyard is then used as a topping lift; however, in this case, when the pole is swung outboard, the halyard will not make a fairlead onto its sheave, which may cause chafe.

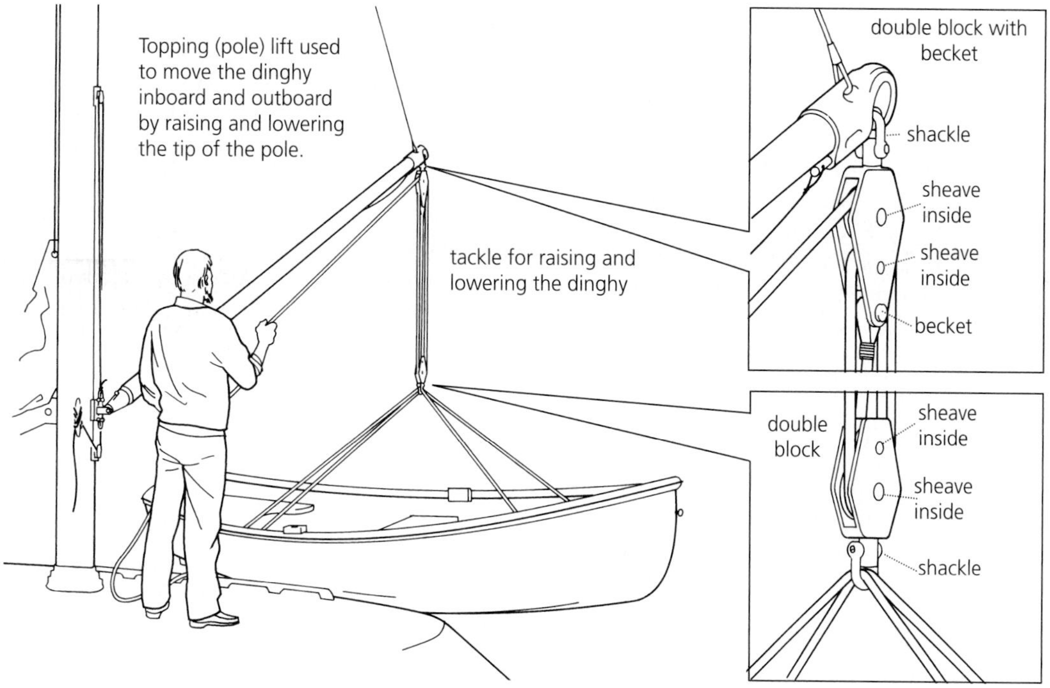

A downwind pole makes a good crane for hoisting a RIB or rigid dinghy onto the foredeck.

In practice, a bridle is normally attached to the dinghy and the main halyard is used to raise and lower the dinghy. While one crew member operates the halyard winch, the rest of the crew fends the dinghy off the topsides and lifelines, and maneuvers it into place once it is on the cabintop. A couple of small fenders hung over the side of a hard dinghy minimize the chances of damage.

The easiest way to stow a dinghy is upright. A bridle attached to lifting eyes inside the bow and on either side at the transom keep the dinghy stable while it is being taken on and off the boat. However, stowed like this, it will catch rainwater and spray (it needs removable drain plugs), create considerable windage, be thoroughly in the way, and be quite difficult to adequately tie down in heavy weather. Therefore, most dinghies are stowed upside down.

Flipping a dinghy over by hand can be hard work and may result in damage to the boat or dinghy, especially in a rolly anchorage. To make the job easier and controllable, the lifting bridle should attach to eyes on the *outside* of the bow and transom, just above the balance point of the dinghy. The bridle will need a spreader bar a couple of inches longer than the dinghy. Rigged like this, it is a piece of cake to roll a dinghy over and back up again.

Wherever a dinghy is placed, it needs solid chocks, if possible, and on an offshore boat immensely strong tiedown points (through-bolted pad eyes with substantial backing blocks). If solid water starts coming aboard, the dinghy and its retaining hardware will be subjected to enormous stresses.

Light-weather dinghy stowage on Nada. *Although the dinghy is tied down forward to a large cleat and lashed across its top aft, this would be nowhere near adequate to resist the impact of boarding waves. For heavy weather, a cat's cradle of lashings needs to be added, or the dinghy deflated to make it less of a target.*

For stowage aft of the mast, it is best to devise a bridle and use the main halyard. This is also an excellent way to stow a dinghy at night in an anchorage where theft may be a problem.

Miscellaneous Dinghy Thoughts

Lastly, some odds and ends concerning dinghies.

- The towing eye on a dinghy should be down near the waterline—this makes the dinghy less likely to shear around and roll its gunwales under when towed at speed. To spread the towing load, an inflatable needs a bridle secured to a couple of eyes.
- Sooner or later, we all suck the towline into the propeller. Polypropylene line floats, eliminating this problem, and therefore is used for some painters, but it rots rapidly in sunlight so it is not recommended. A nylon painter can be buoyed with fishing floats every few feet. Ultimately, the best response is to just get into the habit of shortening the painter before backing down.
- If an inflatable is towed in high winds and/or steep seas, it can come right out of the water and flip over; it can even do this in a squall at anchor! We never tow a dinghy at sea. If you do tow the dinghy, at least take off the outboard motor.
- A noninflatable dinghy needs enough buoyancy to keep the gunwales entirely above water when the dinghy is fully swamped and still has an adult aboard. Without this level of buoyancy, it will be almost impossible to bail out.

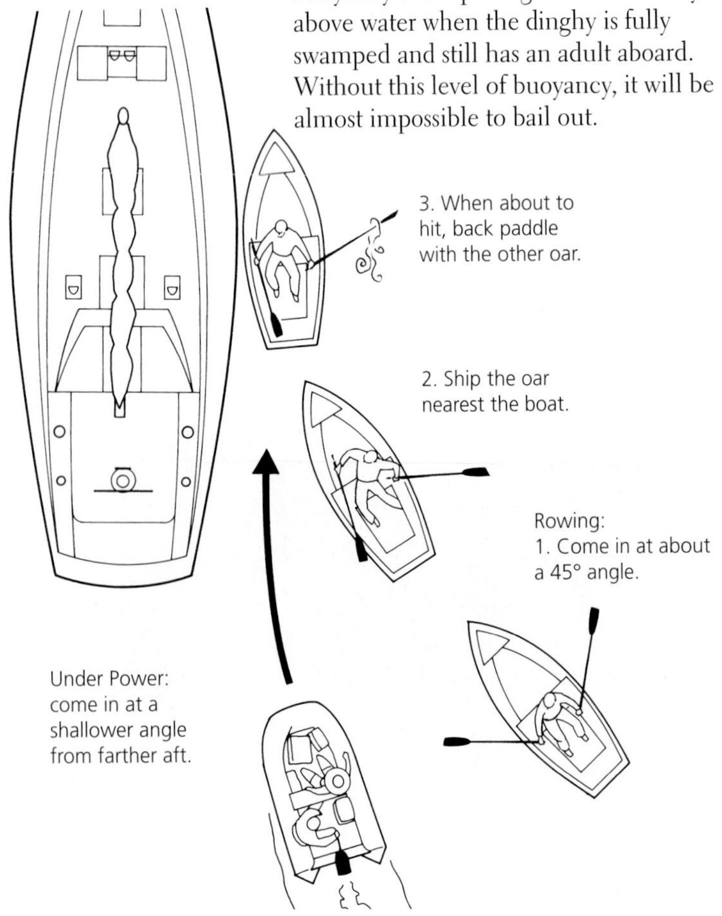
3. When about to hit, back paddle with the other oar.
2. Ship the oar nearest the boat.
Rowing:
1. Come in at about a 45° angle.
Under Power: come in at a shallower angle from farther aft.

Bringing a dinghy alongside a boat under oars and under power.

- At a minimum, the dinghy on a cruising boat needs a good-sized bailer firmly attached to the dinghy, an anchor, and oars. Also, flares and, ideally, a handheld VHF. Consider adding spare spark plugs and a plug wrench for the outboard motor, and a bottle of water in case you get stranded for a while.
- Noninflatable dinghies need excellent fendering so that they don't ding up the topsides.
- Oars must be long enough to be effective; most inflatable oars are not. Oarlocks (rowlocks) should be attached to the dinghy or the oars; if not, the oarlocks will get lost.
- When using oars to bring a dinghy alongside a boat, approach a point just forward of the gate in the lifelines, coming in at about a 45-degree angle. When close enough to get there under the dinghy's momentum alone, ship the oar closest to the boat. Just as you are about to hit, back paddle with the other oar to put you alongside.
- When coming alongside under power, come in at a shallower angle from farther aft.
- If trying to land a rowing dinghy on a beach through surf, be warned that the breakers are twice as big as you think they are! Just outside the line of breakers, turn the dinghy around to put the bow into the waves, watch for a lower set of waves, wait for a crest to pass, and then go in on the backside of the crest. If overtaken by the next breaking crest, the single most important thing is to keep the bow directly into the wave. As soon as the stern hits the beach, the crew needs to pile out and haul the dinghy higher before it gets sucked back and/or rolled by the next wave.
- When powering an inflatable into shore through surf, the idea is to again watch for a lower set of waves, and then get on the backside of a wave and run in at the same speed. Lift the outboard just before you hit the beach and quickly get the dinghy higher or the next wave will break over the transom.
- It can be a backbreaking job hauling dinghies on and off beaches. A pair of flip-up dinghy wheels attached to the transom make all the difference in the world. The wheels should have the largest diameter possible, be as wide as

Landing a dinghy through surf under oars and under power.

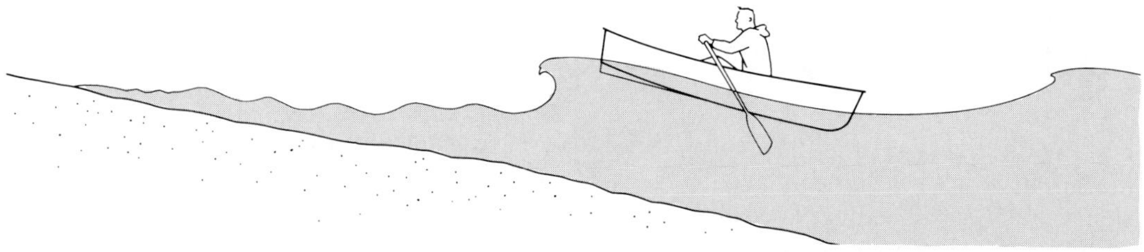

If rowing, go in backward, waiting for a crest to pass so you can move in on its back.

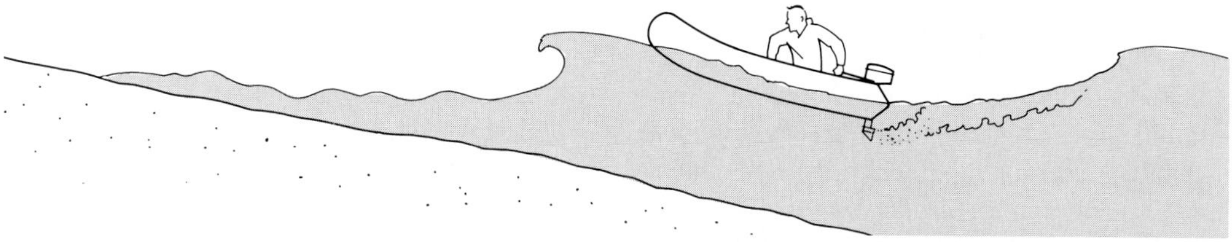

Under power, wait for a crest to pass and then power in on its back at the same speed as the waves are moving.

possible, and preferably have pneumatic tires.

- When single-handing a dinghy with an outboard, you will get a much better weight distribution if you fit an extension to the throttle handle and sit farther forward. A suitably sized piece of PVC pipe generally works well.
- All dinghies are vulnerable to theft. To minimize risks, a stainless steel cable is needed that can be fed through a strong point on the dinghy, the outboard motor handle, any fuel tank, the oars if possible, and life jackets, and still be long enough to be padlocked to the main boat or around a piling or tree onshore. If you have room for two dinghies, leaving one onboard is an excellent way to deter thieves because most assume there is still someone on the boat. At night, we always put our dinghy back on deck or leave it hanging from a halyard and lashed to the lifelines. This has the added benefit of not collecting barnacles and slime.
- One of the major causes of drowning is people falling out of dinghies. You should always wear a life jacket. When using an outboard motor, particularly if single-handing, you should not disable the safety shutdown lanyard. (This is one of those "do as I say, not as I do" things; in practice, that lanyard can be a major inconvenience—however, it is there for a reason.)

An excellent pair of dinghy wheels in the "down" and "up" positions.

FOUL-WEATHER GEAR

Foul-weather gear is another area in which modern materials have brought about a radical change over the past couple of decades, notably in the area of waterproof—yet breathable—fabrics, primarily Gore-Tex's Ocean Technology. This fabric is used by most of the high-end foul-weather clothing manufacturers, including Gill, Henri-Lloyd, and Musto.

Gore-Tex's Ocean Technology fabric is built around a special membrane that is *hydrophobic* (literally, water-hating: it will not absorb water) and also contains an *oleophobic* substance (oil-hating: resistant to contamination). The membrane has nine billion pores per square inch (65 mm^2). Each pore is twenty thousand times smaller than a raindrop, but seven hundred times larger than a molecule of water vapor. In theory, this means Gore-Tex is completely waterproof (you can spray it with a fire hose and the water won't pass through), yet it allows sweat and any trapped moisture to evaporate under body heat and work its way out through the fabric. In practice, after overcoming initial problems in the marine environment, it works!

The Gore-Tex membrane has excellent flexibility and resistance to abrasion. It is further protected and strengthened by being sandwiched between an external polyamide (nylon) fabric treated with a water repellent and an internal polyester layer. When made into articles of clothing, all manufacturers add taped seams over stitching (to prevent water penetration through the stitches), various kinds of special closures at the wrists and other entry points, weather flaps, and specialized linings. The net result is foul-weather gear that is not only significantly better than anything ever produced before, but is also long-lived and remarkably tolerant of abuse. The fabric can even be run through a washing machine and dryer on gentle cycles and low heat. The price, of course, is shocking—it is easy to spend over $1,000 on a jacket and pants!

For those with smaller budgets, there are several excellent alternatives. Generally, the most inexpensive foul-weather gear on the market is PVC-coated cotton. It is heavy and somewhat less comfortable than most other gear, but it is tough, waterproof, and long-lived. This is the gear typically found on commercial fishing boats.

A significant step up in price, comfort, and features (more pockets, better closures) comes with PVC- and urethane-coated nylon, with the price and quality substantially related to the weight of the underlying fabric (the nylon). The PVC coating is more common because it has a higher abrasion resistance; however, urethane is lighter and more flexible, and gets less stiff in cold weather.

Until the advent of the breathable fabrics, high-end foul-weather gear was made of coated nylon; we are still using twenty-year-old Henri-Lloyd clothing in this category. It has given us wonderful service, despite the fact that it lost its waterproofing some years ago and now needs periodic retreatment. Other than replacing one zipper, we've made no repairs and the gear still has many years of useful service left in it.

Features

What makes or breaks all foul-weather gear are the construction features. In addition to ensuring watertight seams, the following points are important:

- *Ease of getting it on and taking it off, both dry and wet.* Our latest-generation breathable gear is not as good in this respect as the old gear; the linings in the sleeves tend to foul up, especially when our hands are wet. It is well worth trying on gear, with several layers of undergarments, before buying. Imagine how it will be at sea in rough weather.

Some otherwise excellent foul-weather gear can be a little difficult to get on and off, especially when wet. The rubberized cuffs on this jacket are especially frustrating.

- *Adequate sealing of all apertures, particularly zippers, wrists, and necklines.* Better-quality gear has a double sealing arrangement at the wrists and high-throated yet comfortable closures at the neckline.
- *Comfort and flexibility in use.*
- A *hood (preferably rollaway)* designed so that it does not flop down over your face obstructing your vision (many do) and that has a drawstring to pull it tight around your face. Some hoods have an adjustable drawstring across the back that alters how far it comes over your head—an excellent feature.
- *Bib-type pants.* The high front and sides are important in keeping water from migrating under a jacket and down the pants.
- *Reinforcement at all stress points* (particularly the seat of the pants and the knees).
- *Corrosionproof zippers.* We had an otherwise excellent (and expensive) lightweight jacket on which the zipper froze in a couple of months of saltwater use.
- *Either an integral harness or a harness channel with an optional harness.* I prefer the former: if the harness is built into the jacket, there is a much greater chance of it being used. Some of the jackets made for Southern Ocean use have no harness channel in order to eliminate a potential water-entry point. For most of us who do not intend to race around the Antarctic in gale-force winds at subfreezing temperatures, the harness is much more important.
- *Attachment loops for an inflatable life jacket* (discussed later in this chapter). Some of these jackets come with toggles on a short length of line. The toggles slip through the loops on the foul-weather jacket, enabling the life jacket to be left attached to the jacket when the jacket is taken off—a handy feature.
- *Yellow, orange, or lime green fabric.* The current fashion for other colors is absurd. If you go overboard, you want to be seen. The one downside to yellow is that sharks seem to be attracted to it, so if you are not rescued quickly, you may get eaten!

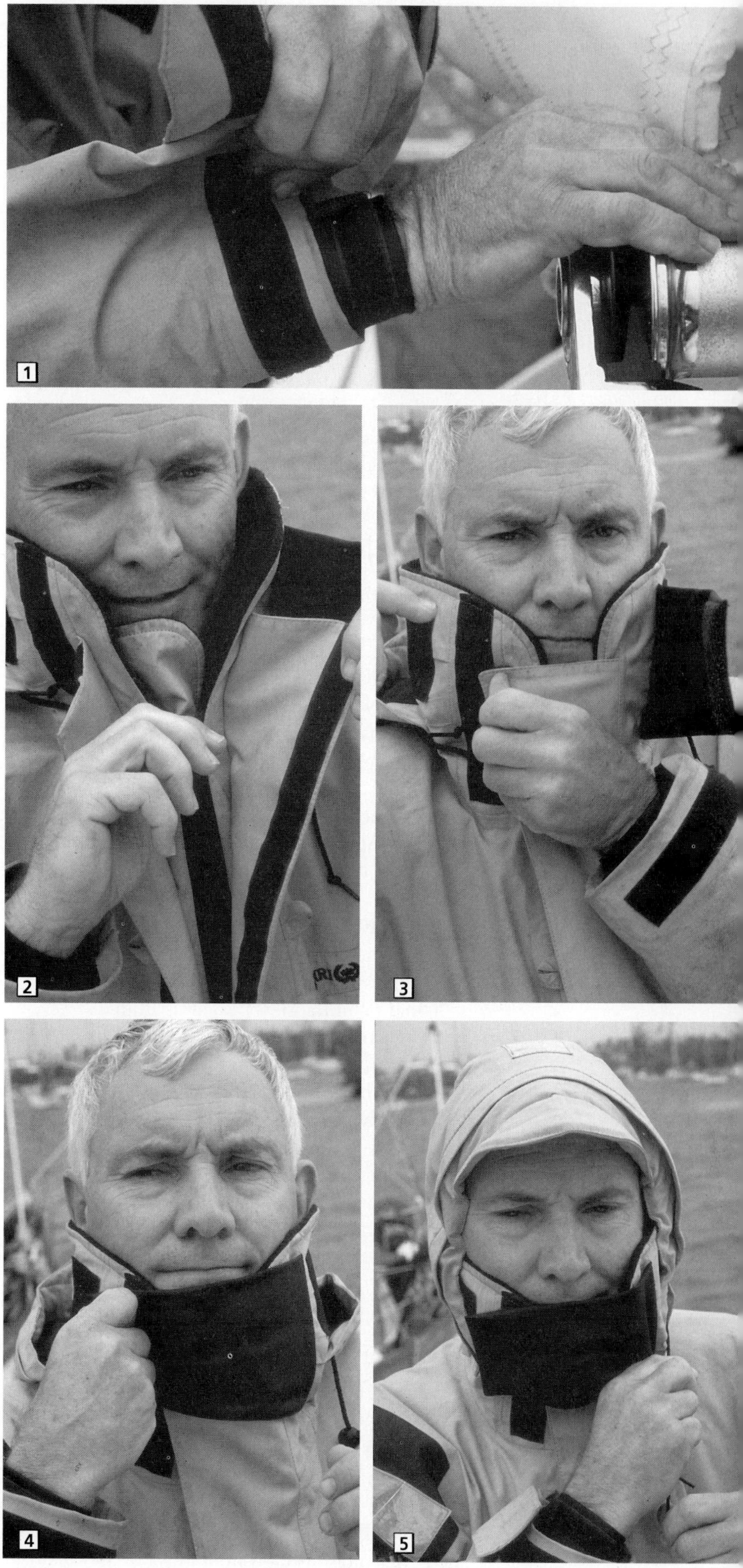

For offshore foul-weather gear, desirable features include (1) near watertight double enclosures at the wrists; (2) double enclosures down the front; (3) and (4) double enclosures at the neck; and (5) a hood that can be tightly cinched up around your face without the visor obstructing your vision.

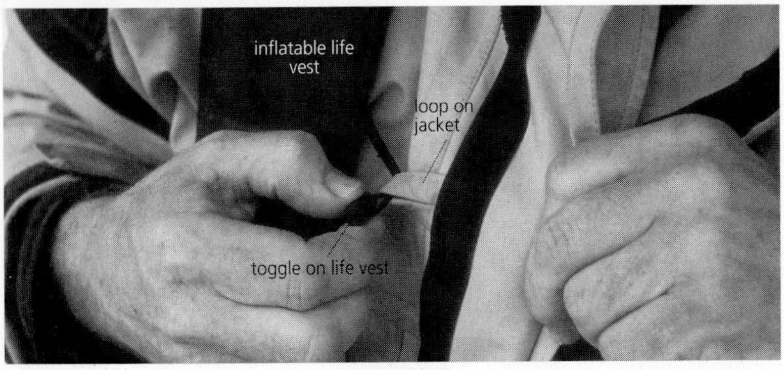

A desirable feature is to have loops on a foul-weather jacket that take a toggle fitted to some (but not all) inflatable life vests or harnesses. This way, the life vest can be left in place when you're taking off the jacket.

- *Reflective tape on the jacket*, to make it easier to find a person overboard at night.
- *Built-in flotation.* Our old Henri-Lloyd jackets have this, which is an excellent feature, but it is difficult to find nowadays. In addition to flotation, the foam provides insulation that we have greatly appreciated on many occasions, including in the tropics.

Layering and the Extremities

Foul-weather gear is only the outer layer of clothing. What you wear beneath is as significant as the choice between breathable and nonbreathable outer fabrics. If you're wearing cotton underwear and sweating in a cold climate, even with Gore-Tex outerwear you are still likely to get cold and clammy, and in extreme conditions to suffer from hypothermia (mountain climbers say that "cotton kills").

Marine and outdoor clothing manufacturers have a two- or three-layer system consisting of

1. Lightweight underwear (the *base* layer), designed to be comfortable next to the skin, with high wicking capability. Given that water transfers heat away from a body up to 30 times faster than air, this ability to remove moisture as fast as possible is critical to staying warm.
2. A midweight inner layer, also with high wicking capability, but with a much higher insulation value. It has to combine an ability to continue transporting moisture away from the body with retaining warm dry air inside the clothing system. *Fleeces* are generally used.
3. Perhaps another insulating layer of heavier weight fleece beneath the outer layer of foul-weather gear.

Underwear and insulating layers are best made from some variant of polyester (commonly known as *polypro* because early high-tech underwear was made from polypropylene; nowadays it's all made from polyester), which will help wick moisture away from the body and keep you warm even when wet. This is especially the case for "technical" fabrics such as Malden Mills's Capilene (from the word *capillary*) and Polartec Power Dry (Capilene is proprietary to Patagonia; Polartec Power Dry, in numerous incarnations with varying trade names, is used by other high-end clothing manufacturers).

Not only are technical underwear and fleeces not cheap, some fabrics and treatments wear out quickly with washing, or else pull into an uncomfortable jumble of small lumps (*pilling*). One reason Malden Mills's fabrics are so widely used is that they have a reputation for not pilling.

Dealing with the Extremities

The hardest parts to keep warm are the head, hands, and feet. The wide variety of watch caps and balaclavas now available in wool or fleece to wear under a foul-weather hood make it a little easier to keep the head warm.

When it comes to gloves, the challenge is to find something that's waterproof, with a high insulating value, and yet compact and supple enough to allow the wearer to handle lines. Traditionally, leather has formed the outer shell, but increasingly a synthetic product called Amara is being used. This is just as waterproof as leather but wears better, dries faster, and doesn't go stiff and hard when it dries out. Lined with fleece, it does a pretty good job. Gill's excellent Helmsman's gloves combine Kevlar palms for wear resistance with Amara sides to the fingers, a nylon back, a waterproof outer liner, and a fleece inner liner.

A layered, breathable system is also ideal for the feet. This can be done, but at a high price. Gill makes Gore-Tex sailing boots, and Musto makes Gore-Tex socks. For those of us on more restricted budgets, a number of companies manufacture heavyweight high-moisture-transport socks with excellent insulation value. These will help to keep your feet warm inside traditional sea boots even though the boots don't allow moisture to evaporate.

Staying Warm and Dry

If you want to dress like a round-the-world racer, you can easily spend $2,000 on layered clothing together with Gore-Tex boots and foul weather gear! For those of us who can't afford this, it's best to invest in decent underwear, intermediate layer clothes, and warm socks and gloves, coupled to a midlevel set of foul weather gear, rather than blowing the budget on Gore-Tex Ocean Technology.

SAFETY-RELATED EQUIPMENT

It needs to be stressed that the primary factors in safety are, on the one hand, an inherently safe boat (comfortable motion; a secure cockpit; wide, unobstructed side decks; excellent nonskid; strong, high lifelines; accessible jacklines; properly installed systems—see part 1 of this book) and, on the other hand, a recognition of the key roles of preparation, conservative seamanship, and personal responsibility. Beyond this, all kinds of gear can be carried to handle emergency situations, some of it legally required in different countries and much of it not.

A lot of money can be spent on safety- and emergency-related gear. In a properly maintained and sailed boat, this gear will likely never be needed. As a result, we all have to choose how far to take this process: balancing the likelihood of something being needed against its cost, but also considering the consequences of not having it. For example, a life raft is almost certainly never going to be needed and is expensive both upfront and to maintain; therefore, it looks like a really bad investment. But if it is ever needed, it may make the difference between living and dying, so the stakes here are high . . . (for more about life rafts, see chapter 11). It is not always easy to make these judgment calls. My preference is to focus on the boat and the gear necessary to its functioning, and to minimize other expenditures.

Regardless of what kind of safety and emergency gear is carried, it is essential that its presence does not result in a false sense of security and a careless attitude toward the operation of the boat. When this happens, the equipment undermines safety instead of promoting it, something that happens much too often.

Life Jackets and Harnesses

Life jackets (PFDs) not only are legally required by the United States and some other countries but are also cheap and address the most frequent cause of loss of life at sea: drownings. Having a life jacket for everyone onboard is a no-brainer.

When to wear a life jacket is a little more complex. We do not use ours as much as we should, primarily because they are uncomfort-

Left: *The first priority in safety at sea is to stay attached to the boat.* Right: *Inflatable life vests with built-in harnesses are the most comfortable way to keep the crew protected. (Courtesy Mustang Survival)*

Many of the inflatable life vests have significantly more buoyancy than almost all other life jackets. (Courtesy Mustang Survival)

able. This makes me believe that it is an excellent investment to purchase at least a couple of high-quality inflatable PFDs with built-in harnesses (more about this later) and to insist that the watchkeeper—especially when in the cockpit alone—wears one at all times. The cost is several times more than that of a cheap life jacket, but is still not high compared to the risk being guarded against.

This brings up a more general point. We have a full complement of cheap life jackets onboard. These comply with the USCG's minimum requirements and so keep us out of legal trouble in the U.S. But the reality is that in a real-life emergency, they don't fit well and they would have minimal buoyancy. In addition, they make it difficult to wear a safety harness. It's one thing to be legal, another to be safe.

From a legal standpoint, the USCG classifies PFDs as follows:

- Type I provides at least 22 pounds (100 N) of buoyancy and is designed to turn an unconscious wearer into the face-up position. These are the best.
- Type II provides at least 15½ pounds (70 N) of buoyancy and may turn an unconscious wearer into the face-up position.
- Type III has the same buoyancy as type II, but will not turn an unconscious wearer into the face-up position.
- Type IV is a throwable device, including horseshoe buoys and some cushions.
- Type V is an inflatable device that can have a performance equal to a type I, II, or III device (noted on the label).

In the United States, boats under 16 feet (5 m) must have at least one type I, II, III, or V device for every person onboard. Above 16 feet, these must be supplemented with a throwable device (type IV).

From a safety standpoint, type II and III PFDs do not keep a wearer's head much above water. In rough conditions, with breaking seas and spray, the wearer may still drown! A type I or better device makes a measurable difference. Many of the inflatable life jackets have more than 30 pounds (136 N) of buoyancy ("high buoyancy"), with some going as high as 60 pounds (275 N), which is considerably better than the type I legal requirement. To be most effective, a life jacket needs a crotch strap (to stop it riding up in the water). Whether worn or not on a daily basis, each member of the crew should have a personal life jacket, with the straps adjusted for his or her use, so that if needed in a hurry it will immediately fit properly.

All of the inflatable life jackets have a cylinder of carbon dioxide for rapid inflation backed up with a tube that can be blown into; the carbon dioxide is either activated manually (by pulling a cord) or automatically (on contact with water). Given that it is rare for someone to be knocked unconscious when going overboard, and given the propensity for unintended inflation with the automatic type, my preference is for the manual cord. However, I would make an exception to this if sailing in cold water because of the shock and disorientation that can occur when falling in (see later in this chapter)—in this case, autoinflate may be a lifesaver.

Life jackets for children should have a "handle" on them (at the collar) so that if a child falls in the water, he or she is easier to lift out. This is also an excellent idea for adults: the handle needs to be strong enough to haul someone who is unconscious out of the water.

Harnesses

Although not legally required by the USCG (they are required under some racing rules), harnesses are just as and maybe more important than life jackets. After all, if you don't fall in the water, you won't need the life jacket.

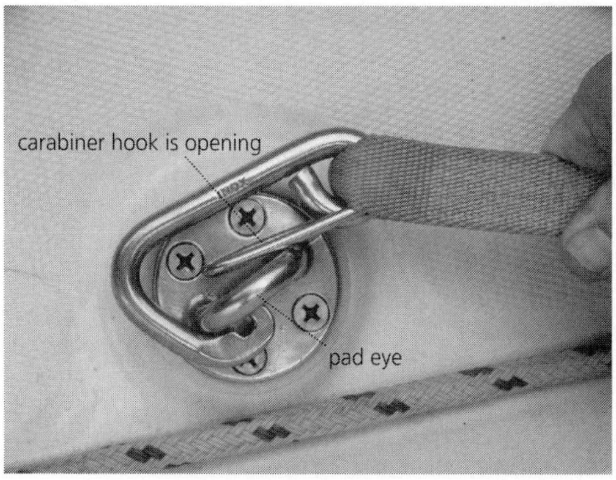

When a carabiner-type (snap) hook twists around a pad eye, it can trip itself loose. Some type of locking hook is much safer.

Harnesses, like life jackets, need to be comfortable to encourage their use and easy to get on and off.

To do the job for which it is designed, a harness and the line (*tether*) and attachments used to anchor it to the boat need to be immensely strong. Six of the fifteen deaths in the 1979 Fastnet race were attributable to harness or attachment failures. The ORC requires chest webbing to be at least 1½ inches (38 mm) wide and to have a minimum breaking strength of 3,300 pounds (1,500 kg), with a WLL of more than 1,575 pounds (716 kg). Tethers must have a minimum breaking strength of 4,950 pounds (2,250 kg); this sounds like a lot—it *is* a lot! However, the shock load of a heavy person thrown across a boat and brought up short on the end of a harness can exceed 2,000 pounds (909 kg).

Tethers commonly have a carabiner-type (snap) hook at both ends. These are relatively cheap and easy to put on. However, when attached to a pad eye, in certain circumstances they can get accidentally opened. In other circumstances, they can be difficult to undo under a load. A better approach is a double-gated (Gibb-type) hook or a Wichard safety hook, although these are harder to clip on and take off using just one hand (the other hand being needed to hang onto the boat). At the chest end, even better is a snap shackle because it can be released under a load—if you find yourself attached to a sinking boat, you will be able to undo your tether.

In summary, *it is obvious that the best set of compromises for cruising sailors in both PFDs and harnesses is an inflatable PFD with a built-in harness*. The cost won't be much more than that of a harness and good-quality life jacket bought separately, and for this you have something that is easy to put on, comfortable to wear, has a harness that meets the demanding ORC standards, and has excellent buoyancy if you go in the water. This represents a good safety investment. One small detail to look for when going this route are toggles on the PFD that enable it to be attached to loops found on some foul-weather jackets—this way, the PFD can be left on the jacket when it is taken off.

Crew Overboard Maneuvers

The single greatest cause of loss of life at sea (approximately 80 percent of deaths) occurs as a result of people falling overboard and drowning (mostly because life jackets were not worn), dying of hypothermia, or simply not being found. The most important measure for preventing loss of life is to *stay on the boat*; specifically, to wear a safety harness and life jacket whenever the going gets rough, whenever on deck alone, and whenever going forward. Beyond this, if someone goes overboard, being able to recover him or her as rapidly as possible may be the difference between life and death. This requires a clearly understood recovery procedure *that has been practiced by all onboard* (it is frequently the skipper who goes overboard; if the crew hasn't been trained in recovery procedures, the skipper is in deep trouble).

If sight of the person in the water is lost, the chances of a successful rescue are *dramatically* reduced; therefore, the number-one priority is always to keep the person in sight or, at the least, to provide visual markers. For example, toss over a COB pole (a Dan buoy), life rings, and a trail of boat cushions, and anything else that floats while the boat is being got under control and turned around. It is an excellent idea to insist that those on deck always carry a small pocket-sized (personal) strobe light to increase the chances of their being seen if pitched overboard. Depending on circumstances and crew size, a rescue procedure should go something like this:

1. If other people are onboard, an immediate cry of "Crew overboard!" gets everybody on deck; at the same time, flotation is tossed to the person in the water. Someone is delegated to keep the person in sight and point in this direction.
2. If a GPS is in use, the "Crew Overboard" button should be pressed; if not, the boat's course should be jotted down as soon as possible, with the wind speed and direction, and (if available) a fix. If sight of the person in the water is lost, this informa-

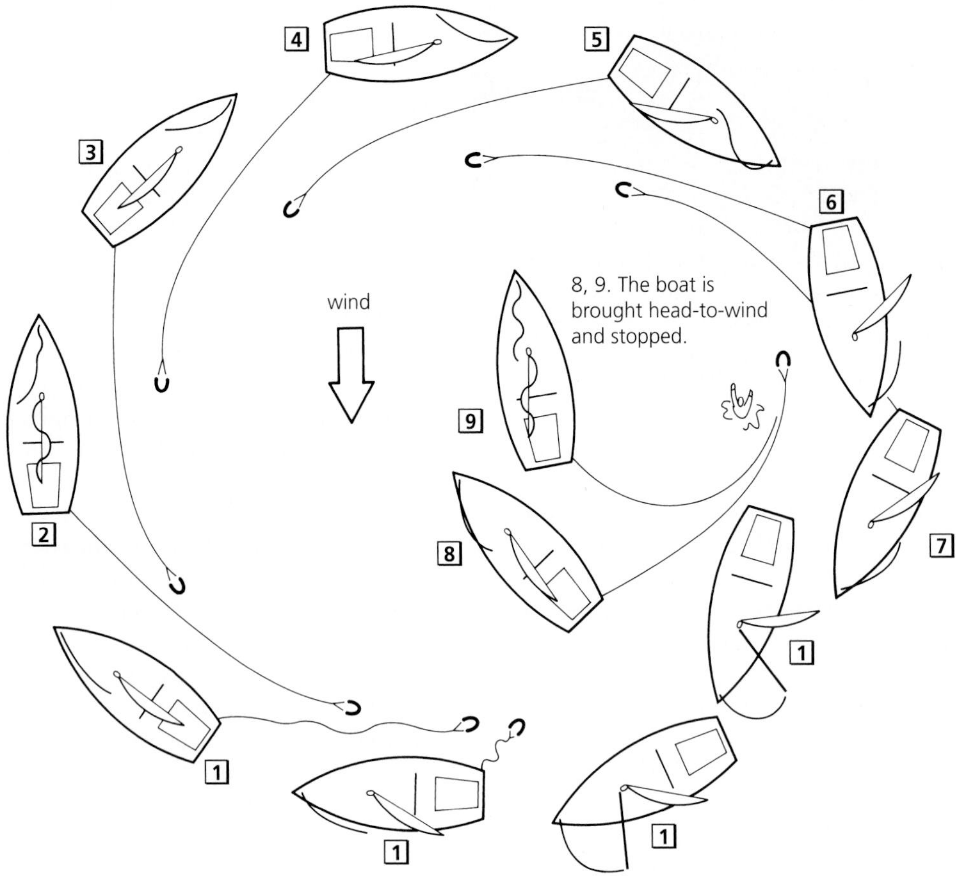

The Quick-Stop method for recovering a COB.

1. Regardless of the point of sail, the boat is brought hard on the wind and the Lifesling (Crew-Link) deployed.

2, 3, 4. The boat is tacked, leaving the headsail sheeted to windward.

5, 6, 7. The boat is jibed around the person in the water until the Lifesling (Crew-Link) is in reach.

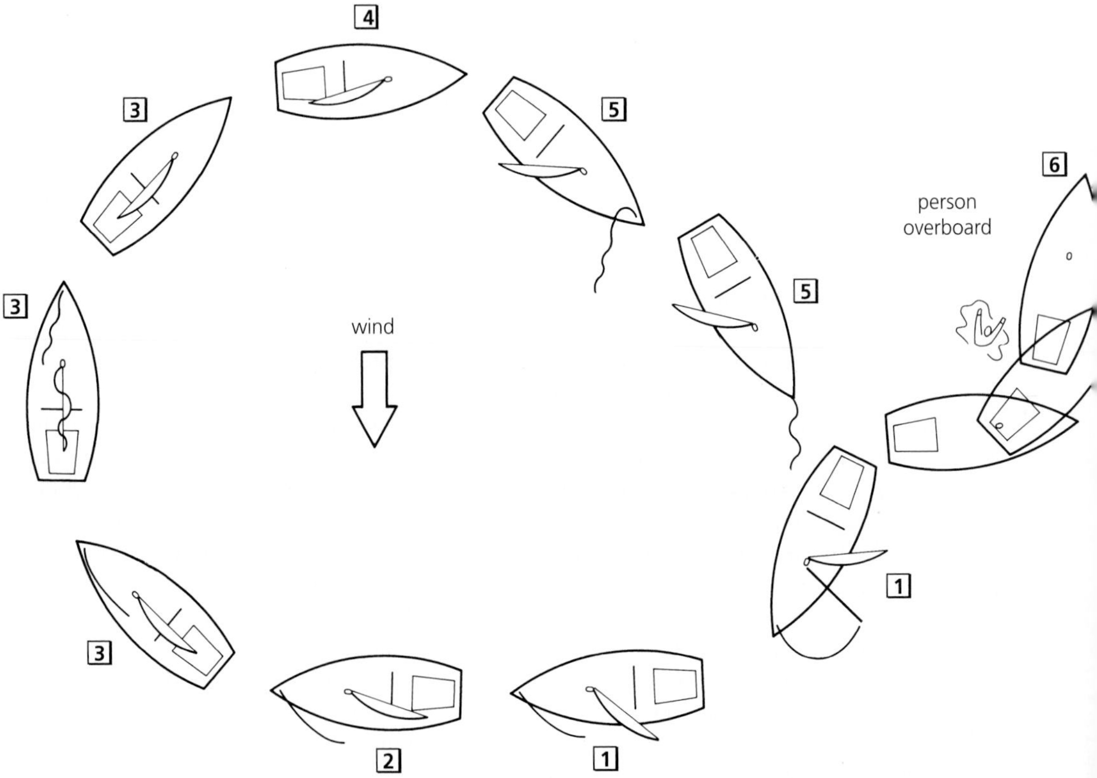

Figure-eight method for recovering a COB.

1. Regardless of the point of sail, the boat is put onto a beam reach.

2. The course is noted when on the beam reach.

3. The boat is tacked.

4. The boat is put on a reciprocal beam reach.

5. Headsail sheet is let fly to slow down.

6. The boat is brought head to wind alongside the person overboard.

tion can make the difference between life and death.

3. Three different approaches can be used to turn the boat around:

   i. The first instinct is generally to crank the motor and power back. Resist this instinct—in all probability, trailing lines may foul the propeller. If this approach is adopted, the boat should be brought head to wind, the sails dropped or rolled up, and a check made for trailing lines before cranking the motor. All this takes time. Extreme care has to be taken to not foul the lines to any trailing life rings, and to *not injure the person in the water with the propeller*. Usually, it is faster and safer to sail back, using one of the next two methods.
   ii. *Quick Stop or Crash Stop (with or without a Lifesling or Crew-Link)*: Regardless of its point of sail, the boat is immediately brought onto the wind, hauling both the main and headsail sheets in tight, and then tacked, leaving the headsail sheeted to windward (i.e., with the sail aback). This slows down or stops the boat and turns it rapidly, minimizing the distance from the person overboard. Either the turn is continued around the person in the water—bearing away onto a reach and run, and then jibing, without loosening the sheets—or the sails are taken down and the motor cranked (this is probably the best option with an inexperienced crew; see previous method). Most cruising boats now have onboard a *Lifesling* (a patented recovery system utilizing a horseshoe buoy on a long line), Crew-Link, or something similar, which is tossed overboard while the other actions are occurring. The objective is to circle the person until either he or she is in reach or the Lifesling (Crew-Link) has been brought into reach.
   iii. *Figure Eight*. Regardless of the point of sail when the person goes overboard, the boat is *immediately* and momentarily put on a beam reach (i.e., if hard on the wind, the helmsperson bears away; if running, the boat is brought closer to the wind). The course is noted because it will always be possible to sail its reciprocal (another beam reach), putting the boat in the vicinity of the person in the water. The boat is tacked and put back on the reciprocal course (toward the person in the water), letting fly the headsail sheet to slow down the boat. The boat is sailed back to the person in the water, a little downwind, and then brought up into the wind to stop alongside him or her. The principal danger with the figure-eight maneuver is the potential for losing sight of the person in the water during the period when the boat continues to sail away on a beam reach. The quick-stop maneuver minimizes the distance sailed and, for this reason, is now preferred by many experts.

The next job is to get the person out of the water. There are many cases of people who have been brought alongside—still conscious and able to help themselves—but who were unable to get aboard and, as a result, succumbed to hypothermia. If the boat has a sugar-scoop-type stern, in reasonably calm seas it should be possible to drag the person onto the lower step and complete the recovery from there. However, in any kind of seas, the stern will be pitching up and down dangerously; *recovery must be made over the side.*

If recovery is made on the leeward side, this puts the person in the relatively protected lee of the boat. The boat will also be heeled to some extent, putting the rail closer to the waterline. It may be possible to roll the crew member aboard, particularly if the lifelines can be disconnected as recommended in chapter 1. However, in many circumstances, some type of a sling with a hoist is required. The Lifesling (Crew-Link) has a built-in sling; harnesses have the necessary attachment points. In the absence of these, another person may have to get in the water to tie a line around the crew member. In that case, a survival suit (if one is on board) and a life jacket and harness, attached to the boat, are essential before going overboard.

Ideally, the necessary block and tackle for hoisting the person onboard is part of the boat's safety gear and can be rapidly deployed. If not, the main halyard, or any available halyard, is likely to be the best bet. A spinnaker halyard gives the best lead from the masthead (its block will swivel into alignment with the load), but brings the person aboard at a location where the freeboard is quite high. If any halyard is too short, a harness tether or something similar can be used to extend it.

Another viable option on many boats is the crane that is used to bring the outboard motor onboard. The hoisting line needs to be long enough to allow the lifting tackle to reach the

SAFETY EQUIPMENT CHECKLIST

- One life jacket per person
- One safety harness and tether per person
- If going offshore in high latitudes or cold water, a survival suit for each crew member
- COB recovery system (Lifesling, Crew-Link, or alternative plus COB pole)
- Life raft or other abandon-ship vehicle large enough to hold the entire crew
- Abandon-ship bag (ditch kit; see chapter 11)
- Emergency water supplies
- First-aid kit
- Flares
- EPIRB (for more information, see chapter 11)
- Foghorn and bell
- Radar reflector
- VHF
- GPS
- Navigation lights
- Basic navigation equipment
- Fire extinguishers
- A fire blanket
- Minimum of two bilge pumps, one of which can be manually operated from the cockpit
- A 5-gallon (19 L) bucket with attached lanyard (two are better)
- A softwood fid (plug) tied with a lanyard to each through-hull
- Waterproof flashlight
- Effective emergency steering
- Rigging cutters

US Sailing publishes an excellent booklet titled *Safety Recommendations for Cruising Sailboats* that is well worth consulting to check that a boat is safely set up for cruising. It can be ordered through its Web site (*www.ussailing.org*) or by calling 401-683-0800.

The Royal Yachting Association also has an excellent booklet titled *Cruising Yacht Safety, Sail and Power*. Contact them at RYA House, Romsey Road, Eastleigh, Hampshire, S050 9YA, U.K.; 44 (0)2380 627400; *www.rya.org.uk/*.

water. In all probability, a person in the water is too heavy to lift, so the other end of the line has to be led through a snatch block to a cockpit winch. This end of the line, too, needs to be long enough. This all should be thought about and planned for before the need arises. Once the person is at deck level, he or she can be dragged inboard.

Clearly, there is much that can go wrong in this situation. Success frequently depends on decisive leadership, a clearly understood procedure memorized by the crew, and an intimate knowledge of the boat's behavior in this kind of crisis situation. *There is no substitute for practice drills in which all crew members are required to take control so that all are capable of leading a recovery attempt.*

Shock and Hypothermia

"You might think drowning is the most immediate danger in falling overboard, but it's not, especially in cold water. The shock of suddenly and unexpectedly plunging into cold water is immense. As the water hits your face, you gasp involuntarily and uncontrollably—sometimes before you get back to the surface—and the muscles controlling the windpipe may contract to stop water getting into your lungs; this leaves you unable to take a breath once you've surfaced. Your chest feels as if it's in a vise, and your heart rate slows drastically. This effect is called the diving reflex.

"As the shock takes effect, the breathing rate increases from about ten to sixty breaths a minute and you begin to hyperventilate. External blood vessels constrict to conserve heat and increase blood flow to the brain and major organs. Blood pressure rises rapidly, increasing the chances of suffering a stroke. In some cases, the combined assault on the heart can result in cardiac arrest. This initial cold shock can kill!

"Elderly or unfit people are most likely to succumb to the initial shock. To increase the chance of survival, you must attempt to control your breathing rate by staying calm and still" (Yachting Monthly, *June 2000*).

Assuming this first rude shock is survived, a person in the water must concentrate on conserving body heat. Once the body's core temperature drops below 95°F (35°C), hypothermia will set in, initially causing uncontrolled shivering and exhaustion, then a loss of muscular control. Shivering ceases as the muscles become rigid, speech becomes slurred, and behavior may become irrational. Finally, stupor and unconsciousness take over. The usual cause of death is heart failure.

The keys to limiting heat loss are as follows:

- Minimize movement. Movement generates heat, which the water removes. In addition, it replaces the already warmed layer of boundary water next to the skin

SUMMARY OF U.S. COAST GUARD MINIMUM LEGAL REQUIREMENTS

PFDs. "At least one readily accessible life preserver or other lifesaving device, of the type prescribed by regulation, for each individual onboard." For boats under 16 feet (5 m), the prescribed type is a correctly sized, USCG-approved (it will say so on the label), wearable life jacket (types I, II, III, and V). Above 16 feet (5 m), an "immediately available" throwable device must be added (type IV).

Fire Extinguishers. Below 16 feet, there is no requirement; from 16 to 26 feet (8 m), at least one B-I; from 26 to 40 feet (12 m), at least two B-Is or one B-II; from 40 to 65 feet (20 m), at least three B-Is or one B-I plus one B-II; above 65 feet (20 m), one or more B-IIs, depending on weight. All fire extinguishers must be USCG-approved (it will say so on the label) and must be "kept in condition for immediate and effective use and so placed as to be readily accessible." (In the United Kingdom, there are no legal requirements, but the Royal Yachting Association [RYA] recommends at least one 5A/34B extinguisher [a U.K. rating] plus a larger 13A/113B extinguisher.)

Navigation Lights. Under sail, red and green sidelights, with a white sternlight; under power, there must be a white steaming light above the sidelights. On sailboats under 66 feet (20 m) in length, the sailing lights can be combined in a masthead tri-color light (see chapter 8).

Noisemakers. Boats under 40 feet (12 m) must be able to make "an efficient sound signal." Above 40 feet, a whistle and bell are required. The whistle must have an audible range of at least a half-mile.

Navigation Rules. Boats over 40 feet (12 m) must carry a copy of the USCG *Navigation Rules, International–Inland.*

Visual Distress Signals. Boats over 16 feet (5 m) must have a minimum of three day-use and three night-use, or three combined day- and night-use pyrotechnic devices (flares) *that are not date-expired* (for more about flares, see chapter 11).

Marine Sanitation Devices (MSDs). Up to 65 feet (20 m), any boat with an installed toilet must have a type I, II, or III MSD device (see chapter 12) *and use it in accordance with local and federal laws.*

Oil and Garbage Placard and Plans. Boats over 26 feet (8 m) must have clearly displayed oil discharge and waste discharge placards. Boats over 40 feet (12 m) must also have a written waste management plan.

with a fresh layer of cold water. Movement increases the rate of heat loss by up to 50 percent.

- If alone and wearing a life jacket, curl up in the fetal position, keeping your arms in to your sides, your legs together, and your knees up toward your chest (the HELP position: *heat escape lessening position*).
- If in a group, get in a huddle, with everyone packed as tightly together as possible.
- Keep your head out of the water—50 percent of heat loss is through the head, and any loss is accelerated by immersion (water is twenty-five times more conductive than air).

The HELP (heat escape lessening position) for individuals and groups.

Once a hypothermic person has been retrieved from the water, the focus is first on restoring heat to the core part of the body. A mildly hypothermic person can be wrapped in a blanket, given a warm (not hot) drink, and given time for the body to do its job. In more severe cases of hypothermia, warm or hot drinks may be dangerous, drawing warm blood away from vital organs. In a hospital, special techniques are used to warm the core body regions. On a boat, the best that can be done is probably to strip the person naked and put him or her in a sleeping bag with another naked person or, at least, in contact with warm (not hot) objects (e.g., warm towels) focusing on the neck, armpits, trunk, and groin, *not* the arms and legs. Having the patient breathe warmed air also helps.

In any case, *do not use massage* (especially of the arms or legs), exercise, or rapid warming to warm a hypothermic person, all of which may start frigid blood flowing from the extremities into the body's core sections, further reducing the core temperature—a condition known as *afterdrop*. Also, *do not give alcohol* because it causes a loss of heat. Again, warm (not hot) drinks can be administered once the person is conscious enough to drink without risk of choking. Rough handling of a severely hypothermic person also can induce life-threatening afterdrop—important to remember when recovering somebody from the water.

Fire Extinguishers

Fire extinguishers are a good investment, given that they are relatively cheap and that an out-of-control onboard fire is one of the two most likely reasons to abandon ship (the other being the boat sinking under you). The most likely sources of fire are something falling against a hot exhaust, galley fires (e.g., a pan of oil catching fire), and electrical fires, which mirror the following three types of fire that can occur (as defined in the U.S.):

- Type A — General combustibles, such as wood, paper, clothing, rubber, and plastics
- Type B — Flammable liquids such as oil, gasoline, diesel, kerosene, alcohol, solvents, oil-based paints, grease, and cooking oil
- Type C — Electrical fires, usually the result of a short circuit of some kind (just turning off the electricity source generally still leaves a type A fire)

(In the U.K., type A and B fires are the same, but type C fires are classified as those involving flammable gases such as propane or butane.) All three fire types require a heat source to initiate the ignition process, a supply of combustible material, and oxygen to sustain the chemical reaction that produces fire. Knowing this, we can see there are three ways to stop a fire: bring the temperature below the combustion point, remove the combustibles, and cut off the oxygen supply (or otherwise interrupt the chemical reaction). However, the ways in which these objectives are achieved vary according to the nature of the fire.

Given a type A fire, water is quite effective. The water is turned to steam, which takes a lot of energy (latent heat of evaporation). This energy is drawn from the fire, hopefully reducing the temperature below the combustion point. Throwing water on a flammable liquid (type B fire), however, may have little effect, and may make the situation worse because the liquid is likely to float on top of the water and continue burning. In this case, the best approach is to cut off the oxygen supply—in effect, smother the fire—or interrupt the chem-

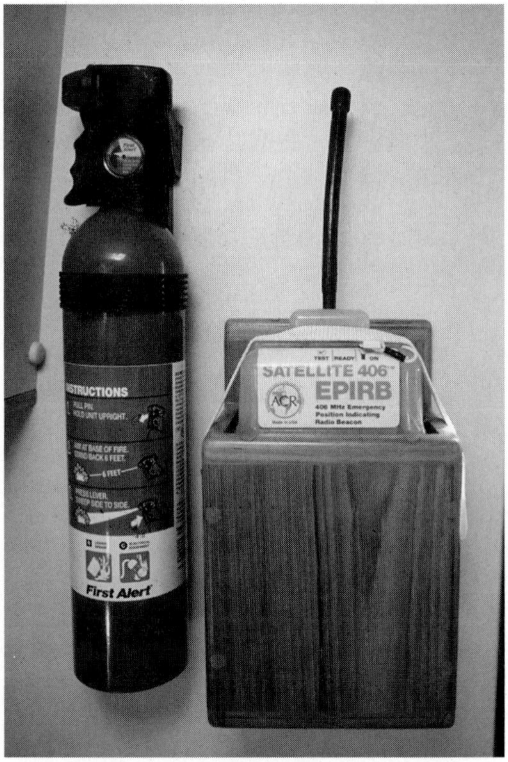

Fire extinguisher for types B and C fires (U.S. categories: see the bottom of the label) that meets minimum USCG standards. From a safety perspective, however, it is better to have something larger. This one is mounted alongside the companionway with a 406 MHz EPIRB (see chapter 11).

ical reaction. A small galley fire, for example, can be readily subdued with a fire blanket. Larger fires may require carbon dioxide, which displaces the oxygen, or dry powder, which interrupts the chemical reaction.

Electrical fires (type C in the U.S.) are a special case inasmuch as water, carbon dioxide, and dry powder may all be effective in reducing fires in surrounding materials (type A fire); however, until the short has been eliminated, the source of the initial heat will not be removed and the fire will continue to break out anew. The primary concern is to break the electrical circuit and then fight the fire. Even then, water is not advised because it may result in new short circuits.

Electrical fires can spread extremely rapidly (sometimes a cable running the entire length of a boat becomes red hot) and they are the most likely to produce noxious smoke (from burning cable insulation). They can rapidly force a boat to be abandoned, which drives home the point that *the first priority is to cut off the electrical energy source*, usually by tripping the main battery switch. In some cases, particularly engine-cranking circuits, it may be necessary to break a red-hot cable physically loose from a battery. It is better to install a disconnect switch and proper overcurrent protection in this circuit in the first place (see chapter 4)!

If the fire is in a contained or semicontained space (e.g., an engine room), about the worst thing you can do is open it up to take a look. This immediately provides a fresh source of oxygen. If possible, the firefighting agent should be blown in without opening any doors or hatches. It is worth having a hole the size of a fire-extinguisher nozzle in the side of an engine compartment through which a carbon-dioxide extinguisher can be discharged.

When fighting a fire, the particular firefighting agent is always aimed *at the base of the fire*. Water, water-based products (e.g., foams), and dry powder all leave a mess to be cleaned up. Carbon dioxide leaves none, but if it fails to subdue the fire, the carbon dioxide is rapidly dispersed and then becomes ineffective.

Dry powder and carbon dioxide are not particularly effective on type A fires, especially deep-seated fires that are likely to keep on smoldering and then break out again. Water is the best bet in this situation. Given the availability of water on a boat, the focus in onboard firefighting is generally on type B and C (electrical) fires, both of which can be fought with carbon dioxide and dry powder. It makes sense to have carbon dioxide as the first line of

Pressure gauge on a fire extinguisher. These need to be regularly checked. Dry-powder extinguishers also should be inverted periodically to keep the powder from caking up.

defense (because it makes no mess), with dry powder as a backup. In addition, an automatic engine-room system is very effective in dealing with engine-room fires, but also is quite expensive.

Dry-powder fire extinguishers use compressed carbon dioxide as a propellant. Over time, both these and regular carbon-dioxide fire extinguishers may suffer from a slow leak, leading to a loss of pressure. The pressure gauge on all such fire extinguishers should be regularly checked. The dry-powder extinguishers also suffer from compaction of the powder over time, so they should be periodically inverted and shaken to make sure the powder is loose.

The USCG has classified portable fire extinguishers in two classes—B-I and B-II—based on size. Assuming no fixed engine-room system, USCG regulations require at least one B-I extinguisher on boats from 16 feet (5 m) (there is no requirement below 16 ft.) to 26 feet (8 m). From 26 to 40 feet (8–12 m), two B-Is or one B-II are required; from 40 to 65 feet (12–20 m), three B-Is or one B-I plus one B-II are required. These are absolutely minimum requirements; common sense dictates that on any cruising boat there should be a fire extinguisher near the engine room and near the galley, and at least one other—with more on larger boats. They need to be readily accessible (on a bulkhead) and located so that it is not necessary to reach through any likely fire (e.g., over the top of the stove) to get them. In a worst-case situation, wherever you are on the boat, you need to be able to knock down a fire to the point that you can escape. The larger the fire extinguishers, the better.

A Dorade vent is a good place to stow small teddy bears, which rarely create safety problems!

We all get caught in nasty weather once in a while.

CHAPTER ELEVEN

WEATHER PREDICTIONS AND HEAVY-WEATHER SAILING

In this era of continuous weather reports on cable TV, regular broadcasts on the radio, real-time satellite pictures of major weather features, numerous weather information sources on the Internet and on ham radio, and Weatherfax, it seems as if the sailor doesn't need to understand the weather—someone else will take care of it, providing accurate forecasts.

To a significant extent this is true, but to some extent it still is not. The crux of the matter lies in the need for accurate weather forecasts *at the precise location in which you happen to be*. Even the most specific of weather forecasts is dealing in generalities. The cruising sailor needs a basic understanding of the driving forces that create "weather" to be able to modify the generalities for local conditions.

For example, in the United States, NOAA continuously broadcasts excellent coastal forecasts on VHF radio, whereas in the United Kingdom the BBC produces regular broadcasts. However, in your particular location, the daily wind and sea patterns may be substantially modified by local topographic features such as hills or by the effect of an estuary. You need to be able to plug these factors into the bigger picture.

The farther offshore you venture, the greater the generalities built into weather forecasts. At times, the forecasts will be dramatically wrong in terms of the weather you are experiencing. The better your understanding of both the forces that create weather and the signs associated with different weather systems, the better your chances are of making favorable use of weather systems and of being properly prepared when conditions deteriorate.

This chapter is intended to give a "feel" for the weather. Ultimately, such a sense will improve not only sailing skills, but also the enjoyment of sailing.

BASIC THEORY

The driving force behind the world's weather systems is the differential absorption of heat from the sun. Of the available heat energy, approximately half is reflected back into space by the atmosphere; the other half is absorbed by the surface of the earth to be discharged back into the atmosphere and into space.

If we assume that heat emanates from the sun in parallel waves and the sun's heat emission is more or less constant, it is easy to see that a given quantity of heat is concentrated into a smaller area of the earth's surface at the equator than it is at the poles. This has nothing to do with the equator being fractionally closer to the sun; rather, it is simply a function of the oblique angle at which the sun's rays hit the earth in higher latitudes. The lower levels of heat absorption at the poles are exacerbated by

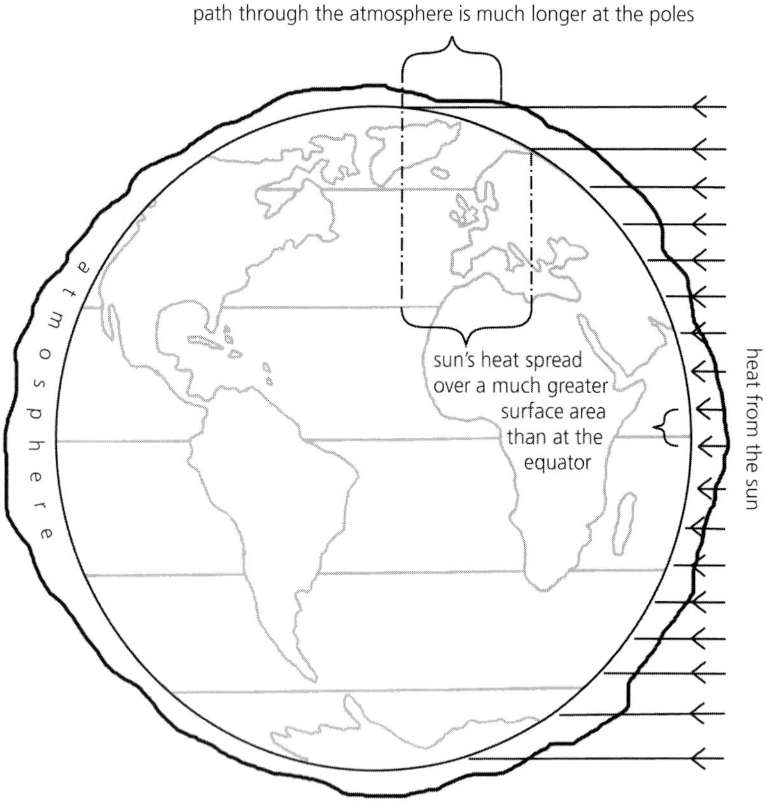

Above: *The sun's heat has a much greater warming effect at the equator than it has at the poles.* Below: *Mechanisms of global heat transfer.*

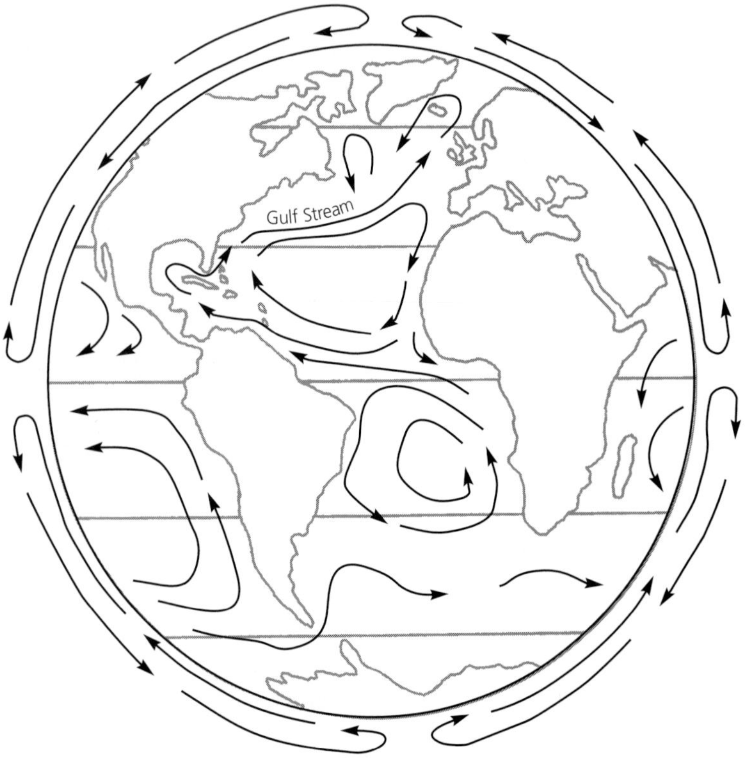

the longer path through the atmosphere and the reflective effect of the snow and ice. The net result is that tropical regions become much warmer than polar regions.

If it were not for other factors, the equatorial regions would heat up and the polar regions would cool down to a point at which neither would be inhabitable. The fact that this isn't the case is the result of a redistribution of heat from the equatorial regions to the poles. This heat is moved in two principal ways—through vast ocean currents, such as the Gulf Stream, and through the movement of air masses.

Currents are present in all of the oceans, although none is as dramatic as the Gulf Stream. It moves from east to west across the South Atlantic Ocean north of the equator, absorbing heat as it goes. It then swings northwestward across the Caribbean Sea, to be funneled through the Yucatan Straits and the Florida Straits into the North Atlantic Ocean. Typically, it is now at about 84°F (29°C) and is considerably warmer than the surrounding ocean. It makes a huge loop around the North Atlantic, dissipating heat as it goes, making northern Europe habitable in the process. Finally, it arcs south down the western coasts of Europe and North Africa, now colder than the surrounding water, again absorbing heat. In making this circle, it has moved vast amounts of heat energy from tropical latitudes to high latitudes.

Something similar is happening in the atmosphere. At the poles, the cold earth cools the lower levels of the atmosphere. As air cools, it contracts, becomes denser, and sinks. This mass of dense, cold air results in relatively high atmospheric pressure. In the tropical regions, the heated earth warms the lower levels of the atmosphere. Warm air expands, becomes lighter, and rises, creating a region of relatively low atmospheric pressure. We end up with a convective cycle in which cold air from the poles moves at low altitudes toward the equatorial regions, becoming warmer along the way; warm air from the tropics moves at high altitude toward the poles, cooling as it goes. In the process, huge amounts of heat energy are again transferred from tropical regions to high latitudes.

The net effect of these phenomena is that a global "heat balance" is achieved in which the heat input to a given region of the earth's surface is balanced by the heat output, resulting in relative stability at the global level. Average surface, water, and atmospheric temperatures vary little from year to year, although there naturally are radical differences from season to season, day to night, and day to day.

Adding Wind and Putting a Spin on These Processes

The global atmospheric circulation is nowhere near as simple as depicted so far. There are all kinds of complicating factors such as the impact of land masses and mountain ranges, and, in particular, the effect of the earth's rotation on the movement of various air masses (the *Coriolis effect*). Instead of one great circulation loop in each hemisphere from the north or south pole to the equator and back, with high pressure at the poles and low pressure at the equator, we end up with three broadly defined loops (*circulation cells*). The first runs from the high-pressure region at the poles to a region of relatively low pressure somewhere around 50 to 60 degrees latitude north or south; the second extends from there to a region of relatively high pressure around 20 to 30 degrees north or south; and the third from there to the equatorial low-pressure region.

These three circulation cells determine not only the movement of air masses, but also the general pattern of surface winds around the world. In the absence of other factors, they would result in winds blowing in a north or south direction from the high-pressure regions toward the low-pressure regions. These north and south flows, however, are distorted by the effect of the earth spinning on its axis.

Given an air mass situated at a particular point over the surface of the earth, friction between it and the earth tends to get it moving at the same speed as the earth, which is approximately 24,000 miles a day at the equator (one revolution every twenty-four hours). Rotational speeds steadily decrease the farther north or south from the equator, declining to nothing at the poles (because the poles are on the axis of rotation).

When an air mass moves away from its source region, it is initially spinning at the same speed as the region from which it came. As it moves into a different latitude, it will have a certain *inertia* (if it moves from the poles toward the equator) or *momentum* (if it moves from the equator toward the poles). In the former case, the earth beneath the air mass will now be spinning faster than the air mass, and slower in the latter case. Relative to the surface of the earth, this results in a deflection of the path of the air mass away from a northerly or southerly direction. In the Northern Hemisphere, if the wind is more or less behind you, this deflection is to the right; in the Southern Hemisphere, it is to the left.

Putting these pieces together, we get a schematic representation of the earth's principal pressure and wind zones, which gives us the following:

- A region of high pressure at the poles (the *polar high*) from which northeast winds blow in the Northern Hemisphere and southeast winds in the Southern Hemisphere (the *polar easterlies*). Note that wind directions are always given in terms of the direction *from which the wind is coming*, not that toward which it is blowing (e.g., a south wind comes from the south and blows to the north).
- A region of relatively low pressure around 50 to 60 degrees north or south (the *temperate low-pressure belt*, also known as the *polar front*), into which the polar easter-

Above: *Basic atmospheric circuation pattern.* Below: *The Coriolis effect on global wind patterns. The generalized pattern in theory.*

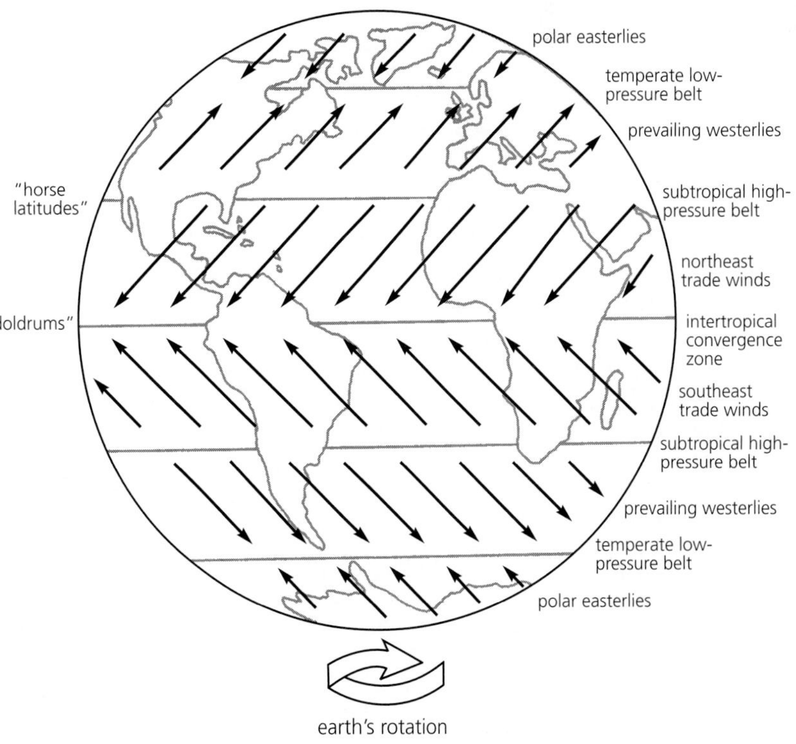

lies blow, along with southwesterly winds in the Northern Hemisphere and northwesterly winds in the Southern Hemisphere. These latter winds are known as the *prevailing westerlies*.

- A region of relatively high pressure at around 20 to 30 degrees north or south (the *subtropical high-pressure belt* or the *midlatitude high-pressure zone*), from which the prevailing westerlies emanate, along with northeast winds in the Northern Hemisphere and southeast winds in the Southern Hemisphere. These latter winds are known as the *trade winds* because in the days of sail, they dominated many world trade routes. The subtropical high-pressure belt is characterized by light winds that, in the days of sail, sometimes resulted in long passages during which drinking water became scarce. Horses were reputably thrown overboard to conserve water for human consumption, resulting in this region being known as the *horse latitudes*.
- A region of low pressure at the equator into which the trade winds blow (the *intertropical convergence zone*, ITCZ). It is also characterized by light winds, and has long been known as the *doldrums*.

The Coriolis effect on global wind patterns. The generalized pattern in practice. (From Bowditch, courtesy DMA)

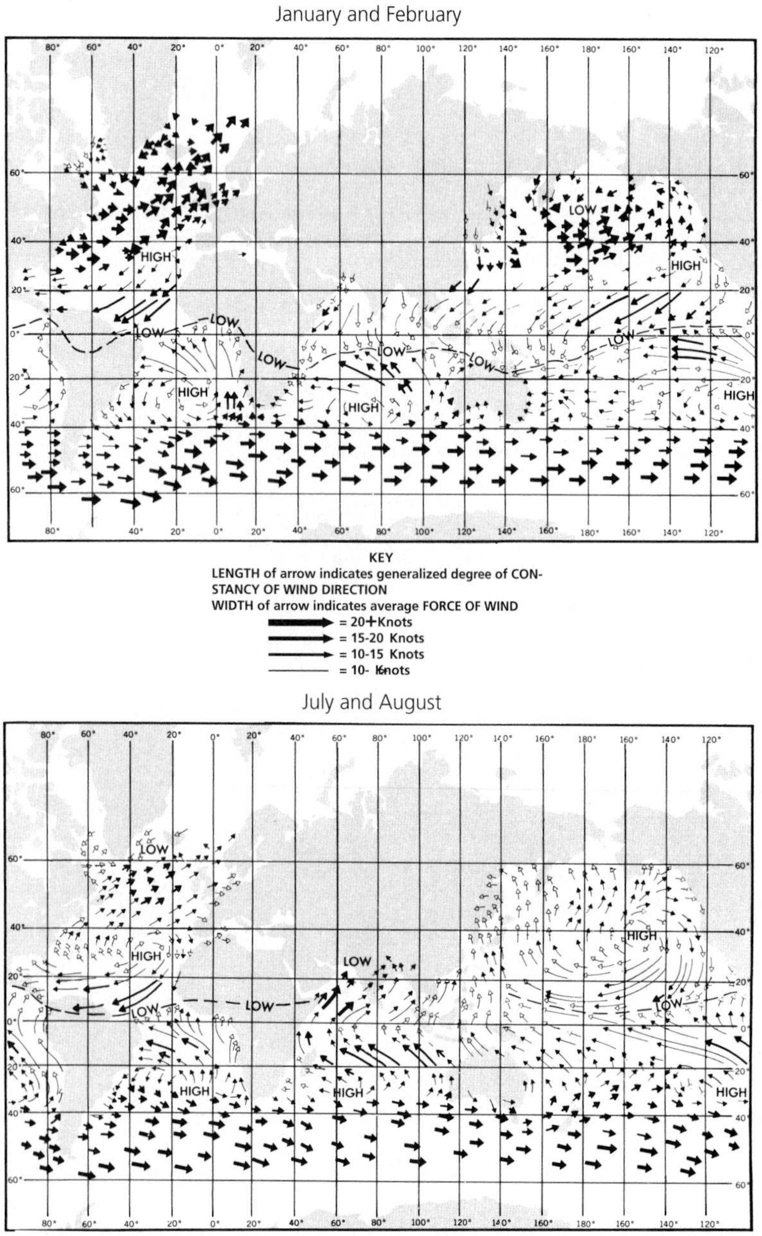

The relative locations of the high- and low-pressure belts and their associated winds move north and south with the seasons. This movement lags approximately two months behind the north and south movement of the sun, which is over the Tropic of Capricorn—23.5 degrees south—around December 22; over the Tropic of Cancer—23.5 degrees north—around June 21; and over the equator on the spring and fall equinoxes—around March 20 and September 21.

Pressure Changes, Isobars, and Wind Direction

This schematic representation of wind and pressure zones is greatly modified in practice. For example, in the Northern Hemisphere the North American, European, and Asian continents fall squarely in the path of the prevailing westerlies, disrupting the global flow; whereas, in the Southern Hemisphere, the only land mass at these latitudes is the tip of South America. As a result, the prevailing westerlies are both stronger and more consistent in the Southern Ocean, to the point that the latitudes in which they occur have been nicknamed the *roaring forties*, the *furious fifties*, and the *screaming sixties*.

Although I have referred to high- and low-pressure belts, in reality there are high- and low-pressure regions more or less strung out along the relevant latitudes, with seasonal changes. For example, in the winter, the oceans near the poles are warmer than the land, creating rising air and intensifying the low pressure over the Aleutian and Icelandic regions; whereas, in the summer, the temperature differences even out and these lows are not so pronounced.

Regions of high and low pressure are shown by meteorologists on special charts—*synoptic charts*—which are constructed by simultaneously taking many pressure readings around the world, reducing the readings to a common datum (sea level), and then joining all those points that have a common pressure to form lines that are known as *isobars*. The end product is a series of more or less concentric circles around high- and low-pressure points.

When moving from a region of high pressure toward a region of low pressure, the synoptic chart will show a steady decrease in pressure as one isobar after another is crossed. The closer together the isobars, the faster is the rate of pressure change (i.e., the steeper the *pressure gradient*) and the stronger are the resulting winds that will be experienced on the ground.

Intuitively, you would expect the winds to blow outward in all directions from areas of high pressure toward areas of low pressure, crossing the isobars at right angles; however, this is not the case. Surface friction, the Coriolis effect, and other influences come into play with the result that the winds more or less follow the lines of the isobars, particularly at higher altitudes. However, surface winds (those experienced by sailors) are deflected by friction from the lines of the isobars into the low-pressure centers by approximately 30 degrees over land and 15 degrees over water.

Because of the Coriolis effect, the winds are again deflected to the right in the Northern Hemisphere and to the left in the Southern Hemisphere. As a result, winds blowing away from a high-pressure region in the Northern Hemisphere

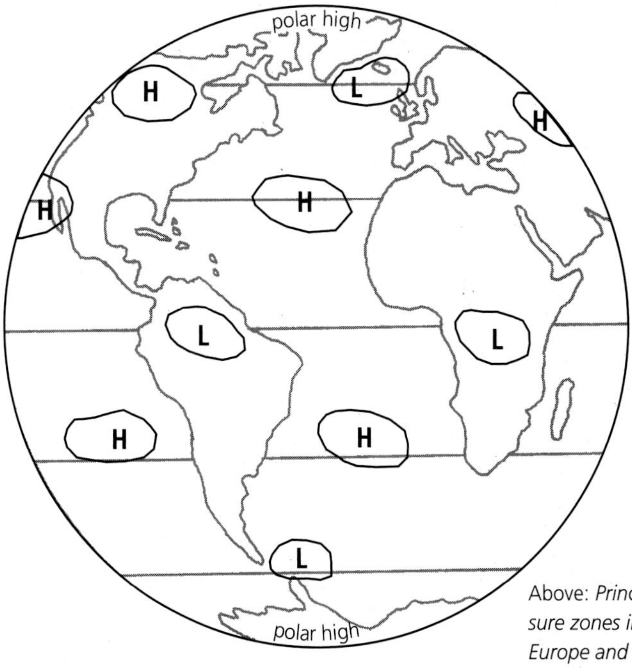

Above: *Principal pressure zones in Western Europe and the Americas.* Below: *Sample synoptic chart for the North Atlantic, 17 June 2000. The symbols are explained later in this chapter.*

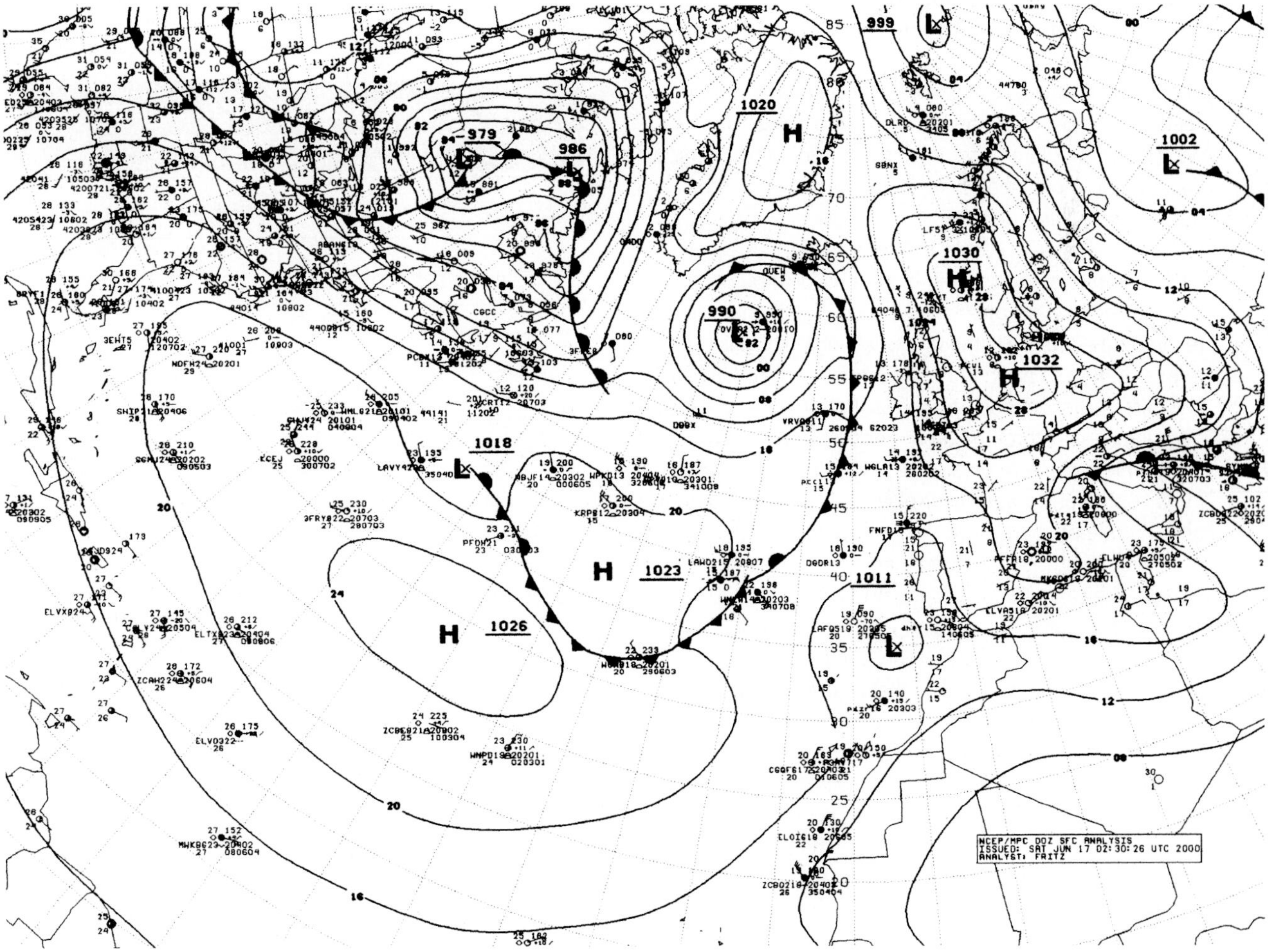

MEASURING ATMOSPHERIC PRESSURE

Atmospheric pressure is measured by a device known as a *barometer*. The most accurate type consists of a tube sealed at the top, filled with mercury (Hg), and then upended over an open container of mercury. The weight of the mercury in the tube causes it to sink down the tube, pulling a vacuum at the top of the tube. This establishes an equilibrium in which the weight of the remaining mercury is balanced by the vacuum. Any change in atmospheric pressure upsets this balance, causing the mercury to move up or down the tube. The tube is graduated in inches, which leads to the traditional method of reading atmospheric pressure in *inches of mercury*, with 29.92 inches (760 mm) Hg being standard atmospheric pressure.

Nowadays, however, inches of mercury are rarely used for measuring atmospheric pressure. The unit that has found universal acceptance is *millibars*. The former is converted into the latter as shown in the following table.

Internationally, another unit of measurement—*kilopascals* or *hectopascals*—is sometimes used. Kilopascals (kPa) equal millibars divided by 10; hectopascals (hPa) equal millibars.

A mercury barometer requires a stable location and, therefore, will not work onboard a boat at sea. Another type of barometer—an *aneroid barometer*—takes its place. An aneroid barometer has a hollow tube of metal coiled into a spring that is partially evacuated of air and then sealed. Changes in atmospheric pressure cause the coil to wind up some more or to unwind. Through a mechanical linkage, this movement is translated into a reading of atmospheric pressure.

A barometer is a basic and essential piece of equipment on an offshore cruising boat. Individual barometric readings don't have great significance, but changes in the reading do—especially the rate of change. For this reason, regular noting of the barometric pressure in the log is a key part of the logkeeping process. Better yet is to have a *barograph*—a recording barometer that makes a trace of atmospheric pressure on a piece of graph paper—providing a continuous graphical display on which any changes and the rate of change are readily apparent.

For accurate readings, barometers require periodic calibration. The easiest way to do this is to call the local airport to obtain a local barometric reading, and then calibrate the barometer accordingly. If the airport is much above sea level, it is important to ask for a reading that is corrected to sea level.

The mechanics of aneroid barometers are such that they tend to "stick" at one pressure reading until pressure changes are sufficient to overcome the resistance of the mechanism to movement. To get an accurate reading, always be sure to first tap the face of the barometer, which provides whatever jolt is necessary to get the pointer to move.

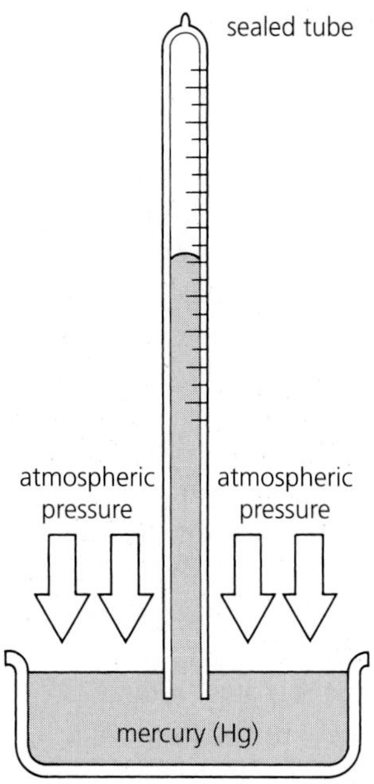

How a barometer works. The weight of the column of mercury pulls a vacuum in the top of the tube. This vacuum is counterbalanced by atmospheric pressure operating on the open dish. Changes in atmospheric pressure cause the mercury to move up and down the graduated tube.

Conversion of Millibars to Inches of Mercury

MILLIBARS	INCHES OF MERCURY
1,050	31.00
1,040	30.70
1,030	30.41
1,020	30.11
1,013.3	29.92—standard atmospheric pressure
1,010	29.82
1,000	29.52
990	29.23
980	28.93
970	28.64
960	28.34
950	28.05
940	27.75

do so in a clockwise circulation, while those blowing into a low-pressure region do so in a counterclockwise circulation. In the Southern Hemisphere, the circulation is reversed.

Relative Humidity, Air Masses, Stability, and Instability

Over time, the temperature of the air mass over any particular region of the earth takes on a similar temperature to that of the surface of the earth below it. Furthermore, if the air mass is over water, especially warm water, it absorbs moisture; if it is over land, it tends to lose moisture. If there were no atmospheric circulation of air masses, we would end up with three static air masses—what are known as polar (P), tropical (T), and equatorial (E)—each of which could be over the ocean (maritime [m]) or land (continental [c]). This gives us the following six fundamental air-mass categories

- Continental Polar (cP)
- Maritime Polar (mP)
- Continental Tropical (cT)
- Maritime Tropical (mT)
- Continental Equatorial (cE)
- Maritime Equatorial (mE)

In practice, at any given time, all six categories are present over different parts of the world. The global atmospheric circulation causes these air masses to move from the regions in which they are generated to other parts of the world. It is the interplay of these air masses that largely determines local weather patterns.

The moisture-carrying capability of air is a function of its temperature: the warmer the air, the more moisture it can carry; the cooler it is, the less it can carry. At any given temperature, the amount of moisture it is carrying, relative to what it is capable of carrying, is expressed as a percentage known as its *relative humidity* (i.e., an air mass with a relative humidity of 50 percent is carrying 50 percent of the moisture content it is capable of carrying at that temperature). If air with a certain moisture content is steadily cooled, its relative humidity will steadily rise *even though the absolute moisture content remains the same*. This is because as its temperature cools, its moisture-carrying capability goes down. At some point, the falling temperature brings the relative humidity up to 100 percent (the *dew point*), after which any further decrease in temperature results in precipitation. Conversely, if air with a given moisture content is heated, its relative humidity will steadily decrease, even though the absolute moisture content remains unchanged.

As warm air rises—all other factors being equal—its temperature declines uniformly with altitude. However, the temperature of the surrounding air typically also declines with altitude. If the relative rates of decline are such as to keep the warmer air warmer so that it rises to ever-higher altitudes, sooner or later its relative humidity will reach 100 percent and precipitation will ensue. In this case, the air mass is described as unstable.

If, on the other hand, the air surrounding the mass of rising warm air cools with altitude at a slower rate than the rising air, at some altitude the temperature difference will even out and the mass of warm air will stop rising. In this case, there is no further cooling, and the relative humidity remains unchanged. The air mass is described as stable.

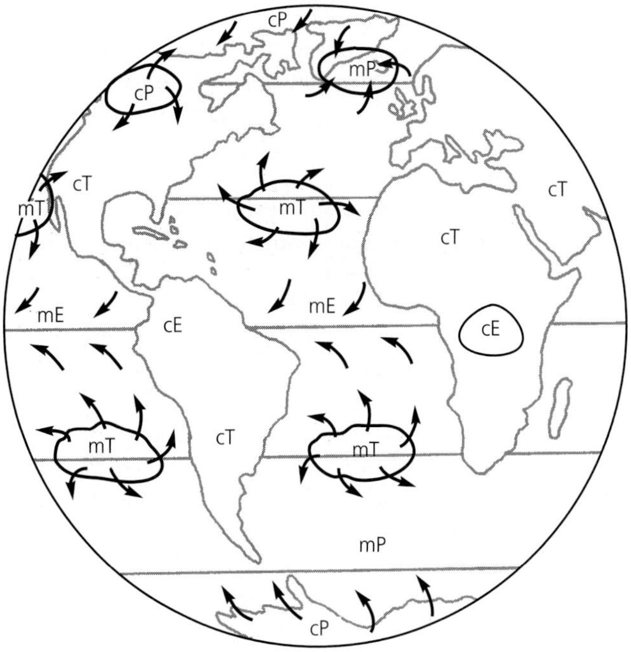

Fundamental air masses on a global scale.

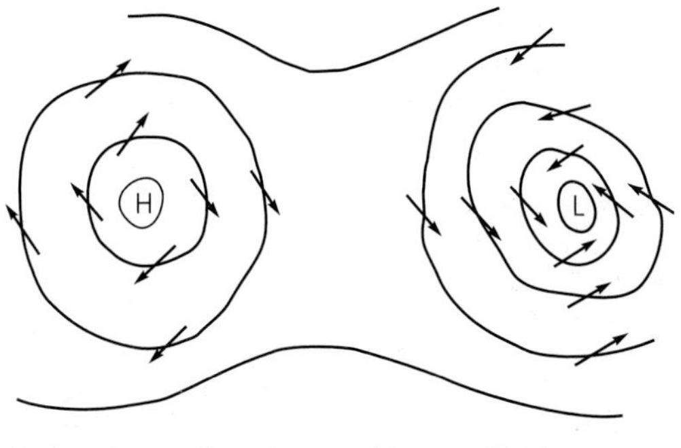

The circulation of winds around low- and high-pressure regions in the Northern Hemisphere (reverse for the Southern Hemisphere).

As discussed previously, in regions of high pressure, air sinks to the surface of the earth and moves outward at the surface. As it sinks, it warms—lowering its relative humidity. As a result, regions of high pressure are often characterized by homogeneous air masses, clear skies, and stable weather patterns. In fact, a number of the world's high-pressure regions are semipermanent.

It is quite different in the low-pressure regions, which have strong ascending air currents. As air rises, it cools. Looking first at the ITCZ, particularly those sections situated over the oceans (and therefore of interest to us), we see that the northeast trade winds are blowing in on one side and the southeast trades on the other. The trade winds will have blown over warm oceans, absorbing moisture—resulting in mT air masses with high relative humidity. In the ITCZ, these air masses ascend to higher altitudes and cool off. The relative humidity goes beyond the *saturation point* (100 percent relative humidity), resulting in frequent showers, squalls, and thunderstorms—some of them quite violent.

As for the low-pressure regions in the temperate low-pressure belt, we typically have two very different air masses drawn in—polar air from the poles (cP or mP) and tropical air from the subtropical high-pressure belt (mT or cT). If the tropical air has passed over water, especially warm water, it will be loaded with moisture (mT) and close to its saturation point. These are all the ingredients for a highly unstable situation with very variable weather conditions; in fact, these are the ingredients for a classic frontal system.

Approximate boundary lines where many major weather systems are spawned.

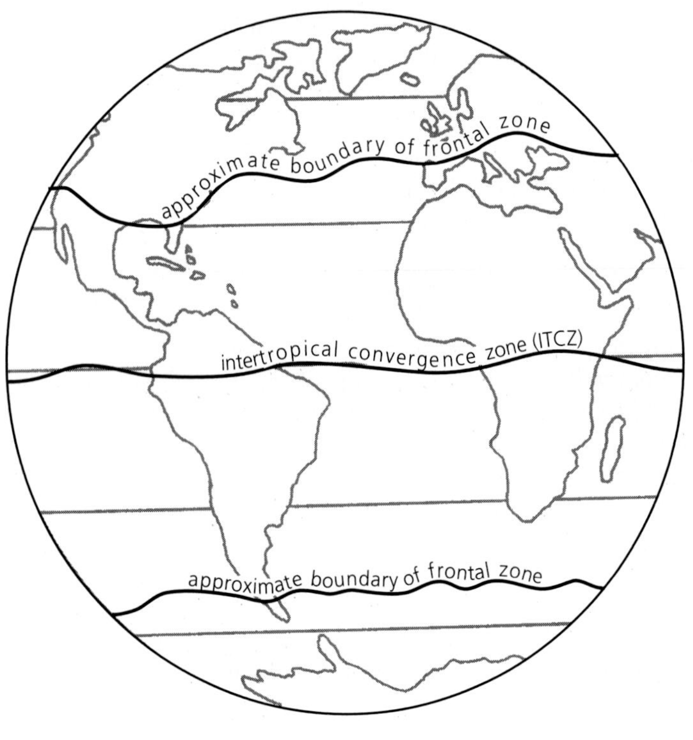

Frontal Systems

When different air masses meet or collide, as they do along the temperate low-pressure belt, little mixing takes place. Instead, what happens is that kinks in the boundary line between the air masses develop into revolving low-pressure systems (*depressions* or *frontal systems*), in which the warm air mass rides up over the cold air mass or the cold air mass forces its way under the warm air mass. These depressions move steadily from west to east as they develop and then fade. At certain times of the year, specifically the winter months in the Northern Hemisphere, they are spawned in large numbers, forming a continuous procession along the temperate low-pressure belt.

Let's look at one of these depressions in the Northern Hemisphere, starting with a polar air mass on one side of the boundary line, with prevailing northeasterly winds, and a tropical air mass on the other side of the line, with prevailing southwesterly winds. Both air masses are moving from west to east. Some mechanism, which I believe is still not well understood, initiates the development of a region of low pressure at a point along the boundary line.

The boundary line becomes kinked. Within a day or two, the depression takes on a "classic" form, with the warm air forming an inverted V-shaped wedge surrounded by cold air on both sides. The lowest pressure is at the tip of the V, and the whole system moves from west to east. Winds spiral into the low in a counterclockwise direction in the Northern Hemisphere and in a clockwise direction in the Southern Hemisphere, at an angle of approximately 15 degrees (over water) to the isobars. The closer together the isobars are, the steeper is the pressure gradient and the stronger are the winds.

As the depression moves from west to east, an observer on the ground to the south of the center of the low (in the Northern Hemisphere) or to the north (in the Southern Hemisphere) will first be in the cold air mass, and then the warm, and then the cold again. Specific weather is associated with the two *fronts* at which the warm and cold air meet. The first front is called a *warm front* (for the observer on the ground, colder air is replaced with warmer); the second

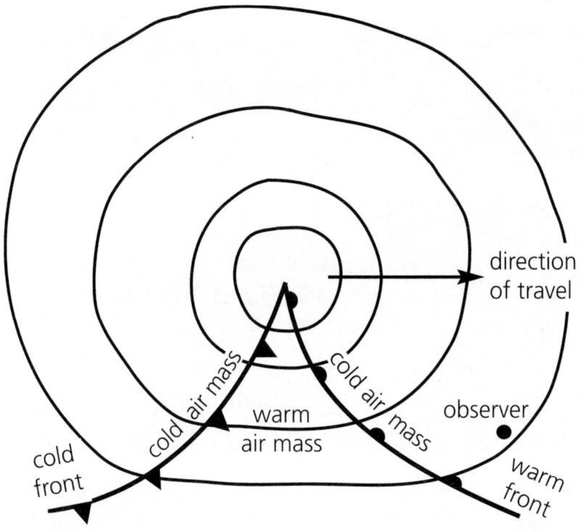

The succession of air masses as a frontal system passes over a stationary observer.

is called a *cold front* (warmer air is replaced with colder).

Cold fronts move faster than warm fronts. Consequently, the cold front steadily overtakes the warm front, starting at the center of the low and moving out along the warm front, resulting in what is known as an *occluded front*. The system then starts to run out of steam and fades away until the usually more or less straight boundary line between the two air masses is restored, while a new depression is spawned somewhere else along the temperate low-pressure belt. At any given time, there may be numerous depressions developing or dying, with highly complex interactions.

Warm Fronts

In a typical warm front, warm, moist tropical air (mT) is driven up over a wedge of cold polar air (cP or mP). As the tropical air rises, it cools below its saturation point. Clouds form and later precipitation develops. The speed with which everything happens is a function of how fast the warm air is overtaking the cold and how steep is the gradient up which the warm air is moving. This is usually a relatively slow process that takes place over many hours, and sometimes a couple of days.

An observer on the ground being overtaken by a warm front will be in the wedge of cold air for some time, while the warm air pushes up the face of the wedge and spreads out overhead. As a result, an entire sequence of cloud types will be seen before the warm air—the front itself—reaches the observer on the ground. Typically, the process starts with a clear sky. Advance warning of the coming front is signaled by high, thin cirrus (Ci) clouds, which gradually increase to

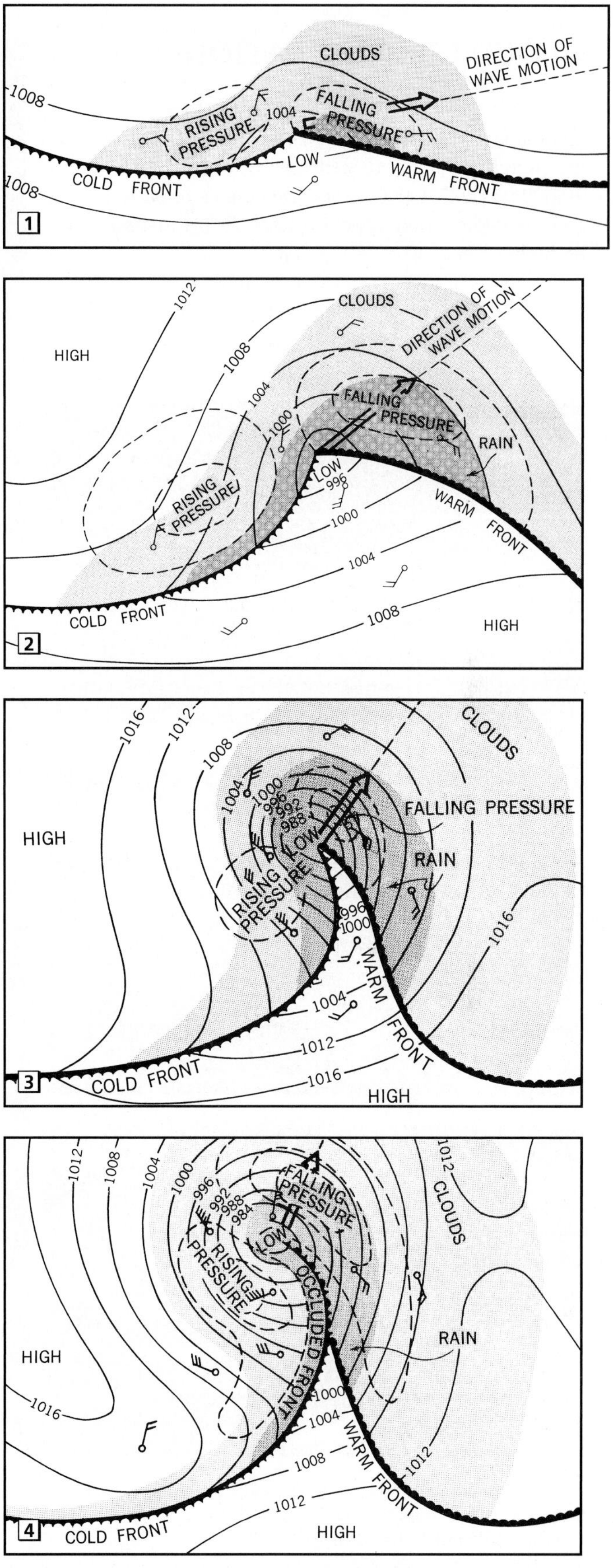

Development and progression of a frontal system. 1. First stage in the development of a frontal wave. 2. A fully developed frontal wave. 3. A frontal wave nearing occlusion. 4. An occluded front. (From Bowditch, courtesy DMA)

CLOUD CLASSIFICATION

Clouds are classified primarily according to their height and shape. High clouds (above 20,000 ft./6,000 m) are given the prefix *cirro*; medium-level clouds (7,000–20,000 ft./2,000–6,000 m) are given the prefix *alto*; and lower-level clouds (below 7,000 ft./2,000 m) have no prefix.

In terms of shape, *stratus* means relatively flat layers and *cumulus* means heaped up or lumpy. The word *nimbo*, or *nimbus*, is then sometimes added to delineate clouds

1

2

3

4

5

6

The succession of clouds during the passage of a frontal system in the Bahamas. 1. *Ahead of the front, the first wispy lines of cirrus clouds move in.* 2. *The cirrus clouds are thickening, and lower-level stratus layers are approaching. Note the jet contrails: when these occur, it is indicative of higher moisture levels in the atmosphere.* 3. *Cumulus clouds are being added to the mix.* 4. *The sky is now totally occluded with clouds. Once there is total cloud cover, you can no longer determine the cloud type (is it stratus, cumulus, or cumulonimbus?).* 5. *There's not much doubt that this weather system has a little punch to it!* 6. *A break in the cover reveals that here we have cumulus clouds that are acquiring considerable vertical elevation (cumulonimbus).*

producing precipitation. These simple categories result in the following cloud types:

- Cirrus (Ci): curly, wispy or fibrous high-level clouds in narrow bands with very little substance, sometimes taking on the appearance of *mares tails*
- Cirrostratus (Cs): cirrus-type clouds, but in more uniform sheets, that sometimes make a halo around the sun and the moon
- Cirrocumulus (Cc): small, high-altitude, puffy balls that are smaller than the sun and moon, and that sometimes take on the appearance of *mackerel scales*
- Altostratus (As): midlevel sheets of clouds, generally thicker than Cs, but nevertheless thin enough for the sun's hazy outline to be seen through them much of the time
- Altocumulus (Ac): darker and thicker than As and Cc
- Stratus (St): dense, gray overcast skies at low altitudes, often with drizzle, that completely blot out the sun
- Nimbostratus (Ns): similar to St, but with heavier precipitation
- Cumulus (Cu): scattered puffy clouds at low levels
- Stratocumulus (Sc): dense blankets of compressed low-level Cu similar to St, but with greater vertical development (difficult to differentiate from stratus from below, but generally with a more patchy appearance)
- Cumulonimbus (Cb): large Cu cells with great vertical development that is associated with squalls and thunderstorms

There is no sharp dividing line between these different cloud forms, so it is not always easy to classify the clouds in view—in addition to which the situation may be confused by the simultaneous presence of several different cloud types. Nevertheless, the clouds that can be seen often fall into one or another category. From a cruiser's perspective, accurately classifying them takes a back seat to getting a sense of the changing cloud forms that occur as different weather systems pass overhead.

7. *Cumulonimbus often produces violent squalls. A few minutes after this photograph was taken, the wind was up to 35 knots and the rain was coming down in buckets (it's time to put the camera away, clean the side decks, and fill the water tanks).* 8. *Following the passage of a front, the cloud cover frequently clears out quite rapidly . . .* 9. *leaving, in most tropical and midlatitude regions, the occasional "fair-weather" cumulus.* 10. *Fair-weather cumulus is particularly likely to form over land masses (including islands) and warm ocean currents (the rising hot air during the day creates the thermal currents that lead to cloud formation). The clouds increase in size and density during the day, sometimes building to spawn midafternoon squalls and thunderstorms, but mostly peaking around sundown (as these are) without producing any weather activity.*

cirrostratus (Cs), perhaps forming a halo around the sun or moon.

The cirrostratus continues to thicken and lower as bands of altostratus (As), nimbostratus (Ns), stratus (St), and stratocumulus (Sc) clouds move in, one after the other. The nimbostratus brings light precipitation (drizzle), which intensifies to the heavier precipitation that comes in with the stratocumulus. The precipitation may continue for as long as twenty-four hours before it tapers off.

If an observer is to the north of the low-pressure center in the Northern Hemisphere (and to the south of it in the Southern Hemisphere), this cycle will be experienced without any significant change in temperature, and with the precipitation tapering off to be replaced with cool or cold clear weather. If the observer is to the south of the low-pressure center in the Northern Hemisphere (north of it in the Southern Hemisphere), there will be a marked warming as the warm front comes through, with quite likely clearing skies. This warm front is soon followed by the cold front. The time between the two, however, is not predictable without a synoptic chart—it all depends on how far you are from the center of the low and how fast the low is traveling: the farther the

Top: *Cloud patterns and weather associated with the passage of a warm front.* Bottom: *Cloud patterns and weather associated with the passage of a cold front.*

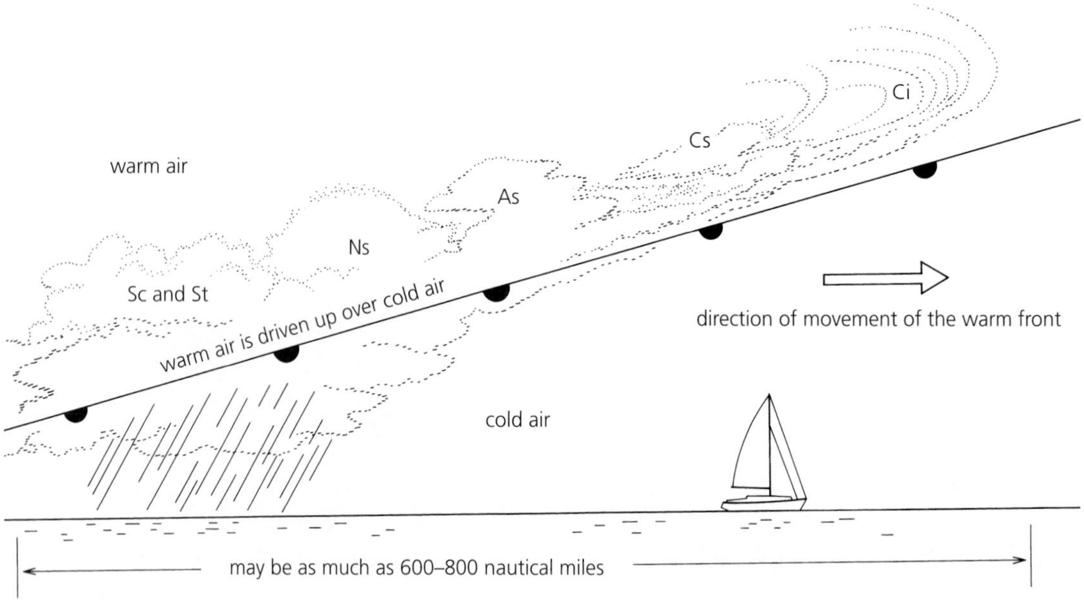

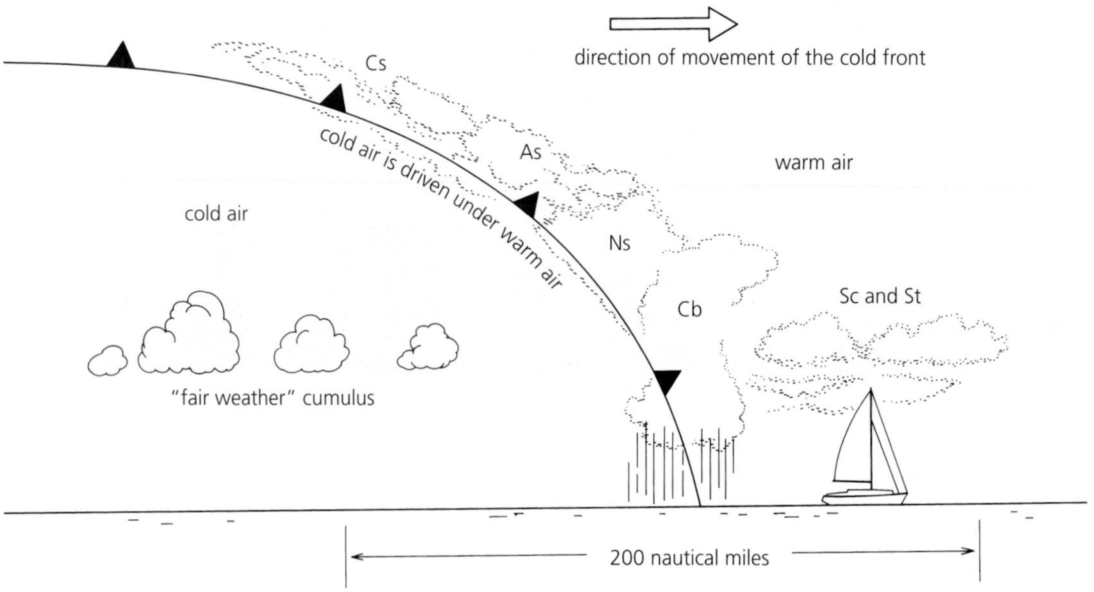

distance and the slower the rate of advance, the longer the interval is likely to be between the two fronts.

Cold Fronts

Cold fronts move faster than warm fronts, with the advancing cold air aggressively driving the warm air aloft up a much steeper gradient than occurs in a warm front (typically, twice as steep). As a result, the kind of weather associated with a cold front is compressed into a shorter time frame and is more dramatic.

A cold front is sometimes preceded (by anywhere from 50 to 300 miles) by a line of violent squalls. This is particularly likely if the warm air preceding the front is unstable. These squalls may trail a large area of stratus clouds with steady rain, or there may be a clearing before the front itself comes through.

The front is likely to bring its own line of squally weather with a sharp wind shift (discussed later in this section) and a sudden drop in temperature. (In extreme cases, the temperature can drop as much as 50°F—approximately 30°C—in less than an hour.) The colder air behind the front generally brings clearing skies, although the front may trail further showers, particularly if the cold air mass is unstable.

In terms of cloud patterns, a receding warm front will trail stratus and cirrostratus clouds, which may clear in advance of the cold front. Any squall line preceding the cold front will be characterized by an advancing line of cumulonimbus clouds. The front itself is also likely to bring a line of cumulonimbus, trailing off into nimbostratus, altostratus, and cirrus over a relatively short period.

Occluded Fronts

When a cold front catches up with a warm front, we have—in succession—the cold air ahead of the warm front, the warm air associated with the warm front, and then the cold air behind the cold front. In other words, the warm air is sandwiched between two cold air masses. If the second cold air mass is the colder of the two, it drives under the first and forces both it and the warm air aloft (a *cold-front occlusion*). However, if the first cold air mass is the colder of the two, the second cold air mass rides up over it, again forcing the warm air aloft (a *warm-front occlusion*).

The passage of both cold- and warm-front occlusions is likely to be accompanied by stratus clouds developing into cumulonimbus, with showery weather, followed by a clearing as the front passes and the colder air mass takes over.

Pressure and Wind Changes Associated with the Passage of Fronts

If we draw a "classic" depression showing the isobars surrounding the low-pressure center and the warm- and cold-front lines, we find that although the isobars are generally circular, they flatten out in the area of the wedge of warm air. There is a relatively sharp angle (a *refraction* of the isobars) where the isobars cross both the warm and cold fronts.

In the Northern Hemisphere, at the surface of the earth, the wind blows into the low-pressure center in a counterclockwise direction at an angle of about 15 degrees (over water) to the isobars; in the Southern Hemisphere, the circulation is clockwise.

If we imagine ourselves to be stationary, north of a depression in the Northern Hemisphere with the depression tracking overhead, we will experience a steadily lowering pressure with the wind first coming from the southeast and then *backing* (changing direction in a counterclockwise manner) into the east as the center of the low moves to the south of us. The pressure then starts to rise as the wind continues to back into the northeast. We will likely run the gamut of the cloud types associated with a warm front, but without any sudden change in air temperature.

If, instead, we imagine ourselves to be south of a depression in the Northern Hemisphere, the sequence of pressure and wind changes is quite different. As the depression approaches, the pressure steadily falls and the wind direction slowly *veers* (changes direction in a clockwise manner) from the southeast into the south. When the warm front arrives, the pressure levels out. At this

Wind and pressure changes associated with the passage of a frontal system in the Northern Hemisphere. Note that north of the center of the depression, the forward speed of the system counteracts the wind speed, resulting in the lightest winds, whereas south of the center the forward speed augments the wind speed, resulting in the strongest winds.

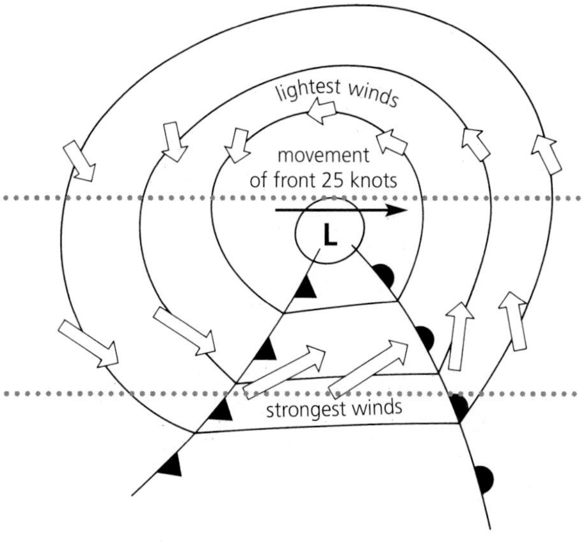

Observer to the north of the depression: the wind backs progressively from SE to NW.

Observer to the south of the depression: the wind veers from SE to NW, with a rapid shift from SW to NW as the cold front comes through.

time, there is likely to be a fairly rapid shift of the wind into the southwest (the first refraction in the isobar is passing over us).

With the arrival of the cold front, the pressure rises quite rapidly and there will be another sharp change in wind direction from the southwest into the northwest. Sometimes this can be quite dramatic with first a calm settling in and then a squall line approaching rapidly, and finally the front itself arriving with a blast of anywhere from 25 to 60 knots out of the northwest.

Once the front has passed through, the winds are likely to blow hard out of the northwest for a couple of days, and then slowly ease as they continue to veer into the north and northeast. The elapse of time from the arrival of the cold front to the restoration of prevailing conditions is likely to be two to four days. However, quite often in the wintertime, the next front is following closely on the heels of the last one, truncating the period before the wind shifts back into the east and the process starts again.

If we happen to be precisely on the track of a depression, we will experience a steadily falling barometer with no appreciable change in wind direction (which, most likely, will be from a southerly direction). The wind typically dies down as the center of a depression moves overhead (sometimes quite dramatically), and then returns from almost the opposite direction (a northerly direction)—again, sometimes quite dramatically.

In the Southern Hemisphere, when to the south of a depression, the pressure will decline and then increase. The wind veers with no appreciable change in temperature occurring. When to the north of a depression, both fronts will pass overhead. The pressure falls, levels out, and rises quite sharply with the wind backing as each front passes.

Note that in both Northern and Southern Hemispheres, the most "active" weather is on the equator side of midlatitude depressions (tropical depressions may be different—see later in this chapter). On this side, the (easterly) forward motion of the system augments the wind speeds, producing the strongest winds. On the pole side, the forward motion reduces the wind speed, resulting in lighter winds.

The Jet Stream and the 500-Millibar Chart

We need to add another piece to this picture, which is the *jet stream*. Jet streams consist of winds that blow at high altitudes, sometimes in excess of 200 knots. In the midlatitude regions, these high-altitude winds have a significant "steering" effect on the weather systems that give rise to surface-level winds. There is a less obvious connection between jet streams and weather systems closer to the equator. Consequently, the jet stream that gets the most attention is the *polar jet stream* (the *temperate-latitude jet stream*) that circles the world more or less around the temperate low-pressure belt.

Jet streams can be deciphered from something known as the 500-millibar (hectopascal) chart, which is a computer-generated chart of the atmosphere at an altitude of about 18,000 feet (approximately 5,600 meters). At this altitude, atmospheric pressure is approximately half of what it is on the surface of the earth; that is, around 500 millibars—hence, the name *500-millibar chart*.

The 500-millibar chart differs somewhat from a surface-level synoptic chart. The lines (isobars) on the latter chart link all points at the same pressure so that the chart as a whole shows pressure differences over the surface of the earth, reduced to a common datum of sea level; the 500-millibar chart shows no pressure differences. Instead, it focuses on a single pressure—500 millibars—and shows the differing heights above sea level at which this pressure occurs.

This can best be visualized in terms of seeing the 500-millibar pressure zone as a blanket wrapped around the world. At times, the blanket sinks down toward the surface of the earth (indicative of low pressure at the surface); at other times, it is lifted up higher than normal above the surface of the earth (indicative of high pressure at the surface). In other words, the 500-millibar chart is a contour or relief map of the 500-millibar zone. Just as with a surface-level contour or relief map, where the contours are close together, the change in elevation is rapid; where the contours are widely spaced, there is little change in elevation.

Embedded within the 500-millibar chart are *short wave troughs* that are shown as bold dashed lines. These indicate surface-level low-pressure systems or developing lows and, as such, are a useful predictive tool.

At the kinds of altitude at which the pressure is 500 millibars, the surface of the earth has no frictional effect on the wind. As a result, instead of deviating from the chart's contour lines by 15 to 30 degrees, jet-stream winds flow along the contour lines. The closer together the contour lines, the stronger are the winds. Wind speeds above 30 knots are shown on charts. A glance at the chart gives us a good idea of what is happening aloft, which in turn helps to under-

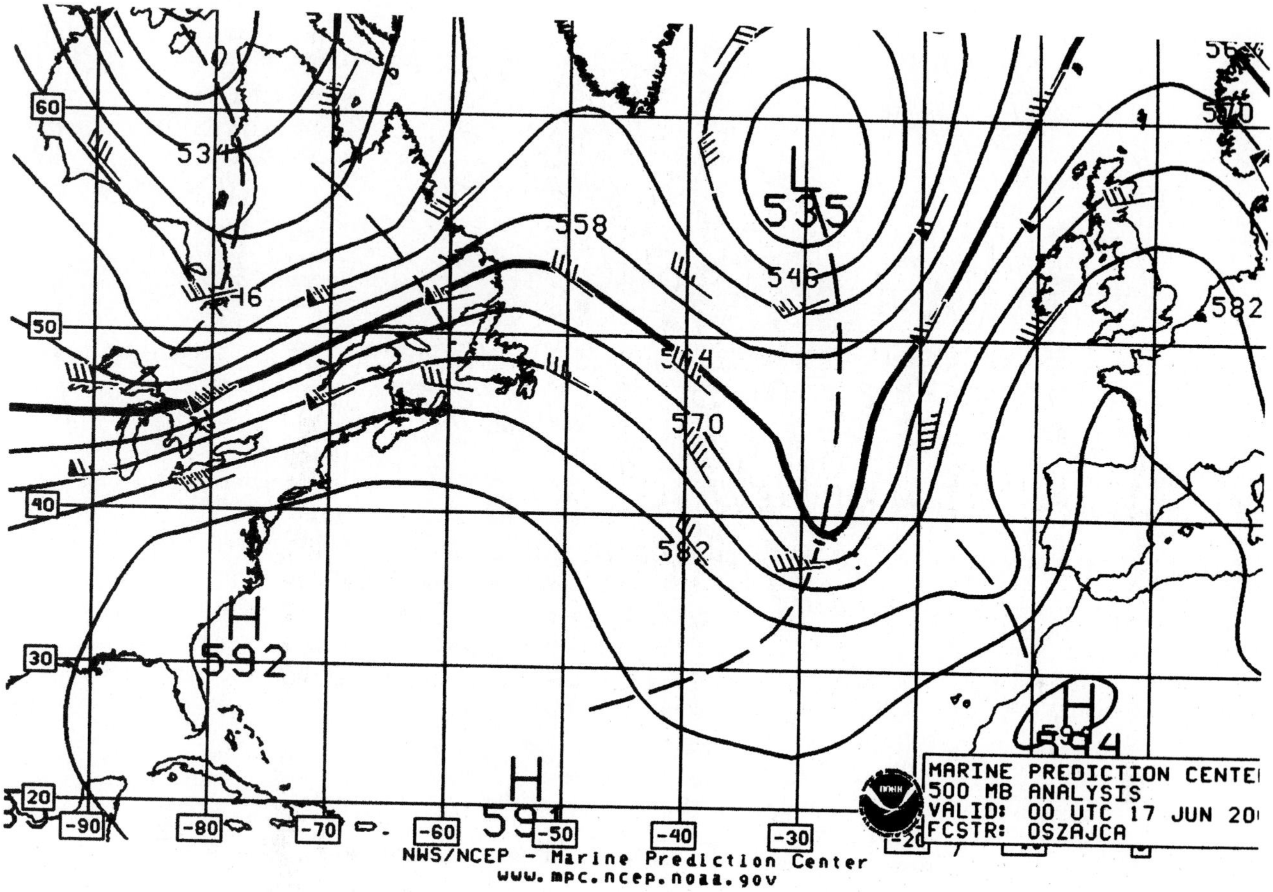

500-Millibar (hectopascal) chart for the North Atlantic for the same period as the synoptic chart on page 485. The dotted line represents the front shown on the surface level chart, bearing down on Europe.

stand what is happening and what is about to happen below.

For example, in the wintertime, the polar jet stream frequently dips southward over the continental United States, bringing frigid arctic air to the central United States and spawning strong cold fronts that reach all the way across the Gulf of Mexico into the Caribbean, sometimes as far south as Honduras. These southerly cold fronts can form as early as November and continue into April, although the greatest incidence is in February when one frequently follows on the heels of another with just two to four days between them. They can make navigation in the Gulf of Mexico and along the northern coast of Cuba quite challenging.

Sure signs that such activity is imminent are the jet stream curving down into the continental United States and the spacing between the contour lines closing up. We will soon see cold fronts spawned that will hook around through Texas and the Gulf of Mexico, following the path of the jet stream up the East Coast and out over the North Atlantic Ocean to arrive in Europe a few days later. If we look at the surface-level synoptic chart and see a cold front already formed at some point on this loop, we can also reasonably project its advancement broadly along the line of the jet-stream loop and across the North Atlantic, *traveling over the ground at between one half and one third* the speed of the upper-level jet-stream *steering winds.* Surface-level wind speeds along the cold front (the strongest winds) are likely to approximate one half the speed of the upper-level jet-stream winds.

The 5,640-meter contour is widely used on the 500-millibar chart as an indicator of surface-level storm tracks and so is generally highlighted. In the Northern Hemisphere, this contour is also considered to represent the southern extent of Force 7 (28–33 knots) or stronger winds in the winter, and Force 6 (22–27 knots) or stronger winds in the summer.

The 500-millibar charts are most useful if viewed every six or twelve hours. The charts then help to display underlying trends in weather systems, giving a sense of what is heading where and at what strength in the near future.

The Big Picture

The information provided to this point skims the surface of the "big picture" as far as understanding weather systems and in terms of being able to read and make sense of the synoptic charts and other materials readily available to

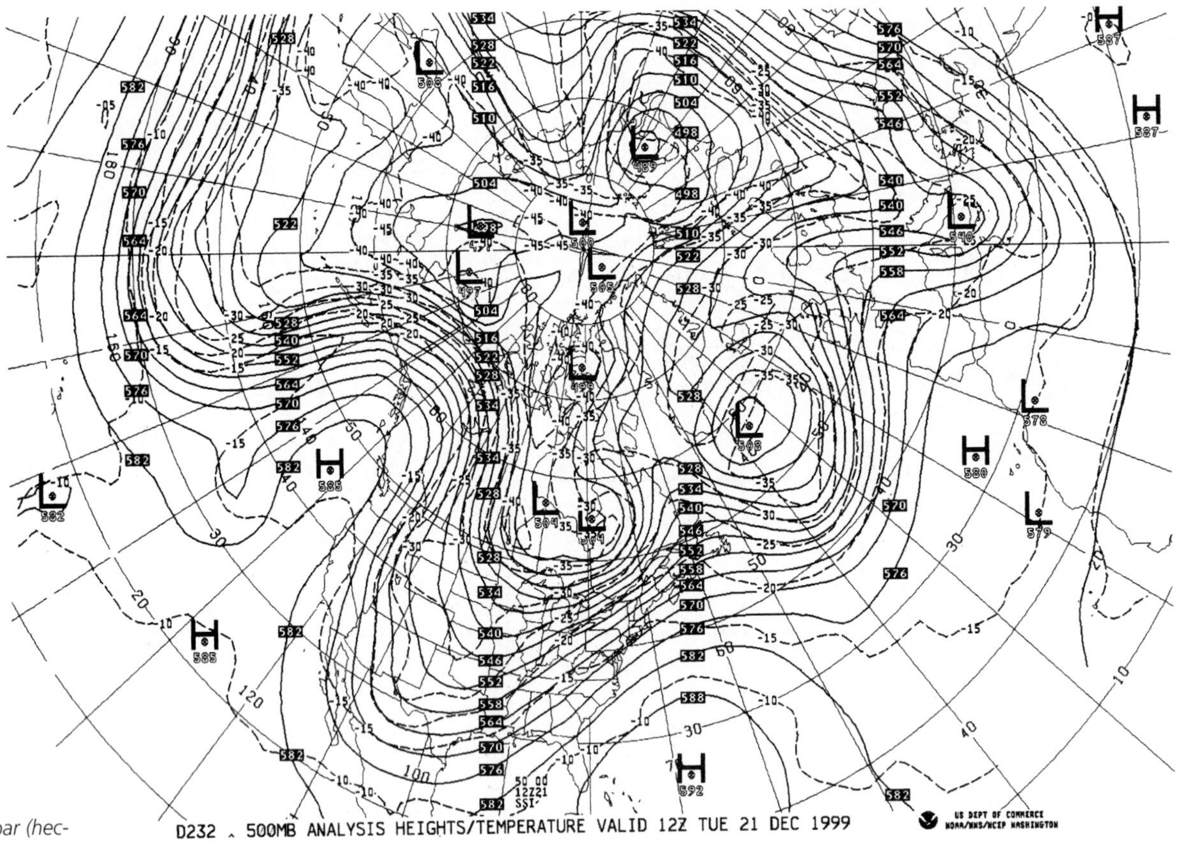

500-Millibar (hectopascal) chart for the Northern Hemisphere in December. Note how the 5,640-meter line pushes southward over the continental U.S.: we can expect a strong cold front to drive across the southern U.S. and into the Gulf of Mexico, before heading across the Atlantic to Europe.

sailors. Some of this big-picture information is directly useful to the sailor, even at this macro level. For example, if planning a round-the-world cruise, information at this level of generality will be used to determine when to be in what part of the world and when to seek a safe refuge. The cruise will be carefully planned to take advantage of trade-wind routes and to keep away from hurricanes and typhoons during the Atlantic and Pacific cyclone seasons.

However, information at this level of generality frequently is not directly useful in terms of the kind of day-to-day decisions that underlie cruising. But it can be useful in helping to analyze and make sense of local and immediate phenomena, thereby playing a vital role in day-to-day decision-making. It is now time to see how this broader understanding of weather situations can be woven into short-term cruise-planning and sailing considerations.

COASTAL CRUISING: PUTTING THEORY TO USE

In *The Weather Book*, Jack Williams, the well-known *USA Today* meteorologist, writes that a good three-day weather forecast needs a view of the weather at a hemispheric level, while a five-day forecast needs a view at the world level—this is assuming a bank of supercomputers running some of the world's most sophisticated weather-prediction software. So what can the rest of us hope to achieve with the relatively puny resources available to us? The answer is, quite a lot at times.

Let's look first at coastal cruising. Most of the time we don't really care what the weather will be in three or five days. All we are interested in is today and maybe tomorrow, and then it's back to work the day after! Mostly what we want to know is the direction from which the wind will be blowing and its strength, and the nature of the waves that it will kick up: a gale-force wind coming from astern and the seas it generates are often more comfortable than a Force 5 (17–21 knots) and the seas it generates on the nose. To a somewhat lesser extent, we will be interested in precipitation.

Coastal forecasts (on VHF radio and from other sources) typically give a fairly accurate pic-

READING SYNOPTIC CHARTS

A tremendous amount of information is condensed onto a synoptic chart. At its simplest, it shows

- Isobars (lines of common pressure) labeled with their pressure (in millibars/hectopascals), but omitting the "9" or "10"—for example, on the chart "84" means "984," whereas "08" means "1008."
- Regions of high (H) and low (L) pressure, generally labeled with the highest or lowest pressure (the full number for the pressure is given, and is underlined—e.g., on this chart, the low pressure at the south end of Hudson's Bay is "979" mb/hPa). Forecast tracks are given for the next 24 hours (the arrow pointing away from the present position of the low pressure center), with the forecast pressure in 24 hours (this time omitting the "9" or "10" in order to distinguish *forecast* pressure from *actual* pressure—e.g., the low is forecast to move to the NE, with the pressure increasing to "82" [i.e., "982"] mb/hPa). An X denotes both the position and forecast position of the low; a circled X is used for highs.

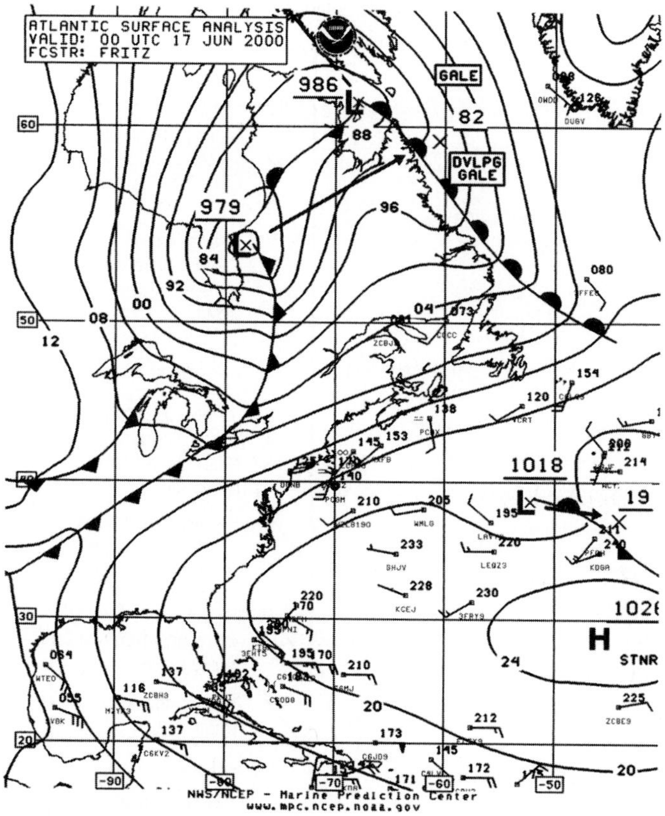

Synoptic chart. A detail from the chart on page 485, showing a low-pressure system moving to the northeast, with a warm front ahead of it, a cold front trailing it, and a gale developing in advance of the warm front. Off to the southeast, we have high pressure associated with the Bermuda high.

- Warm fronts displayed as a series of black semicircles along a line, cold fronts as a series of triangles, and occluded fronts as alternating semicircles and triangles. Stationary fronts have the relevant symbols on both sides of the line. A pair of parallel line segments (=) indicates the junction between one type of front and another (not shown on this chart).

The following abbreviations are used on NOAA products:

DISPT—DISSIPATE	STNRY—STATIONARY
WKNG—WEAKENING	RPDLY—RAPIDLY
FRMG—FORMING	MOVG—MOVING
INLD—INLAND	DVLPG—DEVELOPING
COMB—COMBINED	DCRS—DECREASING
INCRS—INCREASING	INTSFY—INTENSIFY

Beyond this, there may be information from numerous shore- and sea-based reporting stations, which use a common (internationally agreed upon) format. The only way to understand what specific numbers and symbols mean is by reference to their placement relative to a central circle. The circle itself contains symbology that denotes the extent of any cloud cover. Coming out of this circle will be an "arrow" with feathers on it. The direction in which the arrow points into the circle is the direction in which the wind is blowing. The "feathers" give the wind speed (as determined from 10 meters above the surface of the earth).

Arranged around the circle in preordained locations may be the following information:

- air temperature
- dew point
- type and ceiling of any cloud cover
- barometric pressure
- change in pressure over the past three hours
- information about recent precipitation
- information about sea states (from marine stations only)

Bits and pieces of this information are displayed on many synoptic charts, frequently in a manner that makes them somewhat difficult to read! Clearly, the more you understand the way in which this information is displayed, the more you will get from these charts.

The 500-millibar chart is generally easier to read inasmuch as it may only show the 500-millibar contours (labeled in meters, but dropping the last zero; e.g., 564 = 5,640 m), together with the height of high-pressure (H) and low-pressure (L) areas. Sometimes wind directions and speeds are also shown, as well as temperatures at this altitude (often without any minus sign; however, they are always negative at this altitude).

National Weather Service symbology and sample field station report.

Sample Weather Station Plot

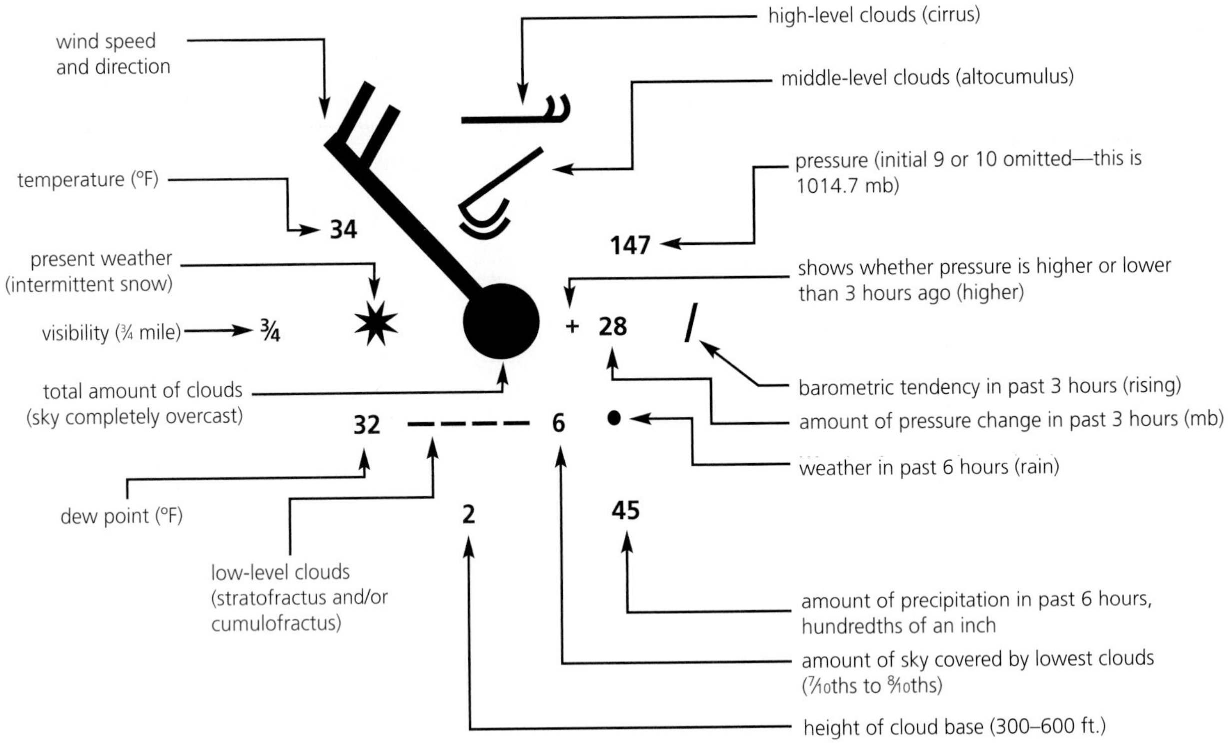

(Courtesy NOAA)

Weather Conditions

Drizzle ❜
Rain ●
Snow ✶
Single symbol (e.g. ❜) = intermittent but slight at time of observation
Double vertical (e.g. ❜❜) = intermittent and moderate at time of observation
Treble vertical (e.g. ❜❜❜) = intermittent and heavy at time of observation
Double horizontal (e.g. ❜ ❜) = continuous but slight at time of observation
Treble (e.g. ❜❜❜) = continuous and moderate at time of observation
Quadruple (e.g. ❜❜❜❜) = continuous and heavy at time of observation

Additional Symbols

▽ = showers
▽ = squall
△ = hail
∞ = haze
= lightning
= thunderstorm, but no precipitation at the station

A square bracket to the right of a symbol (e.g. ❜]) = during the past hour but not at the time of the observation.

Fog Symbols

Fog is depicted by 3 horizontal lines, (e.g. ☰)
If the fog is patchy, the top and bottom lines are intermittent, (e.g. ☰)
A vertical line to the left (e.g. |☰) = the fog is getting thicker
A vertical line to the right (e.g. ☰|) = the fog is getting thinner
Parentheses (e.g. (☰)) = fog is visible, but is not at the observation station

The various symbols can be combined into a composite picture, e.g.:

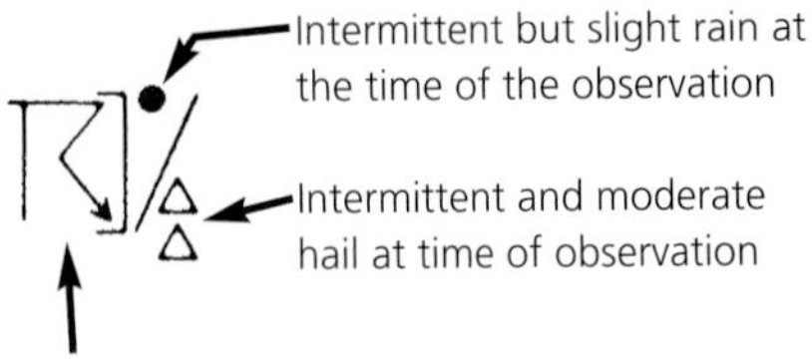

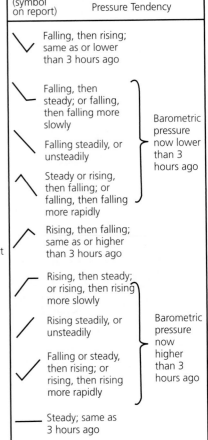

(symbol on report)	Pressure Tendency	
	Falling, then rising; same as or lower than 3 hours ago	
	Falling, then steady; or falling, then falling more slowly	Barometric pressure now lower than 3 hours ago
	Falling steadily, or unsteadily	
	Steady or rising, then falling; or falling, then falling more rapidly	
	Rising, then falling; same as or higher than 3 hours ago	
	Rising, then steady; or rising, then rising more slowly	Barometric pressure now higher than 3 hours ago
	Rising steadily, or unsteadily	
	Falling or steady, then rising; or rising, then rising more rapidly	
	Steady; same as 3 hours ago	

(symbol at center of report)	Total Amount of Cloud Cover	(symbol on report)	Amount of Sky Covered by Lowest Clouds	(symbol on report)	Height of Cloud Base in Feet (m)
	No clouds	0	No clouds	0	0–100 (0–30)
	One tenth or less, but not zero	1	One tenth or less, but not zero	1	100–300 (30–90)
	Two-tenths to three-tenths	2	Two-tenths to three-tenths	2	300–600 (90–180)
	Four-tenths	3	Four-tenths	3	600–900 (180–275)
	Five-tenths	4	Five-tenths	4	900–1900 (275–580)
	Six-tenths	5	Six-tenths	5	1900–3200 (580–975)
	Seven-tenths to eight-tenths	6	Seven-tenths to eight-tenths	6	3200–4900 (975–1,500)
	Nine-tenths or overcast with openings	7	Nine-tenths or overcast with openings	7	4900–6500 (1,500–2,000)
	Completely overcast (ten-tenths)	8	Completely overcast	8	6500–8000 (2,000–2,400)
	Sky obscured	9	Sky obscured	9	At or above 8,000 (2,400), or no clouds

(symbol on report)	**Wind Speed** knots	miles per hour
	calm	calm
	1–2	1–2
	3–7	3–8
	8–12	9–14
	13–17	15–20
	18–22	21–25
	23–27	26–31
	28–32	32–37
	33–37	38–43
	38–42	44–49
	43–47	50–54
	48–52	55–60
	53–57	61–66
	58–62	67–71
	63–67	72–77
	68–72	78–83
	73–77	84–89
	103–107	119–123

(symbol on report)	**Cloud Symbols**
	Cu of fair weather, little vertical development and seemingly flattened
	Cu of considerable development, generally towering, with or without other Cu or Sc, bases all at same level
	Cb with tops lacking clear-cut outlines, but distinctively not cirriform or anvil-shaped; with or without Cu, Sc, or St
	Sc formed by spreading out of Cu; Cu often present also
	Sc not formed by spreading out of Cu
	St or StFra, but no StFra of bad weather
	StFra and/or CuFra of bad weather (scud)
	Cu and Sc (not formed by spreading out of Cu) with bases at different levels
	Cb having a clearly fibrous (cirriform) top, often anvil-shaped, with or without Cu, Sc, St, or scud
	Thin As (most of cloud layer semitransparent)
	Thick As, greater part sufficiently dense to hide sun (or moon), or Ns
	Thin Ac, mostly semitransparent; cloud elements not changing much and at a single level
	Thin Ac in patches; cloud elements continually changing and/or occurring at more than one level
	Thin Ac in bands or in a layer gradually spreading over sky and usually thickening as a whole

(symbol on report)	**Cloud Symbols**
	Ac formed by the spreading out of Cu or Cb
	Double-layered Ac, or a thick layer of Ac, not increasing; or Ac with As and/or Ns
	Ac in the form of Cu-shaped tufts or Ac with turrets
	Ac of chaotic sky, usually at different levels, patches of dense Ci are usually present also
	Filaments of Ci or "mares tails" scattered and not increasing
	Dense Ci in patches or twisted sheaves, usually not increasing, sometimes like remains of Cb; or towers or tufts
	Dense Ci, often anvil-shaped, derived from or associated with Cb
	Ci, often hook-shaped, gradually spreading over the sky and usually thickening as a whole
	Ci and Cs, often in converging bands, or Cs alone; generally overspreading and growing denser; the continuous layer not reaching 45° altitude
	Veil of Cs covering the entire sky
	Cs not increasing and not covering entire sky
	Cc alone or Cc with some Ci or Cs, but the Cc being the main cirriform cloud

Cloud Abbreviations

St—STRATUS
Fra—FRACTUS
Sc—STRATOCUMULUS
Cu—CUMULUS

Cb—CUMULONIMBUS
Ac—ALTOCUMULUS
Ns—NIMBOSTRATUS
As—ALTOSTRATUS

Ci—CIRRUS
Cs—CIRROSTRATUS
Cc—CIRROCUMULUS

ture of what to expect in terms of prevailing weather conditions for the next day or so. The problem is, those prevailing conditions are frequently overcome by local weather influences, resulting in winds and waves often at odds with the forecast. Our understanding of the basic factors that create weather can help us predict these differences.

Onshore and Offshore Winds

The most probable divergence from the forecast is likely to occur as a result of onshore and offshore winds that develop locally. The causative mechanism is the differential heating and cooling of the land and sea that takes place during the day and at night. When the sun shines over land, its heat does not penetrate far into the ground. As a result, the heat content is concentrated on the surface, which warms up quite rapidly. In contrast, when the sun shines over the ocean, the better conductivity of water—in conjunction with the movement of waves—transmits the heat to much greater depths. The surface temperature of water comes up much more slowly than that of land. Once the sun's heat source is removed (through cloud cover or at night), the land will cool down much faster than the water.

Assuming clear skies, by 0900 hours (local time), the land temperature is likely to be rising above that of the sea. The hot air rises, drawing in a surface-level breeze from seaward (a *sea breeze*). As the land continues to heat up, the breeze becomes stronger, generally peaking between 1300 and 1400 hours, and then diminishing until it dies out between 1500 and 2000 hours.

Land and sea breezes.

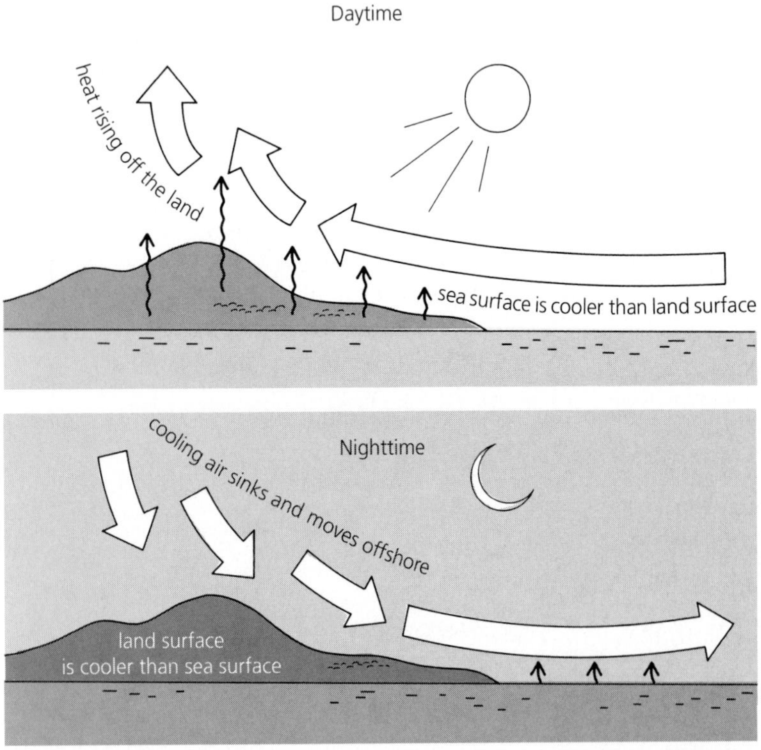

Daytime
heat rising off the land
sea surface is cooler than land surface
Nighttime
cooling air sinks and moves offshore
land surface
is cooler than sea surface

Because the sun is the driving force, this phenomenon requires more or less clear skies. Given clear skies, it is quite consistent along many coastlines. If there is high ground close to the coastline, it is likely to intensify the sea-breeze effect because of the air currents rushing aloft up the face of the high ground.

The strength of an onshore breeze is related to the strength and direction of the prevailing (forecast) wind. If the prevailing wind is blowing offshore, the sea breeze tends to cancel it out, resulting in light and variable winds; however, if the prevailing wind is onshore, the sea breeze augments it. Coupling a prevailing onshore wind with some high ground inland results in consistently strong onshore winds by midafternoon, such as the 25- to 30-knot winds commonly found in San Francisco Bay in the summer. In the Northern Hemisphere, sea breezes are likely to veer during the course of the day; in the Southern Hemisphere, they are likely to back.

At night, the cycle reverses, but offshore breezes are generally nowhere near as strong as the daytime onshore breezes. The exception is when high mountains come close to the coastline. Nighttime cooling over land causes cooler air to sink down the face of the mountains (a *katabatic* wind) and to push out to sea. By midnight, the land breeze may be strong enough to completely stall out and reverse even a 20- to 25-knot trade wind, although the effect will extend only a short distance out to sea (sometimes not much more than a few hundred yards). Onshore wave action also is considerably muted, even for swells and waves that developed over an extended fetch.

We have utilized the katabatic effect to sail comfortably against the prevailing trade winds along the northern coast of the Dominican Republic, the southern coast of Puerto Rico, the coast of Honduras, and the southeastern coast of Cuba. It really does work, although in all cases, we had to stay close to shore, which requires careful navigation. Boats that left in company with us but then headed farther offshore had a rough ride, while we motor sailed and reached in light winds and relatively smooth seas.

Even with less dramatic features ashore, the local onshore-offshore wind pattern will be modified by local topographic features. For example, in our part of Maine (northern New England), there are a number of long, narrow estuaries with

INTERNET WEATHER RESOURCES

The Internet is loaded with potentially useful weather-related Web sites—so many, in fact, that checking them out can become a real sinkhole in terms of time. Following are some of the key U.S. "official" sites that supply the raw data from which many other sites derive their information and analyses, with a few useful "private" sites (I focus on the U.S., because the information is free and has worldwide coverage). The most current addresses are listed; unfortunately, as the Internet and the way we all relate to it continuously evolve, these addresses may not remain current for long. However, many of the sites are linked, so if you can find some of them, they should lead you to the current addresses of the others (and many more).

http://weather.noaa.gov/fax/marine.shtml and *http://weather.noaa.gov/fax/nwsfax.shtml*—Synoptic charts, 500-millibar charts, and associated data and analyses for North America and the entire world, from the NOAA and the National Weather Service (NWS) (the home pages for NOAA and NWS are *www.noaa.gov/* and *www.nws.noaa.gov/*).

www.mpc.ncep.noaa.gov/—NOAA's Marine Prediction Center. Twelve-, twenty-four-, and forty-eight-hour forecasts for the oceans. This is a fabulous free service for the mariner containing an incredible wealth of data and analyses. Go to the Radiofacsimile Charts User's Guide for an explanation of the various products supplied. It is well worth spending some time at this site and familiarizing yourself with many of the products.

www.nhc.noaa.gov—NOAA's Tropical Prediction Center.

www.nws.fsu.edu/wxhwy.html—Weather information superhighway; links to weather information around the globe.

www.weather.unisys.com—A thorough source of graphical weather information (from the NWS) for the United States, including satellite pictures and analysis, and a ten-day 500-millibar forecast.

http://fermi.jhuapl.edu/—Satellite images of sea-surface temperatures, especially the Gulf Stream.

www.nws.fsu.edu/buoy and *http://seabord.ndbc.noaa.gov*—Near real-time weather data from offshore buoys, primarily around the coast of the United States.

http://weather.msfc.nasa.gov—Weather satellite imagery for North America.

http://manati.wwb.noaa.gov/doc/ssmiwinds.html—Ocean surface wind speeds (but not direction).

www.fnoc.navy.mil/—Ocean weather features, including wind speed and direction, for the world.

www.nhc.noaa.gov—National Hurricane Center home page.

www.navcen.uscg.mil/—The USCG Navigation Center home page.

www.franksingleton.clara.net—A very useful explanation of the organization of the U.K.'s official weather forecasting.

www.met-office.gov.uk—The home page of the British meteorological office, with detailed forecasts for the United Kingdom and its surrounding waters, and a page of useful links to other meteorological offices around the world.

www.bbc.co.uk/weather/—The British Broadcasting Corporation (BBC) weather services home page. Click on Shipping Forecast or Inshore Waters for the United Kingdom–regional marine forecasts.

www.weathersite.com—A list of U.K. weather stations and their current weather conditions.

www.ecmwf.int—The European Center for Medium-Range forecasts. European synoptic charts for between three- and six-day forecasts.

www.marineweather.com—A commercial weather site with a great collection of free synoptic charts, satellite images, wind and current analyses, and more, collected from numerous official sources.

Various software packages are also available that automatically connect you to numerous weather-related sites, and perform some incredible analyses and enhancement of the information contained within them. I hesitate to recommend specific packages because this field changes rapidly; however, OCENS (*www.ocens.com*) is currently highly rated. Also see the Weather Forecasts sidebar on pages 506–507.

ridges of higher ground between them. Regardless of the wind and sea patterns even 10 miles down the coast, on a daily basis these estuaries significantly modify the wind and sea states more or less predictably, both within the estuaries and around the headlands between them.

A more noticeable *cape effect* occurs around coastlines with high headlands or islands with relatively high ground. The wind funnels around the headlands or tips of the islands. This is particularly evident, for example, with many of the higher islands in the West Indies (e.g., Dominica, St. Lucia, and Grenada) where the prevailing trade winds are deflected north or south so that as you emerge from the lee of an island, expecting to be on a broad reach, you

Three areas in which we have used the katabatic effect at night to make excellent progress to windward.

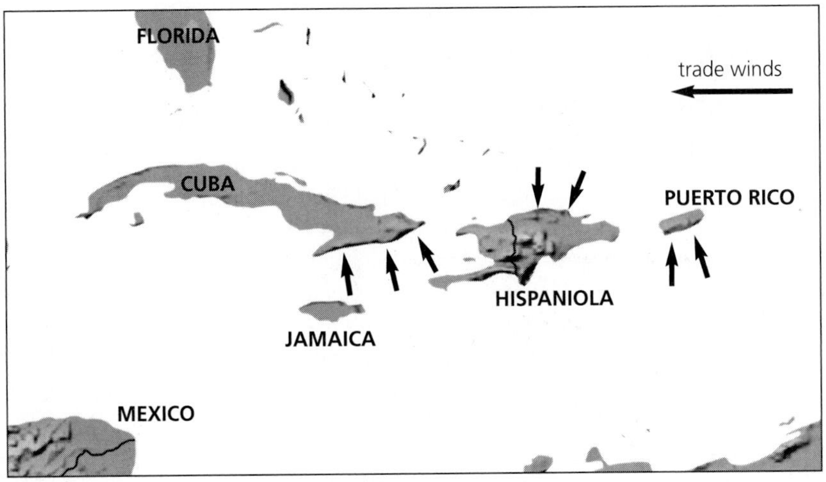

Island and cape effects in the West Indies.

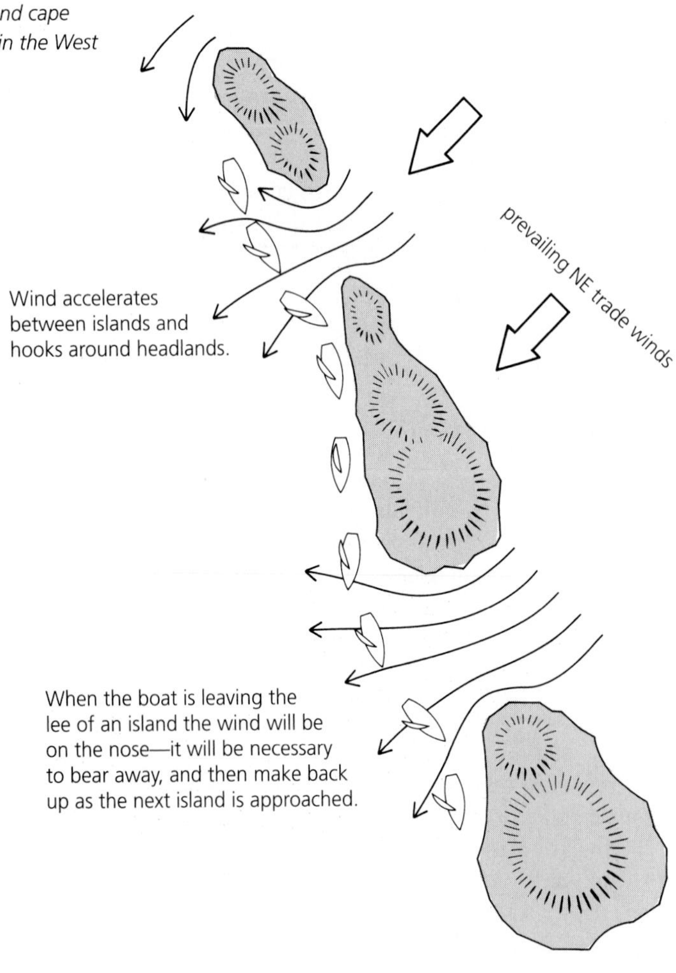

find instead that you are beating into the wind and seas. Similar cape effects are noticeable at Capes Finisterre and St. Vincent in Europe, to name but two.

prevailing NE trade winds
Wind accelerates between islands and hooks around headlands.
When the boat is leaving the lee of an island the wind will be on the nose—it will be necessary to bear away, and then make back up as the next island is approached.

The bottom line is, for coastal cruising, figuring out the daily wind pattern may be just as important as the local weather forecast! This is especially true when the forecast is for light winds, along coastlines where there is higher ground close to the coast, and when there are extended periods of sunlight. The lighter the forecast winds, the more likely it is that the local topographical features will determine the real-life winds.

Thunderstorms

Thunderstorms create their own highly localized weather systems. In many coastal areas of the world, they are closely associated with the same daily heating and cooling cycle that creates onshore and offshore breezes. Heating results in rising air. If this air has a high relative humidity, as it rises and cools, precipitation is likely.

If you think back to high school physics, you may remember something called *latent heat*, which is energy required to bring about a change of state in water. For example, when water is vaporized (and absorbed into the atmosphere), a significant amount of heat energy is needed to bring about the change of state from water to vapor. When the vapor condenses back out of a cloud to form precipitation, that heat energy is released back into the atmosphere.

This heat can reinforce rising air currents while precipitation drags down colder air from aloft. If we start with an air mass with high relative humidity in an unstable state (rising through cooler layers of air), pretty soon on a hot summer day we can get some dramatic

The progression of an afternoon thunderstorm. 1. Cumulus clouds are building some elevation and developing into cumulonimbus. Note how the top of the cloud is indicating the direction of the upper-level winds. 2. The cumulonimbus clouds are beginning to build some power. 3. A well-developed cumulonimbus thunderhead is bearing down on the anchorage. 4. This particular cloud packed enough of a punch to flip over the Tinker dinghy!

updrafts and downdrafts, with violent winds blowing both into and out of this local weather cell from any direction at speeds of up to 60 knots. This is a classic thunderstorm, a mini-weather system that is likely to have wind strengths and directions radically different than those that have been forecast for the area.

A sure sign of the presence of the kind of unstable air masses necessary to spark thunderstorm development is when fair-weather, small, puffy cumulus clouds start to thicken and increase in height. A rule-of-thumb is that as long as the vertical development of the cloud appears to be less than the height of its base above the surface of the earth, it is not likely to produce much in the way of precipitation. However, once its vertical development starts to exceed the height of its base above the surface of the earth, change is on the way.

Given the right conditions, a classic thunderhead—a towering cumulus cloud, perhaps with an *anvil top* (which points in the direction upper-level winds are blowing, thereby indicating the direction in which the thunderstorm is moving)—can blow up in a surprisingly short time and move across the water at speeds of up to 20 knots. A radar, set to its maximum range, is a great tool for spotting thunderstorms and tracking their movement. Without radar, if the storm creates lightning, its distance off (in statute miles) can be judged by timing the interval (in seconds) between lightning flashes and the accompanying thunder, then dividing by five.

Clearly, with thunderstorms it is best to stay out of the way. If it seems likely that you cannot avoid one, sail should be shortened and everything battened down on deck well ahead of time. All crew members should put on life jackets—if this really is a strong storm, visibility may go down to near zero (especially for those wearing glasses if there is driving rain), and the situation may suddenly get out of control.

It is well to remember that the force of the wind goes up with the square of its speed; that is, if the wind speed doubles, its force will quadruple. The strong gusts associated with thunderstorms can easily knock down a boat with more than a minimal sail area set, putting the mast and spreaders in the water and pitching people without harnesses over the side. There are numerous reports of partially furled roller-reefing sails being suddenly opened out—overpowering the boat—when reefing lines failed. Any roller-reefing sail should be tightly rolled up, with several wraps of the sheets around it. To keep it under control, the sheets and reefing lines need to be firmly cleated off.

All sheets and other lines need to be tidied up and secured. Too often, lines get washed overboard and then wrapped around propeller shafts when motors are cranked: I've done it myself, in the midst of a blinding, 50-knot squall! Dinghies need to be especially well secured because of the substantial amount of windage they create. If an inflatable is being towed astern, be sure to take the outboard motor off—a strong squall may render the dinghy airborne and flip it over.

Concerning lightning, the safest place for people is inside the boat—the rigging will form something of a protective cocoon. Those who have to remain on deck need to stay within the envelope provided by the rigging and out of contact with metal objects (including the steering wheel, if possible). Above all, care must be taken not to provide a potential electrical bridge between two different metal objects, such as occurs when hanging onto a shroud and touching the mast or hanging onto the backstay and the steering wheel at the same time.

Fog

Although fog occurs at some places on the high seas (notably the Grand Banks off Newfoundland), it is mostly a coastal phenomenon. It is typically caused by warm, moist air moving over colder water, causing the moisture to condense into surface-level fog. At times, the fog layer may be not much thicker than the mast height on the boat, but this is little consolation for those onboard.

There are certain areas of the world where cold water currents (e.g., the Labrador Current off the coast of Newfoundland and Maine) or cold water upwellings (e.g., occurring off the coast of California in the San Francisco region) result in a high incidence of fog, particularly in the summer months when moist tropical air invades those regions. Then there are other areas (particularly the Gulf of Mexico in the region of the Mississippi River delta) where cold water outflows from rivers, particularly in the winter months, also create a high incidence of fog.

Understanding the causative factors helps in making local predictions. For example, if the jet stream plunges down over the continental United States in the winter, bringing a deep freeze to the Central Plains states, within a few days the temperature of the lower reaches of the Mississippi River will drop as the now-cold water from the central states flows south. When the jet stream moves back up north, allowing moist, tropical air to push back into the southern United States, it is a good bet that there will be surface-level fog on the lower Mississippi and out to sea.

We got caught on the Mississippi in such a situation for four days one year, with not a wisp of fog over the land and the fog sometimes no

Fog on the Mississippi River. A cold spell in the Central Plains states sent a mass of cold water down the river, causing surface-level fog in the lower reaches. One minute we could see nothing, the next we would get a clearing patch. Much of the time, the fog bank was no thicker than our mast height, but it didn't make it any less scary every time it shut down the visibility to a couple boat lengths.

higher than the upper spreaders on the boat, but thick enough on the surface of the water to reduce visibility sometimes to not much more than a boat length. If I had used my brain, I would have foreseen the situation and we would have headed out to sea without any problem using one of two alternative routes.

On occasion, the air and water conditions are such that just a small temperature change in one or the other causes a dense bank of fog to develop and roll in "out of thin air." In Maine in the summer, it is not unusual to see one of the offshore islands suddenly disappear—a sure sign that such a fog bank is on its way. It can travel quite rapidly, turning a gorgeous sailing day into a stressful navigational exercise in a matter of minutes. When warm moist air is moving up a coast with cold-water sources, it is advised to be on top of the navigation at all times and to be ready for a sudden loss of visibility.

SMALL CRAFT ADVISORIES AND OTHER WARNINGS

Definitions:

Small Craft Advisory: Observed or forecast winds of 18 to 33 knots. Small Craft Advisories also may be issued for hazardous sea conditions or lower wind speeds that may affect small craft operations (there is no legal definition of "small craft"). They may be issued up to twelve hours ahead of anticipated conditions.

Special Marine Warning: Observed or forecast winds of 34 knots or more associated with a squall or thunderstorm and expected to last two hours or less.

Gale Warning: Observed or forecast winds of 34 to 47 knots.

Storm Warning: Observed or forecast winds of 48 knots or more.

Tropical Storm Warning: Observed or forecast winds of 34 to 63 knots.

Hurricane Warning: Observed or forecast winds of 64 knots or more associated with a hurricane.

OFFSHORE CRUISING: PUTTING THEORY TO USE

The general global weather picture is of real assistance in overall planning for long-distance cruising, both in terms of picking an appropriate time of year to make a specific passage and in selecting a route that will keep the boat out of regions of semipermanent high pressure, fast-moving (and therefore potentially dangerous) lows, or hurricanes and typhoons. Then, when it comes to specific passages, the weather forecasts can be used to look for a "window" of favorable conditions in which to begin a voyage. This may be accurate for as many as five days out to sea, which in some cases is all it takes to complete the passage.

For example, we have made several midwinter crossings of the Gulf of Mexico from Louisiana south to the Yucatan Peninsula in Mexico. We try to leave just ahead of a strong cold front so that we are out in the Gulf when the front comes through. We reef down the boat for the blow and then expect to run with favorable following winds for at least two days—if we are lucky, for four—which is just enough to complete the 600-mile passage ahead of the prevailing southeasterlies. It can be a fairly wild passage in gale-force following winds, but this is preferred over beating into a typical 15- to 20-knot southeasterly.

Similarly, when making the passage from the East Coast of the United States to Bermuda, a departure on the back of a strong cold front should guarantee several days of favorable winds as the wind steadily clocks around from the northwest to the north and then to the northeast.

In practice, most ocean passages extend well beyond the day-to-day projections of even the best forecast and, as the boat gets farther out to sea, the available forecasts become less specific and less accurate. It is possible to sign up with various weather routing services (at a cost) to get continuous detailed analyses; however, in reality, most of us have to interpret available forecasts in light of the conditions we are experiencing and the clues these conditions provide about what is coming our way.

Things to Monitor

To make the best stab at predicting the coming weather, it clearly helps to have an updated weather forecast, such as a USCG High Seas Forecast or, better yet, a Weatherfax or Internet-derived synoptic chart (i.e., a *surface analysis*, sometimes called a *mean sea level analysis* [MSLP-ANAL] or an *actual surface analysis* [ASXX]), with a 500-millibar chart, sometimes called an *actual upper-air analysis* (AUXX). A single chart is only of limited use—a succession at six- or twelve-hour intervals provides a much better picture of how the situation is unfolding. Of particular interest are areas of high and low

WEATHER FORECASTS

NOAA broadcasts continuous coastal weather forecasts for the United States on VHF radio on the following frequencies (generally accessible by pressing the "WX" button on the radio):

162.400 MHz
162.475 MHz
162.550 MHz

Continuous time signals are broadcast on SSB radio (stations WWV and WWVH) on the following frequencies:

2.5 MHz
5 MHz
10 MHz
15 MHz
20 MHz

Coastal and High Seas Forecasts are broadcast by the USCG on SSB radio at the following times, on the following frequencies:

USCG Coastal and High Seas Forecasts

TIME (UTC)	FREQUENCY (kHz)		
USCG ATLANTIC (NMN PORTSMOUTH VA)			
0330	4426	6501	8764
0500	4426	6501	8764
0930	4426	6501	8764
1130	6501	8764	13089
1600	6501	8764	13089
1730	8764	13089	17314
2200	6501	8764	13089
2330	6501	8764	13089
USCG SAN FRANCISCO (NMC)			
0430	4426	8764	13089
1030	4426	8764	13089
1630	8764	13089	17314
2230	8764	13089	17314
USCG HONOLULU (NMO, HAWAII)			
0600	6501	8764	
1200	6501	8764	
1800	8764	13089	
0000	8764	13089	
USCG MARIANAS (GUAM)			
0300	13089		
0705	2670		
0930	6501		
1530	6501		
2130	13089		
2205	2670		

When writing down a weather forecast from a radio, it is almost impossible to keep up with the flow of information (because it is in a very condensed form) without having a preprepared map of the region and a form designed around the format of the forecast. It also takes a little practice, so this should not be left until the voyage is already underway!

The BBC broadcasts regular forecasts for the coastal waters of the United Kingdom and for northern Europe on the domestic radio channel, Radio 4 (92–95 FM and 198 KHz Long Wave; the schedule of broadcasts is on the BBC's Web site at *www.bbc.co.uk/radio4*, BBC Weather). These broadcasts make *no sense at all* to someone who is not equipped with a chart of the region giving the names and boundaries of the various forecast areas. The relevant chart can be downloaded from the meteorological office Web site (*www.met-office.gov.uk*). It also is extremely difficult to keep up with the rate of information delivery without a preprepared form and some practice.

There are numerous ham-radio nets with regular weather forecasts; for a schedule, get an up-to-date radio guide. The big advantage of these nets is that it is quite possible that another boat is already seeing the weather coming your way and can give a very accurate prognosis.

And then there's Herb Hilgenberg, who runs a daily weather net for cruisers in the Atlantic and Caribbean. He broadcasts on 12359 kHz at 2000 UTC every day (boat log-in starts at 1930 UTC), crafting local forecasts for any boat that cares to log in. It's best to log in a day or two before departing on a voyage (his call sign is *South Bound II*) or e-mail him at *hehilgen@aol.com*. Herb's service is free (and much valued by cruisers), but he does expect a local report from those logged in, which helps him to develop his forecast.

Weatherfax can be picked up with a stand-alone dedicated unit, many of which can be set to automatically download and print out the faxes, or via an SSB radio and laptop computer, using one of a number of software packages and a *demodulator*, which connects the external speaker or headphone socket of an SSB radio to a spare serial port on the computer. Some stand-alone Weatherfax machines use thermal paper and others use plain paper—the thermal-paper machines are generally cheaper up front, but the paper is more expensive to buy, harder to come by in many parts of the world, and the image fades with time and in direct sunlight.

Of the software packages for use with an SSB, the cruiser's favorite appears to be the Coretex system (see the sidebar on page 501 for its Web site address). Downloading Weatherfax information to a computer has significant advantages over a dedicated Weatherfax machine: the charts are clearer, they can be stored in memory, and the images can be edited and otherwise manipulated and enhanced, as with any other computer image.

A cheap high-frequency receiver, a demodulator, a laptop and some software, and we have the most up-to-date weather reports available.

As with a dedicated Weatherfax, an SSB, demodulator, and computer can be set up to download faxes automatically; however, the computer and SSB must be left "on," which can result in a significant power drain (as opposed to the minimal standby drain of a dedicated Weatherfax). Most cruisers prefer to turn on the radio and boot up the computer for each use—it takes just a couple of minutes to acquire a fax and shut everything down again—but you need to know the Weatherfax broadcast schedule. U.S. Weatherfax information is found at *www.mpc.ncep.noaa.gov/* (you can also download synoptic charts from this site); worldwide Weatherfax information is found at *www. hffax.de/* (privately maintained). A complete inventory of worldwide Weatherfax stations is listed at *www.nws.noaa.gov/om/marine/radiofax.htm* (with all kinds of other useful information).

Weather Routing Services—private, commercial services that provide detailed weather forecasts, at a cost, for any area of the world and that are routinely used by round-the-world ocean racers—are provided by, among others, Michael Carr (*mcarr@mitags.org*; *www. mitags.org*) and Jenifer Clark (*gulfstrm @erols.com*; see page 511), especially excellent Gulf Stream analysis, with predictions of warm and cold eddies.

pressure, the associated winds, and what direction and at what speed the highs and lows are moving. The meteorological office has its own projections marked on *mean sea level prognosis* charts (also called *forecast surface* [FSXX] charts) and *forecast upper-air* (FUXX) charts, which project the situation twelve, twenty-four, and thirty-six hours ahead, and sometimes longer.

To plug this information into the local picture, we need to add our own barometer readings, which should ideally be logged every hour, but certainly at least every three hours. What is of importance is not so much any specific reading, but rather the *rate of change* from one reading to another. Forecasters use the following terminology to describe the rate of change over a *three-hour period*:

Less than 0.1 mb change	*stable*
0.1 to 1.5 mb change	*rising* or *falling* (depending on the direction of change) *slowly*
1.6 to 3.5 mb change	*rising* or *falling*
3.6 to 6.0 mb change	*rising* or *falling* *quickly*
more than 6 mb change	*rising* or *falling* *very rapidly*

We can use something known as Buys Ballot's Law to determine the direction in which the center of any low pressure lies. To do this, we stand with our back to the wind. In the Northern Hemisphere, the low pressure is on our left; in the Southern Hemisphere, it is on our right.

In the log, we should also be recording the (true) wind speed and direction. We then add visual information—specifically, the extent of the cloud cover, what kinds of clouds we are seeing, the sequence in which we are seeing them, whether they are increasing or decreasing, and whether they are lowering or lifting. A final piece is the existence of any swell from a direction different from the local seas and the time (in seconds) between the swells.

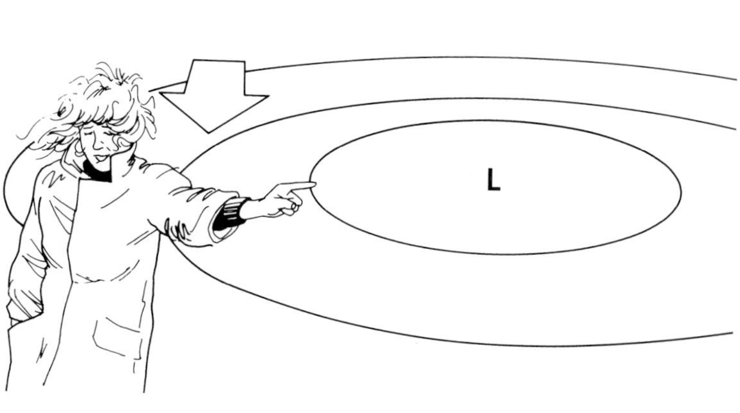

Buys Ballot's Law in the Northern Hemisphere. With your back to the wind, the low pressure lies on your left-hand side (right-hand side in the Southern Hemisphere).

MARINE WEATHERFAX BROADCASTS

Note: For a comprehensive worldwide schedule, refer to the Web site cited on page 507 or the Admiralty List of Radio Signals (ALRS)—available from the British Admiralty—or a similar publication.

When using the upper sideband (USB) mode on an SSB radio, first tune the frequency 1.9 kHz below those listed; when using the lower sideband (LSB) mode, first tune 1.9 kHz above those listed, and then fine-tune for the best reception (USB and LSB are explained in chapter 12).

The various Weatherfax stations broadcast different products (e.g., a surface-level synoptic chart or a 500-millibar chart) at different times of the day. Unfortunately, the schedules tend to change, which is why I haven't included them, and many sites may be shut down in the near future.

Selected Worldwide Weatherfax Broadcasts

CITY	ID	COUNTRY	FREQUENCIES					LATITUDE	LONGITUDE
Auckland	ZKLF	New Zealand	5807.6	9458.6	13550.1	16340.1		36.52S	174.46E
Boston	NMF	U.S.	3240.1	6340.5	7528.1	9110.0	12750.0	42.20N	071.00W
Bracknell	GFA	U.K.	2618.5	4610.0	8040.0	14436.0	18261.0	51.20N	000.42W
Buenos Aires	LRO	Argentina	5185.0	10720.0	18093.0			36.30S	060.00W
Canberra	AXM	Australia	2628.0	5100.0	11030.0	13920.0	20469.0	35.15S	149.08E
Copenhagen	OXT	Denmark	5850.0	9360.0	13855.0	17510.0		55.41N	012.34E
Darwin	AXI	Australia	5755.0	7535.0	10555.0	15615.0	18060.0	12.20S	130.50E
Delhi	ATA	India	4993.5	7403.0	14842.0	18227.0		28.38N	077.17E
Halifax, NS	CFH	Canada	122.5	4271.0	6496.4	10536.0	13510.0	44.38N	063.35W
Hamburg	DDH	Germany	3855.0	7880.0	13882.5			53.32N	009.59E
Honolulu	KVM70	U.S.	9982.5	11090.0	16135.0	2331.5		21.20N	157.55W
Jeddah	HZN	Saudi Arabia	3560.0	5452.0	10294.0			21.29N	039.16E
Kodiak	NOJ	U.S.	4298.0	8459.0				57.30N	152.45W
Moscow	RVO	Russia	2815.0	3875.0	5355.0	7750.0	10980.0	55.45N	037.35E
New Orleans	NMG	U.S.	4317.9	8503.9	12789.9				
Northwood	GYA	U.K.	2374.0 12844.5	3652.0 16912.0	4307.0	6446.0	8331.5	51.32N	000.25W
Pearl Harbor	NPM	U.S.	4855.0 21837.0	6453.0	8494.0	9090.0	9396.0	21.20N	158.00W
Pretoria	ZRO	South Africa	4014.0	7508.0	13538.0	18238.0		25.44S	028.12E
Rio de Janeiro	PWZ	Brazil			12662.0	17142.0		23.00S	043.12W
Rome	IMB	Italy	4777.5	8146.6	13597.4			41.54N	012.30E
San Francisco	NMC	U.S.	4346.0	8682.0	12730.0	17151.2	22527.0	37.35N	122.30W
Saint-Denis	HXP	Réunion	8176.0	16335.0				20.50S	055.30E
Tokyo (1)	JMB	Japan	3622.5 18220.0	4902.0 23522.9	7305.0	9970.0	13597.0	35.45N	139.45E
Tokyo (2)	JMJ	Japan	3365.0	5405.0	9438.0	14692.5	18441.2	35.45N	139.45E
USN Norfolk	NAM	U.S.	3357.0	8080.0	10865.0	15959.0	20015.0	36.52N	076.15W
Valparaiso	CBV	Chile	4228.0	8677.0	17146.4			33.02S	071.40W

Sample Weatherfax Schedule

TIME	CHART	VALID	I.O.C.
03:41	MSLP ANALYSIS FOR 00:00	00:00	288
04:31	500 HPA CONTOUR/TT (1000/500HPA) ANALYSIS FOR 00:00	00:00	288
04:40	MSLP 24-HOUR FORECAST (VT 00:00)	00:00	288
08:06	MSLP 48-HOUR FORECAST (DT 00:00)	00:00	288
08:12	MSLP 72-HOUR FORECAST (DT 00:00)	00:00	576
08:18	NORTHERN HEMISPHERE SURFACE ANALYSIS	00:00	288
09:29	SEA/SWELL ANALYSIS FOR 00:00	00:00	288
09:35	SEA/SWELL 24-HOUR FORECAST	00:00	288
09:41	MSLP ANALYSIS FOR 06:00	06:00	288
10:00	500 HPA CONTOUR/TT (1000/500HPA) T+24 FORECAST	00:00	288
10:10	SEA/SWELL 48-HOUR FORECAST	00:00	288
10:31	NORTH ATLANTIC INFERENCE	00:00	576
10:42	MSLP 24-HOUR FORECAST (VT 06:00)	06:00	288
14:12	UK SEA TEMPERATURE ANALYSIS	00:00	288

TIME	CHART	VALID	I.O.C.
15:41	MSLP ANALYSIS FOR 12:00	12:00	288
16:02	NORTH ATLANTIC SEA ICE CHART	00:00	576
16:22	SCHEDULE: MARINE PRODUCTS	05:00	576
16:30	GENERAL NOTICES (if any)		576
16:41	MSLP 24-HOUR FORECAST T+24 (VT 12:00)	12:00	288
17:08	500 HPA CONTOUR/TT (1000/500HPA) ANALYSIS FOR 12:00	12:00	288
20:12	SEA/SWELL ANALYSIS FOR 12:00	12:00	288
20:18	SEA/SWELL 24-HOUR FORECAST	12:00	288
21:41	MSLP ANALYSIS FOR 18:00	18:00	288
21:52	SEA/SWELL 48-HOUR FORECAST	12:00	288
22:22	MSLP 48-HOUR FORECAST (DT 12:00)	12:00	288
22:30	MSLP 72-HOUR FORECAST (DT 12:00)	12:00	288
22:41	MSLP 24-HOUR FORECAST (VT 18:00)	18:00	288
23:33	MSLP 96-HOUR FORECAST (DT 12:00)	12:00	288
23:40	MSLP 120-HOUR FORECAST(DT 12:00)	12:00	288

Signs of Change

What can this information tell us? Concerning barometer readings, the following generalizations can be made. If, over a three-hour period, the rate of change is:

1 mb/hour, a Force 6 is likely
2 mb/hour, a Force 7 or 8 is likely
3 mb/hour, greater than a Force 8 is likely
5 mb/hour, a storm is likely
10 mb/hour, extreme conditions are likely

In general, the lower the pressure falls, the worse the weather is, and the faster it falls, the stronger are the winds. However, it is also possible to get strong winds with little change in pressure in a stationary front and weak winds with rapid pressure changes in a fast-moving front. This relationship between changes in barometric pressure and wind strength is by latitude. The lower the latitude (i.e., the closer to the equator), the more wind that will be created by a given pressure change.

When Weatherfax charts show a significant pressure change approaching your location, you can use the barometer as a kind of alarm clock by marking a target pressure associated with the advancing weather system on its face, or noting it in the logbook. When the barometer reaches this pressure, you have your warning of the system's imminent arrival.

The skies should be constantly scanned for clues indicating a change in the weather. If we have clear skies or fair-weather cumulus but with cirrus clouds moving in at high levels, we should attempt to gauge the direction of movement of the cirrus relative to the surface winds or low-level clouds. These cirrus clouds are up at the level of the jet stream and, therefore, can provide a clue about what is happening in the higher atmosphere.

Alan Watts, an English meteorologist, developed what he calls his "crossed-winds rule." If, in the Northern Hemisphere, with our back to the surface wind, the high-level winds are moving from left to right, a worsening of the weather is on its way. If, on the other hand, the high-level clouds are moving from right to left, the weather will probably improve. In the Southern Hemisphere, these wind directions are reversed. The closer the angle between the lower- and upper-level winds approaches 90 degrees, the more likely is the change. However, if the upper-level winds are moving in either the same or the opposite direction as the lower-level winds, little change in the weather is likely.

When high-level cirrus clouds start to thicken and lower and the classic cloud sequence preceding a warm front begins, it is fair to assume a depression is on its way and the weather will worsen. Very often, the time it takes

Alan Watt's "crossed-winds rule."

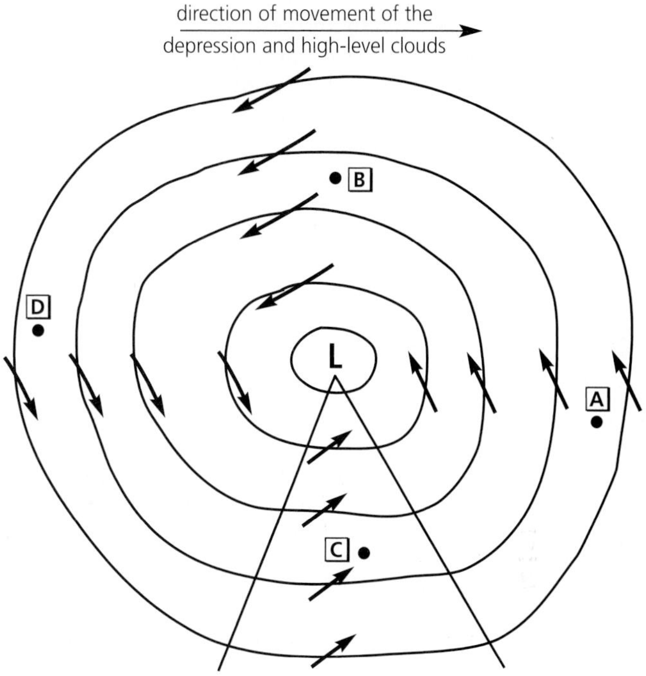

Observer (with back to the wind) at:
A. The high-level clouds are moving left to right—the weather will deteriorate.
B–C. The high-level clouds are moving in the same direction as, or directly against, the surface winds—little change for the time being, especially at "B" (winds moving in opposite directions). However, note at "C" (winds in same direction) the approaching cold front.
D. The high-level winds are moving right to left—the weather will improve.

The cumulus clouds are moving in the opposite direction to the cirrus clouds (the upper-level winds). There will be little change for the time being.

from the first appearance of cirrus clouds to the sun being blotted out is about the same as that from the sun being blotted out to the first rain. The slower the depression moves in, the longer the bad weather is likely to last. The wind generally rises ahead of the rain, but if the rain comes first, the wind is likely to be strong. With all frontal systems, gusts anywhere from 30 to 70 percent above the "steady-state" (forecast) winds are likely. Bearing in mind that a doubling of the wind speed quadruples the force, it is clear that these gusts are a major factor in the situation.

We can use Buys Ballot's Law to determine the center of a depression and the 500-millibar charts to determine its likely track to get a sense of whether it will pass to the south or to the north. If we are on the equator side of the system (the side with the warm and cold fronts, and the most "active" weather) in either the Northern or Southern Hemispheres, the forward velocity of the depression (as it travels from west to east) is added to the speed of the winds generated by the system. This results in significantly stronger winds than on the pole side of the system, where the forward velocity is subtracted from the speed of the winds generated by the system.

On the active (equator) side of the system, in the Northern Hemisphere, the wind will veer as a depression passes by, but it will back in the Southern Hemisphere. On the pole side, the wind will back in the Northern Hemisphere and veer in the Southern Hemisphere. If there is no

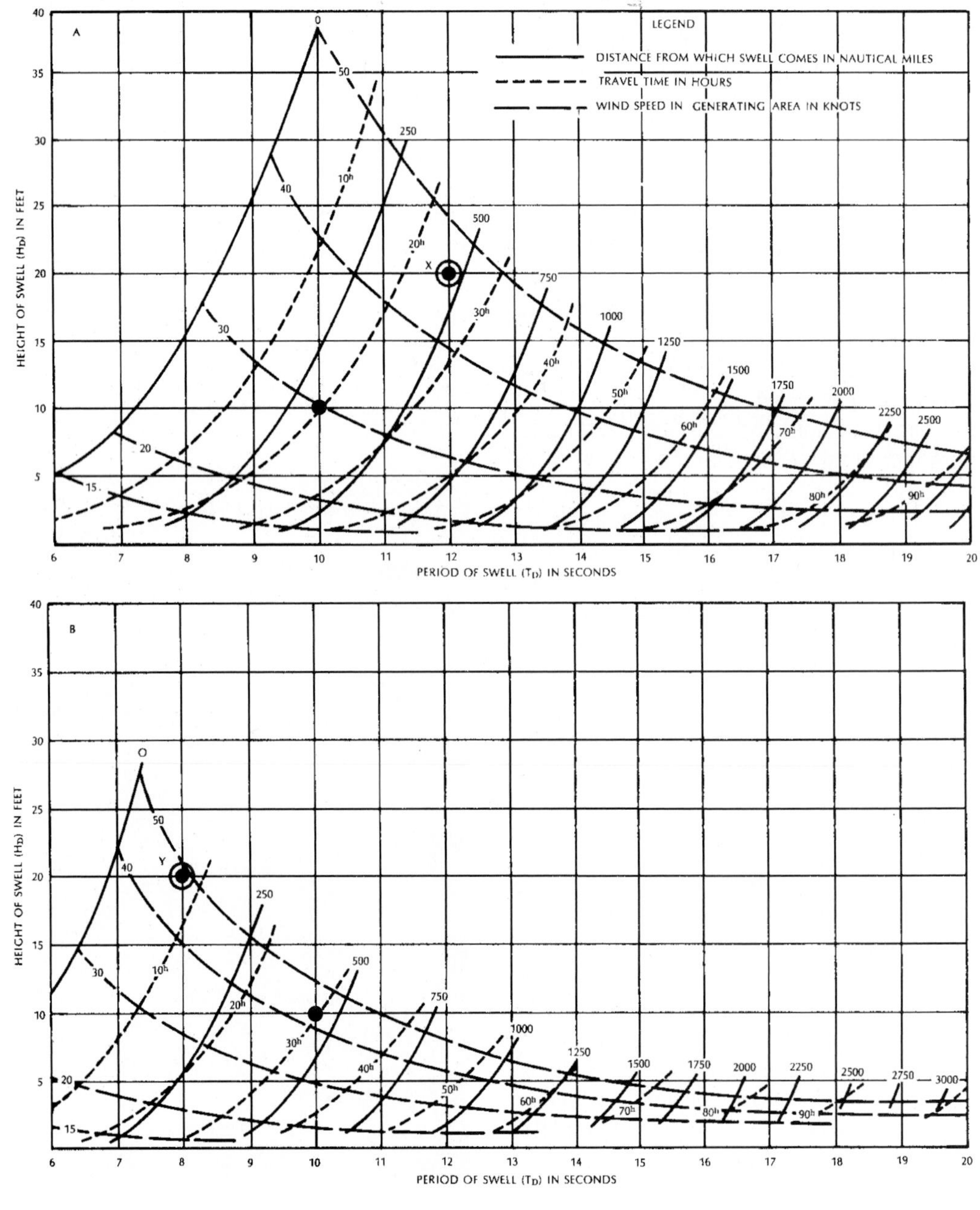

The distance a swell has traveled, the time it took, and the wind speed in the generating area, as a function of the observed height and the period of the swell. The upper graph assumes a less violent storm center closer at hand. When observed swell heights and periods fit both graphs, some intelligent guesswork will be needed to determine which is the most appropriate. (Reproduced from Kotsch, Weather for the Mariner, *courtesy Naval Institute Press)*

change in wind direction, and with a steadily falling barometer, the center of the depression is headed straight for you; no change with a steadily rising barometer, it is headed away from you.

In the open ocean, the advance of large and powerful weather systems is often foretold a day or two ahead of time by long swells that are generated by the storm and move out from its center in all directions, often traveling hundreds and even thousands of miles. The arrival of such swells at a period (interval between crests) of five to twenty seconds is a warning sign. The center of the storm is approximately in the direction from which the swells are coming. Its distance, the strength of the winds, and the time it took for the swells to reach you can be approximately determined from the graphs on the previous page (use whichever one is appropriate):

For example, in the top graph, opposite, a 20-foot swell with a twelve-second period coming from 070 True (point X): the graph tells us the storm is 440 nautical miles away with winds of 46 knots. The swells took twenty-four hours to reach us. At the time they were generated, the storm was on a bearing of 070 True (it may have moved in the twenty-four hours since then). Or, in the bottom graph, opposite, a 20-foot swell with an eight-second period coming from 135 True (point Y): the graph tells us the storm is 120 nautical miles away with winds of 47 knots. The swells took eight hours to reach us. At the time they were generated, the storm was on a bearing of 135 True (it may have moved in the eight hours since then).

The *significant height* of waves (the average height of the highest one third of the waves) that can be expected to develop in your area, given a certain wind speed blowing for a specified length of time over a given distance (fetch), can be determined from the graph below.

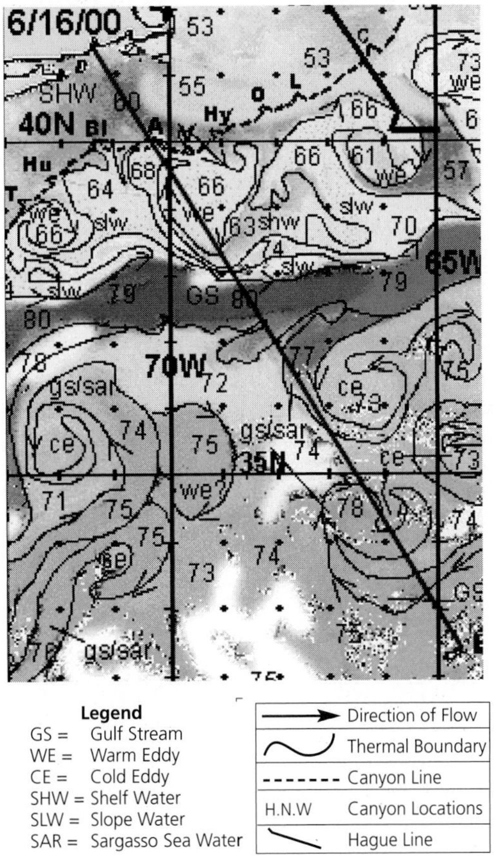

Jenifer Clark's Gulf Stream Analysis. (Courtesy Jenifer Clark)

Ocean Currents

Major ocean currents can result in significantly different local weather and sea states than those forecast. Two factors are at work here: changes in temperature and the interaction of the current with waves.

The Gulf Stream, for example, is warmer than the surrounding water as it pours up through the Gulf of Mexico and into the Atlantic. Just as air masses at different temperatures tend not to mix, so too with water masses: the boundary line between an ocean current and

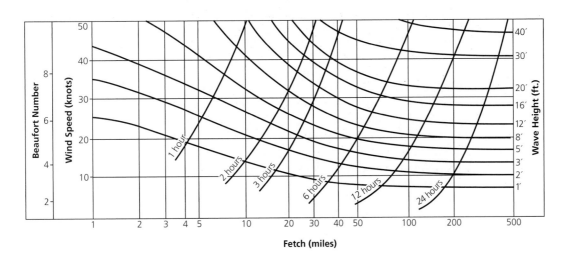

Maximum wave height as a function of fetch, wind velocity, and time. (After graph courtesy Practical Boat Owner*)*

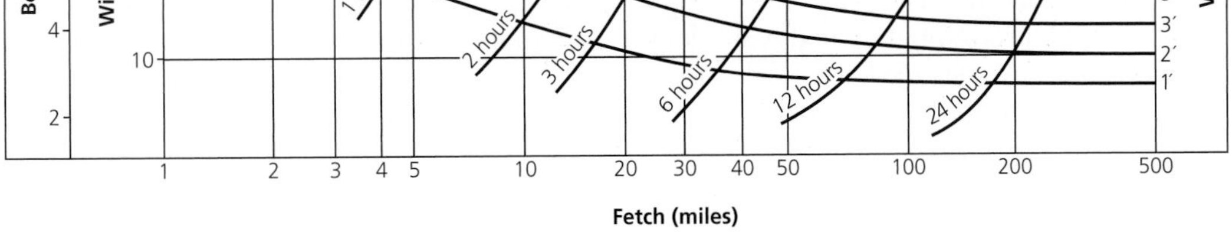

BEAUFORT SCALE

FORCE	WIND SPEED (knots)	WIND DESCRIPTION	AVERAGE WAVE HEIGHT, feet (m)	MAXIMUM WAVE HEIGHT, feet (m)	SEA CONDITIONS
0	0	calm	0 (0)	0 (0)	mirror smooth
1	1–3	light air	¼ (0.1)	¼ (0.1)	small ripples
2	4–6	light breeze	½ (0.2)	1 (0.3)	small wavelets
3	7–10	gentle breeze	2 (0.6)	3 (1.0)	large wavelets
4	11–16	moderate breeze	3 (1.0)	5 (1.5)	waves, some with whitecaps
5	17–21	fresh breeze	6 (2.0)	8 (2.5)	moderate waves, many with whitecaps
6	22–27	strong breeze	10 (3.0)	13 (4.0)	large waves with extensive whitecaps
7	28–33	near gale	14 (4.0)	18 (5.5)	seas heaping up with foam from breaking waves beginning to form streaks
8	34–40	gale	18 (5.5)	25 (7.5)	moderately high waves with edges of crests getting blown off into spindrift
9	41–47	strong gale	23 (7.0)	33 (10)	high waves with dense streaks and some breaking crests and foam reducing visibility
10	48–55	storm	29 (9)	41 (12.5)	very high waves with long, overhanging crests; sea looks white; poor visibility from foam
11	56–63	violent storm	37 (11)	53 (16)	exceptionally high waves that can obscure medium-size ships; wave edges blown into froth, sea completely covered in foam, and visibility seriously impaired
12	64–71	hurricane/typhoon	45 (14)	—	air filled with foam and spray; sea completely white; visibility very seriously impaired

Note: Wave heights are significant wave heights (the average of the highest one third of the waves), assuming open water with no current or other complicating factors. Statistically, one wave in one thousand will be almost twice as high.

the surrounding water is often quite sharp. For example, we have measured a near 30°F (approximately 16°C) change in water temperature in the winter when sailing from Gulf of Mexico water into Gulf Stream water and back out again.

These changes in surface temperature lead to the development of unstable air masses, with warm currents in particular providing a source of heat and moisture. In fact, large ocean currents are, to a significant extent, their own weather-makers, especially if the prevailing regional conditions are relatively light. It is not unusual to have a warm current's perimeter defined by a line of cumulus clouds, developing into cumulonimbus and squalls in certain conditions. Cold currents create fog.

When the prevailing regional winds kick up, they tend to override the local weather-making influences of the current. But now the direction in which the wind blows relative to the current is of key importance to the mariner. Even a moderate Force 4 (11–16 knots) blowing *against* a 2-knot or more current can produce extremely nasty, steep-sided waves. A Force 7 (28–33 knots) and stronger can create survival conditions for small boats. Again, the Gulf Stream is notorious in this respect, as is the Agulhas current off the eastern coast of South Africa.

For these reasons, it is important when in the vicinity of ocean currents to consider the implications for the weather and the sailing conditions before committing to a course that will carry you into the current. Once in it, you may wish you had chosen some other time or route! On the other hand, there is nothing like getting a 3-knot boost when a moderate wind is blowing with the current, producing leisurely swells while you knock off effortless 200-mile days.

EXTREME WEATHER SITUATIONS

Every once in a while, an extreme meteorological event strikes the sailing community to remind us that we have to be ever vigilant. The most obvious is a *hurricane* (a *typhoon* in the Pacific), which in turn can transition into a huge *extratropical storm* in higher latitudes. And then there are *rapidly intensifying lows* (RILs), which have become known as *meteorological bombs*. RILs were responsible for the havoc and loss of life during the 1979 Fastnet race, the 1998 "Queen's Birthday" storm, and the 1998 Sydney to Hobart race. Finally, there is growing recognition of the significance of *microbursts* at the local level.

Hurricanes and Typhoons

Hurricanes and typhoons are *tropical cyclones*—that is, revolving weather systems with low pressure at the center—that develop along the low-pressure region defined by the ITCZ. When the ITCZ is close to the equator, there is insufficient Coriolis effect to get a strong rotation going, so any cyclones tend to be weak: hurricanes and typhoons are unheard of in latitudes below 5 degrees. But when the ITCZ moves into higher latitudes as it migrates north and south of the equator with the seasons, there is more likelihood of a cyclone developing a stronger circulation and building into a tropical storm or hurricane (typhoon).

Meteorologists use the following classification for tropical cyclones:

tropical disturbance: winds less than 28 knots
tropical depression: winds 28 to 33 knots
tropical storm: winds 34 to 63 knots
hurricane or typhoon: winds over 63 knots

Given that the annual migration of the ITCZ tends to lag a couple of months behind that of the sun, and that the sun is over the equator on the spring and fall equinoxes, the ITCZ is close to the equator in May and November. This just about defines the hurricane/typhoon season: June to November north of the equator and November to April south of the equator. With today's technology, hurricanes and typhoons can be detected before they build to lethal strength and then tracked as they move from their birthplace into higher latitudes.

Once a system builds to a certain size and momentum, it tends to be self-sustaining as long as it remains over warm water. Crudely speaking, within the center of the system, rapidly ascending air currents create tremendous instability and torrential rain. As moisture condenses into rain, it releases vast amounts of latent heat energy, which feeds the ascending air currents. These currents suck in air from all directions, which in turn brings in more moisture, evaporated from the warm water over which the air is being drawn. The continuous supply of fresh moisture keeps the cycle going until the system moves over either colder water or land, at which time the moisture input is cut off and the system runs out of steam.

As with any other depression, the direction of circulation is counterclockwise in the Northern Hemisphere and clockwise in the

Areas in which tropical cyclones occur and the storm tracks followed by the cyclones. (From Bowditch, courtesy DMA)

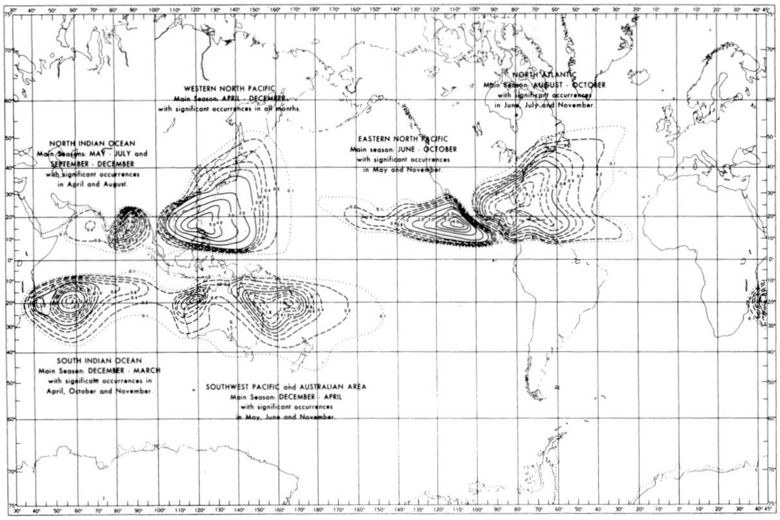

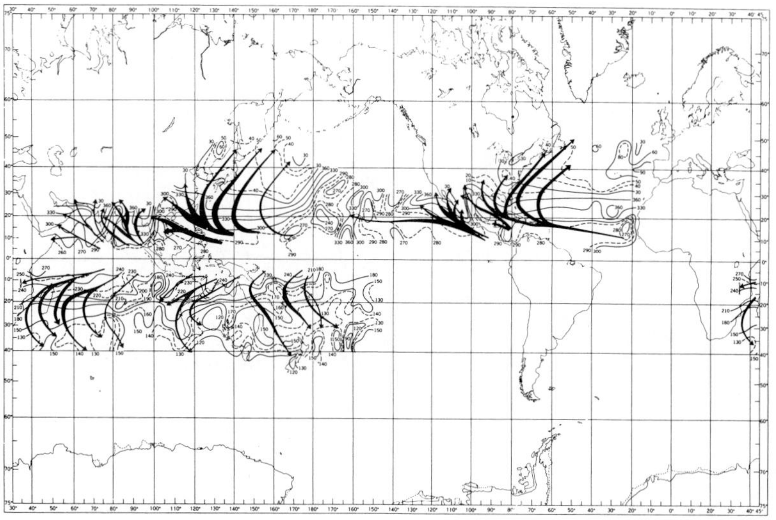

Southern Hemisphere. The sequence of cloud patterns is also similar to a depression in higher latitudes. There may be clear skies the day before a hurricane or typhoon arrives, with perhaps fair-weather, puffy cumulus clouds, giving way to cirrus, cirrostratus, altostratus, altocumulus, cumulus, and cumulonimbus clouds. Long swells generated by the storm, with a period of ten to thirty seconds, will move out from the center in all directions and may be the first indication of the approaching system. As it gets closer, the barometric pressure will start to fall rapidly down below 1,000 millibars.

Buys Ballot's Law can be used to determine the approximate center (the *eye*) of the system. A more accurate determination of the bearing to

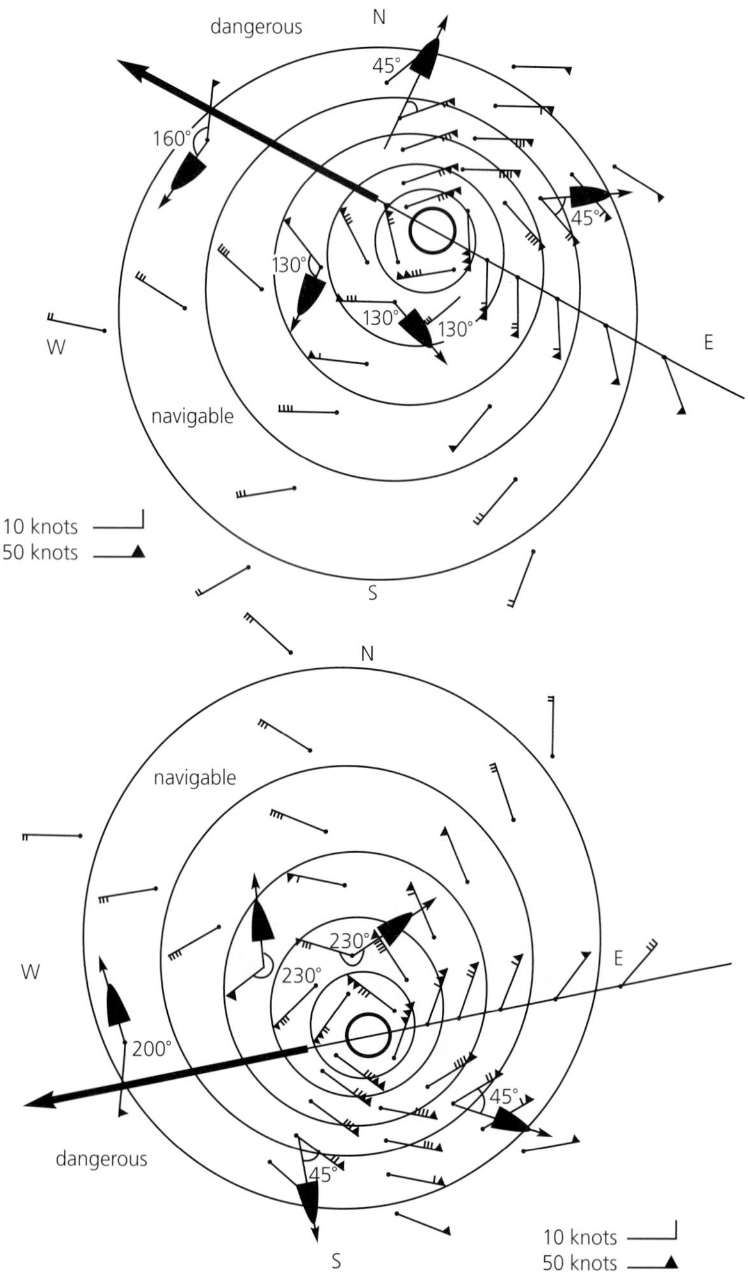

Hurricane avoidance tactics in the Northern (top) *and Southern* (bottom) *Hemispheres. (After Kotsch,* Weather for the Mariner*)*

the eye can be made by measuring the true-wind angle at the present location and then adding 115 degrees. If this produces a number greater than 360 degrees, subtract 360.

When an observer imagines himself or herself to be at the center of a hurricane or typhoon and looking in the direction of travel of the system, in the Northern Hemisphere the semicircle on the right-hand side has its wind speeds augmented by the rate of travel, and thus is known as the *dangerous semicircle*; the left-hand side has its wind speeds to some extent ameliorated by the rate of travel, and so is known as the *navigable semicircle*. In the Southern Hemisphere, the dangerous semicircle is on the left-hand side and the navigable semicircle is on the right-hand side. In addition to higher wind speeds, when a system hits land, the dangerous semicircle just ahead of the eye also experiences the highest *tide surge* (the event that does most of the damage).

In the Northern Hemisphere, if you are in the path of a hurricane/typhoon, a veering wind indicates that you are in the dangerous semicircle. As the storm gets closer, the direction from which the swells are coming will shift clockwise (e.g., swells from the east will become swells from the southeast). When facing the center of the storm (as determined by Buys Ballot's Law), it can be expected to pass from left to right. A backing wind, with the swell direction shifting counterclockwise, indicates that you are in the navigable semicircle. When facing the center of the storm, it can be expected to pass from right to left. If the wind and swell directions remain constant with a steadily falling barometer, the system is headed straight toward you; if the wind and swell directions are constant with a steadily rising barometer, the system is headed away from you.

In the Southern Hemisphere, these directions reverse: the dangerous semicircle brings backing winds and swells whose direction of travel shifts counterclockwise; when facing the center of the storm, it can be expected to pass from right to left. The navigable semicircle brings veering winds and swells whose direction of travel shifts clockwise; when facing the center of the storm, it can be expected to pass from left to right.

Given that hurricanes and typhoons typically travel at between 10 and 30 knots, cruising sailboats cannot outrun them. Given a day or two advance warning and a sense of the direction in which the system is traveling, it is possible to put some distance between yourself and the eye of the storm. Clearly, this is especially important if you are likely to get caught in the dangerous semicircle. However, forecasts of hurricane tracks typically contain errors of up to 100 miles each side of the track per day of advance warning. In other words, if a hurricane is predicted to hit a certain location in twenty-four hours, the track may be in error by 100 miles each side; if the prediction is for forty-eight hours ahead, the error may be 200 miles each side; and so on.

The basic rules of thumb are as follows:

- Get below 10 degrees latitude (e.g., Trinidad or Venezuela in the Caribbean) during hurricane season (hurricanes never develop closer to the equator than this) or stay above 35 degrees.
- If in the dangerous semicircle in the Northern Hemisphere, sail close-hauled (if this is impossible, then heave-to) on the starboard tack away from the projected track of the hurricane, making all speed possible; in the Southern Hemisphere, sail (or heave-to) on the port tack.
- If in the navigable semicircle in the Northern Hemisphere, keep the wind at 130 degrees relative to the boat's heading (i.e., broad reaching with the wind on the starboard quarter) and make all speed possible; in the Southern Hemisphere, keep the wind at 230 degrees relative (broad reaching with the wind on the port quarter).
- If directly ahead of the storm track in the Northern Hemisphere, keep the wind at 160 degrees relative to the boat's heading (i.e., run with the wind on the starboard quarter) and make all speed possible; in the Southern Hemisphere, keep the wind at 200 degrees relative (run with the wind on the port quarter).
- If directly behind the storm track, steer to increase the distance!

Sometimes a hurricane or typhoon makes the transition from tropical latitudes to higher latitudes without running out of steam, in which case it becomes known as an extratropical storm. It loses its well-defined eye and spreads out, creating strong winds ever farther away from its center, and often worsening wind and sea conditions for boats on the periphery of the system. The forward speed of an extratropical storm may accelerate to as much as 50 knots (1,200 miles a day). Hurricane Mitch, after meandering through the Caribbean and stalling out a couple of times, confounding meteorologists' predictions day after day, accelerated and moved from Honduras to the Azores, a distance of 2,400 miles, in less than three days.

For these reasons, sailors in higher latitudes should always keep a close eye on hurricanes and typhoons, and never assume that the system will follow the typical path of making landfall and dying—it may curve back out to sea, rebuild itself, and threaten huge areas of the ocean.

The high forward speed of many extratropical storms intensifies the wind speeds in the dangerous semicircle, but moderates them in the navigable semicircle. If caught ahead of one of these systems and unable to reach shelter, it is clearly desirable to be on the navigable side!

Rapidly Intensifying Lows (Meteorological Bombs)

Once in a while, the meteorological conditions are such as to cause a strong extratropical cyclone (a depression outside the tropics) to suddenly intensify, resulting in dramatic increases in wind speeds—often chaotically—with the development of extremely massive jumbled wave trains with tumultuous breaking seas. These systems are characterized by a sudden drop in barometric pressure of 1 millibar or more an hour over a period of twenty-four hours. These are the RILs, or meteorological bombs, defined previously, and they can become as powerful as a hurricane or typhoon, but without the advance warning—as such, they are perhaps even more dangerous.

Even with today's forecasting techniques, because of the speed with which these bombs can develop and their sometimes localized nature, they are often well developed before they are detected. The unlucky sailor caught in such a system is likely to be aware of it before the forecasters, which is precisely what happened with the Fastnet race, the "Queen's Birthday" storm, and the Sydney to Hobart race.

This is one reason why it is important to keep a close eye on the barometer and to regularly log its readings, especially when sailing in temperate latitudes. Any time the barometer falls a millibar or more an hour for six hours, the potential for a bomb exists.

Given the speed of bomb development, there is not much hope of getting out of the way. Instead, the boat should be battened down and prepared for an extreme blow. The general sequence of the wind and weather patterns follow that of a strong depression, although within the bomb itself there may be, effectively, a whole series of ministorms, resulting in dramatic changes in wind speeds and directions and contributing to the chaotic nature of the seas.

Microbursts

Microbursts are a highly localized phenomenon associated with strong thunderstorm activity. They can occur both with and without rain and squalls. The causative factor is the rapid cooling of air within a thunderstorm cell, leading to the cold air plunging to the ground and then spreading out at the surface of the earth. Wind gusts of up to 130 knots have been recorded. Sailors need to recognize that such things can occur. If thunderstorm activity cannot be avoided, the possibility of microbursts must be factored into the boat's preparedness equation.

HEAVY-WEATHER SAILING

Although hurricane-force winds are likely to be terrifying enough, the breaking waves that accompany them are the big problem in heavy weather. Tank testing by the Wolfson Unit at Southampton University in England has shown that when caught beam on to breaking waves:

- many modern boat designs will get rolled over by breaking waves with a height that is just 40 percent of the boat's LOA
- *no design survived breaking waves with a height of 55 percent of the boat's LOA*
- all designs could be rolled past 130 degrees by breaking waves with a height of just 35 percent of LOA

This means that if hit by the wrong wave at the wrong time, *all boats will capsize*. The essence of heavy-weather sailing, therefore, is to avoid such waves if at all possible or to ensure that the boat is in the most favorable attitude to weather the waves if they cannot be avoided.

The primary avoidance tactic is staying out of weather systems that generate gale-force and stronger winds, particularly in areas where these winds may blow against strong ocean currents, producing fearsome seas. Steve and Linda Dashew point out in *Surviving the Storm: Coastal and Offshore Tactics* that many tropical storms have tightly focused centers—sailing as little as 25 to 30 miles out of the way can mean the difference between hurricane-force and gale-force winds. Even with the larger storm centers of higher-latitude systems, aggressive avoidance tactics can make a big difference. The key to avoidance is to guesstimate the center of the weather system and its likely track, to determine which are the most likely "dangerous" and "navigable" quadrants and which, therefore, is the optimum direction in which to sail to minimize its impact. In the accompanying drawings, note that a typical extratropical depression moves in the direction opposite to a hurricane/typhoon, which reverses the "dangerous" and "navigable" semicircles, resulting in a commensurate change in avoidance tactics.

Avoidance—*driven by an understanding of how the weather system is developing locally*—should be the name of the game until the breaking seas threaten a knockdown or rollover, at which point the focus shifts to dealing with them.

Entire books have been written on the subject of how to handle these seas. The best I can do herein is summarize the recognized techniques, bearing in mind that very few of us ever get into these situations. With a little luck, none of what follows will ever be needed.

Being Prepared

The first essential in coping with heavy weather is to be prepared. This means, among other things, having a well-found boat (see part 1) and a suitable sail inventory. On many cruising sloops, the sail inventory consists of a single roller-reefing headsail and a mainsail. In this case, both sails must be built strongly enough so that when heavily reefed, they can stand up to at least gale-force conditions (Force 8 on the Beaufort scale; 34 to 40 knots). The mainsail will need three reef points to bring it down to a suitable size. On a cutter, the staysail is the heavy-weather headsail and must be built appropriately.

Personally, I don't like all the reefing lines needed to put three reefs in a mainsail and, in any case, I believe an offshore cruising boat should have a purpose-built trysail—a small, heavily built sail that is set in place of the main. A trysail can be set on the same sail track as the main; however, to do so, the mainsail must be removed, which is the last thing you want to be doing in the middle of a howling gale. Consequently, I believe the trysail should be provided a separate sail track. If the track is brought down close to deck level, the sail can be put on well before it is required and then stowed in its bag at the base of the track until needed.

At the time of deployment, a trysail is hoisted with the mainsail halyard or a spare halyard. The trysail should have a long enough pendant to enable it to be hoisted above the headboard of the furled mainsail so that it does not foul the main at any time. A trysail is flown *loose-footed* (not attached to the boom), with twin sheet leads (as with a headsail) led through appropriately placed snatch blocks on the rail well aft (the necessary attachment points need to be available), and then run to the cockpit winches. Ideally, the topping lift and vang (and lazyjacks, if fitted) arrangement will be such that the aft end of the boom can be lowered to the deck and lashed off. A well-reefed headsail—or, better yet, a reefed staysail—with a trysail makes a balanced sail combination that can be flown in most conditions.

As the wind kicks up, everything on deck needs to be firmly lashed down. In a worst-case scenario, the lashings have to stand up to solid water sweeping over the boat. A boat with all kinds of jerricans and other "stuff" on deck is inherently an accident waiting to happen—hopefully all these things have a secure "home" in some locker. Windage should be reduced as much as possible; for example, by taking down roller-reefing sails and mast-mounted downwind and spinnaker poles. If the boat has running backstays, they should be tightly set up.

The anchor deck (navel) pipe must be plugged (this is frequently overlooked, resulting in large amounts of water below decks), ventilators removed and plugged, hatches dogged down, and storm windows fitted (if necessary and if available).

Cockpit lockers and companionway dropboards must be secured. If they are not already in place, jacklines should be rigged and life jackets and harnesses broken out. All loose gear needs to be stowed in secure lockers, particularly winch handles—if the boat gets knocked down and they go overboard, it will be extremely difficult to work the sheets—and the handle for the manual bilge pump, which should be tied to the boat in some way. Make sure that gear in cockpit lockers cannot foul the steering system; the emergency tiller should be accessible.

Down below, all loose gear needs to be stowed. Lockers that do not have secure catches

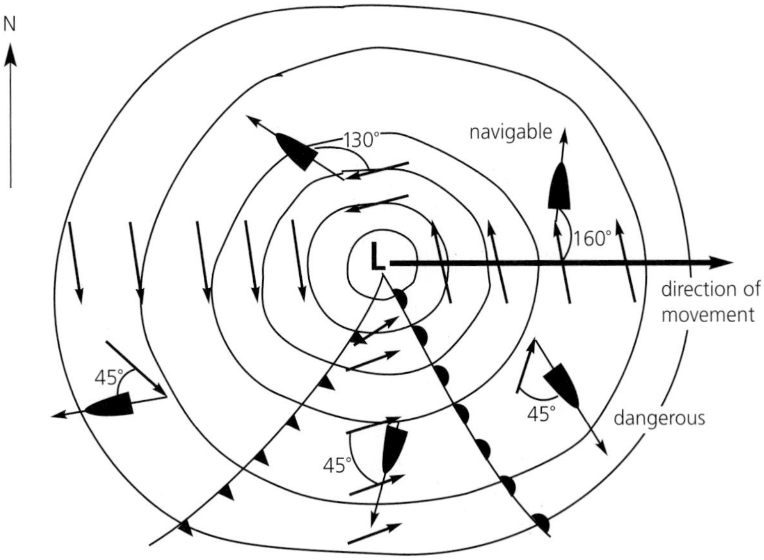

Storm avoidance tactics with a typical easterly moving depression in the Northern Hemisphere. The "dangerous" quadrant, where the forward speed reinforces the wind speed, is on the southern side of the track; the "navigable," where forward speed decreases the wind speed, in on the northern side of the track. 1. If directly in the path of the system, keep the wind at 160° relative to the boat's heading. 2. If in the dangerous quadrant, sail close-hauled, or heave-to if this is impossible, on the starboard tack. 3. If in the navigable quadrant, keep the wind at 130° relative to the boat's heading.

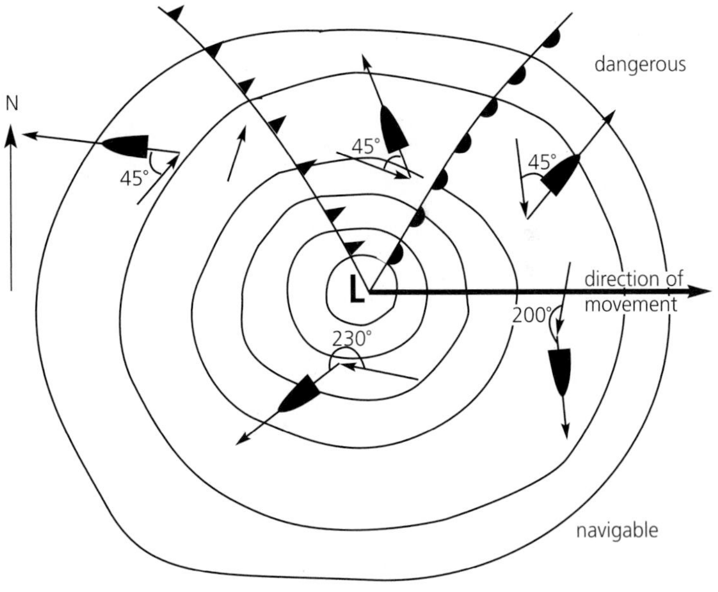

Storm avoidance tactics with a typical easterly moving depression in the Southern Hemisphere. 1. If directly in the path of the system, keep the wind at 200° relative to the boat's heading (i.e., on the port quarter). 2. If in the dangerous quadrant, sail close-hauled, or heave-to if this is impossible, on the port tack. 3. If in the navigable quadrant, keep the wind at 230° relative to the boat's heading (i.e., abaft the port beam).

should be taped shut (duct tape works well). It pays to eat a meal while it is still relatively calm and then to prepare additional food and snacks before shutting down the galley and securing the stove. If the crew is prone to seasickness, it's a good idea to take a preventative pill. If necessary, the batteries should be charged. The navigation lights should be checked and the bilges pumped. Lee cloths should be rigged. On many boats, it is advisable to close toilet and sink seacocks. Appropriate clothing should be put on. Damage-control materials and tools should be close at hand with life jackets and the abandon-ship bag.

Finally, a fix should be plotted and the chart checked with two goals in mind:

- ensuring that there is sufficient sea room to ride out whatever is coming, remembering that the boat may make a considerable amount of leeway or be forced to run off before the gale
- looking for potential safe havens in case they are needed

In general, if there is any doubt about the ability to make a safe haven before the onset of bad weather, it is best to stay at sea, concentrating on ensuring adequate sea room. One or more of the following tactics should then see the boat and crew through the storm.

Heaving-to.

Heaving-To

Heaving-to is the traditional response to heavy weather. By the time it becomes necessary, there are generally a couple of reefs in the main and the headsail (jib) is also well reefed. In the case of a cutter, the jib or genoa will have been taken down or furled and replaced by the staysail, which may in its turn be reefed. A boat should never be heaved-to with an overlapping headsail—it will soon be torn to pieces on the spreaders. If the boat has a trysail, it may have been set in place of the reefed main.

With this kind of sail plan, heaving-to is simplicity itself in principle. The boat is tacked but without releasing the jib or staysail sheet. On the new tack, the mainsail (or trysail) drives the boat up to windward, while the backed jib or staysail knocks the bow off the wind. The idea is to establish a balance in which the boat lies about 45 to 50 degrees off the wind, making minimal forward motion and not much leeway. On traditional long-keeled boats, the desired effect is almost always achieved by lashing the tiller to leeward or the wheel to windward, so that the rudder is turning the boat into the wind.

On many modern boats, it may take a certain amount of experimentation to find a sail and rudder combination that will cause the boat to heave-to effectively. On some, particularly those with minimal fin keels and spade rudders, it is simply not possible—other heavy-weather tactics must be adopted (although taking down roller-reefed sails may reduce the windage up forward to the point at which the boat will heave-to). The boat's ability to heave-to should be determined by testing different sail and rudder combinations in 25- to 30-knot winds rather than waiting for a full-blown crisis.

If a boat can be made to heave-to reliably, it is quite amazing the difference it makes to onboard comfort. A boat that, moments before, was crashing into and off waves will settle down into gently bucking and rolling. Down below, with the noise of the gale outside muted, the crew can relax and rest while they wait for the gale to blow itself out. Many cruisers on a rough passage heave-to from time to time—even when not strictly necessary—just to have a meal in peace or to get a little rest.

In the fifth edition of Adlard Coles' renowned *Heavy Weather Sailing*, Peter Bruce concludes: "For many non-extreme yachts in heavy weather, heaving-to should be the preferred primary tactic, but skippers should be fully prepared to employ other tactics if the time comes when lying hove-to is not sustainable." In particular, heaving-to is a completely passive form of storm management that makes it impossible to actively maneuver around threatening waves.

Forereaching

Forereaching is what might be termed an "actively managed" form of heaving-to. It is most commonly used on modern boats that will not heave-to reliably. When forereaching, sufficient sail area and speed is maintained to provide minimal steerageway. The helmsperson heads up into the wind as each passing wave crest comes by, thereby minimizing the potential for getting rolled, and then falls off in the wave troughs. *The trick is to build up enough steerageway in the troughs to ensure that the boat never stalls or gets set aback on the wave crests.* If it should get set aback, it may fall off broadside to the waves, with the risk of being rolled.

There are numerous instances where the tactic of forereaching has safely brought boats through extreme conditions (e.g., the 1998 Sydney to Hobart race). This tactic seems to be particularly applicable to lightweight, fin-keel, and spade-rudder designs that sail well to windward with a high degree of maneuverability. It may prove advantageous to run the engine and use it to help maintain steerageway, but only after making sure that there are no lines trailing overboard and that none are in a position to come loose and get washed overboard in the future.

The one major disadvantage to forereaching is that it requires constant attention to the helm, which is extremely tiring—this is in contrast to heaving-to, which requires no one on the helm. Although forereaching has almost certainly saved boats and lives on the racing circuit, it is not a suitable tactic for short-handed crews for any length of time.

Lying Ahull

In the past, lying ahull was commonly adopted as an alternative to heaving-to or forereaching. The sails were taken down and stowed, everything on deck lashed down (including the helm), and the boat left to its own devices. Typically, a boat will lie near broadside to the waves or maybe with its head blown off downwind to some extent. In theory, with all the sails off, the motion should be almost intolerable; however, in reality, many practitioners have described lying ahull as being reasonably comfortable.

The big problem is that if a boat is caught lying ahull in large breaking seas, it runs a great risk of being rolled. As noted, the Wolfson research has shown that most hull shapes will get rolled by breaking waves whose height is 40 percent of the length of the boat. No hull will resist getting rolled once the breaking-wave height is 55 percent of the length of the boat. In *Heavy Weather Sailing*, Andrew Claughton, who conducted the research, wrote: "After our tests and calculations examining all these different design features, one must admit to a sense of disappointment that no combination of hull form or ballasting arrangement offered a substantial improvement in capsize resistance." In other words, no matter how resistant to capsize a boat may be, once the breaking waves get to a certain size, the boat is going to roll if it gets caught broadside to such a wave. Larger boats are inherently safer in these conditions simply because it takes bigger seas to roll them.

When a boat gets rolled, the mast generally gets torn off, which reduces the boat's stability and makes further rollings more likely (in addition to which, the motion is now almost intolerable). Lying ahull in extreme conditions is a tactic that has few advocates in this day and age.

Reefed down in heavy weather. The next step is heaving-to. (Courtesy Patrick Roach)

Running Off

Once the situation has deteriorated to the point where heaving-to courts the risk of being rolled and forereaching has been ruled out, it is often preferable to run off before the seas. The apparent wind speed is lessened, the motion is more comfortable, and the stern of the boat presents a relatively small target for advancing waves, although those that do break over the back of

Right: *Trailing a drogue. (Courtesy Para-Tech Engineering)* Below: *Trailing drogues.*

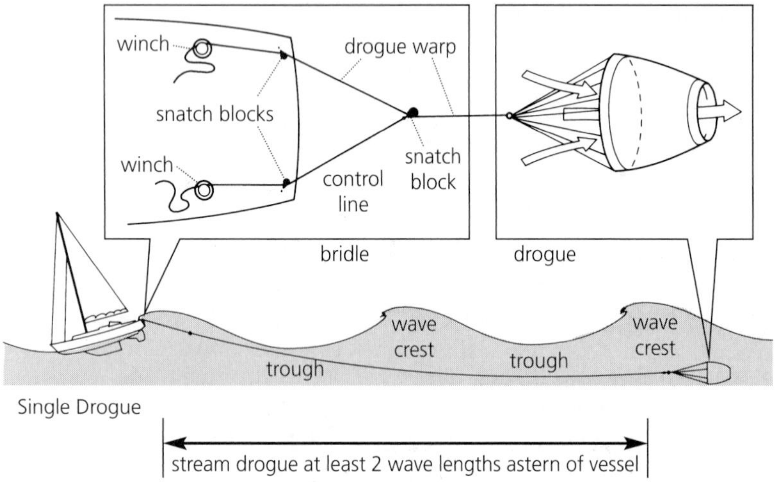

Single Drogue

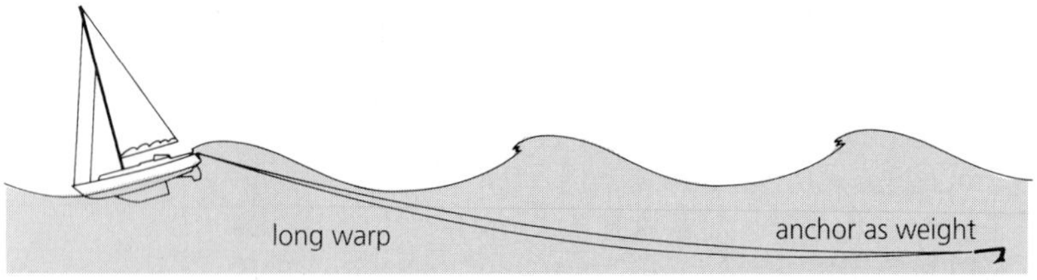

Trailing Warps

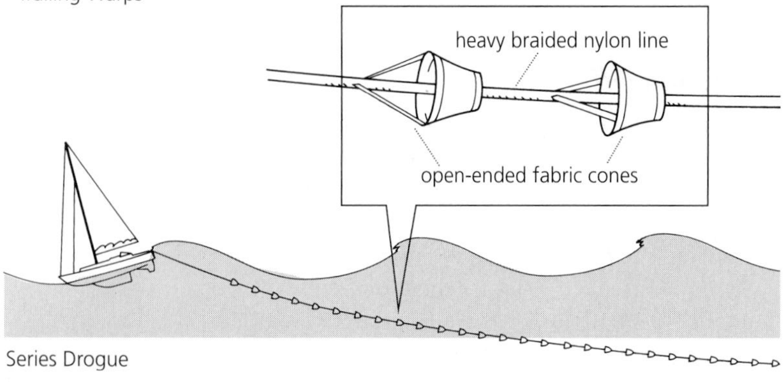

Series Drogue

the boat are likely to hit the cockpit and aft end of the house with some force. (If the engine is not running and there is no exhaust seacock to close, these seas may drive up the exhaust, flooding the engine.) The faster the boat travels, the slower the rate at which waves catch up with it, and the fewer the waves that have to be dealt with. Up to a point, speed can enhance maneuverability and, therefore, the ability to dodge some breaking crests.

When running off, there may be times when waves pick up a boat and carry it forward such that the boat and the water in which it is floating are moving at the same speed, resulting in no flow over the rudder and a complete loss of steerage. There may be other times when the boat accelerates down the face of a wave, the stern lifts, the bow digs in, and the boat wants to broach. With really big waves, the boat will be faced with the full force of the wind on the wave crests and greatly moderated wind in the troughs, exacerbating steering problems. In all these circumstances, running the engine in slow forward may help to maintain steerageway at critical moments by maintaining a flow of water over the propeller.

The key is to keep the stern square to breaking waves—in other words, to keep the boat from rounding up. There has been considerable disagreement over the years as to the best way to ensure this. One school of thought advocates stripping the boat down to bare poles and trailing *warps* and *drogues* (a kind of sea anchor deployed from the stern) to slow the boat to the greatest extent possible. The other school advocates sustaining the maximum boat speed commensurate with maintaining steerageway, which—in many instances—results in the boat surfing at double-digit speeds.

In all probability, what underlies these radically different recommendations are differences in boat designs and in boat-handling characteristics in extreme conditions. Many traditional, heavy-displacement, long-keeled boats with attached rudders become unmanageable when run off under sail at speed, occasionally rounding up uncontrollably with a risk of being rolled by the next breaking wave—they will settle down under bare poles with trailing warps and drogues. In contrast, many modern boats with relatively small keels and rudders maintain excellent steerageway at high speeds in heavy seas, even when surfing down the faces of breaking waves; however, they become quite unmanageable when towing warps and drogues. In this case, speed is reduced only insofar as is necessary to maintain control of the boat.

If warps or a drogue are deployed, it is advisable to rig them to some type of bridle that is then held by lines taken to both stern quarters (i.e., both sides of the boat) and then up to the cockpit winches. Tensioning one bridle line or another will haul the warps or drogue around to one side or another, causing the boat to run off a little differently. In this way, the boat's attitude can be optimized for the conditions.

To be effective, warps or drogues need to be well immersed—some kind of weight is recommended. Even so, at times the warp or drogue may be thrown forward by a wave, losing its effectiveness. This is where a *series drogue* comes into its own. Numerous cones are attached to a single line and trailed astern so that different parts of the drogue are immersed in different wave trains, resulting in a nearly uniform pull on the drogue.

Finally, consider these comments in a letter from E. A. (Ted) Wright of Chobham, England, to *Blue Water Sailing* magazine: "We have a drogue onboard and we have trailed it astern. It slows us from over 7 knots down to less than 2, but there is tremendous strain on the attachments. The warps hum like violin strings, and the effect is the same as driving your boat backwards at 7 knots or more into waves that are overtaking you at 25 knots. Seas run up the transom, you can feel the effect on the rudder, and there is the possibility of rudder damage if the wheel or tiller were to let go. All in all, it is not a comfortable feeling" (Feb. 2000).

Extreme conditions are not the time to find out how your boat behaves with a drogue. Some experimentation with and without warps and drogues is advisable prior to getting caught out in heavy weather.

Sea Anchors

A *sea anchor* (parachute anchor) is the ultimate passive survival tool. It is a large parachute-shaped device (generally with a diameter approximately 35 percent of the boat's LOA) that is streamed from the bow of the boat. The idea is to hold the bow into the wind and breaking seas. Even though green water may regularly be sweeping the decks from bow to stern, chances of structural damage to the boat and of being rolled are minimized. Once set, the sea anchor is more or less self-tending, so the crew can go below and wait for the gale to blow itself out.

Opinions on the efficacy of sea anchors are all over the map. Hiscock wrote: "The widely held belief that if streamed from the bow a sea anchor will hold a yacht's head to the wind has been disproved so often that one wonders how it survives. No matter how large the sea anchor may be, the yacht will range about . . . (and) . . . will soon fall off one way or the other and lie beam on" (*Cruising under Sail*). Contrast this with the following comment from Earl Hinz: "In extreme storms, the parachute sea anchor stands out as the best possible safety device for the offshore sailor" (*Ocean Navigator*, Jan.–Feb. 1999).

What is at issue—at least in part—is the difference in the efficacy of the sea anchors available in Hiscock's time as opposed to those available today. This efficacy is a function of size as well as design and deployment techniques that ensure the parachute remains submerged at all times. Be that as it may, whatever the reasons for this difference of opinion, sufficient anecdotal evidence has been gathered over the last few years to prove that a parachute anchor can be a useful tool of last resort in extreme conditions.

I say "tool of last resort" advisedly because there is also sufficient anecdotal evidence to show that once deployed, many parachute anchors are never recovered! Precisely because of its size, an effective sea anchor offers such extreme resistance to the water that it puts tremendous loads on its rode, with a concomitant risk of chafing through. If it survives its deployment, this resistance makes it extremely difficult to recover when it is time to get it back onboard.

Some sea anchors have a trip line from the crown that is tied off onboard as the anchor is paid out, with the idea that pulling on this line will collapse the anchor for retrieval. Others have shorter trip lines that are buoyed, with the idea of recovering the buoy later and collapsing the anchor for retrieval. In practice, the long trip lines sometimes wrap around the main rode, disabling the trip line, while it may well prove impossible to work the boat up to the shorter trip line.

In a 1999 rally in which a number of boats were hit by the remnants of Hurricane Mitch, resulting in four parachute anchors being deployed, one fouled up on launching (due to crew errors; deploying one of these anchors in a gale is fraught with the possibility of a foul-up) and was cut away, one was lost due to chafe, and a third was cut away after the gale had passed because the crew was unable to get it back onboard. The fourth was recovered only with difficulty after the winds had dropped to 15 knots and the seas had considerably abated (reported in *Ocean Navigator*, Sept.–Oct. 1999).

This is not to say that the sea anchors were not a success. Another boat in the same rally attempted to lie ahull. It was rolled, dismasted, and sank; it would almost certainly have survived if the crew had successfully deployed a sea anchor. The two owners who were unable to retrieve their anchors probably thought this was a fair price to pay for coming through the gale otherwise unscathed.

However, what this does point up is the difficulties inherent in successfully launching, managing, and retrieving such a large piece of fabric with all its attendant lines in extreme conditions. The recommended practice is to rig the anchor long before it is needed, bringing the rode aft to the cockpit where the parachute, recovery float, and so on are stored in a bag ready for deployment. When it is time to deploy the parachute, it should always be set over the windward bow to reduce the chances of fouling the boat.

As with other survival tactics, it is clear that some practice in more peaceful circumstances is highly recommended. Furthermore, a sea anchor should not be deployed in rough weather unless absolutely necessary, and only with the realization that it may well be a one-time use because it might be impossible to recover it. In addition, a boat lying to a sea

Right: *Sea anchor deployed. (Courtesy Para-Tech Engineering)*
Below: *Sea-anchor deployment and use.*

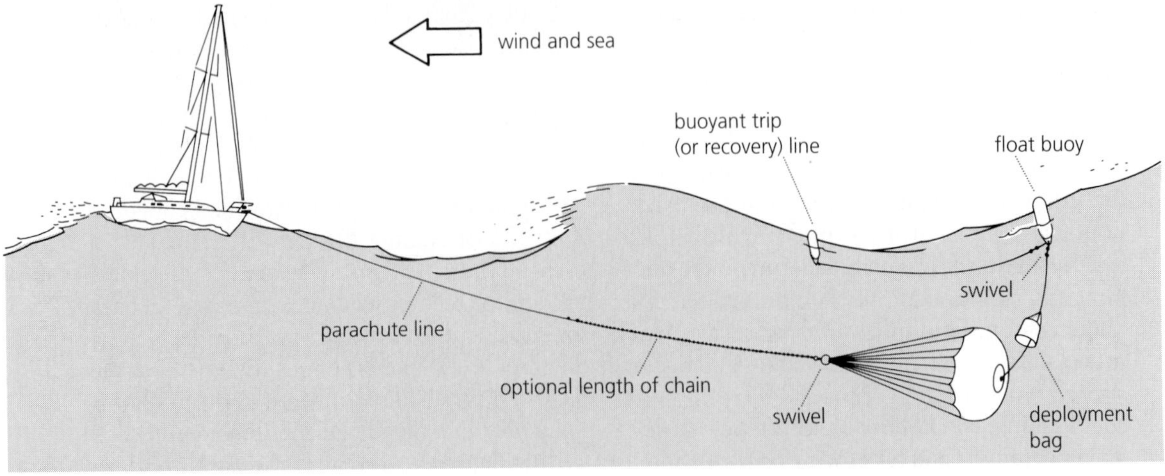

anchor is liable to be thrown back violently from time to time, transmitting severe shock loads to the steering system—the wheel or tiller needs to be strongly lashed off.

Once deployed, it may be found that the braking action of a sea anchor produces an extremely uncomfortable motion. Writing in *Yachting World*, cruiser Tim Trafford reported on his experiences in a severe gale. With the sea anchor deployed (not easy in itself), "the motion was appalling. *Ardevora* was pitching heavily: chafe marks seen later on the stem indicated up to 45 degrees above and below horizontal. She was also rolling her gunwales under and yawing up to 30 to 40 degrees either side of the wind. . . . On large breaking crests, we were surging sternwards at some speed. . . . The strain on the rode was so great that I seriously thought the starboard winch would tear out of its mountings. . . . Almost four hours after deployment, the rode parted. The decklog entry at 0020 records: 'The relief that it had gone was just—I don't know what—but like throwing off a huge weight, stress just went'" (Oct. 1999). He and his wife spent the rest of the night lying ahull. *Ardevora* "was so comfortable that we took turns to sleep—something that had not been possible while lying to the sea anchor."

The Traffords might have found that a tiny riding sail mounted on the backstay would have lessened the yawing; nevertheless, other cruisers who deployed sea anchors in extreme conditions have also reported substantial yawing and wild motion. This seems to be particularly the case with lightweight boats that have deep-fin keels and/or boats that tend to weave around at anchor.

A sea anchor is particularly likely to produce an almost intolerable motion if deployed in a strong ocean current with the wind blowing against the current (the Traffords were in the Humboldt current). The current will physically drag the boat into the oncoming waves. Deployment in these circumstances should probably be an act of last resort.

(Note: A modification to a standard sea-anchor deployment is advocated by Lyn and Larry Pardey. They place a snatch block around the rode with a line attached that is brought back to a cockpit winch. By cranking in on the winch, they can alter the angle at which the boat lies, customizing it for different sea states and maximum safety and comfort. However, a number of reports from cruisers who have attempted this approach attest to the difficulty of rigging the additional tackle in storm conditions—it needs to be figured out and set up well in advance.)

Chafe: The Weak Link

Sea anchors invariably use nylon rodes with a minimum length of 300 feet. Braided nylon should be used rather than three-strand because the constant changes in tension may make three-strand unlay and hockle. The rode needs to be at least as large as that on the main anchor (see chapter 9). According to the Wolfson Research Unit at Southampton University, it may be subjected to loads of up to 80 percent of the boat's weight; therefore, the attachment point on the boat must be immensely strong (there are reports of windlasses, when used as an attachment point, being ripped out of boats). It may be necessary to spread the load over several attachment points.

The weak link with warps, drogues, and sea anchors is chafe at the point where the line exits the boat. In a prolonged gale, the traditional approach of tying a piece of rag around the rode will not provide adequate chafe protection. This is especially true with a sea anchor that, because of its size, will put enormous, constantly changing strains on the rode, causing the rode to saw backward and forward through its fairlead or over the bow.

This chafe is generally ameliorated with a piece of hose (preferably a heavy-duty braided hose) installed over the parachute-anchor's rode with small holes at both ends so that it can be lashed in place. The hose should be long enough to extend several feet back from the chafe point. This way, if the hose starts to chafe, a little more rode and hose can be let out.

Even with this kind of protection, the rode may still chafe, in addition to which the internal

Strong point for the attachment of a snatch block to minimize chafe on a parachute-anchor's rode.

heat generated by the rode working backward and forward may melt it (see chapter 9). There should always be a sufficient length left on deck to be able to ease a little more out from time to time; however, this needs to be done with great care because the rode will be under a tremendous load, with potential to cause major injury if control is lost.

Chafe can be eliminated if a length of chain is used to run the rode over the bow roller. However, if the boat is bucking around wildly—which it almost certainly will be—and the chain is not firmly restrained at the roller, it can end up doing substantial damage to the bow roller and bow pulpit. A better way of reducing chafe may be to add a length of heavy-duty polyester (Dacron or Terylene) line, put some chafe protection on it (a hose), and run it over the bow roller. The polyester, with its low-stretch characteristics, builds up far less heat and, therefore, is unlikely to melt (see chapter 9).

Dealing with Flooding

What if, in the middle of a storm, you find the cabin awash? This has got to be right up there with fires at the top of a sailor's list of worst nightmares. However, in the majority of cases, the cause of the water ingress can be found and cured; in many cases of the boat ultimately sinking, it could have been saved with a more systematic approach to damage control.

Before you do anything else, taste the water and see if it is salt or fresh. If it is the latter, you can relax—you have a leaking freshwater system. If it is salt water and the onboard pumps are not keeping up with the inflow, *the primary concern is to find the source of the leak; pumping out the boat is the secondary concern* (except where it is necessary to lower the water level enough to find the leak). Furthermore, if the water level is rising, *it is essential to check all likely sources low in the boat as soon as possible.* Once the source of a leak is covered with more than a minimal amount of water, it can be extremely difficult to trace it.

If it is salt water, close all the seacocks as fast as possible—starting with the lowest ones—and check the keel bolts (if present) if they can still be checked. Take a close look at any through-hulls that don't have seacocks (there should be none below the waterline, but too often there are). Examine the engine exhaust, propeller shaft seal, and rudder stock seal (often overlooked, it can be a significant source of water).

If the leak stops after closing the seacocks, you have time to pump out the water and inspect the boat's plumbing—somewhere there is a failed hose, hose clamp, or pipe. If the leak continues, think about any other through-hulls that may be underwater and siphoning into the boat. The bilge pump itself may be the problem. Otherwise, if the boat is well heeled or the foredeck is plunging into the waves, it may be the hull-to-deck joint that is leaking or the chain pipe that is taking on water (another potential source of a surprising amount of water).

Try tacking. Wherever the leak is, this may bring it out of the water. If the rate of influx continues but slows, it is a fair indication that the leak is now on the "high" (i.e., windward) side. Whatever you do, don't give up looking for the leak. If it is low down in the hull, the rate of influx will slow as the water level rises inside the boat, equalizing the pressure, which may give your pumps a chance to catch up and at least stabilize the situation.

Once a leak is found, bring it as close to the waterline as possible by heeling the boat. A large leak may require the addition of some type of collision patch (a heavy triangular piece of sailcloth with grommets in each corner, to which lines are attached) to be maneuvered over its outside. Given that a collision patch is unlikely to be onboard (this is recommended in most offshore books and routinely ignored by sailors), a small sail can be pressed into service but will be much more difficult to handle. If the leak is accessible from the inside of the boat, it may be just as productive to jam cushions into it, wedged with anything that comes to hand. If necessary, interior joinery can be ripped out—this is no time to be sentimental.

Once the rate of influx has been slowed, focus on pumping the boat dry, after which a more permanent repair can be made. A person with a 5-gallon bucket can realistically expect to move 30 to 50 gallons of water a minute (1,800–3,000 gph/6,813–11,355 L/h) from a flooded cabin through a companionway hatch, which is significantly more than most bilge pumps (see chapter 5) and much more than you will ever get by plumbing the engine raw-water pump to the bilge and so on. If you have the crew available, bailing is likely the most productive use of their time.

Do not give up on searching for a leak and bailing until the water level in the cabin drives you out. Unless help is immediately forthcoming, your best chance of survival lies in keeping the boat afloat.

Abandoning Ship

If, despite all efforts, the water level in a boat is rising uncontrollably, it is time to think of abandoning ship. However, this should not be done until the last moment—as long as it is afloat, the boat will be a much more visible target for rescuers than a dinghy or life raft; it may surprise you and stay afloat. A life raft, in particular, should not be launched or inflated until it is decided to abandon the boat. The Royal Yachting Association points out that "an inflated life raft cannot be towed or held alongside for any length of time in a seaway without being damaged. When the raft has been launched and inflated it should be boarded by the entire crew as quickly as possible. With only one person on board the raft will be prone to capsize." As soon as everyone is on board, the raft should be set loose to drift clear of the boat.

Long before this happens, all the crew should have put on life jackets and safety harnesses. The abandon-ship bag (*ditch kit*) should be readied with at least all the items listed in the sidebar on page 527. If there is time, gather extra water and clothes (for protection from exposure), and rudimentary navigation equipment (a small-scale chart, pencil, and notepad in a large plastic bag).

What about bringing your boat alongside a rescue ship? This is a highly dangerous prospect. My uncle, an experienced North Sea pilot, was killed boarding a ship in rough weather. At slow speeds, the ship's captain has no maneuverability. The overhanging bow and stern will probably bring down your boat's rigging. Your boat will crash up and down against the side of the ship with each passing wave, easily by as much as 10 to 20 feet (3–6 m). Boarding a ship from a small boat in rough seas should be done only as a last resort if lives are in danger (they certainly will be during the boarding operation).

It is much better to wait for official rescue services or to board a small fishing vessel if one is in the vicinity. If this is not possible, it is preferable to have the ship's captain launch a lifeboat to pick up you and your crew. If a ship has to be boarded directly, do everything possible to keep it to windward, allowing it to drift down slowly on your boat so that it provides partial protection in its lee.

Long before the two boats are close enough to jump for dangling ladders, nets, or ropes, you should be watching the rolling of the ship, gauging the waves, and estimating the point at which your boat is going to be the highest relative to the ship. This is the moment to grab a rope or ladder and start climbing, straining every nerve and muscle in your body to get clear of your boat and its rigging. Try to leave your boat well forward or aft to clear the mast and spreaders. In all cases of rescue at sea, safety harnesses and life jackets should be worn—the rescuers may be able to clip a line to the harness and pull or winch a crew member aboard.

Helicopters require special techniques. Rescue by helicopter generally cannot be done from the deck of a sailboat—the risk of entangling the helicopter's hoisting cable in the mast and rigging is too great. For obvious reasons, no line from a helicopter should ever be made fast to a boat! It may be possible to put the whole crew in a dinghy or life raft and stream it downwind of the boat on a long line to give the helicopter sufficient clearance from your boat. At night, a flashlight should be carried in the dinghy or life raft to illuminate it for the rescue pilot.

Static electricity can build up on hoisting cables and slings. To avoid shock, they should be allowed to ground out on the life raft or in the water before grabbing them. (This might be forgotten in the urgency of the moment!) In any case, if there is any kind of sea running, the dinghy or life raft will bob up and down and the sling, rescuer, or whatever will shoot in and out of reach. Good timing and strong arms are needed—weaker crew members must be helped up first. When the rescue cable is lowered, probably with a rescue swimmer on it, and if it is not possible to be rescued directly from the dinghy or life raft, the boat's crew will have to take to the water one at a time in life jackets.

Life Rafts

Some people won't go to sea without a life raft, and some racing rules require one to be onboard. In Europe, there is a trend toward *requiring* life rafts on offshore boats and *requiring* life-raft replacement every ten years. We have never had one because they are not only expensive to buy (it is easy to spend \$3,000–\$5,000 once all the pieces are assembled), but also relatively expensive to maintain, requiring regular inspections by qualified people. This means the life raft must be gotten to and from the inspection center, which often is not at all convenient, and then there is no guarantee that the inspection was done properly. Although there are many reputable people in this business, there are also too many instances of inspected rafts that turn out to have major deficiencies. Finally, a life raft has a finite life expectancy.

Above: *Life raft in action.* Below middle: *Ocean Liferaft.* Below bottom: *Coastal Liferaft. (All photos courtesy Avon Marine)*

A life raft is a passive form of defense—about all you can do is get in it and wait to be rescued. We've all read harrowing stories of people spending weeks drifting in a life raft. Having said that, the reality is that with an EPIRB (explained later), most people in life rafts are able to alert the relevant authorities within a matter of hours (probably sooner), which ensures a reasonably speedy rescue. It is very unlikely, even in a worst-case scenario, that you will be forced to inhabit a life raft for any length of time.

I justify not having a life raft on the basis that we almost never sail in cold water and that our longest ocean crossing is usually the Gulf of Mexico, which is about 600 miles across at its widest, with water temperatures ranging from 60°F (16°C) to more than 80°F (27°C). We carry an inflated inflatable on deck and a second deflated one (a Tinker folding RIB, which has a sailing rig) also on deck. We have an EPIRB. As long as the inflatable floats and as long as we can hang onto it, we should be able to survive for at least several days, especially if we manage to take our abandon-ship bag with us. The EPIRB should *(continued page 528)*

Features include:

1. Inflation CO_2 cylinder on the side of the buoyancy tube.
2–3. Boarding system: weighted boarding ladder + webbing bridle inside to ease entry into raft.
4. High-visibility self-erecting canopy with reflective tapes.
5. Outside lifelines.
6. Automatically activated lighting: inside and on canopy arch, with battery-save feature.
7. Entrance flap with ties.
8. Ventilation chute/observation port and rain water collection.
9. Inside bracing lines.
10. Weighted stabilizing pockets.
11. Upper and lower independent neoprene/nylon buoyancy tubes.
12. Inflatable double floor for heat retention.
13. Rescue quoit and line.

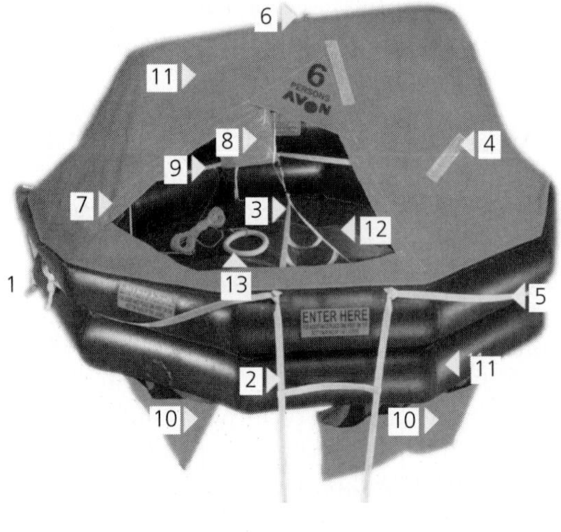

Features include:

1. Inflation CO_2 cylinder on the side of the buoyancy tube.
2. High-visibility self-erecting canopy.
3. Outside lifelines.
4. Inside bracing lines.
5. Observation port/water collector.
6. Independent buoyancy chambers.
7. Weighted stabilizing pockets.
8. Rescue quoit and line.

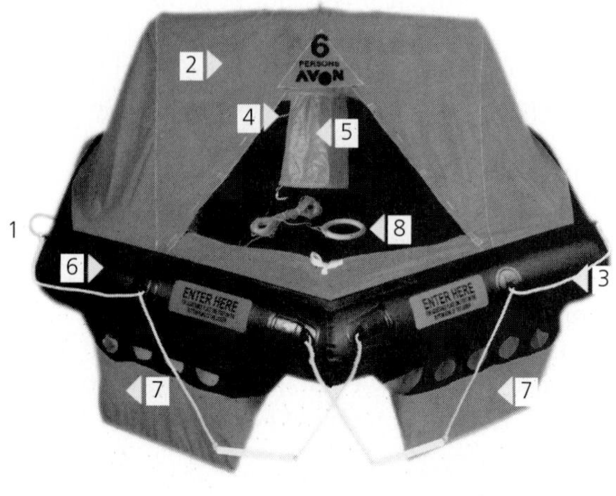

A DITCH KIT

A ditch kit is not something we like to think about, but it's something that every boat going offshore should have. Whether or not the boat has a life raft and regardless of the supposed contents of the life raft, a ditch kit should have the basic elements needed for survival if the boat has to be abandoned. The reason is that there are too many instances of life-raft survival kits being unusable when needed and the life raft itself being swept away in a storm, with only a dinghy left to the crew.

A ditch kit is useless if it is not readily accessible in circumstances of extreme duress—fundamentally, that means being close to the companionway at the top of a locker. We have ours on a shelf in the wet locker between the nav station and the companionway (with the life jackets on another shelf and the safety harnesses hanging there).

A ditch kit should be waterproof (or the contents, at least, should be in waterproof containers), it should float, and it should preferably be highly visible (orange is a good color). It needs an attached lanyard so that it can be rapidly secured to a life raft or dinghy. A basic ditch kit should contain as many of the following items as are appropriate to the type of cruising:

- a 406 MHz EPIRB (we keep ours in a rack beside the companionway) (see sidebar on page 528)
- a *waterproof* handheld VHF
- maybe a SART*
- a *waterproof* handheld GPS with spare batteries
- a flare kit (the ditch kit is as good a place as any on the boat to keep the main flare kit)
- some kind of protection from the weather (in the tropics, this may be no more than space blankets; in higher latitudes and cold water, survival suits may be required, in which case they will be stored separately)
- water or a manual watermaker (we keep a couple of bright yellow 5 gal./19 L jerricans at the top of a cockpit locker, with both cans just two thirds full so that they float, and with an attached lanyard so that they can be tied to our inflatable)
- high-energy, non-thirst-producing foods and multivitamins that are well sealed and have a long shelf life
- a waterproof flashlight and spare batteries
- medicine for seasickness and any other essential prescriptions, treatment for sunburn, and painkillers
- first-aid kit
- waterproof sunblock, lip balm, and skin lotion
- spare eyeglasses if they are necessary to see
- a small-scale chart of the region being cruised, with a compass, pencils, and dividers
- fishing tackle including a knife
- ¼-inch (6 mm) line or smaller and duct tape
- a reasonably sized bailer, to be attached to the dinghy or life raft, and a sponge to mop up residual water
- a drogue of some kind, with a rode of at least 50 to 60 feet (in rough weather, this will be essential to keep the bow of a dinghy into the wind and waves or to keep a life raft from capsizing)
- photocopies of essential documents

With the exception of the jerricans of water, this ditch kit is quite compact. You can get as elaborate as you want, but the ditch kit will get increasingly bulky and less maneuverable.

Ditch kit.

* A *search and rescue radar transponder* (SART) is a battery-powered device that responds to a radar signal from another vessel, sending back a strong and distinctive signal to help you be located in a distress situation. Detection of a sea-level life raft is up to 30 miles (48 km) by a searching aircraft but only about 5 miles by a ship—the range would be greater from the deck of a boat.

send rescuers in our direction well before the several days have passed. If we can take the Tinker and its rig with us, we can row and sail toward shore. In our circumstances, I believe a life raft represents a poor investment.

If we get into a survival situation and I turn out to be wrong in these assumptions, I may find that I have bet all of our lives on a set of false premises. But, in reality, our lives are much more likely to be risked in an onshore car accident than in an emergency at sea. In a car wreck, we would be better protected by a Volvo than by the car we drive now; therefore, if we had the money for a life raft, it would still make more sense to put the money saved into a more robust car. . . . At some point, these things all come down to a cost-benefit analysis that each of us has to make given our specific cruising plans, finances, and assessment of risk. For us, I don't believe the life-raft numbers pencil out, and I resent the interference of legislative bodies in this kind of decision-making (the Hiscocks and other seminal cruisers may have been unable to afford to cruise in today's overregulated environment). Nevertheless, if we sailed across oceans, or into high latitudes, or even in cold water, I might think differently.

EPIRBS

An EPIRB (emergency position-indicating radio beacon) is a transmitter that sends out a distress signal on one or more fixed frequencies that are monitored by various aircraft, vessels, land stations, and—most importantly—a network of satellites (COSPAS-SARSAT: COSPAS is operated by Russia, SARSAT—Search And Rescue Satellite Aided Tracking—is a Canadian-French-U.S. initiative).

Class A and B EPIRBs (the "A" means the EPIRB will float free and automatically activate if the boat goes down; the "B" means it must be manually activated) transmit a signal on a frequency of 121.5 MHz. This signal is not stored by satellites; to be heard, any receiving satellite must also be over a ground station to which the signal is retransmitted. There are holes in the coverage, particularly in the Southern Hemisphere, added to which the precision and power of the system only allow a boat's location to be calculated to within 12 miles, leaving a huge potential search area. Alert time is at least one to two hours.

Every year, the USCG alone receives at least a hundred thousand false alerts from 121.5 MHz EPIRBs (more than a thousand false alerts for every real emergency). For this reason, the USCG is considering the phasing out of these EPIRBs and terminating the processing of the signals.

A 406 MHz EPIRB transmits a signal that is received and stored by satellites until it can be retransmitted to a ground station. This ensures worldwide coverage. The precision and power of the signal are such that a boat's position can be calculated to within 2 miles. The signal also has an embedded code that identifies the transmitting vessel. When cross-referenced with registration information, this provides the owner's name, a vessel description, and a point of contact to ensure that the vessel is in the area from which the signal is coming. This allows rescue services to weed out many false alarms.

Both the COSPAS and SARSAT satellites circle the globe approximately every hundred minutes. When a 406 MHz EPIRB is activated, the authorities are alerted in from thirty minutes to three hours. Because the satellites are in polar orbits, coverage is best in high latitudes and worst at the equator, resulting in the longest alert times at the equator. The average alert time in midlatitudes is thirty to forty-five minutes.

When a distress signal is received, the rescue services attempt to contact the registered owner (or the contact person listed in the registration information) before initiating a search. *If the unit is not properly registered, no search will take place*. Once a search is initiated, the transmitted signal puts the rescue services within 2 miles of the EPIRB, at which point a homing signal, transmitted on 121.5 MHz (one of the frequencies used by class A and B EPIRBs) should enable them to close in on the distressed vessel.

The pinpointing of a vessel in distress can be accelerated by the most recent generation of 406 EPIRBs. Known as "L-band EPIRBs," they contain a GPS that enables them to transmit an accurate fix with the distress signal. The signal from an L-band EPIRB can be picked up and processed by the geostationary GOES weather satellites, which are over the equator, as well as the COSPAS-SARSAT satellites. This significantly reduces alert times in tropical waters.

A 406 MHz EPIRB is the cheapest and best insurance against loss of life that money can buy if confronted by the loss of the boat.

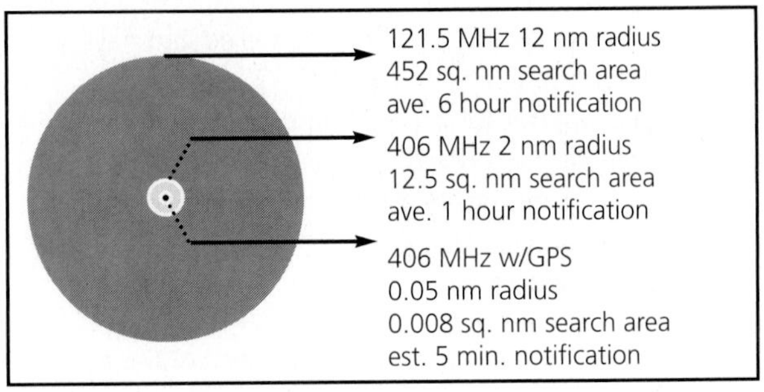

EPIRB response times and search areas as a function of EPIRB type.

Concerning life rafts, several factors must be considered in the following four broad categories:

- rescue platforms: a flat, inflatable disc for people to hang onto or crawl on top of
- rescue pods: a minimal raft with a single tube, no insulation, a lightweight canopy, and little equipment
- coastal life rafts: something between a rescue pod and an offshore life raft
- offshore life rafts

An offshore life raft should have double tubes, an inflated or insulated floor (*very important in cold waters*), a sturdy inflated canopy with a locator light on the top, and *weighted* ballast pockets or a similar device, plus a drogue to

FLARES

Flares (*visual distress signals*) are another means of attracting attention. Flares are red for distress and white to get attention, and they are handheld or fired from a flare gun (either 12 gauge or 25 mm). Of those that are fired into the air, some immediately fall back to earth (meteor-type), others come down slowly on a parachute. Parachute flares can also be hand-launched.

In the United States, red flares (but not white) are made to two standards—a minimum USCG standard and a much tougher SOLAS standard, which requires the flares to be waterproof—*a most important feature*. In Europe, flares are made to the SOLAS standard.

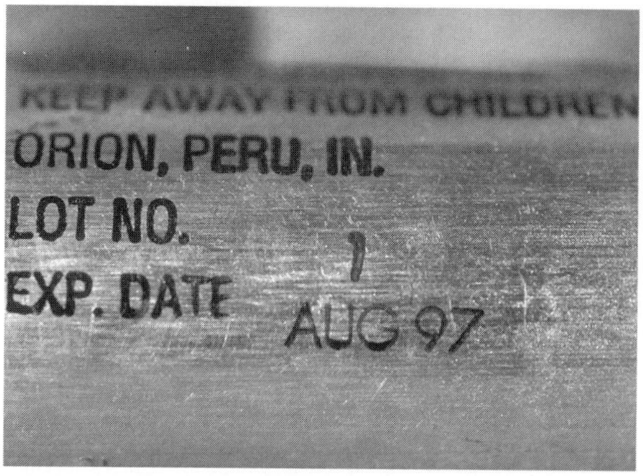

Date stamp on a flare. Replace flares as the expiration date approaches.

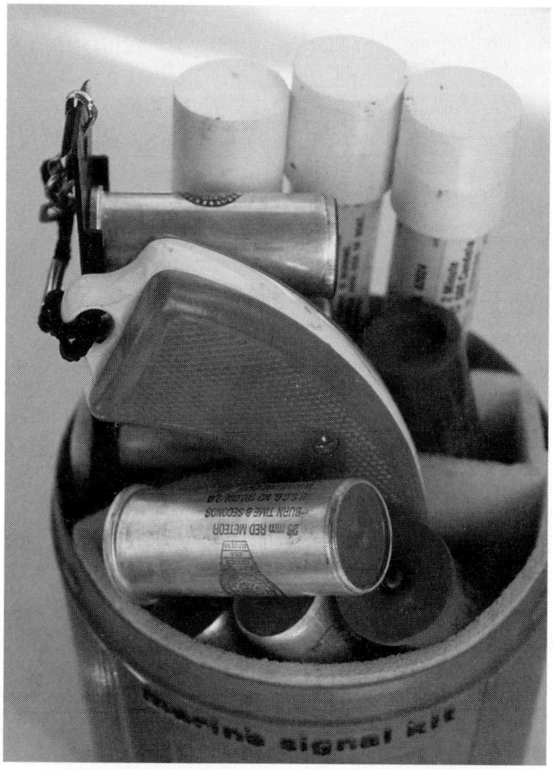

Flare kit. Note that there are many more than are legally required in the United States because we have kept all the out-of-date flares over the years. This is a 25 mm flare gun—greatly preferred to a 12-gauge gun—but the flares are regular "cheapos"—SOLAS-approved flares would be a significant improvement.

From first-hand experience, I know that passing ships do not necessarily keep a watch and see flares. To be sure of getting attention, you need lots of them and they need to be as visible as possible. A minimum of three relatively low-intensity and low-visibility red flares are legally required by the USCG on all boats over 16 feet (5 m) in length. The prudent cruiser will go well beyond this, using a much more powerful 25 mm rather than a 12-gauge flare gun and SOLAS-approved flares rather than those that have only a USCG approval. For offshore cruisers, I suggest a minimum inventory of four handheld red flares and four red parachute flares, preferably conforming to SOLAS standards.

Given that flares legally expire after forty-two months and, therefore, new ones have to be bought to comply with USCG requirements, U.S. sailors will have quite a collection after a few years, most of which will still work. When buying flares, *make sure that they have been recently manufactured or else you very soon will be buying more!*

If flares have to be used, they should be shot off in pairs, a few seconds apart—the first as an attention-getter, the second for confirmation. The flares should be kept in the abandon-ship bag: if you need them on the big boat, you will have time to get them out; if there is not time, there is no risk of leaving them behind. *Make sure a waterproof flashlight is packed with handheld flares so that you can read the operating instructions at night!*

keep it from blowing over and from blowing downwind faster than you can swim. Better quality life rafts meet ORC standards; the best also meet Safety of Life at Sea (SOLAS) "A" standards. The best offshore life rafts come with a twelve-year warranty and three-year inspection intervals (rather than two-year or annual inspections). For those on an extended world cruise, it is important to ensure that the manufacturer has licensed inspection stations at suitable points around the globe.

A life raft is useless if it cannot be deployed when needed. Many larger boats have a custom locker built into the stern, which is probably the best way to go. A sternrail mount makes it easy to release a raft, but also makes it vulnerable to being swept away in the extreme conditions in which it is most likely to be needed. If mounted on deck, the mounting hardware needs to be almost bulletproof. A deck-mounted life raft may be difficult to get over the side (life rafts are heavy and the canisters have no handles and so are not easy to maneuver)—think about designing the lower lifelines so that they can be rapidly disconnected or cut away, enabling the canister to be slid overboard. Lastly, if a life raft is stored in a locker, it is likely to get buried and may end up going down with the boat!

A life raft should not be used until "you have to step up to it"—in other words, it should be used only if the boat goes down. There are too many cases of prematurely abandoned boats surviving while the crew perished in a life raft, including seven people in the Fastnet race. In the same race, twelve life rafts were washed overboard and lost before they could be used, which emphasizes the need to have incredibly secure stowage, yet easy to release when needed.

CONCLUSION

Where does this leave us? The sensible sailor uses available weather-prediction sources before setting sail, whether for a coastal or an offshore cruise. These sources are then supplemented by local knowledge, particularly for coastal cruising, with close attention to local conditions and other clues about how the weather is likely to develop.

When going offshore, weather forecasts can be used to pick a suitable window for departure. In many cruising anchorages around the world, you are likely to find a cluster of boats all waiting for a similar window. Very often, particularly after an extended stay in port, sailors develop a (sometimes unconscious) reluctance to put to sea and a kind of "herd instinct" takes over, holding the fleet back. If you have done your analysis and decided that now is the time to go, do not be deterred by an apparent reluctance to move on the part of your fellow cruisers.

Once at sea, whatever window was used for departure will have been superseded within a few days by the ever-changing weather situation. It is now that your understanding of weather systems will help you combine available weather forecasts with local clues to develop a strategy for continuing the voyage. With good judgment and a little luck, you should be able to make the most of favorable conditions—and minimize the unpleasant consequences of unfavorable conditions—to complete a fast and reasonably comfortable passage safely.

CHAPTER TWELVE

EXTENDED CRUISING AND STAYING IN TOUCH

The thrill of cruising: tied to a palm tree off the Pitons, St. Lucia, in the Caribbean.

For many of us, the ultimate thrill in cruising is to get away on an extended cruise in waters completely new to us: to face fresh navigational challenges, to see new sights, to meet different people, and to immerse ourselves in cultures other than our own (even if still within our own country). The logistics involved in such cruising are significantly different from the logistics of weekend cruising, particularly if the voyage takes the boat and its crew into foreign waters—and there is the problem of maintaining communication with home. In this chapter, I discuss some of these longer-term cruising issues.

LOGISTICAL CONSIDERATIONS

There is a whole grab bag of practical matters that must be dealt with before the dock lines are cast off at the start of an extended cruise. Provisioning requires special attention; then there are environmental, bureaucratic, financial, and health concerns. Even such day-to-day chores as washing clothes are different.

Provisioning

Provisioning for an extended voyage takes preplanning. It's very easy to forget some "must-have" ingredient. The best preparation is to track your grocery shopping for a month or two (list absolutely everything, with quantities) and then look around the pantry and add any other items that are only bought occasionally (e.g., spices). This list is a good starting point, but it will need to be adjusted, remembering that you will quite likely change your cooking and eating habits (e.g., you may bake bread onboard, which dramatically increases your consumption of flour and yeast).

When you do stock the boat, save the shopping list for future reference (noting any changes that developed in the course of the cruise). We have a scruffy old piece of paper that has formed the basis for our provisioning list for the past twelve years.

In many parts of the world, roaches are a problem. To minimize the chances of an infestation:

- Always unload cardboard boxes in the cockpit (never take them below).
- Transfer eggs from cardboard to Styrofoam containers (it is worth saving some from Western supermarkets) or plastic egg boxes (we got some in Mexico—in many parts of the world, you need to take egg boxes with you when shopping).
- Remove as much cardboard packaging as possible from other products.

The dreaded cockroach comes aboard.

To deal with the occasional roach that inevitably makes it onboard, put powdered boric acid in confined spaces that roaches are likely to visit.

In the developing world, rice, pasta, flour, dried beans, dried peas, and cereals are frequently infested with weevils. Once onboard, these little critters can spread rapidly, eating right through heavy-duty plastic containers in the process. We attempt to buy all products likely to have weevils from western supermarkets, stocking up with enough supplies to carry us through to the next big supermarket. If we have to do some intermediate shopping, the following strategies minimize the chances of an infestation:

- Freezing the supplies overnight (they must freeze hard) kills the critters and their eggs.
- Microwaving the supplies for a couple of minutes (until they get hot) does the same. However, all packages must be opened because microwaving releases residual moisture, which must then be allowed to evaporate or the supplies will get moldy.
- Putting bay leaves in all packages is said to help (we've tried it and it seems to work, but I can't tell how effective it is).
- Adding a small piece of cotton soaked in chloroform to all packages and then sealing them is also said to keep weevils at bay (we haven't tried this one).
- Putting flour into strong containers and then pounding it into a near-solid consistency minimizes infestation.
- If all else fails, floating the little buggers out of pastas before and during cooking, or sieving them out of flour, gets rid of most of them. These techniques, however, do not work too well with rice: it is better to have brown rice so that weevils are not as noticeable.

If you find even one live weevil, you need to ruthlessly search out any others as soon as possible.

We bake a fair amount of bread. To do so without having to buy flour locally, we carry a lot of it—especially whole-wheat flour (which is hard to come by)—and dried yeast. We also carry biscuit mix, pancake mix, and cake mixes—in other words, all those things that make life so easy at home.

Breakfast cereal is often a scarce commodity, stale if it can be found, and expensive—substantial stocks should be bought before sailing. There is a tremendous amount of packaging in most cereal—it pays to consolidate using good-sized, *airtight* plastic containers.

Produce should always be bought fresh (unrefrigerated) if possible. Once refrigerated, it does not keep long. We keep most of our vegetables and fruits in a small hammock suspended above the galley table—it looks picturesque, keeps the produce from getting bruised, and provides plenty of ventilation. The principal exception is potatoes, which should be kept cool and in the dark (in our case, in a locker under the cabinsole). New potatoes keep for weeks.

We use the refrigerator for salad items and other perishable produce, as well as all the other things found in the refrigerator at home, including drinks (but on a smaller scale). Salad ingredients bought in third-world countries can be a health hazard (see later in this chapter). They can be at least partially sterilized by soaking in a chlorine or tincture of iodine solution or in a solution of potassium permanganate—put in enough crystals to make the water turn pink. Lettuce should be avoided. Bananas (especially a large bunch) should be dunked in saltwater for a while to float out any bugs and spiders and then stored in the rigging.

When we have access to first-world supermarkets, we consider that the best use of the freezer is to jam it solid with meat, cheese (which may be hard to come by in third-world countries, and may be dubious from a sanitary perspective), and butter (also hard to come by). We divide the meat into meal-sized amounts, put it in resealable plastic storage bags, and then layer everything so that we don't have to dig to the bottom of the freezer for some item. We like fresh milk in our tea, so we also freeze 2 or 3 gallons. When many freezers are stuffed full, the lack of air circulation results in partial defrosting (and eventual spoilage) of produce that is up against the sides of the freezer—it may be necessary to leave some air spaces and/or occasionally rearrange everything. We make ice by putting water in a quart-size resealable plastic bag and putting it in the freezer. It makes a good-sized block that we subsequently break up with an ice pick.

Butter can be acquired in tins in some places. As long as it is the salted variety (regular butter), it seems to keep forever (we have had tins that were fine when opened after seven years!).

When bought fresh (not refrigerated), eggs keep for weeks just as they are—they keep even longer if covered in petroleum jelly (e.g., Vaseline). As the eggs get older, they should be dunked in freshwater (not salt water) before cracking—those that float have gone by. Many salamis and other smoked meats, when bought in sausage form, are extremely tasty and will keep for months simply hung up somewhere without refrigeration.

Here are more items for your supermarket shopping list: spices, sauces (packet soups, gravies, and seasonings come in handy), curry powder, chili powder, ginger, Tabasco sauce (after six years on Gulf of Mexico oil rigs, I take a bottle everywhere), salad dressings, mayonnaise, pickles, ketchup, barbecue sauce, taco fixings (seasoning, sauce, shells, and refried beans), brown rice, spaghetti sauce and pasta, parmesan cheese, other assorted pastas, olive oil, cooking oil, vinegar, balsamic vinegar, peanut butter, honey, jam, dried milk (the low-fat variety, which is often hard to find, tastes more like regular milk than full- or nonfat), tea, coffee, cocoa, drink mixes, canned foods (soups, meats, chili, fish, vegetables, fruit, and tomato paste), night-shift snacks (e.g., chocolate, nuts, raisins, and cookies), and beverages (soft drinks, beer, wine, and liquor).

Canned foods, especially meats, vary enormously in quality. If buying an unknown brand in bulk, first sample a single can to make sure it is edible. We once bought a case of Venezuelan corned beef (how could anybody get corned beef wrong?) because the price was truly excellent—we ended up feeding it to the fish.

Load up with local delicacies whenever the opportunity arises. For example, olives and olive oil in Spain, pâté and wine in France, feta cheese in Greece. . . .

Cleaning and other household supplies are not easy to find in some parts of the world, so it is worth stocking up on dishwashing detergent (Joy works well in salt water), laundry detergent, a floor-washing detergent, scrubbing pads and brushes, stainless steel polish, aluminum foil, resealable plastic storage bags (several sizes), plastic wrap, wax paper; garbage-can liners, trash bags (heavy-duty), paper towels, and toilet paper.

And remember:

- Although plastic grocery bags are becoming common around the world, you still need sturdy shopping bags for hauling groceries (large backpacks work well).
- In many parts of the world, bargaining is the norm. Don't be shy.
- Some countries (e.g., Tonga, Fiji, and Australia) confiscate on your arrival just about all the fresh and frozen food onboard, so check ahead and stock only what you can eat before arriving in one of those places!

Where to Put All This Stuff

When choosing suitable lockers, bear in mind the following:

- It is best to put all the pastas in one place, all the baking supplies in another, and so on—it makes it much easier to find things and to confine weevil outbreaks to one area.
- However, many lockers are somewhat inaccessible, so we maintain the galley lockers as short-term stowage, containing a little of everything. Prior to a passage, we plan some meals (which may be simply boiled rice and canned chili if it looks like seas will be rough) and make sure that everything we need is close at hand.
- If at all possible, lockers should be divided into small spaces—this minimizes the distance things can move, cuts down on breakages, and reduces the area to be cleaned in the event of breakage.
- You can almost eliminate glass breakages

by gluing lengths of PVC sewer piping into a honeycomb matrix within which glass jars are stored (see chapter 3).
- There should be a locker with snacks for the night shift that is readily accessible without disturbing the rest of the crew.
- In case of possible bilge-flooding, nothing that could plug the bilge pump should be stored there —including all cardboard packaging and cans with paper labels that can come unglued.
- It pays to give each locker and stowage space a name or number and to record what is stowed there—it is amazing how fast you can forget. Once a stowage pattern has been established, stick to it. When we bought our new boat, we replicated the same stowage pattern as much as possible as on the old boat—it makes finding things so much easier.

Ensuring Safe Water

The longer a cruise, the more important water management becomes. As discussed in chapter 5, all cruising boats—without exception—should have at least two water tanks. These tanks should not be pumped down sequentially; rather, when one is half empty, the other should be switched online. This way, if one tank becomes contaminated for any reason, or someone leaves a faucet open and pumps the tank dry (it is best to turn off the electric freshwater pump at sea), there is always some clean water remaining in the other tank. If a jerrican of water is part of the abandon-ship supplies, it is the ultimate backup.

These considerations apply whether or not there is a watermaker onboard—always assume that the watermaker will not work when most needed. The watermaker enables many boats to carry less water (space and weight savings) and to consume a lot more (long, hot showers). Still, the watermaker must be backed up with a minimum of two water tanks, with sufficient capacity to complete a passage with on inoperative watermaker.

Away from the first world, many freshwater sources are of questionable quality. Our overriding rule is that if we are in doubt about the purity of the supply, we don't take it onboard. We don't have the ability to test local water supplies, so we are often dependent on our knowledge of the hygiene in that country, some idea of where the water has come from, and recommendations from other cruisers or people we trust.

If you are forced to take on questionable water supplies, sodium hypochlorite (regular household bleach as sold in the U.S.) goes a long way toward eliminating any potential pathogens (although it may cause problems with aluminum water tanks). However, the U.S. Centers for Disease Control (CDC) warns that "chlorine treatment alone, as used in the routine disinfection of water, may not kill some enteric viruses and the parasitic organisms that cause giardiasis, amebiasis, and cryptosporidiosis"—in other words, it is not a completely effective treatment (these bugs are discussed in more detail later in this chapter). Treatment with tincture of iodine is more effective, but the water has to sit for fifteen hours to reliably kill cryptosporidium.

If chlorine is used, the recommended dose is a ½ teaspoon of 5.25 percent solution (typical of what is sold in U.S. grocery stores—check the label) per 5 gallons (19 L) of clear water, and 1 teaspoon per 5 gallons of cloudy or questionable water. The dosage should be adjusted up or down as appropriate for bleach of a different concentration (note that many European bleaches have other substances in them and so should not be used). After treatment, the water should be allowed to stand for at least thirty minutes, with the filler caps off tanks to allow the fumes to dissipate.

If tincture of iodine is used, the recommended dose is five drops of 2 percent solution (typical of what is sold in drugstores) per quart of clear water, and ten drops per quart of cloudy or questionable water. The dosage should be adjusted up or down for iodine of a different concentration. Again, the water should be allowed to stand for at least thirty minutes before use (and longer if possible). One drop is considered to equal 0.05 milliliters; for 5 gallons (19 L) of clear water, the dosage is 5 milliliters.

On a cruising boat, it is well worth designing the side decks, toerails, and tank fills so that most of the surface area can be used for rainwater capture. Alternatively, awnings can be rigged to catch the rain. Where water supplies are questionable, this is an excellent way to fill tanks.

Finally, a note on dealing with the laundry, since few boats have washing machines. For short-term cruises, the laundry accumulates and goes ashore at the end of the cruise. On longer-term cruises, the laundry often has to be dealt with onboard. Many cruisers do it in two buckets—one for washing and one for rinsing. It's a lot of work. We have a raised sill on our shower stall so we can fill the base of the shower with water and detergent in which to soak the clothes. When anyone takes a shower, he or she is expected to tromp up and down on the laundry!

A cruising boat needs a supply of either wooden or plastic clothespins shaped to fit over the lifelines. Clothes should be hung inside the lifelines so that if they get blown loose, there is less chance of them going overboard. Unfortunately, if any of the lifelines are made from uncoated stainless steel (i.e., do not have a plastic sheath), they can leave unsightly rust stains on the laundry, which are almost impossible to remove.

Traditional wooden clothespins last well in a marine environment, but plastic is better.

Laundry day after we forgot to close the forehatch, dove into a wave, and took a load of water down below! The hardest thing is getting salt out of foam cushions.

Environmental Issues

As more people go cruising, it becomes incumbent on all of us to pay more attention to our effect on the environment and to accept our role as stewards of it. This is particularly true with respect to coral reefs—it pains us to see the thoughtless damage caused by some cruisers, both when anchoring carelessly and snorkeling in reefs. Between global climate changes and the assault of humans, coral reefs worldwide are being destroyed at a truly alarming rate.

However, this is not the focus of this section. Rather, I want to concentrate on the legal aspects of environmental compliance, specifically those concerning oil, garbage, and effluent.

Oil

Following the *Exxon Valdez* disaster, the United States enacted some very tough oil-pollution laws (the Oil Pollution Act of 1990, or OPA-90). There is similar, though less draconian, legislation in Europe. Under OPA-90, any kind of oil or fuel spillage that creates a slick or sheen of more than 1 square foot (a thimbleful of diesel is enough) can potentially bring down on a cruising boatowner the wrath of a law designed to deal with supertankers. The USCG and other agencies have broad discretion in deciding how to deal with a spill, with the costs billed to the polluter (in addition to any other legal action). In a worst-case scenario, even a tiny spill can result in a monstrous bill.

The most common source of fuel spills is carelessness when refueling. Most often, the tank is overfilled and diesel either blows back through the fuel fill pipe or spurts out the vent. There are now devices on the market to prevent this from occurring. One is fitted in-line with the fuel fill fitting with the vent coming back into it (available from Vetus, Racor, and others)—this must be installed when the boat is built or must be retrofitted at some cost. Another option is a simple collection device on a suction cup that can be temporarily attached to the hull below any vent fitting when refueling (available from Davis).

On our new boat, I had the fuel fill fitting moved from the side deck to the cockpit—which gives us more chance of catching any blow-back before it gets into the drains—and moved the tank vents from the exterior of the hull to interior locations, where a milk jug beneath the vents catches any overflow when refueling.

If the fuel coming onboard is cold and the boat in the vicinity of the fuel tank is warm, the fuel will expand. If a tank is filled to the brim, it will drive fuel out the tank vent. A small air pocket should always be left at the top of a tank.

Another common source of oil or fuel pollution on a boat is leakage of oil from the engine, or diesel from the fuel system, into the bilges, from where it is pumped overboard by the bilge pump. I strongly recommend an engine drip pan that is completely sealed from the bilge and the addition of oil- and fuel-absorbing "socks" to the bilge. Special bilge water filters are also available that will remove small amounts of hydrocarbons from bilge water as it is being pumped overboard.

The United States requires the posting of a placard close to the engine room warning against the overboard disposal of oil or oily water.

Garbage

At the international level, garbage-dumping at sea is regulated by Annex V of MARPOL (Marine Pollution) 73/78 (commonly known as MARPOL V). Various additions to this regulation have been promulgated by individual countries; the United States is one of the strictest and, therefore, a good benchmark.

In line with MARPOL V, the United States bans the dumping of plastic anywhere—no exceptions. Plastic is defined as including not just the obvious (e.g., plastic bags, milk jugs, and six-pack holders), but also Styrofoam, synthetic fishing lines and nets, synthetic ropes, and biodegradable plastics.

Within 25 miles of the coast, the dumping of dunnage (protective materials for cargo) and any other lining and packing materials that float is also banned. Moving closer to the coast, from 3 to 12 miles out, anything that is allowed to be dumped must be ground to particles of less than 1 square inch (645 mm^2). Inside 3 miles, almost everything is banned except gray water (the discharge from sinks, showers, and laundry) and fresh fish parts.

Storing garbage on a long trip can be a problem. We have found high-quality, heavy-duty trash bags to be the best answer. On larger boats, a good case can be made for a trash compactor run off either an AC generator or an inverter (the electrical load is less than that of a microwave and for only a brief time, so the overall drain on a battery bank is very modest).

Disposal in out-of-the-way places is also a problem. More than once, we had someone offer to dispose of our garbage only to see it carried down the dock and pitched into the sea. We now look for evidence of proper disposal facilities before handing it over.

The United States requires U.S. vessels to have a prominently displayed placard warning against the disposal of garbage overboard. Boats more than 40 feet (12 m) in length that operate more than 3 miles from shore are also required to have a written waste management plan that describes procedures for collecting, processing, storing, and disposing of garbage, and that designates the person responsible for implementation of the plan.

Effluent

Within the international community, the United States for many years also has led the pack on effluent issues; therefore, U.S. regulations provide a useful benchmark.

Discharge of untreated raw sewage is illegal anywhere within the U.S. 3-mile limit. In the United States, any installed toilet (*marine sanitation device* or MSD) in a vessel less than 65 feet (20 m) in length must conform to one of the three following types:

- Type I MSDs break up the sewage so that no visible floating solids remain. The sewage is treated chemically to kill bacteria and then discharged overboard.
- Type II MSDs are similar to type I, but treat the sewage to more exacting standards.
- Type III MSDs eliminate overboard discharge in prohibited areas by storing the effluent in a holding tank and then discharging it either through a dockside pumpout facility or overboard beyond the 3-mile limit.

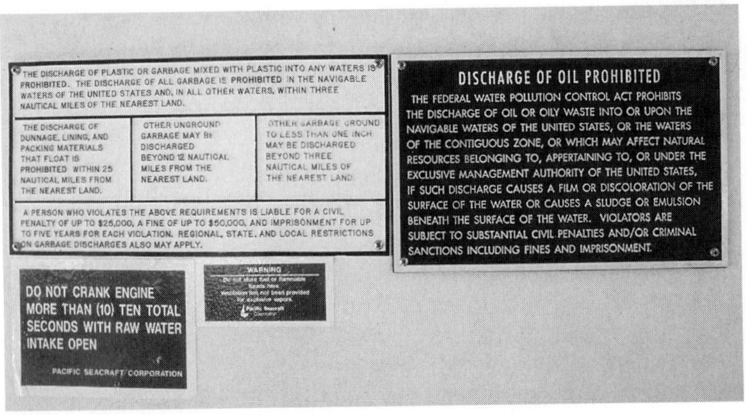

Required waste and oil discharge placards on U.S.-built boats.

Vessels over 65 feet (20 m) can use only type II or III systems. Type I and II devices must be properly certified and have a certification label. Holding tanks require no certification, provided they store effluent only at ambient temperatures and pressures, which is typically provided by venting the tank to atmosphere via a through-hull fitting.

Currently, it is perfectly legal to have a toilet and holding tank with a Y-valve so that the toilet can be pumped directly overboard (beyond the 3-mile limit) or into the holding tank, but it is no longer legal for a U.S. boatbuilder to install such a system. Rather, the toilet must be plumbed directly to the holding tank, with the Y valve installed on the discharge side, so that regardless of where the effluent ends up, it must first pass through the holding tank. However, it is legal for the customer, after buying a boat, to switch a Y-valve from downstream of the holding tank to upstream of it! The Y-valve handle must be secured in the holding-tank position when in territorial waters. Padlocking, removal of the valve handle, or using a plastic wire tie are all considered adequate methods of securing the valve. *The USCG checks these things.*

There is increasing concern that the chemicals used to treat the effluent in many type I and II systems are themselves damaging to the environment. We are already seeing moves to restrict the use of these devices in inshore waters and can expect more restrictions in the future. In the meantime, both in the United States and Europe, considerable resources are being put into developing the network of pumpout stations (in 1992 alone, the U.S. appropriated $40 million for this purpose). *Type III devices are the way to go.*

Finding Crew

A couple of decades ago, most cruising boats were crewed by their owners. As the "average" cruising boat gets larger and more complex, there is a trend toward taking on additional crew, particularly for longer passages. In some cases, insurance companies insist on it.

You would think that it would be easy to find suitable crew for a passage to "paradise." People constantly tell us: "If ever you need crew, just let me know!" But, the reality is that very few people, confronted with the chance to go, are actually able or willing to cut loose from their jobs and shoreside ties. Finding suitable crew can be a headache.

The first question is to determine what constitutes a suitable crew. For us, technical skills are not important; for someone else, the skills issue may be the most important one. What we primarily need is a responsible watchkeeper who does not get seasick (or, at least, not to the point of being incapacitated), who is personable and without offensive habits, who is willing and able to fit into a somewhat cramped family environment, and who does not need to be asked twice to help with onboard tasks and chores. Sail-handling and other skills can be learned along the way.

When you find a potential candidate, it really is important to devise a means by which this person can be put on "probation" until it is determined that he or she is compatible with the boat and its existing crew. This probation might take the form of a shakedown cruise before setting sail on a longer voyage, but it is more likely to be an understanding that if things don't work out on the initial passage, the crew member will be put ashore at the first landfall where transportation home is available. We found out the hard way that someone who is a delight to have around for a week or two can become a complete pain over a longer period (in this case, after the stock of admittedly captivating anecdotes were on their third word-perfect recycling)!

If things melt down, who pays the cost of the crew going home? This needs to be clearly understood beforehand (as part and parcel of discussing the probation arrangements). While on the subject of money, will the crew contribute to the boat's costs and groceries and, if so, how much? If a trip ashore is made, to what extent will the crew contribute to costs? Who pays for visas and other necessary paperwork?

It is important to remember that the skipper is in many ways legally responsible for the crew. As such, the skipper has to check that the crew has proper documentation (e.g., a passport). If the crew smuggles drugs onboard that are found, the skipper will likely be held responsible. If things don't work out and the crew is put ashore penniless, the local authorities are likely to hold the skipper responsible for the crew's upkeep and repatriation.

It is for these and other reasons that we are reluctant to take on crew whom we do not know well. We also have a drug policy of absolutely zero tolerance. And we make sure that one way or another, the crew has the financial resources necessary to get home from the farthest point of the voyage (we also learned this the hard way).

Given these considerations, once it has been determined that someone is a potential crew member, I recommend a frank and amicable discussion along the lines of "If, after a while, you find we have habits that are driving you up the wall, or we find there are things about you that are driving us nuts, we want you to understand that you have the right to quit at any landfall—but we also have the right to ask you to leave, even if you feel the problems are entirely our fault. If this does happen, we want to make it clear that our obligation to you ends as soon as you leave this boat—again, regardless of who you feel is to blame for the situation. We expect you to have the resources to take care of yourself from that point." And so on.

At one extreme, you may agree to pay an airfare home regardless of who is to blame for the meltdown; at the other extreme, before setting sail, you may insist on the crew handing over to you the cost of their airfare home. The key is to discuss these issues amicably before getting underway; if you can't have this kind of frank discussion with a potential crew member, things are likely to get fairly difficult somewhere along the way!

If a crew member does leave, it is important to make sure that he or she is properly removed from the crew list, with the necessary documentation to substantiate it. Some officials can become quite disturbed when checking a boat in or out of a country if the list of those onboard has changed in any way (more about "officialdom" later in this chapter).

Ultimately, other than relatively short visits by friends or relatives whom we know well, we feel it is best to sail without additional crew if at all possible. The longer the voyage, the more this tends to be the case. Long-term cruising is most successfully accomplished by stable couples or family groups.

Financial Matters and Insurance

Getting money when off the beaten track used to be quite a hassle, but it is unbelievable now the extent to which credit cards have penetrated the most obscure corners of the world. With a Visa or MasterCard, you can get cash advances just about anywhere there is a bank, although sometimes only one or the other is honored (it pays to have both). However, you will sometimes get hit with some stiff fees and lousy exchange rates. On a long cruise, there is the problem of keeping track of the account balances and making the monthly payments necessary to avoid delinquency charges.

American Express (Amex) is not as widely accepted as Visa and MasterCard, but it does enable you to get cash or traveler's checks from American Express offices around the world. An Amex card is also the best way to pay for rental cars (you can decline additional insurance charges—Amex picks up the tab if you have an accident). So here's another card to add to the wallet.

Travelers checks are accepted around the world, especially from American Express—without question, these are the best to carry. The cost associated with cashing them is frequently less than with a credit card. For this reason, it is a good idea to keep a stock onboard, including relatively small denominations (e.g., $20) for those times when only small amounts of local currency are needed.

In many countries, a better rate of exchange is found on the black market (i.e., on the street) than in the banks. To change money on the street, cash is usually needed—the almost universally preferred currency being U.S. dollars. To avoid carrying large amounts of cash on an extended cruise, it pays to check exchange rates before setting sail for any given country. If there is no black-market rate, then wait to withdraw money in local currency when you get there. If there is a significant difference between the official and the black-market rates, it may be necessary to obtain the cash dollars you think you need before setting sail from your present port of call.

In addition to the cash required for day-to-day transactions, we also carry a certain amount hidden away (in more than one place so that if one stash is found and raided, we are not left destitute). This is our emergency reserve.

Insurance

Whether to carry insurance is a constant topic of debate among cruising sailors, although in some countries debate is now preempted by a requirement to carry at least third-party coverage. Typically, on a well-found boat with an experienced crew, you can expect to pay an annual premium from 1 to 3 percent of the covered amount, with a deductible from 1 to 4 percent of the insured amount.

If insurance is carried, it is important to ensure that the region being cruised is covered at the time the cruise is taking place. Over a period of ten years, we made frequent cruises to the Caribbean, assuming that we had insurance coverage—only to find when I switched to another carrier that the policy excluded the Caribbean unless a special rider was in force (which we did not have)! All those wasted premiums.... Many policies do not cover tropical regions during hurricane or typhoon season. As with any insurance, it is important to read the fine print.

In many countries, cruisers are increasingly being held liable for their impact on the environment. In the United States and its overseas territories, for example, not only is draconian legislation in force regarding even tiny oil or fuel spills, but also covering damage to coral reefs. Let's say you run aground on a coral head on a falling tide. The boat heels to the point at which a pint or so of diesel dribbles out the fuel-tank vent. The USCG has the power to call out whatever troops it thinks are necessary to contain the spill, put booms around your vessel, take any other actions it sees fit to take, and then bill you for the entire operation while still taking you to court for the initial infraction. The local state or federal authorities may then come after you for damage to the reef (relatives of ours lost their boat on a reef in Florida; they were sued for $500,000 by the government). If insurance is carried, it is important to check whether such risks are covered.

Bureaucracy

Bureaucracy is a worldwide phenomenon that can be as aggravating in first-world countries as it sometimes is in third-world countries. U.S. sailors tend to talk disparagingly of customs and immigration officials in other countries without realizing that for the foreign sailor, the United States can be one of the more frustrating countries to enter!

Every boat needs papers, including the following:

- *Registration papers.* In the United States, most boats carry a state registration, which is generally an unimpressive slip of paper. When "going foreign," it is preferable to be a USCG-documented vessel; however, it takes a few weeks and costs considerably more than a state registration. It also needs renewing every year and expires if not renewed within thirty days, so it is important to have a way to handle this when going on a long cruise. For more information, visit the USCG home page at *www.uscg.mil/* or the vessel documentation center at *www.uscg.mil/hq/g-m/vdoc/nvdc.htm*. Other countries have similar documentation processes.
- A *radio license for the onboard* VHF and, if necessary, for an SSB and other radiotelephone equipment.
- *In Europe, a Value-Added Tax (VAT) receipt* if the boat is being sailed by Europeans or has been in Europe for six months (more information about the VAT, including exemptions, follows).

When going overseas, these documents need to be supplemented with the following:

- *Passports for everyone onboard.* It is also worthwhile to carry copies of other "official" papers such as birth and marriage certificates, plus a few spare passport photos.
- *Visas*, which sometimes have to be obtained in advance but usually can be obtained on arrival. It is best to check the current situation before setting sail because it can change overnight.
- A *valid driver's license* if you intend to rent or drive an automobile.
- A *certificate of insurance* for the boat, although in most countries it is not necessary.
- *Vaccination certificates for any pets* and sometimes for people (particularly for yellow fever in some parts of the world).
- *Licenses for guns.* Guns should be kept in a locked cabinet. The lock should be designed so that the cabinet cannot be opened without breaking any official "seal" that may be put on it.
- Perhaps some type of *boat-handling "certificate of competence."* This is increasingly required in Europe and currently under discussion in a number of states in the United States. If you intend to use the canals in Europe, you are advised to study an up-to-date copy of *EuroRegs for Inland Waterways* by Marian Martin, available from *yachtingbooks@ipc.co.uk* or by telephone (in England) at 0870-444-1110.
- A *crew list* giving full name, nationality, birth date, age, sex, and passport number of each crew member. It pays to have several copies.
- If the boat's medical kit contains prescription drugs, especially narcotics, it is recommended that you have a *letter from a doctor* authorizing their possession.
- If there is diving equipment onboard, *a diving certificate* is required in many parts of the world to get air bottles refilled.
- *An "official" ship's stamp* (a rubber stamp readily available from office supply stores) is a handy tool for stamping paperwork. A stamp makes a great impression in those countries where rubber stamps rule daily life!

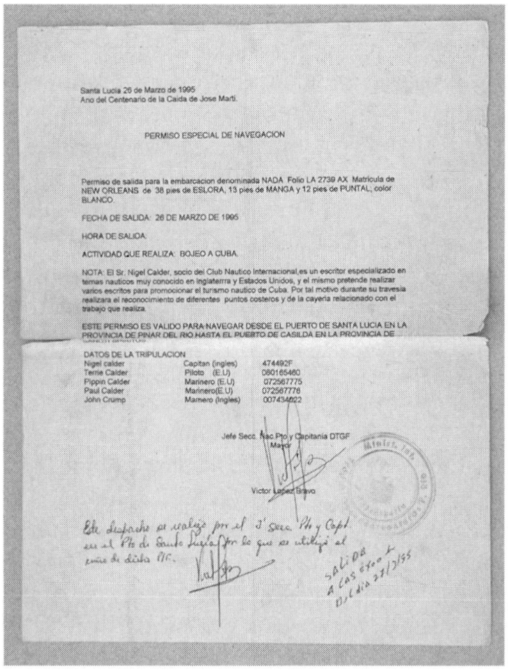
Santa Lucia 26 de Marzo de 1995
Ano del Centenario de la Caida de Jose Marti.

PERMISO ESPECIAL DE NAVEGACION

Permiso de salida para la embarcacion denominada NADA Folio LA 2739 AX Matricula de NEW ORLEANS de 38 pies de ESLORA, 13 pies de MANGA y 12 pies de PUNTAL, color BLANCO.

FECHA DE SALIDA: 26 DE MARZO DE 1995

HORA DE SALIDA:

ACTIVIDAD QUE REALIZA: BOJEO A CUBA.

NOTA: El Sr. Nigel Calder, socio del Club Nautico Internacional,es un escritor especializado en temas nauticos muy conocido en Inglaterra y Estados Unidos, y el mismo pretende realizar varios escritos para promocionar el turismo nautico de Cuba. Por tal motivo durante su travesia realizara el reconocimiento de diferentes puntos costeros y de la cayeria relacionado con el trabajo que realiza.

ESTE PERMISO ES VALIDO PARA NAVEGAR DESDE EL PUERTO DE SANTA LUCIA EN LA PROVINCIA DE PINAR DEL RIO HASTA EL PUERTO DE CASILDA EN LA PROVINCIA DE

DATOS DE LA TRIPULACION

Nigel calder	Capitan (ingles)	474492F
Terrie Calder	Piloto (E.U)	080165460
Pippin Calder	Marinero (E.U)	072567775
Paul Calder	Marinero(E.U)	072567776
John Crump	Marinero (Ingles)	007434622

Jefe Secc. Nac Pto y Capitania DTGF
Mayor

Victor Lopez Bravo

Cuban *zarpe*, giving permission to cruise the northern coast of Cuba.

Clearance procedures for foreign countries vary considerably; nevertheless, there are some constants. When crossing the 12-mile limit into another country's waters, a courtesy flag should be hoisted to the starboard spreaders with a yellow flag (the "Q" flag) below it. The courtesy flag should be of a reasonable size and in reasonable condition (some officials take offense at a shoddy little beat-up flag), and make sure it is hoisted right side up. The Q flag constitutes a formal request for inward clearance, and it is left up until you are told to take it down.

Once in harbor, sometimes it is acceptable to go ashore to find the officials, and sometimes you have to wait for them to come to you. When in doubt and if there are no other cruisers to ask, it is best to wait. If no one shows up, the captain alone goes ashore to check out the situation.

Usually, the boat and crew have to clear with customs (who may search the boat) and immigration (who will check passports and either stamp or issue visas). In addition, there may be agriculture and health officials, the local police, and the local port captain. Most countries issue a cruising permit for the boat (commonly known as a *zarpe* in Spanish-speaking countries). Otherwise, there may be specific paperwork from the customs and other officials. Some countries require clearance papers from the last country visited; others don't. Some countries require boats to clear in and out of every port, province, or region visited; others issue a single clearance for the entire country.

The clearance process can take from a few minutes to all day. The keys are to dress conservatively, act respectfully, keep cool, and don't offer bribes. When we are asked for bribes (it happens), we act dumb if we don't know the language; if that doesn't work, we ask for a receipt, which is usually sufficient to get the official to back off. Occasionally, we just have to pay, although we realize that in doing so, we are making life more difficult for the next cruiser who comes through.

A collection of flags required to cruise the northwest Caribbean.

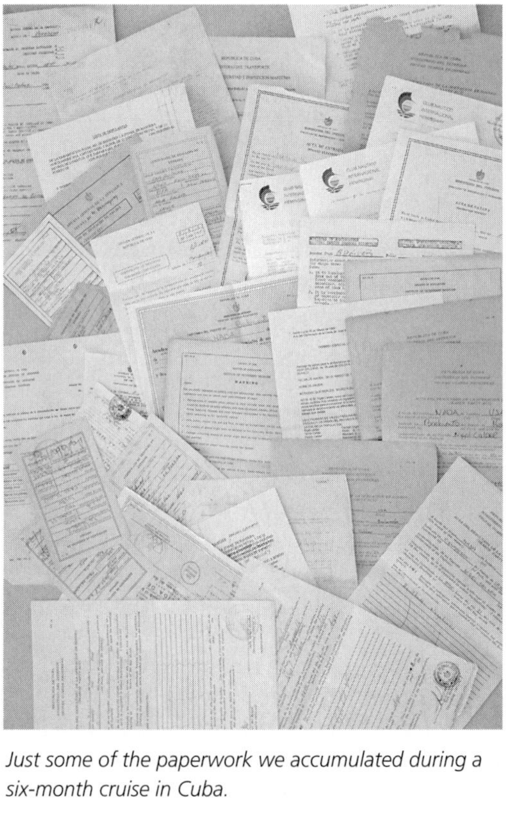
Just some of the paperwork we accumulated during a six-month cruise in Cuba.

Pets and firearms may create difficulties. Pets need valid vaccination certificates. Beyond this, they may be subjected to an extended quarantine period (particularly in many of the ex-British colonies). Firearms should always be declared—if they are hidden and subsequently found, the captain may end up in jail with the boat confiscated. With a lockable cabinet, officials from some countries may simply seal it; in other countries, the firearms will be taken ashore and held until the boat leaves (which means you have to return to this port to depart).

Entry visas and boat clearances are typically valid for a period that ranges from as little as two weeks to as much as a year. In Europe, unless exempted, foreign boats that have not paid the VAT are limited to a stay of six months, after which the boat must be sailed to a country outside the European Union (EU) or the tax paid (from 15 to 25 percent of the value of the boat). If the boat is sold to or used by an EU resident, the tax must be paid anyway. Some European nations can be particularly difficult when it comes to VAT issues.

A longer-term VAT exemption can be obtained from United Kingdom (British) customs and, presumably, other EU countries if the boat is your "normal home." In the United Kingdom, the procedure is described in HM Customs and Excise Notice #8 (April 1996, available at *www.hmce.gov.uk/notices/8.htm*), titled "Customs—Sailing Your Pleasure Craft to and from the United Kingdom." Form #C104A, "Importation of a Private Vessel on a Transfer of Normal Home to the United Kingdom," must be filled out (it will be given to you on arrival). Requirements include the following:

- living outside the EU for at least the prior twelve months
- owning and using the vessel outside the EU for at least six months
- using the vessel solely for private use
- not lending, hiring, or selling the boat in the EU for twelve months after the exemption from the VAT is granted

Children Onboard

Last in this section, but certainly not least, I look at the relationship between children and long-term cruising. We have cruised with very young children (from birth), but I do not recommend it for the following two reasons:

- the difficulty of dealing with diapers (nappies)

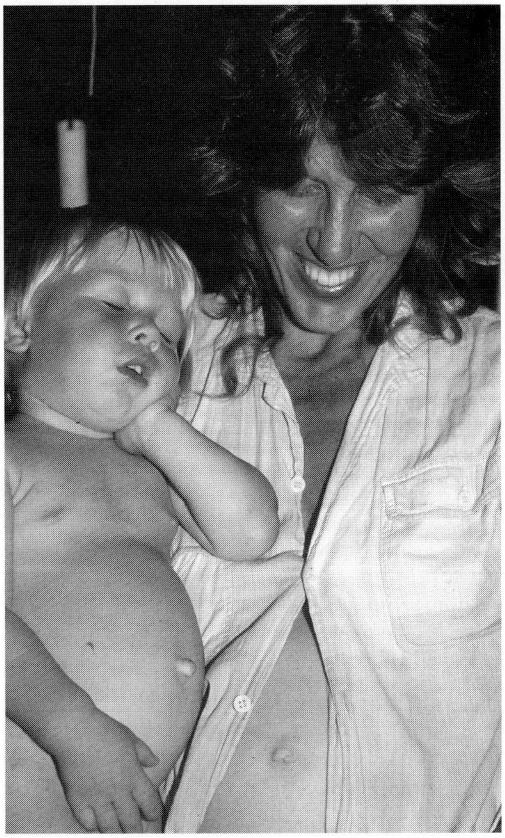

Pippin at fifteen months and Terrie at seven months, anchored out in Saint Lucia!

- the difficulty of dealing with typical childhood illnesses in out-of-the-way places

We also found that both our children experienced seasickness from birth (which the books tell you they don't). We had some quite miserable passages with the children throwing up all over us!

Once children are out of diapers and have somewhat built up their immune system, they are a joy to have onboard and wonderful icebreakers and ambassadors wherever you go. The main issue in this stage of their development is safety. We had extra-high lifelines (36 in./900 mm) on our boat, which were a godsend, and inside these we wrapped a nylon fishing net with a 1-inch mesh. The only spankable offense onboard was climbing the netting, potentially a matter of life and death for the children.

When they were at the crawling and early walking stages, but not yet old enough to respond to rational conversation, we built a sort of pen in one of the berths (like a drop-sided crib). Whenever we needed them safely out of the way so that we could give our undivided attention to the task at hand (e.g., when kedging off after running aground), we locked them in the pen. I recommend this to anyone with toddlers.

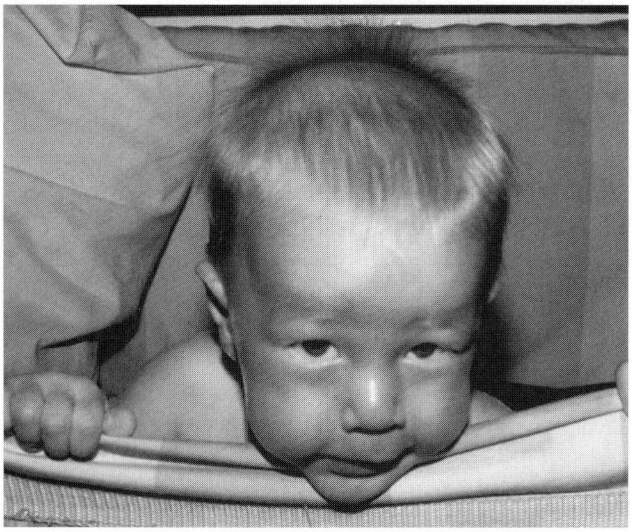

Left: *Paul penned up while we get on with some essential boat tasks.* Right: *It is our experience that cruising brings a family closer together.*

As children get older and more independent, safety at sea becomes an even greater concern. It is uncomfortable to force them to wear life jackets and harnesses at all times in the tropics. Because we had a particularly safe cockpit, we compromised by banning them from leaving the cockpit when underway or even climbing the coamings, but allowing them to sit in the cockpit in calm weather without life jackets. In rough weather, of course, there was no question.

Older still, they were allowed out of the cockpit, but only in calm weather and when wearing life jackets, and not out on the bow pulpit. This is, in fact, the rule that remains today. The next step is full integration into the working of the boat, going forward clipped on in rougher weather.

As children get older, their education becomes an increasing concern. For shorter cruises, we enrolled our children in and out of the state school system, getting curriculum from the teachers before leaving. We don't necessarily cover all the material we should, but what they miss in formal academics they more than make up for with other educational experiences, maturity, and responsibility. For longer cruises, we have bought a curriculum from a professional home-schooling organization (in our case, Calvert). We have found this material to be dry and unrelated to what the children are experiencing, but it does cover the formal academic bases.

More adventurous parents develop their own curriculum around the places they are cruising, often with spectacular results. The bottom line is that until children reach their teen years, there is no problem ensuring that they get at least as good an academic education as their peers in school, with a whole lot more. I never heard of a boat child who did anything other than excel when placed back in the school system.

When they get into their teen years, the education gets more demanding and, in the case of the sciences, needs facilities (i.e., laboratories) that are not available to cruisers. Nevertheless, children raised on boats continue to do exceptionally well; it just takes more effort on the part of everybody involved.

The bottom line is that the lack of educational facilities on a boat should *never* deter a family from going cruising; quite the opposite. Everything we have seen suggests that children benefit enormously, even when their formal education is somewhat haphazard.

Finally, we have found that in the absence of a TV (which we also don't have at home), the children read voraciously. It is a constant challenge to keep them supplied with books—a challenge that Terrie happily assumes!

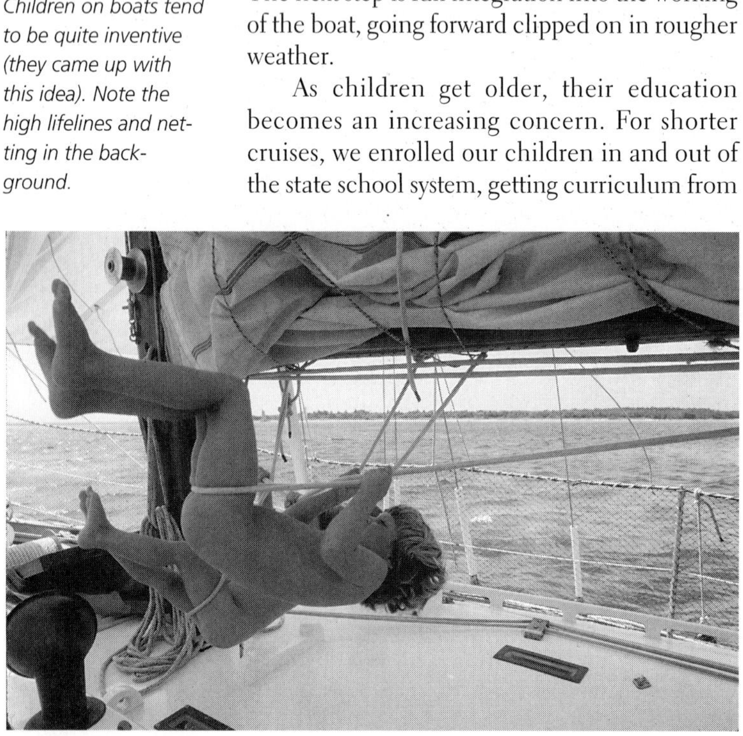

Children on boats tend to be quite inventive (they came up with this idea). Note the high lifelines and netting in the background.

Home-schooling in Cuba with a Cuban friend.

You won't get experiences like this at home—Pippin meets an orphaned spider monkey. However, part of the price that must be paid is an increased risk of getting sick.

SOME HOME SCHOOL RESOURCES AND CURRICULA

National Home School Association, *www.n-h-a.org*

Distance Education and Training Council (information about Accredited Institutions), *www.detc.org*

Home Education Magazine (very useful resource pages), *www.home-ed-magazine.com*

Calvert School (K through 8th grade), *www.calvertschool.org*

Oak Meadow School (K through 12th grade), *www.oakmeadow.com*

Clonlara School (K through 12th grade), *www.clonlara.org*

Sycamore Tree Center for Home Education (K through 12th grade), *www.sycamoretree.com*

Cambridge Academy (6th through 12th grade), *www.cambridgeacademy.com*

Phoenix Special Programs, *www.phoenixacademies.org*

Indiana University Independent Study Program, *www.extend.indiana.edu*

Brigham Young University (high school), *http://coned.byu.edu/is/index2.htm*

Home Study International (preschool through college), *www.his.edu*

CyberSchool (high school), *http://CyberSchool.4j.lane.edu*

Keystone National High School (high school), *www.keystonehighschool.com*

University of Nebraska (interactive, Web-based high school program), *www.unl.edu/conted/disted* and *www.class.com*.

Physics experiments on a boat can go beyond what's possible at a land-based school.

STAYING HEALTHY

The cruising life is fundamentally a healthy life. Nevertheless, it does have certain inherent risks, not the least of which is the possibility of being faced with a serious medical emergency far from professional help. We have had our scares. To some extent, this is simply the price we pay for leading the lifestyle we've chosen. To a considerable extent, however, many of the most likely problems can be anticipated and guarded against. In reality, the single greatest problem faced by cruisers is seasickness.

Seasickness

Both Terrie and I, as well as our two children, suffer from seasickness, so we understand the misery it can cause. The children got sick as babies. We found there is nothing that can spoil a long passage faster than having to hang onto two seasick babies while helming the boat and being seasick yourself!

Over the years, we have tried all kinds of remedies. Some worked; others failed us completely—in the latter category are Sea-Bands, which utilize acupressure; other people swear by them. (We have not tried the latest generation high-tech bands, for which I have received several favorable reports.) The most effective remedies all have side effects that we would rather do without, so we tend to continue without medication unless we feel really queasy. Staying up in the cockpit in the fresh air, focusing on the horizon, and perhaps taking on a responsibility such as helming the boat help considerably. When below, it is recommended to lie down and close your eyes. When you become really nauseated, it is often best to throw up and get it over with.

Prevoyage anxiety is undoubtedly a contributing factor to seasickness. Tests have shown that the simple act of "treating" seasickness with a placebo cures 30 percent of people, which demonstrates that there is a strong psychosomatic component.

Of the available remedies, hyoscine (e.g., Scopolomine, Scopoderm, and Travacalm) is extremely effective, especially the patches that you stick behind your ear—which are back on the market after an absence of several years. (Hyoscine is also available in a gel form that is rubbed directly onto the skin every few hours.) The patches generally confer immunity from sickness for three days, by which time most people have their sea legs. The side effects, however, can be quite pronounced, including a dry throat, restlessness, and difficulty in focusing on books and charts (the words and images tend to dance around).

Antihistamines (the most common is dimenhydrinate; e.g., Dramamine, Nauseatol, and Andrumin) are less effective and induce drowsiness; however, if a crew member is not needed, it might be preferable to have him or her doze below rather than use hyoscine. Another over-the-counter medicine that does not induce drowsiness is meclizine (e.g., Bonine). Many cruisers swear by cinnarizine (e.g., Stugeron and Marzine), but it is not available in the United States; one of its benefits is that it, too, does not induce drowsiness. All these remedies should be taken well before they are likely to be needed (preferably a full day, but at least four hours).

Our choice is a mixture of promethazine (Phenergan) and ephedrine (25 mg promethazine with 50 mg ephedrine), which the Naval Aerospace Medical Research Laboratory at Pensacola, Florida, came up with after extensive testing. It found other drugs to be more effective (e.g., straight amphetamines—"speed") but with unacceptable side effects.

The promethazine-ephedrine combination is at least as effective as hyoscine, much more so than Dramamine and other over-the-counter medications, and has few noticeable side effects. Promethazine is an antihistamine that, if taken alone, makes you extremely drowsy; however, ephedrine is a stimulant, and the two seem to just about cancel out. The advantage of this mixture is that it is taken only when you feel sick (as opposed to the hyoscine patches that are put on before the voyage and stay on throughout); if sick people can keep the pills down for half an hour, it will relieve them of the seasickness.

Promethazine can be obtained only with a doctor's prescription. Ephedrine is available over the counter, although in recent years it has been hard to find because drug addicts buy it and "cook" the speed out of it. If it's not available, pseudoephedrine (e.g., Sudafed) will suffice. A pharmacist can make up combined promethazine-ephedrine pills or you can buy the promethazine and ephedrine tablets separately and just take the necessary dosage. You should only need one dose, with perhaps another eight to twelve hours later if the seasickness is not under control. *Discuss possible side effects of this and all other medications suggested in this chapter with your doctor, considering the individual histories of yourself and your crew.*

When using other over-the-counter medicines, a person prone to seasickness should start taking tablets well before setting sail (some recommend as many as two days before), which results in the maximum possible immunity.

Finally, it should be realized that the greatest danger from seasickness is the increased risk of falling overboard when vomiting (it is essential that people remain tethered to the boat), and the lesser risk of hypothermia from lying out in the cockpit for prolonged periods. In severe cases of seasickness, the person should be taken below and put to bed. It is worth the effort it takes to get him or her undressed and as comfortable as possible.

If vomiting is frequent, dehydration will result; various rehydration drinks are discussed later in this chapter. Even without seasickness, dehydration is common on long voyages, particularly in rough weather. It is simply a result of not drinking enough fluids, and the most immediate side effect is headache. *A conscious effort needs to be made to drink at least 2 to 3 quarts a day.*

Good Health in Tropical Climates

Much long-term cruising is done in the tropics. There is no question that traveling to many parts of the tropics carries with it an increased risk of sickness over that experienced at home. There are a number of reasons for this.

- The higher heat and humidity create a greater tendency to sweat. Combined with the warm atmosphere, this provides an excellent environment for fungi and bacteria to grow on the skin. As a result, various itches, rashes, and vaginal yeast infections are quite common, and even tiny bites and pinpricks have a tendency to become infected. The sun, of course, can also cause serious sunburn; skin cancer is a very real problem for long-term cruisers.
- Many water supplies are contaminated, particularly with pathogens from human and animal fecal matter that cause diarrhea and other intestinal disorders.
- Sanitation is often poor at best. Flushing toilets are rare and even where they exist, the plumbing is often not adequate to handle toilet paper. Used paper is frequently thrown into a bin or the corner of the latrine. Various pathogens find their way from fecal matter onto food via unwashed hands and flies.
- Most food processing is not subject to the same rigorous public health standards as in the developed world.
- There are numerous pathogens to which the local population is relatively immune, but which cause sickness in visitors.
- Finally, diseases that have been all but eradicated in the developed world are still widespread in parts of the undeveloped world. Of these, malaria is probably the greatest hazard, but not to be ignored are dengue fever, hepatitis, cholera, yellow fever, typhoid, and tuberculosis.

Prevention

Despite the previous discussion, there is no cause to be paranoid about sailing into the tropics. What is needed are the following commonsense measures to minimize the chances of getting sick.

- The best preparation for tropical cruising is to complete a full schedule of *prophylactic* (preventive) inoculations (immunizations), which is especially true for children because they have weaker immune systems than adults. Most of us have already received a number of inoculations, but it must be remembered that while some confer immunity for life, the beneficial effects of others fade with time. *Before leaving home, adults need to carefully review their history of inoculations and obtain boosters when necessary* (especially for tetanus and polio). Additional inoculations that are not typically given in the developed world may be desirable when visiting some third-world countries (e.g., for yellow fever and *Japanese encephalitis*). Several inoculations should be obtained that are available today that were not when many of us were immunized (particularly for hepatitis A and B).
- Protection from the sun. Other than the risk of sunburn, excessive long-term exposure is known to cause skin cancer (a particular problem among cruising sailors). Biminis and awnings are essential for tropical cruising, combined with sensible use of suntan lotion, hats, and clothing. Suntan lotion is difficult to find

in much of the third world, so carry a good supply. Sunglasses are needed to protect the eyes, especially from reflected glare off the water surface.

- Shoes should be worn at all times in inhabited areas with poor sanitation because hookworms can be picked up through the soles of the feet; footwear should also be worn when swimming and snorkeling (discussed further later in this chapter).
- Personal hygiene is important. Whenever possible, a freshwater shower (or sponge bath) night and morning, with a regular change of clothes, goes a long way toward eliminating skin irritations caused by bacterial and fungal infections.
- Hygiene of others is a major problem. Because we have no control over the hygiene of the local population, all fresh food—fruit, vegetables, and meat—bought in the tropics should be considered suspect, as should most salads and fresh fruits consumed in restaurants. When eating out, you should look for clean restaurants and eat only well-cooked foods *while they are still steaming hot. Avoid salads at all times*. Fruit must be well washed in uncontaminated water or, better still, peeled. Peeled fruit is only as safe as the hygiene of the individual peeling it; therefore, to be sure, peel any fruit yourself (wash your hands with soap first—you should always travel ashore with soap). Flies are a frequent carrier of parasites from fecal and decaying matter

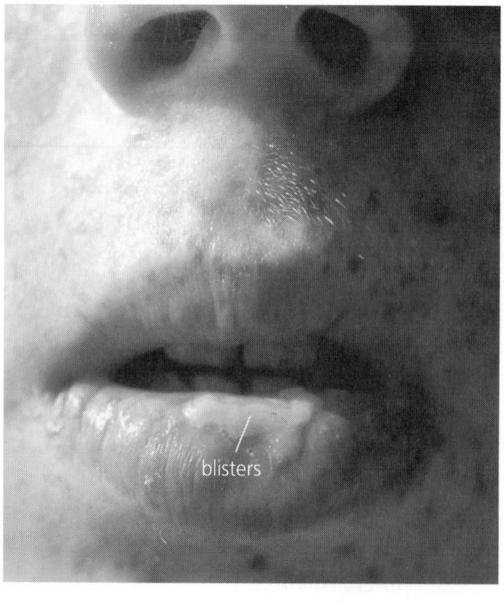

The sun can be dangerous. The unanswered question is to what extent does carelessness at this stage result in skin cancer in older age?

The iceman cometh! But has the ice been made from safe water?

lying around in unsanitary conditions. Avoid eating any food left around fly-infested areas (including your own boat—keep food covered).

- Do not drink the local water, and *don't use ice in your drinks unless you know it is made from purified water*. Don't eat ice cream or other water- or milk-based products (e.g., yogurt and cheese) unless you know they are made from purified water and/or pasteurized milk. When drinking bottled water, have it opened in front of you (it is not unknown for restaurateurs to fill the bottles from a faucet out back). Soft-drink bottling plants almost always have their own water-purification systems making them safe, as are drinks made from boiled water, such as tea and coffee.
- Cooking aboard is the safest way to avoid intestinal problems. Thoroughly wash all uncooked vegetables and fruits. Lettuce should be avoided altogether: it is too hard to clean properly and has very little nutritional value anyway. All meats should be well cooked. Warm milk, yogurt, and soft cheese make a fine environment in which to grow various harmful bacteria. Not only can diseases be transmitted from the cow itself, but also from the dirty hands of the person milking the cow. Use only pasteurized milk, yogurt, and cheese. To pasteurize milk yourself, either boil it or heat it to 144°F (62°C), keep it at this temperature for thirty minutes, and then cool it rapidly. Powdered milk is always safe (as long as

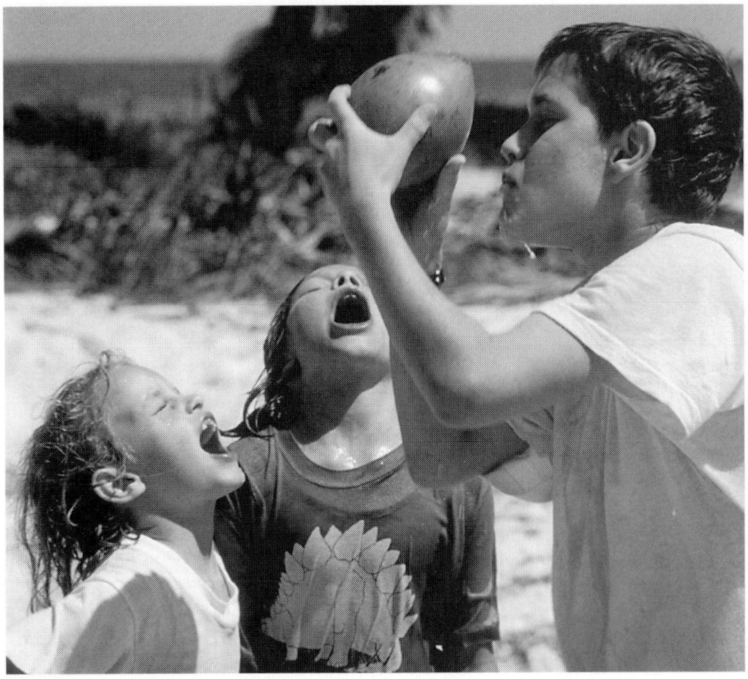

One way to get a safe drink!

the water used to make it is clean). Once mixed, it must be stored in a cool place, just as with regular milk, or it will rapidly sour.

A balance needs to be found between being overly cautious and enjoying the local cuisine and culture. At times, we have been careless and have paid a price: we have had numerous doses of Montezuma's Revenge (attacks of diarrhea); the children have picked up lice, intestinal worms, and hookworms; and Terrie had a serious attack of hepatitis A that almost killed her. These days, we are less adventurous, especially when it comes to eating out at local holes-in-the-wall.

Hepatitis A can be particularly nasty. It is highly endemic throughout the developing world. There is no cure other than resting, drinking a lot of fluids, avoiding alcohol (hepatitis affects the liver, which will have a difficult enough time without giving it extra work), and letting the body take care of itself. Antibiotics do not help and may do real harm. A sufferer is likely to feel very sick for two to four weeks, and to remain weak for one to six months afterwards. In recent years, a vaccine protecting against hepatitis A has become available—it should be given serious consideration.

Diarrhea

Diarrhea is caused by a number of infectious organisms, although the most common is *Escherichia coli* (ETEC). In almost all cases, the sufferer has watery stools with mild to severe stomach cramps for from one to five days, although we once got a bout that took ten days to clear. Occasionally, more serious strains of bacillary or amebic dysentery are contracted, in which case there is likely to be blood and mucus in the stools and/or recurrent bouts of diarrhea. In all these cases, a doctor should be consulted.

The likelihood of getting stricken can be substantially reduced by taking prophylactic doses of bismuth subsalicylate (e.g., Pepto-Bismol or Peptic Relief) at times of high risk (i.e., eating ashore in regions with poor hygiene). Reportedly, a tablespoon or tablet taken four times a day with meals and at bedtime reduces the risk of infection by 60 to 65 percent. However, such high doses are not recommended for long periods (certainly no more than three weeks).

Distribution of hepatitis A worldwide. (Courtesy Centers for Disease Control)

RECOMMENDED INOCULATIONS

The CDC provides the following "vaccine recommendations for most adult travelers." It's worthwhile to check its Web site—see below—periodically for updates.

- Tetanus-diphtheria. After completion of a primary series, a booster should be administered once every ten years for life.
- Polio. After completion of a primary series, an additional dose should be given *once* in adult life if traveling to a country where the disease occurs (many countries in Africa, Asia, the Middle East, and Eastern Europe).
- Measles. A dose of measles vaccine should be given to people born in or after 1957 who have not had two doses on or after their first birthday. Measles remains a common disease in many parts of the world—the risk to travelers may be high.
- Hepatitis B. Long-term travelers to intermediate or high-prevalence areas (many tropical countries) should be immunized, as well as any short-term travelers who have contact with blood or body fluids.
- Hepatitis A. All travelers—except to Japan, Australia, New Zealand, Canada, and developed countries in Europe—should be immunized. It is estimated that protection lasts for twenty years.
- Japanese encephalitis. Long-term travelers to Asia, the Indian Subcontinent, and the Western Pacific should be immunized.
- Typhoid. Recommended for travelers staying in areas of questionable sanitation. An estimated sixteen million cases, with six hundred thousand deaths, occur worldwide every year.
- Yellow fever. Only necessary if going to an area where yellow fever is endemic (parts of Africa and Latin America).
- Cholera. Almost never recommended (the vaccine is only 50 percent effective and is short-lived; cholera is relatively easy to treat in most cases).
- Rabies. Inoculation should be considered if you intend to spend time in the countryside where the incidence of rabies is high (much of Central America and Southeast Asia). If you are bitten by a rabid animal, the risk of infection *even without inoculation* can be significantly reduced by thoroughly cleansing the wound with copious amounts of soap and water.

In the United States, routine childhood vaccinations now include diphtheria, tetanus, pertussis (whooping cough), measles, mumps, rubella, varicella (chicken pox), polio, hepatitis B, rotavirus (the most common cause of gastroenteritis among infants and young children in the U.S.), and Haemophilus influenza B (which causes meningitis and other bacterial infections such as pneumonia). If any of these vaccinations were not received, they should be reviewed with a doctor to see if an inoculation is appropriate. Most of the diseases they protect against are still common in much of the undeveloped world.

For more on the worldwide incidence of disease and precautions that should be taken, consult the CDC's excellent Web site at *www.cdc.gov/travel/*. From there you can download a book called *Health Information for International Travel* (the "Yellow Book"; it is a 1.6 MB file and 225 printed pages). Other useful sites are listed as follows.

- International Society of Travel Medicine, *www.istm.org*
- American Society of Tropical Medicine and Hygiene, *www.astmh.org*
- Pan American Health Organization, *www.paho.org*
- World Health Organization (WHO), *www.who.org*
- Central Intelligence Agency (CIA), *www.odci.gov/cia/publications/pubs.html* (select World Factbook)
- Department of Health, U.K. (44 800 555 777: request booklet T3, *Health Advice for Travellers Outside the European Community*). Also, check the excellent Web site at *www.doh.gov.uk/traveladvice/index.htm*

As for other prophylactic medicines, the CDC advises that "prophylactic use of difenoxine, the active metabolite of diphenoxylate (e.g., Lomotil), actually increases the incidence of traveler's diarrhea, in addition to producing other undesirable side effects. Antiperistaltic agents (e.g., Lomotil and Imodium) are not effective in preventing traveler's diarrhea. . . . Enterovioform and related halogenated hydroxyquinoline derivatives (e.g., clioquinol, iodoquinol, Mexaform, Intestopan, and others) are not helpful in preventing traveler's diarrhea, may have serious neurological side effects, and should never be used for prophylaxis." Although various antibiotics are an effective prophylactic at times, the CDC recommends against their use because the potential drawbacks outweigh the potential benefits. In other words, the only effective prophylactic is good hygiene and watching what you eat and drink!

However, it has been shown that if someone is infected by *Escherichia coli*, a three-day course of double-strength trimethroprim-sulfamethoxazole (TMP-SMX) (e.g., Bactrim,

Septra, and Co-trimoxazole) taken twice a day will cut in half the time a person is sick. In this context, loperamide (e.g., Imodium) or another antidiarrheal (e.g., Lomotil) can be used to control the diarrhea itself while the antibiotics do their thing. A fluoroquinolone such as ciprofloxacin (e.g., Cipro; 500 mg tablets every twelve hours) is suggested by some doctors as an alternative to TMP-SMX, with fewer side effects.

The question is: Do you want to use all those antibiotics to clear up something that almost always clears up on its own in just a little more time? Unless there is blood in the stool or persistent or recurrent diarrhea, often the only treatment necessary is to take it easy and drink lots of liquids to replace the lost fluids. Young children especially can rapidly be put at risk from dehydration.

Studies have shown that a cereal-based rehydration drink is better than a sugar-based (using glucose or sucrose) drink. A preparation can be made with powdered or mashed rice to form a thin gruel, with a half-teaspoon of salt added to every quart (liter).

More commonly, various sugar-based powders (e.g., Oralyte, Dioralyte, and Pedialyte) are mixed with water to replace lost body salts. If the rice-gruel approach is not followed, a homemade rehydration drink can be mixed from 1 quart (32 fluid oz./0.9 L) of safe or boiled water, 8 level teaspoons of glucose powder, ½ of a level teaspoon each of baking soda (sodium bicarbonate) and salt, and ⅓ of a level teaspoon of potassium chloride. If potassium chloride is unavailable, reduce the salt and baking soda to ¼ of a level teaspoon each. If glucose is not available, use sugar or honey in the same amount.

The rehydration gruel or drink should be sipped every five minutes, day and night, in serious cases of loss of body fluids, or until normal urination is established. A large person needs 3 quarts (2.7 L) a day; a small child at least 1 quart (0.9 L), or a glass (8 oz./0.2 L) for every watery stool.

A person with diarrhea should start to eat if the diarrhea lasts for more than a day, because the body still needs nourishment. Try the BRAT diet (bananas, rice, applesauce, and dry toast). Other suitable foods include potatoes, noodles, crackers, sugar cookies, and low-fat milk products. Avoid fatty and greasy foods, raw fruit, highly seasoned food, and alcohol. Unless recommended by a doctor, children should not be given salicylates (e.g., Pepto-Bismol, Kaopectate), as this has been linked to Reye's syndrome, a potentially fatal condition.

Childhood Infections and Infestations

Worms and lice are commonly picked up by small children—ours did it twice (although, to be fair, one of those times the worms were acquired in Louisiana, and not the third world). Hookworms, threadworms, whipworms, and roundworms inhabit the gut. Eggs are variously deposited in feces or around the anus. They are then transferred to the mouth through poor hygiene, through playing in the dirt, or—in the case of hookworms—through the soles of the feet when walking barefoot on infected ground or beaches.

Worm medicines containing piperazine (e.g., Antepar) clear up threadworms and roundworms. When one child is infected, it is recommended to treat all. Thiabendazole and mebendazole are used against whipworms and hookworms; however, thiabendazole has some nasty side effects and mebendazole (e.g., Vermox) must not be given to pregnant women and children under two years old.

Tapeworms and trichinosis can be acquired through eating infected meat that has been insufficiently cooked (this pertains to any meat, not just pork; however, if you have ever seen pigs rooting around in open sewers, you can easily understand why pork is more likely to be infected than other meats).

All forms of lice (head, body, and pubic—the latter is better known as *crabs*) are treated with a lotion containing pyrethrine (e.g., Rid) or gammabenzene hexachloride (e.g., Lindane, Kwell, and Gammazane, which are relatively toxic and should not be used repeatedly). Clothing and bedding should be boiled at the same time if at all possible. Benzyl benzoate cream is used on scabies, a skin eruption caused by mites.

Prickly heat is another common complaint among children. A rash develops into raised red spots, often with a whitehead. Frequent washing (preferably with an antiseptic soap), drying, and exposure to air are needed. A powder of equal parts boric acid, zinc oxide, and talc—with a little camphor—applied after every washing also helps.

Fungus infections may occur on any part of the body, but the most common areas are between the toes (athlete's foot) and around the genitals (jock itch). Most infections grow in the form of a ring (ringworm), and should be regularly washed with soap and water, dried, and kept exposed to air if possible. Change and launder socks and underwear frequently—the fungus can be transmitted to others via infected clothing and towels. Antiseptic soaps such as Phisohex and Betadine should be used if possible. A cream or powder containing tolnaftate (e.g., Tinaderm or Tinactin) is generally effective in clearing up the infection if washing doesn't get rid of it.

Avoiding Mosquito-Borne and Other Transmittable Diseases

Malaria, dengue fever, yellow fever, and Japanese encephalitis—all mosquito-borne diseases—are common in some parts of the world frequented by cruisers. The obvious way to avoid them is to avoid getting bitten: use mosquito screens on the boat; keep your body covered when mosquitoes are active; and use insect repellents, sprays, and mosquito coils to keep them at bay.

Permethrin-containing repellents (e.g., Permanone) are recommended for use on clothing, shoes, bed nets, and camping gear. Permethrin is highly effective at repelling mosquitoes, even after laundering. For skin applications, formulations containing approximately 30 percent DEET (N,N-diethyl-meta-toluamide) work well; above a 30 percent concentration, the CDC advises that "the additional gain in repellent effect with higher concentrations is not significant when weighed against the potential for toxicity."

Malaria

Malaria is caused by a parasite carried in the saliva of the anopheles mosquito, which only bites in the evening and after dark. Currently, there is no vaccine for immunization against malaria, although there is some hope of developing one in the near future. In the meantime, various medicines kill the parasite if you get bitten; however, to be effective, the medicine must already be in the bloodstream—that is, a prophylactic dose must be taken *before* entering a malaria-prone region.

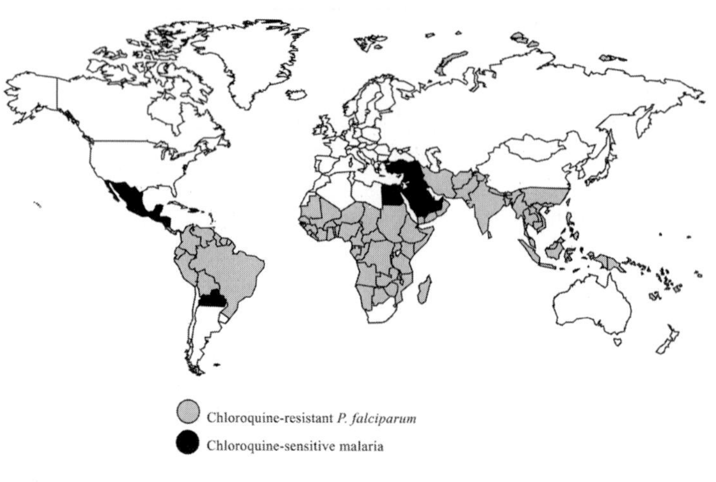

Distribution of malaria and chloroquine-resistant malaria worldwide. (Courtesy Centers for Disease Control)

The most common medicine is chloroquine (e.g., Aralen, Avloclor, Nivaquine, and Resochin), which is taken two weeks prior to entering a malarial area *and continued six weeks after leaving* (this is important). Unfortunately, in some parts of the world, chloroquine-resistant strains of malaria are becoming widespread (e.g., Panama, Venezuela, and much of Asia). Where resistance has developed, mefloquine (e.g., Lariam) is commonly given, but other drugs are also used (e.g., hydroxychloroquine sulfate and doxycycline), sometimes with unpleasant side effects. Clearly, before entering a region with malaria, it is important to find out the best drug for that region.

In the third world, it has been shown that local doctors frequently misdiagnose malaria, even after blood tests, when in fact there is some other condition causing the sickness (e.g., flu or dengue fever). Test kits are now available for self-diagnosis, but they sometimes fail to detect malaria if prophylactic drugs are being taken. Nevertheless, it is definitely worth carrying such a kit when cruising extensively in malarial regions. If nothing else, the test kit can determine whether malaria really is the problem if someone experiences malaria-like symptoms after leaving the region and when no longer on a prophylactic drug.

More than three hundred million people develop cases of malaria each year, of whom one million to three million die: malaria needs to be taken seriously. If there is any question about its possible occurrence, the prophylactic dose should be taken—swallowing one or two tablets a week is a small price to pay for freedom from the disease. As mentioned previously, this dose must be maintained for six weeks after leaving the infected region—*many people have become seriously ill by neglecting this step.*

Dengue Fever

Dengue fever (otherwise known as *breakbone fever* because of the intense aching in the joints it causes) is carried by a mosquito that hangs out in populated areas around cisterns and other stagnant water supplies, and only bites during the day. It is a rapidly expanding disease in most tropical areas of the world with more than 2.5 billion people estimated to be at risk, and an estimated hundred million cases of infection each year (with twenty-five thousand fatalities). Increased transmission is anticipated in all tropical areas for the indefinite future; the worst time of year is during and just after the

▨ Areas infested with Aedes aegypti	■ Areas with A. aegypti and dengue epidemic activity

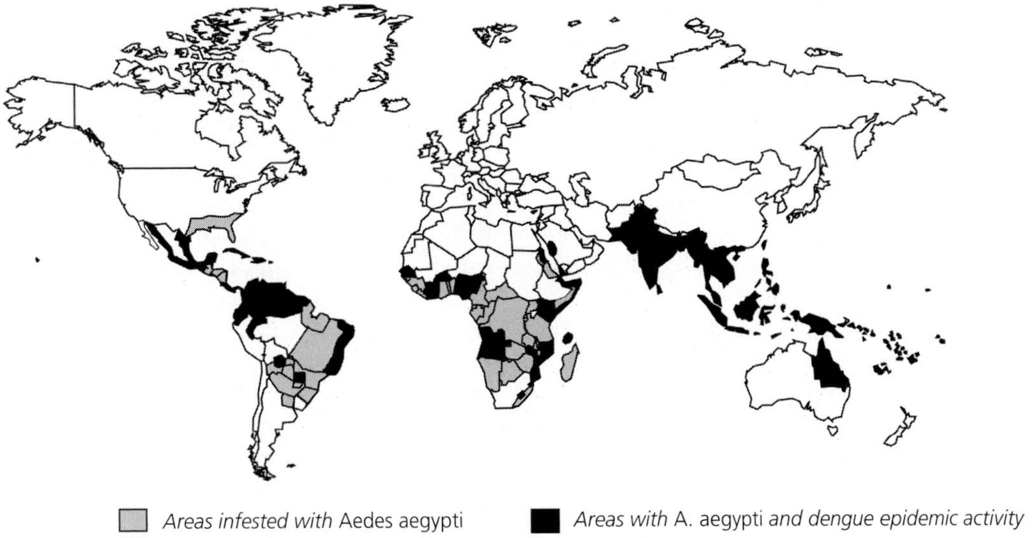

Distribution of dengue fever worldwide. (Courtesy Centers for Disease Control)

rainy season. There is no cure other than time; the best course of action is to take measures to avoid getting bitten.

Yellow Fever

Yellow fever is less widespread and there is an effective inoculation against it. If there is any likelihood of sailing into a region where yellow fever is present, inoculation (which is good for ten years) is recommended.

Japanese Encephalitis

Occurring in Asia, Japanese encephalitis is a common mosquito-borne virus with some nasty side effects. The relevant mosquito feeds in the evening, mostly in the countryside. An effective vaccine is available.

Schistosomiasis

Schistosomiasis (*bilharzia*) needs to be mentioned. It is a particularly nasty disease, carried by freshwater snails, that is endemic in many tropical regions (including parts of the Caribbean, South America, Asia, and Africa—an estimated two hundred million people are infected). Swimming in tropical freshwater lakes and streams should be avoided unless it is certain that the parasite is not present. If it is diagnosed, safe and effective drugs are available for its treatment.

Yellow fever zones in the Americas and Africa. (Courtesy World Health Organization)

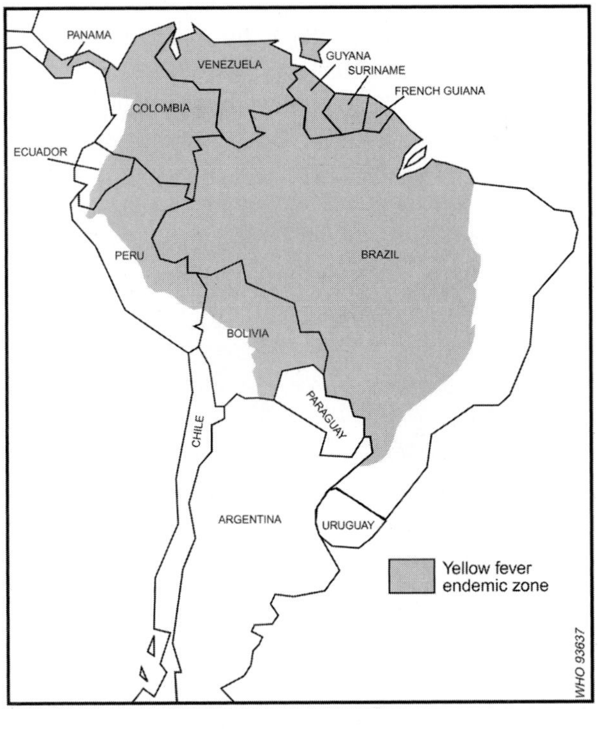

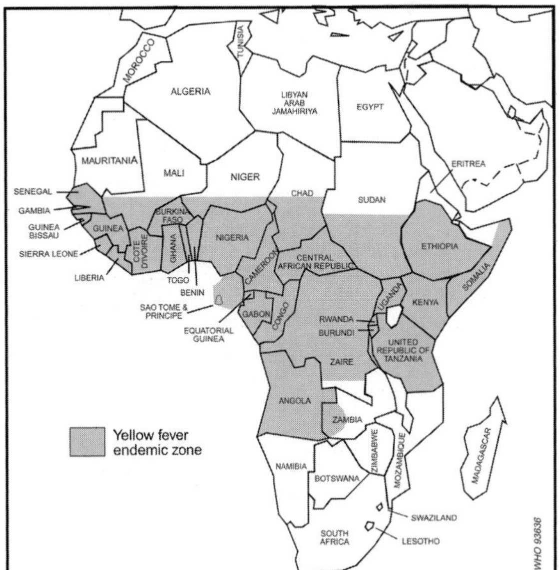

NOTE: Although the "yellow fever endemic zones" are no longer included in the International Health Regulations, a number of countries (most of them not bound by the Regulations or bound with reservations) consider these zones as infected areas and require an International Certificate of Vaccination against Yellow Fever from travelers arriving from those areas. The above map based on information from WHO is therefore included in this publication for practical reasons.

Sexually Transmitted Diseases (STDs)

Of course, it is AIDS that gets all the attention, with good reason: in some parts of Africa, 50 percent of the population is infected with the virus. Haiti and Thailand also have notoriously high levels of infection. As everyone knows, AIDS is transmitted primarily through unprotected sex and dirty needles—the risk to travelers is determined less by their geographic destination than by their sexual and drug-abusing behaviors.

Hepatitis B is another disease transmitted in the same way; however, there is an inoculation that immunizes against it (but it takes up to six months to be fully effective). The obvious way to avoid problems is to practice safe sex and for drug addicts to stay away from shared needles. Cruisers should carry a small supply of sterile hypodermic syringes and needles in case an injection is needed for medicinal purposes in an area that lacks medical facilities.

Cuts, Scratches, Insect Bites, and Marine Hazards

Cuts and scratches have a tendency to become infected quite quickly in the tropics, sometimes developing into nasty abscesses. In addition to being painful, they may need to be drained surgically. All punctures of the skin, however slight, should be cleaned with soap and water and an antiseptic (e.g., hydrogen peroxide) as soon as possible, treated with an antibiotic cream (e.g., Neosporin, Polysporin, or an ointment containing tetracycline), and covered with a clean bandage.

If a cut becomes infected, it should be allowed to drain. Promote healing by soaking the wound several times a day in slightly salted, hot-as-you-can-stand-it water. Change the dressing regularly and continue applying the antibiotic cream. If stronger treatment is required, two effective antibiotics are tetracycline (TNC) and TMP/SMX.

One particular problem sometimes experienced by sailors on long, wet crossings is the occurrence of saltwater boils on the buttocks. Regular washing with freshwater followed by a generous application of zinc oxide ointment (e.g., Desitin) at the first sign of pimples helps to prevent the boils.

Insect bites are generally no more than a nuisance, but in rare cases, an acute allergic reaction occurs requiring immediate medical aid. Otherwise, cold compresses with baking soda and soothing lotions (e.g., Calamine, Caladryl, Benzocaine, and various corticosteroid creams, which should be used sparingly) are all that is necessary. Antihistamines such as diphenhydramine (e.g., Benadryl), dymenhydrinate (e.g., Dramamine) and promethazine (e.g., Phenergan) help to reduce itching, but also induce drowsiness.

As mentioned previously, the best insect repellents are those containing N,N-diethyl-meta-toluamide (e.g., DEET, 6-12, and Off!) or dimethylpthalate (DMP). Various other "folk" remedies that may help repel insects include eating large quantities of garlic, which is more easily taken in capsule form (and is also thought to help in combating stomach ailments), and taking 200 mgs of vitamin B-1 daily for a month before exposure.

Marine Hazards

Sharks are generally attracted by blood in the water or thrashing motions such as might be made by a wounded fish (they have extraor-

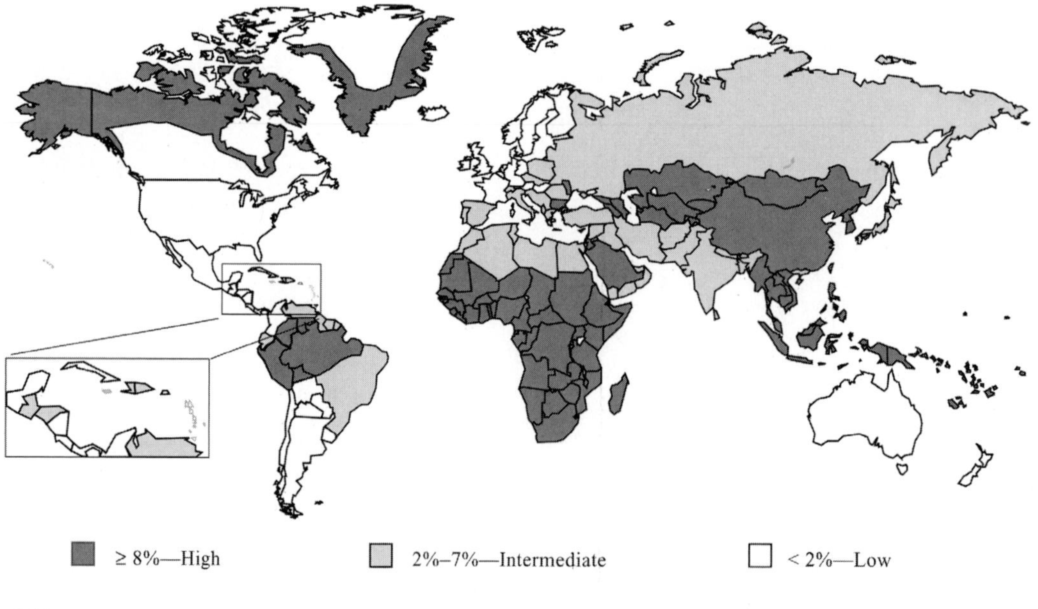

Distribution of hepatitis B worldwide. (Courtesy Centers for Disease Control)

◼ ≥ 8%—High	▨ 2%–7%—Intermediate	☐ < 2%—Low

dinary senses of smell and hearing). The only time they are likely to be dangerous is when you are carrying bleeding fish while spearfishing. Hold the fish well away from your body and get it into your dinghy as fast as possible. If the blood attracts sharks, get out of the water.

Barracuda hunt by sight and are attracted by bright, flashing objects, so don't wear bright wristwatches or jewelry in the water. Barracuda are both curious and bold, and frequently approach very closely, mouths open, displaying their fearsome teeth—which can be unnerving—but you need not be afraid.

Moray eels are shy and rarely venture out of their protective caves in the coral. However, if you incautiously poke your hand into a moray's lair, you may get bitten! The bite is not poisonous, but it is likely to get infected very rapidly—it will need thorough cleaning with an antiseptic (e.g., hydrogen peroxide), and treatment with an antibiotic cream (discussed previously in this chapter).

Stingrays, especially large ones, can inflict a deep and extremely painful venomous cut; infection is very likely. The cut should be bathed in antiseptic ointment and immersed in hot-as-you-can-stand-it water until the pain subsides (the heat breaks down the proteins in the venom); medical aid should then be found. After the pain has gone away (one to three hours), the big risk is a secondary infection developing as a result of infectious material left in the wound. The puncture area needs to be watched for several days—if it reddens and swells, treatment for infection is needed. To avoid such an infection, doctors often recommend a prophylactic course of antibiotics beginning as soon as possible after the injury occurs; TNC works well.

Scorpionfish have venomous spines along the dorsal area. Because the fish are well camouflaged and generally motionless, they can be accidentally trodden on or touched. Stings, which are deep and painful, should be immersed in hot-as-you-can-stand-it water until the pain subsides, and then medical aid should be found. The same considerations as for stingrays apply concerning secondary infection.

Sea urchins have spines that can occasionally penetrate even sneakers and bootees, so watch where you put your feet. The spines are not usually poisonous, but they are sharp and brittle. Once embedded, they tend to break off and it is almost impossible to extract them. Warm lime juice applied to the spines reportedly dissolves them; otherwise, the body generally absorbs them over time.

SELECTED HEALTH-RELATED BIBLIOGRAPHY

Where There Is No Doctor by David Werner, published by Hesperian Foundation, P.O. Box 1692, Palo Alto CA 94302 (*www.hesperian.org/*). This book was first written to encourage medical self-help among Mexican villagers with little or no access to doctors. Because this approximates the situation of cruising sailors in remote areas of the world, it contains much information of outstanding value for us also. With its emphasis on illnesses common in Central America, it is particularly relevant to anyone cruising the northwest Caribbean. Prescription drugs are widely sold "over the counter" throughout much of the world. If you cannot find a doctor, this book helps you diagnose your condition and choose appropriate drugs, where necessary, to deal with the situation. It also has an excellent first-aid section. Highly recommended.

Health Information for International Travel from the CDC and *Health Advice for Travellers* from the U.K. Department of Health; mentioned on page 548.

Preservation of Personal Health in Warm Climates by Ross Institute of Tropical Hygiene, London School of Hygiene and Tropical Medicine, Keppel Street (Gower Street), London WC1E 7HT, U.K. A very good booklet.

Staying Healthy in Asia, Africa, and Latin America by Volunteers in Asia, P.O. Box 4543, Stanford CA 94305.

The Ship Captain's Medical Guide by the United Kingdom Department of Trade and Industry. Written for merchant marine captains, this book contains solid advice on how to handle many serious and life-threatening emergencies. Some of the photographs are not for the squeamish.

Jellyfish are sometimes seen in great concentrations; many can sting. The Portuguese man-of-war, easily identified by its bright blue float, is particularly nasty and can sting long after it is dead. (Paul found this out when he dropped a rock on one and its bursting sack spattered his neck with tentacle parts—years later, he still has small scars). If stung by a Portuguese man-of-war, bathe the affected area with vinegar, which neutralizes the venom. If vinegar is not available, use ammonia or alcohol. Also apply a paste of meat tenderizer mixed with water. Don't try to wash the stings off with freshwater because it causes remaining stinging cells to discharge their poison.

On the U.S. East Coast, the most commonly found jellyfish is the sea nettle. Its sting is best neutralized with a paste made from baking soda and water.

Fire coral is quite common, especially at shallow (i.e., snorkeling) depths. It is generally yellowish brown and relatively smooth. Any contact can produce a painful rash. Bathe the

MEDICAL CHECKLIST FOR LONG-TERM AND TROPICAL CRUISING

Along with the generic name of various medicines, I provide the best-known brand names, but you can often save money by buying a generic drug:

Basic Precautionary Supplies and Measures

Sunglasses, sun hat, suntan lotion, lip balm (e.g., ChapStick)
Insect repellent: DEET or DMP (e.g., DEET, Off!, and 6-12)
Toothbrushes, toothpaste, dental floss, and other dental supplies—it is strongly recommended to get any dental problems fixed before setting sail
Spare eyeglasses for those who wear them

First-Aid Supplies

Adhesive tape, bandages, butterfly bandages to close cuts, gauze, safety pins, cotton swabs, cotton balls; maybe splints
Scissors and tweezers, needle and thread for stitches
Hydrogen peroxide, merthiolate, rubbing alcohol
Antiseptic soap (e.g., Betadine, a nonprescription soap, or Phisohex, by prescription)
Eye bath
Rubber syringe (e.g., for flushing wounds, ears, etc.)
Thermometer

Nonprescription Medications

Over-the-counter ear drops for "swimmer's ear"
Antibiotic cream (e.g., Neosporin, Polysporin, or creams with TNC)
Soothing lotions: Calamine, Caladryl, benzocaine, and Novocain
Hydrocortisone cream (for itching and hemorrhoids)
Pain pills: aspirin; acetaminophen (e.g., Tylenol), especially for children; ibuprofen
Antihistamines, such as promethazine (e.g., Phenergan, by prescription), diphenhydramine (e.g., Benadryl), or dimenhydrinate (e.g., Dramamine)
Typical cold remedies and other medications
Seasickness remedies
Bismuth subsalicylate (e.g., Pepto-Bismol or Peptic Relief) for diarrhea prophylaxis on short trips ashore
Imodium (for diarrhea; refer to the text and use only to bind your bowels for a specific purpose, such as a long bus journey) or Lomotil (by prescription)
Creams and powders with tolnaftate for athlete's foot (e.g., Tinaderm, Tinactin)
Medication for vaginal yeast infections
Pyrethrine (e.g., Rid, Nix) for lice
Piperazine (e.g., Antepar) and/or mebendazole (e.g., Vermox) for various intestinal worms

Prescription Medications

Antibiotics (see text following list)
Strong pain pills for emergencies
Otosporin in reserve for serious ear complaints
Lomotil (see Imodium under Nonprescription Medications)
Promethazine (e.g., Phenargan; see Antihistamines under Nonprescription Medications)
Seasickness medication: add ephedrine to the promethazine; scopolamine patches
Medi-halers and other medicines for asthma and bronchitis sufferers
Silvadene (for more serious burns, which are more prevalent than when ashore due to pots tossed off stoves in rough weather)
Gammabenzene hexachloride (e.g., Lindane, Kwell, and Gammazane) for scabies, and crabs
Antimalaria tablets

Miscellaneous

Vinegar and ammonia (useful on some bites and jellyfish stings)
Boric acid, zinc oxide powder, talcum powder, and camphor, or a medicated talcum powder (e.g., Ammen's)
Rehydration mix: a rice-based gruel, but also glucose, baking soda (useful on many bites), potassium chloride, or Oralyte, Pedialyte, or Dioralyte
Milk of magnesia (laxative)
Bleach (for sterilizing water and cleaning tanks), tincture of iodine, and/or potassium permanganate plus water-purification tablets (Halozone) to take on trips inland

A special word about antibiotics, for which prescriptions are needed, is necessary. There should be several different antibiotics onboard, including penicillin (e.g., Ampicillin and/or Amoxicillin), dicoxacillin, or cotrimoxacillin (e.g., Bactrin or Septra, which may be needed for penicillin-resistant bacteria, particularly staphylococcal); tetracycline; and a fluoroquinolone such as ciprofloxacin. Unfortunately, there are increasingly more antibiotic-resistant bugs around, occasionally necessitating the use of some of the heavier-duty medicines. We had a real scare with Paul one time when a virulent staph infection caused an abscess that was almost growing before our eyes and that was not responding to antibiotics. It took a new, powerful, and expensive antibiotic—cefpodoxime proxetil (e.g., Vantin), which some ear, nose, and throat specialists regard as their "ace in the hole"—to get it under control. With antibiotics comes the responsibility to use them judiciously and with some understanding of what is appropriate (a doctor should always be consulted before use if at all possible). It is our belief that people are too free with their antibiotics. In all our cruising and with various childhood infections, we have used them only a couple of times. Once started, the full course of antibiotics needs to be completed.

The antibiotics and some of the other medicines will be date-sensitive. It is not worth buying large stocks. It is also a good idea to keep a log of expiration dates and to check it occasionally.

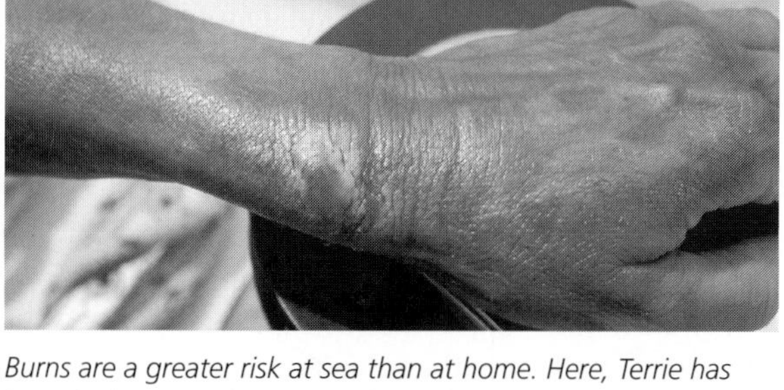

Burns are a greater risk at sea than at home. Here, Terrie has been hit by a pot that came off the stove.

affected area with vinegar or ammonia. This and all other coral scrapes and scratches should be treated with an antiseptic and watched closely for infection.

Ciguatera Poisoning

Ciguatera is a toxin secreted by reef fish and then concentrated in the bodies of those that feed on them. The larger a fish, the greater is the chance of ciguatera poisoning. Barracuda is the most toxic fish and should generally be avoided (especially large barracuda). Red snapper, grouper, amberjack, sea bass, and a wide range of tropical fish contain the toxin at unpredictable times. The potential for poisoning exists in all tropical and subtropical areas of the West Indies and the Pacific and Indian Oceans, although the actual distribution of the toxin is haphazard and sporadic. Local knowledge should be sought before eating fish from any of these regions. Kits are now available for testing fish for ciguatera, although the procedure is somewhat involved and time-consuming and relatively expensive.

Symptoms of ciguatera poisoning include the usual food-poisoning symptoms (nausea, vomiting, and diarrhea); tingling and numbness in fingers, toes, lips, and tongue; joint and muscle pain; hypertension, shock, and (very rarely) paralysis; and coma and death. Reportedly, "the inexpensive laxative Mannitol, given intravenously, reverses the symptoms within minutes and results in a full recovery" (letter to *Ocean Navigator*, June 1993). The same author reports good results from taking orally a powdered form of the laxative (Mannicol). I have been unable to confirm the efficacy of this treatment.

Finally, *Cruising World* magazine published a letter claiming that if a piece of fish is cooked with fresh coconut meat or anything silver (e.g., a silver coin), the coconut or coin will turn black if ciguatera is present (Feb. 2000). If this is true, it is a tremendously useful piece of information. Can any readers corroborate this?

STAYING IN TOUCH

It is no accident that I have left marine communications to the end of this book. Telecommunications is a field that gets increasingly complex, with dramatic changes—both technological and organizational—occurring overnight. The best I can offer is an overview with a sense of the options that are current. Although it may be out of date when this book is published, I hope it provides a helpful framework within which new developments can be categorized. The primary communications options for cruisers are as follows.

- VHF radios
- Medium-Frequency (MF: 1.6–4 MHz) and High-Frequency (HF: 4–30 MHz) radios, either a marine SSB radio or a ham SSB radio
- the International Maritimes Satellite (Inmarsat) system, which comes in various configurations (A, B, C, D, and M)
- various worldwide satellite-based cell-phone developments (e.g., ICO and Globalstar, and maybe the off-again, on-again Iridium)
- cell (i.e., mobile) phones
- e-mail
- of course, the tried and true "snail mail"

Big Ship Developments

Before discussing these developments from the perspective of a cruising sailor, we need to look at the big ship picture, recognizing that as of 2000, the Global Maritime Distress and Safety System (GMDSS)—which was adopted by the International Maritime Organization (IMO) in 1988 as an amendment to the 1974 *Safety of Life at Sea* (SOLAS) convention—was supposed to be fully operational (it was not, but it is getting there). All ships, regardless of when they were built, are now required to be in compliance.

The GMDSS legally requires all commercial vessels to have certain equipment onboard, dependent on how far offshore the vessel goes. Following are the four zones:

1. Within 20 miles of the coast, a VHF radio with *digital selective calling* (DSC) capability must be carried. DSC is a system that allows the equivalent of a telephone number to be assigned to a VHF, which then permits calls to be placed to individual VHFs. The number is called the *Maritime Mobile Service Identity* (MMSI) number. The VHF radio to which the call is addressed sounds an alarm ("rings")

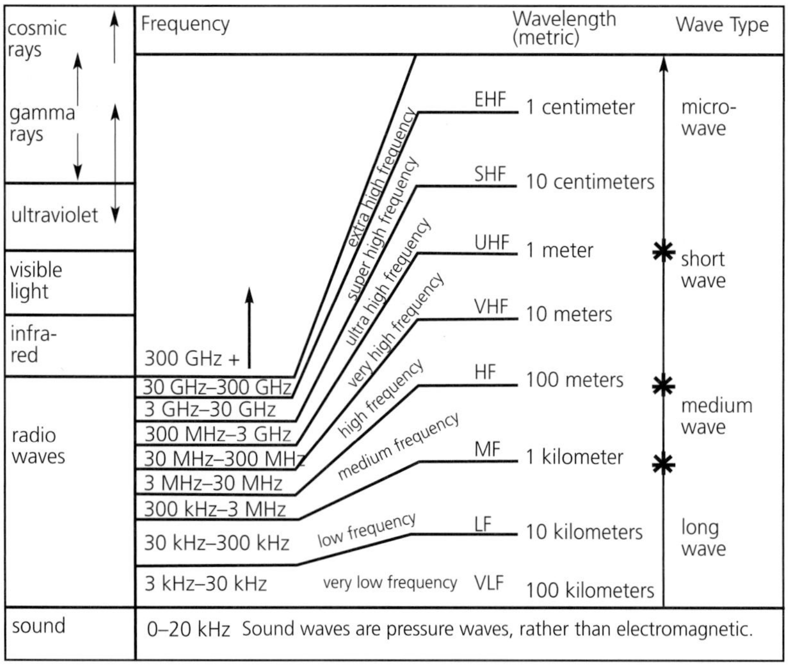

The radio-frequency spectrum.

when it senses an incoming call, just as a regular telephone does. This obviates the need for the receiving vessel to monitor that radio channel to get the message, eliminating what Bowditch—in a classic piece of bureaucratese—calls "dedicated aural watchstanding"! DSC channel 70 has been assigned as an international ship-to-shore, ship-to-ship, and distress-calling channel that serves the same purpose in the DSC world as channel 16 does in the voice world. *Ships are no longer legally required to monitor channel 16.* What this means for the recreational boater is that if a DSC-capable VHF radio is not onboard, it frequently is not possible to contact commercial shipping; therefore, any distress signal sent out on channel 16 or any other channel may not be picked up. Over time, not only ships but also various coast guard agencies around the world will also cease to monitor channel 16 (they can legally do so after February 1, 2005). Commercial DSC-capable radios (known as class A and class B) are very expensive, but they contain various features that radios built for the pleasure-boat market (class D) may not. Of particular interest is a specific piece of code required for automatic ship-to-shore telephony (voice communications—more on this later). When the DSC-capable radio is linked to a GPS unit, pressing a distress button automatically transmits the vessel's identity (MMSI) and position on channel 70.

2. From 20 to 100 miles out, shipping is required to augment the DSC VHF radio with a DSC MF SSB radio. Traditionally, the 2.182 MHz (2182 kHz) frequency has served the same purpose for MF radio as channel 16 has for VHF radio—that is, it has been used to make ship-to-ship and ship-to-shore contact, and has served as a distress-calling frequency. It typically has a range of around 100 miles. All commercial shipping had been legally required to monitor this frequency, but *not any more.* It too has been replaced with a DSC frequency (2187.5 kHz), with the same implications for the recreational boater as discussed previously.
3. From 100 miles out to sea and between latitudes 70 degrees north and south, shipping is required to augment the DSC VHF radio and DSC MF radio with a DSC HF capability and/or Inmarsat (discussed in more detail later in this chapter).
4. Outside these areas (i.e., toward the poles), the DSC VHF radio, DSC MF radio, and DSC HF radio or Inmarsat system must be augmented with a COSPAS-SARSAT capability (an international satellite-based search and rescue system that forms the backbone of the 406 MHz EPIRB system—see chapter 11).

The shift into GMDSS-compliant DSC-capable radio equipment by commercial shipping clearly has tremendous significance for recreational boaters. *At a stroke, it is making much of the equipment currently fitted to boats significantly less useful and ultimately obsolete!* Let's look at some of this equipment.

VHF Radio

The VHF radio has been and will remain the communications workhorse of the recreational boater. It operates on line-of-sight, which means that the higher the antenna, the greater is its range—generally 5 to 25 miles, but up to 50 miles when communicating with high towers ashore (we have picked up NOAA weather forecasts at well over 100 miles). Despite the increasingly widespread use of cell (mobile) phones in coastal waters, a VHF should be considered an essential piece of safety equipment, for the following reasons:

- It is now and will be for the foreseeable future the prime means for ship-to-ship communication and for contacting bridgetenders and lock keepers, marina managers, harbormasters, and boat-towing outfits.
- It has a greater range than cellular (mobile) phones (and you don't get charged for the calls).
- It is the key piece of equipment for getting attention when in distress; despite DSC, the USCG, U.K. Coastguard, and similar agencies around the world will continue monitoring channel 16 for years to come.
- The British Marine Industries Federation (BMIF) has warned that cell (mobile) phones can crash GPS systems or cause them to give false readings, and it cautions that the magnetic field created by a phone can cause magnetic compasses to give false readings.

When looking at fixed-mount VHF radios, the following factors should be remembered.

- The higher the antenna, the better.
- Antennas take the available signal and concentrate it into a focused beam. The more highly focused the beam, the longer is the range, but the greater is the chance of the signal not being received at the other end if the boat is rolling heavily. The degree of concentration is expressed as *decibels (dB) of gain*. A sailboat should generally have an antenna with a 3 dB gain; a powerboat does best with a 6 or 9 dB gain antenna.
- As of 2000 in many parts of the world (including the U.S.), the infrastructure to listen to DSC distress calls did not yet exist, as required by GMDSS. However, it is on its way; the USCG expects to be fully functional by 2004. When you are buying a new radio, it is advisable to get one that is DSC-compliant; in the United States, it should comply with the *Federal Communications Commission* (FCC) SC-101 standard.
- It is now possible to use a VHF radio to dial into a shoreside telephone in the United States and probably soon will be in other parts of the world. The largest operator in this field in the United States is MariTel (*www.maritelusa.com* and *www.mari.com*): by mid-2002, it will have the coastlines of the lower forty-eight states covered from 50 to 100 miles out to sea (depending on the height of the shoreside antennas). Given the height of the antennas (200–700 feet), a VHF radio used in this way generally has significantly more range than a cell (mobile) phone, and often at a cheaper cost (in the U.S., MariTel's annual fee varied in 2000 from $50 to $200, with the cost-per-minute of calls ranging from $1.00 to $1.50). Services include not just voice, but also e-mail and data transmission. This is probably the ideal communications system for the coastal cruiser at the present time and for the foreseeable future. However, it does require a DSC-capable VHF radio, which—if it is a class D radio (most likely)—*must contain the automatic ship-to-shore telephony code* (sometimes called a "D+" radio) and to which an MMSI number can be assigned.
- Although channel usage with VHF radio is broadly defined by international standards, there are some differences between Europe on the one hand and the United States and Canada on the other. Boats that will be voyaging in both European and American waters need a set that has an "International–USA" capability.
- A VHF radio for use in North American waters should have preprogrammed weather channels (WX) to pick up the invaluable NOAA coastal forecasts that are broadcast twenty-four hours a day.
- Many modern VHF radios have an option for a remote "smart" microphone (a *remote access microphone*, RAM) that enables the radio to be controlled from a cockpit microphone—which essentially provides a second waterproof radio at modest cost. This is a great feature, especially if the main unit is installed below in a navigation station.

As for handheld VHF radios, the following factors should be remembered.

- Waterproofness (including the battery compartment) and rugged construction are critical.
- The unit should have sufficient battery life to be left on for the better part of a day. Battery life is generally defined on the assumption that the unit will be on standby 90 percent of the time, receiving for 5 percent of the time, and transmit-

VHF RADIO CHANNELS

Remember, the primary purpose of VHF radio is for safety-related communications. Personal chitchat—except on calls placed via a Marine Operator (discussed below)—is technically illegal. If this is engaged in, it should be confined to the noncommercial (i.e., pleasure-boat) channels defined herein.

When using a VHF radio to communicate with another vessel, the correct procedure is to use one of the hailing channels (channel 16 or 9) to make contact with the other vessel, and *to then immediately agree to a working channel to which both vessels switch*. After the conversation is completed, both vessels return to the hailing channel and monitor it.

Channel allocation in the United States is as follows (there are some minor differences, as noted, in other parts of the world):

- Channel 16: distress and safety; ship-to-ship; and ship-to-CG, hailing
- Channel 9: noncommercial (i.e., pleasure craft) hailing in areas where channel 16 is congested; also used by bridgetenders on some sections of the Intracoastal Waterway
- Channel 6: inter-ship safety information (also channel 72 outside the U.S.)
- Channel 13: commercial hailing and passing intentions between ships, which can also sometimes be used to get the attention of ships at sea if they are not monitoring channel 16 (channel 67 is used for the same purpose in some areas); also used by most bridgetenders
- Channel 22: a working channel used by the USCG (channel 22 in the U.S. is different than channel 22 internationally—the set must be switched to its "USA" mode)
- Channels 68, 69, 71, 72, and 78: noncommercial working channels and also used by many marinas (in the U.K., many marinas use channel 80) (Notes: *do not use channel 70*, which is reserved for DSC distress and other calls; channel 72 is becoming accepted internationally through common usage as a yacht-to-yacht channel)
- Channels 1, 7, 8, 10, 11, 18, 19, 63, 77, 80, and 88: commercial channels that should be avoided by pleasure craft
- Channels 24, 25, 26, 27, 28, 84, 85, 86, and 87: used by Marine Operators ashore to connect VHF radios with shoreside telephone systems. (Note: although not all of these channels are used in all locations, they should be avoided except when placing calls through a Marine Operator.) With the widespread use of cell (mobile) phones and other forms of communication (e.g., the Maritel network), we are seeing the demise of many of these shoreside services.

ting for 5 percent of the time. Any increase in transmitting time *radically* shortens battery life.

- It is preferable to have a unit that accepts standard alkaline batteries in place of the supplied NiCad battery pack. In the event that the battery pack fails or can't be recharged, this makes it easy to change the batteries.
- Given that the boat's inverter often has to run to provide the AC power necessary to use a NiCad battery-pack charger, the charger that comes with the unit should have a fast-charge capability (most don't) to minimize the inverter drain on the boat's DC system.
- The unit should have an antenna socket that accepts the coaxial cable and connector used on the boat's fixed-mount VHF radio. This way, if the main VHF radio goes out in a distress situation, the range of the handheld can be substantially increased by plugging it into the main antenna.
- The unit should have both International and U.S.-Canadian capability.

Marine SSB and Ham SSB Radio

Marine SSB and ham SSB radio (MF and HF radio) have been the cruiser's preferred means of long-distance communication for many years. Despite all the new satellite-based technology, this is likely to remain the case because the costs associated with MF and HF high-seas communications are currently substantially lower than those associated with other systems (e.g., the setup cost is less than $2,000, and there is usually no operating cost). SSB radio is also extremely versatile: with appropriate "add-ons," it can be used not only for voice communications and to connect to international search-and-rescue services, but also for Weatherfax, data transmission, e-mail, and connection to the Internet.

SSB radio transmission utilizes what is known as a *carrier frequency*—a radio wave generated at a particular frequency—on which a voice or other message is superimposed. This gives the following four possible transmission combinations:

- the original carrier frequency
- the superimposed frequency

- the carrier frequency plus the superimposed frequency
- the carrier frequency minus the superimposed frequency

The third and fourth items are a mirror image of one another, containing the same information. If both are broadcast and received, this constitutes *double sideband* (DSB) radio. In practice, only one is needed at the receiving end to "decode" a message; hence, the term *SSB radio*. Marine SSB automatically selects the USB; ham SSB radios can be tuned to either the upper or lower. (If you refer to the table of Weatherfax frequencies in chapter 11, this explains the note at the top of the table on page 508: "When using the USB mode on an SSB radio, first tune the frequency 1.9 kHz below those listed; when using the LSB mode, first tune 1.9 kHz above those listed, and then fine-tune for the best reception.")

Although just about any antenna can be used for SSB (marine and ham) reception, effective transmission requires a fairly elaborate setup. This is not the book to discuss such matters: suffice it to say that if you are installing SSB radio, obtain some expert advice.

Marine and ham SSB radio use the same overall radio frequency spectrum, with each being assigned separate blocks of adjacent frequencies. The principal difference between them is that marine SSB is used for commercial purposes, ham SSB radio is restricted to amateur radio—commercial and business dealings are not allowed.

Although it takes the same radio set to receive and transmit on marine and ham frequencies, the radios are generally internally configured so that they only operate on one or the other set of frequencies. However, with many units, a small (perhaps illegal) internal modification configures a radio for both sets of frequencies. Some newer marine SSB radios are configured for ham radio right "out of the box"; for example, Icom's M-700 Pro Version 2, which—in common with a number of other marine SSB units—also has an automatic 2182 kHz alarm (the SEA 235 and the SGC 2020 and 2000 have similar capabilities). For legal reasons, this ham capability is rarely advertised in the literature. Other features important for a cruising SSB radio are RS232 and NEMA 0183 interfaces, which are necessary to interface with laptop computers and to upload and download data.

A license is required to transmit on any SSB radio (marine or ham—no license is required to receive). The requirements are different for the two licenses. For the marine SSB, it is primarily a matter of filling out forms; for a ham license, a test must be passed, which is much more demanding, although the requirements have been lowered in recent years. Ham radio is generally the preferred way to go from a cruiser's perspective, with the radio reconfigured so that in an emergency, the marine frequencies also can be accessed and used. Although using these channels is illegal, when in distress, it is not likely to be a concern! When using the ship-to-ship, ship-to-shore, and distress-calling frequency of 2182 kHz for anything other than a distress call, *a three-minute silence must be observed on the hour and the half hour*. This is so that any distress calls can be heard and not drowned out by other traffic.

There are numerous ham "nets" around the world that connect cruisers in a given region and provide tremendously useful up-to-date information on a wide range of subjects. In addition, ham radio is a way to chat with other boats and to communicate economically with friends and relatives back home. (If a connection is made with another ham operator living in the same area as the person being contacted in the U.S., you can be "patched" into the local telephone system at local rates; in the U.K., this is not legal.) As discussed previously, with an appropriate demodulator, the MF/HF radio can be used to send and receive e-mail, to receive Weatherfaxes and other faxes, and to connect to the Internet.

The downside to all of this is that there is a significant amount of learning associated with the use of MF/HF radio, which should be accomplished well before setting sail.

PHONETIC ALPHABET

Alfa	November
Bravo	Oscar
Charlie	Papa
Delta	Quebec
Echo	Romeo
Foxtrot	Sierra
Golf	Tango
Hotel	Uniform
India	Victor
Juliet	Whiskey
Kilo	X-ray
Lima	Yankee
Mike	Zulu

DISTRESS CALLS USING VHF AND SSB/HAM RADIOS

The following three levels of distress calls can be broadcast over a radio:

- "Sécurité" (pronounced *sayCURitay*), repeated three times, which is used to preface a warning to other shipping
- "Pan-Pan," repeated three times, which is used to preface a request for help if a boat or its crew is in danger, but the situation is not life-threatening
- "Mayday," repeated three times, which is used to preface a call for immediate help when in grave and immediate life-threatening danger

With an old-style VHF radio, channel 16 is used to broadcast such calls; with a DSC-capable radio, channel 70 is used to automatically transmit a distress signal (see above; channel 70 should not be used for *sécurité* and *pan-pan* messages), after which further information is provided on channel 16, as described below. With an old-style SSB, the distress frequency is 2182 kHz; with a DSC-capable SSB, it is 2187.5 kHz. In many parts of the world, 4125 kHz is used to supplement 2182 kHz; in parts of the Southern Hemisphere, 6215.5 kHz is also used.

In all cases of distress, the procedure is to repeat the relevant distress word three times, followed by

- "This is . . . {boat name, boat name, boat name}"
- "Call sign . . . "
- "{Boat name} position is {degrees and minutes of latitude; degrees and minutes of longitude}"
- "We . . . {nature of the emergency or warning}"
- "We . . . {type of assistance requested or other information}"
- other essential information (e.g., number of people onboard, injuries, state of the boat)
- "We will be standing by on {e.g., channel 16, 2182 kHz} on the hour, every hour, for {five minutes, or whatever the schedule will be}"
- "{Boat name} over"

Pause and then repeat this message, and continue pausing and repeating it until someone responds.

In a Mayday situation, the coast guard or another party coordinating a response may likely order a radio silence with the words "Seelonce Mayday," at which time only those involved in the proceedings can use this radio channel. The radio silence period will be terminated with the words "Seelonce fini." If you are passing on a Mayday message to a third party, your transmission begins with the words "Mayday relay" repeated three times, followed by

- "This is . . . {your boat's name}"
- "Mayday relay; following received from {name of vessel in distress}, call sign {call sign of vessel in distress}"
- repeat the complete message
- "{Your boat name} over"

If you hear a Mayday and are in a position to help, you should respond by twice repeating the name of the boat in distress, followed by "This is (name of your boat, name of your boat), received Mayday." When the boat in distress has acknowledged your response, you can give your position, course, speed and *estimated time of arrival* (ETA). However, take care not to interfere with other radio transmissions—there may be someone else better placed to render assistance.

Distress Calls Using Inmarsat-M

With an Inmarsat-M unit, lift the handset and listen for a dial tone. Lift the flap over the "distress" key and hold it in *for at least six seconds*. Press the pound (#) key. When the Rescue Coordination Center (RCC) comes on the line, give the Inmarsat Mobile Number (IMN) for the phone and the ocean region, followed by the preceding information, and then follow the instructions given by the operator.

Inmarsat

The Inmarsat system is built around geostationary satellites 22,200 miles above the equator. Its primary purpose is to provide maritime safety information for ships (it is part of the GMDSS system), but it has evolved well beyond this.

The components are *ship earth stations* (SES), which communicate via the satellites with *land earth stations* (LES), also known as *coast earth stations* (CES). These stations, in turn, are patched into local telecommunications systems. Because the polar regions are not visible to the satellites, coverage is limited to 70 degrees of latitude north and south.

Inmarsat A and B

The original Inmarsat A system is direct-dial voice, fax, and data capable, although fax and data are at relatively slow transmission rates. Inmarsat A is expensive to install and operate, and requires an antenna that is much too big

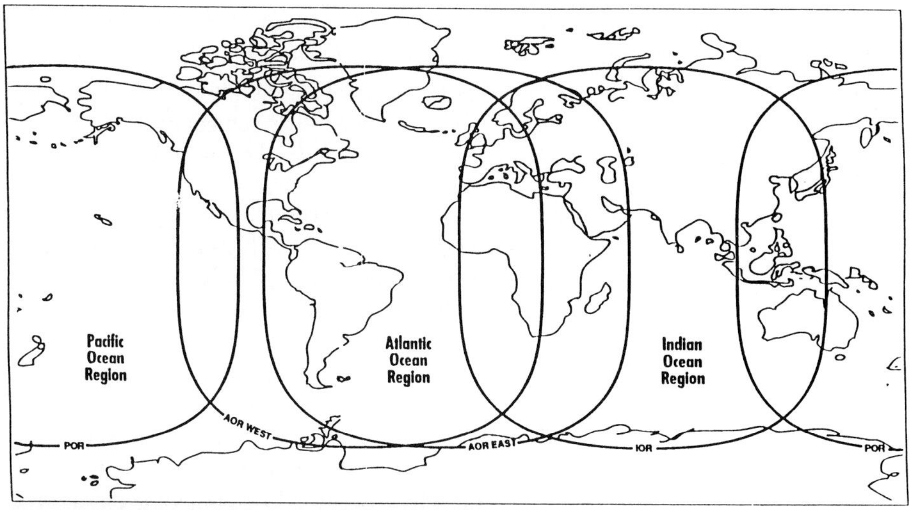

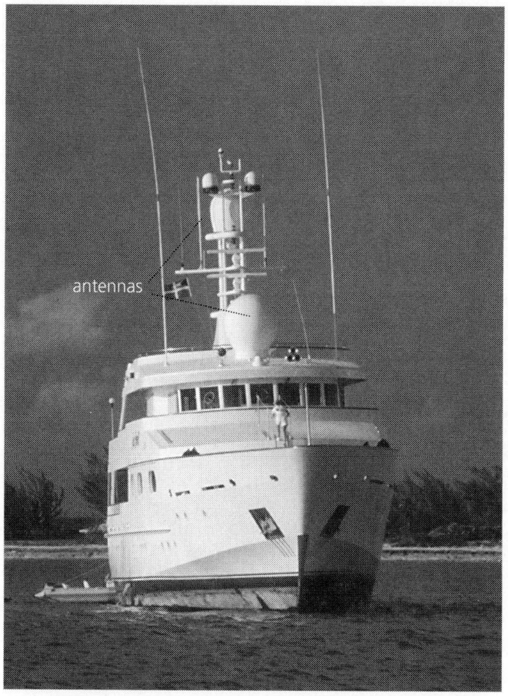

Above left: *Inmarsat coverage worldwide.* Below left: *Inmarsat A antennas.*

for most recreational boats. Inmarsat A is being replaced by Inmarsat B, which has the same capabilities but at faster transmission rates and lower costs. Nevertheless, it is still expensive and, although the necessary antenna is significantly smaller than that for Inmarsat A, it is still large.

Inmarsat C

Inmarsat C provides a store-and-forward data-messaging capability (i.e., it functions like a local Internet service provider, ISP), but at very slow and expensive transmission rates. It has no voice capabilities. It was specifically set up to meet GMDSS requirements for receiving maritime safety information (MSI) data onboard ships and for transmitting distress signals. The hardware is considerably lighter, smaller, and cheaper than Inmarsat A and B, but is limited in its application. It has to be hooked to a personal computer and printer to send and print out messages.

If Inmarsat C is to be used to send and receive e-mail through a local ISP (rather than the Inmarsat center), it is necessary to ensure that the local ISP can connect to Inmarsat (not all do) at local telephone rates—otherwise, you will get long-distance telephone charges when connected to the ISP (this is discussed further later in this chapter). You can't get on the Internet with Inmarsat C. Despite its limitations, many long-distance cruisers like Inmarsat C because of its reliability; its ability to transmit distress signals; getting the weather and other information that is provided free through the system; and the fact that for those who are neither familiar with ham radio nor have a license, it is a much simpler way to get a (limited) high-seas e-mail capability (although every message will cost you).

Inmarsat D

Inmarsat D is a service that permits automatic vessel position reporting. It is a passive system that does not permit two-way communication. It has been used by round-the-world racers but is finding wider acceptance (e.g., many on the Atlantic Rally for Cruisers—ARC—use it to display their position on a rally-organized Web site so friends and family can see where they are; this facility is being made available to the general cruising community).

Inmarsat M

Inmarsat M/Mini M is the latest Inmarsat variant. It has voice, fax, and data capabilities in a much lighter and more compact package and at considerably less cost than Inmarsat A or B. As such, it is a viable option for most cruising boats; however, the upfront cost is still high (approximately $6,000 in 2001), the per-minute operating cost is also relatively high, and the data transfer rate is slow. In addition to the poles, there are also significant areas of the South Pacific and Indian Oceans that have no Mini M coverage. It is not a GMDSS-approved system.

Distress Alerting

All Inmarsat systems are fitted with an automatic distress-alerting mechanism, which is typically a single "distress" key, but is sometimes a special dialing code. With a GPS connection, this not only contacts a shore-based station to raise the alarm, but also transmits the boat's position.

The L-Band EPIRB (see chapter 11) is also part of the Inmarsat system.

High-Seas Safety Information

Over the years, a number of systems have been developed to create and transmit high-seas safety information to ships (*Maritime Safety Information*, MSI). These include NAVTEX (Navigational Telex), which consists of a series of worldwide coast stations broadcasting on 518 kHz (received by MF radios), with a range of up to 200 miles offshore; and SafetyNet, a satellite-based system (using the Inmarsat satellites) that extends the range of MSI beyond NAVTEX. The different Inmarsat systems can be configured to automatically receive MSI, including screening out all MSI except those relevant to the region in which the boat is sailing (this prevents a huge pile of irrelevant messages).

If NAVTEX is all that is wanted, a standalone (dedicated) receiver can be installed at

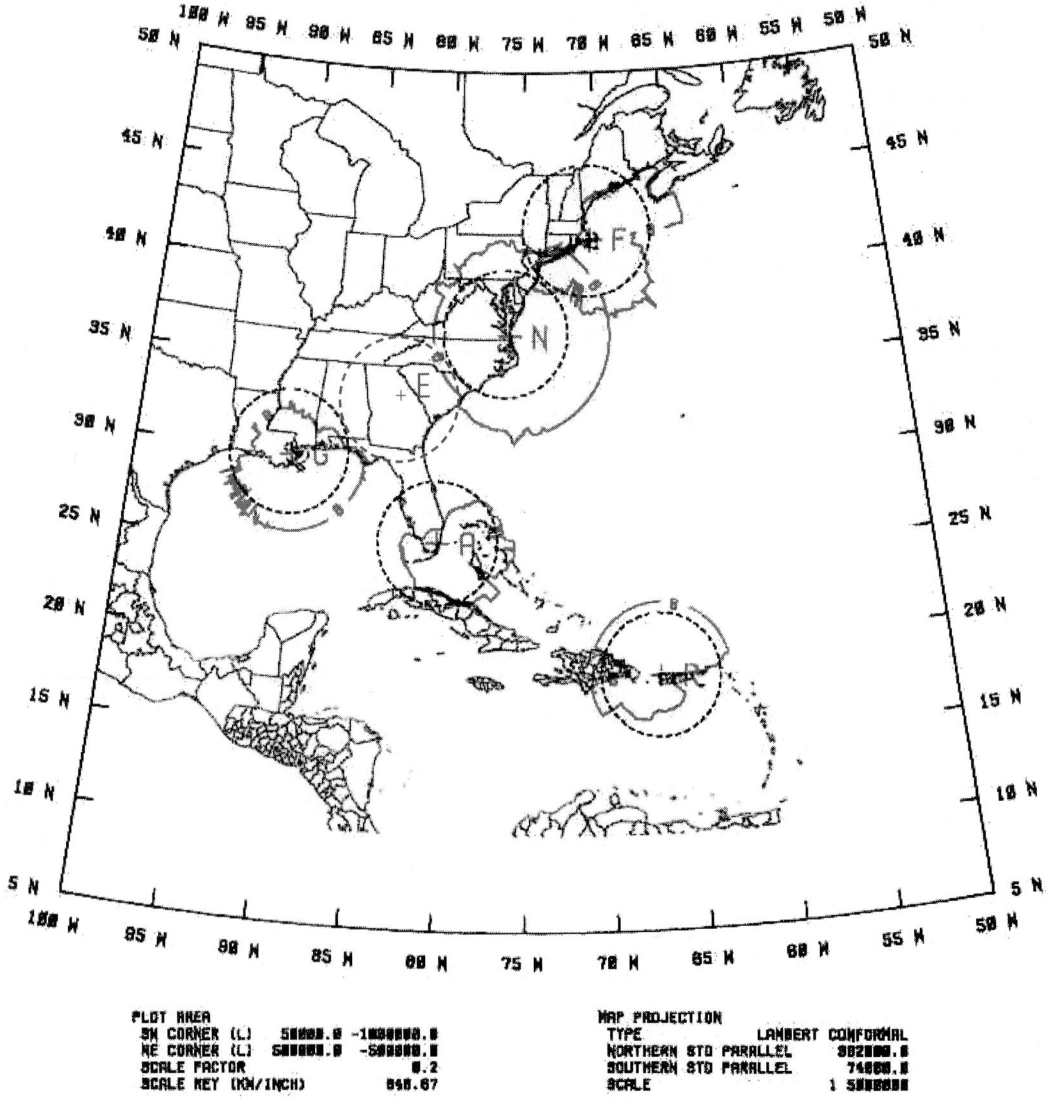

NAVTEX coverage of the Atlantic coast of the U.S.

much less cost ($150 and up; there are no user fees) than any of the Inmarsat systems. NAVTEX receivers are purely passive (receive only). The broadcast stations transmit about every four hours, with gale warnings and search-and-rescue (SAR) information transmitted upon receipt from an SAR coordinator or meteorological office, and then repeated at the regular transmission times. Older receivers simply printed this information; newer ones can print it or store and display it. In either case, the receiver must be left on all the time to get all the transmissions, which can represent a significant power drain, but otherwise can simply be turned on at the scheduled times; the newer display-type receivers use less power.

The IMO has designated NAVTEX as the primary means for transmitting urgent coastal marine safety information to ships worldwide. As such, NAVTEX coverage is theoretically worldwide, up to 200 to 300 miles from coastlines, provided by about 150 stations around the globe. In practice, coverage is good in much of North America (with minor gaps, including Texas's Gulf of Mexico coastline), Europe, the Mediterranean, and the Asian Pacific, but else-

Left: *Inmarsat Mini M antenna—note how much smaller this is than an Inmarsat A antenna. (Courtesy KVH)* Below: *NAVTEX coverage of the Pacific coast of the U.S.*

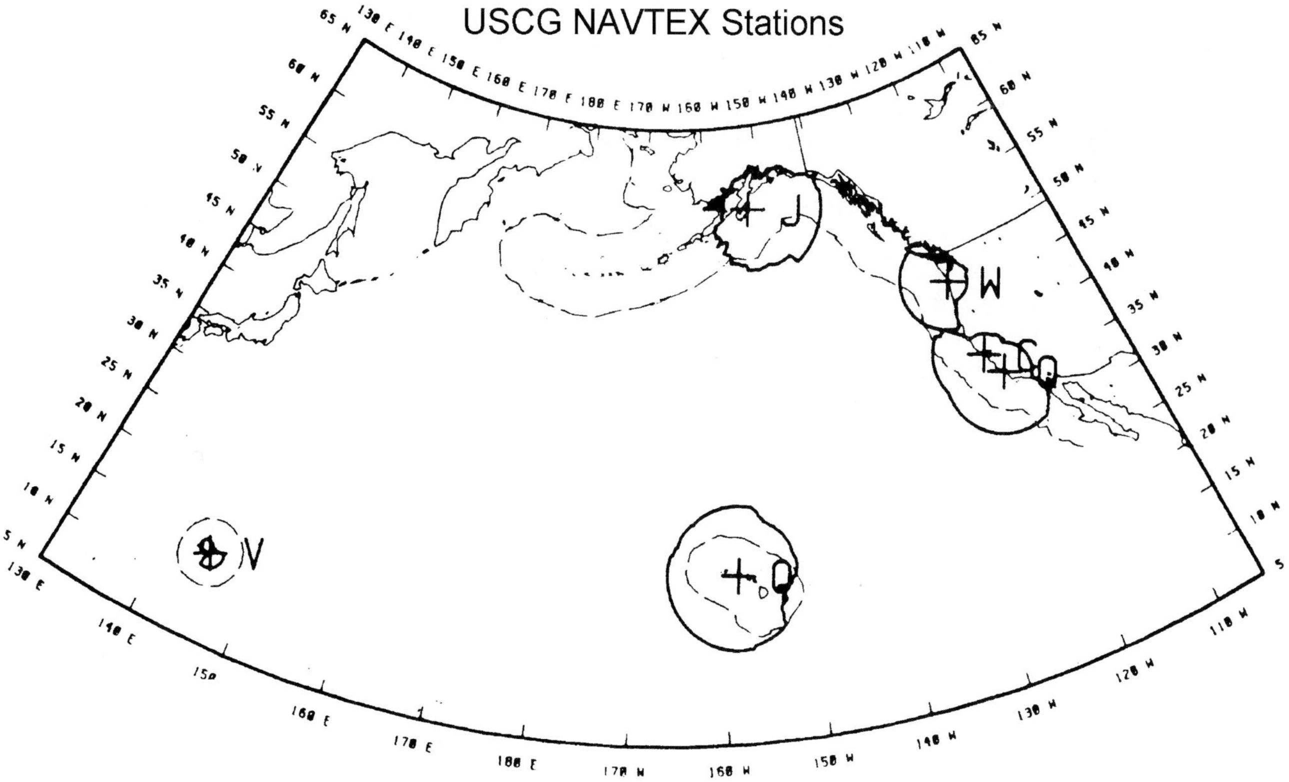

where can be spotty or lacking—not covered is most of the Caribbean, Mexico, much of South America, Australia, New Zealand, and most of the South Pacific. In general, NAVTEX is much more popular among recreational boaters in Europe than it is in North America (mostly, I would think, because of the availability of the excellent 24-hour NOAA coastal forecasts on VHF radio, for which there is no equivalent in Europe). For blue-water cruisers, NAVTEX is no substitute for a high-seas weather forecasting capability such as Weatherfax.

Satellite and Cell (Mobile) Phones

Cellular phones are becoming ubiquitous worldwide. As long as a boat is within range of a shore-based antenna, they work as well on boats as on land. With the addition of a digital modem and a special connecting cable between the modem and the phone, they can be used to connect a laptop computer with an ISP for e-mail; however, transmission is often slow and, because you are paying by the minute for airtime, costs can be high.

In thinly populated areas, coastal coverage is often spotty, in addition to which many phones do not work once outside of the local dialing area (especially in North America). There is also a mismatch between most North American and most European cell phones; however, some cell phone companies are expanding their worldwide coverage, which is often described as *GSM-capable* (global system for mobile communications).

GSM networks now cover most of Europe, the Mediterranean, eastern Australia, New Zealand, South Africa, the eastern seaboard of the United States, and Southern California. However, GSM systems in different parts of the world (particularly the United States) use different frequencies—to have truly global coverage, it is important to check that a phone can operate on all the relevant frequencies. In addition to the large coverage area, GSM networks have much faster data transfer rates than many other cell phone systems.

Clearly, when making cell phone choices, it is important to match the areas in which you intend to cruise with the available systems. An American going to Europe, for example, should wait to buy a European GSM phone and appropriate phone cards on arrival.

Satellite Systems

There are truly global satellite-based cell-phone-type systems, although following the bankruptcy of the grandest of them all—Iridium—the future is questionable in the face of competition from land-based cell phones (there is currently some talk of resuscitating Iridium). These systems use worldwide networks of either *low earth orbit* (LEO) or *medium earth orbit* (MEO) satellites to connect a cell phone with other satellites or with land-based communications networks. They have the potential to provide genuinely global telephone service, with very modest (in terms of size and weight) equipment requirements, but at a significant initial cost and operating cost. For example, when considering all the factors—including amortization of the equipment purchase cost and the setup cost—moderate use of an Iridium phone for a year (when the system was operational) ran up a bill of thousands of dollars. Data transmission rates are also slow and some phones do not work below decks without an additional external antenna.

Iridium was truly global: its satellites could receive a signal from anywhere in the world and then bounce it from satellite to satellite until in "view" of an appropriate ground station (a "gateway"), which forwarded it via traditional means. The other systems use what is known as the *bent-pipe approach,* which is to say the signal bounces off a single satellite back to earth—if there is no satellite "in sight," or the satellite does not have a gateway in sight, there will be no connection.

Of the bent-pipe systems, Globalstar had 52 LEO satellites in orbit by January 2001, with theoretical worldwide shoreside coverage, which in practice includes the coastlines of all the continents and the Caribbean, except Asia, Japan, and much of Africa (the Mediterranean coastline and South Africa are covered). Coverage is typically limited to 100 to 200 miles out to sea, although the entire Mediterranean is covered, and much of the North Atlantic, with technology being deployed that substantially extends this range (notably in the North Pacific) but with somewhat less reliability (depending on the distance from the gateway). The phone cost is around $1,500; the operating cost is around $30 a month and $1.70 a minute.

Other systems of interest still in the deployment stage are ICO and Teledesic (both owned by Teledesic). ICO is designed to use ten MEO satellites to provide worldwide coverage. It is backed by Inmarsat, with years of experience in this field. Teledesic is still very much in the development stage.

Finally, there is Skycell (from American Mobile Satellite Corporation), a satellite-based

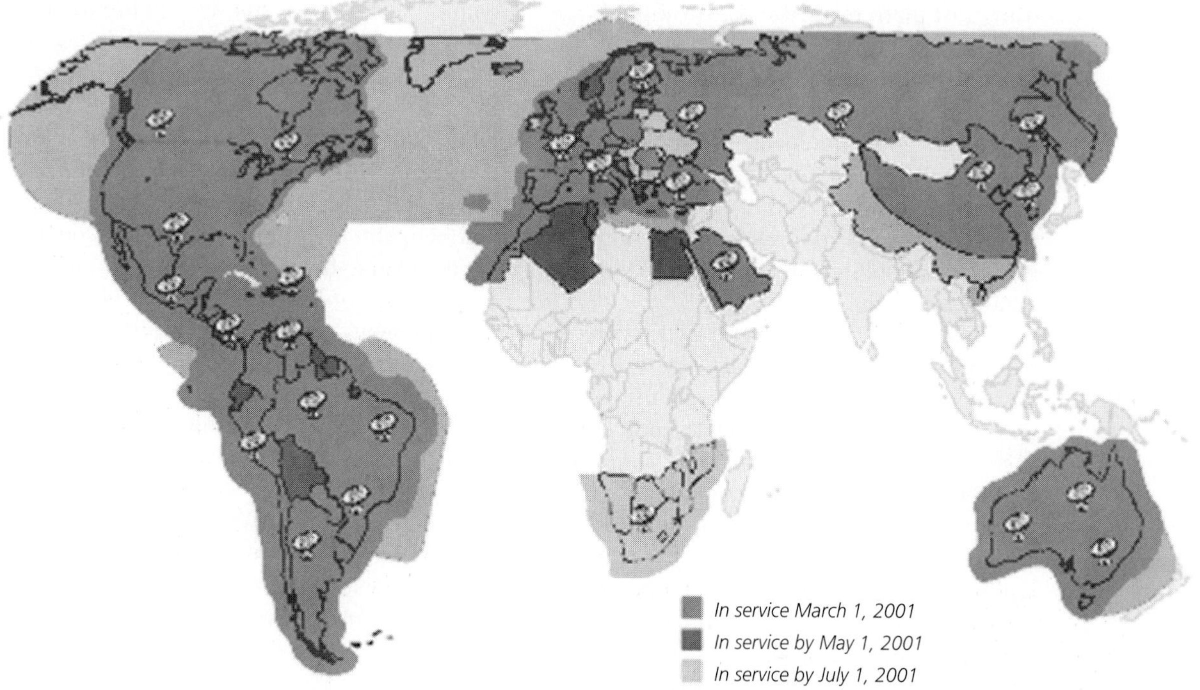

Globalstar coverage. (Courtesy Globalstar USA)

phone system with a single satellite that covers much of North America, Central America, and the Caribbean—although coverage does not reach Bermuda or the southern islands in the Eastern Caribbean. For those cruising within its coverage area, it offers a voice- and data-capable, lower-cost alternative to Inmarsat C, Mini-M, and the worldwide satellite systems, with higher transmission rates for data. However, with Maritel and Globalstar encroaching on its territory, it's not unreasonable to wonder about its future. (As we go to press, Globalstar is deferring some debt repayment, so maybe its future isn't as assured as it seems!)

E-Mail

E-mail is an increasingly popular way for cruisers to communicate with home. High-seas e-mail, using a marine SSB radio, was pioneered by companies such as PinOak Digital (*www.pinoak.com*) and Globe Wireless (*www.globewireless.com*). Assuming the SSB and laptop computer are already onboard, an additional hardware and software package—costing up to $2,000—is needed to make the system operational. There is also an annual fee of approximately $200. Data-transmission costs, at approximately $1 per kilobyte (approximately a page of text), are cheaper than any other commercial service (data-transmission costs quoted by some other carriers are given in *kilobits* rather than *kilobytes*—there are 8 kilobits in a kilobyte).

With appropriate hardware and software, the same kind of e-mail service can be obtained for free on ham radio, assuming a connection can be made through a shore-based ham and a telephone patch-in to the ISP. The land-based "host" station needs to be part of a rapidly expanding worldwide network of volunteer mailbox (MBO) stations, also known as WinLink or NetLink stations. These stations have computers standing by twenty-four hours a day that automatically pick up a message sent by a ham radio and forward it to any e-mail address. (A worldwide list of these stations is at *http://users.iafrica.com/z/zs/zs5s/buls.htm*.) From the boat, use an e-mail address that reads "*<your call sign@domain>*" with the name of the MBO to which you customarily connect, filling in the blank (the call sign is your radio call sign). More information is at *www.winlink.org* and *http://win-net.org*.

The downsides to using ham radio for e-mail are that it cannot be used for any business-related e-mail (activities related to personal financial gain are illegal); the operator must have a General Class ham radio operator's license; during transmission, the data is accessible to anyone with the necessary equipment (don't transmit credit-card information); and there is no guarantee of being able to make the necessary shoreside connection whenever you want to or in an emergency. Furthermore, people sending messages to you have to be educated in certain procedures, including keeping messages short, using just plain text (ASCII), turning off any HTML and MIME switches, turning off the function that returns the original message with a reply, not adding attachments, never passing on jokes and other junk mail, and never adding your e-mail address to widely copied lists that may invite junk and spam mail (keep your boat and regular e-mail addresses separate, and only give the boat address to close friends who are educated in its use).

To use ham radio to send and receive e-mail, you will almost certainly need one of the newer SSB radios listed previously (unless you are technically highly competent), coupled to a special modem (a *terminal node controller*, TNC) that converts the digital output of a computer into a radio signal for transmission and then converts the radio signal back into digital output for reception. The TNC should operate on something called PACTOR II (currently, the latest-generation, fastest, most versatile SSB communications protocol; it has significant advantages over other protocols). The cost of the modem may be as high as $650 (less versatile modems can be purchased for as little as $300). There will probably be a software package with the modem, but a better package—AirMail, written by Jim Corenman—is available at no charge for ham users (download it from *www. airmail2000.com*).

There is a middle ground between the commercial SSB e-mail providers and ham radio that is provided by services such as SailMail (*www.sailmail.com*)—this site includes an excellent primer on SSB e-mail, including hardware, software, and installation requirements (*www.sailmail.com/smprimer.htm*). SailMail was started by Jim Corenman and Stan Honey, with help from West Marine and others. It takes the kind of text-only e-mail services that are available for free to ham aficionados and makes them available on *marine* SSB—which means you don't need a ham license to use the service—on an at-cost (nonprofit) basis. This is great for those who don't want to work for a ham license and/or who need e-mail for business purposes. A similar service is proposed by the 10,000 strong (5,600 boats) Seven Seas Cruising Association (SSCA, *www.ssca.org*).

Currently, there is an annual SailMail membership fee of approximately $200 that varies according to the overall cost of providing the service (the cost is divided equally among all participating boats); there is no charge for use. Clearly, this is much cheaper than the commercial services (e.g., PinOak and Globe), but you don't get the full graphics capability of the commercial systems, special weather information, access to the Internet, and backup services. Of more significance for many users is the fact that SailMail is slow (a half-page of plain text takes ten to ninety seconds to transmit) and has a ten-minute daily time limit (which may be as little as two pages of text). Once this time limit is reached, you are cut off. If you subsequently need e-mail to handle an emergency, you cannot get back online until the next day. All of those previous comments about educating the people sending you messages are even more applicable here.

Similar services are available from the following.

- Shipcom (Foley AB), *http://world.std.com/~msgctr*
- MarineNet (Jupiter FL), *www.marine.net*
- CruiseEmail (Fort Lauderdale FL), *www.CruiseEmail.com*

Looking down the road, broadband (fast) Web access via satellites will be linked to pocket and palm PCs. Sending and receiving e-mail, and even surfing the Web, are likely to become as easy in midocean as they are at home. This will make redundant much of what has been discussed above!

Other current e-mail and messaging options include Orbcomm; the popular PocketMail in conjunction with either a cell phone onboard or a shoreside phone; a telecoupler; and cyber cafés.

Orbcomm

Orbcomm consists of a network of LEO satellites with coverage that provides data communications over much of the world. Magellan manufactures a small Personal Satellite Communicator (the GSC 100), which is a compact, handheld transmitter/receiver that allows brief messages to be entered with a small keypad and then transmitted to shore via the Orbcomm satellites, or received from shore. The GSC 100 has an integral GPS receiver that tags all messages from the boat with its position (a useful safety device).

Messages sent from a boat are routed to your ISP (for e-mail); it is also possible to have messages routed to a shoreside dispatcher who either faxes or telephones them to the intended recipient. Telephone or fax messages for the boat are called in to the dispatcher, who sends them on to the GSC 100 for retrieval. There is an upfront cost for the equipment, a monthly service fee, and a per-character transmission cost—messages are not cheap, especially if you or those sending messages to you are long-winded!

PocketMail

PocketMail utilizes a palm-sized computer, with a miniature screen and keyboard, to send brief messages. Newer versions allow messages to be composed on a regular computer (much easier) and downloaded to the PocketMail unit for transmission. The device includes a built-in acoustic coupler that, when held up to a regular phone and some cell phones, automatically makes an Internet connection and delivers or downloads messages. The system is cheap to buy (not much over $100) and cheap to operate (monthly fee of around $10), but it is limited to short text messages and may result in expensive phone bills.

Acoustic Couplers

You can buy an acoustic coupler, a telecoupler (available from Connect Globally at *www.LaptopProducts.com* and others) to connect a laptop computer to an ISP through a shoreside phone or cell phone in the same manner as the PocketMail device, only with full e-mail and Internet capability. However, if yours is a locally based ISP back home, there may be no available phone connection—and even if there is, you will pay long-distance telephone charges of up to several dollars a minute (so you'd better hope for no junk mail and no graphics on the server!). It is better to have an ISP with an extensive global network (CompuServe is a favorite) or else to use one of the free e-mail services available on the World Wide Web (e.g., Hotmail and WebMail). You can use just about any telephone to get connected at local rates, or persuade the folks at a friendly marina or dock to let you use their phone (as long as it is a local call, they probably won't mind). Of course, if you can persuade them to let you unplug their phone, you can directly plug in your laptop and dispense with the acoustic coupler—assuming you have a suitable phone cable.

Cyber Cafés

If you don't have a laptop and acoustic coupler, there is always the local cyber café, where you can rent a computer with an Internet connection on an hourly basis. Cyber cafés are popping up in even the most remote corners of the world. When the cruiser hits the beach, a cyber café can be used to send e-mail and download whatever is being stored on the server back home. As with a telecoupler, if yours is a locally based ISP back home, there may be no available phone connection, and even if there is, you will pay up to several dollars a minute; try to find an ISP with local phone service in your cruising area.

PocketMail and cell phone in use in the Bahamas. The PocketMail unit has a built-in acoustic coupler on the back, enabling it to be hooked up to the cell phone for transmission and collection of e-mail.

Making Decisions

As can be seen from the previous discussion, the contemporary communications picture for cruisers is extremely complicated. A VHF is an irreducible minimum. Beyond this, to make sensible decisions on what equipment to carry, the cruiser needs to consider available choices in light of the following questions.

- What is the purpose of the communications equipment (e.g., safety, personal communications, business)?
- Where will the boat be cruised (what coverage is needed around the world)?
- What services are needed (voice, fax, e-mail)?
- Whom do you want to contact and have contact you, and how time-sensitive are these contacts (can they wait until you log in once a day or do you need to be on call)?
- What will be the volume of voice and data traffic?
- What are the costs of specific pieces of equipment in terms of capital costs, standing monthly and other charges, usage costs, and maintenance costs?
- What is likely to be your usage of the equipment?
- Based on the previous two questions, what will be the total cost of the

equipment? (Given the rate of technological development and associated obsolescence, I recommend amortizing any capital costs over no more than four years.)

- How complicated is the equipment (how difficult is it to learn to use it)?
- What is its power consumption, in both use and stand-by mode (if it will be needed in stand-by mode)?

This is a lot to think about. Once the answers to these questions have been determined, it is a good idea to draw up a matrix—including all available equipment—to see what fits your needs at what cost. This exercise should clarify the available choices. As far as e-mail is concerned, given current technology,

- if you want to short-circuit this process
- if you don't have SSB or ham radio transmit capability
- if you will only be sending and receiving short messages
- if you don't need midocean capability

set yourself up with an ISP with local service on a worldwide basis, and use PocketMail!

Snail Mail

Despite the electronics revolution, many long-distance cruisers still do not have long-distance communications capability (we don't). For them, there remains a shoreside phone when in port and the postal service.

Receiving mail in out-of-the-way places is not always easy. Mail can be sent to a local post office with instructions that it be held until called for (conspicuously mark it "poste restante"), but there is always the risk of it getting misplaced and lost, or returned to the sender (most post offices do not hold mail for more than a specified length of time). It is generally preferable to find a local yacht club or marina and ask them to hold the mail until called for; however, there is often little to no security associated with how it is held (it could be dropped in a box with mail for other boats, with no control over who is allowed to sift through it).

Even in first-world countries, mail delivery can be appallingly slow. We once waited for almost six weeks for a box of mail to get from the United States to the U.S. Virgin Islands. In some third-world countries, mail can take months to get through, which can really mess up cruising plans.

We have found that the best way to get mail in out-of-the-way places is to have friends come and visit for a week or two and bring it with them. If this is not possible, there is almost always a flow of people in anchorages where cruising boats gather, and other peoples' guests sometimes can be pressed into service as couriers. However, strictly limit this to letters (i.e., no packages) in order not to compromise the courier with today's high levels of airport security. If parts need to be brought in, the person acting as courier must open and repack the boxes to be able to affirm that he or she packed them.

POSTSCRIPT

It is appropriate that the last several chapters of this book deal with the miracles of modern technology. For it is technology that is driving so much of modern boating in the form of new hull materials, new sail fabrics, new gear for handling boats, new ways of navigating, new ways of communicating with one another and with home, and ultimately new ways in which we perceive our relationships with our boats and with this lifestyle we call *cruising*.

We need to recognize, however, that it is easy to get bowled over by this technology so we lose sight of why we go cruising in the first place. Take communications equipment. It is wonderful to have a phone that enables us to contact anybody in the world from *anywhere*, anytime. But the other side to this picture is that with this miraculous device we are equally contactable at any place around the globe, at any time of the day or night.

One of the reasons Terrie and I take our family cruising is to remove ourselves from the daily pressures and stresses of modern life. This is not possible if we cannot isolate ourselves from a communications standpoint. For this reason we *choose* not to have a cell phone, and we *choose* not to have a marine SSB or ham SSB capability. At the time of writing, when cruising we are not even e-mail capable (which frustrates my editors, but the primary reason for not having this capability is so they cannot get hold of me!).

The only communications equipment we have is a trusty VHF (which is of no use for staying in touch with home and work once we are out of sight of land), and a shortwave *receiver* (no transmit capability) to get weather forecasts. The last thing I do before leaving the house for a cruise is to record a message on the telephone answering device saying we will be back in four, or five, or six months. I do not pick up messages, and I don't have e-mail forwarded. Once a month or so we call my mother-in-law to let her know we are still alive and to make sure all is well with our families. With such a regime, I find that almost as soon as we set foot on the boat, the house, work and related cares slip out of my mind and do not resurface until we near home shores once again. Surely this is an important part of what cruising is about.

The other side to this technology picture is the increasing complexity of modern boats, and the resultant systems problems that plague many cruisers. I have made a career out of writing about the technical side of boating, and indeed the justification for this book is, to a considerable extent, the integration of traditional cruising conceptions and skills with modern cruising technology. But at the end of the day, it is important to sense the point at which this technology starts to come between us and our cruising dreams.

In terms of the recreational dollars it attracts from the general public, the sailboat industry has, for years, been losing out to other recreational industries. Among the many reasons for this, a couple stand out. The first is the incredible cost of modern boating; the second is the high incidence of customer frustration arising from systems failures.

There comes a point at which the benefits of the systems that differentiate a modern cruising boat and cruising lifestyle from a traditional cruising boat and cruising lifestyle are quite simply outweighed by the cost, complexity, and associated problems; the systems are no longer worth paying for. Many cruisers have unfortunately passed this point, some by a long shot.

So although much of this book is about the technical side of modern cruising, I would urge all my readers to take a long hard look at the reasons they want to go cruising, and to then review all boat and equipment choices from this perspective, keeping things as simple and economical as is compatible with the fundamental dream. Although Terrie and I have some wonderful systems on our boat, there are many others we could have had that we simply chose not to have (the long-distance communications capability being the most obvious). As a result, we enjoy a wonderfully comfortable cruising lifestyle with a minimum of maintenance and aggravation and a fair degree of separation from the stresses of our workaday world.

I would urge those of you who have set your sights on cruising to minimize your systems aspirations and to focus instead on making your boat seaworthy and on getting away. I repeat what I wrote in the introduction: If, in spite of this admonition, your boat is loaded down with systems, you need to cultivate a mindset that says that the systems are nice to have so long as they are working, but in no way will their loss be allowed to interfere with the basic enjoyment of the cruise.

Ultimately, if a boat is to be considered a cruising boat, it should be able to function and to continue cruising with all the mechanical and electrical systems out of service. And those who are cruising in this boat should be able to continue enjoying the cruise without any of these systems. After all, they will then be in pretty much the same boat as the Hiscocks and all the other pioneers who showed us the way forward, and who had a lifetime of fun in the process.

BIBLIOGRAPHY

Barth, Roland. *Cruising Rules: Relationships at Sea.* Alna ME: Head Tide Press, 1998.

Bruce, Peter. *Adlard Coles' Heavy Weather Sailing.* 30th anniv. ed. Camden ME: International Marine; London: Adlard Coles Nautical, 1999.

Calder, Nigel. *Boatowner's Mechanical and Electrical Manual: How to Maintain, Repair, and Improve Your Boat's Essential Systems.* 2nd ed. Camden ME: International Marine; London: Adlard Coles Nautical, 1996.

Carr, Michael. *International Marine's Weather Predicting Simplified: How to Read Weather Charts and Satellite Images.* Camden ME: International Marine, 1999.

Centers for Disease Control. *Health Information for International Travel.* Washington DC: U.S. Government Printing Office, 1999–2000.

Dashew, Linda, and Steve Dashew. *Offshore Cruising Encyclopedia.* 2nd ed. Tucson AZ: Beowulf, 1997.

———. *Surviving the Storm: Coastal and Offshore Tactics.* Tucson AZ: Beowulf, 1999.

Gerr, Dave. *The Elements of Boat Strength: For Builders, Designers, and Owners.* Camden ME: International Marine; London: Adlard Coles Nautical, 2000.

———. *The Nature of Boats.* Camden ME: International Marine, 1992.

———. *The Propeller Handbook: The Complete Reference for Choosing, Installing, and Understanding Boat Propellers.* Camden ME: International Marine, 1989.

The Glénans Manual of Sailing. Trans. Peter Davison, Jim Simpson, Ruth Bagnall, and Catherine du Peloux Menagé. Rev. reprint. Newton Abbot UK: David & Charles, 1993.

Board of Trade, Great Britain. *The Ship Captain's Medical Guide.* London: H. M. Stationery Office, n.d.

D'Oliveira, Basil, and Goulder, Brian, eds. *Macmillan Reeds Nautical Almanac 2000: European Edition.* London: Nautical Data, 2000.

Hydrographic Department, Great Britain. *Ocean Passages of the World.* 4th ed. Taunton UK: Hydrographer of the Navy, 1987.

Greene, Danny. *Cruising Sailboat Kinetics: The Art, Science, and Magic of Cruising Boat Design.* Newport RI: Seven Seas Press, 1984.

Griffith, Bob. *Blue Water: A Guide to Self-Reliant Sailboat Cruising.* Boston: Sail Books, 1979.

Harris, Mike. *Understanding Weatherfax.* Dobbs Ferry NY: Sheridan House; London: Adlard Coles Nautical, 1997.

Hinz, Earl. "By the Numbers," *Ocean Navigator,* no. 95 (Jan.–Feb. 1999): 76–79.

———. Letters, *Ocean Navigator,* no. 93 (Sept.–Oct. 1998).

Hiscock, Eric C. *Cruising under Sail: Incorporating Voyaging under Sail.* Camden ME: International Marine; London: Adlard Coles Nautical, 1981.

Hubbard, Richard. *Boater's Bowditch: The Small-Craft American Practical Navigator.* Camden ME: International Marine, 1998.

Killing, Steve. *Yacht Design Explained: A Sailor's Guide to the Principles and Practice of Design.* New York: Norton, 1998.

Kotsch, William J. *Weather for the Mariner.* 3rd ed. Annapolis: Naval Institute Press, 1983.

Leonard, Beth. "Moving on Up," *Sail* 31, no. 8 (Aug. 2000): 60–64.

———. *The Voyager's Handbook: The Essential Guide to Bluewater Cruising.* Camden ME: International Marine; London: Adlard Coles Nautical, 1998.

Marshall, Roger. *The Complete Guide to Choosing a Cruising Sailboat.* Camden ME: International Marine, 1999.

Martin, Marian. *The RYA Book of EuroRegs for Inland Waterways.* London: Adlard Coles Nautical, 1998.

Michael on s/v Lookfar. "Ciguatera: The Dime Solution," *Cruising World* 26, no. 2 (Feb. 2000): 8.

Neal, John. *Offshore Cruising Companion.* Friday Harbor WA: Mahina Expeditions, 2000.

Paine, Chuck. Quoted in *The Complete Offshore Yacht.* London: Yachting Monthly, 1990.

Pardey, Lin, and Larry Pardey. *The Care and Feeding of Sailing Crew.* 2nd ed. New York: Norton, 1995.

Reed's Nautical Almanac: North American East Coast 2000. Boston: Thomas Reeds Publications, 2000.

Ross, Wallace. *Sail Power: The Complete Guide to Sails and Sail Handling.* New York: Knopf, 1984.

Ross Institute of Tropical Hygiene. *Preservation of Personal Health in Warm Climates.* 7th ed. London: London School of Hygiene and Tropical Medicine, 1978.

Rousmaniere, John. *The Annapolis Book of Seamanship.* 3rd rev. ed. New York: Simon & Schuster, 1999.

———, ed. *Desirable and Undesirable Characteristics of Offshore Yachts.* New York: Norton, 1987.

Royal Yachting Association. *Cruising Yacht Safety.* Eastleigh US: Royal Yachting Association, 1998.

Schroeder, Dirk G. *Staying Healthy in Asia, Africa, and Latin America.* 4th ed. Chico CA: Moon, 1995.

Sutphen, Hal. "Sea Anchor Survey," *Ocean Navigator,* no. 100 (Sept.–Oct. 1999): 106–10.

Thomas, David. Quoted in *The Complete Offshore Yacht.* London: Yachting Monthly, 1990.

Trafford, Tim. Letters, *Yachting World* (Oct. 1999).

Naval Sea Systems Command, U.S. *U.S. Navy Salvors Handbook.* Washington DC: U.S. Government Printing Office, 1976.

U.S. Sailing. *Safety Recommendations for Cruising Sailboats.* Portsmouth RI: U.S. Sailing Association, 1999.

USYRU/SNAME Joint Committee "Safety from Capsizing," Final Report of the Directors. Society of Naval Architects and Marine Engineers: Jersey City NJ: June 1985.

Watts, Alan. *The Weather Handbook.* 2nd ed. Dobbs Ferry NY: Sheridan House, 1999.

Waugh, Ian. *The Maritime Radio and Satellite Communications Manual.* Shrewsbury UK: Waterline, 1994.

Werner, David. *Where There Is No Doctor: A Village Health Care Handbook.* Palo Alto CA: Hesperian Foundation, 1992.

Whidden, Tom. *The Art and Science of Sails: A Guide to Modern Materials, Construction, Aerodynamics, Upkeep, and Use.* New York: St. Martin's; London: Adlard Coles Nautical, 1990.

Williams, Jack. *The Weather Book.* 2nd ed. New York: Vintage, 1997.

Wright, E. A. (Ted). Letters, *Blue Water Sailing* (Feb. 2000).

METRIC CONVERSIONS AND TRADEMARKS

METRIC CONVERSIONS

(°F – 32) × 0.555 = °C
(°C × 1.8) + 32 = °F
inches × 25.4 = millimeters
ounces × 28.35 = grams
pounds × 0.45 = kilograms
feet × 0.3 = meters
square feet × 0.09 = square meters
U.S. gallons × 3.785 = liters
cubic inches × 0.016 = liters
cubic feet × 28.3 = liters
pounds per square inch × 0.7031 = kilograms per square centimeter
pounds × 4.45 = Newtons

TRADEMARKS

3M, 6-12, Aerogel, AeroRig, American Express, Ammen's, Aquamet, Aralen, Avon, Bactrim, Barrier, Barrier Ultra-R, Benadryl, Betadine, Boeshield T-9, Bonine, Bruce, Caladryl, Capilene, ChapStick, Cipro, Clorox, Cold Machine, CompuServe, Corelle, Corian, C.Q.R., Crew-Link, Cutless, Dacron, Data-Scope, Desitin, Dramamine, Duralac, Dutchman, Dyneema, E-Meter, Forespar, Formica, Fortress, Frigoboat, Gore-Tex, Green Stripe, Harken, Hotmail, Hypalon, Icom, Imodium, John Crane, Joy, Kevlar, Kwell, Lariam, Lifesling, Lomotil, Magellan, Marelon, Martec, Marzine, MasterCard, Max-Prop, Monel, Mylar, Navtec, Neosporin, Novocain, Nylok, Ocean Technology, Off!, Oralyte, Orbcomm, Patagonia, Pedialyte, Pepto-Bismol, Permanone, Phenergan, Phisohex, PocketMail, Polysporin, Profurl, Resochin, Rid, SafetyNet, SailMail, Sailomat, Schaefer, Scotchgard, Sea-Band, SeaGard, Septra, Silvadene, Skycell, Spartite, Spectra, Sta-Lok, Styrofoam, Sudafed, Sunbrella, Tabasco, Tank Tender, Tanksaver, Technicolor, Technora, Tef-Gel, Teflon, Terylene, Thermos, Thin-Lite, Thompson's Water Seal, Tinactin, Treadmaster, Tylenol, Vantin, Vaseline, Vectran, Velcro, Vermox, Vetus, Visa, Vise-Grips, WD-40, Weather Channel, Weatherfax, WebMail, Windpilot, and Yeoman are registered trademarks.

INDEX

Numbers in **bold** refer to pages with illustrations

C

D

E

J

K

L

M

N

O

P

Q

R

S